Developmental Psychopathology

Developmental Psychopathology

From Infancy through Adolescence

Fifth Edition

Charles Wenar
The Ohio State University

Patricia Kerig
Miami University

McGraw Hill

Boston Burr Ridge, IL Dubuque, IA Madison, WI New York San Francisco St. Louis
Bangkok Bogotá Caracas Kuala Lumpur Lisbon London Madrid Mexico City
Milan Montreal New Delhi Santiago Seoul Singapore Sydney Taipei Toronto

The McGraw·Hill Companies

 **Higher Education**

DEVELOPMENTAL PSYCHOPATHOLOGY: FROM INFANCY THROUGH ADOLESCENCE
Published by McGraw-Hill, a business unit of The McGraw-Hill Companies, Inc., 1221 Avenue of the Americas, New York, NY, 10020. Copyright © 2006, 2000, 1994, 1990 by The McGraw-Hill Companies, Inc. All rights reserved. No part of this publication may be reproduced or distributed in any form or by any means, or stored in a database or retrieval system, without the prior written consent of The McGraw-Hill Companies, Inc., including, but not limited to, in any network or other electronic storage or transmission, or broadcast for distance learning.

Some ancillaries, including electronic and print components, may not be available to customers outside the United States.

This book is printed on acid-free paper.

1 2 3 4 5 6 7 8 9 0 DOC/DOC 0 9 8 7 6 5

ISBN   0-07-282019-5

Editor in Chief: *Emily Barrosse*
Publisher: *Beth Mejia*
Senior Sponsoring Editor: *John T. Wannemacher*
Marketing Manager: *Melissa S. Caughlin*
Director of Development: *Judith Kromm*
Managing Editor: *Jean Dal Porto*
Project Manager: *Rick Hecker*
Art Director: *Jeanne Schreiber*
Associate Designer: *Srdjan Savanovic*
Cover Designer: *George Kokkonas*
Art Editor: *Katherine McNab*
Photo Research Coordinator: *Nora Agbayani*
Cover Credit: *© SuperStock*
Production Supervisor: *Jason I. Huls*
Senior Media Producer: *Stephanie George*
Media Project Manager: *Alexander Rohrs*
Permissions Editor: *Marty Granahan*
Composition: *10/12 Times Roman by GTS—York, PA Campus*
Printing: *PMS Black, 45# New Era Matte Plus, R.R. Donnelley and Sons, Inc./Crawfordsville, IN.*

Credits: The credits section for this book begins on p. C–1 and is considered an extension of the copyright page.

Library of Congress Cataloging-in-Publication Data
Wenar, Charles, 1922-
    Developmental psychopathology: from infancy through adolescence / Charles Wenar,
Patricia Kerig.-- 5th ed.
        p. cm.
    Includes bibliographical references and index.
        ISBN 0-07-282019-5 (alk. paper)
    1. Child psychopathology. 2. Adolescent psychopathology. I. Kerig, Patricia. II. Title.
RJ499.W396 2006
    618.92′89—dc22   2005047937

www.mhhe.com

To Mikel, who has been an education and an inspiration—and to all the young people who courageously have shared with us their journeys.

Patricia K. Kerig

About the Authors

Patricia K. Kerig

Patricia K. Kerig received her PhD in clinical psychology from the University of California at Berkeley with a specialization in children and families. After completing an internship at Stanford Children's Hospital, she was a postdoctoral fellow in clinical child psychology at the University of Colorado Health Sciences Center. Currently an Associate Professor in the Psychology Department at Miami University, she previously held faculty positions at Simon Fraser University and the University of North Carolina at Chapel Hill. Her research honors include the Brodsky/Hare Mustin Award from Division 35 of the American Psychological Association and the New Contribution Award from the International Society for the Study of Personal Relationships. She is the author of a number of scholarly works on the topics of risk and resiliency in children exposed to interparental conflict, violence, divorce, and traumatic stress and is a member of the editorial boards of the *Journal of Family Psychology, Journal of Emotional Abuse,* and *Journal of Social and Personal Relationships.* She is also an actively practicing clinician.

Charles Wenar

Charles Wenar is professor emeritus of psychology at The Ohio State University. He headed both the developmental area and the clinical child program in the department of psychology there. A graduate of Swarthmore College and State University of Iowa, Dr. Wenar was both a clinician and a researcher at Michael Reese Hospital, the Illinois Neuropsychiatric Institute, and the University of Pennsylvania. His four previous books and numerous articles, as well as his research on autism and on negativism in healthy toddlers, attest to his long-standing interest in both normal and disturbed children. In 1986, Dr. Wenar received the Distinguished Professional Contribution Award of the Section on Clinical Child Psychology of Division 12 of the American Psychological Association for his meritorious contribution to the advancement of knowledge and service to children.

Contents

Chapter Seven

The Preschool Period: The Emergence of Attention-Deficit/Hyperactivity Disorder and Learning Disorders

Chapter Eight

Middle Childhood: The Anxiety Disorders

Chapter Nine

Middle Childhood to Adolescence: Mood Disorders and Suicide

Chapter Sixteen

Psychological Assessment

Chapter Seventeen

Intervention and Prevention

Preface

The Developmental Approach

The unifying theme in all editions of this text is that childhood psychopathology should be regarded as normal development gone awry. Thus, normal development becomes the point of departure for understanding childhood disturbances. The basic challenge is that of discovering what forces divert development from its normal course and what forces either sustain the deviation or foster a return to normality. Because of this unifying theme, an entire chapter (Chapter 2) is devoted to the contributions made by the biological, family, social, and cultural contexts as well as the normal development of six processes in the individual context: cognition, emotion, attachment, the self, moral development, and gender and sexuality. The roots of a given disturbance in normal development are then presented; for example, autism is related to the normal development of infants, and reading disability is related to the normal process of learning to read. A pedagogical advantage of Chapter 2 is that students from diverse backgrounds in areas such as education or social work can all be equally well informed concerning the development of the 10 crucial variables.

Another consequence of the developmental approach is that, with some exceptions, the psychopathologies can be arranged in a rough chronological order rather than in the usual descriptive categories such as "behavioral disorders" or "emotional disorders." Autism originates in infancy; anxiety disorders, in middle childhood; and eating disorders, in adolescence. This arrangement, in turn, is another way of helping students to "think developmentally."

Not everyone agrees with the developmental approach used here. For some, developmental psychopathology consists of describing a given psychopathology and then dealing with the issues of etiology and prognosis. However, even though such an approach may involve charting the "developmental pathways" of various disturbances, it is basically the same as that used in descriptive psychiatry. In both instances the *crucial connection to normal development* is neglected.

Changes for the Current Revision

1. Each chapter has been extensively revised in the light of *new research* on the prevalence, origins, consequences, and treatment of each of the disorders. In particular, the developmental psychopathology perspective has alerted researchers to the crucial need for *longitudinal research* that allows us to observe patterns of continuity and change over the life span (see Chapter 1). The dilemma, however, is that a life-span study requires the entire life span of the investigator! Nonetheless, the harvest of a number of long-term longitudinal studies is now being reaped. Important new research is emerging about the etiology and course of many disorders, including depression (see Chapter 9) and conduct disorder (see Chapter 10).

2. Given the importance of the developmental perspective to this text, in the current revision the chapters have been reordered to better reflect the *age of onset* of the disorders. For example, the discussion of mental retardation (see Chapter 4) has been moved into the infancy period, just as our discussion of depression (see Chapter 9) has been shifted to the early adolescent transition when rates begin to surge, especially for girls.

3. Given that developmental psychopathology comprises the study of normative and deviant pathways throughout the life span, we have extended our coverage into the *late adolescent/early adult* period with the addition of a chapter on emergent personality disorders (see Chapter 15), in which we focus on important new research on borderline personality disorder.

4. While in the previous edition, issues related to ethnic minorities were segregated into a separate chapter, the current edition integrates discussion of *ethnic, racial, class, and cross-cultural differences* into every chapter. Chapter 2 introduces conceptual issues related to how psychopathology might be affected by ethnicity, culture, and social class. Subsequently, wherever the research and literature allow, diversity is explored within the context of each of the disorders. Unfortunately, the attention paid to these issues in the literature has not kept pace with psychologists' recognition of their importance. Therefore, we will frequently encounter a dearth of research on diversity in childhood psychopathology.

Pedagogical Features

Overall organization. The overall organization in terms of *contexts*—specifically, biological, individual, family, social, and cultural—provides a consistent framework for ordering the sprawling research literature. In addition, each psychopathology is systematically presented in terms of a set *organizational framework:* namely, definition and characteristics (including prevalence, gender, and socioeconomic and ethnic differences), comorbidity, developmental course, etiology, and intervention. *Key terms* appear in bold in the text and are included in a glossary at the end of the book. There are frequent *summaries* throughout each chapter, presented either in written form or as figures. Such summaries have the advantage of being more detailed and relevant than an overall, global summation at the end of the chapter.

In each chapter, *boxes* are used to highlight issues of theoretical interest, to illustrate debates and controversies in the field, or to provide greater depth in our coverage of the relevant research.

Further, in each chapter, a *case study* is presented in the form of a vignette or box to illustrate the disorder under investigation. Wherever possible, the case studies used are real-life cases, many of which are derived from autobiographical material. By the same token, Chapter 17 includes transcripts of actual therapy sessions to illustrate each of the intervention modalities described. Consistent with the developmental psychopathology perspective of a continuum between the normative and the psychopathology, our goal is to put a human face on the disorders and to increase our readers' empathy and understanding for those who experience them.

For the Instructor

An *Instructor's Manual,* prepared by Patricia Kerig, is available on the text's companion Web site (www.mhhe.com/wenar5). It includes additional references for case studies, films, discussion/study questions, and suggested examination questions.

PowerPoint presentation slides, created by Leslie Zeigenhorn (University of San Diego and San Diego State University), are also available to instructors on the companion Web site.

For the Student

The goal of the present edition has not changed—namely, to enable the student to "think developmentally" about psychopathology as it unfolds from childhood through adolescence. A number of features of the new edition have been designed to provide students with a clearer pathway through the material. For example, more figures have been included in order to illustrate research findings and conceptual models, the visual appeal of the book has been increased, and key terms have been put in bold print. In addition, boxes have been added in order to provide more detailed information, to explore issues and questions raised by the research, or to bring the material alive through case studies. Review articles are often cited so that students can have access to more detailed presentations of research than is possible within a given chapter. Also there are references to literature on topics that, while important, had to be excluded because of space limitations.

Acknowledgments

We appreciate the help of many colleagues who contributed information, encouragement, and clarification to the text. We are also indebted to many individuals at McGraw-Hill whose names appear on the copyright page.

Finally, we are grateful to the reviewers of this edition. We were impressed by their thoroughness and we profited greatly from their comments.

Reviewers

Mary Katherine Weibel-Duncan, *Bloomsburg University*

Patricia Metz, *School of Social Work, University of Michigan*

Gregory P. Hickman, *Penn State University, Fayette*

George W. Ledger, *Hollins University*

Annette Mahoney, *Bowling Green State University*

Jennifer Langhinrichsen-Rohling, *University of South Alabama*

Virginia Powers-Lagac, *Westfield State College*

Azmaira Maker, *Marquette University*

Jeanine Vivona, *The College of New Jersey*

Mikal Galperin, *University of Texas, Dallas*

The Developmental Psychopathology Approach

Overview

The three vignettes in Box 1.1 illustrate the key hypothesis that informs this text: that child psychopathology can be understood as *normal development gone awry.* Psychopathology is behavior that once was, but no longer can be, considered appropriate to the child's level of development. Whether the described behaviors are regarded as normal or pathological depends on when they occur in the developmental sequence. All three of the behaviors in the vignettes presented in Box 1.1 are to be expected in toddlers and preschoolers but would be suspect at later ages. In the first example, it is not unusual for a docile infant to become a willful, negativistic, temperamental tyrant during the "terrible twos." If the child were 10, however, his attack on his brother might well represent a serious lapse in self-control. Likewise, in the second example, it is not unusual

for preschool boys to believe that they can grow up to be women, because they have not grasped the fact that gender remains constant throughout life. And finally, ideas of omnipotence and a failure to clearly separate fantasy from reality are part of normal cognitive development in toddlers and preschoolers; their presence from middle childhood on suggests the possibility of a serious thought disturbance and an unhealthy lack of contact with reality.

At the applied level, the *developmental framework* underlies the child clinician's deceptively simple statement, "There's nothing to worry about—most children act that way at this age, and your child will probably outgrow it"; or its more ominous version, "The behavior is unusual and should be attended to, since it might not be outgrown." A considerable

1

Box 1.1 | What Is the First Question You Ask?

You are a clinical child psychologist. A mother telephones your office frantic over the sudden personality change in her boy. "He used to be so sweet and then, out of the clear blue sky, he started being sassy and sulky and throwing a fit if anybody asked him to do the least little thing. What really scared me was last night he got so mad at his brother, he ran at him and started hitting him with all his might. His brother was really hurt and started screaming, and my husband and I had to pull them apart. I don't know what would have happened if we hadn't been there. I just never saw anybody in a rage like that before."

What is the first question you ask?

You are at a cocktail party and, after learning that you are a clinical child psychologist, a former star-quarterback-turned-successful-business-executive takes you aside. After some rambling about "believing in sexual equality as much as the next fellow," he comes to the point. "Last week my son turned to my wife and announced that when he got old enough, he was going to become a girl. When my wife asked him where he got a crazy idea like that, he said that he thought boys were too rough, and he liked to be with girls more. I know he's always been a 'mama's boy,' but I'll be darned if I want any son of mine to have one of those sex changes done on him."

What is the first question you ask?

You are a clinical child psychologist conducting an initial interview with a mother who has brought her daughter to a child guidance clinic. "She has always been a sensitive child and a loner, but I thought she was getting along all right—except that recently she has started having some really strange ideas. The other day we were driving on the highway to town, and she said, 'I could make all these cars wreck if I just raised my hand.' I thought she was joking, but she had a serious expression on her face and wasn't even looking at me. Another time she wanted to go outside when the weather was bad, and she got furious at me because I didn't make it stop raining. And now she's started pleading and pleading with me every night to look in on her after she has gone to sleep to be sure her leg isn't hanging over the side of the bed. She says there is some kind of crab creature in the dark waiting to grab her if her foot touches the floor. What worries me is that she believes all these things can really happen. I don't know if she's crazy or watching too much TV or what's going on."

What is the first question you ask?

The first question is the same in all three cases: *How old is your child?*

amount of information concerning normal development must be mastered before one can judge whether the behavior at hand is age-appropriate or whether a suspect behavior is likely to disappear in the course of a child's progress from infancy to adulthood. Further, knowledge of development alerts us to the fact that some problem behavior is normal in the course of life. (See Figure 1.1.) In fact, the absence of misbehavior might constitute a reason for worry. The 2-year-old who is not distressed by separation from the mother, the 3-year-old who never says no, the adolescent who never experiments with new roles—children such as these might warrant a second look.

Before we set out to analyze child psychopathology as normal development gone awry, we first will set the stage. First, we will present a general *developmental framework* in order to examine various characteristics of development itself. Then we will identify those *processes of development* that are particularly important to the understanding of childhood psychopathology and trace their normal course. Our vignettes, for example, suggest that the variables of self-regulation, gender identity, and cognition should

Figure 1.1

Development is lifelong and problems are a part of normal development.

be included in the list. We also will evaluate *theoretical models* that contribute most to the developmental approach. As we examine various disorders, we shall discover that there are many variations on this theme of psychopathology as developmentally inappropriate behavior; therefore, we shall constantly be seeking the specific developmental scheme that best fits the data at hand. Lastly, we shall examine the **developmental psychopathology** approach, which attempts to integrate these different perspectives.

A General Developmental Framework

Our general developmental framework includes the time dimension along with five *contexts* of development: the biological, individual, family, social, and cultural.

The Biological Context

The biological context involves a number of organic influences that are relevant to understanding deviant development: *genetics, brain chemistry, brain structure, neurological* and *neuropsychological* functioning, and other innate characteristics that are involved in the development of individual differences such as *temperament.* Research in the neuropsychology of childhood disorders has been burgeoning in recent years, and we will consider this work in our exploration of each of the psychopathologies. The effects of psychological disturbances on biology will be central to our examination of the eating disorders bulimia and anorexia nervosa. Reversing the direction of influence, we will also consider the psychological consequences of physical illness and brain damage. Additionally, we will explore the role that genetic factors play in various psychopathologies.

The Individual Context

The individual context concerns psychological variables within the person—personality characteristics, cognitions, emotions, and internalized expectations about relationships. This context will figure most prominently in our discussions of psychopathology, since it provides the greatest amount of developmental data. We must give careful consideration to which variables would be the most useful to study for a particular child. Traditional behaviorists would persuade us to deal exclusively with observable behavior and to avoid all mentalistic or inferential concepts; Freudians urge us to examine the child's ego strengths and monitor the battles between id and superego; Piaget reminds us not to neglect egocentrism and the balancing act between assimilation and accommodation; Erikson points to the centrality of ego identity.

The choice among conceptualizations has important clinical implications. The behavioral viewpoint leans toward a definition of psychopathology based on social norms—since there is nothing in behavior itself that designates it as abnormal, such a judgment must be based on the behavior's infrequency or on the fact that a given society chooses to label certain behaviors as psychopathological. In another society the same behavior might go unnoticed or even be regarded as a special gift, such as the accepting attitudes displayed toward psychotic behavior in certain African cultures. The psychoanalysts' approach, on the contrary, maintains that behavior is important only as it furnishes clues to the child's inner life; psychopathology is not a matter of behavior per se, but of the meaning of such behavior. The frequency of daydreaming in adolescence, for example, is not as important as the stage-appropriateness of the fantasies that accompany the behavior.

Because our primary goal here is to understand the individual context rather than to champion a particular conceptualization of it, we use various theories to the extent that they throw light on the psychopathology at hand. No single theory offers a satisfactory account of all of childhood psychopathology, while various individual theories may offer conflicting but useful accounts of specific disturbances.

The Family Context

The family provides an important—perhaps the most important—context for child development. Among family influences, the greatest amount of attention has been paid to the parent-child relationship. However, it is important to note that most parents in research have been mothers. Fathers have been relatively neglected in child development research, with notable exceptions (Lamb, 1997; Phares, 1992). We will consider different normative patterns of parenting and the child behaviors associated with them, as well as such pathological extremes as neglect and physical and sexual abuse. In addition, we will look at the family systemic perspective, which highlights qualities of the whole family that influence child development.

The Social Context

Broadening our scope, we move from the intimate family context to the world of social relations outside the family, a world that widens incrementally over the course of development. *Peer relations* play a significant role in normal and deviant development and have been given increasing attention in recent years. In our discussions we explore positive peer relations, such as popularity and friendship, and also their negative counterparts, such as rejection and encouragement of antisocial behavior. We will also consider the role of *extrafamilial adults* such as teachers or coaches who might provide children with positive role models and mentorship or, on the negative side, with negative influences and discouragement.

The Cultural Context

In considering the cultural context, we will discuss the role of the larger social and cultural factors that might increase the risk of, or protect against, psychopathology. We will consider *social class* in general and *poverty* in particular. We will also incorporate into our discussions considerations related to *race and ethnicity* and will take into account *cross-cultural* and cross-national differences where the data allow. Cultural background is a superordinate variable that significantly affects all other contexts. Culture may affect the risk for becoming disturbed and moreover may even affect whether a given behavior is considered to be psychopathological. Thus, in some cultures obedience and conformity in children are valued while self-assertiveness and independence are valued in others; in some cultures beliefs in malevolent spirits are normative while in others such ideas would be considered to be a sign of serious disturbance.

Interactions

We have been discussing these contexts of development as if they were static entities, but in fact, they are in constant *interaction* with one another. For example, the context of time interacts with all other contexts, which in turn interact with one another. Parents who are 25 years old when their daughter is born are not at the same stage in their development as they will be at 40 when she enters adolescence. In a like manner, the

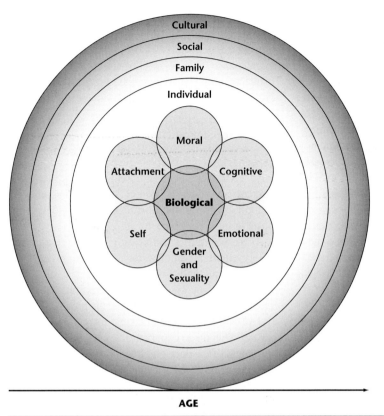

Figure 1.2

A Developmental Framework.

AGE

Note: All contexts and variables interact at each point in time as well as over time.

casual, improvised peer group of the preschool period differs from the adolescent clique, which begins to surpass the parents as the major influence on dress, music, language, and social behavior.

In sum, our developmental framework entails the interaction of variables both at a given point in time and over time. The framework itself is presented schematically in Figure 1.2.

Models of Child Psychopathology

The developmental framework we have presented is designed to be general and comprehensive. It is intended to serve as a means of organizing what might otherwise be a bewildering array of variables used to account for a given psychopathology. It also is sufficiently general to embrace the specific theories of psychopathology that we are about to present.

A variety of theories provide models of the **etiology** (origins or cause) of childhood psychopathology. While they each have distinctive features, the models are not necessarily incompatible. Some share common features. Others are complementary. Still others have irreconcilable differences. Each has merit; none is totally satisfactory. Therefore, we must reconcile ourselves to living with diversity and partial truths. In our own presentation of models, we concentrate on those features that will be relevant to our subsequent discussion of various psychopathologies.

The Medical Model

There are two essential components to the traditional medical model. The first involves the general hypothesis that psychopathologies result from *organic dysfunctions*. The second characteristic of the medical model is its penchant for classifying psychopathological behavior in the same way as physical diseases—namely, in terms of *diagnoses.* Emil Kraepelin, who published the landmark classification of adult psychopathologies in 1833, set the stage by assuming a biological etiology for each disorder in his list. Attempts to construe child behavior problems in medical terms have resulted in some odd classifications indeed. Take, for example, the 18th century concept of "masturbatory insanity," which posited that excessive self-stimulation was the cause of many physical and mental problems in children (Mash & Dozois, 2003). More modern perspectives hold that the body and mind are part of a system, such that each influences the other. While psychopathology may arise out of organic disturbances—whether as a function of neurochemistry, brain structure, or neuropsychological functioning—it is also the case that psychological processes—such as strong emotions, stress, and exposure to trauma—can affect biology.

In Chapter 3, we will take a detailed look at the classification system used to diagnose disorders in children, the *Diagnostic and Statistical Manual of Mental Disorders* (*DSM-IV-TR;* American Psychiatric Association, 2000). Although this classification system remains neutral on the question of etiology—biological origins of the disorders are not assumed—the *DSM* retains the medical model's tendency to view psychopathology as an illness residing within the person, rather than as a product of interactions between the child and the environment.

The Behavioral Model

Three characteristics distinguish behavioral psychology. First is the assertion that scientific psychology must be based only on *observable behavior.* Radical behaviorists would limit psychology to the study of responses organisms make to environmental stimuli, excluding all "mentalistic" variables such as thoughts, images, feelings, and memories since these cannot be observed. More moderate theorists include nonobservable concepts under two conditions: that such terms can be defined behaviorally and that their inclusion assists us to meet the goals of predicting and controlling behavior. Next, behaviorists base their evidence on *empirical research* conducted under highly controlled conditions,

with the laboratory experiment being the ideal method for studying the behavior under investigation. Third, behaviorists believe that the acquisition, maintenance, change, or elimination of much of human and animal behavior can be adequately and concisely accounted for in terms of *learning principles.*

Principles of Learning

The three principles of learning that form the basis of the behavioral approach are respondent conditioning (also called classical or Pavlovian conditioning), operant conditioning (also called instrumental conditioning), and imitation (also called modeling or observational learning). *or classical*

In **respondent conditioning** a stimulus that innately elicits a response (e.g., a snarling dog will elicit fear in a child) is paired with a neutral stimulus (e.g., the sound of the dog-house door opening). After a given number of pairings, the previously neutral stimulus comes to elicit the response, such that the child begins to experience fear upon first hearing the sound of the door. Such associations may explain the origins of phobias (i.e., irrational fears related to an object that is not in and of itself threatening).

In **operant conditioning** the organism operates upon or does something to the environment in order to achieve a given result. In essence, it is a process by which an organism learns to associate certain consequences with certain actions it has taken. These consequences may serve to increase or decrease the likelihood of the behavior's being repeated. The term used to designate an increase in the likelihood of occurrence is **reinforcement.** In *positive reinforcement,* behavior is followed by a reward; for example, the father of an 8-year-old treats his daughter to an ice cream cone after she has completed her chores. In *negative reinforcement* an aversive stimulus is removed; for example, a 10-year-old boy is excused from mowing the lawn for a month after improving his grades. The two methods used to decrease the likelihood of a behavior's being repeated are extinction and punishment. In **extinction** the reinforcement maintaining a response is removed; for example, upon her therapist's advice, a mother no longer gives in to her 4-year-old's demands every time he has a temper tantrum, and the tantrums disappear. In **punishment** a response is followed by an aversive stimulus; for example, a 3-year-old is denied dessert when she colors the walls with her crayons.

One consequence of punishment is particularly relevant to our interest in psychopathology. Once exposed to an aversive stimulus, an organism will try in the future to avoid reexposure, a process called **avoidance learning.** Avoidance learning is a double-edged sword. It protects the organism from a repeated encounter with a possibly harmful situation; for example, once burned, a 2-year-old is not likely to touch again the burner of a stove. But avoidance learning can also lead to unrealistic avoidance of situations after they are no longer noxious; for example, an adult may be terrified of his reasonable, benevolent boss because, as a child, he was brutally beaten by his father. Thus, avoidance prevents the individual from adopting new behaviors that are appropriate to changed circumstances.

The third learning principle is **imitation** or modeling, which involves learning a new behavior by observing and imitating another person's performance of that behavior. Thus, without being directly taught to do so, preschoolers will pretend to clean the house or hammer a nail as their parents do or will answer the phone with the exact words and intonation they have heard adults use. Children whose parents, peers, and communities model nonconstructive behavior are likely to develop antisocial ways of behaving.

Behavioral Perspectives on Psychopathology

The behaviorists believe that—once allowance has been made for genetic, maturational, and temperamental factors—all behavior conforms to the basic principles of learning just described.

How does psychopathology develop in this perspective? Some children grow up with the kinds of learning experiences that maximize their chances of making a successful adaptation to environmental demands, while others have experiences that minimize such an outcome. In the latter instance, behaviorists prefer to talk in terms of *"maladaptive"* rather than "abnormal" behavior. Implicit in their

stand is also a *cultural relativism:* What is adaptive in one society may be maladaptive in another.

Using cultural standards as their guide, behaviorists define psychopathology as deviations in the *frequency or intensity* of behavior. According to such a definition, psychopathologies can be grouped in terms of behavioral deficit or excess. In **behavior deficit,** behaviors occur at a lower frequency or intensity than is expected within society, so the child's social, intellectual, or practical skills are impaired. Autism, learning disabilities, and mental retardation are examples. In **behavior excess,** behavior occurs at a higher frequency or intensity than is adaptive to the standards of society. The hyperactive child who is in a continual state of activity, the obsessive-compulsive child who repeatedly washes his hands, and the anxious child who is constantly terrified by real and imagined dangers all show signs of behavior excess.

The *developmental dimension* is introduced in terms of age-related changes in societal expectations for behavior. In U.S. society, a child should be toilet trained toward the end of the preschool period, should be able to cope with school by the beginning of middle childhood, should function independent of parents by the end of adolescence, and so on. Other societies have different requirements and different timetables.

Social Learning Theory

Social learning theorists such as Bandura (1986) expanded the scope of behavior theory in a number of ways. For one, Bandura countered the radical behavioral assumption that the individual is a mere reactor to environmental stimuli. He proposed a process of **reciprocal determinism,** by which the person and the environment come to influence one another. He also views individuals as having an active role in determining their responses to the environment. Whereas radical behaviorists focused on the stimulus → response relationship, terming what went on between these two events in the person's mind the "black box," Bandura invited us to open that box and peer inside.

Bandura's most significant contribution was to expand behavioral theory to include attention to *cognitive processes,* such as internal representations of experiences, expectancies, and problem solving. Cognitive processes determine how external events will affect behavior by influencing "which external events will be observed, how they will be perceived, whether they leave any lasting effects, what valence and efficacy they have, and how the information they convey will be organized for future use" (Bandura, 1977, p. 160). Bandura also introduced the concept of **self-efficacy,** which reflects the fact that individuals come to anticipate not only that a given behavior will produce a given outcome, but more importantly, whether or not they can successfully execute such a behavior. Thus, people fear and avoid situations they believe exceed their coping skills, and they behave with confidence in those situations which they believe themselves capable of handling. Therefore, self-efficacy influences both the choice of action and persistence in the face of obstacles.

While the cognitive dimension to social learning theory is an important contribution, one significant limitation is the lack of attention to developmental differences. Thus, we must turn to cognitive developmental theory—exemplified by the work of Piaget—to further understand childhood psychopathology.

Cognitive Models

Cognitive Developmental Theory

Piaget is one of the major figures in developmental psychology. Although much of his work focused on the development of cognition, Piaget and others that followed him have applied his research to the understanding of psychopathology. (See Cowan, 1978, and Piaget, 1981.)

Piaget makes the assumption that cognitive development proceeds in a series of orderly, fixed stages. Each stage is qualitatively distinct, and no higher type of thinking can evolve until the child has gone through all the preceding stages. The timetable may differ from child to child, but the order can never vary. (One of the clearest and most succinct expositions of Piaget's theory is found in Chapters 1 and 2 of Piaget, 1967.)

One of the significant contributions Piaget made to our understanding of development is the concept of the schema. A **schema** is a model or blueprint that helps the child to understand and predict the environment. The schema also is the fundamental building block of change over the course of development, as the child's capacity to reason becomes more sophisticated, complex, and abstract. What causes schemas to change? According to Piaget, development is fueled by the child's attempts to adapt to the environment and adaptation takes place through two psychological processes: assimilation and accommodation. **Assimilation** refers to the incorporation of new information into an existing schema. For example, the boy accustomed to playing with his affectionate siblings may approach the first child he encounters in preschool with an enthusiastic hug, assuming this new child fits his schema of "kids just love me!" **Accommodation** refers to the alteration of a schema to take into account new information. Thus, if the new child backs away in alarm at the unexpected hug, the exuberantly affectionate boy may adjust his schema to a more realistic one of "*some kids just love me.*"

In general, cognitive development is characterized by a balance, or **equilibration,** of assimilation and accommodation. Assimilation gives the world some predictability and provides the child some context in which to place new experiences so that they are not bewildering. Accommodation allows the child to take in new information and expand his or her understanding of the world. In Chapter 2 we will detail Piaget's cognitive developmental stages and explore the implications of assimilation and accommodation for understanding how psychopathology develops.

Piaget's theory has generated an impressive body of research that confirms some aspects and disconfirms others. More sophisticated experimental techniques show that Piaget underestimated the infant's cognitive capacities: For example, object permanence is possible earlier in infancy than Piaget postulated. By the same token, when researchers alter tasks to make them more familiar, preschoolers can produce higher levels of reasoning than Piaget would predict. Piaget's concept of stages also is hotly debated. For example, there are those who maintain that cognitive development is gradual and continuous rather than marked by qualitative advances.

There is also a group of neo-Piagetians who prefer to retain and modify the theory, which, they claim, contains too many valuable and valid insights to be discarded (Lourenco & Machado, 1996).

Social Cognitive Theory

More recently, *social cognitive theorists* (also called social information processing theorists) have expanded Piaget's concepts in important ways. For example, Dodge and his colleagues (Dodge, 1993; Crick & Dodge, 1994; Dodge & Petit, 2003) use the concept of the *schema* to study children's behavior in the interpersonal domain, termed *social information processing.*

Dodge emphasizes the fact that schemata are stable mental structures that incorporate children's perceptions of self, their experiences in the past, and their expectations for the future. Therefore, based on the lessons they draw from past experiences, schemata color children's perceptions of new events and thus their response to those events. For example, depressed children display a pessimistic cognitive style that draws their attention to all that is negative and consistent with their low expectations. Consequently, they may behave toward others in ways that promote rejection, fulfilling their worst prophecies; for example, the child who enters the classroom the first day of school expecting to be friendless and rejected may isolate herself and display a scowling affect, thus contributing to her own friendlessness. In a similar manner, conduct disordered children display a *hostile attribution bias* that leads them to perceive others as ill intentioned toward them and thus as deserving a response in kind. For example, the child who accidentally bumps into another in a rush to the water fountain might be perceived as "mean" and deserving of punishment by the child with conduct problems. In turn, when conduct disordered children's aggression does in fact inspire peers to respond negatively to them, their hostile schema is confirmed. As we shall see, the social cognitive perspective makes an important contribution to the understanding of the development of psychopathology, particularly depression and conduct disorder, and has informed a number of highly effective interventions for children.

Psychoanalytic Models

Classical Psychoanalysis

Classical psychoanalysis, also known as drive theory, is concerned with discovering the dynamics—the basic motives, the prime movers—of human behavior. This concern with intrapersonal forces clearly sets psychoanalysts apart from the behaviorists, with their concern for the environmental factors that shape behavior, and cognitive psychologists, who focus primarily on conscious processes and reason. As with the other approaches discussed so far, our coverage of Freud's work will not be comprehensive; instead, we will concentrate on the two aspects of classical psychoanalysis most relevant to understanding childhood psychopathology—the structural and psychosexual models.

The Structural Model Freud's tripartite conceptualization of the human psyche—id, ego, and superego—is known as the *structural model.* (For an interesting overview of Freud's theory and how it was lost in the translation to American English, see Bettelheim, 1983.)

According to classical Freudian theory, originally the human psyche consists of the **id** ("it") which is the source of all biological drives. The drives of the id are primitive, demanding immediate and complete satisfaction, and its thought processes are irrational and magical. At about 6 months of life, the **ego** ("me") arises from the id's need to balance gratification with reality. Unlike the id, the ego is endowed with *ego functions,* such as perception, memory, and reasoning, which enable it to learn realistic means of satisfying the id. The ego also is the source of the **defense mechanisms** that help a child tolerate intense emotions and cope with anxiety, in part by keeping unacceptable thoughts and feelings out of consciousness.

The third structure, the **superego** ("over-me"), comes into its own at about 5 years of age. Also a part of the unconscious, the superego contains the moral standards that the preschooler takes over from his or her parents and that becomes an internalized judge of right and wrong behavior. When the child misbehaves, the superego punishes the child with guilt feelings. The superego can be absolutist and implacable, demanding strict obedience to its standards of proper behavior. From middle childhood on, then, the ego must find ways of obtaining as much id gratification as reality will allow without arousing the superego, which in its way is as irrational and demanding as the id.

In structural terms, therefore, psychopathology is a matter of *internal conflict* and imbalance between id, ego, and superego. If the id is excessively strong, the result is impulsive aggressive or sexual behavior. If the superego is excessively strong, the result is overly inhibited behavior in which the child is tortured by guilt feelings for the slightest transgression, real or imagined.

The Psychosexual Theory   Freud's **psychosexual theory** assumes that there is an inevitable progression in the parts of the body that predominate as sources of pleasure. Equally important, each progression of libido is accompanied by a psychological change in the intimate relations with the parents or primary caretakers.

During the initial **oral stage,** feeding is associated with the first emotional attachment or *object relation.* Sensitive, loving caretaking engenders a positive image both of mother and of self; caretaking marked by distress and frustration will engender an image in which love is mixed with anxiety and rage. In the **anal stage,** conflicts over autonomy and parental control of behavior are primary. If parental discipline is punitive, unloving, or coercive, the toddler may become rebellious and oppositional or anxious and overly compliant. The **phallic stage** in boys is associated with the wish to be the exclusive love object of the mother, which results in rivalry toward the father. This is referred to as the **Oedipus complex.** Resolution of the Oedipus complex requires that the child relinquish this infantile wish for exclusive love and, through identifying with the same-sex parent, content himself with the idea that "I am not your rival; I am like you." (Freud's explanation of female development was never satisfactory, even to himself; see Chodorow, 1989.) The **latency stage** offers a period of relative calm in which attention is turned to mastery of developmental accomplishments other

than sexuality. In the **genital stage** of adulthood, mature sexuality entails a mutuality and appreciation of the partner's point of view that is counter to the egocentricism of the early stages.

Although much of the content of Freud's assumptions about psychosexuality is not now generally accepted, the theory has contributed valuable ideas to the developmental processes by which psychopathology might come about. **Fixations** in development lay the groundwork for psychological disturbances either because they hamper further development or because they increase the possibility that, under stress, the child will return to the fixated, less mature stage. This latter process is called **regression.** Excessive fixations can result either from inadequate gratification, such as inadequate love during the oral period, or excessive gratification, such as an overly involved parent during the Oedipal phase. The stage at which fixation occurs determines both the severity and the kind of psychopathology. In general, the earlier the fixation, the more severe the psychopathology, so a child who is either fixated at or regresses to the oral stage is more disturbed than one who is fixated at or regresses to the anal stage.

Ego Psychology

Ego psychology made a major revision in the classical theory by arguing that the ego initially is endowed with its own energy and can function autonomously rather than being subservient to the id. The emphasis of ego psychologists such as Erikson (1950) is the reality-oriented, adaptive functions of the psyche. In addition, Erikson enlarges the interpersonal context of development from the nuclear family to the larger society.

Briefly, Erikson's developmental model focuses on stages of *psychosocial* development, which closely parallel Freud's stages of psychosexual development. Each of these stages represents a crisis, the resolution of which sets the individual on a particular developmental trajectory.

During the 1st year of life, the quality of the caregiving environment contributes to the child's sense that the world is either a safe and loving place or a disappointing and dangerous one. This is the crisis of *trust versus mistrust.* In the 2nd year, conflicts with caregivers over such emotionally charged issues as toilet training can lead children to develop a sense of either self-pride or self-doubt; this is the crisis of *autonomy versus shame.* In the 4th to 5th year, the way in which the Oedipus complex is resolved can contribute to children's comfort with their own impulses or else the sense that they are fundamentally "bad" for having such desires. This is the crisis of *initiative versus guilt.* At age 6, children begin to confront the tasks of school and socialization with peers, contributing to a sense of either competence or inadequacy; this is the crisis of *industry versus inferiority.* The last stage of Erikson's we will describe is associated with adolescence, in which the tasks are to form a clear sense of identity and a purpose in life. This is the crisis of *ego identity versus role confusion.*

Erikson's framework enhances our understanding of psychodynamic development by laying out a clear progression of stages and the tasks that must be accomplished for the child to proceed through them apace, as well as by pointing out the social context in which child development takes place. We will refer to his work particularly when we consider the developmental challenges associated with adolescence.

Object Relations Theory

A "third revolution" in psychoanalytic thinking is represented by **object relations** theory. Object relations actually refers to a diverse collection of psychoanalytic perspectives that share an emphasis on the importance of affectionate *attachments* in human development. In contrast to Freud, who posited that infants attached to their parents initially because their parents gratify their drives, for object relations theorists it is relatedness—in essence, love—that is the primary motivator of human behavior. The label "object relations" refers to the relationships with people—the objects of our affections—that determine what kind of individuals we become. (For more detail, see Blanck and Blanck, 1986.)

A major figure in this tradition is Bowlby (1988) whose theory of attachment has had a powerful influence on the conceptualization of normal and deviant development and has generated considerable

research. We will refer to his work in subsequent discussions, and we will describe the development of attachment in more detail in Chapters 2 and 6.

A second important figure is Margaret Mahler, whose theory provides a bedrock for object relations theory (Mahler, Pine, & Bergman, 1975). Over the course of the first 3 years of life, Mahler proposes, the "psychological birth" of the child takes place through a series of stages called the **separation-individuation** process.

Initially, at birth, the infant does not distinguish between the self and other (*normal autism*). During the first 2 months of life, however, there is a dawning recognition that there is a caregiver who responds to the infant's needs. Initially, the infant perceives the self and caregiver as two parts of one organism (*symbiotic phase*). Inevitably, however, there are moments when caregiver and child are not in perfect synchrony. By about 4 months of age, such experiences—of delay, frustration, mismatched goals—help the child to recognize that the caregiver is a separate person with her or his own feelings and intentions (*differentiation phase*). At about 8 months of age, the infant begins crawling and is able to move under his or her own steam. The infant explores in ever-widening circles around the caregiver, returning to this "safe base" at regular intervals in order to "emotionally refuel," actively experimenting with separation versus closeness (*practicing phase*). As toddlers advance to the 2nd year of life, the beginnings of symbolic thought provide them with a growing awareness of the vulnerability associated with being separate (e.g., "If I wander too far, I might get lost"). At the same time, the child craves independence, and the parent-child relationship is marked by ambivalence as the infant alternates between clinging to the caregiver and pushing her away (*rapprochement phase*). It is as though the child experiences the caregiver as two separate beings—the "good" mother who is loving and kind and the "bad" mother who is frustrating and disappointing.

The final stage in the separation-individuation process is ushered in by the achievement of emotional **object constancy:** the ability to integrate both positive and negative feelings into a single representation. Thus, it is possible to be angry with the mother and yet still love her, to be disappointed with oneself and yet still believe one is a worthwhile human being. Like Piaget's concept of object permanence, object constancy depends on the *cognitive* capacity to recognize that an object out of sight still exists. However, object constancy requires the recognition that an *emotion* we are not currently experiencing—for example, affection for someone who has just enraged us—still exists. In summary, object constancy allows us to experience ourselves and others as fully fleshed, whole persons, complete with both good and bad qualities.

Central to object relations theory is that the child's sense of self develops in the context of the relationship with the caregiver. The quality of that relationship communicates important messages about the child's own worth and the trustworthiness of others. Thus, through his or her experiences with the caregiver, the child comes to develop an *internal representation* of the relationship. Children who experience warm and sensitive care internalize an image of the loving parent—the "good object"—and of themselves as lovable. In contrast, children who experience poor parenting internalize an image of their caregiver as angry and rejecting—the "bad object"—and perceive themselves as unworthy and incapable of inspiring love.

A criticism of Mahler's work, as indeed of most psychoanalytic theory, is that it is based on clinical observation and speculation rather than objective data. Most recent work on self-development in infancy suggests that revision of this formulation may be in order. For example, evidence suggests that normal infants do not lack a sense of separation between self and other. Rather, from the very beginning of life, infants demonstrate emergent capacities for self-organization and for engaging in the complex choreography of interpersonal relationships (Stern, 1985). While Mahler's theory may not be an accurate depiction of *normal* infant development, it may be a useful way of describing the origins of some forms of *psychopathology* (Greenspan, 2003).

In conclusion, the psychoanalytic models are among the most developmentally oriented of all the theories of psychopathology. Among the most significant contributions they make to our understanding

of normal and pathological development is the uncovering of *unconscious* representations and motives that underlie human behavior, a supposition that modern research supports (Fonagy & Target, 2000). The concept of ego *defense mechanisms* is another important contribution that psychoanalytic theory makes to our understanding of development. The nature of the defenses used to ward off anxiety—whether primitive or sophisticated, rigid or flexible, brittle or robust—gives us important clues about the person's emotional maturity and level of functioning.

However, among the weaknesses of psychodynamic concepts is a tendency to narrowly focus on the first 5 years of life, without attention to later developmental stages. Psychoanalysis is also mentalistic, inferential, exceedingly complex, and riddled with inconsistencies; and its assumptions are difficult to test with the tightly controlled research that behaviorists believe is essential to a scientific psychology (Fonagy, Target, Steele, & Gerber, 1995). But to conclude that psychodynamic concepts cannot be tested empirically is unjustified. Psychoanalytic theory has generated more research than any other personality theory, and empirical support has been found for some of its key assumptions (Fonagy & Target, 2000; Greenberg & Fisher, 1996; Westen, 1998). Modern psychoanalytic theory, integrated with the cognitive perspective, also has inspired a new generation of clinical child psychology researchers (Fonagy, Gergely, Jurist, & Target, 2003).

The Family Systemic Model

The last major theoretical orientation we describe is the family systemic perspective (see Fiese, Wilder, & Bickham, 2000). While many other theories acknowledge the importance of family relationships, what sets the systemic model apart is that it views the entire family as the unit of analysis. The family is conceptualized as a *system,* a dynamic whole that is greater than the sum of its parts. Systems have certain characteristics. For example, they are coherent and stable, and they have a self-righting tendency, termed *homeostasis,* that allows them to maintain their structure even in the face of change. Like psychoanalytic theory, the systemic perspective is composed of many different schools of thought, but in this case the core idea that unites them is that individual personality is a function of the family system. We will concentrate on the work of Salvador Minuchin and colleagues (Minuchin, 1974; Minuchin & Nichols, 1998), whose perspective is called *structural family theory.*

According to Minuchin, one of the ways in which being part of a family helps us to develop is by allowing us to participate in a number of different relationships simultaneously. Within the larger family system, there are naturally occurring *subsystems* that join some family members and differentiate them from others. For instance, the parents form a *marital* subsystem, which is based on the complementary roles that husbands and wives fulfill: to be a romantic couple, to raise their children, and to play a leadership role in the family. *Parent-child* relationships comprise another subsystem, based on the nonreciprocal needs and responsibilities that parents and children fulfill for one another; for example, while children turn to their parents for comforting and advice, and parents expect their authority to be respected, the reverse usually is not the case. *Siblings* form yet another subsystem, based on their shared status as the children in the family. Yet siblings, too, are differentiated from one another; for example, special privileges might be granted to the eldest child and extra latitude to the youngest. Thus, through the various roles they play, family members simultaneously experience feelings of belonging and feelings of independence from others.

What allows these subsystems to function well are the **boundaries** that separate them. Clear boundaries differentiate the subsystems from one another, define the roles of individuals, and allow family members opportunities to meet their appropriate developmental needs. Clear boundaries are also permeable and adaptable; that is, they allow both emotional contact and independence, and change as the needs of family members change over development. For example, the parent-child relationship should become more reciprocal and egalitarian as children enter young adulthood.

Failure to maintain appropriate boundaries can cause families to become confused and dysfunctional.

For example, overly *rigid* boundaries foster separation between family members or maintain strict role differentiation among them: "Father knows best"; "Children should be seen and not heard." While rigid boundaries can foster a sense of independence and self-sufficiency, they can also make it difficult for family members to reach across barriers to communicate their feelings or obtain emotional support. Individuals may feel lonely and unsupported in rigidly structured families and may lack a sense of belonging.

At the other extreme, absent or unclear boundaries result in **enmeshment.** Family members who are enmeshed do not differentiate between one another, even between parent and child. Mutuality and togetherness are emphasized at the expense of individuality and separateness. While family members may enjoy the feelings of belonging and sharing that ensue, extreme enmeshment may interfere with individuals' freedom to have their own autonomous thoughts and wishes. An attempt by a family member to individuate may be perceived as a threat to the harmony of the family system and thus may arouse anxiety or resistance. For example, the youth in an enmeshed family who expresses a desire to go away for college may precipitate a family crisis.

In Minuchin's view of family structure, the heart of the family is the *marital subsystem.* The kind of intimacy, emotional support, and mutuality that characterize a healthy couple's relationship is unique; for example, the emotional needs that an adult romantic partner fulfills are different from those fulfilled by parent-child and sibling relationships. Therefore, Minuchin especially emphasizes a need for clear boundaries around the marital dyad. When this boundary is violated, children become involved in their parents' marital relationship in inappropriate ways, and psychopathology may develop. Minuchin describes the different problematic family systems as *rigid triangles,* which may take one of three general forms, described next (Kerig, 1995).

First, a **parent-child coalition** arises when one parent involves the child in an alliance that excludes the other parent. Such a relationship occurs when a parent encourages the child to behave disrespectfully to the other parent, or it may take the form of an overly intimate and enmeshed relationship between one parent and the child. This family dynamic may create a *parentalized child* who is burdened by the assumption of such developmentally inappropriate tasks as offering emotional support and acting as an intimate confidante to a parent. Minuchin gives the example of a family in which the unhappily married mother becomes depressed. The oldest daughter takes over preparing meals and caring for her younger siblings, covering for the mother so the father won't know the extent of her dysfunction. A number of negative consequences follow from this scenario. Because the daughter has taken on responsibilities beyond her years, she begins to feel stressed and overwhelmed. In addition, because the younger siblings do not have direct access to their mother and cannot receive the care and attention they need from her, they begin to misbehave. Further, because the parents aren't communicating directly with each other, they cannot resolve their marital problems. In sum, while the intentions of the parentalized child are good and her self-sacrifice might help the family to cope in the short term, in the long term the family is an increasingly distressed and unhappy one.

In the second type of rigid triangle, called **triangulation,** the child is caught in the middle of the parents. In this case the child attempts to maintain a coalition with each parent, either to be a peacemaker or go-between or in response to pressure from parents to side with one or the other. Minuchin describes this as the most stressful family dynamic for the child, whose attempts to be close to either parent may be interpreted as disloyalty by the other. This family form may be particularly evident during conflictual divorces, such as in the tug of war over child custody (Buchanan, Maccoby, & Dornbusch, 1991).

The third kind of triangle, **detouring,** is the most subtle of the triangular family forms because there may be no apparent conflict between the parents. Instead, they may insist that their marriage is perfect and that the only problem in the family is their child's disobedience or delicate nature. As Minuchin got to know this kind of family better, however, he noticed that the parents never spent any time together as a couple but rather devoted all their time and energy to caring for their child. Then he began

to observe covert ways in which the parents supported and encouraged their child's problems. Further, the only time the parents acted conjointly was when they were responding to their child's "special needs." It became apparent to Minuchin that in such cases having a troubled child was meeting some need for the parents.

Minuchin concludes that some unhappily married couples attempt to avoid acknowledging their marital problems because they do not know how to resolve them; instead, they try to deflect attention from them or detour around them. Having a troubled child, therefore, serves a function in the family by providing the parents with a problem external to their relationship on which to focus their attention. Because they are united when attempting to respond to their "problem child," detouring allows the couple to maintain an illusion of harmony. Further, detouring couples are motivated to covertly reinforce children's behavior problems in order to maintain the homeostasis in the family system. The detouring may take two forms: *detouring-attacking* when the child is viewed as troublesome or "bad" and *detouring-supportive* when the child is viewed as needy or delicate (Carlson, 1990). (See Figure 1.3.) The child caught in the family triangle is called the *identified patient* because he or she is the one who is overtly symptomatic.

Minuchin's perspective widens our scope of vision to include the larger context in which child development takes place. Not only is the individual psychology of the child important, as well as his or her relationship with parents, but the entire family *system* must be taken into account. Another important implication of the family systemic approach is that the location of psychopathology is not in the child, or even in the parents, but in the *relationship between them.* Lastly, the systemic perspective reminds us to take a *functional* approach to interpreting problem behavior. An aggressive, acting-out child may appear to be disturbed. However, another possibility is that the child's misbehavior serves a function in the family system, perhaps representing an attempt to meet appropriate developmental needs in a pathological environment. Thus, the family systems perspective fits well with our definition of psychopathology as normal development gone awry.

Figure 1.3   Pathological Triangles.

A set of three lines indicates an enmeshed relationship; a broken line indicates a conflictual relationship.

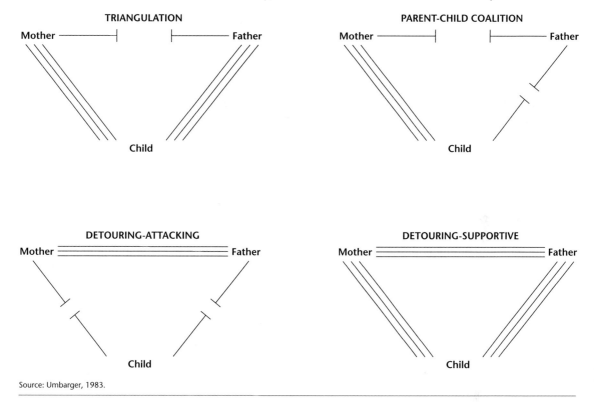

Source: Umbarger, 1983.

Comparing and Integrating Models

There are many points of *divergence* among the models we have presented. (See Table 1.1.) Freud was primarily concerned with drives, the unconscious, and mental events, while ego psychologists concentrate on psychosocial adaptation and object relations theorists emphasize the primacy of interpersonal relations. Traditionally, behaviorists wanted to banish the intrapersonal context with all of its mentalistic baggage, substituting an environmentally oriented objective psychology. Cognitive psychologists reintroduce mental terms such as schemata in order to understand how children interpret their experiences with the environment.

There are also some points of *convergence*. For example, even such apparently opposing models as object relations and family systems theories agree that

relationships are central to personality development. Further, each of these models has undergone its own developmental process, which in many cases has led to an expansion of common ground shared with other theories. The medical model no longer couches issues dichotomously as, for example, heredity versus environment. Instead, there is a recognition that organisms develop in an environmental context that interacts with and affects organic variables. The psychoanalytic model has shifted from emphasizing the intrapersonal to appreciating the interpersonal context, while the behavioral model has changed in the opposite direction. With the increasing overlap and convergence among the different models of psychopathology, the possibility of—and need for—a unified model emerges. Developmental psychopathology represents the beginning steps toward creating such an integrative model.

Table 1.1

Comparing and Integrating Models of Development

	What Develops?	What Are the Processes of Development?	What Is Psychopathology?	How Does Psychopathology Develop?
Medical Model	Biology	Maturation	Mental illness	Organic dysfunction
Social Learning	Behavior	Rewards, punishment, imitation of models	Inappropriate behavior	Reinforcement or modeling of maladaptive behavior
Cognitive Developmental	Schemata	Assimilation, accommodation	Imbalance between assimilation-accommodation	Overstimulation or understimulation
Classical Psychoanalysis	Ego/superego, psychosexuality	Clashes between drives and reality, transfer of libido	Fixation or regression	Conflicts among parts of psyche
Ego Psychology	Ego strengths	Interactions with social world	Inability to resolve stage-related issues	Failures at mastery experiences
Object Relations	Self-other relationships	Separation-individuation	Failure to progress in development	Affective splitting, internalization of bad relationships
Family Systems	Adaptivity	Belonging and separateness	Inappropriate family structure	Boundary dissolution, triangulation
Developmental Psychopathology	The whole child	Hierarchization, organization, integration, adaptation	Development gone awry	Risks, vulnerabilities; potentiating, transactional, and protective processes

Developmental Psychopathology

Developmental psychopathology is not a theory in and of itself; rather, it is an approach to understanding how psychopathology emerges over the life span. (Our review follows Cicchetti and Cohen, 1995, except where noted. The classic paper that launched the field, still well worth reading, is Sroufe and Rutter, 1984.) Developmental psychopathology is an *integrative* approach that incorporates different theoretical perspectives under one umbrella to produce an understanding of the development of the whole person (Achenbach, 1990). (See Figure 1.4.) Instead of focusing only on behavior, cognition, uncon-

scious processes, and so forth, the developmental psychopathologist pays attention to each of these variables in order to understand how they contribute to the formation of psychopathology—or of emotional health. Although a number of definitions of developmental psychopathology have been offered, they often overlook the latter point, that both adaptive and maladaptive development are relevant to the field. Therefore, we offer the following as a concise definition:

> Developmental psychopathology is the study of developmental processes that contribute to, or protect against, psychopathology.

Now we turn to the specific principles that define the developmental psychopathology approach.

Figure 1.4   The "Umbrella" of Developmental Psychopathology.

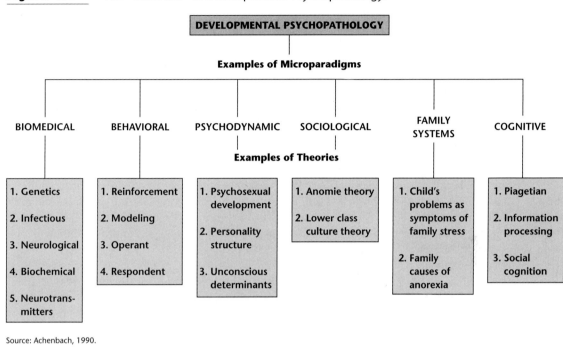

Source: Achenbach, 1990.

The Organizational Perspective

Although developmental psychopathology does not follow any unitary theoretical model, it is guided by an *organizational perspective.* First, the organizational perspective views the human organism in a *holistic* way, as an integrated and dynamic system in which all domains of development—the cognitive, social, emotional, and biological—are in continual interaction with one another. Second, development itself is considered to be *hierarchical;* psychological growth is a process of increasing complexity and organization, such that new structures emerge out of those that have come before.

The key to understanding development in this perspective is to attend to the tasks at each stage of development—termed *stage-salient issues*—that must be confronted and mastered. Whether these issues are resolved in adaptive or maladaptive ways influences future adaptation. Erikson's ego theory provides a good example of this construct; for example,

whether the infant resolves the first developmental crisis by forming an attitude of trust or mistrust toward the world will influence his or her capacity to satisfactorily resolve the salient issues of the next stage.

The implication of the organizational perspective is that stage-salient issues affect the individual in such a way that their effects are carried forward into the next stage of development. Thus, previous areas of vulnerability or strength may influence the way in which individuals handle stress and crisis and may shape the way in which they adapt to future life challenges. However, the consequences of previous stage-salient resolutions are *probabilistic* rather than *deterministic.* In other words, while previous development might have a shaping or constraining effect on subsequent development, such that it tends to increase or decrease the likelihood of psychopathology, such an effect is not predetermined. Many individual, social, or environmental factors might intervene in order to change the course of development. What happened before does not doom us, and what is to come is not written in stone. A nice illustration of this is provided by Bowlby (1988), who argues that, while the quality of attachment between an infant and caregiver has an important influence on child development, it is not an immutable one. A secure attachment may set the child on the pathway to healthy development, but other stresses and traumas might intervene that deflect that child from that course. In turn, and on a hopeful note, the child with a disrupted attachment who gets a poor start in life still has many opportunities to be nudged back toward a healthy pathway, such as by forming a relationship with a caring teacher. Pathways might be particularly amenable to change during key turning points of development, when young people are striving to understand and make choices about their place in the world.

The Continuum Between Normal and Abnormal Development

Another important characteristic of developmental psychopathology is that it assumes that there is a *continuum* between normal and abnormal development. Underlying every life course—whether it is a healthy or maladaptive one—are the same fundamental developmental principles. Therefore, it is important to have a clear conceptualization of adaptive development in order to understand how development might go awry (Sroufe, 1997). The challenge is to understand *why* development takes one path rather than the other. Further, as we will see in Chapter 2, it is *normal* to have some problems in the course of development. In sum, unlike the medical model, developmental psychopathology views psychological problems not as disease processes resident within the individual, but as significant deviations from a healthy developmental course.

Risk, Vulnerability, Potentiation, and Protection

Risk Factors and Risk Mechanisms

A **risk** is any condition or circumstance that increases the likelihood that psychopathology will develop. (Kazdin, Kraemer, Kessler, Kupfer, and Offord, 1997, summarize the literature on risk factors.) There is no comprehensive agreed-on list of risk factors and they span all contexts. (See Table 1.2.) In the biological context risk may involve birth defects, neurological damage, inadequate nutrition, or a parent who has a disorder with a known genetic component. In the individual context risk may be in the form of low intelligence, low self-efficacy, or poor self-control. In the family context risk may take the form of parental neglect, and in the interpersonal context antisocial peers may present a risk. In the cultural context risk may arise from poverty. While single risks have limited predictive power, multiple risks have a cumulative effect; for example, children with two alcoholic parents are more than twice as likely to develop problems as are children with one alcoholic parent.

However, the developmental psychopathology framework goes beyond viewing risks as static causal agents. Simple cause-and-effect relationships (e.g., physical abuse causes depression) do not capture the complex nature of child development. (Consider the lampooning of this simplistic perspective in Mel Brooks's film *High Anxiety,* in which the protagonist's neurosis was cured instantly when he recalled falling from a high chair in infancy.) Instead, the developmental psychopathologist asks, If poverty or intelligence or parental neglect affect development, *how* do they do so? To answer this question, we must look beneath these one-dimensional variables to uncover the *mechanisms* by which these risks exert their negative effects. In Chapter 2, we will detail a number of potential **risk mechanisms** that underlie psychopathology, including insecure attachments, dysregulated emotions, and distorted schemas.

Vulnerabilites and Potentiating Factors

While a risk is a factor that would be expected to negatively affect any child exposed to it, a **vulnerability** increases the likelihood that a *particular* child will succumb to risk. Thus, while risk directly causes disturbance, then, a vulnerability intensifies the child's response to risk. For example, while frequent family moves are significant events in a child's life, not all children will be stressed by

Table 1.2

Examples of Risks, Vulnerabilities, Protective Factors, and Protective Mechanisms

Context	Risks	Vulnerabilities/ Potentiating Factors	Protective Factors	Protective Mechanisms (Across All Contexts)
Biological	Genetic disorders Prenatal influences Neurological damage Inadequate nutrition	Difficult temperament	Easy temperament	
Individual	Low intelligence Low self-esteem Low self-control	Gender Poor planning ability Sociability	Intelligence Competence Physical attractiveness Engaging personality	Reduction of risk impact Reduction of negative chain reactions Self-efficacy and coping skills Opening of opportunities
Family	Insecure attachment Interparental conflict Abuse Neglect Domestic violence Boundary dissolution	Poor parent-child relationships Lack of affectionate care	Positive, stable care Competent adult role models Parental supervision Parental valuing of child attributes	
Social	Antisocial friends	Poor social skills	Positive peer relationships Adult mentors	
Cultural	Poverty Racism Prejudice Community violence	Personal characteristics that clash with societal ideals/expectations	Positive cultural values Positive ethnic identity Cultural tolerance for diversity	

Sources: Masten et al., 1998; Masten and Curtis, 2000; Robins, 1972; Rosenblith and Sims-Knight, 1992; Rutter, 1990, 2000.

them—it is the child with an anxious temperament who is most likely to be negatively affected by disruptions in the home. A helpful way to distinguish between risks and vulnerabilities is in terms of the statistical concepts of main effects versus interactions (Zimmerman & Arunkumar, 1994). A risk factor is associated with an increased likelihood of psychopathology for *all* children exposed to it; thus, it emerges as a main effect in statistical analyses. (See Figure 1.5.) A vulnerability, in contrast, increases the likelihood of psychopathology *particularly* for those children who are susceptible to it; thus, it emerges as an interaction effect.

Rutter (1990) identifies a number of vulnerability factors. Gender is one; for example, while both boys and girls are adversely affected by family stress, boys react with a higher rate of behavior problems than girls. Temperament is another vulnerability factor; children who are difficult to care for are more often targets of parental irritability, criticism, and hostility than are easily managed children

and, in turn, are more vulnerable to subsequent disturbance. Rutter's list also includes the absence of a good relationship with parents, poor planning ability, a lack of positive school experiences, lack of affectionate care, and poor social skills. Further, at the sociocultural level, children whose personal characteristics do not match societal expectations—such as the shy child in a culture that values boldness—may be more vulnerable to risk.

In a similar vein, a **potentiating factor** is one that exacerbates the impact of a risk. For example, exposure to community violence and being a latchkey kid are both potential risks for the development of child behavior problems. However, the child most likely to be negatively affected is the one living in a neighborhood without a strong sense of community who has no friendly or caring neighbors to go to when the sound of gunshots rings out while she is alone during the day after school. Thus, social isolation may potentiate the effects of other environmental stressors.

Figure 1.5   Risk Factors and Vulnerabilities.

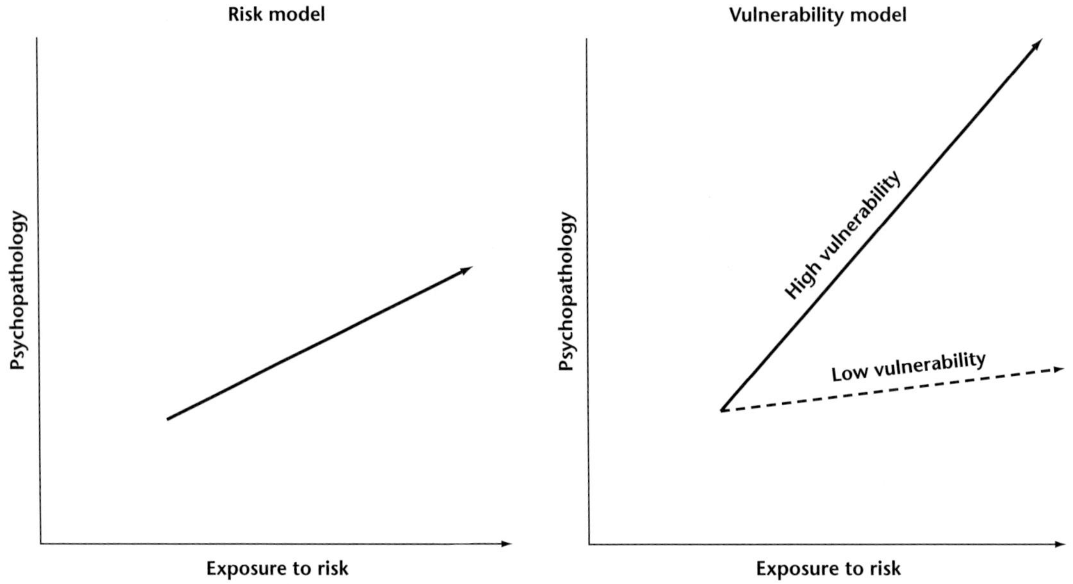

Risk model

Psychopathology

Exposure to risk

Vulnerability model

Psychopathology

High vulnerability

Low vulnerability

Exposure to risk

Protective Factors and Resilience

Since not all children who are at risk become disturbed, the challenge for researchers is to discover the factors that promote or maintain healthy development. These are called **protective factors,** and the children who make a good adjustment in spite of being at high risk are called **resilient.** Protective factors within children might include intelligence, an easygoing disposition, and the presence of competencies valued by themselves or society, whether they be academic, athletic, artistic, or mechanical. Protective factors in the family might include the presence of a loving, dependable parent; a parenting style characterized by a combination of warmth and structure; socioeconomic advantage; and social support from an extended family network. Peers can have a protective influence through providing emotional support and encouragement for prosocial behavior. Protective factors in the cultural context might include involvement with prosocial institutions, such as the church or school (Masten & Coatsworth, 1998).

For example, an in-depth study of resilience was conducted on the Hawaiian island of Kauai. Werner

and Smith (1992) evaluated 505 individuals in infancy, early and middle childhood, late adolescence, and early adulthood. True to the developmental psychopathology model, they conceptualized resilience as the balance between risk and protective factors. Risk factors included poverty, perinatal stress, and parental psychopathology or discord. Most of the low-risk participants became competent, confident, caring adults, while two-thirds of the high-risk participants had delinquency records or mental health or severe marital problems or were divorced. The authors were particularly interested in the remaining third of the high-risk group who became competent, confident, caring adults.

The authors were able to isolate three clusters of *protective factors:* (1) at least average *intelligence* and *personal attributes* that elicited positive responses from family members and other adults, such as robustness, vigor, and a sociable temperament; (2) *affectionate ties* with parent substitutes such as grandparents or older siblings, which encouraged trust, autonomy, and initiative; and (3) an external *support system* in church, youth groups, or school, which rewarded competence.

Protective Mechanisms

Rutter (1990) proposes that we go beyond listing protective factors to attempt to understand what *accounts* for the protective power of such variables; for example, what is it about intelligence or socioeconomic advantage that protects against psychopathology? The term he uses for these processes is **protective mechanisms,** and he has identified four of them on the basis of theory, observations, and empirical research.

The first mechanism, *reduction of risk impact,* means that some variables act to buffer a child from exposure to risk. For example, negative peer influences are powerful risk factors for children growing up in gang-ridden neighborhoods. However, parents who monitor their children's peer group activities and who guide them in their choice of play and friendships can reduce the likelihood of delinquency.

The next mechanism is *reduction of negative chain reactions.* Protective factors may provide their effects through their influences on relationships. For example, a temperamentally easy child is less likely to be the target of his stressed parent's anger; consequently, the child is less likely to develop behavior problems, thereby de-escalating the parent's stress and lessening the anger. Thus, a vicious cycle of negative reaction from parent to child is averted.

Next, factors that *promote self-esteem and self-efficacy* help children feel they can cope successfully with life's problems. These qualities are enhanced by secure and supportive personal relationships and by task accomplishments, such as school achievement, that foster self-confidence.

The fourth protective mechanism is *opening of opportunities.* Development involves many turning points that offer a chance to reduce the impact of risk factors, and the resilient child is the one who takes advantage of these opportunities. Thus, adolescents who choose to stay in school allow themselves more opportunities for growth and achievement than dropouts do, and those who pursue their unique artistic talents or interests have more opportunities for personal fulfillment than do those who deny their talents and follow the crowd.

Table 1.2 provided examples of risks, vulnerabilities, protective factors, and protective mechanisms derived from the literature. However, it is important to keep in mind that no variable *inherently* falls into one category or another. A particular variable can be construed in different ways, depending on how its effects unfold. For example, while poverty acts as a general risk factor for many forms of psychopathology, it may also play the role of a vulnerability factor by increasing the likelihood that a child will react negatively to a stressor: Children whose families have few economic resources may be the most negatively impacted by certain stressful life events, such as a house fire in which all their possessions are lost.

Research in resilience is hopeful and inspiring. However, Luthar (1993) urges a cautionary note. While earlier work referred to resilient children as *invulnerable,* this term implies an imperviousness to harm that does not characterize them accurately. For example, Luthar observed subtle ways in which resilient children in her study still carried a legacy of their adverse upbringing. While resilient individuals were less likely to behave in ways that labeled them as troublesome to others, they still showed signs of being inwardly troubled; for example, 85 percent had significant symptoms in the areas of anxiety and depression. By the same token, many resilient adults in Werner and Smith's (1992) sample had stress-related health problems such as migraines and backaches, as well as feelings of dissatisfaction with their lives. In many cases they reported feeling burdened by the expectation that they care for their nonresilient parents and siblings. Thus, even resilient children are not armor plated and their good social functioning may come at some personal cost (Cicchetti & Garmezy, 1993; Luthar, Cicchetti, & Becker, 2000).

Developmental Pathways

The emergence of psychopathology over the life course is conceptualized in terms of **developmental pathways,** or trajectories. The initial question in constructing a pathway is this: At what point in time and for what reasons does development begin to be diverted from its normal course? Not all at-risk children become disturbed; therefore, both the factors that make children more vulnerable to risk *and* the factors that protect them from risk must be uncovered. In those cases in which protective factors are outweighed by risk and vulnerability, the question becomes, How do the latter two factors work their mischief over time in order to produce a full-blown psychopathology?

Finally, since children grow out of disturbances as well as growing into them, charting developmental pathways involves understanding the factors leading to extinction as well as those leading to persistence of psychopathology; this is the question of *continuity versus discontinuity.* The final challenge is to explain the data in terms of developmental principles and to understand the mechanisms and processes responsible for propelling the child from one step to the next along the path to a particular disorder (Sroufe, 1997). In addition, sometimes pathways cross to produce **comorbidity,** or the co-occurrence of two psychopathologies. In the past, clinicians tended to focus on a single disturbance and researchers tried to study "pure" cases, regarding the existence of other psychopathologies as potential confounds. However, it has become increasingly clear that certain disturbances, such as anxiety and depression or conduct disorders and hyperactivity, frequently occur together.

The implications of developmental pathways for prevention and intervention are significant. The more we learn about the earliest risk factors, the better able we will be to design effective preventive programs. And at least for those psychopathologies showing a progression in seriousness of disturbance, earlier intervention is likely to result in more effective treatment. In our subsequent examinations of specific psychopathologies in the chapters ahead, we will chart developmental pathways and give more detailed accounts of the examples cited above.

Although the terms are not used consistently in the literature, we will reserve *developmental pathways* to refer to research that charts the journey children travel to a disorder; for example, how does a child come to be depressed? In contrast, the term *developmental course* will be used in reference to the progression of the disorder once it has developed; for example, what does the future hold for the child who is depressed? Developmental course is also referred to as *prognosis;* however, *prognosis* is a term derived from the medical model that implies that disorder is a fixed and static state. Because the developmental psychopathology literature suggests that there is much variability and diversity of outcome, we have chosen developmental course as a preferable term.

Equifinality and Multifinality

Equifinality refers to the idea that a number of different pathways may lead to the same outcome (Cicchetti & Rogosch, 1996). For example, a variety of factors may lead to the development of depression, including genetics, environmental stress, and cognitive style. In contrast, **multifinality** states that a particular risk may have different developmental implications, depending on such contextual and individual factors as the child's environment and his or her particular competencies and capacities. For example, loss of a parent may result in depression in a child whose previous relationships with caregivers have been marked by insecurity, but it may result in conduct disorder in a child who faces additional environmental stress such as exposure to community violence.

Multideterminism

Following from the notions of equifinality and multifinality, developmental psychopathology proposes that the etiology of any psychopathology is *multidetermined.* The search for a single cause—as in "juvenile delinquency results from neglectful parents"—is simplistic and erroneous. Rather, psychopathologies have multiple causes.

Continuity and Discontinuity

As we follow children along their unique developmental journeys, we find that, while some stay on a disordered course (continuity), others are deflected onto more healthy pathways (discontinuity).

Continuity in psychopathology has been found in studies following individuals from early childhood through adolescence (Costello, Angold, & Keeler, 1999; Costello, Mustillo, Erkanis, Keeler, & Angold, et al., 2003). The evidence is particularly strong in the case of aggressive behavior. For example,

Fergusson, Lynskey, and Horwood (1996) followed a large sample of New Zealand children from age 3 through adolescence. Children with early disruptive behavior were 16 times more likely to develop later conduct problems than other children, while only 12 percent showed a discontinuous history.

Discontinuity can occur in a number of ways. The first of these is as a function of *development* itself. Problem behavior in the toddler and preschool period tends not to be a good predictor of subsequent disturbances. Such unpredictability is congruent with the fluidity of early development. Around 6 or 7 years of age predictability increases, with children who have many symptoms at one age tending to have many symptoms later as well.

Sometimes the behavior associated with a disturbance changes with age, a phenomenon termed **developmental transformation** (Sroufe, 1990). This means that there is continuity in the underlying disorder while its behavioral manifestations change over time. For example, insecure attachment is evidenced by precocious independence from the mother in infancy but excessive dependence on the teacher in preschool (Carlson & Sroufe, 1995). The underlying insecurity is consistent but is expressed differently at different ages.

Complex *patterns* of continuity and discontinuity also may be found when samples are studied more closely. For example, McGee and colleagues (1992) report other findings from the New Zealand longitudinal sample. They found that girls who demonstrated anxiety or depression at age 11 were 6.2 times more likely to have anxiety or depression at age 15 than were girls without such problems earlier. In contrast, boys who demonstrated anxiety or depression at age 11 were 5.8 times as likely to have conduct problems at age 15. The authors speculate that *mediating factors* associated with gender—peer pressures, societal expectations, the quality of parent-child relationships—may cause these different developmental trajectories to come about. Evidence for other mediating factors comes from Fergusson and colleagues' (Fergusson & Lynskey, 1996; Fergusson, Lynskey, & Horwood, 1996) studies that showed that children whose early behavior problems remitted had fewer of the risk factors—

including economic disadvantage, family conflict, learning problems, and low self-esteem—that predicted continuity in other children.

Discontinuity and continuity may co-occur in other ways. For example, while there may be discontinuity in the particular diagnosis given the child, continuity is seen in the tendency toward psychopathology in general. Further data from the New Zealand study illustrate this point (McGee, Feehan, Williams, & Anderson, 1992). For example, only 10 percent of children who were diagnosed with attention problems were given the same diagnosis in adolescence. However, only 25 percent of these children were problem-free in adolescence, as compared to 75 percent of their peers. Thus, while there may be discontinuity in a *specific* disorder, continuity may be expressed in terms of an underlying vulnerability to psychopathology.

Discontinuity in Well-Functioning Children

If disturbed children can "outgrow" their psychopathology, can normal children "grow into" disturbances as adults? The idea that certain well-functioning children are at risk for becoming disturbed is a perplexing but important one. Just what are the telltale signs indicating that all is not as well as it appears to be? Some insight into this kind of discontinuity can be gleaned from Fergusson and colleagues' (1996) longitudinal study. Those without behavior problems in childhood who went on to develop later conduct disorder were more likely to associate with delinquent peers in adolescence. Therefore, just as with the transition from a pathological to a normative course, unexpected negative outcomes may be accounted for by *mediating factors* within and external to the child.

The Question of Specificity

As we have noted, developmental psychopathology models have become increasingly complex, recognizing the interactions amongst multiple factors in the origins of a disturbance. However, the multiplicity of factors implicated in each psychopathology creates a new problem, that of *specificity*. The specificity question refers to whether a particular risk factor is *specific* to the development of a particular disorder, as opposed to increasing the likelihood of some sort of *global* psychopathology. As we will see, certain risk factors—such as insecure attachment—may be precursors to such various forms of child psychopathology as depression, suicide, anxiety, conduct disorder, and substance abuse. Therefore, the question remains whether knowing about a given risk factor, such as a history of broken parent-child bonds, is helpful in predicting a child's specific developmental outcome beyond a rough notion of "bad input, bad output."

One of the snarls we encounter in attempting to untangle the specificity question is that most of the research devoted to identifying risk factors has focused on only one individual disorder; for example, a particular study might ask, Is insecure attachment a risk factor for childhood depression? The problem with this strategy is that it does not tell us whether that same risk factor might predict other forms of psychopathology equally as well. Thus, one researcher's discovery of a relationship between insecure attachment and depression needs to be interpreted in the light of other research demonstrating that insecure attachment is a risk factor for conduct disorder. There is a need for studies that look at multiple risk and protective factors, as well as multiple outcomes, in order to discriminate between specific and general effects. (For an example of a multifaceted design, see Asarnow, Tompson, Hamilton, Goldstein, and Guthrie, 1994.) This is rarely done, since most researchers focus on one particular disorder or predictor at a time. This strategy leaves us vulnerable to either overestimating—or underestimating—the extent to which knowledge about the past can help to predict a child's developmental outcome.

Transactions

An additional concept that helps us to understand how multideterminism in psychopathology comes about is that of transactions. A **transaction** can be defined as a series of dynamic, reciprocal interactions between the child and his or her social context. Rather than viewing etiology as a matter of simple linear cause and effect—due to organic

factors such as genetics, or family variables such as parenting style—developmental psychopathology views development as a function of a complex interplay between the child and the environment over time (Cicchetti, Toth, Bush, & Gillespie, 1988; Sameroff, 1995).

Let us look at an example. A mother gives birth to a delicate and premature son, which is a source of some anxiety. Her anxiety during the first few months of the child's life causes her to be hesitant and inconsistent in her parenting. Subsequently, the child develops some irregularities in his sleeping and eating habits, making his temperamental style a more difficult one. This difficult child taxes the mother's parenting skills even more, and she begins to withdraw from interaction with him. As he enjoys less interaction and verbal stimulation with his caregiver, the child develops language delays that affect him when he enters preschool, impacting both his academic success and social relations with peers. Thus, a complex developmental sequence can be seen, in which parent and child both influence one another's behavior (Sameroff, 1995). (See Figure 1.6.)

Three important features of transactions help to define them. The first is that the nature of the transaction *changes over time.* Any particular relationship, such as that between the parent and child, is the product of a series of exchanges during which they gradually shape one another's behavior over the course of development. Thus, the observation the clinician makes at any given moment—that the mother responds with helpless distress to her youngster's oppositionality, for example—is the product of a long history of their influence on one another. The second feature of transactions is that they are *reciprocal,* which means that development is not simply a factor of a combination of influences, some arising from the child and some arising from the environment, but rather that the child and environment influence one another, each changing as a function of the other. The third feature of transactions is that they are *dynamic.* There is a live quality to them in that something new happens in the chemistry of the relationship. In the case of

Figure 1.6  An Example of a Transactional Process.

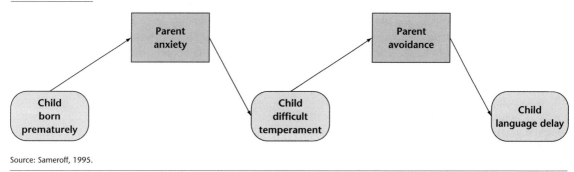

Source: Sameroff, 1995.

parent behavior, for example, Sameroff (1995) states, "In order for a genuine transaction to occur, the parents must be influenced by the infant's behavior to do something they would not have done if the child had behaved otherwise" (p. 7).

Transactional processes do not always lead to negative developmental outcomes. Consider the following clinical scenario concerning a severely depressed mother and her young child: When initially observed, this girl had a tendency to be somber and reserved, showing some signs of emerging depression as is often the case in a child of a depressed parent. However, during her early struggles to learn to dress herself, the toddler discovered that there were behaviors she could perform that could coax a smile from her mother. For example, when her mother was distressed, the child might come into the room in outlandish getups—her father's boots on her feet, her mother's panties on top of her head. The mother began to respond more warmly and positively to the child, who in turn began to increase her repertoire of "silly" yet heartwarming behaviors. The feeling that she was a successful parent helped to lift the mother's depression, while the experience of being "mother's little sunshine" brightened the child's affect. Thus, through the transactions between them, mother and daughter shaped one another's behavior in more adaptive ways. Despite all the risks associated with maternal depression, the mother and child developed a positive relationship, which decreased the mother's depression and increased the daughter's chances of staying on a healthy developmental course.

In sum, like the family systems approach, developmental psychopathology perceives psychopathology not as something a person "has" but rather as the result of a series of successive adaptations to the environment (Sroufe, 1997). Because transactions are observable and malleable, they can provide a powerful tool for intervention.

Conceptualizing Relationships Between Development and Psychopathology

Stages of Development

Piaget's cognitive theory and Erikson's ego psychology are two good examples of theories that associate psychopathology with stages of development. Typically, stage theories make two assumptions: (1) Stages represent significant *qualitative* reorganizations of behavior rather than mere *quantitative* changes or "more of the same," and (2) the sequence of stages is unalterable. Thus, something new emerges at each stage and the order of emergence is fixed. For both Piaget and Freud, the question How old is the child? is not as important as What stage is the child in?

A characteristic of stage theories is that they often regard the *transition between stages* as a time of increased tension, unrest, and even regression to less mature behaviors. Freud's psychosexual stages have this characteristic, and Piaget describes the child's return to immature ways of thinking during cognitive transitions. Stage conceptualizations stand in contrast to radical behaviorism, which claims that stability or instability is primarily the consequence of the experiences the child is having. The important idea here is that normal development may entail built-in times of stress and upset; for example, the transitions from infancy to the preschool period and from middle childhood to adolescence are two potentially stressful periods. Knowing when disturbed behavior is part of normal growth helps the clinician decide when to tell a parent, "Most children act like that and yours is likely to outgrow it."

There is another aspect of stage theories that informs our approach in this text. Our developmental framework implies that in order to evaluate the meaning and import of an event in a child's life, it is essential to know not only what happened but also at *which stage of development* it happened. A lengthy separation from the mother, for example, may have few negative effects in early infancy before an attachment to the mother has developed but may trigger a dramatic reaction after an attachment has been formed. Being hospitalized becomes progressively less upsetting for children between 2 and 12 years of age and also may have different meanings, with the younger children being distressed over separation, for example, and the 4- to 6-year-olds fearing mutilation or death or viewing hospitalization as punishment.

Earlier perspectives on development proposed that there were *critical periods* during which negative effects have pervasive and irreversible effects. For example, it was once believed that infants needed to bond with the mother within the first hours after birth or the relationship would be irrevocably damaged. However, current theories are less deterministic and foreboding. Now it is believed that there are *sensitive* periods during which particular **stage-salient issues** come to the fore and when they are both most vulnerable to disruption and most open to change (Cicchetti, 1993).

How Might Development Go Awry? Conceptualizations of Psychopathology

If psychopathology is normal development gone awry, in what ways might development be disrupted? There are several ways in which psychopathology might relate to stages of development: delay, regression, deviation, asynchrony, and precocity. There also are two nonstage-related conceptualizations of psychopathology that we will encounter in the chapters to come: developmental deviation, and adaptational failure. Next we define these terms and provide some concrete examples.

In **developmental delay** development proceeds at a pace significantly slower than normal, such as the 3-year-old who has not yet learned to talk. **Regression** involves falling off the course of normal development, such as when a formerly articulate 8-year-old suddenly begins to refuse to talk, termed selective mutism. We also might see in a regressed child a return to developmentally early forms of behavior that are no longer appropriate, such as bedwetting or temper tantrums.

Next, in **asynchrony** there are markedly uneven rates of progress among processes of development. This unevenness may result from maturational *delays* in particular developmental variables; for example, children with Asperger's disorder may be on track in the verbal realm and yet far behind their peers in social development. Alternatively, unevenness may result from emotionally painful experiences that cause *fixation* at the stage of development in which the trauma or conflict occurred. For example, the otherwise bright and well-functioning child who, at the end of elementary school, reacts with distress rather than pleasure to the idea of graduation may be one who has had repeated experiences with traumatic separations.

In turn, **precocity** involves an accelerated rate of development that might be associated with psychopathology. Examples of precocity include the attempt by substance-abusing youths to take on adult roles and responsibilities before they are developmentally prepared for them, or the way in which children with generalized anxiety disorder worry excessively about grown-up matters, carrying the weight of the world on their shoulders.

The foregoing definitions of psychopathology are basically *quantitative*: That is, compared to others at this age, is this child displaying too much or too little of the behavior in question? In contrast, a **developmental deviation** involves the emergence of a function that is so *qualitatively* different from normal that it would be considered inappropriate at any stage of development. An example of this is the echolalic speech of the autistic child who purposelessly repeats back what others have said to him or her.

Finally, there is a very different conceptualization of psychopathology that does not concern developmental processes within the child, but rather the goodness of fit between the child and the environment. The concept of **adaptational failure** concerns the child's ability to adapt to the expectations of the environment. When the environment exerts demands that tax the capacities of the child—for example, the adolescent with low verbal abilities who is required to perform in school—dysfunction might be apparent. Should the youth find a better fitting niche—a vocational training program that capitalizes on his or her nonverbal intelligence, for example—good adaptation is possible nonetheless.

Research Strategies in Developmental Psychopathology

We have discussed how the developmental psychopathology framework views the origins of psychopathology as *multiply determined,* incorporating variables within the person, the social environment, and the transactions among them. Consequently, research designs that capture such models must be complex and sophisticated. The two essential techniques of the developmental psychopathology researcher are longitudinal designs and multivariate statistical techniques. To accomplish the task of determining what risks and protective factors lead to disorder or resilience, we need to follow children over time; hence, longitudinal research is essential. Further, in order to assess which variables are significantly related to children's outcomes over time, we need statistical techniques that are able to tease apart their effects; to this end, we use multivariate analytic strategies. Let us take a closer look at the tools in the developmental investigator's toolbox.

Longitudinal Research Designs

The Retrospective Strategy

A time-honored method of gathering developmental data is the **retrospective strategy,** in which inquiry is made about the past history of a disturbed child or adult in order to reconstruct the origins of the psychopathology. An example is Robins's (1966) classic study of adults who had been assessed at a child mental health clinic when they were children. Retrospective studies often rely on interviews, whether of the parent, the child, or other knowledgable adults. (An interesting exception is provided by Poal and Weisz (1989), who asked child clinical psychologists to retrospectively rate their own childhood behavior problems on a standardized behavior checklist.) However, despite the widespread use of interviews among clinicians and researchers alike, the data they produce are colored by the subjective judgments of the respondents and subject to the limitations of human memory for events that happened far in the past. While retrospective data may offer initial leads about which intra- and interpersonal variables may be fruitful to study, questions about their reliability and validity suggest that they should be used only with great caution (Henry, Moffitt, Caspi, Langley, & Silva, 1994).

The alternatives to retrospective designs are those that are *prospective;* that is, they follow children over time. The interval between assessments should be sufficient to capture general developmental trends, and the evaluations should be independently conducted by individuals who are more objective than parents. Three of the most popular strategies are the follow-back, the follow-up, and the cross-sectional models, all of which eliminate a number of the deficiencies of retrospective data, although they have limitations of their own.

The Follow-Back Strategy

Like the retrospective approach, the **follow-back strategy** begins with a population of disturbed children or adults but obtains data from a previous time period via data kept by observers other than parents, such as school records, teachers' assessments, child clinic files, and court records. For example, let's say an investigator examined the medical records of violent children in a child psychiatry inpatient unit to determine whether they were more likely than other children to have suffered head injuries or seizures. A comparison group should also be selected, say, from the next name in the list of classmates or clinic patients, in order to control for other variables that might be relevant to the psychopathology being studied. For example, one might find that the violent children differed from peers not only in rates of head injury, but in social class and exposure to violence in the community.

Advantages of the follow-back design include that it allows the investigator to focus immediately on the target population, and it is flexible enough to permit the investigator to pursue new leads as they emerge. However, the follow-back strategy has a number of limitations. The data may be *uneven* in quality and availability, with some records being comprehensive and reflecting a high degree of professional competence, and others being skimpy and distorted by conceptual or personality biases. The data also tend to be very *general*—for example, number of arrests, decline in school grades, intact or broken family, number of job changes—lacking both the detail and the interrelatedness of variables found in an in-depth evaluation.

Other problems concern design and *population bias* in particular. Clinical populations may not be representative of disturbed children in general. Parents who seek professional help for a child with a school phobia, for example, may be different from those who do not, so findings from a clinical population cannot be generalized to all parents of phobic children. Likewise, children who are arrested may not be a representative sample of all youthful offenders, because police officers have their own biases about whom they arrest and whom they let go.

More important, reliance on data such as child guidance and court records biases the data in terms of *accentuating pathology* and *exaggerating relationships* found at time 1 and time 2. To illustrate, let's say that one follow-back study indicated that 75 percent of alcoholics had been truants, compared with 26 percent of healthy individuals—a highly significant difference—but a follow-up study revealed that only 11 percent of truants and 8 percent of nontruants become alcoholics. Thus, truancy can have a variety of outcomes, and its particular association with alcoholism is too weak for predictive purposes. In general, follow-back studies, which select individuals who have already developed a particular disturbance, tend to show stronger relations between time 1 and time 2 variables than do follow-up studies, the design we turn to next.

The Follow-Up Strategy

The ideal method of charting children's development is the **follow-up strategy,** in which children enter into the study in their early years and are followed into the next developmental period—or even into adulthood. An example of this is the Cambridge Youth Study (Farrington, 1995) in which inner-city boys were initially assessed at age 8 and then reassessed at ages 10, 14, 16, 18, 21, 25, and 32. The resulting longitudinal data can reveal which children develop what psychopathologies, together with how they fared with and without intervention. Instead of being at the mercy of whatever records exist, as with follow-back studies, the investigator can ensure that data will be gathered by well-trained investigators using the best available methods.

A major advantage of the follow-up study is that prospective longitudinal data allow the researcher to sort out the relationships among variables. For example, evidence that psychopathology in children of divorce was present *before* the breakup indicates that the divorce alone was not the cause; rather, the more likely culprit is the long and bitter process of marital dissolution that leads up to divorce (Rutter, 1994). Although no longitudinal design can demonstrate *causal* relationships—a true experiment in which variables are controlled and manipulated is necessary for that—prospective data allow investigators to test the plausibility of hypotheses about antecedent and consequent relationships.

Despite its advantages, the follow-up study has a number of limitations. Such research is extremely *costly* in terms of money and expenditure of effort. A major problem, as Loeber and Farrington (1994) point out, is that of *time:* The investigator ages at the same rate as the participants, and therefore one must live to a ripe old age indeed in order to reap the rewards of a life-span longitudinal study. On the other side of the equation, participants are difficult to retain in a study for such long periods of time. **Attrition** occurs when investigators lose track of participants; worse, participants may drop out selectively, with the most disturbed children and unstable families tending to be the ones who become uncooperative and move without leaving a forwarding address. Thus, researchers may be faced with a dwindling number of people in the very population they are most interested in studying. Population *selectivity* is another problem. Because most psychopathologies are rare, large numbers of children must be evaluated at Time 1 to ensure a reasonable number of disturbed ones at Time 2. As one solution, many investigators begin with a disturbed population or with a population at risk for developing a given psychopathology, such as infants of schizophrenic mothers, who have a greater likelihood of becoming schizophrenic than do infants from an unselected population. However, such selectivity may introduce the same population bias we noted in the follow-back design.

Moreover, the follow-up study is *rigid.* Once having selected variables to study, the design does not allow the investigator to drop some and add others as results from relevant studies come in or as new theories and concepts come to the fore. Moreover, new measurement techniques may be devised that are superior to the ones in use; however, the researcher cannot use them without losing comparability to the old data in the data set.

One final problem with the follow-up studies is the so-called **cohort effect;** one cannot assume that groups born in different eras are equivalent, since the time of birth may significantly affect development. Children born in times of war or depression are not necessarily comparable to those born in times of peace and prosperity, just as children born before the advent of television or the feminist movement grew up in an environment very different from that of those born afterward (Caspi, 1987; Cohen, Slomkowski, & Robins, 1999). Thus, the results of a 30-year longitudinal study may or may not be applicable to the current population of children.

The Cross-Sectional Strategy

The **cross-sectional approach** to gathering developmental data consists of studying different age groups (cohorts) at one point in time. For example, the Cambridge Youth Study might have collected samples of 8-year-olds, 10-year-olds, 14-year-olds, and so forth. The chief *advantage* of this approach is that of time in that age-related differences can be studied without waiting for participants themselves to age. However, among its *disadvantages* is, again, the cohort effect. Although these groups may be equated for all the variables thought to be important, they cannot be equated for differential experiences they might have had because of their time of birth. For example, in a sample of military families, the parent-child relationships of a group of 14-year-old boys who grew up during wartime might differ significantly from those of a group of 7-year-old boys who grew up after the war. Thus, age and environmental events are confounded. The cross-sectional design is not truly developmental in that we do not know whether 2 years from now the 8-year-old participants will respond in the same way as those who are currently 10-year-olds; we can only assume that differences between them are due to age.

The Accelerated Longitudinal Approach

One solution to the confounding of developmental effects with cohort effects is the **accelerated longitudinal approach,** also known as the longitudinal, cross-sectional approach. In this design children at different ages are studied as in the cross-sectional approach but then are subsequently followed. In this design, several age cohorts of children are followed up for the same number of years until the children in the younger groups are the same age as those in the next older groups (Loeber & Farrington, 1994). Thus, the length of time needed to carry out a study spanning a long developmental period is reduced significantly. This strategy was used by Stanger, Achenbach, and Verhulst (1997), who assessed seven cohorts of Dutch children ages 4, 5, 6, 7, 8, 9, and 10 every 2 years for a period of 10 years. In this way, both within-cohort and between-cohort differences could be assessed. For example, the 4-year-old girls were compared with 6-year-old girls at Time 1 and then again at Time 2, and their scores at age 4 were compared to their own scores at age 6.

Among its advantages, such a design allows researchers to compare the age trends obtained cross-sectionally with longitudinal data. The saving in time is obvious: A longitudinal study that would have had to follow the 4-year-olds for 14 years can now be accomplished in half the time. However, as with any design, this one has limitations. These include the difficulty in equating groups and the likelihood of selective loss of participants across groups.

Evaluation of Research Strategies

While the follow-up and follow-back strategies are an improvement over the retrospective approach, neither is a panacea. Because of its flexibility, the follow-back strategy is most suited to generating hypotheses. Leads as to possible significant antecedents can subsequently be accepted or rejected as they are put to further tests. However, follow-up studies, because of their ability to monitor the child's development while it actually occurs, provide the most convincing data concerning change. This strategy also comes closest to testing causal relations among variables, although, because it is correlational rather than experimental, it cannot actually establish causation.

One final cautionary note: The designs of follow-up and follow-back studies have only recently received the attention they deserve. Consequently, our reviews of longitudinal research will include studies using varying degrees of methodological sophistication and thus generating results with varying degrees of conclusiveness. While containing important leads about the developmental course of childhood psychopathology, many of the findings reviewed should be regarded as tentative.

Multivariate Research

Without going too far afield into the realm of statistics, we will briefly describe some essential techniques that are used to test the complex designs that are generated by multifaceted, longitudinal research. This will be helpful given that these methods are the ones used to construct the integrative developmental frameworks that we will feature in our discussions of each of the psychopathologies.

Moderators and Mediators

Research in developmental psychopathology, as we have seen, goes beyond the simple questions of "bad input → bad output" and attempts to discover how the input variable and the output variable are related. For example, a large body of literature has established that exposure to interparental conflict is a risk for child maladjustment (Grych & Fincham, 2001). But *how* and *why* do these effects take place? In other words, we want to identify the mechanisms—such as risk or protective processes—that account for the effects of interparental conflict (the *independent variable,* or IV) on outcome (the *dependent variable,* or DV). These linking mechanisms come in two types (Holmbeck, 1997). A **mediator** is a *causal* variable; it is through and only through the mediator that the IV affects the DV. For example, perhaps children exposed to interparental conflict develop a hostile attribution bias toward others, and it is this distorted cognition that accounts for their poor adjustment. In contrast, a **moderator** is a variable that *affects* the relationship between the IV and DV, but does not cause it. A vulnerability is a good example of a moderator, in that children who are at low levels of the moderator variable will be affected differently than children who are at high levels. For example, perhaps triangulation in interparental conflict moderates the effects of interparental conflict on children, such that it is those who are "caught in the middle" of their parents' battles who are most affected (Kerig, 1998b).

The search for moderators and mediators helps us to create some powerful models of how psychopathology comes about. These linking mechanisms also allow us to identify possible targets for intervention. Because we cannot simply assign children to "happy families," we cannot eradicate family stress from their lives. But if we can interrupt the process by which hostility in the home is carried over into hostility with peers, for example, we can help children to stay on a healthy developmental pathway.

Structural Equation Modeling

Testing complex moderational and mediational models requires sophisticated analytic strategies. We won't attempt to describe them all here, but we will introduce one technique that we will see many times as we review integrative developmental models. Structural equation modeling (SEM) is a method of evaluating how well a complex theoretical model fits the actual relationships among a set of observed variables (Hoyle & Smith, 1994). Rather than examining these relationships one at a time as a correlation does, the advantage of SEM is that it simultaneously assesses the interrelationships among multiple variables, taking each association into account when considering the others.

To make the model more robust, instead of relying on a single measure, the investigator may select a number of different measures of a construct. To

avoid biases, ideally these measures involve dissimilar methods and come from diverse sources. For example, a researcher interested in child anxiety disorders might interview teachers, provide parents with a questionnaire to complete, and observe children in the laboratory in order to come up with a set of measures for the construct "anxiety." The individual measures are termed *observed variables* and the theoretical construct they are assumed to tap is the *latent variable*. If the observed variables indeed relate to one another consistently so as to form a latent construct, the investigator may then proceed to the next step of testing his or her hypothesis regarding the relationships among the constructs.

For example, Davies and his colleagues (2003) theorize that the mechanism by which interparental conflict affects children is *emotional security*—that is, quarrels between parents distress children by threatening their sense of security in the family system. To test this model, the authors wanted to assess three constructs, or latent variables: interparental conflict, emotional security, and child adjustment. *Interparental conflict* was assessed through four separate parent-report questionnaires. The investigators then created measures of three dimensions of *emotional security*. First, observers watched children during a parental quarrel in the laboratory and rated children's *emotional reactivity* (e.g., anxiety, freezing, sadness) and, second, their *regulation of exposure* to the conflict (e.g., attempts to avoid or become actively involved in the quarrel). Third, children's *internal representations of family security* were derived from their responses to interview questions. Finally, *child adjustment* was assessed through parents' ratings on a checklist and children's self-reports on an anxiety questionnaire. After using factor analysis to establish that the individual measures held together to form the constructs they were designed to assess, the authors conducted a SEM analysis to show how the latent variables related to one another. Consistent with their hypothesis, two measures of emotional security—emotional reactivity and internal representations of family security—mediated the relationship between interparental quarreling and child anxiety. (See

Figure 1.7   Structural Equation Model Showing the Links Among Interparental Conflict, Emotional Security, and Child Adjustment.

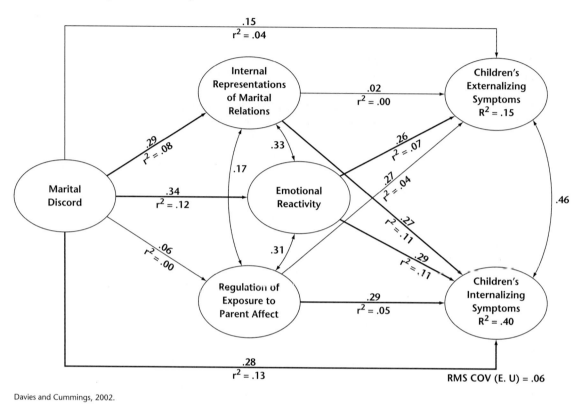

Davies and Cummings, 2002.

Figure 1.7.) In other words, the investigators demonstrated that interparental conflict affects children's adjustment by undermining their emotional security within the family system.

To make matters even more complex, developmental psychopathology models require that we test the interactions among multiple variables over time. Thus, we need techniques that allow us to assess not only whether variables are related to one another, but whether those relations emerge developmentally in patterns consistent with the theory. SEM also has the flexibility to test models of change over time in longitudinal research (Curran & Hussong, 2002).

Having outlined our general developmental framework and the methods used in its study, we are now ready to describe the normal development of the intra- and interpersonal variables that will have a bearing on our subsequent discussions of the various childhood psychopathologies. Then, in Chapter 3, we will build a bridge to the psychopathologies themselves.

(It would be helpful for the reader to have the kind of general familiarity with the major developmental theories that can be gained from an introductory text in child development. For example, see Siegler, DeLoache, and Eisenberg, 2003, or Hetherington and Parke, 2003.)

Normative Development

If we are to understand childhood psychopathology as normal development gone awry, we must first chart normative development. Although development occurs across all psychological and biological processes, we have chosen a few key developmental lines that are so crucial to a child's well-being that, should anything go radically wrong with any one of them, we should seriously consider the possibility that the child will become disturbed.

First, there is a *biological* context to development. The child with a difficult temperament, or whose brain or neurochemical development has gone awry, is vulnerable to the development of psychopathology. Further, the *family* context must be considered: The quality of the parenting the child receives, the structure of the family system, and the extent to which the parent-child relationship is warm and kind versus harsh and rejecting will affect susceptibility to negative developmental outcomes.

Next, there is a group of individual processes binding the child to the human environment. Prominent in this group is the bond of love, which is called *attachment,* that develops between infant and caregiver in the first year of life. Throughout childhood and life the ability to feel deeply about and become attached to another individual lies at the core of the human experience. As development advances, children and youth expand their social horizons to form increasingly meaningful and significant *social relations* with peers and adults outside the family. With the advent of *sexuality* later in development, erotic attachments and truly intimate relationships are formed. If something goes radically awry with any of these bonds—if, for example, the loving overtures of a parent are met with rage or profound indifference, if sexual intimacy is a source of terror rather than pleasure, if the child is socially isolated and friendless—we would rightfully be concerned.

As children form important relationships with others, they are also forming a conceptualization of who they themselves are: Am I loved and therefore

33

lovable? Am I able to win friends and influence people and therefore likely to be able to achieve whatever I set out to do? The *self* is pivotal to many developmental variables that might be related to psychopathology and health, including self-esteem, perceived self-efficacy, mastery motivation, identity, and the ego functions that allow for successful coping with internal and external stress. Attachment and the self also are pivotally linked to the processes of *emotional* development. From the earliest years, when young children are buffeted by the effects of emotional storms over which they can exert little control, responsive environments and sensitive care assist the child to develop the capacity to regulate emotions and engage in increasing degrees of self-control. Socialization often involves curbing children's behaviors; with time, children take over these monitoring and controlling functions themselves. *Moral development* therefore comes into play by guiding the child in regard to the rightness or wrongness of behavior. Morality and self-control also involve the development of defense mechanisms, which help to manage anxiety and serve as one of the principal deterrents to performing socially disapproved actions.

Further, it is essential for the child to understand the physical and social environment as well as himself or herself, a variable we shall call *cognitive development.* Reality can be distorted by magical ideas in the first few years of life because of cognitive immaturity. It is essential that these distortions be replaced by realistic understanding; the persistence of bizarre, magical ideas—such as a 10-year-old's belief that he can hear through his belly button and can control television pictures by his thoughts—is a sign of disturbed development. *Gender* differences interact with all of the other processes we have mentioned, as sex-role socialization affects interpersonal relations and self-perceptions to a significant degree.

Last, but not least, children develop in a larger *cultural* context that must be considered. Cultural attitudes and values, social class, and ethnicity are all variables that affect the child by shaping his or her physical and psychological environment.

In sum, in our developmental approach to childhood psychopathology, we will discuss contributions made by the biological, family, social, and cultural contexts. In addition, we will focus on six processes in the individual context: cognition, emotion, attachment, the self, moral development, and gender and sexuality.

Development in the Biological Context

Genetics

As we discuss each of the specific disorders in the chapters to follow, we will make note of whether there is evidence of genetic transmission within families. Models of genetic heritability involve the *genotype*—the genetic material that is passed on; the *phenotype*—the way the genes are expressed in physical characteristics and behavior; and the *environment*—aspects of the surroundings that might compete with genes as the explanation for behavior. (See Rutter, Silberg, O'Connor, and Simonoff, 1999.)

Instead of engaging in the old-fashioned nature-nurture debate, the modern field of behavioral genetics assumes that all behavior arises as a function of an interaction between genetic and environmental factors (O'Connor & Plomin, 2000). *Heritability* is estimated as the proportion of variability in a given trait within a group of individuals that is attributable to the shared genes, in contrast to variability that is attributable to *shared environments* (e.g., experiences all siblings share, such as being parented by a stressed mother) and *nonshared environments* (e.g., experiences that are unique for each sibling, such as parents' differential treatment of the youngest and eldest child). Interestingly, over the course of development there is a decline in the extent to which siblings in the same family share the same environment. In a process known as *niche-picking,* children increasingly engage actively in shaping their environments by choosing activities, friends, and experiences according to their own individual attitudes and interests (Reiss, Neiderhiser, Hetherington, & Plomin, 2000).

The strongest evidence for genetic influences comes from studies of twins, which compare those who share 100 percent of their genes in common (identical or monozygotic twins) to those who share only 50 percent of their DNA (fraternal or dizygotic twins). The investigator determines the *concordance rate,* the percentage of cases in which a characteristic displayed by one child is also displayed by his or her twin. The ideal behavioral genetics study is one that compares twins reared in the same family to those reared apart. If twins reared apart are more alike then different, this suggests that genes rather than environmental influences are affecting their behavior. For example, the Minnesota Study of Twins Reared Apart (Markon, Krueger, Bouchard, & Gottesman, 2002) sheds light on the genetic contributions to personality development. The investigators evaluated the "normal" and "abnormal" personality traits of 122 monzygotic and dizygotic twin pairs who had been reared in different households. Overall, the data suggested that identical twins were more similar than fraternal twins; thus, the contribution of genetics was significant. However, environment still made a significant contribution to personality type.

In general, the weight of the research suggests that about 50 percent of personality is attributable to genetics (Rende & Plomin, 1995). Therefore, there still is much room for psychological and environmental processes to exert their influences. Moreover, there is an increasing understanding of biological systems as dynamic processes that interact with cognitive, emotional, and environmental factors. Modern thinking in biological psychology, therefore, has turned from the old-fashioned "nature versus nurture" debate, to a more sophisticated set of questions concerning how nature and nurture interact to influence the development of psychopathology.

Neuropsychology

The field of child neuropsychology has been making rapid and exciting advances in recent years, and it will be beyond our scope to review it in its entirety here. But, briefly, important dimensions of neuropsychological development that will concern us include brain structure, function, and chemistry. (For a basic overview of neuropsychological development, see Kolb and Whitshaw, 2003; for excellent reviews of neuropsychology and psychopathology, the reader is referred to Cicchetti and Walker, 2003, and Pliszka, 2002.)

Regarding *brain structure,* or neuroarchitecture, we will make note of whether research shows that various disorders are linked to malfunctions or disconnections among the parts of the developing brain. Next, we want to consider *brain function,* or how differences in brain anatomy are displayed in behavior. In the realm of *brain chemistry,* we will be concerned with the **neurotransmitters** that communicate between nerve cells (neurons) in the brain, including dopamine, serotonin, GABA, and norepinephrine. When these transmissions are disrupted, or they are excessive or deficient in quantity, psychopathology might develop. In addition, stressful experiences overstimulate the release of certain **neuroendocrines** that, in excessive quantity, have toxic effects on the developing brain. For example, in our investigations of anxiety, trauma (Chapter 8), and maltreatment (Chapter 14), we will encounter the *hypothalamic-pituitary-adrenal (HPA) axis,* which plays an important role in the response to stress by regulating the production of the hormone cortisol and stimulating the familiar "flight or fight" response. Children who are exposed to excessive amounts of cortisol in the context of prolonged or repeated trauma may become locked in a state of heightened fear and arousal, with resulting pernicious effects on the developing brain (Beers & De Bellis, 2002).

Brain Development

The development of the infant's brain parallels the advance of evolution in that the first structures to develop are the most primitive. For example, the lowest part of the brain, the *brain stem,* lies just above the

Figure 2.1   Map of the Human Brain.

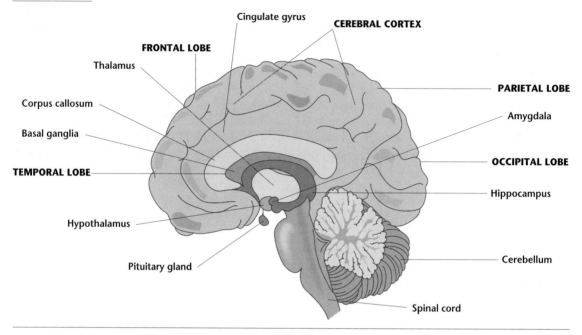

spinal cord and regulates autonomic functions such as breathing, heartrate, motor coordination, and arousal. (See Figure 2.1.) Behind this sits the *cerebellum,* which is responsible for coordination and balance. Atop the brain stem is the *forebrain,* which includes the *limbic system.* Incorporating structures such as the hippocampus, cingulate gyrus, and amygdala, the limbic system governs the basic drives of sex, aggression, and satiety and plays an important role in the regulation of emotion and impulse control. Next, the *basal ganglia,* including the *caudate nucleus,* are involved in the organization and integration of information regarding thoughts, feelings, and behavior.

The last part of the forebrain to develop is the *cerebral cortex,* which is involved in the most complex human operations of reasoning and creativity. The cortex comprises two hemispheres that are specialized for certain functions, a characteristic of the human brain termed *lateralization.* The *left hemisphere* (dominant in most right-handed people) is involved in the processing of verbal information and linear forms of logic, such as reading and mathematics, while the *right hemisphere* specializes in visual and holistic processing, such as that involved in spatial and social perception. However, despite this bilateral specialization, the two sides of the brain are highly integrated and both are involved to some extent in most tasks, with communication taking place through the *corpus collosum,* a bundle of fibers that connects the two hemispheres.

The cerebral cortex is further divided into four areas, or *lobes:* occipital, parietal, temporal, and frontal. The *occipital* lobe, at the very rear of the cortex, is largely involved in visual processing. Above this, the *parietal* lobes are responsible for perception of sensory information, including the recognition of pain, pressure, touch, and the movement of the body through space. The *temporal* lobes, in the temple area on either side of the cortex, are important for memory, auditory perception, and facial recognition. At the very forefront of the brain lie the *frontal lobes,* which are central to the higher mental operations. These include the **executive functions,** so named because they act like executives in a corporation and oversee such tasks as planning, problem solving, decision making, and organization.

Although it was once assumed that the process of brain development was complete around 12 years of age, recent research has revealed that significant changes in the cerebral cortex continue to occur well into adolescence, and even into early adulthood (Giedd, 2003). Two important developmental processes are myelination and pruning. **Pruning** involves the brain's ridding itself of unnecessary, redundant, or nonfunctional cells. The first wave of pruning occurs in the final months before birth, following an explosive growth in prenatal neural development. Recently, scientists have discovered that there is a second, critical pruning stage that begins later in childhood and culminates in the late teens. This second wave involves reducing not only the number of cells but also the number of connections between neurons.

The brain consists of two types of neural tissue, gray matter and white matter. White matter gets its color from the *myelin sheath* that surrounds the axon of the nerve cell and serves much the same function of insulation on a wire, increasing the speed and efficiency of the transmission of information. Increasing **myelination** of the neurons begins around puberty (age 11 for girls and age 12½ for boys) and continues at least into the 20s and perhaps even into the 40s. Myelination proceeds in the same manner as brain development in general: from the rear portions of the brain, where basic and primitive functions are housed, to the front of the brain, where more advanced functions lie. The last part of the brain to be pruned and myelinated is the prefrontal cortex, which is responsible for such higher mental functions as planning, decision making, organization, and weighing alternatives. Therefore, investigators propose that some of the risky behavior and illogical thinking associated with the "storm and stress" of adolescence may have a biological basis: "The part of the brain that makes teenagers more responsible is not finished maturing yet" (*Time,* May 10, 2004, p. 61).

Temperament

Each infant appears to be born with a particular *temperament*—a characteristic tempo and activity level, a particular mood and adaptability, a special set of vulnerabilities and resiliencies, preferences and dislikes. (See Molfese and Molfese, 2000.)

Temperament Types

The pioneers in the study of temperament are Alexander Thomas and Stella Chess (1977), who distinguished among three types of infants: difficult, easy, and slow-to-warm-up. *Difficult* infants are fussy, irregular in their eating and sleeping habits, easy to upset, and difficult to soothe. *Easy* infants, in contrast, generally display positive affect, react in a mild manner to frustration, and are easily soothed by parental comforting. *Slow-to-warm-up* or shy infants have a generally low activity level and, while they may show an initially negative reaction to new stimuli or change, they will adapt over time and begin looking more like the easy infants.

Using data from the New York Longitudinal Study, Thomas and Chess (1977) followed 133 people from infancy into adulthood. While they found no correlation between any single temperamental trait and early adult adjustment, difficult temperament at 3 years of age was negatively correlated with overall ratings of emotional adjustment in adulthood. Further, children who developed psychiatric problems were overwhelmingly more likely to have shown a difficult temperament in infancy.

Another set of temperament researchers used data from the Berkeley Guidance Study, which began in 1928 and followed 214 people from early childhood through adulthood (Caspi, 1987). Based on parent report, young children were classified as temperamentally *dependent, ill-tempered,* or *shy;* and when the participants were 40 years of age, they were interviewed by members of the research team. (Although the term "dependent" sounds negative, keep in mind that dependency on caregivers is normatic for young children; therefore, this was the most adaptive temperament pattern.) Inspired by the personality typology developed by their theorist Karen Horney, the investigators described the children who exhibited these three temperamental patterns, as respectively, moving *toward, against,* or *away* from the world. They found remarkable continuities in temperamental patterns as well as interesting gender differences regarding the consequences of particular temperaments for adults in the 1950s. For example, childhood ill-temper was associated with hostility and irritability in both men and women (Caspi, Elder, & Bem, 1987). On the other hand, while shy men had difficulty with life transitions throughout adulthood, delaying marriage, child-rearing, and the establishment of their careers, shy women's temperament was not associated with a problematic developmental course (Caspi, Elder, & Bem, 1988). While shy girls grew up to be reticent women, their preference for a quiet, domestic lifestyle fit well with the stereotypical expectations for women of their era.

Subsequently, Caspi and colleagues (Newman, Caspi, Moffitt, & Silva, 1997) followed a sample of over 900 children from age 3 to age 21. The investigators identified five distinct temperamental types: *well-adjusted, reserved, confident, inhibited,* and *undercontrolled.* While the first three groups displayed a range of interpersonal behaviors in adulthood, their adjustment was generally good. Inhibited children, in turn, grew up to be adults who experienced lower levels of social support than others, but still enjoyed adaptive relationships with romantic partners and workmates. The undercontrolled preschoolers, however, were significantly more likely than others to display significant adjustment problems across all interpersonal relationships in adulthood. We will revisit the finding from these studies when we discuss psychopathologies of anxiety and aggression in Chapters 8 and 10.

In summary, despite their use of different terminologies and classification systems, temperament studies consistently show that extremely shy/inhibited temperaments and their opposite, extremely difficult/aggressive/undercontrolled temperaments, increase children's vulnerability to the development of psychopathy. The remarkable continuity of child temperament from infancy to adulthood also emerges as a consistent theme. In their attempt to explain the mechanism by which childhood temperament affects

adult behavior, Caspi and colleagues (1988) proposed two valuable concepts. The first of these is *interactional continuity.* For example, they proposed that because shy boys were timid and lacking in social skills, they tended to be neglected by other people: They were overlooked, ignored, the last picked when teams were being formed. We would term this a transaction (see Chapter 1): Through the way that shy boys interacted with others, they inspired others to respond to them in ways that exacerbated their shyness and, consequently, led them to want to withdraw even more. The second concept is a *historical* one. As Caspi (1987) argues, every culture at every historical epoch defines a set of roles that have to be fulfilled by individuals—these identify the competencies individuals are expected to have and specify which behaviors are deemed appropriate to display. Therefore, individual development is in part influenced by how the person negotiates the agenda provided by his or her culture at his or her time in history.

One of the most valuable contributions that Chess and Thomas have made to our understanding of developmental psychopathology is their observation that temperamental characteristics alone do not determine a child's outcome. Instead, it is the *fit* between the child and environment that determines whether development took a healthy or a pathological course (Chess & Thomas, 1999). Next we look at this concept in more detail.

Goodness of Fit

Chess and Thomas (1990) were struck by the individual differences in their longitudinal sample in that some children showed a consistent pathway from infancy to adulthood while others ended up at quite a different destination. Given that Chess and Thomas are clinicians who are interested in how their research can be used to better the lives of the children in their samples, the investigators became intrigued with the question of why one child shows a consistent temperamental course whereas another shows great variability over time. Chess and Thomas proposed that the explanation lay in the **goodness of fit:** the meshing between the child's temperamental style and the demands the environment places on the child. When the environment's expectations, demands, and opportunities are compatible with the individual's temperament, the child is able to master environmental challenges effectively. When there is a poorness of fit, the demands from the environment exceed the child's capacities and the ensuing stress leads to an unhealthy developmental course.

As Chess and Thomas (1990) state, "Goodness of fit does not imply an absence of stress or conflict: quite the contrary. Stress and conflict are inevitable during development, as new expectations and demands for ever-higher levels of functioning occur continuously as the child grows older. Demands, stresses, and conflicts, when they are consistent with the child's developmental potentials and capacities for mastery, will be constructive in their consequences. The issue involved in disturbed functioning is rather one of excessive stress resulting from poorness of fit between environmental demands and the capacities of the child at a particular stage of development" (p. 211). For example, Chess and Thomas describe two cases from their sample, which we present in Box 2.1.

More recently, in a longitudinal study spanning infancy to the 7th year of life, Rothbart and colleagues (2000) assessed a number of dimensions of temperament, including positive reactivity, fear and frustration, span of attention, approach to novel stimuli, and activity level. They found continuity across the 7-year period for a number of characteristics including fear, frustration, and approach. Moreover, these temperamental variables were predictive of psychopathology. While infant fearfulness was predictive of school-age anxiety, frustration and anger were related to behavior problems of both an aggressive and anxious sort.

Therefore, temperament appears to provide a biological predisposition upon which the environment acts in order to moderate or potentiate the development of psychopathology.

Biological Processes and Developmental Psychopathology

To summarize, there are several processes by which biology might contribute to the development of psychopathology: (1) genetically inherited traits; (2) abnormalities in brain structure; (3) dysfunctions in brain function or miscommunication among parts of the brain; (4) imbalances in brain chemistry; (5) difficult temperament; (6) inadequate myelination; and (7) dysfunctions of the pruning process that rids the brain of redundant and nonfunctional pathways. Each of these biological processes evolves in interaction with the environment, and therefore our consideration of organic factors will be conducted with the concept of *transactions* in mind.

Development in the Individual Context

Cognitive Development

As we noted in Chapter 1, Piaget (1967) outlined a series of orderly, fixed stages that children progress through in the process of cognitive development.

During the first two years of life the child is in the **sensorimotor stage,** so called because the vehicles for understanding are sensation and motor action. When presented with a novel object such as a rattle, an infant may determine its properties by placing it in the mouth or shaking it. Incapable of symbolization, except toward the end of the period, infants and toddlers must explore and learn by acting directly on the environment and by using their senses. A significant development in this period is that of **object permanence.** For the first few months, infants give no evidence of missing an object they can no longer see or hold. Thus, the world exists only when they are acting upon it or perceiving it. Only gradually do infants come to realize that objects exist regardless of their own actions or perceptions—objects exist "out there" as part of the environment, while actions exist "in here" as part of the self. This represents a giant step toward separating "me" from "not me."

The **preoperational stage** lasts from approximately 2 to 7 years of age and marks the appearance of *symbolic functions.* The most obvious manifestation of symbolization is language, which develops rapidly in this period. However, the preschooler tends literally to believe what he or she sees. Consequently, something that *looks* different *is* different. Piaget's well-known documentation of this

Box 2.1 | **Case Studies in Temperament and Goodness of Fit: Norman and Carl**

Stella Chess and Alexander Thomas describe two young people who participated in their longitudinal study of temperament and developmental psychopathology, Norm and Carl.

In infancy, Norm showed temperamental traits of shyness, distractibility, and low persistence. However, he was intelligent and did well in school. Norm's father was of a different temperamental type: He was focused and hard-driving and he did not tolerate well Norm's hesitancy and dreaminess. While the investigators did their best to provide the parents with insight into the temperamental basis for Norm's behavior, the father preferred to interpret it as "irresponsibility" and "lack of character," opinions that he expressed openly to his son. Norm grew to recognize that he didn't have his father's drive, but

he also accepted his father's negative judgment about his character. By adolescence he was very self-critical and he told Dr. Chess, "My father doesn't respect me, and let's face it, why should he?" His introspectiveness only increased his negative self-image and led to further discouragement and hopelessness. He dropped out of several colleges for lack of effort and went from job to job without motivation enough to continue with any one of them. He tried psychotherapy but was not helped by it, because his self-defeating tendencies wouldn't allow him to see the possibility that he could make any positive changes.

Carl also had been an infant in the longitudinal study, and when he was 19 years old, he requested an interview with Dr. Chess. He had just finished his first semester in college and

was experiencing feelings of depression and inability to cope with the new academic and social demands pressing on him. He hadn't been able to make any new friends and was having trouble studying, problems that he had not experienced before in his life. He didn't understand what was happening to him: "This just isn't me!"

Looking back at his research profile, Dr. Chess noted that, as an infant, Carl had shown a very difficult temperament pattern, with intense negative reactions to new situations and slow ability to adapt. His mother had worried that she must be doing something wrong as a mother; otherwise, why would Carl behave so differently from other children? Happily, his father was a very patient person who saw Carl's behavior as challenging but not abnormal and reassured

thesis is the *conservation* experiment. If, before their very eyes, water is poured from a wide, squat glass into a tall, narrow glass, preschool children will claim that there is now more water. It looks like more, so it must be more. Lack of conservation also contributes to erroneous beliefs we explored earlier, such as the young child's conviction that by changing her clothes she can change her gender. Preoperational children also are known for magical thinking, also termed **omnipotent thinking.** Because their understanding of causality is limited, they tend to view themselves as the agents causing the events around them.

The **concrete-operational stage** extends from approximately 7 to 11 years of age. The triumph of middle childhood is that children are capable of understanding the world in terms of reason rather

than in terms of naive perception. They grasp the notion that objects conserve or maintain their identity despite changes in appearance. Although realistic, the child's thinking is still tied to concrete reality and bound to the here and now.

The **formal-operational stage** begins around the 12th year and lasts into adulthood. In this period the youth is able to generalize ideas and construct abstractions. The ability to draw conclusions from hypotheses rather than relying totally on actual observation is called *hypothetical-deductive* thinking. Adolescents can go wherever their thoughts lead them. They discuss, they write, they ruminate. They create a philosophy of life and explain the universe. They are also capable of being truly self-critical for the first time because they can reflect on and scrutinize their own ideas.

his wife that they could cope with their demanding infant. Dad interpreted Carl's loud shrieking as "lustiness" and viewed his son's boldness as admirable in comparison to the father's own mild temper. Consequently, the parents handled Carl's tantrums with a patient, consistent, and low-keyed approach.

Throughout his childhood, Carl lived in the same community. He went through school with the same group of friends and had no major disruptions or stressors in his life. Any changes he experienced were slow to occur and he had time to adapt to them. In contrast, college was an abrupt change that simultaneously confronted him with a whole series of stressors: new surroundings, a strange peer group, and a variety of different academic pressures. He experienced an intense negative emotional reaction and fell back on his temperamental pattern of withdrawal from these new stimuli.

Sitting down with Carl, Dr. Chess reviewed the evidence regarding his temperamental pattern. She also gave him some behavioral strategies to help him cope, such as limiting the number of new academic subjects he took per semester and becoming involved with a peer activity group and attending it regularly so that he could develop a consistent set of friends. After this consultation, Carl expressed appreciation and went on his way. Seven years later Carl, now age 26, made another appointment to see Dr. Chess. He was extremely cheerful and talked about the many activities he had under way. He was enjoying a successful career in computers and was planning to start his own business, while at the same time he wanted to take a year off and study music. He was also in an intense relationship and was trying to decide whether to get married, was learning photography, and was actively involved in athletics. She joked with him, "When do you sleep?" He replied, "That's one of my problems. I don't get enough sleep and I'm always tired. But I really came to ask you why I have all these tics." Dr. Chess laughed to herself and pointed out that all these activities, dilemmas, and decisions must be causing tension and fatigue. Carl responded by limiting his activities and, upon returning for a check-up 3 years later, was doing well.

Adapted from Chess and Thomas, 1990.

Cognitive Processes and Developmental Psychopathology

Assimiliation-Accommodation Imbalance   In order to understand the origins of psychopathology in Piaget's scheme, we must consider the processes that account for cognitive growth and progression through these stages. According to Piaget, development is fueled by the child's attempts to adapt to the environment. As we noted in Chapter 1, adaptation occurs through two psychological processes: assimilation and accommodation. **Assimilation** refers to the incorporation of new information into an existing schema and **accommodation** refers to the alteration of a schema to take into account new information. Whereas normative development is characterized by a balance, or **equilibration,** of assimilation and accommodation, problems may arise when accommodation and assimilation are used to the exclusion of one another. Exclusive use of assimilation, for example, might interfere with new learning, leading the child to make erroneous assumptions and to distort information so that it fits with preexisting notions. At the extreme, the child who is overly reliant on assimilation may be lost in fantasy, trying to bend the world to his or her own wishes. On the other hand, exclusive use of accommodation would result in the child's constantly changing his or her schema to fit with new stimuli. In the extreme, the overly accommodating child may lack a cohesive sense of self (Cowan, 1978).

Magical Thinking   An adolescent girl who will not speak for fear that feces would come out of her mouth, or a young man who always sleeps on his back in the belief that, if he did not, he would turn into a woman, would be regarded as psychopathologically disturbed because they are convinced that they can cause events, which, in reality, are beyond their control. While in normal development magical ideas and omnipotence begin to give way to logic during middle childhood, remnants of preoperational thinking may be seen in children whose development is delayed or children who are undergoing regression due to traumatic stress. Omnipotent thinking is problematic particularly for those traumatized children who misattribute to themselves causality—and blame—for their abuse.

Egocentrism   Piaget defines **egocentrism** as conceiving the physical and social world exclusively from one's own point of view. Consequently, characteristics of the self are used to define or interpret characteristics of the objective environment: The me is confused with the not-me.

Egocentric thinking appears at all stages of cognitive development. The infant believes the very existence of objects depends on his or her actions. For preschoolers, egocentrism has an important social consequence in that it prevents them from understanding that each person has his or her own point of view. The ability to view the same situation from multiple vantage points—for example, to see an episode of classroom cheating from the viewpoint of the boy who cheated, the boy who was pressured into helping him cheat, and the teacher responsible for disciplining the classroom—represents a giant step forward in cooperative social interactions.

Social perspective taking has its own progressive stages; for example, 3- to 6-year-olds seldom acknowledge that another person can interpret the same situation differently from the way they interpret it, whereas 7- to 12-year-olds can view their own ideas, feelings, and behaviors from another person's point of view and realize that other people can do the same in regard to them. As we shall see, social perspective taking enters into the discussion of a number of psychopathologies, particularly conduct disorder (Chapter 10).

Egocentrism makes its last childhood stand in early adolescence. Piaget assumed that times of cognitive transition are times when primitive modes of thought are apt to reappear. One aspect of egocentrism may be expressed as *self-consciousness;* if someone laughs on the bus while the adolescent boy is fumbling to find the correct change for the fare, he is certain that he is being laughed at. Another aspect of the adolescent's egocentrism is the belief that ideas alone will win the day and that his or her ideas hold the key to solving the world's problems—if only the world would listen!

Cognitive Delays and School Failure   While formal operations are considered a characteristic of adolescence, not all youths achieve this advanced stage of reasoning. In fact, children with severe cognitive delays may not even progress to concrete operations. There are also learning-disabled children with different learning styles that interfere with their ability to fulfill their potential and achieve in school (see Chapter 7). The child's general level of cognitive functioning has important implications for his or her functioning throughout development. School failure figures prominently in discussions of psychopathology. Both the future delinquent and the future schizophrenic might be variously described as disruptive and inattentive in class, defiant and truant, for example, while the devaluing of achievement in school is an important factor determining drug use in adolescence (see Chapter 12).

Cognitive Distortions   The information processing model we encountered in Chapter 1 also provides leads about how cognition can influence psychopathology. When solving social problems, children go through a series of steps: encoding social cues, interpreting those cues, searching for possible responses, deciding on a particular response from those generated, and, finally, acting on that response (Dodge, 1993; Crick & Dodge, 1994). The second step of cue interpretation involves the important psychological process of *attribution*. An attribution is an inference about the causes of behavior. Dodge's thesis is that in disturbed children the cognitive process is either distorted or deficient. Aggressive children, for example, are predisposed to attribute malicious intent to the behavior of others even when such behavior is benign or accidental. This distorted appraisal is termed a *hostile attribution bias.* We will return to this concept when we discuss aggression in Chapter 10.

Emotional Development

The development of emotions has important implications for our understanding of both psychopathology and normalcy. Although emotions have important adaptive functions, they also might have maladaptive consequences when emotions are not integrated with other systems of development. (Here we follow Izard and Harris, 1995, except otherwise noted.)

Emotion Expression

A number of processes are involved with emotional development, one of which is *emotion expression.* At the very beginning of life, the newborn is capable of displaying a wide variety of emotions, including interest, smiling, disgust, and pain. As early as 2 or 3 months of age, infants exhibit sadness and anger, whereas fear emerges at 6 or 7 months. With increasing cognitive development after the first year of life, children are able to express more complex emotions such as contempt, shame, shyness, and guilt. The emergence of emotion expression is highly influenced by caregivers. Infants directly imitate their caregiver's affect and caregivers, in turn, selectively reinforce the infant's facial expressions. For example, mothers respond differently to expressions of anger in male and female infants (Malatesta & Haviland, 1982).

By 10 to 12 months of age, the role of emotional expression is increasingly social and has an important function in organizing behavior. The 1-year-old judges the meaning of events through studying the caregiver's emotional reaction to them, a phenomenon known as *social referencing.* For example, in a classic study, Klinnert and her colleagues (1983) placed infants on a "visual cliff," a glass sheet underneath which a vividly patterned chasm appeared. The mother stood on one side of the cliff and beckoned the infant to crawl across to her. When the mothers beckoned with a smile, almost all of the infants crossed the cliff, whereas when mothers

displayed a fearful expression, none of the infants ventured out.

As children progress through the second year of life, emotional expression becomes increasingly stable and integrated with cognitive development. In the third year, as self-awareness and representational thought emerge, we begin to see the emergence of *self-conscious emotions,* such as shame, guilt, embarrassment, and pride (Harter, 1999). Preschoolers evaluate their performance and react emotionally to success and failure, appearing to experience pleasure or dissatisfaction not just with the task, but with *themselves* (Stipek, 1995).

In middle childhood, children demonstrate an increasing capacity to determine the *social appropriateness* of emotional expressions and to suppress or disguise their emotional reactions when the situation and social standards warrant. For example, when given yet another used video game at her birthday party, the 10-year-old is better able to smile nonetheless and say thank you than the 5-year-old would be. True to stereotype, research suggests that adolescence actually does bring with it an increase in emotional intensity and lability. Larson and Richards (1994) asked adolescents and their parents to carry pagers and to report their emotions when beeped at random intervals throughout the day. Adolescents were five times more likely to report being "very happy" than their parents but were also three times more likely to report being "very unhappy." While adolescents' emotions were more extreme, they were also more fleeting, suggesting that teenage moodiness is real. On the other hand, their cognitive development provides adolescents with awareness of the social impact of their emotional displays as well as increasing skill at managing them, allowing youths to suppress affects when they might harm relationships or to communicate feelings when they might enhance connections with others (Saarni, 1999).

Emotion Recognition

Klinnert and colleagues' visual cliff experiment also reveals the emergence of another important process in emotional development, that of *emotion recognition.* Children scan the faces of their caregivers in order to obtain clues about the meaning of events going on around them: Is it safe or is it dangerous? Young children often look to the emotional expressions of those around them to interpret even the children's *own* internal experiences: Take, for example, the toddler who takes a fall and, depending on whether the parent's affect expresses alarm or calm, either begins to squall or blithely goes on playing. Emotion recognition plays an important role in the development of healthy social relations and is a prerequisite for the acquisition of empathy and prosocial behavior.

Emotion Understanding

Nowhere is the interplay between cognitive and emotional development as important as in the emergence of children's *emotion understanding* (Case, 1988; Hesse & Cicchetti, 1982). A crucial task for development is to be able to identify, understand, and reason about emotions in oneself and others. Emotion understanding is central to development in the individual context, including the self-concept, and has a central place in interpersonal and moral development, including the emergence of empathy and social competence. Just as emotional expression comes under increasing conscious control over the course of development, the older child is able to reflect on and understand her or his emotions with greater complexity and depth. For example, the school-aged child understands that it is possible to experience more than one emotion at a time ("double-dip feelings," Harter & Whitesell, 1989), that emotions arise out of specific situations, and that the same experience might evoke different emotions in different people (Wintre & Vallance, 1994).

Emotion Regulation

Emotion regulation, also termed *affect regulation,* is the ability to monitor, evaluate, and modify one's emotional reactions in order to accomplish a goal (Thompson, 1994). Emotion regulation requires the capacity to identify, to understand, and, when

Unregulated emotion.

appropriate, to moderate one's feelings. Emotion regulation might involve *inhibiting* or subduing emotional reactions; for example, children might breathe deeply or count to 10 in order to calm themselves in the face of distressing feelings. But emotion regulation also may involve *intensifying* emotional arousal in order to meet a goal. For example, children might "pump up" their anger in order to gather the courage to stand up to a fearsome bully; or children might enhance positive emotions by recalling or reenacting a pleasant experience. In essence, emotion regulation allows the child—in the words of one child client—to be "boss of my own self."

Parents contribute to children's emotion regulation skills by responding sensitively to children's distress and keeping affect at tolerable levels so that it is manageable (Kopp, 2002). Over the course of development, children are able to take over these regulatory functions in order to engage in *self-soothing* and regulation of their own affect. As with other forms of self regulation, the functions that children initially rely on parents to provide become internalized so that the child is able to perform those skills for himself or herself.

Emotion Processes and Developmental Psychopathology

Inaccurate Emotion Expression, Recognition, or Understanding   In our discussions of the psychopathologies, we will encounter children who have deficits in some of the basic emotion functions. For example, with autism (Chapter 5) children may express emotions inappropriately and fail to accurately read and understand them in others. In other cases, the child's ability to develop emotion recognition skills is hampered by a social environment that offers mixed or unclear signals, as we will discover in our discussions of insecure attachment (Chapter 6) and maltreatment (Chapter 14). In other cases, children may hold distorted beliefs that color their ability to interpret emotions in others, as is the case in conduct disorder (Chapter 10). Consequently, when the development of emotion expression, recognition, or understanding goes awry, we will see a major effect on psychological adjustment.

Emotion Dysregulation   The preeminent risk mechanism in emotional development is poor emotion regulation (Bradley, 2000; Cicchetti, Ackerman, & Izard, 1995; Cicchetti & Izard, 1995). As Cole and colleagues (1994) point out, emotion regulation can go awry in two ways: through *underregulation* or through *overregulation*. In other words, the inability to express one's feelings can be as problematic as the inability to control them. Whereas underregulation is related to externalizing disorders associated with poor impulse control, acting-out, and aggressive behavior, overregulation may be related to the development of internalizing problems associated with anxiety, depression, and internal distress.

Emotion regulation is an essential component of many forms of psychopathology that we will discuss. For example, emotion regulation is central to coping with anxiety as well as a key to moderating anger so that it does not give rise to aggression. Similarly, the child's ability to control extreme states of negative and positive emotional arousal allows peer relations to go smoothly. Consequently, we will encounter the concept of emotion regulation in our review of the literature regarding several manifestations of psychopathology, including depression (Chapter 9), conduct disorder (Chapter 10), eating disorders and substance abuse (Chapter 12), as well as the consequences of maltreatment (Chapter 14).

As we noted previously, parent-child relationships play an important role in scaffolding the child's ability to manage upsetting emotions. However, increasingly over the course of development children need to be able to become self-reliant and govern their own emotions in settings where their parents are not available to help them, such as in school and in the peer context. Perhaps the best window into this process—by which children shift from reliance on parents to internalized emotion regulation—is provided by the construct of parent-child attachment.

Attachment

We don't usually think of radical behaviorism and classical psychoanalysis as compatible points of view but, when it comes to parent-child attachment, it seems they are. Both of these perspectives assume that human infants form affectionate ties with their caregivers secondary to those caregivers meeting the child's biological needs. The parent who provides for the infant's primary necessities, such as food, becomes associated with the positive feelings that result from being fed. In essence, this is a classical conditioning paradigm: Food is an unconditioned reinforcer that is paired with the presence of the caregiver. After a number of such pairings, the caregiver comes to be associated with positive feelings and acquires the properties of a conditioned reinforcer.

However, research on primate behavior suggests that there is a fundamental need for affection that is independent of other biological drives and may even supercede them. The preeminent examples of this are the classic experiments conducted by Harry Harlow (1958). Harlow demonstrated that infant macaque monkeys raised in isolation preferred a soft terry-cloth-covered "mother" to the wire-mesh "mother" that fed them. While experiments such as Harlow's certainly are not conducted on human infants, in Chapter 6 we will explore the effects of deprivation of care such as is suffered by children who are raised in bleak, impersonal institutions.

Attachment Theory

Attachment theory originates with Bowlby (1982), who took an ethological perspective on human behavior. Bowlby argued that, given the extreme helplessness of the human infant, it is highly adaptive to remain in close contact with the caregiver early in life. By attaching to the caregiver, the child is assured of safety, food, and ultimately survival. Thus, the "set-goal" of attachment is to maintain proximity to the caretaker. The child's behavior is organized around this goal and is designed to enhance the probability that the relationship with the caretaker will be a strong one. The attachment system becomes activated by distress, either in the form of internal needs, such as hunger, or external stressors, such as danger.

Stages of Attachment

The development of attachment follows a series of clearly identifiable stages over the first 3 years of life. (Our review follows Cassidy and Shaver, 1999, and Carlson and Sroufe, 1995.) Newborns arrive in the world oriented toward and responsive to other people. By 2 weeks of age they prefer the human voice over other sounds, and by 4 weeks they prefer the mother's voice over any other. In the second month, eye contact is established and precursors of attachment are seen as the infant orients toward the caregiver and signals his or her needs. During the next phase, from ages 3 to 6 months, infants begin to express and elicit delight in human interaction through the *social smile.* The fact that adults go through all kinds of antics to elicit such a smile shows just how adaptive and valued this behavior is, as it assures not only that a strong attachment will be formed but that it will be reciprocal. Between the 6th and 9th month, infants increasingly discriminate their own caregiver from other adults and reward this special person with a *preferential smile.* Both *separation anxiety* and *stranger anxiety* signal that the infant is aware that the caregiver has a unique value and function. From 12 to 24 months of age, crawling and walking allow children to regulate their closeness or distance to the caregiver. *Proximity-seeking,* also known as safe base behavior, is seen as infants turn to the caregiver for comforting, assistance, or simply "emotional refueling." Around 3 years of age, the goal of attachment expands beyond the infant's safety and comfort and becomes more reciprocal. In the preschool years, attachment is oriented toward establishing a *goal-directed partnership* with the caregiver, in which the needs and feelings of both participants in the relationship are taken into account.

Patterns of Attachment

Our understanding of variations in attachment relationships has been advanced by the work of Mary Ainsworth and her colleagues (1978). Ainsworth began by observing infants and their mothers in Uganda and noticed that there were distinct differences in the quality of their relationships. Back home in Boston she set up a laboratory for conducting observations of parents and infants. Her observations allowed her to identify three types of attachment relationships that have held up well over 30 years of research, with the more recent addition of a fourth pattern.

In order to activate the attachment system without unduly distressing the infant, Ainsworth created an ingenious strategy called the *Strange Situation.* The laboratory itself is a new and truly strange situation for the child and, first, the parent and child spend time together there while the investigator observes the quality of their interaction. Of particular interest is how the child uses the mother as a source of security in the presence of a new person and as a secure base from which to explore the unfamiliar toys. Subsequently, the mother is asked to leave the room and the infant's reaction to her departure is observed as is the child's ability to settle and engage in play in the mother's absence. The most powerful variable in determining attachment, however, is how the child responds to the mother when being reunited after a separation. Next, we take a closer look at these variations in attachment.

Secure Attachment   Securely attached infants explore the environment freely and interact well with the unfamiliar adults when in the caregiver's presence. They may be distressed by separation and, if so, will protest and limit exploration in the caregiver's absence. Upon reunion, they greet the caregiver positively and seek contact with her, are readily soothed, and can return to play after a period of emotional refueling. Around 65 percent of infants in U.S. middle-class, normative samples are securely attached.

The caregiver's behavior is marked by *sensitivity* to the infant's needs. Specifically, the caregiver correctly reads the infant's signals and responds quickly, appropriately, and with positive affect.

Insecure-Avoidant Attachment   In cases of **avoidant attachment** the infants seem to be precociously independent. They don't seem to rely on the caregiver for security when she is present, exploring the room very independently and responding with equal interest to the parent or the stranger. They react minimally to the caregiver's absence, sometimes not even looking up from their play as she leaves. Upon reunion, these infants avoid proximity

with the caregiver; they may turn away, avoid eye contact, and ignore her. Although they appear indifferent, physiological measures show that they are in fact distressed. Around 20 percent of infants from normative U.S. samples show this avoidant pattern.

The caregiver's behavior is marked by *distance* and an absence of comforting combined with irritability and anger during closeness. Avoidance is believed to be the infant's attempt to cope with the parent's need for distance by keeping a low profile and suppressing emotional displays that might trigger parental rejection (Main & Weston, 1982).

Insecure-Resistant Attachment   In contrast with the avoidant infants, those with **resistant** (also called ambivalent) **attachment** are preoccupied with the caregiver. They tend to be clingy and inhibited from exploring the room or interacting with the stranger even when the caregiver is present. They are highly distressed by separation but, upon reunion, angrily resist attempts at closeness and are not easily soothed. They respond to the mother with an ambivalent pattern of proximity-seeking and rejection. For example, they may demand to be picked up and then angrily push the caregiver away, or cling to her while arching away and refusing to accept her caresses. Around 15 percent of infants from normative U.S. samples show this resistant pattern.

The caregiver's behavior is marked by *unpredictability*—the caregiver is excessively close at some times and uninvolved or irritable at others. Resistance is viewed as infants' attempts to capture the attention of the caregiver, while anger results from the frustration of inconsistent care.

Insecure-Disorganized Attachment   The fourth category, which was added more recently to the typology, is the **disorganized attachment** pattern. Disorganized infants act in an inconsistent or odd manner. They may have a dazed expression or wander around aimlessly or seem to be fearful and ambivalent in the presence of the caregiver, not knowing whether to approach for comfort or avoid for safety. If they seek proximity, they do so in distorted ways such as approaching the caregiver backwards, or suddenly freezing and staring into space. Unlike infants with avoidant and resistant attachments, these infants do not seem to have developed a consistent strategy for dealing with the caregiver. Around 5 percent of infants in a normative population display this pattern.

The caregiver's behavior is marked by the use of *confusing cues,* such as the caregiver's extending her arms to the infant while backing away. Caregivers of disorganized infants also are observed to behave in strange and frightening ways. Disorganized attachment, therefore, appears to represent a collapse of any kind of systematic strategy in the face of an unpredictable and threatening environment (Lyons-Ruth, Zeanah, & Benoit, 1996).

To summarize, the quality of the caregiving relationship—whether it is warm and reliable or erratic and harsh—influences the kind of attachment that will develop. If parents are sensitive in their caregiving, if they are alert to the infant's needs and react quickly and appropriately, the infant is more likely to develop a *secure* attachment. A securely attached infant responds positively to his or her caregivers and, because of their consistency, is confident they will be there when needed. Such infants develop a loving, trusting relationship. Closeness does not result in dependency and clinging, however; on the contrary, securely attached infants explore the environment confidently. Well-cared-for infants are also apt to develop a positive self-image and confidence in their ability to cope successfully with problems as they arise. There is evidence, for example, that the securely attached infant becomes the effective problem solver as a toddler and the flexible, resourceful, and curious preschooler who is enthusiastically involved with school tasks and peers (Bretherton, 1996). Thus, through their experiences with the caregiver, children develop a schema about relationships and about the self in those relationships. This model acts as a template or guide for the child's interpersonal behavior and expectations of the self and other.

Transactional Processes

It is important to examine attachment relationships in the context of a host of other relational variables that affect the parent-child bond and interact with one another over time. Take, for example, child temperament. The child with a difficult temperament is negative, unpredictable, and difficult to read, which might impede even the best-intentioned parent's ability to provide sensitive care. On the other side of the coin, the child who is securely attached expresses positive affect and responds positively to the parent's discipline techniques, setting off a positive chain reaction in which both parent and child are increasingly rewarding to one another (Cummings & Cummings, 2002).

Therefore, attachment should not be regarded as a quality inherent in the parent or the child, but as the product of *transactions* that change over time. Thus, the patterns of attachment are not permanently fixed nor are they due exclusively to the parent's contribution to the relationship. While the various kinds of attachment show stability, for example, they also may change, especially as environmental conditions change. Or again, while there is a relation between attachment security and sensitivity of caregiving, there is still room for the influence of other variables such as infant temperament, parenting style, and socioeconomic and cultural variables (De Wolff & van IJzendoorn, 1997).

Continuity of Attachment over the Life Span

Many short-term longitudinal studies have provided evidence that the quality of infant attachment is related to functioning in preschool, middle childhood, and even adolescence. (These studies are reviewed in Cassidy and Shaver, 1999.) Recently, a number of prospective, longitudinal studies have emerged that explore the question of whether attachment is continuous over the life span. These data are impressive and virtually unprecedented in the developmental psychopathology literature. For example, Waters and colleagues (2000) conducted a study spanning 20 years, in which they investigated the relationship between attachment in infancy and adulthood. While these investigators found consistency across time points, the results of other studies are not consistent. In another prospective study of a high-risk sample, no continuity was found from infancy and adulthood (Weinfield, Sroufe, & Egeland, 2000).

However, the fact that attachment at Time 1 does not predict attachment at Time 2 is not necessarily evidence against the validity of attachment theory. What we need to look for is whether attachments are merely discontinuous or whether they show *lawful discontinuities*—that is, do attachment relationships change with circumstances in ways that attachment theory would predict? For example, one prospective longitudinal study found no continuity in attachment patterns from infancy to adulthood. However, changes in attachments were linked in "lawful" and predictable ways to negative interpersonal events, such as maternal depression and family adversity (Weinfield et al., 2000). In another example, Lewis and colleagues (2000) assessed attachment patterns at 12 months and 18 years of age but also investigated other dimensions of family functioning in the intervening period. While attachment classifications at 1 year and 18 years were not continuous, parental divorce during childhood was predictive of insecure attachment in late adolescence. In other words, the loss of a secure family environment was associated with the development of a less secure internal working model of attachment, as the theory would suggest.

Cross-Cultural Diversity in Attachment

An impressive body of research has investigated the validity of the attachment construct in diverse cultures, including the United States, Japan, Israel, China, Columbia, Germany, and several African countries. Investigators find the same patterns of attachment across samples and are able to link attachment security to sensitive caregiving and good child adaptation, as attachment theory would predict (van IJzendoorn & Sagi, 1999). However, evidence suggests that the proportion of children in each of the classifications differs across cultures, with the percentage of securely attached infants ranging between 56 percent and 80 percent.

Differences in attachment may be in keeping with cultural styles of caregiving. For example, in Japanese samples, when children are rated insecure, it is almost always with the resistant type; the avoidant type is rarely seen. Presumably, this occurs because in Japanese culture, where young children

rarely attend day care, mother-child togetherness is emphasized to the extent that the child would react with outrage to the unexpected and unwelcome event of her leaving (Dennis, Cole, Zahn-Waxler, & Mizuta, 2002).

In addition, Rosen and Rothbaum (2003) point out, the meaning that is associated with child behaviors might vary as a function of culture. For example, in their research in Japan, they find that parents view autonomy and self-assertion in children as a sign of developmental immaturity. Therefore, the investigators argue, attachment researchers must be careful not to impose Western ideals of self-reliance and self-sufficiency on other cultures nor assume that these behaviors are universally signs of a secure attachment.

Attachment Processes and Developmental Psychopathology

It is important to remember that the patterns of attachment described previously represent variations in *normal* patterns of parent-child relationship. Insecure attachment is not equivalent to psychopathology. However, as we will review in detail in Chapter 6, a wealth of research suggests that a secure attachment starts the child off on the right road in life, while insecure attachment increases vulnerability to the development of disorder. Therefore, rather than viewing insecure attachment as psychopathology, attachment relationships are viewed as a *general* risk associated with a host of psychopathologies.

Risk Mechanisms Associated with Insecure Attachment Let us take a closer look at the mechanisms by which insecure attachment increases the risk for psychopathology. (A more extensive presentation of these concepts can be found in Carlson and Sroufe, 1995.)

Insecurity The affective heart of attachment is *felt security*. Our evolutionary history has programmed infants to associate proximity to the caregiver with safety and security and separation from the caregiver with danger and anxiety. The child whose parent reliably provides the child with such security instills in the child the belief that the interpersonal world is a trustworthy place and the self is lovable. As Erikson's theory suggests, basic trust is an important prerequisite to healthy social and psychological development. (See Chapter 1.)

Inhibited Mastery Motivation   While motor skills enable the toddler physically to explore the environment, attachment makes it possible for the child to explore from a secure emotional base. With a home port to return to, the child may venture out while being confident that, in times of danger, distress, and fatigue, the caregiver will be available for protection and comfort. In contrast, insecurely attached infants either are hesitant and uncertain or defensively avoidant of the environment, thereby depriving themselves of many learning opportunities (Kelly, Brownell, & Campbell, 2000; Moss & St. Laurent, 2001). This willingness to engage with and explore the world is linked to **mastery motivation,** the child's drive to interact with the environment for the intrinsic satisfaction of learning about it (MacTurk & Morgan, 1995). Thus, through affecting exploration and mastery motivation, insecure attachment deflects the child from a healthy path of cognitive and emotional growth.

Emotion Dysregulation   The ability to rely on the caregiver as a secure base allows the child to cope successfully with the stresses and frustrations of childhood. Even when the parent is absent, the child can call on the image of the loving caregiver to soothe himself or herself. In early childhood, when children are still developing their representational skills, a physical prop can help; for example, to ease a preschooler's distress at her leave-taking, a sensitive mother may leave her keys with the child if his or her favorite cuddly blanket is not available. As we have seen, over the course of early life, children who have experienced secure attachments are increasingly able to internalize the caregiver's comforting functions, modulate their own emotions, and generate a sense of inner confidence.

Internal Working Models   As symbolic skills develop, the young child internalizes the attachment relationship in the form of an *internal working model.* The model represents not only an image of the caregiver as loving, but also of the self as lovable and love-worthy. Like any other schema, the internal working model reflects past experiences and guides expectations as to future intimate relationships. Thus, for example, the preschooler with a secure attachment will tend to be open and trusting; one with an avoidant attachment will tend to be guarded and standoffish; and one with a resistant attachment will tend to be clingy, demanding, and petulant—not just with the caregiver, but with other adults and children (Urban, Carlson, Egeland, & Sroufe, 1991). Transactionally speaking, these behaviors are likely to bring about just the kind of negative relationship that the insecurely attached child expected. In each case past experiences with caregiving have left their imprint on the children's mental life, and this imprint produces different expectations concerning what future close relations will be like and, consequently, different interpersonal behavior. In later life internal working models of self and other play a part in the quality of friendships (Schneider, Atkinson, & Tardif, 2001) and adult romantic partnerships (Crowell et al., 2002).

In sum, attachment involves core affective and cognitive variables in both the intrapersonal and interpersonal contests. It is therefore reasonable to assume that, if the process goes awry, the child's development might be at risk for being diverted from its normal course. Given the importance of attachment relationships to the child's core sense of identity, we turn next to the development of the self.

Self-Development

For many developmental psychopathologists, attachment and the self are seen to be so inexorably linked in development that they are viewed as part of an organized system (Cicchetti, 1991b; Sroufe, 1990a). Indeed, the object relations theorist Winnicott (1987) asserted, "There is no such thing as a baby. There is a baby *and someone*" (p. 88). Or as George Herbert Mead (1932) wrote, "Selves can only exist in definite relationship to other selves" (p. 285). Remember that the internal working model of attachment is a model not only of the relationship with the caregiver, but of the self. Over the course of childhood, children develop increasingly complex and differentiated models of the self and of relationships. Through their interactions with caregivers, children develop a sense of who they are and what value is placed on their unique personhood and qualities.

The Emergence of Self

Sroufe (1990a) defines the self as "an inner organization of attitudes, feelings, expectations, and meanings" (p. 281), which arises in the context of the caregiving relationship. The emergence of self over the course of childhood is characterized by increasing organization and increasing agency, as the child becomes a more active participant in the process of development (Cicchetti, 1991). Sroufe describes self-organization as proceeding through a series of phases over the course of childhood.

In the first 6 months of life (the *preintentional self*), infants become increasingly socially interactive and aware of their surroundings. They are dependent on their caregivers to modulate states of arousal and provide them with regulation of their inner states. However, they also begin to adapt their behavior to that of their caregivers and can respond to complex patterns of interaction, resulting in mutual delight.

During the next stage, from 6 to 12 months (*the intentional self*), infants are more intentional and goal directed in their behavior and can now coordinate, initiate, and direct exchanges with the caregiver. For example, the infant now engages in a greeting response (smiling, cooing, bouncing, and raising both arms) at the sight of the caregiver while showing negative reactions to strangers. Toward the end of this stage, as we know from attachment research, the infant's emotions, cognitions, and social behavior are organized around the caregiver and the caregiving relationship.

From ages 12 to 24 months (*the separate, aware self*) toddlers increasingly actively pursue their own goals and plans, even when these are contrary to the caregiver's. They initiate separations both physically and psychologically, practicing their independent skills, while still orienting around the caregiver as a "safe base." This phase marks a development shift toward the emergence of self-awareness and agency, the self as the author of its own actions.

The next period, from ages 24 to 60 months (*the self-monitoring self*), is marked by a new level of awareness of both self and other. This change is ushered in with the capacity for representational thought as well as an increasing ability to modulate and regulate their own emotions and behavior. These symbolic capacities allow the child to recognize internal states in the self and others as well as the boundaries between them. For example, not only are children aware of their own plans and intentions, but they are aware that the caregiver is aware of their plan and has opinions about it. The most important attainment here is a sense of **self-constancy,** the recognition that the self is an organized whole that "goes on being" even with shifts in mood and in the relationship with the caregiver.

These processes of internalization, stability, and self-directedness continue to direct self-development over the next years of life. Middle childhood, according to Sroufe, is the era of the *consolidated self,* as the child's internal working model leads to consistency in representations of self and other. In adolescence, we see the emergence of the *self-reflective self,* as formal operations allow the youth to observe and reflect on his or her own perspectives and capacities.

At the core of self, in Sroufe's perspective, is ownership of one's own experience. The mechanism by which children learn that they are the authors of their own actions is *internal regulation* of emotions and behavior. In other words, children initially develop a sense of self through experiencing their actions as effective or ineffective in managing internal and external demands and maintaining equilibrium. "The core of self," states Sroufe, "lies in patterns of behavioral/affective regulation, which give continuity to experience despite development and environmental change" (p. 292).

Self-Regulation

As we have seen, normal development involves the increasing organization and self-directedness of behavior. In short, the child is increasingly in his or her own driver's seat and able to initiate and regulate behavior

The origins of self-control.

and emotions. **Self-regulation** is defined as behavior that is initiated by the self and experienced as voluntary and autonomous (Grolnick & Farkas, 2002). In other words, children who are self-regulated experience themselves as the agents of their own actions. Further, children who are self-regulated are intrinsically motivated, not requiring parents to control and structure their behavior. They are also able to make independent choices and think for themselves without being unduly vulnerable to peer pressure.

Self-regulation has two components: *emotion regulation,* which we introduced previously, and *behavioral self-regulation,* which involves the ability to manage one's own behavior. Place an attractive toy in front of a young child and say, "Now don't touch until I come back," and you will see how difficult it is for children to control their impulses and delay gratification. Self-regulation emerges in the second year of life and is observed when children display self-control and act socially appropriately even in the absence of parental monitoring. In the preschool years, the child's representational capacities allow for increasingly adaptive and flexible self-regulation. Language development assists this process, enabling children to engage in self-talk to cope with temptation. For example, it is not unusual to see the young child look at the desirable toy and repeat aloud the adult's prohibition ("Mustn't touch!").

Self-Concept

Self-concept comprises two components. The first of these concerns the *content* of the self-concept (e.g., "What am I like?"). The second involves *valence,* that is whether those self-perceptions are positive or negative (e.g., "Do I like who I am?"), also termed *self-esteem* or *perceived competence.* Children's self-concept emerges through a series of stages that parallel their cognitive and emotional development.

Development of the Self-Concept

Infancy and Toddlerhood   (Our review follows Harter, 1999, except where otherwise noted.) The infant's dawning recognition of self arises out of experiences of effectiveness in the world: I smile and people smile back; I cry and the food I need appears. Thus, in the earliest years the infant's sense of self is termed the *self-as-agent.* By 2 years of age, children respond with recognition to their reflection in a mirror and are able to pick themselves out of an array of photographs. Perhaps the clearest expression of a sense of self is evident during the "terrible twos" when the toddler asserts his or her own wants, needs, and opinions in sometimes strident tones.

Preschool   In the preschool years, children's conceptions of self are focused on concrete observable characteristics such as their physical appearance ("I'm tall"), play activities ("I play baseball"), preferences ("Pizza is my favorite food"), or possessions ("I have a bike"). This is the time of the *behavioral self.* These concrete descriptors represent discrete behaviors rather than higher-order categories (e.g., "I can run real fast" does not generalize to "I'm good at sports"). Thus, the self-concept of the preschool child is not organized in a particularly logical or coherent way, and contradictory evaluations of the self can coexist quite comfortably. Further, young children are likely to evaluate themselves in unrealistically positive ways,

confusing their hopes and desires with their actual competencies. Children at this age also engage in all-or-none thinking about the self, based on the affective states they are experiencing at the moment ("I'm always happy"; "I'm never scared"). Cognitive limitations also make it difficult for children to understand that they can experience two different feelings at the same time, a phenomenon termed affective *splitting* (Fischer & Ayoub, 1994).

Early to Middle Childhood   Children aged 5 to 7 still show some of the characteristics of the early stage, including a tendency toward unrealistically positive self-perceptions (e.g., "I can also throw a ball real far; I'm going to be on some kind of team when I am older. I can do lots of stuff real good, lots! If you are good at things you can't be bad at things, at least not at the same time. I know some other kids who are bad at things, but not me!" [Harter, 1999, p. 41]). All-or-nothing thinking persists in the form of thinking in terms of opposites and *overdifferentiating*—that is, a child whose learning disability results in low achievement may come to the conclusion that she is "all dumb." In middle childhood, children's self-descriptors focus on specific competencies and skills they have mastered. These now begin to be interrelated and organized into general categories, but these tend to be compartmentalized on the basis of positive and negative valence, and the child still cannot integrate both positive and negative attributes with one another. Although children, before middle childhood, do not have a general self-concept, they do differentiate two sources of self-esteem, one deriving from being socially acceptable; the other from being competent (Harter, Bresnick, Bouchey, & Whitesell, 1997).

Middle to Late Childhood   By age 8 to 11, children's concepts of self involve generalizations that integrate a number of characteristics of the self (e.g., "I'm pretty popular, at least with the girls. That's because I'm nice to people and helpful and can keep secrets" [(Harter, 1999, p. 48]). In late childhood, children view the self not in terms of observable behaviors they perform but in terms of personality characteristics they hold—this is the *psychological self,* which is increasingly stable and integrated. The new ability to form higher-order concepts allows the school-age child to develop a representation of his or her overall self-worth. In addition to a *global* sense of self-esteem, children evaluate themselves in terms of three specific areas of competence: *academic, physical,* and *social* (Harter et al., 1997). From middle childhood on, self-evaluation is also closely related to behavior: Academic self-esteem predicts school achievement, curiosity, and motivation to take on challenges, while social self-esteem is related to confidence with peers. In this period, children also engage in *social comparison,* evaluating their competencies and worth in comparison to others'.

Adolescence   The formal operational skills of adolescence allow the youth to think about the self in increasingly abstract terms, based not only on what one is doing and has done but on what one believes one can be. This is the *abstract, future-oriented self.* In adolescence, the self becomes more complex as, in addition to the global, academic, physical, and social dimensions of self-concept, adolescence brings the additional areas of *close friendship, romantic appeal,* and *job competence* (Harter et al., 1997). However, whether any of these areas affect general self-worth depends on their *salience* or importance to the youth. Making all As or being good-looking may mean everything to one youth but be a matter of indifference to another. Consequently, while children with low self-worth believe they are incompetent in areas that are important to them, children with high self-worth can tolerate perceiving themselves as less competent in areas that are unimportant to them (Harter, 1986). For example, Steele & Eccles (1995) find that African American youths who perceive their school achievement to be devalued maintain a positive self-image by de-identifying with the academic domain. Thus, how the self is valued depends on the discrepancy between the *real self*—how one believes one is—and the *ideal self*—how one feels one should be. The adolescent's representational abilities also can be a source of vulnerability, as egocentricity and

increasing self-consciousness lead adolescents to become preoccupied with what (they assume) others must be thinking of them.

Identity   Although the process of self-concept formation is ongoing throughout childhood, Erikson proposed that in adolescence the youth confronts a crisis of *identity versus identity confusion.* The youth who has successfully navigated this process is termed *identity achieved* (Marcia, Waterman, Archer, & Orlofsky, 1993). Adolescents in this category have explored their options and developed a coherent sense of identity and are more socially mature and motivated to achieve than their peers. However, the identity formation process might go awry in different ways. One relates to *precocious* development (see Chapter 1): The youth who precipitously declares an identity without exploring the options is termed *identity foreclosed.* Research shows that foreclosed youths are rigid and authoritarian in their attitudes. Another deviation relates to *developmental delay:* Youths who are confused and uncertain about their identity and are making no progress toward establishing one are termed *identity diffuse* and tend to be socially isolated, unmotivated, and attracted to substance abuse. In contrast, youths who are in *moratorium* are engaged in actively exploring their options but have not yet made a commitment to any of them. While they are also likely to have experimented with drugs and show some anxiety, they also are high in self-esteem.

Ethnic Identity   Another important task in the process of identity formation is the inclusion of ethnicity into the self-concept. By around age 7, children identify themselves as a member of their ethnic group and by about 10 they understand that their ethnicity is constant (Ocampo, Knight, & Bernal, 1997). Parents and community members make an important contribution to children's understanding of and pride in their culture. However, as youths enter the adolescent years, they are increasingly aware of prejudice and racism in the society around them. Ethnic minority youths might also experience conflict between their family's values and those shared by their peers from the dominant culture (Phinney, Ong, & Madden, 2000). Intergenerational conflicts are particularly evident in immigrant families, where children are being raised in a culture much different from that of their parents. (See Coll and Garrido, 2000.)

Research on ethnically diverse samples also raises a question as to whether the identity status presumed to be ideal in Western society is a culturally specific one. Youths who are raised in subcultures that emphasize the maintenance of traditional communal values, such as Native American tribes, are disproportionately represented among those classified as identity foreclosed. However, for these young people it may be adaptive to early on commit themselves to membership in a cohesive, supportive community rather than estranging themselves by attempting to individuate in the dominant culture's fashion (Spencer & Markstrom-Adams, 1990).

The task of identity formation is complex for the ethic minority youth. It involves forging an identity that incorporates a sense of the self as a member of a unique subgroup as well as a member of the larger culture. Some research supports the notion that the achievement of a *bicultural identity* is associated with the best psychological health (LaFromboise, Coleman, & Gerton, 1993).

While most of the research and theory focuses on children of a single ethnic background, increasing numbers of children in the United States are *multiracial*. While in the 1970s, 1 in 100 children was born to parents who were of different races, in 1999 the proportion had increased to 1 in 19 (National Center for Health Statistics, 1999). The achievement of a multiracial identity requires an added level of fluidity and adaptability and may be associated with a variety of outcomes. "For example, some learn to negotiate the intricacies of more than one social group and become more socially skilled as a result; others resolve their conflicting loyalties by identifying only with one group or by adopting a fused biracial or bicultural identity" (Herman, 2004, p. 732).

Ego Development and the Self

In Chapter 1, we described the evolution of psychoanalytic theory from its early focus on primitive drives to its more modern attention to the adaptive aspects of the person. Two legacies of ego psychology have proven especially helpful to our attempts to understand psychopathology of the self (Hauser & Safyer, 1995). The first concerns the concepts of ego resilience and ego control. The second concerns the development of ego defenses.

Ego Resilience and Ego Control   To set the stage, let us imagine the scene that Jeanne and Jack Block created in their own developmental laboratory. To assess individual differences in children's response to challenge, they brought a series of young children into their lab and presented them with a puzzle to solve that was beyond the child's developmental level. One group of children gave up easily: some with indifference, some with tears, and others with rage. Yet other children persisted at the task despite their frustration and inability to solve it. Some persisters demonstrated a grim, driven style, repeating the same strategy over and over despite its ineffectiveness, while others displayed a scientist-like curiosity and creative problem-solving style. At the end of the day, some children appeared dejected and some angry, while others declared the study "fun."

To explain these individual differences, the Blocks proposed the constructs of ego resilience and ego control (Block & Block, 1980). **Ego control** refers to the degree to which individuals give free expression to their impulses; and, at moderate levels, it is associated with spontaneity, emotional expressiveness, and socially appropriate behavior (Eisenberg et al., 2003). However, children who are ego overcontrolled are inhibited, reluctant to express their feelings, and vulnerable to depression (Block & Gjerde, 1990), while ego undercontrol is related to conduct problems in children and adolescents (Huey, Jr. & Weisz, 1997; White et al., 1994).

Ego resilience, in turn, is defined as "resourceful adaptation" to a changing environment (Block & Block, 1980). Ego resilient individuals are able to analyze situations and flexibly choose from an array of strategies the problem-solving approach that best fits the circumstances. In contrast, *ego brittleness* involves inflexibility and "an inability to respond to the dynamic requirements of the situation, a tendency to perseverate or become disorganized . . .

when under stress, and a difficulty recouping after traumatic experiences" (p. 48). Research has linked ego resilience to secure attachment and problem-solving ability in preschoolers (Carlson & Sroufe, 1995), whereas ego brittleness is related to childhood disorders such as anxiety and depression (Huey, Jr. & Weisz, 1997).

Ego Defenses   Freud stated that internal conflicts can become so painful that we develop strategies to defend ourselves against awareness of them. For example, one such defense mechanism is **repression,** in which both the dangerous impulse and the ideas and fantasies associated with it are banished from consciousness. In essence, the child says, "What I am not aware of does not exist"; for example, a girl who is frightened of being angry with her abusive mother no longer is aware of such feelings after repression. If repression is insufficient, **reaction formation** might be called into play so that the child thinks and feels in a manner diametrically opposed to the anxiety-provoking impulse. Continuing our example, the girl now feels excessively loving toward her mother and would not dream of being angry. In **projection,** the forbidden impulse is both repressed and attributed to others; the little girl might be upset that "all of the other girls" she knows are sassy and disrespectful to their mothers. In **displacement,** the impulse is allowed expression but is directed toward a different object; for example, our little girl becomes angry with her babysitter.

The danger of defense mechanisms is that they might distort an individual's perceptions of the self, the other, or reality in general. The child who represses her hostility toward her parents is as convinced as if, in reality, the relationship were an unusually blissful one. If defense mechanisms prevent reality testing by protecting the child from facing his or her fears, are they then inherently pathological? Not so, said Anna Freud (Freud, 1965), who extended her father's work on the understanding of defense mechanisms. Defenses are a necessary and normal part of psychological development. The healthy child can use defenses flexibly, relying on them to manage a particularly painful episode in development but relinquishing them

when they are no longer needed. When defenses become *rigid, pervasive,* and *extreme* and when the child's repertoire is unduly *limited,* defenses are in danger of jeopardizing future growth.

Recently, research has documented the emergence of the defense mechanisms over the course of development, from preschool to adulthood (Cramer & Block, 1998; Cramer, 2000) and across different levels of psychological maturity in adolescents and adults (Bond, 1995). Taken together, this research suggests that defenses can be construed along a *developmental continuum,* ranging from those that are primitive—and associated with poor adaptation if used exclusively and rigidly—to those that are mature and associated with high adaptive levels. This continuum is represented in the Defensive Functioning Scale, one of the Axes Provided for Further Study in *DSM-IV-TR* (2000). (See Table 2.1.) Defenses at the *high adaptive level* are those that allow for a balance between conflicting thoughts and feelings and maximize their access to conscious awareness. An example of an adaptive defense is humor, which allows a person to acknowledge something painful without being devastated by it. At the *low adaptive level* are those defenses that interfere with the child's perception of objective reality, such as psychotic denial.

Self Processes and Developmental Psychopathology

To summarize, a number of aspects of self are implicated in psychopathological development.

Low Self-Esteem   A *negative self-concept* is a risk mechanism for a number of disorders, most obviously depression and suicide. The child who perceives himself or herself as defective, unworthy, or unable to achieve the cultural ideal is vulnerable to feelings of sadness, hopelessness, and futurelessness. A poor self-concept may also be the product of societal attitudes, such as racism or homophobia; for example, gay, lesbian, and bisexual youths have rates of suicide that are disproportionately high (Rotheram-Borus & Langabeer, 2001). Disturbances in self-esteem may take the opposite form as well. Some disturbed children evidence unrealistically *high* self-esteem, claiming that they are the "best at everything"

Table 2.1

DSM-IV-TR Defensive Functioning Scale and Definitions of Defenses

1. **High adaptive level:** allowing conscious awareness of feelings and ideas and promoting a balance between conflicting motives
   Humor—emphasizing the amusing or ironic aspects of a conflict or stressor
   Sublimation—channeling potentially maladaptive feelings or impulses into socially acceptable behavior

2. **Mental inhibitions or compromise level:** keeping potentially threatening ideas and feelings out of awareness
   Isolation of affect—separating ideas from the feelings originally associated with them
   Repression—expelling disturbing wishes, thoughts, or experiences from conscious awareness

3. **Minor image-distorting level:** distorting one's image of self or others in order to allow one to maintain self-esteem
   Devaluation—attributing exaggerated negative qualities to others in order to minimize their importance
   Omnipotence—perceiving self as being superior to others in order to fend off feelings of vulnerability

4. **Disavowal level:** keeping unpleasant or unacceptable impulses, ideas, affects, or responsibility out of awareness
   Denial—refusing to acknowledge some painful aspect of external reality or subjective experience
   Projection—falsely attributing to another one's own unacceptable feelings, impulses, or thoughts

5. **Major image-distorting level:** creating gross misattributions or distortions in the image of self or other
   Projective identification—falsely attributing to another one's own unacceptable thoughts or feelings and behaving in such a way as to engender in the other person those very thoughts or feelings
   Splitting—compartmentalizing positive and negative experiences in order to block one side of ambivalence from awareness

6. **Action level:** dealing with stress by acting or withdrawing
   Acting out—giving vent to conflicts through action in order to avoid experiencing upsetting feelings
   Passive aggression—presenting a facade of overt compliance that masks covert resistance, resentment, or hostility

7. **Defensive dysregulation:** using defenses involving a pronounced break with objective reality
   Delusional projection—forming a fixed delusional belief system revolving around one's own projections
   Psychotic denial—engaging in extreme denial of perceived external reality resulting in gross impairment in reality testing

Source: Adapted from *DSM-IV-TR.* Copyright 2000 American Psychiatric Association.

(Baumeister, Bushman, & Campbell, 2000). However, in contrast to normal, healthy self-esteem, exaggerated self-esteem is unrealistic, insecure, and easily deflated (Cicchetti & Howes, 1991).

Identity Confusion   As we have seen, youths who have difficulty resolving the crisis of identity are more vulnerable to risk in adolescence. For many youths, this process also involves the task of incorporating ethnicity and/or sexuality into the identity concept. One form identity confusion takes is a lack of *self-continuity,* when youths "lose the thread that tethers together their past, present, and future" (Chandler, Lalonde, Sokol, & Hallett, 2003, p. 2). As we will discuss in Chapter 9, such youths are highly vulnerable to suicide.

Disruptions in Self-Organization   While identity confusion represents a delay in normal develop-

ment, lack of self-organization is a severe deviation from the norm. In contrast to Mahler's view of the infant as essentially autistic at birth, research shows that from the moment of birth the infant is engaged in organizing its experiences in a coherent and cohesive way and that the attachment relationship is fundamental to this process (Stern, 1985). When this process goes awry, it is associated with some of the most severe psychopathologies we will cover in this text.

Disruptions in self-organization are associated either with profound mental illnesses, such as autism and schizophrenia, or with extremes of pathological caregiving. For example, as we saw earlier, severely traumatized adolescents with disorganized attachment histories lack a cohesive sense of self (Ogawa, Sroufe, Weinfield, Carlson, & Egeland, 1997). Instead, their self-image vacillates with their moods and they have difficulty maintaining the boundaries that separate themselves and others—in other words, they have trouble recognizing where the self ends and others begin. These youths also engage in the use of primitive defenses that distort their perceptions of self and other. Such disruptions in self-organization are associated with the development of borderline personality disorder, a deviation in self-development that we will describe more fully in Chapter 15.

Ego Brittleness   In Chapter 1, we introduced the concept of resilience, the remarkable ability to emerge as a psychologically healthy individual despite negative circumstances. The concept of ego resilience describes protective factors that are incorporated into the self. The ego resilient youth is able to "play a bad hand well," while the ego brittle youth has rigid defenses, lacks adaptibility, and is discouraged by obstacles rather than challenged by them.

Poor Self-Regulation   Another accomplishment of normal development is the ability to regulate one's own behavior, emotions, and relationships with others. When this process goes awry, the child is highly reactive, impulsive, and unable to adapt smoothly to changing environmental demands. One of the important developmental processes that contributes to self-regulation is the *internalization* of parental values. Internalization and self-regulation are also directly related to another important developmental task, moral development; we will next turn to that topic.

Moral Development

Under the heading of moral development, we are integrating research on a number of different themes, including conscience, guilt, and moral judgment. In particular, we are concerned with the question of how children come to *internalize* their parents' values and teachings. Over the course of development, children's good behavior comes to be governed less by fear of punishment and more by self-generated moral standards and ideals. First, however, we should look at how children's reasoning about right and wrong progresses as a function of their cognitive development.

The Development of Moral Reasoning

Elaborating on Piaget's (1932) earlier work on children's thinking about moral issues, Kohlberg (1976) constructed a theory of the development of moral reasoning. By presenting children with classic moral dilemmas, such as that of Little Hans, who must decide whether it is right to steal to provide his mother with life-saving medication, Kohlberg determined that children's moral judgment advances through a series of stages.

At the *preconventional* level, during the early preschool years, children evaluate actions in terms of whether they lead to pleasure or punishment. Those resulting in rewards are good; those resulting in punishment are bad. ("He better not or the store owner might get mad at him.") During the *conventional* morality stage, in middle childhood, the child adopts the conventional standards of behavior to maintain the approval of others or conform to some moral authority such as religion. Thinking is absolutist and inflexible—right is right, wrong is wrong, and there are no extenuating circumstances or mitigating considerations. ("It is wrong to steal; it's the law.") In the *postconventional* or principled stage, older children and adolescents judge behavior in terms of the morality of contract and democratically accepted law, of universal principles of ethics and justice, and of individual conscience, holding themselves personally accountable for moral decisions ("Some things have a higher priority than others—like human life is more important than money. So saving his mother's life is more important than obeying rules about property"). Between 6 and 16, the preconventional level gradually declines while the other two levels increase, although only about one-quarter of 16-year-olds achieve the highest level.

One of the shortcomings of research on moral reasoning is that it is not always predictive of moral behavior. Therefore, children's ability to think in sophisticated ways about hypothetical dilemmas is not necessarily linked to the choices they make in real life. Some youths, as we will see in Chapter 10, are perfectly aware of the higher moral principles that they "should" follow, and yet they behave otherwise. What differentiates children who behave prosocially or antisocially is more than a matter of cognition; it also involves emotion—particularly the emotions of guilt and empathy. Before we explore the role of these emotions, let us look at the context in which they emerge: the parent-child relationship.

Internalization

Ultimately, the goal of socialization is that children be guided not merely by concern for external rewards and punishment but rather that they come to *internalize* parental values and therefore be intrinsically motivated to behave in prosocial ways. Internalization leads directly to the development of *conscience* and therefore is an important developmental process underlying moral behavior. In short, through the process of internalization, morality comes to be something that is intrinsic to the self, not something imposed from without.

Kochanska's (2002) line of research on internalization teaches us a great deal about the process by which behavioral regulation is transferred from the parent to the child over the course of development. The standard scenario is to expose the child to temptation—to provide the child with opportunities to cheat on a task or to ignore a parental command or prohibition—and to observe how the child behaves in the parent's absence. Internalization is inferred when the child complies with parental expectations even when the parent is not there to monitor his or her behavior. (See Figure 2.2.)

The first stage in the process of internalization is *committed compliance*—that is, rather than complying solely on the basis of the immediate consequences

Figure 2.2

Internalization, "For Better or Worse".

of behavior, the child appears to share the parent's values and to be as committed as the parent to the goal of good behavior. The committed child not only behaves appropriately without prompts and reminders, but does so enthusiastically. Research confirms that committed compliance is a precursor to internalization: Committed compliance in toddlerhood predicts internalization in the preschool years (Kochanska, Aksan, & Koeing, 1995).

Kochanska and colleagues' research also reveals the qualities of parenting that are most likely to foster internalization. First, observations show that *shared positive affect* is key. Committed compliance is related to shared positive affect between parents and children during free play in the laboratory, presumably via increasing the child's motivation to share the parents' values and goals (Kochanska et al., 1995). Second, internalization is related to a quality of *mutual responsiveness* between parent and child (Kochanska & Murray, 2000). Mutual responsivity is a transactional process in which children who experience their parents as responsive and caring respond in kind by showing consideration for the parents' feelings and wishes. Over time, mothers who engage in mutually responsive relationships with their toddlers have less need to be directive and controlling when the children are preschool-age (Kochanska, 1997b), and in the school-age years their children are less likely to give in to the impulse to cheat (Kochanska & Murray, 2000).

Kochanska's research points to the importance of the quality of the parent-child relationship for moral development. When the relationship is marked by parent sensitivity and responsiveness—qualities that are also related to a secure attachment—the child is motivated to please the parent as well as to adopt the parent's goals and values. Thus, love plays a role in morality. Three other emotions come into play and deserve our attention: shame, guilt, and empathy.

Emotional Dimensions of Morality: Shame, Guilt, and Empathy

The Emergence of Shame and Guilt   In our previous discussion of emotional development, we mentioned that self-conscious emotions emerge after the 3rd year of life. Among these are the two emotions

of shame and guilt. While the terms are often used synonymously, research shows that they have different origins and functions. The experience of *shame* is other oriented, focusing on public disapproval and involving a negative evaluation of the entire self (e.g., "I'm bad"). In contrast, *guilt* is inner oriented, focusing on failure to meet one's own internalized standards and involving a negative evaluation of the behavior (e.g., "I did a bad thing") (Tangney & Fischer, 1995).

Again, parental socialization is key. Parents who are *coercive*—that is, those whose reprimands focus on children's failures and make the children feel badly about themselves—are likely to produce children who are prone to experiencing shame, whereas parents whose discipline calls children's attention to the effect they have on others are likely to help engender guilt. While guilt might sound like an unpleasant emotion from which we would want to spare the child, in fact it is linked with prosocial behavior and consideration for others. In contrast, shame is linked to antisocial behavior and destructiveness (Tangney, 2001).

An integrative study by Kochanska and colleagues (2002) establishes the links among parenting, self, guilt, and moral development. In their laboratory, children were observed after having been told that they had damaged a valuable toy—in fact, the experimenters had rigged the toy to fall apart as soon as the child handled it. Children whose self-concepts were more developmentally advanced at 18 months displayed more guilt for their "transgression" at 22 months of age and, in turn, engaged in more prosocial behavior and exhibited higher levels of moral reasoning at 56 months. Coercive maternal discipline was related to lower levels of guilt in children; however, the relationship was a curvilinear one: The highest levels of guilt were displayed by children whose mothers were either very high or very low in coerciveness.

Empathy   Empathy refers to an emotional reaction to another's experience. A distinction is often made between *empathic concern,* which involves caring about others' welfare and being motivated to help them, and mere *empathic distress* (Endresen & Olweus, 2001). For example, if two children observe another child crying, the empathically concerned child may ask what is wrong, whereas the empathically distressed child may simply start crying as well. As early as 6 months of age children respond to emotional distress in peers, but it is not until the preschool years that children display true empathy, in which they clearly distinguish their own experience from the other person's (Siegler, DeLoache, & Eisenberg, 2003). Research shows that empathy in children evokes feelings of guilt which, in turn, motivate prosocial behavior (Bohart & Stipek, 2001).

Research also shows gender differences in the emergence of empathy over the course of childhood. Generally, at every age, girls score higher on measures of empathy (Eisenberg & Strayer, 1987). However, there are also gender-related differences related to the *recipient* of empathy. For example, Endresen and Olweus (2001) found that as boys approach adolescence, they tend to become increasingly more empathic toward females. The authors suggest that sex-role socialization comes into play, because an acceptable part of masculinity entails being protective and caring toward females but not toward other males.

Moral Processes and Developmental Psychopathology

Relational Deficits   The context in which all the dimensions of morality described previously develop is a caring relationship. When caregivers are harsh and unresponsive, children have little motivation to comply with their expectation or to internalize their parents' values. Similarly, children who experience shaming forms of discipline grow to be deficient in empathy and the appropriate guilt that motivates prosocial behavior. In Chapter 10, we will describe a possible exception to this, a group of children whose callousness toward others does not appear to be a product of poor parenting practices.

Cognitive Deficits   Children who are not able to reason about moral problems are likely to respond merely on the basis of immediate rewards and punishments. Social cognitive variables we discussed earlier are important to understanding how moral judgment results in prosocial or antisocial behavior.

Children who engage in distorted cognitions about others may perceive their own aggression not as bad behavior but as justifiable self-defense—even as an act of heroism (Caprara, Barbaranelli, & Pastorelli, 2001).

Cultural Expectations   Cultural expectations also come into play. As we will discuss in Chapters 10 and 14, children growing up surrounded by brutality learn that this behavior is normative and acceptable. Societal forces also arise in the form of sex-role stereotyped expectations for the display of such qualities as kindness, caring, and empathy in males and females. Let us now turn to look in greater detail at the developmental variables of sex and gender.

Sex and Gender

First, some terminology is in order. While *sex* and *gender* are both used to refer to biological maleness or femaleness, the child's awareness of his or her sex is called **gender identity.** In addition, society prescribes which behaviors and feelings are appropriate for boys and which are appropriate for girls, and children must learn such appropriate **gender-role** behavior. Finally, *sexuality* involves sexual feelings and behavior, while **sexual orientation** refers to the choice of partner, whether same or other sex.

Gender Identity

The typical 2- to 3-year-old male child has grasped the idea that "boy" applies to him, and he can correctly answer the question "Are you a boy or a girl?" However, he does not comprehend the real meaning of the label, nor has he grasped the principle of categorizing people by sex, relying instead on external cues of size, clothing, and hairstyle (Golombok & Fivush, 1994). Remember that preschoolers are still cognitively in the preoperational stage, literally believing what they see, so their categorizations by sex are on the basis of manifest differences. Because children this age are incapable of conservation (understanding that objects remain the same even when their appearance changes), they also believe that as appearances change so do essences—things that look different are different. Consequently, for a child this age it seems perfectly possible for boys to change into girls and vice versa just by altering their clothes, hairstyle, and behavior to that of the other sex. To the boy in our third vignette in Chapter 1, it seems perfectly possible for a child to grow up to be a "mommy" or a "daddy" regardless of his or her present status. Only around age 6 or 7, when conservation is cognitively possible, do children achieve **gender constancy,** grasping the idea that gender is permanent and immutable. They also come to realize that the genitals are the crucial factor determining gender.

Gender Roles

Every society prescribes behaviors and feelings appropriate and inappropriate to males and females. Traditionally in Western society, boys should be dominant, aggressive, unsentimental, stoic in the face of pain, and pragmatic; girls should be nurturing, sociable, nonaggressive, and emotionally expressive. The essential differences between these prescriptions for the masculine and feminine role have been defined as *agency* versus *communion* (Block, 1983). Despite societal changes in the roles of men and women, gender stereotypes have remained remarkably consistent over the past three decades (Ruble & Martin, 1998). Children as young as 3 years of age can classify toys, clothes, household objects, and games according to social stereotypes; and preschoolers do the same with adult occupations. As thinking becomes less concrete and more inferential in middle childhood, children are able to associate gender roles with more subtle psychological characteristics such as assertiveness and nurturance.

In addition to knowing the stereotypes, very early in development children also show a preference for engaging in gender-stereotypical behavior. Children aged 2 to 3 prefer stereotyped toys (trucks for boys, dolls for girls) and would rather play with same-sex peers (Maccoby, 1999). In middle childhood boys increasingly prefer gender-typed behavior and attitudes, while girls shift to more masculine activities and traits. This is an example of boys being more narrowly gender-typed than girls. "Sissies" are teased, whereas "tomboys" are tolerated.

Social learning theorists point to the many ways culturally prescribed gender-typed behavior is reinforced. For example, fathers play more vigorously with their infant sons than with their infant daughters. In the toddler and preschool periods boys receive more physical punishment, are rewarded for playing with gender-typed toys, and are encouraged to manipulate objects and to climb. In middle childhood parents interact more with the same-sex child. Also, boys are reinforced for investigating the community and being independent, while girls are supervised more and rewarded for being compliant. In general fathers are more narrowly stereotyped in their behavior than are mothers, which is one reason boys are punished for deviations more than girls are (Lamb, 1997). Finally, both teachers and peers, in numerous overt and subtle ways, exert pressure on children to conform to social stereotypes.

Sexuality

Our understanding of normal childhood sexuality is surprisingly limited (Sandfort, 2000). Since Freud first opened the Pandora's box of childhood sexuality, many have expressed shock and discomfort with the idea of the child as a sexual being. Moreover, it has been difficult for us to arrive at an understanding that is based on empirical research. If parents are uncomfortable with the idea that children have sexual feelings, they are hardly likely to allow them to participate in a study that inquires about these. Childhood sexuality is not only sensitive to study but methodologically difficult. Children's capacity to understand their private experiences is limited, as is their ability to put those experiences into words. And even young children are aware that certain topics are not appropriate for discussion with a strange adult. However, an understanding of normative sexual development is valuable to us. Sexual feelings are a part of life and a motivator of behavior. Further, as we consider the continuum between normal and abnormal development, we will want to know what sexual behaviors in a child are signs of psychopathology and which are part of normal childhood sexual exploration.

For example, age-inappropriate sexual knowledge is often used as evidence that a child has been molested. Therefore, it is important to know what children of various ages normally understand about sex (Volbert, 2000). Before the age of 4 girls tend not to have a specific term for their genitalia, referring generally to that entire region of their body as their "bottom." Before the age of 7 children generally do not report a sexual function for their genitalia beyond a vague notion that "babies are made there." It is only by the age of 9 that children normally begin to associate procreation with the sex act. Volbert (2000) conducted one of the rare studies of young children's knowledge of sexuality by interviewing a sample of 147 two- to six-year-olds. Until the age of 5, no children demonstrated knowledge of adult sexual behavior, and only three of the older children described overtly sexual actions, the most knowledgeable boy revealing that he had seen this activity in a movie.

Children's understanding of sexuality also is a function of their level of cognitive development. True to Piaget, children will transform the facts they are taught to fit with the schemas they already have. Therefore, when children provide wild explanations about where babies come from, Bernstein and Cowan (1975) argue, the source may not be misinformation but the process of assimilation at work on information that is too complex for the child to understand. Children's knowledge about sex also varies across cultural contexts, determined by norms for adult openness about sexual matters and how accessible sex-related information is to children.

Other research focuses on what kinds of sexual behaviors children display in the course of normal development. Curiosity about their own and others' genitals is quite common in children in the preschool years (Schuhrke, 2000). Beginning in the second year, children look, play with, expose, and comment on their bodies and invite caregivers to do the same, while the object of their interest begins to shift from parents to peers in the school-age years. Sandfort and Cohen-Kettenis (2000) asked a group of Dutch mothers about the behaviors they observed in their own children, including 351 boys and 319 girls ranging in age from 0 to 11. Mothers reported that 97 percent of children

touched their own genitals, 60 percent played "doctor" with friends, 50 percent masturbated, 33 percent touched others' genitals, 21 percent displayed themselves to others, 13 percent drew sex parts, 8 percent talked about sex acts, and 2 percent imitated sexual behavior with dolls. A number of these behaviors increased in frequency across the child's age, whereas some were more common in boys (e.g., masturbating) and others in girls (e.g., sex play with dolls).

Despite the interest children show in learning about sex throughout development, normally it is not until adolescence that sexuality takes center stage. *Puberty* ushers in physiological maturity, the period extending from around 8 to 18 years of age for girls and from around 9½ to 18 years of age for boys (Conger & Galambos, 1997). Ideally, for those youths who reach sexual maturity in their teens, these new biological urges arrive in tandem with the advances in cognitive, emotional, and social development that will allow them to successfully navigate the stage-salient issues of adolescence. In turn, youths whose sexual development is premature, whether spurred on by precocious hormones or inappropriate sexual stimulation, will not be ready to face the complex challenges and responsibilities of burgeoning adult sexuality. Ultimately, in late adolescence sexuality is part of the questions Whom can I love? and With whom can I share my life? and the search for a physically and psychologically fulfilling relationship with another person.

Sexual Orientation Recent estimates are that 1 percent to 2 percent of high school students in the United States identify themselves as gay, lesbian, or bisexual (Rotheram-Borus & Langabeer, 2001). The issue of sexual orientation is bound up in important ways with the process of identity development that we described earlier. Although some gay, lesbian, bisexual, and transgendered youths report having known their orientation from an early age, it is in adolescence that most grapple with the question of whether to confirm or closet these feelings and whether to incorporate them into their image of "who I am."

Savin-Williams (2001) conducted a series of interviews with sexual-minority youths and described the process by which their identity developed. The first step, *recognition,* involves the realization that one is different, sometimes accompanied by feelings of alienation and fear of discovery. On average, youths come to label themselves as gay, lesbian, or bisexual around 15 to 18 years of age. Recognition is followed by a phase of *test and exploration,* marked by ambivalence and curiosity. The third phase is *acceptance,* which is evidenced by a positive attitude and openness about one's sexual orientation. The final stage, *integration,* involves a firm commitment to a sexual object choice, accompanied by pride and open identification with one's community.

Not all individuals progress through all the stages, particularly when negative attitudes in the larger culture make the process of coming out uncomfortable—or even dangerous. After revealing their sexual orientation, from 20 percent to 40 percent of sexual-minority youths are rejected or threatened by family members and 5 percent are physically injured (D'Augelli, Hershberger, & Pilkington, 1998). Many report losing at least one friend after disclosing their sexuality (Pilkington & D'Augelli, 1995). Lack of acceptance in Hispanic and Asian American families may make the process of coming out even more difficult (Dube, Savin-Williams, & Diamond, 2001).

Gender and Sexual Processes Involved in Developmental Psychopathology

Exaggerated Sex-Role Characteristics   In Bakan's (1966) original formulation, healthy psychological development requires a balance between the opposite poles of *agency* and *communion.* The agentic, or masculine, side of human nature is competitive, aggressive, and egocentric, while the communal, or feminine, side is empathic, altruistic, and interpersonally oriented. Unmitigated agency, in Bakan's view, may lead to self-serving destructiveness. Unmitigated communality is problematic as well because it fails to equip the person to meet the developmental challenges of individuation. Assertiveness, a sense of self-esteem, and a willingness to defend oneself when wronged all are essential to the development and protection of the self (Kerig,

2004). Therefore, while agency must be tempered with considerations of "mutuality, interdependence, and joint welfare," communality also must be amended to "include aspects of agentic self-assertion and self-expression—aspects that are essential for personal integration and self-actualization" (J. H. Block, 1973, p. 515).

Bakan's theory suggests that a *hypermasculine* identification, an exaggerated notion of what it means to be a "real man," might contribute to a propensity for antisocial and violent behavior (Berry, 2001). As we will see in Chapter 10 when we discuss conduct problems, this idea has garnered some support. Similarly, exaggerated notions of *femininity* might increase the risk of certain disorders, given that the individual's focus is on pleasing others at the expense of the self. In Chapter 12, we will review evidence of the role of sex-role socialization and feminine identification in the development of eating disorders.

Precocious Sexuality   Mature sexuality involves not only physical intimacy, but also interpersonal sensitivity and self-understanding. Children who engage in sexual behavior precociously—those whose cognitive, emotional, and interpersonal development does not keep pace with their physical development or life experience—are at risk for maladjustment. We will encounter at least two examples of this: the increase in inappropriate behavior associated with early maturation in girls (Chapter 10) and the negative effects of sexual abuse on children (Chapter 14).

Sexual-Minority Orientation   Gay, lesbian, bisexual, and transgendered youths who are developing in a culture that is judgmental or hostile to their orientation may face additional stresses that affect the process of identity formation as well as family and peer relations. Feelings of isolation and lack of acceptance may increase the risk of maladaptation in sexual-minority youths, including suicide (D'Augelli, Hershberger, & Pilkington, 2001; see Chapter 9) and substance abuse (Jordan, 2000; see Chapter 12). However, caution must be exercised when interpreting these studies, given that they tend to be based on samples of troubled youths rather than being representative of the larger population (Rotheram-Borus & Langabeer, 2001).

Development in the Family Context

The Development of the Family

When we consider development, we often only think of it as relevant to children. However, all members of a family are in the process of development throughout the life span, as is the family as a system (McGoldrick & Carter, 2003). For example, at the first stage of the family life cycle, adults must differentiate from their families of origin and form a new marital partnership. As children are born, the couple relationship must adjust to make room for these new members. Next, as children advance into the teenage years, the parent-child relationship must become more flexible in order to allow adolescents to move in and out of the family system. The next stage of family development involves launching children into the world and reinvesting in the marital relationship, as well as realigning the family in order to include children's significant others and in-laws and, ultimately, the grandchildren. The developmental tasks for parents at the stage of middle adulthood are complex because, just when their own children have achieved adult status, they often have to become caregivers to their own aging parents.

Appreciation of family developmental processes suggests an important insight, that the parenting strategies that are most adaptive at one time in development (e.g., the close supervision of a 2-year-old) are not ideal at another stage (e.g., consider the average adolescent's reaction to such monitoring). Thus, parenting strategies must be flexible as well as developmentally sensitive. Let us take a look at the major dimensions of parenting that are implicated in healthy and pathological development.

Parenting Style

One of the most influential typologies of parenting style is the one developed by Baumrind (1991a, 1991b). She views two independent dimensions of parenting as essential: *warmth/support* and *control/structure*. By assessing parents on these two dimensions, she derives four parenting styles.

The **authoritarian parent** is high on structure but low on warmth; consequently, this parent is demanding, controlling, and unreasoning. The implicit message is "Do what I say because I say so." If parents discipline in a punitive, rejecting manner, their children tend to become aggressive; uncooperative; fearful of punishment; and low on initiative, self-esteem, and competence with peers. The **permissive/indulgent parent** is high on warmth without accompanying structure. This parent is undemanding, accepting, and child centered and makes few attempts to control. The result may be a dependent, irresponsible, aggressive, spoiled child. **Authoritative parents,** in contrast, are high on both warmth and structure. They set standards of mature behavior and expect the child to comply, but they are also highly involved, consistent, loving, communicative, willing to listen to the child, and respectful of the child's point of view. Their children tend to be self-reliant, self-controlled, secure, popular, and inquisitive. Lastly, the **neglectful parent** rates low on both warmth and structure; consequently, this parent is described as indifferent, uninvolved, or self-centered. Lax, unconcerned parenting is the breeding ground for antisocial behavior. Self-centeredness on the parents' part is associated child impulsivity, moodiness, truancy, lack of long-term goals, and early drinking and smoking.

For example, Steinberg and colleagues (1994) used Baumrind's system to assess parenting style in families of over four thousand 14- to 18-year-olds. Adolescents from authoritative homes were better adjusted than the others on measures of psychosocial development, school achievement, internalized distress, and problem behaviors, while youths from neglectful families fared the poorest. Youths from authoritarian families were doing fairly well in school and were refraining from delinquency, but their self-concepts and self-reliance were poor. In turn, adolescents from indulgent homes engaged in misconduct, achieved poorly in school, and abused drugs, but tended to perceive themselves positively. One year later, the investigators reassessed 2,000 of the youths and found that differences accounted for by parenting style were generally maintained or even increased. Youths from authoritative homes continued to outshine their peers, while youths from authoritarian homes not only showed continued poor self-image but increasing internalized distress. Adolescents from indulgent homes presented a mixed picture. While their self-concepts were positive, their school behavior and achievement had worsened. Youths from neglectful families showed continued significant declines in functioning over the year, including disinterest in school, drug and alcohol use, and delinquency.

However, research in ethnic diverse samples suggests that an authoritarian parenting style has different meanings and consequences in different cultures. For example, Lindahl and Malik (1999) found that an authoritarian parenting style was associated with increased externalizing behavior in European American families, but not in Hispanic American families. They suggested that the term *hierarchical* better describes the normative Hispanic family, in which the parents, particularly the fathers, play a strong leadership role.

Parental Sensitivity

When we discussed attachment, we saw the importance of parental sensitivity to the child's signals, emotions, and developmental needs. Sensitive parents engage in a careful choreography with the child, providing structure and guidance when needed and stepping back and allowing children the pleasure of doing for themselves those things that they have mastered. Following from the work of the Russian psychologist Vygotsky (1978), this process is known as *scaffolding* (Wood, 1980). Like the scaffold that is erected to support a building under construction, parental support should be available but nonintrusive, allowing the child to grow strong and resourceful under its protection—it would be a poor scaffold indeed that never could be removed without collapsing the

Sensitive caregiving involves stimulation as well as comforting.

building underneath. On the contrary, in Vygotsky's view, development is essentially a process of internalization in which the child is increasingly able to take over for him- or herself competencies that parents have scaffolded for them. For example, mothers' scaffolding of children's problem solving leads to greater self-regulation and competence in the academic setting (Neitzel & Stright, 2003). Scaffolding takes place not only in the cognitive realm, but also in the realms of social and emotional development (Denham, Mason, & Couchoud, 1995).

Parent-Child Boundary Dissolution

According to Minuchin's (1974) family systems theory, clear boundaries in the family are crucial to healthy psychological development. While in Chapter 1 we described the pathological triangles that might result when children are inappropriately involved in the marital subsystem, here we will describe three forms of boundary problems that may arise in dyadic parent-child relationships. Indeed, single parents and their children may be particularly vulnerable to boundary violations (Kerig, 2003a, 2005).

Enmeshment

At the extreme end of boundary dissolution is *enmeshment,* characterized by a lack of acknowledgement of the autonomy or separate selfhood of the child. The enmeshed parent and child are "two halves of the same person," at least as far as the parent is concerned. As developmental theory would predict, children with enmeshed parent-child relationships have difficulty individuating in adolescence. They also, in comparison with youths whose parents allow psychological autonomy, are more depressed (Jewell & Stark, 2003) and have less secure working models of attachment (Allen & Hauser, 1996).

Intrusiveness

Intrusive, or *psychologically controlling* parenting (Barber, 2002) is characterized by the parent who is overly controlling, not of the child's behavior but of the child's thoughts and feelings. In short, a psychologically controlling parent strives to manipulate the child's thoughts and feelings in such a way that the child's inner life will conform to the parent's wishes.

The parent may use subtle techniques such as indirect hints, guilt induction, and withdrawal of love to coerce the child into complying. Longitudinal data show that infants of intrusive mothers later demonstrate problems in academic, social, behavioral, and emotional adjustment (Egeland, Pianta, & O'Brien, 1993), including anxiety and depression (Barber, 2002).

Role-Reversal

Role-reversal, also termed *parentification,* refers to a relationship in which a parent relies on the child for emotional support and care, rather than providing it (Jurkovic, 1997). A parent engaged in role-reversal may be ostensibly warm and solicitous, but the relationship is not a truly nurturing one because the parent's emotional needs are being met at the expense of the child's (Chase, 1999). Children who fulfill their parents' emotional needs exhibit more internalizing, behavioral, and social problems in the early years (Jacobvitz, Hazan, Curran, & Hitchens, 2004; MacFie, Houts, McElwain, & Cox, in press), as well as depression, anxiety, low self-esteem (Jacobvitz & Bush, 1996), and eating disorders (Rowa, Kerig, & Geller, 2001) in later development.

Seductiveness

Seductiveness, also termed *spousification* (Sroufe & Ward, 1980) occurs when a parent turns to a child for an adult-like intimate partnership, perhaps even to the extent of seeking sexual gratification (Jacobvitz, Riggs, & Johnson, 1999). For example, Sroufe and Ward (1980) found that emotionally troubled mothers, many of whom were survivors of incest, engaged in seductive behaviors with their young sons, which included being overly physically affectionate, flirtatious, and seeking excessive affection from the child. Sroufe and colleagues' (Shaffer & Sroufe, in press) longitudinal research shows that children of seductive parents are inattentive and overactive in kindergarten, violate boundaries with peers in middle childhood, and exhibit more behavior problems in adolescence.

Divorce and Interparental Conflict

While in the early 1960s almost 90 percent of children spent their childhood in a home with two biological, married parents, the stereotypical nuclear family is a reality for only 40 percent of children today (Hetherington & Stanley-Hagan, 1999). Recent estimates are that 1 million children in the United States experience the divorce of their parents each year (U.S. Bureau of the Census, 2003).

Research confirms that children are negatively affected by family dissolution. Recently, Amato (2001) conducted a meta-analysis of studies published in the 1990s and found, consistent with the results of a meta-analysis conducted a decade earlier (Amato & Keith, 1991), that children of divorce score lower than children of married parents on measures of psychological adjustment, self-esteem, and academic achievement and demonstrate more conduct problems and difficulties in interpersonal relationships. However, other investigators have noted that there is great diversity in children's reactions to parental divorce. For example, the majority of children cope with the stress of family disruption without developing significant mental health problems. Therefore, research needs to be directed toward uncovering the risk and resiliency factors that account for the variability in children's reactions (Hetherington, Bridges, & Insabella, 1998; Hetherington & Stanley-Hagan, 1999).

Risk Factors for Children of Conflictual Marriages

Divorce is not a discrete event in the life of a child; it is the culmination of a long process. The majority of couples report years of marital acrimony leading up to the decision to divorce. The children, therefore, are exposed to significant levels of *interparental conflict,* sometimes even interparental violence. As we saw in Chapter 1, evidence is strong that children are affected by quarreling between their parents even in the absence of divorce (Davies et al., 2003; Grych & Fincham, 2001) and that it is this conflict rather than the act of divorce per se that accounts for the deleterious effects on children (Buchanan & Heiges, 2003; Kelly, 2003). Divorce even may benefit children when it results in relief from exposure to marital hostilities. However, counterintuitively, children are highly distressed by divorce when there have been *low* levels of

interparental conflict during the marriage, presumably because the divorce is a surprising and unwelcome change in a family that seemed to the child to be "not so bad" (Morrison & Coiro, 1999). Unfortunately, divorce does not necessarily bring an end to interparental conflict and may even increase it. The separation process itself brings up many heated issues (e.g., child custody, visitation, alimony, and child support) that spark parental hostilities. Children may feel "caught in the middle" (Buchanan, Maccoby, & Dornbusch, 1991) when they are asked to take sides with one parent against the other, to inform parents of one another's activities, or to act as a messenger between parents who are not on speaking terms. As we saw in our discussion of Minuchin (1974) in Chapter 1, this kind of *triangulation* is highly stressful for children. Exposure to these stressful family processes may last far longer than the divorce. For example, Maccoby and Mnookin (1992) found that even as long as 3½ years after marital separation, 26 percent of parents experience ongoing hostilities.

Divorce also is accompanied by a number of *life stresses:* Children may have to move, change schools, separate from friends, lose contact with grandparents, and suffer many other disruptions. For the 85 to 90 percent of children who live primarily with their mothers after divorce (Thompson & Amato, 1999), there is a significant decline in economic circumstances (White & Rogers, 2000); in fact, divorce is one of the principal ways by which children enter poverty.

In addition, for many parents divorce represents a painful failure at one of life's most important accomplishments, that of sustaining a love relationship. All of the life changes and stresses that affect children are felt keenly by parents. Consequently, divorce is associated with a number of signs of *parental distress,* including depression, anxiety, irritability, and substance use (Tein, Sandler, & Zastra, 2000). When parents' emotional difficulties spill over into the *parent-child relationship,* there are negative consequences for children's development. Parents may become emotionally unavailable to children and their parenting skills may be disrupted; fathers in particular may become distant or even absent from their children's lives (Hetherington & Stanley-Hagen, 2002).

Protective Factors for Children of Conflictual Marriages

Despite the risks and emotional distress accompanying divorce, within two to three years most children are able to adapt successfully. What protective factors account for this? Many of the *individual characteristics* related to resilience in other contexts also emerge as protective factors in studies of divorce: intelligence, easy temperament, and perceived competence. Young *age* may also be protective, particularly when parents remarry; while older children do not adapt easily to remarriage, younger children benefit from the return to an intact family structure (Chase-Lansdale, Cherlin, and Kiernan, 1995). Children's own *coping strategies* also can serve to exacerbate or alleviate divorce-related stress. Sandler, Tein, and West (1994) found that children of divorce who distracted themselves or used active coping strategies demonstrated fewer internalizing or externalizing problems than those who coped through passive withdrawal. Further, as children approach adolescence, they increasingly are able to look outside the family to peers and other adults as sources of *social support*. Young people's finding prosocial support systems to turn to can be beneficial. However, many adolescents of divorce precociously seek independence and disengage from their families, increasing the risk of involvement in antisocial activities (Hetherington, 1999).

Just as parent-child conflict and poor parenting are risk factors for maladjustment, a *positive parent-child relationship* and *authoritative parenting* style can help to buffer children from family stress (Hetherington, 1999). Children in joint custody arrangements especially benefit when they are able to enjoy positive involvement with both parents (Bauserman, 2002). Finally, despite their difficulty getting along with one another, many parents are able to set aside their differences when it comes to raising their children. Consequently, *coparenting cooperation* buffers children from the negative effects of interparental conflict in both divorces (Ahrons & Wallisch, 1987; Whiteside, 1998) and

intact marriages (McConnell & Kerig, 2002; McHale, Kuersten-Hagen, Lauretti, & Resmussen, 2000). Currently, in an effort to increase coparental cooperation and prevent children from being inveigled in interparental conflicts, many states mandate that divorcing parents work with a mediator to resolve any potential custody disputes.

Single-Parent- and Grandparent-Headed Homes

It is increasingly the case that children in the United States are growing up in families that are not the stereotypical nuclear form comprised of a father, a mother, and 2.2 children. Rising rates of divorce and teenaged pregnancy have resulted in a rise in *single-parent families,* mostly mother headed. Single-parent families are, on average, economically more stressed and the children are vulnerable to a number of negative behavioral and emotional outcomes (Hetherington & Stanley-Hagen, 2002; Mistry, Vandwater, Huston, & McLoyd, 2002). Moreover, this is not the only so-called nontraditional family form that is on the rise. The 2000 census found that more than 2.4 million *grandparents*—42 percent of those surveyed—were the primary caregivers of at least one grandchild. Among children under age 18, 6.3 percent are living in a grandparent-headed home, an increase from 5.5 percent in 1990 and 3.6 percent in 1980. Grandparents often step in when a parent dies, is incarcerated, loses employment, is too young to assume responsibility for childrearing, or simply abandons the child to the grandparents' care. The prevalence of grandparent-headed homes was highest in the South and rural areas of the country. In our reviews of the disorders to come, we will be attendant to the risks associated with the financial and emotional stresses associated with single-parent- and grandparent-headed homes, but we also will be sensitive to the sources of resilience and strength that nonetheless can lead to positive development (Brodsky, 1999; Murry, Bynum, Brody, Willert, & Stephens, 2001).

Maltreatment and Family Violence

Children do not need to grow up in an ideal family to emerge as psychologically healthy persons. The "average expectable environment" for infants includes protection and nurturance from adult caregivers, while older children require a supportive family as well as opportunities to relate to peers and master the environment (Scarr, 1992). Families can meet those needs of children in a variety of ways without impeding their development, as long as the home environment falls within the range of expectable conditions. In contrast, home environments that are violent, abusive, or neglectful fall outside this range and send the child on a pathological developmental course.

Maltreatment is implicated in the development of many of the psychopathologies that we will investigate (Cicchetti & Lynch, 1995) and will receive extensive coverage as a topic of its own in Chapter 14. Moreover, maltreatment can take many forms. Children do not have to be the direct victims of abuse in order to be negatively affected by family violence. Consequently, in Chapter 14 we will review research regarding the experience of children who are innocent bystanders to violence between the adults in the home.

Family Processes and Developmental Psychopathology

To review, in this section we have uncovered several processes by which family relationships may contribute to the development of psychological health or pathology: (1) overly harsh or lax parenting; (2) parental insensitivity; (3) inappropriate parent-child boundaries; (4) family dissolution, interparental conflict, and single-parenting; and (5) victimization or exposure to violence in the home. Given its importance, in the chapters to follow we will many times return to consider the quality of the family context in which child development takes place.

Development in the Social Context

Peer Relations

Peer relations are a potent predictor of subsequent psychopathology (Cicchetti & Bukowski, 1995). In our discussions we distinguish a general interest in peers, which we call *sociability,* from *groups,* which

are organizations of individuals possessing norms or values regulating the behavior of the individual. (For further reading, see Parker, Rubin, Price, and DeRosier, 1995.)

Infancy to Preschool

Many dramatic developments occur in the first 6 years of a child's life, but we will not make them a focus of our attention because they have yet to be linked with psychopathology. Two-month-old infants are interested in looking at one another, and by 10 months of age there is a more varied and sustained reaction expressed in mimicking, patting, hitting, and imitation of laughing. By 15 months of age affection appears, and by age 2 there is participation in games, although the toddler's short attention span and limited ability to communicate and to control the behavior of others gives sociability a fleeting, improvisational quality.

Clearly, all early social behaviors are less stable and intense than attachments, and for good reason. Peers have no interest in assuming the caregiving role of relieving distress and providing stimulation, nor do they have the caregiver's skill in responding quickly and appropriately to needs. However, they have one inherent advantage over adults in that, being at comparable developmental levels, they are naturally attracted to one another's activities. Whereas a parent may love a child for what he or she is, peer attraction is based on mutual interests. Peer relations are important not because they represent diluted versions of attachment but because they add a new dimension to development.

A number of changes take place in the preschool period. Positive exchanges such as attention and approval increase, although sharing and sympathy do not. Competition and rivalry are also on the rise, while quarrels are fewer but longer. More important, immature or inefficient social actions are becoming more skilled; for example, there is greater speaker-listener accommodation so that a child begins to talk *to* rather than *at* another child; and collaboration begins to emerge in social problem solving. Cooperativeness, respect for property, constructiveness, and adaptability are the bases of general social attraction. The preschooler who is highly aggressive,

Peer relations are an important influence on children's development.

quarrelsome, or dictatorial; who refuses to play with others; or who is dependent on adults for attention and affection rates low on attractiveness and sociability (Musun-Miller, 1993). Friendships now have that combination of sharing and quarreling that will characterize them throughout childhood.

Middle Childhood

Sociability, the interest in the larger world of peers, comes to the fore in middle childhood. Research on sociability often is based on an assessment of children's *sociometric status*: that is, the way that they are perceived by peers. (See Bukowski and Cillessen, 1998, for a comprehensive review.) Four types of children emerge from sociometric studies: accepted, rejected, neglected, and controversial. The child who is *accepted* by other children is resourceful, intelligent, emotionally stable, dependable, cooperative, and sensitive to the feelings of others. *Rejected*

children are aggressive, distractable, and socially inept in addition to being unhappy and alienated. Moreover, they are at risk for being school dropouts and for having serious psychological difficulties in adolescence and adulthood. *Neglected* children, who are neither liked nor disliked by peers, tend to be anxious and lacking in social skills. Finally, *controversial* children are perceived both positively and negatively by others. These children are often troublemakers or class clowns, yet they possess interpersonal skills and charisma that attract or impress other children.

Among the many determinants of sociability, two social-cognitive and one affective variable will figure in our future discussions. We have already dealt with the role of *social perspective-taking* in the development of conscience, and it is easy to see how it would also facilitate sociability by countering self-centeredness. The second social-cognitive variable is *social problem solving,* which is concerned with conflict resolution. As we have seen, it involves a number of social-cognitive skills: encoding and accurately interpreting social cues, generating possible problem-solving strategies and evaluating their probable effectiveness, and, finally, enacting the chosen strategy. Young children's strategies are impulsive and designed to meet their own needs; such strategies include grabbing, pushing, and ordering other children about. Older children take the needs of others into account and are inclined toward persuasion and compromise (Selman, Schultz, & Yeates, 1991). Empathy, the affective component of sociability, involves both an awareness of the feelings of others and a vicarious affective response to those feelings. Toddlers have been observed to respond empathetically to the distress of others, for example, by giving a crying child a favorite toy (Thompson, 1987). Empathetic responses increase with age. The range of eliciting stimuli also increases, broadening eventually to include general life conditions rather than immediate distress, as in concern for the poor or the sick. As for the psychological significance of peer relations, Sullivan (1953) claims that the shift from "me" to "we" is aided by the mutuality and equality of peer relations. In the context of sharing, children learn what Sullivan calls accommodation: Instead of thinking of themselves as unique or special, as they might at home, they begin to learn how to get along with others.

There is another important dimension that sociability adds to the child's development. At home the child has to be love-worthy because affection and obedience lie at the heart of the parent-child relationship. With peers the child must be respect-worthy, which is a matter of proven *competence.* Children must expose themselves to comparisons with other children in regard to athletic ability, manual skills, resourcefulness in suggesting and implementing interesting activities, and so on. They are valued in terms of their actual contributions to the activities that peers themselves value.

The insubstantial, play-oriented groups of the preschool period become the middle childhood friendship network, which, by the time children are 8 to 10 years of age, is sufficiently potent to compete with the family in terms of interest, loyalty, and emotional involvement. The child begins to subordinate personal interests to the goals of the group, tries to live up to group standards, and criticizes those who do not. Thus, "we" becomes more important than "I." The friendship group no longer needs to rely on stereotyped games and activities such as hopscotch or jump rope but is sufficiently autonomous to respond to general suggestions such as "Let's make a clubhouse" or "Let's give a party." Names, insignia, and secret passwords help give the group a special identity. In addition to being identifiable social units, friendship groups traditionally have been segregated by sex, with boys being action oriented and girls being sociable in their interests.

The friendship group advances the sense of belonging. It offers training in interdependent behavior, encourages venturing out further than the individual could go alone, and through its cohesiveness buttresses the individual member's self-control.

Adolescence

Group involvement reaches a high point in adolescence. The adolescent group is an autonomous social organization with purposes, values, standards of behaviors, and means of enforcing them. In its stability and differentiation it resembles adult groups rather than those of middle childhood. Conformity peaks in 11- to 13-year-olds and gradually declines; it is greatest in those adolescents low in status among their peers and high in self-blame.

Adolescent groups vary in structure and nature. There is the small, close-knit clique, whose members are bound together by a high degree of personal compatibility and mutual admiration. The crowd, a larger aggregate than the clique, is concerned with social activities such as parties and dances and does not demand the same high personal involvement that the clique requires. Crowds vary in status, and being a member of a high-status crowd is one of the surest ways to gain popularity. An important function of the crowd is to provide a transition from unisexual to heterosexual relations. The clique still survives and requires more loyalty than the crowd. It is often hostile to adult society and has a specific goal: sexual, athletic, delinquent, and so on. It retains its emphasis on adventure and excitement as well as on the formal trappings of organization, such as name, dress, and initiation ritual.

These groups serve as the adolescent's primary bridge to the future. They provide a sense of belonging, which is especially important during the period of transition between being a child and being an adult. They help adolescents master uncertainty by prescribing behavior, right down to what clothes to wear, what music to listen to, and what language to use. They provide both provocation and protection in changing from same-sex to heterosexual relations. Finally, they support individuals in their opposition to their parents. This does not imply that the majority of adolescents are rebellious and alienated; the battle of the generations is fought only fitfully, and many values of the group, such as cooperation, self-control, and dependability, are congruent with or even reflections of parental values (Conger & Galambos, 1997).

What mars adolescent groups is their rigidity and demands for conformity. Adolescence is a high-water mark for group prejudice, when caste and class lines are sharply drawn and inclusions and exclusions are absolute. For all their rebelliousness against adult society, adolescents are more slavishly conforming to the group than they have been before or will be in the future. In short, in middle childhood and especially in adolescence there is a narrow group-centeredness, which is the counterpart of the child's earlier egocentrism. Perspective and flexibility, evaluation of individuals in terms of personal worth, loyalty without chauvinism, social commitments that transcend immediate group interests—all these lie in the future.

As we shall see, peer relations play an important role in both conduct disorder and substance abuse. However, there is a question about whether they play a leading etiological role. Does the juvenile gang pressure its members to defy the law, or do angry, defiant youths seek out juvenile gangs? Does peer pressure cause drug abuse, or are adolescents who become addicted those who are particularly disturbed to begin with? We will return to these questions in Chapters 10 and 12.

Extrafamilial Adults

As children move through the school years into adolescence, adults outside the family increasingly play a role in shaping their behavior and attitudes about themselves. Potential mentors and sources of support outside the family include teachers, coaches, tutors, school counselors, camp leaders, clergy, godparents, neighbors, and other adult friends of the family. The quality of children's relationships with *teachers* contributes in important ways to children's sense of well-being. For example, teachers who blatantly treat differently the students they perceive as high and low achievers inculcate in children not only perceptions of low self-efficacy but actual lowered school performance, the so-called Pygmalion effect (Weinstein, 2002). Peers also are sensitive to differential teacher treatment and are likely to reject the child they perceive as ill favored (Donahue, Perry, & Weinstein, 2003). On the other hand, teachers who relate to children with warmth, structure, and personal interest increase children's well-being and sense of security as well as children's capacity to cope with stress (Brody, Dorsey, Forehand, & Armistead, 2002; Little & Kobak, 2003). Similarly, *school environments* that are perceived as dangerous, unsafe, or uncaring can lead to student negativity, alienation, misbehavior, and poor attendance (Stipek, 2001).

Social Processes and Developmental Psychopathology

To review, the social context involves several processes that might influence psychopathology. These include (1) peer rejection, (2) poor social skills, (3) social problem-solving deficits, (4) negative peer influences, and (5) weak or negative attachments to schools and extrafamilial adults.

Development in the Cultural Context
Poverty and Social Class

Children growing up in poor families are at increased risk for a range of behavioral, emotional, health, and academic problems (Bornstein & Bradley, 2004;

Figure 2.3   Environmental Relationships Between Poverty and Educational Failure.

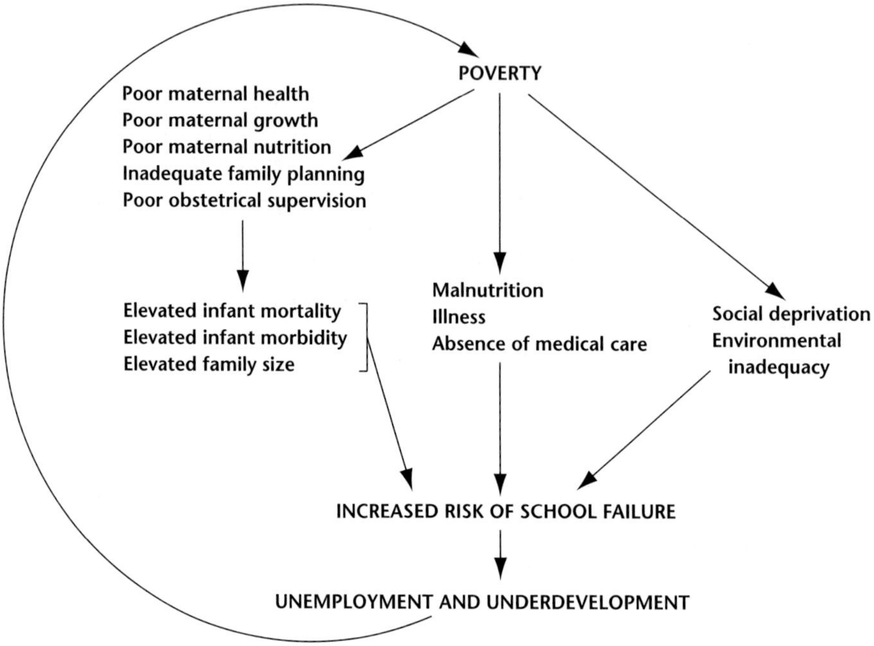

Source: Birch and Gussow, 1970.

Bradley & Corwyn, 2002). (See Figure 2.3.) Poverty may exert its effects on child development through a number of mechanisms. Some of these are *environmental* (Evans, 2004); for example, economically deprived neighborhoods are bleak and unattractive, lacking in child-friendly amenities such as yards and playgrounds; and marked by high rates of violence, drug-dealing, and models of antisocial behavior. The homes of children reared in poverty are crowded, noisy, unsafe, and poorly maintained; the air they breathe and water they drink are more polluted. Children from poor families also have less access to cultural amenities and cognitively stimulating activities than do children from more privileged backgrounds (Bradley, Corwyn, Burchinal, McAdoo, & Coll, 2001). Low SES, moreover, may exert its effects indirectly through the *parent-child relationship*. For example, poverty is associated with lower levels of warmth and maternal responsiveness,

which in turn are associated with increased child behavior problems (Bolger, Patterson, & Thompson, 1995).

A compelling study recently conducted in Finland demonstrated the effects of economic stress on children and their families. Solantaus, Leinonen, and Punamäki (2004) began studying a sample of 527 families at the time the children were 8 years of age, shortly before a severe economic recession hit the country. Following the children into their 12th year, the investigators found that the economic downturn was associated with increased parent distress, interparental conflict, and negative parenting, which, in turn, were associated with a significant rise in youth depression, aggression, and oppositional behavior. These data replicate previous findings reported in European American and African American samples (Conger et al., 2002), pointing to their cross-cultural relevance.

Other neighborhood characteristics frequently associated with poverty also may affect child development. One of these is a lack of *community cohesion:* Neighborhoods in which neighbors do not know one another and do not provide mutual support and a sense of belonging are not the villages in which one would wish to raise a child. A second risk factor is *community violence,* to which children in poverty are exposed to an alarming degree and which they mimic and rationalize increasingly as development proceeds (Guerra, Huesmann, & Spindler, 2003).

Whereas poverty may increase the risk for psychopathology, it far from ensures it. Therefore, we must be careful not to rush to pathologize children and families on the basis of their social class. There are many sources of strength and resilience among economically challenged families that can protect children from the risks (Murry et al., 2001). For example, social support increases the mother's positive involvement with the child and confidence in her parenting abilities, thus buffering children from the effects of poverty (Hashima & Amato, 1994; Runyan et al., 1998). As Kim-Cohen, Moffitt, Caspi, and Taylor (2004) report, maternal warmth and provision of cognitive stimulation serve to protect children from the negative effects of economic adversity, as does the child's possession of a calm temperament.

Ethnic Diversity

While the terms are not used consistently in the literature, the American Psychological Association (2003) defines *race* as a "category to which others assign individuals on the basis of physical characteristics, such as skin color or hair type, and the generalizations and stereotypes made as a result" while *ethnicity* is used to refer to "the acceptance of the group mores and practices of one's culture and the concomitant sense of belonging" (p. 380). Whichever of these terms is used, there is no doubt that the United States is a highly diverse society and is becoming more so. Recent census data indicate that 36 percent of the U.S. youth population belongs to a racial or ethnic minority group; further, the proportion of non-European American youth is projected to increase to 48 percent by the year 2020 (U.S. Bureau of the Census, 2003). Thirteen percent of U.S. residents are of Hispanic origin, 12.7 percent are African American, 3.9 percent are Asian American, and 1 percent is Native American (American Indian or Alaska Natives). An additional 4.1 percent belong to more than one ethnic group, termed *biracial* or multiracial (Gibbs, 2003).

However, these statistics obscure the great diversity within ethnic and racial categories. For example, the label Hispanic includes many races (White, Black, and Indian) and such divergent families as Mexican Americans whose ancestors' residence in California predates European Americans, recent poor immigrants fleeing from political strife in Central America, and upper-class Cuban Americans who came to this country a generation ago to escape from communism. Similarly, African American families range widely in income levels, religiosity, and the extent to which they adopt majority cultural values.

Thus, there are two additional dimensions that must be considered when we discuss ethnicity. First, within ethnic groups there are important differences related to *social class.* Members of minority groups are disproportionately likely to live in poverty, which increases the risk for a variety of negative outcomes, including school dropout, substance use, and delinquency (Parke, 2004). However, there also exist middle- and upper-class minority families to whom these stressors do not apply. Second, there are significant differences in the level of *acculturation,* or adoption of the values of the majority culture. Acculturation is related to language use, customs, and ties to the community outside the ethnic enclave. Because of such differences, first- and third-generation Chinese Americans, for example, may have less in common with one another than do middle-class, acculturated Chinese and European Americans (Gibbs & Huang, 2003).

Racism and Prejudice

Racism is defined as "beliefs, attitudes, institutional arrangements, and acts that tend to denigrate individuals or groups because of phenotypic characteristics or ethnic group affiliation" (Clark, Anderson, Clark, & Williams, 1999, p. 805). The experience of systematic, chronic racism has been identified as a significant risk factor for physical and mental health. Responses to perceived racism include anger, anxiety, paranoia, helplessness, hopelessness, poor self-esteem, frustration, resentment, and physiological reactions such as elevated blood pressure (Clark et al., 1999).

Children appear to have some awareness of racial differences in physical appearance as early as 6 months of age. (See Katz, 2003, for an overview of longitudinal research on the topic.) However, the valence associated with perceived difference is influenced in major ways by parental attitudes. Attitudes about race may be conveyed through direct instruction or more subtle behaviors (Coll and Pachter, 2002). Between the ages of 2½ to 3½, young children demonstrate knowledge of prevailing stereotypes associated with race. Young children may shy away from those with a different skin color or refuse to play with a peer who has a physical disability or speaks a different language. By the time they are in preschool, children have labels for ethnic groups and can express their own theories about what causes racial differences. In the early school years, children have formed a core sense of individual ethnic identity and actively seek out information about their own group. Moreover, by middle childhood, attitudes about other races tend to have consolidated and are unlikely to change without a significant influential event or intervention. Throughout childhood and into adulthood, individuals receive messages from peers, family members, and the media that reinforce already formed attitudes and beliefs (Aboud, 1987).

Racism is not the only form of *prejudice* that increases the risk of psychopathology. Misogyny, nationalism, and religious intolerance—the list of forms that hatred takes is vast. Prejudiced attitudes are held not only by bigoted individuals but may be socially sanctioned by belief systems that place certain outsiders beyond the pale. For example, one particular form of prejudice that presents a risk to some developing adolescents is *homophobia*. Gay and lesbian teens whose environments are hostile to their sexual preference are vulnerable to the development of depression and may be at increased risk for attempted suicide (Savin-Williams & Ream, 2003).

Sources of Risk and Resilience in Ethnically Diverse Families

It is beyond our scope to present a comprehensive overview of the various racial, ethnic, and cultural groups that comprise the U.S. population. (For descriptions of parenting and family life in ethnically diverse samples in the United States, as well as cross-cultural differences across the world, see the four-volume *International Encyclopedia of Marriage and Family* (Ponzetti et al., 2003). The attempt to describe ethnic groups as a homogenous category also runs the risk of stereotyping and pigeon-holing, implying that all families of a particular cultural background or race are alike. Our understanding of ethnic differences in developmental psychopathology is also hampered by the dearth of research that systematically attends to issues such as race, ethnicity, and culture in the children and families under investigation (Coll, Akerman, & Cicchetti, 2000). However, in order to be culturally competent, psychologists need to have sensitivity to the different worldviews and experiences that contribute to child development in our diverse society (American Psychological Association, 2003; Sue, 1998). An important advance in psychological research with ethnic minority families is the shift from a deficit/pathology perspective to one of strength and resilience (Coll & Garrido, 2000; McLoyd, Cauce, Tanauchi, & Wilson, 2000). With this in mind, therefore, we will present brief snapshots of the particular challenges and sources of resilience that may be associated with membership in four of the largest groups that contribute to the U.S. cultural mosaic.

African American Families   Parke (2004) notes a number of characteristics of the African American family that provide protection against psychopathology: (1) Extended family members tend to live near one another; (2) the family is highly valued and the sense of family obligation is strong; (3) household boundaries are fluid, with great willingness to welcome relatives and others into the family; and (4) there is a secure system of mutual aid. Such extended support is particularly important given the large proportion of single-mother-headed and grandparent-headed households in the lower-income African American community, which rely on family members for assistance with child care and economic needs. The church also often is a bulwark of African American social life and values. On the other hand, challenges to the development of African American youths include high rates of poverty and racial discrimination, which increase the likelihood of a range of emotional and behavioral problems, including school dropout, juvenile delinquency, substance abuse, and teenaged childbearing (Gibbs, 2003).

Typically, African American parents use more physical punishment than European American parents in the discipline of children, even after accounting for social class (Deater-Deckard & Dodge, 1997). However, as we will explore in greater depth in Chapter 14, physical discipline is not predictive of externalizing in African American children as it is in European American children, suggesting that the cultural context gives a different meaning to parental behaviors. Instilling close adherence to parental authority may be adaptive for parents who are raising their children in a dangerous environment (McLoyd et al., 2000).

Hispanic Families   Although many Mexican Americans were residents long before their lands became part of the United States, recent immigrants and their families are the fastest-growing group in the Hispanic community (Parke, 2004). Mexican Americans comprise the largest group of Hispanic Americans, followed by Central and South Americans, Puerto Ricans, and Cubans. Characteristics of the Hispanic family include *familismo,* the sense of a strong identification and interdependence with the family over the course of the life span. (Our review follows Organista, 2003, except where noted.) Family members tend to remain close, both emotionally and economically, and form extended family ties

A multigenerational Mexican American family.

through intermarriage, the enfolding of friends into the family system, and a sense of connectedness with the larger Hispanic community. Other important values include *respeto* (respect), deference to those with more status in the family system; *simpatia,* the emphasis on interpersonal harmony and the avoidance of conflict; and *personalismo,* the valuing of the personal dimension in relationships. As it does in the African American family, economic and racial discrimination poses risks to Hispanic children, who are four times more likely than European American children to live in poverty.

Traditional values in childrearing are reflected in the anticipation that children will respect the authority of their parents and adhere to cultural protocols, such as refraining from disagreeing with an elder even when the child is "right." In addition, there is the expectation that children will remain close to their families throughout their lives (Parke, 2004). The typical family is arranged hierarchically, with the father as a clear authority figure. However, unlike the negative connotations associated with the term *authoritarianism,* the hierarchical Hispanic family is described as warm and supportive rather than harsh and unresponsive (Lindahl & Malik, 2001). (For further reading, see Vlach, 2003, on Central American children and their families, and Inclan and Quinones, 2003, on Puerto Rican families.)

Asian American Families   Asian American families comprise a highly diverse group, including people from 28 countries or ethnic groups (Parke, 2004). These groups speak different languages, have different traditions, have been in the United States for varying numbers of generations, and immigrated to this country for many different reasons. Currently, the largest Asian groups in the United States are Chinese, Filipino, and Indo-Chinese (e.g., Vietnamese, Cambodian, and Laotian). Even with acculturation, Asian families tend to retain traditional Confucian attitudes toward childrearing, which emphasize the obligation of parents to guide and control their offspring and of family members to put the good of the family above their individual needs (Chao & Tseng, 2002). The family system typically is patriarchal, with the father acting as an authority figure who maintains some emotional distance from the other family members and is responsible for the family's economic well-being and social status. While the mother may be stereotypically deferential to her husband and devoted to the home and children, she is likely to be a powerful force behind the scenes (Huang, Ying, & Arganza, 2003). Respect for elders, obedience to parents, and family loyalty are highly valued in children.

Although Asian American parenting styles have been termed authoritarian, recent thinking has questioned whether this construct translates adequately across cultures. Unlike European American children, whose behavior and academic achievement are negatively affected by authoritarian parenting style, Asian American children whose parents rate high on authoritarianism are well adjusted and academically high performing (Steinberg, Dornbusch, & Brown, 1992). Consequently, investigators propose that what is defined as authoritarian in the U.S. context is reflection of a different set of childrearing values and styles in Asian American culture. Rather than being conceptualized as controlling and restrictive, Asian American parents are more accurately described as deeply involved and concerned with training their children to fit into the roles they will take in society (Chao, 2001; Stewart, Rao, Bond, McBride, Chang, Fielding, & Kennard, 1998). (For further reading, see Agbayani-Siewert and Enrile, 2003, on the Filipino American family, and Ida and Yang, 2003, on Southeast Asian children and their families.)

Native American Families   The term *Native American* is used to refer to all indigenous peoples of the United States, including natives of Alaska, Aleuts, Eskimos, Metis (mixed bloods), and members of 561 federally recognized tribes. (Our review here follows LaFromboise & Dizon, 2003.) The resilience of the Native American family is remarkable, given a history of genocide, forced residential schooling, and ostracism. At present, approximately 36 percent of Native Americans live on designated tribal reservations and about 26 percent of these families live in poverty. Impoverished Native American children have the highest dropout rates among ethnic groups:

From 35 to 50 percent never complete high school. High rates of parental unemployment, family dissolution, poverty, and substance abuse lead to increased child exposure to family violence and maltreatment. Despite these challenges, the majority of Native American youths enter adolescence with a strong sense of identity and family ties.

Native American childrearing traditionally is governed by a view of the child as a "beloved gift," whose development should be allowed to unfold rather than being controlled or directed by the parents. Autonomy and self-discipline are highly valued, and therefore children are expected to make their own decisions and to function independently at an early age. Consequences for breaching the norms of acceptable behavior are likely to be indirect. Children simply may be allowed to experience the natural consequences of their misbehavior; or, to protect the parent-child bond, an aunt or uncle who has assumed responsibility for guiding the youth's character development may intervene on behalf of the extended family. Because parental control is not overt, Native American parenting styles historically have been misjudged as lax or negligent by social service agents.

Ethnic Processes and Developmental Psychopathology

As these brief snapshots suggest, ethnicity is a crucial variable for us to consider as we attempt to chart a pathway of normative development. First and foremost, ethnicity influences *norms* for child development: What is normative in one ethnic group may not be in another and may even be an indication of psychopathology. We will need to keep in mind that race is not a sufficient index of ethnic identity, which is also a product of *social class* and *acculturation.* Perhaps one of the most significant differences we will need to keep in mind is that of *parenting styles* that are prevalent and considered appropriate in various ethnic groups, driven as they are by different philosophies and values regarding childrearing, family, and attitudes toward the larger society. Overt *racism* and *prejudice,* the regrettable accompanying overlap between ethnic minority status and *poverty,* as well as simple *ignorance* about

minority groups' norms and belief systems also at times will complicate the process. For example, although we will strive to consider issues of diversity in all of the disorders we will study, in many cases the relevant research has not been done and therefore few if any studies have paid attention to race, ethnicity, or social class in the prevalence, etiology, course, or treatment of the disorder under question.

Cross-Cultural Norms and Expectations

In addition to attending to ethnic subgroups within the United States, we also will be interested in exploring how psychopathology might develop in different cultures around the globe. Beliefs about what constitutes psychopathology and how it arises vary across cultures. Some conceptualizations are quite unique to their context. For example, consider the concept of *zar,* or spirit possession, found in North Africa and the Middle East; *amok,* a Malaysian dissociative experience involving a period of brooding followed by an outburst of violence; or *taijin kyofusho,* the Japanese fear that one's body or bodily functions are offensive to others. (A further list of culture-bound syndromes is given in *DSM-IV-TR.*) In other cases, culturally specific syndromes have clear relationships to those that are defined by Western taxonomies such as *DSM-IV-TR,* but cross boundaries in ways that reflect a different underlying meaning. For example, consider the Latin American syndrome of *nervios,* characterized by a generalized sense of emotional distress, physical symptoms, including heart palpitations and body aches, irritability, insomnia, nervousness, inability to concentrate, trembling, and dizziness; this syndrome is conceptualized as resulting from a loss of significant personal relationships (Castillo, 1997). While this syndrome includes features of Western diagnostic entities such as anxiety, depression, and somatoform disorder, applying to a child these multiple diagnoses does not do justice to the larger gestalt of symptoms and the meaning that they have within the culture.

Cross-cultural research also teaches us that whether a child's behavior is considered normal or disordered depends on adult *expectations* about appropriate behavior, which vary across societies

(Weisz, Weiss, Suwanlert, & Chaiyesit, 2003; Harkness & Super, 2000). For example, an oft-cited cultural distinction is the one between an emphasis on *individualism,* the promotion of self-expression, independence, and individual achievement in children, and *communalism,* the valuing of social relations, interdependence, and the placement of one's own interests second to those of the larger group (Kitayama, 2000). Precociously independent behavior, for example, may earn a child delighted praise in one context and parental disapproval in another. A crucial factor is the *fit* between the child's characteristics and those the culture values. Consider the expectation that a 6-year-old child sit quietly and attentively in the classroom for six hours a day (Silk, Nath, Siegel, & Kendall, 2000). Some would criticize this expectation as a developmentally inappropriate one, fostered by a culture that is in a rush to "hurry" us through childhood (Elkind, 1981). However, because certain cultures expect this behavior, those children whose activity level is on the high end of the normal continuum are at risk for being labeled as hyperactive (Carey & McDevitt, 1995).

Cultures collide in the case of recent *immigrant families,* a growing group that has been relatively neglected in the research literature. Nearly one in five children in the United States has a parent who was born in another country (Federal Interagency Forum on Child and Family Statistics, 2002). Effects of immigration on children vary as a function of social class and circumstance. For impoverished immigrants fleeing economic hardship or war or civil unrest, the process may be fraught with danger and peril, resulting in trauma for parents and children alike. Once settled in the United States, children of immigrant families may be exposed to new stresses and developmentally taxing expectations, such as the children's translating for their parents and helping their elders navigate social service bureaucracies. Generational strains may develop when parents hold to the cultural beliefs and values of the home country while their children are being exposed to and adopting the values of the new country, particularly as adolescence approaches and American norms of freedom and experimentation for youth challenge the old ways.

The individual family's level of *acculturation* plays a role, as does whether the immigrant culture values assimilating into the American "melting pot" versus maintaining its distinct identity. Such values and practices vary. For example, Bornstein and Cote (2004) conducted a study in which they examined the parenting beliefs and practices of immigrant Japanese American and South American mothers and compared them to those of European American mothers as well as those in the home countries of Japan and Argentina. Consistent with previous research, the investigators found that Japanese American immigrant mothers tended to maintain traditional values and beliefs, with their ratings closely corresponding to those of mothers in the home country. In contrast, South American immigrant mothers' attitudes were closer to those of European Americans than to those of Argentinians.

Cultural Processes and Developmental Psychopathology

According to Castillo (1997), culture influences psychopathology in five key ways. The first of these is *culture-based subjective experience,* the way in which culture influences one's view of psychopathology and one's perceptions of self. For example, cultures that emphasize internal processes as causal in psychopathology might lead depressed persons to perceive themselves as ill, whereas, in contrast, non-Western conceptualizations might locate the problem in a misconnection between the self and others and therefore construe depression as a family or interpersonal issue. Second are *culture-based idioms* of psychological distress, which refer to the ways in which psychopathology is evidenced in behavior. Culture may influence the symptoms that individuals exhibit as well as those that others focus on in determining mental health or illness. For example, Asian beliefs regarding the interconnectedness of the mind and body may contribute to the expression of emotional distress in the form of physical ailments (Ho, 1992). Third, *culture-based diagnosis* involves the categories and language that people use to understand and explain psychopathology. For example, we described earlier several examples of culturally specific syndromes that have meaning only within their unique context. Fourth, *culture-based treatments* determine who are the potential healers and what are the mechanisms through which healing takes place: for example, whether a psychiatrist is sought for medication, a faith healer is visited to reconnect the spirit to the body, or the symptom is hidden to protect the honor of the family. Fifth are *culture-based outcomes,* the results that ensue when a psychopathology has been conceptualized and treated in a particular way. For example, the child's response to treatment may be influenced by the degree to which society emphasizes the need to provide familial support to the individual who is suffering from mental illness.

As Harkness and Super (2000) point out, culture provides an important context for child development, influencing the physical and interpersonal settings, the styles of childrearing, the psychology of parenting, and the social relations that the child will need to adapt to over the course of childhood.

Developmental Integration

Now we will integrate the information about developmental pathways presented in Chapter 1 with the 10 developmental processes just discussed. To do this we use the case of a hypothetical girl named Zoey. (See Figure 2.4.)

Zoey is an African American, lower-middle-class child growing up in a suburban area in the southeastern United States. Zoey's mother went through a postpartum depression when Zoey was born; consequently, Zoey's attachment to her mother was tainted by insecurity (*attachment, slight deviation*). While this did not constitute a major problem, she tended to react strongly to changes in her environment (*temperament, vulnerability*). She showed some anxiety about beginning school and struggled academically throughout her elementary school years (*cognitive development, deviation*). When Zoey was 8 years of age, she experienced an increase in familial disharmony when her parents began arguing heatedly (*interparental conflict, risk*). However, her good relationship with her father enabled her to take the stress in stride (*parent-child relationship, protective factor*).

When she was 10 years old, Zoey's parents divorced (*family dissolution, risk*), and she was placed in her mother's custody. Mother and child moved from the family home to a small apartment closer to the inner city. The two spent more time apart as the mother returned to the workforce, sometimes working two jobs because the pay her unskilled labor earned was poor (*socioeconomic disadvantage, risk*). At this point, a number of behavior problems began to develop. Zoey's principal problems were angry outbursts and argumentativeness with the teacher (*affect regulation, severe deviation*). Although initially a friendly child, Zoey began to be regarded as a troublemaker by peers. As peers rejected her, Zoey began acting out in an increasingly hostile manner toward other children (*transactional process*). Consequently, her popularity declined (*peer relations, moderate deviation*). However, two positive events occurred when Zoey was age 12. First, a hitherto undiagnosed learning disorder in reading was uncovered by a perceptive and supportive school psychologist, and Zoey was made eligible for special educational services. As a consequence, Zoey was transferred to the special education classroom where she made friends with two other girls who formed a special clique of "outsiders" (*social relations, protective factor*).

As a preteen, with her mother, Zoey was chronically sullen (*attachment, continued moderate deviation*), although there were outbursts of more serious temper tantrums and name-calling, especially after she came home from visits with her father. Her angry outbursts were usually overreactions to ordinary frustrations of everyday life. She was not spoiling for a fight by imagining everyone else was against her (*cognition, adaptive* since there was no distortion in regard to attribution). She went from being a B student to being a C student at school, and, while she acted bored and sardonic, she did not give up on school entirely (*mastery motivation, moderate deviation*). Rather than doing homework, she concentrated on drawing and sketching, a hobby she had shared with her father, becoming quite skilled and covertly enjoying being praised (*self-esteem and self-efficacy, protective mechanisms*). She and her friends talked about sex, masturbation, and other

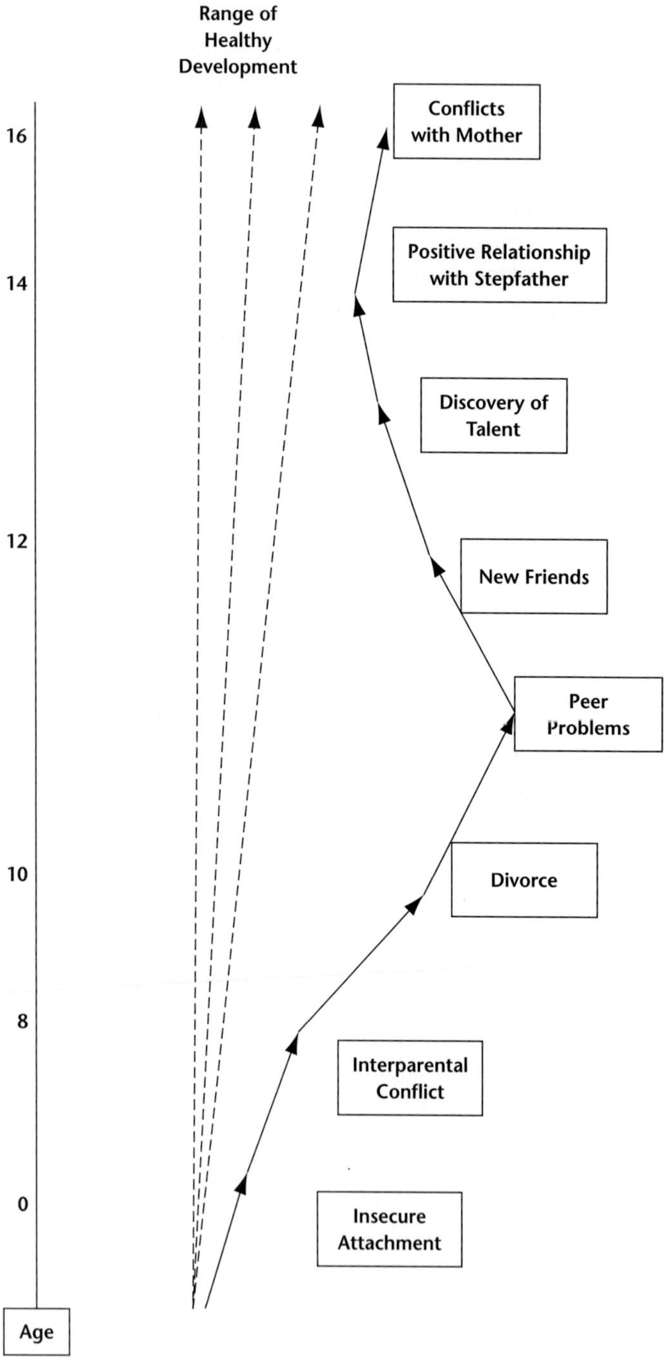

Figure 2.4

Zoey's Developmental Pathway.

Range of Healthy Development

Conflicts with Mother

Positive Relationship with Stepfather

Discovery of Talent

New Friends

Peer Problems

Divorce

Interparental Conflict

Insecure Attachment

Age

16
14
12
10
8
0

Adapted from Bowlby, 1988.

pubertal changes, and, while wary of boys, she was no more so than a number of other shy preadolescent girls (*sex and gender, adaptive*). She was properly but not excessively troubled over her outbursts (*moral development, adaptive*). Finally, while her self-regulation had declined significantly, it had not collapsed altogether. She was not an impulse-ridden child, driven to strike out at the slightest provocation; rather, she was basically a good kid in the grips of a problem too big for her to handle (*emotional development, moderate deviation*).

When she was 14 years old, her mother remarried and, after some initial storminess, Zoey established a good relationship with her stepfather (*protective factor*). Her problem behaviors gradually subsided and her development began to shift toward a more healthy pathway. However, she continued to be cool and standoffish toward her mother and made a point of finishing high school early so that she could move away from home as soon as possible (*attachment, continued deviance*).

This vignette suggests that the degree of deviation from normative development is a function of the *severity* of the disturbance both within and across the developmental variables and the *duration* of the disturbance. It is also a function of the *balance* between risk, vulnerability, and protective factors. Zoey's story also demonstrates that a disturbance may not envelop all of the child's personality— or even all of a given developmental process. As we have noted, it is important for the clinical child psychologist to assess areas of competence and resilience as well as deviations, especially when planning interventions.

Our challenge in the coming chapters is to construct developmental pathways for the various classifications of childhood psychopathologies. First, for a given classification we must discover which of the developmental and contextual variables have been adversely affected and to what degree of severity. Then we must discover both the balance between risk, vulnerability, and protective factors that produces psychopathology and the balance that enables the child to overcome the disturbance.

Before doing this, however, we must become acquainted with the psychopathologies themselves and develop a general understanding about which are apt to continue into adulthood and which are apt to be outgrown. These are the matters that will occupy us next.

Chapter **Three**

The Bridge to the Psychopathologies

In Chapters 1 and 2 we established a general developmental framework and provided a working knowledge of the variables we will use to investigate psychopathology as normal development gone awry. In this chapter we begin to focus on the psychopathologies themselves. We first discuss the way normality shades gradually into psychopathology both conceptually and empirically, then discuss the major psychopathologies of childhood, and finally summarize longitudinal studies of normal and disturbed children to show which psychopathologies tend to persist and which tend to be outgrown. In Chapters 4 through 15 we go on to explore selected psychopathologies.

First, however, we must investigate the methods that are used to determine whether a child should receive the psychopathological labels we are about to describe.

Diagnosis and Classification

One purpose classification systems serve is to organize a myriad of descriptors and observations into meaningful units. However, they do more than help place a given child in a given category: They are points of departure for exploring *etiology* on the one hand and *prognosis* on the other. Thus, the diagnosis of adolescent schizophrenia should carry with it implications about causative factors and consequences, both in regard to the chances of outgrowing the disturbance and the effectiveness of therapeutic intervention. At present, we are far from realizing such an ideal goal.

Another goal of classification systems is *differential diagnosis*—that is deciding which disorder best captures the child's presentation and which alternative disorders should be ruled out. The correct diagnosis is invaluable in determining how treatment should proceed; for example, the child whose inattentiveness is a product of attention-deficit hyperactivity disorder (ADHD) needs a very different intervention than the child whose inattentiveness is due to anxiety. However, children rarely fit neatly into a single diagnostic category. Disorders in children are often *comorbid;* that is,

they occur together. Consequently, multiple diagnoses are often used rather than a single diagnostic
label. The clinician also should take into account
acuteness or chronicity based on the history of the
disturbance, evaluate the severity of disturbance,
specify the developmental period the child is in, and
describe the specific behaviors that comprise the
psychopathology.

We will start by reviewing the traditional method
of diagnosis used in the United States. However,
clinicians concerned with the adequacy of traditional systems for diagnosing children have raised
a number of criticisms, particularly in regard to
whether such systems pay sufficient attention to
developmental considerations. As part of our discussion we will examine alternative strategies for
clinical diagnosis.

The DSM

The various editions of the *Diagnostic and Statistical Manual of Mental Disorders* (DSM) are in the
tradition of classification based on naturalistic
observation. The tradition has primarily been carried on by psychiatrists and relies heavily on the
observational skills of the clinician for its imple-
mentation. The current version of the DSM is the
fourth, with a recent text revision: DSM-IV-TR
(American Psychiatric Association, 2000).

Features of DSM-IV-TR

The Development of the DSM-IV-TR

As with all the editions of the DSM, the selection
and definitions of the disorders to be included in
DSM-IV-TR were the product of 13 work groups,
each of which took responsibility for revising a
section of the manual. The work groups were composed of at least five members and often more.
For example, the group that developed the section
on Disorders Usually First Diagnosed During Infancy, Childhood, or Adolescence included 12 MDs
and four psychologists. Their recommendations
in turn were critiqued by 50 to 100 advisers,
selected to represent diverse nationalities and

diverse disciplines, including both clinicians and
researchers. The work groups were charged with
conducting comprehensive and objective reviews
of the relevant literature on each of the disorders
under their purview and, where empirical research
was lacking or contradictory, to conduct reanalyses
of existing data or to carry out field trials to determine the reliability and utility of the diagnosis in
the real world. As might be expected, this was a
lengthy process. The DSM-IV (American Psychiatric Association, 1994) was 12 years in the making, and the current text revision took 3 years to
produce. The DSM-V is expected to take even
longer than its predecessors, and therefore the text
revision was undertaken to bridge the gap by up-
dating the manual in the light of more recent
research findings. The most recent version of the
DSM also was developed in close collaboration
with the developers of the *International Statistical
Classification of Diseases and Related Health
Problems,* ICD-10 (World Health Organization,
1996), the diagnostic scheme used most preva-
lently in Europe, in order to increase compatibility
between the two systems.

Definition of Psychopathology

There is no generally accepted definition of psychopathology, as our survey of models has shown.
The authors of the DSM do not pretend to resolve
the knotty issue of conceptualizing psychopathology but settle for stating their own criteria for
what is termed a mental disorder. According to
DSM-IV-TR, a mental disorder is a *"clinically
significant behavioral or psychological syndrome or
pattern that occurs in an individual and that is
associated with present distress (e.g., a painful
symptom) or disability (i.e., impairment in one or
more areas of functioning) or with a significantly
increased risk of suffering death, pain, disability, or
an important loss of freedom"* (p. xxxi).

The authors of DSM-IV-TR are careful to state
that disorders, not individuals, are being classified.
Thus, the manual never refers to "a schizophrenic"
or "an alcoholic," as if the psychopathology were
the person; instead, it uses such phrases as "a child

with schizophrenia" or "an adult with alcohol dependency." The distinction is a simple but a significant one, which we also have adopted in this text.

Objectivity and Behavioral Specificity

DSM-IV-TR strives to avoid the use of terms that are inferential, theoretical, and open to multiple interpretations. Instead, *behaviorally specific* terms are used that can be objectively described and operationally defined. For example, "Fights more frequently than agemates" is more specific than "Has destructive impulses." To take only one example, separation anxiety disorder is defined in terms of 10 behavioral criteria, including unrealistic worry about possible harm befalling major attachment figures, repeated nightmares involving the theme of separation, and persistent reluctance to be separated from major attachment figures.

Reliability

Reliability refers to the consistency of results obtained from using a diagnostic instrument. An instrument that would place the same child in different categories when used by two different clinicians would not be very useful. One criterion of reliability is the consistency with which a diagnostic instrument functions at two points in time, or *test-retest reliability*. More frequently, however, diagnostic systems use *interobserver agreement,* in which two experts are asked to evaluate the same child at the same point in time.

In his review of reliability studies of DSM-IV, Cantwell (1996) concludes that acceptable reliability has been demonstrated for most of the major diagnostic categories. However, reliability is greater for more general categories, such as anxiety disorder, than for more narrowly defined subcategories such as social phobia or generalized anxiety disorder. There is also evidence that clinicians are less reliable than are researchers who undergo specific training to use the diagnostic system in a standardized way. One reason for poorer reliability in practice is that, while DSM provides lists of various criteria that must be met to diagnose a particular disorder, there are no precise rules for determining

when a criterion is met, nor are there guidelines for how to evaluate and integrate various sources of information. Thus, if one clinician uses a parent report to judge whether a symptom is present, another interviews the child, and a third relies on a score on a formal psychological test, they might well reach different conclusions.

Validity

Validity is crucial to the utility of a measure. It indicates the extent to which the measure assesses what it claims to assess or, in this case, the extent to which a diagnostic system does, in fact, correctly classify disturbed children. There are a number of different ways in which evidence for validity might be demonstrated. There is *content* or *face* validity, which is the degree to which the content of a diagnostic category has an obvious relation to what is being evaluated. In the case of separation anxiety disorder, the three behavioral criteria mentioned make sense on the face of it. Ideally, the criteria should also be analyzed statistically to test whether they do, in fact, cluster together. *Concurrent* validity compares the current evaluation with some other contemporary criterion; for example, the diagnosis of a reading disability based on parental report could be compared with scores on a reading achievement test. *Predictive* validity compares current evaluations with some future criterion; for example, children diagnosed with schizophrenia in middle childhood should continue to be more disturbed as young adults than children diagnosed with school phobia. *Construct* validity is the relationship between a diagnostic category and other variables that should be related to it theoretically; for example, children diagnosed with conduct disorder should perform poorly on measures of self-control, such as the ability to delay gratification. And, finally, *discriminative* validity is the extent to which clinical features are unique to the disorder in question and differentiate it from other similar disorders. For example, the diagnostic criteria should help to distinguish children with separation anxiety disorder from those who are depressed. This corresponds to the important clinical task of *differential diagnosis,* and a DSM-IV-TR *Handbook of Differential*

Diagnosis (First, Frances, & Pincus, 2002) is available to assist the clinician with this process.

Validity is difficult to establish, given that there are few independent criteria that can be used for predictive or concurrent validation studies. However, Cantwell (1996) notes that advances have been made in the attempts to obtain external validation of the DSM-IV disorders, although the study of child psychopathology has lagged behind that on adults in this regard. DSM-IV has a stronger *empirical basis* than its predecessors and thus corresponds better to the research evidence regarding different forms of psychopathology. This evidence was obtained from comprehensive reviews of published literature, from reanalysis of studies containing information concerning diagnosis, and from field trials in which data on 6,000 participants were analyzed in terms of reliability and validity of diagnostic criteria. The resulting five-volume DSM-IV sourcebook provides documentation of the decisions reached concerning the classifications and their behavioral components.

Other evidence for external validity is suggested by the fact that there are different predictors and correlates of certain syndromes of disorders, as well as studies demonstrating continuities over time. For example, research has shown that the three kinds of depression described in DSM-IV-TR—Major Depression, Dysthymia, and Adjustment Disorder with Depressed Mood—have a different age of onset, course, and recovery during childhood. In addition, the fact that individuals diagnosed with a particular disorder respond differentially to treatments designed specifically for that disorder lends credibility to the system used to diagnose them.

Comprehensiveness

DSM-IV is substantially more comprehensive than previous versions in its coverage of childhood disorders. In addition, DSM-IV-TR supplies updated information concerning a host of characteristics of a given disorder where such information is available: for example, prevalence; age of onset; course; predisposing factors; differential diagnosis; laboratory findings; and specific age, cultural, or gender-related features.

Multiaxial Classification

Five Dimensions

Instead of assessing only in terms of the presenting problem, DSM-IV-TR uses a **multiaxial classification** system to evaluate the child comprehensively in terms of five dimensions.

Axis I: Clinical Disorders; Other Disorders That May Be a Focus of Clinical Attention   This axis contains most of the disorders with which we will be concerned. The DSM criteria for those disorders will always be included in our discussions.

Axis II: Personality Disorders; Mental Retardation   This axis is concerned with conditions that affect functioning in a pervasive manner, including personality disorders and mental retardation. It can also be used to indicate problematic personality characteristics that do not meet the criteria for a full-blown personality disorder, such as maladaptive and rigid use of defense mechanisms.

Axis III: General Medical Conditions   This axis includes general medical conditions that are potentially relevant to the understanding or management of cases: for example, injuries and infectious diseases, diseases of the nervous system or digestive system, and complications of pregnancy and childbirth.

Axis IV: Psychosocial and Environmental Problems   This axis includes negative life events, stresses, and environmental deficiencies that provide the milieu within which the child's problems developed. Categories include problems related to the *primary support group* (e.g., death of a family member, divorce, abuse); the *social environment* (e.g., inadequate social support, acculturation difficulties, discrimination); *education* (e.g., illiteracy, discord with teachers or classmates); *occupation* (e.g., stressful work schedule, discord with boss or coworkers); *housing* (e.g., homelessness, unsafe neighborhood); *economics* (e.g., poverty, insufficient welfare support); *health care* (e.g., transportation difficulties, inadequate health insurance); *legal system* (e.g., arrest, criminal victimization); and

Table 3.1

Selected Levels of the Children's Global Assessment Scale for DSM-IV Axis IV

100–91	Superior functioning in all areas (at home, at school, and with peers); involved in a range of activities and has many interests (e.g., has hobbies or participates in extracurricular activities or belongs to organized groups such as Scouts). Likable, confident, "everyday" worries never get out of hand. Doing well in school. No symptoms.
80–71	No more than slight impairment in functioning at home, at school, or with peers. Some disturbance of behavior or emotional distress may be present in response to life stresses (e.g., parental separations, deaths, birth of a sibling), but these are brief and interference with functioning is transient. Such children are only minimally disturbing to others and are not considered deviant by those who know them.
50–41	Moderate degree of interference in functioning in most social areas or severe impairment of functioning in one area, such as might result from, for example, suicidal preoccupations and ruminations, school refusal and other forms of anxiety, obsessive rituals, major conversion symptoms, frequent anxiety attacks, frequent episodes of aggressive or other antisocial behavior with some preservation of meaningful social relationships.
30–21	Unable to function in almost all areas (e.g., stays at home, in ward, or in bed all day without taking part in social activities) OR severe impairment in reality testing OR serious impairment in communications (e.g., sometimes incoherent or inappropriate).
10–1	Needs constant supervision (24-hour care) due to severely aggressive or self-destructive behavior or gross impairment in reality testing, communication, cognition, affect, or personal hygiene.

Source: Rapoport and Ismond, 1996.

other psychosocial and environmental problems (e.g., exposure to natural disaster or war).

Axis V: Global Assessment of Functioning This is the clinician's judgment of the overall level of functioning. Such information is useful in planning treatment and measuring its impact. The judgment is made in terms of a Global Assessment of Functioning (GAF) Scale, which goes from superior functioning (100 points) to persistent danger of hurting self or others or persistent inability to maintain minimal personal hygiene (1 to 10 points). (See Table 3.1 for a condensed version of the GAF adapted for children.)

Strengths and Limitations of DSM from a Developmental Psychopathology Perspective

In many ways DSM-IV-TR represents an impressive accomplishment. However, as its authors note, it is difficult to accurately place individuals into discrete diagnostic categories. Even individuals with the same disorder present in slightly different ways, and there is some fuzziness to the boundaries between the different classifications.

Consequently, the DSM requires a high level of clinical judgment and is vulnerable to the subjectivity of the diagnostician. Classification systems such as DSM also have not coped well with the *comorbidity* problem that frequently arises in studies of childhood psychopathology (Cantwell, 1996). It is difficult to know whether multiple diagnoses are accurate—whether they result from a lack of clear distinctions between diagnostic categories or whether they arise from different early expressions of various forms of psychopathology during development.

The Heterogeneity Dimension

One of the reasons why it is difficult to place individuals into discrete diagnostic categories is that they do not fit very neatly. The children who are categorized within a given disorder may be extremely heterogeneous. Take for example two children given the diagnosis of conduct disorder: One is a 7-year-old who engages in cruelty to animals, fighting, and bullying peers, while the other is a 17-year-old boy who engages in vandalism, truancy, and theft. Although the symptoms and their behavioral manifestations differ, both children receive the same

DSM code—and by implication, according to the medical model, should receive the same treatment (Douchette, 2002).

The Developmental Dimension

Another significant shortcoming of the DSM is its failure to acknowledge the *developmental dimension* within disorders. With some exceptions, DSM-IV-TR assumes that the diagnostic criteria are essentially identical across development, whereas research increasingly indicates that this is not the case (Silk, Nath, Siegel, & Kendall, 2000). Evidence suggests that the symptom picture of a disorder changes with age. For example, younger children with separation anxiety disorder worry excessively about separation from their attachment figure and have nightmares, while older children primarily have physical complaints and are reluctant to go to school. Motor disturbances are more characteristic of younger boys with attention-deficit hyperactivity disorder, while older boys with the disorder are characterized by inattention.

Developmentally oriented clinicians have been offering similar criticisms across several generations of DSM revisions. As long ago as 1965, Anna Freud observed that the two criteria fundamental to diagnosing clinical disorders in DSM—*subjective distress* and *impairment of functioning*—are not appropriate for children. The most seriously disturbed children—for example, those with autism, schizophrenia, or conduct disorder—may be oblivious to the fact that they have problems and may experience no subjective distress. Instead of being disturbed, such children are better characterized as disturbing to others. Regarding the second criterion, children do not have a consistent level of functioning. Given that they are still in the process of developing, it is normal for their abilities to wax and wane and fluctuate significantly. Therefore, Anna Freud proposed that only one criterion could help to determine whether a particular behavior or symptom was an indication of psychopathology in a child: *whether it interferes with the child's capacity to move forward in development.*

A classic paper by Garber (1984) proposes a developmental framework for the classification of psychopathology in childhood, arguing against the "adultomorphism" inherent in DSM's tendency to apply adult categories to the problems of children. In attempting to avoid all theory, the authors of DSM also ignore the developmental perspective, overlooking the point that development is not a theory but a basic fact (Bemporad & Schwab, 1986). Further, not only do children change over time, but one of the child's tasks throughout development is to respond in age-appropriate ways to a changing environment. By focusing on superficial descriptions of behavior, DSM ignores the complex nature of the transactions and adaptations that affect individuals as they move through development (Jensen & Hoagwood, 1997).

Cantwell's (1996) conclusion echoes that of Garber 12 years earlier: "Developmental aspects of child and adolescent psychopathology will have to be given much greater consideration in future classification systems" (p. 9).

The Transactional Dimension

Given how dependent children are on their caregivers, the interpersonal context needs must play a significant role in childhood psychopathology. However, problems arising from troubled relationships are not considered clinical disorders in the DSM (Volkmar & Schwab-Stone, 1996). Although DSM avoids taking any overt stand on etiology, by focusing on the disorder as something the child "has," it reveals that an underlying assumption is a static and unidetermined one. This is a far cry from the transactional perspective of developmental psychopathology, in which problems arise in the context of relationships and are a product of reciprocal influences of individuals on one another (Jensen & Hoagwood, 1997). Consequently, some of the most significant concerns that bring children to the attention of mental health professionals—abuse, family conflict, bereavement, family dissolution— are placed in DSM-IV-TR in a somewhat vaguely defined category of V-Codes, which may not be seen as priorities for treatment.

In a move toward acknowledging the significance of relationships for psychopathology, DSM-IV-TR includes the Global Assessment of Relational Functioning (GARF) Scale in the Axes Provided for Further Study. Like the GAF, the GARF allows the clinician to rate the overall adaptive functioning of a relationship on a scale of 0 to 100. The ability of the family to meet the instrumental or emotional needs of its members is rated by consideration of the three following areas: *problem solving* (e.g., adaptability to stress, ability to resolve conflicts and negotiate), *organization* (e.g., maintenance of appropriate boundaries, appropriate distribution of control and responsibility), and *emotional climate* (e.g., empathy, attachment, mutual affection, and respect). Although not yet widely used, the GARF has shown promise as a strategy for assessing the ways in which psychopathology affects relationships and the ways in which relationships elicit and maintain psychopathology (Yingling, 2003).

Family systems-oriented clinicians also have proposed alternative ways to conceptualize and classify psychopathologies as *relational disorders* (Kaslow, 1996). To date these intriguing ideas have not been incorporated into the DSM system, although a working group currently is in the process of developing a Classification of Relational Diagnoses (CORE) that it hopes to see included in the next version of the DSM (Group for the Advancement of Psychiatry Committee on the Family, 1996).

Cross-Cultural and Ethnic Diversity

In response to calls that the field of mental health be more culturally informed and sensitive to ethnic diversity, DSM-IV-TR attempts to deal with *multicultural* considerations in several ways. First, there is a section describing culturally specific symptom patterns, prevalence, and preferred ways of describing or exhibiting distress; for example, in certain cultures depressive disorders are characterized by a preponderance of somatic symptoms rather than by sadness. Next, there is an index of culture-bound syndromes that are found in one or only a few of the world's societies. The index includes the name of the condition, the cultures in which it is found, a brief description of the psychopathology, and a list of possibly related DSM-IV-TR disorders. Examples include *brain fog,* a West African condition primarily experienced by male high school or university students, in which a feeling of mental fatigue is accompanied by neck pain and

blurring of vision; *falling out,* a Caribbean and Southern American phenomenon characterized by a sudden collapse, loss of vision, and an inability to move; and *taijin kyofusho,* a Japanese phenomenon involving intense fear that one's body or bodily functions are displeasing, embarrassing, or offensive to others.

Nonetheless, it is the case that the diagnostic categories contained within DSM are creations of a particular Western cultural perspective, and it is far from certain that they are universally valid. There are a number of ways in which culture might affect diagnosis. A particular concern is that a culturally naïve diagnostician may perceive as pathological behavior that is normative in the context of the child's culture. For example, Tharp (1991) describes the preferences of certain Native American children for allowing time to pass before responding to a question as well as for avoiding direct eye contact with the speaker: A clinician who did not understand the meanings of these behaviors in their cultural context might make the error of assuming that the child is anxious or depressed. (We will revisit this issue in Chapter 16 on psychological assessment.) Another example is that styles of childrearing in the African American community that involve physical discipline and sharp verbal admonitions have historically been interpreted as abusive by investigators lacking in cultural understanding. (We will explore this issue in more detail in Chapter 14 when we discuss child maltreatment.)

Fundamentally, there is the inescapable problem that all diagnostic systems call for clinical judgment, judgment that might be colored by issues of race, social class, ethnicity, religion, and the personal characteristics and predilections of the diagnostician. The developers of the DSM have made efforts to ensure that clinicians remain cognizant of these issues just as the American Psychological Association (2003) mandates that all psychologists should be clinically competent. Nonetheless, prejudices often are hidden, even from those who hold them (McIntosh, 1998), and so we will need to take care in our review of the psychopathologies to take into account ethnic and cultural considerations, wherever the data exist that allow us to do so. (see Box 3.1 on pp. 100–101.)

potentially stressful situations listed are disrupted attachment relationships, domestic violence, psychiatric disturbance in a parent, sexual abuse, social discrimination and/or family isolation, inadequate school resources, homelessness, unsafe neighborhood, and natural disaster. For each situation, the clinician is provided with a developmentally sensitive list of protective and potentiating factors that might moderate the child's response to the stressor.

Child Manifestations   The second section contains the classifications of child behavior problems, divided into 10 categories. The disorders generally follow the DSM-IV-TR; however, because the DSM-PC includes behaviors that are on the normative spectrum, the terminology differs and additional distinctions are made:

1. *Developmental Competency* (e.g., mental retardation; difficulties acquiring motor, speech, or academic skills).
2. *Impulsive, Hyperactive, Inattentive Behaviors* (e.g., overactivity, difficulty sustaining attention).
3. *Negative/Antisocial Behaviors* (e.g., negative emotional behaviors, aggressive/oppositional behaviors, secretive antisocial behaviors).
4. *Substance-Related Behaviors* (e.g., substance use or abuse).
5. *Emotions and Moods* (e.g., anxiety, sadness, obsessive-compulsive behaviors, suicidal ideation).
6. *Somatic Behavior* (e.g., pain, daytime sleepiness, sleep problems).
7. *Feeding, Eating, and Elimination* (e.g., soiling, purging-binge eating, body image dissatisfaction, irregular eating).
8. *Illness-Related Behaviors* (e.g., excessive fearfulness of medical procedures, noncompliance with medical regime, denial of physical illness).
9. *Sexual Behaviors* (e.g., wishing to be, or believing one is, the other gender; cross-dressing; discomfort with one's own sexual anatomy).
10. *Atypical Behaviors* (repetitive or bizarre behaviors, absence of normal social relatedness).

Within each of these classifications, child behavior problems are further subdivided into three levels of severity: developmental variations, problems, and disorders. The *developmental deviations* include behaviors that may concern parents but that are still within the normal range of age expectations. For example, an 18-month-old who still speaks in one-word sentences is by no means precocious but is still within the normal range. Often such variations are brought to the pediatrician's attention by parents who lack accurate information about normal child development, and their concerns are quickly resolved with a consultation and parent education. In contrast, a *problem* refers to behavior that is significant enough to disrupt the child's functioning in school, family, or peer relationships, but is not serious enough to warrant the diagnosis of a disorder. For example, a developmental/cognitive problem would be coded when a preschooler evidences a mild delay in acquisition of speech and language skills. Generally, such problems can be treated with a short-term intervention. Lastly, the *disorders* are those defined by DSM and represent clinically significant behavior problems that are distressing and disruptive to functioning, such as the child's whose stuttering interferes with school performance. The disorders generally require referral to a child mental health professional. The DSM-PC manual also describes how problems at each level of severity would present in infancy, early childhood, middle childhood, or adolescence. An example of classifications related to sadness is provided in Table 3.3.

Strengths and Limitations of the DSM-PC

The DSM-PC has not taken us far afield from the medical model, given that it retains the focus on classifying the disordered behavior with which children present. However, DSM-PC offers a number of

Table 3.3

Example of DSM-PC Categories: Sadness

Classification	Common Developmental Presentations
V65.49 Sadness Variation: Transient depressive responses to stress are normal in an otherwise healthy population. **V62.82 Bereavement:** Sadness related to a major loss that typically persists for less than 2 months after the loss. Children in hospitals or institutions often experience some of the fears that accompany a death or separation. These fears may be demonstrated in actions that mimic normal grief responses.	**Infancy:** Brief expressions of sadness, which normally first appear in the last quarter of the first year of life, manifest by crying, brief withdrawal, and transient anger. **Early Childhood:** Transient withdrawal and sad affect occur after losses; bereavement due to the loss of a parent, pet, or treasured object. **Middle Childhood:** Transient loss of self-esteem after experiencing failure and feelings of sadness with losses. **Adolescence:** Similar presentation to that of middle childhood but may also include fleeting thoughts of death. Bereavement includes loss of a boyfriend or girlfriend, friend, or best friend.
V40.3 Sadness Problem: Sadness or irritability that begins to include some symptoms of major depressive disorders in mild form: • Depressed/irritable mood • Diminished interest or pleasure • Weight loss/gain or failure to make expected weight gains • Insomnia/hypersomnia • Psychomotor agitation/retardation • Fatigue or energy loss • Feelings of worthlessness or guilt • Diminished ability to think/concentrate These symptoms are more than transient and have a mild impact on the child's functioning. However, the behaviors are not sufficiently intense to qualify for a depressive disorder.	**Infancy:** Developmental regressions, fearfulness, anorexia, failure to thrive, sleep disturbances, social withdrawal, irritability, and increased dependency, which are responsive to soothing and engagement by caregivers. **Early Childhood:** Sad affect becomes more apparent. Temper tantrums may increase, as well as physical symptoms such as soiling, constipation, bedwetting, and nightmares. **Middle Childhood:** Some sadness that results in brief suicidal ideation with no clear plan of suicide, some apathy, boredom, low self-esteem, and unexplained physical symptoms such as headache and abdominal pain. **Adolescence:** Some disinterest, decrease in motivation, and daydreaming in class may lead to deterioration of schoolwork. Hesitancy in attending school, apathy, and boredom may occur.
300.4 Dysthymic Disorder: Depressed/irritable mood for most of the day, for more days than not, for at least 1 year. Also the presence of two or more of the following: • Poor appetite/overeating • Insomnia/hypersomnia • Low energy or fatigue • Poor concentration/difficulty making decisions • Feelings of hopelessness Because of the chronic nature of the disorder, the child may not develop adequate social skills.	**Infancy:** Not diagnosed. **Early Childhood:** Rarely diagnosed. **Middle Childhood and Adolescence:** Feelings of inadequacy, loss of interest/pleasure, social withdrawal, guilt/brooding, irritability or excessive anger, decreased activity/productivity. May experience sleep/appetite/weight changes and psychomotor symptoms. Low self-esteem is common.

advantages to the clinician with a developmental psychopathology perspective. First, the DSM-PC is *transactional,* viewing problems as arising from the relationship between the child and the environment. Consequently, the diagnostician is asked to consider a host of environmental, social, and interpersonal factors that might have affected this child's development. Risks, vulnerabilities, and protective factors are to be weighed. Second, the DSM-PC appreciates the *continuum* between normal and abnormal development and provides the diagnostician guidelines for determining when development is slightly deviant or has indeed fallen off the normal course. Third, the DSM-PC is explicitly *developmental,* placing its definitions of variations, problems, and disorders in the context of age-appropriate norms and behavioral manifestations. On the other hand, this diagnostic system also requires even more complex clinical judgments than the other two systems. The boundaries between the categories of deviation, problems, and disorder are often fuzzy; and, because normal development is so varied, there can be no firm criteria for deciding whether behaviors exceed the normal range. Finally, data on its reliability and validity are not yet available.

The Empirically Based Approach

In contrast to the top-down approach exemplified by systems based on the medical model, such as the DSM and ICD, the empirically based approach can be termed "bottom up" (Achenbach, 2000). (See Table 3.4.) Instead of starting with a theoretical construct, such as Oppositional Defiant Disorder and then collecting data to determine how well the label applies to children, the empirical approach starts by collecting data in the real world. The empiricist begins by measuring a large number of specific behaviors exhibited by disturbed children; eliminates those that are infrequent, redundant, and obscure; and subjects the rest to statistical techniques designed to determine which are highly related to one another. The statistical technique employed is called *factor analysis,* and the behavior items that relate to one another form *factors.* After examining the content of the interrelated items, the investigator assigns each factor a label. Such labels may resemble the theoretical constructs used in traditional diagnosis, such as "oppositionality" or "neurosis"; however, what the factors actually mean is a question that can only be answered by further empirical research.

Another important difference between the empirical approach and DSM is that, while DSM is

Table 3.4

Comparison of DSM and Empirically Based Approaches

Similarities Between Paradigms
Explicit statements of problems to be assessed
Some DSM categories and empirically based syndromes describe similar problems
Statistically significant agreement between some diagnoses and syndromes

Differences Between Paradigms	
DSM	**Empirically Based**
Categorical	Dimensional
Problems judged present or absent.	Problems scored on a continuum.
"Top-down" approach: Categories and criteria are chosen by committees.	"Bottom-up" approach: Syndromes are derived from empirical data.
Clinical cutpoints are identical for both genders, all ages, and all informants.	Clinical cutpoints and norms are derived separately by gender, age, and informant.
Individual clinician chooses sources of data, data to obtain, and assessment procedures to use.	Standardized procedures for obtaining data.
No procedures specified for comparing data from different sources.	Statistical methods available for comparing scores across informants.
End products are diagnoses.	End products are syndrome scores and profiles compared against norms for age and gender.
Many separate diagnostic categories.	Specific problems are grouped into a smaller number of statistically robust syndromes.

Source: Achenbach, 2000.

categorical, classifying children in terms of whether or not they "have" a disorder, the empirical approach is *dimensional,* rating children on the extent to which they show symptoms or problem behavior consistent with a particular diagnosis. One objection to categories is their all-or-none quality; for example, a child either is or is not depressed; and if he or she is, the clinician must decide whether the degree of disturbance is mild, moderate, or severe. The dimensional approach is compatible with the idea of continuity between normality and psychopathology, with the number of symptoms providing a measure of the severity of the deviation from the norm.

The preeminent proponent of the empirically based approach is Thomas Achenbach. His Achenbach System of Empirically Based Assessment (ASEBA) (Achenbach & Rescorla, 2001) consists of a set of carefully developed measures to assess children's behavior problems from the perspectives of parents, teachers/caregivers and, in the case of adolescents, the youths themselves. Here we will focus on the parent-report measure, the Child Behavior Checklist (CBCL).

Achenbach's first step was to collect descriptions of pathological behavior from psychiatric case histories and from the literature. Through a series of preliminary studies these were reduced to 112 items that form the current CBCL. Here are some examples of items on the checklist: argues a lot, complains of loneliness, doesn't eat well, runs away from home, has strange ideas. To obtain norms, the CBCL was filled out by parents of 4,994 children derived from a national survey encompassing 40 U.S. states, as well as Australia and England. The analyses yielded both narrow-band and wide-band factors. The narrow-band factors included specific **syndromes,** or behavior problems, such as Withdrawn/Depressed, Somatic Complaints, Social Problems, Attention Problems, and Aggressive Behavior. The Withdrawn/Depressed syndrome contains the following behavioral items: would rather be alone than with others, secretive, shy, sad, and withdrawn. The Aggressive Behavior scale includes these behavioral items: destroys own and others' things, disobedient in home and school, argues, fights, and threatens others.

Several of the narrow-band syndromes were grouped together to form two wide-band factors. The

Internalizing factor comprises Anxious/Depressed, Withdrawn/Depressed, and Somatic Complaints, and the **Externalizing** factor comprises Rule-Breaking Behavior and Aggressive Behavior. The internalizing-externalizing distinction describes two very different symptom pictures. Anxious children, for example, generally are well behaved but are tormented by fears or guilt. They suffer inwardly, internalizing their distress. On the other hand, some children act out their problems in relation to others, thereby externalizing their distress. It is important to note, however, that internalizing-externalizing is a dimension of behavior, not a typology of children. While some children fall at either extreme, many of them demonstrate mixtures of both elements; that is, children can be both sad and aggressive or have a "nervous stomach" and steal.

By comparing data from normal and clinical populations, it is possible to determine cutoff scores, below which the child is considered within the normal range and above which the child would be considered disturbed. Children whose scores are higher than those of 98 percent of children in the normative population are considered to be above the clinical cutoff. These norms differ by age and gender. For example, girls generally are rated lower than boys on aggressiveness and therefore the cutoff score for girls is lower.

After scoring all eight narrow-band scales, the clinician can obtain a profile indicating which scales are within normal limits and which exceed them. A hypothetical child might be within the normal limits for the internalizing scales of Anxious/Depressed, Withdrawn/Depressed, and Somatic Complaints, while exceeding the norm in the externalizing scales of Rule-Breaking Behavior and Aggressive Behavior. Figure 3.1 presents the profile of a 15-year-old boy's behavior based on the parent-report version of the CBCL.

In an innovation for the most recent version, Achenbach has included profiles that relate children's CBCL scores to DSM-oriented categories: affective problems (items reflecting depression and suicidality), anxiety, somatic problems, attention deficit/hyperactivity, oppositional defiance, and conduct problems. Thus, the CBCL can be used to assist the clinician in determining whether

Figure 3.1   CBCL Profile of a 15-Year-Old Boy.

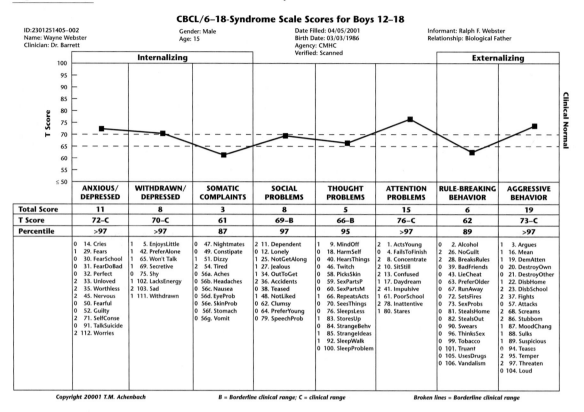

CBCL/6–18-Syndrome Scale Scores for Boys 12–18

ID:2301251405–002
Name: Wayne Webster
Clinician: Dr. Barrett

Gender: Male
Age: 15

Date Filled: 04/05/2001
Birth Date: 03/03/1986
Agency: CMHC
Verified: Scanned

Informant: Ralph F. Webster
Relationship: Biological Father

Internalizing ... **Externalizing** ... **Clinical Normal**

	ANXIOUS/ DEPRESSED	WITHDRAWN/ DEPRESSED	SOMATIC COMPLAINTS	SOCIAL PROBLEMS	THOUGHT PROBLEMS	ATTENTION PROBLEMS	RULE-BREAKING BEHAVIOR	AGGRESSIVE BEHAVIOR
Total Score	11	8	3	8	5	15	6	19
T Score	72–C	70–C	61	69–B	66–B	76–C	62	73–C
Percentile	>97	>97	87	97	95	>97	89	>97

ANXIOUS/ DEPRESSED	WITHDRAWN/ DEPRESSED	SOMATIC COMPLAINTS	SOCIAL PROBLEMS	THOUGHT PROBLEMS	ATTENTION PROBLEMS	RULE-BREAKING BEHAVIOR	AGGRESSIVE BEHAVIOR
0 14. Cries	1 5. EnjoysLittle	0 47. Nightmates	2 11. Dependent	1 9. MindOff	2 1. ActsYoung	0 2. Alcohol	1 3. Argues
1 29. Fears	1 42. PreferAlone	0 49. Constipate	0 12. Lonely	0 18. HarmSelf	0 4. FailsToFinish	2 26. NoGuilt	1 16. Mean
0 30. FearSchool	1 65. Won't Talk	1 51. Dizzy	1 25. NotGetAlong	0 40. HearsThings	2 8. Concentrate	2 28. BreaksRules	1 19. DemAtten
0 31. FearDoBad	1 69. Secretive	2 54. Tired	1 27. Jealous	0 46. Twitch	2 10. SitStill	0 39. BadFriends	0 20. DestroyOwn
0 32. Perfect	0 75. Shy	0 56a. Aches	1 34. OutToGet	0 58. PicksSkin	2 13. Confused	0 43. LieCheat	0 21. DestroyOther
2 33. Unloved	1 102. LacksEnergy	0 56b. Headaches	2 36. Accidents	0 59. SexPartsP	1 17. Daydream	0 63. PreferOlder	1 22. DisbHome
2 35. Worthless	2 103. Sad	0 56c. Nausea	0 38. Teased	0 60. SexPartsM	2 41. Impulsive	0 67. RunAway	2 23. DisbSchool
2 45. Nervous	1 111. Withdrawn	0 56d. EyeProb	1 48. NotLiked	0 66. RepeatsActs	1 61. PoorSchool	0 72. SetsFires	2 37. Fights
0 50. Fearful		0 56e. SkinProb	0 62. Clumsy	0 70. SeesThings	2 78. Inattentive	0 73. SexProbs	0 57. Attacks
0 52. Guilty		0 56f. Stomach	0 64. PreferYoung	0 76. SleepsLess	1 80. Stares	0 81. StealsHome	2 68. Screams
2 71. SelfConse		0 56g. Vomit	0 79. SpeechProb	1 83. StoresUp		0 82. StealsOut	2 86. Stubborn
0 91. TalkSuicide				0 84. StrangeBehv		0 90. Swears	1 87. MoodChang
2 112. Worries				1 85. StrangeIdeas		0 96. ThinksSex	1 88. Sulks
				1 92. SleepWalk		0 99. Tobacco	1 89. Suspicious
				0 100. SleepProblem		0 101. Truant	0 94. Teases
						0 105. UsesDrugs	2 95. Temper
						0 106. Vandalism	2 97. Threaten
							0 104. Loud

Copyright 20001 T.M. Achenbach   *B = Borderline clinical range; C = clinical range*   *Broken lines = Borderline clinical range*

From Achenbach and Rescorla, 2001.

one of the subjective DSM categories actually fits the data.

Limitations of the Empirical Approach

The empirical approach offers significant advantages over more subjective diagnostic systems, including increased precision, reliability, and behavioral objectivity. However, those benefits come at some cost. One of the prices paid is in comprehensiveness. For example, Achenbach's system provides us with eight narrow-band and two broad-band dimensions for rating children's problems, and these map onto six DSM-oriented diagnoses. In contrast, DSM-IV-TR and ICD are more differentiated; for example, they distinguish between degrees of depression (e.g., major depression and dysthymia) and have separate diagnoses for subtypes of

anxiety disorders such as separation anxiety and phobia. DSM-IV-TR and ICD also contain diagnoses not found among Achenbach's syndromes, most notably anorexia nervosa, bulimia, specific learning disabilities, and autism. Because the empirically based approach starts with descriptors that occur frequent in clinical populations, it has difficulty capturing rare but important disturbances.

Further, while the empirical approach is more behaviorally specific and objective, subjective judgments still enter into informants' ratings (Drotar, Stein, & Perrin, 1995). While it is true that the statement "Is disobedient at home" is more objective than "Has a problem with authority figures," the former still requires a judgment. Thus, the same behavior a mother might regard as disobedient in her son might be dismissed by the father as being "just the way boys are." Behavioral ratings depend on who does the rating and the situation in which the behavior occurs. Parents, teachers, and professionals may disagree in rating a particular child either because they evaluate the same behavior differently or because they observe the child in different settings. An oppositional girl may respond to the teacher's firm discipline and thus not display the problem behavior she does at home, while the inattentive child's problems may emerge in the school setting but not be noticeable to parents. Achenbach's system takes into account the perspective of different raters by providing methods for integrating and comparing scores across informants. However, when raters disagree, clinical judgment is needed in order to interpret the meaning of these discrepancies. Are the mother's ratings high due to the fact that she is stressed and intolerant of even ordinary misbehavior, or are the father's low ratings due to the fact that the child indeed behaves differently when he is present?

The fact that information providers often have discrepant views of the same child is not a problem confined to multivariate statistical assessment but is present in all assessment procedures that rely on multiple sources of information. However, we do have a few leads about what sources would be most valid for some particular psychopathologies. There is some evidence that parents and teachers are better informants in regard to *externalizing* symptoms, such as disruptive behavior, hyperactivity, inattentiveness, and oppositional-defiant disorders than are children, who tend to underreport them. In turn, children's own reports are more informative about *internalizing* symptoms such as anxiety and depression (Cantwell, 1996). This is an issue we return to in Chapter 16, when we discuss strategies for coping with multiple sources of data and divergent information about the same child.

Normal Problems and Normal Problem Behavior

If we are to treat psychopathology as normal development gone awry, we must anchor our thinking in a definition of normality. Moreover, we must have an idea of the problems and problem behaviors inherent in normal development, since normality never means problem-free.

Normal development involves both problems and problem behaviors (see Figure 3.2). To take one example of the latter: One study found that about

Figure 3.2

Abnormally normal behavior?

Calvin and Hobbes   by Bill Watterson

Box 3.1 | **Case Study: Comparing Diagnostic Systems**

In Chapter 2, we introduced the case of Zoey, whose development we tracked from birth to age 14. Recall that when Zoey was age 10, after experiencing her parents' divorce, a move to the inner city, and her mother's return to the workforce, Zoey began exhibiting a number of behavior problems. These included angry outbursts and argumentativeness with the teacher, poor peer relationships, and sullenness with her mother. Further, she was struggling with school, hampered by a reading difficulty that had long gone undiagnosed. While our knowledge of Zoey's eventual good outcome points out one of the major limitations of diagnosis—it takes a static snapshot of a child whose developmental trajec-

tory is still in motion—let us look at how different diagnostic systems might have classified her 10-year-old behavior.

DSM-IV-TR

Axis I (Clinical Disorder): 313.81 Oppositional Defiant Disorder; 315.00 Reading Disorder
Axis II (Personality Disorder/Mental Retardation): V71.09 No diagnosis
Axis III (General Medical Conditions): None
Axis IV (Psychosocial and Environmental Problems): Parent–Child Problem (divorce, mother-child conflict); Educational Problems (conflict with teachers and classmates);

Economic Problems (inadequate finances)
Axis V (Global Assessment of Functioning): 65

DSM-PC

Axis I (Clinical Disorder): 313.81 Oppositional Defiant Disorder; 315.00 Reading Disorder; V40.3 Sadness Problem; V65.49 Hyperactive/Impulsive Variation
Axis II (Personality Disorder/Mental Retardation): V71.09 No diagnosis
Axis III (General Medical Conditions): None
Axis IV (Psychosocial and Environmental Problems): V61.20 Challenges to Attachment Relationship; V61.0 Divorce; V60.2 Inadequate Financial Status;

---

half the children in kindergarten through grade 2 were described as "restless," while another study found that a similar percent of 6- to 12-year-olds were described as "overactive." While both of these behaviors are part of the syndrome of hyperactivity, it would be incorrect to assume that half the children were hyperactive, since they have neither the clustering nor the intensity and chronicity of problems that would interfere with adaptive functioning. On the other hand, it would be equally foolish to deny that restlessness and overactivity constitute a problem both at home and in school. (See Box 3.2.)

Campbell (1989, 2002) outlines some typical nonpsychopathological developmental problems during the infancy and preschool period:

The "Difficult" Infant Studies of individual differences in infants, or infant temperament, have shown that some infants are easy to care for while others are difficult. The latter tend to

be irritable, slow to adapt to change in routine, intense and negative in their reactions, and irregular in their biological functioning. If cared for sensitively, infants can outgrow this difficult phase; however, if caretakers are impatient and intolerant, or change routines abruptly and often, the chances of behavior problems in the toddler period are increased.

The Defiant Toddler Disciplinary problems and uncertainty about when and how to set limits are the major concerns of parents of toddlers. In most instances the problems are stage-specific, leaving no residue. However, parental mismanagement, say, in the form of overcontrol, may increase the likelihood that problems will develop and persist.

The Insecurely Attached Child We have already described the concept of secure and insecure attachment and reviewed the evidence

V62.3 Discord with Peers/Teachers

Axis V (Global Assessment of
Functioning): 65

ICD-10

Axis One (Clinical Psychiatric
Syndrome): F92.8 Mixed
Disorder of Conduct and
Emotions; Rule out F91.3
Oppositional Defiant Disorder

Axis Two (Specific Disorders of
Psychological Development):
F81.0 Specific Reading Disorder

Axis Three (Intellectual Level): 4

Axis Four (Medical Conditions): None

Axis Five: (Associated Abnormal
Psychosocial Situations):

1.0   Lack of warmth in parent-
child relationships

1.5   Intrafamilial discord among
adults

5.4   Living conditions that
create a potentially
hazardous psychosocial
situation

6.6   Negatively altered pattern
of family relationships

8.0   Discordant relationships
with peers

Axis Six: Global Assessment of
Psychosocial Disability: 5

**Achenbach System of Empirically
Based Assessment** (Based on Teacher
Report Form)

Syndrome Scale Scores

Anxious/Depressed:	Normal
Withdrawn/Depressed:	Borderline
Somatic Complaints:	Normal
Social Problems:	Clinical
Thought Problems:	Normal
Attention Problems:	Borderline
Rule-Breaking Behavior:	Normal
Aggressive Behavior:	Clinical

Factor Scores

Internalizing:	Normal
Externalizing:	Borderline

DSM-Oriented Scales

Affective Problems:	Borderline
Anxiety Problems:	Normal
Somatic Problems:	Normal
Attention Deficit/ Hyperactivity Problems:	Borderline
Oppositional Defiant Problems:	Clinical
Conduct Problems:	Borderline

that the insecurely attached infant may be at risk for problems in the area of initiative and social relations. However, such problems are not inevitable and can be minimized by sensitive caregiving. In Chapter 6, we will review the evidence.

The Aggressive or Withdrawn Preschooler
Aggressive behavior toward peers is a common complaint of parents and teachers of preschoolers, with boys being more aggressive than girls. However, as with other behavior problems, there is no need to read ominous portents into such aggressiveness unless it is coupled with mismanagement by parents or a discordant family situation. Social withdrawal, unlike aggression, is relatively rare and has not been satisfactorily studied. There is tentative evidence that the shy, quiet child is less at risk for developing behavior problems than is the

disruptive one, but such risk may be increased in extreme cases when combined with other internalizing problems such as separation anxiety or dysphoric mood.

Next, at the other end of our developmental spectrum the American Psychological Association (2002) outlines some normal behavior problems of adolescence.

The Oppositional Adolescent   Adolescents often practice their new higher reasoning skills by engaging adults in debates, arguing persistently and taking an oppositional stance over matters that may seem trivial to their parents. By the same token, they are often highly critical of the adults around them, seeming to intentionally search for discrepancies, contradictions, or exceptions to what adults say. Parents who take personally this excessive fault-finding might experience

Box 3.2 | Are the Problems of America's Children Getting Worse?

We frequently hear it said that things are worse now than in the past. Is this true when it comes to childhood psychopathology? Achenbach and Howell (1993) set out to answer this question by comparing rates of maladjustment in children over a 13-year period. Parents' and teachers' reports on the CBCL were obtained from large samples collected at multiple sites across the United States from 1976 and 1989. The authors found that there were significant increases over time in all problems reported, and that these were not limited to a particular area of functioning; children demonstrated increases in both internalizing and externalizing disorders over the 13-year period. In addition, the proportion of children in the clinical range increased on all scales,

particularly Attention Problems, Internalizing, and Externalizing. Over 18 percent of the sample scored in the clinical range in 1989, as compared to only 10 percent in 1976. Children's average competence scores also decreased.

The investigators also compared the rates of maladjustment shown by the U.S. sample with those found in other countries, including Thailand, Australia, Puerto Rico, and Holland, and found that cross-culturally the 1989 U.S. rates were not significantly higher. Further, demographic variables did not account for problem behavior, which did not differ according to child age, gender, ethnicity, or socioeconomic status.

While this study showed evidence that changes have occurred, it does

not answer the question of why they occurred. Subsequently, Stanger, Achenbach, and McConaughy (1993) examined the risk factors associated with the development of adjustment problems over a 3-year period in a large national sample of children. Disturbance was accounted for by the presence of multiple risk factors, the most powerful of which were child attention problems, parental stress, and a need for mental health services on the part of any family member. Whether these risk factors increased in prevalence and intensity during the period from 1976 and 1989 is not known; if so, that would provide one potential explanation for the increase seen in children's problem behavior. What other factors do you think might have come into play?

raising an adolescent as a highly frustrating experience. However, the teenager's argumentativeness is best viewed as a form of cognitive exercise that helps adolescents to develop their critical thinking skills.

The Overly Dramatic/Impulsive Youth   The teenage years are a time of heightened emotionality and, sometimes, rash thinking. Adolescents may appear to jump to conclusions, stating extreme opinions that startle and concern the adults around them. Such bravado, however, may be an attempt to cover anxiety and uncertainty. By the same token, adolescents may have a tendency toward overexaggeration and dramatics because they are experiencing their world in a particularly intense way. While adults may complain that everything seems to be a big deal to teens, to the youths themselves, what is happening in the moment indeed appears dire.

The Egocentric Teenager   As adolescents focus inward in order to explore such stage-salient issues as identity, gender role, and sexuality, they may appear to adults to be excessively "me-centered." With time, they can be expected to develop a more reciprocal orientation. Where perspective-taking abilities do not develop naturally, these skills can be taught.

The DSM-IV-TR Disorders

While keeping in mind its limitations, throughout this text, we will be utilizing the DSM-IV-TR classifications of the disorders. Here we provide summaries only of those specific psychopathologies that we will subsequently discuss in detail in later chapters.

Adjustment Disorders

We describe **adjustment disorders** first because they form a link between the normal problems just described and the more serious psychopathologies to come. The symptoms of an adjustment disorder emerge in reaction to a recent identified stressor. The symptoms are significant enough to interfere with social, academic, or occupational functioning and are in excess of the normal expected reaction. Adjustment disorders may occur with *depression* (sadness, hopelessness), *anxiety* (nervousness, separation fears), disturbance of *conduct* (aggression, truancy), or a combination of these. However, the symptoms do not persist longer than 6 months after the termination of the stressor, thus marking the boundary between adjustment disorders and other more persistent disorders.

Disorders Usually First Diagnosed in Infancy, Childhood, or Adolescence

As for the more serious psychopathologies, DSM-IV distinguishes between disturbances that are specific to children and those that are essentially the same for children and adults. We present those in the former category first.

Mental Retardation

Mental retardation is defined as significantly below-average intellectual functioning (i.e., an IQ of 70 or below) combined with deficits in adaptive functioning such as self-care, social skills, and personal independence.

Learning Disorders

Learning disorders include *reading disorder, mathematics disorder,* and *disorder of written expression.* In each instance, the academic ability is substantially below what is expected given the child's chronological age, measured intelligence, or age-appropriate education.

Pervasive Developmental Disorders

The primary disorder here is **autism,** which is marked by a qualitative impairment in social interaction (e.g.,

lack of social or emotional reciprocity, impaired use of nonverbal behavior such as eye contact and gestures to regulate social interaction); gross and sustained impairment in communication (e.g., delayed or total absence of spoken language, stereotyped language, absence of imaginative play); and restricted, repetitive, and stereotyped patterns of behavior, interests, and activities.

Attention-Deficit and Disruptive Behavior Disorders

The disorders included here were formerly listed under separate categories. They have been subsumed under a single classification because of the frequency with which they overlap.

Attention-deficit/hyperactivity disorder is characterized by a number of inattentive behaviors (e.g., being easily distracted, having difficulty in following through on instructions, frequent shifting from one uncompleted activity to another) and/or by hyperactivity-impulsivity (e.g., acting before thinking, fidgeting, having difficulty waiting in line or taking turns).

Conduct disorder is characterized by repetitive and persistent patterns of behavior in which either the basic rights of others or major age-appropriate societal norms or rules are violated (e.g., initiating fights, using weapons that can cause serious physical harm, stealing, setting fires, truancy).

Oppositional defiant disorder is marked by a pattern of negativistic, hostile, defiant behavior (e.g., loses temper, argues with adults and defies their requests, deliberately annoys others, lies, and bullies).

Elimination Disorders

In this category we will only be discussing **enuresis,** which is defined as repeated voiding of urine into bed or clothes at a chronological age of at least 5 years, and **encopresis,** which involves soiling.

Other Disorders of Infancy, Childhood, or Adolescence

Separation anxiety disorder is characterized by excessive anxiety concerning separation from those to whom the child is attached: for example, unrealistic worry about harm befalling an attachment figure, refusal to go to school in order to stay with an attachment figure, refusal to go to sleep without being near an attachment figure.

Reactive attachment disorder is characterized by disturbed social relatedness (e.g., excessive inhibition or ambivalence, or diffuse attachments manifested by indiscriminate sociability with relative strangers) due to grossly pathogenic care, such as neglect or frequent change of caretakers.

Disorders Diagnosed in Children, Adolescents, and Adults

The following disorders either have the same manifestations in children as in adults or can be made applicable to children with a few specific modifications.

Substance-Related Disorders

Substance-related disorders are specific to a specific substance (alcohol, cocaine, cannabis, amphetamines, etc.) and involve clinically significant distress or impairment of function relating to its use. The classifications involve substance use disorders, including **substance abuse** and **substance dependence,** or **substance induced disorders** that are caused by ingestion (e.g., intoxication, anxiety, mood disorder, psychosis).

Schizophrenia

Schizophrenia is a severe, pervasive disturbance consisting of delusions, hallucinations, disorganized speech, bizarre behaviors, and the so-called negative symptoms of flat affect, avolition, and alogia. Among the different types of schizophrenia are the *paranoid type,* marked by delusions or hallucinations, and the *disorganized type,* marked by disorganized speech and behavior and inappropriate affect.

Mood Disorders

Major depression is defined in terms of a depressed mood, weight loss, insomnia, psychomotor agitation or retardation, feelings of worthlessness or

guilt, indecisiveness, recurrent thoughts of death, and markedly diminished interest or pleasure in activities. It occurs in single or repeated episodes. **Dysthymic disorder** designates a chronic state of depression lasting at least one year. The third major category, **bipolar disorder,** is characterized by mood swings from depression to mania.

Anxiety Disorders

There are many anxiety disorders, but here we describe only those we will be discussing in later chapters.

Specific **phobia** is a fear provoked by the presence or anticipation of a specific object or situation (e.g., flying, heights, animals). The phobic stimulus is avoided or endured with marked distress. While adults recognize the unreasonable nature of the fear, this is not true of children.

Social phobia, also known as social anxiety disorder, involves excessive anxiety and avoidance of situations in which one might be exposed to unfamiliar people or required to perform in front of them. Typically, the child fears that he or she will be embarrassed or negatively evaluated in a public setting.

Obsessive-compulsive disorder is characterized either by obsessions, defined as recurrent thoughts, impulses, or images that are intrusive and inappropriate and cause marked anxiety or distress, or by compulsions, defined as ritualistic behaviors (e.g., hand washing) or mental acts (e.g., counting, repeating words silently) that a person feels driven to perform in response to an obsession or according to rigidly applied rules.

Posttraumatic stress disorder results when a person has experienced an event involving actual or threatened death or injury to the self or others. Among the many symptoms are persistent reexperiencing of the traumatic event (e.g., through recurrent, intrusive, distressing recollections), persistent avoidance of stimuli associated with the trauma (e.g., inability to recall aspects of the trauma or a diminished range of interests or activities), and persistent symptoms of increased arousal (e.g., difficulty falling asleep, irritability, difficulty concentrating).

Generalized anxiety disorder involves excessive worry and tension that is uncontrollable and pervasive across stimuli and situations.

Eating Disorders

Anorexia nervosa is an intense fear of gaining weight even though the individual is underweight, an undue influence of body weight on self-evaluation or denial of the seriousness of current low body weight, and a body weight less than 85 percent of that expected. **Bulimia nervosa** is marked by recurrent episodes of binge eating along with a sense of lack of control over eating during the episode. Self-evaluation is unduly influenced by body shape and weight, while weight is often normal.

Gender Identity Disorders

Gender identity disorder is evidenced by a strong and persistent desire to be, or insistence that one is, a member of the other sex. The child displays an intense discomfort with the gender roles and anatomical features associated with his or her own biological sex.

Personality Disorders

Personality disorders are inflexible patterns of behavior and inner experience that deviate significantly from social expectations and lead to distress or impairment. Their onset is seen in adolescence and early adulthood and they are rarely applied to children. However, increasing attention has been drawn to a particular personality disorder whose precursors appear to manifest themselves early enough in life to warrant diagnosis in young persons. **Borderline personality disorder** involves a pervasive instability in interpersonal relationships, self-image, and affect. We will explore its manifestations as we discuss the transition from late adolescence to adulthood.

Integration of Normal Development and Psychopathology

In Table 3.5, we present an outline of the developmental variables associated with each developmental period, as described in Chapter 2, and show how these are related to the emergence of the various psychopathologies. This developmental timeline is approximate. With some exceptions, most of the disorders can be seen in children of any age. Even infants, for example, can exhibit symptoms of depression. However, what we have done is to display the age that is associated with an increased *prevalence* of the disorder, since this indicates that the risk of developing this psychopathology is associated with this developmental stage. Consequently, we place depression in the early adolescent period, given that this age is associated with a dramatic increase in the diagnosis of mood disorders, particularly for girls.

We are now ready for a detailed exploration of selected psychopathologies. As much as possible we will take them in chronological order from a development standpoint. In all cases we will use the information about normal development provided in Chapter 2 to answer the question, How can this psychopathology be understood in terms of normal development gone awry? How deviations from normality at one point in time affect future development will also be discussed. This dual concern requires reconstructing the natural history of the psychopathology. Finally, the issue of the efficacy of psychotherapeutic measures in curtailing further deviance will be addressed. However, a systematic examination of psychotherapy will come only after we conclude our exploration of the psychopathologies.

Table 3.5

The Relationship Between Psychopathology and Normal Development

Developmental Process	Infancy (0–12 months)	Toddlerhood (1–2½ years)	Preschool-Age (2½–6 years)	
Stage-Salient Issues	Biological regulation, secure attachment	Affect regulation, autonomous self-hood	Self-regulation, formation of interpersonal relations outside family	
Psychosexual Development (Freud)	Oral	Anal	Phallic → Oedipal	
Ego Development (Erikson)	Trust *vs.* mistrust	Autonomy *vs.* shame and doubt	Initiative *vs.* guilt	
Separation Individuation (Mahler)	Normal autism → Symbiosis	Differentiation → Practicing	Rapprochement → On the road to object constancy	
Cognitive Development (Piaget)	Sensorimotor		Preoperational	
Attachment	Preferential smile → Separation reactions	Caregiver as secure base	Goal-directed partnership	
Self-Development	Self-as-agent	Self-constancy emerges	Behavioral self: defined "all-or-none" by abilities and actions	
Emotional Development	Emotions driven by immediate experience; labile, primary, and intense	Emotion language expands, displays heightened (temper tantrums, fears)	Emotions viewed as caused by external events; emotion regulation increases	
Moral Development			Preconventional: absolute, rigid, literal	
Gender and Sexuality		Gender identity Curiosity about own body	Gender constancy; stereotyped interests Curiosity about others' bodies	
Peer Relations	Focused on relations with caregivers, egocentric	Recognition of others' emotions, empathy	Increasing peer interactions, social comparison; cooperative play	
Family Relations	Dependent on parents to define meaning of events and provide safety	Parents must tolerate vacillation between dependency and independent strivings		
Emergence of Psychopathologies	Autism	Reactive Attachment Attention-deficit/ Hyperactivity Disorder	Separation Anxiety Disorder Oppositional Defiant Enuresis/Encopresis	

Middle Childhood (6–11 years)	Preadolescence (11–13 years)	Adolescence (13–17 years)	Late Adolescence-Young Adulthood (17–20 years)
Mastery of academic and social environments	Individuation, identity, sexuality	Independence from family, formation of intimate relationships	Work, purpose and meaning in life, formation of lifelong romantic attachments
Latency		Genital	
Industry *vs.* inferiority		Identity *vs.* role diffusion	Intimacy *vs.* isolation
Concrete operations	Formal operations begin	Metacognition and abstraction continue to develop	
Internal working model of self and other guides relationships	Re-emergence of conflict over closeness *vs.* independence	Formation of new attachments opens opportunities for the reworking of old ones	
Psychological self: stable internal representation	Abstract, future-oriented self	Self increasingly stable, integrated, self-reflective	
Affects more stable, affective "style" emerges, capacity for internally generated emotions	Labile emotions, negative affect common	Stable affect regulation, capacity for full range of emotions and defenses against them	
Conventional: rule-bound, right *vs.* wrong	Perspective taking; considerations of mutuality	Post-conventional: Self-determined moral principles	
Sex-segregated play Understanding of relationship between genitals and procreation	Increasing flexibility of gender roles Knowledge of adult sexuality, combined with misinformation	Gender stereotyped behavior reemerges Sexual experimentation, awareness of sexual preference	Stable gender role adherence Commitment to sexual preference and intimate partner
Sustained friendship; relations with adults outside family; social perspective taking	Group-oriented relationships with peers increasingly important, social problem-solving	Peers have increasing importance over family	Stable, deep, meaningful friendships and romantic relationships
Family's functioning viewed in increasingly public realms	Boundaries must become more flexible to allow adolescent independence	Realignment of relationships to allow adolescent to function as young adult	
Conduct Disorder Social/School Phobia Learning Disorders Anxiety Disorders	Substance Abuse Depression Bipolar Disorder Gender Identity Disorder	Eating Disorders Schizophrenia	Personality Disorders

Infancy: The Developmental Consequences of Mental Retardation

In this chapter, we have our first encounter with a disorder that is not coded with the other Clinical Disorders on Axis I of the DSM-IV-TR (see Chapter 3). Mental Retardation is coded on the DSM Axis II, reflecting its pervasive effect on functioning and the need to take its presence into account when considering any other diagnosis that might be present for the individual.

Is Mental Retardation a Psychopathology?

Why include *mental retardation* (MR) in a discussion of psychopathology? Just because a child has a low score on an IQ test, should he or she be placed in the company of children who have a conduct disorder or a phobia or attention-deficit hyperactive disorder? On the surface,

such a child does not seem to be "troubled" in the way those other children do—he or she is just cognitively slower than others. As we shall soon see, this question has been of concern to the experts, who have made the definition of MR increasingly contingent upon factors other than IQ scores alone.

On the other hand, MR indeed may be related to psychopathology. It was once believed that mental retardation excluded an individual from a psychiatric diagnosis, under the misapprehension that an individual with a low IQ score was not capable of developing a full-fledged neurosis. Consequently, the emotional problems of those with MR were dismissively attributed to their cognitive limitations or to underlying medical problems. However, we now know that not only may individuals with MR develop the full range of psychopathologies, but they are at

109

three to four times the risk for developing psychological disturbances when compared to members of the general population.

Returning to the question that opened our discussion, the answer is clearly no; MR is not a psychopathology. However, MR should be considered a deviation in development that increases the risk for psychopathology (Sachs & Barrett, 2000). All the factors that come into play in the developmental psychopathology of disorder—biology, emotion, cognition, family relationships, peers, and sociocultural factors—also affect the developing individual with an MR diagnosis.

Definition

Historical Background

Prior to 1959, the original definition of MR was in terms of *subaverage intelligence,* as measured by a standardized **intelligence test.** Numerically, an IQ (**intelligence quotient**) score that is more than two standard deviations below the mean is regarded as a significant deviation from average intelligence, which means that an IQ of 70 was considered to be the cutoff score for the MR range.

In 1959, **adaptive behavior** was added as a criterion. If a person were adapting adequately to the environment, why regard him or her as dysfunctional or abnormal just because the score on a cognitive test was below a given cutoff point? For example, there is a group called "6-hour retardates" who do poorly in school (which is approximately 6 hours per day) but function well, say, in a rural or inner-city environment. Thus, the key to MR became not a test score but the way an individual *functioned.*

The American Association of Mental Retardation (AAMR) Adaptive Behavior Scale (Nihira, Foster, Shelhaas, & Leland, 1974) is an example of an instrument that assesses adaptive behavior. Factor analyses showed that the scale contains three dimensions: personal self-sufficiency, community self-sufficiency, and personal-social responsibility (Nihira, 1976). *Personal self-sufficiency* is found at all ages and involves the ability to satisfy immediate personal needs such as eating, toileting, and dressing. *Community self-sufficiency* involves independence beyond immediate needs, along with self-sufficiency in relation to others: for example, using money, traveling, shopping, and communicating adequately. *Personal-social responsibility* involves initiative and perseverance— the ability to undertake a task on one's own and see it through to completion. These last two factors represent higher-level behavior than the mere satisfaction of immediate needs and emerge at around 10 years of age.

A Controversial Revision

> Mental retardation is not something you have, like blue eyes or a bad heart. Nor is it something you are, like being short or thin. It is not a medical disorder . . . nor is it a mental disorder. . . . Mental retardation is present when specific intellectual limitations affect the person's ability to cope with the ordinary challenges of everyday living in the community. If the intellectual limitations have no real effect on functioning, then the person does not have mental retardation. (American Association on Mental Retardation, 1992, pp. 9, 13)

These statements represent the latest in a series of reconceptualizations by the American Association on Mental Retardation (AAMR). In 1992 the AAMR proposed a new definition of MR that takes the concept of adaptation further than had been done in the past. Adaptation itself is not some kind of trait or absolute quality individuals possess. Rather, adaptation is always *in relation to an environment.* Therefore, the characteristics of the environment to which the individual is adapting must be scrutinized before one can determine whether that individual is mentally retarded.

The new conceptualization of MR is represented schematically in Figure 4.1. Note that the criterion of *functioning* is at the base of the triangle, signifying that it is the basic, or fundamental, construct. Thus, how well or how poorly a child can function in a given environment is more important than intellectual level. Functioning, in turn, is determined by two factors: *capabilities* and *environments.*

Figure 4.1   General Structure of the Definition of Mental Retardation.

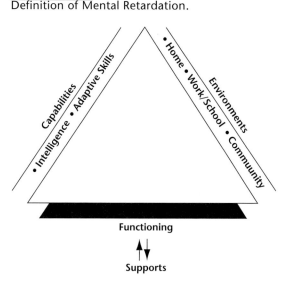

Functioning

Supports

Source: American Association on Mental Retardation, 1992.

Capabilities (or competencies) are variables in the intrapersonal context. There are two kinds of capabilities, intelligence and adaptive skills:

1. *Intelligence* encompasses both cognition and learning. The AAMR identified an IQ of 75 or lower as the cutoff criterion for MR.
2. *Adaptive skills* are made up of practical and social intelligence. *Practical* intelligence involves the skills needed to maintain one's independence in managing the ordinary activities of daily living (e.g., bathing, dressing, or feeding oneself). *Social* intelligence involves the ability to comprehend appropriate social behavior, social skills, and good ethical judgment in interpersonal situations.

Environments are conceptualized as the *specific settings* in which the person lives, learns, plays, works, socializes, and interacts. The environment must be typical of the child's same-age peers and appropriate to the child's socioeconomic background. MR quite literally does not exist when the individual is able to function well in the community

without special support services. However, if the individual requires special supports or services, such as a sheltered workshop or institutional care, that person can be considered mentally retarded.

The AAMR further requires that the diagnosis specify the child's *level of impairment* by indicating the extensivenesss of the *support services* that would be needed to allow the child to function in the environment. There are four such levels: intermittent, limited, extensive, and pervasive. For example, one child might only need special tutoring in academic courses, while another might need 24-hour custodial care.

According to the AAMR revision, duration of MR need not be lifelong. If the environment becomes less demanding—say, in the case of a child's leaving school—and the child adapts to it, then MR is "outgrown." Here it is important to note that intellectual functioning as measured by an IQ score is fairly stable from childhood on; however, it is the impact of intellectual limitations on functioning that may change over the course of development. An adult may find his or her niche and function well in a job that does not require the same kinds of skills that caused that person to fail in school. Therefore, the individual may not be limited or handicapped in any identifiable way despite a low IQ.

Finally, the AAMR conceptualization explicitly states that MR is *not* a psychopathology. In addition, the definition in no way implies that MR places the child at risk for behavior problems. The essence of the definition is the child's adapting or failing to adapt to the environment. This definition also offers a new way of conceptualizing psychopathology, as an *adaptational failure*.

DSM-IV-TR Criteria

The DSM-IV-TR (2000) criteria include three features: (1) subaverage intelligence defined as an IQ score below 70, (2) deficits in adaptive behavior, and (3) early onset typically defined as below 18 years of age. (See Table 4.1.)

Intellectual Deficits

The first criterion for MR involves significantly subaverage general intellectual functioning. The DSM

Table 4.1

DSM-IV-TR Criteria for Mental Retardation

A. Significantly subaverage intellectual functioning: an IQ of approximately 70 or below on an individually administered IQ test (for infants, a clinical judgment of significantly subaverage intellectual functioning).
B. Concurrent deficits or impairments in present adaptive functioning (i.e., the person's effectiveness in meeting the standards expected for his or her age by his or her cultural group) in at least two of the following areas: communication, self-care, home living, social/interpersonal skills, use of community resources, self-direction, functional academic skills, work, leisure, health, and safety.
C. Onset is before age 18 years.

Code degree of severity reflecting level of intellectual impairment:

Mild Mental Retardation: IQ level 50–55 to approximately 70
Moderate Mental Retardation: IQ level 35–40 to 50–55
Severe Mental Retardation: IQ level 20–25 to 35–40
Profound Mental Retardation: IQ level below 20 to 25

Source: Adapted from DSM-IV-TR. Copyright 2000, American Psychiatric Association.

establishes an IQ cutoff score of 70 to define intelligence that is in the mentally retarded range.

The DSM also uses IQ scores to make finer classifications according to levels of retardation (see Box 4.1 for more detailed information):

1. *Mild* mental retardation: IQ 55 to 70. This level comprises as many as 85 percent of all persons with retardation. These individuals acquire academic skills up to approximately the sixth-grade level by their late teens and can live successfully in the community either independently or in supervised settings.
2. *Moderate* mental retardation: IQ 40 to 54. While some of these individuals require few supportive services, most require some help throughout life. They adapt well to community life in supervised settings.

3. *Severe* mental retardation: IQ 25 to 39. These individuals have limited ability to master academic skills, although they can learn to read certain "survival" words. As adults they may perform simple tasks under supervision and adapt to the community by living with their family or in group homes.
4. *Profound* mental retardation: IQ below 25. These individuals require lifelong care and assistance; and intensive training is needed to teach basic eating, toileting, and dressing skills. Almost all show organic causes for their retardation.

Adaptive Behavior

The second criterion in the DSM-IV-TR requires that the individual be unable to function according to the age-appropriate norms of his or her cultural group in areas such as communication, self-care, and social skills.

Comparison of the AAMR and DSM Approaches

The AAMR's 1992 revision was controversial from the start and to this date has not been universally accepted by other organizations nor by practitioners and researchers. We can see that not all of its recommendations were adopted by the DSM-IV-TR.

The first difference we should note is the defining score used to establish MR in the two definitions. AAMR's decision was a highly contentious one in that, when determining the level of intelligence that defined MR, the AAMR raised the cutoff IQ score from 70 to 75. This may seem to be a slight adjustment; however, because IQ scores form a bell curve, it actually doubles the number of individuals in the MR category. The developers of the DSM-IV-TR, like most clinicians and researchers in the field, have ignored this recommendation.

Another criticism of the AAMR's definition is that, while it requires deficits in 2 of 10 domains of adaptive behavior, these were not identified on any empirical basis and no normed and standardized scales exist that measure these particular domains (State, King, & Dykens, 1997). Also problematic is the AAMR's elimination of the usual classifications of levels of retardation (mild, moderate, etc.) and

Box 4.1	**Developmental Differences in Mental Retardation and Down Syndrome**

Level	Preschool Age (birth to 5 years)	School Age (6 to 21 years)	Adult (over 21 years)
Mild Retardation (IQ of 50–70)	Can develop social and language skills; less retardation in sensorimotor areas; seldom distinguished from normal until older	Can learn academic skills to approximately sixth-grade level by late teens; cannot learn general high school subjects; needs special education, particularly at secondary school levels	Capable of social and vocational adequacy with proper education and training; frequently needs guidance when under serious social or economic stress
Moderate Retardation (35–49)	Can talk or learn to communicate; poor social awareness; fair motor development; may profit from self-help; can be managed with moderate supervision	Can learn functional academic skills to approximately fourth-grade level by late teens if given special education	Capable of self-maintenance in unskilled or semiskilled occupations; needs supervision and guidance when under mild social or economic stress
Severe Retardation (21–34)	Poor motor development; speech is minimal; generally unable to profit from training in self-help; little or no communication skills	Can talk or learn to communicate; can be trained in elemental health habits; cannot learn functional academic skills; profits from systematic habit training	Can contribute partially to self-support under complete supervision; can develop self-protection skills to a minimal useful level in controlled environment
Profound Retardation (20 or below)	Gross retardation; minimal capacity for functioning in sensorimotor areas; needs nursing care	Some motor development present; cannot profit from training in self-help; needs total care	Some motor and speech development; totally incapable of self-maintenance; needs complete care and supervision

Source: Adapted from Sattler, 1982.

substitution of *levels of impairment* as defined by the need for support services. While there are criteria listed for defining these levels, there are no objective ways of measuring them. Since assigning levels depends on clinical judgment, the chances of unreliability and misdiagnosis are increased. Moreover, there is evidence that levels of retardation and need for supportive services *cannot* be equated, especially for mildly retarded children who vary in their need for support across different contexts.

On the other hand, the AAMR's attempts have been lauded as an attempt to reduce the stigma associated with mental retardation.

Some other conceptual issues have arisen since either of these diagnostic systems were developed and with which neither has yet grappled. Increasingly, models of intelligence are becoming multifaceted, requiring the assessment of cognitive abilities in a multidimensional framework for which a single summary score may not be a reliable index. The concept of IQ itself has been called into question, in part because of the popular misinterpretation that this number is immutable and sets an absolute limit on an individual's potential. Indeed, a recent version of one of the commonly used intelligence tests for children—the Stanford-Binet

Fourth Edition (1986)—abandoned the term IQ entirely. While the most recent Weschler Intelligence Scale for Children-IV (2003) retains an overall IQ score, its developers advocate focusing more on domain-specific index scores. We will have more to say about both of these tests and the reconceptualizations of intelligence from which they derive when we discuss assessment in Chapter 16. In the meantime, it is interesting to speculate about how the definition of MR might have to be revised in the light of newer conceptualizations of multiple intelligences.

Characteristics

Prevalence

The question of how many children fall into the MR category depends, of course, on how MR is defined. Using IQ scores alone as the criterion, prevalence changes significantly if one raises the cutoff score from 70 to 75, as we have seen. Using the DSM criterion of 70 and below, 3 percent of the population can be classified as in the mentally retarded range of intelligence.

However, IQ scores ignore other factors critical to the diagnosis of MR, the most important one of which is adaptive behavior. Particularly at the level of mild retardation, IQ and adaptive behavior are not highly correlated, so IQ scores alone would overestimate the prevalence of MR. In turn, overestimation might occur due to the instability of IQ scores, since some children who now are in the mildly retarded range will, upon retesting, score in the lower bound of average intelligence.

Finally, our ability to detect MR is related to children's age, and may become more sensitive and accurate later in development. In particular, children with mild mental retardation are likely not to be identified until the school years when academic performance serves to highlight their limitations. Therefore, the prevalence rate tends to be low in the preschool years, then gradually rises in the school years, peaks in early adolescence, and declines subsequently.

Consequently, when all of the above factors are taken into account, the prevalence of MR is estimated to be about 2 percent of the population (Hodapp & Dykens, 2003).

Gender

As many as three times more boys than girls qualify for a label of mental retardation (Stromme & Hagberg, 2000). The gender difference probably largely is due to the fact that genetically linked disorders in general affect males more than females.

Socioeconomic Status and Ethnicity

While MR is more prevalent among socieconomically disadvantaged samples, which disproportionately include ethnic minorities, this is true only for those children with mild MR. The more severe levels of MR occur about equally in different economic and racial groups (Hodapp & Dykens, 2003). With regard to social class, genetic and environmental effects probably contribute to the fact that parents with low socioeconomic status tend to have lower IQs, as do their children.

Explanations for racial differences include cultural factors (e.g., a relative lack of emphasis on individual achievement) and environmental factors (e.g., poverty and lack of access to resources; Turkheimer, Haley, Waldron, D'Onofrio, & Gottesman, 2003). For example, Brooks-Gunn and colleagues (2003) found that the effects of economic deprivation, an understimulating home environment, and maternal youth and lack of education accounted for 71 percent of the difference in IQ between European American and African American children.

In addition, there is concern that standardized IQ tests might be biased in ways that underestimate the intelligence of children from minority backgrounds. In recognition of this possibility, some school systems have moved away from the use of IQ tests in evaluating children's needs for educational support services. For example, in the 1970s, parent advocates brought a suit against the San Francisco school system, arguing that the use of culturally biased IQ tests was resulting in an overrepresentation of minority children in special education. The suit was successful, and California school systems are now prohibited from using IQ tests for educational placement decisions involving minority students.

Differential Diagnosis

Children with MR must be differentiated from those who have *low intellectual abilities* but no deficits in adaptive skills. Indeed, as some higher-functioning children with MR learn to care for themselves and perform tasks independently, they may lose their MR label as they advance in development. Similarly, MR is differentiated from simple *learning disorders* that are confined to a specific academic skill (see Chapter 7); the deficits in MR are more pervasive. Lastly, although MR may co-occur with *autism* (see Chapter 5), the two can be distinguished primarily because of the limited social interest and odd repetitive behaviors of the autistic child; children with MR are often quite sociable and friendly (First, Frances, & Pincus, 2002).

Comorbidity

There is good evidence that MR increases the risk of developing psychological disturbances. Estimates of comorbidity in the MR population range from 10 percent to 50 percent (Hodapp & Dykens, 2003). Studies find that, among those in the MR range, the risk of developing a psychiatric disorder is three to four times that in the typically modifying developing population (Sachs & Barrett, 2000). Comorbid disorders include a wide spectrum, including *aggression, inattention/hyperactivity, schizophrenia, autism, depression,* and *anxiety.*

However, the likelihood of comorbidity is related to the *degree of retardation* (Einfeld and Tonge, 1996). Those in the profoundly retarded group have considerably lower rates of comorbidity, probably because their behavioral repertoire is more limited as is their capacity to communicate emotional problems. Level of retardation also affects the kind of disturbance seen, with those in the mildly retarded range having a predominance of disruptive and antisocial behavior and the severely retarded group being characterized by withdrawn and autistic-like behavior.

Einfeld and Aman's (1995) summary of factor-analytic studies is instructive in regard to how comorbidity differs in the MR and typically developing populations. While both groups develop

withdrawal, aggression, and hyperactivity, *anxiety* is less common in children with MR than the typically developing population. In addition, *stereotypic and self-injurious* behaviors are often seen in children with MR but are rare in those who do not have MR. Consequently, withdrawal in children with MR generally is not accompanied by anxiety as it is in other children, while aggression is more often accompanied by self-injurious behavior in those with MR. In short, there seems to be a different mix of problems in children with MR.

Difficulties in Detecting Psychopathology in MR

Hodapp and Dykens (2003) point out that the nature of MR makes it difficult to detect and measure psychopathology. For example, while certain behavior problems are common to children with MR, such as temper tantrums, overactivity, and withdrawal from others, they may not reflect psychiatric illness per se. Limitations in the ability of individuals with MR to reflect on and articulate internal emotional states particularly hinder the diagnosis of internalizing disorders such as depression, which often rely on self-reports of subjective experience. In turn, observers' ratings usually require a judgment about the appropriateness of behavior for a person of this individual's chronological age, when the individual with MR might display behavior that actually is appropriate for his or her mental age. For example, an adolescent functioning at a preschool level could be expected to show some of the magical reasoning and poor reality testing that are typical of the preoperational period. Future work in this area will benefit from the development of measures that are designed for and normed on the MR population.

The Biological Context: Organic MR

Mental retardation comes in two general types with two distinct etiologies. The first, **organic MR,** which will be our focus in this section, comprises a mixed group. It is estimated that there are over 1,000 different biological causes of mental retardation.

These include genetic anomalies, prenatal insults, and neuropsychological abnormalities. Most children with organic MR are severely impaired; for example, 77 percent of cases in the moderate-to-profound range are due to organic factors.

Genetic Factors

Many genetic anomalies result in mental retardation—over 750, in fact—each of which may be associated with a different phenotype consisting of a unique set of physical, cognitive, and behavioral features. (Here we follow Hodapp and Dykens, 2003.) Next we describe three of the more commonly seen syndromes.

Down Syndrome

Down syndrome is the most common of the genetic birth defects related to MR, with a prevalence of 1 to 1.5 per 1,000 births. Children with the disorder have three number 21 chromosomes instead of the normal two; hence, the condition is also called trisomy 21.

Recently, a critical region on chromosome 21 has been identified, and the available markers for this and flanking regions have enabled clinicians to confirm cases of Down syndrome in the context of subtle translocations and chromosomal abnormalities other than trisomy (King, State, Shah, Davanzo, & Dykens, 1997). Thus, the genetic basis for the syndrome has been expanded.

This disorder was originally called mongoloidism because of the characteristic facial features of wide face, slanted eyes, and flattened nose. (See Box 4.2.) The cognitive picture of children with Down syndrome includes a decelerating rate of mental growth, and the mean IQ of the group as a whole is around 50. Their social intelligence tends to be high, but their speech and comprehension of grammar are low.

In regards to behavior, the typical Down syndrome child is a friendly, sociable one, although some studies suggest that this picture becomes less positive with age, with aggression sometimes emerging in adolescence. However, generally, the

A child with Down syndrome can be an enjoyable playmate.

Box 4.2 | **Case Study: Down Syndrome**

Dan's mother was 37 and his father was 40 when he was born in an isolated, rural area of the mountains. At the birth, the midwife immediately recognized Dan's physical characteristics—disproportionate and odd-appearing eyes, ears, hands, and feet—and suggested that Dan's mother have him checked out at the Mountain Medical Clinic. There, the doctors diagnosed Dan with Down syndrome.

While most parents would have been very upset at having a Down syndrome child, Dan's parents were surprisingly unmoved by it all. They did not especially value intellectual achievement, and Dan, like many Down syndrome children, did not have behavioral problems. Dan was generally content to play in the woods behind their house, and when inside was content to sit with his toys in front of the television set for hours. Also, fortunately, Dan did not have many of the medical handicaps from

which most other Down children suffer. He did have some liver problems that were not too severe, and he also seemed prone to respiratory problems.

He was never enrolled in day care or kindergarten. When he was brought to school for the first grade, his intellectual deficiency was quickly evident to the teacher. She immediately referred Dan to the school psychologist for testing. The psychologist administered a Wechsler Intelligence Scale for Children, and Dan attained an IQ score of 61. This score would place him in the "mild" level of mental retardation and is a higher score than would be attained by the average Down syndrome child. However, it was clear he could not compete in the standard classroom, so he was placed in special education classes. Dan enjoyed the school and made reasonable progress, although he never made it beyond the second grade in any academic skill area, in part because his parents never

really encouraged him at home in academic work.

By the time he was 14, he was 40 pounds overweight. He was put on a strict diet and exercise plan that was way overdue. His health was obviously declining. However, when Dan lost weight and became more active, his health improved. Dan made it through his school years and on into young adulthood without major difficulty, and he was even doing some easy part-time work for some neighbors.

Dan continued to live at home. When he was about 30, he started showing signs of emotional deterioration. He became irritable and had tantrums for no reason that he could explain. Other times he would not communicate at all. He was also having more medical problems and, at 36 years of age, Dan succumbed to a bout of pneumonia.

Source: Adapted from Meyer, 1989.

---

children tend to have a low level of behavioral disturbance. (See Box 4.2.)

Fragile-X Syndrome

The prevalence of this syndrome is 0.73 to 0.92 per 1,000 births. The condition is due to a fragile site on the X chromosome and occurs more often in males than in females. New work in the advancing field of molecular genetics suggests that some of the features of the Fragile-X phenotype can be attributed to the amount of protein produced by the affected (FMR-1) gene. The less protein that is produced, the greater the level of MR (Tassone et al., 1999).

Cognitively, boys show a moderate level of retardation, with development slowing from puberty on,

whereas, when girls are affected, there may be no MR apparent. The children do well on tasks requiring the processing of holistic, Gestalt-like information, such as picture recognition, but do poorly on those requiring linear reasoning, such as auditory short-term memory. Behaviorally, the children tend to be hyperactive or to show autistic-like features, such as perseverative or stereotyped behaviors, social withdrawal, and gaze avoidance.

Prader-Willi Syndrome

This condition is due to anomalies in a region of chromosome 15 and occurs in 1 per 15,000 births. In 70 percent of cases those with the syndrome have a microscopic or submicroscopic deletion on the paternal chromosome 15, while the remaining cases have two copies of the maternal chromosome and no paternal contribution. In either case, the child is missing genetic material from the father.

The cognitive picture of children with Prader-Willi syndrome involves a mild degree of retardation. However, the deficits are largely in the verbal realm while some nonverbal skills are left intact. For example, a peculiar characteristic of children with the disorder is a remarkable facility with jigsaw puzzles, which they can complete more quickly than even typically developing children of the same age (Dykens, 2002).

Behaviorally, the picture changes with age. In infancy, children may show significant developmental delays and problems with feeding that can lead to failure to thrive. Beginning at ages 2 to 6, children begin to become preoccupied with eating (termed *hyperphagia*) and are vulnerable to obesity. While earlier in development, young children with the syndrome generally were described as affectionate and pleasant, the onset of hyperphagia is associated with increasing behavior problems, including stubbornness, temper tantrums, impulsivity, and underactivity. Obsessive-compulsive symptoms also are often seen, including hoarding, compulsive talking or questioning, excessive ordering and rearranging, and repeating rituals (Dykens, Leckman, & Cassidy, 1996).

Recent evidence suggests that the two different genetic mechanisms underlying Prader-Willi syndrome have different behavioral phenotypes. Those with the deletion on the paternal chromosome 15 tend to have more maladaptive behavior and cognitive deficits than those with the duplicate maternal chromosome. However, it turns out that only children in the former category have the unique splinter skill of solving jigsaw puzzles so adeptly (Dykens, 2002).

As these descriptions illustrate, different genetic origins result in a different kind of MR, complete with relative strengths and weakness in various areas of functioning. As Hodapp and Dykens (2003) argue, the advancement of research in the field will require that investigators acknowledge that there are various types of MR rather than treating the disorder as a single entity.

Prenatal and Postnatal Factors

A host of prenatal and postnatal factors can damage the central nervous system and result in MR. Rubella (German measles) contracted by the mother during the first trimester of pregnancy can cause a number of impairments, MR being one. Syphilis is another cause of MR. Exposure to massive doses of radiation in the first few months of pregnancy, chronic alcoholism, age (35 years or older), and severe emotional stress throughout pregnancy are among the numerous maternal factors that increase the risk of MR in the infant. Pediatric AIDS, fetal alcohol syndrome, and exposure to substances in utero also may be associated with MR.

Prematurity and prenatal anoxia (oxygen deprivation during or immediately after delivery) are hazards of birth that can lead to MR. Postnatal causes of MR include encephalitis and meningitis (inflammations of the brain resulting from infections by bacteria, viruses, or tuberculosis organisms), particularly if they occur during infancy. Throughout childhood, head injuries (most commonly resulting from automobile accidents and child abuse), infections, seizure disorders, and exposure to toxic substances may contribute to mental retardation.

Neuropsychological Factors

Studies of brain structure and development are beginning to pinpoint various anomalies in the different types of MR. For example, in Down syndrome, neuroimaging studies indicate a normal-appearing brain at birth with a declining brain volume over the course of development. (Here we follow Pennington, 2002.) In the first few months of life, children with Down syndrome evidence delayed myelination and reduced growth in the cerebellum and frontal lobes. By adulthood, the brain appears microcephalic, with many of the features of Alzheimer's disease.

In contrast to the microcephaly seen in Down syndrome, children with Fragile X have a large brain volume, which suggests a failure of the brain to "prune" redundant and inefficient neuronal connections as it does in normal development.

Interestingly, this is also a feature of the autistic brain, and children with Fragile X often show autistic-like behaviors. Fragile X also is associated with decreased size of an area of the posterior cerebellum, which may be related to impairments in sensory motor integration, as well as ventricular enlargements that could be the result of oversecretion of cerebrospinal fluid.

The Cultural Context: Familial MR

Familial Mental Retardation

In contrast to the organically derived types of MR described in the foregoing section, approximately half of all cases of MR have no clear biological cause and are called **familial** or **familial-cultural retardation.**

The characteristics of this kind of MR include a level of retardation that is usually mild, with IQs rarely lower than 45 to 50. Individuals are likely to blend into the general population before and after they reach school age. Familial retardation is more prevalent among minorities and individuals of low socioeconomic status, and one or both parents are likely to qualify for a diagnosis of MR.

However, the causes of familial retardation are hotly debated. On the biological side, it is hypothesized that these individuals have minor, difficult-to-detect neurological problems that have not yet been identified. In contrast, environmentalists emphasize the features of low socioeconomic status that place intellectual growth in jeopardy—prenatal and postnatal risk, inadequate health care, large families, and a disorganized home environment lacking in personal attention and growth-promoting objects such as books and school-readiness games. Finally, statisticians claim that familial retardation simply represents the lower end of the bell-shaped curve of intelligence. However, the prevailing wisdom suggests that both environmental and genetic factors are involved, the contribution of each being about equal (Pennington, 2002).

Whatever its true origins, familial MR clearly can be contrasted with organic MR. Children with organically based MR tend to be moderately to severely retarded and come from all ethnic groups and socioeconomic levels, while those in the familial-cultural category tend to be mildly retarded and come from minority groups and low socioeconomic levels. Further, the mental retardation of children in the genetic category has a clear organic etiology, whereas for children in the familial-cultural category both organic and environmental factors are involved.

Risk Factors

While the causes of familial retardation are not known, there are data concerning environmental variables that place children at risk for MR. Sameroff (1990) hypothesized that it was not the kind but the number of risks that determined intellectual functioning in children of comparable biological status. He extracted 10 such risk factors from previous research, including maternal mental illness, rigid values in regard to child development, large family, and minimal education. Using longitudinal data, he found that, when they were 4 years old, children with no risks scored more than 30 IQ points higher than children with eight or nine risks. In general, IQ declined as risk factors increased; for example, in multiple-risk families, 24 percent of the children had IQ scores below 85, while none of the children in the low-risk families did.

Further analysis of Sameroff's (1990) data revealed that no single risk variable and no one pattern of variables reduced intellectual performance; rather, different families had different constellations of risk factors. While the low socioeconomic status group had more high-risk families, high-risk middle- and upper-class families were equally damaging to their children's intellectual growth. Finally, Sameroff found that the same lack of environmental support that undermined the children's competence at an early age would continue to do so when they were 13 years old.

The picture was not totally pessimistic, however, since 20 percent of the high-risk children escaped the fate of the group at large. The variables responsible for a more favorable outcome were parental restrictiveness, clarity of rules, and emotional warmth. This pattern of authoritative parenting was sufficiently potent to counteract environmental risks.

The Family Context

Parent-Child Relationships

Recent studies of parents of a child with MR have shifted from a focus on pathology to a *stress and coping* orientation. For example, parental reactions used to be described in terms of depression and mourning. Currently, researchers regard retardation as an added stressor on the family system and explore the coping techniques used by parents. This new approach allows for positive as well as negative consequences, such as parents being brought closer together or siblings developing an empathy with and concern for children with handicapping conditions. (Here we follow Hodapp, 2002.)

A model for conceptualizing this approach is called the *Double ABCX* (Minnes, 1988). *X* represents the *stress* of having a child with MR, and that stress is a function of the *specific characteristics* of the child, or *A*; the family's internal and external *resources,* or *B*; and the family's *perception* of the child, or *C*. *Double* refers to the *developmental* dimension that takes account of the fact that all the components may change with time. It will be worthwhile to examine this model in greater detail.

Child Characteristics

As we have seen, children with different types of MR can behave differently and, in keeping with the developmental psychopathology concept of *transactions,* these differences can affect parental behavior. In families of children with Prader-Willi syndrome, for example, parental stress is related to such syndrome-specific behaviors as overeating, skinpicking, sleeping more than usual, and hoarding objects (Hodapp, Dykens, & Masino, 1997). Initially, investigators believed that families of children with Down syndrome were more cohesive and harmonious than families of children with other kinds of MR, with the mother experiencing less stress and having a more satisfactory social network. However, there is now evidence that, when methodological flaws in previous studies are eliminated, the stress related to rearing children with Down syndrome is no different from that of rearing children with other disabilities (Cahill & Glidden, 1996). However, this study also found that the average adjustment of all families was quite good, being at or near the norm for families with children who were not retarded. Specific characteristics of the Down syndrome phenotype—including a happy disposition, affectionate nature, and sociability—may contribute to positive parent-child relationships and, in turn, to a lower incidence of family stress.

Internal and External Resources

Some of the factors enabling parents to cope are obvious: Affluent parents cope better than do poor ones, two-parent families cope better than singleparent families, and mothers in harmonious marriages cope better than those in conflicted marriages. More interesting are the findings that parents differ in the kinds of support they find helpful. Mothers request more social-emotional support along with more information about the child's condition and help in child care, while fathers are more concerned with the financial cost of rearing the child. Mothers are helped by a close, supportive social network, while fathers cope better when they have an extended, noncritical social network.

Perception of the Child

Our example comes from research on communication between mother and child. (See Hodapp and Zigler, 1995.) Both mothers of children with MR and mothers of typically developing children shorten their sentences and emphasize and repeat key words when the children are learning to speak. However, unlike their counterparts, mothers of children with MR are more directive, initiating bids more often and overriding the child's speech. By contrast, the interaction between mothers and children without MR is more playful and spontaneous and is less goal oriented. The behavior of mothers of children with MR is motivated by their perception of the child as needing to be taught, along with their anxiety concerning the child's ability to learn to speak. Ironically, the mother's intrusiveness runs the risk of further increasing the child's communicative difficulties. In fact, some intervention programs aim at helping the mothers to become less directive and to imitate the child more, thus allowing the child to take a more active role in learning to speak.

The Developmental Dimension

Parents' reactions and successful adaptation to parenting a child with MR may change over the course of development. Parents may go through a phase of mourning at each developmental transition, when they are struck anew with a sense of loss when the child fails to achieve a significant developmental milestone. For example, depression may appear in a mother of a child with Down syndrome when the child is about 4 months old, at which time the child's inconsistent smiles and dampened affect contrast with the vigorous and gleeful responses of the typical infant (Hodapp & Zigler, 1995). A depressive reaction may appear again in the parent when the child is 11 to 15 years of age (entering puberty) or at 21 years of age (entering adulthood). Parents also may begin distancing themselves from the child from middle childhood on in order to prepare the child for becoming independent.

The Social Context

There is evidence that children with MR often are not accepted by their typically developing peers, although they tend to be ignored rather than actively rejected (Nabors, 1997). Their friendship patterns in preadolescence also differ. Friendships among typical preadolescents are marked by a high level of engagement, evidenced by frequent verbal communication, shared decision making, and mutual responsiveness at a high affective level such as laughing together. Friendships between a preadolescent who is typically developing and one who has mild retardation have a low level of engagement, with the children often working independently and rarely laughing together. In short, the children look more like acquaintances than friends (Siperstein, Leffert, & Wenz-Gross, 1997).

Social Cognition

The lack of peer acceptance is usually attributed to a low level of social competence in children with MR. While social competence has been conceptualized in a variety of ways and involves a number of variables, research has primarily been concerned with the variable of social cognition, which lies at the juncture between intelligence on the one hand and adaptive behavior on the other.

There is evidence that children with MR, as compared with those who are not retarded, have less developed perspective-taking, are less skilled in interpreting social cues, and have less advanced social strategies for dealing with problem situations (e.g., joining a group or responding to provocative behavior). (For a summary of the literature, see Leffert and Siperstein, 1996.)

Siperstein and Leffert (1997) also studied the difference between mildly retarded fourth and sixth graders who were socially accepted and those who were socially rejected. The findings concerning social behavior and social cognition seem paradoxical. Accepted children favored submissive goals and generated few positive, outgoing strategies. In contrast, the rejected children favored assertive goals and positive, outgoing strategies. One explanation for this unexpected finding is that low-key, deferential, and accommodating goals and strategies protect children against being rejected by making them "blend in" with the others, whereas socially assertive and intrusive goals and strategies do not. Since peer rejection and indifference are more likely than acceptance, children with MR have more to lose if assertiveness goes wrong than do children without MR.

The Individual Context

Answering the question What has gone awry with normal development in the case of mental retardation? has resulted in an impressive body of research addressing both the cognitive and the personality-motivational factors involved.

Cognitive Factors

Two different questions have been raised concerning the cognitive factors involved in MR. One is a general question: Is the *development* of intelligence in children with MR the same as or different from its development in children with normal intelligence? This is known as the *difference versus development* issue. The second question is a specific one: What *particular deviations* underlie the subnormal intellectual functioning of individuals who are retarded?

The Difference Versus Development Issue

Historically, there have been two points of view concerning the nature of MR. One is that MR is due to a *basic cognitive deficit* that results in thinking that is *fundamentally different* from that found in typically developing populations. The term "mental *deficiency*" epitomizes this view. The second point of view is that thinking in mental retardation is the same as it is in normal intelligence, the only difference being a *developmental* one, which results in *slower progress* and a *lower level of final achievement*. (See Figure 4.2.) There are data supporting both sides of the controversy.

Zigler has been the principal advocate of the developmental approach, proposing two hypotheses to test it. One is concerned with similar sequencing of cognitive development; the other with similar structure. (A detailed account of these hypotheses and the research testing them can be found in Hodapp and Zigler, 1995.)

The Similar Sequencing Hypothesis   This hypothesis states that children with MR will proceed through the same *stages* of cognitive development and in the same *order* as do children who are not retarded. For example, children with MR will go through the same Piagetian stages in the same invariant order from sensorimotor to preoperational to concrete operational thought. (They rarely reach the final level of formal operational thinking.) Retardation is the result of slower progress and a lower level of achievement.

A considerable body of research supports the similar sequence hypothesis, which holds for retardation

Figure 4.2   Developmental Model of Cognitive Growth.

The single vertical arrow represents the passage of time. The horizontal arrows represent environmental events impinging on the individual, who is represented as a pair of vertical lines. The individual's cognitive development appears as an internal ascending spiral, in which the numbered loops represent successive stages of cognitive growth.

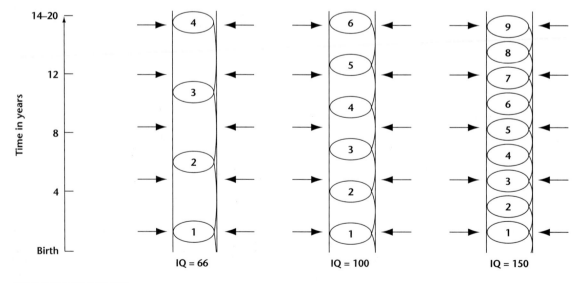

due to both organic and nonorganic (or familial) causes. Thus, the same sequential development has been found in Piagetian tasks, moral reasoning, symbolic play, geometric concepts, and language, to name some of the specific areas. Moreover, when strict sequencing does not hold for the retarded population, as in the more advanced stages of moral reasoning, it tends not to hold for typically developing populations as well.

Finally, there is suggestive evidence that children with some kinds of retardation exhibit a less solid grasp of the kinds of thinking involved at the higher levels. Thus, they are more apt to show a mixture of higher and lower levels of thinking than are their typically developing counterparts. This variability can be evidenced from month to month or even within a single testing session (Hodapp & Zigler, 1995).

The Similar Structure Hypothesis This hypothesis states that, when matched for overall mental age, children who are retarded will be at the same level of functioning on a variety of intellectual tasks (other than those used to measure intelligence) as are children who are not retarded. Thus, this hypothesis is concerned with *intertask* functioning. It runs counter to the idea that there are specific areas of deficit in thinking in MR.

The support for the similar structure hypothesis is more qualified than that for the similar sequencing hypothesis. When they are doing Piagetian-based tasks, the performance of children with familial (i.e., nonorganically determined) retardation is comparable to mental-age-matched typically developing children. However, in performance on information-processing tasks of learning, memory, learning set formation, distractibility, and selective attention, the MR group tends to be inferior. The reason for this puzzling finding is not clear.

The performance of children whose retardation is due to organic factors does *not* support the similar structure hypothesis. Not only is such performance worse than matched mental-age controls, but there are also specific areas of deficit. For example, children with Down syndrome have deficits in grammar relative to other abilities, while boys with Fragile-X

syndrome are particularly weak in sequential thinking such as remembering a sequence of digits. (See Hodapp and Zigler, 1995, for details.)

In sum, there is good support for the similar sequencing hypothesis, but the support for the similar structure hypothesis is limited to Piagetian tasks in children with nonorganically determined retardation. The similar structure hypothesis is not supported when information-processing tasks are used and retardation is due to organic factors.

Specific Deviations in Thinking

Having discussed the general developmental question concerning cognitive factors involved in MR, we now turn to the research on specific deviations underlying subnormal intellectual functioning. The findings can be grouped under five categories.

1. Attention to Relevant Cues The basic research paradigm here is called *discrimination learning*. The child is presented with a succession of stimuli, such as objects differing in color, shape, and size, two or three at a time, and is asked to choose one. On the basis of being told that a choice is either right or wrong, the child must learn what dimension—color, shape, or size in this instance—is the key to making a correct choice. To illustrate: A girl is presented with a red circle and a blue square. Guessing that "circle" is the correct response, she chooses the first figure and is told she made a correct choice. Next time a green circle and a blue triangle are presented and she is told her choice of the circle is incorrect. She must now change her hypothesis. If she remembers that the original circle was also red, she strongly suspects "red" to be the solution, which she verifies when another red object is shown. If she does not remember, she must adopt another hypothesis such as "triangle" or "green."

In discrimination learning situations the learning curve for children of normal intelligence rises quickly at first and then levels off. For children who are retarded, choices are no better than chance for a number of trials, but then there is rapid improvement.

Further investigation reveals that children with MR often do not attend to relevant aspects of the situation; for example, they are not asking themselves, Is it color or shape or size? On the contrary, they have a strong initial preference for position, such as the first object, which they persist in using despite being told that their choice is frequently incorrect. Once they can break this irrelevant set, they learn rapidly. Given a task in which position is the relevant cue, they learn as fast as or faster than children with normal intelligence. Thus, in a special sense they are not slow learners, but they are slow to catch on to the relevant question. (See Hale and Borkowski, 1991.)

The preference for position responses seen in children who are retarded has its counterpart in normal development, since position habits have been observed to interfere with discrimination learning in 1-year-olds. Such habits no longer seem to affect discrimination learning in the toddler and pre-schooler, although the evidence is not conclusive on this point. If the preference in children who are retarded does in fact represent a fixation, it is one that goes back to earliest childhood and may significantly interfere with subsequent learning.

2. Attention   Children who are mentally retarded may have a basic attentional deficit. For example, they have slower reaction times in simple reaction-time experiments. These experiments involve a preparatory signal, such as a buzzer, followed by a stimulus, such as a light, to which the subject must respond as quickly as possible (e.g., by pressing a button). Another kind of evidence of a decreased ability to maintain adequate attentional levels is the increase in off-task glancing both in simple and complex tasks.

3. Memory   There is no evidence that children who are retarded have a deficit in short-term memory, as tested in tasks involving repeating back digits. The findings concerning a possible deficit in long-term memory are contradictory and inconclusive because it is exceedingly difficult to control all the prior processes in order to obtain an unconfounded evaluation of this one alone. The situation is also complicated by the fact that long-term memory depends on the use of a number of *strategies* designed to aid retention and organize the incoming information. Such strategies include rehearsal, clustering, and mediation.

3a. Rehearsal   *Rehearsal* typically consists of repeating each new item along with all the prior ones; for example, in remembering a series of numbers, a child may think, "six, six-three, six-three-eight," and so forth. Rehearsal is clearly evidenced by the third grade in children who are not retarded. Research indicates that children who are retarded are deficient in rehearsal. If they are trained, their performance improves, but in most cases they will not spontaneously use such aids. As with discrimination learning, they fail to do what they are capable of doing. And again, as with discrimination learning, this failure has its counterpart in normal development, since first-graders also make no use of their ability to rehearse.

3b. Clustering   Remembering improves if incoming information is organized in a meaningful manner, a strategy called *clustering*. Present the average child with, say, a list comprised of three categories of words arranged in random order, and the child will tend to recall them by categories; for example, the words the child remembers and says following "dog" will tend to be other animal words in the list, and those following "apple" will be the other food words. Both children who are retarded and young children of normal intelligence show little evidence of using the strategy of clustering. While children who are retarded can be taught to do so, once again they fail to use this aid spontaneously.

3c. Mediation   Memory is also facilitated by mediation strategies. The research paradigm here is paired-associate learning. Initially, two stimuli are presented, and subsequently, only the first is shown, and the child is asked to recall the second. Paired-associate learning can be facilitated if the child ties the two stimuli together in a meaningful manner; for example, "sun" and "bird" are more readily associated if related by something such as "The sun shines on the bird." While 5- to 6-year-olds can produce and use mediational strategies, younger children and those who have mental retardation do not use them. If the latter children are provided with mediators or even instructed to generate them, their learning is significantly improved. However, if the experimenter no longer instructs the children, they may fail to continue using mediators on their own. Training them to get into the habit has met with only limited success, being effective primarily with the mildly retarded. Thus, it is not that children with MR are deficient in the sense that they are incapable of grasping higher-level strategies; rather, for some unknown reason, they fail to use spontaneously the abilities they possess.

3d. Retrieval   There is evidence that the same deviation in categorization that hampers memory also adversely affects the retrieval of information that has been learned. It makes sense to assume that items stored singly in memory would be more difficult to retrieve than items stored by categories that represent superordinate organizations of the individual items. As was the case in regard to rehearsal and clustering, the deficit seems to be one of lack of *use* of category knowledge rather than lack of category knowledge itself.

3e. Metamemory   *Metamemory* refers to children's understanding of how memory works, such as knowing it takes more time and effort to memorize a long list of words than a short one. While metamemory improves dramatically with age in children of normal intelligence, the rate of improvement is variable in populations with MR. For example, their understanding of the relation between amount of study time and remembering or the effect of delay of recall on performance is commensurate with mental-age-matched peers; however, even children with higher levels of intellectual functioning lack awareness of the fact that it is easier to relearn old material than to learn new material.

4. Problem Solving   Problem solving typically requires attention, abstraction, planning, and logical thinking. The same failure to generate relevant hypotheses that mars discrimination learning in children with MR also affects the more complex task of solving problems. For example, even when the classic "20 questions" task has been modified so that, in the simplest case, only one question is sufficient to supply the information necessary to make a correct

choice, children who are retarded ask noncritical questions as frequently as critical ones. Once the information is supplied, they can use it effectively, however.

5. Generalization   Finally, while children with MR can be trained to do a specific problem successfully, they characteristically do not generalize to similar problems. It is as if each task is a new one that must be mastered in its own right. The impediment to learning is obvious.

Summary   Children with MR perform poorly on discrimination learning tasks, although once their position set is broken, they learn as fast as typically developing children. The same failure to generate relevant hypotheses that hampers discrimination learning also adversely affects problem solving. Children with MR have a basic deficiency in attention and generalization, but their short-term memory is intact. While they are not incapable of grasping the strategies of rehearsal, mediation, and clustering that facilitate long-term memory, they neither spontaneously generate such strategies nor assimilate them to the point of habitually using them after being instructed or taught to do so. In a similar manner, children with MR do not use their categorizing ability to facilitate the retrieval of information. For unknown reasons, their performance in regard to metamemory tasks is variable, being a mixture of adequate and low-level functioning.

Personality-Motivational Factors

The Similar Reaction Hypothesis

Zigler's third hypothesis, called the *similar reaction hypothesis,* states that there is no basic difference between children who are and are not retarded when it comes to their reactions to life experiences. However, since these experiences might well be different for children who are retarded, such as repeated failure or institutionalization, the children with MR may have special motivational and personality characteristics. A number of these characteristics have been investigated. (Our presentation follows Hodapp and Zigler, 1995.)

Dependency and Outerdirectedness

Children with MR are more attentive to and dependent on adults. For example, because of their need to gain positive reinforcement from adults, institutionalized children will play a boring, repetitive game longer than will noninstitutionalized children matched for mental and chronological age. Zigler calls this need for positive reinforcement the *positive reaction tendency*. Along with this tendency goes outerdirectedness, or *an exaggerated need to look to others* for clues about how to solve problems. Such clues will subsequently be used even when they are extraneous or misleading. Outerdirectedness contrasts with the behavior of children who are not retarded, who are more self-reliant and use their own judgment more.

Lower Expectancy of Success

Because of repeated experiences with failure, children who are retarded have a lower expectancy of success that makes them give up more readily than children who are not retarded. In certain instances this can lead to a vicious cycle, with the self-protective need to avoid yet another failure experience, resulting in a premature abandoning of the attempt to solve problems—which in turn further reduces the likelihood of success.

Lower Mastery Motivation

Finally, there is a decrease in mastery motivation, or initiative, in children who are retarded. There is less interest and pleasure in tackling new tasks or meeting new challenges, and less intrinsic reward in achievement for its own sake.

The Self

In regard to personality, the self of a child with MR is less differentiated than it is for children in the typically developing population. Recall that, while there is a generalized self-concept, it is also divided into various domains such as intellectual, social, and athletic. Thus, a child might say, "I don't do well in school, but I have lots of friends." Compared with children matched for chronological age, those with MR have fewer specific domains and a more impoverished concept of the self.

Individuals also have an ideal self and a real self—a "me as I would like to be" and a "me as I am." Compared with typically developing children, those with MR have a lower ideal self, perhaps due to their greater number of failures and to their being treated as incompetent. (See Hodapp and Zigler, 1995.)

We now see that the child with MR has two handicaps—one intellectual, the other motivational. The problem may further be compounded in institutional settings where docility and conformity to a drab routine are rewarded, while assertiveness and initiative are punished. The challenge to researchers is to disentangle basic intellectual handicaps from those that result from motivational and environmental influences. The therapeutic challenge is to find ways our society can accommodate the realistic limitations while maximizing the assets of the child who is retarded. Meeting this challenge will result in a more balanced mixture of successes and failures for those with MR than presently exists. It is helpful to remind ourselves that in certain societies MR is not stigmatized or even viewed as a problem that needs to be corrected. Our achievement-oriented society might profit from such examples of acceptance.

Developmental Course

The potential developmental outcomes associated with MR are as diverse as are the causes of the disorder. While children with more profound levels of retardation may need 24-hour supervision and care, requiring them to live their lives in an institutional setting, children with mild MR may lead adaptive and successful lives in the mainstream.

Stability and Change

First, any generalizations about the developmental course of MR must be tempered by the recognition that their functioning may wax and wane over time, depending on the level of retardation and the type. Regarding level, while severe MR is relatively stable from childhood to adulthood, children with mild MR may show IQ changes in an either upward or downward direction. Developmental course is also affected by the type of MR. For example, the IQ of children with Down syndrome continues to develop, but at a decelerating rate, making smaller and smaller gains over time, while children with Fragile-X syndrome, show a steady or near-steady gain in IQ until they are 10 to 15 years old, at which point the development slows considerably. (See Hodapp and Dykens, 2003.)

Type of retardation also affects the developmental trajectory of adaptive behavior. Children with Down syndrome reach a plateau during middle childhood, making few advances between 7 and 11 years of age. A longitudinal, cross-sectional study of boys with Fragile-X syndrome, on the other hand, showed the most striking gains in the toddler and preschool periods, less marked but still significant gains up until 11 years of age, and no age-related gains into early adulthood (Dykens et al., 1996).

Stage-Salient Issues

Infant Development

MR may affect the child's accomplishment of the major stage-salient issues of infancy, namely attachment, self-regulation, and exploration of the environment. (Here we follow Sachs and Barrett, 2000.) Many children with MR show delayed or absent eye contact, cooing, and social smiling, all of which may interfere with the development of a secure attachment relationship, as may the frequent hospitalizations of children who have accompanying physical disabilities. By a similar token, on the parents' side, attachment may be complicated by grieving in the parent whose child has received the MR label or frustration and irritation in the parent whose child's more subtle deficits have not yet allowed the diagnosis to be made.

Early Childhood

MR also runs the risk of interfering with the child's development of mastery, self, and peer relationships in early childhood. By this point in development, most children's developmental delays have been identified. Parental reactions play a crucial role in the child's outcome and may range from mobilization of resources in a campaign to "beat the odds," to denial and unrealistic expectations at one extreme, or sadness and resignation at the other. Early and intensive intervention is important at this stage in order to assist the child with language and communication skills, which are strongly predictive of the development of behavior problems. Children who are unable to communicate their needs or desires are at risk for becoming aggressive, destructive, or withdrawn. Self-care skills may be disrupted by MR, interfering with the child's capacity to participate in mainstream activities unless intervention is initiated. MR similarly might interfere with the child's ability to engage in meaningful play behavior and communicate socially with peers. Self-esteem, interpersonal trust, and perceived competence all emerge from the successful mastery of these tasks.

Middle Childhood

In the school-age years, mainstreaming, particularly of children with mild mental retardation, introduces a new set of challenges. Many have difficulty adapting to the transition from the supportive, flexible, child-focused day at home to the more structured school setting. For the first time, children may have to cope with interacting with nondevelopmentally disabled peers and with hearing labels applied to them such as "retarded," "slow learner," or "special ed." Unfortunately, one of the downsides of mainstreaming is the too-frequent incidence of teasing and rejection by peers. The self-aware child with MR may respond with withdrawal, isolation, and depression or begin to act out his or her frustration in the form of externalizing behavior. Similarly, as school progresses and subjects become more abstract and complex, children with MR begin to fall further behind and to recognize their differences from others. The physical disabilities that often accompany MR also interfere with the child's ability to participate in important socializing activities, such as sports and scouts. A protective factor, however, is the parent who has access to and knowledge about special activities for developmentally disabled children, such as Special Olympics or community programs.

Adolescence

The strivings for independence, self-esteem, and social awareness that preoccupy adolescents are additionally challenging for the child with MR. Poor social skills and lack of adherence to social norms, such as a lack of attention to personal hygiene, can contribute to peer rejection. The emphasis on physical appearance in adolescence is a further challenge to the self-esteem and social acceptance of the youth with physical anomalies. The youth with MR also is likely to have difficulty keeping up with the verbal repartee, changing styles, and complexities of social relationships in the peer group. Friendships with typically developing peers may languish as those peers begin dating, working, driving, and engaging in more independent behaviors. Youths with mild MR may have the same dreams and aspirations as their peers, but be unable to reach these goals. Consequently, depression and withdrawal may emerge. Suicidal ideation is not uncommon.

Sexuality is another developmental challenge for the adolescent with MR. Girls with moderate to severe levels of retardation may have difficulty comprehending menstruation and engaging in appropriate self-care. Youths who do not comprehend rules related to sexual touching may engage in inappropriate physical behavior. However, it is important to note that youths with MR are not likely to be perpetrators of sexual abuse but rather to be the victims of sexual mistreatment by others. This is a particular risk for those who are living in institutional settings, such as group homes.

The academic realm brings further challenges and potential protective factors. In adolescence, youths with MR are likely to be routed out of the academic mainstream and into vocational classes, a boon to the youths who find their niche, but a bane to the youths who feel stigmatized and bored by the repetitive tasks such training often involves.

Finally, adolescence brings a new set of challenges to the family system, which must cope with weighing the developmentally appropriate needs of the youth for independence with the needs for structure and, in some cases, lifelong care.

Intervention

Government Regulations

One unique aspect of programs for the mentally retarded is the involvement of the federal government. PL 94-142, known as the Education for All Handicapped Children Act of 1975, assures that all handicapped children have a free public education tailored to their unique needs, assures the rights of handicapped children and their parents or guardians, assists states in providing education, and assesses and assures the effectiveness of efforts toward education.

Two specific requirements have had far-reaching effects. The first is that an *individualized education program (IEP)* must be devised for each child with special needs. Implementing an IEP involves assessing the child's present level of functioning, setting goals, and providing educational services and procedures for evaluating educational progress. Parents as well as various professionals participate in the decision-making process.

The second requirement is that handicapped children be educated in the *least restrictive environment*. This requirement reversed the 75-year-old tradition of placing children who are retarded in self-contained special settings, such as special classrooms for the educable mentally retarded (EMR). The contention was that such classes were ineffective in helping many EMR children learn basic academic and occupational skills, that minorities were overrepresented, and that advances in education have made individualized instruction in regular classes feasible (Beyer, 1991).

Special Education

Children classified as *educable mentally retarded (EMR)* have IQ scores between 55 and 80 and are expected to perform at least at a third-grade level and occasionally as high as a sixth-grade level by the time they finish school. The *trainable mentally retarded (TMR)*, who have IQ scores between 25 and 55, are taught to function in a restricted environment and are not expected to master traditional academic skills.

In special education classes, EMR pupils are taught academic subjects as tools to enhance social competence and occupational skills. Small classes with individualized attention are recommended. Between 6 and 10 years of age, the EMR child, whose mental age is between 3 and 6 years, is given the kind of readiness programs usually found in kindergarten: The emphasis is on language enrichment and self-confidence, along with good health, work, and play habits. EMR children between 9 and 13 years of age, whose mental age is about 6 to 9 years, can master the basic academic skills involved in the three Rs. At the junior and senior high school levels the applied emphasis continues; for example, the children are trained to read the newspaper and job application forms and to make correct change. Occupational education stresses appropriate work habits such as punctuality and following directions, since most vocational failures are due to poor adjustment rather than low mental ability. After formal schooling, sheltered workshops and vocational rehabilitation centers help the mildly retarded adjust to our complex society.

The curriculum for TMRs emphasizes self-care and communication skills, work habits, following directions, and rudimentary social participation. Reading instruction, for example, is likely to include recognizing signs such as "Stop," " Men," and "Women," while arithmetic is limited to making change. The majority of these children do not achieve social or economic independence as adults, although they can engage in useful work and adjust well in the protective setting of the family.

Mainstreaming   Educating children with MR in regular classrooms is called *mainstreaming*. In keeping with the civil rights movement in the 1960s and 1970s, special classes were labeled another form of discrimination and segregation. The majority of children and adults appear to benefit from inclusion into mainstream educational settings (Freeman & Alkin, 2000).

Behavior Modification

By far the most successful and widely used therapeutic technique for children with MR is behavior modification. This technique involves the operant principles of changing undesirable behaviors by altering the specific consequences that reinforce them and by reinforcing new, more socially acceptable responses. It has been used to increase a wide array of behaviors: self-help behaviors (toileting, feeding, dressing), work-oriented behaviors (productivity, task completion), social behaviors (cooperation, group activities), nonacademic classroom behaviors (attending, taking turns, talking at appropriate times), academic learning (arithmetic, sight vocabulary), as well as decreasing undesirable behaviors such as attention-getting and aggressive or self-injurious behaviors. An important benefit is that parents can actively participate in the therapeutic program in the home setting. Most important of all, more than any other single therapeutic technique, behavior modification has been responsible for changing the prevailing attitude of hopelessness among professional and nonprofessional caregivers. (See Carr et al., 1999.)

Didden, Duker, and Korzilius's (1997) meta-analysis of 482 published studies covering a period of 26 years provides some specific details in regard to treatment outcomes. As to overall effectiveness, 26.5 percent of all behaviors can be treated quite effectively, 47.1 percent can be treated fairly effectively, while treatment effectiveness of the remaining 26 percent are questionable or poor. In regard to kinds of treatment, response contingent procedures (i.e., those based on the operant principle of immediate reinforcement) are significantly more effective than are other techniques.

Prevention

The most challenging population to involve in prevention consists of mothers who have mental retardation, 40 percent of whose children will develop familial MR. While most of these mothers are socioeconomically deprived, the basic problem is not so much poverty itself but impaired parenting skills. This group has been the target of myriad preventive programs, including parent education or placing the child in a more stimulating environment, or both.

One of the more successful and better-designed prevention programs was initiated by Ramey and

Figure 4.3   Growth Curves in Reading Achievement for Groups from the Abecedarian Project.

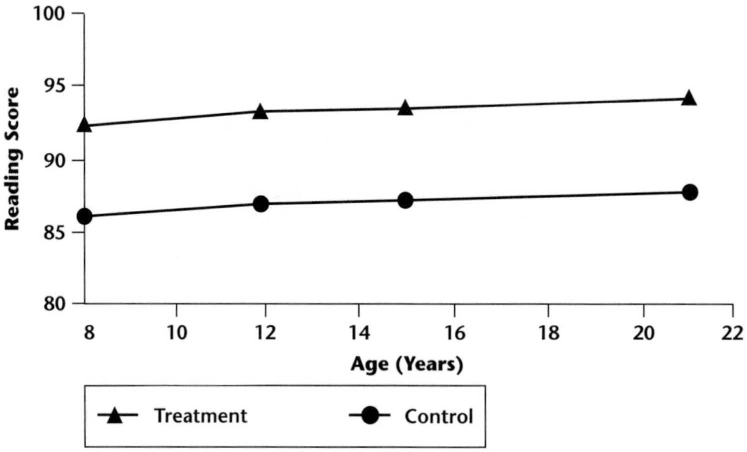

From Campbell, Pungello, Miller-Johnson, Burchinal, & Ramey, 2001.

colleagues (1991). Called the Abecedarian Project, the intervention took its name from a term referring to the literate individual—the abecedarian is one who knows his or her ABCs. Evidence shows that, without early intervention, infants of mothers with low IQs are particularly at risk for poor intellectual outcomes. The lower the mother's IQ, the greater the risk. The Abecedarian Project was designed to counter the early decline in infant IQ by placing preschoolers in a special early childhood education program. The preschool was intensive, involving a full day 5 days a week for 50 weeks a year for the first 5 years. Each child received an individualized program of educational activities that addressed cognitive, social, and emotional development but emphasized language most of all.

By the time the children were 3 years old, those receiving the educational intervention scored 20 IQ points higher than children in the control group, putting 95 percent of them in the average range as compared with 49 percent of the control children. Moreover, the programs had a particularly powerful preventive effect on children whose mothers had the lowest IQs—the group most at risk for developing mental retardation.

To date, follow-up analyses have been conducted on the children at ages 12, 15, and 21. In contrast to an untreated control group, the children who received the intervention had higher reading achievement scores throughout their school years (see Figure 4.3). In addition, they had higher intelligence test scores and better academic achievement and were significantly more likely to attend a 4-year college (Campbell, Ramey, et al., 2002). The intervention also had positive benefits for the mothers. Because their children were in the preschool program, the mothers were able to work at higher-paying jobs and to better their own life situations.

Our next topic involves another disorder with its roots in the infancy period. However, unlike organically based mental retardation, which usually is apparent right from birth, autism is an insidious disorder whose effects begin at birth but may not reveal themselves until much later in development.

Infancy: Disorders in the Autistic Spectrum

What lies at the heart of human development in the first 2 years of life? The establishment of the bond of love is certainly important, as are curiosity, and symbolic communication culminating in speech. But what if all were wrenched from their normal course? We would rightly predict severe psychopathology. One such psychopathology that could result is one of the pervasive developmental disorders, the subject of this chapter. In this chapter, we will concern ourselves with two of these profound psychopathologies, both of which are in the *autistic spectrum.* We will first outline *autistic disorder*'s behavioral manifestations and effects on subsequent development, and then we will describe the related disorder of *Asperger's disorder.* After that we will raise the seemingly simple question mentioned in previous chapters—how can this psychopathology be understood in terms of normal development gone awry?—and find out how complex the answers are. As we shall see, the study of disorders in the autistic spectrum also illustrates one of the other important issues in developmental psychopathology that we have been considering throughout this text—the continuum between normal and pathological development.

Autism

Definition

Early Descriptions

The term *autism* derives from the Greek word *autos,* meaning "self." The term was first coined by the psychiatrist Eugen Bleuler at the beginning of the 20th century to refer to an extreme withdrawal from social life into the self that he saw in some of his severely disturbed patients. In a classic paper, Leo Kanner (1943), a Baltimore psychiatrist, used the term to refer to an unusual group of patients who shared three essential features.

The first feature identified by Kanner was *autistic aloneness:* "There is from the start an extreme

The social imperviousness and manneristic behavior of the autistic child.

autistic aloneness that, whenever possible, disregards, ignores, shuts out anything that comes to the child from the outside. . . . He has a good relation to objects; he is interested in them, can play with them happily for hours (p. 242). [But] the child's relation to people is altogether different. . . . Profound aloneness dominates all behavior" (p. 246).

The second characteristic of autism identified by Kanner was a pathological *desire for sameness.* "The child's noises and motions and all his performances are as monotonously repetitive as are his verbal utterances. There is a marked limitation in the variety of his spontaneous activities. The child's behavior is governed by an anxiously obsessive desire for the maintenance of sameness" (p. 245).

Third, Kanner noted that these children evidenced significant language problems characterized by delayed language development, echolalia, pronoun reversals, and extreme literalness.

A fourth observation made by Kanner was that these children exhibited what he termed *islets of ability.* That is, in spite of severe overall deficits in their functioning—particularly in the area of communication, which was often severely impaired—specific skills might be preserved or even enhanced.

Among these, he noted, were the "astounding vocabulary of the speaking children, the excellent memory for events of several years before, the phenomenal rote memory for poems and names, and the precise recollection of complex patterns and sequences" (p. 247).

Kanner proposed that deficits so profound must be the signs of an inborn disturbance, the core of which is a failure of normal attachment. "We must, then, assume that these children have come into the world with innate inability to form the usual biologically provided affective contact with people, just as other children come into the world with innate physical or intellectual handicaps" (p. 250). Interestingly, he later abandoned this view in favor of a theory that attributed autism to psychodynamic factors, a wrong turn that the field took with him for several generations, as we shall see. (See Box 5.1.)

DSM-IV-TR Definition

The DSM-IV-TR places Autistic Disorder in the category of the Pervasive Developmental Disorders, a group of syndromes characterized by severe and pervasive impairment in several areas of development: social interaction, communication, and the

Box 5.1 | The "Refrigerator Mother": Theories of Autism Take a Wrong Turn

Although Kanner (1944) originally proposed that autism was a biologically based disorder, he later revised his theory in favor of a psychodynamic one, in keeping with the tenor of the times. The belief that autism was caused by maladaptive parenting caught hold with clinicians as well as the general public. The parent of the autistic child was described as cold, rejecting, and emotionally absent: the "refrigerator mother."

For example, in his book *The Empty Fortress* (1967), Bruno Bettelheim wrote, "Throughout this book I state my belief that the precipitating factor in infantile autism is the parent's wish that his child should not exist" (p. 241). He described one mother as follows: "About other people she spoke with animation and clarity. But when the conversation turned to Joey, she immediately became impersonal,

detached, and was soon unable to keep her mind on him, switching to other topics. When she told us about his birth and infancy, it was as if she were talking about some vague acquaintance, some person or event she had heard about and noted without interest. Soon her thoughts wandered away to other people, or herself. It seemed that Joey simply never got through to his mother" (p. 241).

Viewed through a critical lens, the behavior of a mother or father trying to parent an unresponsive child indeed might look less than ideal. However, the refrigerator parent theory represented a tragic wrong turn in the study of autism, which we now know to be a biologically based disorder. Many generations of parents bore the burden, not only of parenting an extremely disabled child, but of misplaced guilt for causing the

problem. Research has shown that mothers of children with autism are not significantly different in their personality characteristics and attitudes toward their children from mothers of children with other handicaps (McAdoo & DeMyer, 1978). Further, despite the indifference and lack of reinforcement with which their overtures are met, mothers of children with autism are observed to be highly adept at adjusting their behavior in order to socially engage their children (Doussard-Roosevelt et al., 2003). Therefore, in contrast to other attachment disorders that are secondary to pathological caregiving that we discuss in Chapter 6, autism can be considered a *primary* attachment disorder in that the child comes into the world lacking in normal response to others.

presence of stereotyped behaviors, interests, and activities. Table 5.1 summarizes the basic diagnostic features of autism. Note that three of Kanner's observations—social isolation, impaired speech, and a pathological need for sameness—have stood the test of time. Next, we describe the deficits characteristic of autism in each of these areas of functioning.

Impairment in Social Interaction   Children with autism exhibit extreme *social isolation* and an inability to relate to people. For example, in a face-to-face situation a girl with severe autism will not look at you or even away from you; rather, she will look *through* you. If you put her on your lap, her body will not accommodate to yours; instead she will sit as if you were a chair. If she needs you to do something, say, open a door, she will take your hand

(rather than taking *you* by the hand) and bring it in contact with a doorknob. It is as if you do not exist as a person but rather as a thing.

Wing and Attwood (1987) described the social impairments of the children with autism in their study as falling into one of three types (see Figure 5.1). The first includes *aloof* children, who seem to be isolated in their own bubble. These children are withdrawn and do not respond to the social overtures of others. They do not seek eye contact and often actively attempt to avoid it. They also dislike physical contact, refusing to be cuddled, and do not respond to caregivers with interest or excitement. While they will approach others, it is only to get instrumental needs met, such as to be fed, and not to meet emotional needs, such as for comfort or affection. The second group includes the *passive* children, who accept

Table 5.1

DSM-IV-TR Criteria for Autistic Disorder

A. A total of six or more items, with at least two from category 1.
  1. Qualitative impairment in social interaction, as manifested by at least two of the following:
     a. Marked impairment in the use of multiple nonverbal behaviors such as eye-to-eye gaze, facial expression, body postures, and gestures to regulate social interaction
     b. Failure to develop peer relationships appropriate to developmental level
     c. A lack of spontaneous seeking to share enjoyment, interests, or achievements with other people (e.g., by a lack of showing, bringing, or pointing out objects of interest)
     d. Lack of social or emotional reciprocity
  2. Qualitative impairments in communication as manifested by at least one of the following:
     a. Delay in, or total lack of, the development of spoken language (not accompanied by an attempt to compensate through alternative modes of communication such as gesture or mime)
     b. In individuals with adequate speech, marked impairment in the ability to initiate or sustain a conversation with others
     c. Stereotyped and repetitive use of language or idiosyncratic language
     d. Lack of varied spontaneous make-believe play or social imitative play appropriate to developmental level
  3. Restricted repetitive and stereotyped patterns of behavior, interests, and activities, as manifested by at least one of the following:
     a. Encompassing preoccupation with one or more stereotyped and restricted patterns of interest that is abnormal either in intensity or focus
     b. Apparently inflexible adherence to specific, nonfunctional routines or rituals
     c. Stereotyped and repetitive motor mannerisms (e.g., hand or finger flapping or twisting, or complex whole body movements)
     d. Persistent preoccupation with parts of objects
B. Delays or abnormal functioning in at least one of the following areas, with onset prior to age 3: (1) social interaction, (2) language as used in social communication, or (3) symbolic or imaginative play

Reprinted with permission from the *Diagnostic and Statistical Manual of Mental Disorders,* Fourth Edition Text Revision. Copyright 2000 by the American Psychiatric Association.

others' social overtures but in a submissive and indifferent manner. While they interact with others, they do so as a matter of daily routine rather than as a source of spontaneous pleasure. They also are compliant and even overly so; for example, they may be easily led into mischief by peers because they do whatever they are instructed to do. The third group includes the *odd* children, who are very interested in other people but are lacking in social comprehension and appreciation for the norms of behavior. They might approach strangers and indiscriminately touch them or ask inappropriate questions, without registering the feedback that their behavior is discomfiting to others.

Wing and Gould (1991) observed the children over the next 16 years of their lives and found that many changed from one category to another. In particular, there was a strong tendency for children in the aloof group to become passive or odd over the course of development, probably as a result of interventions that encouraged socialization.

Impairments in Communication   *Communicative deficits* are commonly seen in autism and often are severe. They may range from *mutism*—as many as half of children with autism will never learn to speak—to *noncommunicative* speech. Characteristics of noncommunicative speech may include *echolalia,* the exact repetition of words or phrases spoken by others with no effort to comprehend their meaning (e.g., a child who had been scolded for eating butter out of the butter dish repeatedly stated, "Don't do that, Gregory"). Speech also may be used *idiosyncratically,* such as the utterance of phrases or sentences that are irrelevant to the situation (e.g., while repeatedly flushing the toilet, a girl with

Figure 5.1

Three Types of Social Impairment.

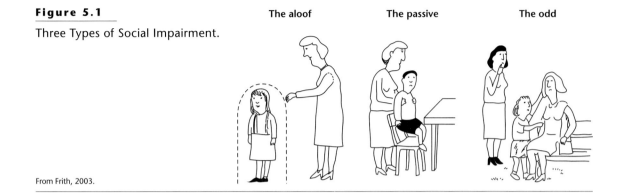

From Frith, 2003.

autism suddenly said, "The hamburgers are in the refrigerator!").

The speech of autistic children is often extremely *literal* and *pedantic,* with speech used in an overly formal and stilted manner as if they had memorized by rote phrases in a foreign language (e.g., one British child always requests, "May I extract a biscuit from this tin?"; another young man, each time he phones his favorite aunt, announces himself by saying, "This is J. M. Wright, your nephew, speaking"). Children with autism also tend to comprehend speech in an overly literal way. Such literalism can be scary: A girl with autism was terrified when a nurse asked her to "Give me your hand" because she thought the nurse literally wanted her to remove her hand (Frith, 2003).

Children with autism often have difficulty understanding the correct use of first and third person. They may engage in *pronoun reversal,* using "you" instead of "I" (e.g., "You want to go out") or referring to themselves by name (e.g., "Jack wants to eat" rather than "I want to eat").

Another commonly seen characteristic of autistic speech is that it lacks *prosody,* the changes in rhythm and intonation that gives normal speech its melody. Instead, the child with autism speaks in a monotone without the proper stress on words or rise and fall in tone that help to convey emotion and meaning. Correspondingly, children with autism also seem to lack an understanding of what others are communicating through the prosody of their speech. Consider how comprehension of humor,

irony, or sarcasm relies on attention to the *way* something is said (e.g., imagine that an exasperated parent walks into a room strewn with toys and says, "Well, thanks very much for cleaning up in here!" While the typically developing child would likely pick up on the dripping sarcasm—and respond by beginning to pick up the room—the child with autism is likely to be bewildered, unable to grasp that the literal meaning is not the intended one).

Play is another modality through which children communicate. However, unlike typically developing children, the play behavior of those with autism is lacking in social and symbolic functions. In particular, children with autism do not tend to initiate make-believe play. For example, when given blocks to play with, a typically developing preschooler might use them to represent a car ("Vroom! Vroom!") or to create an airport landing strip. The child with autism, in contrast, is more likely to become fixated on lining the blocks up in a precisely straight row or, if they are striped or brightly colored, spinning them and staring as they whirl. However, most of this research has required children with autism to produce pretend play spontaneously. When they are provided with prompts, such as the investigator's asking, "What can you do with these [toys]?" or "Can you pretend to give dolly a drink [from an empty cup]?" the performance of children with autism is comparable to that of children with mental retardation (Charman & Baron-Cohen, 1997). These findings suggest that there is not a basic inability to pretend in children with autism but rather that they are not as *motivated* to pretend as are other children.

Restricted and Stereotyped Interests and Behavior   The *need for sameness* applies both to the child's own behavior and to the environment. Often the child's activities are simple, such as sitting on the floor and rocking back and forth for long periods of time, or twirling his or her shoelaces, or running up and down a hall. Sometimes the activities resemble complex rituals, such as the activities of a 5-year-old who takes a toy truck, turns it on its side, spins a wheel while making a humming noise, goes over to the window, looks out while drumming his fingers on the sill, and then returns to the truck, only to repeat the exact same sequence over and over. The need for sameness can be expressed in a number of other ways; for example, the child must have the exact same food and plate and utensils, or wear the same article of clothing, or have the furniture arranged in a specific way. The intensity of the need is evidenced not only by the rigidity of the behavior but also by the child's panic and rage when attempts are made to alter the environment even in minor ways, such as providing a different food or moving a chair to a different part of the room.

Associated Features

Sensory Processing   Other behaviors that may be present in autism are not essential to the diagnosis. For example, children with autism often respond to sensory stimulation in unusual ways. They may smell every object that comes into their hands, even an inert object, or place it in their mouths. Children with autism may be hypersensitive or hyposensitive to stimuli, often with an unpredictable fluctuation between the two. For example, they may be *hypersensitive* to touch and find unbearable the feel of certain fabrics on their skin, or highly reactive to sounds, such that the noise of a telephone is agonizing. Autobiographical accounts of adults with autism also contain references to a generalized sensory overload, such as feeling bombarded by bright lights and unpredictable movement or being overwhelmed by the noise and confusion of large gatherings. It

may be that, when faced with such an environment, the children seek the safety of repetitive, low-intensity sensory stimulation, such as humming the same note over and over or concentrating their attention on the movement of a spinning coin. In short, the pathological need for sameness may provide a defense against being overwhelmed by ordinary environmental stimuli.

Hyposensitivity may take the form of an unusual tolerance of cold or imperviousness to pain, which may be related to the fact that many children with autism engage in self-injurious behavior such as head banging or hitting, slapping, scratching, or biting themselves. Hyposensitivity to sound may be so profound that the child is mistakenly thought to be deaf and peculiarly, hyposensitivity may exist for some sounds at the same time that the child is hypersensitive to others. Thus, the same child who shrieks in fear and rage at the sound of the telephone may be entirely unresponsive to the sound of a fire alarm.

In other ways, children with autism appear to be *cortically understimulated* and may engage in odd behaviors that serve to increase cortical arousal, such as staring at spinning objects, flashing lights off and on, flicking their fingers in the corner of their eyes, or compulsively masturbating.

Autistic Savants   Although a popular image of children with autism is that they are *savants,* possessing a rare talent or genius or the ability to perform remarkable feats such as memorizing the phone book, calculating complex equations, reproducing melodies, knowing the day of the week on which any date ever fell, or learning foreign languages. However, such splinter skills are seen in only about 10 percent of children with the disorder. (For more on these fascinating individuals, see Hermelin, 2001.) For most children with autism, the disorder is associated with significant cognitive deficits in all areas. (See Box 5.2.)

Characteristics

Age of Onset

According to the DSM-IV-TR criteria, autistic behavior must be present before the 3rd year of life in order for the diagnosis to be valid. Although the

Box 5.2 | **Conceptualizations of Psychopathology: Qualitative Differences and Asynchrony**

Note that DSM-IV uses the term "qualitative" when describing impairment in social interaction and communication (see Table 5.1). Whether psychopathology represents a quantitative or a qualitative difference from normality is a perennial question. Generally speaking, the *quantitative* view is more prevalent: Phobias are regarded as extremes of normal fears; delinquency is viewed as an exaggeration of normal adolescent rebelliousness. The three major developmental models of psychopathology—fixation, regression, and developmental delay—are quantitative. DSM-IV's description of autism in terms of *qualitative* impairments implies that autistic behavior has no counterpart even in the behavior of younger normal children and that the developmental sequencing of behavior does not follow that charted for normal children.

To evaluate the quantitative versus qualitative issue, Wenar and colleagues (1986) compared the development of 41 children with autism between 5 and 11 years of age with that of 195 normal children between 3 months and 5 years of age, using a standardized observational technique called the Behavior Rating Instrument for Autistic and Other Atypical Children (BRIAAC). The investigators found that severely autistic children's obliviousness to caretaking adults, their minimal expressiveness, their disinterest in or fleeting exploration of objects, their unresponsiveness or negative reaction to sound, and their indifference to social demands all indicated an imperviousness to the social and physical environment that had little counterpart in normal behavior and development. In a like manner Dawson (1991), in discussing early socioemotional development, concludes that in certain cases both the surface behavior and the function or need it fulfills may be unique to the autistic child, and parallels in normal developmental patterns may be difficult to find.

Our review of research on autism also suggests another new conceptualization of normal development gone awry. In autism, deviance lies in the relationships among variables rather than within a single variable itself. We will call this deviation *asynchrony*. Progress among variables is disjointed, with some variables proceeding at a normal pace while others lag or follow an idiosyncratic course. While asynchrony has been noted in the clinical literature (see A. Freud, 1965), it is now being verified in objective studies of language development in children with autism (e.g., in the discrepancy between understanding of syntax and language semantics).

disorder is believed to be present at birth, the diagnosis is complicated by the fact that many of the diagnostic criteria concern functions that emerge later in development. For example, it is not until 18 months that we would expect a typically developing child to demonstrate the first rudiments of pretend play. The timing of the diagnosis also is likely related to the degree of deficit. The diagnosis might come later for the child who is higher functioning, because the disparity between the child and his or her normally developing peers only becomes apparent as development proceeds. A diagnostic dilemma also exists for the low-functioning child, who might languish with an incorrect diagnosis of mental retardation.

However, just because adults did not notice or label the child's autism, that does not mean it was not present throughout infancy. Geraldine Dawson and her colleagues (Osterling & Dawson, 1994) came up with the ingenious idea of watching old family videos of the first birthday parties of children who later were diagnosed with autism. Comparing 11 typically developing infants with 11 infants with autistic disorder, the investigators found that children with autism consistently less often looked at the faces of others, showed or pointed to objects of interest, or oriented to their names when called. These behaviors allowed raters to correctly classify 91 percent of the children correctly as being in the autistic or nonautistic group.

In a subsequent study, Dawson and colleagues (Werner et al., 2000) found that they could reliably detect oddities in behavior even earlier in development. At 8 to 10 months of age, infants later diagnosed with autism were less likely than a matched cohort of typically developing children to orient to the speaker when their names were called and were slightly less likely to look at another person while smiling. Interestingly, developmental pediatricians performed no better than chance when attempting to classify the 8- to 10-month-olds as autistic or nonautistic. However, the raters were able to place children in the correct group 78 percent of the time when provided videotapes made when the children were 12 months of age, a mere few months later. Consequently, the investigators conclude, autism may be extremely difficult for observers to detect prior to 1 year of age even though subtle signs of the disorder are emerging.

Prevalence

Officially, DSM-IV-TR places the median prevalence rate at 5 per 10,000 individuals but notes that there is wide variation from study to study. While earlier reports suggested that autism was an extremely rare phenomenon, more recent surveys have revealed a surprising increase. Statistics recently compiled in the United States show that autism is 10 times more prevalent now than it was 20 years ago (Yeargin-Allsop et al., 2003). While the rates in the 1980s were 4 to 5 in every 10,000 children, the most recent rates were 3.4 in every 1,000 children ages 3 to 10. Similarly, Wing and Potter (2002) reviewed 39 population-based studies derived from a dozen different countries and found that, in the past decade, prevalence rates for autistic disorder ranged between 3.8 and 60 per 10,000 children, a rate many times greater than those reported 30 years ago. The prevalence of more broadly defined *autistic-spectrum disorders* was estimated at around 60 per 10,000 children. No systematic differences in prevalence are found among different social classes or races, lending credence to the idea that autism is a biologically based disorder that strikes all with equal impunity.

If rates of autism are increasing, does this signify an epidemic? Most likely not. Experts in the field generally believe that the rise in prevalence is due to increasing awareness of autism among physicians and the general public. In addition, there has been a widening of the diagnostic criteria, which are more sensitive than previously to detecting the disorder. For example, Frith (2003) notes that a survey in California reported a 250 percent increase in the diagnosis of autism between 1987 and 1994, while rates of the diagnosis of mental retardation decreased by exactly that amount in the same time period. Rather than indicating an increase in the prevalence of autism, a more likely explanation of these data is that, as the accuracy of the diagnostic system increases, more children with autism are being correctly diagnosed.

Gender

The sex difference in autism is significant. On average across studies, boys outnumber girls at a ratio of 4 to 1. However, the ratios change when we look at children with varying levels of cognitive ability: Boys predominate less at the lower end of the IQ range. For example, in a large-scale study conducted in the United Kingdom, Wing (1991) found that at the lowest IQ levels, the ratio of boys to girls was 2 to 1, whereas at the highest levels it was 15 to 1. The explanation for this gendered pattern is not yet known.

Social Class, Ethnicity, and Culture

While earlier studies hypothesized that autism was more prevalent among the upper classes, more recent research shows that this simply was due to a sampling bias in the populations that made their way to diagnostic clinics. The prevalence of autism is not related to social class nor to ethnicity. Studies conducted in many different nations reveal a similar picture of the disorder (Evans & Lee, 1998; Schriebman & Charlop-Christy, 1998).

Comorbidity

Many children with autism also qualify for a diagnosis of *mental retardation*. (However, mentally retarded children without autism differ in numerous and profound ways from children with the disorder, as we shall see, and thus the two clearly are distinct disorders.) Whereas earlier studies reported that 75 percent of children with autism were mentally retarded, with IQ scores falling below 70, these studies were based on clinical populations and included only the most severely disturbed. A population-based study in the UK, which sampled the entire range of the autistic spectrum, found that only 35 percent of children affected by autistic spectrum disorders had cognitive skills in the mentally retarded range (Baird et al., 2000).

Anxieties are evident in 7 to 84 percent of autistic children (Lainhart, 1999), particularly related to stimuli to which they are hypersensitive. At times, these may reach phobic proportions, interfering with the child's ability to function. For example, Klinger et al. (2003) describe the child afraid of blacktop who consequently was unable to walk across the parking lot, street, or school playground.

Autism also coexists with *seizure disorders* in 11 to 39 percent of cases. Those most likely to be affected are females and those with mental retardation (Ballaban-Gil & Tuchman, 2000).

Asperger's Disorder

Definition

Early Descriptions

Unbeknown to Kanner, at the same time that he was studying autism in Baltimore, Hans Asperger was writing about a similar group of children in Vienna. Asperger's classic paper, published in 1944, was long forgotten until it was reintroduced to the profession by Lorna Wing (1981). Asperger's words were translated by Frith (1991) as follows: "In what follows I will describe a type of child which is of interest in a number of ways: the children have in common a fundamental disturbance which manifests itself characteristically in all behavioural and expressive phenomena. This disturbance results in considerable and typical difficulties of social integration. In many cases, the failure to be integrated in a social group is the most conspicuous feature, but in other cases this failure is compensated for by a particular originality

of thought and experience, which may well lead to exceptional achievement in later life" (p. 37).

Asperger noted a number of features these children had in common: They avoided eye contact, their speech lacked melody and was often monotone or sing-song, they engaged in odd stereotypic movements, and they did not respond to positive emotional displays from others.

Although Asperger in fact described children whose symptoms ranged widely, his name became associated with a particular subset of children in the autistic spectrum. Currently, the label Asperger's Disorder is reserved for children whose deficits are more subtle and whose intellectual and language functioning is higher than that of those children who fit the Autistic Disorder label.

DSM-IV-TR Definition

The separate diagnostic category of Asperger's Disorder (AD; also known as Asperger Syndrome) was first added to the DSM-IV in 1994. The DSM-IV-TR criteria are listed in Table 5.2. As we see, the key difference with autism is that children with AD show no delays in language development and no significant cognitive deficits. It must be said that even though the diagnosis is part of the official nomenclature, experts disagree about whether AD truly represents a different category of disorder from autism (Volkmar & Klin, 2001). Many in the field tend to the view that the two are variants of the same underlying developmental disorder, with AD at the less severe end of the autistic spectrum (Frith, 2003).

Associated Features

Although not part of the DSM-IV-TR criteria, there are a number of other characteristics often seen in children with AD. For example, they frequently show a number of *obsessive-compulsive* tendencies, including behavioral and verbal rituals such as the accumulation and recitation of facts.

While children with AD may be highly verbal, they show a number of deficits in the social use of language, or *pragmatics*. For example, their communications with others may be restricted to monologues in their narrow specific area of interests, not

Table 5.2

DSM-IV-TR Criteria for Asperger's Disorder

A. Qualitative impairment in social interaction, as manifested by at least two of the following:
  1. Marked impairment in the use of multiple nonverbal behaviors such as eye-to-eye gaze, facial expression, body postures, and gestures to regulate social interaction
  2. Failure to develop peer relationships appropriate to developmental level
  3. A lack of spontaneously seeking to share enjoyment, interests, or achievements with other people (e.g., by a lack of showing, bringing, or pointing out objects of interest to other people)
  4. Lack of social or emotional reciprocity
B. Restricted repetitive and stereotyped patterns of behavior, interests, and activities as manifested by at least one of the following:
  1. Encompassing preoccupation with one or more stereotyped and restricted patterns of interest that is abnormal either in intensity or focus
  2. Apparently inflexible adherence to specific, nonfunctional routines or rituals
  3. Stereotyped and repetitive motor mannerisms (e.g., hand or finger flapping or twisting, or complex whole-body movements)
  4. Persistent preoccupation with parts of objects
C. The disturbance causes clinically significant impairment in social, occupational, or other important areas of functioning
D. There is no clinically significant general delay in language (e.g., single words used by age 2 years, communicative phrases used by age 3 years)
E. There is no clinically significant delay in cognitive development or in the development of age-appropriate self-help skills, adaptive behavior (other than in social interaction), and curiosity about the environment in childhood

Reprinted with permission from the *Diagnostic and Statistical Manual of Mental Disorders,* Fourth Edition Text Revision. Copyright 2000 by the American Psychiatric Association.

including the other as an active participant in the conversation; and they lack the social niceties of turn-taking, sharing the floor, and using appropriate nonverbal communication such as eye contact and facial expression.

Although children with AD are intact cognitively, their verbal skills are preserved while they still may have difficulties in the area of *nonverbal intelligence* (Lincoln, Courchesna, Kilman, & Elmasian, 1988). Indeed, children with AD are remarkably similar to those with nonverbal learning disabilities (Rourke & Tsatsanis, 2000).

Characteristics

Prevalence

Because Asperger's Disorder has only recently been officially recognized, little is known about its prevalence. In addition, because of their good intelligence, children with AD may go long undetected. However, recent studies using good diagnostic criteria suggest that AD appears in a larger segment of the population than previously thought. For example, studies of children in the mainstream school system in Sweden have estimated the prevalence between 36 and 48 per 10,000, amounting to 0.4 percent of the child population (Kadesjo, Gillberg, & Hagberg, 1999).

As Frith (2003) notes, if these initial investigations of the prevalence of autism and AD are replicated across cultures and stand the test of time, we may be looking at a prevalence rate of disorders in the autistic spectrum that is near 1 percent of the total population, akin to the prevalence of schizophrenia.

Gender

As we noted in our description of autism, boys are disproportionately represented amongst those with high cognitive abilities. Consequently, we would expect to see more boys than girls with AD and this is the case. Based upon the available studies, Frith (2003) estimates that the gender ratio in AD is approximately 15 boys for every girl.

Age of Onset

For many with Asperger's Disorder, the disorder is not detected until late in development because recognition of their deficits is obscured by their good cognitive and verbal skills. Far from being seen as disordered, these precocious children may have even delighted the adults around them with their "little professor" demeanor, their lack of interest in peers shrugged off as an eccentricity. Some with AD are not assessed until adolescence, when stage-salient tasks begin to demand just those abilities that the youth has failed to develop. For example, the young person's social difficulties may begin to interfere with the development of normal intimacy to a degree that they no longer can be explained away. Yet others with AD are not diagnosed until adulthood, in part because the disorder simply was not known when they were children. However, AD is believed to be an innate disorder that is present from birth, just as is autism.

Comorbidity

Particularly in adolescence and adulthood, mood disorders such as *anxiety* and *depression* frequently are seen in individuals with AD (Howlin, 2000). Clinical reports recount that young persons with AD may become painfully self-aware of their social deficits and exclusion from the mainstream of human society. These negative appraisals may lead to dysphoria and hopelessness.

Are Autism and Asperger's Separate Disorders?

As we have noted, researchers in the field are not in agreement about whether autism and AD represent truly distinct disorders. Complicating the picture is the fact that many investigators disagree with the DSM criteria for the AD diagnosis, and instead base their research on their own definitions of Asperger Syndrome. In one of the few studies to directly compare the two, Ozonoff and colleagues (2000) compared 23 children and adolescents with autism to 12 with AD, all diagnosed according to DSM criteria. The investigators found that as preschoolers the children with autism had had more severe

symptoms. However, currently, the two groups were similar in their social behavior and communicative ability. One clear difference was in the area of repetitive behavior: In contrast to the autistic insistence on sameness, the children with AD were described as having intensely circumscribed interests. Although the children with autism were more impaired in verbal comprehension, they did not score significantly lower than those with AD on verbal intelligence. The investigators speculate that the children with autism had "caught up" with their AD peers by the time they entered their teenage years.

Etiology of Disorders in the Autistic Spectrum

In the review that follows, we will describe research exploring the origins of both autism and Asperger's Syndrome. Perhaps reflecting the belief of many researchers that the two are manifestations of the same underlying disorder, studies do not always differentiate the two. Additionally, researchers have just begun to turn their attention to AD, and so most of the evidence is based on studies of autism. Therefore, in each section we will begin with a description of research on autism and/or the autistic spectrum and will end with a description of the research specific to AD, where it is available.

The Biological Context

Environmental Factors

In recent years, a number of environmental factors have been posited to play a causal role in autism. One of these involves birth complications. However, recent investigations have found birth complications to be either minor or no greater than those found in nonautistic infants with congenital anomalies. A second proposed environmental factor was congenital rubella. Initial studies suggested that rubella in pregnant mothers increased the incidence of autism in their infants. However, further research indicated that both the clinical description and the course of the children's disturbance were atypical; for example, such children tended to outgrow their presumed autism.

One alarming suggestion was that the combined measles, mumps, and rubella vaccine was a culprit. Many parents responded by declining to have their children immunized against these devastating diseases (Frith, 2003). However, investigators have assessed the association between the incidence of autism and the introduction of the vaccine in several different countries and at several different time points and, to date, have found no discernable pattern (Fombonne & Chakrabarti, 2001). However, it remains possible that the vaccine potentiates the onset of autistic spectrum disorders in children who are genetically vulnerable to them (Wing & Potter, 2002).

Genetic Factors

There is little doubt that genetics plays an etiological role in autism. Although it is rare for parents to have two children with autism, the risk of having a second child with the disorder is 15 to 30 times higher for parents with an autistic child versus those with a typically developing youngster. (Here we follow Rutter, 2000.)

As is always the case, the most convincing genetic data come from comparing monozygotic (MZ) with dizygotic (DZ) twins, one of whom has autism. General-population twin studies yield concordance rates ranging from 36 percent to 91 percent for the MZ twins and from 0 to 5 percent for DZ twins. Further evidence for a strong genetic component in autism comes from the finding that the nonautistic MZ twins have some autistic characteristics but to a lesser degree, termed the *broader autism phenotype*. Characteristics of the phenotype include some type of cognitive deficit, usually involving language delay, and persistent social impairment. Only 8 percent of the MZ co-twins were without such cognitive or social disorders compared with 90 percent of the DZ pairs. These studies suggest that the autistic phenotype extends well beyond the traditional diagnosis, involving characteristics similar to autism but markedly different in degree.

Because of its complexity it is not likely that autism is caused by a single genetic abnormality, but is more likely due to *genetic heterogeneity*—that is, different genetic abnormalities that all lead to the same clinical picture. The model of transmission, therefore, would involve multiple interacting genes rather than a single gene operating in a Mendelian fashion.

The search for genetic factors in AD is only beginning and the number of available studies is small (Folstein & Santangelo, 2000). In one of the larger investigations to date, Volkmar and colleagues (1997) surveyed 99 families of individuals with AD. The investigators found that 46 percent of the families reported symptoms consistent with AD in first-degree relatives, generally male family members. Rates of autism also were higher among the siblings and cousins of children with AD than would be expected in the normative population, suggesting a genetic link between autism and AD, if indeed they are separate disorders.

Neuropsychological Factors

The task of bridging the gap between brain and behavior is easiest when there is a circumscribed disturbance in behavior that can be related to a known characteristic of brain structure or functioning. Autism is a far cry from this model of simplicity. Autism is a pervasive disorder and the many psychological functions are affected. In light of this complexity, we cannot expect simple and certain answers to the question of the relation between brain and behavior, but many suggestive leads are emerging.

Neurochemical Findings   Neurochemical studies of autism search for abnormalities in **neurotransmitters** (the "chemical messengers" responsible for communication among nerve cells). Findings in regard to serotonin, dopamine, norepinephrine, and endorphins have been suggestive but inconsistent and inconclusive. Studies using positron-emission tomography (PET) have identified higher brain glucose metabolism of individuals with autism (Chugani, 2000).

Neuroanatomical Findings   Neuroimaging studies of the brains of individuals with autism have been inconsistent to date. Many different structures have been implicated in the different studies. Many investigators have found abnormalities in the temporal lobe and cerebellum, but these findings have not been replicated in all studies (Dawson et al., 2002). Interestingly, even when the *specific* brain areas differ, studies have converged on the finding that there are abnormalities in the various parts of the brain involved in social cognition. In particular, several neuroimaging studies have found that individuals with autism have an abnormally large *amygdala,* an area of the medial temporal lobe that is specialized for processing information about emotions (Schultz et al., 2000). Further, the extent of the abnormality in the amygdala is directly proportional to the degree of impairment in recognition of facial expressions and joint attention, two of the social cognitive functions that are most affected by autistic disorder (Sparks et al., 2002).

Much of the available evidence suggests that there is diffuse damage to widespread parts of the brain rather than one localized deficit (Johnson et al., 2002). One consistent finding is that individuals with autism have a larger cerebral volume or brain weight than those who are typically developing. Interestingly, this increased volume is not present at birth but is observed later on in development. The larger size is due to an excess of *white matter* in the brain (Filipek, 1999), which consists of connective tissue involved in the communication between areas of the brain. Normally, the connections proliferate early in development only to be pruned later, eliminating redundant or inefficient pathways and making for quicker and more efficient connections. Therefore, the deficits in autism may have less to do with any specific area of the brain and more to do with abnormalities in *pruning* and the development of connections between the parts of the brain.

Researchers have only begun to investigate whether there are differences in neuroanatomy that are specific to AD. So far findings are preliminary and only suggestive. One speculation has been that **brain lateralization**—the differentiation of function between the left and right hemispheres—differs between AD and autism. Schultz and colleagues (2000) note that there are two areas of functioning—motor skills and visuospatial abilities—that differentiate AD from autism. Because these are functions related to the right side of the brain, as are socioemotional processes and facial recognition, some in

the field have speculated that AD is related specifically to a right hemispheric dysfunction. However, autistic children, too, evidence right hemispheric deficits, just as children with AD evidence left hemispheric deficits (Ozonoff & Griffith, 2000), so the answer may not lie in brain lateralization alone.

As in those with autism, individuals with AD are found to have increased brain size associated with abnormal white cell growth. Neuroimaging also shows that those with AD typically have abnormalities in two other areas of the brain, the limbic-temporal lobe system (which includes the amygdala) and the frontal lobes (Schultz et al., 2000). In one of the rare neuroanatomical comparisons of autism and AD, Lincoln and colleagues (1998) found that individuals with AD had less pathology in the cerebellar region, a thinner posterior (at the back of the head) corpus callosum, and a larger anterior (at the front of the head) corpus collosum.

Clearly, more research is needed in the neuropsychology of autism. Future research will benefit from the newer imaging technologies that allow us to watch the brain in action, such as functional MRI and positron-emission tomography.

The Intrapersonal Context

What Is the Essential Deficit?

One of the conundrums in the study of autism has been arriving at a clear understanding of what the disorder essentially *is:* That is, what is the core deficit that underlies this extreme deviation from normal development? As we review studies that have examined developmental processes within the child—attachment, emotions, cognitive development, joint attention, theory of mind—consider how each of these reflects a different emphasis, even a different construal of the essential nature of autistic disorder.

Attachment

Because the lack of affectionate ties to caregivers is such a core feature of autism, it stands to reason that a fundamental disorder of attachment might lie at the heart of autistic disorder. Indeed, attachment took center stage in Kanner's (1943) original depiction of autism.

However, it is an exaggeration to say that children with autism are incapable of forming an attachment. Studies using Ainsworth's Strange Situation paradigm (see Chapter 2) show that 40 to 50 percent of children with autism were securely attached, which comes close to the 65 percent found in the typical population (Capps, Sigman, & Mundy, 1994). It may be that attachment-related behaviors, such as seeking proximity during times of stress, are so critical to the survival of the species that they have been programmed into the infant by evolution. Thus, they are preserved even in the most psychopathologically disturbed infants.

Nonetheless, there are qualitative differences between autistic and typically developing children in regard to attachment. Attachment-related behaviors are not accompanied by the same kind of emotional pleasure and reciprocity as they are in typically developing children. Behaviorally, attachment in children with autism is interspersed with characteristic repetitive motor movements such as hand flapping, rocking, and spinning. Their attachment-related behavior is also more variable over time than it is in other children (Dissanayake & Sigman, 2001).

Further, attachment involves more than behavior aimed at maintaining a secure base. It also involves an *internal working model,* or mental image, of the parent and of the parent-child relationship. This kind of complex mental image is probably not existent in young children with autism (Capps et al., 1994). Thus, while the child with autism may have a working model of mother as someone who is a source of security and fulfillment of concrete needs, it is doubtful that this child can evolve an image of the mother as a person in her own right, with her own unique thoughts, motives, desires, and personality.

Emotional Development

A number of deficits in the area of emotional development point toward this as a potential key to the mystery of autism.

Emotion Recognition   Children with autism, in contrast to typically developing children or those with mental retardation, have difficulty decoding the basic emotions as they are displayed on the human face (Baron-Cohen, Wheelwright, Spong, Scahill, & Lawson, 2001). They particularly have difficulty discriminating negative emotions, such as fear (Pelphrey, Sasson, Reznick, Paul, Goldman, & Piven, 2002). The problem is not with processing visual information—they are as adept as others at recognizing objects—but is specific to the human face. This is a significant deficit given that the recognition of emotions is essential to forming meaningful relationships with others, which is the ability that is most absent in autism.

Further, detailed studies of gaze patterns show that even individuals with autism who *can* discern emotional expressions do not look at faces in the same way that others do. Normally, when looking at a human face, people's gaze first focuses on the eyes of the other person. This is a good strategy, given the amount of social information that is presented in the facial expressions of the eyes—it is for good reason that they are known as the windows of the soul. Studying someone's affect can give us clues about their inner state, just as following someone's gaze can alert us to their intentions (Emery, 2000). Individuals with autism, however, spend as much time looking at others' chins as at their eyes (Pelphrey et al., 2002). (See Figure 5.2.) It is as if they do not perceive that any useful information is to be obtained from reading others' facial expressions. The lack of interest in faces appears to be peculiar to disorders in the autistic spectrum, in that it sets apart these children not only from typically developing children but also from those with mental retardation or other disorders of brain development.

Deficits in face perception may even be hardwired into the autistic brain. Dawson, Munson, and colleagues (2002) compared the eventual-related potential (ERP) responses to visual images of 4-year-old typically developing children, those with autistic spectrum disorders, and those with developmental delays. Both typically developing and developmentally delayed children showed different responses when viewing their mother's face versus that of a stranger, as well as when observing their favorite toy versus an unfamiliar one. Children with autism, in contrast, showed no difference in responding to

Figure 5.2   Facial Processing in Autism.

Sample Scanpaths from Phase II of the Experiment for Three Autistic Participants (First Column) and Three Control Participants (Second Column).

Participants were instructed to identify the emotion portrayed in each face.

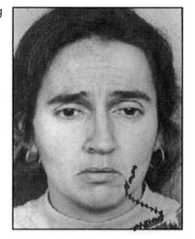

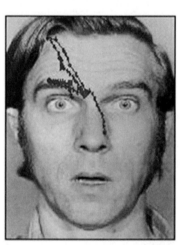
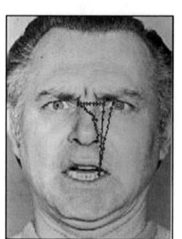

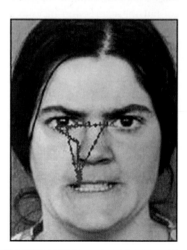

From Pelphrey et al., 2002.

their mother's face versus a stranger's face, but did respond differently when viewing their favorite toy versus an unfamiliar toy. Further, Schultz and colleague's (2000) functional MRI studies indicate that the part of the brain that is specialized for facial recognition in typically developing people is not so specialized in those with autism or Asperger's Syndrome. While most individuals use the fusiform gyrus when perceiving faces, those in the autistic spectrum show activity in the inferior temporal gyrus, the area of the brain usually used for the perception of objects.

Emotional Expression   While children with autism are less affectively communicative than other children, careful observation has shown that the stereotype of the autistic child as flat, wooden, and without emotional expression is incorrect. They giggle when happy, throw temper tantrums when angry, express delight when tickled or bounced, and in fact are capable of displaying quite intense emotions—frenetic glee, distress, frustration, fury, and panic. However, what differentiates them from typically developing children is that children with autism are more likely to show negative emotions and odd blends of affect (Kasari, Sigman, Baumgartner, & Stipek, 1993). Children with autism also are less likely to direct affect at a partner or to reciprocate it, such as by mirroring another's social smile. Therefore, what is missing is not emotion expression per se, but the expression of emotions that would be expected as part of a reciprocal interaction. For example, one study showed that children with and without autism alike displayed pleasure at learning a new task; however, the typically developing children displayed their pride in a way that was uncharacteristic of those with autism: Typical children turned around to check their observer's reaction (Kasari et al., 1993). In short, children with autism do not *share* emotions with others.

Joint Attention

Another feature of autism that has been proposed as the core of the disorder is a deficit in shared or *joint attention*. The typically developing 6- to 9-month-

old will look between an object and the caretaker, as if to say, "Look what I am looking at." This is called *referential looking*. Toward the end of the first year of life, the infant starts using *referential gestures*, such as pointing to an object when a caregiver is present or holding an object up for the caregiver to see. Rather than attending to the object alone, the infant now tries to attract the adult's attention so that the interest can be shared. Note that the goal is a social one, to share a feeling or interest, rather than merely an instrumental one, such as to meet a concrete need. The infant is not signaling in order to get an adult to do something the infant cannot do, such as bring a toy that is out of reach, but rather to share with the parent the infant's delight in the toy. When the adult responds with interest, the interaction is a highly rewarding one.

In children with autism, shared attention behaviors are deficient or even absent, as the home video studies reported earlier illustrated (Osterling et al., 2002). While children with autism may point to objects when they want them, or show that they need a toy mended, these *instrumental* gestures are not accompanied by the *expressive* gestures that communicate the desire that the parent join them in appreciating or recognizing the toy. Such deficits in shared attention are seen in all developmental periods. For example, Attwood, Frith, and Hermelin (1988) found that adolescents with autism were no different from normal and retarded children matched for mental age in regard to using or understanding instrumental or action-oriented gestures. However, they never used gestures expressing *feelings* concerning the self or others, such as hugging and kissing another child, putting an arm around another to console or as a sign of friendship, or putting the hand over the face to express embarrassment. Such social gestures, unlike instrumental ones, require knowledge of how another person feels along with an expression of one's own feelings and desires.

By the same token, when shared attention behavior occurs in children with autism, it is not accompanied by the sharing of positive affect as it is in typically developing children or those with Down syndrome (Roeyers, Van Oost, & Bothuyne, 1998). Thus, autism robs shared attention behaviors of the affective signals of smiling and laughter that play such an important role in reinforcing the social interplay.

Language Development

We have described a number of qualities that differentiate autistic speech from normative language development; for example, autistic speech tends to be echolalic, literal, and lacking in prosody. We also know that there is great variation, ranging from mutism to speech that is odd in content. We also know that language development is a defining distinction between autism, in which language development is delayed, and Asperger's Disorder, in which language skills are preserved.

Tager-Flusberg (2000) and her colleagues carried out a longitudinal study of language development in which they compared children with autism, children with Down syndrome, and typically developing children. As the toddlers were just learning to talk, the investigators found that syntax and grammar developed similarly across the three groups. While their results showed no deficits in the formal *structure* of language, there were significant differences in the way in which children with autism *used* language. Specifically, children with autism appear to talk *at* rather than *with* their listeners, seeming to lack the interest or need to share communication with others. They are prone to using bizarre idiosyncratic phrases and language that reflect their own private meaning and associations, to which they are not concerned about cluing in the listener. Children with autism also have difficulty differentiating between the information that is relevant or irrelevant for the listener and determining whether their meaning has been comprehended by others (Frith, 2003).

Even when children with high-functioning autism or AD have adequate language development, they have difficulty with *language pragmatics,* the social rules of communication that require understanding the point of view of the speaker (Landa, 2000). For example, typically we learn to mark a change in topic ("Well, anyway . . ." "Oh, speaking of that . . .") so that our listener is not confused. However, the subtleties in communication that assist others to understand our meaning are not available to individuals with autism or AD. They are likely to interpret

and respond in literal ways that make for awkward conversation, to miscommunicate and misinterpret the intended meaning of utterances, and to fail to provide the cues and references that will keep the listener oriented to the topic.

However, it is interesting to note that even among those children who never speak, there is evidence of written language development. For example, Frith (2003) describes a case of a young man who had been mute all his life but who quickly mastered the use of a computerized communicator. Many individuals in the autistic spectrum are able to read fluently even when they display delays in spoken language. However, their processing of the information they read is unusual. Typically developing children read for the gist, or meaning, of a sentence or passage, while children with autism focus on the individual words. Therefore, children with autism are unable to recognize when silly words or nonsense phrases have been inserted into a passage (e.g., "The hedgehog could smell the scent of the *electric* flowers" [Frith, 2003, p. 125]). Further, although they are better able than children with dyslexia to identify whether a sentence presented to them is exactly the same as the one in a passage they read, children with dyslexia surpass those with autism when told the gist of the story. Consequently, because children with autism focus on the words rather than the content, the underlying meaning of what they read escapes them.

Perspective-Taking   Many of the deficits seen in autistic language appear to reflect a deficit in *perspective-taking.* Language pragmatics are a prime example of the way in which good communication requires understanding the perspective of the listener. For another example, take the confusion of pronouns "you" and "me" in autism and the tendency to refer to the self in the third person. While this might seem to signify a deep confusion of personal identity, a lack of a sense of self, in fact, children with autism recognize their own names and identify others by name. The key to the riddle is that, while names are constant, pronouns change. The person called "I" by Charles is not the person referred to as "I" by Patricia. The use of pronouns is a matter of *perspective:* The correct pronoun depends on who is the speaker and who is the listener, and it is just this ability to shift perspective that is absent in autism.

Echolalia offers yet another example. While echoing another's speech is a highly socially awkward form of communication, it has a certain logic for the child focused only on his or her own perspective. The child with autism is essentially a behaviorist—his or her knowledge of others is acquired through observing cause and effect. When mother asks, "Do you want a cookie?" and one is given to the child, a logical conclusion is that those words are the magic spell for making another treat appear.

Cognitive Development

As we have seen, children with autism range widely in intelligence, with scores in the average to the severely mentally retarded range. One concern about these data is that IQ tests may not be sensitive to measuring nonstandard forms of intelligence, some of which may be intact in autism (Frith, 2003). In contrast, children with AD have average to superior cognitive abilities. However, a concern is that these data do not accurately reflect whether this intelligence is *functional*. For example, a savant with an extraordinary memory who is able to memorize and recite the bus schedules of every route in London may still have difficulty finding the way to the bus stop or negotiating a ticket purchase with the conductor.

Even when intelligence is intact, children in the autistic spectrum tend to show a particular *pattern* of scores that is consistent across different ability levels. Generally, children with autism score low on tests that assess their *social reasoning,* such as is assessed by the Comprehension subtest on the Wechsler Intelligence Scale for Children, which asks children questions such as what they should do if they find a lost wallet. In contrast, children with autism perform best on tasks that assess reasoning about *concrete* objects, such as on the Block Design subtest, which requires children to solve a visual puzzle (Frith, 2003).

An interesting cognitive difference between typical children and those in the autistic spectrum is in their use of *context* to solve a problem. Generally, people find it useful to place a problem in a real-world context: for example, to translate the arithmetic

equation $5 - 4$ into a word problem ("If you have 5 cents and spend 4 cents, how much will you have left?"). In contrast, individuals with autism do not benefit from contextual information. In fact, they perform better than their peers on tasks that require ignoring the context. An example of this is an embedded figures task, in which the image of a common form or object is embedded in a complex geometric display. (See Figure 5.3.) While typically developing children have trouble ignoring the context in order to pick out the object, children with autism do quite well at the task. These data, as Happé (1999) points out, show us that differences in autistic thinking do not necessarily represent deficits.

This characteristic of autistic thinking, of focusing on details and ignoring the big picture, is termed a *lack of central coherence* (Frith, 2003). While ordinarily humans strive to generalize across contexts, make associations, extract underlying meanings, and otherwise integrate the information they receive into a coherent whole, this propensity is lacking in the child with autism. It is as though the child is detached cognitively in the same way that he or she is detached socially.

Executive Functions   Children in the autistic spectrum also have difficulties in the area of *executive functions* involving planning, organization, self-monitoring, and cognitive flexibility. For example, one task assessing executive functions is the Wisconsin Card Sorting Test (WCST), in which the child first learns by feedback from the experimenter whether color, shape, or number is the "correct" criterion on the basis of which to sort 10 cards into piles. Then the experimenter changes the "correct" category without telling the child. The critical measure is how long the child persists in the incorrect sorting when it is no longer accurate. For example, after the child has learned that color is the "correct" way to sort the cards, the experimenter shifts to shape as the "correct" sort and records how many sorts it takes the child to make the shift. The WCST is regarded as a measure of set shifting or flexibility. Another executive functions task is the Tower of Hanoi, a measure of planning ability. This is a ring transfer task requiring children to plan a sequence of

Figure 5.3

Examples from the Children's
Embedded Figures Test.

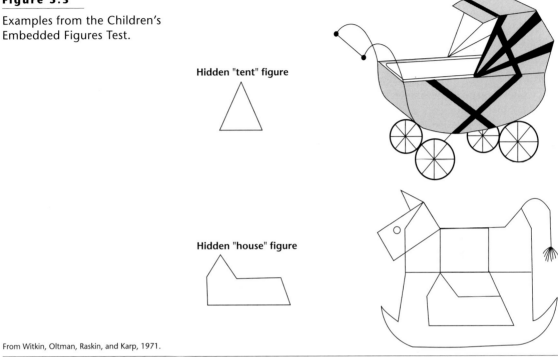

Hidden "tent" figure

Hidden "house" figure

From Witkin, Oltman, Raskin, and Karp, 1971.

moves transferring an initial configuration of rings on a peg into a tower of rings of decreasing size on another peg. When the rings are moved, larger ones cannot be placed on top of smaller ones. A third task, the Stroop Color-Word Test assesses inhibition by requiring the child to ignore the color in which a word is printed: for example, to read as "blue" the word "blue" that is colored in red ink.

At all ages and levels of severity, children with autism consistently show deficits in performing executive functions tasks assessing set-shifting and planning. Children with autism make more perseverative mistakes than do children with conduct disorder or attention-deficit hyperactivity disorder (ADHD), even though these two groups are also deficient in executive functions. Ozonoff et al. (1991) found that children with mental retardation and autism had more difficulty with the WCST and the Tower of Hanoi when compared to learning disabled children with the same IQ level. At a 3-year follow-up, the investigators found that learning disabled children's performance on the

executive functions tasks improved, whereas the children with autism did not change over the course of development (Ozonoff & MeEvoy, 1994).

While executive functions deficits also are seen in a number of other disorders, there are some qualitative differences that are specific to individuals in the autistic spectrum (Ozonoff & Griffith, 2000). For example, while individuals with autism show deficits in flexibility and planning, they do not evidence the difficulties in inhibition that are seen in children with ADHD. However, research to date has not been consistent, especially in identifying executive functions deficits in preschoolers with autism.

Theory of Mind

On the cover of her classic text on autism, Uta Frith (2003) reproduces a painting that depicts a scene in which, with gestures and significant glances, a group of card players convey to the observer that one of their members is cheating. In the text, Frith explains the many clues to the painting's meaning and what intuitive knowledge is required of the viewer to extract their meaning. However, not everyone is able to interpret this social information. A. C., a young woman with high-functioning autism, sent Frith an e-mail in which she commented on the cover of the book, stating, "I remember looking at the picture for something like an hour, figuring out how smooth the pigments of the paints the artist [used] had to be, and the quality of brushes . . . and of reproduction of the actual textures of the fabrics in the character's clothes, and of course this is the most obvious thing about the painting, the realism and the skill of the artist, and then I read inside the book, and I was like, What the . . . There's this whole 'soap opera' that the 'normal' person is supposed to pick [up] on first, and this person cheating, and that person knows, and that other person doesn't, etc. It's nuts!" (pp. 78–79).

In a similar vein, Sir Michael Rutter (1983) describes a young man with autism who "complained that he could not mind-read. Other people seemed to have a special sense by which they could read other people's thoughts and could anticipate their responses and feelings; he knew this because they managed to avoid upsetting people whereas he was always putting his foot in it, not realising that he was doing or saying the wrong thing until after the other person became angry or upset" (p. 526).

One of the most profound deficits in autistic spectrum disorders—and one that some experts believe underlies and integrates all the others we have described—is what Baron-Cohen (1995) has referred to as "mind-blindness": the lack of recognition of mental states in oneself and others. The formal name for this important human function is **theory of mind.** It is called a theory because, while we cannot feel, smell, or otherwise directly observe the minds of other people, we *believe* they have one. How do we prove our theory is correct—that other people have minds? Well, for one thing, we can play tricks on them.

For example, Baron-Cohen, Leslie, and Frith (1985) created the "Sally-Anne" scenario in which dolls act out the following sequence: Sally and Anne are in a room together; Sally puts a marble in a basket and leaves the room; Anne transfers the marble to a box; Sally returns. (See Figure 5.4.) The experimenter then asks the child the crucial question: "Where will Sally look for the marble?" The child must understand that Sally will act on her belief that the marble is in the basket even though the child knows it is no longer valid. A correct answer indicates that the child has distinguished what he or she knows from what the doll knows. This test of theory of mind is called a *false belief* task and requires the child to infer what another person knows and does not know and to predict his or her behavior accordingly. Significantly, while typically developing children *and* those with Down syndrome are able to perform the task correctly, children with autism can not, no matter how high their intelligence. Similar results are found with another task, the "Smarties" scenario, in which children are shown a candy box with a pencil inside and are asked to predict what another child would expect to find inside the box.

Since these classic experiments were conducted, more recent research has not been quite as clear-cut (Yirmiya et al., 1998). It appears that, later in development, many children with autism may be able to solve false belief tasks correctly. Happé (1995) found that the majority of typically developing children were able to pass false belief tests by age 5, as were learning disabled children by a mental age of 5. However, children with autistic spectrum disorders typically could not pass false belief tasks until age 10, if at all. This may suggest that, in autism, there is a 5-year developmental delay in the understanding of mental states in others. However, it is also possible that children arrive at the correct answer to these questions via two different routes. The first way, available to typically developing children, is an intuitive theory of mind. The second way, available to the bright autistic child, is to compensate for a lack of intuitive understanding by learning about mental states through observing and applying logic. (See Box 5.3.)

Happé (1994) supposed that the compensatory theory of mind—one that is acquired the hard way, so to speak—might be fragile and prone to error. To test this hypothesis, she constructed scenarios that required more sophisticated understanding of others' mental states than the Sally-Ann task. These included scenarios depicting sarcasm, white lies,

Figure 5.4   The Sally-Anne Experiment.

From Frith, 1989.

Box 5.3 | **Case Study: An Autobiographical Account of Autism**

Jim, a university student studying anthropology, was diagnosed with autism in his childhood but was only informed by his parents when he was 19 years old. He agreed to tell his story in a remarkable collection of autobiographies written by college students with autism and compiled by Dawn Prince-Hughes (2002), a university professor diagnosed with Asperger's Disorder.

Autism, for me, is just the way things are. It means I don't receive and process information in the same manner as other people, not that I am stupid. It means that I don't share the general neurotypical population's innate receptive and expressive communication skills; it doesn't mean I am unable to have feelings and emotions or am unable to share those emotions with others.

Let me give some examples here. As a child, I didn't understand the terms used to describe emotions. For the first seven years of my life, "happy" meant my blue toy truck. "Afraid" meant the Wizard of Oz poster on the

wall of my bedroom that I was unable to ask to have removed; "sad" meant rainy weather. I didn't generalize that the emotion I felt when I was playing with my blue truck was the same as when my father came home.

Sometime—before I had a sense of time—I learned to read. I read the cards I received for my birthday. When I was five and six years old I read the *Encyclopedia Brittanica* in hopes of understanding why I was not like everyone else. I read a lot of interesting facts, but found no explanation. When I was seven years old, on a visit to see a great-aunt, I discovered a collection of about fifty years of *National Geographic* in her basement. I spent most of the summer reading them. The articles described strange cultures and far-away lands in terms very similar to the way I thought about the world around me . . . I can remember thinking that the worlds they studied were as strange to them as the world around me was to me—so the same methodology should teach me about my world . . .

What was "weird"? Let me just say that at age 10 I had a list of several pages of areas of behavior where I differed substantially from the norms I had identified around me. And I had no idea why . . . I considered a lot of approaches to dealing with the differences . . . The first idea that came to mind was suicide. In retrospect, I can understand the discomfort people have when they consider that a ten-year-old boy actually did a cost/benefit analysis on suicide . . . One of the positive benefits of suicide was that I would no longer have to deal with a world I couldn't understand. It was outweighed by my curiosity about the world around me. The next possibility was to change myself to better fit into the society around me. Anyone who has ever dieted or tried to stop smoking has an idea how difficult it is to institute permanent changes in one's behavior—imagine changing literally everything about your behavior, when you don't understand any of it. I actually tried to do this for about a year.

pretense, and other forms of social communication that require inferring another's intentions, perceptions, or feelings. As predicted, individuals with autism struggled to comprehend these more advanced theory of mind tasks even when they were able to correctly respond to the Sally-Ann scenario.

Ozonoff and Miller (1995) investigated whether they could directly teach individuals with autism about theory of mind. They devised an intervention that, in addition to teaching specific social communication skills, directly instructed average-IQ adolescents with autism in the social cognitive skills

needed to understand mental states in others. For example, they taught perspective-taking by having participants walk a blindfolded leader through a maze, describing obstacles to be avoided along the way, and had children engage in role-plays modeled after the false belief tasks on theory of mind measures such as the Sally-Ann scenario. Following the intervention, participants performed better on laboratory tasks assessing theory of mind. However, no meaningful change was seen in their social competence as rated by parents and teachers. Therefore, while children with autism can be taught theory of

While I was busy trying to institute permanent changes in my behavior, I developed an interest in lithic technology—stone tools. Writers spoke of "tool kits"; . . . I began to consider adapting this to my needs. Such a "tool kit" would consist, for my purposes, of a package of cognitive skills and behaviors to meet the needs of a situation . . . This was a real breakthrough for me, but it was obvious that it would take me forever to gain the skills and understanding I would need. I realized this after my first attempt at developing a behavior module failed miserably. My first attempt was at developing a module that would allow me to participate in recess activities with my peers.

I was playing basketball with my classmates at noon recess. Someone shot the ball and missed. I moved for the rebound. I was focused on the ball in typical autistic fashion and injured one of the other players—I just ran him over. I didn't understand why the others were upset. By my understanding of "success" in this situation, I

succeeded—I had recovered the ball for my team. In study hall after lunch, I asked a classmate what I had done wrong. She said I should have apologized to the student I had injured. After a bit, she said, "You don't understand—you really don't understand, do you?" (This was the first time any of my classmates directly asked me about my differences.)

I told her what I was doing. She sat down and helped me develop what has evolved into the most successful of my behavior modules— ethics. Under this heading, we classified things that most would consider "manners." None of it made any sense to me, despite her attempts to explain, so we set some tentative rules and some default modes. If I'm unsure how to behave, I can follow those rules. I may seem strange, but I won't be breaking any of the formal rules of society. I tend to be very polite with strangers, that way I won't offend people. Regardless of responsibility, I apologize. (I do realize that many people find these habits annoying, but I

consider that better than to be seen as incredibly rude.) . . .

Emotionally, I get by. I realize that isn't very descriptive, but I am still working on correlating the vocabulary with the actual emotions. Most of the time I can pass as normal, when I am under stress people begin to notice I am not. If I am happy or excited, my body rocks and my voice changes but very few people know what this means. If I am really stressed I try to escape to someplace safe, usually home. I live alone so no one is bothered if I pace for 36 hours . . . As time goes on the times when I engage in self-injurious behavior grow farther and farther apart.

I realize my life is not what a lot of parents would want for their children, but it's a life. I have my studies, my work, and a few friends. I have a degree of satisfaction in life. It's important to remember that while my mind is different from the neurotypical population around me, it's my mind— and it's the only thing I know.

mind, just as they can be taught social skills, they may continue to lack an intuitive grasp of others' mental states and be unable to apply their acquired knowledge in a flexible and socially adept manner.

The implications of a lack of theory of mind are profound. It will affect children's social relationships and language development, given the lack of interest and motivation in sharing their experience with others. It will affect their emotional development, given the lack of understanding of the correspondence between inner states and affective expressions. It will affect their ability to communicate,

given their difficulty adjusting their perspective to that of the listener. In short, as we ourselves seek central coherence in our study of autism, we see that many of the core features of the disorder can be organized under the concept of theory of mind.

On the other hand, while her review of the research evidence suggests much merit to the theory of mind hypothesis of autism, Tager-Flusberg (2001) points out that there remain features of the disorder that are not well explained by the model. For example repetitive behaviors, stereotyped and limited interests, and superior visual spatial skills also are seen in

the disorder and are not clearly linked to the absence of theory of mind. Again, the complexity of autism defies simple explanations. Most likely, there are a series of deficits—perhaps linked to different genes—that combine to create the autistic phenotype.

Systematizing

A remarkable new theory about the essential deficit in autism has been proposed by Simon Baron-Cohen (2003). Baron-Cohen follows up on a suggestion that Asperger (1944) had made 60 years ago, in which he likened autistic intelligence to an extreme masculine turn of mind. Developing this theme, Baron-Cohen states that those with autism (who, he reminds us, are mostly male) are specifically lacking in just those characteristics that are associated with stereotypical femininity—empathy and sensitivity to relationships—and have strengths in those tasks that require skills associated with stereotypical masculinity—objectivity and systematic analysis. He calls this masculine form of intelligence *systematizing*. Systematizing requires a drive to understand the laws that govern cause and effect relationships, as well as detachment, attention to details, and deductive thinking. Baron-Cohen is careful to point out that, in the normative population, the differences between males and females are small and there is a large overlap in their distributions. However, he proposes, at the greatest extremes of the continuum we may see individuals who exemplify one characteristic to the exclusion of the other. Extreme systematizers he describes as follows:

> These are the people (mostly men) who may talk to others only at work, for the purposes of work alone, or talk only to obtain something they need, or to share factual information. They may reply to a question with the relevant facts only, and they may not ask a question in return because they do not naturally consider what others are thinking. These are the people who are unable to see the point of social chit chat . . . Why bother? And what on earth about? How? For these people it is both too hard and pointless . . . The object or system in front of them is all that is in their mind, and they do not stop for a moment to consider another person's knowledge of it. These are the people with the extreme male brain. (p. 133)

To illustrate his theory, Baron-Cohen points to the autistic preference for attending to things rather than relationships, particularly things that are orderly, predictable, and controllable. Individuals with autism are fascinated and even obsessed with mastering closed systems, such as understanding computers or collecting facts on obscure topics such as the pressure points of the human body or the mathematics of juggling. However, when they are required to deal with the unpredictable and less controllable social world, they are out of their element and may attempt to impose order through rigid insistence on sameness, the use of repetition and rituals, or, ultimately, temper tantrums.

As evidence for this *extreme male brain* theory of autism, Baron-Cohen cites evidence from studies assessing empathy and the reading of facial expressions, which show that on average females score higher than males, while individuals with high-functioning autism or AD score lower than the average male. A similar pattern of results is found for tasks assessing language pragmatics, theory of mind, and interpersonal sensitivity. By the same token, on tests assessing systematizing, such as one devised by Baron-Cohen (e.g., "When I look at an animal, I like to know the precise species it belongs to"; "When I cook, I think about exactly how different methods and ingredients contribute to the final product"), males on average score higher than females, while those with AD score higher than the average male.

This is a provocative proposal and one that is sure to generate much discussion and research.

Developmental Course

Initial Detection

As we noted previously, data on age of onset reveal a great deal of variability in the time when the symptoms are first detected. Interestingly, there are two different pathways to detection. (Here we follow Klinger et al., 2003.) In the majority of cases, there is a clear developmental *delay*. Symptoms appear in the child's 1st year of life, although parents may only retrospectively recognize them as signs of the disorder. The most common first symptoms to be noticed include the child's failure to look at others' faces, to share his or her interests by looking or gesturing, or

to engage in pretend play. The second route to detection involves *regression.* In 20 to 47 percent of cases, parents report that the child's development was initially on track until some point—generally 16 to 24 months of age—when the child suddenly loses previously attained developmental achievements. Most commonly, it is language development that is gained and then lost. It appears, however, that in at least half the cases, there were preexisting deficits that were simply not noticed by the parents.

As Zelazo (1991) notes, our knowledge of the developmental unfolding of autistic spectrum disorders is hindered by the fact that developmental psychologists have rarely identified the children during the critical first years of life.

Developmental Outcome

The developmental course of autistic spectrum disorders was investigated in a large-scale study conducted in Japan that followed 197 individuals with autism who were treated in childhood (Kobayashi, Murata, & Yoshinaga, 1992). When the individuals with autism reached adulthood, the investigators found that 27 percent were living independently (i.e., had employment) or were on their way to doing so (i.e., they were enrolled in a college or technical school). Approximately 47 percent had developed good language skills and were able to communicate verbally with others. However, 73 percent required close supervision and were not able to function on their own. Further, adolescence was a time of transition, for better or worse. While about half showed a deterioration of functioning in adolescence, almost half showed a marked improvement.

The developmental outcome for individuals with autism depends greatly on how many cognitive deficits are present and how much language development is affected. A lack of communicative speech by 5 years of age and an IQ below 70 are poor prognostic signs, as is the presence of a seizure disorder (Gillberg, 1991). Another major factor influencing outcome is whether early intervention was initiated. As we will see when we discuss treatment, there is hope for significant gains for children who receive intensive intervention in the first few years of life.

The prognosis for children with AD is generally more favorable, although again this depends on the degree of dysfunction. Even among high-functioning individuals with AD, only between 5 to 44 percent are employed and only 16 to 50 percent live independently (Howlin, 2000). In one study of 20 adolescents with AD, Green, Gilchrist, Burton, and Cox (2000) found that, according to parent report, only 50 percent performed daily self-care activities (e.g., washing, grooming, eating) independently, only 15 percent used the phone without assistance, and only 5 percent planned their activities without guidance and supervision. None had a social life outside the home and 90 percent had difficulty making friends.

Is Asperger's *Necessarily* a Disorder?

One of the implications of the idea of an autistic spectrum is that children may be placed at various places on the continuum—in other words, some might have "just a touch" of autism. This is most clearly seen in the case of high-functioning individuals with AD, who, despite their social oddities, may never be considered disabled in any significant way. Characteristics of AD might be subtly present in many individuals who are able to function in the mainstream at school, at work, and in the community.

For example, Baron-Cohen and his colleagues (2001) developed a screening tool for Asperger's Disorder, which they administered to four groups: 58 adults diagnosed with AD or high-functioning autism, 174 randomly selected adults from the community, 840 Cambridge University students, and 16 winners of the UK Mathematics Olympiad. They found that, overall, males scored higher than females and that students studying mathematics and the physical sciences scored higher than those studying humanities or social sciences. Award-winning mathematicians evidenced the most Asperger-like symptoms, replicating an earlier study that showed a tendency in individuals with AD to show an interest in and penchant for mathematics, physics, and engineering (Baron-Cohen et al., 1998).

One of the implications of the finding that AD may be found among university students and award-winning mathematicians is that AD need not be an impediment to very high achievement in life (Baron-Cohen, Wheelwright, Spong, Scahill, & Lawson, 2001). Many of those who study and treat individuals with AD are struck with the myriad strengths those with the disorder exhibit. Indeed, Baron-Cohen (2000) has argued that we should consider AD a "difference" rather than a "disability." For example, he argues, consider the child who prefers to remain in the classroom poring over the encyclopedia instead of playing outside with the other children at recess: Just because this child is doing something different, who are we to assume it is less legitimate or valuable?

Researchers in the field have used psychobiography to retrospectively diagnose a number of famous high achievers throughout history, including Isaac Newton and Albert Einstein (Baron-Cohen, 2003). More currently, we have the benefit of autobiographical accounts from such remarkable individuals as Temple Grandin (1996), who went on to earn a PhD in the study of animal behavior. Her specialization, designing facilities for livestock, is greatly assisted by her ability to visualize complex systems, a talent that she calls "thinking in pictures."

However, Frith (2003) counters that it is important not to paint too optimistic a picture. A lack of social awareness can affect a person's ability to function in many spheres. Many adults with AD never leave the family home and, if they work, end up in careers that are far below their intellectual ability (Tantam, 2000).

Integrative Developmental Model

Given the many different deficits associated with autistic spectrum disorders, and the many different tacks that researchers have taken in describing them, it can be no surprise that there is as yet no holistic integrative model to account for the development of autism. Klinger, Dawson, and Renner (2003) make the important point that affective development, social development, cognitive development, and language development are all intrinsically linked during early development. Impairment in one area is likely to have significant consequences for all the others. Therefore, it is impossible to discern whether any *specific* area of development is more centrally causal than the others.

Klinger and colleagues (2003) propose that a comprehensive theory must account for the links among biological abnormalities, information processing deficits, and the behavioral symptoms of autistic spectrum disorders. (See Figure 5.5.) To date, the available research has focused on some links in the model to the exclusion of others. For example, while MRI evidence of cerebellar abnormalities may be linked to slow attention orienting in individuals with autism, the link to social and behavioral impairments has not been made. By the same token, while other investigators have made links between the cognitive and behavioral features of the disorder, the underlying neuroanatomical mechanism has not been demonstrated. Thus, we still await the research that will support a comprehensive, integrative theory of the developmental psychopathology of autism.

Figure 5.5   Theoretical Links Among Genetic, Neuropsychological, Cognitive, and Behavioral Development in Autism.

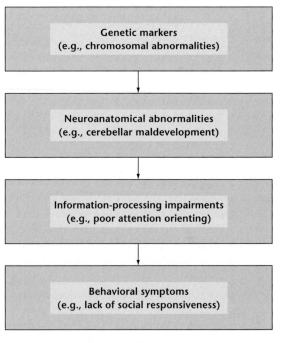

From Klinger, Dawson, and Renner, 2003.

Intervention

Interventions for children with autism come in two types. The first involves focal interventions designed to address specific deficits, such as social interaction or symbolic play skills, reports of which abound in the literature. The second type involves comprehensive programs designed to increase the child's general level of functioning in all areas, which have the greatest likelihood of making a significant difference in the life of a child with autism (Rogers, 1998).

All the programs have five particular features in common (Dawson & Osterling, 1997): (1) Treatment focuses on a broad range of autistic behaviors, including attention and compliance, motor imitation, communication, appropriate use of toys, and social skills; (2) in light of the difficulty children with autism have with generalization, specific strategies are needed for generalizing newly acquired skills to a wide range of situations; for example, skills learned with the therapist would be implemented by the parent at home and then by the teacher in school; (3) the teaching environment is highly structured with a low staff-to-student ratio. In addition, the daily schedule is highly predictable. This emphasis on structure and predictability is necessary because of the children's stormy affective reactions to novelty and change; (4) there is a high level of family involvement, with parents serving as therapists or cotherapists; (5) particular attention is paid to developing the skills needed to make the transition from the program to a regular preschool or kindergarten classroom.

Lovaas's Behavior Modification Program

Among the comprehensive programs, Lovaas and his colleagues (see Lovaas and Smith, 2003) pioneered the use of intensive behavior modification in the treatment of autism. Treatment in the Lovaas model is both intensive and extensive. Children enter the program in the preschool years and remain for 2 years or longer, receiving 40 hours a week of intensive behavioral therapy. Initially, treatment takes place mostly in the home, with parents trained to use operant conditioning to reinforce children for demonstrating appropriate social, cognitive, and language skills. Later in treatment, the investigators strive for generalization by shifting the treatment into community and typical preschool settings.

In order to empirically demonstrate the effectiveness of their treatment, Lovaas and colleagues (McEachlin, Smith, & Lovaas, 1993) compared the outcomes achieved by 19 treated children to those in two control groups. The first control group consisted of children who were eligible for services in the clinic but for whom there were no available therapists; consequently, these children received a minimal exposure to the treatment, consisting of less than 10 hours per week of individual therapy and community services. The second control group consisted of children who received interventions solely from the community. All children were matched on chronological and mental age, and their autism diagnoses were confirmed by independent clinicians. The treatment was manualized and close supervision was provided to the university students who directly implemented it in order to assure treatment fidelity. At the end of 2 years, 47 percent of the treated group were functioning well in a regular school setting, with no need for special services, in contrast to 2 percent of children in the control groups. Further, intelligence tests revealed a whopping 30-point difference in IQ between the treated and control groups. Only 10 percent of the treated children had IQs in the mentally retarded range, whereas 53 percent of children in the control groups had IQs in the mentally retarded range.

At a follow-up conducted when the children were in adolescence, the investigators found that 47 percent of the treated children were performing well in regular schools, while this was true of none of the control children. The 30-point IQ difference remained stable and similar gains emerged for the treated group on measures of adaptive behavior. Overall, the children who benefited most from the intervention were those whose mental ages were higher before the treatment began. While a number of independent replications of Lovaas's treatment have been published, they are plagued by methodological limitations and, in many cases, have failed to obtain results quite as dramatic or long lasting as those reported by Lovaas and his colleagues (Rogers, 1998).

TEACCH

Another well-respected comprehensive treatment program is TEACCH (Treatment and Education of Autistic and Related Communication Handicapped CHildren), which was developed 30 years ago at the University of North Carolina at Chapel Hill for the treatment of children at all points along the autistic continuum. The core element of TEACCH's approach is called Structured Teaching (Mesibov, Shea, & Adams, 2001). In recognition of the significant deficits that children in the autistic spectrum demonstrate, the TEACCH program highly structures the child's environment in order to build on strengths and minimize deficits. For example, because of their receptive verbal communication problems, children with autism and AD are presented with visual information whenever possible (e.g., chores may be presented as pictures, or as a written list; choices of strategies for self-calming may be written on a cue card). Another structuring technique used is the "social story," in which a series of brief, written sentences is developed to explain situations that are puzzling or upsetting to the child. Examples include "Why we put on different clothes each day," "What happens at a birthday party," "Why we sometimes have substitute teachers." Structuring of the environment also helps individuals with autism to cope with their hypersensitivity to sensory stimulation, and reduces the emotional distress and tantrums that arise out of cognitive confusion and anxiety. Further, TEACCH's interventions are developmentally sensitive, focusing on stage-salient issues such as social skills in the school-age years and vocational issues in late adolescence.

Although the TEACCH program has not yet published empirical data from its preschool intervention research, clinicians who have used aspects of the TEACCH curriculum have reported good results in well-controlled studies. For example, Ozonoff and Cathcart (1998) added a daily TEACCH home-teaching session to their intervention for preschoolers with autism and found significant gains in comparison to a group of control children.

Comparing the Programs

While having a number of features in common, Lovaas's program and TEACCH use different techniques. For illustration, we describe here two contrasting methods of remedying the language deficiencies in autism, both of which have an impressive record of success.

Lovaas (1977) employs an operant conditioning model that relies heavily on imitation and reinforcement. For example, the therapist models and reinforces words and phrases until the child gradually acquires a repertoire of language. The meaningful use of language is accomplished by two techniques. In *expressive discrimination* the child is reinforced for making a verbal response to an object, such as correctly labeling a cup when it is presented. In *receptive discrimination* the stimulus is verbal and the response nonverbal, such as correctly responding to "Give me a cup." Sequences are carefully graded so that new ones are based on mastered material.

By contrast, TEACCH's interventions are based on principles of normal language acquisition and development. The motivational aspect of teaching is handled by making language relevant to the children's own interests and showing them that words are powerful means for getting people to act in a desired way. For example, "ride" is taught as a means of obtaining a favored bicycle, *not* as a rewarded label to a picture, as it would be in the Lovaas program. Comprehension is aided by teachers' simplifying their language and supplementing it with gestures. Finally, as is done with normal children, language is integrated into ongoing activities and is supported by as many contextual cues as possible rather than being taught as an isolated skill.

While this concludes our discussion of autism, we are not ready to conclude discussion of the infancy period as yet. A considerable body of research deals with attachment disturbances as a risk factor for psychopathology. We need to examine this research before going on to disorders of the toddler and preschool periods.

Infancy Through Preschool: Insecure Attachment, Oppositional-Defiant Disorder, and Enuresis

As noted in the previous chapter, we have more to explore concerning the infancy period in order to do justice to the literature on **insecure attachment,** a topic that has generated an impressive body of research. While there is one attachment disorder listed in DSM-IV-TR, we will also consider the ways in which insecure attachment alone is a risk factor for other disorders.

Later in the chapter we will turn to the toddler period, first presenting an overview of normal developments that will be germane to understanding the psychopathologies that follow—namely, **oppositional-defiant disorder** and **enuresis.**

Attachment Disorders

In Chapter 2, we described the development of normal attachment and reviewed the ways in which secure attachment provides a basis for healthy cognitive, emotional, social, and self-development. Attachment is such an important evolutionary adaptation that, as we saw in Chapter 5, it is seen even in some of the children who are most psychopathologically disturbed, albeit in distorted forms. Therefore, while many troubled children may show signs of *insecure* attachment, *absence* of attachment is very rare. The first disorder we review in this chapter indicates just such an

Table 6.1

DSM-IV-TR Criteria for Reactive Attachment Disorder of Infancy or Early Childhood

A. Markedly disturbed and developmentally inappropriate social relatedness in most contexts, beginning before age 5 years, as evidenced by either:
   (1) Persistent failure to initiate or respond in a developmentally appropriate fashion to most social interactions, as manifest by excessively inhibited, hypervigilant, or highly ambivalent and contradictory responses (e.g., the child may respond to caregivers with a mixture of approach, avoidance, and resistance to comforting, or may exhibit frozen watchfulness)
   (2) Diffuse attachments as manifest by indiscriminate sociability with marked inability to exhibit appropriate selective attachments (e.g., excessive familiarly with relative strangers or lack of selectivity in choice of attachment figures)
B. The disturbance is not accounted for solely by developmental delay (as in Mental Retardation) and does not meet criteria for a Pervasive Developmental Disorder
C. Pathogenic care as evidence by at least one of the following:
   (1) Persistent disregard of the child's basic emotional needs for comfort, stimulation, and affection
   (2) Persistent disregard of the child's basic physical needs
   (3) Repeated changes of primary caregiver that prevent formation of stable attachments (e.g., frequent changes in foster care)
D. There is the presumption that the care in Criterion C is responsible for the disturbed behavior in Criterion A.

Specify Type:
Inhibited Type: if Criterion A1 predominates in the clinical presentation
Disinhibited Type: if Criterion A2 predominates in the clinical presentation

extreme disruption in the formation of attachment relationships that develops in reaction to a pathological environment.

Reactive Attachment Disorder

Reactive attachment disorder is diagnosed when, before the age of 5, the child shows a markedly disturbed and developmentally inappropriate pattern of social relatedness. (See Table 6.1.) The child's disturbed relatedness may take two forms: (1) the *inhibited type,* in which the child persistently fails to initiate and respond to social interactions; and (2) the *disinhibited type,* in which the child is indiscriminately sociable and is not selective in the choice of attachment figures. The key to the diagnosis is that the relational problems are the result of severely inadequate caregiving; hence, the disorder is a *reaction* to a pathological emotional environment. Pathogenic care is evidenced either by significant emotional neglect of the child or by repeated changes of caregivers, either of which interferes with the child's ability to form a secure, deep, and abiding attachment relationship.

Prevalence and Characteristics

The diagnosis of reactive attachment disorder is rarely given, due to the extremely pathological care associated with it, which happily is rare. Children with reactive attachment disorder often first come to the attention of their pediatrician because of *failure to thrive,* a term that describes an infant or child who is failing to develop physically. The differential diagnosis is made when physical causes for the child's growth deficiency are ruled out and observations of parenting behavior reveal disregard for the child's basic physical and/or emotional needs. However, historically the one caregiving environment that significantly increases the risk of reactive attachment disorder is the cold, impersonal institution that we will describe later.

Gender, Race, and Social Status

Because the disorder is so rare, no information has been gathered about ethnic, gender, or cultural differences in its prevalence or manifestations.

Course

Again, due to its rarity and the lack of research attention given to it, there are no data on the developmental course of reactive attachment disorder. However, interesting case studies can be found in Robertson and Robertson, 1971, 1989.

Etiology

In contrast to other disorders, the DSM makes an explicit statement about the origins of reactive attachment disorder. The definition specifies that the disorder is caused by pathogenic care; therefore, the culprit clearly is in the interpersonal context.

Institutionalized Children

The concept of reactive attachment disorder emerged from studies of the effects of maternal deprivation on children raised in institutions. For example, in the 1940s, Rene Spitz began studying infants separated from their parents and raised in what were then termed foundling homes. In one such orphanage in Mexico Spitz discovered that 37 percent of the infants died within a few weeks of admission. These children were given proper nutrition and were fed and bathed and clothed—there was no physical reason for them to fail to thrive. Spitz made careful observations of these children and described a clinical picture characterized by loss of interest in their environment, poor weight gain, rocking and stereotypic behavior, and extreme listlessness. He made a film of his observations, heartrending to watch, which is entitled simply *Grief.* Spitz termed this disorder in children *anaclitic depression,* a term that refers to the loss of that on which one depends—for the young child, this traumatic loss was the loss of loving care (Spitz, 1946). Spitz argued that, if children do not receive human affection, despite adequate food and shelter, they literally wither away and die.

Further evidence for the importance of attachment came after the Second World War, when there was a great problem with orphaned and homeless children throughout the world. In the 1950s John Bowlby worked on a World Health Organization report on the mental health of these orphans. His report made a resounding impact on the world community. He argued that in the first 3 years of life even the most clean, well-run institution would increase the risk for physical and mental illness and could possibly damage children irreparably. His

classic work is the three-volume series entitled *Attachment, Separation,* and *Loss.*

Bowlby (1982) identified three stages of grief and mourning in young children undergoing separation. The first was *protest,* as the child vigorously attempts to elicit a response from a caregiver with tears and cries. The second stage, *despair,* was characterized by sadness and grief and appeared to be akin to mourning in adults. The third stage, *detachment,* is evidenced by a kind of learned helplessness as the child becomes passive and unresponsive even to adults who attempt to engage the infant.

More recently, studies of children raised in large, impersonal, depriving institutions in Romania have confirmed the relationship between lack of affectionate care and developmental psychopathology (O'Connor et al., 2003). While, generally, children recover when placed in a more nurturing environment, previously institutionalized children often continue to show odd social behavior as long as 3 years after adoption into a normal family. As many as two-thirds develop insecure attachments with their caregivers (Zeanah, Boris, & Lieberman, 2000). A particular behavior problem that persists is *indiscriminate friendliness,* a component of the disinhibited type of reactive attachment disorder described earlier. For example, in a longitudinal study of children adopted from Romania into Canadian families, investigators found indiscriminately friendly behavior was evident both 11 months and 39 months postadoption (Chisholm, Carter, Ames, & Morison, 1995). Although indiscriminate friendliness was related to insecure attachment at the first assessment, this problematic style of social interaction did not decrease even as attachments became more secure over the 2-year period.

Fortunately, the kind of complete loss of a nurturing relationship that institutionalization represents is a relatively rare occurrence. Instead, the bridge from attachment to psychopathology most often takes the form of *variations* in the quality of relationships between parents and children. The DSM-IV classification refers to an extremely impaired subgroup of infants whose insecure attachments are due to neglect or frequent changes in caregiving. However, as we will see next, most insecure attachments are not so extreme in their manifestations nor are they a product of such deviant caregiving (Zeanah, 1996).

Insecure Attachment and Psychopathology

As we explored in Chapter 2, a secure attachment provides children with a sense of comfort, self-worth, and self-reliance. Securely attached children are emotionally expressive and responsive to others, are flexible and resourceful in response to challenges, and are able to cope with distressing emotions. In contrast, avoidantly attached children display brittle independence and affective overcontrol while resistantly attached children are dependent, fearful, and angry. Another piece of evidence confirming the relationship between attachment and psychopathology is that insecurely attached children are more prevalent in clinical populations. While cross-culturally about 40 percent of children in normative samples are classified as insecure, as many as 70 to 80 percent of children seen in mental health centers are insecurely attached (van IJzendoorn, 1995).

In summary, although insecure attachment is not in itself a form of psychopathology, it can be considered to be a risk mechanism for psychological disturbance. Next, we consider whether there is evidence that attachment patterns are related to specific psychopathologies.

Limitations to Continuity

First, we need to make some comments on the methods we use to investigate the relationship between attachment and the development of specific disorders. One of the factors that complicates the attachment-disorder link is that attachments themselves are not always stable across development. One longitudinal study, for example, found that only half the infants maintained the same classification by 4 years of age (Goldberg, 1997). Therefore, whether an avoidant attachment in infancy predicts school-age anxiety depends on whether the child's attachment pattern is continuous across that developmental period. This is the *continuity-discontinuity* distinction we introduced in Chapter 1. What the research evidence suggests is that, when the family environment is stable, so is attachment. But when the family environment changes, for better or worse, so may the quality of the child's attachment. (See Chapter 2.)

Further, and in keeping with the multi-determined, transactional developmental psychopathology model, it is unlikely that one variable alone—even one so significant as attachment—can predict the complex etiology of a disorder. Radke-Yarrow and coworkers' (1995) research nicely illustrates this point. First, they found that insecure attachment at 1.5 and 3.5 years of age *alone* was not directly related to disturbance when the children were 6 and 9 years of age; however, it was related *in interaction* with other variables—in this case, the mothers' depression. Further, styles of attachment could serve either as risk or protective factors depending on how they interacted with other variables. Interestingly, secure attachment in the context of severe maternal depression predicted the child's developing a depressive disorder; *insecure* attachment to a depressed mother was associated with an *absence* of child anxiety at 6 years of age. Thus, while, in general, security and insecurity can be regarded as protective and risk factors, respectively, under special circumstances their roles may be reversed.

Cross-Cultural Differences

Cross-cultural differences also might come into play. As we reviewed in Chapter 2, although the central tenets of attachment theory appear to hold up well across diverse cultures, the proportions of securely attached children do vary. In addition, there is as yet little research to confirm that the implications of insecure attachment are consistent across these different cultures. For example, while almost half of the children in samples taken in certain countries are judged to be insecurely attached (van IJzendoorn & Sagi, 1999), we did not yet have evidence that their rates of psychopathology are higher (Rosen & Rothbaum, 2003). Behavior that is considered maladaptive and indicative of insecure attachment in a U.S. sample may be adaptive in another cultural context.

Empirical Evidence

Evidence concerning the relation between insecure attachment and subsequent disorders is beginning to emerge from a series of longitudinal studies. Table 6.2 summarizes the findings on the relationship between attachment types and psychopathology.

Table 6.2

Developmental Findings Regarding Attachment and Psychopathology

	Secure	Avoidant	Resistant	Disorganized
Infancy				
With caregiver	Uses caregiver as secure base from which to explore	Precociously independent	Clingy, inhibited exploration	Inconsistent
During separation	If distressed, protests	Minimal reaction	Highly distressed	Odd behaviors
Upon reunion	Seeks contact, easily soothed	Avoids proximity	Hard to soothe, seeks and rejects proximity	Distorted attempts at proximity seeking
Caregiver behavior	Responsive, nonintrusive	Unresponsive, rejecting	Inconsistent	Coercive, frightening behavior, mixed signals
Preschool	Competent with peers	Unempathic and negative with peers	Passive, immature, easily victimized by peers	Aggressive, oppositional
School-age	Socially skilled, self-confident, harmonious friendships	Interpersonally insensitive, more likely to be alone	Dependent on teachers, negative biases toward peers	Externalizing problems
Adolescence	Sociable, insightful, ego resilient	Hostile toward peers, low in social support	Anxious, distressed, poor self-concept	Personality disorganization, dissociation
Adulthood	Autonomous	Dismissing	Preoccupied	Unresolved

Resistant Attachment   One study confirming a relation between infant attachment and subsequent psychopathology was conducted by Warren and colleagues (1997). They hypothesized that resistant attachment in infancy would predict subsequent *anxiety disorders* since inconsistent caregiving would result in a chronic concern about whether needs would be met. In addition, this anxiety would be more overtly displayed by resistant children than it would be by those with an avoidant attachment. The data confirmed the hypothesis. Resistant attachment at 12 months of age was significantly related to anxiety disorders at 17.5 years of age. Moreover, the relation was a specific one. Resistant attachment predicted anxiety disorders in particular rather than a variety of other disturbances while, on the other hand, avoidant attachment did *not* predict later anxiety problems.

Avoidant Attachment   In a longitudinal study of infants medically at risk, Goldberg (1997) found that there was a significant relation between avoidant

attachment in infancy and subsequent *internalizing and externalizing* problems at age 4 years of age. In contrast, in this study other forms of insecure attachment were not predictive of psychopathology.

Disorganized Attachment   Research on disorganized attachment yields mixed results, perhaps because this is the newest and least well-studied classification. While Goldberg (1997) did not find disorganized attachment to represent a special risk for future disturbance, Lyons-Ruth and colleagues (1993) found that disorganized attachment in infancy predicted *aggressive behavior* in kindergarten. The relationship was especially strong when the mother evidenced psychiatric problems such as depression, which increased her hostility and intrusiveness with the child. Further, another longitudinal study found that disorganized attachment in infancy predicted clinical levels of *externalizing* behavior problems in elementary school (Lyons-Ruth, Easterbrooks, & Cibelli, 1997).

Shaw and coworkers' (1996) longitudinal study also found that disorganized/disoriented attachment in infants differentially predicted *aggression* at 5 years of age. However, this risk was not sufficient in itself but had to be potentiated by the mother's perception of the child as being difficult to cope with. In fact, disorganized/disoriented attachment, childrearing disagreements between parents, maternal personality (aggression, depression, and suspiciousness), and child aggression at 3 years of age were *equally* predictive of aggression at 5 years of age.

Finally, studies of adolescents with disorganized attachment patterns show that they are vulnerable to severe forms of psychopathology involving *personality disorganization* and *dissociation*. These effects also were linked to a history of traumatic abuse in the home (Ogawa, Sroufe, Weinfield, Carlson, & Egeland, 1997).

Given the pervasive and wide-ranging effects of attachment, we will return to the relation between insecure attachment and specific psychopathologies many times in subsequent chapters.

Intergenerational Transmission of Insecure Attachment

In Chapter 2, we described the different behaviors exhibited by parents of securely and insecurely attached infants. Interest in understanding what accounts for these different parenting styles has led to a body of research on the parents' own internal working models of relationships. The method used is an interview that asks parents to reflect on their own childhood attachment experiences. The Adult Attachment Interview classifies mothers into four types that parallel the child attachment categories (see Table 6.2): autonomous, preoccupied, dismissing, and unresolved (Main & Goldwyn, 1988). Prospective studies conducted before the birth of the child show that mothers' internal working models of attachment predict their 1-year-old children's attachment security with uncanny accuracy. A meta-analysis of 18 separate studies found a 75 percent correspondence rate between mother and child security/insecurity. Further, across studies, mothers with insecure attachments are highly prevalent among

those whose children develop psychopathology: Among mothers of children being treated for psychiatric disorders, only 14 percent had secure internal working models (van IJzendoorn, 1995).

Continuity in attachment patterns has been observed even into the third generation. One study interviewed pregnant women and their mothers and then later observed the new mothers with their infants in the Strange Situation. The investigators found that, in 64 percent of the families, mothers, grandmothers, and children were classified into the same attachment pattern (Benoit & Parker, 1994). However, the results are qualified by the fact that most of the individuals in this well-functioning, middle-class sample were securely attached; dismissing or preoccupied mothers often had children with a different attachment pattern than theirs.

Proposed Disorders of Insecure Attachment

Research indeed suggests that, over time, insecure attachment is a significant risk factor for psychopathology. However, most of this work is not reflected in the DSM-IV-TR. Charles Zeanah and his colleagues (1996, 2000) argue that the DSM diagnosis of reactive attachment disorder describes only the extreme end of a clinically significant continuum. These authors characterize the current diagnostic systems as "oddly detached" from the extensive research literature on insecure attachment and developmental psychopathology. Therefore, based on their observations and clinical work with disturbed children, they propose an alterative classification of attachment disturbances that integrates the DSM-IV and ICD classifications with the research evidence. The disorders are of three general types: nonattachment, distortions, and disruptions.

Disorders of Nonattachment

In keeping with the DSM and ICD, Zeanah and colleagues propose two disorders in which there is an absence of a preferred attachment figure: (1) *Nonattachment,* evidenced by emotionally withdrawn and inhibited behavior toward the caregiver; and (2) *Indiscriminate Sociability,* in which the child seeks comfort and affection from strangers, without demonstrating developmentally appropriate discrimination of the attachment figure from others. Children who display these patterns are likely to have serious problems with self-regulation and self-protection.

Secure Base Distortions

What distinguishes the disorders in this category is that the child has a preferred attachment figure, but the relationship is severely disturbed. Moreover, these disturbances are specific to a *particular* relationship, in keeping with research evidence that children form different kinds of relationships with different caregivers.

Attachment Disorder with Self-Endangerment The child boldly and uninhibitedly explores the environment without seeking proximity or reassurance from the safe haven of the attachment figure. The child may engage in dangerous or provocative behavior such as running into traffic, running away in crowded places, or climbing on ledges. The child may also engage in aggression that is directed toward self or the caregiver, particularly in the context of comfort-seeking.

Attachment Disorder with Clinging/Inhibition At the opposite extreme, the child does not venture away from the attachment figure in order to explore the environment in an age-appropriate fashion, instead clinging and showing extreme dependence. Just like aggression in the first child, the inhibition in this child is seen only in relation to the caregiver. There may be no such anxiety or inhibited behavior in other contexts, such as when the child is with another familiar trusted adult.

Attachment Disorder with Vigilance/Hypercompliance Like the aforementioned child, this child is inhibited from exploring the environment while in the caregiver's presence. However, rather than clinging, this child appears emotionally constricted, hyperattentive, and overly compliant with the caregiver, seeming to fear the caregiver's displeasure. All spontaneity is gone from the child's be-

havior. This is similar to the pattern of "compulsive compliance" observed in children of harsh, intrusive parents (Crittenden, 1988).

Attachment Disorder with Role Reversal In this pattern the child, rather than seeking emotional support, nurturance, and caregiving, provides it to the parent. Consequently, the child bears a developmentally inappropriate burden of responsibility for the caregivers' well-being and is deprived of having his or her own emotional needs met (Zeanah & Klitzke, 1991).

Disrupted Attachment Disorder

This category is reserved for cases in which the child experiences the sudden loss of the attachment figure. Following from Bowlby, the child evidences the reaction sequence of protest, despair, and detachment. Although not well studied due to its rarity, case reports paint a compelling picture of the distress exhibited by children who lose their attachment figures through death, illness, or foster care placement (Gaensbauer, Chatoor, Drell, Siegel, & Zeanah, 1995; Robertson & Robertson, 1971). (See Box 6.1.)

Because these categories are still in the proposal stage, we do not yet have evidence for their reliability, validity, or clinical utility. As Zeanah and colleagues (2000) note, more research is needed to clarify how different types of relational disturbances relate to psychopathology.

Intervention

Parent-Child Therapies

A characteristic of attachment interventions is that it is neither the child nor the parent but their *relationship* that is the "identified patient" (Lieberman, 1992). Examples of this approach include the Steps Toward Effective and Enjoyable Parenting (STEEP) program developed by Egeland and colleagues (2000) and the Infant-Parent Program developed by Lieberman and Pawl (1993). The majority of the families in these programs are considered high risk, due to socioeconomic disadvantage, cultural uprooting, mental illness, and/or substance abuse. Many times the mothers have a history of being abused as children. The focus of the intervention is on changing the parent's internal

Box 6.1 | **Case Study in Attachment Disorder: John at 17 Months**

In the 1950s it was not thought unusual to place a child in an institution when the mother went into hospital to give birth to a sibling. While this may have been accepted practice, two colleagues of John Bowlby, James and Joyce Robertson, thought differently. They requested permission to observe a group of five children who were placed either with foster families or in a residential nursery (i.e., an orphanage). One child in the latter group was John, who at 17 months was a bright and happy child with an easy temperament. He slept and ate well and was developing normally in all spheres. His father was a young professional man at a crucial point in his training, and it was considered impractical for him to care for John on his own. So, on their family doctor's advice, the parents dropped John off at the nursery the night his mother went into labor.

On the first day, John woke in a strange setting, surrounded by the clamor of other children. When a nurse approached him with a smile, he responded in a friendly way and interacted as she dressed him. At breakfast a different nurse fed him and he was friendly to her as well as to the two others who cared for him in the course of the day. When his father came to visit, he was slow to respond but finally blossomed into a smile of recognition.

While John continued to cope well on the 2nd day, by the 3rd day he was visibly distressed. He cried little, but sat forlornly at the end of the room or played with his back to the group. He made tentative approaches to the various nurses but was often overlooked in the noisy bustle. By the 4th day, he had ceased to eat and drink and was listless, with lengthy spells of sad crying. On the 5th day, the nurses noticed his constant misery but were not able to comfort or distract him. He continued to refuse to eat and cried in quiet despair, sometimes rolling about and wringing his hands. He made fewer attempts to get close to the nurses and lay on the floor, burrowed under a giant teddy bear. While Nurse Mary tried to make herself more consistently available to him, she came and went with the duty roster and not according to John's need of her.

On the 6th day, John was miserable and inactive. He cried a great deal. When his father came to visit, John pinched and smacked him. Then his face lightened and he went to the door, gesturing his wish to go home. He fetched his outdoor shoes and when his father humored him by putting them on, John broke into a little smile. But when his father did not move, John returned to the nurse and gave his father an anguished expression. He then turned away from the nurse and sat forlornly in a corner.

working model of relationship through changing her relationship with her child.

Components of the intervention include weekly home-based visits in which the therapist provides the parent with gentle guidance and information about normal development, as well as fostering a trusting and close relationship in which the parent is encouraged to reflect on her own childhood experiences and how they influence her interactions with the child. The therapist also helps the mother to become a more developmentally sensitive and empathic observer of the child, expanding the parents' understanding of attachment-related behavior, separation anxiety, and the centrality of the parent-child relationship in the infant's world. (We will take a closer look at this intervention in Chapter 17.)

A review of attachment-based interventions found that, while they were effective overall, the best results were obtained for studies that focused on increasing *parental sensitivity* toward the child (van IJzendoorn, Juffer, & Duyvesteyn, 1995). Further, although change in the parent's behavior was seen, this was not always accompanied by a change in her internal working model. (See also Bakermans-Kranenburg, IJzendoorn, and Juffer, 2003.)

Child Therapies

Sometimes the focus of intervention is on the individual child, especially in the case of children in foster care or group homes whose connections to attachment figures may have been severed. Unstructured *play therapy* may be used to provide the child

On the 7th day, John cried weakly but continually all day long. He did not play, did not eat, and did not respond for more than a few seconds to the attempts of the nurses to cheer him. His expression was dull and blank and he stumbled when he walked. Toward the end of the day, he would walk toward an adult, then either turn away to cry in a corner or fall on his face on the floor in a gesture of despair. On the 8th day, John was even more miserable. For long periods he lay in apathetic silence on the floor. When his father tried to feed him, John was so distraught that he could neither eat nor drink.

On the 9th day John cried from the moment he awoke. He was slumped motionless on a nurse's lap when his mother came to take him home. His response was immediate and dramatic. He threw himself about, crying loudly, and, after stealing a glance at his mother, looked away from her. Several times he looked and then turned away with loud cries and a distraught expression. After a few minutes, his mother took him in her arms, but John continued to struggle and scream, arching his back away from his mother. Eventually, he got down and ran crying to Joyce Robertson, who calmed him down and passed him back to his mother. John then cuddled into his mother, clutching his blanket but not looking at her. When the father entered the room, John struggled away from his mother and into his father's arms. His crying stopped and for the first time he looked at his mother directly. It was a long hard look. His mother said, "He has never looked at me like that before."

After returning home (and remember that home now included a new sibling who shared his mother's attention), he had more frequent temper tantrums, went through periods of refusing food, slept badly, and was more clingy. Seven weeks after he returned home, Joyce Robertson visited and John reacted strongly to her presence—he began refusing food, rejecting his parents' attention, and aggressing against his mother, an episode that lasted for 5 days. Even 3 years later, when John was 4½, his parents worried that they could see some long-lasting effects of the separation. Although he was generally a happy and competent child, he was very fearful of losing his mother and became extremely upset any time she was out of sight. Also, every few months he had bouts of aggression against her that seemed to come out of the blue and lasted for several days.

Adapted from J. Robinson and Robinson, 1971.

with a safe environment in which to explore his or her thoughts and feelings and to experience a positive relationship with a caring therapist. (We will describe play therapy more fully in Chapter 17. For more information on interventions for attachment disorders, see Brisch, 2002 and Box 6.2.)

In summary, as we have seen, the origins of attachment disorders are clearly in the family context, particularly the quality of caregiving received in the first 3 years of life. However, the *consequences* of attachment disorders span all developmental contexts and place the child at risk for taking a deviant pathway in development. Attachment is a crucial stage-salient issue of the toddler years that affects the child's ability to master developmental issues at each subsequent stage. Attachment is concerned with balancing between the need to cling and the need to let go. When the child has difficulty resolving that dilemma, one possible consequence is the development of an overly rigid, controlling, and oppositional stance toward the world.

Oppositional-Defiant Disorder

The toddler period is a time of increased expansiveness on the child's part and increased restrictions on the part of the socializing adults. It is natural that these two should go hand in hand. Toddlers who are now physically able to explore vast new regions of the environment inadvertently damage valued household items, leave chaos in their wake, and occasionally endanger themselves.

Box 6.2 | **Controversies in the Diagnosis and Treatment of Reactive Attachment Disorder**

In recent years, clinicians and researchers have seen a dramatic increase in the number of children diagnosed with reactive attachment disorder. On the one hand, this may reflect greater awareness and sensitivity to the devastating effects on pathological caregiving and may serve children well by placing the blame or their disturbed environments rather than labeling the children themselves as "bad seeds" or "defectives." Correct diagnosis also is helpful because it can lead to the proper treatment to alleviate the child's difficulties. But when is the diagnosis correct and what is the proper treatment? Investigators in the field are far from unified on these points (Hanson & Spratt, 2000).

In regard to diagnosis, perhaps the most thorny issue is that, unlike almost every other disorder in DSM, the criteria for the diagnosis of reactive attachment disorder are specific as to

etiology: The disorder must arise as a function of pathological caregiving. This requires a high level of inference on the part of the diagnostician, who must determine not only that inadequate care has been given to the child, but that it is this care—and no other cause—that is responsible for the disorder. While child maltreatment may result in a number of pathological disturbances, as we will discuss in Chapter 14—including such suggestive symptoms as withdrawal, passivity, and the avoidance of attachment figures—not all young children who receive inadequate parenting develop reactive attachment disorder. However, in actual practice, Hanson and Spratt find in their review, clinicians concerned to highlight the issue of maltreatment and avoid pathologizing the child frequently apply the reactive attachment disorder label to children who have been abused but whose

symptoms go far beyond the criteria specified in the diagnostic criteria.

What harm is there, really, in erroneously diagnosing a child with reactive attachment disorder? The other controversy in the field concerns the treatment of the disorder. Many alternative therapies that have been developed for this disorder are theoretically ungrounded and lacking in empirical support. Further, some of these treatments may be damaging or traumatizing for children. They may even be fatal. For example, "rebirthing" is a technique used to simulate the physical and psychological birth of the child in order to foster the development of attachment afresh. In one widely publicized case in Colorado, a child died during the process. She suffocated when wrapped in a blanket and held down by the rebirthing therapists, while her foster mother looked on unawares.

Such unfettered initiative must be limited by "No" and "Don't." Socializing parents want to teach their toddlers control of unacceptable behavior while the enterprising toddlers brazenly assert their autonomy. The ensuing battles are fought over the issue of who is going to control whom. The sometimes stormy confrontations are responsible for the entire period being humorously called the terrible twos.

If all goes well in the confrontations between expansive toddlers and the restricting parent, the toddlers will emerge as socialized preschoolers who can both control themselves and be assured of their autonomy. In short, they are both self-controlled and self-reliant.

However, there is also the possibility that this normal development will go awry, resulting in psychopathological deviations. The healthy need for self-assertion evidenced in negativism can be carried to an extreme of *oppositional-defiant* behavior, which disrupts relations with caregiving adults while blocking the child's own growth.

Definition and Characteristics

Definition

The manifestations of Oppositional-Defiant Disorder (ODD) include outbursts of temper; arguing; defying and deliberately annoying others and blaming others for the child's own mistakes; and being

Oppositional-defiant behavior.

touchy, angry, and spiteful (see Table 6.3 for the DSM-IV-TR criteria). However, unlike conduct disorder (CD), there are no violations of the basic rights of others or of major societal norms and rules, such as persistent lying, aggressiveness, and theft.

Prevalence and Characteristics

Costello and colleagues (2003) gathered data from a representative community sample of 1,420 children assessed annually from ages 9 to 16. Using a standardized diagnostic interview, the authors found that the prevalence of the ODD diagnosis ranged from 2.1 percent at age 9 to 4.1 percent at age 15 to 2.2 percent at age 16. Across the age range, overall prevalence rates were 2.1 percent for girls and 3.1 percent for boys. Reviewing the available studies from around the world, Lahey and colleagues (1999) report prevalence rates from 0.3 percent to 22.5 percent, with a median of 3.2 percent. Findings are likely to be inconsistent across studies due to differences in the age, sex, and socioeconomic status of the groups studied as well as to the use of different assessment methods. Nevertheless, ODD is one of the most frequently reported problems of clinically referred children in the United States; for example, one-third of all clinically referred preadolescent and adolescent children are diagnosed as

Table 6.3

DSM-IV-TR Criteria for Oppositional-Defiant Disorder

A. A pattern of negativistic, hostile, and defiant behavior lasting at least six months, during which four (or more) of the following are present:
 (1) often loses temper
 (2) often argues with adults
 (3) often actively defies or refuses to comply with adults' requests or rules
 (4) often deliberately annoys people
 (5) often blames others for his or her mistakes or misbehavior
 (6) is often touchy or easily annoyed by others
 (7) is often angry and resentful
 (8) is often spiteful or vindictive
 NOTE: Consider a criterion met only if the behavior occurs more frequently than is typically observed in individuals of comparable age and developmental level.
B. The disturbance in behavior causes significant impairment in social, academic, or occupational functioning.
C. The behaviors do not occur exclusively during the course of a psychotic or mood disorder.
D. Criteria are not met for Conduct Disorder.

Reprinted with permission from the *Diagnostic and Statistical Manual of Mental Disorders,* Fourth Edition Text Revision. Copyright 2000 by the American Psychiatric Association.

ODD (Rey, 1993). Moreover, rates of oppositional behavior increase in youths as they enter adolescence (Keenan et al., 1999).

Gender, Ethnicity, and Social Status   Regarding *gender,* ODD appears at similar rates in boys and girls in early childhood. However, by late childhood, ODD is overwhelmingly more predominant in boys. *Social class* is an important factor, and surveys consistently find that ODD is more prevalent in groups who are socioeconomically disadvantaged (Lahey, Miller, Gordon, & Riley, 1999). *Racial and ethnic differences* are not consistently examined; when they are, they are found in some studies but not others (Lahey et al., 1999). Further, seldom have the effects of social class been controlled in studies of the ethnic diversity of ODD, making these data difficult to interpret.

Comorbidity and Differential Diagnosis

ODD and Conduct Disorder

Both in the descriptive psychiatric literature and in objective studies there is a strong association between ODD and conduct disorder (CD). DSM-IV-TR groups them under the more general rubric of *disruptive behavior disorders* just as the empirical approach classifies both as *externalizing disorders.* In fact, some have argued that the overlap is so extensive that ODD should be regarded as a mild form of CD rather than being a psychopathology in its own right.

However, there are a number of reasons why ODD is regarded as a separate disturbance from CD. (For a detailed discussion see Hinshaw and Lee, 2003.) As we have seen, DSM-IV-TR differentiates the disorders on the basis that children with ODD do not violate the basic rights of others or major societal norms. Moreover, in ODD the deviant behaviors are more commonly, although not exclusively, limited to parents and the home environment, whereas, in CD, deviant behaviors frequently involve peers, teachers, and others outside the home. While both ODD and CD are related to antisocial behavior and adverse events in the family, the severity of such problems is less in ODD children (Walker et al., 1991). In general, children with ODD are less disturbed than those with CD.

Frick and colleagues (1993) provide some of the best evidence of the independence of ODD and CD. In a meta-analysis of factor analytic studies of disruptive behaviors, they found that items congruent with ODD belonged in a cluster of *overt nondestructive behaviors,* such as defies, annoys, argues, shows temper, and is stubborn. By contrast, items congruent with CD belonged to three other clusters: overt destructive, such as assaults, fights, and bullies; covert destructive, such as steals, lies, and sets fires; and covert nondestructive, such as truants, uses controlled substances, and swears. The main overlap between ODD and CD was mildly aggressive behavior. (The comorbidity of ODD and CD will be discussed again in Chapter 10.)

Developmental data provide additional reasons for regarding ODD as being independent of CD. ODD emerges in the preschool period, whereas CD typi-cally does not appear until middle childhood. While it is true that in the majority of cases CD is preceded by ODD, longitudinal research shows that approximately two-thirds of children do *not* go on to develop CD (Biederman et al., 1996). There are some data on why certain oppositional children develop the more serious psychopathology of CD while others do not. A high level of *aggression* seems to be the most important determinant of subsequent CD. However, family variables such as parental antisocial behavior, neglect, lack of parental monitoring, and father separation also play a role (Loeber, Lahey, & Thomas, 1991).

ODD and Attention-Deficit Hyperactivity Disorder

There is considerable overlap between ODD and attention-deficit hyperactivity disorder (ADHD), with a comorbidity of approximately 50 percent (Hinshaw & Lee, 2003). ADHD increases the risk of early onset of ODD and, in children with *both* ADHD and CD, there is an increase in the severity of ODD symptoms (Biederman et al., 1996). Thus, ADHD appears to potentiate ODD. This ODD-ADHD comorbidity is also associated with significant impairment in the personal, interpersonal, and family domains (Hinshaw & Lee, 2003).

ODD and Learning Disabilities

ODD *by itself* is not associated with learning disabilities (LD). When such a relationship is found, it is due to the presence of ADHD as a comorbid disturbance (Hinshaw & Lee, 2003).

ODD and Internalizing Disorders

Interestingly, ODD also is prevalent in children diagnosed with anxiety and depression (Hinshaw & Anderson, 1996). One explanation for this may lie in the irritability and bad temper that accompany internalizing disorders, which lead children to respond in a negativistic manner to their parents. However, clinical observations suggest that anxious children often attempt to bind their anxiety by controlling the world around them (Lieberman, 1992). Therefore oppositional behavior may be the child's method of trying to make the interpersonal world less intrusive and unpredictable.

Etiology

There is general agreement that ODD is on a continuum with normal behavior. In fact, normal children fail to comply with parental commands about one-third of the time (Webster-Stratton & Herbert, 1994). Thus, normal problem behaviors in toddlers include disobedience, defiance, tantrums, and negative mood. (See Chapter 1.) The terrible twos are aptly named except that the behaviors can also extend into the preschool period. Psychopathology enters the picture when there is an increase in *frequency* and *intensity* of such behaviors or when they *persist* into later periods (Gabel, 1997).

The Individual Context

Oppositionality in Normal Development   If psychopathology can be understood as normal development gone awry, then it is reasonable to look to studies of normal development for clues to answering the etiological question of why it becomes diverted. The relevant literature concerns negativism, or noncompliant behavior.

In their longitudinal study of toddlers and preschoolers, Kuczynski and Kochanska (1990) conceptualize negativistic behavior in terms of *social strategies*. Direct defiance is the least skillful strategy because of its openness and aversiveness to parents. Passive noncompliance is also considered unskillful but not so aversive to parents. Negotiation, which attempts to persuade parents to modify their demands, is relatively indirect and nonaversive, so it is the most skillful. The investigators found that direct defiance and passive noncompliance decreased with age, while negotiation increased, reflecting a more active and adroit way of expressing resistance to parental requests. Of particular interest to us is the finding that only the least skillful forms of resistance were predictive of externalizing problem behaviors at 5 years of age.

Kuczynski and Kochanska also make a point concerning compliance that clinical child psychologists should note. Although noncompliance may be problematic, *excessive compliance* is of concern as well. A rigid and compulsive form of compliance develops among infants of abusive parents, with fear

of the parent's reaction inhibiting the child from normal expressions of self-will and spontaneity. In their study, these investigators found that overly compliant young children were at risk for the development of internalizing problems.

Oppositionality in Clinical Populations   Recently there has been some interest in studying the association between ODD and attachment. DeKlyen (1996) found more *insecure attachment* in a group of 25 preschool boys referred for disruptive behavior disorder than in normal controls. Speltz and coworkers (1995) also found that attachment classification discriminated clinically referred ODD preschoolers from normal controls better than measures of maternal behavior such as the number of commands and criticisms. In particular, prospective studies show that *avoidant* attachment in infancy is linked to oppositional-defiant behavior in the preschool years (Lyons-Ruth, Alpern, & Repacholi, 1993). The authors of all these studies are careful to point out that attachment should not be regarded as the sole cause of ODD but rather as a factor that interacts with other risk variables (Greenberg, DeKlyen, Speltz, & Endriga, 1997).

There is also some evidence that a *difficult temperament* in 7-year-olds predicts ODD in adolescence (Rey, 1993). However, as is the case with attachment, temperament should be regarded as one of many risk factors producing ODD.

The Family Context

Research on the characteristics of parents of ODD children describes them as more negative toward and more critical of their children than are mothers of other children. They also engage in more threatening, angry, and nagging behaviors. Both parents give their children significantly more commands and instructions while not allowing enough time for the child to comply. (See Webster-Stratton and Hancock, 1998, for a summary of the research.) As is always true of interactional studies, there is the "chicken and egg" problem of the direction of causation. Parents either may be generating or reacting to their children's behavior, and only additional studies can help distinguish the direction of effects.

Looking at more specific parental behaviors, McMahon and Forehand (2003) found that noncompliant behavior is maintained by parental attention. Attention serves as a reinforcer even when it is negative and takes the form of anger and punitiveness. In addition, McMahon and Forehand discovered the types of parental commands that are most apt to elicit noncompliance. The so-called *alpha commands* are specific and clear and are less likely to produce noncompliance. They include commands that have a clear, explicitly stated objective: for example, "Eat your peas or there will be no dessert" or "You may finish watching this program, but then the TV goes off." The so-called *beta commands* are vague and interrupted. They are difficult or impossible to obey, either because of their ambiguity or because the parent issues a new command before the child has a chance to comply: "Do you think that you might want to do something not so noisy—or not?" or "Quit picking on your. . . . Now help Mommy find her pocketbook." Beta commands are more characteristic of parents of noncompliant children than are alpha commands.

Parents' *attributions* for their children's noncompliance also influence their parenting behavior and, subsequently, the likelihood that the child will respond positively to discipline. Parents who view their children's misbehavior as intentional and malicious—or view themselves as helpless and incompetent to manage it—respond more harshly to their children and thus engender more misbehavior (Geller & Johnston, 1995).

New research looking at multiple risk factors suggests that ODD is a product of interactions among a number of factors in both the intrapersonal and family contexts, including child temperament as well as poor attachment, family conflict, and low SES (Campbell, 2002). But again, we are left with the question of how these general risk factors *specifically* result in the ODD diagnosis. We turn next to a model that attempts to address this question.

Integrative Developmental Model

In a thoughtful review paper, Greene and Doyle (1999) propose that there are multiple developmental pathways to ODD. While the social learning model focuses on faulty parenting practices as the major determinant, children bring to the interaction their own characteristics that can contribute to the problem. The proof is in the pudding, the authors suggest, when one considers the limited effectiveness of treatments that focus only on changing the parents' behavior. Therefore, their model incorporates both child characteristics and parent-child transactions that may increase the risk of oppositional-defiant behavior.

Child Characteristics That Contribute to ODD

Poor Self-Regulation Children with problem behavior are generally found to be impulsive and reactive and to have poor control over their emotions and behavior. This poor self-regulation underlies both ADHD and ODD and may in fact account for the comorbidity between them. As Greene and Doyle point out, compliance is a skill that is acquired over the course of development. In order for the child to be able to delay gratifying his or her own goals in response to a caregiver's goals or standards, the child needs the capacity to adapt, internalize, self-regulate, and modulate his or her emotions. Deficits in self-regulation, therefore, might lead to ODD. Indeed, infants with poor emotion regulation are found to be the most noncompliant during the toddler years (Stifter, Spinrad, & Braungart-Rieker, 1999).

Executive Functions Another deficit that ADHD and ODD may share is in the area of executive functions: cognitive skills that are necessary for planning, monitoring, and correcting one's own performance; adapting and shifting set; and flexible problem solving. Children who are lacking in these capacities may have difficulty, for example, reflecting on previous experiences and anticipating the likely consequences of further noncompliance, or shifting quickly from one mind set to another as is required by the parental command, "Turn off that video game and get ready for bed." Indeed, children with these kinds of deficits may appear intentionally defiant to parents, when the actual culprit is their inability to process information and choose a response pattern in an organized, adaptive manner.

Mood and Anxiety Disorders   As noted previously, ODD is comorbid with depression as well as some anxiety disorders, particularly obsessive-compulsiveness (Garland & Weiss, 1996). The underlying mechanism here again may be poor emotion regulation. Children who are not able to modulate their reactions to affectively charged situations are likely to become overaroused and respond with emotion rather than reason in what are termed "affective storms." Thus, irritability, mood instability, anxiety, and obsessiveness can compromise the child's capacity to respond adaptively to adult commands.

Language Processing Problems   Language is crucial to development in many ways, including the emergence of self-regulation. The toddler's language skills enable him or her to label, categorize, and communicate needs and to identify appropriate behavioral responses. Language also allows children to receive feedback about the behaviors they choose and to reflect and consider their actions. Oppositional behavior may ensue when a child with language problems has difficulty labeling and communicating about feelings, engaging in cooperative give-and-take interactions, and developing a flexible repertoire of problem-solving skills.

Cognitive Distortions   Children with poor emotion regulation skills are vulnerable to interpreting social information in biased, inaccurate, incomplete, or distorted ways that are colored by the affect they are experiencing in the moment. This sets the stage for the child's viewing the parent's limit-setting in a hostile light—and responding in kind.

Transactional Patterns in ODD

Children's self-control, emotion regulation, and cognitive capacities do not develop in a vacuum; parents are pivotal to the acquisition of these skills. Parents model and teach, but also may elicit compliant or noncompliant behavior from children by the tone of their commands and the harshness of their responses to child disobedience. The quality of parent-child transactions is particularly crucial during the stage of development when oppositional behavior begins to

emerge. As Greene and Doyle state, "It is at this point in development where two important forces—a child's capacity for compliance and adults' expectations for compliance—are thought to intersect" (p. 137). In sum, if the parent responds to the child in a way that exacerbates the child's frustration and cognitive and emotional difficulties, a maladaptive transactional pattern will ensue. Quoting DSM-IV-TR, there may develop "a vicious cycle in which the parent and child bring out the worst in each other" (p. 100).

Therefore, in the transactional approach, no one characteristic of the child or parent accounts for ODD. Rather, the problem arises out of what the authors term *parent-child incompatibility,* akin to the concept of goodness of fit we discussed in Chapter 2. For example, if a boy whose language processing problems interfere with his ability to express frustration in a socially appropriate manner were paired with a parent who lacked understanding and attempted to motivate the child by offering rewards for behaviors of which the boy was incapable, frustration and oppositionality might develop. Or, to take another example, if a parent with poor emotion regulation skills were paired with a child with similar temperamental deficits, their incompatibility might also increase the risk of ODD.

Developmental Course

The onset of ODD is usually gradual, emerging over the first 8 years of life. There is evidence that ODD declines in frequency during middle childhood but increases again in the adolescent period (Lahey, McBurnett, & Loeber, 2000). Prognostically, ODD is one of the most stable diagnoses and one with the poorest rate of recovery. And, as we have seen, ODD is associated with the development of other disorders, notably conduct disorder, attention-deficit/hyperactivity disorder, and learning disorders.

Intervention

Behavioral strategies for the treatment of ODD are the most widely used and researched. For example, McMahon and Forehand (2003) focus first on improving the quality of the relationship between parent and child by helping parents to attend to children's behavior and interact with them in a warm, noncoercive manner. They then teach parents specific behavioral skills, such as to replace their vague, interrupted beta commands with firm, specific alpha commands; to shift from punishing noncompliant behavior to rewarding compliance with praise, approval, and positive physical attention; and to employ a "time-out" procedure of isolating the child for a brief period after noncompliance. It is also helpful to teach parents the general principles of operant conditioning rather than providing them solely with techniques for handling specific problems. Modification of one behavior tends to affect other behaviors within the home; for example, one girl who was reinforced for picking up her toys spontaneously began to keep her clothes tidy. Moreover, there is evidence that the compliance of untreated siblings undergoes the same positive change, since the parents alter their behavior to them as well. Suggestions also are made for including teachers in the behavioral program in order to generalize successes from home to school. Finally, there is evidence that gains made in middle childhood are sustained in adolescence.

Webster-Stratton (1998) has adapted these methods and introduced the innovation of including videotapes that provide parents with models of both adaptive and maladaptive techniques. The empirical support for this approach is strong and has been established in studies of ethnically diverse, low SES populations. We will describe her intervention in more detail in Chapter 17.

Over a period of two decades, the behavioral approach has proven effective, although, as Greenberg and Doyle (1999) point out, not for all children. Instead, Greenberg and Doyle suggest that we move to designing treatments that are tailored toward the *specific* mechanisms that are driving oppositional behavior in each individual child and family who present to the consulting room.

The disorders of attachment and oppositionality we have just discussed arise from normal developmental challenges that children face in the period from infancy through preschool. Among the other developmental tasks the child must accomplish in this period, those that concern bodily functions are particularly important—not only to the child but to the caregiver. We turn to these next.

Enuresis

While the requirements for self-control affect many aspects of the toddler's life, they are keenly felt when they intrude upon bodily functions. The young child lives close to his or her body, and eating and elimination hold special pleasures and special fascinations. The socializing parents' demands can, therefore, trigger some of the most intense conflicts of early childhood. We will be exploring a major disturbance in regulating elimination—namely, enuresis.

Definition and Characteristics

Definition

Enuresis has a long history: It was mentioned in Egyptian medical texts as early as 1550 B.C. (Thompson & Rey, 1995). In current usage *enuresis* is defined as repeated involuntary or intentional discharge of urine into bed or clothes beyond the expected age for controlling urination. According to DSM-IV-TR, this age is 5 years or a comparable developmental level. The behavior is clinically significant if it occurs twice a week for at least three consecutive months. However, it may also be regarded as significant if there is considerable distress or impairment in important areas of functioning. Another qualification is that enuresis is not due to a general medical condition or to drugs that affect urination. (See Table 6.4.)

There are three different types of enuresis. In *nocturnal* enuresis passing urine occurs only during nighttime sleep. In *diurnal* enuresis urine is passed during waking hours. In *mixed,* or nocturnal and diurnal enuresis, urine is passed during both waking and sleeping hours. These three distinctions are not always made in the research literature, however, resulting in a certain ambiguity in the findings.

There is another important classification. *Primary enuresis* refers to children who have never been successfully trained to control their urination. *Secondary enuresis* refers to children who have been successfully trained but revert back to wetting—for example, in response to a stressful situation in the family. In our developmental terminology, primary enuresis represents a *fixation,* whereas secondary enuresis represents a *regression.*

Table 6.4

DSM-IV-TR Criteria for Enuresis

A. Repeated voiding of urine into bed or clothes (whether involuntary or intentional)
B. The behavior is clinically significant as manifested by either a frequency of twice a week for at least 3 consecutive months or the presence of clinically significant distress or impairment in social, academic (occupational), or other important areas of functioning
C. Chronological age is at least 5 years (or equivalent developmental level)
D. The behavior is not due exclusively to the direct physiological effect of a substance (e.g., diuretic) or a general medical condition (e.g., diabetes, spina bifida, a seizure disorder)

Specify Type:
   Nocturnal Only: passage of urine only during nighttime sleep
   Diurnal Only: passage of urine during waking hours
   Nocturnal and Diurnal: a combination of the two subtypes above

Reprinted with permission from the *Diagnostic and Statistical Manual of Mental Disorders,* Fourth Edition Text Revision. Copyright 2000 by the American Psychiatric Association.

Prevalence and Characteristics

In the United States, approximately 15 to 20 percent of 5-year-old children will develop symptoms of enuresis. Fischel and Liebert (2000) summarize prevalence rates across several studies and find that the prevalence of enuresis changes significantly with *age.* It is found in 33 percent of 5-year-olds, 25 percent of 7-year-olds, 15 percent of 9-year-olds, 8 percent of 11-year-olds, 4 percent of 13-year-olds, and 3 percent of 15- to 17-year-olds. Of these children, 75 percent showed only nocturnal enuresis; diurnal enuresis is much less common. There is a *gender difference:* Overall, 60 percent of enuretic children are male. However, this too changes with age. Between ages 4 and 6 years the number of boys and girls with enuresis is about equal. However, the ratio changes so that by 11 years of age there are twice as many boys as girls. There is evidence that the incidence of enuresis varies with *social class;* in the United States it is more prevalent among those who are socioeconomically disadvantaged (Walker, 1995). There is no evidence at present for *ethnic differences.*

Comorbidity   Attention problems and hyperactivity co-occur frequently with enuresis (Ornitz, Hanna, & Traversay, 1992). Children with enuresis also are more likely to display behavior problems such as misconduct, anxiety, immaturity, and underachievement in school. Enuresis also has been implicated in studies of encopresis (fecal soiling), learning disabilities, and developmental delays in intelligence (Biederman, Santanpelo, Faraone, Kiely, Guite, Mick, et al., 1995; Walsh & Menvielle, 1997).

Developmental Course

Both noctural and diurnal enuresis appear to be self-limiting; that is children tend to outgrow them even without treatment. There is some evidence that remission rates for girls may be higher than those for boys: 71 percent of girls and 44 percent of boys between the ages of 4 and 6 spontaneously stop wetting themselves (Harbeck-Weber & Peterson, 1996). Since there are also effective treatments, as we shall see, the prognosis is quite favorable for enuresis.

Etiology

The Biological Context

Enuresis can be caused by a number of purely medical problems such as anomalies of innervation of the bladder that result in an inability to empty it completely, illnesses such as diabetes insipidus or urinary tract infections, and drugs such as diuretics. The clinical child psychologist should make sure that these factors have been ruled out by a medical examination.

There are two leading contenders in biologically focused theories of etiology. The first involves deficiencies in the nighttime secretion of antidiruetic hormone, which normally reduces the amount of urine produced at night. However, evidence in support of this hypothesis is questionable, since not all enuretic children produce excessive urine, and not all children who produce excessive urine are enuretic (Ondersma & Walker, 1998). The other leading theory involves the absence of learned muscle responses that inhibit urine flow during sleep (Mellon & Stern, 1998).

There appears to be a strong *genetic* component to enuresis. For example, when both parents have a childhood history of enuresis, the risk of the child's developing the disorder is estimated to be 80 percent.

In contrast, if one parent had the disorder, the risk for the child is 45 percent, whereas if neither parent were enuretic, the child's risk is only 15 percent (Fischel & Liebert, 2000). Furthermore, there is a 68 percent concordance rate for monozygotic twins and only a 36 percent concordance rate for dizygotic twins (Harbeck-Weber & Peterson, 1996).

The Individual Context

Developmental Status   Although we might tend to take toilet-training for granted, it is actually quite a developmental accomplishment. Communication skills are needed to convey to the parents that the toilet is needed, social and emotional development must have advanced to the point that the child recognizes the importance of adhering to social expectations, fine and gross motor skills are needed to accomplish the physical tasks involved, and cognitive skills are needed to engage in planning and self-control. Therefore, a child whose overall development is delayed in any of these areas may be more vulnerable to enuresis (Fischel & Liebert, 2000).

Psychosocial Stress   On one hand, there is evidence that secondary enuresis may be a response to stress, especially in 4- to 6-year-olds (Walsh & Menvielle, 1997). On the other hand, studies have failed to find a relation between enuresis and a variety of psychosocial factors such as economic background, family intactness, and the quality of the family environment (Biederman et al., 1995).

It may be that the negative findings regarding psychosocial variables were due to a failure to take into account the interaction between intrapersonal and interpersonal factors. Also, none of the studies was developmental in nature. The research of Kaffman and Elizur (1977), although conducted a number of years ago, is unique in taking both interaction among contexts and development into account. It is worth describing in detail.

An Integrative Developmental Study

A rare longitudinal study was conducted by Kaffman and Elizur (1977), set in a kibbutz in Israel. In the kibbutz, four to six infants are cared for by a trained caretaker, or *metapelet* (plural, *metaplot*), in a communal children's house. Each child spends 4 hours daily with his or her parents. Generally speaking, the children's development and the parent-child relationships are similar to those in traditional Western families. Toilet training in particular is nonpunitive and child centered.

Kaffman and Elizur assessed 153 children on a number of physiological, interpersonal, and intrapersonal variables from infancy to 8 years of age. The investigators regarded enuresis as beginning at 4 rather than 5 years of age. While they found the usual genetic and physiological predisposing factors in the 4-year-olds with enuresis (siblings with enuresis, smaller functional bladder capacity, impaired motor coordination), the intrapersonal and interpersonal factors are of greater interest.

In the *individual context,* the children with enuresis had a significantly greater number of behavior symptoms than the nonenuretic ones, indicating that they were more disturbed. Within this general context, two high-risk personality patterns could be distinguished. Around 30 percent of the children were hyperactive, aggressive, and negativistic in response to discipline, had low frustration tolerance, and resisted adjusting to new situations. One can imagine how difficult it must have been for these children to sit or stand still when being potty trained! A smaller group of children with enuresis were dependent and unassertive, had low achievement and mastery motivation, and masturbated frequently, perhaps to compensate for their lack of realistic pleasures. In contrast, the children who were *not* enuretic were self-reliant, independent, and adaptable; and they had a high level of achievement motivation.

In the *family context,* the clearest relation was between parental disinterest and enuresis. In addition, temporary separation from the parents was the only stress related to increased bedwetting, for the kibbutz children took in stride the stresses of a sibling's birth, hospitalization, and even war. Interestingly, absence of the *metapelet* produced no such reaction, suggesting that the parent-child relationship was central. While not statistically significant, a relationship between bed-wetting and the *metapelet*'s behavior was suggested. Permissiveness, low achievement demands, and insecurity on the part of the metapelet tended to be related to enuresis, whereas structured, goal-oriented, and directive toilet training in the context of a loving relationship enhanced early bladder control.

The authors draw some general conclusions from the data. For low-risk children the *timing* of toilet training does not matter. In the high-risk group, *delayed* training *increases* the likelihood of enuresis in the motorically active, resistive, and aggressive infant. Such an infant is difficult enough to socialize, but the difficulties are compounded during the terrible twos and threes. In the interpersonal realm, a *permissive* attitude, combined with noninvolvement or uncertainty, tends to perpetuate bedwetting, since there is neither sufficient challenge nor sufficient support for the child to take this particular step toward maturity. Such a finding is congruent with studies of normal development that show that a child's competence is maximized when parental affection is combined with challenges and an expectation of achievement. Overall, the children's *personality characteristics* were more highly correlated with enuresis than were interpersonal variables.

In the longitudinal phase of their study, Kaffman and Elizur (1977) found that 50 percent of the children with enuresis were identified as problem children when they were 6 to 8 years of age, in contrast to 12 percent in the nonenuretic group. Learning problems and scholastic underachievement were the most frequent symptoms, although some of the children also lacked self-confidence and felt ashamed, guilty, or depressed. Unfortunately, Kaffman and Elizur did not analyze their data further to determine *which* children were more apt to develop problems.

These longitudinal findings have important implications for developmental course. Looking at a graph showing the progressive decline of enuresis, one would opt for the prediction that children would outgrow their problem. Such graphs are based on cross-sectional data. But longitudinal studies that include intrapersonal and interpersonal variables alert the clinician to the possibility that enuresis in some 4-year-olds may be the first sign of other problems that will persist and perhaps escalate. In short, while most children may "grow out of" a psychopathology, a substantial subgroup might "grow into" other problems.

It is essential for the clinical child psychologist to have a good understanding of such longitudinal information when helping parents decide whether or not their child with enuresis is in need of intervention. After all, why subject a child to treatment for a problem that is apt to disappear? Parents should be made aware that the prognosis is not so favorable when the focus shifts from enuresis alone (which is apt to be "outgrown") to problem behavior in general, so they can then make an informed decision about treatment by considering both sets of information.

Intervention

The *urine alarm* is a behavioral treatment that has a proven record of effectiveness and of superiority to drug treatments. Essentially, this is a classical conditioning paradigm. A device the size of a stick of gum is worn on the child's body and an attached urine-sensitive probe is placed in the child's underwear. This device activates a buzzer when the child wets, awakening the child, who then goes to the bathroom to finish voiding. Eventually, the child begins to awaken in *anticipation* of the alarm, allowing the child to get up before urinating. (See Figure 6.1.) Studies have shown the urine alarm to be effective in the majority of cases; 65 to 75 percent of bedwetters are able to stay dry within 3 months, especially those of the primary enuretic type. However, the alarm takes 12 weeks or more to achieve an effect, and the patience and compliance of parents with the treatment is not always high (Fischel & Liebert, 2000). In addition, there is significant relapse rate within the year after treatment.

Full Spectrum Home Training (Houts, 2003) combines the urine alarm with three other interventions: cleanliness training, retention control training, and overlearning. In *cleanliness training,* the child is provided with a wall chart with which to track "wet" and "dry" nights. The child is rewarded with a sticker each time the child wakens in response to the alarm. To ensure that the child fully awakens, parents are encouraged to have the child wash his or her face and hands or work on some arithmetic homework. *Retention control training* involves rewarding the child over a 2-week period for holding his or her urine for incrementally large periods of time, up to 45 minutes. Finally, *overlearning* is designed to prevent relapse. After the child has enjoyed 14 consecutive dry nights,

Figure 6.1

Anticipatory awakening.

he or she is required to drink a gradually increasing amount of water each night before bedtime. For every two nights the child remains dry, the amount of water increases by 2 ounces a night until the maximum amount for that child's age is reached. Again, this procedure continues until 14 consecutive dry nights are achieved. This procedure has reduced relapse rates up to 50 percent, with 45 percent of children showing a lasting benefit (Mellon & Stern, 1998).

Recently, cognitive techniques have been added to the clinician's repertoire for treating enuresis. For example, children are encouraged to make self-efficacious statements such as "When I need to urinate, I will wake up all by myself, urinate in the toilet, and return to my nice, dry bed" (Miller, 1993). Additionally, visualization techniques may be used such as teaching children to picture themselves as if they are on videotape as they sleep, feel their bladders filling, and awaken to use the bathroom. They may also be encouraged to visualize their bladders as they expand and fill, sending "beeper signals" to the brain and triggering the brain to awaken the child (Butler, 1993).

Our presentation of various psychopathologies will now move from the preschool years to disorders that are risks for the child entering the school years. From regulating bodily functions and the relationship with the caregiver, the focus will shift to the ability to pay attention and to work up to one's academic potential. As we will explore in Chapter 7, both of those can go awry, producing hyperactivity on the one hand and learning disabilities on the other.

The Preschool Period: The Emergence of Attention-Deficit/ Hyperactivity Disorder and Learning Disorders

As we have just explored in Chapter 6, when the development of self-regulation goes awry in the toddler period, the child may start down the pathway to an oppositional-defiant disorder. However, adaptive development involves not only self-reliance and autonomy but also curiosity and exploration. As Piaget has taught us, even infants are problem solvers, implicitly asking, "What is that?" and "How does it work?" until, by the end of the 1st year, they are actively experimenting with the physical and social environment. In a like manner, toddlers have a remarkable ability to give their undivided attention to the tasks involved in exploration. In the preschool period, children begin to experience the academic setting that channels intrinsic curiosity into the work of learning specific subjects.

Yet this ability to concentrate on school work in the preschool period can be seriously curtailed by hyperactivity and inattention, which prevent children from keeping their minds on the task at hand. When schooling begins in earnest, a different deviation can appear in intelligent, motivated children: the inability to achieve at an appropriate level in one or another academic subject such as reading or arithmetic. In this chapter we will first discuss attention-deficit/hyperactivity disorder and then consider learning disorders and their consequences for development.

Attention-Deficit/ Hyperactivity Disorder

Definition and Characteristics

Definition

We will begin by presenting and discussing the DSM-IV-TR criteria for Attention-Deficit/Hyperactivity Disorder (ADHD) because they capture the restless history of the attempt to define this psychopathology. (See Table 7.1.)

Note that there are three major types of ADHD: one featuring inattention, one focusing on hyperactivity/impulsivity, and one based on a combination of the two. Children with the *inattentive* type are unable to sustain attention at an age-appropriate level. Parents and teachers might complain that the children cannot concentrate, are distractible, go from one activity to another, are disorganized, and are forgetful and prone to daydream. With *hyperactivity,* children are continually "on the go" as if "driven by a motor." This drive to move may be evidenced by their climbing or running about, excessive talking, or continually and inappropriately leaving their seats during class. *Impulsivity* is "acting without thinking." Children may blurt out answers rather than taking time to think a problem through, they may interrupt or intrude on others by butting into conversations and games, or they may have difficulty waiting for their turn. Many of these behaviors can be found in typically developing young children, and therefore the diagnosis requires that the child demonstrate them at a level that is significantly age-inappropriate. (See Box 7.1.)

Historically, diagnoses have emphasized the most obvious manifestation of the disturbance, which is hyperactivity. For example, DSM-II (American Psychiatric Association, 1968) labeled the condition "hyperkinetic reactions of childhood," characterizing it by overactivity, distractibility, restlessness, and a short attention span. Subsequent research, particularly that conducted by Virginia Douglas (1983), suggested that attention, rather than motor activity, was the crucial deficit. This research led to the primary diagnosis of Attention-Deficit Disorder (ADD) in DSM-III (American Psychiatric Association, 1980), which could be either with or without hyperactivity. More recent research questioned the centrality of the attention defect while showing that hyperactivity and impulsivity were so highly correlated that they should be combined into a single category. Thus, we now have DSM-IV-TR's tripartite diagnosis of ADHD Predominantly Inattentive Type, ADHD Predominantly Hyperactive-Impulsive type, and ADHD Combined type, which includes both behaviors.

Three other features of the DSM-IV classification deserve further comment: (1) the specific times defining age of onset, (2) duration of symptoms, and (3) the importance of setting.

Age of Onset   Age of onset of symptoms is defined as before 7 years in DSM-IV-TR. However, a study of a clinical sample of 380 youths 4 through 17 years of age showed that children who met this criterion were predominantly the hyperactive-impulsive type. Forty-three percent of the inattentive type and 18 percent of the combined type did not manifest symptoms until after 7 years of age (Applegate et al., 1997). Thus, the age of onset appears to differ with the type of ADHD. The hyperactive-inattentive type emerges in the preschool years, the combined type emerges in the early primary school years (ages 5 to 8), while the primarily inattentive type emerges later (ages 8 to 12) (Barkley, 2003). Whether these age effects reflect true differences in onset or merely recognition of the disorder is not clear. Certainly hyperactive and impulsive behaviors are more disruptive to the family and the classroom and are therefore more readily identified than the more subtle symptoms of inattentiveness.

Subsequent research has not consistently shown differences between children with early onset versus late onset of the disorder, although there is some evidence that the earlier the symptoms manifest themselves, the more severe the developmental consequences (McGee et al., 1992).

Duration of Symptoms   In regard to duration of symptoms, there is evidence that the 6-month period required by DSM-IV-TR is too short, particularly for young children. Research data show that a 12-month

Table 7.1

DSM-IV-TR Criteria for Attention-Deficit/Hyperactivity Disorder

A. Either (1) or (2):

   (1) *Inattention:* Six (or more) of the following symptoms of inattention have persisted for at least 6 months to a degree that is maladaptive and inconsistent with developmental level:

      (a) Often fails to give close attention to details or makes careless mistakes in schoolwork, work, or other activities

      (b) Often has difficulty sustaining attention in tasks or play activities

      (c) Often does not seem to listen when spoken to directly

      (d) Often does not follow through on instructions and fails to finish schoolwork, chores, or duties in the workplace (not due to oppositional behavior or failure to understand instructions)

      (e) Often has difficulty organizing tasks and activities

      (f) Often avoids, dislikes, or is reluctant to engage in tasks that require sustained mental effort (such as schoolwork or homework)

      (g) Often loses things necessary for tasks or activities (e.g., toys, school assignments, pencils, books, or tools)

      (h) Is often easily distracted by extraneous stimuli

      (i) Is often forgetful in daily activities

   (2) *Hyperactivity/Impulsivity:* Six (or more) of the following symptoms of hyperactivity/impulsivity have persisted for at least 6 months to a degree that is maladaptive and inconsistent with developmental level:

   Hyperactivity

      (a) Often fidgets with hands or feet or squirms in seat

      (b) Often leaves seat in classroom or in other situations in which remaining seated is expected

      (c) Often runs about or climbs excessively in situations in which it is inappropriate (in adolescents and adults, may be limited to subjective feelings of restlessness)

      (d) Often has difficulty playing or engaging in leisure activities quietly

      (e) Is often "on the go" or often acts as if "driven by a motor"

      (f) Often talks excessively

   Impulsivity

      (g) Often blurts out answers to questions before the questions have been completed

      (h) Often has difficulty awaiting turn

      (i) Often interrupts or intrudes on others (e.g., butts into conversations or games)

B. Some hyperactive-impulsive or inattentive symptoms that caused impairment were present before 7 years

C. Some impairment from the symptoms is present in two or more settings (e.g., at school and at home)

Code based on type:

   Attention-Deficit/Hyperactivity Disorder, Combined Type: If both Criteria A1 and A2 are met for the past 6 months

   Attention Deficit/Hyperactivity Disorder, Predominantly Inattentive Type: If Criterion A1 is met but Criterion A2 is not met for the past 6 months

   Attention-Deficit/Hyperactivity Disorder, Predominantly Hyperactive-Impulsive Type: If Criterion A2 is met but Criterion A1 is not met for the past 6 months

period is more appropriate duration of symptoms for preschoolers (Barkley, 2003).

Setting   Although the DSM-IV-TR criteria specify that the symptoms of ADHD must be present in two settings, for some children they may be evident only in one, such as the home or at school, while for other children they may be pervasive across environments. For example, a clinical child psychologist, after having read the referral on a hyperactive child, may be braced to deal with the "holy terror" the mother described, only to find the child to be a model of

Box 7.1 | Case Study in Attention-Deficit Disorder

Ricky S. is a 7-year-old African American boy referred by his school psychologist to an outpatient mental health clinic. At the time of the assessment, Ricky was in second grade. During her initial call to the clinic, Mrs. S. stated that her son was "out of control." When asked for specifics, she said that Ricky was "all over the place" and "constantly getting into trouble." As a single mother, she felt overwhelmed by his behavior and was unable to manage him.

As part of the evaluation, Ricky and his mother were interviewed separately by a doctoral intern in clinical psychology. Ricky was interviewed first and presented as polite, reserved, and a little socially anxious. He reported having difficulty adjusting to his new school and especially to his new teacher, Mrs. Candler, who was always yelling at him and sending notes home to his mother. When asked why the teacher was yelling at him, Ricky said at first that he did not know, but then admitted that it was mostly about not paying attention or following class rules. Ricky said he was often "on red"; the classroom had a discipline system in which students had to change their name card from green to yellow to orange to red for each infraction of the rules. A red card meant an automatic call home to the child's parents. In the past month alone, Ricky had accumulated five red and seven orange cards.

When asked if he liked school, Ricky shrugged and said that he liked science, especially now when the class was studying the growth of tadpoles. He said he had a few friends but often he had to keep to himself because

Mrs. Candler had him spend so much time in a corner of the classroom in order to complete his work. Ricky said he felt bored, sad, tired, and angry in the classroom. He felt happiest in the afternoons after school when he would go riding his bicycle for hours. "Then nobody yells at me and I can go wherever I want." Ricky denied other emotional or behavioral problems, but did acknowledge that he felt bad about being "a pain to my mom" and was confused about why he was doing so poorly in school.

A subsequent interview with Mrs. S. confirmed most of Ricky's report, with added detail. For example, Mrs. S. revealed that Ricky was almost intolerable in the classroom, in that he often threw tantrums or cried when forced to do his work and was even disrespectful to the teacher, which resulted in many of the calls home. At home he was fidgety and disorganized and tended to lose things and either did not listen to or did not understand some of what was said to him. Mrs. S. had already attended four conferences with the teacher at school, including one with the principal and school psychologist. Ricky had recently undergone cognitive and educational testing, which revealed an average level IQ and achievement scores commensurate with his abilities. The teacher wanted to refer Ricky to a classroom for behaviorally and emotionally handicapped children, but Mrs. S. opposed this and came to the clinic in order to seek an independent evaluation.

After carrying out a classroom observation, obtaining parent and

teacher behavioral ratings, and conducting more detailed neurocognitive testing of Ricky's attentional skills, the intern came to the conclusion that he fit the criteria for a diagnosis of Attention-Deficit Hyperactivity Disorder. His mother was introduced to the idea of multimodal treatment and, after some hesitation, agreed to give stimulant medication a try. Ricky's teachers also were trained to implement a behavior modification program in which they rewarded successively longer periods of time of on-task behavior by allowing Ricky to participate in an enjoyable activity, including playing a new video game on the classroom computer. Next, attention and self-monitoring were targeted, with rewards given when Ricky made eye contact, listened to Mrs. Candler's instructions, and repeated them to himself. As he mastered these skills, the goals of treatment shifted to organizational and study skills, such as keeping his desk neat, handing his homework in on time, raising his hand to ask questions, and telling his mother what supplies he needed for school. Although Ricky benefited from treatment, showing less disruptive behavior and increased attention over the next 6 months, his mother discontinued abruptly, saying that she felt he had improved enough to be maintained only on drug treatment. Telephone contact a year later revealed that Ricky's misbehavior was still manageable but that his school performance remained mediocre to poor.

Source: Adapted from Kearney, 2003.

cooperativeness in the consultation room. Research suggests that the children's ability to sustain attention and control their impulses is more problematic (1) later in the day; (2) when tasks are more complicated and require more organizational skills; (3) when behavioral restraint is required, such as sitting in church or a restaurant; (4) when levels of stimulation are low; (5) when there is a delay in feedback or reward for task completion; (6) in the absence of adult supervision; and (7) when the task requires persistence. Children with ADHD also tend to evidence fewer behavioral problems when their fathers are at home, perhaps because of the additional structure that fathers' presence provides. Taking all these factors into account, it is no surprise that the classroom is the single most problematic setting for children with ADHD, given that it requires all of the skills and aptitudes that are most challenging for the child with the disorder (Barkley, 2003).

The inconsistency of the child's behavior from setting to setting also might mislead adults about the willfulness of the child's inattentiveness and overactivity. Because children with ADHD may demonstrate relatively few behavioral problems in unstructured or stimulating settings, such as during the lunch period, free play, or during novel events such as field trips, adults may erroneously assume that the children's behavior is a matter of choice and that ADHD is within their control: "He can behave when he wants to!"

Prevalence

In a study of a representative community sample of 1,420 children, Costello and colleagues (2003) found that the prevalence of the ADHD diagnosis ranged from 2.2 percent at age 9 to 1.4 percent at age 12 to 0.3 percent at age 16. Across the age range, overall prevalence rates were 0.3 percent for girls and 1.5 percent for boys. Averaging across, the prevalence of ADHD is generally estimated at 3 to 5 percent of the school-age population. There is also evidence of a decline with age, especially for boys. However, it is not clear whether this is a true decline or an artifact of the developmentally insensitive assessment techniques used; for example, the diagnostic criteria might not be as appropriate for adolescents as they are for those in middle childhood (Barkley, 2003).

Gender Differences

Determining the extent of sex differences in ADHD is complicated by referral bias. Since more boys than girls have the comorbid conditions of oppositional defiance and conduct problems, boys are more likely to be referred for an evaluation. For example, the ratio of boys to girls in the clinical population is 6:1 to 9:1, while the ratio ranges between 2:1 to 3:1 in nonclinical samples. Further, the behavioral criteria used to diagnose ADHD appear to be more relevant to boys than girls; consequently, girls must meet a higher threshold in order to qualify for the diagnosis (Barkley, 2003). Therefore, there is some question about the true nature and extent of the gender difference in ADHD.

In clinical samples, when girls are diagnosed with the disorder, they show a similar level of impairment as boys and the same pattern of comorbidity, but even greater deficits in intelligence. However, samples drawn from the community show that girls with ADHD are less likely to have comorbid conduct problems and oppositionality but are as socially and academically impaired as boys (Gershon, 2002).

Socioeconomic Status, Ethnicity, and Culture

There is some evidence that ADHD is more prevalent in *socioeconomically disadvantaged* groups; however, the data are not consistent and the association seems to disappear when comorbid disorders are taken into account (Barkley, 1998). Similarly, while some studies show a disproportionate percentage of ADHD in lower-SES African American and Hispanic children, this may be due to the increase in the comorbid conditions of aggression and conduct problems in these populations rather than to ADHD itself (Szatmari, 1992).

Ethnic differences in the prevalence of ADHD are unclear and a topic of some debate. While disconcertingly few studies have included ethnically diverse samples, one finding of note is that teachers tend to rate African American children higher on symptoms of ADHD than they do European American children (Epstein, March, Conners, & Jackson,

1998). Whether these ratings are related to actual behavioral differences or biased perceptions is an important question for future research. Within the Asian American community, in contrast, rates of ADHD are lower than in other ethnic groups (Serafica, 1997).

Looking *cross-culturally,* we find that discrepant prevalence rates are reported in international studies comparing samples derived from diverse cultures, including the United States, Germany, New Zealand, Canada, Japan, India, China, the Netherlands, Brazil, Columbia, the United Arab Emirates, and Ukraine. Rates have been found ranging from a high of 29 percent in India to a low of 2 percent in Japan (see Barkley, 2003). While much of the variability probably is due to differences in the diagnostic criteria, measures, and sampling methods used, culturally derived differences in expectations for children's behavior and the interpretation of symptoms

also may contribute to these discrepancies. For example, while Chinese children in Hong Kong were found to have higher rates of hyperactivity than comparison children in the United States and the United Kingdom, Chinese parents appeared to be less tolerant of a high activity level in children, and therefore might have been more inclined to rate their children's behavior as troublesome (Evans & Lee, 1998). In fact, some critics have questioned whether ADHD is anything *but* a culturally derived disorder. (See Figure 7.1 and Box 7.2.)

Comorbidity and Differential Diagnosis

Comorbidity affects many of the clinically relevant features of ADHD as well as the effect of ADHD on later development. (Comorbidity of ADHD and learning disorders will be discussed in more detail in the section of this chapter that discusses learning disorders.)

Figure 7.1

TOLES Copyright © 2000 *The Washington Post.* Reprinted with permission of UNIVERSAL PRESS SYNDICATE. All rights reserved.

Box 7.2 | **Is ADHD a "Real" Disorder? The International Consensus Statement**

In the history of clinical child psychology, perhaps no disorder has been more challenged and subject to scrutiny than ADHD. Indeed, the very existence of the disorder has been called into question by some who dismiss it as a myth or even a fraud. As the cartoon in Figure 7.1 suggests, some critics have argued that the mental health establishment is quick to label as psychopathological exhuberant and energetic behavior in children merely because it is inconvenient to the adults around them. Further, it is argued, earlier in human evolution, impulsive thinking, snap judgments, and vigilance to every distraction in the environment were adaptive traits for human beings (Hartmann, 1997)—and perhaps still are in our fast-paced world of quick sound bites and instant gratification (Hallowell & Ratey, 1994).

In response to these challenges, an international consortium of 70 ADHD investigators, spearheaded by Russell Barkley (2002), published an International Consensus Statement to counter media dismissals of the authenticity of the ADHD diagnosis. Excerpts from the statement will best illustrate the urgency of their argument and the heat the controversy has generated:

- "We cannot overemphasize the point that, as a matter of science, the notion that ADHD does not exist is simply wrong. All of the major medical associations and government health agencies recognize ADHD as a genuine disorder because the scientific evidence indicating it is so overwhelming . . . As attested to by the numerous scientists signing this document, there is no question among the world's leading clinical researchers that ADHD involves a serious deficiency in a set of psychological abilities and that these deficiencies pose serious harm to most individuals possessing the disorder" (p. 89).
- "ADHD is not a benign disorder. For those it afflicts, ADHD can cause devastating problems . . . Yet, despite these serious consequences, studies indicate that less than half of those with the disorder are receiving treatment. The media can help substantially to improve these circumstances. It can do so by portraying ADHD and the science about it as accurately and responsibly as possible while not purveying the propaganda of some social critics and fringe doctors whose political agenda would have you and the public believe there is no real disorder here" (p. 90).
- "To publish stories that ADHD is a fictitious disorder or merely a conflict between today's Huckleberry Finns and their caregivers is tantamount to declaring the earth flat, the laws of gravity debatable, and the periodic table in chemistry a fraud" (p. 90).
- "ADHD should be depicted in the media as realistically and accurately as it is depicted in science—as a valid disorder having varied and substantial adverse impact on those who suffer from it through no fault of their own or their parents and teachers" (pp. 90–91).

ADHD/Disruptive Behavior

There is a strong association between ADHD and disruptive behavior disorders. By 7 years of age, 54 to 67 percent of clinically referred children with ADHD will also be diagnosed as having oppositional-defiant disorder (ODD). From 20 to 50 percent will develop comorbid conduct disorder (CD) in middle childhood and 44 to 50 percent will be diagnosed with CD in adolescence. Conduct problems persist into adulthood in as many as 26 percent of cases (Fischer, Barkley, Smallish, & Fletcher, 2004).

ADHD/CD has an earlier onset than ADHD alone and a higher ratio of boys to girls. In general, the combination results in a more severe disturbance, adversely affecting a wide array of developmental variables within the children, in their relations with parents, and in their performance at school and in other settings (Kuhne, Schachar, & Tannock, 1997). Aggressive boys with ADHD also report more depression and lower self-esteem than do non-aggressive boys with ADHD (Treuting & Hinshaw, 2001). Adolescent substance abuse is a particular risk for those with comorbid ADHD and conduct disorder, as is adult criminal activity (Satterfield & Schnell, 1997).

Both environmental and genetic factors may contribute to the comorbidity of ADHD and disruptive behavior. While these disorders all tend to co-occur in families, suggesting an underlying genetic base, family adversity also is a risk factor they have in common, suggesting an environmental influence (Barkley, 2003).

ADHD/Anxiety Disorder

There is an overlap between ADHD and anxiety disorders in 10 to 40 percent of the clinical population (Tannock, 2000). The presence of an anxiety disorder, unlike that of conduct disorder, tends to diminish rather than intensify the negative effects of the disturbance. Specifically, children with comorbid ADHD and anxiety evidence lower externalizing behaviors in general and less impulsivity in particular (Pliszka, 2002). In this way, anxiety appears to act as a buffer against ADHD symptoms. The primarily inattentive children are the most likely to have comorbid anxiety disorders (Milich, Balantine, & Lynam, 2001).

While anxiety disorders may be comorbid with ADHD, *differential diagnosis* is important in the case of Posttraumatic Stress Disorder (PTSD). (See Chapter 8.) ADHD and PTSD have in common a number of symptoms such as distractibility, inattentiveness, and difficulty concentrating. However, the origins, implications, and interventions for the symptoms are significantly different for the two disorders. Therefore, it is important to assess for the presence of trauma in the lives of children who are suspected of having ADHD (Kerig, Fedorowicz, Brown, & Warren, 2000).

ADHD/Mood Disorders

ADHD also tends to co-occur with depression, both in its mild and severe forms (Spencer et al.,

2000). While the prevalence range differs from study to study, most find the comorbidity to be between 20 and 30 percent. However, the relationship between ADHD and depression is complicated by the presence of other disorders. For example, one follow-up study (Fischer et al., 2004) found that by young adulthood, 26 percent of a sample of children with ADHD had developed a major depression, but the risk was largely accounted for by a comorbidity with conduct disorder. There also is a significant overlap between ADHD and bipolar disorder (manic-depression), but there is a question about whether this is an artifact of the similarity in the symptoms used to diagnose the two disorders (Kim & Miklowitz, 2002).

ADHD/Learning Disorders (LD)

The majority of clinically referred children with ADHD have difficulty with school performance, which can be detected as early as the preschool years (Barkley et al., 2002). From 19 to 26 percent of children with ADHD have difficulties severe enough to qualify for a diagnosis of learning disorder, and as many as 80 percent have learning problems significant enough to cause them to lag two years behind their peers in school (Barkley, 2003). Low academic achievement seems to be a natural consequence of children with the inattentive type of ADHD because of the difficulty in sustaining attention on tasks, distractibility, failure to follow through on instructions, and problems with organization. There is also a small but significant relation between lower IQ and the hyperactive-impulsive type of ADHD, which in turn plays a role in lower academic achievement.

Rapport, Scanlan, and Denney (1999) proposed two pathways by which ADHD might be linked to academic underachievement. In one pathway, ADHD symptoms increase the risk of conduct problems in the classroom that lead to academic problems. In the other pathway, cognitive deficits associated with ADHD, including poor attention, lower general intelligence, and deficits in executive function, directly affect academic achievement.

Associated Developmental Problems

Frequently, children with ADHD evidence problems in a number of areas of development. For example, they often have difficulties with fine and gross motor coordination, nonverbal reasoning, executive functions such as planning and organization, verbal fluency, and emotion regulation. They also often evidence social problems and present teachers, parents, and peers with a difficult interactional style characterized by intrusiveness, demandingness, negativism, and excessive emotionality (Barkley, 2003). While not disorders in and of themselves, these associated characteristics increase the risk for negative transactions, maladaptation, and the development of comorbid psychopathology.

Etiology

The Biological Context

Unsupported Hypotheses   We will note here a number of biological hypotheses that were once popular but have failed to stand up under the scrutiny of objective studies.

An influential etiological hypothesis around 50 years ago was that ADHD was due to *brain damage*. This is understandable given that attention problems are a frequent consequence of traumatic brain injury (see Chapter 13). However, subsequent research using more advanced technology for exploring the brain showed that fewer than 5 percent of the children with ADHD have suffered neurological injury or seizure disorders, and therefore brain injury is not implicated in most of the children with the disorder (Barkley, 1990).

Some studies have targeted *diet* and *neurotoxins* as causes of ADHD. Sugar and food additives such as artificial coloring have been regarded as the culprits by some researchers, and special diets have been devised as treatment. However, subsequent objective studies indicated that the diets were largely ineffective in changing the symptoms of ADHD (Richters et al., 1995).

Elevated blood lead levels have been implicated as causing ADHD, but studies relating lead poisoning to the symptoms of ADHD have yielded conflicting results. While it is clear that lead blood level is not a primary etiological agent for ADHD, there is a small but significant relation between the two; for example, one estimate is that lead poisoning accounts for approximately 4 percent of the variance in ADHD symptoms (Fergusson et al., 1988).

Genetic Factors   There is compelling evidence that heredity plays a major role in causing ADHD. Results from studies of twins provide the most convincing evidence. In such studies the heritability for symptoms ranges from .75 to .97 (Levy & Hay, 2001). For example, Levy and colleagues (1997), using a cohort of 1,938 families with twins and nontwin siblings ages 4 through 12, found a heritability quotient of .75 to .91. The finding was robust, holding across familial relations (i.e., between twins, between siblings, and between twins and other siblings) as well as across definitions of ADHD. Estimates of the contribution of nonshared environmental (nongenetic) factors is between 9 and 20 percent.

Neuropsychological Factors   A host of characteristics of ADHD implicate impairment within the brain: the early onset and persistence of symptoms, the dramatic improvement with medication, deficient performance on neuropsychological tests such as working memory and motor coordination, and the genetic risks just described. Data from direct examination of the brain have yielded suggestive findings.

Studies using EEGs have found a consistent pattern of increased slow-wave activity in the frontal lobes, suggesting underarousal and underreactivity in children with ADHD. (Here we follow Barkley, 2003.) Further, stimulant medication directly corrects these abnormalities.

Investigations of cerebral blood flow using single-photon emission computed tomography (SPECT) show decreased blood flow to the prefrontal regions, particularly the right frontal area, as well as to pathways connecting these areas to the limbic system, particularly an area known as the caudate nucleus, and the cerebellum. The frontal and frontal-limbic areas are of special interest because one of their functions is the inhibition of motor responses. The prefrontal lobes also are suspected to be involved in ADHD because this is the area of the brain that is primarily involved with the executive functions of planning, organization, self-regulation, and impulse control that are so lacking in the child with ADHD. The degree of blood flow in the right frontal area can be directly correlated with the severity of the disorder, just as that in the cerebellum is related to motor problems in children with ADHD (Gustafsson et al., 2000).

Magnetic resonance imaging (MRI) techniques have revealed that children with ADHD have a smaller splenium, which is the posterior portion of the corpus callosum (the structure connecting the two hemispheres of the brain). In addition, studies have also found a smaller left caudate nucleus, consistent with the blood flow studies described earlier. This latter finding is particularly interesting given that it represents a reversal of the usual asymmetry of the caudate, in which the right side is generally smaller. While other studies have implicated other areas of the brain, the results have not been as consistent as those pointing to the prefrontal area, the caudate, and the cerebellum.

Advances in methodology have allowed us a peek into the brain at work. Studies using functional MRI (fMRI) show that, when asked to do tasks requiring attention and inhibition, children with ADHD show abnormal patterns of activation in the right prefrontal region, the basal ganglia (that includes the striatum), and the cerebellum.

Neurotransmitters   There also has been interest in investigating central nervous system neurotransmitters, particularly dopamine and norepinephrine, which are thought to be important to the functioning of the frontal-limbic area of the brain. Neurotransmitters also are implicated because stimulant medications, which are so effective in treating ADHD, act by increasing the availability of dopamine and norepinephrine in the brain (DuPaul, Barkley, & Connor, 1998).

The Developmental Dimension   Seidman and associates (1997), who conducted one of the few studies yielding developmental data, were concerned

with changes in neuropsychological functioning as assessed by tests of attention and executive functions. The 118 ADHD and control male participants, who were between 9 and 22 years of age, were divided into two age groups, one younger than 15, the other older. The investigators found both ADHD groups to be neuropsychologically impaired, attesting to the enduring nature of such deficits. In regard to development, older boys with ADHD performed better than younger ones did; however, this improvement was seen in normal controls as well. Consequently, while older boys with ADHD become less impaired, they still are not able to catch up with the normal group, which also has improved over time.

The Family Context

DSM-IV-TR classifies ADHD as a *disruptive behavior disorder,* signifying that its symptoms of aggression, oppositionality, intrusiveness, and disorganization interfere with the normal give-and-take of social interaction. As might be expected, such negative behavior has a transactional effect on family relations, bringing out the worst in both parent and child. Parents of ADHD children report more stress and maladaptive strategies for coping with the demands of parenting and tend to respond more negatively to their children than do parents of control children (DuPaul, McGoey, Eckert, & VanBrakle, 2001).

Johnston and Mash (2001) reviewed the literature on the family relationships of children with ADHD and found that, although the research is often mixed and complicated by comorbidity with conduct problems, several trends emerge consistently. One is that parents and children with ADHD engage in more negative and coercive behavior with one another, a dynamic that is particularly salient when observations are made of mothers' interactions with young boys. Parents of ADHD children also report higher levels of stress and psychological symptoms across numerous studies. Another consistent theme is that parents' attributions for their children's behavior differ as a function of ADHD. Parents of children with ADHD are more likely than those of typical children to view the child's behavior as caused by uncontrollable and stable factors within the child, while they perceived their child's positive behavior as less dispositional, and the parents themselves as having less responsibility for how their child behaved. On the other hand, the available research does not support the assumption that parents of children with ADHD have more marital problems or are more likely to divorce than parents of typically developing children.

Given the heritability of ADHD, we also must keep in mind that many of the parents also struggle with ADHD, which might interfere with their ability to consistently implement good parenting techniques. Mothers of ADHD children who themselves have ADHD also report more personality and psychiatric problems, including depression, anxiety, low self-esteem, and poor coping, than do mothers of ADHD children who do not themselves have ADHD (Weinstein, Apfel, & Weinstein, 1998).

There also is strong evidence that it is not the presence of ADHD per se but of the comorbid ODD and CD that is associated with many of the problematic family relations. This same comorbidity is associated with a greater degree of parental psychopathology, marital discord, and divorce than is found in ADHD alone (Loeber, Green, Lahey, Frick, & McBurnett, 2000).

Protective Factors   On the side of protective factors, research shows that among children at high risk for ADHD, positive parenting can provide a buffer. Tully and colleagues (2004) conducted a study of 2,232 five-year-old twins, half of whom had low birth weight. Using a measure of expressed emotion (EE), in which mothers were tape recorded while they answered open-ended questions about their children, raters coded parental warmth as a function of mothers' tone of voice, empathy, and positive feelings expressed toward the child. While low-birth-weight children of mothers high in warmth were less likely to exhibit ADHD symptoms on scales completed by teachers and parents, low maternal warmth appeared to exacerbate the effects of low birth weight on children's attention.

The Social Context

The annoying, intrusive, and insensitive behaviors of children with ADHD significantly increase the chances of peer rejection and social isolation. They interact with peers in a more negative and socially unskilled way than do control children (DuPaul, McGoey, Eckert, & VanBrakle, 2001). Moreover, when introduced to a peer with ADHD, children take only minutes to notice and react negatively to the ADHD child's behavior. Parental behavior also plays a role in the peer status of children with ADHD. Hinshaw et al. (1997) found that authoritative parenting, with its combination of firm limits, appropriate confrontations, reasoning, warmth, and support, promoted social competence in children with ADHD.

The Cultural Context

Television Viewing   For some time, concerns have been raised in the professional and popular media about the potential effects of *television* and *video games* on children's attention. In contrast to the natural pace of life, Christakis and colleagues point out, television presents children with a rapidly changing series of images, scenes, and events that can be interesting and stimulating but requires only a limited span of attention. The investigators set out to determine whether television viewing in the early years, when the brain is developing in crucial ways, increases the risk of ADHD symptoms. The researchers followed a group of 1,345 children from age 1 to age 7 and asked parents to report on the number of hours a day children spent in front of the television screen. Among 1-year-olds, 36 percent watched no TV while 37 percent watched 1 to 2 hours daily and 14 percent watched TV 3 or more hours. The risk of attention problems by age 7 increased directly as a function of the number of hours spent in front of the television during the preschool years. Two hours daily was associated with a 10 to 20 percent increased risk, and 3 to 4 hours daily was associated with a 30 to 40 percent increased risk when compared to the children who watched no TV at all.

While the data are suggestive, the investigators acknowledged that they did not track the kinds of

Figure 7.2   An Integrative Model of Hyperactivity-Impulsivity.

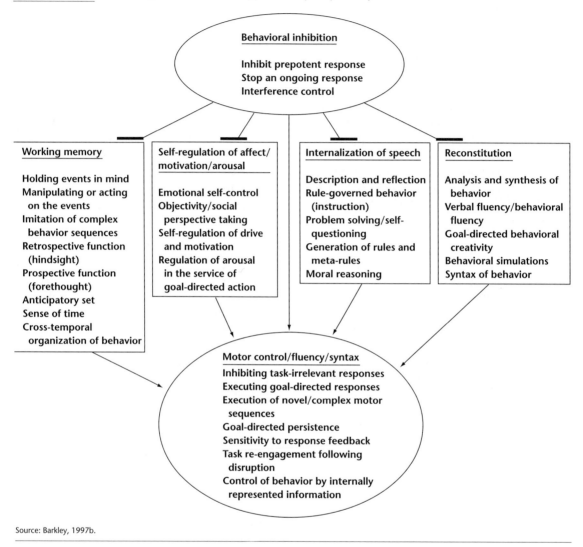

Source: Barkley, 1997b.

television programs the children were watching. Whether the findings would hold true for children who view educational programs is not certain. Another question concerns other possible differences among the families and households in which young children were protected from television viewing: These might have been more highly educated parents or affluent families who had access to alternative activities in which to engage their young children.

An Integrative Developmental Model: The Hyperactive-Impulsive Type

Russell A. Barkley (1997, 2003) has developed a model that integrates research findings concerning the hyperactive-impulsive type of ADHD. (See Figure 7.2.)

The cornerstone of Barkley's model is *behavioral inhibition* or the ability to delay motor response. There are two component processes to behavioral inhibition: (1) the capacity to delay an initial response (response inhibition), and (2) the capacity to protect this response delay from interference by competing events that might tempt the child to become disinhibited (interference control).

Behavioral inhibition, in turn, allows for the adaptive development of *executive functions*. There are four such functions. The first of these is *nonverbal working memory,* which allows the child to hold information "on-line" while performing an operation on it, such as by comparing it to previously learned information. Working memory is essential for planning in that it allows the child to activate past images ("hindsight") in order to guide a future response ("foresight"). Working memory also has a role in sustained attention in that it allows the child to keep in mind an intention or plan in order to engage in goal-directed activity in the face of distractions, obstacles, or even boredom. Impairments in working memory may be a culprit in many of the deficits that are characteristic of ADHD, including forgetfulness, poor time management, reduced hindsight and forethought, and problems with sustaining long chains of organized behavior. To date, research has confirmed that children with ADHD have difficulties with working memory, temporal sequencing, and forethought, although the model's predictions regarding sense of time have yet to be tested.

The second executive function is *internalized speech,* which is related to verbal working memory. As children enter the preschool years, language becomes a vehicle not only for communicating with others, but for communicating with the self. Young preschoolers often provide a running commentary about their own activities, both for the edification of themselves and others. By the time they enter first grade, for most children self-talk becomes more quiet and private and is used specifically for the purposes of self-instruction and self-control. For example, children might repeat aloud to themselves the rules of a game or their parents' inhibitions about touching a fragile object. However, Barkley proposes that children with ADHD exhibit a delay in the internalization of speech, resulting in excessive talking in public, less mental reflection before acting, poorer

self-control, and difficulty following rules and instructions. While research has offered confirmation for some of these suppositions, it is unclear to what extent such deficits might be accounted for by the overlap of ADHD with learning disorders (Willcutt et al., 2001).

The third executive function necessary for adaptive development is *self-regulation of affect,* which involves the ability to moderate the expression of feelings and to delay responding in reaction to them. Such self-regulation occurs internally, moderating the intensity of the emotional experience, as well as externally, allowing the child control over the public display of emotion. As we know from our discussion of emotion regulation in Chapter 2, the child who is able to regulate emotions can dampen as well as heighten them as needed. Therefore, affect regulation allows children to "psych up" and increase arousal as needed, such as to motivate themselves in order to keep working on a tedious task. The child with ADHD, in contrast, lacks this kind of emotional self-control, Barkley posits, leading to greater emotional reactivity to events, less objectivity, and poorer perspective-taking in that their perceptions are colored by their immediate emotional reactions, and dependence on external motivators to sustain their efforts to meet a goal. Research has demonstrated that children with ADHD have poorer emotion regulation, but this appears to be true particularly of those children who have comorbid oppositional-defiant disorder.

The fourth executive function is *reconstitution,* which involves high-level mental operations, such as analysis, synthesis, and creative thinking. The child who can delay responding long enough to sustain a mental image of a problem is a child who is better able to study it, explore its component pieces, and perhaps even put it together in a different way. Barkley surmises that these higher-level mental processes arise out of the internalization of play: Just as internalization of language goes from overt (talking aloud) to covert (thinking it through in one's mind), so does mental play. The capacity for reconstitution is essential to the child's ability to shift set and engage in flexible problem solving in order to overcome obstacles. In contrast, the model suggests that children with ADHD would have difficulty with analysis and synthesis, verbal and nonverbal fluency, and strategy development. To date, little research is available on this facet of Barkley's model.

The final outcome of executive functions is *motor control and fluency,* which relates to the planning and carrying out of actions. Given that Barkley's model assumes that the deficits in behavioral inhibition arise in the brain's motor system, the executive function dysfunctions described previously should show their effects in developmental difficulties in motor coordination and the planning and execution of complex chains of goal-directed behavior.

Barkley believes that the primary deficit in ADHD is the weakened ability to *inhibit behavior.* All other deviations characteristic of ADHD are secondary to this reduced capacity for behavioral control. Thus, when the development of behavioral inhibition goes awry, this deficiency is primarily responsible for the deficits in the subsequent executive functions that emerge later over the course of development. Further, Barkley's model assumes that the primary deficit in behavioral inhibition arises as a product of biological factors, whether genetic or neuropsychological. While interpersonal factors may influence the expression of the disorder, they do not cause it.

Barkley's is a complex model that integrates many of the findings regarding children with the hyperactive-impulsive type of ADHD. One of its particular strengths is that it accounts for many of the associated characteristics that reflect underlying cognitive, social, and emotional developmental problems in ADHD beyond simple inattention or disinhibition. The model also has a developmental component that helps to explain the temporal ordering of the emergence of ADHD symptoms. On the other hand, many of the elements of the model have yet to be tested, and so it remains a promising hypothetical construction of the developmental psychopathology of ADHD.

Developmental Course

In keeping with our thesis that psychopathology is normal development gone awry, we will first present relevant material on normal development. This material, in turn, will serve as a point of departure for presenting the deviations evidenced by the symptoms of ADHD.

The Toddler/Preschool Period

Campbell (2002) makes the point that normal development shades imperceptibly into ADHD, especially in the first 6 years of life. One expects toddlers to be "all over the place and into everything," for example, and if they have a high energy level along with a determination to do what they want to do when they want to do it, it may not be easy to decide whether or not they are disturbed because these are age-appropriate behaviors. In addition, the fluidity of early development makes it difficult to predict if a child will outgrow the behavior when it is deviant.

Normal preschoolers are expected to be sufficiently task oriented to complete what they start and monitor the correctness of their behavior. They are also sufficiently cooperative to accept tasks set by others and participate in peer activities. As in the toddler period, deviations from expectation may be part of normal development, perhaps because of temporary difficulties in adjustment or temperament or unrealistic adult requirements. The main clues to disturbance lie in the severity, frequency, pervasiveness, and chronicity of the problem behaviors.

Now we consider ADHD itself. Before 3 years of age, toddlers evidence an undifferentiated cluster of behaviors that has been called an *undercontrolled* pattern of conduct. However, at around 3 years of age this pattern becomes differentiated, making it possible to distinguish between hyperactive and impulsive behavior on the one hand and aggressive and defiant behavior on the other. Thus, at age 3 to 4 years we are able to detect ADHD properly (Barkley, 2003).

Hyperactive and impulsive preschoolers who continue to be difficult to control for a year or more are highly likely to have ADHD in middle childhood (Campbell, 2002). This persistence of ADHD, in turn, is more apt to occur if parent and child are locked into a pattern of negativism and overcontrollingness on the mother's part and defiance on the child's. In fact, parental stress is at its highest during the preschool period (Campbell et al., 1991).

Middle Childhood

By middle childhood the standards for self-control, task orientation, self-monitoring of appropriate and inappropriate behavior, and cooperation in family and peer groups are sufficiently clear that the difference between typical variability of behavior and ADHD is more readily apparent. Thus, a persistent constellation of disruptive behavior at home and in the classroom, along with disorganization and inability to follow routines, raises serious questions of psychopathology (Campbell, 2002).

Hyperactive-impulsive behavior is likely to persist throughout middle childhood. In addition, there are two new developments. One is the appearance of problems with **sustained attention,** or the ability to continue a task until completed. These problems appear at around 5 to 7 years of age (Loeber et al., 1992). *Inattention,* in turn, gives rise to difficulties with work completion, forgetfulness, poor organization, and distractibility, all of which may adversely affect the children's functioning at home and at school.

There is evidence that inattention remains stable through middle childhood whereas hyperactive-impulsive behavior declines (Hart et al., 1995). As has been noted, it is not clear whether the latter effect represents a true developmental phenomenon or whether it is an artifact of increasingly inappropriate behaviors used to define hyperactivity/impulsivity (e.g., inappropriate running around and climbing) (Barkley, 2003).

The second important development in middle childhood is the increased prevalence of comorbid conditions (Barkley, 2003). Early in the period ODD may develop in a significant number of children, and by 8 to 12 years of age such early forms of defiance and hostility are likely to evolve into symptoms of CD in up to half of the children (Hart et al., 1995). Comorbid disruptive behaviors are most likely to develop among the children whose ADHD symptoms are more pervasive across situations (McArdle, O'Brien, & Kolvin, 1995).

Adolescence

The previously held idea that ADHD is outgrown in adolescence has proved to be incorrect. From 50 to 80 percent of clinically referred children will continue to have ADHD into adolescence. While it is true that adolescence marks a decline in the symptoms of hyperactivity and inattention, the same decline is noted in normal controls. There may also be a change in the expression of symptoms; for example, driven motor activity may be replaced by an inner feeling of restlessness, or reckless behavior such as bike accidents may be replaced by automobile accidents (Cantwell, 1996).

Perhaps because of the cascading effects of previous developmental failures in school and peer relations, adolescents with ADHD engage in a number of problem behaviors. Klein and Mannuzza (1991), in their review of longitudinal studies, found that a substantial subgroup (25 percent) of adolescents with ADHD engaged in antisocial activities such as stealing and fire setting. Between 56 and 70 percent were likely to repeat grades, and the group as a whole was more likely to be expelled or drop out of school, as compared with controls. In addition, Whalen, Jamner, Henker, Delfino, and Lozano (2002) found that higher levels of ADHD symptoms were related to increasingly negative moods in adolescents, less time spent on achievement-oriented tasks, and more tobacco and alcohol use.

In sum, adolescents with ADHD are significantly more disturbed than those without ADHD and must face the normative adolescent challenges of physiological changes, sexual adjustment, peer acceptance, and vocational choice burdened by the cascading deficits arising from poor resolution of stage-salient issues in past developmental periods.

Adulthood

Cantwell (1996) estimates that around 30 percent of adolescents outgrow ADHD; 40 percent continue to have the symptoms of restlessness, inattention, and impulsivity while 30 percent develop additional disturbances. The chances for recovery seem particularly good for the symptoms of hyperactivity and impulsivity. For example, in his longitudinal research, Barkley and his colleagues (1992) have found that a subset of young adults with childhood ADHD-Combined Type meet criteria only for the inattentive type in young adulthood, seeming to have outgrown their hyperactive-impulsive tendencies.

Box 7.3   **Dilemmas in the Assessment of ADHD: Whose Report Is Valid?**

The attentive reader will have noted that at a number of junctures we offered cautions regarding the possibility that some findings may in fact be artifacts of problems with the measures used to assess and diagnose ADHD. These include the fact that measures are generally developmentally insensitive and thus do not capture well the differential appropriateness of the relevant behaviors across the life span; in addition, the measures are not sensitive to gender differences in the ways that girls and boys display symptoms of the disorder. Barkley (2003) adds to these concerns the fact that the diagnostic criteria do not require the clinician to obtain information from reporters who know the child's behavior well. This can lead to erroneous assumptions, such as that ADHD symptoms decrease over the course of late adolescence and adulthood. For example, Barkley and his colleagues (2002) conducted a follow-up study of adults

who had been diagnosed with ADHD in childhood. Based upon self-reports of behavior, the investigators found that only 5 percent of these individuals still met DSM criteria for the disorder. Does this mean that they had outgrown their ADHD? It depends on whom you ask. When the interviewers asked parents to provide ratings, the number of adults who still met DSM criteria for ADHD rose to 46 percent—a nine-fold increase.

Whose report is the most valid? To answer this question, the investigators compared how well self-reports and parent reports predicted individuals' educational, social, and occupational functioning, as well as their antisocial behavior. The results showed that parents' reports made a larger contribution to predicting almost all domains of functioning than did self-reports, suggesting that parents' ratings might indeed be more valid.

Another diagnostic dilemma results from DSM-IV-TR's requirement

that the child exhibit symptoms in at least two of three settings, in which his or her behavior is likely to be rated by different observers. The perspectives of teachers, parents, pediatricians, employers, and so forth often do not agree, precisely because they are seeing the individual in different environments. What draws the observer's attention to the child and raises his or her concern also might differ according to setting. For example, parents might be more reactive to disruptive behavior, whereas teachers might be more sensitive to inattentiveness that interferes with school performance. Further, observers' ratings might be colored by comorbidity of the child's ADHD with other disorders that call attention to themselves, particularly conduct problems and ODD (Costello, Loeber, & Stouthamer-Loeber, 1991). Ideally, the clinician will seek multiple sources of information, "triangulating" them the way that a surveyor does (Cowan, 1978).

The *continuity* of ADHD across the life span is addressed by four large-scale studies that followed children with ADHD into adulthood. For example, in a study based in Montreal, Weiss and Hechtman (2004) found that 67 percent of their now 25-year-old sample reported that symptoms of the disorder continued to interfere with their functioning. Thirty-four percent reported moderate to severe hyperactivity, inattention, and/or impulsivity. Similar results were obtained in Sweden by Rasmussen and Gillberg (2001), who found that 49 percent of those diagnosed with ADHD in childhood had symptoms of the disorder at age 22, in comparison to 9 percent of controls. Both of these studies were based on

symptom rating scales rather than official DSM criteria. A more exacting methodology was used in a study based in New York (Mannuzza et al., 1998) that found that 31 to 43 percent of their sample met DSM-III criteria for ADHD in adolescence, whereas 4 to 8 percent met the newer DSM-III-R criteria in adulthood 8 years later. A possible reason for this remarkable disparity is that, as the research participants reached adulthood, the source of information about symptoms shifted from parents and teachers to the individuals themselves. (See Box 7.3.)

Longitudinal studies of children with ADHD indicate that as adults they have a higher prevalence of ADHD, antisocial behavior, and substance abuse than do other adults (Klein & Mannuzza, 1991). However, while the risk for criminal behavior increases in adulthood, this holds only for those who have both ADHD and CD or other antisocial behaviors; there is no direct connection between ADHD and criminality.

While no cognitive deficits have been documented in adults, academic achievement and educational history both suffer. Children with ADHD complete about 2 years less schooling than do controls. As can be expected, when they enter the work world in adulthood, they have lower-ranking occupational positions (Mannuzza et al., 1998).

Summary of Developmental Course

In the preschool period hyperactive-impulsive behavior and aggressive and defiant behavior become differentiated out of a generalized pattern of uncontrolled behavior. Consequently, children begin to clearly exhibit behavior that allows for the diagnosis of ADHD at around 3 to 4 years of age. Persistent ADHD in the preschool period is predictive of its continuation into middle childhood. Early middle childhood sees the addition of the inattentive type of ADHD. Moreover, comorbid ODD emerges early in the development, while CD emerges later on. Whereas inattention remains constant throughout middle childhood, hyperactivity/impulsivity declines.

ADHD persists into adolescence and adulthood. While hyperactivity may decline in those with ADHD, it is still significantly greater than in non-ADHD controls, with impulsive behavior being replaced by feelings of restlessness. The adolescent with ADHD may engage in antisocial behavior and do poorly academically. Adults may have problems with alcoholism and drug abuse, as well as with antisocial behavior. However, antisocial behavior is related to comorbid CD rather than to hyperactivity itself. While the rate of employment for ADHD adults is no different from that of non-ADHD adults, those with ADHD have lower-ranking occupational positions.

The Inattentive Type

Comparatively little is known concerning the predominantly inattentive type of ADHD. The diagnosis itself was not established as a separate type until DSM-III, and systematic etiological research has been conducted only recently. Perhaps the fact that the symptoms are relatively subtle and unobtrusive has made the study of the disorder seem less urgent than in the case of the obstreperous hyperactive-impulsive type. However, the emerging evidence suggests that the inattentive subtype has different correlates and consequences than the hyperactive-impulsive or combined subtypes.

Descriptive Characteristics

In contrast to their hyperactive peers, who are described as noisy, messy, and disruptive, children with the inattentive type of ADHD are described in terms such as dreamy, "in a fog," "spaced out," passive, withdrawn, or lethargic (Barkley, 2003). Compared with typical children they are more often "off task," are less likely to complete their work, are less persistent in correctly performing boring assignments, work more slowly, and are less likely to return to an interrupted task (Barkley, 1997a). With peers, inattentive children are withdrawn, shy, and apprehensive rather than aggressive (Milich et al., 2001).

Recently, speculation has been increasing that the inattentive type actually represents a separate disorder from the hyperactive-impulsive type. In contrast to their hyperactive peers, the inattentive children exhibit a sluggish cognitive style, poor *selective* rather than sustained attention, less comorbidity with ODD and CD, more passivity in social relationships, and, as we will discuss in more detail next, a more benign developmental course (Milich et al., 2001). In addition, inattentive children appear to have more problems with verbal memory and visual-spatial processing than do children with the hyperactive-impulsive type.

As was true of the hyperactive-impulsive children described earlier, questions have arisen about the accuracy of the DSM criteria for describing the inattentive subtype. In particular, the sluggish cognitive tempo characteristic of children with the inattentive subtype is not well captured in the DSM description of inattentiveness. Carlson and Mann (2002) identified a subset of inattentive children who exhibited this slow cognitive tempo and found that, in comparison with other inattentive children, they were more likely to have problems with anxiety, depression, and social withdrawal. Therefore, it is possible that future diagnostic systems will need to take into account the possibility of a separate disorder—inattention—with two subtypes: slow and fast cognitive tempo (Barkley, 2003; Milich et al., 2001).

Prevalence and Gender Differences   The inattentive type of ADHD appears to be less prevalent than the hyperactive-impulsive type, at least during the school-age years. For example, one epidemiological study (Szatmari et al., 1989) found that 1.4 percent of boys and 1.3 percent of girls had the inattentive type (in contrast to 9.4 percent of boys and 2.8 percent of girls with the hyperactive-impulsive type). There was a shift in adolescence, however, with 1.4 percent of boys and 1 percent of girls having the inattentive type (in contrast to 2.9 percent of boys and 1.4 percent of females with the hyperactive-impulsive type).

Associated Disturbances   The inattentive type of ADHD particularly is associated with anxiety and mood disorders (Barkley, 2003). Because of such internalizing tendencies, children with the inattentive type are at less risk than are children with the hyperactive-impulsive type for adolescent delinquency and substance abuse, as well as for school suspensions or expulsions (Barkley, Fischer, Smallish, & Fletcher, 2004). Some studies have found that inattentive children are more likely to have poor school achievement or learning disorders, but the data are inconsistent (DuPaul, McGoey, Eckert, & VanBrackle, 2001).

Developmental Course of the Inattentive Type

While the majority of preschool children with ADHD are diagnosed with the hyperactive-impulsive type, it is in the school-age period that both the inattentive type and the combined hyperactive-inattentive type of ADHD begin to emerge. Thus, the age of onset is later for disorders involving primarily inattention.

The reasons for this developmental difference are unclear. Whether the later emergence of attention problems is due to the increasing developmental demands for attentiveness in school, because these represent two different developmental stages of the disorder, because these in fact represent two different disorders, or whether the explanation lies in the natural unfolding of the developmental variable of attention is not yet known.

What is clear, however, is that the developmental consequences differ for children whose ADHD is not accompanied by hyperactivity-impulsivity. Inattentiveness alone is not related to antisocial behavior, as is hyperactivity; but inattentiveness is predictive of poor academic achievement, particularly in reading. Symptoms of inattention also are more stable over the course of development, whereas hyperactivity and impulsivity decline in the transition from middle childhood to adolescence. However, Barkley (2003) offers a caveat: The behavioral measures used to assess hyperactivity-impulsivity appear to be more appropriate for younger children, whereas the measures used to assess inattention appear relevant across the age span. Therefore, it is possible that the stability of inattentiveness is an artifact of the methods we use to assess it.

Intervention

Pharmacotherapy

Medication is the most powerful and best-documented intervention for ADHD. (Our review follows the AACAP Official Action, 1997, which provides a more comprehensive discussion.)

Stimulants   Stimulants are the first choice for medication and the literature on them is voluminous. Stimulants are clearly effective, the onset of their action is rapid, and the side effects generally considered mild. The most popular stimulant is methylphenidate (Ritalin) followed by amphetamines (e.g., Dexedrine) and Pemoline (e.g., Cylert).

Most children with ADHD improve on stimulants, with the percentages ranging from 70 percent to as high as 96 percent. Stimulants not only affect the major symptoms of ADHD but also affect a host of social, cognitive, and academic problems. In regard to interpersonal problems, stimulants improve the mother-child and family interactions, reduce bossiness and aggression with peers, and increase the ability to work and play independently. Cognitively, short-term memory is improved along with the use of strategies already in the children's repertoire. Academically, classroom talking and disruptions decrease, while both the amount and accuracy of academic work completed increase. Incidentally, improvement is not specific to ADHD, since normal children given these stimulants improve as well.

In regard to comorbid conditions, stimulants are as effective in children with ADHD and aggression as with those who have ADHD alone. Evidence concerning the effectiveness of stimulants in ADHD with comorbid anxiety is mixed. Finally, research on the comorbid conditions of ODD and CD is sparse.

In general, stimulants have an extremely high margin of safety, and there is little evidence of increased tolerance that would necessitate increased dosage. However, there are side effects. Mild appetite suppression is almost universal, while individual children might also respond with irritability, headaches, and abdominal pains. Proponents of stimulants argue that concern about other side effects is exaggerated (Barkley, 2003). Children do not become "zombies" when medicated; on the contrary, they are alert and focused. Adverse effects on height and weight are rarely large enough to be clinically significant, although prolonged appetite suppression may be associated with delayed growth. Nor is there an increased risk of substance use or abuse later in development (Biederman, 2003). However, a general problem with all stimulant medications is that their positive effects are not sustained after they are withdrawn.

Tricyclic Antidepressants   While far less studied than stimulants, tricyclic antidepressants (TCSs) have demonstrated effectiveness in treating children and adolescents with ADHD. They are second-line drugs for children who do not respond to stimulants or who develop significant depressive or other side effects. Children with comorbid anxiety disorders, depression, or tics may respond better to TCSs than to stimulants.

However, there are drawbacks to TCSs. Efficiency in improving cognitive symptoms is not as great as for stimulants; there is a potential for cardiac side effects, especially in prepubertal children; and there is a possible decline in effectiveness over time.

Limitations to Medication

Scope of Research   While the quantity of research on medication is impressive, its scope is limited. Most of the research consists of short-term studies of European American boys in middle childhood. Relatively little is known about long-term effects or about possible gender and ethnic differences. Comorbidity has also been neglected, as was noted. The few studies of other age groups suggest that adolescents and children in middle childhood respond well but that preschoolers do not (Spencer et al., 1996).

Nonmedical Dangers   The twin dangers of pharmacotherapy for treating ADHD are the belief that drugs are a cure-all and that "one size (dosage) fits all." These dangers have little to do with the positive effects of the drugs themselves, but they can significantly obstruct progress in helping the children.

As we have seen, ADHD is accompanied by a wide variety of comorbid problems. Medication, in spite of its effectiveness, does not solve them all. It can not magically produce the social and academic skills that the children have failed to acquire, it leaves learning disorders untouched, and it does not resolve all the difficulties arising from the attempts of parents (who themselves often have ADHD) to deal with their disturbed children. Moreover, the illusion of the pill-as-cure-all provides an excuse for parents and professionals alike not to undertake the often arduous demands of other forms of treatment.

The "one size fits all" illusion ignores the fact that, while medication is generally effective, individual children vary widely in their response. For a particular child some symptoms and some attendant problems may improve while others are not helped at all.

There is also variability in compliance. Parents may be resistant to using medication and adolescents in particular may fear stigmatization by peers. For physicians there is the danger of overprescribing medication and a subsequent failure to conduct the necessary but time-consuming monitoring of effectiveness of dosage.

Medication Without Assessment   One of the other concerns about the way in which medications are used to treat children with ADHD is that too often they are prescribed by pediatricians or psychiatrists without a thorough assessment to confirm the diagnosis. Because ADHD is such an eminently treatable problem, it may be tempting for a physician to view all child behavior problems in its light and to prescribe the cure. However, it is important to first determine that it is in fact this disorder that is causing the parents' or teachers' complaints of poor school work, inattentiveness, uncontrolled behavior, and so forth rather than a competing explanation such as a learning disorder, anxiety, or parenting problem. In response to this concern, the American Academy of Pediatrics (2000) has issued a set of guidelines requiring that physicians conduct a careful assessment of ADHD before a prescription is written, including gathering information from parents, ruling out other conditions, and inquiring directly of teachers regarding the child's behavior in the classroom—the setting, which we know, in which ADHD is most likely to evidence itself.

Medication-Related Attributions   What do children with ADHD make of the fact that they must take medication in order to be able to function in structured settings? Some critics have suggested that these children are being set up to become substance abusers in that they are being given the message that drugs can solve their problems, although the weight of the evidence has not supported this supposition (Barkley, 2003). However, the attributions that children make about medication can have an impact on their developmental outcomes. For example, Treuting and Hinshaw (2001) presented children with ADHD a series of hypothetical scenarios involving a boy who has good and bad experiences during his school day. In some of the stories, the boy receives his medication and in other stories his mother forgets to give it to

him. Their results showed that children largely gave medication the credit for the boy's good outcomes, more so than the boy's own efforts or abilities. Moreover, children with ADHD were highly likely to ascribe bad outcomes to a lack of medication, even when the mother in the story *had* remembered to give it (e.g., "His medication wore off"; "He needs a higher dose"). Further, children who gave medication-related attributions for good outcomes in the story gave significantly higher self-reports of depression and low self-esteem. Thus, it appears that it is important for children with ADHD to have perceived self-efficacy and an internal locus of control in regard to their disorder and not to credit all their successes to medication. The investigators suggest that clinicians and parents think carefully about how to introduce children to the idea of medication treatment, and emphasize the role of medication as a *facilitator* rather than a determinant of good behavior, one that will allow the child's true potential to shine through.

Psychosocial Interventions

As we have seen, medication does not remedy all the problems that beset children with ADHD. Specifically, it may not affect comorbid conditions, parental psychopathology, academic and social skills, and peer popularity. Therefore, other remedial measures are needed. We will describe some of these briefly.

Behavior Management   In the operant approach, environmental rewards and punishments along with modeling are used to decrease problem behaviors and increase adaptive ones. In the short term, behavioral interventions improve social skills and academic performance in the setting in which they are implemented. There is evidence that the operant approach in the classroom significantly improves the behavior of children with ADHD (Pelham, Jr., Wheeler, & Chronis, 1998). The greatest weakness of behavior modification is that gains often are not maintained over time and do not generalize to other situations.

Cognitive-Behavioral Therapy   Cognitive behavioral interventions were developed to remedy the previously-mentioned shortcomings of behavior modification. In order to increase the transfer of learning to new situations, children are taught cognitive strategies that they can take with them wherever they go, such as stepwise problem solving. While initial studies of effectiveness were promising, subsequent results have been disappointing (Pelham, Jr., Wheeler, & Chronis, 1998). However, Shapiro, DuPaul, and Bradley-Klug (1998) point out that the interventions that gave a poor showing relied on purely cognitive strategies, such as teaching children cognitive control, whereas the impulsive response style of ADHD children interferes with their ability to engage in such cognitive processing. Instead, interventions that combine cognitive techniques with behavioral techniques, such as contingency management, have proven more effective.

Contingency management involves helping children to evaluate their own behavior and to apply the appropriate consequences. For example, in order to shape and reward children's ability to monitor their own behavior, Hinshaw (2000) utilizes the "Match Game" in which children are asked to rate their behavior on a skill or concept that needs to be learned or practiced, such as paying attention or cooperating. (See Figure 7.3.) The adult also rates the child and the two discuss the reasoning that went into their ratings, giving specific examples of desirable or undesirable behavior. The child receives points based on how high the adult's ratings were, but the points are *doubled* if the child's ratings agreed with the adults—in other words, if there was a match. Over time, children not only become more accurate in their self-evaluations, taking over the monitoring required by the supervising adult, but also come to require less external reinforcement as self-monitoring becomes a reward unto itself.

Anger Management Training   Because of the high comorbidity with conduct disorder, children with ADHD often benefit from cognitive-behavioral training in anger management to provide them with alternatives to aggression (Hinshaw, 2000). (These are described in more detail in Chapter 10.)

Social Skills Training   Children with ADHD often have interpersonal problems and could benefit from learning better social skills (Hinshaw, 2000).

Figure 7.3   The Match Game.

From S. P. Hinshaw, 2000.

One empirically supported social skills intervention was developed by Pfiffner & McBurnett (1997), in which girls and boys with ADHD meet in groups of 6 to 9. Groups are designed to systematically address (1) children's social knowledge, (2) performance deficits, (3) recognition of verbal and nonverbal social cues, (4) adaptive responding to problem situations, and (5) generalization, including bringing parents into the treatment in order to promote and support children's use of their newfound skills in other settings.

Parent Training   Parent training aims at substituting adaptive for maladaptive ways parents deal with their children. The parents are trained to focus on specific problematic behaviors and to devise strategies for changing them. Behavioral parent training has a well-documented record of effectiveness (Anastapoulos 1998; Pelham, Jr., Wheeler, & Chronis, 1998).

Academic Skills Training   Academic skills training involves specialized individual or group tutoring that teaches children to follow direction, become organized, use time efficiently, check their work, take notes, and, more generally, to study effectively. Remediation of comorbid learning disorders may also be necessary. The effectiveness of academic skills training for children with ADHD has received little systematic evaluation.

Comparison of Treatment Effects

One of the most comprehensive treatment effectiveness studies was carried out by the Multimodal Treatment (MTA) Cooperative Group (1999), a consortium of prominent ADHD researchers at several different sites who pooled their resources in order to provide a more definite answer to the question, What works for ADHD? The study involved a sample of 579 children aged 7 to 9.9 years, all of whom were diagnosed with ADHD Combined Type. Children were randomly assigned to one of four treatments, each of which lasted 14 months: (1) medication with stimulants; (2) intensive behavioral treatment, involving the child, the parent, and the school; (3) a combination of medication and behavioral treatment; or (4) standard community care provided by outpatient mental health agencies. The design allowed the investigators to answer a number of specific questions:

Which is more effective, medication or behavioral treatment? Results strongly indicated that medication resulted in a more significant improvement in ADHD symptoms, according to parents' and teachers' reports of inattention and teachers' ratings of hyperactivity/impulsivity. (See Figure 7.4.)

Does the combination of medication and behavioral treatment result in increased effectiveness? Somewhat surprisingly to many in the field, the multimodal treatment was not superior to medication alone. The combined treatment showed no difference in effectiveness when compared to medication alone, but was superior to behavioral treatment alone in reducing parents' and teachers' ratings of inattention, parents' reports of hyperactivity/impulsivity, as well as parents' reports of oppositional/aggressive behavior, internalizing symptoms, and reading difficulty.

Are the three MTA treatments superior to traditional community care? Again, the addition of medication to the mix generated the best results. Children who received medication alone or the combined treatment improved more than those in traditional community care, according to both parents' and teachers' reports, whereas children who received behavioral treatment alone did not.

Conclusions

The most parsimonious conclusion from these data is that medication is the treatment of choice for ADHD. However, the authors note that medication's effectiveness is specific to a relatively narrow range of ADHD symptoms, whereas, as we know, the disorder is accompanied by a host of related deficits, such as oppositional behavior, poor social skills, and internalizing problems, which might benefit from behavioral, cognitive, or parenting interventions. The investigators also note that, since medication is typically a part of traditional community treatment for children with ADHD, it is not clear what mechanism explains the superiority of medication treatment in the MTA study. However, one suggestive fact is that parents and teachers had regular monthly contact with the MTA clinicians, who provided training, guidance, and readings as needed. These collateral interventions are not part of routine pill-dispensing and may have helped parents and teachers to stay better informed, to engage in a collaborative relationship with the treating clinician, and ultimately to provide higher-quality support to the

Figure 7.4   Results of the MTA Cooperative Study Comparing Treatments for ADHD.

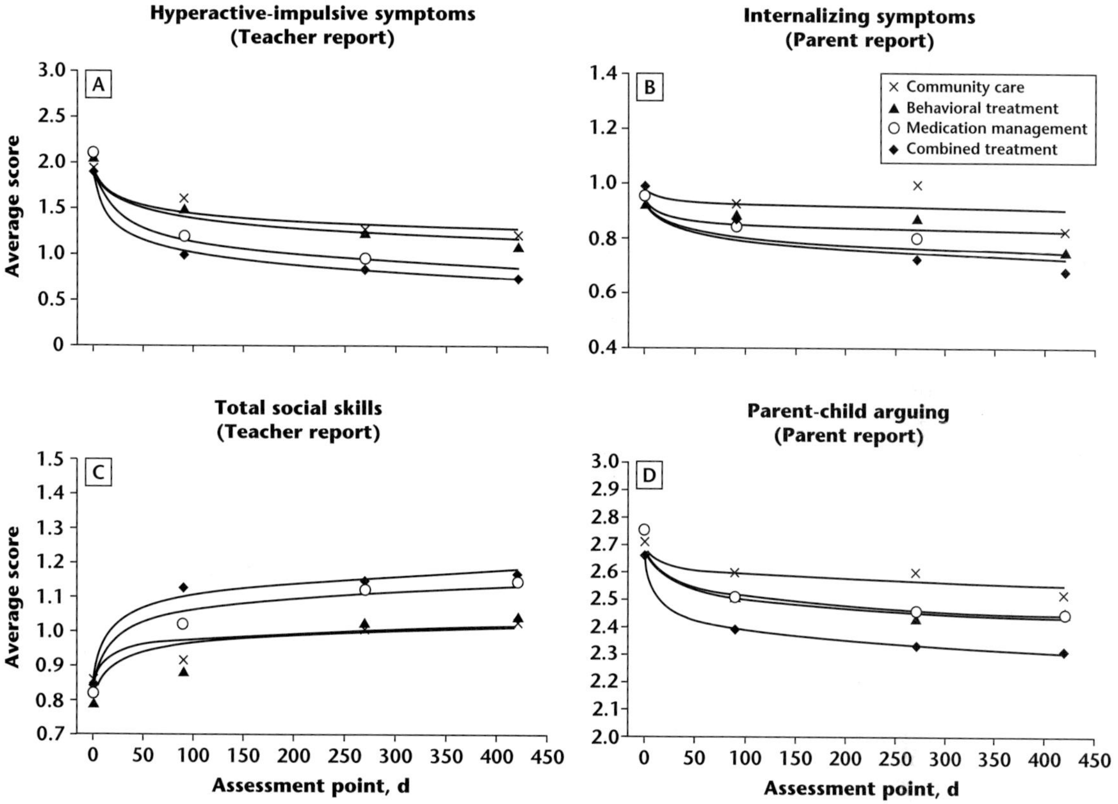

From MTA Cooperative Group, 1999.

children. Lastly, it is intriguing that by the end of the study the children in the combined treatment were receiving lower levels of medication than those in the medication-only condition, which potentially is good news for parents concerned about the side effects associated with large doses of stimulants.

Learning Disorders

Definition and Diagnosis

As we turn our attention to *learning disorders* (LD), we must consider the two questions basic to understanding any psychopathology: How should LD be defined? and How should the definition be operationalized?

Conceptualizing Learning Disorders

In regard to conceptualizing LD, matters got off on the wrong foot in the first widely adopted legal definition. In the Education for All Handicapped Children Act of 1977 (PL 94-142), LD was defined as a disorder in one or more of the *basic psychological processes* involved in understanding and using spoken or written language. It may manifest itself in a severe *discrepancy between age and ability levels* in one or more of the following areas of academic achievement: oral expression, listening comprehension, reading, writing, or arithmetic. According to this definition, LD does not include children who have learning problems that are primarily the result of visual, hearing, or motor handicaps, mental retardation, emotional disturbances, cultural or economic disadvantage, or limited educational opportunities. This definition is reflected in the federal law currently governing special education, the Individuals with Disabilities Education Act (IDEA), which was most recently reauthorized in 1997.

A core problem with this definition is that the "basic psychological processes" are not specified, and, indeed, it is only now becoming clear what some of these processes might be. The exclusion of a number of other groups of disturbed and deprived children has been criticized on two counts: First, LD can co-occur with conditions excluded from the definition, such as physical handicaps or emotional disturbances; and second, it is not always possible to disentangle LD from these excluded conditions. (See Shaw et al., 1995.)

Definitions prepared subsequently by the National Joint Committee on Learning Disabilities (NJCLD) and DSM-IV-TR come closer to hitting the mark, although they are not without problems. NJCLD (1988) defines LD as a heterogeneous group of disorders manifested by significant difficulty in the acquisition and use of listening, speaking, reading, writing, reasoning, or mathematical abilities. The specification of "underlying processes" has been deleted. NJCLD also states that the disorder can occur concomitantly with other handicapping conditions, such as sensory impairment, emotional disturbance, cultural differences, or insufficient instruction but that LD is not the result of these conditions. The disorder is presumed to be due to a central nervous dysfunction.

DSM-IV-TR does not have a general definition for LD, which it calls Learning Disorders; rather it lists the diagnostic criteria for three such disorders: Reading Disorder, Mathematics Disorder, and Disorder of Written Expression. Since the criteria are essentially the same for all three, we will present only those for Reading Disorder (see Table 7.2).

DSM-IV-TR's definition is more precise in that it substitutes discrepancies between objective measures of achievement on the one hand and IQ, age, and grade on the other for NJCLD's somewhat nebulous "significant difficulty in acquisition and use" of an academic skill. DSM-IV-TR is also more

Table 7.2

DSM-IV-TR Criteria for Reading Disorder

A. Reading achievement, as measured by individually administered standardized tests of reading accuracy or comprehension, is substantially below that expected given a person's chronological age, measured intelligence, and age-appropriate education.
B. The disturbance in Criterion A significantly interferes with academic achievement or activities of daily living that require reading skills.
C. If a sensory deficit is present, the reading difficulties are in excess of those usually associated with it.

Source: DSM-IV-TR. Copyright 2000 by the American Psychiatric Association.

concerned with the effects of LD on the child's adjustment. However, NJCLD has a broader spectrum of concurrent conditions than does DSM-IV-TR.

Assessing and Diagnosing Learning Disorders

Satisfactorily assessing LD has proved to be an even more thorny undertaking than conceptualizing it. At the heart of the matter is the use of the **discrepancy model**—the difference between what students should be able to do (ability) and how they actually are performing in school (achievement). Typically, children's ability is operationalized by their score on a standardized intelligence test, while their achievement is measured by an educational test battery, such as the Woodcock-Johnson-III Tests of Achievement (2001). A learning disorder is indicated when a child's achievement falls significantly below what would be expected on the basis of his or her intelligence test score. Generally, children with LD are found to have low average to superior intelligence, which clearly differentiates them from the children with mental retardation whom we encountered in Chapter 4.

However, a basic practical problem is that there is no general agreement about how large a discrepancy should be in order to classify children as LD. Because local criteria differ, a child can change from being LD to being non-LD simply by moving from one state to another. Moreover, professionals differ among themselves about what scores on achievement and IQ tests constitute a significant discrepancy.

Another problem with the discrepancy model that particularly concerns clinicians is that it requires the children to fail academically before being diagnosed. This requirement impedes early detection and intervention. It is not unusual, for example, for children to be in the third grade before explanations other than LD are exhausted; for example, "He doesn't like the teacher" or "Girls just don't do well in math." The delay is important because the longer it persists the less amenable the child is to remedial measures (Lyon, Fletcher, & Barnes, 2003).

A final limitation of the discrepancy model is that, at least in the case of reading, it does not serve the basic diagnostic function of differentiating a unique population of children. For example, there is evidence that children classified as LD in reading because their achievement is lower than their IQ are no different from children who are classified as "slow readers" because their poor achievement in reading is congruent with their IQ level. This lack of differentiation of the two groups applies to a number of variables: information processing, response to instruction, genetic variability, and neurophysiological markers (Lyon et al., 2003).

Even with all its shortcomings and with the at times heated controversies that the concept of LD has sparked, it also has had a number of positive consequences. It has called attention to a population of children who are neither "stupid" nor "lazy" in regard to schoolwork, as they tended to be regarded in the past. The concept of LD has also stimulated research into cognitive skills involved in learning specific subjects, the possible biological roots of such cognitive processes, and the consequences of LD for general adjustment.

Race, Social Class, and Lack of Opportunity

There are two ways in which considerations of ethnic diversity and social class complicate our understanding of learning disorders. Interestingly, these lie at opposite ends of a continuum: One argument is that minority children might be *underrepresented* among those identified as LD, whereas the other suggests that they might be *overrepresented*.

Underidentification   DSM-IV-TR stipulates that learning disorders must not be due to other factors, including economic disadvantage, race, ethnicity, lack of opportunity, or other cultural characteristics. However, this creates a diagnostic dilemma. These factors may well co-occur with learning disorders and even have a contributing influence on them. For example, children who grow up in economically deprived circumstances often are behind their peers in language development when they enter school, which in turn will interfere with their mastery of reading and math skills. Further, parents who are undereducated or who themselves have reading problems will find it difficult to foster their children's literacy. While learning disorders occur in children from all social classes, the exclusionary criteria may have the undesirable effect of depriving underprivileged children of the special education services that would help to remediate their difficulties.

As Kavale (1988) states, "Since culturally disadvantaged children have been shown to exhibit the behavioral characteristics included as primary traits in definitions of LD, it is difficult to determine why the culturally disadvantaged group is categorically excluded from the LD classification. Yet, children from lower SES levels with LD-type behaviors have little chance for receiving LD diagnosis and treatment with an increased likelihood of being labeled retarded in spite of the fact that LD and [culturally disadvantaged] groups are not clearly identifiable as separate entities" (p. 205).

Overidentification   At the opposite end of the spectrum are those who argue that, in fact, children from ethnic minority and lower SES families are overrepresented among those in special education classrooms, which suggests some bias in the identification and referral process. At the center of this debate is the question of whether standardized intelligence and achievement tests—which were developed by and often normed on middle-class European Americans—might underestimate the abilities of minority, disadvantaged, or immigrant children (Kaminer & Vig, 1995; Valencia & Suzuki, 2000). (See Chapter 16.) Children who have not had the same sorts of cultural experiences as those from the majority culture, as well as those whose language skills are limited or whose use of English simply differs from the standard, might be unfairly assessed by the very instruments that are key to identifying LD. Unfortunately, there has been little research to inform us about what extent the LD label is applied in a biased or inequitable manner. However, we should keep this possibility in mind as we review the available literature.

Alternative Models

Response to Intervention   Currently, efforts are under way to modify the IDEA, with bills placed before both the United States Senate and the House of Representatives that would change the language in the federal law governing the LD designation. Rather than focusing on the IQ-achievement discrepancy as the main method of identification, advocates are promoting an alternative model called "response to intervention" (RTI). In this model, which is used in a handful of school systems nationwide, children with academic difficulties are routed through a series of levels of intervention before being diverted to special education. First, children are given the opportunity to succeed in the regular classroom. Those who struggle are offered a secondary intervention, generally utilizing intensive, small-group instruction that is individualized to each student's needs; and in some school systems an even more intensive tertiary intervention is offered. Only those students who fail to respond to each successive level of intervention are placed in special education.

Advocates argue that this system increases the likelihood that scarce special education resources will be reserved for those truly in need of them and that the continual assessment of the child provided in the model will provide a more accurate and competency-based index of the child's abilities. However, critics argue that such a system requires the child to fail at multiple levels before special education services are offered. Further, critics point out that RTI does not specify how assessments are to be conducted in order to identify the cognitive processes that might be interfering with an individual child's classroom learning (Bailey, 2003).

Empirically Derived Learning Disorders   Other experts in the field of learning disorders who question

Table 7.3

Subtypes of Learning Disorders Supported by Empirical Research

Reading Disorder: Word Recognition
Reading Disorder: Comprehension
Reading Disorder: Fluency
Mathematics Disorder
Mathematics Disorder—Reading Disorder
Disorders of Written Expression: Handwriting, Spelling, and/or Expression of Ideas

Source: Adapted from Lyons et al., 2003.

the basis for the DSM and federal definition's categorizations of LD offer a different typology based on empirical research. Table 7.3 lists the learning disorders that have emerged from empirical investigations. These include three separate disorders of reading, involving word recognition, comprehension, or fluency; two of mathematics, depending on the presence or absence of word recognition problems; and one of written expression, which includes difficulties with spelling, handwriting, or expression of ideas.

Reading Disorder

The recent trend in research is to study specific learning disorders rather than the heterogeneous population that makes up LD as a whole. This approach is proving fruitful in uncovering core etiological variables and, in the case of reading disorders, in forcing a rethinking of the nature of LD itself. We will concentrate on reading disorder (RD) because it is the most frequent of the various disorders and because the research findings are particularly substantial and revealing.

Definition and Characteristics

Definition   Most definitions of RD utilize the discrepancy model. In the case of reading this means a significant discrepancy between reading accuracy, speed, or comprehension and chronological age or measured intelligence. (Our presentation follows Lyon, Fletcher, and Barnes, 2003, unless otherwise noted.) Children with RD are assumed to be different from children whose reading, while significantly

Box 7.4 | **Case Study in Learning Disorders**

When University of Rochester basketball player Todd Rosseau opens his political science textbook, the first line looks something like this: "We hop thes turths to be sefl eivdent."

But this is not just another "jock" who can't read. Rosseau in fact is very bright. But he suffers from a reading disorder that does not discriminate between the mentally gifted and the disabled.

"When I was growing up, I used to think I was just dumb," the college senior said. "I thought that for a long time. I didn't know I was different from anyone else. I just wondered why my sister was so much smarter than I was. It was all so confusing."

The first hint that something was wrong came in a kindergarten play group. "It was on my report card," he recalled. "The teacher wrote, 'Good with blocks and not much else.'" By

fourth grade, Todd was leaving class for special tutoring in language arts several times a week. When that didn't help, he went to Massachusetts General Hospital in Boston to be tested for learning disorders. "The tests showed that I had a superior IQ, but I was severely dyslexic," he said. "I see what everyone else sees on the paper, but somehow in the translation to the mind, it shows up wrong. And it's a random thing. I can read the same sentence perfectly the second time."

Todd attended seventh and eighth grades at the Carroll School in Lincoln, Massachusetts, a special facility for children with reading disorder. He went on to a private high school in Cambridge, Massachusetts, which was founded as a prep school for Harvard but offered extensive assistance for youths with learning

problems. The University of Rochester was a good college choice in that it too offers special assistance to students with special needs—as well as an excellent basketball program. "School never was as easy for me as other people. There were times when I worked real hard with no results. It would be easy to say, 'There's no point in trying, I'm dyslexic.' But basketball has helped," he said. "It gave me something to work for outside school." Todd's talent in basketball is one source of his resilience, but so is his stick-to-itiveness when it comes to overcoming his difficulties with reading. "I'm learning the ropes and getting better at it. As a matter of fact, I even read for pleasure, something I didn't do much in high school."

Adapted from Meyer, 1989.

below average, is in keeping with their lowered IQ. This latter group is sometimes called "garden variety reading disordered," and we will designate it as GRD.

RD was thought to be different from GRD for another reason. A number of years ago data showed that performance in reading, rather than being normally distributed, has a "hump" at the lower end of the curve. This hump was believed to be due to the addition of a group of children with a special kind of reading problem. It was further assumed that these children with RD were qualitatively different from children with GRD.

Recent studies have cast doubt on the validity of the discrepancy model, as we have seen. For example, studies show that there is no difference between RD and GRD in the reading skills of word recognition and knowledge, on nine cognitive variables such as vocabulary and memory that are related to reading

proficiency, and on teachers' behavioral ratings. Moreover, subsequent population studies of school children have failed to find the hump at the lower end of the distribution of the reading curve. Rather than indicating a qualitatively different group, the data show that performance in reading is continuously distributed throughout the school population. On a practical level this means that trying to establish a cutoff point that will distinguish the RD population from other slow readers is doomed to fail.

Empirically Derived Types of Reading Disorder
Although they are lumped together in DSM-IV-TR, research suggests that there are two distinct types of reading disorder: one involving problems with *word recognition* (commonly termed dyslexia; see Box 7.4) and the other involving *reading comprehension*. Most of the research has been devoted to

the first type of reading disorder, while relatively little is known about the latter.

Prevalence   RD affects approximately 10 to 15 percent of the school-age population. RD also is the most common form of learning disability, comprising 80 percent or more of children served in special education programs. While schools tend to identify more boys than girls, epidemiological and longitudinal studies show no *gender differences*. Boys tend to demonstrate comorbid externalizing problems, which cause them to be referred at a greater rate than girls (Lyon et al., 2003).

The question of whether there are *social class* or *ethnic differences* in the prevalence of LD is an important one to which, unfortunately, little attention has been given. While children from lower income and minority groups are disproportionately assigned to special education classrooms, it is not clear whether this is a product of a true higher prevalence of learning disorders or whether these differences reflect biases in identification and referral (Sattler, 2002).

Comorbidity and Differential Diagnosis

RD and Other Learning Disorders   While some children have difficulty only in the domain of reading, other children evidence multiple learning disorders, including difficulties with oral language, written expression, or mathematics. Children with more pervasive learning problems may comprise a different subtype with a different etiology (Lyons et al., 2003).

RD and ADHD   Around 20 to 25 percent of students with RD also have ADHD (Beitchman & Young, 1997). However, the reasons for this overlap are not known. There is evidence suggesting a shared genetic variation between the two conditions. One can also argue that problems with attention along with restlessness interfere with learning to read. It is equally plausible to argue that persistent academic failure can lead to restlessness and inattention in the classroom.

RD and Behavior Problems   Three longitudinal studies throw light on the relation between RD and behavior problems: Sanson, Prior, and Smart's (1996) study going from infancy to middle childhood; Smart,

Sanson, and Prior's (1996) study of the middle childhood period; and Maughan and colleagues' (1996) study going from adolescence to early adulthood.

In general, the results indicate a lack of any direct causal relation between RD and behavior problems. For example, there was no evidence that RD in middle childhood was the precursor of behavior problems in general or externalizing problems in particular in adolescence and adulthood. In addition, adolescents who had RD had no higher rates of alcohol problems, antisocial personality disorders, or crime when they became adults. While there was an increase in delinquency in teenagers, this was due to poor school attendance (and, inferentially, increased opportunities for delinquent behavior) rather than to RD itself. Thus, whatever relation exists between RD and behavior problems is due to the comorbid condition of ADHD.

Reversing the direction of causation, we can ask whether behavior problems and ADHD can be precursors of RD. The longitudinal data indicate that they can. For example, there was evidence that problem behavior in the period of infancy through the preschool increased the likelihood of RD plus behavior problems in middle childhood. Moreover, while behavior problems in general were not a precursor of RD in the middle-childhood period, hyperactivity in particular was.

The developmental data also indicate that there were important sex differences. Boys followed a different developmental course from girls, evidencing more externalizing problems such as hyperactivity, which, as we have seen, can be a precursor of RD. However, girls develop RD in the absence of behavior problems in general and hyperactivity in particular.

More recent studies have investigated whether the relationship between RD and problem behavior might be due to the contribution of a third variable: ADHD. Indeed, Willcutt and Pennington (2000) found that the comorbidity of RD and ADHD explained the association between externalizing behavior and reading problems. Once ADHD was accounted for, the association between RD and misbehavior was no longer significant.

RD and Social Skills Deficits   The relation between learning disorders and social skills deficits has been well established empirically. In a meta-analysis of 152 studies over the past 15 years, Kavale and Forness (1996) found that 75 percent of students with LD manifested significantly greater social skills deficits than did comparison groups. The finding was robust, being consistent across different evaluators (teachers, peers, and the students themselves) and across most of the major components of social skills.

In terms of peer evaluations, children with LD were considered less popular and cooperative, were selected less often as friends, and were avoided more than non-LD peers. These negative evaluations, in turn, were attributed to a perceived lack of communicative competence and reduced empathetic behavior. LD students themselves, like their peers, perceived their social functioning as adversely affected by a lack of competence in communication as well as deficient social problem-solving skills. There were two pervasive attitudes underlying their perceptions. The first was a general feeling of inferiority due to a poor self-concept and a lack of self-esteem. The second was an external locus of control that made them view success and failure as due to luck or chance rather than to their own effort.

RD and Internalizing Problems   Children with RD are vulnerable to the development of internalizing problems, including low self-esteem, social isolation, anxiety, and depression, many of which can be attributed directly to their frustrations and failure experiences in school. Internalizing problems are a particular risk for girls with RD (Willcutt & Pennington, 2000).

The Direction of Effects   Do behavioral and emotional problems co-occur with learning disorders, or are they causally related to them? Evidence suggests that the direction of effects is from learning problems to socioemotional problems. For example, large-scale clinical trials show that effective interventions for reading and math difficulties in first grade are associated with lower levels of behavioral and emotional problems in middle school (Kellam et al., 1994). In short, children who fail in school are likely to act out or to feel badly about themselves, but remediation of their academic problems can moderate the risk.

Etiology: The Biological Context

Genetic Influences

There is a strong genetic component in reading achievement. Grigorenko's (2001) review of this research shows that 25 to 60 percent of parents of RD children also have reading difficulties, and this is more true of the fathers than the mothers. Further, twin studies find that concordance rates are high for monozygotic twins (80 percent) versus dizygotic twins (50 percent). More complex statistical analysis estimates that 50 to 60 percent of the variance in reading achievement is attributable to genetic factors. Advances in genetic research are beginning to allow investigators to locate the area of dysfunction. Currently, the best evidence implicates an area of chromosome 6, a finding that has been replicated in several different laboratories.

Neuropsychology

As our techniques for viewing the brain in action advance, so does our understanding of the neuropsychology of reading disorders.

For example, studies using technology that measures magnetic activity in the brain have found consistent differences in the activation patterns of children with and without RD. For example, Simos and colleagues (2000) observed brain activity while children completed tasks in which they listened to words or were asked to recognize either real words or nonsense syllables. Both groups of children showed activation primarily in the left hemisphere when listening to words, as would be expected. However, on the word recognition tasks, brain activation patterns were remarkably different for the two groups. Typically developing children showed activation in the occipital lobes, which are specialized for visual recognition, followed by activation of the left temporoparietal region (including the angular gyrus, Wernicke's area, and the superior temporal gyrus). In children with RD, however, the temporoparietal region of the *right* hemisphere was activated. This altered pattern of lateralization is consistent with findings based on other brain-imaging methodologies, including positron-emission tomography and functional MRI.

Etiology: The Individual Context

Normal Reading Development

Before discussing the etiology of RD it is essential to present the normal process by which children learn how to read. Reading is obviously a complex skill involving the entire gamut of psychological processes, from visual and auditory perception to the higher-order thinking processes of abstraction and conceptualization. Our discussion will concentrate on the very early stages of learning to read, since these will be the most germane to our interest in the etiology of RD. (A more comprehensive presentation can be found in Lyon, Fletcher, and Barnes, 2003.)

Consider this hypothetical situation: A friend shows you, a non-Arabic reader, a sentence in Arabic and challenges you to find the name David, which is pronounced "Dah-oo-dah" in the Arabic language. (See Figure 7.5.) Confronted with a swirl of graceful lines, dashes, dots, and curlicues, how would you go about it? One way is to assume that Arabic uses a phonetic alphabet as does English. Analyzing the sound of the word, you note that it begins and ends with the same sound, "dah." Next, you assume that the written Arabic reflects the sounds of the oral language on a one-to-one basis. Consequently, you look for a visual pattern that begins and ends with the same squiggle, with a different squiggle in between. While any or all of your assumptions may be wrong, you are using a process of reasoning that serves you well in comprehending your native written language. What you are doing is proceeding from the known oral word to the unknown written representation of that word and trying to "break the code" of the latter. ("Dah-oo-dah" are the letters of the word on the far right.)

Many psychologists regard *breaking the code* as an essential first step in learning to read; specifically, the preschooler must find the relation between the *meaningless visual pattern* of the written language and the *meaningful auditory patterns* of words and sentences.

The major problem in breaking the written code is that spoken words are directly perceived as units; for example, "cat," when spoken, registers as a whole. The fact that "cat" is really made up of three separate sounds, or **phonemes,** does not occur to children. Written language is different. Written words do not register as wholes. Understanding that individual words are composed of units—the letters—and understanding that different letters represent different phonemes is crucial to learning how to read. Awareness of and access to the sound structure of language is called **phonological awareness,** which, stated simply, is the awareness that words are made up of separate sounds, or phonemes.

Identification of the individual phonemes in words is called *phonological analysis,* while combining a sequence of isolated speech sounds in order to produce a recognizable word is *phonological synthesis.* One measure of phonological analysis involves orally presenting children with words containing two to five blended phonemes and asking them to tap out the number of phonemic segments. One measure of synthesizing skills is a word-blending task that consists of presenting individual phonemes at half-second intervals and asking the child to pronounce the word as a whole.

Phonemic awareness shows a developmental trend. At age 4 years few children can segment by phonemes, although half can segment by syllables. By 6 years of age 90 percent can segment by syllables and 70 percent can segment by phonemes. By 7 years of age 80 percent can segment syllables into their component phonemes, but between 15 and 20 percent still have difficulty understanding the alphabetic principle underlying the ability to segment words and syllables into phonemes—which is approximately the same percentage of children manifesting difficulties in learning to read.

Figure 7.5   Find the Name David.

لما كنا في كندا قابلنا داوود في شلالات نياغرا .

Box 7.5 | **A Piagetian Approach to Understanding Underachievement**

Philip Cowan (1978), in his pioneering book on developmental psychopathology, *Piaget with Feeling,* describes his experience offering consultation to teachers regarding children who had been identified as underachievers. A good Piagetian, he began by interviewing the children in order to gain their perspective on just where the problem lay. He discovered that the children were able to articulate quite clearly that they had made a conscious decision to disengage from the learning process, and they were very aware of their motivations for doing so.

Some wanted to win a power struggle with their parents and teachers—whether or not the child learned was something the child alone had control over.

Some avoided learning because they wanted to reject adults' expectations of what they should be like, or to avoid being ridiculed by their classmates for being "nerds" or "teacher's pets" if they did well in school.

Others Cowan described as having a "Peter Pan" syndrome: With increased learning comes increased responsibilities and expectations from others, and the best way to avoid these unwanted demands is to fail to achieve or to deliberately give the wrong answers on tests.

Yet another group wanted to avoid the experience of failure and therefore didn't want to risk trying to succeed for fear that they would feel badly about themselves if they made an effort that missed the mark. As long as they did not try, their failures could be chalked up to being "too cool to care."

Phonological Processing and RD

A deficit in phonological processing is the major culprit that impedes learning how to read (Lyons et al., 2003). Approximately 80 to 90 percent of children with RD have a defect in phonological processing, with the gender ratio being no different from that in the population as a whole. For example, studies show that children with RD have difficulty with segmenting phonemes, storing phonological codes in short-term memory, categorizing phonemes, and producing some speech sounds. Moreover, the research indicates that the relation is a causal one; that is, there is evidence that the deficit precedes the difficulty in learning to read.

There are two cautions in regard to the research findings. First, all of the studies used single words or word recognition as the measure of reading, and it remains to be seen whether differences exist on other measures of reading disorder such as comprehension or response to instructions. Second, we are dealing with the weight of evidence rather than with universal findings, since there are some contradictory data and some support for alternative etiological hypotheses.

Locating the origin of RD in the ability to decode and read single words runs counter to the idea that RD represents a defect in reading comprehension. However, comprehension itself is dependent on the ability to decode single words rapidly and automatically. If words are not rapidly and accurately processed, children's ability to understand what they read is likewise hampered.

Emotional Development and School Achievement

While we tend to focus on cognitive factors when we think about the skills and qualities needed for school achievement, the child involved in the learning process is engaged emotionally as well. When the task is difficult, is the child intrigued by the challenge, driven to overcome it, or humiliated by failure and easily discouraged? For all children, and even for adults, learning requires some ego resilience in that we may well feel "dumb" while we are struggling to master a new task. For children with learning disabilities, the challenges to self-esteem and motivation are amplified, as they watch their age-mates surpass them; and they may even suffer the wounds of teasing by peers and the stigmatization of placement in the special education classroom. For some LD children, such negative experiences may turn them off the learning process entirely. (See Box 7.5.)

Figure 7.6

Differential teacher treatment.

Another important contribution to children's attitudes toward school and the learning process is made by teachers. Children as young as first grade appraise the way that teachers behave toward them and their classmates and learn to differentiate themselves according to who is a high and low achiever. (See Figure 7.6.) *Differential teacher treatment* (Weinstein, 2002) subsequently affects children's self-image, their choice of which peers to play with and study with, and how receptive or responsive they are to future teachers' attempts to educate them. Further, children who are turned off to learning, dislike school, and react as if the teacher is torturing them are, in the transactional model, not going to inspire her to do her best teaching.

Grade retention is another consequence of poor school achievement that has a significant effect on children's socioemotional functioning. For example, in a longitudinal sample of children followed from kindergarten to age 12 in Quebec, Pagani and colleagues (2001) found that children's academic performance worsened; and their anxiety, inattention, and disruptive behavior persisted or even increased after being held back a grade. Boys were more vulnerable than girls to the negative effects of grade retention on achievement and externalizing behavior, but both long- and short-term negative effects were striking for all children. Indeed, Stipek (2001) points to the pernicious effects of unsupportive school environments that

"demoralize and discourage children" (p. 228), leading to negative attitudes toward the self and others.

Rethinking LD

Let us review certain relevant findings concerning RD.

1. Children with RD do not form a distinct qualitatively different group of readers. Rather, performance in reading is normally distributed with children with RD and children with GRD at the lower end of the continuum. Moreover, children with RD do not differ from children with GRD in regard to numerous cognitive dimensions.
2. Accurate, fluent reading, with appropriate comprehension, depends upon rapid and automatic recognition and decoding of the printed word—in short, on phonological processing. The basis of RD is a specific defect in this processing.
3. Phonological defects impede the normal progress of learning to read *regardless of the children's level of general intelligence*—that is, regardless of whether they have adequate intelligence and are labeled RD or whether their intelligence is below average and they are labeled GRD.

It is this last point that hides a demon. If the core difficulty in learning how to read exists regardless of IQ level, what happens to the concept of LD as a discrepancy between achievement and ability? In regard to reading, at least, the disorder has little to do with phonological defects. In short, the discrepancy model is invalid. At the very least, the conceptualization of LD must be broadened to recognize the fact that the discrepancy model is not universally applicable. Instead, there may be core deficiencies that impede academic progress regardless of children's general ability.

Developmental Course

A number of well-designed longitudinal studies attest to the continuity of RD from childhood into adulthood. (Our presentation follows Maughan, 1995.) Not all aspects of reading are equally affected, however. Comprehension continues to improve well into adulthood, for example, while phonological processing (i.e., understanding the sound structure of words) is highly resistant to change.

A number of factors determine the developmental course of RD. As might be expected, initial severity of RD and general intelligence are the most potent predictors of progress; however, context factors also play an important role. Socially advantaged children who are given special attention at school and support at home can make good progress even though they take longer to achieve a given level of competence and they tend to avoid reading-intensive courses. However, school systems are inequitable and there are significant differences between schools in affluent and impoverished neighborhoods in terms of the length of waiting lists for LD assessments, classroom size, resources for special education, and the like. Consequently, the picture of the disadvantaged student with RD is a bleak one characterized by early dropout along with a negative attitude toward formal schooling. For example, one study showed that 40 percent of poor readers remained without any academic or vocational qualifications in their 20s. Educational attainment, in turn, is the strongest predictor of occupational outcome, so it is not surprising that disadvantaged students with RD experience more unemployment, tend to work at semiskilled or unskilled tasks, and have lower vocational aspirations. (See Maughan, 1995.)

In terms of adult self-perception, childhood reading problems adversely affect only the specific area of literacy, where adults tend to blame themselves for their problem. The level of overall self-esteem of such adults, however, is on a par with that of their more literate peers. In terms of general psychological well-being, the functioning of young adults shows little traces of the problems that had formerly characterized their behavior. Where problems exist, they seem to be related to other difficulties, such as immaturity or personality disturbances, rather than to RD per se.

Summary

The severity of children's RD and their general intellectual level are the most powerful predictors of RD's developmental course. Advantaged children who receive support at home and special education at school and who, as adults, select vocations that maximize their strengths and minimize their limitations can have a positive view of their general self-worth (although still blaming themselves for their reading failure) and tend to outgrow their childhood problems. On the negative side, being disadvantaged increases the likelihood of dropping out of school at an early age, which, in turn, limits vocational choice and increases the likelihood of unemployment.

Intervention

Assessment and the Educational Plan

Intervention with learning disorders begins with a careful educational assessment that details the child's deficits as well as strengths that might be capitalized on to help the child overcome the challenges. Next, the parents, teachers, and school psychologist meet to discuss the findings and devise an Individualized Educational Plan that will provide the least restrictive and most supportive educational modifications that will increase the child's chances of success in school.

Mainstreaming

Increasingly, due to the Individuals with Disabilities Act (IDEA, 1997), children with special educational needs are mainstreamed with other children. Mainstreaming, also known as inclusion or regular education, is intended to reduce stigma or the denial of educational opportunities that might result from segregation in a separate classroom. Instead, children either receive specialized tutoring in the regular classroom or are pulled out for part of the day in order to receive services.

Educational Interventions

Educational interventions utilize a number of modalities, including the following (here we follow Elliott, Busse, and Shapiro, 1999, except where otherwise noted).

Instructional Interventions   Instructional interventions include the use of specially designed educational materials that are devised to target the specific deficits that are interfering with the child's ability to perform in school. For example, in the case of reading disorder, the child might be provided with exercises and practice with letters, words, and a variety of specialized reading materials. Other interventions attempt to maximize children's ability to learn by presenting information in the children's preferred sensory modality, such as vision or hearing, or presenting material in a multisensory manner that combines sight, touch, hearing, and kinesthetic cues.

Phonological Training   Phonological training that specifically helps children with word identification is particularly helpful in the case of reading disorders and has been proven effective (Lovett et al., 2000). Remarkably, Simos and colleagues (2002) demonstrated that an 8-week intensive course of phonologically based intervention was successful in changing patterns of brain activation. Children with severe word recognition difficulties, ranging in age from 7 to 17 years, received an intense phonologically based intervention 2 hours a day, 5 days a week, over an 8-week period. While prior to treatment all of the children exhibited the atypical pattern of activation in the right hemisphere, after the intervention not only were their reading scores in the average range, but their brain images had shifted to the more typical left-dominated activation pattern. (See Figure 7.7.) Clearly, this is a powerful intervention. While special phonological instructional materials have been developed for the classroom,

parents also are able to work on these skills with home-based programs. Materials are presented in an attractive and game-like way, including opportunities for hands-on manipulation of objects, such as using colored alphabet blocks to break words up into their constituent sounds.

Behavioral Strategies   *Classroom contingency management* involves teachers' providing children with rewards for adaptive learning behaviors such as completing work, handing in assignments on time, and checking work for accuracy. The focus may be specifically academic, such as increasing the legibility of handwriting, or it may be a more general academic one such as increasing on-task behaviors. *Performance feedback* involves providing children with frequent direct feedback about their task performance, in order to increase awareness and self-monitoring.

Cognitive Interventions   Cognitive strategies include *self-instruction* to help children to talk themselves through problem-solving steps. For example, in the case of reading, young children might be encouraged to remind themselves to sound out the words, while more advanced readers might be provided with a series of questions with which to quiz themselves on the text (e.g., 'What is the main point here? How does this sentence follow from the one that came before?'). Another cognitive technique is *self-monitoring,* which, as we saw in the treatment of ADHD, helps children to learn to monitor, regulate, and reward their own academic efforts.

Computer-Assisted Learning   Children find computers inherently interesting and rewarding and therefore may benefit from special computer programs for reading, math, and spelling. Such programs may keep children engaged in the sometimes tedious processes of decoding speech and learning word-attack skills, for example.

Peer Interventions   Peer interventions include *peer tutoring,* in which children help one another on academic tasks; *cooperative learning,* in which students complete assignments together; and *group contingencies,* in which the entire class is rewarded for good effort by all class members.

Figure 7.7   Brain Activation Patterns in Reading Disorders Before and After Phonological Training.

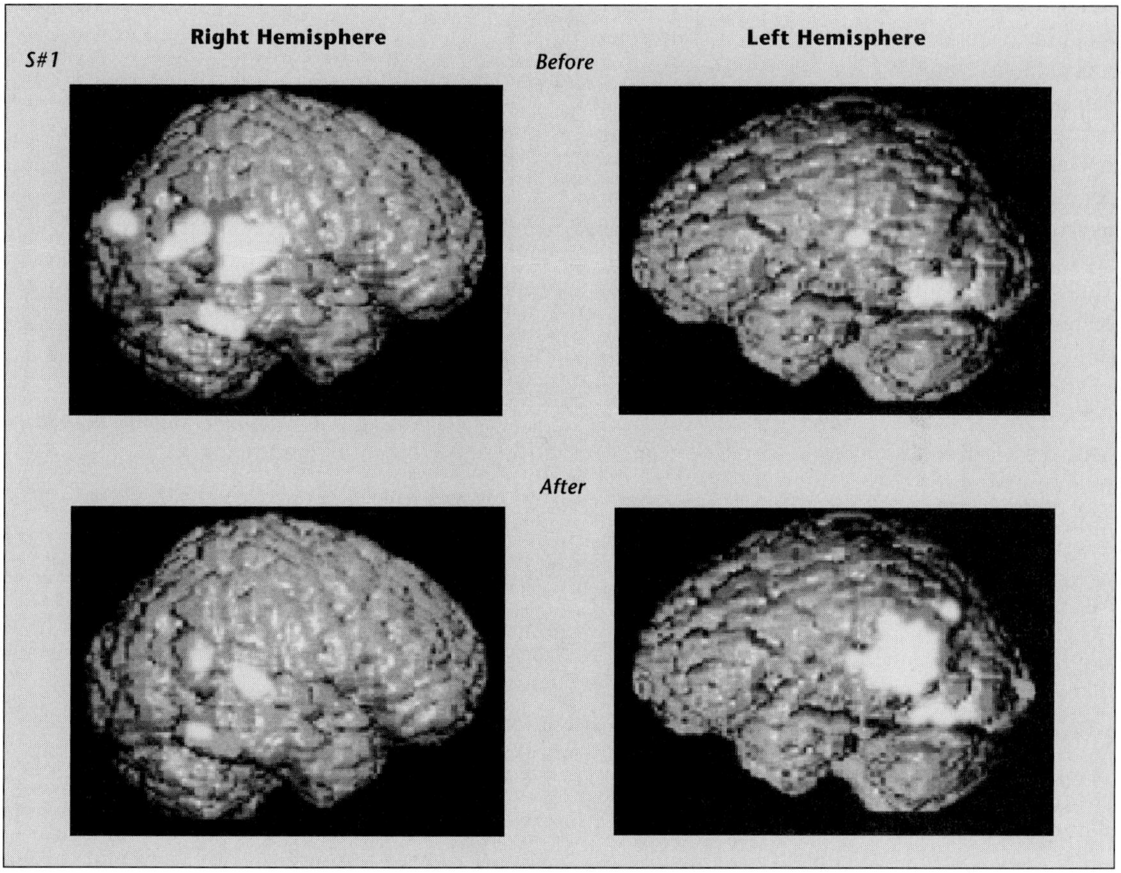

From P. G. Simos, et al., 2002.

Collaborative Partnerships with Parents

At a minimal level, teachers may utilize *school-to-home journals* in order to maintain good communication with parents. Teachers may use the journals to keep parents aware of what work needs to be done, and parents may use them to alert teachers to areas of homework in which children particularly are struggling.

However, even more active involvement of parents in their children's education has been touted as a strategy for remediating or even preventing early learning problems from developing into full-blown disorders. The goal of this movement is for parents and teachers to work together as collaborative *educational partners* (Christenson & Buerkle, 1999), who meet together to discuss problems as they emerge and to arrive at mutually agreed goals and means for meeting them. Empirical support for collaborative partnerships is promising. Results are particularly good when efforts are made to reach out to and empower low-income parents, some of whom may feel intimidated by or disengaged from official institutions such as schools.

Effectiveness of Interventions

Despite their appeal and the good intentions behind them, the empirical evidence for learning disorders interventions is only modest to date. In a review of dozens of educational intervention studies, Kavale and Forness (2000) found that most yielded only medium to small effect sizes. Further, there is considerable debate about whether children with special needs are best served by inclusion in mainstream classrooms, where they still may be stigmatized by other students, and where teachers might not have the training or time to provide the children with the individualized accommodations they need in order to succeed in school (Kavale & Forness, 2000).

One thing is certain, however, and that is that early assessment and intervention are key. For example, children at risk for reading problems benefit most when they receive phonological training beginning in the preschool period (Foorman et al., 1997).

One consequence of various psychopathologies may be feelings of anxiety. Consider children with LD, who are forced to go to school every day and face failure in reading or math or spelling while being helpless to do anything about it; who are unpopular with peers; who must face parents or teachers who might regard them as "just lazy"—all of these are enough to make any child feel tense and worried. However, such natural reactions are different from the psychopathology of anxiety, which is more than worrying about worrisome things. Exploring anxiety disorders will be our concern in Chapter 8.

Middle Childhood: The Anxiety Disorders

In the course of his psycho-analysis, a middle-aged man recalls, "When I acted up as a kid my grandmother would scold me, saying, 'You're too young to have nerves!' For a long time after that I kept wondering, 'Am I old enough now?' like having nerves was one of the signs of being grown up." Grandmother, unknowingly, was a good Freudian. According to classical psychoanalytic theory, excessive anxiety is a hallmark of neurosis and neurosis itself is a developmental achievement. However, both modern research and theory belie this. Anxiety is an experience that is normative and moreover serves a function in development. But, when development goes awry, even preschoolers can suffer from debilitating anxieties that interfere with their functioning and cause them significant emotional distress.

In our presentation of the anxiety disorders, we proceed as follows. First we describe the characteristics of anxiety and fears as they are manifest over the course of development.

Then, we describe general features common to the anxiety disorders before exploring several specific anxiety disorders in turn: generalized anxiety disorder, specific phobias, social anxiety, separation anxiety disorder, obsessive-compulsive disorder, and posttraumatic stress disorder. For each disorder, we offer a clinical vignette that will help to inform differential diagnosis. After that we raise the question that lies at the heart of developmental psychopathology: Why does normal development go awry and produce anxiety disorders? To answer this question, we consider an integrative developmental model that integrates the major research findings concerning etiology.

The Nature of Anxiety

Fears in Normal Development

Fear is usually defined as a normal reaction to an environmental threat. It is adaptive and even essential to survival because it warns the individual that a situation may be physically or psychologically harmful. In the early years of life, infants learn to anticipate when a noxious stimulus is imminent and experience *signal anxiety,* an internal red flag that warns, "Danger ahead!" With such warning, the child can take steps to avoid the feared situation, including crying out to the parent for help.

Fears are common in childhood. For example, Muris, Merckelbach, Gadet, and Moulaert (2000) found that fears are prevalent among preschoolers (71 percent), peak between the ages of 7 to 9 (87 percent), and then decline from age 10 to 12 (68 percent). There also were age differences in the content of children's fears. (See Table 8.1.) Preschoolers were most likely to report fears of ghosts and monsters, while in middle childhood these imaginary fears begin to be replaced by more realistic fears, such as the fear of bodily injury and physical danger. However, school-aged children continue to show some irrational fears, such as fears of snakes and mice, as well as nightmares. Adolescence brings with it a new set of age-appropriate fears, such as social anxieties, concerns over money and work, and fear of war or destruction of the environment. The fear of failure looms particularly in the teenage years. Irrational fears are less frequent but do not disappear altogether; teenagers can be afraid of the dark, of storms, of spiders, or of cemeteries (Vasey, Crnic, & Carter, 1994).

Table 8.1

Common Fears in Childhood

Age Range	Worries and Fears
0–12 months	Loud noises, looming objects, loss of support.
12–24 months	Separation, strangers.
24–36 months	Separation, animals, dogs.
3–6 years	Separation, strangers, animals, darkness, imaginary beings.
6–10 years	Darkness, injury, being alone, animals.
10–12 years	Injury, school failure, ridicule, thunderstorms.
12–18 years	Social failure, peer rejection, war, natural disasters, the future.

From Normal Fears to Anxiety Disorders

In the process of normal development, children are able to master their fears by the use of increasingly adaptive defense mechanisms (see Chapter 2) and sophisticated coping strategies. For example, as children enter concrete operations, they are able to use logic and reasoning to calm their fears, as exemplified by the coping strategy of positive cognitive restructuring (e.g., "I'll remind myself that it is just a dream; it's not real." "Even if I goof up, it really isn't the end of the world; I'll do better next time"). By the same token, children are able to "dose" their exposure to a feared stimulus until they feel ready to approach it (e.g., "That makes me too nervous, so I'm not going to think about it right now").

However, the overwhelming nature of pathological anxiety suggests a failure in these adaptational mechanisms. Anxiety disorders are distinguished from normal fears on the basis of their *intensity,* which is out of proportion to the situation; their *maladaptiveness;* and their *persistence.* They are also *beyond voluntary control* and cannot be explained or reasoned away. Ultimately, our task will be to understand how it is that development goes awry and leaves some children unable to master their fears.

The Anxiety Disorders

Common Features

As the name implies, **anxiety disorders** are a group of disturbances characterized by intense, persistent anxiety. They also have other characteristics in common: The symptoms are distressing and unwanted, reality testing is relatively intact, the disturbance is enduring, and the symptoms do not actively violate social norms. Descriptively, Freud was correct in locating the origins of anxiety disorders in middle childhood, for the most part.

Children with anxiety disorders are **internalizers;** that is, their suffering is turned inward. Recall that in Chapter 3 we described Achenbach's (2000) factor analysis of a symptom checklist for children, which yielded a principal factor that he labeled "internalizing-externalizing." Among internalizing symptoms were phobias, worrying, stomachaches, withdrawal, nausea, compulsions, insomnia, seclusiveness, depression, crying—all indicating an inwardly suffering child.

In terms of *prevalence,* anxiety disorders are among the most common childhood and adolescent disorders. In community samples, they are found in 10.7 percent to 17.3 percent of the population (Weiss & Last, 2001). In clinical samples, prevalence rates are much higher: As many as 45 percent of children in mental health clinics are diagnosed with an anxiety disorder (Last, Perrin, Hersen, & Kazdin, 1992). However, this overall figure masks a developmental trend of increased prevalence. For example, one prospective study found an increase in prevalence from 7.5 percent of 11-year-olds to 20 percent of 21-year-olds (Kovacs & Devlin, 1998). To complicate the developmental picture even further, certain specific disorders increase while others decrease in prevalence, as we shall see. The reasons for these different developmental patterns are not clear.

There also are *gender differences* in the prevalence of anxiety disorders in general (although, as we shall see, these gender differences do not hold for all the anxiety disorder subtypes). For example, Lewinsohn and colleagues (1998) found a predominance of females in their study of 1,079 adolescents with anxiety disorders. Although there was no sex difference in *age of onset,* by the age of 6 females were already twice as likely as males to have experienced an anxiety disorder. As age increases, so does the gender gap. Girls are increasingly more likely than boys to become diagnosed with anxiety disorders throughout childhood and into adolescence and early adulthood (Roza, Hofstra, van der Ende, & Verhulst, 2003). Although data on *ethnic* and *cross-cultural* differences are sparse, we will find that they exist for a number of anxiety disorders.

Anxiety disorders are unlikely to occur alone. Some studies show *comorbidity* rates as high as 65 and even 95 percent (Kovacs & Devlin, 1998). While externalizing disorders such as ADHD and conduct disorders can also be present, they are relatively infrequent. Most commonly, anxiety disorders occur with another type of anxiety. Depression is the next most frequently seen comorbid condition.

Are Anxiety Disorders and Depression Distinct?

Because of the close relation between anxiety and depression, their comorbidity has been conceptualized as a function of an underlying factor, termed negative affectivity. **Negative affectivity** includes moods such as fear, sadness, anger, and guilt. Initially some investigators speculated that negative affectivity was an underlying unifying construct, so anxiety and depression should be placed on a continuum rather than being considered independent disorders. However, subsequent research has not confirmed this. While negative affectivity is a common element in anxiety and depression, each disturbance also has distinctive features. Specifically, Lonigan, Carey, and Finch (1994) found that depressed children reported more problems related to loss of interest and low motivation and had a negative view of themselves, while anxious children reported more worry about the future, their well-being, and others' reactions to them. In addition, depressed children, unlike anxious ones, had low scores on measures of positive affect. Joiner, Catanzaro, and Laurent (1996), using a somewhat different procedure, added to the picture of anxiety disorders the characteristic of physiological hyperarousal, a characteristic that is not part of depression. In sum, both studies agree that anxiety and depression are distinct disturbances that share a common characteristic of negative affectivity.

Next, we turn to a detailed consideration of several of the specific forms that anxiety disorders take in childhood: generalized anxiety disorder, specific phobia, social anxiety, separation anxiety disorder, obsessive-compulsive disorder, and posttraumatic stress disorder.

Generalized Anxiety Disorder

Eleven-year-old Arantxa's parents say that she is a child who "always worries about everything." She doesn't like to try new things and will "work herself into a state" for weeks before a special event, ruminating about all the things that might go wrong. At school, her teachers report that she repeatedly asks for reassurance about whether her answers are correct and she worries excessively about making mistakes, being late, or breaking a rule. Even though she often knows the right answer, she seldom raises her hand in class because she worries that it will "come out wrong." However, her schoolwork often is just as "perfect" as Arantxa wants it to be, given that she hits the books as soon as she gets home from school and does her work extremely neatly, even if that means tearing up the paper and starting again several times. At night, she frequently has difficulty falling asleep, spending as long as 2 hours fretting about the events of the day that has passed and worrying about the day ahead. She worries about robbers getting into the house at night and trying to hurt her family, and she will often get up at night to investigate noises and to check that her little brother is okay.

Definition and Characteristics

Definition

In previous editions, the DSM provided a separate category of Overanxious Disorder of Childhood. However, in the most recent edition, the DSM-IV-TR includes both children and adults in the diagnosis of Generalized Anxiety Disorder (GAD). (See

Table 8.2.) The hallmark of GAD is *worry*. Unlike other anxiety disorders, in which the worry is related to a specific situation (such as separation) or a specific object (such as a phobia of snakes), the child with GAD can turn anything into an occasion for worry. (See Figure 8.1.)

The worries of children with GAD focus particularly on their competence and the quality of their performance in activities such as in school or sports. These worries are present even when they are not being evaluated by others—children with GAD are their own worst critics. They tend to perfectionism and self-judging, redoing tasks over and over in order to get them "just right." They also may worry excessively about catastrophes, such as the possibility of a natural disaster or war, and seek reassurance repeatedly without benefiting from it. Small imperfections, such as not being punctual, may be raised to the level of catastrophe in their minds.

Observable manifestations of generalized anxiety include muscle tension; trembling; feeling shaky; somatic symptoms such as stomachaches, nausea, or diarrhea; nervous habits, such as nail biting

Table 8.2

DSM-IV-TR Criteria for Generalized Anxiety Disorder

A. Excessive anxiety and worry (apprehensive expectation), occurring more days than not for at least 6 months, about a number of events or activities (such as work or school performance).
B. The person finds it difficult to control the worry.
C. The anxiety and worry are associated with three (or more) of the following six symptoms (with at least some symptoms present for more days than not for the past 6 months). **Note:** Only one item is required in children.
  (1) restlessness or feeling keyed up or on edge
  (2) being easily fatigued
  (3) difficulty concentrating or mind going blank
  (4) irritability
  (5) muscle tension
  (6) sleep disturbance (difficulty falling or staying asleep, or restless, unsatisfying sleep)
D. The focus of the anxiety and worry is not confined to a particular situation or event (as in other anxiety disorders).
E. The anxiety, worry, or physical symptoms cause clinically significant distress or impairment in social, occupational, or other important areas of functioning.

Figure 8.1

A child with generalized anxiety disorder can transform any event into an occasion for worry.

ing or hair-twirling; and a tendency to startle easily. Younger children may find it difficult to make the connection between these physical sensations and their emotional state. Further, very young children may not yet have a verbal label for such feelings as "anxiety" or "worry." Thus, it may be left to the astute adult to infer what it means when a physically healthy preschooler frequently declines to go out to play because she or he is "feeling sick."

Cultural Variations   Symptoms of anxiety also may vary across cultures. For example, while individuals from Western cultures may express more *cognitive* symptoms (e.g., excessive worrying), individuals with GAD from Asian cultures may evidence anxiety more in *somatic* forms (e.g., muscle tension) (APA, 2000).

Characteristics

Prevalence   Although there is not much research on children diagnosed with GAD, prevalence rates are generally estimated between 2 and 19 percent of children and adolescents (Silverman & Ginsburg, 1998). One sample of adolescents in 9th, 10th, and 12th grades found a lifetime prevalence rate of 3.7 percent (Whitaker et al., 1990). *Gender differences* also were found, with 4.6 percent of girls and 1.8 percent of boys developing the disorder. *Ethnic differences* are virtually unexplored.

Comorbidity and Differential Diagnosis   While GAD is characterized by a global and diffuse state of anxiety, children with GAD also are vulnerable to developing other *anxiety disorders,* such as specific phobias. Although the disorders are distinct, GAD also often co-occurs with *depression* (APA, 2000). It is easy to see why. The mind of the child who is worrying about his or her performance ("I'm not going to do it right. I'm gonna mess up") is teeming with negative thoughts and self-doubt. Chronic perfectionism and self-criticism can lead to a sense that one is not and never will be "good enough." Similarly, excessive worry about bad things that might happen contributes to a child's sense of hopelessness and helplessness.

Developmental Course

The majority of adults with GAD report that they have been anxious all their lives (APA, 2000). Many remained undiagnosed until they sought help in adulthood, suggesting that anxiety symptoms in children are difficult to detect or that they are easy to chalk up as being "just a stage." However, the truth of the matter is quite the opposite, given that the course of Generalized Anxiety Disorder tends to be chronic. However, the severity of symptoms is variable over the course of the life span, diminishing at some points only to flare up again in times of stress.

Intervention

Cognitive-behavioral treatments have proven effective for relieving children of the symptoms of Generalized Anxiety Disorder. One of the most well established of these is Kendall's (2000) Coping Cat program, which we will explore in greater detail in Chapter 17. The essential features of the program include teaching children to recognize the physiological cues that indicate that they are becoming anxious, identify maladaptive appraisals that turn a neutral event into an anxiety-arousing one, and develop cognitive restructuring and active coping strategies to counter their fears. Children practice their new skills during exposure tasks, in which contact with the anxiety-arousing situation takes place in a series of graduated steps according to the child's pace and comfort level. As a graduation project, children create a picture, videotape, or performance that teaches other children what they have learned about conquering anxiety.

This intervention has proven effective cross-culturally, having been adapted successfully by clinicians in the Netherlands, Ireland, and Australia (where it was renamed Coping Koala) (Kendall, Chu, Gifford, Hayes, & Nauta, 1998). Its effects over the long term appear to hold. In a longitudinal study, Kendall and colleagues (2004) found that children who successfully completed the treatment for anxiety disorders during childhood had maintained their gains 7.4 years later and were significantly less likely to engage in substance abuse. However, there were no longitudinal effects of the treatment on the development of later depression.

Specific Phobias

Twelve-year-old Mei's soccer team is having such a successful year that they have been invited to participate in an exhibition match in another state. It is a 3-hour plane ride away and Mei is devastated because she knows she cannot go. The very thought of being in a plane makes her feel shaky, begin to sweat, and fear that she is going to be sick. She is so terrified of planes that she dreads the part of the drive to school that takes her past the airport, where the sound of the jets roaring past sends a shot of anxiety running through her like an electric current. Mei is bewildered by this fear and critical of herself for being unable to "just get over it." In fact, she has ridden on a plane before, when the family took a vacation in Vancouver 2 years ago, and nothing bad happened. Now, however, her mind paints horrific images of the jet falling through the sky, the oxygen failing, or terrorists taking over the plane.

Definition and Characteristics

Definition

According to DSM-IV-TR, the defining feature of a specific **phobia** is a marked and persistent fear that is excessive or unreasonable, cued by the presence or anticipation of a specific object or situation. Table 8.3 provides a listing of the major symptoms. Phobias may develop in relation to many different objects or situations, such as fear of snakes, enclosed places, water, or flying on airplanes. *School phobia* is a common example, although the diagnosis is a controversial one, as we will see.

Common phobias among clinically referred children include the dark, school, and dogs (Stark & Last, 1993). However, childhood phobias sometimes take forms that are bewildering to adults, such as a fear of clowns or people wearing masks. Imagine the dismay of a parent at Disney World whose daughter reacts to Mickey Mouse's greeting with shrieks of terror, or the parent of a son who hides in his room every Halloween because he is horrified by the sight of trick-or-treaters wearing costumes.

Table 8.3

DSM-IV-TR Criteria for Specific Phobia

A. Marked and persistent fear that is excessive or unreasonable, cued by the presence or anticipation of a specific object or situation (e.g., flying, heights, animals, receiving an injection, seeing blood).

B. Exposure to the phobic stimulus almost invariably provokes an immediate anxiety response which may take the form of a situationally bound or situationally predisposed panic attack. **Note:** In children, the anxiety may be expressed by crying, tantrums, freezing, or clinging.

C. The person recognizes that the fear is excessive or unreasonable. **Note:** In children, this feature may be absent.

D. The phobic situation(s) is avoided or else is endured with intense anxiety or distress.

E. The avoidance, anxious anticipation, or distress interferes significantly with the person's normal functioning, social activities, or relationships, or there is marked distress about having the phobia.

F. In individuals under age 18 years, the duration is at least 6 months.

Specify type:

Animal Type
Natural Environment Type (e.g., heights, storms, or water)
Blood-Injection-Injury Type
Situational Type (e.g., airplanes, elevators, enclosed places)
Other Type (e.g., fear of choking, vomiting, or contracting an illness; in children, fear of loud sounds or costumed characters)

Reprinted with permission from the *Diagnostic and Statistical Manual of Mental Disorders*, Fourth Edition Text Revision. Copyright 2000 by the American Psychiatric Association.

Developmental Considerations   It is not uncommon for young children to have transient fears and phobic reactions. For example, a 3-year-old boy was in the car with his father when a blowout forced his father to pull over to change a tire on the freeway. Although the boy expressed no fear at the sound of the tire bursting, the erratic swerving of the car, or the sight of his father kneeling on the verge with cars whizzing past him inches away, the boy startled when, as they pulled away, he spied a lit flare continuing to burn at the side of the road. For several days after the event he reacted fearfully to flames and repeatedly requested reassurance that the "fire had gone out." Such fearful reactions may come and go in childhood and, for this reason, the DSM criteria for phobias specify that in children the duration must be at least 6 months.

Characteristics

Prevalence   In regard to the *prevalence* of phobias, estimates range from 2 to 9 percent in community

samples and 30 to 40 percent in clinical samples of children (Weiss & Last, 2001). There is evidence for *gender differences*, with girls tending to outnumber boys. Almost no research has been conducted to investigate *social class, racial,* or *ethnic* differences (Silverman & Ginsburg, 1998).

Comorbidity and Differential Diagnosis   Comorbidity with both *internalizing* and *externalizing* disturbances is high, as is the comorbidity among specific types of phobias (Weiss & Last, 2001). Phobias are specific to a particular stimulus, clearly distinguishing them from the more generalized anxiety of GAD. A separate disorder, which we will review next, is specific to children whose phobias are focused on social relationships.

School Phobia

A common example of a specific phobia is school phobia, which is estimated to occur in 1 percent of the general population and 5 to 7 percent of clinically

Box 8.1 | School Refusal in Japan

Kameguchi and Murphy-Shigetmatsu (2001) discovered that there is a pervasive problem of school refusal amongst Japanese youths and set about to discover why. Following Minuchin's (1974) structural family theory, they believe that a strong boundary or "membrane" around the parental subsystem is essential to the healthy organization of the family. However, amongst Japanese families of school-refusing youths, Kameguchi and his colleagues observed a common pattern of excessive closeness between mother and child and disengagement in both the marital and father-child relationships. These patterns, the authors argue, are promoted by features of Japanese society, including the demanding work lives of men that often require them to spend their evenings and vacations with their colleagues rather than their families, and the expectation that women will devote themselves exclusively to the care of their children. Kameguchi and his colleagues propose that "vague generational boundaries between a parental dyad and a child interfere with the developmental tasks of adolescents . . . The child is thus deprived of experiences that accelerate his or her psychological separation from the parents and that also assist the parents in separating from the adolescent" (p. 68). Ultimately, both parent and child collude in behaviors—such as the child's staying home from school—which interfere with individuation.

referred children. In school phobia, a child experiences an irrational dread of some aspect of the school situation accompanied by physiological symptoms of anxiety or panic when attendance is imminent, resulting in a partial or total inability to go to school. School phobia in childhood is associated with increased risk of anxiety and depressive disorders in adulthood. For example, approximately a third of such children will need additional treatment for these disorders as adults (Blagg & Yule, 1994).

However, it is important to differentiate true school phobia from the many different disorders that might result in the unwillingness to attend school, known as *school refusal*. For example, children may refuse to attend school due to depression or disturbances that have little to do with anxiety, such as oppositional-defiant disorder. For children with these nonanxious disorders, the reaction lacks the intensity necessary to be a truly phobic response and is mixed with other negative affects such as sadness and low self-esteem. The most common disturbance that may masquerade as school phobia is separation anxiety disorder (Albano, Chorpita, & Barlow, 1996). Nonetheless, it is possible to distinguish between the two. Children who fear separation are generally female (when gender differences are found), younger than 10 years of age, and from families of low socioeconomic status, whereas children with a school phobia tend to be male, older than 10 years, and of a high socioeconomic status (Blagg & Yule, 1994). Children with SAD are more severely disturbed in that they have more additional symptoms and their overall functioning is more disrupted. Children with SAD always remain at home with an attachment figure when not in school, whereas children with a school phobia are comfortable in many settings, as long as it is not the school. Finally, there is evidence that mothers of children with SAD have more emotional problems, particularly in the form of depression (Last & Francis, 1988). (See Box 8.1.)

Developmental Course

Specific phobias have different *ages of onset*. Evidence suggests that animal phobia begins around 7 years of age, blood phobia around 9, and dental phobia around 12. Fear of enclosures and social phobias begin in adolescence or early adulthood (Silverman & Rabian, 1994). Over the course of childhood, specific phobias show a modest level of continuity across intervals varying from 2 to 5 years. This finding contradicts a previously held view that they were outgrown for the most part.

control group. Gains were still evident 6 months after treatment had ended.

In another study, Spence and colleagues (2000) investigated the effectiveness of a group treatment for children that combined exposure therapy and social skills training with relaxation, problem solving, and cognitive restructuring. The authors also assessed whether treatment was more effective when parents were involved. Children aged 7 to 14 were assigned either to a waiting list, or the child group alone, or the child group plus parental involvement. In the latter group, parents received training in management of child social anxiety and observed their children's sessions while the therapists modeled and reinforced the treatment goals. The results showed that children in both treatment groups benefited significantly. Eighty-seven percent of those in the child plus parent group were free of their diagnosis at follow-up, whereas this was true of 58 percent of those in the child-only group and 7 percent of those on the waiting list. Although the difference between the two treatments was not significant, it may be that parental involvement is important particularly for younger children (Sweeney & Rapee, 2001) or in families in which the parents themselves are anxious (Cobham, Dadds, & Spence, 1998).

Separation Anxiety Disorder

Seven-year-old Lili has always had difficulty separating from her parents. When her parents go out to run even a brief errand, Lili begs them to take her or asks repeated questions about where they are going, what route they will take to get there, and when they will return. When it is Lili who needs to leave the house in order to go to school or attend an activity, she frequently reports "feeling funny" and pleads to be allowed to stay home. At times, she becomes so distressed by impending separation that she clings to her parents, cries, and has to be dragged kicking and screaming to the car. When she is at home, she does not like to be alone in any room of the house, preferring to follow her mother around and play in whatever room her mother is in. While her parents try to be understanding, they find this clinginess to be exasperating ("I can't move

without finding her underfoot!") but, if they do not give in to it, the intensity of Lili's tantrums is unnerving. Consequently, her parents vacillate between pushing her to "be a big girl" and giving in to her neediness in order to avoid a battle. Lili is able to play comfortably with peers—as long as they play at her house—and can even participate in activities such as dance class—as long as one of her parents is with her. She has never been willing to spend a night away from home and tends to have trouble sleeping, awakening from nightmares in which she has gotten lost or something bad has happened to her parents.

As we have seen, the development of the bond of love to the caregiver and the fear of loss of the loved one go hand in hand in normal infant development. Normally, separation anxiety emerges between 9 and 12 months, peaks at 13 to 20 months, and then declines. Although a number of factors are responsible for the mastery of this separation anxiety in the toddler period, for some children the panic over separation returns from the preschool period through adolescence, producing separation anxiety. Separation fears may present themselves as school phobia; however, careful evaluation of the child reveals that it is not a pathological fear of school that is the problem, but rather that the child's school avoidance is motivated by fear of being away from the caregiver.

Definition

The core characteristic of Separation Anxiety Disorder (SAD) is excessive anxiety over separation from people to whom the child is attached, typically the parents. The DSM-IV-TR criteria provide a comprehensive listing of symptoms. (See Table 8.5.)

Characteristics

Prevalence

SAD is found in 2 to 12 percent of the general population and in 29 to 45 percent of the clinical population (Weiss & Last, 2001). It is the most prevalent of all the anxiety disorders and ranks third among childhood disorders in general (Tonge, 1994). While some evidence suggests that separation anxiety is

Box 8.2 | **Case Study: Separation Anxiety, School Phobia, or Generalized Anxiety Disorder?**

Leilani Greening, a psychology intern at the UCLA Neuropsychiatic Institute, and her supervisor, Dr. Stephen Dollinger, describe the case of Bradley A., a 9-year-old European American boy. Bradley's parents brought him to a university psychology clinic due to their concerns about his fears of the dark and unwillingness to sleep alone in his bedroom. According to his mother, Bradley's fears first emerged when he was 6 years old. Mrs. A. had brought Bradley and his sister Janet, 3 years his elder, to see the movie *Jaws*. Bradley was very frightened by the movie and refused to sleep alone in his bedroom that night. His sleep problems continued intermittently over the next several months and

intensified in the following summer when he began to complain about monsters in his room and people trying to kill him. He began to refuse to go to sleep unless there was a light left on in his room. Bradley's parents attributed his fears to the movie he had seen and believed that his anxieties would fade over time. While Bradley's symptoms indeed did lift when he returned to school in the fall, they recurred in an even more intense form the next summer. He frequently woke during the night crying out for his parents because he was scared. His parents would comfort Bradley until he fell asleep and return to their bedroom only to be awakened again a few minutes later by his screaming.

Bradley's problems continued with intermittent remissions and relapses over the next 3 years. The family tried a number of solutions, including reassuring Bradley, having a family member sleep in his room, and praying for guidance. At the time they sought professional help, Bradley's mother was sleeping in a cot in his room. The entire family's functioning was organized around appeasing Bradley's anxiety, and each episode would inevitably end up with everyone yelling at each other. The family conflicts were so stressful that one night Bradley cried and said, "I would do anything in the world not to be like this!" It was then that Bradley's mother determined to seek professional help.

Table 8.5

DSM-IV-TR Criteria for Separation Anxiety Disorder

A. Developmentally inappropriate and excessive anxiety concerning separation from home or from those to whom the individual is attached, as evidenced by three (or more) of the following:
   (1) recurrent excessive distress when separation from home or major attachment figures occurs or is anticipated
   (2) persistent and excessive worry about losing, or about possible harm befalling, major attachment figures
   (3) persistent and excessive worry that an untoward event will lead to separation from a major attachment figure (e.g., getting lost or being kidnapped)
   (4) persistent reluctance or refusal to go to school or elsewhere because of fear of separation
   (5) persistently and excessively fearful or reluctant to be alone or without major attachment figures at home or without significant adults in other setting
   (6) persistent reluctance or refusal to go to sleep without being near a major attachment figure or to sleep away from home
   (7) repeated nightmares involving the theme of separation
   (8) repeated complaints of physical symptoms (such as headaches, nausea, or vomiting) when separation from major attachment figures occurs or is anticipated
B. The duration of the disturbance is at least 4 weeks
C. The onset is before the age of 18 years
Specify If:
Early Onset: if onset occurs before age 6 years

After evaluating Bradley and his family, the clinicians working on the case were struck by two things. One was Bradley's high level of overall anxiety. The other was his parents' anxiety. In an interview, Bradley's parents described him as a fearful child who often worried about harm befalling his family. He fretted about burglars and was particularly afraid that his father, who worked the night shift at a dangerous manual labor job, would be killed at work or during the long drive home. What was interesting, however, was that Bradley's parents shared his fears. Mrs. A. too worried that her husband would be hurt at work and related a number of stories about coworkers who had been killed on the

job. Furthermore, she kept a loaded pistol in the house because she and her husband were fearful of robbers coming into the house at night while Mr. A. was working. To cope with their anxiety, family members had developed a number of rituals. Both Bradley and his father reported that each time Mr. A. left for work they felt that they would never see each other again and engaged in long goodbyes as though each were their last. The parents worried about their children's safety to the extent that they were not allowed to ride their bikes outside of the yard. Later, Mr. A. provided the basis for this fear when he related his feelings of guilt following the death of his younger brother, who died in

childhood after being hit by a truck while riding Mr. A.'s bicycle.

As an initial step, the clinicians worked to increase Bradley's sense of self-mastery by teaching him relaxation exercises to counter his anxiety. When these interventions were only moderately successful, they turned to working with the whole family in order to help the parents cease from reinforcing Bradley's anxiety with their own. One of the family's strengths turned out to be their sense of humor, and they were able to recognize and ultimately to change their patterns of interaction.

Source: Greening and Dollinger, 1989.

more prevalent among *lower SES* groups, the little research available regarding *ethnicity* to date reports no differences (Silverman & Ginsburg, 1998).

The evidence is conflicting in regard to *gender differences,* with some studies finding no evidence of difference and others finding that girls outnumber boys. However, Last et al. (1992) found that, in a clinical sample of children with anxiety disorders, 48 percent diagnosed with SAD were boys. SAD is more prevalent in low-income samples and among children whose parents have lower-than-average education. The families tend to be caring and close, but the incidence of SAD appears to be higher in children of mothers with anxiety disorders (Crowell & Waters, 1990).

There is some evidence that children from *lower SES* families have higher prevalence rates for SAD (Silverman & Ginsburg, 1998). Although data concerning *ethnicity* are limited, symptoms of SAD tend to be higher in African American (Compton,

Nelson, & March, 2000), Hispanic (Silverman & Ginsburg, 1998), and Native American children (Costello, Farmer, Angold, Burns, & Erklani, 1997) as compared to European American children.

Comorbidity and Differential Diagnosis

One-third of the children with SAD have a secondary diagnosis of *GAD* while, later in development, another third also will be diagnosed with *depression.* The child with SAD fears separation from the caregiver as opposed to fearing other people, as in the case of social phobia, or fearing going to a specific place, as in the case of school phobia. See Box 8.2 for a case requiring a differential diagnosis of separation anxiety, school phobia, and GAD.

Developmental Considerations

SAD appears more often in the preschool period than in adolescence, as one would expect. Certain symptoms of separation anxiety show a developmental progression. Symptoms characteristic of 5- to 8-year-olds are excessive worry about harm befalling an attachment figure, nightmares involving separation themes, and school refusals because of separation anxiety; 9- to 12-year-olds are distressed at separation itself; and somatic complaints such as headaches and stomachaches and school refusals are characteristic of 13- to 16-year-olds (Albano, Chorpita, & Barlow, 1996).

Developmental Course

The average *age of onset* ranges from 7.5 to 8.7 years, although the mean age at which children with SAD are presented for treatment is 10.3 years, suggesting a delay in the recognition of the disorder (Weiss & Last, 2001).

There are few studies of the developmental course of SAD, although there is some evidence that the course is a variable one. Periods of remission often are followed by recurrences either in response to stressors or "out of the blue." Finally, there is evidence that SAD increases the risk of anxiety or depressive disorders in adulthood and, for females, increases the risk of panic disorder or agoraphobia in adulthood (Albano, Chorpita, & Barlow, 1996).

Intervention

Kendall's (2000) cognitive-behavioral Coping Cat program, which we described under Generalized Anxiety, is also a treatment of choice for SAD (Kendall et al., 2003). For example, Levin, Ashmore-Callahan, Kendall, and Ichii (1996) describe the case example of Allison, a 9-year-old girl whose parents brought her for treatment because she insisted on sleeping in their bed every night. Her need to sleep with her parents was interfering with her social development, because she was unable to tolerate attending sleep-overs with her friends. The therapist was able to help Allison connect her "fidgety" behavior (nail-biting, chewing on her hair) to the emotional experience of anxiety. The therapist also attempted to help Allison counter her negative cognitions with more adaptive ways of thinking. However, although Allison was able to identify her negative

thoughts, she became so overwhelmed by them that she could not consider alternative ideas. Therefore, using the treatment manual flexibly, the therapist shifted the focus in treatment to actions ("What can you do to feel better?") rather than cognitions. For her homework, Allison was assigned a series of graduated tasks, beginning with spending time alone in her room every day. Her parents were given tasks of their own, including redecorating Allison's room so that it was comfortable, pleasant, and safe and rewarding her for making attempts—even if unsuccessful—to master her fears. At the end of treatment, Allison no longer met criteria for the SAD diagnosis.

Obsessive-Compulsive Disorder

For the past 4 months, 10-year-old Oskar has been late for everything. It isn't that he does not care about being on time, but there is so much to do before it is safe to leave the house. First, the toys on his shelf have to be exactly right, arranged by height and lined up straight. Then, he has to check that the lights are off in every room and then go back and check them a second time—but, of course, the third time is the charm. Although Oskar's teachers had previously described him as a "joy," the most neat and well-organized child in the classroom, recently they have been complaining that Oskar is turning his homework in days late, if at all. Oskar's parents are bewildered, given that he spends several hours a night working intently on his homework. When asked to describe his homework strategy, Oskar explains that he gets three sheets of lined paper, three sheets of unlined paper, three newly sharpened pencils, and his textbook. Everything has to be placed in exactly the right spot on his desk before he can begin. When he writes his answers, the letters have to be exactly the same size and the distance between the lines of writing exactly the same height. If he makes the smallest mistake, he has to tear up the paper and start over from scratch. When asked why he cannot simply erase the error and continue on, Oskar becomes visibly upset and states, "I could never do that. I just couldn't stand it."

Table 8.6

DSM-IV-TR Criteria for Obsessive-Compulsive Disorder

A. Either obsessions or compulsions:

Obsessions as defined by:
  (1) recurrent and persistent thoughts, impulses, or images that are experienced, at some time during the disturbance, as intrusive and inappropriate and that cause marked anxiety or distress
  (2) the thoughts, impulses, or images are not simply excessive worries about real-life problems
  (3) the person attempts to ignore or suppress the thoughts, impulses, or images, or to neutralize them with some other thought or action
  (4) the person recognizes that the obsessional thoughts, impulses, or images are a product of his or her own mind (not imposed from without as in thought insertion)

Compulsions as defined by:
  (1) repetitive behaviors (e.g., hand washing, ordering, checking) or mental acts (e.g., praying, counting, repeating words silently) that the person feels driven to perform in response to an obsession, or according to rules that must be applied rigidly
  (2) the behaviors or mental acts are aimed at preventing or reducing distress or preventing some dreaded event or situation; however, these behaviors or mental acts either are not connected in a realistic way with what they are designed to neutralize or prevent or are clearly excessive
B. At some point during the course of the disorder, the person has recognized that the obsessions or compulsions are excessive or unreasonable. **Note:** This does not apply to children.
C. The obsessions or compulsions caused marked distress, are time consuming (take more than 1 hour a day), or significantly interfere with the person's normal functioning, social activities, or relationships.

Reprinted with permission from the *Diagnostic and Statistical Manual of Mental Disorders,* Fourth Edition Text Revision. Copyright 2000 by the American Psychiatric Association.

Definition and Characteristics

Definition

Obsessive-Compulsive Disorder (OCD) is marked by intrusive ideas (**obsessions**) and behaviors (**compulsions**). Further, these thoughts and actions (1) arise from sources over which the child has no control, (2) are irresistible, and (3) are often recognized as irrational. (The DSM-IV-TR criteria are presented in Table 8.6.)

The most frequent *obsessions* involve fear of germs or contamination, fears of harm to the self or someone else, and excessive religiosity (Chang & Piacentini, 2002). Not all obsessions are related to anxiety. Children might complain of intrusive thoughts, feelings of disgust or discomfort, or a vague sensation that something is just not right, termed the *just-right phenomenon*. (See Table 8.7.)

The most common *compulsions* in children include handwashing, repetitive checking (such as continually checking the doors to make sure they are

locked), preoccupation with orderliness, and repeatedly counting to a particular number or touching objects a given number of times (Chang & Piacentini, 2002). It is not unusual for a child to combine a number of rituals. An 11-year-old boy who was terrified of germs used his magic number 4 for protection in a variety of ways: He touched his fork 4 times before eating, counted to 4 when entering the locker room in the school gym, got in and out of bed 4 times before going to sleep, and lined up his perfectly sharpened pencils in groups of 4. When he became worried that a ritual might not have worked, he repeated it 4 times.

It is easy to see how crippling OCD can become; the disorder interferes with children's personal, social, and academic lives as well as becoming burdensome to their families. For example, Piacentini and colleagues (Chang & Piacentini, 2002) found that, among 162 children with OCD, parents reported that symptoms interfered with functioning in a number of areas: completing assigned chores at home (78 percent of children), settling to bed at

Table 8.7

Common Obsessions and Compulsions
in Childhood OCD

Obsessions	Compulsions
Contamination	Washing
Harm to self or others	Repeating
Aggression	Checking
Sex	Touching
Religion, morality	Counting
Forbidden thoughts	Ordering/arranging
Symmetry	Hoarding
Need to tell, ask, confess	Praying

Source: March and Mulle, 1998.

night (73 percent), concentrating on schoolwork (71 percent), and getting along with family members (70 percent). Over 85 percent of children reported that OCD impaired their ability to function in all three areas of school, home, and peer relations.

Children's symptoms are likely to increase at times of stress, such as at the beginning of the school year, moving to a new home, or separation from a family member. With great effort, children with OCD are able to control their behavior for short periods in specific situations, such as the classroom or social situations; and therefore teachers and others may remain unaware of the difficulty for quite some time.

Characteristics

Prevalence   In regard to lifetime prevalence, rates of 1 to 3 percent have been reported in the general population of children, consistent with rates for adults, while 15 percent of the child clinical population is affected (Weiss & Last, 2001). However, these prevalence rates might be underestimates—OCD in children appears to be difficult to detect. For example, one epidemiological survey of high school students found that few of the children who had OCD were in treatment and, most remarkably, *none* of the children, including those in treatment, had been correctly diagnosed with OCD (Flament et al., 1988).

There is a *gender difference* in childhood, with boys starting earlier than girls and outnumbering

girls (Rapoport et al., 2000). However, by adolescence this difference has all but disappeared.

Ethnic and Social Class Differences   Although *ethnic minorities* and children from *disadvantaged social classes* are underrepresented among those treated for OCD (Rasmussen & Eisen, 1992), these statistics may be a result of the fact that children from these communities are referred less often to clinicians. March and Mulle (1998) confirm this, reporting that large-scale epidemiological studies find no differences in prevalence rates based on race and ethnicity, while European American children are disproportionately more likely to receive treatment than are African American children. Strikingly, native Hawaiian adolescents are diagnosed with OCD at rates that are twice as high as those from other ethnicities, a finding that appears to be related to both environmental and genetic factors (Guerrero et al., 2003).

Comorbidity   The comorbidity rate of OCD is high. In community samples, around 84 percent of the children with OCD have comorbid conditions (Douglass et al., 1995), while in clinic samples the figure is around 41 percent. Common comorbid conditions are *depression* and other *anxiety disorders,* particularly social phobia, tic and habit disorders (e.g., nail-biting or hair pulling), as well as *substance abuse. Learning disorders* also are common among children with OCD, particularly those involving problems with nonverbal reasoning.

Differential Diagnosis   While ruminative thinking and rigid behavioral patterns might be seen in children with other anxiety disorders, what characterizes OCD is a debilitating level of obsessive thinking and compulsive behavior that dominates the child's life, interfering with other more adaptive activities.

Developmental Considerations   Early in development, some obsessiveness or compulsiveness is commonly seen in children as they attempt to navigate stage-salient issues involving mastery and control. For example, preschoolers frequently want things done "just so" or insist on elaborate bedtime rituals to help them to sleep (March & Mulle, 1998).

True OCD is distinguished by the fact that it is not time limited or developmentally appropriate and results in significant distress or dysfunction rather than mastery.

When the disorder does develop, the symptoms generally look the same in children and adults. However, Geller and colleagues (1998) found that there also are a number of differences. For example, although some studies show that males predominate among children, there are no gender differences among adults. Child OCD is comorbid for disruptive disorders such as ADHD, which is not true for adults. Finally, children with OCD perform more poorly on intelligence tests than do adults, and there is a stronger genetic loading. The authors suggest that childhood OCD might be a developmental subtype rather than being essentially the same as the adult disturbance. As we know, behaviors that look the same in children and adults might, in fact, represent different underlying processes.

Developmental Course

The *age of onset* can be as early as 7 years, although the mean age is 10 to 14 years (Weiss & Last, 2001). Once OCD develops, there is no doubt concerning the *chronicity* of OCD. Follow-up studies have found that 43 to 68 percent of young people treated for OCD continued to meet criteria for the disorder 2 to 14 years after the initial diagnosis, while 32 percent had some other comorbid condition (Bolton, Luckie, & Steinberg, 1995).

Developmental Pathways to OCD

Using data from the Dunedin Multidisciplinary Health and Development study, which evaluated a large cohort of New Zealand children every 2 years from age 3 to 18, Douglass and colleagues (1995) investigated the predictors of OCD in a sample of 933 youths. They found no evidence that OCD was predicted by perinatal problems or abnormal birth events, to poor performance on neuropsychological tests, to eating disorders, or to tics. However, the researchers did find that, when they were 11 years old, 18-year-olds with OCD had been significantly more

depressed than the healthy group; and when these OCD adolescents were 15 years old, they had been significantly more *anxious* than the healthy group and had a higher level of *substance abuse*. Eighty-four percent never sought help for their psychological difficulties. Although this study is valuable in focusing on the pathways that lead to OCD, it still leaves unanswered the question of how depression, anxiety, and substance abuse lead to OCD rather than any other disturbance.

Intervention

Pharmacotherapy

Among medications used to treat OCD, selective serotonin reuptake inhibitors in particular have been found to be effective. Although response rates are positive, with as many as 55 percent of children reporting some symptom relief, the reduction in symptom severity is only 20 to 50 percent, and many children continue to experience a significant disruption in functioning due to their OCD (Grados et al., 1999). Accordingly, medication is considered an adjunct rather than the sole treatment for OCD.

Cognitive-Behavioral Treatment

Cognitive-behavioral treatment has proven to be a highly effective treatment for OCD in children (March & Mulle, 1998). Treatment takes place in five steps. First, the therapist provides *psychoeducation* regarding OCD, firmly framing the problem as the disorder rather than the child. Child-friendly metaphors are introduced, such as the idea that obsessions are "brain hiccups," and children are invited to externalize their symptoms by giving it a name, such as "Germy." In the second step, the therapist introduces the child to cognitive strategies for "bossing back" OCD, such as constructive self-talk. The third step involves "mapping" the child's symptoms by identifying situations in which the child feels he or she "wins" against OCD or those in which OCD renders the child helpless. The middle zone, in which the child has partial success against the symptoms, becomes the work zone in which the therapist will stand side by side with the child to increase his or her ability to resist the obsessions and compulsions. At the fourth step comes the core of the intervention, exposure with response prevention, or ERP. *Exposure,* as the term implies, involves exposing the child to the feared stimulus. This is usually done gradually, with the child moving stepwise through a symptom hierarchy, but sometimes it is done abruptly in a variant termed *implosion therapy.* For example, a child who fears contamination may be required to remain in contact with a "germy" object until the anxiety decreases. In *response prevention,* the compulsive ritual is blocked so that, for example, this same child would be prevented from washing his or her hands. While children benefit from graduated exposure in therapy, the most significant gains from treatment come from practicing in the natural environment. Research on the effectiveness of this treatment has yielded impressive results, with positive response shown by 60 to 100 percent of children (March, 1995).

Posttraumatic Stress Disorder

Although several months have passed, 6-year-old Abby still awakens frequently from nightmares about the car accident her family experienced when their car was forced off the road by another vehicle whose driver had fallen asleep at the wheel. Although Abby and her 2-year-old brother Andy were safe in their car seats in the back, their mother hit her head on the windshield and was badly injured. The car rolled over several times and finally came to rest in a ditch. Abby initially seemed only confused and disoriented, until her mother turned around to check on the children in the back seat and Abby saw the blood streaming down her mother's face. Since that time, Abby has reacted with distress to the color red and repeatedly asks why her mother had paint on her face, even though the family members have many times explained to her about the blood from her mother's head wound. In fact, as often as not Abby holds her hands over her ears if anyone tries to talk to her directly about the accident. Her parents also have noticed that Abby is more withdrawn and irritable and appears to take

no joy in the artwork that once gave her such pleasure. She is extremely reactive to whatever is going on in her environment and startles at loud, unexpected sounds.

Definition and Characteristics

Definition

Traumatic Event   The first criterion for the diagnosis of **Posttraumatic Stress Disorder** (PTSD) is that the child has experienced a *traumatic event,* which DSM-IV-TR defines as an event involving actual or threatened death, serious injury, or a threat to the self or others. Further, the individual's reaction to that event is one of intense fear, helplessness, or horror or, in children, agitation or disorganized behavior. (See Table 8.8.) This is one respect in which PTSD differs from all other anxiety disorders—it lacks the element of irrationality. If a boy is terrified of riding the school bus when nothing out of the ordinary has happened, we are puzzled; however, if a boy is terrified of riding a school bus after being in one that has skidded off the road and turned over, we might say, "Of course!"

However, in order for an event to be traumatic, it must be perceived as such (Pynoos, Steinberg, & Wraith, 1995). In other words, the child's *appraisal* of the event is important to determining whether it results in PTSD. A boy who views a car accident as a thrilling adventure with which to regale his friends, for example, is not likely to be traumatized no matter how real the actual threat of harm. By the same token, the child whose cognitions about an event involve negative appraisals, such as shame, helplessness, and self-blame, is likely to experience a more severe posttraumatic reaction.

Traumatic events can be of two types (Terr, 1991). *Type I* traumas involve sudden, anticipated single events—"short, sharp, shocks" such as car accidents, natural disasters, house fires, or school shootings. *Type II* traumas, in contrast, involve long-standing, repeated exposure to horrific events, such as those experienced by children who are victims of chronic child abuse. We will focus here on Type I traumas and in Chapter 14 we will return to the study of Type II PTSD in the context of child maltreatment.

Table 8.8

DSM-IV-TR Criteria for Posttraumatic Stress Disorder

A. The person has been exposed to a traumatic event in which both of the following were present:
   (1) the person experienced, witnessed, or was confronted with an event or events that involved actual or threatened death or serious injury, or a threat to the physical integrity of self or others
   (2) the person's response involved intense fear, helplessness, or horror. **Note:** In children, this may be expressed instead by disorganized or agitated behavior
B. The traumatic event is persistently reexperienced in one (or more) of the following ways:
   (1) recurrent and intrusive distressing recollections of the event, including images, thoughts, or perceptions. **Note:** In young children, repetitive play may occur in which themes or aspects of the trauma are expressed
   (2) recurrent distressing dreams of the event. **Note:** In children, there may be frightening dreams without recognizable content
   (3) acting or feeling as if the traumatic event were recurring (includes a sense of reliving the experience, illusions, hallucinations, and dissociative flashback episodes, including those that occur on awakening or when intoxicated). **Note:** In young children, trauma-specific reenactment may occur
   (4) intense psychological distress at exposure to internal or external cues that symbolize or resemble an aspect of the traumatic event
   (5) psychological reactivity on exposure to internal or external cues that symbolize or resemble an aspect of the traumatic event
C. Persistent avoidance of stimuli associated with the trauma and numbing of general responsiveness (not present before the trauma) as indicated by three (or more) of the following:
   (1) efforts to avoid thoughts, feelings, or conversations associated with the trauma
   (2) efforts to avoid activities, places, or people that arouse recollections of the trauma
   (3) inability to recall an important aspect of the trauma
   (4) markedly diminished interest or participation in significant activities
   (5) feeling of detachment or estrangement from others
   (6) restricted range of affect (e.g., unable to have loving feelings)
   (7) sense of a foreshortened future (e.g., does not expect to have a career, marriage, children, or a normal life span)
D. Persistent symptoms of increased arousal (not present before the trauma) as indicated by two (or more) of the following:
   (1) difficulty falling or staying asleep
   (2) irritability or outbursts of anger
   (3) difficulty concentrating
   (4) hypervigilance
   (5) exaggerated startle response
E. Duration of the disturbance (symptoms in Criteria B, C, and D) is more than 1 month.

Specify If:
Acute (duration of symptoms less than 3 months)
Chronic (duration of symptoms is 3 months or more)
Delayed Onset (onset of symptoms is a least 6 months after the stressor)

Reprinted with permission from the *Diagnostic and Statistical Manual of Mental Disorders,* Fourth Edition Text Revision. Copyright 2000 by the American Psychiatric Association.

Symptom Clusters   Three clusters of symptoms define the disorder: reexperiencing, avoidance, and numbing (APA, 2000).

First, children who develop PTSD following a traumatic experience exhibit persistent *reexperiencing* of the event, characterized by intrusive, distressing recollections of the incident. Reexperiencing may occur at unexpected moments throughout the day, but often occurs when the child is exposed to traumatic reminders. For example, while in a restaurant 3 weeks after undergoing a series of extremely painful treatments for a burn on her chest, a 5-year-old girl erupted in tears upon spying the white latex gloves on the hands of a food service worker replenishing a salad bar, because the gloves reminded her of those that the doctor had worn during the medical procedure. Sometimes the traumatic reminders are so subtle that their connection to the distressing event is hard to discern. Sounds, colors, and the quality of the light at a certain time of day all might act as triggers for emotions of distress that, to the child and others, seemingly come out of nowhere. Reexperiencing also might take the form of dreams about the traumatic event or, in children, nightmares with nonevent-related content such as getting lost or being attacked by monsters. Particularly in younger children, reexperiencing takes the form of posttraumatic play in which aspects of the event are reacted. Although "playing it out" can be therapeutic for children, posttraumatic play is differentiated by the fact that it is repetitive, compulsive, and anxiety arousing rather than relieving. For example, a 5-year-old girl who was attacked and bitten by a monkey at the zoo repeatedly played out this theme with her dolls, although the play did nothing to help her master her fright.

The second cluster of symptoms involves persistent *avoidance* of stimuli associated with the trauma or numbing of general responsiveness. Children with PTSD may actively avoid thoughts or activities and people that arouse recollections of the trauma. For example, the girl who had been burned covered her ears anytime her mother attempted to talk to her about the scar on her chest and insisted, when mention was made of it by curious peers, "I don't know what you're talking about." Avoidance may also take the form of numbing, which is evidenced by a markedly diminished interest in activities that previously were pleasurable. The child with PTSD may no longer show enjoyment of play.

The third cluster of symptoms is characterized by increased *arousal*. Heightened emotional arousal in children may take such forms as sleep disturbance, irritability, difficulty concentrating, heightened physiological reactivity, and hypervigilance. The hypervigilant child is overly sensitive to the environment, scanning constantly for signs of danger and reacting intensely to unexpected stimuli. A classic sign of posttraumatic arousal is the *exaggerated startle response*—for example, the child who jumps

out of her skin and begins to tremble when a door slams suddenly down the hallway.

Characteristics

Prevalence   Though the incidence of PTSD in children who undergo traumatic events is estimated to be high—ranging from 12 percent (March et al., 1997) to 60 percent (Pynoos & Nader, 1987)—many children with symptoms of PTSD are never identified and never receive treatment, despite the distress they experience. An estimated 6 percent of children will meet the criteria for PTSD by the age of 18 years (Pfefferbaum, 1997). The data in regard to *gender differences* are contradictory. A number of studies with large samples have found girls exposed to trauma to be more symptomatic than boys, but other studies have found the opposite (Pfefferbaum, 1997).

Ethnic and Cultural Factors   Data on ethnic differences are very sparse but indicate that, among those referred to clinics, African American children are more likely to have a history of PTSD when compared to European American children (Last & Perrin, 1993).

Studies of refugee populations, who commonly suffer the stresses of political violence, displacement, and immigration, suggest the importance of cultural factors in symptom *expression*. Cambodian refugee children, for example, while suffering from PTSD and comorbid anxiety and depression, do not show the increase in conduct disorders or substance abuse seen in European American samples. They are respectful of authority, have a positive view of school, and function at a high level (Pfefferbaum, 1997).

Comorbidity and Differential Diagnosis   Comorbid conditions are common, with PTSD significantly increasing the risk of *depression, anxiety,* and *disruptive behavior disorders* (Amaya-Jackson & March, 1995). PTSD can be differentiated from other anxiety disorders by virtue of the fact that there is a specific precipitating event, a unique symptom constellation, including such symptoms as reexperiencing, and a definitive timeline.

Developmental Considerations The kinds of symptoms children manifest after being exposed to traumatic events vary with age (Kerig et al., 2000). Young children may regress to a previous level of functioning, such as losing bowel and bladder control, collapsing into tears at small frustrations, sucking their thumbs, and developing fears and eating problems. Separation anxiety is apt to reappear. Avoidance and numbing may lead children to become inattentive, "spaced out," quiet, and withdrawn.

While children rarely exhibit total amnesia for traumatic events, preschoolers are particularly vulnerable to cognitive distortions that exacerbate their distress. For example, one young boy was distressed by the memory of the SWAT team members who came to rescue him and his classmates during a sniper attack, because he misperceived these booted, weapon-carrying men as a second wave of assailants. Young children may also confuse the ordering of events. The reversal of cause and effect can result in *omen formation,* the mistaken belief that they could have predicted and therefore prevented the catastrophe.

For school-aged children *fears and anxieties* are the predominant symptoms. These children also more often complain of headaches and visual and hearing problems, fight with or withdraw from peers, and have sleep disturbances such as nightmares and bed-wetting. Younger children reexperience through *behavior,* such as by engaging in elaborate reenactments of the traumatic event, while older children might reexperience in *thoughts.* For example, they may have repetitive fantasies of being rescued or avenging themselves against the perpetrator (Terr, 1988).

Preadolescents and adolescents, like school-age children, may develop various physical complaints, become withdrawn, suffer from loss of appetite and sleep, and become disruptive or fail at school. Numbing may result in a feeling of estrangement from others, leading to withdrawal, truancy, and even aggression.

Although listed as criteria for both children and adults, some symptoms of PTSD are particularly evident in children. For example, children and adolescents may exhibit a sense of *futurelessness,* or foreshortened future, in that they do not expect to grow up, marry, or achieve happiness in adulthood (Saigh, 1992).

Developmental Course

The meager prospective data suggest that the developmental course depends on the chronicity of trauma. Children tend to outgrow their reactions to single-occurrence stressors, but (not surprisingly) continue to be disturbed by exposure to repeated, multiple stressors.

Risks, Vulnerabilities, and Protective Factors

Characteristics of the child as well as the nature of the traumatic event help to determine whether PTSD will develop and whether it will take a prolonged course (Kerig et al., 2000). *Risk* is increased when traumas are intense and repeated and involve human aggression, particularly when violence is perpetrated toward the child or a person to whom the child looks for security, such as a parent. The events with the most impact also will be those experienced directly by the child. Although vicarious traumatization does occur, the child most likely to be distressed is the one who actually witnessed a family member being shot, for example, rather than the child who merely heard about it. On the other hand, the risk is reduced when the event is an acute one with a specific end point so that, once life has returned to normal, the child will have the opportunity to outgrow its effects. Factors that increase a child's *vulnerability* to trauma include previous traumatization, a difficult temperament, and poor emotional adjustment. *Protective factors* include a resilient temperament, affect regulation skills, internal locus of control, a history of learning how to cope with and master stressful events, as well as a supportive family environment (Pynoos et al., 1995).

Intervention

Crisis intervention strategies are described by Nader and Pynoos (1991), who offer "psychological first aid" to children exposed to disaster or community violence. By taking the treatment directly to the school, the clinicians are able to reach children early in the process and act quickly in order to prevent psychopathological reactions from forming. The central goals of treatment are to normalize PTSD re-actions, minimize confusion and fear contagion, and to engage in therapeutic reexposure. For example, following a sniper attack in which a classmate was shot, children were encouraged to draw a picture and tell a story about their experience of the event. The drawings had the most therapeutic benefit when children were able to depict healing or repair of the damage that had been done.

Amaya-Jackson and colleagues (2002) empiri-cally tested a *cognitive behavioral* group interven-tion for children and adolescents exposed to single-incident stressors, such as hurricanes, car accidents, or gunshot wounds. The sessions begin with psy-choeducation regarding PTSD in order to normalize the symptoms that sometimes make children feel that they are "going crazy." Children are then invited to tell the story of their trauma to the other group members and to begin constructing a narrative of their recovery in the form of a storybook entitled *"My Scary Story with a Good Ending."* In subsequent sessions, children are taught anxiety-management strategies and cognitive skills for "standing up to the bully" of PTSD. As children talk about their trauma, they are helped to identify degrees of fear on their "stress thermometer." The therapist then guides the development of graduated exposure tasks to help children face the trauma-related stimuli that they are avoiding. Exposure to mildly stressful reminders is paired with relaxation strategies until the child can tolerate them comfortably. Parents often play key roles in helping children carry out exposure tasks, and adolescents are even encouraged to involve close friends in their practices. The investigators re-ported that the intervention provided children significant relief. After treatment, 57 percent of the children no longer met criteria for PTSD, and 86 percent did not meet criteria at a follow-up eval-uation 6 months later. There was a 40 percent reduc-tion in PTSD symptoms immediately after treatment and a further 40 percent reduction in symptoms at follow-up.

Developmental Pathways to Anxiety Disorders

Until recently it was erroneously believed that child-hood anxiety need not be taken seriously because the symptoms were unstable and liable to be out-grown. As we have seen in our discussion of each of the DSM-IV-TR categories of anxiety, data using di-verse methods and populations show that, on the contrary, having an anxiety disorder increases the risk for future anxiety disorders or related distur-bances (Kovacs & Devlin, 1998). Moreover, anxiety disorders in childhood can be the beginning of a longtime pattern of disturbance.

An Integrative Developmental Psychopathology Model

Vasey and his colleagues (Vasey & Dadds, 2001; Vasey & Ollendick, 2001) developed a dynamic, transactional model that integrates the research on the etiology of anxiety disorders. This integration involves four elements:

I. Predisposing factors.
II. Two pathways to the onset of anxiety disorders.
III. Factors maintaining or intensifying anxiety.
IV. Factors contributing to desistance.

The model is presented schematically in Figure 8.2. We will now discuss it, point by point.

I. Predisposing Factors

The Biological Context

Genetic Risk There is good evidence that anxiety disorders run in families—that is, that there is *genetic risk*. The most convincing data come from twin stud-ies, which show that the risk of developing anxiety disorders is higher for monozygotic twins than it is for other siblings due to the greater similarity of genetic material. Evidence for a genetic link is particularly strong in the case of OCD (Chang & Piacentini, 2002). However, for anxiety disorders in general, the studies show that heritability accounts for only about one-third of the variance, whereas there is still a significant role played by the shared environment (Eley, 2001).

Figure 8.2   Integrative Model of the Development of Anxiety Disorders.

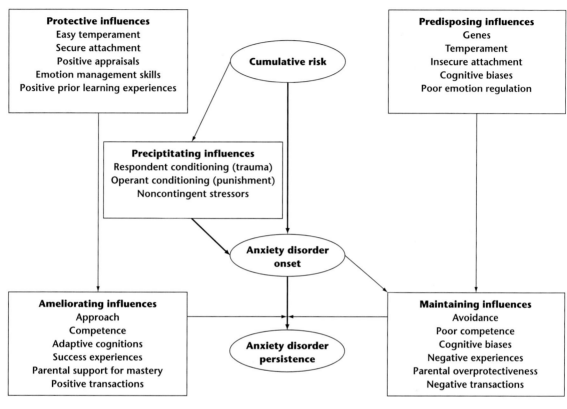

From M. W. Vasey and M. R. Dadds, 2001.

Further, it is important to note that what is inherited is not a specific anxiety disorder per se but rather a *predisposition* to develop disorders in the anxiety spectrum. For example, the Virginia Twin Study of Adolescent Behavioral Development (Eaves et al., 1997; Hewitt et al., 1997) assessed 1,412 twin pairs aged 8 to 16 years. The authors found that separation anxiety and generalized anxiety disorder were genetically linked, but each disorder showed a specific time course: The same child might be vulnerable to developing separation anxiety disorder in the early years and generalized anxiety disorder in adolescence.

Temperament. Currently, one of the most promising leads concerning the biological precursors of anxiety disorders is the temperament variable of **behavioral inhibition** (Lonigan & Phillips, 2001). (See Chapter 2.)   Because inhibited infants are characterized by high motor activity and irritability, they also react to novelty with restraint, withdrawal, avoidance, or distress. In addition they are shy, withdrawn, and fearful, and they avoid challenges. Research suggests that around 20 percent of children inherit the inhibited temperament type.

However, not all infants with inhibited temperament are "doomed" to develop anxiety disorders. It is only among the approximately 10 percent of children whose inhibition is *stable* from the early years into middle childhood that the risk for developing anxiety disorders is heightened (Turner, Beidel, & Wolfe, 1996). These are the children whose behavioral inhibition is most extreme. They also tend to develop two or more anxiety disorders; for example, they are more likely than other children to have phobias such as the fear of being called on in class or the fear of strangers or crowds.

Neurobiological factors. Evidence is beginning to emerge pointing to neurobiological processes underlying the development of anxiety-proneness (Sallee & March, 2001). During moments of fear, stress hormones are released and lead to enhanced excitability of the HPA (hypothalamic-pituitary-adrenocortical) brain circuit associated with fearfulness. When these brain circuits are habitually excited, the child develops an increased susceptibility to anxiety (Gunnar, Bruce, & Donzella, 2001). In support of this idea, studies show that children with a stable inhibited temperament have a lower threshold of arousal in the HPA circuit and react with an activated sympathetic nervous system (Oosterlaan, 2001). Further, parents of inhibited children are disproportionately likely to exhibit social phobia and to have histories of childhood anxiety disorders, suggesting a biological link (Biederman et al., 1995). However, research support is mixed, with some studies showing that shy and anxious children evidence *suppressed* levels of cortisol in response to threat.

Other evidence of neuropsychological factors comes from studies of PTSD, which show that exposure to extreme levels of anxiety affects brain chemistry, which in turn affects the interconnections among neurons, brain structure, and brain functioning (De Bellis, 2001).

The Family Context

Attachment   There are a number of reasons for hypothesizing that an *insecure attachment* increases the probability of developing an anxiety disorder (Thompson, 2001). Recall that insecure infants have caregivers who are either insensitive or nonresponsive to their needs. This, in turn, engenders a view of the world as unreliable and unpredictable and a view of the self as helpless to control the ensuing anxiety. Secure attachment also is fundamental to the development of such important capacities as emotion regulation, which allows children to approach new situations with confidence in their ability to cope and manage any strong emotions that might arise.

Research shows that insecure infants are more fearful than secure ones in free-play situations and in exploring the environment and are also more shy and withdrawn with peers. Evidence also suggests that insecure attachment is predictive of the development of anxiety disorders. In a prospective study of 172 children, Warren et al. (1997) found that, of those who had been rated as insecurely attached in infancy, 28 percent reported having either current or past problems with anxiety at age 17. In contrast, only 13 percent of those in the securely attached group reported such symptoms. The insecure-resistant and insecure-disorganized attachment patterns in particular have been found to increase the risk of anxiety disorders—in some studies, by as much as 100 percent (see Manassis, 2001).

The Individual Context

Cognitive Biases   Children with anxiety disorders display a number of *information processing biases* (Vasey and Dadds, 2001). First, there is an *attentional* bias in that children with anxiety disorders are particularly sensitive to potentially threatening events; for example, they selectively attend to threatening versus nonthreatening words in an experimental task, as compared with nonanxious children. Children with anxiety disorders also interpret ambiguous situations as *threatening;* for example, they are more apt to interpret a noise in the house as an intruder than as an unlatched window rattling. Lastly, children with anxiety disorders show *unrealistic cognitive beliefs* such that they perceive the world as a dangerous place and perceive themselves as incompetent to deal with its threats. Thus, they are lacking in a sense of self-efficacy. (For a detailed discussion of information processing in childhood anxiety, see Vasey and MacLeod, 2001.)

While these cognitive distortions may arise from the child's negative experiences in the environment, they also lead children to shape their own environments in maladaptive ways. Children with low self-efficacy and perceived powerlessness give up more

Middle Childhood to Adolescence: Mood Disorders and Suicide

In this chapter we will cover a spectrum of disorders related to mood, ranging from the darkest depths of major depression—Winston Churchill's "black dog" (Storr, 1989)—to the "slow, black, oily anger" (Godwin, 1994) of dythymia and the "giddy, intoxicating highs" (Redfield-Jamison, 1995, p. 54) of bipolar disorder. As we shall see, depression may emerge in children at any age, even during infancy. However, we have placed our coverage of depression during the transition to adolescence because of an extraordinary increase in prevalence during this period of life. Our task is to identify what in the context and stage-salient tasks of adolescence acts on vulnerable youths to bring about this increased risk. In this chapter we will also discuss the risks associated with child and adolescent suicide, which, we will discover, is related to but independent of depression in some surprising ways.

Depressive Spectrum Disorders

Most of us have times of experiencing something we call depression—being in low spirits, feeling "down," having "the blues." It is even appropriate to feel dejection or despair in response to loss of a loved one or another painful life event. Thus, depression as a *symptom* is relatively common, even normative. Depression as a *syndrome* is a constellation of symptoms that co-occur, including feelings of sadness and loneliness, as well as worry and nervousness. Depression as a *disorder* (sometimes referred to as "clinical depression" or unipolar depression) refers to profound levels of these symptoms and has a specific etiology, course, and outcome (Petersen et al., 1993). As with all disorders defined by the DSM, the key is that the combination of symptoms is significant enough to cause distress and/or to interfere with functioning.

In decades past, professionals did not believe that depression existed in childhood, partly because it was assumed that children did not have the cognitive complexity required for depression. This idea also had credibility because of the wide range of nondepressive responses children show in reaction to traumatic losses, such as rebelliousness, restlessness, and somatic symptoms. Such behaviors were thought to be "masking" an underlying depression. However, while the concept of **masked depression** was once widely accepted, investigators find that child depression shares many of the same characteristics as adult depression and can emerge at any point in the life span. Rather than *masking* depression in childhood, therefore, behavior problems actually *accompany* the symptoms of depression (Hammen & Compas, 1994).

Definitions, Characteristics, and Differential Diagnosis

DSM-IV-TR provides us with four major categories for diagnosing depression, which can be viewed as lying along a continuum of severity. The least severe form of a depressive spectrum disorder is **Adjustment Disorder with Depressed Mood** (see Table 9.1). The essential feature of adjustment disorders (see Chapter 3) is the development of short-term emotional or behavioral problems—in this case, sadness, tearfulness, and hopelessness—in reaction to a recent identified stressor.

Dysthymic Disorder is characterized by the presence of depressed mood that has persisted for at least 1 year in children (as opposed to 2 years in adults). DSM-IV-TR differentiates between child and adult dysthymic disorder in yet another way: In children and adolescents negative mood may take the form of *irritability* rather than depression. At least two specific symptoms must accompany the periods of depression, such as loss of pleasure in activities, feelings of worthlessness, and fatigue. (See Table 9.2.) Dysthymia has an earlier onset than other forms of depression and also has a more protracted course.

Major Depression is a more debilitating disorder. It requires the presence of five or more symptoms during a 2-week period (see Table 9.3), one of which must be depressed mood or irritability in children. Major depression is an acute condition in that the onset is relatively sudden and, while recovery is more likely than from dysthymia, recurrence is likely as well. Recurrent, or *chronic,* major depression is diagnosed when an individual suffers from multiple repeating episodes. Severe depressive episodes may even be accompanied by psychotic symptoms, such as auditory hallucinations, which are seen in one-third to one-half of preadolescents diagnosed with major depression (Mitchell et al., 1988). *Double depression* is a term used for

Table 9.1

DSM-IV-TR Criteria for Adjustment Disorder with Depressed Mood

A. The development of symptoms (depressed mood, tearfulness, or feelings of hopelessness) in response to an identified stressor(s) occurring within 3 months of the onset of the stressor(s).

B. These symptoms or behaviors are clinically significant as evidenced by either of the following:
   (1) Marked distress that is in excess of what would be expected from exposure to the stressor
   (2) Significant impairment in social, occupational, or academic functioning

C. The stress-related disturbance does not meet the criteria for another specific mental disorder and is not merely an exacerbation of a preexisting disorder.

D. The symptoms do not represent bereavement.

Adapted from the *Diagnostic and Statistical Manual of Mental Disorders,* Fourth Edition Text Revision. Copyright 2000 by the American Psychiatric Association.

Table 9.2

DSM-IV-TR Criteria for Dysthymic Disorder

A. Depressed mood for most of the day, for more days than not, as indicated either by subjective account or observation by others, for at least 2 years. Note: In children and adolescents, mood can be irritable and duration must be at least 1 year.

B. Presence, while depressed, of two (or more) of the following:
   (1) poor appetite or overeating
   (2) insomnia or hypersomnia
   (3) low energy or fatigue
   (4) low self-esteem
   (5) poor concentration or difficulty making decisions
   (6) feelings of hopelessness

C. During the 2-year period (1 year for children or adolescence) of the disturbance, the person has never been without the symptoms for more than 2 months at a time.

D. No Major Depressive Episode has been present during the first 2 years of the disturbance (1 year for children and adolescents), unless that episode was in full remission with no signs or symptoms for 2 months before the development of the Dysthymic Disorder.

E. There has never been a Manic Episode or Hypomanic Episode.

Specify If:
Early onset: if onset is before age 21 years
Late onset: if onset is age 21 years or older

Adapted from the *Diagnostic and Statistical Manual of Mental Disorders,* Fourth Edition Text Revision. Copyright 2000 by the American Psychiatric Association.

Table 9.3

DSM-IV-TR Criteria for Major Depressive Episode

A. Five (or more) of the following symptoms have been present during the same 2-week period and represent a change from previous functioning; at least one of the symptoms is either (1) depressed mood or (2) loss of interest or pleasure.
   (1) depressed mood most of the day, nearly every day, as indicated by either subjective report (e.g., feels sad or empty) or observation made by others (e.g., appears tearful). **Note:** In children and adolescents, can be irritable mood
   (2) markedly diminished interest or pleasure in all, or almost all, activities most of the day, nearly every day (as indicated either by subjective account or observation made by others)
   (3) significant weight loss or weight gain when not dieting (e.g., more than 5 percent of body weight in a month), or decrease or increase in appetite nearly every day. **Note:** In children, consider failure to make expected weight gains
   (4) insomnia or hypersomnia nearly every day
   (5) psychomotor agitation or retardation nearly every day (observable by others, not merely subjective feelings of restlessness or being slowed down)
   (6) fatigue or loss of energy nearly every day
   (7) feelings of worthlessness or excessive or inappropriate guilt (which may be delusional) nearly every day (not merely self-reproach or guilt about being sick)
   (8) diminished ability to think or concentrate, or indecisiveness, nearly every day (either by subjective account or as observed by others)
   (9) recurrent thoughts of death (not just fear of dying), recurrent suicidal ideation without a specific plan, or a suicide attempt or a specific plan for committing suicide

B. The symptoms are not better accounted for by bereavement and are not due to the effects of a substance or medical condition.

Adapted from the *Diagnostic and Statistical Manual of Mental Disorders,* Fourth Edition Text Revision. Copyright 2000 by the American Psychiatric Association.

Box 9.1 | **A Case Study in Depression**

Mary, a young woman in her early 20s, is currently experiencing her second major depressive episode. She recalls a childhood marked by tension and fighting between her parents, who were frequently critical of her or simply seemed disinterested. Her mother herself was depressed much of the time and was overwhelmed by the responsibilities of raising four children on her husband's limited income. As a consequence of her parents' unavailability and disparagement, Mary perceived herself as less important and less competent than other children.

She did relatively well at school early on. However, her academic achievements rarely increased her confidence. Instead, Mary interpreted her good grades as a sign that the teacher was being nice to her out of pity, and she began to worry that the other students would dislike her for getting better grades than they did. As she entered puberty, she experienced increasing family conflict at home, more demanding courses at school, and increasing self-consciousness about whether she was popular or attractive enough. Consequent to all these

worries, her concentration and motivation declined. She had friends, but still felt like an outsider, dubious that peers really liked her for herself or would be there for her if she were in need. When conflicts arose with her peers, she would typically acquiesce to their demands, keeping her anger and frustration to herself. In high school, her experience of misery grew more acute. Mary was more preoccupied with unhappy thoughts and worried a great deal about her future and her appearance, fearing that life didn't hold much for her. The one hope she held was to

individuals who experience chronic dysthymia punctuated by periods of major depression. (See Box 9.1 for a case example.)

Virtually none of the literature on the developmental psychopathology of depression addresses adjustment disorders. Therefore, we will focus our discussion on dysthymic disorder and major depression. Distinctions between the two disorders will be made whenever possible, although much of the research literature is based on studies of *symptoms* of depression (e.g., a significant score on a measure such as the Child Depression Inventory [Kovacs, 1992]), rather than a specific psychiatric *diagnosis*.

Prevalence

Prevalence estimates vary widely, depending on the criteria and assessment instruments used. Many epidemiological studies only index whether children score above a certain point on a depression rating scale, failing to differentiate amongst the various diagnostic categories.

When viewed as a *symptom* (depressed mood), the prevalence is high in community populations. (Here we follow Hammen and Rudolph, 2003, and

Compas, 1997, unless otherwise noted.) Large-scale studies in the United States and Canada have found that, according to parent reports, 10 to 20 percent of boys and 15 to 20 percent of girls in the general population go through periods of depressed mood. Among adolescents, from 20 to 46 percent of boys and 25 to 59 percent of girls report experiencing depressed mood.

When depression is viewed as a *disorder*, prevalence rates are lower. Depressive disorders are rare in the preschool period, more frequent in middle childhood, and most prevalent in adolescence. A distinction is made between point prevalence (how many children in the population are depressed) and lifetime prevalence (how many children will become depressed at some time in their lives). Regarding *point prevalence*, the largest U.S. study conducted to date found that, among children aged 9, 11, and 13, rates were 0.03 percent for major depression, 0.13 percent for dysthymia, and 1.45 percent for the catch-all category of Depression Not Otherwise Specified (Costello et al., 1996). Limited data are available on depression in preschool children, but the prevalence is estimated to be less than 1 percent (Kashani & Carlson, 1987).

meet a man who would love her and make her feel happy and secure.

She met Jack in her first year of college. He was exciting, outgoing, and seemed capable of taking good care of her. He was also more handsome and popular than any man she thought she could attract and, out of fear of losing him, she accommodated to him when he insisted on sexual intimacy. When she became pregnant, the families pressured them to marry, and Mary dropped out of college to become a homemaker and mother. Soon afterward, Mary experienced a major

depression in the wake of discovering that Jack wouldn't provide financial or emotional support for her and that she was stuck at home with a small child and no job prospects.

The marriage limped along for another 2 years, while, with another child, the couple struggled to make ends meet. Jack began to complain that Mary was no fun to be with, owing to her depressed mood, lack of energy, and pessimistic outlook. He spent much of his free time with his friends and was verbally abusive to her if she complained. Mary devoted

herself to being as good a parent as possible, although she often found the children a burden and couldn't bring herself to play with them or suppress her irritation. The older child suffered terrible separation anxiety upon starting preschool. Just recently—prior to her current depressive episode—she found out that Jack was having a serious affair with another student, and she knew that their relationship had to end.

Source: Adapted from Hammen, 1992.

Regarding *lifetime prevalence*, estimates for major depression have ranged widely. One large-scale longitudinal study of 386 nonreferred children found that over 9 percent had developed major depression by the time they reached age 18 (Reinhertz et al., 1993). Among adolescents, a nationally representative sample of 15- to 18-year-olds found a lifetime prevalence of 14 percent for major depression and 11 percent for dysthymia (Kessler & Walters, 1998). In contrast, Lewinsohn and colleagues (1998) found a lifetime prevalence of 25 percent for major depression.

When clinical populations are studied, studies show that 10 to 57 percent of children in mental health centers have a depressive disorder. School-aged children referred to treatment have higher rates of major depression (about 13 percent) when compared to younger children (about 1 percent).

Of particular concern is the fact that prevalence rates for child and adolescent depression have been increasing significantly in recent decades (Kessler et al., 2001). While no direct evidence is available about the cause, speculations have focused on societal pressures and stresses, which we will return to when we discuss sociocultural factors.

Ethnicity, Culture, and Socioeconomic Status

As has been found with adults, rates of depression are highest in children who come from *low-income,* underprivileged homes (Conger et al., 1994; Costello et al., 1996). Stressors associated with low SES, including family disruption, low income, lack of access to educational and cultural resources, unsafe and unattractive neighborhoods, and other forms of adversity, potentially contribute to the risk.

Among the limited number of studies that have directly investigated *ethnic* differences in the prevalence of depression, results have been inconsistent. While some studies find higher rates in African American than European American adolescents (Garrison, Jackson, Marsteller, McKeown, & Addy, 1990), others report the opposite (see Sagrestano et al., 2003). In a large-scale study of a sample of 5,423 schoolchildren in grades 6 through 8, Roberts, Roberts, and Chen (1997) investigated ethnic differences while controlling for effects associated with social class. These authors found comparable rates of depression among European American and African American children; however, the rates for Mexican American children were higher. Hill, Bush, and Roosa (2003) also found that Mexican American children had higher levels of depression than European American children in their sample of 344 school-agers.

The Developmental Dimension

Developmental Differences in Depressive Symptoms

The question is often raised about whether depression in children can be regarded as the same disorder as that in adults, or whether developmental differences necessitate modifications in our diagnostic criteria (Carlson & Garber, 1986; Weiss & Garber, 2003). If this is so, age-related differences in reported prevalence rates could be an artifact of the use of developmentally insensitive measures and conceptualizations of depression. At one extreme are those who maintain that children's cognitive, language, and emotional functioning is so different from that of adults that depression in children must be distinct. At the other extreme are those who point to the similarities in the manifestations of depression in children and adults as evidence that the syndrome is essentially the same across the life span. For example, Kovacs and Beck (1977) find that a comparable set of symptoms are demonstrated in both depressed children and adults. They describe these as *emotional* (e.g., feels sad, cries, looks tearful), *cognitive* (e.g., anticipates failure, says "I'm no good"), *motivational* (e.g., achievement declines, shows no interest in pleasurable activities), and *physical* (e.g., loss of appetite, somatic complaints).

In general, developmental psychopathologists take a middle position, acknowledging that, while there is a significant correspondence between adult and childhood depression, children also have certain unique characteristics.

This middle position was bolstered recently by Weiss and Garber (2003), who conducted a meta-analysis of developmental differences in depression. While their ability to draw firm conclusions was hampered by extreme variability in the effects reported from study to study, they identified six symptoms that differed as a function of age: Developmentally advanced children displayed more anhedonia (loss of

pleasure), hopelessness, hypersomnia (oversleeping), weight gain, and social withdrawal. However, the analysis was not fine grained enough to determine at what point in development these symptoms emerge. Turning to the question of developmental differences at the *syndrome* level (i.e., Do the symptoms of depression cluster together differently for children of different ages?), the results were a three-way tie: Two studies supported consistent syndromes across age, two supported developmental differences, and one provided support for either.

Integrating Hammen and Rudolph (2003), Shafii and Shafii (1992), and the individual studies reviewed by Weiss and Garber (2003), we can summarize the findings to date regarding developmental differences in the symptoms of depression.

Infancy and Toddlerhood   Signs of depression in very young children might include delays or losses of developmental accomplishments, such as toilet training, good sleeping habits, and intellectual growth. A sad facial expression and gaze aversion may be seen. Children may engage in self-harming behavior such as head banging, and self-biting occurs, as well as self-soothing behavior such as rocking or thumb sucking. Clinging and demanding behavior may alternate with apathy and listlessness.

Preschool   Depressed preschoolers are unlikely to verbalize feelings of dysphoria and hopelessness, but instead tend to be characterized by a sad appearance. The depressed preschooler may experience a loss of interest in pleasurable activities or achievements. Developmental backsliding may be evident, such as loss of cognitive and language skills, social withdrawal, and excessive anxiety about separation from the caregiver. Vague somatic complaints, irritability, and sleep problems and nightmares also are seen.

School Age   As children approach school age, their symptom picture is more similar to that of adults. Depressed mood becomes evident, as do expressions of low self-esteem, self-criticism, and guilt. Loss of motivation may affect the child's interest in participating in social or school-related activities. In addition, depressed school-aged children may engage in disruptive and aggressive behavior that negatively affects their peer relationships and academic performance. Eating and sleep disturbances may be seen, as well as developmental delays. As children advance in age, symptoms become more severe, and there is a greater loss of interest or pleasure in previously enjoyed activities (anhedonia), and suicide is a possibility.

Adolescence   Adolescents are the most likely to directly verbalize their sad feelings and distress. Other symptoms of depression in adolescence include sharp mood swings and negativity, frequently accompanied by truancy, misbehavior, and a drop-off in academic achievement. Hypersomnia (sleeping too much) is another symptom seen more frequently in adolescents than in younger children (Kovacs, 1996). Changes in eating behavior also increase with adolescence.

To summarize, while developmental trends in depressive symptoms exist, age-related differences are not absolute. Studies generally find that depression can be reliably assessed in young children using criteria consistent with DSM-IV-TR. Therefore, despite some age-related differences in symptoms, the existing criteria for depression appear to be valid for use with children.

Age and Gender Differences in Depression

Adolescence and Depression   Although depression may be seen in children at any age, most typically, the onset for major depression is in mid- to late adolescence. There also are differences related to the type of depression shown. Large-scale epidemiological studies show that the mean *age of onset* of the first major depressive episode is 15 years, while the onset of dysthymic disorder is in younger children, beginning at about age 11 (Lewinsohn et al., 1994). In fact, the marked increase in prevalence that comes with *puberty* is probably the most significant developmental trend in the phenomenon of depression. There is a dramatic rise in depression between the ages of 13 and 15, a peak at ages 17 and 18, and a subsequent decline to adult levels.

Why the increase in depression in adolescence? Part of the explanation may lie with the emotional and cognitive factors that come into play during this developmental period. *Emotionally,* adolescents are capable of experiencing intense sadness and of sustaining this experience over time. *Cognitively,* they can think in terms of generalizations about themselves and their circumstances and can project these negative expectations into the future. They can consciously evaluate the self and judge it as helpless or inept.

In addition, the developmental *context* of adolescence differs from that of childhood. Children have the basic security of knowing they are an integral part of the family unit. By contrast, adolescents are faced with the task of giving up their place within the family and developing a new status as an independent person. Even in a healthy adolescent, therefore, one might expect to see some transitory depressive states when closeness to the family is taboo but mature sources of love have not yet been found. Thus, depression may be an exaggeration of the normal separation-individuation process in adolescence (Weiner, 1992). If moderate levels of depression appear as part of the expected turmoil of the adolescent period, the question becomes how to differentiate normative from pathological symptoms.

Gender and Adolescent Depression   While prior to adolescence sex differences in depression are small and not reliably found, around age 13 to 15 there is an increase in the prevalence, severity, and recurrence of depression in girls, especially among those who are referred to mental health clinics (Lewinsohn, Pettit, Joiner, & Seeley, 2003). By the time they reach age 16, girls are twice as likely as boys to be diagnosed with depression (Hankin et al., 1998). (See Figure 9.1.)

Why are more girls depressed? Hormonal changes accompanying puberty are one possible explanation that has recently garnered some evidence (Angold, Costello, Erkanli, & Worthman, 1999). On the other hand, a provocative set of findings suggests that there are different psychological predictors of depression in males and females. A prospective study by Block and Gjerde (1990; Gjerde & Block,

Figure 9.1   Prevalence
Rates of Major Depressive
Disorder by Gender.

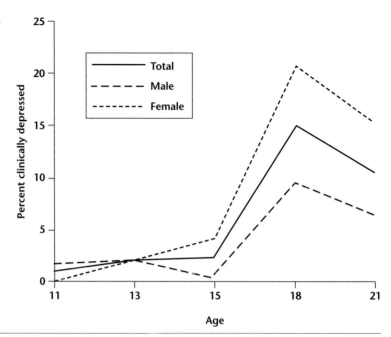

Source: Hankin et al., 1998.

1991) found striking sex differences in the symptom picture leading up to depression in 18-year-olds. At 14 years of age, girls who later became depressed were described as vulnerable, anxious, worried, somatizing, and concerned with their adequacy—characteristics associated with *internalizing*. By contrast, at age 14 boys who became depressed were seen as antagonistic, aggressive, antisocial, self-indulgent, deceitful, and mistrustful of others—characteristics associated with *externalizing*. Further, depression was associated with low self-esteem only in girls. While female adolescents described themselves as aggressive and socially unskilled, observers found those traits only in males. These sex differences in precursors to depression were in evidence as early as the preschool period. In subsequent work, Gjerde (1995) followed these same subjects to age 23. Consistent with previous findings, adult depression in males was predicted by preschool ratings of undercontrolled, aggressive behavior. For females, predictors of depression were not reliably identified until adolescence but included overcontrolled behavior and introspective self-concern.

How are we to understand these results? Gjerde (1995) and Nolen-Hoeksema (2002) argue that adolescence is a developmentally sensitive period that may have different implications for males and females. First, while both boys and girls undergo significant biological changes, girls are more likely to evidence dislike of the changes they are going through and dissatisfaction with their bodies (see Chapter 11). Second, social relationships are particularly important to girls, who have higher needs for affiliation with others and are more attuned and sensitive to the opinions of peers (Rudolph, 2002). Therefore, girls may be more reactive to some of the stressors associated with adolescence, such as increasing peer pressure and the dynamics of social inclusion and exclusion. Moreover, as they move into mid-adolescence, girls are more sensitive than boys to interpersonal stressors in the home, such as maternal distress and interparental conflict, to which they are more likely to react with depressed mood (Crawford, Cohen, Midlarsky, & Brook, 2001). Third, adolescent girls are more likely than boys to experience certain kinds of psychosocial stressors, such as unwanted sexual attention and sexual assault (see Chapter 14). Fourth, because gender roles and the expectation that one will conform to them increase in adolescence, girls may believe that they will be disliked if they act in ways counter to their gender-role stereotype, such as by being assertive and independent minded or by beating a boy in a competition (Brown & Gilligan, 1992). Therefore, girls also are more likely than boys to hide their competence in order to avoid others' negative opinions, a phenomenon termed "silencing the self" (Crowley-Jack, 1999). Research has indicated that silencing the self and adherence to a traditional feminine gender role are associated with increased risk for depression in adolescent females (Aube, Fichman, Saltaris, & Koestner, 2000; Obeidallah, McHale, & Silbereisen, 1996) as well as males (Hart & Thompson, 1996). In summary, both gender role and developmental stage come into play in girls' depression.

Comorbidity

From 40 to 70 percent of depressed children and adolescents have at least one other disorder as well (Cicchetti & Toth, 1998). Symptoms of *anxiety* and depression are highly correlated, with 60 to 75 percent of depressed children having comorbid anxiety disorders. While some authors have used this comorbidity to argue that the distinction between depression and anxiety should be abandoned for children, the general consensus is that the two syndromes are sufficiently distinct to justify classifying children as having one disorder or the other, or a combination of the two (Laurent & Ettelson, 2001). Anxiety symptoms typically predate depression, suggesting a developmental relationship between these two forms of internalizing (Avenevoli et al., 2001) such that early-onset anxiety acts as a risk for later depression (Cole et al., 1998).

Depressive disorders also may be comorbid with one another, with some children developing "double depression." The combination of dysthymia and major depression is associated with the most severely negative outcomes (Goodman et al., 2000).

Anger and aggression also play a significant role in childhood depression, especially among boys.

Fourteen to 36 percent of depressed boys also have *conduct disorder* and engage in aggressive antisocial acts such as setting fires, fighting, or stealing (Mitchell et al., 1988). Although this observation is compatible with the idea of masked depression described earlier, again, these misbehaviors are in addition to, rather than instead of, the symptoms of depression. Comorbid conduct disorder and aggression are associated with a more negative outcome and are cause for particular concern (Harrington et al., 1991). Indeed, the International Classification of Diseases (ICD-10) (see Chapter 3) includes a specific category of Depressive Conduct Disorder (DCD). In a test of its validity, Simic and Fombonne (2001) found that, among inpatient children and adolescents in the UK, those with the DCD diagnosis had lower levels of depression and anxiety than the depression-only group, but were more likely to engage in self-harming behavior. In turn, children with DCD were more depressed and less overtly aggressive than the conduct disorder-only group and were more likely to have been abused.

The explanation for the link between depression and conduct problems is not yet known, but several speculations have been offered: (1) Both disorders may arise from a single general underlying developmental deficit, such as in emotion regulation; (2) depression may arise as a consequence of the negative events, stresses, and disruptions that conduct disorders generate in a child's life; or (3) the two disorders may be brought about by shared risk factors and genetic vulnerabilities (Hammen & Rudolph, 2003).

Gender Differences in Comorbidity

There are a number of gender differences in patterns of comorbidity, as we have seen. While girls' depression is more likely to be accompanied by anxiety, boys' depression is more likely to be associated with disruptive behavior, including ADHD and conduct disorder (Kessler, Avenevoli, & Merikangas, 2001).

Age Differences in Comorbidity

Patterns of comorbidity also change with age. Depressed preschoolers are likely to demonstrate separation anxiety; depressed school-aged children may also have conduct disorder; and depressed adolescents tend to show comorbid substance abuse or eating disorders (see Hammen and Rudolph, 2003).

Etiology

The Biological Context

Genetics   Familial concordance rates provide evidence for a *genetic* component in depression. (Here we follow Rutter et al., 1999.) Children, adolescents, and adults who have close relatives with depression are at higher risk for developing depression themselves, with a genetic component generally estimated at about 20 to 45 percent. Parent depression is a particular risk factor for the development of child depression, as we will explore in more detail later. The familial loading is higher for those whose depression began before the age of 20; therefore, it is proposed that childhood-onset depression is a variant with a particularly strong genetic component.

However, simply showing that depression runs in families fails to disentangle the relative influence of heredity and environment. For this, twin and adoption studies are needed. In one large-scale study, O'Connor and colleagues (1998) compared MZ and DZ twin pairs and reported an overall heritability estimate of 48 percent. Another study, the Virginia Twin Study of Adolescent Behavior Development, obtained interviews and self-report ratings of depression from both parents and children (Eaves et al., 1997). The correlations between MZ twins were 0.66 while those for DZ pairs were less than half as large, suggesting a genetic contribution. A puzzling finding emerging from this study was that estimates varied as a function of whose report was used. Whereas the genetic component was estimated to be 54 to 72 percent when findings were based on parent interviews, it shrunk to 11 to 19 percent when children's reports were used. The reasons for these discrepancies are not clear.

In contrast, some adoption studies have found *no* genetic component to depressive symptoms in middle childhood, which may reflect the significant effects of environmental factors on the unfolding of depression (Eley et al., 1998). For example, one study of adolescents compared monozygotic and dizygotic twins, biological siblings, half-siblings, and biologically unrelated step-siblings and found significant genetic influences for those with low levels of depression, but significant environmental influences for those with high levels of depression (Rende et al., 1993).

Silberg and colleagues (1999) used the Virginia twin data to attempt to tease out the relative contributions of nature (genes) and nurture (environmental stress) to the developmental psychopathology of depression. Using two waves of data collection conducted 19 months apart, they found that genetic factors contributed to the consistency of depression over the course of the study, and that life stress also had a direct effect on depression, but particularly for adolescent girls. About 30 percent of the variance in adolescent girls' depressive symptoms was attributable to genetics, with the remainder attributable to environmental factors. In addition, genetic effects tended to increase the likelihood of experiencing negative life events. In conclusion, the authors suggest that an increased genetic liability to depression emerges in adolescence, particularly for girls, which interacts with the experience of life stress in order to produce the disorder.

A limitation of much of the research on genetics is that it often does not consider the issue of *specificity*. In fact, the genetic liability appears to be not specific to depression, but to all internalizing disorders, including anxiety and phobia. It may be that what is inherited is an underlying trait such as negative emotionality. Further, depression and conduct problems frequently co-occur in families as well as in children. For example O'Connor and colleagues (1998) reported a correlation of 0.47 between measures of depression and antisocial behavior in their sample of twin pairs. Using statistical modeling, the investigators estimated that about 45 percent of this relationship could be attributed to genetic factors, while 30 percent was attributable to shared environment, and 25 percent was contributed by nonshared experiences specific to the individual.

Neurochemistry   Research with depressed adults points to disorders of the hypothalamic-pituitary-adrenal (HPA) system, which is activated in response to stress. When the system goes awry, a *neuroendocrine* imbalance may result, particularly hypersecretion of the hormone *cortisol*. A connection between neuroendocrines and mood disorders is plausible, given that hormone production regulates mood, appetite, and arousal, all of which are adversely affected by depression. To date, however, there are only inconsistent data for the role of cortisol in child depression (see Kaufman et al., 2001).

Although studies in this area are just beginning, one promising hypothesis is that difficulties in regulating stress hormones may be a result of early adversity. Cortisol is released when an individual is under severe stress, and excessive levels can have a negative effect on the developing brain. Once sensitized to cortisol, the brain is overreactive to further stress, thus increasing the vulnerability to psychopathology in general and perhaps depression in particular (Heim & Nemeroff, 2001; Pliszka, 2002).

Theories of adult depression point to suppressed levels of the neurotransmitter *serotonin*. Antidepressant medications that act to increase serotonin availability include the new generation of selective serotonin reuptake inhibitors (SSRIs), such as fluoxetine (Prozac) and sertraline (Zoloft), as well as serotonin-norepinephrine reuptake inhibitors (SNRIs), such as venlafaxine (Effexor). While these medications have been proven effective in combating depression in adults, evidence in support of the neurotransmission mechanism in children is mixed. Studies of the efficacy of SSRIs in child and adolescent depression have yielded some promising results (Wagner & Ambrosini, 2001). However, effect sizes are still small, and in some studies results emerge only for ratings of global improvement and not for symptoms of depression specifically, as we shall see when we revisit this issue in our discussion of treatment.

In summary, research on child depression, while limited, suggests that organic theories of etiology derived from studies of adults cannot be applied easily to children (Kaufman et al., 2001). Further, without prospective data demonstrating that biological indicators predate the onset of depression, some question remains about whether these are the cause or *result* of depression. Ultimately, the picture is likely to be a complex and transactional one. Experiences and mood act on biology, and, in turn,

biology reciprocally affects cognitions, emotions, and memory (Post & Weiss, 1997).

Brain Structure and Function   Brain-imaging research with adults suggests that depression is related to low levels of activation of the left hemisphere. Interestingly, the left hemisphere appears to be more involved in the processing of positive affect; when it is underactivated, the right hemisphere may become more active, generating excessive negative affect (Pliszka, 2003). This pattern of left hemispheric hypoactivation also has been found in infants and toddlers of depressed mothers (Dawson et al., 1997). Whether this intergenerational transmission is a function of genetics, or to the children's greater stress and exposure to maternal negative affect, remains to be determined (Hammen & Rudolph, 2003).

The Individual Context

Attachment   As Cicchetti and Toth (1998) note, evidence has accumulated regarding a link between *internal working models of attachment* and depression in infants, children, and adolescents. Children who internalize an image of themselves as unworthy and others as unloving are more vulnerable to the development of the cognitive, emotional, and biological processes that are associated with depression.

Blatt (2004; Blatt & Homann, 1992) relies on attachment theory for his model, which distinguishes between two different kinds of depression. The first, *dependent* or *anaclitic* depression, is characterized by feelings of loneliness and helplessness as well as fear of abandonment. Individuals with dependent depression cling to relationships with others and have unmet longings to be cared for and nurtured. Thus, they have difficulty coping with separation and loss and are uncomfortable expressing anger for fear of driving others away. In contrast, *self-critical* or *introjective* depression is characterized by feelings of unworthiness, inferiority, failure, and guilt. Individuals with self-critical depression have extremely high internal standards, resulting in harsh self-scrutiny and evaluation. They have a chronic fear of others' disapproval and criticism, and they worry about losing the regard of significant others. They are driven to achieve and to attain perfection and thus make excessive demands on themselves. While they may even accomplish a great deal, they do so with little experience of lasting satisfaction or pleasure.

Blatt and Homann (1992) hypothesize that these different kinds of depression are due to particular kinds of attachment experiences affected individuals have in early childhood. The quality of their relationships with caregivers leads to the development of internal working models of self and others that leave these individuals vulnerable to depression. Inconsistent parental availability, associated with the *resistant/ambivalent* attachment pattern, may be more likely to result in depression related to issues of dependency, loss, and abandonment. In contrast, controlling and rejecting parenting associated with *avoidant* attachment would lead to self-criticism and low self-worth, as angry feelings about the caregiver are redirected against the self.

To date, research has offered some support for the model. Much of the research has focused on adults; however, Blatt and associates (1996) were able to differentiate the two types of depression in a sample of adolescents. Further tentative support for the dual model of depression in children comes from Harter's (1990) research, which revealed two groups of depressed children and adolescents. In the larger group depression was due to low self-esteem, while in the smaller group it was due to the loss of a significant person. However, the necessary developmental research—showing that dependent depression and self-critical depression in childhood are predicted from different kinds of attachment relationships in infancy—has not yet been conducted.

Cognitive Perspectives   Cognitive theories about childhood depression follow directly from Beck's (1987, 2002) classic adult model. The cognitive model centers on the **cognitive triad,** which consists of attributions of *worthlessness* ("I am no good"), *helplessness* ("There is nothing I can do about it"), and *hopelessness* ("It will always be this way").

First, evidence regarding the *worthlessness* dimension comes from extensive research documenting the relationship between childhood depression and feelings of low self-esteem or perceived competence

(Harter, 1999; Harter & Whitesell, 1996). Harter finds a strong relation between self-worth and mood, the correlations running as high as 0.82 in children 8 to 15 years of age. Longitudinal research has also demonstrated that low self-esteem is a specific predictor of depression (Lewinsohn, Gotlib, & Seeley, 1997). Moreover, children's negative view of the self leads to a biased interpretation of information in such a way that it "confirms" their belief in their inadequacy. For example, depressed youths recall more negative adjectives describing themselves on a memory test (while nondepressed children recall more positive traits) and are more likely to seek out information that validates their negative view of themselves.

Second, Bandura's (1986) concept of **self-efficacy** provides us with insight into the *helplessness* dimension. Perceived self-efficacy refers to children's belief in their ability to affect the world around them in order to obtain a desired result. Without a sense that they can produce effects by their actions, children have little incentive to take action or to persevere in the face of challenges. Bandura and colleagues (1999) propose that a low sense of self-efficacy contributes to depression via three pathways. The first involves feelings of self-devaluation and despondency that arise when children perceive themselves as being unable to live up to their expectations and fulfill their aspirations. The second involves perceived social inefficacy, which arises when children believe they are unable to form satisfying relationships, leading children to withdraw from others and be deprived of the social support that could help to buffer them from stress. The third mechanism involves perceived inability to control depressive thoughts themselves. While rumination and negative thinking contribute to depression, and interventions that change these thought patterns alleviate depression, research suggests that depressed individuals lack a sense of efficacy about their ability to regulate their negative thinking. In a prospective study of 282 middle school students, Bandura and colleagues (1999) confirmed that perceived social and academic inefficacy influenced children's depression over a period of 2 years. As expected, depressed children had more nonefficacious beliefs about their skills than their actual performance warranted.

Third, Seligman and his colleagues (Abela & Seligman, 2000; Abramson, Seligman, & Teasdale, 1978) contribute to our understanding of the *hopelessness* dimension by adding the variable of **causal attribution.** Three dimensions are involved in the causal attributions leading to depression: They are *internal* ("It is because of me"), *stable* ("I will always be like this"), and *global* ("Everything about me is this way"). When negative events are attributed to characteristics of the individual rather than to external agents, self-esteem diminishes as helplessness increases. When the negative events are attributed to factors that persist over time, then helplessness is stable. And when negativity is generalized to a host of situations, helplessness is global. Stable and global negative attributions are clearly linked to the cognition of hopelessness, which has a significant role in child and adolescent depression (Gladstone & Kaslow, 1995; Harter & Whitesell, 1996).

How do these attributional styles develop? According to Rose and Abramson's (1991) theory, negative events during childhood—such as traumatic loss, maltreatment, or guilt-inducing parenting—set in motion a vicious cycle. As the child attempts to interpret these events and find meaning in them, cognitions are generated related to the events' causes and solutions. When events are negative, uncontrollable, and repeated, hopelessness-inducing cognitions are likely. A number of other factors might facilitate or interfere with the development of negative cognitions, including the extent to which the negative events challenge the child's self-esteem, the child's level of cognitive development, and the reactions and interpretations of events offered by parents (see Figure 9.2). For example, Stark and colleagues (1996) found that children with the depressive cognitive triad had parents who themselves evidenced depressive attributional styles and who communicated negative messages to the child about the self, the world, and the future. As parents disconfirm more hopeful-inducing cognitions and negative events are repeated, a depressed mind-set is formed.

These negative cognitive *schemata* affect not only the child's present state of mind but also the child's future orientation toward the world. Schemata are stable mental structures that incorporate children's perceptions of self, their experiences in the past, and their expectations for the future (Dodge, 1993). Therefore, based on the lessons they draw from past experiences, children's perceptions of present and future events are colored by depressive schemata as if by a pair of grimy gray glasses. Children who look at the world through the lens of depression focus their attention on whatever is negative and consistent with their pessimistic point of view, ignoring the disconfirming evidence offered by positive events. As children develop negative patterns of thinking and engaging with the world, as well as a stable negative cognitive style, the likelihood increases that depression will emerge. One of the strengths of the cognitive model is that these negative attributional styles appear to be specific to the development of internalizing disorders, including anxiety and depression, and are not characteristic of child psychopathology in general (Hankin & Abramson, 2002).

However, there are some important limitations to cognitive models of child depression. Some studies of children's attributional styles have produced mixed results; for instance, some longitudinal research has found negative attributions to be *correlates* of youth depression rather than *predictors* of it (Bennett & Bates, 1995). Hammen (1991) also cautions that depressive cognitions appear to be state dependent, coming and going as depression waxes and wanes, rather than comprising an underlying trait that would serve as a "marker" of vulnerability. There is still much to be learned about the causal role of the cognitive triad in the etiology of depression.

Another limitation of the cognitive model is a *developmental* one. While depression can be detected in very young children, not all the cognitive markers theoretically associated with depression can be (see Shirk, 1988). The research methods for assessing the cognitive triad require children to understand complex language in interviews or questionnaires, which makes it difficult to investigate attributions prior to the late-preschool and middle childhood periods. Moreover, our understanding of cognitive development makes it difficult to imagine complex

Figure 9.2   A Model of the Development of Negative Cognitive Style.

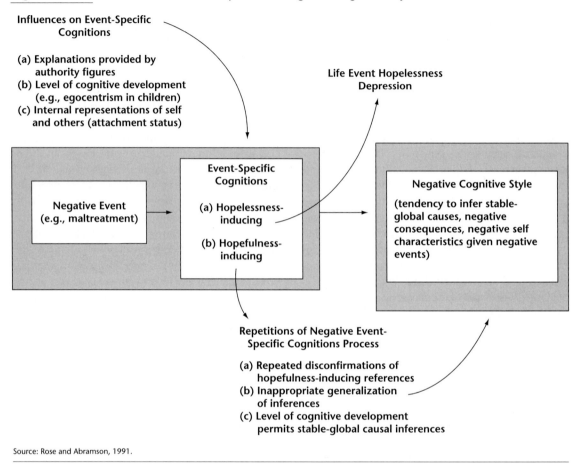

Source: Rose and Abramson, 1991.

cognitions involving worthlessness, helplessness, and hopelessness in infancy, even though the markers of depression can be seen at that early age. In an attempt to resolve this developmental dilemma, Rose and Abramson (1991) offer an intriguing speculation. While the onset of a depressive attributional style may indeed develop in early childhood, the cognitive components of depression may not become evident until years later. The authors theorize that negative experiences only result in the cognitive triad of depression *if* those stressors persist into the period of concrete operations when the child is able to make causal inferences that are stable and global in nature. In other words, while negative attributions indeed may underlie the development of depression from an early age, investigators may only be able to detect them later in childhood.

Emotional Development   One of the underlying developmental processes that contributes to child depression is difficulty with *emotion regulation*. Not only do depressed children have poor general skills for coping with life challenges, including interpersonal problems, but they have more difficulty moderating their emotions in the face of stress (Rudolph et al., 1994; Zahn-Waxler, Klimes-Dougan, & Slattery, 2000). For example, Zeman, Shipman, and Suveg (2002) found that depression in school-aged children was predicted by difficulty identifying their emotional states, suppression of angry emotions, and dysregulation of anger and sadness. In face of poorly regulated emotional distress, depressed children respond in ineffective ways, such as withdrawal or excessive reassurance seeking, that alienate them from their peers and further exacerbate their difficulties (Joiner, Metalsky, Katz, & Beach, 1999). While emotion dysregulation may arise as a function of temperamental qualities of the child, family patterns of interaction also are implicated, particularly for children of depressed mothers, as we discuss in more detail in the next section.

The Family Context

Families of Depressed Children An emotionally aversive family environment predicts the development of depression in children and adolescents (Sheeber et al., 1997). Depressed children describe their families as more conflictual, negative, and controlling and as less cohesive and supportive (Kaslow, Deering, & Racusin, 1994). Families of depressed children report experiencing more acute and chronic stressors than do others, and they have fewer supportive social relationships to buffer them. *Interparental conflict* also increases both parent and child depression (Davies, Dumenci, & Windle, 1999).

Observations of the interactions of depressed children and their parents confirm that the families display high levels of negativity and low levels of nurturance, as well as harshness and excessive control (Messer & Gross, 1995). Observational studies of *expressed emotion* indicate that families of depressed children are critical and emotionally overinvolved (Asarnow et al., 1994). Further, not surprisingly, depression is linked to child *maltreatment* (Toth, Manly, & Cicchetti, 1992; see Chapter 14), including emotional, physical, and sexual abuse (Lizardi et al., 1995). A dysfunctional family environment may undermine the child's self-esteem, which in turn contributes to a sense of failure and depression. All these negative childhood events also interact with the other risk factors we have identified, such as by generating the attributional style of helplessness, hopelessness, and worthlessness

that is characteristic of depression (Rudolph, Kurlakowsky, & Conley, 2001).

Longitudinal research supports the idea that negative family interactions are associated with increases in child depression over time. Sheeber and colleagues examined the effects of family support and conflict over a 1-year period in a sample of 420 mostly European American adolescents and their mothers. While decreased family support and decreased conflict were associated with increases in adolescent depression, adolescent depression did not predict worsening family relationships, lending credence to the idea that the effects are transmitted from the family environment to the child. In turn, Sagrestano and colleagues (2003) found a similar pattern of results in a 2-year longitudinal study of 302 low-income African American school-aged children. Interestingly, their data showed that increases in family conflict and decreases in parental involvement were associated with increases in *both* child and parent depression.

It is worth noting that the previously cited research shows that children become depressed specifically in relation to *interpersonal stressors*, rather than to other kinds of negative events that might affect adults, such as achievement-related failures (Rudolph & Hammen, 1999). Perhaps the single most traumatic interpersonal stressor for children is the loss of a parent, which we consider next.

Parental Loss Our review of the concept of attachment in Chapter 5 demonstrated that adequate caregiving in infancy is not a sentimental luxury but an absolute necessity for optimal development. Although relatively rare, complete loss of a parent is an experience with dramatic effects on child functioning and clear links to depression.

The classic research on *maternal deprivation* was conducted by Spitz (1946) and Bowlby (1960), who studied infants in institutional settings such as hospitals, orphanages, and foundling homes. Despite the fact that their physiological needs were met—they received adequate food, warmth, and hygiene—these infants lacked any kind of affectionate care. As a consequence, many wasted away, and even died—as many as 37 percent in one orphanage. Spitz termed these infants' reaction **anaclitic depression** (meaning, essentially, loss of that on which one depends) and believed that it represented a prototype of adult depression. Bowlby (1960) asserted that the loss of this important relationship—the infant's secure base—is so profound that it should be viewed on the same level as war and natural disaster.

The hypothesized link between maternal loss and depression has received empirical support (Weller et al., 1991). An important fact to keep in mind, however, is that Spitz's and Bowlby's research confounds loss of a parent with *institutionalization.* These variables were teased apart in a series of studies conducted by Joyce and James Robertson (1971). They observed young children who had been temporarily separated from their mothers and found that the ill effects of parental loss were more severe for children who were placed in institutions as opposed to those who were placed in foster families. While large, impersonal orphanages provided children with minimal care and attention from an ever-changing series of nurses, children in loving foster families had available to them surrogate caregivers with whom they readily formed attachments. Children in foster care also demonstrated significantly less distress about the separation from their mothers, and they overcame their distress more readily when reunited with their own families. Therefore, it is not separation per se that is so devastating, but rather the extended stay in a strange, bleak, or socially insensitive environment with little or no contact with the mother or other familiar figures.

Brown, Harris, and Bifulco (1986) examined other factors that can mediate the effect of loss of the mother. These investigators interviewed women who were bereaved as children and also those who underwent a significant period of separation from the mother. Loss of the mother before the age of 11, whether by death or separation, was associated with subsequent depression for most women. Thus, maternal deprivation acted as a *vulnerability factor.* However, loss of the mother had no effect in the absence of a *provoking event,* such as poverty or life stress.

Further research from these investigators uncovered additional mediators. The rate of depression was twice as high in women who had experienced *traumatic* separations from their mothers, such as

being neglected, abused, or abandoned, than it was in women separated by death or by other causes such as maternal illness or divorce (Brown, Bifulco, & Harris, 1987). And, in a subsequent study, Bifulco, Harris, and Brown (1992) found that the rate of adult depression was particularly high in women whose mother died before they were 6 years old and even greater if death occurred before they were 3 years old. However, it was not the early timing of the death per se that was important. Rather, it was the fact that the death came at the end of a long sickness, which, the authors infer, prevented the development of a secure *attachment.*

In sum, both in infancy and childhood, the idea that loss of a caregiver per se leads to depression is too simplistic to be accurate. Rather, depression is contingent on the interaction of a host of factors, including the individual (e.g., helplessness), interpersonal (e.g., lack of social support), sociocultural (e.g., socioeconomic level), and developmental (e.g., the child's level of cognitive sophistication). Therefore, the task of investigators is to tease out the interactions among variables and to examine the ways in which such interactions change as loss occurs at different points in development.

Children of Depressed Mothers   In a major review article in the *American Psychologist,* Peterson and colleagues (1993) state that "the need for services for children of depressed parents as closely approximates a prescriptive recommendation as can be found in the mental health professions" (p. 163). The enormity of the concern is matched by the volume of literature on the topic (e.g., Cummings et al., 1999; Goodman, 2003; Goodman & Gotlib, 2002; Hammen, 1999; Radke-Yarrow, 1998). Approximately 40 percent of children of depressed mothers are themselves diagnosed with depression. Maternal depression more than doubles the risk of a child's developing depression across the life course, with episodes that are particularly severe and long lasting. Further, longitudinal research by Hammen, Burge, and Stansbury (1990) showed that children of depressed mothers had a worse outcome than children of bipolar, medically ill, well, or even schizophrenic mothers. Perhaps, in contrast to the guilt-inducing qualities of parental depression, children readily understand that the overtly bizarre behavior associated with mania and psychosis is not under their control and not of their doing (Anderson & Hammen, 1993).

It is not clear how the intergenerational transmission of depression from parent to child takes place. Although the link may be a genetic one, another likely explanation is *parenting style.* Two dimensions of depressed parenting have been identified: withdrawal and intrusiveness (Malphurs et al., 1996). In terms of *withdrawal,* depressed mothers are observed to be less psychologically available to their children: They offer less positive affect, warmth, praise, and positive feedback. Regarding *intrusiveness,* depressed mothers also are more likely to be controlling, impatient, and irritable; to use coercive discipline techniques; to make more negative attributions about child behavior; and to be less accurate in reading children's affect (Cicchetti & Toth, 1995). Stein et al. (2000) confirm that children of depressed mothers perceive their mothers to be overprotective—and they perceive their fathers to be less caring as well.

The clearest evidence for the effects of maternal withdrawal comes from studies in which mothers' affect has been experimentally manipulated, a rare thing in the literature on psychopathology. While playing with their toddlers, nondepressed mothers were asked to simulate depressed affect by keeping a "still face" and remaining emotionally inexpressive, uninvolved, and unresponsive to their children. Children reacted to their mothers' emotional unavailability with clear distress, physically withdrawing, making more negative bids for attention, and becoming disorganized and oppositional (Seiner & Gelfand, 1995).

Field (1992) reports that infants of depressed mothers develop a depressive mood as early as 8 months of age. These depressive characteristics appear not only during interaction with the mothers but also with a nondepressed stranger, indicating the development of a stable interpersonal style. If maternal depression persists over a year, adverse effects on infant growth and intellectual development are seen, while in the toddler and preschool periods maternal depression is associated with the development of an insecure attachment (Teti et al., 1995).

What is the developmental process by which children of depressed parents become depressed? One proposal is that coping with a depressed parent prevents children from developing adequate strategies for *emotion regulation* (Cicchetti & Toth, 1995). Emotion regulation, as we saw in Chapter 2, allows children to calm themselves in the face of upsetting circumstances. Healthy mothers aid the development of emotion regulation by soothing their children and helping to build their competency to soothe themselves. However, depressed mothers' inability to modulate their own negative feeling states interferes with the ability to modulate their children's moods. Thus, children of depressed mothers are exposed to chronically high levels of negative affect and fail to develop effective strategies for managing these distressing feelings (Garber, Braafladt, & Weiss, 1995).

Alternatively, there is evidence that *cognitive* factors come into play. As young as 5 years of age, children of depressed mothers express depressive cognitions such as hopelessness, pessimism, and low self-worth when observed responding to a mild stress in the laboratory, such as the threat of losing at a card game (Murray, Woolgar, Cooper, & Hipwell, 2001). Similarly, children of depressed mothers are more likely than other children to show a poor self-concept and to engage in negative forms of information processing when their depressive cognitive schemas are primed (Taylor & Ingram, 1999). Depressed mothers may model such depressed cognitive styles for their children as well as reinforce them through maladaptive parenting styles. For example, Langrock et al. (2002) found that children of depressed mothers engaged in maladaptive strategies for coping with stress that were reminiscent of depressive thinking (e.g., rumination and intrusive thinking).

Clinical observations of depressed mothers and toddlers also demonstrate *transactional* processes through which they exert negative influences on one another's behavior (Radke-Yarrow, 1998). For example, children of depressed mothers are more irritable and difficult to soothe and exhibit more negative affect, anger, sadness, and distress, thus taxing the mother's parenting skills and increasing her stress and irritation. Children of depressed mothers, in turn, are highly attuned to their mother's negative affect and may attempt to comfort and nurture the parent, engaging in a process of role reversal or parentification (Cicchetti, Rogosch, & Toth, 1997). Parentified children are burdened by the developmentally inappropriate expectation that they meet the parents' emotional needs at the expense of their own (Kerig, 2005). In these ways, children's attempts to cope with and respond to their mothers' depression might perpetuate problematic cycles of interaction. Over the long term, maternal depression and child depression have been shown to mutually affect one another, as research shows significant relationships between the onset and succession of depressive mood in at-risk mothers and their children (Hammen, Burge, & Adrian, 1991).

There is also research to indicate that the effects of maternal depression vary as a function of *gender;* when the mother is depressed, the risk of developing depression appears to be higher for girls than for boys (Sheeber, Davis, & Hops, 2002). For example, a 7-year longitudinal study by Hops (1992) shows stronger relationships between mother and daughter depressed mood than exists among other family members. Similarly, Davies and Windle (1997) report that maternal depression is associated with subsequent depression in female, but not male, adolescents. The emotional closeness of mother-daughter relationships (Chodorow, 1978) may place girls at particular risk for the effects of maternal depression.

As Goodman and Gotlib (1999) argue, the transmission of depression from parent to child may occur as a function of a number of processes: (1) genetic vulnerability; (2) a shared underlying neurological dysfunction in emotion regulatory mechanisms; (3) exposure of the child to the parent's maladaptive cognitions, behavior, and affect; and (4) the larger context of stress and family conflict with which both parent and child must cope. As a consequence of these mechanisms of risk, children of depressed parents may experience difficulty with the mastery of many developmental tasks, including attachment security, emotion regulation, interpersonal relationships, and problem solving. In Table 9.4, we present Goodman's outline of the ways in which depressed parenting might interfere with the child's

Table 9.4

Effects of Depressed Parenting on Stage-Salient Issues Throughout Development

Developmental Stage	Depressed Mothers[1]

Infancy
  Fostering an attachment relationship
  Facilitating the development of emotional self-regulation
	Less sensitive;
	Less responsive (slower and less contingent);
	Less reciprocal vocalization; and affectionate contact;
	Lower amounts and quality of stimulation

Toddlers and preschool-aged children
  Providing the external support necessary for children to develop:
  • An accurate understanding of social and emotional situations
  • Effective autonomous functioning
  • The ability to manage emotionally arousing situations
  • The ability to organize and coordinate environmental resources
	Spend less time mutually engaged with their children in a shared activity;
	Initiate and terminate their children's attention to objects more frequently (rather than encouraging sustained attention);
	Respond to children's resisting their influence by dropping their demands or persisting less effectively or engaging in coercive mutual influence

School-aged children and adolescents
  • Providing general social support or stress buffering
  • Helping children to maintain their focus on the cognitive-intellectual and social environment
  • Monitoring children's behavior
  • Providing consistent discipline
	Reinforce children's misbehavior by suppressing their dysphoric affect in response to children's aggressive affect;
	More critical, more negative appraisals, and lower tolerance of their children's behavior

[1] Compared with nondepressed controls.

Source: Goodman, 2003.

mastery of stage-salient issues through the course of childhood.

Moreover, many confounding factors conspire to prevent simplistic explanations about the intergenerational transmission of depression. First, maternal depression is associated with a number of other forms of psychopathology in mothers, including anxiety and personality disorders, as well as family stressors such as marital conflict and economic distress, many of which have similar effects on children's development (Cummings & Davies, 1994a). Thus, it is hard to tease apart the effects of parental depression alone. In addition, parental depression is associated with the development of disorders in children other than depression, including ADHD, anxiety, substance abuse, bulimia, and conduct disorder. Therefore, the concept of *multifinality* applies here; maternal depression is a risk factor not specific to child depression, but rather predictive of a variety of poor outcomes.

On the positive side, recent longitudinal research also points toward potential *protective mechanisms* and sources of resiliency. For example, the NICHD Early Child Care Research Network (1999) found that *maternal sensitivity* in infancy moderated the effects of maternal depression on preschoolers' cognitive and behavioral development. For the parent who is sensitive to the child's needs, depression does not necessarily spill over onto child development.

Children of Depressed Fathers   While almost all of the research has focused on mothers' depression, recently investigators have begun to recognize the importance of studying *fathers* as well. While adult men are diagnosed with depression at rates 2 times less than those of adult women, from 3.8 percent to 12.7 percent of men will experience major depression in their adult lives, and many more will experience depressed mood, particularly during the childrearing years (Blazer et al., 1994). In a recent meta-analysis, Kane and Garber (2004) reviewed the available albeit limited research and found that paternal depression was associated with significant increases in children's internalizing and externalizing symptoms as well as father-child conflict.

Patterson and Dishion (1988) propose that parental depression strains fathers' ability to cope with everyday stresses in the family and leads to more irritability and conflict with children. Consistent with this hypothesis, Conger and colleagues (1995) found that *father-child conflict* mediated the association between paternal depression and child psychopathology; specifically, paternal depression led to increases in father-conflict, which in turn led to an increase in adolescent externalizing behavior. In turn, father-child conflict is related to increased depression in children of depressed men (Ge et al., 1994). In the larger family context, interparental conflict also might be a by-product of paternal depression, leading to indirect negative effects on children (Downey & Coyne, 1990; see Chapter 2). On the side of protective factors, fathers' *positive affect and approval* buffers children from the effects of paternal depression (Jacob & Johnson, 1997).

The Social Context

Parents are not the only sources of negative evaluation that can result in depressed mood. Peers can be relentless in their taunting of the child who is different or socially awkward. Therefore, it is no surprise that low social support from peers, lack of perceived social competence, and loneliness are significant predictors of child and adolescent depression (Harter & Marold, 1994), particularly for females (Oldenburg & Kerns, 1997). Children who are victims of peer teasing and aggression score higher on measures of depression and low self-esteem, although positive relationships with close friends can help to buffer them from the risk (Prinstein, Boergers, & Vernberg, 2001).

Consistent with cognitive models, depressed children have overly negative perceptions of their social competence, in that they rate their social status more negatively than peer reports would warrant. However, evidence also suggests that this is not *entirely* a matter of distorted self-perception: Depressed young people actually are less socially skilled than other children. Teachers report that depressed children are less prosocial and more aggressive and withdrawn, and the perceived social incompetence of depressed

Relational aggression.

children may not be entirely invalid (Rudolph & Clark, 2001). Therefore, it has been proposed that depression arises as a function of deficits in *interpersonal problem-solving skills* (Stark, 1990). While good interpersonal skills act as a protective buffer against the impact of negative life events, depressed youths are less able to generate effective solutions to social problems. Consistent with this hypothesis, depressed children have poorer social skills (Bell-Dolan, Reaven, & Peterson, 1993; Rudolph & Clark, 2001), and they are less often chosen as playmates or workmates by other children (Rudolph, Hammen, & Burge, 1994).

Are depressed children the *victims* or the *initiators* of negative social relationships? An ingenious study by Altmann and Gotlib (1988) investigated the social behavior of depressed school-aged children by observing them in a natural setting: at play during recess. The authors found that depressed children initiated play and made overtures for social contact at least as much as did nondepressed children and were approached by other children just as often. Yet depressed children ended up spending most of their time alone. By carefully observing the sequential exchanges between children, the researchers discovered the reason for this. Depressed children were more likely to respond to their peers with what was termed "negative/aggressive" behavior: hitting, name-calling, being verbally or physically abusive. In this way, depressed children may be generating some of their own interpersonal stress (Rudolph & Hammen, 1999).

These observations fit well with the model developed by Patterson and Capaldi (1990), in which peer relations are posited to play the role of *mediators* of depression. According to this model, a negative family environment leads children to enter school with low self-esteem, poor interpersonal skills, aggressiveness, and a negative cognitive style. Consequently, the children are less able to perceive constructive solutions to social problems and are more likely to be rejected by peers because of the way they behave. Peer rejection, in turn, increases their negative view of self and thus increases their depression.

In order to test this model, Capaldi (1991, 1992) differentiated four groups of boys depending on whether they demonstrated aggression, depressed mood, both aggression and depression, or neither. Boys were followed over a 2-year period from grades 6 to 8. While depression and adjustment problems tended to abate over time in the depressed group, no such improvement occurred in the two other disturbed groups. While, in general, aggressive behavior

Figure 9.3   Mediators of the Effects of Child and Family Factors on Depression.

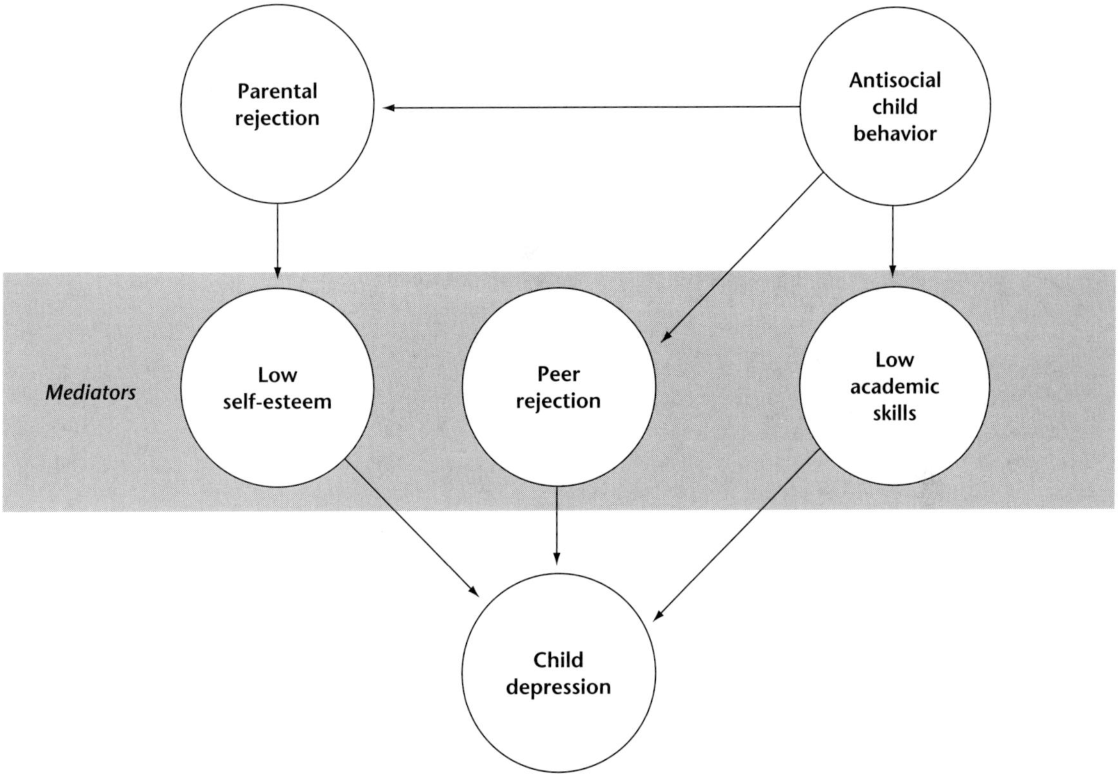

Source: Adapted from Patterson and Capaldi, 1990.

was more stable than depressed mood, conduct problems increased the risk of subsequently having a depressive mood. In fact, aggression in grade 6 predicted depressed mood in grade 8, while earlier depression did not predict later conduct problems.

Capaldi conceptualizes the process leading from aggression to depression as follows. (See Figure 9.3.) Aggression and negative behavior alienates parents, peers, and teachers, resulting in more interpersonal conflict and rejection. Further, aggression makes children oppositional and negativistic in the classroom, which leads to learning deficits and poor skill development. Both of these factors result in profound failure experiences in the social and academic realms. Failure and rejection, in turn, produce low self-esteem. The impact of peer rejection, low

academic skills, and low self-esteem is associated with increasingly serious deficits in adolescence, ultimately resulting in depression.

Interactions and Transactions   Depressed children evidence a number of interpersonal skill deficits, but are these causes or consequences of depression? The longitudinal research available to date supports both sides of the transactional equation. On the one hand, social difficulties lead to increased depression over time (e.g., Cole et al., 1996), and the interpersonal problems of depressed children remain evident even when the depression has lifted (Lewinsohn et al., 1994). On the other hand, depression in turn predicts increases in social difficulties (Rudolph et al., 1994). For example, Steele and

Forehand (2003) found that increases in depression predicted decreased social competence over a 3-year period in a sample of African American boys. As Hammen and Rudolph (2003) suggest, the social difficulties of depressed children generate negative interpersonal experiences, such as peer rejection, which exacerbate the symptoms of depression.

The Cultural Context

Poverty   Widening our scope to include the larger context of child development, we find that depression has been linked to a number of variables in the sociocultural context, including economic disadvantage (Costello et al., 1996; Conger et al., 1994). Other community characteristics associated with poverty, such as neighborhood violence and criminal victimization, leave both parents and children feeling anxious and depressed (Richters, 1993).

Life Stress   In addition to poverty as a specific stressor, there is abundant evidence that general *life stress* has an important role in depression. Longitudinal data show that stress exposure precedes the development of depression in children and exacerbates the severity of depressive symptoms (Ge et al., 1994; Goodyer et al., 2000). Although the data are mixed, some studies suggest that girls are more vulnerable to developing depression in reaction to stress, particularly interpersonal stress (Rudolph & Hammen, 1999).

However, evidence is accumulating that the children most negatively reactive to stress are those who are cognitively vulnerable to it. The vulnerable children are those with negative attributional styles (Hankin & Abramson, 2002), maladaptive beliefs about the self (Rudolph et al., 2001), and dysfunctional problem-solving orientations (Spence et al., 2002). Stressful events, in turn, contribute to the development and consolidation of negative cognitive styles. Again, we need to keep transactional, multidimensional models in mind.

Ethnicity   Given that low SES ethnic minority youths are disproportionately exposed to the above-described kinds of stressors, it is somewhat surprising

that the prevalence data presented earlier reveal few consistent differences among racial groups.

However, one stressor unique to minority youths that is associated with increased depression is *racial discrimination* (Rumbaut, 1994). Simons and colleagues (2002) note that middle childhood is a crucial time for the development of perceptions of the self and the social world. Further, during the school years children begin to turn their attention to the world outside their family and are affected increasingly by the community in which their development is embedded. Racism might interfere with healthy development by negatively affecting children's self-esteem and leaving them with a sense of helplessness and discouragement about their ability to redress the inequities they experience. With these considerations in mind, Simons and colleagues (2002) compiled a list of factors in the family and community contexts that might increase the risk for depression in all children—such as low social support, family poverty, neighborhood crime, and lack of parental involvement—as well as processes that are unique to children of color—such as racial discrimination and lack of ethnic identification. In a sample of 810 African American children, they confirmed that, at the individual level, uninvolved parenting, racial discrimination, and being the victim of crime were associated with increased depression, while, at the community level, high rates of racial discord and low levels of pride and identification within the ethnic group also contributed to youth depression.

However, recall that in our review of epidemiology we learned that Roberts, Roberts, and Chen (1997) found that Mexican American youths had higher rates of depressive symptoms when compared to either African American or European American children and that these results held regardless of social class. Therefore, neither the effects of poverty nor of racism would seem to be an entirely satisfactory explanation. Roberts and colleagues propose two possible explanations for their findings. First, cultural differences may come into play. For example, Mexican society has been described as promoting *fatalism,* the belief that one is helpless in the face of external forces, a belief system that has been associated with impaired coping and depressive symptomatology

(Neff & Hoppe, 1993). Alternatively, *gender differences* may provide an explanation. Roberts and colleagues note that the higher rates of depression were seen particularly in Mexican American girls; females are known to be more likely to use ruminative coping styles, which also are associated with depression (Nolen-Hoeksema et al., 1991). As intriguing as these ideas are, however, no research yet has linked these hypothesized processes to depression in ethnically diverse youths.

On the positive side, evidence also suggests that a *positive family environment* can act as a protective factor that buffers ethnic minority children from the negative effects of neighborhood dysfunction (Richters & Martinez, 1993).

Developmental Course

Although it was once believed that depression was a transitory phenomenon, certainly in contrast to the stability seen in externalizing behavior problems (see Chapter 10), evidence is accumulating regarding the *continuity* of depression. Studies of normative populations show that ratings of child depression taken at the beginning of the school year predict depressive symptoms 3 (Ialongo et al., 1993) and 6 (Achenbach et al., 1995a) years later. In prospective studies of clinical samples, childhood depression has been found to increase the likelihood of depression as long as 15 years later (Weissman et al., 1999).

On an encouraging note, evidence suggests fairly high rates of *recovery* from a given episode of depression. Kovacs and colleagues (1994) followed a group of children diagnosed with depression, assessing them every few years until late adolescence or early adulthood. Most children rebounded from their initial depressive episode. Rates of recovery were highest from a major depressive episode, second highest from adjustment disorder with depressed mood, and lowest from dysthymia. Children took longest to recover from dysthymia, while adjustment disorder required the shortest time for recovery.

However, the news is not as good as it looks at first glance. Although youths are likely to recover from an episode of depression, *relapse* rates are also high, with about 40 percent of children and adolescents experiencing another depressive episode over the course of the next 3 to 5 years (Asarnow et al., 1988; Lewinsohn et al., 2000). For example, in Kovacs and colleagues' (1994) study, within a period of 5 years, children with major depression or dysthymia had a high probability of suffering a new depressive episode. About two-thirds developed a new episode of depression while they were still in their teens. Early-onset dysthymia was a particularly negative indicator, with 76 percent of the children in this category going on to develop a major depressive disorder.

In another large-scale prospective study, Weissman and colleagues (1999) followed a group of 108 clinically depressed children over the course of a decade. About one-third of those with recurrent childhood depression continued to have major depressive episodes in adulthood. Among the adolescents in the study, continuity was even stronger, with 63 percent experiencing at least one major depressive episode over the next 10 years. Similar results concerning continuity have been reported in other longitudinal studies. For example, Harrington and his colleagues (1996) followed 80 children diagnosed with depression into adulthood and compared them to community children matched for age and sex. Those depressed as children were at significantly greater risk for developing affective disorder in adulthood: 84 percent of those depressed as children were depressed in adulthood, as opposed to 44 percent of those who had not had childhood depression. The prospects for later-onset depression may be somewhat less grim, but still are negative. Lewinsohn and colleagues (2000) found that over half of those who were depressed in adolescence met criteria for major depression at some point over the next 5 years.

Early *age of onset* also is a negative prognostic sign. Onset of depression prior to puberty is associated with more severe dysfunction in general and an even greater likelihood of continuity to adult depression (Harrington et al., 1996). This likelihood is the result of the cumulative effects of recurrent depressive episodes, of which more will be experienced by children who are early starters on the developmental pathway to depression. Recently, Lewinsohn and colleagues (2003) found that a bout of major depressive disorder in adolescence is associated with pervasive deficits in adult psychosocial functioning, including job performance, relationship functioning, physical well-being, and life satisfaction. Remarkably, these negative effects pertained even when the depression did not extend into adulthood. The authors liken the experience of early-onset depression to a "scar" that has a pernicious impact on later development.

Some forms of depression might be precursors to others. Dysthymic disorder is an antecedent to major depression for many youths, with the course of dysthymia often punctuated by episodes of major depression. In addition, a significant number of depressed children and adolescents are later diagnosed with bipolar disorder (Akiskal, 1995).

A key reason for the continuity of depression is that mood disorders have the potential to interfere with the child's mastery of developmental tasks in a number of spheres, including the capacity to perform at school, to form satisfying relationships at school, and to form secure bonds within the family (Hyman, 2001). Thus, the effects are cumulative and interact with all other contexts of development.

Specificity

Is depression in childhood a *specific* predictor of later depression? As Harrington and colleagues (1996) point out, there are some limitations to the evidence concerning the continuity of depression. *Looking backward* we find that, while childhood depression predicts adult depression, not all depressed adults were depressed as children; in fact, many of them displayed externalizing disorders. *Looking forward* we find that childhood depression is associated with a number of poor adult outcomes, including interpersonal problems, substance abuse, anxiety, personality disorders, and suicide attempts, but not necessarily depression (Weissman et al., 1999).

However, some investigations suggest that, at least in adolescence, depression is a risk factor specific to the development of adult depression. Bardone and colleagues (1996) compared a sample of well-adjusted 15-year-old girls with a group of same-age girls who had been diagnosed with either depression or conduct disorder. At age 21, while conduct-disordered girls generally demonstrated antisocial personality disorder, depressed girls tended to become depressed women. Further, depression in

the earlier years specifically predicted symptoms of depression in adulthood.

Again, gender differences complicate the picture. Depression in childhood may have different consequences for males and females. For example, Achenbach and coworkers (1995a) found that depression in school-aged girls predicted depression 6 years later, whereas depression in boys predicted diverse symptoms, including depression as well as withdrawal, thought problems, and inattention. These results echo the findings reported earlier on gender differences in the factors that predict depression in males and females.

To summarize, the prognostic picture suggests that, while the recovery rate from depressive disorders is high, so is the relapse rate. Major depression and dysthymia tend to be chronic and recurring disorders and tend to put children at risk for a number of disorders later in development. Of those children with depression who go on to become disturbed, the great majority show depression as part of their adult disorder. Therefore, once on a depressed trajectory in development, a child is likely to stay on this course.

Integrative Developmental Model

A comprehensive developmental psychopathology model of depression has been put forward by Hammen (1991, 1992; Hammen & Rudolph, 1996, 2003) and is presented in Figure 9.4. The case study presented in Box 9.1 also illustrates the elements of this model.

While acknowledging that there are many pathways to depression, Hammen's model places *dysfunctional cognitions* at the forefront. First, however, the stage for the development of these negative cognitions is set by *family factors,* such as a depressed parent, insecure attachment, and insensitive or rejecting caregiving. Adverse interpersonal experiences contribute to the child's development of negative schemata: of the self as unworthy, others as undependable and uncaring, and relationships as hurtful or unpredictable. The depressive cognitive style also involves the belief that others' judgments provide the basis for one's self-worth, as well as a tendency to selectively attend only to negative events and feedback about oneself.

Eighty-eight percent of all eligible students in the school participated in the study. To avoid "contamination," for the first year of the study, the investigators merely administered measures to all of the 9th graders. The second year, all 9th graders participated in the intervention. After the intervention and at 10-month follow-up, youths in the two treatment conditions reported lower levels of depression and hopelessness than the control children.

Bipolar Disorder

Definition and Characteristics

Bipolar Disorder, commonly know as manic depression, is a severe form of psychopathology in which periods of depression alternate with manic episodes involving expansive mood, overactivity, irritability, or increased risk-taking behavior (see Table 9.5).

Bipolar disorder is further differentiated according to type. Type I involves the presence of manic episodes, with or without periods of depression. Type II involves depression interspersed with periods of *hypomania,* a milder form of euphoria or overactivity that is below the threshold for the diag-

nosis of a mania. Because it is at a lower level of intensity, hypomania is defined as causing a *change* in functioning in contrast to the severe *impairment* in functioning associated with full-blown mania. A third type of bipolar disorder, termed *cyclothymia,* is characterized by small, rapidly shifting changes in mood during which the individual experiences hypomania punctuated by depressive symptoms. (See Figure 9.6 for a graphic comparison of the different mood disorder diagnoses.)

The study of bipolar disorder in children is relatively new but is revealing some intriguing findings. (For more extensive coverage, see Geller and DelBello, 2003.)

Prevalence and Age of Onset

Diagnostic Dilemmas   The diagnosis of bipolar in children is rare, although with increasing recognition of the disorder, investigators are beginning to suspect that it is more prevalent than previously thought. For example, retrospective reports of members of a manic-depression self-help organization found that 60 percent of adults with bipolar recalled experiencing symptoms of the disorder in childhood or adolescence (Lish et al., 1994). (See Box 9.3 for a case example.)

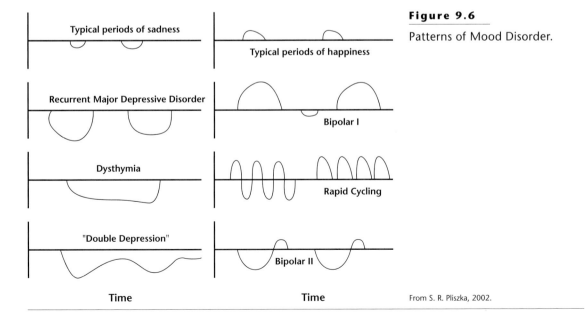

Figure 9.6

Patterns of Mood Disorder.

From S. R. Pliszka, 2002.

Box 9.3 | **Case Study in Bipolar Disorder: Kay Redfield-Jamison Writes**

Kay Redfield Jamison, a professor of psychiatry at Johns Hopkins school of medicine, is one of the most respected authorities on bipolar disorder—and for good reason. Not only has Dr. Jamison made the study of the disorder her life's work, but she has lived personally with its devastating effects. Although in her autobiography she recalls experiencing the crushing lows and giddy highs of the disorder throughout her childhood, it was only when she became a faculty member at the UCLA Neuropsychiatric Institute that she sought professional help and became properly diagnosed and treated.

There is a particular kind of pain, elation, loneliness, and terror involved in this kind of madness. When you're high it's tremendous. The ideas and feelings are fast and frequent like shooting stars, and you follow them until you find better and brighter ones. Shyness goes, the right words and gestures are suddenly there, the power to captivate others a felt certainty . . . Feelings of ease, intensity, power, well-being, financial omnipotence, and euphoria pervade one's marrow. But, somewhere, this changes. The fast ideas are far too fast, and there are far too many; overwhelming confusion replaces clarity. Memory goes. Humor and absorption on friend's faces are replaced by fear and concern. Everything previously moving with the grain is now against—you are irritable, angry, frightened, uncontrollable, and enmeshed totally in the blackest caves of the mind. You never knew those caves were there. It will never end, for madness carves its own reality.

It goes on and on, and finally there are only others' recollections of your behavior—your bizarre, frenetic, aimless behavior—for mania has at least some grace in partially obliterating

---

As Hammen and Rudolph (2003) point out, there are three distinct impediments to the diagnosis of bipolar disorder in children and to the compilation of accurate estimates of its prevalence. First, the symptoms are easily misidentified and may even be shrugged off as mere exaggerations of the typical adolescent moodiness and behavioral dysregulation, especially when they are obscured by comorbid disorders such as substance abuse, conduct problems, or ADHD. Second, bipolar disorder often first evidences itself as depression, and therefore youths must be followed over time for the true nature of their disorder to reveal itself. Third, adolescent bipolar disorder often presents with a rapid-onset mania, sometimes with psychotic features, that may be confused with schizophrenia or other severe forms of psychopathology (Weller, Weller, & Fristad, 1995). Between 30 and 60 percent of youths with bipolar disorder have prominent psychotic symptoms.

Finally, Carlson and Kelley (1998) express concern that the increasing acceptance of the bipolar diagnosis in children has led to its overuse as a catch-all category for severely disruptive behavior that does not clearly fit any other diagnostic classification. For example, the category of Bipolar Disorder—Not Otherwise Specified may be used when children are suspected of having the diagnosis but do not meet the DSM criteria (National Institute of Mental Health Roundtable on Prepubertal Bipolar Disorder, 2001). Diagnoses may become trendy, leading clinicians to view all children through this new set of lenses.

Differential Diagnosis   Misdiagnosis of bipolar disorder is a serious matter because improper diagnosis leads to improper and even damaging treatment. Medications used to treat ADHD may increase irritability in bipolar children, and psychostimulants and antidepressant medications both may potentiate mania (Lombardo, 1997). In turn, the major tranquillizers used to treat schizophrenia will negatively impact the functioning of children who are not correctly diagnosed. Therefore, careful attention to *differential diagnosis* is needed. (See Kim and Miklowitz, 2002.)

For example, children with bipolar disorder often are diagnosed with ADHD, which has similar

memories. What then, after the medications, psychiatrist, despair, depression, and overdoses? All those incredible feelings to sort through. Who is being too polite to say what? Who knows what? What did I do? Why? And most hauntingly, will it happen again? Then, too, are the bitter reminders—medicine to take, resent, forget, take, resent, and forget, but always to take. Credit cards revoked, bounced checks to cover, explanations due at work, apologies to make, intermittent memories (what *did* I do?), friendships gone or drained, a ruined marriage. And always, when will it happen again? Which of my feelings are real? Which of the me's is me? The wild, impulsive, chaotic, energetic, and crazy one? Or the shy, withdrawn, desperate, suicidal, doomed, and tired one? Probably a bit of both, hopefully much that is neither . . .

At this point in my existence, I cannot imagine leading a normal life without both taking lithium and having had the benefits of psychotherapy. Lithium prevents my seductive but disastrous highs, diminishes my depression, clears out the wool and webbing from my disordered thinking, slows me down, gentles me out, keeps me from ruining my career and relationships, keeps me out of a hospital, alive, and makes psychotherapy possible. But, ineffably, psychotherapy heals. It makes some sense of the confusion, reins in the terrifying thoughts and feelings, returns some control and hope and possibility of learning from it all . . . Psychotherapy is a sanctuary; it is a battleground; it is a place I have been psychotic, neurotic, elated, confused, and despairing beyond belief. But, always, it is where I have believed—or have learned to believe—that I might someday be able to contend with all of this.

Reprinted from Redfield-Jamison, 1995.

symptoms of overactivity, heightened energy, distractibility, and impulsivity (Hammen & Rudolph, 2003). However, "pure" ADHD can be distinguished from bipolar by virtue of the fact that children with ADHD show a *consistent* pattern of overactivity or distractibility, in contrast to the *change* from usual behavior that is typical of bipolar children (Weller et al., 1995).

Children with bipolar also often are diagnosed with conduct disorder or oppositional-defiant disorder, which share features of irritability and dysregulated behavior (Hammen & Rudolph, 2003). However, the misbehavior of the "pure" conduct disordered child is more likely to be vindictive, intentional, and without guilt, whereas the child in a manic state acts more out of impulsivity and a sense of omnipotence: "Nothing can hurt me!" Further, children with conduct disorder or ODD do not display the psychotic symptoms, such as delusions, pressured speech, and flight of ideas, that frequently are seen in mania (Weller et al., 1995).

In turn, children with schizophrenia present with an insidious onset of their illness, in contrast to the more acute onset of mania, and are less likely to show the pressured speech and flight of ideas that are typical of the bipolar child (Weller et al., 1995).

Prevalence Estimates With these caveats in mind, we now turn to the sparse data available on prevalence. Studies of the prevalence of childhood disorders have rarely included bipolar disorder. However, an exception was a school-based survey of 1,700 adolescents in Oregon conducted by Lewinsohn, Klein, and Seeley (1995) that found a lifetime prevalence rate of 1 percent, mostly comprised of Bipolar II and cyclothymia. An additional 5.7 percent of the youths reported subclinical levels of hypomania that negatively affected their functioning. In a subsequent study, Lewinsohn and colleagues (1996) found that, among youths with a history of depression, hypomanic symptoms exacerbated their disturbance and were associated with higher levels of comorbidity and more frequent suicide attempts.

Prevalence rates for younger children are difficult to determine, although the disorder appears to be rare before adolescence (Fristad, Shaver, & Holderle, 2002).

The prevalence, age of onset, and course of the disorder do not appear to differ by gender (Lewinsohn et al., 1995). There are as yet no data available on differences related to ethnicity or social class.

Comorbidity

Children with bipolar disorder almost always carry at least one other diagnosis or will do so over the course of their lifetime (Kessler et al., 2001). Because there is not good agreement about the diagnosis of bipolar in children, it is not clear whether comorbidity is genuine or is an artifact of the overlap between diagnostic categories. However, despite the fact that differential diagnosis is needed to eliminate invalid diagnoses, it is possible for children to suffer genuinely from comorbid disorders. Among those most frequently codiagnosed are ADHD, conduct disorder, and oppositional-defiant disorder. There also is a population of children with comorbid bipolar disorder and pervasive developmental disorder (National Institute of Mental Health Roundtable on Prepubertal Bipolar Disorder, 2000). Depression and anxiety also are commonly seen in children with bipolar (Hammen & Rudolph, 2003). Comorbid substance abuse, which is often seen in adolescents (Akiskal, 1995), may comprise attempts to self-medicate or to be reflective of the poor judgment and risk-taking that accompany manic episodes. Youths who truly suffer from these comorbid disorders present particular challenges to treatment.

The Developmental Dimension

As implied in the previous section, there appear to be developmental differences in the symptoms of bipolar disorder in childhood and adulthood. We should be cautious in interpreting this literature, given that there remains considerable debate over whether and how bipolar disorder should be diagnosed in young people. However, we can summarize the available evidence to date.

First, unlike adult bipolar, manic episodes in children are not usually so distinct, nor are episodes characterized by an acute onset with intermittent periods of good functioning. Instead, children tend to show a history of chronic mood symptoms that include extremely rapid shifts, known as *rapid cycling*. For example, Geller and colleagues (2000) found that 77.4 percent of children and early adolescents with bipolar disorder demonstrated mood cycles that vacillated many times a day, while this is a phenomenon seen in only 20 percent of bipolar adults. Children also are more likely than adults to have mixed episodes, in which both depression and mania occur simultaneously (National Institute of Mental Health Roundtable on Prepubertal Bipolar Disorder, 2000). Other adult symptoms, such as grandiosity and euphoria, are rare in children; instead, young people's manic episodes are more often characterized by irritability and rage.

Etiology

The Biological Context

Genetic studies estimate that the heritability of bipolar disorder is high, with estimates in the 20 to 45 percent range (see Rutter et al., 1999). A number of studies have focused on high-risk children—those whose parents are diagnosed with bipolar disorder. Lapalme, Hodgins, and La Roche (1997) conducted a meta-analysis of the available studies and found that bipolar disorder occurred in 5.4 percent of children of bipolar parents, whereas none of the children of healthy parents met criteria for the diagnosis. However, that does not mean that 94.6 percent of the children of bipolar parents were doing well. Fifty-two percent met criteria for at least one psychiatric diagnosis, compared to 29 percent of control children. Mood disorders were the most common, with 26.5 percent of the children of bipolar parents displaying major depression, dysthymia, manic episodes, hypomania, and cyclothymia, whereas these diagnoses were seen in only 8.3 percent of control children.

The Family Context

As we have seen, children with bipolar disorder are disproportionately more likely to come from families in which at least one parent also suffers from the disorder. However, the heritability quotients are less than 100 percent, and therefore other aspects of the family environment may affect children's development, as well. Chang, Blasey, Ketter, and Steiner (2001) investigated the family relations of 56 children diagnosed with bipolar disorder. In comparison to a normative group, parents of children with bipolar disorder reported that their family was less cohesive and organized and higher in conflict. While it is not known whether family dysfunction was a cause or consequence of the disorder, aversive patterns of exchange may affect the child's developmental course. For example, Miklowitz and colleagues (1998) found that family *expressed emotion*—criticism, overinvolvement, and high negative affect—predicted relapse in adolescents and adults with bipolar disorder.

A large-scale study in Denmark utilized national population data to identify 2,299 individuals with bipolar disorder and to retrospectively examine family factors associated with the diagnosis (Mortensen et al., 2003). Not surprisingly, bipolar disorder or schizophrenia in parents or siblings increased the risk 13.63-fold. The only other factor that was associated with bipolar disorder was an unexpected one—parental loss, particularly of the mother. Children who, prior to their 5th birthday, experienced the loss of their mothers had a 4.05-fold risk of developing bipolar disorder. Loss of the mother may reflect a shared genetic vulnerability—these mothers may have suffered from mood disorders that contributed to their deaths, such by increasing their involvement in unsafe behaviors or suicide—but also may comprise a severe psychosocial stressor that acts upon the vulnerable child and produces the disorder.

Developmental Course

Bipolar disorder emerges earlier in development than other disorders in the depressive spectrum. While adolescents in Lewinsohn and colleagues' (1995) study reported a mean *age of onset* of 15 years for major depression, those with bipolar reported a mean age of onset of 11.8 years.

There appear to be at least two distinct pathways to bipolar disorder in children. On the one hand,

many children initially present with symptoms of ADHD. For example, in one follow-up study, Biederman and colleagues (1996) found that over a period of 4 years, 22.8 percent of children diagnosed with ADHD developed bipolar disorder. Geller et al. (1998) have speculated that ADHD might be a developmental precursor to bipolar disorder, with both disorders arising from an underlying excessive level of energy that is expressed in its true bipolar form only later in development.

The second pathway is through depression. As we have noted, children and adolescents with unipolar depression are at significant risk for developing bipolar disorder. For example, in a retrospective study 61 percent of adolescents interviewed by Lewinsohn et al. (1995) reported having had an initial episode of depression. In prospective research, a review of seven studies comprising 250 severely depressed youths found that over a 2- to 4-year period 25 percent had switched their presentation from depression to bipolar disorder (Faedda et al., 1995). Similarly, Geller, Fox, & Clark (1994) found that 32 percent of children with major depression developed bipolar over a period of 5 years, whereas Weissman et al. (1999) found that 5.5 percent of depressed youths went on to develop bipolar disorder over a 10-year period. Akiskal (1995) theorizes that for many youths depression may represent a protracted dysphoric phase in a bipolar cycle that has yet to reveal itself.

There are few data on the course of bipolar disorder, but the evidence to date suggests that the course is protracted and chronic. In the study by Lewinsohn et al. (1995) adolescents reported on average that the duration of the illness was 48 months, with their most recent episode lasting from 0.2 to 96 months. One prospective study found stability in symptoms over a 6-month period and consistency in the diagnosis over the period of a year (Geller, Zimmerman, & Williams, 2000). Retrospective accounts by adults indicate that manic symptoms in childhood persist into adulthood in 90 percent of cases (see Kessler, Avenevoli, and Merikangas, 2001). Thus, there is evidence for continuity in the disorder.

Early-onset bipolar disorder appears to be more severe, persistent, and treatment resistant (Geller &

Luby, 1997). Once a youth has experienced a bipolar episode, it is been speculated that the brain is altered in such a way that it is sensitized and more likely to react with mood disturbance to increasingly milder stressors, a phenomenon termed "kindling" (Post, 1992). Consequently, each subsequent episode over the life span will be more easily triggered but more intractable and harder to treat. In order to attempt to stave off this cascading effect, some clinicians recommend beginning treatment with mood stabilizers as soon as bipolar disorder is even *suspected* (Hammen & Rudolph, 2003).

Children with bipolar disorder are at increased risk for maladaptation in all areas of functioning, including school, peer, and family relationships, and show more functional deficits than children with unipolar depression (Geller et al., 2000; Lewinsohn et al., 1995). They also are at increased risk for suicide. Clearly, this is a disorder with devastating effects on development.

Intervention

Pharmacotherapy

Given the assumption that bipolar is a biologically based disorder, medication is usually the first line of treatment. Generally, children are prescribed the same medications that are effective in adults, such as lithium carbonate, which is derived from a naturally occurring salt. Although the effectiveness and safety of lithium have been reported in a number of clinical trials with children and adolescents, carefully conducted, double-blind, controlled studies are extremely rare (Kowatch, 2001).

As reviewed by Fristad et al. (2002), frequently prescribed alternatives to lithium include anticonvulsant medications, such as carbamazepine (Tegretol) and valproic acid/divalproex sodium (Depakote). While there is evidence that carbamazipine is effective in reducing conduct problems in severely disturbed children, there are no controlled studies of its effectiveness in treating bipolar disorder. One open trial with a sample size of 6 reported marked improvement in adolescents with acute mania. Valproic acid has been studied in a handful of open trials that have revealed a number of unpleasant side effects,

including sedation, nausea, increased appetite and weight gain, and potentially lethal liver failure. Another class of medication administered to bipolar children is comprised of atypical antipsychotics, including resperidone (Risperdol), quetiapine (Seroquel), and olanzapine (Zyprexa). Studies of their effectiveness in children and adolescents are limited to a single retrospective chart review that found that risperidone helped to control mania, aggression, and psychotic symptoms in the majority of children.

One study investigated the effectiveness of three different mood stabilizers in the treatment of bipolar disorder in 42 children and adolescents aged 8 to 18 years (Kowatch et al., 2000). Children were randomly assigned to 6 weeks of treatment with lithium, valproic acid, or carbamazepine. Response rates were positive for all conditions, ranging from 34 to 50 percent, and there were no significant differences among the groups.

Family Therapy

The behavior of the bipolar child can be confusing, frustrating, and even frightening for parents and other family members. Consequently, family treatment is likely to be of benefit. Fristad and colleagues (2002) developed a multifamily psychoeducational group for children with mood disorders, including both depression and bipolar disorder. While investigations of its effectiveness are in the early stages, preliminary results with a sample of thirty-five 8- to 11-year-olds suggest that, posttreatment, families report having gained knowledge, skills, support, and a more positive attitude toward the child's disorder.

Miklowitz and colleagues (2003) developed and tested a family intervention for adults with bipolar disorder. Their family-focused therapy includes all available family members (spouses, parents, and siblings) and provides psychoeducation about bipolar disorder, as well as training in communication and problem-solving skills. Results with adults aged 18 years and older are promising, with the family intervention associated with fewer relapses, lower mood disorder symptoms, and better adherence to medication. The investigators currently are involved in extending the treatment to families of adolescents with bipolar disorder.

Child and Adolescent Suicide

Definitions and Prevalence

As we begin our discussion of suicide, we must immediately distinguish among five categories: suicidal thoughts, suicidal intent, suicidal gestures, suicide attempts, and completed suicide.

Suicidal thoughts, once considered to be rare in childhood, are in fact disconcertingly prevalent. According to the Youth Risk Behavior Survey (Centers for Disease Control [CDC], 2004), a nationally representative sampling of 11,631 high school students, 24.9 percent of females and 13.7 percent of males had "seriously considered" suicide in the past year.

Suicidal intent is more serious in that it involves not just a thought (e.g, "I wish I were dead") but a specific plan and the motivation to carry it out. According to the Youth Risk Behavior Survey (CDC, 2004), 18.3 percent of female high school students and 10.9 percent of males reported that in the past year they had made a specific suicide plan.

Suicidal gestures, also known as **parasuicidal behavior,** involve nonlethal self-harming actions such as making cuts on the arms or legs. Parasuicidal behavior often is motivated by a desire to communicate one's distress to others and acts as a red flag that help is needed. But self-injury also is characteristic of severely disturbed youths who use physical pain as a method of affect regulation—we will encounter these individuals in Chapter 15 when we explore borderline personality disorder. Moreover, suicidal gestures may represent "practice runs" that are precursors of more serious attempts and so remain cause for concern.

Suicide attempts vary by lethality. *Low-lethality* attempts typically involve using a slow-acting method under circumstances in which discovery is possible, such as a youth who ingests drugs at home. Because of the length of time needed for the method to take effect, the likelihood is greater that someone will find the attempter before it is too late to resuscitate. The act most often is in reaction to an interpersonal conflict or significant stressor and, even though the attempt is unsuccessful, it may nevertheless be serious. *High-lethality* attempts involve a potentially deadly method (e.g., a gun) that is quick acting and utilized under conditions in which it would be difficult for others to intervene, such as when the youth is alone. As many as 10.9 percent of high school girls and 5.7 percent of boys report having made a suicide attempt in the past year (CDC, 2002), and there are rare reports of serious attempts at suicide even among preschoolers (Rosenthal & Rosenthal, 1984). Further, as few as 2 percent of attempters seek medical or psychological help. Consequently, since many suicide attempts go unreported, it is likely that our prevalence statistics are underestimates of the actual rates.

Completed suicide is a significant problem among adolescents. In the United States, suicide is the third leading cause of death among 15- to 19-year-olds and the fourth leading cause of death among 10- to 14-year-olds, in line behind accidents and homicides (CDC, 2004). Further, in the previous two decades, suicide among the young has increased more dramatically than in the general population, leveling off somewhat in recent years. Rates for younger children are lower than for adolescents. For example, in 1999 only two children under the age of 10 are known to have committed suicide in the United States. A protective factor for younger children may be that they have more difficulty accessing lethal means; consequently, there are more attempts than completions in children age 10 and below (Pfeffer et al., 1994). Firearms are the most frequent method used by both males and females, followed by hanging for males and drug ingestion for females. (See Box 9.4.)

Gender Differences

In all age groups, females are more likely than males to *attempt* suicide, while males are more likely to *succeed.* Females attempt suicide at least 3 times more often than males do, whereas males age 15 to 19 complete suicide almost 6 times as often as females (CDC, 2002). Over the course of adolescence, the ratio of males to females steadily increases. The explanation for this appears to lie in the choice of method. In contrast to male suicides, two-thirds of whom die by self-inflicted gunshot wounds, the typical young female attempter utilizes low lethality methods, such as drug overdose. It should not be assumed, however, that young women necessarily are

Box 9.4 | **Youth Suicide: Why the Changes over Time?**

Data from across the world showed a marked rise in youth suicide over the course of the past few decades, whereas rates have declined significantly in recent years. The Centers for Disease Control and Prevention's (CDC) latest statistics show that, through 2001, suicide rates among U.S. children and adolescents declined 25 percent. What accounts for these changes over time? In their review of the literature, Gould and colleagues (2003) find that many factors have been implicated, but chief among these are changes in the rates of substance abuse and accessibility of firearms. For example, as rates of youth suicide grew, suicides involving firearms increased at a disproportionate rate; tellingly, guns were twice as likely to be found in the homes of suicide victims as compared to the homes of youths with other kinds of psychiatric disorders. In turn, in the past few years there have been more efforts to restrict firearms in the United States, and the recent decrease in youth suicide appears to largely be accounted for by a decrease in suicide by firearm, according to the CDC. However, Gould and colleagues find these explanations unconvincing for a number of reasons. They point out that youth suicide rates have recently decreased 20 to 30 percent in other countries in the world where guns are rarely used, including England, Germany, and Sweden. Moreover, the decline in youth suicide has not actually been accompanied by a reduction in substance use. Instead, Gould and colleagues propose, a more likely explanation is improvement in availability and effectiveness of treatments for depression. For example, during the period in which youth suicide has declined, prescriptions for the newer class of antidepressants have risen. Exceptions to this expanded availability of treatment, however, include populations such as the African American and Native American communities that have more difficulty accessing mental health services.

less serious about wanting to die. Females are more likely to have an aversion to violent methods, and sometimes young people's understanding of how deadly a drug can be is simply inaccurate. Further, suicide statistics often come from mental health clinics and ignore one very important group: incarcerated males. If we included males in juvenile detention facilities in these statistics, the gender differences in suicide attempts might not be so great.

Cross-Cultural Differences

Table 9.6 displays statistics for youth suicide across the globe. As these data indicate, rates vary widely as does the gender ratio. According to World Health Organization (2002) data, more male adolescents commit suicide in the United States, Canada, Western Europe, Australia, and New Zealand, while the sex ratio is nearly equal in some Asian countries (e.g., Singapore) and reversed in others. For example, in rural China, the majority of adolescent suicide completers are female. This may be because

methods females prefer, such as drug ingestion, are not low lethality in underdeveloped rural settings where modern emergency medicine is not readily available (Gould, Shaffer, & Greenberg, 2003). As with data from the United States, these statistics show an increase during earlier decades. For example, in England and Wales, suicide rates among adolescent males increased 78 percent between 1980 and 1990 (see Flisher, 1999).

Ethnic Diversity

Within the United States, prevalence estimates for ethnicity are hampered by the fact that, until recently, statistics were maintained only on "white" and "nonwhite" youths, later expanded to include a category of "other." In addition, most of these data were cobbled together from unreliable sources. Since 1999 we have detailed statistics for *completed suicide* available from a national database regarding many of the ethnic groups that comprise the U.S. population (National Center for Health Statistics,

Table 9.6

Youth Suicide Rates Around the World (per 100,000)

| Country | Year | 5–14 years | | | 15–24 years | | | 15–24: 5–14 Ratio | |
		Males	Females	M:F	Males	Females	M:F	Males	Females
Australia	1997	0.5	0.5	1.0	30.0	6.6	4.5	60.0	13.2
Austria	1999	0.4	0.2	2.0	20.3	5.3	3.8	50.8	26.5
Canada	1997	1.9	0.6	3.2	22.4	4.5	5.0	11.8	7.5
Chile	1994	0.1	0.3	0.3	10.9	1.5	7.3	109.0	5.0
China (urban)	1998	0.3	0.4	0.8	3.4	4.4	0.8	11.3	11.0
China (rural)	1998	0.9	1.0	0.9	8.4	15.2	0.6	9.3	15.2
Finland	1998	0.9	0.6	1.5	29.5	7.9	3.7	32.8	13.2
France	1997	0.3	0.3	1.0	13.4	4.3	3.1	44.7	14.3
Germany	1998	0.7	0.4	1.8	12.7	3.5	3.6	18.1	8.8
Hungary	1999	1.8	0.2	9.0	19.1	3.9	4.9	10.6	19.5
Ireland	1996	1.3	—	—	25.4	4.5	5.6	19.5	—
Israel	1997	0.4	—	—	12.6	1.6	7.9	31.5	—
Italy	1997	0.2	0.2	1.0	8.5	1.8	4.7	42.5	9.0
Japan	1997	0.5	0.3	1.7	11.3	5.5	2.1	22.6	18.3
Mexico	1995	0.5	0.3	1.7	7.6	2.0	3.8	15.2	6.7
Netherlands	1997	1.1	—	—	11.3	4.4	2.6	10.3	—
New Zealand	1998	3.0	1.4	2.1	38.1	13.3	2.9	12.7	9.5
Norway	1997	1.0	—	—	20.2	4.7	4.3	20.2	—
Poland	1996	1.6	0.4	4.0	17.2	2.9	5.9	10.8	7.3
Republic of Korea	1997	0.9	1.1	0.8	12.5	8.0	1.6	13.9	7.3
Russian Federation	1998	3.0	0.7	4.3	51.9	8.6	6.0	17.3	12.3
Scotland	1997	—	—	—	19.5	5.3	3.7	—	—
Singapore	1998	1.2	—	—	13.4	10.9	1.2	11.2	—
Sweden	1996	0.2	0.4	0.5	12.0	4.6	2.6	60.0	11.5
Switzerland	1998	0.9	—	—	24.8	5.6	4.4	27.6	—
U.K. of Great Britain and Ireland	1998	0.1	0.1	1.0	10.4	2.9	3.6	104.0	29.0
United States	1998	1.2	0.4	3.0	18.5	3.3	5.6	15.4	8.3

Source: World Health Organization, 2001.

2002). As displayed in Table 9.7, the highest rates by far are found for Native American youths. European American males far surpass males from other ethnic groups, while females, particularly African American girls, have the lowest rates. Extremely low reported rates for other subgroups of girls led to their being excluded from the analysis.

As the data show, the mean prevalence rate of suicide completion for African American youths is lower than for European Americans. Nonetheless, suicide rates for African American boys have been

increasing at an accelerated pace. Between 1980 and 1992 suicide among European American boys aged 10 to 14 increased 86 percent, whereas for African American boys in that age group rates increased 300 percent. Similarly, for adolescents age 15 to 19, there was a 22 percent increase for European American males but a 164 percent increase for African American boys. The pattern was different for females. In the 10 to 14 age group, rates increased 233 percent for European American girls and 100 percent for African American girls, whereas in

Table 9.7

U.S. Youth Suicide Rates for 15- to 19-Year-Olds by Race and Gender

Race	Sex	Year	Number of Deaths	Population	Crude Rate
White	Males	1999	1,286	32,202,540	3.99
		2000	1,330	32,313,190	4.12
		2001	1,324	32,386,820	4.09
		2002	1,268	32,440,797	3.91
			5,208	**129,343,347**	**4.03**
	Females	1999	264	30,470,494	0.87
		2000	278	30,578,408	0.91
		2001	273	30,653,511	0.89
		2002	254	30,724,163	0.83
			1,069	**122,426,576**	**0.87**
Black	Males	1999	177	6,562,663	2.70
		2000	185	6,608,630	2.80
		2001	148	6,652,216	2.22
		2002	140	6,685,362	2.09
			650	**26,508,871**	**2.45**
	Females	1999	31	6,375,857	0.49
		2000	27	6,415,686	0.42
		2001	29	6,443,355	0.45
		2002	23	6,472,958	0.36
			110	**25,707,856**	**0.43**
Am Indian/AK Native	Males	1999	45	559,553	8.04
		2000	40	583,692	6.85
		2001	48	575,294	8.34
		2002	38	568,197	6.69
			171	**2,286,736**	**7.48**
	Females	1999	9	539,706	1.67
		2000	11	563,265	1.95
		2001	16	556,030	2.88
		2002	10	550,383	1.82
			46	**2,209,384**	**2.08**
Asian/Pac Islander	Males	1999	33	1,699,627	1.94
		2000	40	1,739,699	2.30
		2001	39	1,776,275	2.20
		2002	33	1,805,784	1.83
			145	**7,021,385**	**2.07**
	Females	1999	14	1,629,532	0.86
		2000	17	1,670,695	1.02
		2001	13	1,702,315	0.76
		2002	11	1,729,747	0.64
			55	**6,732,289**	**0.82**
Total			**7,454**	**322,236,444**	**2.31**

Source: CDC, 2002.

the 15 to 19 age group, the increase was 12 percent and 19 percent, respectively (CDC, 1995).

In contrast to the CDC data concerning suicide completion, some individual studies have found that youths from Hispanic families are twice as likely as other youths to make suicide *attempts* serious enough to require medical attention. Finally, one study investigated suicide attempt rates among a more diverse sample of adolescents, including 5,000 youths of European, Mexican, Vietnamese, and Pakistani extraction (Roberts, Chen, & Roberts, 1997). Pakistani youths were 2 times more likely than European Americans to engage in suicidal ideation, to have made suicidal plans, or to have made a suicide attempt in the past 2 weeks. Youths of mixed ancestry also were at elevated risk for suicidal thoughts or plans. The findings were unexpected and the reasons for these ethnic differences were not evident; however both racial discrimination and cultural beliefs regarding the acceptability of suicide might come into play.

Etiology

The Individual Context

Depression   Psychological autopsies show that the majority of suicidal adolescents—as many as 90 percent—have a diagnosable psychopathology (Gould et al., 2003; see Berman, 2003, for some striking case studies). *Depression* is the most common diagnosis for both completers and attempters, including between 30 and 60 percent of adolescent suicide attempters (Apter & Wasserman, 2003). Many depressed children and adolescents experience suicidal ideation—as many as 60 percent in some samples. Further, suicide attempts occur at a higher rate among depressed youths than depressed adults (Mitchell et al., 1988). (For a case example, see Box 9.5.) Some studies indicate that among suicide completers, more girls than boys meet criteria for a mood disorder (Flisher, 1999).

Aggression and Impulsivity   However, there are other significant predictors of youth suicide besides depression. First, *anger and aggression* emerge as an important part of the suicide constellation (Apter &

Wasserman, 2003; Wolfsdorf et al., 2003). About 70 percent of suicidal youths exhibit conduct disorder and antisocial behavior (Berman & Jobes, 1991). Childhood conduct disorder also has been shown to predict adult suicide independently of depression (Harrington et al., 1994). In fact, Achenbach and colleagues' (1995) 6-year longitudinal study also shows that suicidal ideation is predicted not by depression but by earlier signs of externalizing disorders: for boys, in the form of aggressiveness, and for girls, in the form of delinquent behavior. The link between conduct disorder and suicide may also be strongest for boys, with the combination of depression and conduct problems particularly toxic (Apter & Wasserman, 2003). Capaldi (1992) found that, among boys who showed a combination of depression and aggression, school failure, poor relationships with parents and peers, and low self-esteem resulted in suicidal ideation 2 years later. Therefore, conduct problems—which often are associated with poor relationships, emotion dysregulation, and disinhibition of aggression—are highly related to suicide.

Conduct problems also may contribute to suicidality through increasing peer rejection, association with antisocial peers, substance abuse (Prinstein et al., 2000), and school dropout, as well as precipitating legal problems that often are a catalyst for suicide (Gould et al., 2003).

Second, *impulsivity* is implicated in suicide (Esposito et al., 2003). Impulsivity may be seen in many ways, including low frustration tolerance and lack of planning, poor self-control, disciplinary problems, poor academic performance, and risk-taking behavior. *Substance abuse* is found in 35 percent to 100 percent of suicidal youths, with suicidal thoughts increasing after the onset of substance use (Mehlenbeck et al., 2003). Substance abuse may play a role in suicide by increasing impulsivity, clouding judgment, and disinhibiting self-destructive behavior.

Other Psychopathologies   In addition to depression, conduct disorder, and substance abuse, as described in the previous section, suicide also co-occurs with a number of other forms of psychopathology, including anxiety, borderline personality disorder,

Box 9.5 | **Case Study: A Suicide Attempt**

Dr. Anthony Spirito (2003) and his colleagues at Brown Medical School in Rhode Island present the case of Amy, a 13-year-old girl who was evaluated in the emergency room following a suicide attempt in which she overdosed on 20 over-the-counter medications she found in her medicine cabinet at home. When interviewed, Amy said that she made the attempt on the spur of the moment, without premeditation. After taking the pills, she secreted herself in her room until she began to feel nauseated, at which time she told her mother what she had done. Amy reported that she truly wanted to die and that she believed that the overdose she had taken was genuinely lethal. She further stated that the

stressor that led to her suicide attempt was an argument with her mother. Although they generally got along well, in recent weeks Amy and her mother had been arguing more, particularly in regard to Amy's poor grades and increasing irritability. Amy also acknowledged long-term stressors, including rejection by peers and falling school performance. The purpose of her suicide attempt, she stated, was to escape from the stressors she was experiencing.

Upon obtaining Amy's history, the assessment team learned that she had made two previous suicide attempts, neither of which were viewed as serious by her parents, given that they did not require medical attention. Consequently, the family had never sought

professional help. Amy reported that she was exposed to models of suicidal behavior in her environment, including classmates who had attempted suicide in the previous year. There was a family history of depression in her father and paternal grandmother.

The team asked Amy to complete a number of measures. These included a measure of suicide intent, on which she scored above the norm for other suicide attempters, indicating the sincerity of her wish to die. On a measure of suicidal ideation, her score was in the 85th percentile, reflecting a high frequency of thoughts about ending her life. The team was most struck by Amy's scores on measures of depressed mood and hopelessness, on which her scores were extremely

schizophrenia, and eating disorders (Apter & Wasserman, 2003). It appears that these diagnoses alone do not increase the risk, but rather do so in combination with depression and one another (Apter & Freudenstein, 2000).

Cognitive Factors   Among cognitive variables related to suicidal behavior, *hopelessness* and *poor problem-solving skills* emerge as major contributors to both suicidal ideation and attempts (Esposito et al., 2003; Nock & Kazdin, 2002). However, hopelessness does not predict suicide independent of depression (Gould et al., 2003). A better predictor of suicide than hopelessness is the youth's endorsement of *reasons for living* (Guiterrez et al., 2000).

Disinhibition of Suicidal Behavior   Once a youth has crossed the line dividing suicidal thoughts/intentions from actions, inhibitions against reattempting suicide appear to decrease. Consequently,

previous suicide attempts are a strong predictor of future suicide. Between one-fourth to one-third of youth suicide completers have made a prior attempt (Gould et al., 2003).

The Family Context

The family context also is important, although, as is often the case, a significant weakness of many family studies is that they are *retrospective* rather than *prospective*. An assessment of the family after a suicide attempt has taken place cannot provide convincing evidence that family factors led to the suicide.

Parent psychopathology is associated with increased risk of youth suicidal ideation, attempts, and completions. Among the most potent risk factors are parent substance abuse and depression (Brent et al., 1994), particularly maternal depression (Klimes-Dougan et al., 1999).

Perhaps as a consequence of parental dysfunction, a number of studies have confirmed that elevated. A structured clinical interview showed that Amy met criteria for a major depressive episode, including symptoms of dysphoric mood and irritability, sleep disturbance, change in appetite, psychomotor slowness, fatigue and loss of energy, and feelings of worthlessness. She met criteria for no other psychiatric diagnosis and scored within the average range on measures of anxiety, anger, and substance abuse.

The assessment team concluded that Amy was an adolescent who had been suffering for some time with an undiagnosed major depression. Her irritability and the increased conflicts with parents were obscuring the family's recognition of her underlying deep unhappiness and were contributing to their escalating negativity toward her.

At the end of the evaluation, Amy remained quite depressed and hopeless. She continued to express a wish to be dead and was not able to guarantee that she would not attempt suicide again. Similarly, when asked how she would handle any future stressors that might result in suicidal ideation, she was not able to report any adaptive coping strategies and at one point said that she might simply use a more lethal method. Consequently, an inpatient hospitalization was recommended.

Initially, Amy reacted negatively to being in the hospital, and after several days her parents removed her against medical advice. She agreed to outpatient therapy, however, as well as a trial of antidepressant medications. Nonetheless, within a month she was again threatening suicide and was re-hospitalized. During this second hospital stay, Amy was more amenable and engaged more actively in her treatment. The dosage of her antidepressant medication also was increased. At a 3-month follow-up, Amy's mood was more positive. In addition, her school performance had improved, she had become involved with previously enjoyable activities, and she had developed relationships with some same-age peers. She continued to attend outpatient psychotherapy and receive careful monitoring of her medications. There were no repeated suicide attempts.

---

suicidal youths experience *poorer parent-child relationships* (Gould et al., 2003; Hollenbeck, 2003). Prospective studies show that suicidal ideation and suicide attempts are predicted by low levels of parent warmth, communicativeness, support, and emotional responsiveness, and high levels of violence, disapproval, harsh discipline, abuse, and general family conflict. Retrospective studies show that attempters, ideators, and their parents describe the family as more globally dysfunctional (Prinstein et al., 2000), with lower cohesion, less support, and poorer adaptability to change.

Perceived *lack of support* from parents also has been implicated as a significant predictor of adolescent suicidal thinking (Harter & Marold, 1994). Further, Harter and Whitesell (1996) found that the depressed youths exhibiting the least suicidal ideation were those who perceived themselves to have more positive relationships with parents and more parent support. Thus, supportive parent-child relationships may provide a buffer against suicidality in at-risk children. Parental loss before the age of 12 also increases the risk of suicide (Brent & Mann, 2003).

Within the family system, suicidal children are more likely to be exposed to *interparental conflict, family violence, and abuse* (Brent & Mann, 2003; Pfeffer, 2000). The link between suicide and physical or sexual abuse has been confirmed in a host of studies using diverse ethnic samples (de Wilde, Kienhorst, & Diekstra, 2001). While suicidal youths are somewhat more likely to come from nonintact families, parent depression accounts for the modest association between divorce and youth suicide (Brent et al., 1994).

Finally, children who are exposed to suicide, especially in peers or adults in their immediate social network, are at greater risk for suicide (Gould et al., 2003). This has been referred to as the *contagion effect*. It is estimated that every year as many as

12,000 children and adolescents in the United States experience the suicide of a close family member (Gallo & Pfeffer, 2003). While there is some inconsistency among studies showing that youths exposed to the suicidal behavior of a family member are more likely to attempt it themselves (Brent & Mann, 2003), the data are consistent in showing the profoundly negative psychological effects of suicide exposure (Gallo & Pfeffer, 2003). Such exposure should be regarded as accelerating the risk factors already present rather than being a sufficient cause of suicide.

The Biological Context

The fact that suicide runs in families may not be solely a function of parent-child relationships or imitation. Some have proposed that it has genetic roots, based on studies showing higher concordance rates in twin, adoption, and family studies (Brent & Mann, 2003). For example, Statham and colleagues (1998) report results of a twin study in which the heritability quotient was 55 percent. Schulsinger (1980) conducted a classic adoption study and found a higher concordance rate for suicidal behavior in biological relatives than adoptive family members. However, it would be interesting to know what proportion of the adopted children knew that a biological family member had committed suicide. Clinical observations suggest that the contagion effect is a powerful one and can exert its influence through hearsay even in the absence of direct observation. Attempts to identify the mechanism through which genes effect behavior have focused on serotonin metabolism and receptivity (Apter, 2003).

The Social Context

Perceived *lack of peer support* (Harter & Marold, 1994) and *poor interpersonal skills* (Asarnow et al., 1987) have been identified as risk factors. Suicidal youths are more likely than others to feel ignored and rejected by peers and to experience victimization (Prinstein, 2003). They also report having fewer friends and are concerned that their friendships are *contingent*—that they must behave a certain way in order to be accepted by agemates. *Interpersonal stresses,* such as being rejected by peers or breaking up with a boyfriend or girlfriend, are common catalysts for suicide in youths at risk (Overholser, 2003). Perceived social failures, rejection, humiliation, and romantic disappointments are common precipitants of youth suicide. In fact, peer difficulties lead to as many as one-third of youth suicide attempts (Prinstein, 2003).

The school context also provides a number of stressful life events that precipitate youth suicide, including academic failures and disciplinary problems (Gould et al., 2003).

The Cultural Context

SES   Socioeconomic disadvantage has also been associated with suicide, with youths growing up in poverty being at greater risk for suicidal thoughts, attempts, and completions (Kessler, Borges, & Walters, 2001).

Ethnicity   The prevalence rates cited earlier point to important interethnic differences in the risk for suicide, which may be the consequence of different developmental influences. Cultural factors have been cited to explain lower rates of suicide among *African American* youth, such as an increased role of religion in African American families, support provided by extended family networks, and a tendency to direct aggression outward rather than toward the self (Gould et al., 2003). On the other side of the coin, Zayas, Kaplan, Turner, Romano, and Gonzalez-Ramos (2000) point to social and cultural factors that might contribute to suicidal behavior among *Hispanic* youths, including socioeconomic disadvantage, restrictiveness of the traditional authoritarian family, conflicts between parents and children related to differences in acculturation, and loss of extended family support due to immigration.

The extraordinary rates of suicide among *Native American* youths have been the source of great concern and research attention (Chandler et al., 2003). Rates vary enormously across tribes and geographic locations (CDC, 2004) but poverty, substance abuse, cultural disenfranchisement, the legacy of forced internment of children in residential schools—and the accompanying high rates of sexual and physical abuse—are all important to understanding the context in which Native American children develop (Malley-Morrison & Hines, 2004). In general, as Cicchetti and Toth (1998) note, cross-cultural data suggest that suicide is a greater risk for those minority youths whose connections to traditional values and sources of support have been severed.

Sexual Orientation   Youths with alternative sexual orientations also are at increased risk for suicide (Faulker & Cranston, 1998). In a 21-year prospective longitudinal study conducted in Christchurch, New Zealand, Fergusson and colleagues (1999) found that *gay, lesbian, and bisexual* adolescents had higher rates of both suicidal ideation and attempts. Further, in a sample of 350 gay, lesbian, and bisexual youths in the United States, D'Augelli and colleagues (2001) found that nearly half had experienced suicidal thoughts and a third had made at least one attempt. Many of them attributed their suicidality to a lack of acceptance by others following disclosure of their sexual orientation, with reactions ranging from rejection to verbal harassment and even violent assault. However, those who are suicidal also have more mental health problems than other gay and lesbian youths (Hershberger et al., 1997), as well as having higher rates of life stress and substance abuse (Savin-Williams & Ream, 2003). Among protective factors, family support and self-acceptance can buffer youths from the negative effects of victimization related to sexual orientation (Hershberger et al., 1995).

The Media   Evidence has accumulated that media reports of suicides are followed by a significant upsurge in suicidal behavior, particularly in young people (Stack, 2000). Given concerns about the contagion effect and the possible glamorizing of suicide in media reports of pop stars whom youths identify with and idolize, the CDC (1994) called together a panel of experts to compile a list of recommendations for the reporting of suicide. First, the panel points out that overly simplistic explanations of suicide are misleading and do not accurately portray the serious and cumulative psychological and social problems that lead individuals to make this terrible choice. Second, repetitive and inflated media coverage of a suicide may contribute to youths' becoming preoccupied with the issue; and third, sensationalized reporting should be avoided for the same reason. Fourth, reportage needs to avoid presenting suicide as a problem-solving strategy, but instead to highlight the psychopathology that triggers it. A fifth danger is the glorification of those who commit suicide such as through eulogies and public memorials that suggest that the act is honorable and admirable. Sixth, excessive praise for suicide completers' positive characteristics, unless balanced by a portrayal of their psychological troubles, similarly may make suicide attractive to youths who are longing for admiration and attention.

Modernization   At a larger societal level, rising rates of suicide in the developing world have led some to implicate *modernization,* which brings with it increasing social fragmentation, individualism, and loss of traditional values and support systems. Such values may undermine a youth's sense of belonging and meaning, leading to a state of existential despair (Kelleher & Chambers, 2003).

Developmental Course

The question often arises about whether young children who attempt suicide really are trying to kill themselves and, therefore, whether their attempts warrant serious concern or presage future suicidality. Doubt about whether young children really intend to die is supported by cognitive-developmental research on children's limited understanding of the concept of death, as well as studies showing that suicidal children have a limited understanding of the permanency of death (Cuddy-Casey & Orvaschel, 1997). However, longitudinal research is consistent in showing that childhood suicide attempts are a strong predictor of subsequent attempts and completions. For example, 8 years after their first attempt, suicidal children were 6 times more likely than other children to have made another suicide attempt (Pfeffer et al., 1984). Most subsequent attempts occurred within 2 years of the initial attempt, and over half of those who continued to be suicidal made multiple attempts. Therefore, suicide attempts in children should not be dismissed as mere attention-getting behavior, since those who engage in them are at risk for more serious attempts and possible completions in the future.

While little prospective research is available regarding the long-term outcome for adolescent suicide attempters, Boergers and Spirito's (2003) review of the literature indicates that they are at risk for continued psychological problems and subsequent repeated suicide attempts. One 11-year follow-up found that 29 percent of adolescent attempters and their parents reported improved adjustment, whereas 22 percent were unchanged and 33 percent were rated as more psychologically maladjusted than at the time of the attempt (Granboulan et al., 1995). Not surprisingly, the most improvement is seen in youths whose family relationships and living conditions

change for the better following the attempt. School dropout, "drifting," and engagement in violent and risk-taking activities also are seen over the longer term.

Integrative Developmental Models

Suicidal Ideation

A comprehensive account of the development of suicidal ideation is offered by Susan Harter (Harter, Marold, & Whitesell, 1992; Harter & Marold, 1991, 1994), who integrates her own research with that of others. Her model reconstructs the successive steps that ultimately eventuate in suicidal ideation in a normative sample of 12- to 15-year-olds. (See Figure 9.7.)

Immediately preceding and highly related to suicidal ideation is what Harter calls the *depression composite,* which is made up of three interrelated variables: low global self-worth, negative affect, and

Figure 9.7   Risk Factors for Adolescent Suicidal Ideation.

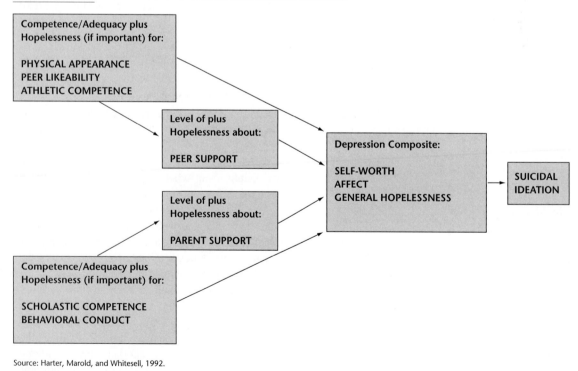

Source: Harter, Marold, and Whitesell, 1992.

hopelessness. The first two are highly correlated—the lower the perceived self-worth, the greater the feelings of negative mood.

Moreover, the depressive composite is rooted both in the adolescents' feelings of *incompetence* and in their *lack of support* from family and friends. These two variables of competence and support are, in turn, related in a special way. In regard to competence, physical appearance, peer likeability, and athletic ability are related to peer support, while scholarly achievement and behavioral conduct are related to parental support. Finally, adolescents identify more strongly with peer-related competencies, with the others being regarded as more important to parents than to themselves.

Analyses of the data revealed that peer-related competencies and support were more strongly related to the depressive composite than were parental-related competencies and support, perhaps because the former are more closely connected with the adolescents' own self-concept. However, parental support was important in differentiating the adolescents who were only depressed from those who were depressed and had suicidal ideation. Further, the *quality* of support was crucial. Regardless of the level, if adolescents perceived they were acting only to please parents or peers, their self-esteem decreased and depression and hopelessness increased. On the other hand, unconditional support helped adolescents minimize the depressive composite.

In regard to the question of which came first, lowered self-worth or depression, the data indicate that causation can go in either direction. Some adolescents become depressed when they experience lowered self-worth, while others become depressed over other occurrences such as rejection or conflict, which in turn lower self-worth.

To answer the question *Why adolescence?* Harter and colleagues (1997) marshal a number of findings concerning this period. In adolescence, self-awareness, self-consciousness, introspection, and preoccupation with self-image increase dramatically, while self-esteem becomes more vulnerable. Peer support becomes significantly more salient, although adolescents still struggle to remain connected with parents. For the first time, the adolescent

can grasp the full cognitive meaning of hopelessness, while affectively there is an increase in depressive symptomatology. Suicidal ideation is viewed as an effort to cope with or escape from the painful cognitions and affects of the depressive composite.

Suicide Attempts

A classic reconstructive account is provided by Jacobs (1971), who investigated fifty 14- to 16-year-olds who attempted suicide. A control sample of 31 youths, matched for age, race, sex, and level of mother's education, was obtained from a local high school. Through an intensive, multitechnique investigation, Jacobs was able to reconstruct a five-step model of the factors leading up to suicidal attempts:

1. *Long-standing history of problems from early childhood.* Such problems included family instability, death of a family member, serious illness, parental alcoholism, and school failure. Subsequent research has shown that it is a high level of intrafamilial conflict along with a lack of support for the child that is the risk factor, not a particular family constellation such as divorce or single parenthood (Weiner, 1992).

2. *Acceleration of problems in adolescence.* Far more important than earlier childhood problems was the frequency of distressing events occurring within the last 5 years for the suicidal youths; for example, 45 percent had dealt with divorce in the previous 5 years as compared to only 6 percent of the control group. Termination of a serious romance was also much higher among the suicidal group, as were arrests and jail sentences. Recent school failure and parent-child conflicts were other precipitants.

3. *Progressive failure to cope and isolation from meaningful social relationships.* The suicidal and control groups were equally rebellious in terms of becoming disobedient, disrespectful of authority, and defiant. However, the coping strategies of suicidal adolescents were characterized much more by withdrawal, including avoiding others and engaging in long periods of silence (see also Spirito, 2003). The isolation in regard to parents was particularly striking. For example, while

70 percent of all suicide attempts took place in the home, only 20 percent of those who reported the attempt had informed their parents about it. In one instance an adolescent telephoned a friend who lived miles away, and the friend, in turn, contacted the parents who were in the next room.

4. *Dissolution of social relationships.* In the days and weeks preceding the attempt, suicidal adolescents experienced the breaking off of social relationships, leading to the feeling of hopelessness.

5. *Justification of the suicidal act, giving the adolescent permission to make the attempt.* This justification was reconstructed from 112 suicide notes of adolescents and adults. The notes contain certain recurring themes; for example, the problems are seen as long standing and unsolvable, so death seems like the only solution. The authors of such notes also state that they know what they are doing, are sorry for their act, and beg indulgence. The motif of isolation and subsequent hopelessness is prevalent. More recently, Overholser and Spirito (2003) note that most suicidal adolescents are ambivalent. They would prefer to go on living, but feel unwilling or unable to endure the pain that they are experiencing.

Jacobs' model was replicated in a study conducted in Sweden (Hultén & Wasserman, 1995). The stage for suicide is set by long-standing suffering and lack of support, which produce hopelessness and ineffective coping strategies. Recent stressors resonate with these earlier losses and disappointments, leading to suicide.

Intervention

The vast majority of suicidal adolescents provide clues about their imminent behavior; one study found that 83 percent of completers told others of their suicidal intentions in the week prior to their death (Berman & Jobes, 1991). Most of the time such threats are made to family members or friends, who do not take them seriously, try to deny them, or do not understand their importance. Friends, for example, might regard reporting the threats as a betrayal of trust. Thus, not only do adolescents themselves not seek professional help, but those in whom

they confide tend to delay or resist getting help. Consequently, an important goal of prevention is to educate parents and peers concerning risk signs.

Once an adolescent comes for professional help, the immediate therapeutic task is to evaluate the risk of suicidal behavior (Pfeffer, 2003) and to protect the youth from self-harm through *crisis intervention.* This might involve restricting access to the means of committing suicide, such as removing a gun from the house or pills from the medicine cabinet; a "no harm contract" (Johnson & Maile, 1987) in which the adolescent agrees not to hurt himself or herself for an explicit time-limited period; decreasing isolation by having sympathetic family members or friends with the adolescent at all times; giving medication to reduce agitation or depression; or, in more serious cases, hospitalization.

Psychotherapy

Many different types of intervention have been developed for suicidal youths. Those that have mustered empirical support include cognitive-behavioral (Harrington & Saleem, 2003) and family therapies (Donaldson, Sprito, & Overholser, 2003). Cognitive approaches focus on altering pathogenic ways of thinking such as catastrophizing, while family therapy works to increase family communication and support. An alternative approach is Dialectical Behavior Therapy (DBT; Linehan, 1993b), which recently has been applied to suicidal and parasuicidal adolescents (Rathus & Miller, 2002). DBT targets important skills such as emotion regulation and stress tolerance, interpersonal problem solving, and impulse control. The practice of mindfulness, derived from mediation techniques, is at the core of the intervention.

Suicide Prevention

Turning to Garland and Zigler's (1993) review, we find that two of the most commonly used suicide prevention efforts—suicide hot lines and media campaigns—are only minimally effective. Communities with suicide hot lines have slightly reduced suicide rates; however, hot lines tend to be utilized by only one segment of the population, Caucasian females. Even less helpful, well-meaning efforts to call media attention to the problem of suicide among teenagers may have the reverse effect. Several studies have shown increased suicide rates following television or newspaper coverage of suicide, particularly among teenagers.

School-based suicide prevention programs are extremely popular, with the number of schools implementing them increasing 200 percent in recent years. Goals of these programs are to raise awareness of the problem of adolescent suicide, train participants to identify those at risk, and educate youths about community resources available to them. However, a number of problems have been identified with school-based suicide prevention efforts. For one thing, they may never reach the populations most at risk because incarcerated youths, runaways, and school dropouts will never attend the classes. Even when students do attend the programs, there are questions about their benefits. The programs tend to exaggerate the prevalence of teenage suicide, while at the same time deemphasizing the fact that most adolescents who attempt suicide are emotionally disturbed. Thus, they encourage youths to identify with the case studies presented, ignoring evidence for the contagion effect. By trying not to stigmatize suicide, these programs may inadvertently normalize suicidal behavior and reduce social taboos against it.

Large-scale, well-controlled studies provide some basis for these concerns. For example, one study of 300 teenagers showed that attending a suicide-prevention program slightly increased knowledge about suicide, but was not effective in changing attitudes about it. Boys in particular tended to change in the undesirable direction: More of them reported *increased* hopelessness and maladaptive coping after exposure to the suicide program (Overholser et al., 1989). Another study of 1,000 youths found no positive effects on attitudes toward suicide. In fact, participation in the program was associated with a small number of students responding that they now thought suicide was a plausible solution to their problems. The students most at risk for suicide to begin with (those who had made previous attempts) were the most likely to find the program distressing (Shaffer et al., 1991).

If school-based suicide prevention programs are not the solution, what might be? While suicide is rare, the stressors and life problems that may lead some youths to it are not. Therefore, successful prevention programs might be aimed toward such risk factors for suicide as substance abuse, impulsive behavior, depression, lack of social support, family discord, poor interpersonal problem-solving skills, social isolation, and low self-esteem, as well as critical underlying developmental capacities such as insecure working models of relationship, self-identity, emotion dysregulation, ego brittleness, and maladaptive coping (Orbach, 2003).

Our previous two chapters have described children who internalize their distress in such forms as anxiety and depression. Next, we will encounter children who are externalizers in the sense that they act out their problems via antisocial behavior. We have already discussed externalizers in earlier chapters in conjunction with oppositional-defiant disorder and attention-deficit hyperactivity disorder; in the next chapter we will focus on the development of antisocial behavior. Far from the excessive self-control of depressed and anxious children, here we will see the reemergence in middle childhood of an issue we encountered earlier in the toddler-preschool period—inadequate self-control, which lies at the heart of conduct disorder.

Middle Childhood to Adolescence: Conduct Disorder and the Development of Antisocial Behavior

onduct disorder has a unique place among the psychopathologies. Not only is the development of the individual with this disorder disrupted, but along the way enormous costs are borne by society and the victims of antisocial acts. (See Box 10.1.) Therefore, it is not surprising that more attention has been paid to understanding the development of aggression and antisocial behavior than any other childhood psychopathology. In this chapter, we will review conduct problems across the life span and their various manifestations, ranging along the continuum of seeming exaggerations in normal misbehavior to the extremes of cold-blooded murder and violence.

Definition and Characteristics

DSM-IV-TR defines **Conduct Disorder** (CD) as "a repetitive and persistent pattern of behavior in which either the basic rights of others or major age-appropriate societal norms or rules are violated." (See Table 10.1.) Conduct problems may occur in four categories: *aggression to people and animals, destruction of property, deceitfulness or theft,* and *serious violations of rules.*

Severity is specified as *mild* (few conduct problems beyond those necessary to make the diagnosis, and those present cause only minor harm to others); *moderate* (an intermediate

Box 10.1 | **Case Study: The Columbine Killers**

At 11:21 A.M., April 20, 1999, two teenagers pulled out sawed-off shotguns and fired on their classmates in the library at Columbine High School in Littleton, Colorado. Even though the homemade pipe bomb they left in the cafeteria did not go off, 15 minutes later, 21 people were wounded and 15 were dead—including the shooters, Eric Harris and Dylan Klebold, who had turned their guns on themselves.

Little forewarning was given for this horrific attack, although in hindsight perhaps some indicators were there. Rewinding the videotape, so to speak, we can see a number of foreboding signs. Both boys were widely known to harbor animosity toward their school and to express alienation from their classmates. Eric often complained that a group of "jocks" were bullying him—pushing him into lockers, throwing things at him, calling him rude names—while school authorities looked the other way. Both he and Dylan emulated a group of boys, the Trench Coat Mafia, who had banded together to counter the social system by wearing combat boots and thrift store grunge. However, Eric and Dylan remained only on the fringes of this group of self-proclaimed outcasts.

A year before the massacre, bored with their usual pastimes of breaking bottles and setting off firecrackers, the two had broken into a vehicle and had been caught with the items they stole. The boys were sentenced to 45 hours of community service, anger-management classes, and regular drug screens, but they so positively impressed their juvenile diversion counselor that they were released a month early. This was despite the fact that, days before their court hearing on the theft charges, the concerned parent of a classmate had presented detectives with excerpts from Eric's web log that revealed that he and Dylan were sneaking out at night to set off homemade bombs. "You all better hide in your (expletive) houses because I'm coming for EVERYONE soon and i WILL be armed to the (expletive) teeth and i WILL shoot to kill and i WILL (expletive) KILL EVERYTHING!" Eric had written. "I am the law, if you don't like it you die. If I don't like you or I don't like what you want me to do, you die. God I can't wait til I can kill you people."

Are there clues in the boys' childhood histories? Were they subject to psychological or physical abuse, or were they witnesses to violence in their homes or communities? Bartels and Crowder (1999) did some investigative reporting and here is what they found:

Dylan had grown up in Littleton, a quiet residential community. Both of his parents hailed from Ohio, his mother from a privileged family and his father from a tragic childhood: He suffered the death of his mother at age 6 and the loss of his father at age 12. Dylan's parents fell in love as undergraduates, married, and determined to raise their two sons in a home that stressed nonviolence: the boys were not even allowed to play with toy guns. When the family moved into a new home in a canyon near to wildlife, little Dylan worried that the cougars would eat his beloved cats. The family honored the mother's heritage by observing Hanukkah and the father's family background by celebrating Christmas, but struggled to find an organized religion that fit their beliefs. As a child, Dylan was described by neighbors as a "gawky," "nerdy" kid, who was marked as a gifted student, particularly in math. In his 1st year in high school, Dylan drifted toward a

number and severity of problems); and *severe* (many conduct problems *or* their effect causes considerable harm to others). DSM-IV-TR further differentiates between conduct problems with a *childhood onset* (prior to age 10) or *adolescent onset* (absence of criteria characteristic of CD prior to age 10), which is an important distinction, as we shall see.

Problem Behavior Versus Conduct Disorder

Misbehavior is part of normal development, as we know. Therefore, our first task is to determine when behavior problems warrant a diagnosis of CD. DSM-IV-TR specifies that the category should be used only in cases in which the behavior is symptomatic of an *underlying dysfunction in the person* rather new set of friends who devoted hours of their time watching violent computer games and reveled in their capacity to surreptitiously ridicule their teachers and classmates. Dylan even used his computer skills to hack into the school's computer system to learn the locker combination of a disliked peer so that he could leave a nasty note inside. In his sophomore year, he briefly found acceptance with a group of nonconformists who were passionately involved in theatre. However, Dylan showed a melancholy side. He continued to express his hatred of the school and took up a new interest in drinking alcohol. He rarely dated. Still, he was described as "shy but nice." As a senior in high school, Dylan often returned home in the afternoons to spend time with his father, who thought that he and his son had become very close. Dylan had been accepted to the University of Arizona to study computer science in the fall.

Eric, in contrast, grew up in a military family and moved many times until his seventh-grade year, when his father decided to retire and return to his native state of Colorado. A much-decorated Air Force test pilot, Eric's father spent long hours at his new job while his mother worked as a caterer. Both parents emphasized to their sons the value of hard work and education. As a child, Eric was described by the girl next door as "preppy and a dork," but otherwise nice and extremely polite. Eric loved the family dog and would take time away from other activities to care for Sparky when he got sick. In high school, he began to favor music with brooding and violent lyrics, which he copied out and sent to his friends; and he retained a fascination with violent video games long after his friends had outgrown them. Eric began taking anger out on those around him, with friendship turning to hate for no reason the other boys could discern. He began dressing all in black and complained that he was being harassed for it. In a psychology class, he reported a dream in which he and Dylan retaliated against someone who "dissed" them in a mall by firing guns and spilling blood. For an economics project, Eric created a marketing video for the "Trench Coat Mafia Protection Service," which, for $10, would kill someone for the consumer. Concerned about their son, his parents sent Eric to a psychiatrist who prescribed an antidepressant. Nevertheless, his supervisor at the fast food restaurant raved about Eric, calling him a "real nice kid . . . kind of quiet but everyone got along with him." After he and Dylan went to court on their theft charge, Eric began keeping a journal that he kept hidden from his parents. Reading the journal after Eric's death, investigators learned that for a year Eric had been mulling plans to blow up his high school on April 20, Adolph Hitler's birthday. Finally, on April 15, 1999, 5 days before the massacre, Eric had learned that his psychiatric history would prevent his acceptance into the Marines, his lifelong ambition. He had been rejected and had no plans for the future.

How well do our theories of the developmental psychopathology of conduct disorder help us to explain the Columbine massacre?

Source: Adapted from Bartels and Crowder, 1999.

than being a reaction to the immediate social environment. DSM-IV-TR suggests that in order to make this judgment the clinician should consider the *social and economic context* in which problem behavior occurs. For example, aggressive behavior may arise out of a need to protect oneself in a high-crime neighborhood or out of a need for survival in immigrant youths from war-torn countries. Therefore, some youths' misbehavior might represent an adaptation to a deviant environment, rather than a mental disorder.

Some concern has been expressed about whether this guideline is sufficient to prevent misdiagnosis of behaviorally troublesome but otherwise normal youths. For example, Richters and Cicchetti (1993) are concerned about the ease with which the CD criteria can be applied to children who do not fit the

Table 10.1

DSM-IV-TR Criteria for Conduct Disorder

A. A repetitive and persistent pattern of behavior in which either the basic rights of others or major age-appropriate societal norms or rules are violated, during which at least three of the following are present in the past 12 months:

Aggression to people and animals
  (1) often bullies, threatens, or intimidates others
  (2) often initiates physical fights
  (3) has used a weapon that can cause serious physical harm to others (e.g., a bat, brick, broken bottle, knife, gun)
  (4) has been physically cruel to people
  (5) has been physically cruel to animals
  (6) has stolen while confronting a victim (e.g., mugging, purse snatching, extortion, armed robbery)
  (7) has forced someone into sexual activity

Destruction of property
  (8) has deliberately engaged in fire setting with the intention of causing serious damage
  (9) has deliberately destroyed others' property (other than by fire setting)

Deceitfulness or theft
  (10) has broken into someone else's house, building, or car
  (11) often lies to obtain goods or favors or to avoid obligations (i.e., "cons" others)
  (12) has stolen items of nontrivial value without confronting a victim (e.g., shoplifting, but without breaking and entering; forgery)

Serious violations of rules
  (13) often stays out at night despite parental prohibitions, beginning before 13 years of age
  (14) has run away from home overnight at least twice while living in parental or parental surrogate home (or once without returning for a lengthy period)
  (15) is often truant from school, beginning before 13 years of age

B. The disturbance in behavior causes clinically significant impairment in social, academic, or occupational functioning.

Reprinted with permission from the *Diagnostic and Statistical Manual of Mental Disorders,* Fourth Edition Text Revision. Copyright 2000 by the American Psychiatric Association.

norm. They point out that some of the best-loved characters in fiction, such as Huckleberry Finn—and even such real-life characters as Huck's creator, Mark Twain—could be considered deserving of the CD label. Clearly it is important to identify those youths who are emotionally disturbed and whose behavior presages more trouble to come. However, Richters and Cicchetti argue that it is equally important not to pathologize youths who might get into trouble because of characteristics—such as nonconformity, independent-mindedness, and "mischievousness"—that represent potential sources of resiliency in the long term.

However, evidence is mounting that a large proportion of youths who engage in antisocial behavior have significant mental health problems. For example, the National Center on Addiction and Substance Abuse (2004) reports that as many as 75 percent of incarcerated 10- to 17-year-olds have a diagnosable mental health disorder. (See Box 10.2.)

Prevalence

Lahey, Miller, Gordon, and Riley (1999) did an impressive job of compiling statistics on *prevalence* derived from 39 population studies from around the world, 22 of which were conducted in the United States. They report a wide range of prevalence estimates, ranging from 0.0 to 11.9 percent, with a median of 2.0 percent. The data are complicated by the fact that different definitions and

Box 10.2 | **A Developmental Dilemma: When Should Children Be Held Legally Responsible?**

During the past decade, spurred by concerns about youth violence, legal reforms have lowered the age at which adolescents can be tried as adults in criminal court. According to the U.S. Department of Justice, 200,000 youths under the age of 18 are tried as adults each year. However, developmentally, are adolescents ready to be held to the same standards as adults? Are they competent to participate in the legal process, assist in their own defense, and comprehend the nature of the charges laid against them? To answer these questions, Steinberg and Scott (2003) administered a structured interview to nearly 1,000 juveniles aged 11 to 17, and 500 young adults aged 18 to 24, half of whom were incarcerated and half of whom were drawn from the community. Their results showed significant age differences in children's ability to comprehend their rights, understand courtroom procedures, and reason about the information relevant to launching their legal defense. Approximately one-third of the 11- to

13-year-olds and one-fifth of the 14- to 15-year-olds scored in the *impaired* range on these variables. Further, young offender's immaturity influenced their behavior in other ways that might negatively affect a legal defense. They were more likely to recommend confessing to the police rather than waiting for the advice of an attorney and to accept a plea bargain rather than standing up for themselves in court. Consequently, the investigators came to the conclusion that adolescents' capacity to participate in legal proceedings was diminished by virtue of their deficient decision-making skills, heightened vulnerability to being coerced, and reactivity to their environments. As the authors state, the results of their study confront lawmakers with "an uncomfortable reality": Under the constitutional restrictions that prevent the state from adjudicating those who are incompetent to stand trial, many young offenders are not equipped to participate effectively in their own defense. Further, the authors note that

the characters of youthful offenders are still in the process of being formed. In contrast to adult criminals, the antisocial behavior of adolescents may be limited to that time period and shaped by environmental and developmental forces, rather than by immutable and fixed personality characteristics. Thus, even though both the adult and adolescent criminal may be characterized by immaturity and poor decision making, these are developmental deficits that the adolescent might have the capacity to grow out of. Given these factors, the authors raise serious concerns about the application of the death penalty to youthful offenders. In response to these concerns, in March 2005, the United States Supreme Court ruled that the Constitution's Eighth Amendment, which prohibits "cruel and unusual punishment," precluded the use of capital punishment for crimes committed before the age of 18. With that ruling, the United States joined the rest of the nations in the developed world that bar the death penalty for children.

criteria were used to establish the diagnosis of CD. In a more rigorously designed study in the United States, Costello and colleagues (2003) collected a representative community sample of 1,420 children and assessed them annually from ages 9 to 16 using a standardized diagnostic interview. The prevalence of the CD diagnosis ranged from 2.7 percent at age 9 to 3.3 percent at age 13 to 1.6 percent at age 16. Across the age range, overall prevalence rates were 1.2 percent for girls and 4.2 percent for boys.

CD is even more prevalent in *clinical samples:* Referrals for conduct problems, aggressiveness, and antisocial behavior make up about one-third to one-half of all child and adolescent treatment cases. Because they are observable, disturbing to others, and difficult to ignore, Weisz and Weiss (1991) note, conduct problems are among the most "referable" of childhood disorders.

Gender differences are significant. The diagnosis of CD is about 4 times more common in boys than in girls, although the gap may begin to narrow in later adolescence (Zoccolillo, 1993). For example, the National Center on Addiction and Substance Abuse (2004) study cited earlier reports that arrest rates for female juveniles have increased 7.4 percent over the past decade even while arrest rates for male juveniles decreased almost 18.9 percent. Girls and boys also tend to display different symptoms: Boys are more likely to engage in overt aggression while girls earn the CD label through more covert antisocial behavior such as skipping school, running away, and abusing substances (Loeber & Stouthamer-Loeber, 1998).

Ethnicity and Social Class

Consistent evidence is found that CD is more prevalent among youths from economically underprivileged groups (Lahey et al., 1999). We will have much to say about the risks associated with growing up in an impoverished neighborhood when we explore the cultural context later in this chapter. Once social class is controlled, there is no consistent evidence for ethnic or racial differences in the prevalence of CD.

Typologies of Conduct Disorder

Childhood Onset Versus Adolescent Onset

As noted previously, DSM-IV-TR distinguishes between two types of CD. *Childhood-onset* CD, also termed "life-course persistent" CD (Moffitt, 1993), "aggressive-versatile" CD (Loeber, 1988), or the "early starter pathway" (Shaw, Bell, & Gilliom, 2000) begins prior to age 10, is associated with overt aggression and physical violence, and tends to be accompanied by multiple problems, such as neuropsychological deficits, inattention, impulsivity, and poor school performance. It occurs most often in males and is predicted by antisocial behavior in parents and disturbed parent-child relationships. The childhood-onset type is the one most likely to show persistence across the life span.

Adolescent-onset CD, also termed "adolescence-limited" CD (Moffitt, 1993), "nonaggressive-antisocial" CD (Loeber, 1988), or the late-starter pathway, is characterized by normal early development and less severe behavior problems in adoles-

cence, particularly in the form of violence against others. In contrast to the higher prevalence of childhood-onset CD in males, adolescent-onset youths are just as likely to be female (Fergusson, Lynskey, & Horwood, 1996). Fewer comorbid problems and family dysfunctions are seen in comparison to the childhood-onset type.

Moffitt and colleagues (Lahey, Moffitt, & Caspi, 2003) have demonstrated that there are different developmental predictors and consequences of these two subtypes. Longitudinal data were obtained in New Zealand from a representative sample of males who were assessed every 2 years from ages 3 to 18 (Moffit et al., 1996). The investigators were able to establish a number of ways in which youths with childhood-onset CD could be distinguished from their "late-blooming" peers. A *difficult temperament* at age 3 was a predictor of childhood-onset CD, as was an early history of *aggressiveness* and antisocial behavior. In adolescence, in contrast to other youths, the early starters were more likely to describe themselves as *self-seeking, alienated, callous* toward others, and *unattached* to families. They were also more likely to have committed a *violent crime*: Early starters were disproportionately convicted of such offenses as assault, rape, and use of a deadly weapon. Further, few of those on the childhood-onset pathway evidenced recovery—less than 6 percent avoided developing conduct problems in adolescence.

Patterson and Yoerger (2002) suggest that these late starters might be best termed "marginal"—that is, they have marginally elevated levels of antisocial behavior and marginally low levels of social competency, in contrast to the more severely maladjusted early-starting cohort. Thus, they could be perceived as lying halfway along the continuum between the normative and psychopathological. However, Moffitt (1993) argues that the majority of those with adolescent-onset CD do not deserve a diagnosis at all. In their longitudinal research in Dunedin, New Zealand, which has been replicated in several different cultures, Moffitt's group finds that the late-starting youths can be clearly distinguished from their early-starting peers by virtue of the lack of significant psychopathology or violent offending, and the absence of the neuropsychological, cognitive, familial, and temperamental factors that predict early-onset CD (Moffitt & Caspi, 2001). The investigators propose that the behavior of late-onset youths is best conceptualized as an "exaggeration" of the normal adolescent developmental process of rebellion and independence seeking or as a product of "*social mimicry*," in that they imitate the antisocial actions of others in order to gain status in the peer group (Moffitt, 1993). As they reach adulthood and have more opportunities to gain status in legitimate ways, their conduct problems generally desist.

However, the most recent data from the Dunedin longitudinal study, which assessed the now 26-year-old men, are not so reassuring (Moffitt et al., 2002). Adult males with adolescent-onset CD (who were matched with the early-onset group in terms of rates of offending) were, overall, functioning better in life than their early-starting peers. They were less likely to engage in seriously violent behaviors, including spousal battering and child abuse, and exhibited fewer psychopathic traits and better overall adaptation. Nonetheless, the late starters differed from their non-CD peers on a number of variables, including higher rates of substance abuse, impulsivity, poor employment histories, and psychological problems. Borrowing a concept from one of Rutter's (1990) protective mechanisms (see Chapter 1), involvement in an antisocial lifestyle, even when it begins later in adolescence, may have the effect of closing down opportunities and ensnaring young men in a network of maladaptive influences from which it is difficult to disentangle themselves.

Destructive/Nondestructive and Overt/Covert

Another line of research has pointed to a distinction based not on age of onset but on the kinds of acts perpetrated by the youths. Frick and colleagues (1993) conducted a meta-analysis of data from 60 factor-analytic studies involving more than 28,000 children. They identified two dimensions on which children's behavior could be distinguished. One dimension concerned whether misbehavior was *destructive* (cruelty to others, assault) or *nondestructive*

(swearing, breaking rules). The second dimension concerned whether behavior problems were *overt* (hitting, fighting, bullying) or *covert* (lying, stealing, destroying property), a distinction that has reliably been made in a number of studies.

Taking these two dimensions into account, the investigators were able to identify four subtypes of conduct-disordered youths, depending on the kind of misbehavior in which they engaged (see Figure 10.1). These were labeled *oppositional* (overt and nondestructive), *aggressive* (overt and destructive), *property violators* (covert and destructive), or *status violators* (covert and nondestructive).

Frick and colleagues (1993) also found that these types could be differentiated in terms of *age of onset*. Those who were primarily oppositional were identified by parents as early as 4 years of age. Aggressive children, in contrast, demonstrated problems after their 6th year. Those who engaged in property violations showed an average age of onset of about 7½ while those whose misbehavior took the form of status violations had an average age of onset of about 9. Interestingly, the status violations are reminiscent of the kinds of behaviors we noted earlier that tend to earn girls the CD label, and girls tend to be later starters than boys, suggesting that there may be an unexamined gender dimension to the typology.

Proactive Versus Reactive Aggression

Although not part of the diagnostic criteria, the distinction between proactive and reactive aggression has emerged as very important in studies of children's interpersonal behavior. *Reactive,* or retaliatory aggression, is a defensive reaction to perceived threat and is accompanied by anger and hostility. *Proactive,* or instrumental aggression, is unprovoked, cold blooded, and generally used for personal gain or to influence and coerce others (Dodge, Bates, & Pettit, 1990). Research demonstrates that there are different predictors and consequences for the two forms of aggression. Reactively aggressive children are more likely to come from physically abusive families, to be temperamentally irritable and dysregulated, to have poor interpersonal problem-solving skills, to misperceive others' motives as hostile, and to be socially rejected than their proactive

Figure 10.1   Meta-Analytic Factor Analysis of Child Conduct Problems.

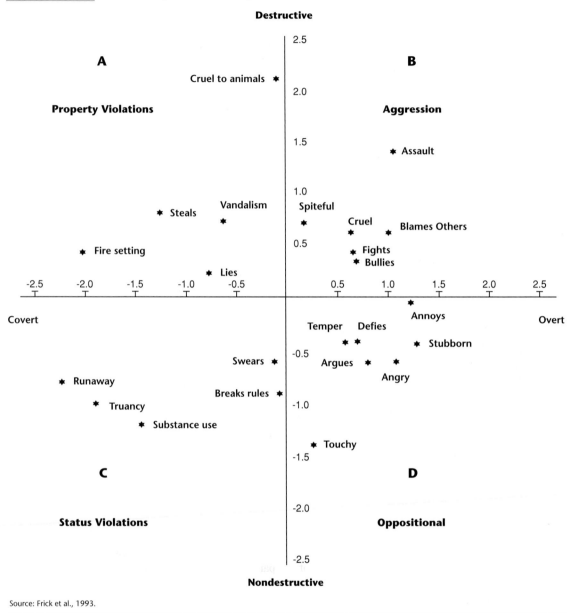

Source: Frick et al., 1993.

peers. Proactively aggressive children, in contrast, expect more positive outcomes to their aggression, are less anxious, and are more likely to emerge as delinquents in adolescences.

Bullies

The study of proactive aggression is important for understanding the development of one kind of miscreant who has made miserable the lives of many throughout childhood: the *bully*. From 15 to 20 percent of U.S. children are estimated to experience some form of bullying during their school years (Batsche, 1997). The victims suffer from more than hurt feelings: Significant anxiety, somatic problems, low self-esteem, inattention, and even suicide can result (Olweus, Limber, & Mihalic, 1999). Whereas in some cases there is validity to the stereotype of the lone bully as a "social oaf"—socially unskilled, verbally limited, and alienated from peers (Crick & Dodge, 1999)—that is not the only kind of bully on the playground. Investigators have identified a second type of bully who is in fact socially and cognitively skilled (Kaukiainen et al., 2002). The socially adept bullies are more likely to be identified as *ringleaders,* whose cruelty to victims serves to secure their status and popularity within the peer group (Sutton, Smith, & Swettenham, 2000). In fact, one of the most frequent reasons children give for bullying is to "look cool"; the other is to "feel powerful" (Farrington, 1992). The tactic may work. Indeed, Rodkin and colleagues (2000) found that highly aggressive boys were among the ones with the highest social status in their samples. These data suggest that the dynamics of the peer group have an important role in the development of bullying; therefore, bullying must be understood not just as a function of intrapersonal variables but also as a social process. Where the peer group rewards bullying with admiration, victimization will flourish.

Callous/Unemotional Traits and Juvenile Psychopathy

An additional important typology, inspired by research on adult **psychopaths,** has recently been extended downward to childhood. In his studies of criminal populations, Hare (1996) found that, among those with antisocial behavior, there is a subset who exhibit psychopathic personality traits. These traits include *callousness* (a lack of remorse, empathy, or guilt), egocentricity, superficial charm, impulsivity, shallow emotions, manipulativeness, and an absence of meaningful relationships. Psychopaths are individuals who commit antisocial acts against others, not out of necessity—they do not rob because they

are poor or strike out at others to defend themselves—but because they derive pleasure from hurting or manipulating other people. They exhibit a lack of awareness of other people as fellow human beings deserving of consideration or compassion. They are, in short, "without conscience" (Hare, 1993).

For example, after the Columbine shootings, Robert Hare was one of the experts the FBI called upon to help perform a "psychological autopsy" of the killers (Cullen, 2004). Although the media were quick to characterize the boys as victims of bullying, Hare's analyses of Eric's private journal showed that the "jocks" were not the only people Eric held in contempt: "YOU KNOW WHAT I HATE!!!? STUPID PEOPLE!!! Why must so many people be so stupid!!? . . . YOU KNOW WHAT I HATE!!!? When people mispronounce words! Learn to speak correctly you morons . . . YOU KNOW WHAT I HATE!!!? STAR WARS FANS!!! GET A FaaaaaaRIGIN LIFE YOU BORING GEEEEEKS!" Far from expressing a sense of victimization, Eric's journal writings suggest grandiosity—someone who is out to punish the entire human race for its appalling inferiority.

Another characteristic consistent with psychopathy was Eric's deceitfulness. "I lie a lot," he wrote to his journal. "Almost constantly, and to everybody . . . Let's see, what are some of the big lies I told? . . . No I haven't been making more bombs. No I wouldn't do that. And countless other ones." Lying for the pleasure of manipulating others is a key characteristic of the psychopathic profile.

Eric also evidenced a total lack of remorse or empathy—another distinctive quality of the psychopath. Hare and his team were solidly convinced of his diagnosis when they read Eric's response to being punished after being caught breaking into a van. After participating in a diversion program involving counseling and community service, both killers feigned regret to obtain an early release. However, Eric seemed to relish the opportunity to perform. While Eric wrote an ingratiating letter to his victim offering empathy, remorse, and understanding, at the same time he wrote down his real feelings in his journal: "Isn't America supposed to be the land of the free? How come, if I'm free, I can't deprive a stupid **** from his possessions if he leaves them sitting in the front seat of his **** van out in plain sight and in the middle of **** nowhere on a Fri****day night. NATURAL SELECTION. **** should be shot."

In summary, Eric's pattern of grandiosity, glibness, contempt, lack of empathy, and superiority read like the bullet points on Hare's Psychopathy Checklist.

Hare believes that ordinary antisocial behavior and psychopathy have different developmental origins. For example, while antisocial behavior generally is predicted by childhood adversity, psychopathy is not. This has led Hare to suspect that psychopathy derives from an innate predisposition. For example, brain scan imagery shows that psychopaths process information about emotions differently than do nonpsychopaths. Ordinarily, when people process information about emotionally meaningful words such as "love," the frontal cortex is activated, showing that the information is being processed at a deep level and many complex associations are being made. In contrast, the processing of a word with little emotional significance, such as "lamp," will not be associated with frontal activity. However, psychopaths process words having to do with feelings and relationships at the same shallow level that they do words about inanimate objects (Williamson, Harpur, & Hare, 1991). Consequently, Hare hypothesizes, psychopathy may have its origins in the "hard wiring" of the brain.

Can children be psychopaths? Most researchers in the field abjure applying that label to children, given that it implies a fixed and rigid personality pattern whereas, as we know, children's characters are still in the process of forming. However, evidence is accumulating that traits akin to the disorder can be identified in certain youths whom Lynam (1997) terms "fledgling psychopaths."

For example, Frick and associates (2000) developed a child version of Hare's device for detecting psychopathic traits, the Psychopathy Checklist. Just as with Hare's studies of adults, the investigators found two separate dimensions of behavior, one concerned with antisocial behavior, termed *impulsivity/conduct problems* (e.g., "acts without thinking," "engages in risky or dangerous behaviors") and the other reflecting *callous-unemotional* (CU) traits (e.g., "does not show emotions," "is not concerned about the feelings of others," "does not feel bad or

guilty"). They also identified a third factor that was labeled *narcissism* (e.g., "brags excessively," "thinks he or she is more important than others"). It is the CU dimension that is the most stable and predictive of serious misbehaviors (Barry et al., 2000). Consistent with the adult research, CU traits in children and adolescents are related to the violence of their offenses and are predictive of the likelihood that they will reoffend (Forth, Hart, & Hare, 1990). Further, consistent with Hare's hypothesis about the distinct etiology of psychopathy, while ordinarily conduct problems in children are predicted by ineffective parenting, in children with callous-unemotional traits, they are not (Wootton et al., 1997).

Subsequent studies in clinical samples have shown that, while children with "garden variety" CD tend to have cognitive deficits, particularly in verbal intelligence, this is not true of conduct-disordered children with CU traits. Children with CU traits also score higher than their non-CU peers on measures of thrill- and sensation-seeking, are less anxious, and show a decreased sensitivity to punishment (Barry et al., 2000; Frick et al., 1994). They are lower in empathy and are less distressed by the negative effects of their behavior on others; have lower levels of moral reasoning; expect to gain more benefits from their aggressive acts; and engage in more proactive, predatory forms of aggression (Frick et al., 2003). While all children with CD are characterized by emotional and behavioral *dysregulation,* Frick and his colleagues conclude, what sets apart the conduct disordered children with CU traits from their peers is behavioral *disinhibition.*

In the light of this research, Frick and Ellis (1999) argue that the childhood-onset CD type should be further differentiated into two groups: those with and without CU traits. They suggest that the different developmental pathways underlying these two types of aggression warrant their being considered separate disorders. While most children's misbehavior develops as a function of high emotional reactivity and poor verbal intelligence, and arises in the context of dysfunctional parenting, the callous-unemotional child's misbehavior arises as a function of low emotional reactivity, particularly to the distress of others. A next stage in this program of research will be to look at the unfolding of CU traits over the life course in order to establish whether CU traits in children truly represent a precursor to the development of adult psychopathy.

Comorbidity and Differential Diagnosis

CD frequently co-occurs with other disturbances. (Here we follow Hinshaw and Lee, 2003, except where noted.) *Attention-deficit hyperactivity disorder* (ADHD) and *oppositional-defiant disorder* (ODD) are the diagnostic categories most commonly associated with CD. Youths with comorbid ADHD and CD also are among the most disturbed. They display higher rates of physical aggression, more persistent behavior problems, poorer school achievement, and more rejection from peers than the "pure" CD type. In a longitudinal study following a sample of mostly African American, inner-city boys from first to seventh grade, Schaeffer and colleagues (2003) found that attention/concentration difficulties were one of the most powerful predictors of persistent or increasing levels of aggression. These data are consistent with the speculation that CD is related to the same underlying neurodevelopmental deficits that are responsible for inattention.

Learning disorders are associated with CD, particularly reading disorder. In some youths, learning problems may lead to frustration, oppositional attitudes, and misbehavior in school and thus to a diagnosis of CD. However, as we saw in Chapter 7, the weight of the evidence argues that learning disorders do not lead to CD, but rather that a third variable accounts for the relationship between them. Youths with *ADHD* are overrepresented among those who have both conduct and learning disorders, and it may be the overlap of these disorders with ADHD that accounts for their co-occurrence. A third variable that may account for the association is socioeconomic disadvantage. CD also co-occurs with *substance abuse* and may be a precursor to it, as we discuss in Chapter 12.

Although internalizing disorders might seem to be diametrically opposed to externalizing problems, *depression* is highly correlated with CD. As we saw in Chapter 9, Capaldi's (1992) longitudinal research suggests that antisocial behavior in boys leads to

academic failures and peer rejection, which lead, in turn, to depression. Comorbid depression and CD are of particular concern because they are disproportionately associated with suicide and substance abuse in later adolescence (Loeber, Stouthamer-Loeber, & White, 1999).

The relationship between CD and *anxiety* is a complex one. While anxiety of a fearful/inhibited type appears to protect children against the development of externalizing problems, anxiety that is characterized by social isolation and withdrawal is associated with an intensified risk of aggressive behavior.

There is a *gender difference* in that comorbidity is most common in girls. Although girls develop CD less often than boys overall, when they do, it is more likely to take a comorbid form (Loeber & Keenan, 1994). In particular, while *depression and anxiety* frequently occur in conduct-disordered youths, girls demonstrate higher rates of comorbidity with these internalizing problems. As we saw in our discussion of depression (Chapter 9), these different comorbidities might in fact represent different subtypes of CD.

Developmental Course

Continuity

There is a high degree of *continuity* in conduct-disordered behavior. Large-scale epidemiological studies in the United States and other countries have established stability from preschool age to middle childhood (Campbell, 1997), from childhood to adolescence (Lahey et al., 1995), from adolescence to adulthood (Farrington, 1995), and, most impressively, from infancy to adulthood (Newman et al., 1997). Thus, the developmental course is a persistent one and the prognosis poor. For example, Fergusson, Horwood, and Lynskey (1995) found that, over a 2-year period, only 14 percent of children diagnosed with CD evidenced remission.

One of the most impressive data sets on the continuity of conduct problems comes from a large, multinational collaboration (Briody et al., 2003). Recently this group compiled data derived from their studies based in Quebec, Canada (1,037 boys followed from ages 6 to 17); Montreal, Canada (1,000 boys and 1,000 girls assessed from ages 6 to 15);

Figure 10.2   Multinational Data on Aggression in Boys.

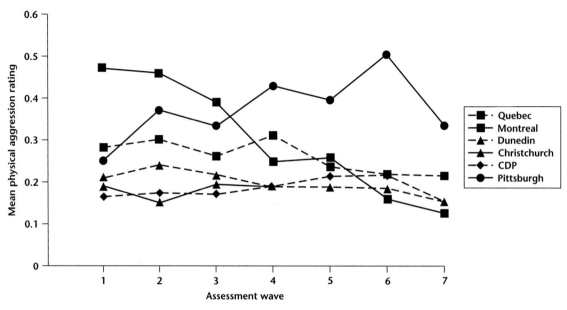

From Broidy, Nagin, Tremblay, Bates, Brame, Dodge, et al., 2003.

Christchurch, New Zealand (635 boys and 630 girls studied from birth to age 18); Dunedin, New Zealand (535 boys and 502 girls followed from ages 3 to 26); and two U.S. samples: one based in Pittsburgh (1,517 boys followed for 12 years, half of whom were African American); and the Child Development Project (CDP), a multisite collaboration based in Tennessee and Indiana (304 boys and 280 girls followed from kindergarten to age 13).

Overall, the data revealed significant differences in the levels and trajectories of aggressive behavior across sites and developmental periods. For boys, there was a trend toward increasing aggression in the U.S. samples, stability in the New Zealand samples, and decline in the Canadian samples (see Figure 10.2). Even within the group patterns of change, however, there was individual stability: Within each cohort, even though the absolute level of aggression might change over time, the relative ranking of individuals tended to stay the same. (So, for example, even though Jean Louis is less physically violent at age 16 than he was at age 6, he is still the most aggressive child in his Montreal classroom.) The investigators also were able

to identify individual trajectories of aggressive behavior, with some youths evidencing moderate levels of aggression that desisted over time, and others—the majority in all samples—rarely being aggressive. Only in the U.S. samples a subset of about 10 percent of the boys followed a course of increasing aggression over the course of childhood. Finally, childhood aggression was the most powerful predictor of adolescent violent and nonviolent delinquency. This prediction held true even when the investigators accounted for the influence of other kinds of disruptive behavior, such as oppositionality, ADHD, and nonaggressive conduct problems. Thus, childhood aggression begets adolescent violence.

Results for girls were quite different. Patterns of trajectory were more difficult to discern in girls and were more variable across the samples than they were for boys. Overall, girls' levels of physical aggression were lower than boys' across all four of the sites that included females (see Figure 10.3). However, in three of the samples, a small group of girls were chronically aggressive over the life course (3 percent in Quebec, 10 percent in Christchurch, and 14 percent in the CDP

Figure 10.3   Multinational Data on Aggression in Girls.

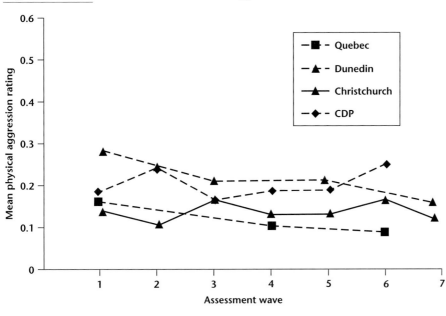

sample), and some of these girls exhibited higher mean levels of aggression than their male peers! But, in contrast to that of boys, girls' adolescent delinquency was not better predicted by childhood aggression than by other forms of disruptive behavior. Thus, despite the fact that the relation between physical aggression and later offending was strong and consistent for boys, it was weak and inconsistent for girls. Although part of the problem may be a statistical one—rates of violent delinquency in girls were so low that there was little variability to predict—the data also suggest that there may be a different pathway to female adolescent offending. As we shall see later in this chapter, other investigators agree.

Interestingly, there was no evidence of a sudden, late-onset type in these studies of the emergence of physical aggression. Does this suggest that the late-onset type does not exist? Probably not. Another interpretation is that while *some* forms of delinquent behavior may emerge only in adolescence in previously well-functioning youths—for example, stealing, truancy, or experimentation with drugs—the

propensity to be physically *violent* has its roots in childhood aggression.

Developmental Pathways

Researchers also have looked more closely at the developmental unfolding of problem behavior. Generally, a sequential progression is found such that one form of problem behavior virtually always occurs before the emergence of another. Relying on reconstructive data, Loeber and colleagues (1992) found an *"invariant sequence"* across development: from *hyperactivity-inattention* to *oppositional* behavior, and then to *conduct problems*. Combining Loeber's research with other work on the precursors and sequelae of conduct problems, we can construct a developmental model tracing the sequencing of behavior problems from difficult temperament in the early years to antisocial personality in adulthood. (See Figure 10.4.)

As youths progress through this sequence, they tend to maintain their prior antisocial behaviors; therefore, because behaviors are retained rather than

Figure 10.4   Developmental Transformations in Antisocial Behavior from Infancy to Adulthood.

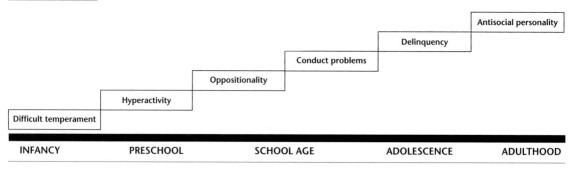

replaced, the developmental progression is better described as one of *accretion* rather than succession. However, the fact that this sequence exists does not mean that all individuals are fated to go through all the steps. On the contrary, while most individuals progress to different stages of increasing seriousness of antisocial behavior, few progress through all of them.

On the other hand, as Loeber and Stouthamer-Loeber (1998) note, *discontinuity* in CD also can be found. For example, some studies show desistance rates from preschool to school age of about 25 percent. Although it appears that these are youths with less serious behavior problems, little is known about the factors that account for their ceasing their antisocial behavior. However, as longitudinal research on the precursors and consequences of CD has emerged, distinct developmental pathways have been identified over the life span, which we describe next.

Early Childhood: Pathways from ADHD to Conduct Disorder

As noted in the previous section, a number of studies have confirmed the link between CD and ADHD (Lahey et al., 1995). Symptoms of ADHD appear to increase the risk for childhood-onset CD, to be associated with more severe behavior problems, and to result in greater resistance to change. Thus, ADHD propels youths to an earlier onset of behavior problems, which is predictive, in turn, of a longer-lasting antisocial career.

ADHD does not lead irrevocably to CD, however. Only those children whose ADHD symptoms are accompanied by *antisocial behavior* such as aggression and noncompliance are at risk for future CD (Loeber & Keenan, 1994). Thus, in this case it appears that ADHD potentiates early conduct problems, hastening them on the way to full-blown CD.

Middle Childhood: Pathways from Oppositionality to Conduct Disorder

ODD, as described in Chapter 6, is characterized by persistent age-inappropriate displays of anger and defiance. While ODD and CD share some similar behavioral features and risk factors, the two syndromes can be distinguished from one another. As we saw in Figure 10.1, large-scale meta-analyses of children's problem behavior reveal a unique factor comprising the kind of overt, nondestructive behaviors that define ODD. ODD also emerges earlier in development than CD, with an average age of onset of 6 years for oppositionality compared to 9 years for conduct problems (Loeber et al., 1992).

Loeber and colleagues (1993) found that CD was almost universally preceded by ODD. In addition, the most severely disturbed children were likely to retain features of oppositionality in addition to acquiring CD symptoms (Lahey et al., 1995). Therefore, there is convincing evidence for a developmental progression from ODD to CD.

Late Childhood and Adolescence: Divergent Pathways

Loeber and colleagues (1993) used prospective data from a longitudinal study of high-risk boys in order to investigate the *developmental pathways* predictive of later problem behavior. Basing their thinking on previous research differentiating CD along the dimensions of overt/covert and destructive/nondestructive, they derived three distinct types (see Figure 10.5).

The first identified was the *authority conflict* pathway. The behavior of these youths was characterized by defiance, stubborn and oppositional behavior, and rule violations such as truancy and running away. While disruptive, these behaviors were considered to be less serious because they did not inflict direct harm on others. Those whose behavior escalated in the authority conflict pathway tended to have continual conflicts with adults, but they were not likely to develop other forms of aggressive and antisocial behavior. They also were the least likely to become labeled delinquent.

The second was termed the *covert* pathway. These youths engaged in minor and nonviolent acts such as shoplifting, joyriding, and vandalism. Escalation in this pathway involved progressing to more serious forms of property crime and theft in later

Figure 10.5   Developmental Pathways to Conduct Disorder.

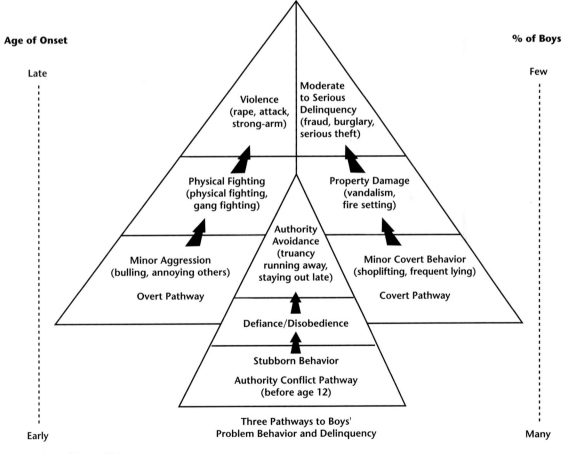

Source: Loeber and Keenan, 1994.

adolescence, but was rarely associated with violence or more severe kinds of antisocial behavior.

The third, the *overt* pathway, was composed of children who exhibited aggression early in childhood. Escalation in this pathway was associated with progression from aggression to fighting to more serious assaults and violence against others. The overt pathway was linked to high rates of criminal offenses in adolescence. In addition, these youths were likely to add covert forms of aggression to their repertoire as their careers proceeded. *Dual overt/covert* pathway youths were more likely to become delinquents; however, the worst outcomes were seen in *triple-pathway* youths—those who showed a combination of overt and covert aggression as well as authority conflict.

Patterson and Yoerger (2002) raise an interesting question about how the kinds of misbehavior that characterize childhood conduct disorder transform into the kinds of delinquent acts that are described in adolescents' police reports. Breaking into a house is different than taking money from a mother's purse, they suggest, just as physical assaults seem to belong to a different class from temper tantrums. What explains this metamorphosis? During the transition from late childhood to early adolescence, they point out, there is a developmental shift in the importance of peer relationships to youths. Noting that involvement in deviant peer relationships is a powerful predictor of antisocial behavior, and that the vast majority of juvenile crimes are committed in groups, the authors argue that peer group processes contribute to the *developmental transformation* of childhood misbehavior into adolescent delinquency.

Finally, Loeber and Stouthamer-Loeber (1998) point out that not all adolescents who demonstrate conduct problems have a childhood history of aggression or antisocial behavior. Thus, in this developmental period arises the *adolescent-onset*, or late-onset, type. Research shows that *peer influences* are crucial in attracting these late-starting youths away from a normative pathway and toward an antisocial lifestyle (Simons et al., 1994; Patterson & Yoerger, 2002), an issue we will return to and focus on in greater detail later in this chapter.

Late Adolescence: Pathways to Antisocial Personality and Criminality

Two conclusions can be drawn from the research linking CD to adult *antisocial personality disorder* and criminal behavior. First, *looking backward,* we find that antisocial adults almost without exception met the criteria for CD earlier in their development. However, one of the criteria for the diagnosis of antisocial personality disorder is onset of problem behavior before age 15, so this is a link that is structured into the diagnostic criteria. Secondly, *looking forward,* we find that only a minority of conduct-disordered youths go on to develop the chronic and disabling patterns characteristic of the adult diagnosis.

The characteristics predictive of those who do go on to develop antisocial personality disorder are early age of onset and diverse, persistent conduct problems in childhood, including aggression and antisocial behavior. As we have seen previously, *age of onset* is one of the most significant predictors of the subsequent seriousness of antisocial behavior. Children with early onset have both a higher level of disruptive behavior and progress more rapidly to more serious problems (Loeber et al., 1992; Reid, Patterson, & Snyder, 2002). There is clear evidence that those who begin their antisocial activities before the teenage years will continue to commit a large number of offenses at a high rate over a long period of time. Further, association with antisocial contemporaries contributes to the continuation of adolescent delinquency into young adulthood. Using longitudinal data from the Oregon Youth Study, Shortt and colleagues (2003) showed that adult antisocial behavior was predicted by adolescents' involvement, not only with deviant friends, but also with antisocial siblings and romantic partners.

Discontinuity and Protective Factors

Not all aggressive youths go on to become antisocial adults. While most adult antisocial behavior is rooted in childhood, only half of the at-risk children grow up to be antisocial men and women (Loeber & Hay, 1997). It is important to understand the factors that account for this discontinuity. With this in mind, Kolvin and coworkers (1989) conducted a longitudinal study of the *protective factors* shielding high-risk boys from adult delinquency. They found that a number of factors were important and that they played different roles in different developmental periods. For the first 5 years, good parental care, positive social circumstances, and few adverse experiences (e.g., accidents) were protective. Protective factors in the preadolescent period included parental supervision, absence of developmental delays, relatively good intelligence and academic achievement, easy temperament, good peer relations, and prosocial activities. Subsequently, Hoge, Andrews, and Leschied (1996) compiled a virtually identical list of protective factors in adolescence.

More recently, Shaw and colleagues (2003) identified factors that contributed to desistance of aggression in children between the ages of 2 and 8. Specifically, high levels of child *fearfulness* and low levels of *maternal depression* differentiated children whose levels of aggression remained low or did not persist. While fearfulness may reflect a temperamental variable that the child brings to the equation, it is worth noting that the investigators measured fearfulness as a function of toddlers' expressions of fear and hesitancy to approach a cabinet in which played a tape recording of gorillas howling in a threatening manner. Recalling our earlier reviews of research on the Strange Situation (Chapters 2 and 6), a 2-year-old's clinging to the mother and requesting reassurance in this context also might reflect security of attachment.

Gender Differences in Developmental Pathways

It is notable that almost all of the longitudinal studies cited have been based exclusively on males. What about *female* developmental trajectories? Because most CD is diagnosed in boys, the greater attention focused on males is justified to some extent. However, only by including girls in the research can we determine whether or not they are at reduced risk or have a different developmental course. (See Moffitt, Caspi, Rutter, & Silva, 2001.)

Although most studies agree that the development of CD in girls is more heterogeneous than that of boys, one finding with some consistency is that girls are more likely to show the *adolescent-onset* form of CD (McCabe et al., 2004; Silverthorn & Frick, 1999). While boys and girls tend to go through the same sequence of behavior problems in the progression toward CD, these misbehaviors generally have a later onset in girls than in boys. Antisocial behavior usually starts at age 8 to 10 for boys, while for girls it generally does not appear until age 14 to 16 (Kazdin, 1997a). One possibility is that this delayed-onset represents a "sleeper effect": Perhaps girls with CD have the same underlying temperamental and cognitive deficits as boys, but do not manifest these problems until adolescence (Silverthorn & Frick, 1999).

Developmental factors also come into play in other gender-differentiated ways. For example, *sexual maturation* is a powerful predictor of antisocial behavior for girls. Girls who mature early tend to engage in more norm-violating behavior, such as staying out late without parental permission, cheating on exams, being truant, taking drugs, and having unprotected sex (Simmons & Blyth, 1987). The reason for this appears to be that early-maturing girls spend more time with older peers who involve them precociously in risk-taking behavior, as we will explore further when we discuss peer influences.

However, as we saw in the multinational data compiled by Briody et al. (2003), girls exhibit lower levels of aggression in nearly all studies, and models of CD need to be able to account for this. Perhaps the explanation lies in the developmental mechanisms underlying conduct disorder. Of interest is the fact that girls are underrepresented among virtually all of the disorders that co-occur with—or are precursors to—CD, including oppositional defiance, attention deficit, and learning disorders. Various theoretical perspectives have been offered to explain this gender difference, summarized by Eme and Kavanaugh (1995). Some have argued that males are more biologically vulnerable to the neuropsychological deficits that underlie all these disorders. Others point to socialization factors, including parental reinforcement of aggressive behavior in boys and nurturance in girls, same-sex role modeling of aggression, and the influence of the peer group, which enforces sex-role stereotypic behavior such as an assertive-dominant style in males.

Others hypothesize that we simply are not doing a good enough job of catching girls in the act: Girls might misbehave in less overt ways than those that are captured by the measures used routinely in our investigations. For example, conduct-disordered girls and boys tend to be identified on the basis of different kinds of behavior problems. Fighting and theft are the most frequent reasons for referring boys, while *covert antisocial activities* such as truancy are more often the cause for concern about girls (Zahn-Waxler, 1993). Another fascinating line of research has focused on gender-differentiated expressions of aggression. While boys are more likely than girls to display physical aggression, both boys and girls engage in *relational aggression* (also termed social aggression): attempting to hurt others by ridiculing them, excluding them from the peer group, withdrawing friendship, or spreading rumors (Crick & Grotpeter, 1995; Underwood, 2003). Over the course of development, such behaviors may lend themselves to hidden forms of cruelty—such as the teenaged mother who psychologically abuses her child in the privacy of the home—that are not routinely captured by measures of antisocial behavior.

Despite the gender differences in prevalence, there is evidence that for those girls who do develop CD, the risk factors and consequences are equivalent to those seen in boys (McCabe et al., 2004). For example, Fergusson and Woodward (2000) found that among girls conduct problems at age 13 predicted association with deviant peers, substance use, academic problems, and risky sexual behavior, which in turn predicted antisocial behavior, mental health problems, sexual victimization, as well as poor achievement in young adulthood.

Etiology

The Biological Context

Recent attention has been drawn to the possibility of uncovering neurodevelopmental factors underlying the emergence of CD. Although much of this research is still in progress, and little of it is definitive, a number of suggestive leads have been identified.

Temperament may reflect a biological underpinning to CD. For example, Moffit and Lynam (1994) propose that underlying the development of disruptive behavior disoders are neuropsychological dysfunctions associated with a difficult temperament, which predisposes children to impulsivity, irritability, and overactivity. Consistent with this, Newman and colleagues (1997) found that children who showed a difficult, undercontrolled temperamental type at age 3 were more likely to be rated as antisocial in adulthood. However, other longitudinal research indicates that the link between aggression and difficult temperament is not a direct one; instead, it is mediated by family factors (McMahon & Estes, 1997).

Genetics also have been considered. One of the best predictors of conduct problems in children is parental criminality or antisocial behavior, especially when research focuses on fathers and sons. This may well be due to a genetic factor; however, environmental explanations cannot be ruled out. In general, there is evidence for both (Pike et al., 1996). For example, Ge and colleagues (1996) collected data on biological and adoptive parents of adolescents adopted at birth. Antisocial behavior in biological parents was significantly related to the aggressiveness of children adopted out of the home, providing evidence for a genetic influence. However, the adoptive parents' parenting practices also predicted children's aggression, suggesting that environmental influences also exist. However, a shortcoming of the genetic research is that most of it has not attended to the subtypes of CD that have emerged as so important in our review of the literature. While adolescent-onset conduct problems show little evidence for continuity across the generations, evidence for heritability has been demonstrated for the childhood-onset version of the disorder (Frick & Jackson, 1993).

Exposure to *toxins* also is implicated in the development of conduct problems. Fetuses exposed to opiates in utero are at increased risk for aggressive behavior 10 years later, as are those exposed to alcohol, marijuana, cigarettes, and lead poisoning (see Dodge & Petit, 2003).

Psychophysiological indicators also set early-onset youths apart from their peers. These children demonstrate overall lower autonomic arousal, demonstrated by low heart rate and galvanic skin response. Youths with low heart rates are likely to fight and bully others at school and are more likely to become violent adults. Low autonomic arousal leads to stimulation-seeking and behavioral undercontol on the one hand, and diminished reactivity to punishment on the other. Investigators concerned with the callous-unemotional subtype have been particularly interested in uncovering a physiological basis, given that this form of CD is not well predicted by environmental factors. For example, Frick and Ellis (1999) hypothesize that the behavioral disinhibition seen in these children arises from an *underreactive sympathetic nervous system,* leading to impulsive responding, heightened reactivity to reward, and insensitivity to negative feedback—such as the cry of another's distress—that might curb the aggressive impulses of others.

A number of *biochemical* correlates have also been investigated (Hinshaw & Lee, 2003). Testosterone is a likely candidate because of its relation to aggression in animals. However, research on humans indicates that hormone levels do not account for aggressive and antisocial behavior, although they may serve a mediating role in individual responses to environmental circumstances. Low levels of serotonin and cortisol also have been linked to aggression in children, although it is worth noting that these deficits have also been identified as factors in the development of a quite different disorder, depression.

Those pursuing research in the biological domain argue that the existence of organic factors in no way rules out or discounts the importance of social and psychological influences. In fact, there is a general appreciation of the complex interplay between psychology and biology (Dodge & Pettit, 2003). For example, Brennan and colleagues (2003) investigated the combined and interacting effects of biological and social processes in the development of aggression in an Australian sample of 370 children, followed from 6 months to 15 years of age. Consistent with other researchers, the investigators identified three pathways: early-onset persistent, adolescent-onset, and nonaggressive. For the early-onset boys, biological risks (perinatal and birth complications, maternal illness during pregnancy, difficult infant temperament, and neuropsychological defects such as poor executive functioning) predicted aggression

only in *interaction* with high social risk (parental rejection, harsh discipline, poor monitoring, parent-child conflict, family poverty, and divorce). In turn, the adolescent-onset aggressive boys differed from their nonaggressive peers by virtue of being exposed to a greater number of cumulative social risks. Gender differences once again raised their heads, in that biological risk factors did not significantly differentiate the aggressive patterns in girls.

The Individual Context

As we have seen, there is a continuum between normalcy and psychopathology, and deviations in fundamental developmental processes underlie many disorders. Indeed, aggression is part of normal development, and there is no reason for assuming that a "hothead" or a "scrapper" has CD if other aspects of his or her personality are proceeding apace. Therefore, to better understand what has gone awry in the development of those children who come to be labeled "conduct disordered," it will be helpful to review what is known about some of the major developmental variables underlying problem behavior: self-regulation, emotion regulation, empathy, and social cognition.

Self-Regulation

Self-regulation is essential to normative functioning, and the society's expectations that children control their impulses increase with age. While we might not be surprised to see a 4-year-old have a temper tantrum on the floor of the grocery store when denied a candy bar, such behavior in a 14-year-old would raise a few eyebrows. However, the 4-year-old is still expected to refrain from attacking a sibling in a rage, masturbating in a restaurant, or trying out a new toy hammer on the computer screen. Early socialization of self-control is particularly important because toddlers and preschoolers have a strong desire for immediate gratification of their aggressive, sexual, and exploratory urges; and they tend to be egocentric and self-seeking. However, objective studies confirm that conduct-disordered children evidence a limited ability to delay impulses and tolerate frustration (Hinshaw & Lee, 2003).

Kochanska and her colleagues (2001) have conducted studies devoted to uncovering the roots of self-control in young children, which they view as an outgrowth of the internalization of parental values (see Chapter 2). The researchers placed young children in a laboratory situation in which they were given time alone in a room with an attractive toy that their mothers had forbidden them to touch; self-control was indicated by their ability to resist the temptation. Those children who showed "committed compliance"—an eager and wholehearted endorsement of their mother's values, as opposed to mere obedience—were those who had experienced the most *mutually positive* affect in the parent-child relationship (Kochanska & Askan, 1995).

Further, Kochanska's (1997b) research has shown that specific parenting styles are optimal for promoting self-control in children with different temperaments. Using longitudinal data, she found that for children assessed as fearful in toddlerhood, a gentle maternal discipline style was most effective. However, for children assessed as fearless, gentleness was not sufficient. Instead, mothers needed to heighten their emotional bond with children in order to foster the motivation to accept and internalize parental values. Therefore, the development of self-regulation in temperamentally difficult children, who are at risk for CD, may require the most *intensely involved* and *emotionally available* parenting—the kind they are least likely to receive.

Emotion Regulation

Emotion regulation is a specific aspect of self-control that has been implicated in the development of CD (Cole et al., 1996). Children chronically exposed to family adversity, poor parenting, and high levels of conflict are overwhelmed by strong emotions and receive little help in managing them from stressed and unskilled parents. Therefore, they are at risk for failing to develop adequate strategies for coping with their negative emotions and regulating their expression. Consistent with this idea, research has shown that conduct-disordered children have difficulty managing strong affects, particularly anger, and that children with poor emotion regulation skills are more likely to respond aggressively to interpersonal problems (Eisenberg et al., 1997).

As was pointed out in Chapter 2, however, emotion regulation may involve not only underregulation but also overregulation. A good example of this can be found in Cole, Zahn-Waxler, and Smith's (1994) study. In order to obtain a sample of preschoolers at risk for developing CD, they specifically recruited children who were noncompliant, aggressive, and hard to manage. As expected, at-risk boys were more likely to respond to frustration by directing displays of negative affect to the experimenters, and they had more difficulty managing their anger. Poor emotion regulation, in turn, was related to symptoms of disruptive behavior and oppositionality. For girls, however, *overcontrol* of negative emotions predicted CD symptoms. Attempting to put too tight a lid on anger may cause it simply to spill over at a later time.

Prosocial Development: Perspective-Taking, Moral Development, and Empathy

Piaget (1967) observed that one of the pivotal developments in the transition to middle childhood is decentering: that is, shifting from cognitive egocentrism—in which the world is viewed primarily from the child's own vantage point—to cognitive perspectivism—in which a situation can be seen from the diverse views of the individuals involved and their rights and feelings taken into account. *Perspective-taking,* the ability to see things from others' point of view, is fundamental to the development of moral reasoning and empathy, both of which can counter the tendency to behave in antisocial and aggressive ways.

Research attests to the fact that aggressive and conduct-disordered youths are delayed in the development of these cognitive and affective variables. In contrast to their nondelinquent peers, juvenile delinquents are more cognitively immature in their *moral reasoning* (Smetana, 1990). In addition, conduct-disordered youths are less *empathic,* as well as being less accurate in reading the emotions of others when compared to their nondisturbed peers (Cohen & Strayer, 1996). Happé and Frith (1996) go so far as to propose that a conduct-disordered youth's lack of social insight and understanding of other people's mental states is akin to the deficits in *theory of mind* seen in autistic children. Accordingly, conduct-disordered youths tend to misperceive the motives of others and to exhibit distortions in their reasoning about social situations, both of which increase the likelihood that they will respond in an aggressive manner. We next turn to these social cognitive dimensions underlying problem behavior.

Social Cognition

Eron and Huesmann (1990), in musing about the stability of aggression across time and generations, state: "The frightening implication of this intractable consistency is that aggression is not situation specific or determined solely by the contingencies. The individual carries around something inside that impels him or her to act in a characteristically aggressive or nonaggressive way" (pp. 152–153). They conclude that underlying aggressions are *cognitive schemata:* scripts for interpreting and responding to events that are derived from past experiences and are used to guide future behavior (Huesmann & Reynolds, 2001).

Selman and Schultz (1988) have proposed a model of the cognitive developmental processes underlying the ability to resolve interpersonal problems without resorting to aggression. Parallel to Kohlberg's stages of morality, the development of *interpersonal negotiation strategies* (INS) proceeds from lower to higher levels of cognitive complexity and comprehensiveness. Selman and Schultz delineate four stages of INS, which have both a thinking (cognitive) and a doing (action) component. (See Table 10.2.) The stages progress from physical aggression or withdrawal at Stage 0, to assertive ordering or submissive obedience at Stage 1, to persuasion and deference at Stage 2, and, finally, to collaboration at Stage 3. Children with conduct problems tend to display immature INS strategies and to fail to progress through the stages as quickly as their peers.

Evidence also suggests that in addition to their deficiencies in interpersonal problem-solving strategies, children with CD have distinctive *social-information processing styles* (Crick & Dodge, 1994). For example, aggressive children misattribute aggressive intent to others when in an ambiguous situation, termed *hostile attribution bias*. They also are insensitive to social cues that might help them more correctly interpret others' intentions and respond impulsively on the basis of their faulty assumptions. In this way, they are ripe for misinterpretation and overreaction to seeming slights. In addition, these children are able to generate few alternatives for solving interpersonal problems, and they have positive expectations of the outcomes of aggression. Therefore, aggression is their preferred option.

These social-information processing patterns have also been shown to account for the relationship

Table 10.2

Selman and Schultz's INS

Stage 0: Impulsive. The strategies are primitive—for example, based on fight or flight—and show no evidence of perspective taking. Either extremes of aggressiveness (e.g., "Tell him to screw off!") or passivity (e.g., "Just do what he says!") would be at this level.
Stage 1: Unilateral. Strategies here show an awareness of the other person's point of view and of the conflict that exists, but strategies are based on assertions of the child's needs or wants (e.g., "Tell him you are not going to show up") or simple accommodation (e.g., "He's the boss, so you've got to do what he says").
Stage 2: Self-reflective and reciprocal. Strategies are now based on reciprocal exchanges, with an awareness of the other party's point of view. However, negotiations are designed to protect the interests of the child: for example, "He'll help the boss out this time, and then the boss will owe him one."
Stage 3: Collaborative. The child or adolescent is now able to view the situation objectively, taking his or her own and the other person's perspective into account and recognizing that negotiations are necessary for the continuity of the relationship: for example, "The boss and he have to work it out together, so they might as well talk out their differences."

Source: Selman and Schultz, 1988.

between early experiences of maltreatment and later childhood aggression (Dodge et al., 1995). Harsh and abusive parenting appears to instill in children a generalized belief that others are hostile and have malicious intent toward them, an assumption that is verified each time they engage in negative exchanges with parents, peers, and others. Therefore, children come to internalize their experiences of family mistreatment in ways that are deeply ingrained in their personalities and behavioral repertoires, replete with cognitive rationales that insure consistency in their behavior.

Substance Abuse

Involvement in *substance abuse* also may contribute to the onset of serious criminal behavior (see Chapter 12). For example, the National Center on Addiction and Substance Abuse (2004) reported that 4 out of every 5 youths currently in the juvenile justice system had a prior history of substance offenses or were under the influence of drugs or alcohol while committing their crimes. The relationship between CD and substance abuse is likely to be complex and transactional. On the one hand, youths who are behaviorally and emotionally dysregulated may be more attracted to the thrills and sensations accompanying substance use. Once involved with illicit substances, the youth is increasingly likely to engage in illegal activities in order to obtain the drugs and to be a part of the antisocial subculture that surrounds their use. Further, alcohol and drug substances have a disinhibiting effect that increases the likelihood of engagement in risky and illegal behavior.

The Family Context

Attachment

Insecure attachments with parents in infancy have been linked prospectively to preschool behavior problems such as hostility, oppositionality, and defiance. However, insecure attachment relationships predict elementary school aggression in girls but not boys, and these predictions are influenced by a number of other factors related to family adversity and environmental stress. As Greenberg, Speltz, and Deklyen (1993) conclude, the research to date has not established a direct effect of attachment on antisocial behavior, although a poor parent-child relationship is a clear risk factor for the development of psychopathology in general.

Family Discord

First, looking at whole-family processes, we find that family discord is fertile soil for producing antisocial acting out, especially in boys (Shaw et al., 1994). In particular, children exposed to *domestic violence* are likely to develop behavior problems (Graham-Bermann & Edleson, 2001; Geffner et al., 2003). Children exposed to violence in the home also start delinquent careers at an earlier age and perpetrate more serious offenses (Kruttschnitt & Dornfeld, 1993). Further, the children are often the targets of their parents' aggression—e.g., youths with CD are more likely to have been victims of *child maltreatment* (Dodge, Petit, & Bates, 1994).

CD is also associated with nonviolent forms of *interparental conflict* (Cummings & Davies, 1994b) and *divorce* (Emery & Kitzmann, 1995). Boys growing up in single-parent households are particularly at risk. Vaden-Kiernan and colleagues (1995) found that once family income, neighborhood, and earlier aggressive behavior were taken into account, boys without a father or father figure in the home were more likely to be rated as aggressive than boys in two-parent families. No such relationship between family type and aggression was found for girls. However, it is not coming from a "broken home" per se that matters, but rather disruptions in the emotional quality of family relationships that may lead to child behavior problems. For example, boys are rarely juvenile delinquents in mother-headed household families if the mother has good parenting skills and the parent-child relationship is a supportive one (McCord, 1990).

Family stress also increases the likelihood of CD. Children who develop behavior problems are more likely to come from families that have experienced more negative life events, daily hassles, unemployment, financial hardship, moves, and other disruptions. In addition, the family members of disruptive children have few sources of social support and engage in chronic conflict with others in the community

(McMahon & Estes, 1997). However, it may be that family stress is not a direct cause of antisocial behavior, but rather that it acts as an amplifier of other problematic parent-child relationship processes (Dishion, French, & Patterson, 1995).

Parent Psychopathology

Parental *substance abuse,* especially in fathers, is predictive of CD in children. *Maternal depression* has also been linked to child conduct problems, as well as a number of other kinds of maladjustment (Cummings & Davies, 1994a).

The most powerful parent-related predictor of CD in children is parent *antisocial personality disorder,* which increases both the incidence and the persistence of the CD. For example, Lahey and colleagues (1995) conducted a 4-year prospective study of 171 children diagnosed with CD. Parental antisocial personality disorder was correlated with CD at the first assessment and, in combination with boys' verbal intelligence, predicted the continuation of conduct problems in later development. How does parent personality translate into child behavior problems? This question concerns us next.

Harsh Parenting and the Intergenerational Transmission of Aggression

There is strong evidence for the *intergenerational transmission* of aggression. Aggression is not only stable within a single generation but across generations as well. Eron and Huesmann (1990) conducted a 22-year prospective study, compiling data on 82 participants when they were 8 and 30 years of age, as well as collecting information from their parents and 8-year-old children. Strong associations were seen between grandparents', parents', and children's aggressiveness. The correlation between the aggression that parents had shown at age 8 and that was displayed by their children was remarkably high (0.65), higher even than the consistency in parents' own behavior across the life span.

While the mechanisms responsible for the continuity of this behavior are not clear, Eron and Huesmann believe it is learned through *modeling*. As noted before, children who have antisocial parents are ex-

posed to models of aggressive behavior, including interparental violence and child maltreatment. However, the aggression need not be so extreme in order to provide a model. For example, adult antisocial behavior is predicted by *harsh punishment* received as a child (Eron & Huesmann, 1990). In adulthood, those punished harshly as children were more likely to endorse using severe discipline in childrearing—in fact, their responses to parenting style questionnaires were strikingly similar to the ones given by their own parents 22 years earlier.

Corresponding results have been obtained regarding the relationship between *spanking* and child aggression. Straus, Sugarman, and Gile-Sims (1997) followed a nationally representative sample of over 800 children ages 6 to 9 over a 2-year period and found that spanking was associated with increased aggression and antisocial behavior. Similar results have been found in clinical populations, establishing a link between corporal punishment and the development of externalizing disorders (Mahoney et al., 2003). Later in development, childhood corporal punishment also increases the risk that males will grow up to become spousal batterers (Straus & Yodanis, 1996). In sum, through their observations of their own parents, children learn that the rule governing interpersonal relationships is "might makes right."

Parenting Inconsistency and Lack of Monitoring

Other research indicates that it is not only the severity of parental discipline but also a pattern of *parental inconsistency*—an inconsistent mix of harshness and laxness—that is related to antisocial acting out. Laxness may be evidenced in a number of ways, particularly lack of parental *monitoring:* failing to provide supervision, to stay knowledgeable about the children's activities and whereabouts, and to enforce rules concerning where the children can go and whom they can be with. These are parents who, when phoned by researchers and asked, "It is 9 P.M.; do you know where your child is right now?" do not know the answer. Patterson and his colleagues (Reid, Patterson, & Synder, 2002) refer to the unsupervised behavior of youths as *wandering* and find that it is a strong predictor of involvement in delinquent activities.

Coercion Theory

Patterson and his colleagues (1982; Reid et al., 2002) have carried out an important program of research on the family origins of conduct disorder. Based on social learning theory, they set out to investigate the factors that might train antisocial behavior in children. They found that parents of antisocial children were more likely than others to *positively reinforce* aggressive behavior—for example, by regarding it as amusing. They also observed that these parents exhibited inconsistent outbursts of anger and punitiveness and made harsh threats with no follow-through, both of which were ineffectual in curbing negative behavior. On the other side of the coin, children's prosocial behavior was either ignored or reinforced noncontingently. Therefore, the investigators conclude that CD is initiated and sustained in the home by maladaptive parent-child interactions.

Patterson's most important contribution was to analyze the interactions of antisocial children and their parents in terms of what he calls coercive family processes. By **coercion,** Patterson means negative behavior on the part of one person that is supported or directly reinforced by another person. These interactions are transactional and reciprocal;

they involve both parent and child, whose responses to one another influence each other's behavior. For example, Patterson notes that the families of typical and CD children have different ways of responding to each other. When punished by parents, CD children are twice as likely as normal children to persist in negative behavior. This is because their family members tend to interact through the use of *negative reinforcement*. Unlike punishment, in which an unpleasant stimulus is applied in order to decrease a behavior, negative reinforcement increases the likelihood of a behavior by removing an unpleasant stimulus as the reward.

To illustrate this concept, consider the scenario presented in Figure 10.6. Who is reinforcing whom? The children have learned that if they behave aversively when their mother says no, they can get their way; their mother has inadvertently *positively reinforced* them for whining. Their mother, in turn, has been *negatively reinforced* for giving the children what they want when they misbehave—she is rewarded by the fact that the children cease their misbehavior.

The cartoon mother has fallen into what Patterson calls the *"reinforcement trap"*: She obtains a short-term benefit at the expense of negative long-term consequences. The trap is that, by giving in, she has ended the children's immediate negative behavior,

Figure 10.6

Coercion.

but has inadvertently increased the likelihood that they will behave the same way in the future. Through the reinforcement trap, children are inadvertently rewarded for aggressiveness and the escalation of coercive behavior, and parents are rewarded for giving in by the relief they experience when children cease their obstreperousness. However, the parents pay a heavy price. Not only are their socializing efforts negated, but their children's behavior will become increasingly coercive over time.

Transactional Processes

Another significant aspect to Patterson's observations is that it involves *transactional* processes between parents and children, such that they affect and shape one another's behavior. A number of investigators agree. For example, Campbell (1997) has observed the relationship between parenting stress and preschool children's aggressiveness and noncompliance. She infers a bidirectional process whereby the stressed mother becomes more restrictive and negative when trying to cope with her impulsive, noncompliant child; this, in turn, makes the child more difficult to handle.

On a similar note, Dumas, LaFreniere, and Serketich (1995) studied the interactions between mothers and their children, who were categorized as being socially competent, anxious, or aggressive. Surprisingly, they found that, overall, aggressive children and their mothers shared a positive emotional tone. However, in comparison to other dyads, aggressive children were more likely to use *aversive control techniques,* and their mothers were more likely to *respond indiscriminately* and to *fail to set limits* on their children's more extreme forms of coercion. Thus, they conclude, both parents and young children are active agents in the interaction and reciprocally influence one another.

Others take a different view of who is in the driver's seat. Lytton (1990) describes a provocative experiment that tested the hypothesis that problematic parenting is a functioning of children's behavior. The investigators observed mothers of conduct-disordered boys and normative boys interacting with their own sons, an unrelated conduct-disordered boy or an unre-

lated well-behaved child. As hypothesized, all mothers were more negative and demanding with conduct-disordered boys, with the highest rates of negativity displayed by mothers of antisocial children when interacting with their own sons. However, when interacting with a normative child, mothers of conduct-disordered children behaved like any other mother. Lytton points to this study, as well as to evidence indicating that some children have a constitutional bias to be aggressive, difficult to manage, and underresponsive to rewards and punishments, in order to argue that we should not underestimate the child's contribution to aversive parent-child relationships.

In general, while attending to the child's contribution is a healthy antidote to parent-blaming, the prevailing opinion seems to be that transactional parent-child processes are more likely to provide an accurate explanation than is either a child-only focus or a parent-only focus (Dodge, 1990).

A Developmental Perspective on Parenting and Conduct Disorder

Shaw and Bell (1993) reviewed the available evidence regarding how various qualities of parenting contribute to the early-starting developmental pathway to conduct disorder and constructed a transactional account of how they might each come into play over the course of childhood. In particular, their model integrates Patterson's (1982) *coercion theory* with research on parent-child *attachment* (Greenberg, Speltz, & DeKlyen, 1993).

Focusing on attachment during the first phase, from birth to 2 years of age, Shaw and Bell (1993; Shaw et al., 2000) propose that the most important factor is likely to be *parental responsiveness.* Through inconsistent and neglectful caregiving, nonresponsive parents may contribute to the development of irritable, impulsive, and difficult infants who perceive the parent as unsupportive and unavailable to help them manage upsetting feelings. These conditions set the stage for the 2nd year of life, when the child high in negative emotionality further stresses the parent's tolerance for the "terrible twos'" oppositionality and fits of anger. By age 3, the pattern of relationship between parent and child has coalesced into an internal working model that guides their expectations and behavior. During this phase, *parental insistence* is hypothesized to take on greater importance. Rather than forming a goal-directed partnership based on mutual negotiation and compromise, parents and children who expect negativity from one another are more likely to initiate coercive and punitive patterns of exchange, which, in turn, contribute to children's further noncompliance and irritability. In the third phase, from 4 to 5 years, the most important factor is *parental inconsistency* in discipline. At this stage, as children's negative models of self and other are carried over into their peer relationships and school behavior, conduct problems intensify and their ramifications become more serious, requiring increasing parental firmness and consistency. Instead, however, the parents of conduct-disordered children are likely to vacillate between ignoring misbehavior and employing— or merely threatening—harsh punishment.

In summary, Shaw and Bell's model proposes that a poor attachment in toddlerhood sets the stage for the development of coercive transactions between parent and child, which lead to escalating harshness, conflict, and emotional disharmony between the child and the social environment.

Over the past decade, Shaw and colleagues have initiated a program of research to test this developmental model. In an initial study, they followed a sample of children from infancy to age 5. Consistent with the model, they found that disorganized attachment was a predictor of disruptive behavior during the 1st year, while from the 2nd year onward, maternal personality problems and parent-child conflicts also contributed (Shaw et al., 1996). In a second study, they found that maternal rejection at 24 months was related to externalizing problems at 42 months. Children contributed to negative patterns of exchange, in that child noncompliance interacted with parenting style in order to produce the most powerful predictor of conduct-disordered behavior (Shaw et al., 1998). Subsequently, following these children into school age, the investigators found that risk factors identified at age 2 predicted conduct problems at age 8. Early problem behavior, maternal depression, low social support, and rejecting parenting

contributed in an additive and interactive manner to the escalation of child misbehavior, negative parenting, and conflictual parent-child relationships (Shaw, Bell, & Gilliom, 2000).

Specificity of Parenting Effects

Kim and colleagues (2003) conducted a rare study that addressed the question of *specificity* regarding how parenting contributes differentially to the development of conduct disorder, depression, or a combination of the two. The investigators gathered a community sample of 897 African American children and assessed them in two waves, at ages 10 and 12. Results showed that children with both CD and comorbid CD/depression received less nurturant and involved parenting than did depressed children. In turn, children with co-occurring problems reported higher levels of parenting hostility than did those with depression alone. However, unique to children in the CD-only group, in contrast to those with depression, was a lower level of parental *warmth.*

The Social Context

Children with CD are readily identified by peers. They are argumentative, easily angered, resentful, and deliberately annoying to others (Kazdin, 1997a). As early as the preschool period, habitual child aggression is associated with subsequent *peer rejection,* which leads, in turn, to further aggressive behavior (Capaldi & Patterson, 1994; Coie et al., 1995). Aggressive children also gain a *negative reputation* with peers that continues to follow them even when their behavior improves. Therefore, interactions between conduct-disordered children and their peers can contribute to further aggression and problem behavior.

Caprara and his Italian colleagues (2001) present an interesting transactional perspective on peer reputation and why it is associated with such stable and unalterable effects: In short, reputations change children's self-perceptions. Their research suggests that children's behavior leads them to gain a reputation among peers and teachers, but that the child's subsequent behavior is filtered through these expectations. Whereas peers and teachers might ordinarily dismiss as accidental a child's bumping into another child on the playground, the child with a reputation as a bully

Troubled youth may seek a sense of belonging and acceptance in an antisocial peer group.

is more likely to be perceived as purposeful and to receive a reprimand. This feedback from others, in turn, comes to influence the child's self-image and behavior. Consequently, the child labeled as a bully is more likely to see him- or herself as such and to behave accordingly. In summary, the expectations of others influence the child's behavior so that he increasingly comes to confirm those very expectations, a process they term "shared consensus building."

By middle childhood, while aggressive children may be rejected by their prosocial agemates, they are apt to be accepted into *antisocial peer groups* that tolerate or even value problem behavior. Antisocial youths spend most of their time in peer groups with no adult supervision, "hanging out" on the streets and engaging in risky behavior. Thus, antisocial youths tend to gravitate toward one another and reinforce one another's behavior.

Consistent with this, Dishion, French, and Patterson (1995) found that *peer rejection* at age 10 (along with academic failure) predicted involvement with antisocial peers at age 12, more so than did parental discipline or monitoring practices. Involvement with antisocial peers, in turn, predicts escalating misbehavior (Kupersmidt, Burchinal, & Patterson, 1995). Similarly, Fergusson and Horwood's (1996)

longitudinal research showed that association with antisocial peers had a reinforcing and sustaining effect on youth misbehavior from childhood to adolescence. Notably, one of the characteristics that accounted for the 12 percent of their sample of disruptive children who did not go on to develop adolescent CD was their lower rates of affiliation with delinquent peers.

Peer factors can be seen clearly in the development of CD in girls during late childhood and adolescence. As noted previously, *early sexual maturation* is a powerful predictor of antisocial behavior for females. Although at first blush sexual maturation might be assumed to be a strictly biological factor, the onset of menarche has important social implications. Puberty results in noticeable secondary sexual characteristics, such as breast development, which, for the first girl in her class to need a bra, can be a source of teasing from same-sex peers and unwanted sexual attention from males. In fact, evidence suggests that heterosexual peer relations mediate the link between sexual maturation and norm violation. Early-maturing girls attract the attention of older males who engage in norm-violating behavior and, in turn, involve the girls precociously in risk-taking behaviors and sexual activity (Simmons

& Blyth, 1987). Late maturers evidence similar behavioral problems after they biologically "catch up" with their early-maturing peers. However, early maturation is only a risk factor for girls who attend mixed-sex schools (Caspi et al., 1993). Those who attend all-female schools are not exposed to the social pressures that make early maturation a predictor of conduct problems for other girls.

Not all children and youths are equally susceptible to peer influences, however. Vitaro and colleagues (1997) followed a sample of almost 900 boys from age 11 to age 13. Based on teacher reports, they typologized boys and their friends as moderately disruptive, highly disruptive, or conforming. Moderately disruptive boys who associated with disruptive peers engaged in more delinquent behavior as time went on. However, friends appeared to have no impact on the development of behavior problems in highly disruptive or conforming boys. For these latter two groups of youths, *individual characteristics* seem to be steering their development—in a positive direction when associated with prosocial skills but in a negative direction when associated with antisocial traits.

In sum, research on the influence of peers indicates that they are a contributing factor but not a determining one. Two different processes seem to be at work that we might term "pushing" versus "pulling." While early aggression may cause a child to be pushed away by prosocial peers, positive attachments to antisocial peers may pull a youth in the direction of engaging in misbehavior. This latter influence may be particularly important for understanding adolescent-onset CD. In fact, association with antisocial peers has a direct effect on delinquency only in the *adolescent-onset type*, while *parent socialization* is a more significant causal factor in the *child-onset* form of the disorder. For adolescent-onset conduct-disordered youths, then, antisocial peer influences appear to be essential, while for early-onset youths the picture is more complicated.

The Cultural Context

The Neighborhood

A number of neighborhood factors are associated with the risk of CD. In particular, children growing up in communities marked by *poverty* and *violence*

are more likely to develop antisocial behavior and CD (Osofsky, 1995). The impact of exposure to community violence is significant (Lynch, 2003). For example, while most of the children who developed CD in Campbell and colleagues' (2000) study experienced multiple risk factors, one sizable cohort evidenced risk in only one domain: They lived in dangerous neighborhoods. Impoverished inner-city children in the United States are routinely exposed to shocking degrees of violence: By age 5 most have seen a shooting, and by adolescence one-third have witnessed a murder (Bell & Jenkins, 1993). Chronic exposure to violence may desensitize children to these experiences. For example, Lorion and Satzman (1993) found that fifth- and sixth-grade children living in high-crime neighborhoods described the shootings, police raids, and dead bodies they had seen in blasé terms, as "nothing special." Further, in their study of 4,458 inner-city school children, Guerra, Huesmann, and Spindler (2003) found that from ages 5 to 12, exposure to community violence was associated with increasing levels of aggressive behavior, engagement in aggressive fantasies, and beliefs that aggression is normative and justified.

Also, it is in the neighborhood that children are most likely to be exposed to models of antisocial behavior and aggression (Ingoldsby & Shaw, 2002). In particular, the *gang culture* of the inner cities offers few alternatives to youths, who may feel they must join in order to survive. Tolan and colleagues (2003) examined the relationships among community characteristics (poverty, crime, lack of available resources, absence of neighborliness and social support), parenting, gang membership, and youth violence. The investigators collected longitudinal data from 294 African American and Latino boys, who were assessed annually over a period of 6 years. The results showed that good parenting was able to partially buffer children from the effects of community disorganization. However, when parenting was poor, youths were more likely to become gang involved, which in turn led to escalating violence over the course of adolescence. Gangs, the authors argue, set a stage for "deviancy training," which is quite apart from other influences; therefore, prevention efforts for inner-city youths should concentrate on diverting adolescents from recruitment into gangs in the first place.

Ethnicity

Socioeconomic disparities must be taken into account when interpreting data on the relatively higher prevalence of conduct disorder in African American versus European American youths. A large proportion of African American inner-city families live in segregated communities characterized by high crime, poor housing, lack of resources, and poverty (Shaw et al., 2000). However, while social class has been found to account for ethnic differences in the prevalence of antisocial behavior in many studies (Hinshaw & Park, 1999), there are some racial effects that persist. For example, even when SES is controlled, African American youths demonstrate more of a hostile attribution bias than European American children (Dodge, Lochman, Harnish, Bates, & Petit, 1997b). Rather than representing a cognitive "error," such reasoning may reflect the experience of growing up in a racially hostile environment and may accurately reflect the way that minority children are treated by peers.

School Environment

The *school* is another aspect of the social environment that can contribute to antisocial behavior. Kasen, Johnson, and Cohen (1990) found that a school environment characterized by a high degree of conflict (fighting, vandalism, defiant students, and teachers unable to maintain order) was related to an increase in CD over a 2-year period. Schools may also contribute to the development of antisocial behavior in more subtle ways. Children quickly determine whether they are perceived by teachers as high or low achievers and develop attitudes toward school in keeping with the attitudes they believe their teachers harbor toward them (Kuklinski & Weinstein, 2001). Those who experience school failure early in their careers develop negative self-perceptions, which lead to hostility and aggression (Stipek, 2001). Further, as they approach adolescence, youths who feel disenfranchised in school develop increasingly negative attitudes toward education and low expectations for themselves, leading them to leave school early and thereby limiting their prosocial opportunities for achieving success. Antisocial behavior becomes a likely option.

Media Influences

At a larger social level, the *media* may also play a role in promoting—and even glamorizing—antisocial behavior. Violence has become a mainstay of American television and movies. Further, violence is perpetrated by heroes as much as by villains and is seldom met with negative consequences (Eron, 2001). Instead, the lesson is largely communicated that violence is an effective method of solving problems and will be rewarded. Research bears out the relationship between television violence and children's behavior. Children with strong preferences for viewing violent television programs are more aggressive than their peers, and laboratory studies also show that increased viewing of aggressive material leads to subsequent increases in aggressive behavior. Further, longitudinal studies also show that children who prefer violent television programs during elementary school engage in more violent and criminal activity as adults (Huesmann et al., 2003). These effects are enhanced by children's identification with TV characters and their belief that fictional TV violence reflects reality; are consistent across gender, social class, and intellectual ability; and are unaffected by parents' aggression, TV viewing habits, or attitudes.

Sex-Role Socialization

Further insights into specific cultural influences have also been offered, particularly regarding the role of *masculine socialization* in the development of male aggression. For instance, Cohen and colleagues (1996) describe the masculine ethic of the American South as a "culture of honor," which requires that males use physical force in order to defend against perceived insults to their own or their family's reputation. The investigators demonstrated this empirically by instructing a research assistant to purposely bump into male college students and then to make a profane and personally disparaging comment. While Northerners were relatively unaffected by the insult, those participants who originated from the South were more likely to feel that their masculinity was threatened, to show heightened physiological arousal and signs of distress, to be more cognitively primed for aggression, and to be more likely to retaliate with violent behavior. The investigators interpret this response as a product of social learning, such that their cultural upbringing leads Southern men to experience interpersonal problems as threats to masculine honor that must be defended through physical aggression.

In sum, opportunities for learning antisocial behavior—and reinforcements for engaging in it—abound in the school, neighborhood, and the culture at large.

Integrative Developmental Model

Patterson and his colleagues have been studying and theorizing about the origins of child conduct problems for over two decades. They provide an integra-

tive developmental model based partly on research and partly on their own observations and experience. (Our presentation is based on Capaldi and Patterson, 1994; Dishion, French, and Patterson, 1995; Patterson, DeBaryshe, and Ramsey, 1989; Patterson, Reid, and Dishion, 1992; and Reid, Patterson, and Snyder, 2002.)

The process of "growing" a conduct-disordered youth takes place in a series of hierarchical stages that build on and elaborate one another, consistent with the organizational hypothesis of developmental psychopathology. (See Figure 10.7.) The process begins with a host of risk factors, some of which are in place before the birth of the child. These include low socioeconomic status, living in a high-crime neighborhood, family stress, antisocial parents, and the parents' own history of being reared by unskilled

Figure 10.7   Patterson's Model of the Development of Conduct Disorder.

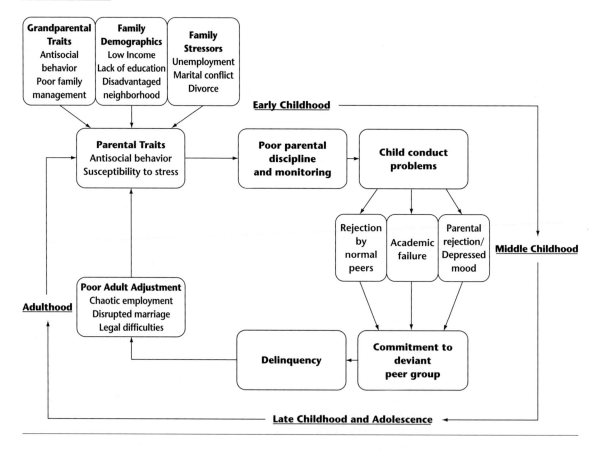

caregivers. However, these risk factors do not directly lead to antisocial behavior. Rather, their effect is mediated by family variables: The basic training camp for antisocial behavior is the home.

The first stage begins in early childhood and involves *poor parental discipline strategies,* with initial coercive interactions escalating into increasingly punitive exchanges. Other poor parent management skills include little involvement and monitoring of children, inconsistent discipline, lack of positive reinforcement for prosocial behavior, and an absence of effective strategies for solving problems. The products of these dysfunctional family interactions are antisocial, socially unskilled children with low self-esteem.

The next stage occurs in middle childhood when children enter school, where their antisocial behavior and social incompetence result in *peer rejection* and *poor academic performance.* Failures in these important developmental tasks also contribute to a *depressed mood.* Further, children who chronically bring home negative reports from teachers are more likely to experience *parent-child conflict* and *parental rejection.*

In adolescence, the youths are drawn to an *antisocial peer group* that has a negative attitude toward school and authority and is involved in delinquent activities, including substance abuse. These antisocial peers support further problem behavior. As development proceeds, adolescents with an antisocial lifestyle are more likely to have similar difficulties in adulthood, including *chaotic employment* careers, *disrupted marriages,* and *institutionalization* for crimes or psychiatric disorders. In late adolescence and adulthood, a process termed *assortative mating* increases the likelihood that antisocial individuals will form relationships with partners with similar personalities and conduct problems. As stressed, unskilled, and antisocial individuals form families and have children of their own, the *intergenerational cycle* is recapitulated.

Intervention

The continuity of CD from childhood to adulthood indicates that this is a psychopathology that becomes entrenched in early development and has long-lasting consequences. Further, other individuals and society pay a high price, in terms of both personal suffering and the dollars-and-cents costs of violence, property destruction, theft, and incarceration. Thus, there is an urgent need for prevention and treatment. Yet the multiple roots of CD—cognitive and affective dysfunctions within the child, psychopathology and discord within the family, encouragement from similarly disordered peers and society at large—present major obstacles to success in both undertakings. As Eron and Huesmann (1990) state, intervention with CD "will take all the knowledge, ingenuity, talent, and persistence we can muster" (p. 154).

Behavioral Approach: Parent Management Training

Parent management training (PMT) is one of the most successful and best-documented behavioral programs. PMT was developed by Patterson (see Forgatch and Patterson, 1998) based on his model of maladaptive parent-child relationships as central to the etiology of CD. PMT focuses on altering the interactions between parent and child so that prosocial rather than coercive behavior is reinforced. As the name implies, this is accomplished by training the parents to interact more effectively with the child, based on the principles of social learning theory. Parents learn to implement a number of behavior modification techniques, including the use of *positive reinforcement* for prosocial behavior and the use of *mild punishment* such as the use of a "time-out" chair. This is a technique with a large body of empirical research behind it, and we will describe it in more detail when we discuss intervention in Chapter 17.

Cognitive-Behavioral Intervention: Anger Coping Program

Larson and Lochman (2002) developed a group intervention for schoolchildren that has demonstrated effectiveness in reducing anger and aggression in a series of investigations. Following from the empirical literature on the developmental psychopathology of aggression, the groups are designed to address core issues such as anger management, perspective-taking, social problem solving, awareness of emotions, relaxation training, social skills, dealing with peer pressure, and self-regulation (Lochman et al., 2003). For example, in the groups, children learn self-control techniques such as calming self-talk and practice them *in vivo* while other children in the group attempt to taunt and tease them into losing their cool. The intervention takes place in the school setting and involves both teachers and parents so that they can reinforce children's use of these new skills outside of the groups. Follow-up studies show that the intervention is effective in reducing aggression and disruptive behavior at both home and school, increasing on-task behavior and perceived self-competence. Gains have been maintained for as long as 3 years after children attended the groups.

Systemic Family Treatment

In keeping with the origins of structural family therapy that Minuchin developed in his work with inner-city African American families, systemic approaches have been featured in a number of interventions designed to address the specific needs of ethnically diverse populations. An example of a culturally sensitive approach to family therapy is *Familias Unidas,* which was developed to reduce the risk for problem behavior among Hispanic immigrant youths (Coatsworth, Pantin, & Szapocznik, 2002). In a nutshell, the intervention is directed toward engaging parents in a participatory process that will assist them in overcoming the stresses of immigration and acculturation to a new society, increase their understanding of risk and protective factors in their child's social world, and help them to develop skills needed to cope effectively with their new cultural environment. In order to address feelings of marginalization and to empower parents, the primary intervention is implemented in small, supportive multiparent groups, called Parent Support Networks. One of the goals for these groups is "Bicultural Effectiveness Training," which promotes and honors the home culture's strengths while educating parents about mainstream culture in order to help them better understand and cope with the social contexts their children will encounter. In working with the family as a system, the clinicians strive to reduce conflict, increase cohesion, and improve both structure and warmth in the parent-child relationships. Parents are encouraged to become actively involved in their youth's school, to monitor peer activities, and to model prosocial skills for their children. Initial investigations of the intervention's effectiveness are promising, with increased parental involvement and decreased behavior problems over a 1-year period.

Multisystemic Therapy

Multisystemic therapy (MST) is recognized as the most well-supported intervention for conduct disorder and has produced an impressive rate of success with some of the most seriously disturbed antisocial youths (Henggeler et al., 2002). MST takes to heart the lesson learned by previous investigators—namely, that there are multiple roots of antisocial behavior. While focused on the family system and grounded in family systems theory, the treatment is individualized and flexible, offering a variety of interventions depending on the special needs of the particular youths. Thus, treatment may focus on family disharmony and school underachievement in one case and lack of social skills and parental unemployment in another. The therapist models an active, practical, and solution-focused approach: "You say you didn't understand the teacher's feedback on Casey's school report? Let's give him a call right now and ask for more information."

Empirical studies show the efficacy of the multisystemic approach with severely conduct-disordered youths, including chronically violent adolescents and sex offenders (Bourdin et al., 1995). Family communication is improved, with a reduction in family patterns of triangulation and lower levels of conflict between parents and children and between parents themselves. Follow-up studies have shown that for as long as 5 years following treatment, youths who receive MST have lower arrest rates than those who receive other forms of treatment.

Culturally Informed Intervention

Jamie Berry, a young African American psychologist, developed an intervention for incarcerated youths—the majority of whom are African American. Called MALE (Male Attitude Adjustments in Order to Lead

More Effective Lives), the program directly addresses problematic notions about masculinity that can lead to deviant behavior and violence, such as the hypermasculine ideal that violence makes you "more of a man." The intervention involves youths in group sessions in which they discuss portrayals of men in rap and hip-hop songs, movies, biographies, and poetry. The goal is to help the youths begin to consider the choices they make and the prices to be paid for those choices. In addition, youths are challenged to question whether the definition of being a "real man" requires being callous, violent, or derogatory to women. For his doctoral dissertation, Berry (2001) conducted an empirical test of the intervention and found that, compared to a control group, youths who participated evidence reduced hypermasculine attitudes, a more positive ethnic identity, and better social problem-solving skills.

Prevention

As Kazdin (1997b) notes, prevention efforts need to be as multifaceted and broad based as are the risk factors for CD. A combination of family management training for parents and interpersonal problem-solving skills training for children has been used to good effect in aggression prevention programs for kindergarteners and at-risk school-age children (McCord et al., 1994; Tremblay et al., 1995). Five, and even ten years later, those who had undergone these programs were achieving better in school and demonstrating less antisocial behavior than untreated youths.

Prevention of School Violence

A particular area of great concern for prevention efforts is the prevention of school violence—not only of the horrific massacres such as the one we introduced this chapter, but also of the ordinary, run-of-the-mill bullying that might provoke such

outbursts (U.S. Department of Education, 2002). By the end of the 1990s, national antibullying programs had been implemented in Norway, Finland, England, Ireland, and the Netherlands (Smith & Brain, 2000), while in the United States efforts remain on a local scale. Flannery and colleagues (2003) describe the development of PeaceBuilders, a violence prevention program for elementary-school children that aims to alter the climate of the school by improving children's social competence and providing alternatives to aggression as a means for solving interpersonal problems. The investigators selected eight schools, matched on the basis of social class and ethnic makeup, and randomly assigned half to the intervention. Among the over 4,000 children included in the study, those involved in PeaceBuilders were consistently rated higher in prosocial behavior and lower in aggression over the next 2 years. An even larger effort is described by Aber and associates (2003), who report positive results from the provision of their Resolving Conflicts Creatively Program to 11,160 first- to sixth-grade children in the New York City public schools. A benefit of the program is that the teachers were trained to implement it and thus could provide immediate reinforcement of the program's teachings in the classroom and on the playground throughout the school day.

In the previous five chapters, we have been concerned with disorders whose symptoms lie somewhere along the continuum between normal and abnormal. Depressed feelings, misconduct, anxiety, oppositionality, and inattentiveness all can be seen in well-functioning individuals across the life span. Our next chapter concerns a disorder that, like autism, lies at the extreme end of the continuum. The pervasive and erratic symptoms of schizophrenia lie far beyond the pale of normal development and thus present a major challenge to our ability to understand and treat the disorder.

Severe Deviation in Late Childhood and Adolescence– Schizophrenia

Like autism, schizophrenia is a severe, pervasive psychopathology that, in its extreme form, is incapacitating. However, in many other ways the two disorders differ. In this chapter we first present schizophrenia's descriptive characteristics and reconstruct its developmental pathway, including both risk and protective factors.

Definition and Characteristics

Definition

The relevant DSM-IV-TR criteria for Schizophrenia are presented in Table 11.1. The symptoms of schizophrenia have been clustered into three groups: positive, negative, and disorganized. *Positive symptoms* involve the presence of thought disorders, delusions, and hallucinations. *Negative symptoms* involve the absence of sociability, pleasure, energy, and affect. A third cluster of symptoms, *disorganized behavior,* includes disorganized speech, bizarre behavior, and poor attention. Next, we define and illustrate these various psychotic symptoms.

Hallucinations are sensory perceptions occurring in the absence of any appropriate external stimuli. Auditory hallucinations, such as hearing a voice saying "You are evil and should die," are more frequent than visual hallucinations, such as seeing a ghost with a burned and scarred face. The structure of hallucinations increases in complexity with age, while the content reflects age-appropriate concerns; for example, younger children have hallucinations about monsters and pets, while older children's hallucinations may involve sex. (See Russell, Bott, and Sammons, 1989.)

Table 11.1

DSM-IV-TR Criteria for Schizophrenia

A. *Characteristic symptoms:* Two (or more) of the following, each present for a significant portion of time during a 1-month period:
(1) Delusions
(2) Hallucinations
(3) Disorganized speech (e.g., frequent derailment or incoherence)
(4) Grossly disorganized or catatonic behavior
(5) Negative symptoms (i.e., affective flattening, alogia, or avolition)
B. *Social/occupational dysfunction:* When the onset is in childhood, failure to achieve expected level of interpersonal, academic, or occupational achievement.
C. *Duration:* Continuous signs of disturbance persist for at least 6 months.
D. *Relationship to a pervasive developmental disorder:* If there is a history of autism or other PDD, the diagnosis of schizophrenia is added only if prominent delusions or hallucinations are present for at least a month.

Adapted with permission from the *Diagnostic and Statistical Manual of Mental Disorders,* Fourth Edition Text Revision. Copyright 2000 by the American Psychiatric Association.

Hallucinations are not unique to schizophrenia. They may occur in response to drugs, but also are found in a number of other psychiatric disorders. For example, Altman, Collins, and Mundy (1997) found that 33 percent of psychiatrically disturbed but nonschizophrenic individuals reported hallucinations. They were particularly frequent in individuals with posttraumatic stress disorder. Hallucinations also can be found in typically developing populations. Preschoolers, for example, can have transient hallucinations in response to acute situational stress; for example, they may feel bugs crawling over their skin or see bugs in their beds (Volkmar et al., 1995).

Delusions are firmly held irrational beliefs that run counter to reality. As with hallucinations, delusions become more complex over the course of development, while their content reflects age-appropriate concerns; for example, a younger boy might believe his stepfather wants to poison him, while an older girl might think children at school are plotting to kidnap and molest her. These two examples illustrate delusions of *persecution*. There are *somatic* delusions, such as believing the body is emitting a foul odor or feces will come out of the mouth if the child speaks, and there are also delusions of *grandeur,* as in the example of a boy flipping through the pages of a book he has never seen before and claiming he knows everything the books says. Like hallucinations, delusions can also be found in disturbed but nonschizophrenic populations. For example, Altman, Collins, and Mundy (1997) found that 24 percent of disturbed, nonschizophrenic individuals had delusional ideas.

Disorganized speech often involves loose associations and illogical reasoning in which the child's language may be fragmented, dissociated, and bizarre. For example:

> It's open in front but closed behind. I'm open in front but closed behind. Did you see me today? I think I was here, but Mommy wasn't. They don't take it away from Mommy. My dolly won't mind. I won't mind. [Enumerates all the family members who won't mind.] I was here yesterday. Was I here today?

The primary irregularities in the speech of those with schizophrenia involve *pragmatics,* or the social use of language; *prosody,* or the melody of speech; *auditory processing,* or attending to what others say while ignoring irrelevant information; and *abstract language.* However, it is important to note that these peculiarities are seen in autism as well as in children with schizophrenia. (See Baltaxe and Simmons III, 1995.)

Disorganized behavior may be expressed by facial grimaces; odd postures and movements, such as persistent rocking while standing or sitting; disheveled or bizarre dress, such as wearing multiple coats, scarves, and hats on a hot day; unpredictable agitation; or bizarre, repetitive actions such as incessantly rubbing the forehead or slapping the wrist or scratching the skin to the point of producing bleeding sores. *Catatonic behavior* involves a marked lack of reactivity to the environment, which may include long periods of immobility (catatonic stupor); assuming inappropriate and bizarre poses (catatonic posturing); or purposeless excessive motor activity (catatonic excitement).

Social dysfunction may take a number of forms. Withdrawal is common, with children with schizophrenia often being oblivious to others, excessively preoccupied with their own thoughts, or puzzled by things happening around them. Lack of social skills may contribute to social isolation, particularly in regard to peers.

Subtypes of Schizophrenia

Subtypes are based on the prominent symptoms that are displayed. The *paranoid* type is characterized by the presence of significant delusions and sometimes auditory hallucinations of a persecutory or grandiose nature. This is the type with the best prognosis (Walker et al., 2004), but is rarely seen in childhood. The *disorganized* type, in contrast, has the worst prognosis and is more often seen in children. It is characterized by flat affect or emotions that are not appropriate to the content of the child's speech (e.g., silly laughter while talking about a lost pet); and disorganized behavior and disorganized speech that is odd, tangential, and not goal oriented. The *catatonic* type mainly displays psychomotor disturbances, including excessive rigidity, immobility, mutism, echolalia (parrot-like repetition of the words just spoken by another), or echopraxia (repetitive imitation of another's movements). The *undifferentiated* type includes none of the above features. In the *residual* type, the individual has undergone at least one psychotic episode in the past, but at present is not actively psychotic but shows some symptoms of the disturbance (e.g., flat affect, disorganized speech, odd beliefs).

Characteristics

Age of Onset

For our purposes the most important descriptive characteristic of schizophrenia is that it has two ages of onset: early onset (or childhood onset), which means it occurs prior to 14 to 15 years of age, and adolescent onset, which occurs between 14 to 15 years and young adulthood.

Prevalence

Childhood-onset schizophrenia is very rare. It is estimated that only 1 child in 10,000 will become schizophrenic (Remschmidt et al., 1994). Because this diagnosis is so rare in children, it is also difficult to study, which prevents us from drawing firm conclusions from the research. After childhood the number of cases of schizophrenia rises dramatically, with one study showing an approximately 10-fold increase in children between 12 and 15 years of age. This dramatic increase seems specific to schizophrenia, since it is not found in the other childhood psychotic reactions, such as those that occur in severe major depression or manic episodes (Häfner & Nowotny, 1995). (See Figure 11.1.)

Gender Differences

There is an interesting gender shift with age: Males predominate in early-onset cases, with a male-to-female ratio between 2 to 1 and 5 to 1, while the rates for males and females are more even in adolescence (Asarnow & Asarnow, 2003). The reasons for this shift are not known, but might reflect differences in etiology across gender or else the unfolding of normative maturational changes that emerge earlier for boys (Spauwen, Krabbendam, et al., 2003).

Socioeconomic Status, Ethnicity, and Culture

While studies of adults with schizophrenia show an excess of cases from *socioeconomically underprivileged* groups, studies of children and adolescents have yielded equivocal findings (Asarnow & Asarnow, 2003). No evidence exists for different prevalence for children and adolescents from different *ethnic* groups (Yee & Sigman, 1998). A World Health Organization collaborative study shows that the symptoms and incidence of schizophrenia in adults are highly similar across countries and cultures (Leff et al., 1991), but comparable data on children are not available.

Comorbidity

Taking child- and adolescent-onset schizophrenia together, there is evidence of a high rate of comorbidity. Russell, Bott, and Sammons (1989), for example, found that 68 percent of cases had another diagnosis, with *depression* being the most frequent

Figure 11.1

Increase in Schizophrenia
in Adolescence.

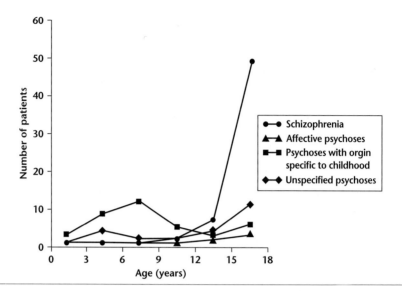

Source: Remschmidt et al., 1994.

(37 percent) followed closely by *conduct disorder* or *oppositional-defiant disorder* (31 percent).

Obsessive-compulsive disorder (OCD) appears to commonly co-occur in adolescents. Nechmad and colleagues (2003) found that in a sample of 50 adolescents with schizophrenia, 26 percent met DSM-IV criteria for OCD.

In addition, youths with schizophrenia also often show *suicidal* ideation and behavior (Asarnow, Neuchterlein, et al., 2001). The highest risk for suicide appears to be in the 2 years following the first psychotic episode. Suicide during this period is predicted by a history of self-harming behavior, prolonged duration of psychosis, a deteriorating course, and substance abuse—for example, Verdoux and colleagues (2001) found that youths who abused substances during the first 2 years after a psychotic break were 7 times more likely to attempt suicide. Aguilar and colleagues (2003) found that among adolescents and adults with schizophrenia who attempted suicide, two distinct clinical types could be differentiated based upon the reasons that predominated: *psychotic* (e.g., rationales derived from delusional thinking) and *depressive*. To understand how psychosis might lead to suicide, it is important to

recognize how terrifying and bewildering a psychotic episode can be, and how devastating to confront the fact that one has a chronic mental illness in which such episodes are likely to recur. (See Box 11.1.)

Differential Diagnosis

As we mentioned at the outset of this chapter, schizophrenia must be differentiated from *autism*. In the past, it was believed that both schizophrenia and autism should be regarded as two manifestations of the same underlying psychopathology. The data, however, have not supported this assumption. While it is true that some children with autism later develop schizophrenia, they do so at no higher rate than children in the general population (Klinger & Dawson, 1996). The clinical picture of the two is different also in that autism lacks the delusions and hallucinations, the loose associations, and the mood disturbances that characterize schizophrenia. The age of onset and developmental course are also different. Autism appears in the first 30 months of life, whereas schizophrenia begins in later childhood or adolescence. Schizophrenia also is marked by progressive declines in functioning, whereas

Box 11.1 | **Case Study: A First-Person Account of Adolescent-Onset Schizophrenia**

"During the second semester of my senior year, I had only a three-hour carpentry course at South Side High School, so in the afternoon I took a job at the pizzeria as a cook. One day at the pizzeria, when I started doing the cooking and the prep work, Pat, Kelly, and the boss started talking around in circles. It seemed as though the devil was taking over their bodies when they talked to me. Kelly started talking on the phone, and it seemed he was using a voice other than his own. That confused me. I was even more confused when he told me that I didn't have to work for the rest of the day.

"I drove home and found no one there. I tried to sleep on the couch, but I couldn't. I got up and went to my car. I started it up and drove to my high school. I met Scott, a friend, there and tried to tell him what was bothering me, but he was between classes and didn't have much time to talk. I went to the school library where I found Bill. But he wasn't much help either. Then I

walked over to the school office where I decided to call the police and tell them of my problem of hearing strange voices. I asked if the Police Chief would come and listen to what I had to say.

"He did. He picked me up at school, drove me around, and listened to me. Finally, he had me drive my car to the police station where I talked with another police office. The police officer called my parents. Soon the four of us were in a room. My father seemed to understand me. My mother and the police officer were talking with me, but it seemed my father was playing with them with his thoughts . . .

"At home, my brother Alex and our pets appeared different, as though my father was using them with his brain. My father could take over people's minds and bodies with his brain waves. My father and I would watch television together and communicate without saying a word. My father's friends from work had a club of people who prac-

ticed brainwashing different people. They wanted to practice on me. They took over the entire household except for me and my father. My father and I would think of different people or objects. We did this to block out minds so they couldn't capture our minds or bodies. They gave up the next day.

"My parents took me to the Lake City Hospital to find out what was happening to me. At the hospital we met my family doctor and a couple of other people, none of whom could figure out what was happening to me. They asked questions, took my blood pressure, and took blood samples. I tried to leave that night. I was urged on by a song from ABBA, but two big guys in white coats took me back to my room. The next morning when I was served my breakfast, I tasted and smelled my food a little before I ate it all."

Source: Emmons, Geiser, Kaplan, and Harrow, 1997.

autism is highly stable. (See Table 11.2 for further detail.)

Schizophrenia is not the only disorder in which psychotic symptoms are seen. Therefore, it is important to distinguish between schizophrenia and severe mood disorders, including *major depression with psychotic features* and *bipolar disorder* (see Chapter 9), both of which involve the acute onset of psychotic symptoms consequent to a dramatic shift in mood state. However, there appear to be relationships among these disorders in that longitudinal research shows that some youths who initially present

with schizophrenia go on to develop bipolar illness (McClellan et al., 2001).

DSM-IV-TR also includes a diagnosis of *schizoaffective disorder,* which stands at the boundary between mood disorder and psychosis, including some but not all of the characteristics of each. The prognosis for schizoaffective disorder also lies on the middle of the continuum, better than schizophrenia but worse than a simple mood disorder (Walker et al., 2004).

A recently identified group of children are diagnosed with atypical psychosis or *multidimensionally impaired disorder* (MDI) (Jacobsen & Rapoport,

Table 11.2

Summary of Premorbid Developmental Predictors of Schizophrenia

Developmental Deviations	Developmental Periods			
	Infancy	Toddler-Preschool	Middle Childhood	Adolescence
Motor and Sensory	Lags in gross and fine coordination; movement abnormalities	Lags in gross and fine coordination	Deviant but not specific to or predictive of schizophrenia	Clumsy but no longer deviant
Passivity	Underaroused and unresponsive; poor muscle tone	Low energy level		
Speech	Little babbling and imitation	Delayed; poor communication	Vague, confused, unclear	
Social Adjustment	Socially odd, unresponsive, flat affect, poor eye contact	"Loner," "hyper"; anxious and hostile with peers	Increased disturbance in boys only	
Attention			Attention deficits	Distractible
Cognitive and Achievement Scores			Below average	Significant declines

1998). These children do not meet the full criteria for schizophrenia, but exhibit symptoms in the spectrum such as delusions, hallucinations, affect dysregulation, poor impulse control, and inattention. Longitudinal research shows that children with MDI have an earlier age of onset and more severe cognitive and behavioral difficulties than do children with schizophrenia. Further, results of a long-term follow-up showed that half of the children with MDI later developed severe mood disorders, with or without psychotic symptoms, while the other half went on to develop disruptive behavior disorders with no signs of psychosis. These findings have suggested to investigators in the field that MDI is a separate diagnostic entity from schizophrenia, with different precursors and consequences.

The Developmental Dimension

Is all schizophrenia one? Evidence to date suggests that child-onset schizophrenia and adolescent-onset schizophrenia share essentially the same features with the adult disorder and can be diagnosed with

the same criteria (Asarnow, Tompson, & McGrath, 2004). The similarities include not only the symptoms that characterize the disorder but also the findings concerning genetic transmission, autonomic functioning, and brain structure and function. While the data regarding childhood schizophrenia are meager, however, a number of developmental differences have emerged. (Here we follow Asarnow and Asarnow, 2003.)

Onset

First, childhood schizophrenia typically has a slow, insidious onset rather than an acute one. Therefore, children show a course of chronic impairment preceding the diagnosis of the disorder, complicating the delineation of the precise age of onset of the disorder as well as making it difficult to differentiate premorbid (preexising) or comorbid symptoms. For example, children often present with symptoms of ADHD prior to and during psychotic episodes. Does this mean that ADHD is a developmental precursor to schizophrenia, an earlier manifestation of the illness, a comorbid disorder, or merely a mislabeling of the disorganized thinking and behavior characteristic of schizophrenia? As yet, we do not know and further prospective longitudinal research will be essential to answering these questions.

Symptoms

In regard to clinical manifestations, there are differences between the symptoms of child-onset and adult schizophrenia. Delusions, hallucinations, and formal thought disorder are rarely seen prior to age 7. Delusions in particular are less frequent in children than in adults. While all subtypes of schizophrenia may be seen in adolescence, young people are more likely to present with the disorganized or undifferentiated subtypes and more rarely with the paranoid subtype.

The symptoms and social impairment are also more severe in children than they are in adults, while the outcome is less favorable. In regard to sex differences, the shift to a comparable number of males and females in adolescence is not typical of adults, for which males outnumber females.

Because the signs and symptoms differ across development, there is concern that diagnosticians may overlook children who are beginning to show early signs of the disorder but do not meet the full adult criteria. Ideally, the diagnostic criteria would be adjusted to account for such developmental trends in clinical presentation.

Normative Developmental Processes

The diagnosis of schizophrenia in young children also is complicated by immaturities in language and cognitive skills. Children's inability to describe their inner experiences makes it difficult for the clinician to evaluate their internal states and perceptions. Further, as we know, young children are in the preoperational stage of development, during which magical beliefs abound and the boundary between reality and fantasy is diffuse. (For example, consider the third scenario presented in the opening to Chapter 1.) Consequently, careful thought must be given to discriminating between psychotic thinking or delusional ideas and the normative magical thought processes of early childhood. Similarly, children

lagging in language development may communicate in ways that strike the listener as illogical and disorganized, but that should not be confused with true thought disorder.

Developmental Pathways to Schizophrenia

Identifying Precursors to Schizophrenia

The developmental unfolding of schizophrenia is divided into three phases: the *premorbid* phase, prior to the onset of the disorder; the *prodromal* phase, during which the early signs of the disorder begin to emerge; and the *acute* phase, in which the full-blown syndrome is evident. Subsequently, phases of recovery, residual, and/or chronic symptomatology may be seen. (See Figure 11.2.) Discovering precursors to the disorder is important both to understanding the nature of the psychopathology and to developing programs aimed at preventing its occurrence. While prospective longitudinal data provide the best evidence for isolating causal factors, gathering such data is a difficult undertaking in the case of schizophrenia. Let us consider why.

Methodological Challenges

For one thing, longitudinal data that follow children from their earliest years to the onset of the disorder are few and far between—and for good reason, given the daunting methodological difficulties of locating cases in such a rare disturbance. With schizophrenia occurring in less than 1 percent of the population, one would have to follow 10,000 randomly selected infants in order to obtain approximately 10 adolescents who will develop the disorder. While such a study is extremely rare, we will in fact encounter some impressive examples. For example, the National Child Development Study (NCDS) included 98 percent of all births in England, Scotland, and Wales registered from March 3 to March 9, 1958, and evaluated the participants again when they were 7, 11, 16, and 23 years of age (Crow, Done, & Sacker, 1995). But consider the effort and cost involved. Of the 12,537 individuals in the final sample, the investigators identified 57 with schizophrenia.

Figure 11.2   Natural Course of Schizophrenia Showing the Time Frame for Critical Phases of the Schizophrenic Illness.

The horizontal line represents the time dimension; the vertical dimension represents functional decline.

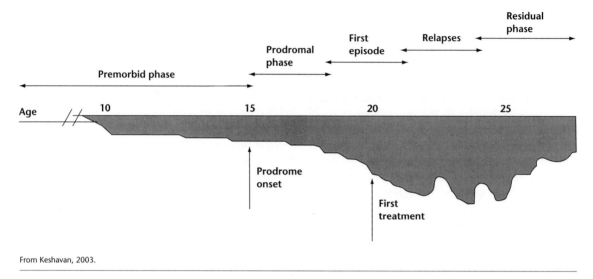

From Keshavan, 2003.

Even with such impressive prospective longitudinal data, the premorbid and prodromal stages are difficult to distinguish. The onset of the disorder is preceded by a long period of behavioral deviations, some of them subtle and some of them with origins in the very early stages of life. To what extent are these deviations in early childhood truly premorbid, and to what extent do they represent a prodrome of the full disorder? This remains a matter for debate and further research.

Diversity in Schizophrenia

The nature of schizophrenia itself further complicates matters, given that the disorder is not a single entity but rather is a family of disturbances with a number of subtypes. This complexity gives rise to a research dilemma: Either study subtypes, thereby reducing the typically small number of cases even further, or combine the data from the entire group and risk obscuring findings concerning subtypes. Further, both the symptom picture and the definition of schizophrenia itself change over time, presenting the researcher with a moving target. The problem of attrition, although common to all longitudinal studies, is even more acute in severely disturbed populations who are the most likely to drop out of the research as time goes on, either because of uncooperativeness or because they have drifted on to other locations without leaving a way to be reached.

Last, there is evidence that not all children who will become schizophrenic travel the same path; on the contrary, they may take distinctly different routes. Therefore, we will also need to examine these differences among pathways.

With these challenges and limitations in mind, we now review the available evidence.

Premorbid Development

Infancy

Motor and Sensory Deviations   Deviations in motor and sensory development along with passivity and deviant speech characterize infants at risk for becoming schizophrenic (Gooding & Iacono, 1995). More specifically, there is a lag in motor and sensory development and deficiencies in gross and fine motor coordination. Walker, Savole, and Davis (1994) also found in at-risk children limb position and movement abnormalities, including choreoathetoid movements (i.e., involuntary twisting and slow, irregular, snakelike movements). All of these motor abnormalities are at their height in the first 2 years of life and subsequently diminish. *Passivity* is evidenced by the at-risk infant's being underaroused and unresponsive to external stimuli, by poor alertness and orientation, and by poor muscle tone. There is some evidence that passivity may be predictive of adult schizophrenia (Gooding & Iacono, 1995).

Speech Delay   Finally, there is deviant speech development evidenced by the paucity of babbling and slowness in imitating sounds (Cantor, 1988; Watkins, Asarnow, & Tanguay, 1988).

Attachment Disturbances   Only two studies concern attachment, and their findings are inconclusive. A special subgroup of at-risk neonates were found to be less cuddly and consolable, but this did not characterize the group as a whole (Watt et al., 1984). There is evidence that separation from the caregiver in the 1st year increases the risk for schizophrenia, but only in infants already at genetic risk (i.e., whose mothers are also schizophrenic) (Olin & Mednick, 1996).

Toddlerhood Through Preschool

Motor and Language Deficits   Many of the deviations in infancy continue into the toddler-preschool period: the abnormality in gross and fine motor coordination, the passivity and low energy level, seriously delayed speech, and poor communication. The most significant impairments are seen in children who have an early onset of psychosis; for example, Nicholson and colleagues (2000) found premorbid deficits in speech and language and motor development in 50 percent of those who developed schizophrenia by 12 years of age.

Socioemotional Deviations   Cantor (1988) and Watkins, Asarnow, and Tanguay (1988) found social oddities, including a preference for being alone,

perseverative play, and being "hyper" with peers, along with bizarre responses to the social environment. The children may be anxious and hostile with others and yet be affectively flat, withdrawn, and isolated in their relationship with their mothers. The meager data on parenting by mothers who are schizophrenic suggest that they are less affectionately involved, more hostile, and less stimulating than mothers in control groups.

In an ingenious study, Walker and Lewine (1990) obtained home movies of 5 adult-onset schizophrenic patients and their healthy siblings taken during infancy and early childhood. The films were viewed by 19 judges who were blind to the psychiatric outcome of the participants. Although none of the participants had any identified psychiatric disorders in childhood, those who went on to develop schizophrenia were reliably identified by virtue of their lack of responsiveness, poor eye contact, flat affect, and poor fine and gross motor coordination.

Middle Childhood

Motoric Deficits   As is found in the toddler years, children at increased risk for schizophrenia display more neuromotoric deficits, particularly those reflecting motoric "overflow" (e.g., tremors, involuntary repetitive movements). Further, in their study of 6-year-olds at risk for schizophrenia, McNeil and colleagues (2003) found that children with neuromotoric deficits were more likely than their peers to display a host of other psychiatric diagnoses, anxiety proneness, interpersonal difficulties, and poor general functioning. Thus, motor difficulties potentially identify a subgroup that is particularly vulnerable to the development of schizophrenia and other disorders.

Attention Deficits   Attention deficits are both temporally stable and predictive of future development of schizophrenia. These deficits are evidenced on a number of tasks: the ability to repeat numbers forward and backward, letter cancellation, and the ability to detect a given letter in an array of other letters presented at a very brief interval (Gooding & Iacono, 1995).

Social Deficits   The social deficits in child- and adolescent-onset schizophrenia are pervasive and significant, more so than in the adult-onset version of the disorder (Hollis, 2003). As a matter of fact, many of these children demonstrate symptoms consistent with Asperger syndrome, autism, or other forms of pervasive developmental disorder during the premorbid phase.

Premorbid social withdrawal, poor interpersonal relationships, and social skills deficits are specifically predictive of negative symptoms in early-onset schizophrenia, including affective flattening, asociability, and poverty of speech (McClellan et al., 2003). The evidence concerning positive symptoms of schizophrenia is inconsistent, with one study finding schizophrenia to be related to excitability, aggression, and disruptive behaviors in childhood and two other studies finding no relation. Thus, negative symptoms may reflect enduring predispositions and have roots in the premorbid phase of the disturbance, while positive symptoms may not have such roots (Walker et al., 1996).

Cognitive and Achievement Deficits   In regard to general intelligence and academic achievement, Crow, Done, and Sacker's (1995) NCDS found widespread impairment in children who went on to develop schizophrenia. Not only was a measure of general intelligence below that of all other groups, but reading and arithmetic achievement also significantly lagged. Further, studies show that premorbid intelligence, language, reading, and spelling are more negatively affected in those with early-onset schizophrenia than those with the adult-onset form of the disorder (Hollis, 2004; Vourdas et al., 2003). When we describe studies of brain development in children with schizophrenia later in this chapter, the likely reason will become clear.

General Psychopathology   Children destined to develop schizophrenia stand out from their peers in ways that often will call them to the attention of mental health professionals. Roff and Fultz (2003) conducted a study of 148 boys who were seen in mental health clinics prior to the onset of schizophrenia. Those who later went on to receive the diagnosis were distinguished from other clinic boys by virtue of having more problems in the areas of attention, memory, and motor coordination. They were also more generally disturbed than the other boys. The authors suggest a developmental pathway by which poor motor coordination and attention are associated with impulsive, inappropriate behavior, which results in peer rejection and increasing secluciveness in adolescence.

Using data from the New York High-Risk Project, a longitudinal study of the children of schizophrenic parents, Ott and colleagues (2002) analyzed videotapes made when the children were about age 9 to determine whether subtle signs of schizophrenia-related disturbances could be seen. Among those who went on to receive a schizophrenia diagnosis, raters observed significantly more signs of thought disorder and positive and negative symptoms. Here again, we see the fuzziness of the boundaries between the premorbid and prodromal stages. Long before the signs and symptoms are clear enough to warrant a diagnosis, children destined for schizophrenia have taken an aberrant path through development.

Adolescence

Inattention   Distractibility, or a deficit in selective attention, emerges as a strong precursor to schizophrenia in adolescence. It also may be an important prognostic indicator (Harvey, 1991).

Motor Difficulties   In regard to motor development, Crow, Done, and Sacker's (1995) NCDS found that prior signs of deviant development were no longer present in adolescence and motor coordination was age-appropriate. However, the at-risk group was rated as clumsy when compared with the other groups.

Cognitive Deficits   Finally, there is a decline in IQ scores that is greater than the decline found in the test scores of children whose mothers are depressed. Achievement test scores of adolescents destined for a schizophrenia diagnosis also decline significantly between 13 and 16 years of age (Fuller et al., 2002). In Vourdas and colleagues' (2004) study comparing early- and late-onset schizophrenia, the investigators found increasing declines in functioning across the board during adolescence, particularly in boys.

Summary of the Premorbid Stage

As the available evidence shows, when schizophrenia begins in childhood, it has a profound effect on emerging competencies in all spheres of development, including the emotional, cognitive, social, and academic. Further, premorbid childhood- and adolescent-onset schizophrenia are characterized by more pervasive and severe developmental impairments than is adult-onset schizophrenia (Hollis, 2004). Motor deviations are present from infancy on but tend to be "outgrown" by adolescence, while deviations in speech and communication seem to be important throughout the entire developmental period. Passivity (a possible precursor of the negative symptoms of schizophrenia) has been documented in the infancy through preschool period, but its subsequent fate has not been charted. Problems in social adjustment are present as early as the toddler period and continue through middle childhood, particularly for boys. Deviations in attention, which are predictive of schizophrenia, have been found from middle childhood on, as have cognitive deficits. In addition to widespread developmental delays, poor general adjustment and the presence of schizophrenia spectrum traits characterize children who will go on to earn a schizophrenia diagnosis.

Are these premorbid variables risk factors for, or precursors to, the development of schizophrenia? The fact that some individuals develop schizophrenia in the absence of these early cognitive and social deficits suggests that the developmental impairments accompany but are not causally related to or necessary to the emergence of the disorder (Hollis, 2004).

Prodromal Phase

Childhood-onset schizophrenia is typically prefaced by a gradual and insidious deterioration in functioning prior to the onset of psychosis. Changes may include social isolation, bizarre preoccupations, deteriorating self-care skills, dysphoria, and alterations in sleep and appetite (McClellan et al., 2001). This prodromal phase may last from days and weeks to months and years.

For example, Hollis (2000) describes the Maudsley study of adolescent psychosis, in which approximately 100 youths ranging from 10 to 17 years were assessed over the course of 11 years. Retrospectively examining case notes at the time of the first psychotic break, the investigators identified a prodromal phase averaging a year in length previous to the onset of positive symptoms. During the prodromal phase, the youths evidenced increasing social withdrawal, declining school performance, and uncharacteristically odd behavior, which in hindsight were recognized by the investigators as early negative symptoms of schizophrenia. Because the prodromal phase is ushered in by these relatively more subtle negative symptoms, which only later shade into more overt psychotic behavior such as hallucinations and delusions, early recognition of the disorder is made exceedingly difficult.

Moreover—and complicating the diagnostician's task further—positive psychotic symptoms in children are not necessarily predictive of schizophrenia, but rather are associated with the development of a number of disorders. In contrast, negative symptoms are associated specifically with schizophrenia as well as mood disorder-related psychotic reactions. Negative symptoms also are predicted by more severe developmental impairments, predict a more pathological course of illness, and are related to the familial risk of schizophrenia, suggesting an underlying genetic and developmental mechanism (Hollis, 2004).

Acute Phase

As we know, while the acute phase is characterized by overtly psychotic behavior and symptoms, child- and adolescent-onset schizophrenia presents differently than the adult-onset version of the disorder. Child-onset schizophrenia is characterized by more evident negative symptoms (e.g., flattened or inappropriate affect, withdrawal, odd mannerisms), and more disorganized behavior. Well-formed delusions, such as persecutory beliefs, are rarer in young people, although other features of thought disorder (loose associations, illogical thinking) are generally present (McClellan et al., 2001). The acute phase generally lasts from 1 to 6 months, or longer depending on the youth's response to treatment.

Recovery Phase

For the next several months following the acute phase, there usually is a period of continued but less severe impairment, characterized by negative symptoms such as lack of energy and social withdrawal (McClellan et al., 2001). Some will develop a postschizophrenic depression in which they display dysphoria and flat affect.

Residual or Chronic Phase

At this stage of the disorder, we see a divergence of pathways. Although still affected by negative symptoms, many youths will experience periods of several months or longer during which they are not acutely psychotic. In contrast, other youths will be unresponsive to treatment and will remain chronically symptomatic. Generally, chronic schizophrenia follows a pattern of cycling through the above phases, with a further deterioration in functioning following each acute episode (McClellan et al., 2001).

Multiple Pathways to Schizophrenia

So far we have raised the question, What are the precursors of child- and adolescent-onset schizophrenia? The best answers come from research designed to compare populations at risk for schizophrenia with populations at risk for affective psychosis, as well as with a normal control group. But there is a further question: Do all at-risk children follow the same path to the ultimate psychopathology, or are there different ways of arriving at the same end point? Answering this question requires a *within-group* analysis of data obtained on at-risk children.

Walker and colleagues (1996) provide such a within-group analysis using a statistical technique called cluster analysis. They found that their follow-back data clustered in two groups. Cluster I children showed more behavioral and attentional problems and more rapid escalation of problems than did Cluster II children. For example, Cluster I children were both more withdrawn and delinquent and had more social problems than children in Cluster II. Moreover, Cluster I children were significantly different from their healthy siblings on all behavioral and attentional problems, whereas Cluster II children were not.

Cluster I children had more motor abnormalities and a higher rate of obstetrical complications. This latter finding helps explain why some investigators, such as Crow, Done, and Sacker (1995), found no difference in obstetrical complications while others did—namely, the data depend on what proportion of Cluster I and Cluster II children one happens to capture in the population.

Walker and colleagues (1996) conclude that there are two premorbid subtypes, one showing early, persistent, and escalating deviations, and the other showing no difference from healthy children. These groups correspond to two different kinds of anecdotal information from parents, some saying that the child with schizophrenia was "different from the beginning," and others saying they were particularly dismayed by the onset because their child had been "perfectly normal." Both may be right. Incidentally, this finding is important for clinical child psychologists to know so that they will not suspect parents of covering up deviations when they paint a picture of a well-adjusted childhood for a child who has been diagnosed with schizophrenia.

Next Walker and colleagues (1996) analyzed their data on precursors in terms of gender differences, with equally important findings. As have other investigators, they found that males had a predominance of both externalizing problems (i.e., acting out, disruptive behavior) *and* internalizing problems (i.e., social isolation), while the females had predominately internalizing problems (i.e., anxiety and depression). Thus, only girls conform to the stereotype of the preschizophrenic as being withdrawn; boys are more apt to be described as being emotionally unstable and having a "stormy" time.

Summary

In sum, there is no single path to schizophrenia; rather, there are different routes to the same outcome.

Some children will be disturbed in many areas of functioning from an early age and become increasingly so, while others will be essentially normal before schizophrenia makes its appearance. In a like manner, the route will be different for males than for females—the former having both externalizing and internalizing problems; the latter having primarily internalizing ones. The finding that different disturbances can lead to the same outcome is an example of **equifinality.**

Etiology

The prevailing theories of the etiology of schizophrenia rely on a **diathesis-stress** model. "Diathesis" is another term for a vulnerability or a predisposition to develop schizophrenia. Stressors increase the likelihood that schizophrenia will actually appear. Among the diatheses, biological factors are most prominent.

The Biological Context

There are four sources of evidence concerning the organic etiology of schizophrenia: genetic studies, neurobiological studies (including studies of the brain, autonomic nervous system, and neurochemistry), studies of neuropsychological variables such as inattention and poor executive functioning, and studies of prenatal and birth complications.

Genetic Factors

Familial Transmission There is little doubt that genetic factors play an etiologic role in schizophrenia. More than 40 family studies spanning several decades of research show that risk to different relatives of individuals who are schizophrenic is considerably greater than the general population risk. Moreover, risk varies as a function of the degree of genetic relatedness to the affected individual. Thus, the highest concordance is between monozygotic twins, who have 100 percent of their genes in common. The specific risk in this case is 48 percent, which is approximately 3 times the 14 percent concordance rate for dizygotic twins (Moldin & Gottesman, 1997).

For example, the UCLA Family Study (Asarnow et al., 2001) compared the likelihood of schizophrenic spectrum disorders in the first-degree relatives of 148 children with schizophrenia as compared to 368 children with ADHD and 206 community controls. The investigators used careful methodology, utilizing structured diagnostic interviews conducted by clinicians who were blind to the diagnoses of the proband. The results showed a significantly higher prevalence of schizophrenia among the parents of children with the disorder, and these parents generally had an early age of onset. The relative risk (the ratio of risk for parents of children with schizophrenia versus parents of community children) was 17, considerably higher than the three- to six-fold increase seen in families of adults with schizophrenia. Similarly, Nicolson and colleagues (2003) found that 24.74 percent of parents of patients with childhood-onset schizophrenia had disorders in the schizophrenia spectrum, in contrast to 11.35 percent of those with adult-onset schizophrenia and 1.55 percent of parents of typically developing children. Taken together, these findings suggest that childhood-onset schizophrenia may be an even more familial, genetically driven version of the disorder than the adult-onset type.

Mechanism of Transmission Exactly which genes are involved in the transmission of schizophrenia is not known at present. The strongest current evidence implicates microdeletions on chromosomes 22q11, which occur more frequently among individuals with schizophrenia, especially childhood-onset schizophrenia (Usiskin et al., 1999).

However, the challenge of detecting and isolating a disease gene is considerable; for example, the time between establishment of linkage to identification of the precise disease gene for Huntington's disease was 10 years (Moldin & Gottesman, 1997). Moreover, genetic influences likely reflect the impact of "many genes of small probabilistic effect rather than the sledge hammer effect of single deterministic genes" (Rende & Plomin, 1995, p. 302). Rende and Plomin also caution that symptoms influenced by genes do not necessarily coincide with symptoms used to define a disorder. Genetic influences can cut across different disorders, such as depression and anxiety, or can influence areas of functioning not considered as core symptoms, such as attention. This lack of a nice correspondence between genes that transmit the psychopathology and the defining clinical manifestations of the psychopathology itself adds just one more complication to research on genetic etiology.

Gene-Environment Interaction   The genetic loading still allows for environmental factors to play a major role in the final production of schizophrenia. One example of the interaction of genetic and environmental factors is a classic Finnish study (Tienari et al., 1983) in which 92 children of mothers who were schizophrenic and mothers who were not were adopted into healthy or disturbed family environments. All the children who subsequently became schizophrenic were in the schizophrenic-mother, disturbed-family group. Schizophrenia did not develop when children of mothers who were not schizophrenic were adopted into disturbed families. Thus, the psychopathology was the result of the combination of a genetically vulnerable child being raised in a disturbed family environment. Equally important, the nondisturbed family protected the at-risk child from becoming schizophrenic.

Another example of gene-environment interaction is the finding that the incidence of schizophrenia increased seven-fold in African-Caribbean children whose parents had immigrated to London (Hutchinson et al., 1996). Possible environmental risks include prenatal rubella infection, drug abuse, and factors associated with assimilation. However, pinpointing which variables in the environment are critical stressors for schizophrenia is as daunting a task as discovering which genes are crucial for its production.

Central Nervous System Dysfunctions

The lion's share of research on central nervous system (CNS) dysfunctions has been conducted on adults with schizophrenia. A number of areas of the brain have been implicated, particularly the hippocampus, frontal cortex, and selected left hemisphere structures. However, in spite of vigorous research efforts, one specific pathogenic brain

mechanism has not yet been identified. No one brain lesion is found in all individuals with schizophrenia, and those that have been found are not unique to schizophrenia (Asarnow & Asarnow, 2003). Further, in contrast to the research on adults, research on children with schizophrenia is meager, consisting at times of the study of a single individual (Jacobsen & Rapoport, 1998).

Cerebral Volume   One highly consistent finding in the research to date points to a smaller total *cerebral volume* in children and adults with schizophrenia. This reduction is greater than that found in adults, and the reduction is strongly correlated with negative symptoms in the children. The reduction appears to be accounted for by loss of *gray matter,* particularly in the cerebellar and frontal areas. For example, Thompson and colleagues (2001) conducted a longitudinal study in which they obtained MRI scans from youths with early-onset schizophrenia and compared them to typically developing adolescents. Repeat scans were conducted at three time points, separated by 2-year intervals. The results showed that over the 5-year period, there was a dynamic wave to the loss of gray matter in the early-onset youths, which progressed toward the anterior of the brain into the temporal lobes, engulfing the sensorimotor and prefrontal cortical areas, and the frontal visual areas. While the temporal lobes were virtually unaffected at the time of onset of the disorder, loss of gray matter in this area became pervasive over the 5-year period. (See Figure 11.3.) The patterns of change were associated with the severity of psychotic symptoms and mirrored the neuropsychological impairments shown by the youths in auditory, visual, and executive functions. Loss of gray matter appears to be specific to schizophrenia, given that it is not seen in children with multidimensional impairment or atypical psychosis (Gogtay et al., 2004).

As gray matter shrinks, there is a concomitant increase in the size of the *ventricles,* the fluid-filled cavities in the brain (Kumra et al., 2000; Sowell et al., 2000). For example, over a 2-year period, one study documented that the ventricular volume increased more rapidly in children with schizophrenia

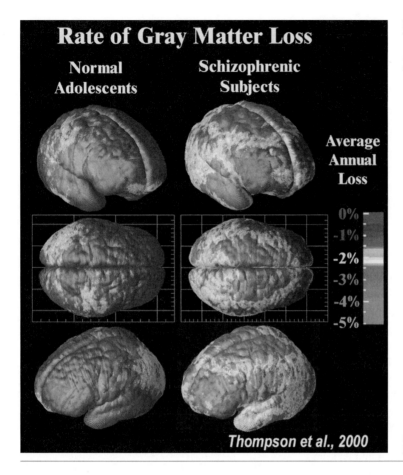

From Thompson, Vidal, Giedd, Gochman, Blumenthal, Nicolson, et al., 2001.

Figure 11.3

Rate of Gray Matter Loss in Early-Onset Schizophrenia Versus Typical Adolescence.

than in typically developing children (Sporn et al., 2003).

Recent data suggest that there are *gender differences* in gray matter loss. Collinson and colleagues (2003) found that females with early-onset schizophrenia tended to have smaller right hemispheres than did typically developing females, whereas males with early-onset schizophrenia had asymmetry of the left hemisphere.

Further, a provocative recent study by Lenane and colleagues (2003) discovered that smaller cerebral volumes and loss of gray matter are also found in the healthy siblings of patients with childhood-onset schizophrenia. Thus, these brain abnormalities may be an important genetic marker for the disorder.

Are these changes in gray matter causes or consequences of schizophrenia? An important longitudinal study by Pantelis and colleagues (2003) provides some insight. Individuals displaying prodromal symptoms underwent MRI scans and were followed up 12 months later. At the initial assessment, those who went on to develop schizophrenia differed from their peers by virtue of having less gray matter in the right medial temporal, lateral temporal, inferior frontal, and cingulate cortex. At the follow-up evaluation, those who had developed schizophrenia evidenced a loss of gray matter in the left parahippocampal, fusiform, orbitofrontal and cerebellar cortices, as well as the cingulate gyrus. These data suggest that some of the changes in gray matter associated with schizophrenia predate the disorder, while others emerge at the time of its onset and progressively worsen over the course of the disorder.

Jacobsen and Rapoport (1998) conclude that the progressive changes in the brain after the onset of schizophrenia, coupled with the evidence of continued intellectual deterioration both before and after the appearance of schizophrenia, suggest that the pathological underpinnings of childhood schizophrenia do not consist of a single static lesion or event but rather a continuous or multievent process of neurodegeneration. These massive CNS changes provide a convincing explanation for the declines in cognitive and academic performance over the course of early-onset schizophrenia.

Brain Morphology   In another MRI study, White and colleagues (2003) examined the brain surface of 42 children and adolescents with schizophrenia and compared them to those of 24 healthy controls. The investigators found a reduction in cortical thickness in those with schizophrenia, particularly in the tissue underlying the sulci, the furrows of the cortex. In addition, the sulci were more flattened, while the gyri, the areas of raised surface of the brain, were more steeply curved in the young people with schizophrenia. The authors suggest that these abnormalities in brain morphology may affect communication and interconnectivity within the parts of the brain.

Corpus Collosum   Another developmental brain scan study documents progressive changes in the corpus collosum, the structure that interconnects the two hemispheres of the brain, in individuals with childhood-onset schizophrenia. Keller and colleagues (2003) obtained MRI scans from 55 children at the time of diagnosis and at 2-year intervals throughout adolescence and young adulthood. These scans were compared to those of 113 typically developing children matched for age and gender. While there were no differences at the time of the initial scan, longitudinal data showed a significant difference in the developmental trajectory of the splenium, which became progressively smaller in those with childhood-onset schizophrenia, even after adjusting for the overall decrease in total cerebral volume.

Neurochemistry

Neurotransmitters   Because of its proven efficacy in treatment, *dopamine,* a monoamine neurotransmitter ("chemical messenger") essential to normal nerve activity, plays a prominent role in neurochemical research concerning the etiology of schizophrenia. Specifically, drugs that block the transmission of dopamine control psychotic symptoms, while those that produce excessive release of dopamine are associated with the intensification of psychotic symptoms. However, the effect is not specific to schizophrenia but applies to a number of psychoses. Moreover, therapeutic effectiveness in controlling symptoms cannot be taken as proof of an etiological hypothesis because cures are not necessarily related to causes (Häfner, 1995). Recent research has begun to examine other neurochemicals, including glutamate, an excitatory neurotransmitter, and GABA, an inhibitory neurotransmitter (Walker et al., 2004).

Neurohormones   Walker and Walder (2003) outline research on the role of cortisol and the hypothalamo-pituitary-adrenal (HPA) system in the development of schizophrenia. They argue that stress results in heightened release of cortisol, which exacerbates psychotic symptoms by increasing dopamine activity. Hormonal changes associated with adolescence might act on the vulnerable brain to intensify the risk of schizophrenia. Interestingly, they suggest that the chronic stress inherent in having a psychotic illness itself might further contribute to brain degeneration.

Neuropsychological Deficits

While brain-imaging techniques help us to discern changes in the structure of the brain, neuropsychological assessment allows us to determine whether the brain functions differently in children with schizophrenia. Evidence consistently points to such differences. When asked to complete neurocognitive tasks, adolescents with schizophrenia generally are found to function more poorly across the board than their typically developing peers (Kravariti et al., 2003). The findings can be summarized as follows.

Attention   The most robust research finding on schizophrenia in children, adolescents, and adults is that they share a dysfunction in selective and sustained attention. This dysfunction is evidenced by studies of span of apprehension in which participants have to identify a target letter (a T or an F) embedded in an array of other letters and displayed for 50 milliseconds. When the number of letters to be identified is large—specifically 5 to 10 rather than 1 to 3—the performance of schizophrenic children is worse than that of typical children or ones with ADHD. Thus, the dysfunction is evidenced in those with schizophrenia when the task involves a significant burden for processing information. Finally, direct evaluation of the participants' brain activity while performing the task showed a comparable deviation in event-related potential, a measure of the brain's electrical activity (Asarnow et al., 1994).

Speed of Processing   Consistent findings show that young persons with schizophrenia have difficulty processing information in a speedy and efficient manner (Asarnow et al., 1994).

Visual-Motor and Motor Functions   Both visual-motor coordination and fine motor speed are impaired in individuals with schizophrenia (Niendam et al., 2003). There is also evidence that, while performance in these areas improves over the course of development in typical children, it does not do so in children with schizophrenia. This lack of improvement suggests either a delay in or failure of normal brain maturation (Jacobsen & Rapoport, 1998).

Executive Functions   As with adults, executive functions (those responsible for planned, flexible, goal-directed behavior) are impaired in children and adolescents with schizophrenia. (See Chapter 7 for a more detailed presentation of executive functions.) For example, individuals with schizophrenia are perseverative in their thinking, a deficit that is related to damage to the frontal lobes, where higher-level executive processing takes place. A number of the findings detailed previously also suggest deficits in the executive function of *working memory,* the ability to hold information in mind while

performing an operation on it. In fact, Niendam and colleagues (2003) compared the childhood test scores of individuals who did or did not go on to develop schizophrenia and found that working memory problems were one of the few deficits that were unique to those who developed the disorder.

In line with the idea of a dysfunction in processing complex information is the paradoxical finding that providing strategies for or information about performing a task to individuals with schizophrenia can interfere with their performance at times. Instead of being helpful, the added information is too much to be assimilated. In regard to relating this finding to brain functioning, it suggests that children and adolescents with schizophrenia have difficulty with processing complex information regardless of the hemisphere involved in the function assessed by the task. In other words, the dysfunction is not localized in one hemisphere or the other.

Prenatal and Birth Complications

Studies regarding the impact of prenatal and birth complications are inconsistent and opinions in the field vary. Some investigators conclude that pregnancy and birth complications are strongly associated with schizophrenia, but only of the childhood-onset type (Rosso & Cannon, 2003). Evidence also points to an increase in prenatal difficulties in high-risk children (e.g., children of schizophrenic mothers) who went on to develop the disorder (Brown & Susser, 2003). Prenatal exposure to viral infection also has been implicated. For example, Mednick and colleagues (1988) found that adults with schizophrenia were more likely to have been exposed to influenza during the 2nd trimester of gestation, but not during the 1st and 3rd trimesters, suggesting that the virus interferes with neural developments that are specific to that critical period. However, other large-scale studies have reported that the links to prenatal and birth complications are weak or even nonexistent (Nicholson, Giedd, & Lenane, 1999). Moreover, the direction of effects might be reversed: Abnormal neurodevelopment in the fetus may be the *cause* rather than the consequence of prenatal and birth complications in schizophrenia (Hollis, 2004).

Puberty

Although the convergence between the onset of puberty and the upsurge in the incidence of schizophrenia has led some to suspect a causal connection, research has failed to make such a link. In a large-scale study conducted by NIMH, no relation was found between childhood-onset schizophrenia and the advent of puberty (Frazier, Alaghband-Rad, & Jacobsen, 1997).

Substance Abuse

Although youths with schizophrenia may abuse substances, evidence of a hypothesized causal relationship between schizophrenia and substance abuse is elusive. Phillips and colleagues (2002) followed a group of high-risk youths (those who showed subthreshold psychotic symptoms or were relatives of someone with psychosis and recently showed a decline in functioning) over a period of 12 months. Thirty-two percent of the youths developed an acute psychotic episode over the year, but the likelihood of psychosis was not predicted by cannabis use. Similarly, Arseneault and colleagues (2002) conducted a prospected longitudinal study of the relationship between adolescent cannabis use and schizophrenia and found that those who used cannabis by age 15 were 4 times as likely to develop psychosis in adulthood, but this effect was no longer significant once psychotic symptoms in childhood were accounted for. Thus, it may be the case that youths with early-onset symptoms utilize substances in an attempt to self-medicate, but that these substances do not in fact precipitate psychosis.

Integration of Biological Factors

We have presented the variables in the biological context in isolation from one another, although it is more likely that they are interconnected. For example, an influence model that guides much of the thinking is Weinberger's (1987) neurodevelopmental model of schizophrenia. Weinberger proposes that a brain legion in the limbic system and prefrontal cortex occurs early in life, but remains "clinically silent" until the brain matures and the neural systems involved in schizophrenia have adequately developed. In particular, Weinberger suspects that schizophrenia involves deficits in the mechanisms involving the neurotransmitter dopamine, which has a major role in the response to stress.

A number of research findings to date indirectly support the *neurodevelopmental hypothesis* (McGrath et al., 2003). For example, long before the disorder reveals itself, retrospective data indicate that development of expressive language, motor skills, and interpersonal relationships—all skills mediated by the frontal cortex—are negatively affected in children who go on to develop schizophrenia, consistent with the idea of a fundamental deficit whose true nature only later reveals itself. Support for the dopamine-stress connection is supported by research showing that stress often brings on an exacerbation of psychotic symptoms in individuals with schizophrenia, as well as the fact that medications that target dopamine result in dramatic alleviation of psychosis.

Rather than being static entities, abnormal brain development and neuropsychological deficits interact with behavior and environment in early-onset schizophrenia. For example, Hollis (2004) notes the importance of executive functions during the preadolescent period (approximately age 8 to 15), the developmental period during which preschizophrenic symptoms begin to emerge. At this stage of life, executive functions are central to many important developmental capacities. For example, social relatedness requires the youth to integrate different sources of information, comprehend others' perspectives, inhibit inappropriate responses, and shift attention and mental set in order to respond to changing circumstances. The young person whose development is impaired in these areas will be unprepared for the increasing social and academic demands of adolescence. And when the youth in question is one who is genetically vulnerable to the development of schizophrenia, the stress of these social and academic failures may be the catalyst that pushes him or her over the threshold. This *executive functioning risk model* predicts that the greater the deficits in executive functioning, the earlier the onset of psychotic symptoms. Thus, we see interactions between risk factors, vulnerabilities, and potentiating factors in the development of schizophrenia.

Familial Links A fascinating line of research shows that the parents of children with schizophrenia, who are themselves without a diagnosis, share some of the same neuropsychological deficits as their children. In comparison to parents of children with ADHD or controls, Asarnow and colleagues (2002) found that parents of children with schizophrenia performed significantly worse on tests of attention and executive functions. By a similar token, unaffected *siblings* of children with schizophrenia show similar, albeit not as severe, patterns of deficit on neurocognitive tasks (Niendam et al., 2003), as well as showing similar patterns of reduction in gray matter (Gogtay et al., 2003). Once again, these findings suggest an underlying genetic liability to schizophrenia that is expressed in gross or subtle ways in different family members.

The Individual Context

Thought Disorder

The disorganized speech that characterizes schizophrenia is a reflection of disorders in thinking. Thought disorders are not only diagnostic indices of schizophrenia, but they have ominous implications for prognosis as well. However, certain of these disorders can be found in the typically developing population of younger children. Loose associations, for example, can be observed up to the age of 7 years, after which time they are infrequent. Illogical thinking also decreases markedly after that time. Therefore, the appearance of loose associations and illogical thinking in schizophrenia may be due to a developmental delay, fixation, or regression, although this possible etiology is only speculation. (See Volkmar et al., 1996, which also contains a detailed summary of the literature on delusions, hallucinations, and other thought disorders.)

Controlled studies have been conducted on loose and illogical thinking underlying disorganized speech. Loose thinking is defined as an unpredictable change of topics, such as answering the question "Why do you like Tim?" with "I call my mother Sweetie." Illogical thinking is defined as contradictions or inappropriate causal relations, such as "I left my hat at home because her name is Mary." These thinking disorders may be specific to

schizophrenia since they are not found in children diagnosed with ADHD, conduct disorder, or oppositional disorder.

The two kinds of thought disturbances are not correlated. Loose thinking is related to distractibility, while illogical thinking is related to a short attention span (Caplan & Sherman, 1990). This latter attention deficit may underlie schizophrenic children's digressive speech, since they are deficient in the short-term attentional processes required for coherent conversation. In sum, we have two hypotheses concerning the etiology of loose and illogical thinking: fixation or regression on the one hand and an attentional deficit on the other.

The Family Context

While poor family relations were at one time considered to be a causal factor in schizophrenia, the evidence clearly shows that family dysfunction constitutes a stressor that increases the probability of schizophrenia in an already vulnerable individual. There is no evidence that a dysfunctional family can produce schizophrenia in a nonvulnerable child. Three aspects of family relationships have been studied: communication deviance, affective quality, and caregiving disruptions.

Communication Deviance

Communication deviance concerns the degree to which relatives' communication lacks clarity as measured by the number of unclear, amorphous, disruptive, or fragmented statements they make in response to projective tests. The construct derives from the work of Lyman Wynne (1984), who regards schizophrenia as the result of a diffuse or fragmented family structure. In a *diffuse* structure, patterns of interaction are marked by vague ideas, by blurring of meaning, and by irrelevancies. Thus, the drifting or scattered thinking of individuals who are schizophrenic represents the internalization of such a family structure. As an example of amorphous thinking, note the following responses of a mother being interviewed for the developmental history of her child who has schizophrenia:

Psychologist: Was it a difficult delivery or did everything go OK?

Mother: I know just what you mean. And I can say for certain that I'm not one of those women you read about where they are so brave and natural childbirth is just the greatest thing in their life (laughs). Believe me, when the time comes, I want the works when it comes to pain.

Psychologist: But did everything go OK?

Mother: Well, there was this Dr. Wisekoff that I never liked and he said all kinds of doom and gloom things, but I told my husband I was the one that had the baby and I was the one that ought to know, so my husband got into this big fight and didn't pay the bill for a whole year and the doctor threatened to hire one of these collection agencies, and what that was all about don't ask me—just don't ask me.

Psychologist: I see, but I'm still not sure . . .

Mother (interrupting): That's just what I mean.

Later the psychologist, who was just beginning his clinical internship, told his supervisor that he wanted to shake the mother and yell at the top of his lungs, "But was the delivery difficult or easy?" One can only imagine how difficult it would be for a child to grow up surrounded by such diffuseness, accompanied by an obliviousness to the diffuseness itself.

Just as the child's amorphous thinking derives from a diffuse family structure, *fragmented* family communication leads to fragmented thinking in Wynne's perspective. In this case communication is marked by digression from topic to topic; non sequitur reasoning; and extraneous, illogical, or contradictory comments. While attention can be focused for brief moments, bits and pieces of memories become intermixed with the current train of thought. The technical term for this abrupt shift from one topic to another is overinclusive thinking, or **overinclusiveness.**

Wynne delineates other faults in the family structure. The family members cannot maintain appropriate psychological **boundaries,** and thus detached impersonality unpredictably alternates with highly personal remarks and confrontations. However, there is a concerted effort to act as if

there were a strong sense of unity, resulting in what Wynne calls *pseudo-mutuality.* There is a great pressure to maintain a facade of harmony, and the child is not allowed to deviate from or question his or her prescribed role. Beneath this facade lie pervasive feelings of futility and meaninglessness.

Objective studies have confirmed that communication deviance reliably differentiates parents of individuals with schizophrenia from parents of persons without schizophrenia but not from those with bipolar (manic-depressive) disorders (Miklowitz, 1994). Communication deviance also predicts the adult onset of schizophrenia spectrum disorders. For example, a 15-year follow-up study of 64 families with mild to moderately disturbed adolescents found that the incidence of schizophrenia or schizophrenia spectrum disorders was highest in families initially classified as having high communication deviance. Moreover, there were no cases of schizophrenia in families with low communication deviance, and adding measures of negative affect increased the predictive power (Goldstein, 1990). These results suggest that, for vulnerable children, disturbance in the family climate in the form of unclear or negative communication presages the appearance of schizophrenia and related disorders in adulthood.

Next, there is evidence supporting Wynne's clinical observation that communication deviance in parents interferes with the development of attention and logical thinking in their children. Mothers with high communication deviance and their offspring with schizophrenia perform poorly on measures of attention and vigilance, as well as on tasks evaluating the ability to integrate and organize complex social information into a coherent whole. Finally, there is evidence that communication deviance in parents is associated with the severity of the psychopathology. While communication deviance is also found in some parents of children with depression, it is not associated either with attentional problems or severity of disturbance in depression, suggesting that it is particularly important for the development of schizophrenic disorders (Asarnow & Asarnow, 2003).

Affective Quality

One of the most extensively studied aspects of shared affect in family interaction is *expressed emotion* (EE), which involves dimensions of *criticism* and *overinvolvement*. Research on adults shows that high EE is a good predictor of relapse after a schizophrenic episode; for example, for hospitalized adults with schizophrenia who return to a high-EE family, relapse within 9 months to a year is 2 to 3 times higher than for those who return to a low EE family (Miklowitz, 1994). Evidence is somewhat mixed for the role of family EE for children with schizophrenia, but is stronger for the effects of criticism as opposed to overinvolvement (Asarnow et al., 1994). In observed interactions, parents of children with schizophrenia spectrum disorders are more likely to express harsh criticism toward their child and to respond to the child's negative verbal behavior with a reciprocal negative response. Further, observed EE during adolescence predicts an increased risk of developing schizophrenia-related disorders in young adulthood (Goldstein, 1987). However, high EE also is found among parents of children with depression or other nonschizophrenic spectrum disorders and thus is not specific to schizophrenia (Asarnow et al., 1994).

Disruptions in Caregiving

There is some suggestive evidence that children who develop schizophrenia have experienced more disruptions in the caregiving environment, including loss and separation from the primary caregiver (Niemi et al., 2003). Whether this constitutes a stressor that precipitates the disorder, or whether the link is a genetic one—with the caregiving disruptions being consequences of the poor functioning of a parent who also has traits of the disorder—is not known.

Transactions

It is difficult in family interactional research to disentangle precursors from consequences. For example, in observed family interactions, children with schizophrenia or schizotypal disorders evidence a higher level of thought disorders and attentional drift (difficulty in maintaining attention to a task) than do children with major depression (Asarnow et al., 1994). This finding raises these questions: Are the harsh critical comments of high EE parents one of the factors *responsible* for their children's disturbance or do they arise in *response to* the frustration of having such a child? Or do both processes occur in a *transactional* model of reciprocal effects? These questions can best be answered by the kind of longitudinal data that are not presently available.

However, King and colleagues (2003) offer one attempt to investigate family relationships in schizophrenia in a more transactional way. Although the patients were largely adults (41 outpatients with a mean age of 31 years), the results are suggestive for our understanding of family relationships in child and adolescent schizophrenia. The investigators set out to determine the extent to which mothers' EE was associated with characteristics of her schizophrenic child, versus those she brought to the situation. The investigators found that mothers' critical comments were predicted by increased symptoms of excitability in the child and lower levels of neurotic symptoms and greater feelings of subjective burden in the mother. Maternal overinvolvement, in turn, was predicted by greater conscientiousness and burden in the mother and, indirectly, by her child's level of depression. Thus, it appears that characteristics of the child interact with those of the mother in order to produce negative affect in the family.

The fact that parenting a severely mentally ill child is challenging would be hard to deny. Schizophrenia is a chronic and debilitating disorder that taxes the emotional and economic resources of the family, increasing the risk of *caregiver burden*. Parents of youths with schizophrenia report that negative symptoms (apathy, asociability, lack of affect) are the most difficult to cope with. Moreover, schizophrenia is a socially stigmatized disorder, a factor that may add to the caregivers' burden. For example, parents report that they often experience an absence of support from their social networks in addition to receiving inadequate help from the mental health system (Knudson & Coyle, 2002).

The Cultural Context

Environmental Stress

As we noted earlier when we discussed prevalence, the association between low SES and adult schizophrenia has not been clearly established for children. Should this finding hold in future research, it would not be surprising. The myriad emotional and instrumental stressors that accompany poverty might well act as precipitants to the disorder in an already vulnerable individual. While it is known that increased life stress precedes the onset of psychotic symptoms and precipitates relapse in adults with schizophrenia (Walker et al., 2004), the corresponding research in child-onset samples has yet to be conducted.

Stigma

Also as noted in the previous section, schizophrenia appears to occur in every nation around the globe. Nevertheless, there are cultural differences in the way in which the disorder is perceived and the extent to which a negative *stigma* is attached to those who suffer from it. For example, in some traditional societies, the bizarre behavior of the individual with schizophrenia is tolerated or even honored as a sign that the individual has been "touched" by a benevolent spirit. (For more on cross-cultural differences in perceptions of schizophrenia, see Jenkins and Barrett, 2004.) Perhaps the issue of stigma versus cultural tolerance explains the results of a WHO study that discovered that individuals with schizophrenia have a more favorable outcome in developing countries than they do in the more highly industrialized nations (Jablensky et al., 1992).

Integrative Developmental Model

Asarnow and Asarnow (2003) outline a multifactorial, transactional model of the developmental psychopathology of schizophrenia. (See Figure 11.4.) The model specifies three etiological factors— vulnerabilities, stressors, and protective factors— and the dynamic relations among them.

In this model, the roots of schizophrenia lie in genetic risk factors that lead to central nervous system dysfunctions and the accompanying impairments in attention and information processing. These deficits interact with environmental stressors, which potentiate the disorder, and protective factors, which mitigate against its development. Acting in concert, these factors influence the likelihood that an individual will develop schizophrenia over the course of development.

Vulnerabilities for schizophrenia are enduring characteristics of individuals that predispose them to the development of the disorder. Current research implicates both constitutional and environmental factors, including genetic markers; CNS abnormalities, either caused by or concomitant with prenatal and birth complications; and disturbed family patterns of affect and communication. While certain vulnerabilities may be specific to the development of schizophrenia, such as a genetic loading for the disorder, other vulnerabilities, such as family discord, may be predictive of an increased likelihood of psychopathology in general.

Stressors involve internal and environmental demands that exceed the capacity of the individual. These may include traumatic life events, such as the death of a parent, as well as more chronic stresses and strains, such as those associated with living in poverty. Furthermore, stresses interact with vulnerabilities so that events that are manageable for one child are experienced as debilitating by the child at risk for schizophrenia. For example, consider the youth whose CNS deficits interfere with the development of executive functions, who consequently will be unprepared for and stressed by the normative social and academic demands of adolescence.

Protective factors, in turn, comprise characteristics of the environment or the person that reduce the risk of schizophrenia. Those suggested in the literature include intelligence, social competence, social support, and healthy patterns of family communication. One of the challenges to identifying protective factors is that if an individual does not develop a disorder, how will we know that they were protected from doing so? On the other hand, the benefits to identifying protective factors are great in that they

Figure 11.4   Vulnerability-Stress Model of Childhood-Onset of Schizophrenia.

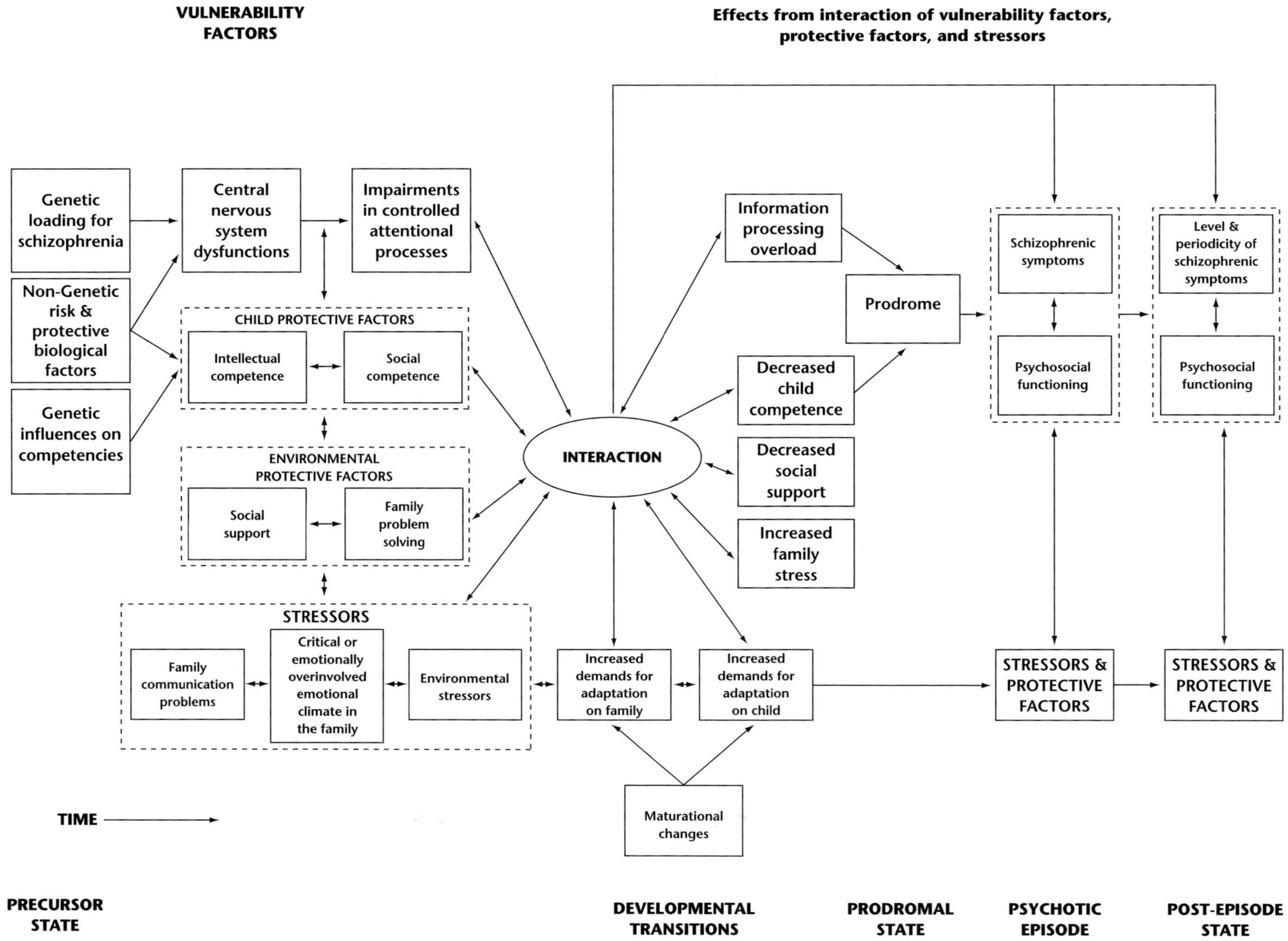

VULNERABILITY FACTORS

Effects from interaction of vulnerability factors, protective factors, and stressors

Genetic loading for schizophrenia

Non-Genetic risk & protective biological factors

Genetic influences on competencies

Central nervous system dysfunctions

Impairments in controlled attentional processes

CHILD PROTECTIVE FACTORS
Social competence
Intellectual competence

ENVIRONMENTAL PROTECTIVE FACTORS
Family problem solving
Social support

STRESSORS
Critical or emotionally overinvolved emotional climate in the family
Environmental stressors
Family communication problems

INTERACTION

Information processing overload

Prodrome

Decreased child competence
Decreased social support
Increased family stress

Increased demands for adaptation on child
Increased demands for adaptation on family

Maturational changes

Schizophrenic symptoms
Psychosocial functioning

Level & periodicity of schizophrenic symptoms
Psychosocial functioning

STRESSORS & PROTECTIVE FACTORS

STRESSORS & PROTECTIVE FACTORS

TIME →

PRECURSOR STATE

DEVELOPMENTAL TRANSITIONS

PRODROMAL STATE

PSYCHOTIC EPISODE

POST-EPISODE STATE

From Asarnow and Asarnow, 2000.

353

can lead to the development of preventative and intervention programs.

As we have come to expect from a *transactional* developmental psychopathology model, these vulnerabilities, stressors, and protective factors interact with one another over the course of development. While a predisposition to schizophrenia is genetically transmitted, the disorder is hypothesized to occur only in those individuals who are exposed to threshold levels of stress. In turn, the interaction between biological vulnerability and environmental stress is moderated by competencies in the individual (e.g., intelligence and social skills) and family responses (e.g., support and positive emotion).

Asarnow and Asarnow (2003) acknowledge that the state of knowledge in the field is not sufficiently well developed to identify with confidence protective and vulnerability factors that are specifically linked to schizophrenia. Rather than providing a precise theory of the origins of schizophrenia, therefore, this model is proposed as a helpful heuristic with which to integrate and organize the existing research findings.

Developmental Course

Short-Term Outcome

In the short term, the prognosis for a first psychotic episode is not good; in fact, the expected outcome is worse for children and adolescents than it is for adults. In the Maudsley study (Hollis, 2000), only 12 percent of the youths achieved full remission at discharge from the hospital, in contrast with 50 percent of those with mood-disorder related psychosis. For youths with schizophrenia, the likelihood of full recovery was greatest within the first 3 months following the onset of symptoms. After 6 months, those who were still symptomatic had only a 15 percent chance of full recovery.

Long-Term Outcome

The longitudinal data are consistent in indicating a high degree of continuity and a poor prognosis for childhood-onset schizophrenia. Remission rates range from 3 to 27 percent depending on the particular study, while 61 to 90 percent of the youths develop chronic schizophrenia with recurring episodes. In the Maudsley study, Hollis (2000) also found a high level of stability in children and adolescents diagnosed with schizophrenia, with 80 percent retaining the diagnosis into adulthood. Further, those who had been diagnosed with schizophrenia in adolescence displayed the most impairments in adult social relationships, independent living skills, educational achievement, and occupational functioning. Eggers, Bunk, & Ropcke (2002) followed up 57 patients who had been diagnosed with schizophrenia prior to age 14. Approximately 16 years later, 27 percent were in remission, 24 percent were slightly remitted, and 49 percent were doing poorly. Similar results were found in a 3- to 7-year follow-up of children first diagnosed with schizophrenia between the ages of 7 and 14, 67 percent of whom continued to display a disorder in the schizophrenic spectrum in adolescence (Asarnow et al., 1994). On a measure of global functioning, 56 percent showed improvement over time, while 44 percent either showed minimal improvement or deterioration.

Later in development, there is evidence that child- and adolescent-onset schizophrenia adversely affect employment, independent living, and intimate relationships (Häfner & Nowotny, 1995). For example, at follow-up 42 years after the initial assessment, Eggers et al. (2002) found that about one-third of those with early-onset schizophrenia were floridly psychotic and many were severely impaired in the social and occupational realms: 27 percent were unable to work, 59 percent were unmarried and lived alone, and only 7 percent were in stable relationships. Considering the fact that social roles in regard to independent living and intimate partnership are in the process of being formed during childhood and adolescence, it is easy to see why these roles are particularly vulnerable to disruption by the insidious effects of early-onset schizophrenia.

Finally, there is an increased risk of mortality from various causes, including violent death, adverse medication-related reactions such as seizures (Hollis, 2004), and suicide, which occurs at a rate of

Figure 11.5   Distribution of Outcome Categories of Chronic- and Acute-Onset Psychotic Patients.

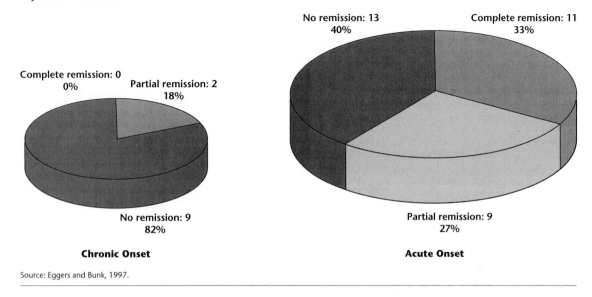

Source: Eggers and Bunk, 1997.

approximately 10 percent among those with early-onset schizophrenia (McClelland et al., 2001).

Protective Factors

Protective factors identified in the literature include higher premorbid social and cognitive functioning, early intervention, short duration of the first psychotic episode, and fewer negative symptoms of psychosis (Hollis, 2004). As with adults, later age of onset and rapid development of the disorder also are associated with a better outcome. For example, Eggers and Bunk (1997), in their 42-year follow-up study, found that none of the patients with a slow, insidious onset experienced a complete remission, whereas 33 percent of those with an acute onset remitted completely. (See Figure 11.5.) Acute onset was significantly more likely in youths aged 12 and older; younger children were more likely to have a chronic onset and thus a more negative outcome. Nonetheless, it is important to recognize that, with early treatment and positive prognostic signs, a young person with schizophrenia may go on to lead a productive and creative life. (See Figure 11.6.)

Intervention

The lack of well-designed objective studies that has hampered our understanding of the nature and origins of childhood and adolescent schizophrenia continues to characterize the literature on intervention. For example, in spite of the widespread use of neuroleptics (dopamine receptor blockers) in the treatment of children with schizophrenia, and in spite of the serious and sometimes toxic side effects that can develop, there are few controlled studies of drug treatment. The literature on psychosocial interventions with children consists largely of clinical reports, with a dearth of controlled studies (Asarnow & Asarnow, 2003).

Psychopharmacology

Antipsychotic medication is the therapy of choice with adults, although there is limited carefully controlled research concerning the effectiveness of neuroleptics with children (McClellan et al., 2001). Two randomized double-blind studies report that haloperidol (Haldol) alleviated symptoms better than placebo in children and adolescents with

Figure 11.6

Artwork by a Young Person with Schizophrenia.

M. Ramell, a painter and aspiring musician, was recently a featured artist in the Brushes with Life: Art, Artists and Mental Illness gallery developed by the Schizophrenia Treatment and Evaluation Program (STEP) at the University of North Carolina Department of Psychiatry.

schizophrenia (Hollis, 2004). Other studies have supported the use of the atypical antipsychotic clozapine (Clozaril) with children, but few are methodologically sound. However, preliminary results suggest that clozapine may be more effective than haloperidol while also being safer and avoiding its negative side effects, such as sedation, parkinsonism, and seizures (Jacobsen & Rapoport, 1998).

Individual Psychotherapy

Because schizophrenia may have such widespread effects on the individual as well as on the family, pharmacological treatment must be supplemented by various other kinds of remedial and rehabilitative measures. Weiner (1992) describes a program of *individual psychotherapy* aimed at counteracting the social isolation and impaired reality contact

found in schizophrenia through relationship building and reality testing. The former involves a combination of warmth and nurturance for those who have been deprived of love, and firmness without anger or punitiveness for those who cannot control their aggressive acting out. To correct delusions and hallucinations, the therapist must point out that, while they are real to the patient, they are not real to the therapist. The next step involves identifying the needs giving rise to the cognitive distortions and dealing constructively with them. At a more practical level, the therapist helps the patient develop more effective social skills to counter social isolation.

Recent approaches to treating individuals with schizophrenia rely on *cognitive behavioral models*. Essential features of treatment include using cognitive strategies to cope with symptoms and counter irrational beliefs, as well as social skills training to normalize interpersonal relationships.

The majority of research establishing the effectiveness of cognitive-behavioral treatments has been conducted with adults (Bustillo et al., 2001). A notable exception is Power and colleagues' (2003) LifeSPAN, a cognitively oriented treatment specifically designed to prevent suicide among youths with early-onset psychosis. The program is initiated by a collaborative risk assessment in which the youth and clinician work together to formulate an understanding of the factors involved in the youth's suicidality. Subsequent treatment modules explore the rationale for suicide, hopelessness, and reasons for living. Following this, the youth is helped to develop specific skills to counter the belief that suicide is the only option, including problem-solving training, strategies for tolerating emotional pain, stress management, self-esteem, help-seeking, social skills, and psychoeducation regarding psychosis. To assess the effectiveness of the intervention, the investigators randomly assigned 21 youths to the treatment group and an equal number to standard clinical care. While both groups improved over the course of the study, those in the treatment group improved more on measures of hopelessness and suicidal ideation. Tragically, 2 participants in the study were lost to suicide, one of whom was from the treatment group.

Family Therapy

While there is extensive clinical literature regarding *family treatment* in schizophrenia—indeed, the early family systems models arose in the context of treating "schizophrenogenic families" (e.g., Bateson, Jackson, Haley, & Weakland, 1956)—randomized, controlled empirical research with children and adolescents is sparse (Wright, Casswell, White, & Partridge, 2004). Nevertheless, it is easy to perceive how involving the family in the treatment process would help family members correct the communication and affective patterns that can precipitate a relapse. There is evidence from studies of adults that family-based interventions for adults help to prevent relapse and lead to improved

adherence to medication treatment (Pilling et al., 2002). Linszen and colleagues (1998) investigated whether adding a family component would boost the effectiveness of intensive medication and individual treatment in an adolescent treatment facility. Results were highly promising for the 1st year, with only 16 percent of the youths relapsing, but the effects appeared to erode in the years to follow, with 64 percent relapsing between 17 and 55 months later. The major predictors of relapse were high EE in the family and heavy cannabis use, both of which indicate the necessity of ongoing family intervention and parental guidance for young people with schizophrenia.

Prevention

Efforts to prevent schizophrenia are hampered by the fact that it is difficult to identify children who are at risk for the disorder before the onset of florid psychotic symptoms. For example, to date, efforts to identify prodromal youths have found that only one-fifth of those suspected of early-onset schizophrenia go on to develop the disorder (Hollis, 2004). Early detection and early intervention in the acute phase, therefore, appear to be more achievable goals. Early intervention also prevents the occurrence of a long duration of untreated psychosis, and thus leads to a much better prognosis. (For a model early intervention program, see Box 11.2.)

An alternative approach to prevention focuses on reducing the negative stigma associated with schizophrenia. Schulze and colleagues (2003) initiated a project with secondary school students aged 14 to 18 that was designed to reduce the negative stigma associated with schizophrenia by providing opportunities for personal contact between students and youths with the disorder. Attitudes toward individuals with schizophrenia were assessed before and after the program for 90 students and were compared to the attitudes expressed by 60 controls who did not undergo the intervention. The investigators found that the intervention significantly reduced negative stereotypes and the effects were still present at a 1-month follow-up. The title of their study sums up the change in attitude nicely: "Crazy? So

Box 11.2 | A Comprehensive Approach to the Treatment of Schizophrenia

Given the progressive and cascading effect of schizophrenia on all areas of functioning, clinicians involved in treating the disorder urge that early detection and intervention are essential (McGorry & Yung, 2003). Malla and colleagues (2003) describe a model program developed in Canada that uses an assertive model for the identification, treatment, retention, and follow-up of young people who are undergoing a first psychotic break.

The first stage of the program strives to reduce delays in treatment by launching a community wide informational campaign regarding the signs and symptoms of psychosis. Once a youth is identified, treatment consists of a comprehensive array of services, including assessment, medication management, individual supportive therapy, family support, and liaison with the community. In addition, youths are engaged in psychosocial group interventions geared to their stage of recovery.

Initially, youths still experiencing psychotic symptoms attend Recovery through Activity and Participation (RAP) groups that involve normalizing activities such as cooking, games, sports, art, and community field trips. In the next stage of recovery, youths are involved in Youth Education and Support (YES) groups, a more intensive intervention focused on psychoeducation about psychosis, self-identity, coping with peer relations, medication compliance, social skills, and strategies for dealing with stigma. Finally, Cognitively Oriented Skills Training (COST) addresses cognitive deficits that interfere with functioning in schizophrenia, such as attention, concentration, memory, and study strategies. Individual cognitive-behavioral therapy is offered when indicated, such as to youths who exhibit anxiety or depression during their recovery. Ultimately, the goal is to normalize the youth's functioning by returning him or her to the community, reestablishing peer relations, and reengaging in occupational or academic activities as soon as possible.

Initial results of the first 2 and a half years of the program are promising. The number of cases treated increased significantly over time, just as the delay in seeking treatment declined 50 percent, indicating that the outreach efforts were successful. Most of the youths were treated with low doses of atypical antipsychotic medications, and retention and treatment adherence were good. At follow-up, three-quarters of the youths treated were in remission and the majority of the remaining youths had only moderate symptomatology.

what!" Currently, the World Psychiatric Association is developing plans to initiate a worldwide initiative to counter the negative stigma regarding schizophrenia (see Thompson et al., 2002).

As we have noted, research on child and adolescent schizophrenia is sparse, and many questions remain unresolved regarding the developmental dimension. By contrast, the psychopathologies we will discuss next—substance abuse and eating disorders—have been well researched and are closely tied to the developments characterizing the adolescent period.

Psychopathologies of the Adolescent Transition: Eating Disorders and Substance Abuse

Normative Adolescent Development

Adolescence marks a major life change. The transition between childhood and adulthood is accompanied by changes in every aspect of individual development and every social context. In addition, adolescence is unique in that it involves two distinct phases: into the stage as one moves from childhood to adolescence, and out of the stage as the adolescent enters adulthood (Ebata, Peterson, & Conger, 1990). Thus, the developmental picture is a complex one.

The *body* itself sets the stage with physical changes more rapid than those of any other developmental period except infancy, including the attainment of a mature size and body shape, hormonal changes associated with puberty, and the advent of adult sexuality. *Society* follows suit by requiring the youth to master more complex tasks, relinquish dependence on the family, and assume responsibility for making decisions regarding the two major tasks of adulthood, love and work. This transition is facilitated by the increasingly important role *peer relations* play and by the newfound cognitive sophistication that enables the adolescent both to think abstractly and to envision future possibilities, expanding the situation-specific self-perception of childhood into the overarching question, Who am I?

Adolescence gives special meaning to many of the personality variables we have been discussing. *Self-regulation* allows for experimenting with new experiences while avoiding the extremes of inhibition and impulsivity. The intimacy of *attachment* merges with burgeoning *sexuality,* and *social relations* with peers take on a new importance. Because of physiological changes, the psychological representation of the body, or the *body image,* is more salient than it has been since the early years. Increased *cognitive* complexity allows the adolescent both to entertain hypothetical possibilities and to ask abstract questions concerning the self and the future. Cognitive development also allows the adolescent a more sophisticated level of self-exploration and a more realistic grasp of the options that society offers. Finally, the *family context* is changing, as parents must readjust their expectations and parenting styles to allow for the youth's needs for increasing independence and autonomy.

Psychopathology in Adolescence

Western society has traditionally viewed the adolescent transition as one of turmoil, the inherent instability of the period being epitomized by the phrase "storm and stress." Psychoanalysts characterize the period as marking the return of primitive impulses and unresolved conflicts from the early stages of psychosexual development while, according to Erikson, a weakened ego struggles to master an identity crisis and role diffusion. However, it is becoming increasingly clear that the image of adolescence as a time of turmoil is applicable primarily to a minority of troubled teens. Most adolescents make the transition without significant emotional problems. Parent-adolescent relationships are generally harmonious, and for most adolescents the search for identity goes on unaccompanied by crises.

The revised picture should not be taken to mean that adolescence is uniformly serene. Moodiness, self-depreciation, and depression reach a peak in adolescence; and other psychopathologies also show a sharp rise, including suicide, schizophrenia, alcohol and drug abuse, and eating disorders. The overall rate of psychopathology increases only slightly, since other disturbances are on the decline; however, the new disturbances are far more serious than the ones they replace, making the picture an ominous one.

As Ebata, Peterson, and Conger (1990) point out, a developmental psychopathology perspective on adolescence needs to attend to (1) the *normative developmental capacities* that can serve as either risk or protective mechanisms for the individual, (2) the *social context* in which individual development takes place, and (3) the dynamic and *transactional processes* that characterize the relationship between the individual and the social context. For example, while peer relations and academic expectations might become more challenging in adolescence, adding sources of stress that can undermine adjustment, adolescents are increasingly able to choose and influence their social contexts and in this way to have more control over their own development. In addition, adolescents have an expanded ability to draw on their own inner resources, as well as those in the environment, in order to adapt and cope. (See Zahn-Waxler, 1996.)

Erikson's concept of **identity** integrates many of the diverse strands of adolescent development as well as provides leads to potential sources of protection and vulnerability. Identity involves both inner continuity and interpersonal mutuality; it is a process of coming to terms with oneself and finding one's place in society. Adolescence is marked by an identity crisis because it is a "turning point, a crucial moment" (Erikson, 1968, p. 16) in which the adolescent must master the challenges of finding a fulfilling vocation, sexual role, and ideology in order to avoid stagnation and regression. Youths approach the task of achieving an identity in ways that are influenced by how they have resolved previous stages of psychosocial development. Trust, autonomy, initiative, and industry act as protective factors, while mistrust, shame, doubt, guilt, and inferiority act as vulnerabilities.

The two psychopathologies we will discuss represent different ways in which developmental processes can go awry. In some youths' relentless pursuit of thinness associated with eating disorders, the body image becomes a destructive tyrant, while the self-defeating need for autonomy is reminiscent of the oppositional behavior of the toddler period. In substance abuse, precocity propels the adolescent into assuming adult roles and freedoms for which he or she is ill prepared.

Eating Disorders: Anorexia Nervosa

Definition and Characteristics

Anorexia Nervosa involves at least a 15 percent loss of body weight through purging and/or voluntary restriction, as well as an active pursuit of thinness. DSM-IV differentiates two types based on the different means used to achieve thinness. The first relies solely on strict dieting and is called the *restricting type*. The second, the *binge-eating/purging type,* alternates between dieting and binge eating, followed by self-induced vomiting or purging (Table 12.1).

Youths with anorexia have a normal awareness of hunger but are terrified of giving in to the impulse to eat. Unlike an ordinary dieter, the individual wastes away to a dangerous state of emaciation in pursuit of some ideal image of thinness. As the condition

Table 12.1

DSM-IV-TR Criteria for Eating Disorders

Anorexia Nervosa

A. Refusal to maintain body weight at or above a minimally normal weight for age and height (e.g., weight loss leading to maintenance of body weight less than 85 percent of that expected; or failure to make expected weight gain during period of growth, leading to body weight less than 85 percent of that expected).

B. Intense fear of gaining weight or becoming fat, even though underweight.

C. Disturbance in the way in which one's body weight or shape is experienced, undue influence of body weight or shape on self-evaluation, or denial of the seriousness of the current low body weight.

D. In postmenarcheal females, amenorrhea (i.e., the absence of at least three consecutive menstrual cycles).

Specify Type:

Restricting Type: During the current episode of Anorexia Nervosa, the person has not regularly engaged in binge-eating or purging behavior (i.e., self-induced vomiting or the misuse of laxatives, diuretics, or enemas).

Binge-Eating/Purging Type: During the current episode of Anorexia Nervosa, the person has regularly engaged in binge-eating or purging behavior.

Bulimia Nervosa

A. Recurrent episodes of binge eating, characterized by both of the following:

(1) Eating, in a discrete period of time (e.g., within any 2-hour period), an amount of food that is definitely larger than most people would eat during a similar period of time and under similar circumstances.

(2) A sense of lack of control over eating during the episode (e.g., a feeling that one cannot stop eating or control what or how much one is eating).

B. Recurrent inappropriate compensatory behavior in order to prevent weight gain, such as self-induced vomiting; misuse of laxatives, diuretics, enemas; fasting; or excessive exercise.

C. The binge eating and inappropriate compensatory behaviors both occur, on average, at least twice a week for 3 months.

D. Self-evaluation is unduly influenced by body shape and weight.

E. The disturbance does not occur exclusively during episodes of Anorexia Nervosa.

Specify Type:

Purging Type: During the current episode of Bulimia Nervosa, the person has regularly engaged in self-induced vomiting or the misuse of laxatives, diuretics, or enemas.

Nonpurging Type: During the current episode of Bulimia Nervosa, the person has used other inappropriate compensatory behaviors, such as fasting or excessive exercise, but has not regularly engaged in self-induced vomiting or the misuse of laxatives, diuretics, or enemas.

Source: American Psychiatric Association, 2000.

advances, diets become increasingly restrictive. For example, one girl ate only two chicken livers a day, while another ate only celery sticks and chewing gum for a year before her death (Bruch, 1973). People who have anorexia often take extreme pride in the control they demonstrate over their food intake.

Among the secondary symptoms of anorexia, *excessive activity* is one of the most common. (Our review follows Foreyt and Mikhail, 1997, and Wilson, Heffernan, and Black, 1996, except where noted.) At times the intensity of the activity is masked by a socially acceptable form, such as participation in sports. *Amenorrhea* is another common secondary symptom, with menstruation often ceasing prior to weight loss.

Anorexia is one of the few psychopathologies that can lead to death. Mortality estimates suggest that about 5 percent die due to suicide or medical complications secondary to the disorder. Semistarvation can affect most major organ systems, resulting in anemia, renal system impairments, cardiovascular problems, osteoporosis, and an irreversible shortness of stature. Chronic dehydration and depletions in serum potassium lead to imbalances in the electrolyte system that is crucial to heart functioning; cardiac arrhythmia and sudden death may ensue.

Prevalence and Onset

Two peak periods of *onset,* ages 14 and 18, correspond to the transitions into and out of the adolescence phase.

Prevalence rates in normative populations have generally sampled children and adolescents in school and have arrived at estimates ranging from 0.2 percent to 0.58 percent (Doyle & Bryant-Waugh, 2000). However, some evidence suggests that these rates are underestimates, given that those with eating disorders appear to be disproportionately likely to decline to participate in prevalence studies (Wilson, Becker, & Heffernan, 2003).

The problem of how to identify cases is a general problem in epidemiological research. Large-scale epidemiological studies of anorexia generally have approached this problem by focusing on health care records, assuming that a dramatic weight loss is likely to bring the youth to the attention of a medical or mental health practitioner. A wide range of results is reported. For example, Joergensen (1992) conducted a study in Denmark in which he identified all females in a single county who over a period of 10 years had sought any form of psychiatric or medical treatment. The incidence rates for anorexia were 9.2 females per 100,000 for 10- to 14-year-old girls and 11.9 per 100,000 for 15- to 19-year-olds. Another large-scale study examined health care records of all individuals living in Rochester, Minnesota, over a period of 50 years (Lucas et al., 1991). Between the ages of 10 and 14, 25.7 females and 3.7 males per 100,000 met criteria for anorexia. In the 15- to 19-year-old age group, 69.4 females and 7.3 males per 100,000 were identified.

As these data suggest, there is a significant *gender difference,* with gender ratios of males to females between 1:29 and 1:10 (Doyle & Bryant-Waugh, 2000). However, these data include the entire age span, and when one looks specifically at *children,* the gender ratio may not be as imbalanced. Small-scale studies of clinical populations of children report that between 19 percent and 30 percent are boys.

Finally, while there is a common belief that the prevalence of anorexia is rising, evidence to support this is clouded by the fact that few good data are available, especially in regard to children. Increasing rates also may be accounted for by the growing awareness of eating disorders and availability of treatment.

Ethnicity and Social Class

Early evidence suggested that anorexia was disproportionately prevalent among youths from the middle and upper social classes. (Here we follow Doyle and Bryant-Waugh, 2000.) However, it is important to keep in mind that prevalence data often come from clinical samples, and more privileged members of society may have better access to treatment facilities. Studies of normative samples of children in London and Norway fail to find an association between social class and the development of eating disorders.

Although there is a dearth of studies including *ethnic minority* populations in the United States (Smolak & Striegel-Moore, 2001), evidence is growing that eating disorders are found across racial and ethnic lines. However, there are subcultural differences. While youths from Hispanic backgrounds have rates equivalent to those of European American youths, Asian American and African American youths are less likely to develop disordered eating (Crago, Shisslak, & Estes, 1996).

Cross-culturally, the assumption that eating disorders are exclusively the purview of Westernized European Americans does not appear to be borne out. For example, during the communist era, equivalent rates were found in Western and Eastern European countries. However, eating disorders are more prevalent in industrialized nations than in developing nations and increase as a function of exposure to Western ideals of thinness and the importance of physical appearance (Lake, Staiger, & Glowinski, 2000).

Comorbidity

Depression is often present in adolescents with anorexia, with one study reporting a comorbidity rate of 73 percent (Herzog et al., 1992). Such high comorbidity has led to the speculation that anorexia and depression share a common etiology. However, subsequent research indicated that, while they occur together, they are independent disturbances. For example, improvement in the eating disorder does not necessarily relieve the depression. Also, depressed mood tends to accompany any form of starvation.

Anxiety disorders are prevalent, particularly obsessive-compulsive disorder. Some longitudinal research suggests that obsessive traits predate the development of anorexic symptoms (Rastam, 1992). Other anxiety disorders are commonly seen, including social anxiety disorder. *Substance disorders* are most likely to occur in the binge-eating/purging subtype (Wilson, Becker, & Heffernan, 2003). *Personality disorders* co-occur in as many as 74 percent of those with anorexia (Skodol et al., 1993), also particularly among those who binge and purge.

Etiology

The Biological Context

Genetics   Anorexia tends to run in families. For example, Strober and colleagues (2000) found that individuals with anorexia were 11.3 times more likely to have a family member with anorexia and 4.2 times more likely to have a family member with bulimia when compared to normative controls. Twin studies reveal some evidence of a genetic component in anorexia. For example, the concordance rate for monozygotic twins has been found to be approximately 10 times greater than for dizygotic twins (Lask, 2000). However, the results of twin studies are highly inconsistent, with heritability estimates ranging from 0 percent to 70 percent (Fairburn, Cowen, & Harrison, 1999). A specific genetic mechanism has not been identified.

Neurochemistry   Speculation has implicated in anorexia an endocrine disorder that affects the hypothalamic-pituitary-gonadal axis. However, many of the biological correlates of anorexia appear to be secondary to weight loss and are reversible with weight gain. Therefore, it is unclear whether these abnormalities are causal or are secondary to starvation, dieting, bingeing, and/or purging (Lask, 2000).

Kaye and colleagues (2003) have focused attention on *serotonergic* functioning in anorexia nervosa. These authors speculate that premorbid imbalances in serotonin precipitate dysphoric mood, which is accompanied by anxiety, obessional thinking, and perfectionism. Self-starvation, as those with anorexia subsequently discover, reduces brain serotonin overactivity and lifts dysphoric mood, thus making this behavior highly reinforcing.

Brain-Imaging Studies   Although a number of abnormalities in brain structure and function have been found in individuals with eating disorders, these also generally appear to be consequences of self-starvation and reverse when normal weight returns (Lask, 2000). An exception to this may be the finding of an asymmetrical reduction of blood flow in the anterior temporal lobe of children and adolescents with anorexia (Gordon et al., 1997), suggestive of an abnormality in the limbic system (Christie et al., 1998).

The Individual Context

The Body Image   Along with menstruation and breast development, females undergo a "fat spurt" during puberty, an accumulation of large quantities of subcutaneous fat that adds an average of 24 pounds of weight. The physical changes associated with puberty force the adolescent to make a fundamental reorganization of her body image, which—coupled with her increased capacity for self-reflection—may result in a preoccupation with her body and with the responses of others to it. There is evidence that these pubertal changes are linked to preoccupation with weight and dieting in normative populations (Howard & Porzelius, 1999). In addition, *early-maturing* girls are more likely to develop eating disorders than those who begin to physically develop later (Swarr & Richards, 1996).

Studies of individuals with anorexia have suggested a developmental sequence in which body dissatisfaction leads to typical dieting attempts, which give way to preoccupation with food and weight and the use of increasingly more maladaptive methods of weight control. Therefore, *ordinary dieting,* in the context of other psychological risk factors, may be the first step in a trajectory toward psychopathology (Wilson, 2002).

Bruch's (1973) clinical observations suggest that girls with anorexia often have *inaccurate perceptions* of their bodies. They literally do not perceive how thin their bodies have become. One patient had difficulty discriminating between two photographs of herself even though there was a 70-pound difference in her weight. Another said she could see how emaciated her body was when looking in a mirror, but when she looked away, she reverted to her belief that she was larger. Thus, the image of the body, which is a reasonably accurate psychological construction in normal development, borders on a somatic delusion in anorexia. Perception is determined not by reality but by emotional conflicts. According to Bruch's (1973) classic theory, the anorexic's pursuit of self-respect

Anorexia involves a distortion of the body image.

through food refusal is expressed in the vain pursuit of a body that literally is never perceived as sufficiently thin. More recent research confirms the relationship between eating disorder symptomatology and distortions in body image (Foreyt & Mikhail, 1997).

Bruch (1973) also suggests that anorexic girls are unable to accurately identify and discriminate between *proprioceptive* (internal body) states, such as hunger, satiety, anger, and sadness. Therefore, they are likely to mislabel their feelings or to confuse emotions such as anger with the desire to eat. Measurement of poor proprioceptive awareness is included in screening assessments for anorexia and has been found to be associated with increased risk for the development of the disorder (Lyon et al., 1997).

Personality Characteristics   *Low self-esteem* is commonly seen in youths with anorexia, who describe themselves in such terms as bad and unworthy (see Box 12.1). *Anxiety, obsessionality,* and *perfectionism* are particularly salient characteristics of those with anorexia and, moreover, seem to predate the onset of the eating disorder and persist even after recovery (Deep et al., 1995).

While both types of anorexia are characterized by their pursuit of thinness, those who *restrict* tend to be more rigid and conforming, socially insecure, obsessional, and lacking in insight.

Those who *binge-purge,* who make up about half the population of those with anorexia, are more extroverted and sociable but are more emotionally dysregulated and alternate between rigid overcontrol and undercontrol. They also tend to have problems with *impulsivity* and are prone to using maladaptive strategies to cope with unpleasant emotions, such as substance abuse or self-harming behavior, including suicide attempts (Garner, 1993). Overall, those who binge-purge have more extreme and overt psychopathology. For example, in their study of 50 women hospitalized for anorexia, Casper, Hedeker, and McClough (1992) found that restricters were higher in self-control, inhibition of emotion, and conscientiousness. By contrast, binge-purgers were more impulsive; and while they shared the restricters' belief in moral family values, they were emotionally more adventurous and had more characterological problems.

In one of the few studies to focus on *males,* Carlat, Camargo, and Herzog (1997) investigated the records of all males who had been treated for eating disorders at Massachusetts General Hospital over a 14-year period. Of the 135 identified, 22 percent were anorexic. Over half of these suffered from major depression, and personality disorders and substance abuse were also common.

Cognition   Fairburn, Shafran, and Cooper (1999) give cognitions a central role in their theory of the origins of anorexia, particularly an *excessive need for control.* Control over food intake and weight become essential to escape from intolerable underlying perceptions of the self as ineffective and inadequate. However, the intense urge to eat that follows from self-starvation threatens to reinstate perceived powerlessness, thus motivating further dietary restriction. Other *cognitive distortions,* such as perfectioninsm, "catastrophizing," overgeneralizing, and personalizing, have been found in those with anorexia to a much greater degree than in controls, as have dysfunctional cognitive styles such as obsessional thinking and negative self-judgments (Foreyt & Mikhail, 1997).

The fact that cognitive factors are also important in regulating eating behavior has been demonstrated in studies of normative dieters. Adherence to a diet is cognitively controlled, often in the form of quotas on food intake, carefully counting of calories, and assiduous self-monitoring. However, chronic dieters are vulnerable to black-and-white thinking that can lead to *counterregulatory eating,* or binge eating on high-calorie food; for example, the belief that one has transgressed one's diet can break the dieter's resolve and trigger increased food consumption (Foreyt & Mikhail, 1997). Such findings on normative populations are relevant to understanding the binge-purge cycle.

One of the cognitive factors that makes anorexia difficult to treat is that the disorder is *ego syntonic;* that is to say that those with anorexia view the symptoms as consistent with their self-image and personal goals. Unlike other disorders, in which youths are unhappy with their symptoms and desire to free themselves of them, those with anorexia view achieving an extremely low weight as "a triumph of self-discipline, upon which their self-esteem depends" (Wilson, Becker, & Heffernan, 2003). Consequently, the motivation to change may be weak or completely absent.

The Family Context

Family Systems Theory   Minuchin, Rosman, and Baker's (1978) observations of "anorexic families" provided the basis for much of the theorizing about the influence of the family system on psychopathology. They describe four characteristic patterns of interaction in families of adolescents with anorexia:

1. *Enmeshment.* Members of the pathologically enmeshed family are highly involved and responsive

Box 12.1 | A Case Study in Anorexia

"At 5 years of age I began to suffer from compulsive behaviour. That meant that I would take my socks on and off up to four or five times before I was satisfied. When walking along the pavement it was imperative that I avoided the cracks. This obsession with ordinary habits meant that I was late for everything and my parents would leave me behind as a punishment. Psychiatrists advised my mother to ignore my 'negative behaviour' and reward only 'good behaviour.' As a result I felt rejected and loved only for the 'good' me.

"When I was 8 we visited my grandfather in Tuscany, and a chance remark deeply affected me. I shall never forget sitting on the grass and looking out at the glistening ocean as I experienced the last few moments of childhood innocence. My grandfather strolled past with my father and remarked, 'Tara is a cute little girl, but when she loses her puppy fat she will be really beautiful!' Presumably my grandfather meant well, but he was unaware of the power his poisonous words were to have. I was sensitive and remember desperately wanting to be perfect in every way.

"Before reaching my ninth birthday I had begun dieting. Along with a drastic reduction in my food intake were some rather unusual habits. I started drinking from a baby bottle and using a baby knife and fork. I found clothes from my early childhood in the attic and began wearing them. This baby syndrome was a desire to be a loveable baby again, like my brother who was a year old and loved by everyone. . . .

"In school during lunch a child in my class tormented me: 'Every bite of food you eat is making you fatter,' he teased. Dieting fads filtered all the way down to the playground. Parents who slimmed passed a 'thin is best' message to their children, encouraged by the media. It is no coincidence that I obtained the starring role in my school play in the midst of my weight loss. The more I suffered from anorexia nervosa the more determined I became to be the best. . . .

to one another but in an intrusive way. As we saw in Chapter 1, enmeshed families have poorly differentiated perceptions of each other, and roles and lines of authority are diffuse (e.g., children may assume parental roles).

2. *Overprotectiveness.* Family members of psychosomatically ill children are overly concerned for each other's welfare. A sneeze can set off "a flurry of handkerchief offers," and criticism must be cushioned by pacifying behavior. The family's overprotectiveness and exaggerated concern for the child retard the development of autonomy, and the child, in turn, feels responsible for protecting the family from distress.

3. *Rigidity.* Pathological families resist change. Particularly during periods of normal growth, such as adolescence, they intensify their efforts to retain their customary patterns. One consequence of rigidity is that the child's illness is used as an excuse for avoiding problems accompanying change.

4. *Lack of conflict resolution.* Some families deny conflict; others bicker in a diffuse, scattered, in-

effectual way; and yet others have a parent who is conflict-avoidant, such as a father who leaves the house every time a confrontation threatens.

Minuchin, Rosman, and Baker (1978) describe the family of the future anorexic as overly concerned with diet, appearance, and control. The family's intrusiveness undermines the child's autonomy, and both her psychological and bodily functions are continually subject to scrutiny. Adolescence is a particularly stressful time for the enmeshed family, which is unable to cope with the developmental task of separation. The youth, sensing the stress, responds with troubled behavior such as self-starvation. Perhaps even more important, being symptomatic helps to maintain the youth in an ostensibly dependent role in relation to her parents, while at the same time her refusal to eat allows her a covert form of rebellion.

Some empirical support can be found for the family model. For example, Fosson and coworkers (1987) found that the families of girls with anorexia evidenced overinvolvement, failure to

"I was convinced that the thinner I was the more loveable I would be to the rest of the world. Fashion spreads filled the walls of my bedroom and the emaciated figure of the average fashion model became the god I worshipped. . . . I insisted I was eating—it just happened when no one was around. When the school doctor weighed me I stole some kilogram weights and hid them in my pocket. . . .

"The way forward only emerged when I entered . . . long-term treatment and lived there for 10 months. My parents came in for meals and family therapy. During these meals my parents practiced working as a team. This was a major change from previous meals, which were filled with arguments and anxiety. They learned how to listen and communicate when there was tension. Weekends were spent at home where the skills we learned during the week were practiced. . . . The goal treatment was particularly effective. If I behaved and ate properly I would achieve my goal in the form of a special treatment. . . . From the beginning of my hospitalisation I had individual therapy sessions. . . . Therapy became a constant and stable part of my life. . . .

"So, what does cause anorexia nervosa in children? It seems to me that there are a variety of contributing factors: parental relations, school pressures—including academic expectations and relationships with other children, media images that are often absorbed unconsciously, and an extremely negative self-image. As an anorexic child I struggled daily with intense feelings of negativity that seemed to confirm my unworthiness. In my mind I was not valuable enough to be fed properly. From personal experience I believe that one of the greatest needs during anorexia is reassurance and the continual confirmation that the sufferer is loveable and worthy."

Source: Haggiag, 2000.

resolve conflicts, and poor communication, while Kog and colleagues (1985) found high levels of enmeshment in families of both anorexic and bulimic patients. Rowa, Kerig, and Geller (2001) similarly found evidence for enmeshment in the relationships between girls with anorexia and their parents. Humphrey (1989) compared the observed interactions of the families of typically developing female adolescents and girls with eating disorders. In support of Minuchin's ideas, parents of daughters with anorexia tended to communicate a double message of nurturance and affection and to discount the daughter's expressions of her own thoughts and feelings. The daughters, in turn, vacillated between asserting their feelings and yielding to their parents.

While other studies have failed to support Minuchin's hypotheses, empirical evidence does consistently show that families with an anorexic member exhibit conflict and dysfunctional communication patterns, particularly between the parents (Kog & Vandereycken, 1988). However, it is not clear whether these are predictors or consequences of the disorder. Further, these family dynamics are not unique to the development of anorexia; they are found in families of children with other forms of psychopathology. A similar case can be made for other family factors associated with anorexia. For example, a family history of depression—especially maternal depression—has been linked not only to an increased risk of anorexia (Lyon et al., 1997), but to several other disorders as well (see Chapter 9). Consequently, a number of authors have refuted the idea that there is one "anorexogenic" family type (Rastam & Gillberg, 1991).

Child Maltreatment   Looking beyond the larger family system, researchers have investigated whether other factors in the parent-child relationship are related to the development of anorexia. For example, studies of the prevalence of *sexual abuse* in those with eating disorders range from 34 percent to 85 percent, depending on the definitions and methods used (Bryant-Waugh & Lask, 1995). However, these studies are generally drawn from clinical populations where maltreatment rates are likely to be high. More carefully designed research has established that sexual abuse is a general risk factor for psychopathology, but not a *specific* risk factor for anorexia (Fairburn et al., 1999). Nonetheless, it is possible that, for some women, an unwanted sexual experience is indeed a precipitating factor in the development of anorexia (Lask, 2000).

A well-conceived study by Romans and colleagues (2001) investigated the factors that differentiated between women with a history of childhood sexual abuse who did and did not go on to develop an eating disorder. Those who went on to develop disordered eating were likely to be younger, to have started menstruation early, and to describe their fathers as overcontrolling. No variables associated with sexual abuse per se (e.g., its frequency, duration, and type) contributed to the prediction of eating-disordered behavior.

The Social Context

Females with anorexia often report that they were *excessively shy,* or even friendless, as children. In adolescence they are also reluctant to form close relationships outside the family, thereby isolating themselves from the important growth-promoting functions of peer relations in the adolescent period. *Sexual relations,* in particular, are avoided. For example, Leon and associates (1985) found that both restricting and binge-purging females had a markedly negative evaluation of sex and lacked interest in developing sexual relationships; and Carlat, Camargo, and Herzog (1997) report that 58 percent of males with anorexia were described as "asexual" in that they eschewed any interest in sexual activity.

There may actually be a *developmental shift* in the sexual behavior of eating-disordered girls. Cauffman and Sternberg (1996) found that girls with disordered eating matured sooner and were involved in sexual activity earlier than other girls. Although they appear more mature than their years, these girls may be emotionally unprepared for the social pressures associated with sexuality. Over time, anxiety about their appearance, lack of pleasure derived from sex, and the withdrawal associated with self-starvation

lead them to withdraw from the sexual activities that contributed to the disorder in the first place.

Research on anorexia is complicated by the fact that starvation per se significantly affects behavior, producing depression, irritability, social isolation, and decreased sexual interest. Starvation can also alter relationships with family members and friends, who are helpless to intervene in eating patterns that produce striking emaciation and might result in death. Thus, the problem of distinguishing causes from consequences is a knotty one.

The Cultural Context

Femininity and Body Ideals   In our society the ideal of feminine beauty has changed from the curvaceous figure epitomized by such icons as Marilyn Monroe to the lean and svelte look admired today. For example, contestants in Miss America pageants have steadily decreased in weight over the past decades. Currently the average weight of beauty pageant contestants is 13 to 19 percent below normal—the "ideal" woman, in other words, meets the first criterion for an eating-disorder diagnosis (Attie & Brooks-Gunn, 1995).

Few young women are able to achieve the exaggeratedly tall and thin proportions exemplified by pageant contestants and high-fashion models. But cultural norms dictate that "fat" is ugly and what is ugly is bad, while thin is beautiful and what is beautiful is good. Moreover, the message is more powerful in certain settings; for example colleges and boarding schools, where beauty and dating are emphasized, and professions such as dancing and modeling, which dictate certain body weights, are breeding grounds for anorexia.

Further, there is evidence that *physical attractiveness* is central to the female sex-role stereotype but is peripheral to the masculine sex-role stereotype, which may account for the fact that far fewer men become anorexic. There are two exceptions to this. First, males who endorse feminine sex-role characteristics appear to be as vulnerable as females to developing disordered attitudes toward eating (Meyer, Blissett, & Oldfield, 2001). Another exception may be found in the gay community, where the greater attention to physical appearance is believed to act as a risk factor for eating disorders in homosexual males (Carlat, Camargo, & Herzog, 1997).

Ethnicity and Culture Some evidence suggests that ethnic minority status in the United States might be a protective factor against eating disorders. African Americans and Hispanics express less dissatisfaction with their bodies than do European Americans and endorse ideals of body shape that are both more generous and more flexible (Smolak & Striegel-Moore, 2001). On the other hand, when viewed cross-culturally, eating disorders are increasingly found across social strata and ethnicities as Western values exert their influence (see Nasser, Katzman, & Gordon, 2001).

A contrasting view is offered by Doyle and Bryant-Waugh (2000), who report that in their clinical work the ethnic minority youths most likely to develop eating disorders are not those who are more exposed to Westernization, but rather those who experience more conflict between the values of their families and the wider culture. Children whose parents rigidly maintain traditional cultural practices and socialize exclusively with members of their own group are more likely to have difficulty reconciling the disparities between their home lives and the norms and expectations of their peers and schools. These internal conflicts, the authors suggest, may represent a risk factor for the development of eating disorders.

Developmental Course

Follow-up studies show that as few as 25 percent of those with anorexia fully recover (Neiderman, 2000). Therefore, anorexia is considered to be a highly intractable disorder that is resistant to treatment (Garner, Vitousek, & Pike, 1997). While almost half may show *partial recovery,* many continue to be seriously impaired. Even in treated populations, depression, anxiety, obsessive-compulsive disorders, and substance abuse tend to persist (Niederman, 2000). While symptoms of depression and anxiety generally predate the onset of the eating disorder, those with a worse outcome at follow-up are those who were more anxious prior to the development of

anorexia (Toner, Garfinkel, & Garner, 1988). Anorexia may also be a precursor to *bulimia* for some; almost a third of Strober and colleagues' (1997) sample of 95 adolescents with anorexia went on to develop binge eating within a 5-year period.

Considering the stage-salient issues of adolescence, long-term follow-ups show that educational and occupational achievement are generally unaffected, while social relationships outside of the family—particularly with other-sex peers—remain problematic for adolescents recovering from anorexia. Individuation from the family is a particular area of conflict and concern for these youths (Neiderman, 2000).

Early onset (i.e., before 16 years of age) may be associated with a less negative prognosis in that the disorder has yet to become chronic and an entrenched pattern of behavior (Lock et al., 2002).

Protective factors that increase the likelihood of recovery include good family functioning and early, intensive intervention (Neiderman, 2000).

Eating Disorders: Bulimia Nervosa

Definition and Characteristics

Bulimia Nervosa is characterized by recurrent episodes of binge eating, or the rapid consumption of large quantities of food in a brief period of time. Binge eating is followed by attempts to prevent weight gain, such as through self-induced vomiting and the misuse of laxatives or diuretics (the *purging type*) or by fasting and excessive exercise (the *nonpurging type*). Although individuals with bulimia may be either under- or overweight, their weight is usually within the average range. (See Table 12.1 on p. 361.)

A binge should be distinguished from normal overeating. True bingeing involves ingestion of food irrespective of actual hunger, consuming to the point of discomfort or even pain, and subsequent feelings of self-disgust or depression. While it was once thought that a binge involved eating a large quantity of food, and this misconception remains in the DSM-IV-TR criteria, subsequent research has disconfirmed this (Guertin, 1999). Instead, individuals with bulimia are

Binge eating.

terrified of losing control over their eating, and this feeling of loss of control, rather than the amount of food consumed, differentiates a binge from ordinary overindulgence. In their all-or-none way of thinking, young women with bulimia fear that even eating a small amount of a forbidden food could result in catastrophic intake. In a less extreme form, they also share the anorexic fear of becoming obese and perceive themselves as fat even when their body weight is normal. Thus, the desire to gorge traps the adolescent between anxiety over anticipated loss of control and obesity on the one hand and guilt, shame, and self-contempt following a binge on the other hand.

Although less often associated with death than self-starvation, purging also represents a serious risk to *physical health*. Bingeing and vomiting can harm the stomach and esophagus, and the repeated wash of stomach acids can erode the enamel of the teeth, causing permanent damage. (See Box 12.2.) Overuse of laxatives can result in dependence and severe constipation upon withdrawal as well as permanent colon damage. Frequent purging causes electrolyte and fluid imbalances, leading to weakness, lethargy, and depression, as well as kidney problems, irregular heartbeat, and sudden death. Habitual vomiting is also associated with broken blood vessels in the face,

blotchy skin, excessive water retention, and enlargement of the salivary glands, producing a "chipmunk cheek" appearance; also, the odor of vomitus may linger on the purger. Thus, the goal of being physically attractive is defeated by the maladaptive strategies used to pursue it.

Prevalence and Onset   Bulimia has a later age of *onset* than anorexia. With a mean age of onset of 18, bulimia may begin in the adolescent or early adult years (Lewinsohn, Striegel-Moore, & Seeley, 2000). The *prevalence* of bulimia in female adolescents and young adults overall is about 1 percent, but this rises to an estimated 4 percent in college females. Larger percentages are found when studies inquire about binge-purging without reference to DSM criteria. For example, almost 20 percent of one sample of college students admitted to engaging in such behavior.

As with anorexia, our statistics may represent underestimates of the actual prevalence rates. A particular concern is that data on prevalence, as well as the characteristics and correlates of bulimia, are often drawn from clinical populations. However, a carefully designed series of studies conducted by a group at Oxford University (Fairburn, Cooper, Welch, & Doll, 1999) utilized a case-control design to recruit a representative sample of 102 bulimic, 204 matched controls, and 102 psychiatric controls and uncovered the fact that 75 percent of those with bulimia had never sought treatment for their disorder.

The *gender differences* for bulimia are not as extreme as those in anorexia. While most bulimia is seen in females, it is estimated that 10 to 15 percent of those with bulimia are male. Evidence suggests that, in comparison to females, males show a later onset (between ages 18 and 26), a higher prevalence of childhood obesity, and less involvement with dieting (Carlat, Camargo, & Herzog, 1997).

There are *social class* and *ethnic differences* in prevalence rates. Bulimia is more often diagnosed in higher SES and in European American girls than in those from other social classes and ethnic groups (Attie & Brooks-Gunn, 1995). *Cross-culturally,* bulimia is most prevalent in highly industrialized societies, such as the United States, Canada, Europe,

Box 12.2 | **A Case Study in Bulimia**

"I no longer clearly remember the first time I forced myself to throw up. What I do remember is how inexpert I was and how long it took before I succeeded in actually vomiting instead of just gagging and retching. . . . In my mid-teens I was too young to believe I was anything but immortal. It didn't occur to me that what I was doing was dangerous—instead, it seemed a smart and practical way of coping with things. I went through months of throwing up once or twice a day, then brief periods when I did not throw up at all, when I seemed to have broken the pattern. Surely this meant I was in control. But by the time I turned 18, the months of not throwing up had diminished to weeks, and when I was vomiting I was doing it four, five, six times a day. I had become addicted to the sensation. It was no longer a penance I had to perform after eating, but the reward at the end of a binge. I loved the feeling I had after purging, of being clean and shiny inside like a

scrubbed machine, superhuman. I would rise from the bathroom floor, splash my face with cold water, vigorously brush the acid from my mouth. I would take a wet cloth, wipe off the vomit that had spattered my arms, and feel as energized as someone who had just woken from a nap or returned from an invigorating jog around the block. I felt as if everything inside me had been displaced so that it was now outside myself. Not only all the food I had eaten, but my entire past. No one could tell me to stop, not even my friends, who eventually knew what I was doing. They could not control this part of my life or any other. This was mine alone. . . .

"I finally stopped being bulimic nearly two years ago, when I was 22. It ended not because of willpower or therapy. . . . It ended because the pain from throwing up rendered the pleasure slight by comparison. It ended when my softened teeth cringed at every mouthful and when I woke

several times each night with cramps wracking my stomach. . . . It ended when I arrived at the point where I could no longer feel my feet. Months later, when I went to the doctor, he would diagnose it as an electrolyte imbalance caused by the vomiting up of so many vitamins and minerals. . . . By then I had also developed a hiatal hernia—a portion of my stomach protruded through my esophagus—and my teeth became so compromised that one day one of them simply disintegrated under pressure. . . .

"The last time I forced myself to throw up, it felt like internal surgery. Grief, love, rage, pain—it all came pouring out, yet afterwards it was still there inside me. I had been bulimic off and on for eight years, and in all that vomiting I had not purged myself of any of the things that were making me sick."

Source: Lau, 1995.

Australia, and Japan (American Psychiatric Association, 2000).

Comorbidity

Anxiety disorders are found in as many as 70 percent of females with bulimia in the clinical population (Wonderlich & Mitchell, 1997) and in 58 percent of those in community samples (Garfinkel et al., 1995). These include obsessive-compulsive disorder, social phobia, generalized anxiety, and posttraumatic stress disorder. Symptoms of *depression* are frequently seen: Between 25 and 80 percent meet criteria for an affective disorder at some point in their illness (Wonderlich & Mitchell, 1997). *Substance abuse* frequently co-occurs; for example, alcohol abuse is found in 30 to 50 percent of individuals

seeking treatment for bulimia (Dansky, Brewerton, & Kilpatrick, 2000). These two disorders also share in common particular predisposing personality factors, including the inability to regulate negative feelings, the need for immediate gratification, and a fragile sense of self. It is estimated that between 21 and 77 percent of those with bulimia also meet criteria for one or more *personality disorders* (Wonderlich & Mitchell, 1997), particularly borderline personality (Skodol et al., 1993).

Differential Diagnosis

Both bulimia and anorexia may involve bingeing and purging. However, bulimia is differentiated from anorexia by virtue of the fact that only in

Box 12.3 | **Dysregulation as Excess Versus Insufficiency: The Role of Serotonin in Eating Disorders**

The serotonin (5-HT) neurotransmitter system is familiar to us as a suspect in the developmental psychopathology of depression (see Chapter 9). In addition, serotonin plays an important role in the modulation of appetite, which makes it a prime candidate in the search for factors leading to eating disorders. If there are problems with the modulation of serotonin in eating disorders, are they a matter of excess or insufficiency?

On the excess side of the equation, Kaye and colleagues (2003) propose the theory that individuals with anorexia have increased activity of brain serotonergic systems. Typically, increased brain serotonin activity leads to a feeling of satiety and cessation of eating, which might account for the anorexic avoidance of food consumption. However, excessive serotonin can lead to dysphoric mood states, particularly anxiety, which is commonly seen in individuals with anorexia even prior to the onset of their eating disorder. Noting that starvation is associated with reduced levels of 5-HT activity, Kaye and colleagues propose that extreme dieting in anorexia serves the function of reducing anxiety and dysphoric mood by lowering levels of serotonin in the brain. To test this theory, the investigators depleted brain levels of serotonin by administering to research participants an amino acid mixture that was free of tryptophan (a precursor to serotonin that directly affects serotonergic functioning). In support of their hypotheses, the investigators found that both women with acute anorexia and those who had recovered from the disorder reported a significant decline in anxiety after undergoing the tryptophan depletion procedure, whereas this was not true of a sample of nonanorexic controls. Thus, the authors of the study suggest that, due to an innate disturbance of serotonin, those with anorexia turn to restricted eating in an attempt to regulate dysphoric mood. The effects are only fleeting,

anorexia does the individual maintain an extremely low body weight.

While binge eating is a hallmark of bulimia, not all who binge meet criteria for the bulimia diagnosis. The DSM-IV-TR includes another category, *Binge Eating Disorder* (BED), which is listed among the diagnoses proposed for further study and possible inclusion in future editions of DSM. BED is characterized by the consumption of large amounts of food in a short time, accompanied by a feeling of lack of control over eating as well as subjective distress and self-disgust. Unlike bulimia, however, those with BED do not use inappropriate compensatory mechanisms (e.g., vomiting, laxatives, excessive exercise) to rid themselves of the calories they have consumed.

Bingeing, whether or not it is accompanied by purging, may result in weight gain and even *obesity*. However, despite the popular conception that obesity is a sign of psychological problems, it is important to note that obesity per se is not considered to be a form of psychopathology nor an eating disorder (Wilson, Becker, & Heffernan, 2003). Troubled people may overeat in an attempt to soothe themselves and obese persons may develop eating disorders, but obesity itself is best considered to be a metabolic problem.

Etiology

The Biological Context

Genetics   As does anorexia, bulimia tends to run in families. For example, Strober and colleagues (2000) found that rates of bulimia were 4.4 times higher and rates of anorexia 12.3 times higher in female relatives of those with bulimia as compared to normative controls. Genetic studies comparing concordance rates between monozygotic and dizygotic twins reveal highly inconsistent findings, with heritability estimates ranging from 0 to 83 percent (Fairburn, Cowen, & Harrison, 1999).

There is likely to be a history of *maternal obesity* in the families of adolescents diagnosed with bulimia. Therefore, there is speculation that a constitutional predisposition makes weight loss difficult for these however, as compensatory mechanisms in the brain attempt to right the imbalance and dysphoria resumes with the onset of eating.

In sum, for anorexia, the equation might look as follows:

Innate Excessive Serotonin → Anxiety → Dieting → Lowered Serotonin → Temporary Reduction in Dysphoria

The case of bulimia is quite a different story, one that leans toward the insufficiency side of the equation. Lowered levels of serotonin have been shown experimentally to lead to excessive eating and dysfunction of satiety

mechanisms as well as to depressed mood. Further, dieting itself lowers plasma tryptophan, and in the vast majority of cases, dieting is a precursor to bulimia. Noting these facts, Smith, Fairburn, and Cowen (1999) proposed that insufficient serotonin levels might play a role in bulimia. Their test of this theory involved the same tryptophan depletion procedure used by Kaye and colleagues (2003) in order to lower plasma levels of serotonin in a sample of women who had recovered from bulimia and a comparison group of nonclinical controls. Women who had previously suffered from bulimia were more likely than controls to respond to tryptophan depletion by an increase in

reported depressive symptoms, concerns about body image (i.e., feeling fat), and fear of losing control over their eating. The authors also noted that the greatest increases in depression were seen in those participants with bulimia who had a history of co-morbid major depression, suggesting that this subgroup may be particularly vulnerable to relapse when serotonin neurotransmission is lowered.

In sum, for bulimia the equation might look as follows:

Dieting → Insufficient Serotonin → Depressed Mood and Urge to Overeat → Binge/Purging

individuals. The tendency toward being overweight increases the likelihood that they will be dissatisfied with their body shape and that they will attempt excessive weight-loss strategies such as purging (Stice & Whitenton, 2002). However, extreme dieting strategies tend to backfire, resulting in weight gain rather than loss, further perpetuating the problem.

Neurochemistry   Bulimia is associated with disturbances in both the *noradrenergic* and *serotonergic* systems. Serotonin is a particularly likely prospect, given its important role in eating and satiety. While serotonin agonists tend to produce feelings of satiety and reduce food intake, serotonin antagonists lead to increased eating. (Here we follow Wilson, Becker, and Heffernan, 2003.) A number of studies have found that individuals with bulimia have low serotonergic activity. However, it is unclear whether these imbalances are causes or consequences of disordered eating. For example, Jimerson and colleagues (1997) note that deficient serotonin levels in those with bulimia were related to the number of

binge episodes participants reported engaging in prior to their study, thus leaving open the question of cause and effect. As bingeing becomes more frequent, serotonin levels decrease, while recovery from bulimia is associated with elevated serotonin metabolite activity.

As we know from our discussion of depression in Chapter 9, serotonin is clearly implicated in the development of mood disorders. One supposition is that underlying bingeing, purging, and restricted food intake is an attempt to regulate mood associated with depleted serotonin (Ferguson & Pigott, 2000; Kaye et al., 1998). (See Box 12.3.)

It is also important to note that *dieting* has both psychological and physiological effects that increase the likelihood of food cravings and binge eating (Leon, Fulkerson, Perry, & Early-Zald, 1995). Food restrictions lead to a decrease in plasma tryptophan, which directly affects brain serotonin levels, mood, and perceived satiety (Anderson et al., 1990). Restricting food intake thus contributes to both further weight gain and disordered eating.

Prospective research clearly links dieting to the development of bulimia. Indeed, in almost all cases, the onset of the disorder follows a period of dieting (Wilson, 2002). For example, in a population-based study in Australia, Patton and colleagues (1999) found that over a period of 6 months those who were "severe dieters" were 18 times more likely to develop an eating disorder than those who did not diet, and even moderate dieting increased the risk.

Taken together, these studies suggest a biological underpinning to bulimia, such that dieting decreases serotonergic activity in vulnerable individuals, which in turn leads to disordered eating in an attempt to correct the imbalance (Wilson, Becker, & Heffernan, 2003).

The Individual Context

Personality Characteristics   Although there is no clear bulimic personality, among the intrapersonal factors associated with bulimia are perfectionism, a need for approval, self-criticism, and low self-esteem. *Perfectionism* in particular appears to be a risk factor for the development of bulimia, and feelings of inadequacy and low self-worth are associated with disordered eating as early as in the sixth and seventh grades (Killen et al., 1994). Further, the self-esteem of youths with bulimia is dependent on the opinions of others. They seem to be willing to neglect their own needs and feelings in order to devote themselves to winning others' approval. *Anxiety* is also a common feature of bulimia, and some studies have shown that anxiety precedes the onset of bulimia and may precipitate eating problems (Schwalberg et al., 1992).

Further, adolescents with bulimia are described as being *sensitive to rejection* and being *high achievers,* with their strivings channeled into their dogged pursuit of thinness. They are likely to have a history of *childhood maladjustment* and to be emotionally unstable (Rodin, Striegel-Moore, & Silberstein, 1990).

Regarding *males,* Carlat and colleagues (1997) found that 42 percent of adolescent males in treatment for bulimia identified themselves as gay or bisexual. Over half suffered from major depression

and substance abuse, while personality disorders and anxiety were also common.

Emotion Regulation   In many ways the behavior of those with bulimia, like their eating pattern, suggests a basic difficulty in *self-regulation.* Research has begun to point toward emotion regulation as a motivator for disordered-eating behavior, particularly purging.

For example, in order to study the psychological processes associated with binge-purging, Johnson and Larson (1982) came up with an ingenious strategy. They asked women with bulimia to carry a pager so that the investigators could cue them to write down their thoughts, feelings, and behavior at random intervals throughout the day. Two hours before an episode of binge eating, women with bulimia reported feeling anger and guilt, while their perceptions of self-control and adequacy were low. During the binge, feelings of anger, guilt, and loss of control intensified. After the binge, feelings of depression, disgust, and self-deprecation dominated. Purges were associated with a reestablishment of a sense of calm, self-control, and adequacy— described in terms such as being "clean," "empty," "spaced out," and "ready to sleep." See Box 12.1 for an illustration of this in author Evelyn Lau's description of her own 8-year battle with bulimia.

Purging, therefore, seems to have certain reinforcing properties in itself. In fact, some researchers have speculated that individuals with bulimia binge so they will be able to purge (Heatherton & Baumeister, 1991). Purging seems to act as a form of *self-sedation,* allowing the adolescent to escape from negative affects and regulate her mood (Stice et al., 1996).

Stice, Burton, and Shaw (2004) examined the associations between bulimia and depression in a prospective study of 496 girls followed over a period of 2 years. The investigators found that depressive symptoms predicted the onset of bulimia but that bulimia, in turn, also increased the risk of depression. Thus, it appears that bulimic behavior begins as an attempt to self-soothe and regulate negative emotions; however, the biological changes (e.g., serotonin depletion) and psychological consequences (e.g., shame, guilt, poor self-image) associated with bingeing and purging ultimately only serve to exacerbate dysphoric mood.

Cognition   Like those with anorexia, young women with bulimia tend to have a *rigid* cognitive style marked by black-or-white, all-or-none thinking. Thus, they view themselves as completely in control or helpless, absolutely virtuous or slovenly (Wilson, Becker, & Heffernan, 2003).

Girls who develop bulimia, like those with anorexia, are more likely to buy into cultural ideals regarding thinness and to view their own body shapes as dissatisfactory (Stice, 1999). Cognitive conceptualizations of bulimia identify rigid and maladaptive beliefs in three domains: *unrealistic expectations* for her body weight and shape (e.g., the belief that weight loss will result in a figure of supermodel proportions); *distorted outcome beliefs* about body weight and shape (e.g., the belief that obtaining the desired weight is crucial to achieving success in life and will earn her the self-esteem she seeks); and *inaccurate conceptualizations of food and eating* (e.g., erroneous ideas about the digestive system, the caloric values of certain foods, and the biological mechanisms underlying weight loss) (Spangler, 1999). These distorted cognitions, along with a poor body image and perceived pressure to be thin, inspire her to utilize extreme efforts at weight control, which, in turn, set in motion the maladaptive physiological and psychological processes associated with bulimia.

Unlike anorexia, however, bulimia tends to be more *ego-dystonic,* or inconsistent with one's goals and self-perceptions. Those with bulimia are more likely to recognize that they suffer from a disorder and, despite some fear or ambivalence about giving up their maladaptive eating patterns, are more willing to try to change their behavior (Wilson, Becker, & Heffernan, 2003).

The Social Context

One way in which peer influences play a role is in terms of *initiating* the adolescent into bulimic behavior. Many adolescents are introduced to vomiting or use of laxatives as a weight-control technique by friends. (One young woman stopped giving in-

spirational talks about her own recovery from bulimia when she found that the high school girls who attended were only interested in learning the techniques she'd used for purging herself of food!) While most young women ultimately abstain from these maladaptive techniques, others become caught in the repetitive cycle of binge-purging.

Qualities of peer relationships also differentiate anorexia and bulimia. Adolescents with bulimia are more *socially extroverted* and outgoing and are thus more likely than those with anorexia to appear on the surface to be functioning adequately in their academic and social worlds. Further, adolescents with bulimia tend to be more *sexually active* than those with anorexia, and some are even promiscuous (Garfinkel & Garner, 1986). However, there is also evidence that they enjoy sex less than do other youths. Rather than seeking out sex for self-gratification, adolescents with bulimia are overly compliant with pressure to engage in sexual activities because of their strong need for social approval and difficulty identifying and asserting their own needs.

In the longer term, when the binge-purge cycle is well established, the shame and secretiveness associated with these activities tends to *social isolation* from peers. The adolescent with advanced bulimia is preoccupied with thoughts of food, eating, and purging to the point that all other matters fall by the wayside. Such adolescents spend less time socializing and more time alone than other youths. Many describe spending most of their time and energy planning and amassing food for their binges, as well as seeking seclusion in order to purge. As one remarked, "Food has become my closest companion" (Johnson & Larson, 1982).

The Family Context

In contrast to the family members of the adolescent diagnosed with anorexia, who may present themselves as untroubled except for the problems of the "identified patient," the family members of youths with bulimia are more likely to be overtly disturbed. *Parental psychopathology* is often observed, particularly depression and substance abuse (Fairburn et al., 1997).

As with anorexia, family relationships of those with bulimia have been described as enmeshed and rigid (Leon et al., 1994). However, more characteristic of bulimia is *family discord,* including parent-child conflict and overt hostility (Fairburn et al., 1997). Humphrey's (1989) observations indicate that, in contrast to those of nondisturbed female adolescents or those with anorexia, families of bulimics show less affection in their interactions. They are also "hostilely enmeshed," with family members blaming or controlling each other. When mothers thwart their efforts to assert their individuality, daughters submit in a petulant and passive-aggressive way. Other family characteristics that act as specific risk factors for bulimia include frequent parental absence, uninvolvement, high expectations, criticism, and interparental discord (Fairburn et al., 1997).

Family attitudes toward weight and dieting also appear to play a role in disordered eating. As early as 5 years of age, maternal concern about the daughter's weight and restricting her access to food are associated with lower perceived competence in girls (Davison & Birch, 2001). Consequently, eating disorders are more prevalent among girls whose parents make critical comments about their weight, body shape, or eating habits (Fairburn et al., 1997) and among those whose mothers and fathers diet (Pike & Rodin, 1991).

The Cultural Context

The same societal influences that contribute to the development of anorexia have been implicated in the development of bulimia, including Western culture's emphasis on slenderness and the tendency to judge females on the basis of their physical appearance. Striegel-Moore (1993) emphasizes two aspects of Western feminine sex-role socialization that contribute to the risk of bulimia: the emphasis placed on *beauty* as an essential component of femininity, and the *communal orientation* that leads girls to base their self-evaluations on the opinions and perceptions of others.

Empirical evidence in support of these ideas is available. Much less so than for males, the self-esteem of female children and adults is based on body image and is influenced by the opinions of others. Dissatis-

faction with body weight and maladaptive eating habits are endemic among young females in North America, even in the preadolescent years. Strikingly, as early as 5 years of age, girls whose weight is above average have a more negative self-image—not only of their bodies but of their cognitive abilities (Davison & Birch, 2001). Moreover, dieting, fear of fatness, and binge eating have been found in 31 to 46 percent of 9-year-old girls and in 46 to 81 percent of 10-year-old girls (Mellin, Irwin, & Scully, 1992). We live, Rodin, Striegel-Moore, and Silberstein (1990) claim, in "the age of eating disorders" (p. 361), and dissatisfaction with their appearance (see Figure 12.1) is women's "normative discontent" (p. 362).

However, not all individuals exposed to these social forces go on to develop eating disorders. Therefore, there must be an *interaction* between sociocultural and individual factors. For example, individuals with bulimia report greater perceived pressure from their peers and parents to be thin, and they are more likely to believe that society in general requires them to be slender (Stice et al., 1996). In this way, they seem to have internalized these larger social dictates more than other girls.

Developmental Course

When compared to anorexia, rates of *recovery* from an episode of bulimia are relatively high; Herzog and colleagues (1993) found that 56 percent of young women treated for bulimia were without symptoms after a period of 1 year. However, in a longer-term study, Keel and colleagues (1999) followed up 177 females treated at an eating disorders clinic after at least 10 years had passed and found that approximately 30 percent continued to engage in binge eating and/or purging. Unfortunately, over the course of the disturbance, periods of recovery are punctuated by episodes of *relapse*. So, like anorexia, bulimia tends to be a chronic disorder (Keller et al., 1992) although a more treatable one (Wilson & Fairburn, 2002).

Illustrating this, Fairburn and colleagues (2000) followed a group of women with bulimia over the course of 5 years. The participants, ranging in age from 16 to 35, underwent an assessment every 15 months. At the first 15-month follow-up, the

Figure 12.1

Concern about weight and dieting begins early in female development.

group as a whole showed improvement in their bulimic symptoms, and this was followed by continued gradual improvement in subsequent years. However, there was marked instability in their symptom picture, with each year approximately one-third remitting and one-third relapsing. At the final assessment 5 years later, 15 percent continued to meet DSM criteria for a diagnosis of bulimia, 2 percent met criteria for anorexia, and 35 percent met criteria for a nonspecific eating disorder. Strikingly, 41 percent of the participants now also met criteria for a major depressive disorder.

Thus, even when the symptoms of bulimia remit, disordered eating and body dissatisfaction in early adolescence are predictors of depression in girls (Stice & Bearman, 2001). The attempt to solve life problems via the attainment of slimness is doomed to fail.

A Comparison of Eating Disorders

Table 12.2 compares the diagnostic criteria and empirical findings concerning anorexia and bulimia. When compared with those who restrict their food intake, those with anorexia who binge and purge are more likely to have family or personal histories of obesity, experience more emotion dysregulation and substance abuse, characteristics that are also descriptive of bulimia. However, while families of adolescents with anorexia are characterized by rigidity and enmeshment, families of those with bulimia are more openly hostile, noncohesive, and nonnurturing.

Table 12.2

Comparison of Eating Disorders

Anorexia: Restricting Type	Anorexia: Binge-Purging Type	Bulimia	
Typical onset age 14		Typical onset age 18	
Excessive thinness		Average or overweight	
Intense fear of gaining weight		Fear of losing control overeating	
Disturbance of body image (self-perception as fat)		Self-evaluation unduly influenced by weight	
Amenorrhea		Normal menstruation	
Voluntary food restrictions	Binge eating and purging		
Family enmeshed, overprotective, rigid, poor conflict resolution	Family history of psychological problems, substance abuse; family discord and overt hostility		
Socially isolated	Socially insecure	Low self-esteem; rejection-sensitive	
Disinterested in sex		Sexually active with little enjoyment	
Overcontrolled	Emotionally labile		
Comorbid with depression, anxiety disorders, including social phobia and obsessive-compulsiveness	Comorbid with depression, anxiety, substance abuse, personality disorder		
Maternal history of anorexia	Family history and predisposition to overweight		
Ego syntonic (disinterested in treatment)	Ego dystonic (motivated to change)		

In general, bulimia and the binge-purging type of anorexia may have more in common with each other than either does with restricting-type anorexia. In fact, it has been suggested that it might be preferable to regard binge-purging anorexia as a special subgroup of bulimia rather than as a special subgroup of anorexia. However, more comparative studies must be done before the issue of classification can be resolved.

Integrative Developmental Models

Two of the more comprehensive accounts of the developmental psychopathology of eating disorders are those offered by Rodin, Striegel-Moore, and Silberstein (1990) and Attie and Brooks-Gunn (1995). As noted before, Rodin and colleagues emphasize *sociocultural* factors, including society's emphasis on thinness as a mark of beauty, and beauty as essential to the feminine ideal. However, clearly not all females exposed to these pressures develop eating disorders. Therefore, a number of predisposing, pre-

cipitating, and sustaining factors come into play in the various domains of development, interacting with one another in significant ways.

First, in the *biological* domain, a *temperament* characterized by a tendency toward obsessional thinking, rigidity, and poor adaptability to change may, in turn, leave the young woman poorly equipped to cope with the *stresses* of adolescence (Strober, 1995). Further, girls on the pathway to eating disorders typically begin *puberty* earlier than their peers (Fairburn et al., 1997), leading to increased unhappiness with their bodies because of the weight gain that naturally occurs at menarche. In addition, particularly in the case of bulimia, these girls may be genetically programmed to be heavier than the svelte ideal. Thus, the young woman predisposed to eating disorders is more vulnerable to societal pressures for thinness because she finds it physically difficult to achieve a slender body shape. Moreover, the girl headed toward disordered eating also is more likely to have internalized the belief that her appearance will determine how successful she will be in life, and so her natural form is unacceptable to her.

In the *family* domain, the parents are likely to be conflicted and insecure. In the case of anorexia, they are perfectionistic and judgmental, while, in the case of bulimia, they are emotionally disturbed and impulsive. Their care of the infant, therefore, while on the surface devoted and attentive, is marred by insensitivity, taking the form of intrusive overprotectiveness or excessive control. The result is a hostile-dependent relationship in which the exploited child cannot express her rage because of the fear that the mother will leave her alone and helpless. Because feeling states are given the labels acceptable to parents—rather than those accurate for the child—poor recognition of feelings, and difficulty regulating and expressing them, develops.

Strober and Humphrey (1987) propose that these family interactions undermine the daughter's development of a sense of *self-efficacy* and interfere with her development of strategies for coping with negative emotions. Thus, the parents overcontrol their daughter and ignore and negate her self-expression, which undermines her efforts to individuate and keeps her in a dependent state. When the normal development of healthy initiative and self-assertiveness (see Chapter 6) is blocked, the only alternative is self-destructive opposition. Also included in the individual domain are factors such as a *lack of autonomy* and sense of mastery, which contribute to a fear of maturation and impending adulthood. Other personality characteristics may include a strong need for social approval and immediate need for gratification, poor impulse control, rigid thinking, obsessionality, depression, and a fragile sense of self.

As Lask (2000) articulates, the issue of *dieting* comes into play because it offers one aspect of her life and her body over which the adolescent can exert control. However, while rigid control over eating restores a sense of control, achievement, and self-esteem, the results are only temporary and fuel ever more desperate and extreme dieting behaviors. (See Figure 12.2.)

Development comes into play in specific ways. Attie and Brooks-Gunn (1995) emphasize the signif-

icance of the fact that eating disorders tend to occur at two developmental transitions: at entry into adolescence and at the boundary between adolescence and young adulthood. The *stage-salient tasks* of adolescence, then, present a number of challenges. Tasks of early adolescence involve establishing a stable self-structure and regulating emotions, impulses, and self-esteem; resolving identity issues; developing sexual relationships and coping with the implications of reproductive capacity; renegotiating relationships with parents in order to develop autonomy while still remaining connected; and establishing achievement goals and a meaningful life trajectory. During the transition to adulthood, tasks include establishing intimate relationships, determining and pursuing one's own values and goals, and developing an independent identity.

However, for females especially, a number of factors conspire against the easy resolution of issues related to sexuality, identity, and achievement. By middle childhood, a girl's self-esteem begins to depend on others' opinions of her. In addition, a girl's perception of her own attractiveness, popularity, and success is often related to a thin body image. However, the pubertal fat spurt, coupled with increasing social sensitivity and the equating of self-worth with physical appearance image, may well cause distress and lead to preoccupation with weight and dieting.

Because of her prior history and psychological makeup, the young woman vulnerable to eating disorders is particularly ill equipped to cope with the normative demands of adolescence. Although she cannot halt the changes occurring in her body or in her interpersonal world, food becomes one realm in which she can exert some control. Anorexia is thus a distorted attempt to resolve the conflict between the uncontrollable and rapid changes associated with the onset of puberty on the one hand, and the need for order and predictability on the other (Strober, 1995).

Intervention

Adolescents with eating disorders are difficult to treat successfully. Half of those treated continue to have eating difficulties and psychological problems. Even recovered patients continue to have distorted attitudes toward eating and weight, along with depression and

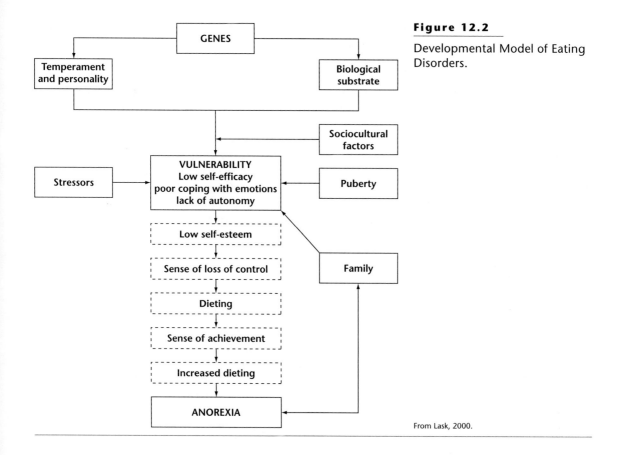

Figure 12.2

Developmental Model of Eating Disorders.

From Lask, 2000.

unsatisfactory social relations. Thus, there is a tendency toward chronicity even with long and intensive treatment. Many different interventions have been proposed. (See Miller and Mizes, 2000, for a fascinating comparison of how various treatment approaches would be applied to a single case.)

Pharmacological Intervention

Some promising results in the treatment of bulimia have been found with *antidepressants,* particularly the newer type of SSRIs (see Chapter 9). However, while medications may be helpful in alleviating comorbid psychopathologies such as anxiety or depression, they have little effect on eating behavior or weight gain (Lock et al., 2002). Therefore, medications are generally used as an adjunct to, rather than as a replacement for, other forms of therapy.

Psychodynamic Psychotherapy

Central to the psychodynamic perspective on eating disorders is poor ego functioning. Without adequate defenses and ego strengths, the adolescent is unable to identify, articulate, and modulate internal affective states, thus experiencing them as "intolerable, dangerous, and overwhelming" (Fallon & Bunce, 2000, p. 86). The goals of therapy are to strengthen ego functions and to allow the adolescent to achieve insight into, tolerate, and express these unacceptable feelings. Conflicts related to family relationships are also at the core of the disorder, with the eating-disordered symptoms viewed as a compromise between the drive to meet the parents' needs by remaining childlike and dysfunctional, and the adolescent's need to individuate and express her autonomy. Important goals for therapy in this respect are to use the therapeutic alliance to increase the adolescent's awareness of the function of her symptoms and improve her self-esteem and differentiation of self. Little empirical research speaks to the efficacy of psychodynamic approaches. Because of the long-term nature of this intervention and the ego syntonic and intractable nature of the disorder, the process is a challenging one.

Behavior Modification

Behavior modification is often the treatment of choice for the adolescent hospitalized with anorexia, because the urgent need is to save her life by restoring her body weight. *Operant conditioning* techniques include rewarding eating through such individualized reinforcers as permission to watch a favorite television show or receive visits from friends, and withholding rewards when there is noncompliance. For bulimia, *behavior modification* focuses on discontinuing the dieting behavior that contributes to food cravings and disordered eating, as well as encouraging more adaptive strategies for mood regulation, such as physical exercise. However, there is evidence that the behavioral approach, while effective in achieving the goal of immediate weight gain in anorexia, does not have long-lasting effects. It does not address faulty notions concerning eating, nor does it help the adolescent improve personality and interpersonal problems. These may be addressed by cognitive therapy.

Cognitive Therapy

Cognitive therapy aims at changing cognitive distortions, overgeneralizations, negative self-perceptions, and erroneous beliefs about eating and about the self, such as "If only I were thin, I would be perfect" (Spangler, 1999). Techniques include engaging the adolescent in treatment as a "scientist" who will collaborate with the therapist in the process of uncovering and disputing automatic thoughts and irrational beliefs (Williamson & Netemeyer, 2000). Among the techniques, *self-monitoring* is used to increase awareness of the situations, thoughts, and emotions that trigger disordered eating. *Behavioral contracting* is used to monitor and reinforce small steps toward larger goals of normalizing eating behavior. *Cognitive re-*

structuring goes beyond thoughts about eating and extends into more general maladaptive schema the youth harbors in regard to the self, relationships with others, and the need to be perfect. Cognitive approaches for bulimia have been generally proven to be successful, with full recovery reported in 50 to 90 percent of cases and low rates of relapse over a year (Lewandowski et al., 1997). And, while other approaches may reduce binge eating and enhance general psychological well-being, the cognitive approach is more effective in changing attitudes about the body and maladaptive dieting behavior as well as being more successful in preventing relapse (Fairburn et al., 1995).

Family Therapy

Structural family therapy aims at reconfiguring family interactions in order to break the patterns of enmeshment and rigidity. A classic technique used is the "*family lunch session,*" in which the therapist involves the entire family in sharing a meal together in order to observe their interactions (Minuchin, 1974). In one example, when an overprotective mother and father immediately began the session by nagging their daughter to eat—which she, in response, steadfastly refused to do—the therapist distracted their attention by engaging the parents in a lively discussion of their religion's dietary laws and cuisine. While they were busy feeding the therapist this interesting information, he pointed out, their daughter had begun to eat her lunch.

More recently, family approaches have incorporated behavioral techniques and strive to help parents to develop better *parent-management skills* as a method of assisting their daughter to change her problematic eating. In addition, the therapist fosters changes in the family system that will counter maladaptive strategies such as conflict avoidance, overprotectivenes, and enmeshment. Empirical investigations show the intervention to be highly effective in the treatment of anorexia, with 68 percent showing positive results immediately after treatment and at a 1-year follow-up (Robin et al., 1999). A manualized family treatment developed by Lock and colleagues (2001) appears to be highly effective and is currently being evaluated in controlled studies in the United States.

Substance Abuse

We turn next to a very different psychopathology that emerges during adolescence; however, there are some parallels between this and our previous topic. While eating disorders represent problems with the regulation of food intake, substance abuse involves problems with controlling the consumption of alcohol and illicit drugs.

Viewed in a historical context, we know that substance use has been a part of human society throughout time. Most cultures have used alcohol: Mead was possibly used around 8000 B.C., the biblical Noah became drunk, and the Indians who met Columbus had their own home brew. Drugs have been used in religious ceremonies, to medicate, to counteract fatigue, to increase fierceness in battle, as well as for recreation. Cultures have applied different sanctions to drugs; one drug may have multiple uses, while another is strongly prohibited.

In modern times, there were more opiate addicts in the United States at the turn of the century than there are now, many being women using opiate-based patent medicines to treat various physical complaints. Some physicians considered opium as a cure for alcoholism, while heroin was regarded as less harmful still, with medical journals stressing its nonaddictive properties. After the Harrison Narcotics Act of 1914 banned opiates, the number of women addicts decreased, while male addicts turned to crime in order to obtain the now illegal drugs.

In the late 1960s and 1970s use of illicit drugs burgeoned into what some described as a drug epidemic, as marijuana, stimulants, sedatives, and analgesics joined the traditional drugs of nicotine, alcohol, and caffeine (Johnston, 1985). By the early 1970s the majority of adolescents had experimented with one or more of these illicit drugs by the end of high school. Concern about the phenomenon spurred the "war on drugs," which brought an increasing number of substances under the regulatory control of the federal government as well as increased surveillance and penalization of the drug trade. The fact that the so-called epidemic spread primarily among adolescents and young adults suggests that the teens and early 20s are particularly important developmental stages for the establishment of drug behavior.

Overall use of most drugs increased from the mid-1970s to 1981, while from 1981 through 1992 adolescent use of drugs declined steadily (Johnston, O'Malley, & Bachman, 1995, 1996). This positive trend turned around, with adolescent drug use rising again in the 1990s only to begin leveling off in the current decade (Johnston et al., 2001). The level of drug use in the United States is the highest of any industrialized nation. From 1992 to 1995 the number of high school seniors who report using marijuana in the past 30 days increased 78 percent (from 11.9 to 21 percent), while among 10th-graders it more than doubled (from 8.1 to 17.2 percent). Upward trends have also been noted in the use of other drugs, including LSD and cocaine. Use of multiple drugs also has increased so that regular use of a variety of psychoactive substances has become typical.

Definition and Characteristics

DSM-IV defines **Substance Abuse** (also called drug abuse) by the presence of one or more symptoms indicating the excessive use of a substance to the extent that it interferes with work or school and interpersonal relationships (see Table 12.3). **Substance Dependence,** in turn, is characterized by abuse in the presence of *tolerance* for the drug, leading to the need for ever-increasing doses in order to achieve the desired effect; *withdrawal* in its absence; *inability to desist using,* despite the desire or attempt to do so; and *preoccupation* with obtaining the substance such that little time or energy is available for other pursuits. (See Box 12.4 on pp. 384–385.)

The Developmental Dimension

Concern has been expressed that the DSM criteria do not accurately reflect the nature of substance-abuse disorders in adolescence. (Here we follow Chassin et al., 2003). For example, many studies report a large proportion of "diagnostic orphans": youths who endorse only some symptoms of substance abuse or dependence and therefore do not meet criteria for a diagnosis despite problematic usage.

Table 12.3

DSM-IV-TR Criteria for Substance Disorders

Substance Abuse

A maladaptive pattern of substance use, leading to clinically significant impairment or distress, as manifested by one (or more) of the following, occurring within a 12-month period:

(1) Recurrent substance use resulting in a failure to fulfill major role obligations at work, school, or home (e.g., repeated absences or poor work performance related to substance use; substance-related absences, suspensions, or expulsions from school; neglect of children or household).
(2) Recurrent substance use in situations in which it is physically hazardous (e.g., driving an automobile or operating a machine when impaired by substance use).
(3) Recurrent substance-related legal problems (e.g., arrests for substance-related disorderly conduct).
(4) Continued substance use despite having persistent or recurrent social or interpersonal problems caused or exacerbated by the effects of the substance (e.g., arguments with spouse about consequences of intoxication, physical fights).

Substance Dependence

A maladaptive pattern of substance use, leading to clinically significant impairment or distress, as manifested by three (or more) of the following, occurring at any time within the same 12-month period:

(1) Tolerance, as defined by either of the following:
  a. A need for markedly increased amounts of the substance to achieve intoxication or desired effect
  b. Markedly diminished effect with continued use of the same amount of the substance
(2) Withdrawal, as manifested by either of the following:
  a. The characteristic withdrawal syndrome for the substance
  b. The same (or closely related) substance is taken to relieve or avoid withdrawal symptoms
(3) The substance is often taken in larger amounts or over a longer period than was intended.
(4) There is a persistent desire or unsuccessful efforts to cut down or control substance use.
(5) A great deal of time is spent in activities necessary to obtain the substance (e.g., visiting multiple doctors or driving long distance), to use the substance (e.g., chain smoking), or to recover from its effects.
(6) Important social, occupational, or recreational activities are given up or reduced because of substance use.
(7) The substance use is continued despite knowledge of having a persistent or recurrent physical or psychological problem that is likely to have been caused or exacerbated by the substance (e.g., continued cocaine use despite cocaine-induced depression; continued drinking despite alcohol-aggravated ulcer).

Specify Type:

With Physiological Dependence: Evidence of tolerance or withdrawal.
With Psychological Dependence: No evidence of tolerance or withdrawal.

Adapted from the American Psychiatric Association, 2000.

There are a number of reasons why the diagnostic criteria might not do an adequate job of capturing problematic substance use in adolescence. First, adolescents in general are more likely than adults to exhibit difficulties in occupational functioning and romantic relationships, which may be independent of substance abuse. Second, there is evidence that youths are less likely than adults to evidence physiological dependence, with its accompanying symptoms of tolerance, withdrawal, and physical ill effects. Further, adolescents, especially girls, are less likely than adults to encounter legal difficulties in connection with illicit drugs. However, it may also be the case that it is just a matter of time: With continued long-term use, the physical and legal ramifications may catch up with substance-abusing youths.

The symptoms that are more commonly and reliably seen in youths, particularly in the realm of alcohol abuse, include blackouts, mood problems, reduced activity level, cravings, and engagement in risky sexual behavior.

Box 12.4 | **A Case Study in Substance Dependence**

Robert was born in 1965, the son of a filmmaker and an actress. Raised in Greenwich Village with his older sister, Robert made his film debut at the age of 5 playing a puppy in a film *Pound,* directed by his father, in which actors played dogs. His parents divorced when he was 13, and Robert ended up living in Los Angeles with his father. He dropped out of high school to pursue acting, and at the age of 16 moved back to New York to live with his mother.

Robert started off with good roles in several feature films and spent a year as a regular cast member of the popular comedy program *Saturday Night Live.* He then began being cast in leading roles in movies that attracted a great deal of popular and critical acclaim. His breakthrough performance was a starring role as a cocaine addict.

However, life was imitating art. By the time he played this role, Robert had developed a serious drug problem himself. The actor reportedly began using substances at age 6, when his father introduced him to marijuana. He completed a drug-rehabilitation program in 1987 but continued to struggle with his addictions. After several forgettable movies during the late 1980s, his acting career took wing as he turned in a number of well-received performances in films by famous directors. In 1992, Robert received an Academy Award nomination for Best Actor for his starring role in *Chaplin.* That year he also married his wife Deborah, after dating her for only 6 weeks, and a year later they had a son, Indio.

By this time, the 27-year-old Robert had come to be seen as one of the most gifted actors of his generation, but had also earned a reputation as a troubled and controversial figure in Hollywood. Although the actor was enjoying steady work, his off-screen life was becoming increasingly troubled.

In April of 1996, Robert separated from Deborah. In June of that year, he was stopped for speeding and a police search of his car uncovered heroin, crack, and cocaine, along with an unloaded gun. He was arrested again a month later when, under the influence of a controlled substance, he passed out on a neighbor's lawn. He was rearrested just 3 days after the second arrest after he walked out of a drug treatment center where he had been ordered to stay. In November 1996, a judge sentenced Robert to 3 years' probation. His probation was revoked in December 1997, however, after he was found to have used drugs again, and the judge sentenced him to 6 months in prison.

Prevalence and Onset

First, recent data revealing the prevalence of substance *use* were compiled by the Monitoring the Future (MTF) study (Johnston, O'Malley, & Bachman, 2003), a survey distributed to over 48,500 children in 8th, 10th, and 12th grades in 392 schools across the United States. (Note that while the inclusiveness of the study is impressive, it fails to capture students who have dropped out of school or are in detention, youths who might be disproportionately representative of those heavily involved with substances.) The latest published data from 1991 to 2003 reveal that 70.1 percent of youths had consumed alcohol by the end of high school, while rates were 59.3 percent and 37.2 percent for 10th- and 8th-graders, respectively. Further, 48 percent of 12th-graders, 34.7 percent of 10th-graders, and 14.5 percent of 8th-

graders had been drunk at least once in their lives. Lifetime use of any illicit drug was admitted by 51.1 percent of 12th-graders, 41.4 percent of 10th-graders, and 22.8 percent of 8th-graders; further, 24.1 percent of high school seniors had used an illegal drug within the past 30 days. Marijuana was the most common of the substances used and youths reported decreasing levels of concern with its risks, decreasing disapproval of its use, and rather high ratings of its easy availability in contrast to previous decades (see Figure 12.3 on p. 386). The investigators noted that while the 2003 data reveal decreases in the use of some substances such as MDMA (ecstasy), these most recent statistics also indicate that previous trends toward decreasing substance abuse have halted, particularly for the youngest children in the sample.

While in prison, Robert was allowed to leave several times to complete work on his film projects. He entered another drug rehab program, but in June of 1999 admitted he was using drugs again. "It's like I have a shotgun in my mouth, and I've got my finger on the trigger, and I like the taste of the gunmetal," he told the judge. Unmoved by this testimony, the judge sentenced Robert to 3 years in state prison. By that time, the actor had been in and out of seven rehabilitation programs since late 1996 and had repeatedly missed mandatory drug tests.

In jail Robert suffered from deep depression and was diagnosed with bipolar disorder, leading many of his friends and colleagues to publicly give voice to the opinion that he belonged in a psychological treatment facility, not in prison. Robert was released from prison in August of 2000 and immediately entered a residential drug rehabilitation facility. His career seemed to be back on track, as he began a guest-starring stint on the TV show *Ally McBeal* and managed to make a few screen appearances, winning praise for his work.

In November of 2000, however, Robert was again arrested, this time in a Palm Springs hotel room, and charged with felony drug possession after police allegedly found cocaine, Valium, and methamphetamine in his room. The highs and lows continued for Robert, when Deborah sued him for divorce the same week that the actor picked up a Golden Globe and Screen Actor's Guild award for his work on *Ally McBeal*.

While awaiting trial, Robert was arrested for being under the influence of a stimulant. Officials later confined him to 6 months in drug rehab for violating his parole. He was then fired from his job on *Ally McBeal*. Robert's lawyers reached an agreement with prosecutors that required Robert to plead no contest to cocaine-related charges. He was sentenced to 3 years' probation, but the ruling allowed him to continue live-in drug treatment instead of returning to prison.

In 2003, Robert became engaged to a producer he met on the set of his new movie *Gothica*. He wears his newfound sobriety well. "Once I finally got committed [to sobriety]," he said, "I discovered all sorts of hidden talents . . . it's like a revelation to me."

Studies reporting specific prevalence rates for the diagnosis of substance *abuse* in adolescents are harder to find. Prevalence rates are estimated to be 3 to 4 percent for alcohol abuse and 2 to 3 percent for drug abuse (Chassin et al., 2003). As we might expect, rates vary with *age*. For example, Costello and associates (2003) conducted diagnostic interviews with a representative sample of 1,420 youths in North Carolina. Virtually no substance-abuse disorders were found among children 12 years of age or younger. The prevalence began increasing in mid-adolescence with rates of 1.4% at age 14, 5.3% at age 15, and 7.6% at age 16. Across development, rates for boys were 2.8 percent while rates for girls were 2.0 percent.

Age of onset appears to be steadily decreasing. For example, first initiation into alcohol use now occurs between 7th and 10th grades (Johnston et al., 2001). Further, there seems to be a shrinking time span between first use and the onset of substance abuse (Fitzgerald et al., 1994).

Gender

Prevalence data reveal a consistent *gender difference* in that substance use is more commonly found in males than females. For example, in the 2000 MTF data, 12th-grade boys were 1.5 times more likely than girls to have engaged in the use of marijuana, alcohol, heroin, steroids, and smokeless tobacco. However, at younger grades the gender ratios were more balanced and girls even surpassed boys in the use of some substances, such as tranquilizers and amphetamines (Johnston, O'Malley, & Bachman, 2001). Whether this represents a true developmental

Figure 12.3   Prevalence of Use and Attitudes Toward Marijuana in the Monitoring the Future Study.

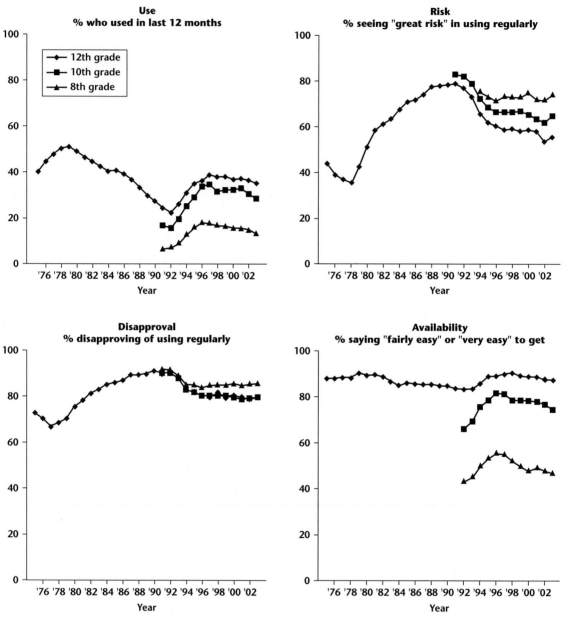

From Johnston, O'Malley, & Bachman, 2003.

shift or merely a cohort effect, such that young girls are beginning to become initiated into the use of illicit substances at the same rate as boys, is not yet clear (Chassin et al., 2003).

In regard to substance *abuse,* the same gender difference prevails and increases with age. For example, Cohen and colleagues (1993) conducted diagnostic interviews with a sample of approximately 500 youths. While 4 percent of boys and 3 percent of girls met criteria for alcohol abuse disorder between the ages of 14 to 16, among 17- to 20-year-olds rates for alcohol abuse were 20 percent for boys and 9 percent for girls, and rates for other forms of substance abuse were over 5 percent for boys and less than 3 percent for girls.

Ethnicity

The MTF data show that African American youths have lower usage rates for all substances than do European American and Hispanic adolescents (Johnston, O'Malley, & Bachman, 2003). While rates for European American youths are the highest among the three largest ethnic groups identified, Hispanic youths are a close second. Further, Hispanic youths are the most heavily involved with substances early in life; the fact that rates are equal later on suggests either that European American youths catch up by their senior year or that substance-abusing Hispanic students drop out of school and are no longer represented in the survey.

Rates of substance use also are high among Native American youths. For example, Plunkett and Mitchell (2000) compared the rates of substance abuse among 407 high school seniors from several American Indian communities to those obtained by the MTF study. Further, these authors improved on the MTF methodology by sampling youths in the community in order to capture in their net those who might have dropped out of school. Overall, Native American youths in Plunkett and Mitchell's sample were more likely than youths in the MTF database to have used illicit substances in the past 30 days. However, the authors point out that the rates vary widely across geographic region and tribal group of origin.

Finally, there appear to be ethnic differences associated with the substance of choice: European American adolescents have the highest rates of barbituate, amphetamine, hallucinogen, and alcohol abuse (with Native Americans a close second in the abuse of alcohol), while Hispanic youths use more heroin, cocaine, and crack (Vik, Brown, & Myers, 1997). Native American youths, in turn, have higher lifetime rates of marijuana and cocaine use, but lower use of inhalants and cigarettes when compared to adolescents of other ethnicities (Plunkett & Mitchell, 2000).

Social Class

There are relationships between substance use and *social class;* for example, in the MTF study, 21 percent of eighth-graders in the lowest SES category had used an illegal drug in the past month, whereas this was true for only 9 percent of those in the highest SES group (Johnston, O'Malley, & Becker, 2001). However, the association between drug use and social class was not significant for the older youths in the sample (although here, too, differential dropout rates of low SES students might have influenced the results). Overall, the influence of social class on drug use is not strong and sometimes even is reversed, with higher rates exhibited by *affluent* youths in some studies (Luthar & Becker, 2002). The links between social class and substance-abuse disorders may emerge only in tandem with other risk factors, such as extreme levels of poverty, poor parental monitoring, and childhood disruptive behavior (Hawkins, Catalano, & Miller, 1992).

Sexual Orientation

Some evidence suggests that sexual-minority youths are at increased risk for substance abuse, associated with the stresses of coming out in the context of a family, peer group, and culture that is unaccepting of their orientation (Jordan, 2000). However, as we noted previously, caution must be exercised when interpreting these studies, given that they tend to be based on samples of troubled youths rather than being representative of the larger population (Rotheram-Borus & Langabeer, 2001).

Comorbidity

Youths who abuse one substance are highly likely to engage in abuse of other substances, behavior termed *polydrug abuse*. Substances that are easily obtainable—those that are illegal only for the underaged to purchase, such as alcohol and cigarettes—often act as "gateway" drugs that lead to the use of harder substances such as marijuana or cocaine (Kandel, Yamaguchi, & Chen, 1992).

By far the highest level of comorbidity is between substance abuse and *conduct disorder,* especially among boys, with some studies reporting comorbidity as high as 95 percent (Brown, Gleghorn, Shuckit, Myers, & Mott, 1996). Such a link is inevitable, given that use of illicit substances is the very kind of norm-violating and illegal behavior required for the diagnosis of conduct disorder. Substance-abusing youths are more likely to associate with deviant peers (Hawkins, Catalano, & Miller, 1992) and display many of the other functional deficits seen in conduct-disordered youths, such as learning disabilities and poor social skills (Tarter et al., 1999; see Chapter 10). Substance use and delinquency may have reciprocal influences on one another, each increasing the risk for the other disorder. For example, Loeber and Keenan (1994) reviewed the available longitudinal research in order to determine whether substance use leads to antisocial behavior or vice versa. While the direction of effect is far from clear, the preponderance of evidence suggests that the onset of conduct disorder precedes substance use and abuse.

Attention deficits are also frequently seen in youths who abuse substances, but may be accounted for by the links among conduct disorder, substance abuse, and ADHD (Costello et al., 1999). (See Box 12.5.)

Anxiety disorders (Kaplow et al., 2001) and *depression* (Costello et al., 1999) are common correlates of substance abuse. Moreover, these internalizing problems appear to predate the onset of drug taking (Wilens et al., 1997). The combination of drugs and depression may be a particularly toxic one: Windle and Windle (1997) followed a group of 975 adolescents and found that the combination of substance abuse and depression leads to an increased risk for *suicide* over time. As many as 42 percent of suicide attempters report having problems with drugs, particularly those who make lethal attempts (Mehlenbeck et al., 2003). It may be that, like purging in bulimia, substance use is an attempt to "self-medicate" against other sources of emotional distress. Intriguingly, the link between substance abuse and depression appears to be stronger for girls than boys (Tarter, Kirisci, & Mezzich, 1997; Zilberman, Tavares, Blume, & el-Guabaly, 2003).

Etiology

By the age of 18 almost all adolescents have had some exposure to substance use. Since substance use is so common, perhaps even normative, our first questions about etiology are What sets some adolescents on the pathway from use to abuse? and Why does it occur in adolescence? In seeking answers we will reintroduce the psychopathology of conduct disorder (see Chapter 10), which can occur with substance use and can play a determining role in escalation. We will then round out our developmental picture by describing the effect of adolescent drug abuse on adjustment in early adulthood.

The Biological Context

Genetics   Although environmental factors play a dominant role in substance abuse, *genetics* may be a contributing factor in some individuals. For example, the risk for alcohol abuse in teenaged children of alcoholics is increased 2 to 9 times. (Here we follow Chassin et al., 2003.) However, the family members of drug addicts also are more likely to demonstrate other kinds of psychopathology, including depression and antisocial personality disorder. Therefore, it is not clear whether the family link is *specific* to substance abuse.

Twin studies offer the best evidence of heritability and suggest that the influence of genetics varies with the type of substance under investigation. For example, McGue, Elkins, and Iacono (2000) studied a sample of 626 seventeen-year-old twins and found that heritability estimates ranged from 10 to 25 percent for illegal drugs to 40 to 60 percent for tobacco use and nicotine dependence. *Shared environment effects* (living in a household where drugs are available, having the same circle of friends as those who

Box 12.5 | **Do Prescription Medications in Childhood Increase the Risk of Substance Abuse in Adolescence?**

One of the concerns with prescribing psychotropic medications to children is that it might be communicating a problematic message, one that suggests that taking pills is the way to solve one's psychological problems. If this is true, it would suggest that those who take psychoactive medications in childhood are at increased risk for developing a substance-abuse problem in adolescence. The concern has emerged particularly concerning the stimulant medications used to treat ADHD (see Chapter 7), given their close links to illegal substances such as methamphetamines. The *sensitization hypothesis* suggests a possible biological underlay in that exposure to prescribed stimulants in childhood might increase sensitivity to the reinforcing effects of the drug, thus motivating illicit use and abuse. Three longitudinal studies have investigated this theory.

Mannuza, Klein, and Moulton (2003) report an investigation of school-aged children with developmental reading disorders and no other psychiatric diagnosis, who were randomly assigned to receive methylphenidate treatment or an inert placebo for 12 to 18 weeks. Sixteen years later, the participants and a sample of nonclinical controls were interviewed by clinicians blind to their group and treatment status. There were no significant differences among the groups on ratings of the prevalence, incidence, age of onset, or duration of substance abuse or dependence. Further, significantly more of the nonclinical controls had used stimulants at any time in their lives (60 percent) when compared to those in the methylphenidate or placebo conditions (46 percent and 41 percent, respectively). Shortcomings of this study include that the participants were not diagnosed with ADHD, as are most children who are prescribed stimulants, and they received a very short course of stimulant exposure in comparison to the years of treatment that children with ADHD typically undergo.

However, more naturalistic prospective longitudinal studies have recently been reported as well. For example, Fischer and Barkley (2003) followed into adulthood 147 individuals who were diagnosed with ADHD in early childhood and interviewed the participants about their use of substances in both adolescence and adulthood. The authors found that stimulant treatment in childhood was not associated with an increase in experimentation with substances, frequency of use, or the risk of abuse. In fact, stimulants prescribed in the high school years appeared to have a protective effect against the abuse of hallucinogens in adulthood. Similar results were reported by Biederman (2003) from a longitudinal study comparing 140 adolescents with ADHD to 120 non-ADHD controls. Not only did those treated with stimulants fail to evidence higher rates of substance disorders, but youths with ADHD who did not receive stimulant medication were 3 to 4 times *more* likely to develop a substance-abuse problem than those who were prescribed stimulants in childhood.

In short, it appears that receiving appropriate medication for psychological disorders may buffer youths from engagement in maladaptive forms of self-medication, such as substance abuse.

indulge in substance use) had the most significant effect on adolescent substance-related behavior, explaining 41 to 66 percent of the variance. However, the investigators note that as the participants grow into adulthood, the heritability estimates appear to increase in size: For males in their sample, the heritability of illicit drug dependence rose to 52 percent in adulthood.

Prenatal Exposure   *Prenatal exposure* to alcohol and tobacco also increases the risk of adolescent use of those substances. The mechanism of effect is not yet known. One hypothesis is that brain receptors may become sensitized by exposure, which in turn causes the child to be more reactive to the substance and to crave its effects. Alternatively, prenatal exposure may precipitate irritability and dysregulation which, in turn, increase the risk for substance abuse (Chassin et al., 2003).

Temperament   A predisposition to general *biobehavioral dysregulation,* under particular environmental circumstances, might move an individual along the pathway to substance abuse (Tarter, Moss, & Banukov, 1996). One index of dysregulation is *difficult temperament,* which involves poor adaptation to change, negative mood, social withdrawal, and high intensity of emotional reactions (see Chapter 2). The link to substance abuse is indicated by findings that, for example, adult cocaine addiction is predicted by ratings of difficult temperament in adolescence (Kagan, Reznick, & Snidman, 1988).

Evidence for a *brain mechanism* involved in behavioral dysregulation comes from brain wave studies of the P3 component in event-related potentials. (Here we follow Chassin et al., 2003.) When exposed to a novel or task-relevant stimulus, individuals with a variety of disorders involving behavioral undercontrol—including aggression, ADHD, and substance abuse—evidence reduced P3 amplitude in comparison with controls. This diminished P3 reaction also is seen in young children of alcoholic parents and predicts the likelihood of the children to engage later in alcohol abuse.

Thus, biobehavioral dysregulation might underlie individuals' likelihood to develop a drug habit, or even their attraction to trying drugs in the first place. However, the genetic studies indicate that exposure to an environment that allows or encourages substance abuse is necessary to turning the propensity into a reality.

The Family Context

Parental Substance Abuse   Parental *modeling* of drug use and children's direct involvement in their parents' drug use are a robust predictor of substance abuse and are particularly important in the early years. Thus, the more adult family members use alcohol or marijuana, the more likely it is that children will use them. This is particularly the case when the parent-child relationship is a close one: Youths are less likely to model their parents' substance

Parental modeling of substance use.

abuse when their relationships with parents are poor (Andrews, Hops, & Duncan, 1997).

However, a number of negative indicators co-occur in families in which parents use drugs and alcohol, the effects of which are difficult to untangle. Substance-abusing parents not only model maladaptive drug use but also engage in more *antisocial activity* in general, are more physically and emotionally *abusive* to their partners and children, have more *economic problems,* and are more likely to *divorce.* Thus, children exposed to substance abuse are being raised in environments that are stressful in a variety of ways.

Parental Depression   In general, parent psychopathology increases the risk for substance abuse in offspring (Mowbray & Oysterman, 2003).

Interestingly, Luthar, Cushing, and McMahon (1997) have demonstrated that *maternal depression,* but not maternal alcoholism, is predictive of youth substance abuse. Because mothers are often the primary care-givers, the negative effects associated with emotion-ally unavailable and negative parenting may play an important role in the development of problem behav-ior. In contrast, *paternal alcoholism,* but not depres-sion, predicts substance use specifically for African African youths. More research will be needed to ex-plain these gender and ethnic differences.

Child Maltreatment Ballon and colleagues (2001) report the results of clinical interviews with 287 youths between the ages of 14 and 24 years who sought treatment for substance-abuse problems. A striking 50 percent of the females reported having been sexually abused and 50.5 percent also reported being physically abused, while, among the males, sexual abuse was found in only 10.4 percent and physical abuse in 26 percent. A similar gender differ-ence emerges in regard to the relationship between childhood maltreatment and the onset of substance use: 64.7 percent of the females reported that they used drugs to help them cope with the trauma, while this was true for only 37.9 percent of the males.

Parenting Style On the *protective* side, a number of studies have indicated that positive parent-child relationships can decrease the risk of substance abuse in young people. For example, Baumrind (1991b) found that *authoritative* parenting (see Chapter 2)—defined as warmth in the presence of structure—was associated with a lower likelihood of drug use. Similarly, lower substance use is found when parent-youth relationships are emotionally supportive and warm and allow children to partici-pate in decision making—and when parents them-selves are abstainers (Hundleby & Mercer, 1987).

Moreover, parental socialization practices *specifi-cally* in regard to substance use might protect youths against involvement with drugs. For example, youths are less likely to use tobacco when parents discuss with their children reasons not to smoke, establish rules about the use of tobacco and other substances,

and enforce these rules by levying consequences for misbehavior (Chassin et al., 1998).

On the other hand, low levels of parental support, discipline, and monitoring of children are predictive of adolescent substance abuse, as are high levels of family conflict and disorganization (Ary et al., 1999; Reid, Patterson, & Snyder, 2002). Children of single parents also are at greater risk for developing substance-use problems, and this may be because of the greater exposure of single-parent families to poverty and the negative influences of crime- and drug-ridden neighborhoods, but may also be due to the difficulty of monitoring and supervising an ado-lescent when there is only one parent in the home (Hops et al., 2000).

It is important to note, however, that family vari-ables were weaker predictors of teenage drug use than were peer influences in the studies just described. The same finding is reported in O'Donnell, Hawkins, and Abbott's (1995) longitudinal study of substance-abusing boys. Therefore, it behooves us to turn next to the important variable of peer relations.

The Social Context

Peer Relationships *Peer relationships* have emerged as one of the most powerful predictors of adolescent drug involvement in both longitudinal and cross-sectional studies (Catalano & Hawkins, 1995). Heavy drinkers, for example, are more likely to have friends—especially best friends—who also drink. In addition, peer relations may interact with other variables and risk factors. Adolescents with low self-esteem may be more attracted to drug use as a means of boosting self-image and gaining status in the peer group (Maggs & Galambos, 1993). In ad-dition, adolescents are more vulnerable to peer pres-sure to use drugs when they live in single-parent homes and their relationships with their mothers are conflictual (Farrell & White, 1998).

Longitudinal data show that there are two mech-anisms by which peer relationships contribute to substance use (Curran, Stice, & Chassin, 1997). One is *peer influence,* in which friends introduce peers to drugs, normalize substance use, and provide models and opportunities for continued use. The other is *peer selection,* in which youths who abuse substances seek out friends with a similar lifestyle. The idea of peer selection is related to Scarr's (1992) concept of *niche picking:* As children enter adolescence, they act as increasingly active agents in their own development, choosing and influencing their environments by gravitating toward contexts that are compatible with their personal characteristics.

For example, in the Oregon Youth Study, Dishion and Owen (2002) followed a sample of 206 youths from early adolescence to young adulthood. The investigators found that, over time, both peer selection and peer influence contributed to the prediction of adult substance use. In addition, there were *bidirectional* effects: Substance use appeared to influence friendship selection in that youths increasingly associated with peers who fostered and reinforced activities and conversations related to drugs.

Peer modeling is a risk factor for substance use.

Sexual Maturation   Another interpersonal variable linked to substance use in girls is *sexual maturation.* As with the data we reviewed related to conduct disorder (see Chapter 10), drinking and drug abuse are two forms of problem behavior seen more often in early-maturing girls than in late-maturing girls (Simmons & Blyth, 1987). Early maturers spend more time with older peers, who introduce them to norm-violating behaviors such as substance use.

The Individual Context

Conduct Problems   With the majority of drug use beginning in junior high school, we must seek its precursors during the elementary school period. Among variables within the person, early childhood *conduct problems* and *aggression* are strong predictors of adolescent experimentation with drugs, escalation in use, and graduation to a full-blown substance-abuse disorder (Chassin et al., 1999; Costello et al., 1999; Hill et al., 2000). The early-onset conduct-disordered child we encountered in Chapter 10 is particularly vulnerable to the development of substance dependence in adulthood (Moffit et al., 2002). Impressively, Block, Block, and Keyes' (1988) longitudinal sample identified predictors of teenage substance abuse that were present as early as 3 years of age. These personality attributes included antisocial behavior, rebelliousness, poor frustration tolerance, lack of motivation and goal-directedness, lack of concern for others, and unconventionality.

There are some indications of *gender differences* in these effects. While behavior childhood problems increase the likelihood of adolescence substance use, as was found in a 4-year prospective study, the effects are stronger for girls. Because aggression is less prevalent and less socially acceptable for girls, those who violate social norms may be at risk for escalating behavior problems with increasingly serious consequences, such as substance abuse (Hops et al., 2000).

Do conduct problems lead to substance abuse, or does substance abuse lead to misbehavior? As noted previously, early-onset conduct problems predict substance abuse; however, evidence for the other direction of effect can be found as well. The National Center on Addiction and Substance Abuse (2004) recently reported than 4 out of every 5 youths currently in the juvenile justice system had a prior history of substance offenses or were under the influence of drugs or alcohol while committing their crimes. In comparison to youths who have not been arrested, those arrested within the past year were twice as likely to use alcohol, 3.5 times more likely to have used marijuana, 3 times more likely to have used illicit prescription drugs, 7 times more likely to have used ecstasy, 9 times more likely to have used cocaine, and more than 20 times more likely to have used heroin. Further, almost 2 million of the 2.4 million youths arrested in the United States have substance-abuse problems, and yet only 68,600 are receiving any form of treatment. Involvement with illicit substances is inherently an illegal activity, and, moreover, substance use may have a disinhibiting effect on the behavior and judgment of the young person.

Unconventionality   A classic longitudinal study by Jessor and Jessor (1977) focused on personality correlates of drug use in high school and college students over a period of 4 years. Adolescents who did not use drugs were likely to value academic achievement, to be unconcerned with independence from their families, to be accepting of the social status quo and involved in a religion, and to regard transgressions as having more negative than positive consequences. Those with high proneness to drug use had the opposite characteristics, including tolerance of deviance, nonreligiousness, the valuing of independence over achievement, and a critical attitude toward society. The Jessors characterized the personality dimension underlying their findings in terms of *conventionality versus unconventionality.*

However, unconventionality may not always be associated with negative outcomes. Shedler and Block's (1990) longitudinal study examined substance use among 101 eighteen-year-olds who had been extensively evaluated since preschool. The adolescents fell into three groups. Abstainers had never tried marijuana or any other drug, experimenters had used marijuana a few times and no more than one drug other than marijuana, and frequent users had used marijuana at least once a week and had tried a drug other than marijuana.

The personality picture of the *frequent user* was one of a troubled, manifestly unhappy adolescent who was interpersonally alienated and emotionally withdrawn and who expressed his or her disturbance through overly antisocial behavior. In terms of our variables, these adolescents were deficient in peer relations, being mistrustful, hostile, and withdrawn; in the realm of mastery, they were neither invested in school nor in channeling their energies toward meaningful vocational goals; finally, their self-control was weak, resulting in antisocial acting out.

The picture of *abstainers* was a surprising one. Far from being well adjusted, they were relatively tense, emotionally constricted individuals who were prone to delay gratification unnecessarily. They avoided close interpersonal relationships and were not liked and accepted by others. While not as disturbed as the frequent users, they shared the quality of social alienation, but were overcontrolled rather than impulsive.

The *experimenters* were the most well adapted, in that they were sociable and warm, evidenced the least distress, and had stable self-control. They also felt the freedom to experiment with values, beliefs, and roles as part of the process of forging a new identity. Thus, the authors conclude that in adolescence a certain amount of behavior that society judges as being a problem may be part of the normal growth process. They also show that in this period abstainers should not be regarded as the "normal" group, either statistically or psychologically.

Shedler and Block's (1990) analysis of their longitudinal data showed that the personality characteristics of the three groups were present in early childhood. Thus, as early as 7 years of age, frequent users were insecure, emotionally distressed, and unable to form good relationships. Abstainers were relatively overcontrolled, timid, fearful, and morose. The mothers of both groups of children were cold and unresponsive, giving their children little encouragement while pressuring them to perform. The authors conclude that abstinence, experimentation, and frequent use represent three relatively distinct personality constellations that are established early in life.

A cautionary note is needed, however. Luthar, Cushing, and McMahon (1997) point out that Shedler and Block's data were derived from normative youths, rather than those with substance abuse or dependence, and focused on the use of marijuana, a relatively socially acceptable drug in the teen culture of the time. In contrast, studies of opiate addicts demonstrate that youthful experimentation with drugs is a strong predictor of later substance-abuse disorder and psychopathology.

Sensation-Seeking   Another personality variable that has been proposed to account for substance use, especially in the early years, is *sensation-seeking* (Zukerman, 1994). Youths who are high on sensation-seeking are more likely to engage in risky behavior such as substance abuse because they are attracted to the thrill and stimulation it provides (Pilgrim et al., 1999).

Cognitive Skills   Cognitive and educational skill deficits are proposed to increase the risk of substance abuse in many theoretical models. There are several mechanisms by which this effect might take place. For example, school failure may increase stress and negative affect, increase alienation from mainstream social institutions, and increase the tendency to affiliate with antisocial peers, all of which are associated with substance use. (Here we follow Chassin et al., 2003.)

Many factors are associated with poor school performance, however, so it would behoove us to look at more specific cognitive skills that might be associated with substance abuse. In keeping with the theory that underlying substance abuse is a tendency toward behavioral dysregulation, youths with substance problems might be expected to evidence poorer skills on cognitive tasks assessing self-regulatory processes such as inhibitory control, planning, flexibility, set-shifting—in other words, *executive functions*. Indeed, poor executive functioning predicts earlier onset of problem drinking and greater frequency of drinking to excess in late adolescent and college student populations.

In addition, executive function deficits are seen in children of alcoholics prior to the onset of drinking and predict the extent of alcohol abuse. For example, Atyaclar and colleagues (1999) assessed executive functioning and behavioral activity levels in a sample of 10- to 12-year-olds at high risk (those whose fathers had a substance-abuse disorder) and low risk (those whose fathers had no psychiatric diagnosis) and followed them over a period of 2 years. High-risk children had higher initial levels of behavior problems and executive functioning deficits and, by early adolescence, had become more involved with drugs than those at low risk. What was striking however, is that the executive function deficits, over and above behavioral problems or paternal substance use, predicted tobacco and marijuana use, number of drugs sampled, and substance abuse in adolescence.

Cognitive Schemas: Expectations and Motivations   Youths' impulse to abuse substances may be driven by their *expectations* of the positive results that will ensue. Cox and Klinger (1990) identified four motives or expectations that might underlie adult alcohol use: (1) *enhancement* (i.e., to stimulate positive mood or feelings of general well-being); (2) *social* (i.e., to obtain positive social rewards such as being the "life of the party"); (3) *coping* (i.e., to reduce or regulate negative emotions); and (4) *conformity* (i.e., to avoid peer pressure or social rejection). Cooper (1994) tested the applicability of this model to a sample of 2,544 adolescents, approximately half of whom were African American. The results showed that enhancement, coping, and social motives were strong predictors of the quantity and frequency of alcohol consumption in adolescents, regardless of gender or race. Coping and enhancement motives, in turn, were the best predictors of alcohol abuse and problem drinking.

In a subsequent study, Cooper and colleagues (1995) further refined the model by demonstrating the different predictors and consequences of enhancement and coping motives. Youths' expectations that drinking would enhance their pleasure were related to a measure of sensation-seeking, while expectations that drinking would help them cope with negative emotions were related to measures of depression and maladaptive coping. Further, while both cognitions predicted alcohol use, coping motivations were more strongly predictive of problem drinking.

In short, the adolescents most at risk for developing a substance-abuse problem are those who believe that substances will relieve them of uncomfortable feelings or emotional pain. The youths who take substances for social reasons may be better able to confine their use to specific social contexts and to be less likely to rely on drinking or drugs to get them through an ordinary day.

Further, there are interactions between youths' and *parents' expectations* regarding youth substance use. For example, Simons-Morton (2004) followed a group of 1,009 sixth-graders over a period of a year to determine the risk factors for early-onset alcohol use. Among youths who had positive expectations regarding alcohol, those whose parents had low expectations for their behavior were 2.6 times more likely to have started drinking than those whose parents had high expectations for the youths' behavior.

Emotion Regulation   Whereas the self-medicating properties of bingeing and purging we discussed previously may not have been immediately apparent, this function is more intuitively obvious in the case of substance use. It is easy to see how an illicit substance might be used as a stand-in for psychoactive medication. But why would youths feel the need to self-medicate? As implied in Cooper's (1994) research described previously, one of the prevailing theories of the developmental psychopathology of substance abuse is that it arises from an attempt to escape and/or to regulate negative emotional states.

One such negative mood state is *anxiety,* which is frequently comorbid with substance-abuse disorders in adolescents and predates their onset (Christie et al., 1988). In an intriguing study, Kendall and colleagues (2004) reported that successful treatment of anxiety disorders in children was associated with decreased risk for substance abuse in adolescence. However, the data are mixed, with a number of prospective studies failing to confirm that anxiety is a predictor of future substance use.

Depression, on the other hand, has fared better as a predictor of the development of substance abuse

(Newcomb & Bentler, 1988; Hussong & Chassin, 1994). However, the support is not unequivocal. For example, Stice, Burton, and Shaw (2004) followed 496 adolescent girls over a period of 2 years. The hypothesis that depressive symptoms predicted the onset of substance abuse was confirmed in univariate tests, but not in the more stringent multivariate tests they conducted, thus providing only mixed support. In contrast, there was strong support for the hypothesis that substance abuse was a predictor of increased depression. Thus, just like disordered eating, drug abuse defeats its purpose by exacerbating the very negative mood states it is intended to reduce.

One of the reasons for the mixed findings in support of the emotion regulation hypothesis may be that this relationship holds true for only a *subset* of youths who abuse substances. Negative emotional states may prompt ingestion of drugs or alcohol for those who have difficulty regulating physiological and psychological distress (Chassin et al., 2003), and, as our review of research on cognitions suggests, for those who also harbor the belief that substances will relieve them of these feelings.

Second, emotion regulation may represent only one factor in a more complex model of the developmental psychopathology of substance abuse. For example, Brody and Ge (2001) report results of a longitudinal study of 120 twelve-year-olds followed over a period of 3 years. Their data showed that harsh and conflictual parent-child relationships contributed to youths' increased difficulty with self-regulation, which in turn predicted increases in the use of alcohol.

Third, Hussong and her colleagues (2001) have argued that studies of global anxiety and depression are too crude to effectively test the emotion regulation hypothesis. Instead, they argue for the use of moment-by-moment ratings of mood and behavior, termed *experience sampling.* Similar to Johnson and Larson's (1982) study of daily mood and bulimic behavior described earlier in this chapter, experience sampling methods may give us a better window into the motivations underlying substance use in youths that might lead to abuse or dependence.

Moreover, there may be important *gender differences* in the relationship between mood and substance abuse. As noted earlier, maltreatment features as a predictor of substance abuse more often for girls than for boys. Further, some data suggest that the relationship between substance use and dysphoric mood is significant for teenage girls but not boys (National Center on Addiction and Substance Abuse, 2003). While boys appear to initiate smoking, drinking, and substance use for the thrill of it, girls ingest substances to relieve stress and depression.

The Cultural Context

Social Class   One stereotype of the adolescent substance abuser is an economically disadvantaged youth who lives in a crime-ridden inner-city neighborhood. While such negative neighborhood and sociological variables predict delinquency and other forms of problem behavior, however, the opposite seems to hold for the relationship between SES and substance abuse. Higher rates of substance use and substance abuse have been found among more *affluent* youths (Luthar & Becker, 2002). Factors that appear to be related to drug use in affluent youths are *achievement pressure* and *alienation from parents* (Luthar & Latendresse, 2002).

Nonetheless, features of *low SES,* including poverty, prejudice, unemployment, deviant role models, and gang influence might contribute to one risk factor that follows from involvement in drugs, and that is participation in *drug dealing*. Dealing may appear to be the easiest—and perhaps the only—way out of poverty for disadvantaged youths (Feigelman, Stanton, & Ricardo, 1993). Negative consequences of dealing are profound and include exposure to violence, legal entanglements, and incarceration.

The Media   The media and the larger social context also influence young people's attitudes by conveying permissive attitudes, presenting glamorous models of substance use, or promoting its beneficial effects. Consequently, communitywide efforts have been recommended to reduce substance abuse in teens by restricting advertising for and access to cigarettes and alcohol (Institute of Medicine, 1994).

Cross-Cultural and Ethnic Differences   Cross-cultural studies show that the developmental psychopathology of substance abuse is similar in widely discrepant societies. For example, Pilgrim and colleagues (1999) examined the influences of personality characteristics, parenting, and peer relationships on drug use among adolescents in the United States and mainland China. Across cultures, the adolescents most likely to engage in using substances over a period of a year were those high in *sensation-seeking* and whose parents were low in *authoritativeness*. One ethnic difference that did emerge was that, while *friendships* with substance-abusing friends were associated with more drug use among Chinese and European American youths, African American youths were less influenced by the behavior of their peers.

Bray and colleagues (2001) report similar results across ethnic groups in their 3-year study of 6,522 European American, Mexican American, and African American adolescents. While African American youths had a slower rate of increase in alcohol use over the time span, in all ethnic groups *family conflict* and lack of cohesion were related to increases in alcohol use, while ratings of adolescents' *individuation* and achievement of a developmentally appropriate sense of identity acted as a protective factor.

Certain risk factors for substance abuse are unique to certain minority groups, however. For example *acculturation stress*—distress resulting from a perceived clash between the values of the family of origin and the dominant culture—has been found to be associated with increased drug use in Hispanic adolescents (Vega et al., 1993).

Developmental Course

The Early Years: The Early-Starter, Early-Escalating Pathway

As with the other problem behaviors we have discussed (see Chapter 10), early onset of substance use is predictive of a more negative developmental course. Early initiation into substance use (i.e., before age 14) is associated with a steep escalation in use and more problematic outcomes, including substance abuse and dependence disorders (Chassin, Pitts, & Prost, 2002; Hill et al., 2000). The long-term consequences of the early-starter pathway are clear. In longitudinal studies spanning adolescence and adulthood, Hops and colleagues (2000) found that early starters were more likely to become cigarette, alcohol, and marijuana users in adulthood. Further, the early-starting youths were likely to have more health problems and to experience aggression and conflict in their relationships with partners and friends.

The early starters are more typically male, demonstrate more antisocial behavior, and are more likely than other youths to come from families with a history of substance problems (Chassin, Pitts, & Prost, 2002; Hill et al., 2000).

The typical developmental sequence of the pathway proceeds from initiation of alcohol use at the beginning of high school, to tobacco and marijuana, then to other illicit substances (Hops et al., 2000).

Developmental Pathways in Early Adolescence: Risk and Protection

Jessor and colleagues (1995) tested a multidimensional model of the factors predictive of drug and alcohol abuse during the transition to adolescence. The investigators followed almost 2,000 students in grades 7, 8, and 9 over a period of 3 years. Risk and protective factors were identified in three systems of development: personality, environment, and behavior.

Risk Factors   In the *personality* domain, the investigators assessed risk factors, including low expectations of success, poor self-esteem, hopelessness, and alienation. In the *environmental* realm, risk factors included peer models for problem behavior and orientation toward peers rather than parents as guides for behavior and life choices. Risks in the *behavioral* realm included poor school performance.

Results of Jessor and colleagues' study showed that the single most powerful predictor of substance use was the presence of *antisocial peer models,* followed by the personality variables of low expectations of success, poor self-esteem, and hopelessness.

Protective Factors   In regard to protective factors in the *personality* domain, the investigators targeted positive orientation toward school, concern about personal health, and intolerance toward deviance. In the *environmental* domain, protective factors assessed included positive relationships with adults, regulatory controls imposed by adults on youth behavior, and peer models for prosocial behavior. Protection in the *behavioral* domain was represented by engagement in prosocial activities.

Ultimately, the results showed that the protective factors that had the greatest impact on reducing youth substance abuse were an attitude of *intolerance toward deviance* and a *positive orientation toward school.* Further, over the 3-year period, those whose problem behavior diminished over time were not those who were exposed to fewer risk factors, but rather those who had available to them more protective factors at early stages in development. Thus, the authors conclude that "antecedent protection has a stronger relation to change . . . than antecedent risk" (p. 931). This suggests that prevention efforts directed at bolstering resistance to the temptations of drug use may be the most effective, a thread we will pick up later when we discuss intervention.

Developmental Pathways in Mid-Adolescence: From Use to Abuse

Newcomb and Bentler's (1988) 9-year prospective study of 654 adolescents provides information about the transition to the late adolescent period. The authors summarize the results in terms of the following developmental tasks faced in the transition to adulthood:

1. *Social integration.* Drug use interferes with this development by reducing social support and increasing loneliness.
2. *Occupation.* Teenage drug use accelerates involvement in the job market, while impeding successful functioning at work. Traditional

educational pursuits are abandoned, thereby limiting the range of career opportunities.

3. *Family and heterosexual relations.* Drug use has both an accelerating and detrimental impact, leading to early marriage and childbearing on the one hand and divorce on the other.

4. *Criminal behavior.* Youthful drug use is differentially related to criminal behavior. Multiple substance use is predictive of increased stealing and drug law violation, such as driving while intoxicated or selling drugs.

5. *Mental health.* Multiple drug use is related to a small but significant increase in psychosis and a decreased ability to plan, organize, and direct behavior. Hard-drug use increases suicidal ideation in young adulthood, while alcohol increases depression.

Newcomb and Bentler (1988) conceptualize their findings in terms of *precocious development.* While precocity is generally viewed positively—in a child with musical talents, athletic abilities, or intellectual capabilities beyond his or her age level, for example—a significant discrepancy between developmental level and aspirations may also jeopardize healthy development. By taking on adult functions for which they are poorly prepared, adolescent drug abusers push themselves toward a maturity that they are incapable of assuming effectively because they have not given themselves time to accumulate the needed skills and experience. Premature involvement in adult roles prior to acquiring adequate competence to handle such challenges leads to a likelihood of failure. The use of drugs directly interferes with social integration and acceptance of adult civic and societal responsibilities while at the same time increasing feelings of social isolation from peers. Finally, drug use can affect cognition by making thinking more disorganized and bizarre, sometimes resulting in increased suicidal ideation. In short, substance use diverts the adolescent from mastering developmental tasks that are critical to healthy adjustment in adulthood.

On the positive side, Elliott, Huizinga, and Menard's (1989) prospective study of drug use in 1,725 youths found that the pull to *desistence* was stronger than the pull to escalation. Substance use generally levels off in young adulthood, and delinquency usually declines after mid-adolescence. Only cautious optimism is warranted, however, since alcohol use often increases in adulthood.

The Transition to Young Adulthood: The Late-Starter Pathway

Finally, a subgroup of late starters has been identified whose substance use begins only after the end of high school (Chassin et al., 2002). The transition to college or the work world provides a new level of independence and freedom from adult supervision to which drinking and drugs might be used as a "rite of passage." As Chassin et al. (2003) point out, in general, alcohol and substance use peak during the ages of 18 to 25 years, the same age range during which substance abuse and dependence are most prevalent. However, for the majority of young adults this time of experimentation is followed by a decline in substance use, commensurate with the increase in adult responsibilities associated with work, marriage, and parenthood. Thus, for most young people substance ingestion is a developmentally limited phenomenon.

In fact, those who successfully make the transitions to these adult roles are the least likely to develop a substance problem (Chilcoat & Breslau, 1996). In contrast, the late starters who go on to become substance dependent demonstrate more overall psychopathology and negative affectivity and have difficulties functioning at work and maintaining satisfying relationships with partners. Once again, we encounter the issue of developmental preparedness but in a different guise: While some youths might push themselves to take on adult roles *precociously,* and in doing so increase the risk for substance abuse, also at risk are the young adults who are developmentally *unprepared* for adulthood and have not mastered the stage-salient issues that will equip them to forge happy marriages, raise children, and launch productive careers.

Integrative Developmental Model

Illustrating the complexity of the factors involved in predicting substance abuse, Fitzgerald and colleagues (1994) have compiled a list of risks derived

Figure 12.4   Antecedents of Adolescent Substance Abuse.

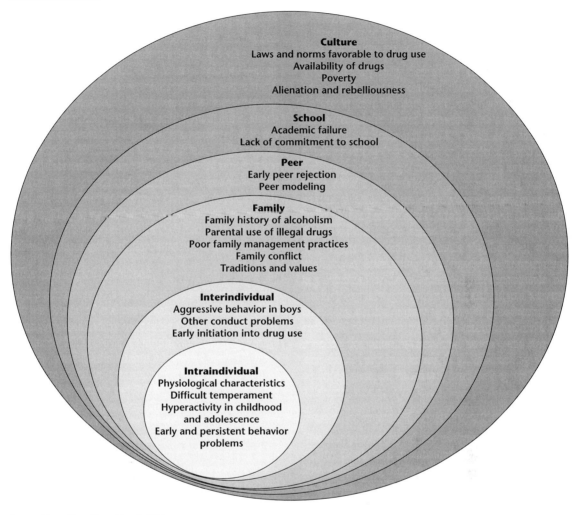

Source: Adapted from Fitzgerald et al., 1994.

from various studies. (See Figure 12.4.) As these authors note, substance abuse is best conceptualized as a life-span problem, with origins spanning as far back as the preschool years. They conceptualize the risks as falling within five domains, which map nicely onto our own dimensions: *intraindividual, interindividual, family, peer,* and those in the larger context such as *school* and *culture.* Thus, drug use is not due to any single cause but to a number of variables. In addition, many of these factors interact with one another, thus contributing in complex ways to the development of substance-related problems.

An important question that remains is one we posed at the beginning of this chapter: *Why adolescence?* Jessor and Jessor (1977, 1995) provide a developmental framework that addresses this issue. Their model regards behavior as a result of interactions between personality and the perceived environment. According to the Jessors, the transition to adolescence takes place in a societal context that affects individuals differently. While prized roles and rewards come with age in our society, the adolescent, especially the early adolescent, has limited access to the valued goals of adulthood, such as autonomy, prestige, sex, and mobility. In addition, societal expectations and rules are based on chronological age alone, which ignores individual differences in adolescents' desire or readiness to pursue adult goals. While some "late bloomers" may feel pushed to take on responsibilities for which they are not prepared, other adolescents who are ready to make the transition may feel frustrated and tantalized by the unattainable attractiveness of mature status. The result is *precocious* engagement in adult-oriented activities—a constellation including alcohol use, cigarette smoking, substance use, sexual intercourse, and delinquency.

The transition from a less mature to a more mature adult status, the Jessors state, is often marked by problem behavior. Adolescence is just such a time of transition in which stage-salient issues related to identity formation and the assumption of adult roles come to the fore. Adolescence is also a time of increasing experimentation, exploration, and risk-taking. Some experimentation with drugs, therefore, is relatively normative for the majority of adolescents. In general, Jessor, Donovan, and Costa (1991) argue, as development proceeds from adolescence into early adulthood, these kinds of problem activities will decline in most young people.

Thus, when viewed within a developmental context, problem behavior is not necessarily deviant or psychopathological. Many problem behaviors, such as drinking and sex, are regarded as acceptable and will even be encouraged by society when the adolescent is old enough to be considered an adult. In essence, the Jessors regard adolescence as a period in which departure from accepted norms is not only to be expected but also may be a sign of healthy development. "Problem behavior may be viewed, at least in part, as an aspect of growing up" (p. 238).

What about those for whom substance abuse and dependence result? Recall that in discussing *oppositionality* (Chapter 6) we saw that psychopathology can result when an exaggeration of normal problem behavior threatens to jeopardize future growth. The same principle can be applied here. When rebellion, defiance, and antisocial behaviors become ends in themselves rather than means for promoting autonomy, adolescents may be in a state not of transition but of stagnation. Or, again, if problem behaviors seem primarily directed against the parents—if adolescents seem to be going out of their way to defy and upset parents, if unconsciously they are behaving like "bad children" in order to prolong their status as children—then we begin to suspect that fixation rather than transition is calling the tune.

Erikson's (1968) writings on *identity* are useful at this point. He states that youths often go to extremes in order to test the "rock bottom of some truth" before committing themselves to a particular way of life (p. 236). These extremes may include not only rebelliousness but also deviant, delinquent, and self-destructive behaviors. Only when such tendencies defeat the purpose of experimentation by fixating the adolescent in this behavior do they become psychopathological. Take, for example, a *negative identity,* which in many ways is the adolescent counterpart of the toddler's negativism. Here the adolescent perversely identifies with all the roles that have been presented as undesirable or dangerous by others. Despairing of ever realizing the unattainable positive roles, the adolescents become the last thing in the world the parents would want them to be. Thus, the psychopathology underlying substance abuse represents not only a more extreme form of adolescent rebellion, but a retreat from the struggle to establish an identity rather than a progression along the way toward reaching that goal.

Further, as substance abuse becomes consolidated as part of an adolescent's behavioral repertoire and preferred method of coping, Caspi and Elder's (1988) concept of *cumulative continuity* is useful. Essentially, this concept posits that actions or events are maintained by the very consequences that they bring about. In the case of substance abuse, we see a cascading series of effects and life choices that close down opportunities to shift life to a more healthy developmental pathway. For example, the substance-abusing youth is increasingly likely to have difficulties succeeding in work or school, to be involved with deviant social networks that are defined by or revolve around substance use, to experience conflict and dissatisfaction in intimate relationships, and to encounter legal difficulties (e.g., charges for possession, driving under the influence, etc.), all of which act as stressors that are likely to serve to increase substance use.

Finally, the fact that substance use and abuse is largely associated with the *male gender* is worth considering. Just as adolescent females may feel pressure to become the epitome of femininity, thus increasing their concern with body shape and dieting, males may feel pressure to fulfill a masculine archetype by being audacious, risk-taking, and fearless. The cachet attached to illicit substance use—in its extreme, the image of the hypermasculine "player" who is both feared and admired—may be attractive to those thwarted in their attempts to find more prosocial ways of achieving a masculine identity.

A Different Model for Girls?

As we have noted, substance-abuse disorders are more common in males than females, which may explain why attention to girls as a unique group is quite rare. However, some evidence suggests that girls are beginning to catch up to their male peers when it comes to initiation into substance abuse. Therefore, more attention to females is warranted. Recent data suggest that there may be important gender differences in the precipitants and consequences of substance abuse. Recently, the National Center on Addiction and Substance Abuse (2004) released results of a 3-year study including 1,200 females ages 8 to 22. Compared to their male peers, girls who abused substances were more likely to enter puberty early, to suffer from depression, to have an eating disorder, and to have a history of sexual or physical abuse. In addition, girls fell into addiction more quickly than boys, even when ingesting the same amount of substances; and girls suffered more adverse consequences, including smoking-related lung damage and alcohol-induced brain and liver damage. Significantly, boys and girls appeared to initiate smoking, drinking, and substance use for different reasons: boys for the thrills or enhanced

peer status, and girls to relieve stress and alleviate depression.

These data suggest that different models might be needed for the developmental psychopathology of substance abuse in males and females. In particular, models that focus on emotion regulation, while equivocal in mixed-gender samples, may be particularly applicable to girls. Furthermore, once a girl has become involved with illicit substances, the consequences for her physical and emotional health are particularly serious. Consequently, models of causality and treatment need to be better informed by recognition of gender differences.

Intervention

Although much of the research is focused on intervention for adult substance abusers rather than adolescents, a general conclusion is that *psychodynamic* treatment for substance abuse is relatively unsuccessful. This approach often requires a willingness to change and the formation of a positive relationship between youth and therapist, neither of which may be present or workable for the drug abuser (Copans & Kinney, 1996). *Behavioral* therapies, which often involve pairing the drug with a noxious stimulus (such as a nausea-inducing chemical or a painful electric shock), have not proven effective either.

Family Systems Approaches

Intervention with adolescents also needs to take into account the family context in which substance abuse develops. Indeed, *family therapy* has been recommended as a treatment of choice for adolescence substance abuse. Empirical research bears this out: In seven out of eight studies comparing family treatment to other forms of intervention, family therapy was found to be the most effective in reducing substance use (Waldron, 1997). Participants are also more likely to engage in family therapy and to remain in treatment longer than those assigned to other interventions (Stanton & Shadish, 1997).

Santisteban and his colleagues (2003) have empirically demonstrated the effectiveness of a brief, strategic family therapy for reducing substance use and other problem behaviors in Hispanic adolescents. Derived from Minuchin's structural family therapy, the focus of the intervention is on restructuring maladaptive patterns of interaction between parents and children. The investigators obtained youths' self-reports of substance use and substantiated them by urine toxicology screens after treatment. Youths were randomly assigned either to the family therapy condition or to a youth-only group therapy condition modeled after the prevention programs that are commonly offered to adolescents in the school setting. Following treatment, which ranged between 4 and 20 weekly therapy sessions, depending on the severity of the presenting problem, the results showed that marijuana use reduced significantly more for those youths who received family therapy, although the effects on alcohol use were not significant. In the family therapy condition, 41 percent were no longer using substances at termination of treatment, whereas this was true for only 13 percent of those who received group therapy.

Multisystemic therapy (Henggeler et al., 2002), which we encountered in Chapter 10, expands treatment beyond the family to include the school and community contexts in which substance abuse develops. This is an intervention with proven success with even the most difficult to treat substance-abusing and -dependent youths (Randall & Cunningham, 2003).

Self-Help Groups

Another form of intervention is the *self-help group*. Twelve-step programs such as Alcoholics Anonymous, Cocaine Anonymous, and Narcotics Anonymous are widely accepted by adolescents. In fact, Brown (1993) found that these groups are the method most widely used by those adolescents who find a pathway out of substance abuse.

Prevention

School-Based Efforts   Prevention is generally less costly than treatment and may be particularly important in the case of substance abuse. As our review of the research has shown, providing protection early in development is more effective than reducing risk factors later: Once established, substance use may be difficult to reverse even as early as in the

sixth grade (Perry et al., 1996). Further, if there is a stepwise progression from less to more serious involvement in drugs, efforts at preventing substance use are well worthwhile (Durlak, 1997).

A common feature found among school-based prevention efforts is *resistance skills* training, which takes its cue from the fact that peers are one of the most powerful influences on initiating substance use. Therefore, they teach students how to recognize, handle, and avoid situations in which they experience peer pressure to smoke, drink, or use drugs. In addition, the programs emphasize developing social skills that will allow youths to decline to participate in substance use while still maintaining their membership in the social group. Students role-play and practice ways of delivering specific refusal messages effectively. Many programs use peer leaders, who often have higher credibility with adolescents than do adults. Evaluation studies show that resistance skills training is effective in reducing smoking, alcohol, and marijuana use by 35 to 45 percent.

Psychoeducation is also a common feature and is directed toward countering misinformation and false beliefs that might make a youth more easily influenced by others. For example, youths might be helped to resist pressure to adopt attitudes and behaviors favorable to smoking by being provided with correct information about the prevalence, acceptability, and health consequences of cigarette use.

A third common feature is *life skills training,* which teaches a broad range of general skills for coping with challenging situations. Among the components are problem-solving and decision-making skills, self-control and self-esteem enhancement, general interpersonal skills, and assertiveness training. These skills are taught by a combination of instruction, demonstration, feedback, reinforcement, and practice. Life skills training is initiated in the early school years and has demonstrated positive effects (Botvin et al., 2003).

Skara and Sussman (2003) evaluated the results of 25 school- and community-based programs designed to prevent substance use in the junior high school and high school period. Overall, the majority of studies yielded significant effects for their target goals of reducing tobacco or other drug abuse. In some studies, effects were maintained as long as 15 years. "Booster shots," periodic refreshers of the program curricula, appeared to be particularly helpful to maintain long-term benefits. However, the reviewers note a number of methodological problems with the studies that were conducted that limited their confidence in the results.

Comprehensive Prevention Programs   *Comprehensive prevention programs* are informed by the research implicating multiple risk factors in the etiology of substance abuse and consequently target a number of different domains for intervention. A prime example is the Preparing for the Drug Free Years program (Kosterman et al., 1997), which aims to reduce the risk for early substance abuse by increasing positive relations within the family. Interventions include increasing family members' prosocial involvement with one another, improving parenting skills, helping parents teach peer resistance skills, reducing family conflict, and increasing expression of positive emotion. Another comprehensive family-focused preventative effort is the Iowa Strengthening Families Program (Kumpfer, Molgaard, & Spoth, 1996). This program, too, aims to increase family protective factors by improving the quality of the parent-child relationship and helping parents to develop good disciplinary practices, but it also addresses children's coping and problem-solving skills. Hourly family skill-building sessions are followed by an hour in which parent and child practice together the skills they have learned. Studies have documented the effectiveness of both of these programs for reducing alcohol use trajectories over the course of childhood and adolescence (Guyll et al., 2004).

Culturally Informed Prevention   Preventive efforts are most successful when they are culturally informed and competent (Loue, 2003). For example, skills training needs to be adapted to reflect the life situations in which ethnic minority youths live and the *bicultural competencies* that they need to develop (Hawkins, Cummins, & Marlatt, 2004). One of these competencies is the ability to cope with the realities of racial oppression without succumbing to a sense of despair and hopelessness, which in

turn contributes to the development of substance-abuse disorders (Gibbons, Gerrard, & Lane, 2003; Gibbons et al., 2004). For this reason, Brody and colleagues (2004) included *adaptive racial socialization* among the parenting variables addressed by their Strong African American Families Program for the prevention of substance use in rural African American families.

Community involvement in the program also is essential to its acceptance and ultimate success (Hawkins, Cummins, & Marlatt, 2004). For example, Hawkins and colleagues (2004) describe their work partnering with Pacific Northwest tribes to develop an intervention based on the principles of the Canoe Family. The Canoe Family is a traditional rite of passage in which, over the course of a year, tribal elders prepare youths to act as representatives of their tribe during canoe trips to neighboring Native communities, a privilege for which the youths must commit to remaining clean and sober. Like the Canoe Family, the prevention program provides youths with strategies to cope with life challenges, both through individual effort and drawing on the strengths of the community, so that the tribe as a whole can arrive safely at its destination.

Developmentally Informed Prevention   Prevention programs that are *specific* to substance use may also be more effective than those that are more broadly directed toward promoting a healthy lifestyle in general. Further, Johnson, MacKinnon, and Pentz (1996) propose a prevention regime sensitive to *stage-salient issues* of development, targeting diet and exercise in middle childhood, smoking in late childhood, alcohol and marijuana use in middle adolescence, and cocaine and hard-drug use in later adolescence. (Hall and Zigler, 1997, review prevention efforts with preschoolers.)

Discussions of psychopathology usually assume that the developing child is not deviant either intellectually or physiologically. The assumption has not always proved correct; in the instance of autism, for example, both mental retardation and organic brain pathology are present. This assumption is absent with our next two topics: brain injury and chronic illness.

The Developmental Consequences of Brain Injury and Chronic Illness

In our discussion of mental retardation in the previous chapter, we learned that there are many ways in which the brain might be damaged, resulting in various kinds of cognitive deficits and psychopathologies. In this chapter, we will consider more specifically the ways in which brain injury affects development. We also will explore the field of pediatric psychology, which is concerned with the effects of chronic medical illness on child development and psychopathology.

Brain Damage

Definition

Brain damage can be defined in three different ways. A strictly *neurological* definition concerns itself with the nature, site, and size of damage to the brain. A *behavioral* definition is concerned with the functions impaired by the damage: motor and communication disorders, sensory and perceptual deficits, intellectual impairment, and so on. Brain damage can also be conceptualized in terms of a wide array of *etiological factors,* such as traumatic injury, anoxia, encephalitis, epilepsy, cerebral palsy, and lead poisoning, to name a few. Each approach is valid, but the complex interrelations among them have yet to be worked out. Therefore, it is important for us to realize at the outset that "the brain-damaged child" is an abstraction that glosses over crucial distinctions among children.

Assessment

While *autopsy* is the surest technique for establishing brain damage, it is, of course, no help in diagnosing a living child. Diagnosis of brain damage frequently relies on the child's *history,* covering factors such as pregnancy and delivery complications; developmental milestones such as sitting up, walking, and speaking; and illnesses. Not only is there evidence that such information is often unreliable, but there is also no direct relation between the information and brain damage. Paradoxically, developmental histories are the least useful yet most frequently used of all diagnostic procedures.

Neurological Examination

The *neurological* examination covers such classic signs as failure of the reflexes, restriction of the visual field, and loss of sensation and function in any part of the body. An important part of the neurological exam is the assessment of the sensory and motor functioning of the 12 sets of cranial nerves (Kolb & Whishaw, 2003). Generally, all the muscles of the body are assessed from the head to the foot and the status of each recorded on a chart. Motor tone and strength are assessed on both sides of the body, as are tremors or other involuntary movements. The examiner tests coordination by asking the child to walk heel to toe in a straight line, touch his or her fingers to his or her nose, and so on. The intactness of the sensory system is assessed by asking the child to smell or taste substances, identify the location of stimulation such as a pinprick on the arm, and identify objects that are placed in the hand while the child's eyes are closed. While valuable for identifying gross neurological deficits, the exam may not be sensitive enough to detect more subtle anomalies in children with head injuries or other forms of brain damage.

Neuroimaging Techniques

Remarkable progress has recently been made in techniques for *visualizing* brain structure and functioning. (See Kolb & Whishaw, 2003.) The traditional **electroencephalogram** (EEG), which measures electrical activity of the brain, can detect gross damage, but is not specific and is prone to error. In fact, 10 to 20 percent of normal children also display abnormal records.

However, two advances in electroencephalographic techniques have resulted in increased sensi-

tivity to brain damage. The first is the **event-related potential,** or **ERP.** When a stimulus such as a light or sound is presented, the brain produces a characteristic response, or ERP. Knowing the ERP in the intact brain allows diagnosticians to detect malfunctions such as visual disorders and deafness in very young or mentally retarded children who cannot be tested by the usual techniques. Next, developments in *computer analysis* and *computer graphics* have made it possible to use many recording leads simultaneously rather than using just the few recording leads of traditional EEGs. Consequently, a detailed computer-drawn picture of the brain is now available.

There have also been advances in imaging techniques for visualizing brain structure deriving from the *X-ray* technique. Traditional X rays were limited by the fact that they could detect only gross abnormalities. **Computerized axial tomography (CAT) scans**—also called computer-assisted tomography (CT) scans—use computer-driven X-ray machines to produce exceptionally detailed images both of the brain's surface and of the levels below, making it possible to localize lesions at any level of the brain. An imaging method called **magnetic resonance imaging (MRI)** produces even clearer images. Use of images from successive layers of the brain makes it possible to generate an MRI-based three-dimensional image of various brain structures.

Functional magnetic resonance imaging (fMRI) is one of the most rapidly growing methods for imaging the living brain. It tracks subtle increases and decreases in oxygen on a moment-to-moment basis as a person performs a given task, such as attending to a visual stimulus. Then, by taking consecutive slices of the brain in various orientations, the MRI scanner reconstructs where in the brain the greatest areas of activation occur. For example, fMRI has been used to map areas of the brain used for the visual system, working memory, learning, and problem solving.

Positron-emission tomography (PET scans), unlike imaging techniques, which produce static pictures of the brain and reveal only structural or anatomical deficits, can detect abnormal functioning in brains that might look structurally intact. Because brain cells metabolize glucose, radioactive glucose

Figure 13.1   Views of the Brain Obtained with Various Imaging Techniques.

The CT, PET, and MRI scans shown here were created by three different techniques for imaging a slice of the brain. The fourth image is a photograph of a brain removed from a cadaver. (After Posner and Raichle, 1994.)

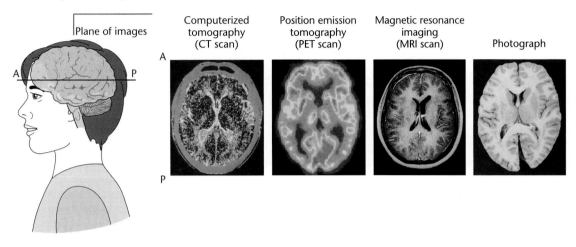

From Kolb and Whishaw, 2003.

is introduced into the cerebral artery and the rate at which it is metabolized in various parts of the brain is recorded. The resulting PET images can then be compared with those of a normally functioning brain. Figure 13.1 contrasts the images obtained by these different techniques.

Neuropsychological Testing

Neuropsychological tests are used to pinpoint and describe the specific cognitive deficits in children with brain damage. Two of the more commonly used comprehensive test batteries for children include the NEPSY Developmental Neuropsychological Assessment (Psychological Corporation, 1998) and the Woodcock-Johnson-III Tests of Cognitive Ability (Riverside Publishing, 2001). While based on different models of cognitive functioning, both of these tests assess important cognitive processes that may be disrupted by brain damage, including attention; memory; speed and fluency; processing of visual or auditory information; and **executive functions** such as organization, planning, self-monitoring, and cognitive flexibility.

Typically, a neuropsychological battery is administered to the child in tandem with a standardized intelligence test, which assesses the child's overall level of ability, and an educational test battery, which assesses the child's mastery of school-related tasks. Testing is repeated at regular intervals over the course of childhood in order to track changes in functioning and to adjust interventions in order to better meet the needs of the child at each stage of development. (See Box 13.1 for a case example involving comprehensive assessment of brain damage.)

Psychopathology in Brain Damage

There is evidence that brain damage increases the risk for psychological disturbances. In his two classical studies, Rutter (1977, 1981) compared 99 children ages 5 to 14 who had cerebral palsy, epilepsy, or other clearly established brain disorders with 189 children from the general population of 10- and 11-year-olds and with 139 children ages 10 to 12 who had physical disorders not involving the brain, such as asthma, diabetes, heart disease, and orthopedic injuries. The rate of psychological disturbance in the brain-damaged group was 34.3 percent of the population, while the rate of psychological disturbance in the group with other physical handicaps

Box 13.1 | **Case Study: Traumatic Brain Injury**

Gordon was a 9-year-old boy who received a severe traumatic brain injury when he was involved in a serious car accident. Upon his admission to the emergency room, the medical team noted that he had a large laceration on his scalp and his right pupil was dilated and unresponsive. He underwent emergency surgery for a depressed skull fracture and injury to the left side of his head. His stay in the hospital was lengthy, lasting several weeks. During his hospitalization he received a series of CT scans, which revealed multiple fractures of the skull and contusions, especially of the frontal lobes. The bleeding from the injuries placed pressure on his brain, encased as it is in the rigid skull with nowhere for this excess fluid to go. As a consequence of this pressure, over time enlargement of the ventricles was seen, indicating some atrophy of brain tissue. Gordon also had a series of EEGs with abnormal results, suggesting seizure activity, and he began taking medication for seizure control.

While Gordon had previously been described as a happy, bright-eyed, sociable child, his behavior was markedly different postinjury. Both his parents described him as a "different child" and said that they felt like they needed to get to know him all over again. Now, they reported, Gordon was sullen, irritable, easily frustrated, and quick to anger. Gordon's social and emotional functioning was formally assessed, using behavioral observations and rating scales completed by his parents and teachers. His parents were asked to fill out the rating scales twice—once for his current functioning and once for his behavior prior to the injury. Both his mother and his father rated his behavior in the average range preinjury, and both also rated his behavior postinjury in the clinically elevated range on scales assessing conduct problems, overactivity, disorganization, and psychosomatic complaints. Consistent with his parents' reports, teachers also rated Gordon as showing hyperactivity, conduct problems, and poorly regulated emotions in the classroom.

In terms of his cognitive development, Gordon's early developmental history had also been normal, and his parents described him as a healthy child with no academic problems. Because Gordon's overall functioning was good, therefore, he had never before been referred for an evaluation and no preinjury IQ scores were available for comparison. However, 6 months postinjury, his cognitive test scores suggested that his overall intellectual abilities were in the low average range. While he demonstrated relatively intact skills on tasks assessing his verbal reasoning, he demonstrated weakness in a number of areas, including attention and concentration, organization of visually presented

was 11.5 percent—which still was almost twice that of the normal population.

Rutter's findings do not mean that all children with brain damage are at risk, however; on the contrary, only when biological factors result in major brain disorders is the risk of psychopathology significantly increased, although, even in this case, it is not inevitable. Aside from this special group, the risk of psychopathology is minimal and difficult to detect. The functions most powerfully affected by brain damage are cognition, sensory and motor functions, and seizure thresholds. (For a more recent confirmatory study, see Max, Sharma, and Qurashi, 1997.)

In light of the importance of the brain, many of the findings mentioned may seem unexpectedly mild. However, it is important to remember the remarkable recuperative powers of the brain—for example, from injuries, strokes, or infections. Two mechanisms aiding recuperation are sprouting and vicarious functioning. In *sprouting,* an undamaged neuron makes synaptic contact with neurons beyond the damaged area (lesion), while in *vicarious* functioning another area of the brain takes over the functions served by the damaged area (such as the transfer of speech from the left to the right hemisphere). Also, as we will soon see, the ameliorating potential of the social environment has been underestimated until relatively recently.

It is important to note that there is no evidence that brain damage leads to a characteristic clinical picture that can be labeled "the brain-damaged information, and expressive language. His performance on educational testing also showed a strength in reading, but poor math and written expression. Further neuropsychological testing of his memory showed that his ability to recall previously learned information was intact, but his ability to remember new information was significantly low. Tests of executive functions revealed that he had severe difficulties with flexibility, planning, and speed of mental processing. Because it is unlikely that a child with these deficits would have been performing as well in school as Gordon had been prior to his injury, the clinicians suspected that they were related to his TBI. Further, his profile was not only consistent with a generalized pattern of brain injury, but pointed to specific location of damage: the frontal lobes.

The clinicians also evaluated the family as a whole and found that they all were greatly traumatized by the accident, even though Gordon was the only one who was physically injured. His older brother had begun showing some behavior problems recently, and his mother was seeking individual therapy to help her with an acute depression.

Over time, as Gordon healed from his injuries, he evidenced recovery of his general cognitive abilities and remote memory. However, he continued to show problems with learning and remembering new information, attention and concentration, processing visual information, organizing, and problem solving. He also continued to show poor self-control and had behavior problems at home and at school.

The treatment team made a number of recommendations to ease Gordon's transition back into the regular school day. They suggested that teachers use compensatory strategies to help Gordon deal with his difficulties with memory, learning new material, and processing visual information. These included such strategies as providing him with all directions both verbally and in writing, keeping instructions short and visible throughout the task, and being willing to repeat directions to Gordon as many times as necessary. To cope with his lack of mental flexibility and poor organizational skill, teachers were advised to provide Gordon with warm-up time before any new activity and to provide him with organizational tools, such as an outline of daily activities. To help with his behavioral and emotional problems, the treatment recommended parent training in behavior management strategies, as well as family therapy to help all family members to adjust to the trauma and the presence of this "new child" in the home.

Source: Adapted from Snow and Hooper, 1994.

child." Effects tend to be nonspecific, with psychopathologies ranging widely as they do in other disturbed populations.

We will now turn to the specific kind of brain damage called traumatic brain injury.

Traumatic Brain Injury

Definition and Characteristics

Traumatic Brain Injury (TBI) is defined as "an acquired injury to the brain caused by external physical force, resulting in total or partial functional disability or psychosocial impairment" (U.S. Office of Education, 1992, p. 44842). Children with TBI have recently been added to the list of children mandated by the federal government to receive special education services under the heading of exceptional children.

There are two kinds of TBI: penetrating head injury and closed head injury. *Penetrating head injury* involves penetration of the skull, dura (the protective layer beneath the skull), and the actual brain tissue. Penetration can be produced by a small object moving rapidly, such as a bullet, or a large, dull object such as a baseball bat. *Closed head injury* is the more common of the two and occurs when a blow to the head does not penetrate the dura—for example, when a child is propelled violently forward in an automobile accident and the head strikes a solid object. In general, over 90 percent of child TBIs involve closed head injuries (Snow & Hooper, 1994).

The two kinds of injuries have different effects on the brain. Penetrating head injuries produce specific and focal deficits at the point of impact, whereas closed head injuries of equal severity produce more extensive neurologic disruption and consequently are more serious. This widespread damage is generally due to tearing, twisting, or shearing of fibers in the brain. Another common characteristic of closed head injury is that there is damage on the opposite side of the brain from the blow, when violent movement of the head causes the child's brain to be thrown against the skull as it moves in the direction of the blow—this is termed a *contra coup* injury. The frontal lobes are particularly vulnerable during closed head injuries because the inside of the skull in the front of the brain contains a number of bony protrusions that cause damage when the brain is thrown against them.

The seriousness of head injury is directly proportional to the extent of unconsciousness (coma) and loss of memory (amnesia) suffered by the child. The Pediatric Coma Scale (Simpson & Reilly, 1982) is a commonly used measure that assesses three aspects of consciousness: eye opening in response to stimulation, verbal responsiveness, and motoric responses. As one might expect, a deeper and long-lasting coma is an indictor of more severe head injury. In regards to amnesia, severe posttraumatic amnesia (difficulty learning and retaining new information) for a week or longer is a predictor of poor outcome.

Prevalence   It is estimated that as many as 1 million children sustain head injuries a year in the United States (Teeter & Semrud-Clikeman, 1997). Further, TBI is the leading cause of death or permanent disability for children and adolescents (Snow & Hooper, 1994).

Gender, Race, and Socioeconomic Status
Males with head injuries outnumber females more than 2 to 1, and the gender difference is even more marked in the adolescent years. (See Figure 13.2.) Males also are disproportionately likely to suffer

Figure 13.2

Incidence of Traumatic Brain Injury in one Minnesota County, 1964–1971.

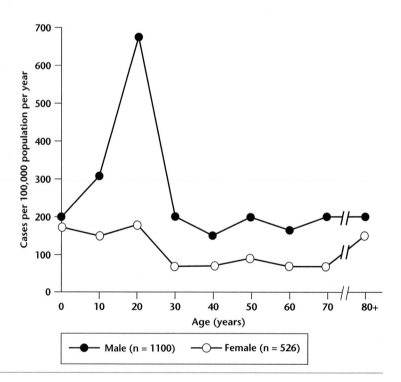

Source: Annegers, Grabow, Kurland, and Laws, 1980.

fatalities. The little information available concerning the role of race and social class suggests that minority and low SES children are more vulnerable to TB (Snow & Hooper, 1994).

Age The incidence of head injuries increases between 3 and 8 years of age, with another dramatic increase at 15 to 16 years of age, probably because at this age youths are allowed to drive or ride with other young drivers. Falls are the predominant injury for younger children. For school-age children, the most prevalent risks are being hit with a car while walking or riding a bicycle, or being hurt during a sports activity. Motor vehicle accidents are the principal cause of TBI in adolescents over the age of 16. The chances of a child's suffering a significant head injury before he or she is old enough to drive is 1 in 30 (Kolb & Whishaw, 2003).

TBI and Psychopathology

Preinjury Functioning

TBI does not occur randomly in the population. Therefore, we must look at characteristics of the child and family that precede the injury (also termed *premorbid functioning*).

Children at risk for brain injury are those who are active and risk-taking, have academic difficulties, and experience other life stresses. Further, there is a high rate of preexisting psychopathology: As many as 52 percent of children met criteria for a psychiatric disorder prior to suffering brain injury, ADHD being one of those most frequently seen (Bloom et al., 2001).

Further, the families of children at risk for TBI tend to be poorly functioning and the parents often fail to provide adequate supervision. Severe head injuries often happen when the children are not being monitored by caregivers either because the caregivers are absent or are negligent. Finally, the parents are apt to have psychiatric and marital problems (Boll & Stanford, 1997).

Lastly, a significant risk factor for TBI is a *previous* TBI. Probably because of the negative effects of the brain injury on judgment and functioning, children who sustain a TBI are at a three-fold risk

for sustaining another head injury (Snow & Hooper, 1994).

Knowing what we do about psychopathology, we could infer that such children are at risk for developing some kind of psychiatric disorder *regardless* of whether there was brain injury. In fact, research has shown a high correlation between children's preinjury behavior and their subsequent psychiatric difficulties. Therefore, the blow to the head is not the only factor involved in determining the outcome of TBI; and all the contexts of development, including individual and interpersonal factors, still come into play.

Psychopathology Postinjury

Studies also show a high rate of new psychiatric diagnosis following child TBI. Psychopathology is related to the severity of injury: A new psychiatric diagnosis is 3 times more likely in children with severe head injury (62 to 69 percent of cases) than those with mild head injury (20 to 24 percent of cases). Depression and ADHD are among the most common new diagnoses given (Bloom et al., 2001), and these disorders are likely to persist over time.

The Biological Context

There are three primary physical forces by which TBI exerts its negative effects: *tension* (tearing apart of tissues), *compression* (pushing together of tissue), and *shearing* (rubbing and abrasion of tissues against one another). (Here we follow Snow and Hooper, 1994.) Another dimension concerns whether the injury results from *acceleration* (the moving head hitting a stationary object, such as a head hitting the windshield in an auto accident), *deceleration* (the stationary head being hit by a moving object, such as a baseball bat), *rotation* (the head being twisted around), or *crushing*. Surprisingly, the latter type of injury is the most rare and least severe, given that skull fracture does not necessarily result in injury to the brain. Of more concern is the diffuse damage that is caused by twisting, tearing, or breaking of the connecting fibers of the nerve cells, which is termed *diffuse axonal injury*.

In addition, certain areas of the brain appear to be more sensitive to damage regardless of the point of impact or severity of injury. Thus, there is a *selective vulnerability* among areas of the brain. One such sensitive area is the hippocampal formation, the most critical limbic system structure for memory functions. This would help explain why one of the most common symptoms of traumatic brain injury is a disturbance of memory functions.

Trauma also may bring about *biochemical changes* such as an excessive release of potassium (an ion critical for neural transmission) in the intracellular fluid. Excessive release, in turn, may lead to prolonged overexcitation that impairs metabolic cell functions and may eventuate in cell death.

Finally, *secondary brain-damaging* effects may contribute to the initial injury. These secondary effects include cerebral edema (swelling) and brain hemorrhaging (bleeding), both of which can put pressure on the brain by pressing it against the skull, thereby causing further damage. Hypoxia (poorly oxygenated blood) or ischemia (obstructed blood flow) may also damage the brain by depriving the cells of essential nutrients. Cerebral atrophy may occur when brain tissue dies, leaving a tell-tale enlargement of the ventricular system (the fluid-filled cavities of the brain). In addition, children are particularly vulnerable to the development of postinjury seizures, which interfere with functioning.

The Individual Context

Severe brain injury can have widespread effects on all areas of intrapersonal functioning. (Here we follow Snow and Hooper, 1994, unless otherwise noted.)

Cognitive Development

Intelligence   Generally, children with head injuries show declines in their performance on intelligence tests that are commensurate with the seriousness of the injury. There also is a specific pattern of deficits, with nonverbal skills being more affected than verbal skills. The likely explanation for this fact is that the verbal scales of intelligence tests assess older, well-rehearsed knowledge (crystallized intelligence), while the nonverbal subtests tend to require speed and accuracy in the solving of novel

problems (fluid intelligence). It is this new learning that is most disrupted by TBI. Children with TBI also tend to show a slow rate of mental processing, which will negatively impact their ability to accomplish timed tasks on intelligence scales. Although IQ scores may improve over time, they rarely return to preinjury levels: Children continue to show deficits as long as 5 years after the injury.

Attention   Many studies have found that children have difficulties sustaining attention and concentration postinjury. These deficits also have been found to persist for years after the injury and can contribute to significant difficulties in school.

Language   Children who suffer TBI often show global difficulties with speech and language, but specific effects are commonly seen. These include problems with naming objects, verbal fluency, word and sentence repetition, and written production. The developmental dimension comes into play, in that the type of language impairment is related to the skills that are emergent in the child's language development at the time of the injury.

Memory   Memory problems are one of the most common effects of TBI, particularly in regard to memory for recently learned information. Poor attention may interfere with children's initial encoding of information into memory (Walker, 1997).

Motor and Sensory Effects   Common effects of TBI include fatigue, reductions in gross and fine motor coordination, visual and tactile problems, and headaches, all of which may impact problem solving, school performance, and mood (Walker, 1997).

Executive Function   Deficits in organization, judgment, decision making, planning, and impulse control are often seen in children who have suffered TBI and are often the result of damage to the frontal lobes (Walker, 1997).

All of the cognitive changes we have just described may adversely affect schooling. Impaired ability to learn new information, concrete thinking, and language disturbances all impede academic progress, while the increased distractibility and poor impulse control and judgment may make the child more of a behavior problem in the classroom.

Emotional Development

Even a mild TBI is typically followed by a change in the child's emotions. Frequently, irritability and poor frustration tolerance are seen in children following head injury. Severely injured children are likely to demonstrate longer-lasting and more significant negative emotions and behavioral problems, which may warrant a diagnosis such as conduct disorder. Very severely injured children may exhibit grossly disinhibited emotions and behavior, associated with damage to the frontal lobes, which are critical to self-monitoring and the exercise of good judgment.

Children who have suffered TBI also frequently show depressed affect, withdrawal, and apathy. While this negative mood might be related to their awareness of the deficits caused by the injury, it also may be related to the location of the injury itself. Children with right hemispheric damage are the most likely to develop postinjury depression (Walker, 1997).

The Self

Children's insight into the injury and its effect on their sense of self vary as a function of age. While younger children typically deny the injury and express a lack of concern about its effects on their functioning, children ages 9 and older report a more negative self-concept and awareness of the way in which their lives and their ability to function have been affected by the injury.

The Family Context

The family may experience increased stress as it struggles to respond to the new and difficult challenges of coping with the child's deviant behavior. It may have to alter its previous lifestyle—for example, by devoting financial resources to medical treatments rather than to vacations or by turning part of the home into a rehabilitation environment rather than a playroom. Families that are adaptable and

loving can take these stresses in stride. Those that are rigid and resentful are at risk for becoming increasingly dysfunctional while at the same time impeding the child's recovery and rehabilitation (Taylor et al., 1995).

The Social Context

The children's increased impulsivity, irritability, and aggressiveness may jeopardize peer relations. Old friends may become impatient, while new friendships may be difficult to make. Thus, there is an increased risk of social isolation (Andrews, Rose, & Johnson, 1998). Further, TBI may interfere with cognitive functions that are key to social interactions, such as pragmatic communication. For example, one study found that, following moderate to severe head injuries, adolescents had difficulty recognizing emotions and understanding social cues, which leads to difficulties in social relationships (Kersel et al., 2001).

Developmental Course

There are many sources of variability in the outcome of brain injury. We have already discussed two of them: type and severity of injury. In regard to *type* of injury, penetrating injuries have effects different from closed head injuries, as we have seen. In addition, the prognosis of recovery from head injury is directly related to the *severity* of the injury. As we know, the duration of coma is an important index of severity; the shorter the duration, the more complete the recovery. However, there are a number of other sources of variability, some organic and others psychological.

Age of the child at the time of injury is another important factor. Preschoolers and infants in particular are at risk for severe and long-lasting effects. Why might this be? Recall that TBI disproportionately affects *new* learning, and the learning of the child in the earliest stages of development is virtually *all* new. Older children may be able to fall back on some old learning to compensate for deficits as well as having a broader cognitive and adaptive repertoire to help them to evolve alternative strategies for coping with challenges that arise due to

TBI. The *developmental status* of affected skills matters as well. Skills that are in the process of being acquired are more vulnerable to damage than are fully developed ones.

Another factor to consider is *rate of recovery*. Most recovery that is going to take place emerges in the first year postinjury; therefore, the more rapidly a function begins to improve, the more hope that it will return to a level close to that existing preinjury.

Lastly, *intra- and interpersonal variables* must be considered. The individual characteristics of the children and their interpersonal relations with family and peers serve to individualize the effects of brain injury. Thus, the adjustment of the child and the family has a significant impact on the effectiveness of coping with the effects of the injury.

A number of *risk and protective factors* have been identified. (Here we follow Walker, 1997.) For example, while denial of the injury may do the child a disservice, children are also poorly served when they or others focus unduly on the injury and make unfavorable comparisons to the child's previous level of functioning. Lack of information is another critical factor. Often, children and their families do not have a good understanding of TBI or the normal recovery process—in fact, many report that they have never had their injury explained to them and do not know what is realistic to expect in terms of recovery of function. Without accurate information, families are vulnerable to unrealistically high—or pessimistic—expectations. Teachers and school personnel also often lack understanding of the TBI and its sequelae, contributing to the child's frustration, poor self-image, and misbehavior.

Further, it is common for social support networks to rally around in the crisis stage immediately following an injury, but to drift away over time, leaving the family alone and unsupported. Peer relationships particularly may suffer when the injury is severe and has significantly changed the child's appearance, personality, and cognitive level, resulting in a child who truly seems to have become a different person.

Finally, youths who have suffered TBI are at significant risk for substance abuse. It is possible that in some cases the substance abuse predated the injury: for example, the adolescent whose TBI was a result of driving while intoxicated. However, the aftereffects of TBI also may include impairment in judgment and impulse control, leaving the youth vulnerable to the influence of negative peer models. Further, some TBI survivors use illicit substances to self-medicate their depression and low self-esteem.

Intervention

Interventions with youth survivors of traumatic brain injury must be as diverse and multifaceted as are the effects of the injury. Intervention begins with a careful assessment, which documents the child's strengths, deficits, and special needs. Intervention with the school is particularly important, in order to ease the child's transition back into the classroom and to help the teachers to design compensatory learning strategies in order to insure the child's continued success and positive attitude about the educational process (Walker, 1997). Psychoeducation, counseling, and social services support for parents and the whole family often are advised. Individual work with children might focus on helping them to come to terms with the injury emotionally or to learn practical strategies for coping with the changes it has wrought (Hooper & Baglio, 2001). For example, *cognitive rehabilitation* may involve (1) analyzing and restructuring the child's daily routine in order to minimize frustrations and failures; (2) providing visual clues, such as photographs of activities, to help the child stay organized and on-task; and (3) rehearsing prior to each step in the routine and reviewing the child's performance. With such supports in place, clinicians have found that they can significantly improve children's task performance at the same time that they decrease aggression and other maladaptive behaviors (Feeney & Ylvisaker, 1995).

Chronic Illness

It is estimated that there are approximately 10 million children with chronic illnesses in the United States, with 10 percent of children in the population affected (Melamed, 2002). The sources of stress for severely ill children and their families are numerous: the pain of the illness and of medical procedures; hospitalization; and the disruption of family life, peer relations, and schooling, to name only a few. In the past the focus was on such negative aspects and the toll they were expected to take on the child's psychological well-being. The fact that such expectations often were not realized forced researchers to turn attention to protective factors such as the resilience of children, the resources and adaptability of family members, and the support of health care professionals.

The study of the effects of chronic illness on youths is under the purview of the field of **pediatric psychology** (which is also known as *behavioral medicine*). (See Ollendick and Schroeder, 2003; Ammerman and Campo, 1998.) Pediatric psychology views both sickness and health as resulting from the interplay among biological factors on the one hand and psychological, social, and cultural factors on the other. Thus, pediatric psychology conforms to our now familiar *transactional model*. This interplay among factors is present at every stage of the disease process, from etiology to course to treatment, although at different points one or another factor may predominate. In addition, the field includes the psychological and social variables involved in *prevention* and *health maintenance*. Finally, pediatric psychology is primarily concerned with chronically ill children, as the life spans of children with once-lethal illnesses increasingly are being expanded.

Definition and Characteristics

Dimensions of Chronic Illness

Generally, an illness (disease, disorder, disability, or medical condition) is considered to be *chronic* when it persists 3 months or more. (Here we follow Fritz and McQuaid, 2000.) Chronic illnesses differ from those that are acute in a number of ways. While an acute illness may be curable, a chronic illness will need to be managed over a period of months, years, or even the life course. Further, while medical personnel often take over the care of the child with an acute illness, the parents of a chronically ill child—and, increasingly with age, the children themselves—usually bear a large part of the responsibility for the management of the condition.

Chronic illnesses comprise a very diverse group of disorders, which have a variety of implications for the child's psychological development. Table 13.1 presents a number of dimensions on which medical illnesses can be categorized, each of which might differentially affect the child. For example, consider the boy whose cerebral palsy creates a visible disfigurement that announces itself every time he walks into the classroom versus the boy whose physical appearance is unaffected by his illness; or the girl with a highly stigmatized disorder such as AIDS that leads peers to shy from her versus the girl with

Table 13.1

Dimensions of Chronic Medical Conditions in Children

Duration	Brief	....	Lengthy
Age of Onset	Congenital	....	Acquired
Limitation of Activities	None	....	Disabled
Visibility	Not Visible	....	Highly Visible
Expected Survival	Usual Life Span	....	Immediate Life Threat
Mobility	Unimpaired	....	Extremely Impaired
Physiological Functioning	Unimpaired	....	Extremely Impaired
Cognition	Unaffected	....	Extremely Affected
Emotional/Social	Unaffected	....	Extremely Affected
Sensory Functioning	Unimpaired	....	Extremely Impaired
Communication	Unimpaired	....	Extremely Impaired
Course	Stable	....	Progressive
Uncertainty	Episodic	....	Predictable
Stigma	None	....	Extremely Stigmatized
Pain	Painless	....	Extremely Painful

Source: Adapted from Perrin et al., 1993.

cancer whose peers respond with an outpouring of sympathy and support.

Prevalence of Chronic Illness

The prevalence of chronic illness in childhood varies widely depending on whether samples are drawn from the community or the clinical setting, based on parents' reports or medical records, and how they are defined. (Here we follow Fritz and McQuaid, 2000.) Because of these methodological differences, prevalence rates range from 5 to 30 percent. However, it is important to note that prevalence rates of chronic illnesses are rising, ironically because better medical care is increasing the life span of medically ill children who, in an earlier age, might not have survived. Also contributing to

the rising prevalence is the increasing survival rate of extremely premature infants, who are more likely than infants brought to term to demonstrate congenital defects.

A large-scale national health survey conducted in the United States provides us with an overview of the prevalence of many chronic medical disorders of childhood (Newacheck & Taylor, 1992). Data from 17,100 children under age 18 produced a prevalence rate of 31 percent for chronic health conditions. (See Table 13.2.) While 20 percent of the children evidenced mild conditions that interfered little with their daily activities, 9 percent experienced conditions with moderate severity and 2 percent had severe conditions that significantly interfered with their functioning in life.

Table 13.2

Prevalence of Childhood Chronic Illnesses (Cases per 1,000)

Condition	Overall N = 5,332	Age		Gender	
		Under 10 Years	10 to 17 Years	Boys	Girls
All children with chronic conditions	307.60	302.20	315.00	326.20	288.20
Impairments					
Musculoskeletal impairments	15.20	10.90	20.90	16.70	13.60
Deafness and hearing loss	15.30	14.10	17.00	18.30	12.30
Blindness and vision impairment	12.70	10.30	16.00	11.40	14.20
Speech defects	26.20	31.60	18.90	35.30	16.70
Cerebral palsy	1.80	2.20	1.2*	2.00	1.5*
Diseases					
Diabetes	1.00	0.6*	1.5*	1.50	0.5*
Sickle-cell disease	1.20	1.3*	0.9*	0.9*	1.40
Anemia	8.80	11.00	5.80	8.40	9.10
Asthma	42.50	39.30	46.80	50.70	33.90
Respiratory allergies	96.80	71.80	130.30	196.50	86.70
Eczema and skin allergies	32.90	31.10	35.20	30.10	35.80
Epilepsy and seizures	2.40	1.7*	3.30	1.7*	3.10
Arthritis	4.60	1.5*	8.70	4.20	4.90
Heart disease	15.20	13.60	17.40	16.40	13.90
Frequent or repeated ear infection	83.40	120.60	33.60	88.50	79.10
Frequent diarrhea/bowel trouble	17.10	22.60	9.60	13.10	15.90
Digestive allergies	22.30	23.20	21.10	25.60	18.90
Frequent or severe headaches	25.30	9.90	45.80	22.80	27.90
Other	19.80	12.10	30.00	19.30	20.30

Source: Original tabulations of the 1988 National Health Interview Survey. Modified from Newacheck and Taylor, 1992.

*Standard error exceeds 30 percent of estimate value.

Common Chronic Illnesses of Childhood

Asthma   Asthma, a disorder of the respiratory system, is the most prevalent childhood chronic illness in the United States; approximately 4 to 9 percent of children suffer from its effects. (In this section, we follow Melamed, 2002.) In asthma, hyperresponsiveness or hypersensitivity of the trachea, bronchi, and bronchiole produces a narrowing of air passages and reduction of lung function. The result may be intermittent episodes of wheezing and shortness of breath called *dyspnea.* Severe prolonged attacks, known as *status asmaticus,* can be life-threatening and may require emergency medical treatment. Asthma is the most frequent cause of emergency room visits and hospitalizations and is the leading cause of school absences among children.

Cystic Fibrosis   Cystic fibrosis (CF) is a genetic disease that is common in European American children, with a prevalence rate ranging from 1 in every 1,700 births in Ireland to 1 in 7,000 in Sweden. CF is a devastating disease, cutting short the child's life expectancy due to pulmonary and gastrointestinal dysfunctions. However, as treatment has improved, so have survival rates, and many children with CF can expect to live into their adult years. Maintenance of the child with CF places heavy demands on the family, which must carefully monitor the child's food intake and insure compliance with medications, particularly enzyme replacement. A particularly challenging task for parents is to engage the child's cooperation with intensive daily physical treatment that involves percussion to the chest to loosen and expel excessive fluid.

Cerebral Palsy   Cerebral palsy (CP) involves a group of disorders caused by damage to the developing brain, generally in utero or during the birth process. Affected children have awkward and poorly controlled movements, difficulty making voluntary movements, or they suffer from rigidity. Speech often is impaired, and some, but not all, may suffer mental retardation. The prevalence of CP has increased 15 percent over the past 20 years, coinciding with the increased survival rate of extremely premature infants. The challenges presented by the disorder vary with the degree of impairment. Some individuals will require a wheelchair while others will be able to navigate on their own, just as some individuals will be able to communicate orally while others will require the use of electronic devices such as speech synthesizers.

Diabetes Mellitus   Type I (insulin-dependent) diabetes is the most common endocrine disorder in childhood, affecting 1 in 800 children under the age of 18 years in the United States. While it can appear at any age, the peak incidence occurs around puberty. Diabetes is a chronic, lifelong disorder that results when the pancreas does not produce sufficient *insulin,* which is essential for metabolizing carbohydrates. The destruction of insulin-producing cells within the pancreas appears to be an autoimmune process; however, the mechanism that triggers this autoimmune process is unknown. The results can be devastating: Individuals with poorly managed diabetes are at risk for blindness, kidney dysfunction, nerve damage, heart disease, and gangrene, resulting in the need for amputation of the lower extremities and even coma and death. Thus, the stakes are high in regard to compliance with medical regimens.

Treatment of the child requires heavy parental involvement. Blood glucose must be monitored daily to prevent hypoglycemia (too little blood sugar) or hyperglycemia (too much blood sugar). Insulin dosages must be adjusted accordingly. Monitoring is accomplished by obtaining a small sample of blood from a finger stick, placing it on a strip that changes color, and comparing the color with colors on a chart showing the glucose levels. Children who are insulin-dependent must take injections three or more times a day and observe a careful diet and program of physical activity.

Sickle Cell Disease   Sickle cell disease (SCD), also known as sickle cell anemia, is an autosomal recessive disorder that causes a number of aberrations in the blood, including the irregularly shaped platelets that give the disorder its name. SCD disproportionately strikes African Americans with about 1 in 500 being affected. SCD is usually detected early in life, and the course of the disorder involves a vulnerability to infection and recurrent episodes of intense pain in the bones and joints due to vasoocclusion (blockages) of the small blood vessels.

Juvenile Rheumatoid Arthritis   Juvenile arthritis is another disorder that involves chronic pain. The child may experience swelling, tenderness, warmth, or acute pain at the joints. It is a highly heritable disorder. The onset is 16 years of age or younger and can have a profound effect on development, including school, peers, and family relationships.

Cancer   Cancer includes a heterogeneous group of conditions, the common characteristic being a *proliferation of malignant cells.* Hematological malignancies involving the blood-forming tissues (i.e., leukemia and lymphoma) account for approximately half of the cancer diagnoses; tumors of the brain and central nervous system make up the second-largest group; and tumors affecting specific tissues and organ systems, such as bone or kidney, come in third. Acute lymphoblastic leukemia (ALL) is the most commonly seen in children. Despite its overall low prevalence rate, cancer accounts for a large number of disease-related deaths in persons under 16 years of age. However, a heartening increase in the survival rate is expected to accelerate as more effective treatments are developed.

However, treatment of cancer is often painful, invasive, and prolonged. For example, treatment of ALL is a heroic undertaking involving four phases. The first phase is designed to eliminate all evidence of leukemic cells. This phase is followed by radiation therapy to prevent the spread of the disease to the central nervous system. Next comes a consolidation phase designed to eliminate leukemic cells that may have developed drug resistance, and, finally, a maintenance phase lasting 2 to 3 years. Many of the procedures involved are painful, involving finger sticks, intramuscular intravenous (IV) injections, lumbar punctures (spinal tap), and bone marrow aspirations (a procedure in which a large needle is inserted into the hip and bone marrow is withdrawn). Moreover, the side effects of treatment are themselves noxious (e.g., vomiting, diarrhea, pain) or socially embarrassing (e.g., loss of hair, weight gain).

Risk for Psychopathology

A number of population-based studies show that children with chronic illnesses are at increased risk for developing psychopathology (Fritz & McQuaid, 2000). Reviews of the available research indicate that the range of psychopathologies covers the entire spectrum, from internalizing to externalizing disorders. Depression and anxiety are particularly common. In addition, children with chronic illness are more likely than their physically healthy peers to develop social and academic problems and to have a poor self-concept, placing them at further risk for more serious psychopathology over the course of development.

DSM-IV-TR Diagnosis

While not all chronically ill children will develop a psychopathological disturbance, the risk is there. When a medically ill child does come to the attention of a mental health professional, DSM's multiaxial system allows the clinician three ways to consider the interplay between the medical condition and psychopathology.

First, the illness itself is documented on Axis III as a *general medical condition,* which reminds the clinician to consider how the child's psychological functioning and response to treatment might be affected.

Second, the clinician must evaluate whether the child meets criteria for a *comorbid clinical disorder,* above and beyond the effects of the physical illness. In some cases, the psychopathology precedes the illness: for example, the conduct-disordered child who develops arthritis. In other cases, the onset of the psychopathology follows the medical condition and may even be causally related to it. For example, has sadness over a shortened life expectancy in CF developed into a major depression? Has fear of needle sticks in the child with cancer transformed into a full-blown phobia? Has the noncompliance of the diabetic child generalized into an oppositional-defiant disorder? In each case, the clinician must decide whether the child's behavior meets all of the criteria for the comorbid psychiatric diagnosis, including that it interferes with the child's functioning to a clinically significant degree.

Third, the clinician may consider whether to give an Axis I diagnosis of *Psychological Factor Affecting*

Table 13.3

DSM-IV-TR Criteria for Psychological Factor Affecting Medical Condition

A. A general medical condition (coded on Axis III) is present.
B. Psychological factors adversely affect the general medical condition in one of the following ways:
   (1) The factors have influenced the course of the general medical condition as shown by a close temporal association between the psychological factors and the development or exacerbation of, or delayed recovery from, the general medical condition.
   (?) The factors interfere with the treatment of the general medical condition.
   (3) The factors constitute additional health risks for the individual.
   (4) Stress-related physiological responses precipitate or exacerbate symptoms of the general medical condition.

Choose name based on the nature of the psychological factors:

Mental Disorder Affecting [the General Medical Condition] (e.g., an Axis I disorder such as Major Depressive Disorder delaying recovery from episodic pain in sickle cell disease).

Psychological Symptoms Affecting [the General Medical Condition] (e.g., depressive symptoms delaying recovery from surgery; anxiety exacerbating asthma).

Personality Traits or Coping Styles Affecting [the General Medical Condition] (e.g., pathological denial of the need to take insulin in diabetes).

Maladaptive Health Behaviors Affecting [the General Medical Condition] (e.g., overeating, lack of exercise, risk-taking behaviors).

Stress-Related Physiological Response Affecting [the General Medical Condition] (e.g., stress-related exacerbations of hypertension, arrhythmia, or tension headache).

Other or Unspecified Psychological Factors Affecting [the General Medical Condition] (e.g., interpersonal, cultural, or religious factors).

Source: Adapted from DSM-IV-TR, copyright 2000 by the American Psychiatric Association.

Medical Condition (see Table 13.3). This diagnosis reflects the presence of psychological or behavioral factors that have a significant adverse effect on the course or outcome of a medical illness. For example, a comorbid emotional problem, such as depression or anxiety, might exacerbate the negative effects of the medical condition or interfere with the child's compliance with treatment. The psychological problems may take the form of full-blown Axis I or Axis II diagnoses or may represent subclinical symptoms, personality traits, maladaptive coping strategies, or susceptibility to emotional stress that complicates the medical illness. The diagnosis also allows the clinician to indicate whether sociocultural factors, such as ethnicity or religion, affect the course or treatment of a child's medical condition.

Developmental Course of Psychopathology in Chronic Illness

The few longitudinal studies that have been done suggest that overall rate of psychological maladjustment is moderately stable in children with chronic illnesses. The exception to this generalization is disturbances involving the central nervous system, which tend to be very stable over time. Chronic illness also may have different effects during the various stages of the life course, as challenges of the illness interact with stage-salient issues of development (Fritz & McQuaid, 2000).

The Developmental Dimension

Clinical child psychologists who became interested in helping pediatric patients tended to ask the clinician's questions: How is physical illness related to traditional disturbances such as anxiety disorder, depression, and conduct disorders? What traditional treatments would benefit such children? While these are legitimate questions, they are too narrow to capture essential features of physical illness in children. Our preference is to ask the developmental psychopathologist's questions: What is the child's experience and understanding of illness at various developmental levels? How do these affect the intrapersonal and interpersonal variables (particularly the family) that have concerned us all along? In short, what we are searching for is a *developmental psychopathology of illness*.

For example, go back to Figure 1.2 and, instead of visualizing a healthy child in the center, substitute a physically ill one. How would physical illness reverberate throughout all of the contexts? In the individual context, how would it be understood and coped with, and how would it affect the child's personality and adjustment? In the interpersonal context, in what ways would illness alter parental and peer relations? At the sociocultural level, how would the ill child fare in school and in occupations, and how would cultural values shape the perception of illness and its management? To the familiar list of interpersonal variables we must add *health care professionals,* such as pediatricians, nurses, and therapists, just as we must add the *hospital* to the list of social institutions.

Finally, and most important of all, we must ask, How do all of these variables change with time? In addition we should know what risk factors are pressing to divert development from its normal course and what protective factors can counter such a diversion.

Infancy and Toddlerhood   Medical management of chronic illness frequently involves separations from parents and invasive, painful medical procedures that may interfere with the development of secure attachment, interpersonal trust, and self-regulation in infancy. (Here we follow Fritz and McQuaid, 2000.) Children between the ages of 1 and 4 show the most severe reactions to hospitalization, including inconsolable crying, apprehension, somatic complaints, and regression in the form of loss of previously attained developmental accomplishments such as toilet training.

As children enter toddlerhood, chronic illness may interfere with socialization outside the family. Restrictions of children's activities and repeated hospitalizations might limit their opportunities to develop the skills and experiences needed to negotiate early peer relations. As negativism increases during the famous "terrible twos," children may become increasingly noncompliant with necessary medical procedures. A challenge for parents at this stage is to resist perceiving the child as fragile or too sick for appropriate limit-setting.

Middle Childhood   Chronically ill school-age children are particularly vulnerable to negative effects in the academic and peer contexts. While the majority of medically ill children do not have intellectual disabilities, with the exception of those with disorders involving the central nervous system, there may be sub-

tle neuropsychological effects related to their illness. Further, some treatments, such as radiation, may have enduring effects on cognitive processing and learning.

Frequent absences from school due to the illness or its treatment can interfere with the development of social and academic competence. Children may be unable to participate in routine peer activities; for example, consider the diabetic child who cannot have cake at a friend's birthday party or eat the spoils of an evening's trick or treating. However, an important variable in this period is the response to peers of the medically ill child. When peers are supportive and accepting, chronically ill children may experience no lack of friends.

Cognitive developmental level may provide an intriguing protective factor for the school-age child. The concrete, rule-oriented thinking of middle childhood fosters a belief that recovery results from strict adherence to medical regimens, and this belief promotes compliance with treatment.

Adolescence   Chronic illness presents a challenge to the teenager who is concerned with stage-salient tasks of the developing autonomy, a positive self-image, and peer and romantic relationships. Self-consciousness about physical appearance and being different from peers also arise for the adolescent with chronic illness, and body image concerns may interfere with the development of dating relationships.

At particular risk is the adolescent whose attempts to assert his or her independence take the form of denial of the disease and resistance to the medical regimen. For example, research on diabetes shows that parents generally begin to give over responsibility to their teenagers for management of their illness, but that teenagers fail to respond accordingly by accepting the responsibility. An increase in noncompliance during the adolescent years is found in many other chronic illnesses as well, including cancer and asthma. Murphy, Thompson, and Morris (1997) found that poor compliance among adolescents with diabetes was related to (1) a negative perception of their bodies, (2) a perception that what they did would not alter their health status, and (3) the belief that negative events were due to external forces rather than being of their own making.

On the side of protective factors, cognitive development in adolescence can provide more effective and sophisticated strategies for coping with chronic illness. For example, teenagers are more likely than younger children to understand the distinction between controllable and uncontrollable stressors and to use the appropriate kind of strategy (i.e., attempting to change the situation versus adjusting to circumstances as they are) in order to adapt to their illness.

The Biological Context

Characteristics of the Illness

Generally speaking, there is no consistent relation between type of illness and psychological adjustment. One exception to this concerns conditions involving central nervous system disorders or brain damage, in which case children show more behavior problems as well as poor peer relations and school difficulties.

Surprisingly, severity of illness also is not usually associated with an increase in behavior problems; however, there are exceptions. Severity of central nervous system disorders does adversely affect peer relations regardless of how severity is operationalized—in terms of degree of medical intervention required, functional impairment such as being ambulatory versus nonambulatory, neuropsychological impairment, or school placement in a regular or mainstreamed classroom. Moreover, adolescents with three or more severe impairments are likely to have very restricted social lives, with the combination of an IQ below 85, walking problems, and obesity being particularly detrimental. (See Nassau and Drotar, 1997.) In addition, there is some evidence of a relation between duration of illness and adjustment in that the longer children are ill, the more adjustment problems they are apt to have.

The Individual Context

Children's response to their illness can have a significant impact on its course. Children's *perception* of illness is more strongly related to adjustment than are the characteristics of the illnesses themselves. Perceived stressfulness of the illness predicts increased anxiety and depression, as well as lower self-

esteem. Low self-esteem further contributes to poor adjustment, increasing depression and behavior problems. The child's level of anxiety is particularly important. Anxiety and stress might exacerbate the symptoms of certain disorders, for example, by increasing the frequency or intensity of asthma attacks.

The child's developmental level also has a major impact on the child's understanding of and reactions to illness. We will explore cognitive factors in two aspects of chronic illness: understanding of the nature of illness itself and comprehension of pain.

Cognitive Development: Children's Understanding of Illness

A child's adaptation to an illness is likely to be affected by his or her comprehension of the disease, what caused it, and how it is that the sometimes painful and unpleasant treatments are in fact helpful. As we know, children's cognitive development changes with age. With some exceptions, research shows that the understanding and explanation of illness follows the Piagetian stages of cognitive development. (Our presentation is based on Harbeck-Weber and Peterson, 1993, and on Thompson and Gustafson, 1996, unless otherwise noted.)

The Preoperational Period   Recall that, in this period, thinking is based on naive perception—in a literal sense, seeing is believing. Thus, the perceived cause of illness tends to be *external* events, objects, or persons that the preschooler has associated with the illness through experience. These causes may be remote from the child ("A cold is caused by trees") or in physical proximity ("You get a cold when somebody stands near you"). As seen in the latter instance, preschoolers may begin to grasp the idea of *contagion,* but their thinking is still at an unsophisticated level, since they do not understand the reasons why proximity is related to illness.

Finally, in this period *causes* can be confused with *consequences;* for example, preschoolers may think that a bowel movement is caused by going to the toilet or you get a stomachache through vomiting.

The Concrete Operations Period   While children in middle childhood still focus on external events, they now can grasp the idea of *contamination* in that there is something harmful that causes the illness; for example, you get a cold from playing with a dirty toy. Later in this period children explain illness in terms of *internalization,* such as swallowing or breathing something that affects the inside of the body. In sum, the children can now make inferences: It is not the perceived object per se but an inferred quality of the object (its harmfulness) that causes illness. Moreover, invisible objects (germs and internal organs) play a role in sickness.

The Formal Operations Period   Adolescents can grasp *internal* causes at two levels. First, they can understand *physiological* causation in terms of the functioning of body organs. Next, they can also understand *psychological* states such as fearfulness as causes. Thus, illness is now *multidetermined,* with a number of external and internal factors playing a role. Finally, adolescents can grasp *abstract* causes such as "poor nutrition."

However, it would be a mistake to assume that, because formal operations tends to appear in adolescence, all adolescents have a sophisticated, abstract concept of the causes of illness. Such is not the case. Crisp, Ungerer, and Goodnow (1996), for example, were interested in the effect of experience on the level of understanding the causes of illness. They called children with little experience with illness "Novices" and those with a good deal of experience "Experts." They then compared a younger group (ages 7 to 10) of Novices and Experts with an older group (ages 10.7 to 14) of Novices and Experts in terms of whether their explanations of causation fell in the preoperational, concrete operations, or formal operations stage of development. Analysis of their data showed that experience did affect level of understanding. However, what interests us is that there is *not* a total shift from concrete to formal operations in adolescence. While there is a statistically significant increase in such thinking, concrete operations thinking still predominates. When we discuss compliance with medical treatment, we will examine the danger of assuming that adolescents are more sophisticated about illness than they really are.

Cognitive Development: Children's Understanding of Pain

The Infant and Toddler Periods   At one time pediatricians widely held the view that newborns could not experience pain; consequently, procedures such as circumcision often were performed without amnesia. However, that assumption is erroneous. The healthy infant announces pain with loud crying, dramatic facial grimaces, tightly clenched fists, limb thrashing, and torso rigidity. (Our presentation follows Craig and Grunau, 1991, unless otherwise indicated.)

The infant's response to painful stimuli—for example, to a hypodermic injection—is global, diffuse, and prolonged. Moreover, the infant neither localizes the region of distress nor engages in self-protective behavior. Cognitive elements soon enter the picture, between 6 and 8 months, when the infant begins to display anticipatory fear—for example, at the sight of a hypodermic needle. Thus, learning and memory add anticipation to the painful response itself. In addition, the infant engages in rudimentary behavior designed to ward off the threatening stimulus.

During the 2nd year of life, toddlers become more competent in their response to pain. They scream for a shorter period, orient toward the site of the injection, attempt to protect themselves or pull away, and use language to communicate their feelings. They also visually scan their mother's face, indicating an integration of the pain experience into the social environment. As the period progresses, the response to pain becomes more localized and efforts to relieve pain become more purposeful and versatile, while expressions of anger and verbal demands for aid increase.

The Preschool Period   As was the case with the understanding of illness, research on children's understanding of pain has been heavily influenced by Piaget's theory of cognitive development. (Our presentation follows Thompson and Gustafson, 1996, unless otherwise noted.) In the preschool period pain is viewed more as an unpleasant physical entity, a *thing* that hurts or is sore. Pain is caused by external events such as having an accident. In coping with pain children are passive in that they rely on concrete methods of relief such as medicine or food, or they turn to parents to care for them.

Middle Childhood   In middle childhood pain is viewed as a feeling rather than as a thing one has. Children's understanding is more differentiated in two respects. First, pain itself is differentiated in terms of intensity, quality, and duration. Second, localization of pain within the body is more differentiated. Physical and psychological causes are now recognized, although the children refer to one or the other, rather than to both. Finally, children take more initiative in coping with pain, such as diverting themselves by exercising or talking with friends. Level of understanding, however, is dependent on the kind of pain; for example, children have the least understanding of the cause of headaches and the most advanced and precise understanding of pain caused by injections.

Adolescence   Cognitively, adolescents are capable of giving sophisticated descriptions of pain and of its causes. (Our presentation of the adolescent period follows McGrath and Pisterman, 1991.) Descriptions can involve the use of physical analogies, such as "It's like a sharp knife slicing my insides." Causation includes both physiological and psychological factors, and adolescents are aware that psychological factors such as anxiety may intensify the purely physical reaction. Finally, adolescents are capable of understanding the adaptive purpose of pain, such as signaling the presence of disease.

Summary   The *concept of pain* goes from its being a physical entity in the preschool period to its being a feeling differentiated as to components and localization in middle childhood to sophisticated descriptions in adolescence. The *understanding of the cause of pain* goes from external events in the preschool period to either physical or psychological causes in middle childhood to both physical and psychological causes in adolescence. *Coping with pain* goes from passive reliance on pills or parents in the preschool period to taking initiative, such as diverting the self in middle childhood. The adaptive purpose of pain is not grasped until adolescence.

The Family Context

Chronic illness confronts families with a host of challenges and problems. (Our presentation follows Melamed, 2002.) Parents are responsible for interacting with the sometimes daunting medical system, processing complex information concerning the nature and treatment of the illness, and implementing the medical regimens. Family routines must accommodate to changes ranging from such minor ones as providing special diets, to major ones such as having to be with the child during lengthy hospital stays. Parents must strike the proper balance between sympathizing with the child's distress and encouraging healthy coping strategies and age-appropriate behavior. Parents must also find ways of dealing with added financial burdens as well as with their own anxieties, frustrations, and heartaches.

Most families, like most children, do meet such challenges successfully. Some even find the experience brings a new sense of closeness; yet, again, as with children, families do not emerge unscathed (Kazak, Segal-Andrews, & Johnson, 1995).

Parental Contributions to Children's Adjustment

Asthma provides a good case in point of how parental responses either may help to alleviate or exacerbate the disorder. Asthmatic children often feel anxious during an attack, or even in anticipation that one might occur; and the natural concern of parents may become exaggerated anxiety and overprotection. These parental behaviors may in turn lead to age-inappropriate dependency on the parents, isolation from peers, and an increase in behavior problems. The causal loop is completed when overdependence or social isolation negatively affects the child's emotional adjustment and becomes yet another trigger mechanism for an asthmatic attack. Figure 13.3 depicts this complex interaction of the biological, intrapersonal, and interpersonal contexts in asthma.

Parenting Stress

The importance of parenting stress should not be overlooked, because not only the parent's well-being

Figure 13.3   Transactional Effects in the Development of Asthma.

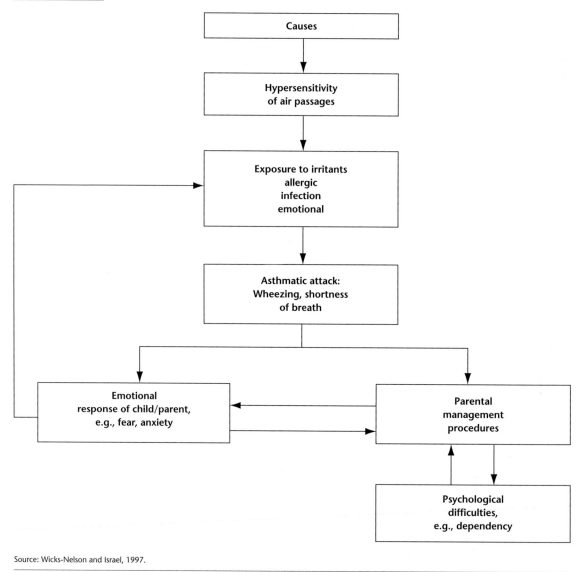

Source: Wicks-Nelson and Israel, 1997.

but the child's is affected. Prospective longitudinal research shows that parenting stress in families of chronically ill children is a better predictor of the development of child behavior problems than other variables, including the severity of the illness or the quality of the parent-child relationship. Coping with a medical illness makes a lot of demands on the parent, and the parent who is stressed and overwhelmed will find it hard to meet those challenges (Melamed, 2002).

Parental Adjustment

Generally few differences exist between families with a child who is chronically ill and comparison families in regard to parental adjustment. An exception to this is maternal adjustment. Probably because they take on the majority of child care responsibilities, mothers of medically ill children are likely to experience a high degree of stress, be prone to feelings of depression, and feel a lack of emotional and practical support (Kazak, Segal-Andrews, & Johnson, 1995).

In regard to risk factors, maternal adjustment is adversely affected by disability-related stresses such as hospitalization and by daily hassles of coping with the child's illness. As for protective factors, these include the mother's perception of herself as competent in solving problems, the amount of social support she receives from family and friends, and the degree to which she remains hopeful (Wallander & Varni, 1998).

Social Support

There is evidence that, in general, social isolation increases the risk of psychological disturbance in families of children with chronic illnesses. Social support, on the other hand, functions as a protective factor (Kazak, 1992).

Unfortunately, well-meaning relations and friends may not provide support when it is most needed in the process. When a chronic illness is diagnosed, families often receive an outpouring of sympathy and assistance. However, the amount of support provided is likely to dwindle as time goes on, even as the family's anxiety, stress, and practical difficulties increase over the course of the chronic illness (Melamed, 2002).

There also are intriguing ethnic differences in the way that social support contributes to family adjustment. For example, Williams, Lorenzo, and Borja (1993) found that social support was helpful to families coping with a child's cancer. However, African American families valued the provision of *instrumental* support (e.g., help with practical matters such as picking up a sibling from school while the parent attends a medical appointment), while European American parents valued *emotional* support from others. Interestingly, although the European American families described their social support networks as twice as large, African American families perceived their networks as more supportive.

The Social Context

Chronic illness may adversely affect peer relations. Severe illness may disrupt the child's life and limit opportunities for social interaction; for example, frequent hospitalizations may be associated with loneliness, sensitivity, and isolation. Boys may be at greater risk than girls in regard to negative effects on peer relations. On the positive side, family cohesiveness, support, and expressiveness serve as protective factors.

Intervention

Psychotherapeutic interventions for children with chronic illness will be as various as the effects of the disorder and the comorbid psychopathologies that accompany it. As we have seen, these encompass the full spectrum from internalizing disorders (anxiety, depression) to externalizing (conduct disorder, oppositional defiance). Some interventions focus on the child, while others involve parents, the whole family system, and even the medical staff. Because in other chapters we discuss treatments for the comorbid psychopathologies, here we will focus on two interventions that are specific to children and families facing chronic illness: family systems pediatric treatment, and pain management skills training. (For a more extensive presentation, see Varni, La Greca, and Spirito, 2000.)

Family Systems Pediatric Interventions

Kazak, Simms, and Rourke (2002) developed a model for intervening in the family system based on their work with children with cancer. Treatment is aimed at helping families to master three major tasks: to manage upsetting feelings in the face of the challenges the disease presents, to develop trusting relationships that allow for collaboration over the course of treatment, and to manage conflict among family members and between the family and the medical staff.

The first step in the process is *joining,* which requires that the clinician empathize with the family and strive to understand their perspective with an attitude of respect, curiosity, and honesty. Second, the clinician will *focus* the work on solving a specific problem that is collaboratively identified with the family. Third, the intervention emphasizes a *competence*

Box 13.2 | **Case Study: Family Systems Pediatric Intervention in Chronic Illness**

Kwame is an 11-year-old African American boy whose recurrent leukemia has left him with chronic fatigue and a small stature in comparison to his peers. During a visit to the oncologist, his mother expressed concern about his increasing aggressiveness, culminating in two arrests at school for physically assaulting peers. The pediatric psychology consulting team considered how best to understand Kwame's behavior. Unlike a traditional orientation, which tends to view behavior through a lens of psychopathology, their competence-based approach led them to assume that Kwame's symptoms represented an attempt at adaptive functioning that was being thwarted by his illness. Their sensitivity to developmental issues suggested that they should consider the challenges faced by a boy entering adolescence, just as their awareness of social ecology suggested that they should consider

neighborhood and ethnic issues. When they asked about the family's life situation, Kwame's mother explained that they lived in a tough, inner-city neighborhood where violence was prevalent and males earned respect through displaying physical power.

The clinician's formulation focused on the stage-salient tasks associated with becoming an adolescent male in a culture of violence. They surmised that Kwame's physical limitations were presenting him with significant developmental challenges to meeting the goal of asserting a positive masculine identity in a context that prized size and power. Consequently, Kwame was left to solve this developmental problem in the best way he knew how: with his fists.

Using the techniques of ARCH (Acceptance, Respect, Curiosity, and Honesty), the clinicians conveyed *Acceptance* by showing an interest and

appreciation for Kwame and his mother, and by communicating their belief that Kwame was using the best strategies he had available to manage his distress about his small stature. They communicated *Respect* by identifying Kwame's strengths, including his willingness to work hard to find solutions to his problems. They evidenced *Curiosity* by inquiring about the neighborhood and how the mother had attempted to help Kwame to deal with difficulties in the past. *Honesty* was conveyed by their openly sharing with the family their reactions and feelings, including their concern about Kwame's behavior and their sincere commitment and belief that they could help him to find more adaptive strategies for asserting his masculine identity.

Source: Adapted from Kazak, Simms, and Rourke, 2002.

based approach, which views symptoms as misguided but understandable attempts to meet developmental needs when more adaptive avenues for doing so have been thwarted. The task then is to harness the child's and family's strengths in order to develop a more adaptive response. Last, the model is *collaborative*, including not only the child, the family, and the clinician, but also the other members of the medical team. (See Box 13.2 for an example of this approach in action.)

Coping with Pain

Pain often is significant for children faced with chronic illness. There are two sources of pain. One is the illness itself: for example, the sometimes

debilitating joint pain that accompanies rheumatoid arthritis. The other source of pain may be the treatment: for example the repeated bone marrow aspirations (BMAs) that children with leukemia must undergo. Consider what the BMA procedure entails. A needle is inserted deep into the child's hipbone and marrow is suctioned out with a syringe. The marrow is then examined to determine whether prior treatment has successfully destroyed the cancer cells. While lasting only a few minutes, BMA is a painful and anxiety-provoking procedure. Anticipatory anxiety can cause nausea, vomiting, insomnia, and crying days before the procedures are scheduled. Young children in particular often kick, scream, and physically resist to the point of having to be carried into the treatment room and strapped in a "papoose" to keep them still during the procedure. Because of the traumatic nature of the procedure, it may take as long as 2 to 3 years for some children to learn to cope with it.

Procedure-Related Pain   Powers (1999) reviewed the literature on treatments for procedure-related pain in pediatric psychology. Many different cognitive behavioral techniques (CBT) have been tried with great success. Common strategies include *breathing exercises,* such as teaching the child to pretend to be a leaky tire filling with air on the in-breath, and then slowly breathing out with a hissing sound as the air leaked out. For younger children, practicing deep breathing by blowing into a party blower adds a bit of enjoyment. *Relaxation training* typically includes breathing combined with progressive muscle relaxation. An example of *imagery* is to invite the child to come up with a story about a favorite superhero or cartoon character using special powers to help the child cope with the medical procedure. Alternatively, imagery can be used to come up with a pleasant image that is incompatible with anxiety and pain (such as walking on a beach or going to an amusement park) and have the child hold that image in mind while breathing slowly and deeply. To be most effective, the imagery should be highly individualized such that each child chooses a unique image that is associated in his or her mind with relaxation. The results can be surprising. While adults might tend toward passive scenarios such as lying on a beach, children's images of relaxation may involve waking up on Christmas morning, attending an exciting football game, or swimming with the dolphins at Sea World.

Other CBT techniques include *distraction,* such as having children play games or do puzzles, or use humor to take their mind off of their anticipatory anxiety. Sometimes *coping models* are used, such as films depicting a child explaining each step of the procedure to be done and modeling adaptive coping. *Cognitive coping skills* include making positive self-statements ("I can do this"; "I'm a brave boy"; "It will be over with soon"). *Reinforcement for compliance* may include presenting the child with a trophy on which his or her name is engraved as a reward for

having the courage to lie still and use deep-breathing skills during the procedure. The child's ability to master and utilize the coping skills taught is enhanced by *behavioral rehearsal and role-play* prior to the procedure, and by *direct coaching* by the clinician or parent during the procedure itself.

Well-designed, controlled studies of treatment packages including several of these procedures show that CBT is generally superior to medication alone in reducing reported pain, observed distress, and physiological indicators of anxiety.

Illness-Related Pain   Unlike medical procedures, which are generally time limited and planned, allowing the child to prepare and practice pain management strategies, the pain associated with illness is often unpredictable and recurrent. Further, because the pain is not limited to the doctor's office, the child and family have even more need of tools that they can take home with them and pull out of their toolbox when needed. Sickle cell disease provides a good example of this kind of pain. Although children's experience varies, on average a child with SCD can expect to experience pain episodes once or twice a month, and these episodes become severe enough to require hospitalization once or twice a year (Powers et al., 2002). Such pain may interfere with school and social activities and be associated with symptoms of depression and anxiety.

Gil and colleagues (2001) developed a CBT intervention for pain in children with SCD and assessed its effectiveness with a group of school-age African American children. First, children were brought into the laboratory and trained to use three coping strategies: deep breathing/counting relaxation, calming self-statements, and pleasant imagery. Each strategy was explained, modeled, and rehearsed by the child. The child then practiced the use of the strategies in two trials that simulated a pain episode by placing a light weight on the child for up to 2 minutes. To help the child to generalize the coping strategies outside of the laboratory, each child was provided with audiotaped instruction, a tape player, and homework assignments for daily practice. As an encouragement to compliance, the investigators telephoned the children at home each week to remind them to practice.

Figure 13.4   Factors Influencing Child Coping and Distress During Painful Medical Procedures.

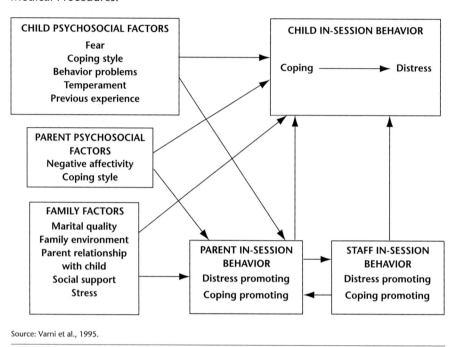

Source: Varni et al., 1995.

A booster review session was provided a week after the initial training session.

Results showed significant reductions from before treatment to after treatment in children's use of negative coping strategies and sensitivity to pain. Four weeks after the treatment had ended, comparisons to an untreated control group showed that children who underwent CBT training used more active coping attempts, had fewer school absences and health care contacts, and were more involved in daily activities even on those days when they were experiencing pain.

Inclusion of the Parents   As we have seen, chronic illness takes a toll on the entire family system, and parents' ability to cope with the stress has a major impact on their child's behavioral, emotional, and even physical well-being. Figure 13.4 displays a comprehensive model of the ways in which characteristics of the child, parent, and family might promote distress or adaptive coping in children's undergoing painful medical procedures. With this in mind, a number of clinicians have emphasized

the importance of working with the whole family in order to prevent the development of psychological problems.

For example, Powers and colleagues (2002) expanded CBT intervention for SCD by including family members in the treatment. Children and parents met once a week for 6 consecutive weeks in separate groups, in which they received psychoeducation about pain and its management, including the side effects of pain medication; education about how to assess and measure pain; training in the use of techniques such as deep breathing, distraction, and positive self-talk; and the use of other physiological methods for reducing pain, such as heating pads and warm baths. A pilot study based on three African American families showed improvements in coping and daily functioning.

We will now shift our focus from the body to the interpersonal context and examine two risk conditions arising from family interactions—child maltreatment and interparental violence.

Risks in the Family Context: Child Maltreatment and Domestic Violence

According to the United Nations Convention on the Rights of the Child (1989; Limber & Wilcox, 1996), each child the world over is entitled to "a standard of living adequate for the child's physical, mental, spiritual, moral, and social development" (p. 6). In the developmental psychopathology literature, these basic necessities for well-being are referred to as the *average expectable environment* (Cicchetti & Lynch, 1995). Perhaps the most profound failure of the interpersonal environment to provide these growth-promoting opportunities occurs when the child's home is a source of fear rather than a place of solace. While others may maltreat a child, abuse that takes place at the hands of parents—the very people that children turn to for comfort and

protection—has the most pervasive and long-lasting effects on development. Therefore, we will focus on maltreatment in the family context.

The "discovery" of child **maltreatment** (also called child abuse) also represents one of the most sensational chapters in the history of child psychology. The very existence of physical and sexual abuse of children was largely denied until early in the 1960s when C. Henry Kempe and colleagues brought the problem of the "battered child syndrome" to the nation's attention (Helfer, Kempe, & Krugman, 1997). Kempe found that, while most physicians and mental health professionals honestly believed that they had never encountered a case of child abuse, this was because they simply could not

429

Figure 14.1   Prevalence of Child Maltreatment in the United States, 1995–1999.

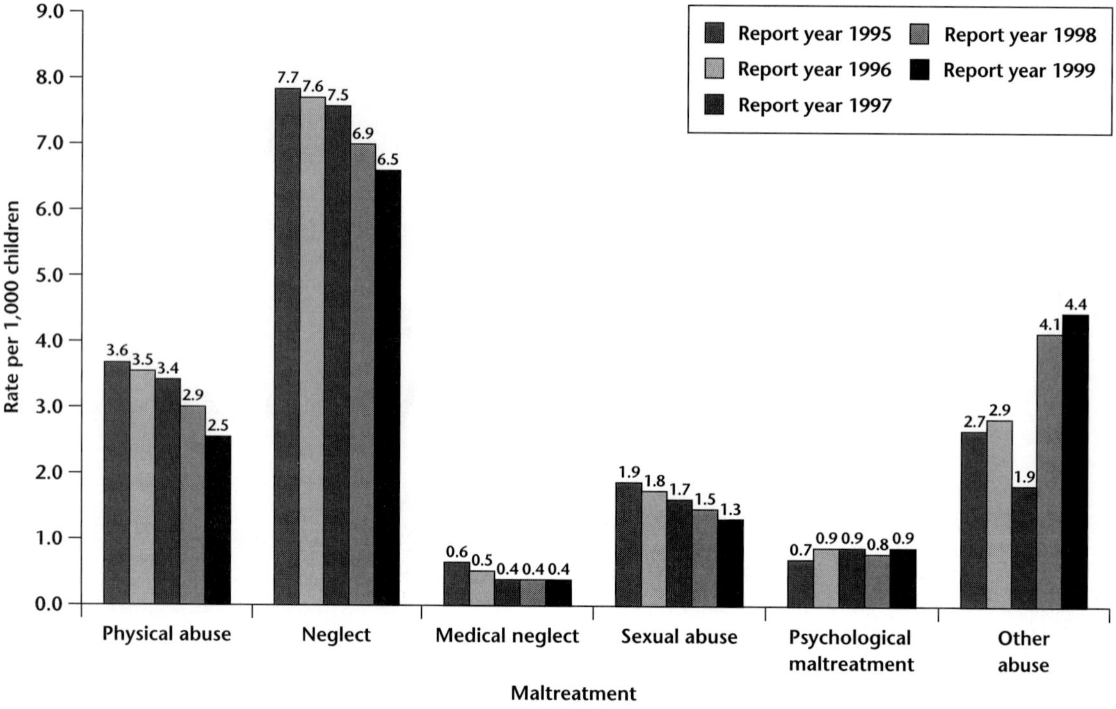

From U.S. Department of Health and Human Services (DHHS), 2001.

bring themselves to acknowledge that such a thing took place.

While rates of child maltreatment in the United States doubled from 1986 to 1993, indications are that the rates have been declining somewhat in the past decade. Nonetheless, maltreatment is highly prevalent. The most recent national data in the United States, compiled from child protective services reports from each individual state, indicate that in 1999 almost 3 million children were reported due to suspected abuse and 826,000 of these cases were substantiated (National Center on Child Abuse and Neglect, 2001). Of those children with confirmed maltreatment, 58.4 percent were neglected, 21.3 percent were physically abused, 11.3 percent were sexually abused, less than 1 percent were psychologically abused, and a further 35.9 percent were maltreated in other ways, such as being abandoned,

threatened with harm, or born drug addicted. (See Figure 14.1.) The mortality rate was 1.6 children per 100,000 and was largely accounted for by infants suffering from severe neglect. Rates of unreported abuse are likely much higher. In a recent national telephone survey of 2,030 U.S. families, Finkelhor, Ormond, Turner, and Hamby (2005) found that 1 in 8 children (136 per 1,000) had experienced some form of maltreatment.

The gradual uncovering of the prevalence of child maltreatment has sent shock waves throughout the nation. Professionals have been galvanized into seeking ways of protecting the child from further abuse, as well as searching for causes that could serve as the basis for intervention and prevention. The search has proved difficult. The initial assumption that abusing parents must be psychologically deviant was overly simplistic and ultimately erroneous. Child maltreatment came to be viewed as multidetermined, involving the interaction among variables from all of the contexts with which we have been concerned.

As our understanding of the determinants of child maltreatment has become more complex and multidimensional, so has our view of what constitutes maltreatment. Maltreatment occurs in a variety of forms, not all of which leave signs as blatant as bruises or broken bones. Along with this broader definition has come a growing recognition of the importance of developmental, interpersonal, and sociocultural variables that determine the effects of a particular abusive act on a child.

Recently, perspectives on child abuse have diverged again, with some questioning the extent to which the phenomenon truly exists. These questions have been spurred by sensational cases of false allegations and spurious "recovered memories" of abuse. However, just as repressed memories of childhood abuse do not lurk underneath every problem in living, it is equally remiss to think that all reports of child maltreatment are fabricated. Our review will navigate this territory with the help of empirical research that offers us signposts for assessing the authenticity and implications of the various forms of maltreatment that do, unfortunately, occur in the lives of some children.

Defining Maltreatment

One of the first hurdles we have to overcome is the problem of defining maltreatment. Unfortunately, no universally accepted definition exists. In actual practice, most professionals base their definitions on the laws governing mandated reporting of child abuse in their jurisdiction. However, since local laws vary significantly from place to place, such laws do not provide a satisfactory definition. Further, while some forms of maltreatment may be overt, with immediately detectable effects (e.g., a physical blow resulting in a red, angry welt), other forms are more subtle, with effects emerging only after some time (e.g., chronic parental indifference resulting in a lack of self-esteem). Additionally, cultural differences in childrearing attitudes and norms make it possible for one parent's "tough love" to be another's "abuse."

The World Health Organization Consultation on Child Abuse Prevention (1999) drafted the following definition:

> Child abuse or maltreatment constitutes all forms of physical and/or emotional ill-treatment, sexual abuse, neglect or negligent treatment or commercial or other exploitation, resulting in actual or potential harm to the child's health, survival, development or dignity in the context of a relationship of responsibility, trust, or power. (p. 5)

Types of Maltreatment

Another complication with defining maltreatment is that there are various kinds of abuse that may have different effects on children's development (Cicchetti & Olsen, 1990). It is unlikely that the child who is emotionally rejected by a parent is affected in exactly the same way as the one who is habitually beaten. Therefore, much attention has been paid to the need to distinguish among types of maltreatment.

A comprehensive typology of maltreatment is proposed by Barnett, Manly, and Cicchetti (1993). These authors distinguish between *physical* abuse (e.g., beating, scalding, slapping, punching, kicking) and *sexual* abuse (e.g., fondling, intercourse, exposure to sexual acts, involvement in pornography). Another category is *neglect,* which may take such form as failure to provide basic necessities (e.g., not ensuring that adequate food, medical care, or shelter is available) or lack of supervision (e.g., leaving a young child unattended or in the care of an unreliable person). The fourth category is *psychological* or emotional abuse (e.g., failing to meet a child's needs for emotional security, acceptance, or autonomy, such as by ridiculing, terrorizing, or excessively controlling the child). Psychological maltreatment is the most recently proposed category and is the one about which there is the least agreement (see Cicchetti, 1991a).

Recent research has suggested that we need to add a fifth category to this typology: *exposure to domestic violence* (McGee, Wolfe, & Wilson, 1997). Children do not have to receive a blow in order to be traumatized by violence in the home, especially when the violence they witness is perpetrated on a parent whom they love and depend on.

The task of identifying the kind of maltreatment children have experienced—for example, physical versus sexual abuse—is complicated by the fact that these different forms of abuse often co-occur. This is known as *multiple victimization* (Rossman & Rosenberg, 1997). For example, Barnett, Manly, and Cicchetti (1993) found that three-quarters of their sample evidenced multiple forms of maltreatment, particularly the combination of physical abuse, neglect, and psychological abuse. In sum, multiple victimization may be the norm for maltreated children.

Assessing Maltreatment

Because definitions of maltreatment vary from jurisdiction to jurisdiction, it is difficult to compile accurate statistics that allow comparisons to be made across states and across countries. In addition, as we describe the prevalence data, we will need to keep in mind that it comes from a number of different sources: cases *reported* to child protection agencies; cases *substantiated* by authorities, which generally amount to a third or fewer of those reported; and *self-reports* of parents or children, which are often based on small and idiosyncratic samples. The strongest data come from nationally representative samples, and so we will rely on these whenever possible. Only recently has a national database been established in the United States, which provides comprehensive information about both reported and substantiated cases.

The Developmental Dimension

Cicchetti and Toth (1995b) argue that in order to define maltreatment it is necessary to place it in a developmental context. A developmental psychopathology perspective focuses our attention on the needs children have at each stage of development, as well as the potential for harm inherent in a parent's failure to meet those needs. As Barnett, Manly, and Cicchetti (1993) state:

The parental acts that are judged to be unacceptable by society change as a function of the child's age. Moreover, the types of parental acts that can enhance development, or that can result in psychological harm to children, also change over the course of development. Thus, acts that might be maltreatment for a toddler would not be for an adolescent, and acts that are maltreatment for an adolescent might not be for a preschooler. (p. 24)

For example, because young children are utterly dependent on caregivers for their physical and emotional well-being, inattentive, lax, or indifferent parenting might have the most severe consequences in infancy. In contrast, the opposite—overprotective, intrusive, or controlling parenting—would be more disruptive for adolescent development. Therefore, a developmental perspective alerts us to the need to define maltreatment in terms of the potential impact of parental behavior on the adjustment of a child at a particular age and stage.

Further, perhaps the most significant aspect of child maltreatment is that it often takes place in the context of the family, perpetrated by the very adults on whom children rely for protection (Trickett & McBride-Chang, 1995). Consequently, the literature focuses on the major developmental capacities that emerge in the context of the parent-child relationship—emotion regulation, interpersonal trust, and self-esteem—that might interfere with the child's ability to master stage-salient issues and move forward in development.

Cross-Cultural and Ethnic Differences

A Global Perspective

Efforts to compile international data regarding child abuse are complicated by the fact that there are major cross-cultural differences in how abuse is defined and perceived in various parts of the world. For example, corporal punishment (e.g., spanking), while defined as physical abuse in many Western countries, is not so defined in the United States and Canada. In fact, corporal punishment is allowed in the public school systems of 23 states (National Coalition to Abolish Corporal Punishment in Schools, 2003). Beatings are accepted as a form of child discipline in many countries, including Sri Lanka, Kenya, Romania, and India (Schwartz-Kenney & McCauley, 2003). On the other hand, behaviors considered normative in Western cultures might be considered abusive in other societies. For example, the expectation that young children sleep alone in a separate room might be considered a form of emotional maltreatment in societies that practice use of a family bed.

The World Health Organization (WHO, 1999) has called for worldwide data collection regarding child abuse and has begun compiling statistics from the countries for which they are available. Overall, WHO (1999) estimates that 40 million children around the world suffer from abuse and neglect. In turn, the United Nations Children's Fund (UNICEF, 2003) has recently reported data on child *fatalities* due to maltreatment in the industrialized world and reports rates ranging from 0.1 per 100,000 children in Spain to 2.2 per 100,000 children in Mexico and the United States. According to their estimates, 2 children die from abuse and neglect every week in Germany and the United Kingdom, 4 a week in Japan, and 27 a week in the United States. Rates are 2 to 3 times higher among low-income versus high-income countries. The association between poverty and child maltreatment has been substantiated in many countries, including the United States, Mexico, India, Bangladesh, and the United Kingdom (WHO, 2002).

As the examples provided in Table 14.1 show, what gets reported to authorities varies widely across cultures (Schwartz-Kenney & McCauley, 2003). Are these discrepancies due to different definitions, different tolerance levels, or actual differences in incidence? As yet, we do not know. However, another important consideration is that cultural practices may influence whether child abuse is reported in the first place. For example, in cultures that emphasize obedience to adults, children may be inhibited from coming forward, while in cultures that emphasize family privacy, a report to authorities might be seen as an act of disloyalty (Comas-Diaz, 1995). In some cases, the consequences of reporting abuse may be so prohibitive that for the child's sake no mention of the experience is ever made. Sexually abused girls may fear ostracism—or even death, in some societies—because of the irrevocable shame their violation brings to the family (Shaloub-Kevorkian, 1999).

Therefore, reliance on officially reported incidents may give a misleading picture of what actually goes on in the homes of children. While parent and child self-reports are not free of bias, they may shed a different light on the subject. Table 14.2 shows cross-national data based upon mothers' reports of their discipline tactics during the past 6 months in Chile, Egypt, India, the Philippines, and the United States (WHO, 2002). A strength of the study is that the investigators presented the items neutrally, without labeling them as "abusive." Many parents reported hitting their children with objects, and blows defined as "moderate" forms of physical punishment were also commonly used.

Ethnic Differences

Within each nation, there also exist subcultural differences related to *ethnicity.* For example, in the United States, reports to Child Protective Services range from a low of 4.4 per 1,000 Asian American children to a high of 25.2 per 1,000 African American children (DHHS, 2001). (See Figure 14.2.) The correspondence between social class and race may account for the ethnic differences in the prevalence of abuse (Morton, 1999). *Poverty* and its correlates— single parenting, parental youth and lack of education, life stress, limited resources, and a large number of young children in the home—all increase the

Table 14.1

Rates of Reported Abuse in Different Areas of the World

	Country		
Type of Abuse	Australia	Ireland	United States
Physical	28%	11%	25%
Sexual	16%	34%	16%
Neglect	24%	47%	45%
Psychological	31%	8%	6%

Source: Schwartz-Kenney and McCauley, 2003.

Table 14.2

Parental Discipline Tactics in Five Countries

	Incidence (%)				
	Chile	Egypt	India	Philippines	USA
Severe Physical Punishment					
Hit child with object (not on buttocks)	4	26	36	21	4
Kicked child	0	2	10	6	0
Burned child	0	2	1	0	0
Beat child	0	25	—[a]	3	0
Threatened child with gun or knife	0	0	1	1	0
Choked child	0	1	2	1	0
Mild Physical Punishment					
Spanked buttocks (with hand)	51	29	58	75	47
Hit buttocks (with object)	18	28	23	51	21
Slapped face or head	13	41	58	21	4
Pulled child's hair	24	29	29	23	—[a]
Shook child	39	59	12	20	9
Hit with knuckles	12	25	28	8	—[a]
Pinched child	3	45	17	60	5
Verbal/Psychological Punishment					
Yelled or screamed at child	84	72	70	82	85
Called child names	15	44	29	24	17
Cursed at child	3	51	—[a]	0	24
Refused to speak to child	17	48	31	15	—[a]
Threatened to kick child out of house	5	0	—[a]	26	6
Threatened abandonment	8	10	20	48	—[a]
Locked the child out of the house	2	1	—[a]	12	—[a]

[a] Item omitted from survey.

Source: World Health Organization, 2002.

likelihood of maltreatment. And these are just the circumstances in which many ethnic minority families live in the United States. Among African American families, for example, 30 percent fall into the lowest income bracket in which the maltreatment prevalence rates are highest (47 per 1,000). Further, 52 percent of African American children are living only with their mothers as compared to 18 percent of European American children (Morton, 1999), another risk factor for abuse. Therefore, statistics on ethnicity always must be interpreted in the context of social class and economic disparity. (For a detailed discussion of child maltreatment in various cultural contexts in the United States—Native American, African American, Hispanic/Latino, and Asian American—see Malley-Morrison and Hines, 2004.)

Disproportionate rates of abuse in ethnic minority samples also may be a product of differential reporting. Zellman (1992) presented hypothetical vignettes to almost 2,000 professionals who are legally required to report suspected abuse, and found that their likelihood of reporting the case and belief that the family would benefit from a report increased when the families were described as African American and low SES.

Another explanation for these discrepancies is that culturally derived preconceptions might lead investigators to define as abusive tactics that are sanctioned and even functional in their context. Parenting styles that are judged negatively by white middle-class psychologists might be conceived as adaptive in disadvantaged communities.

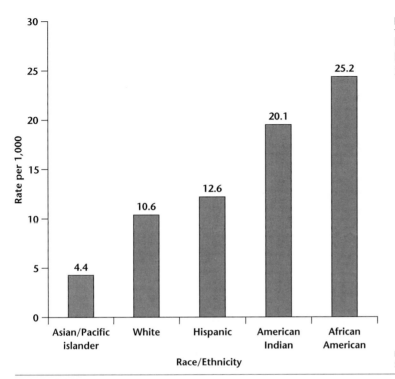

Figure 14.2

Ethnic Differences in Child Maltreatment in the United States, 1999.

From U.S. Department of Health and Human Services (DHHS), 2001.

For example, it may be that in low SES African American families, parenting that emphasizes control over warmth is appropriate for children growing up in dangerous, high-risk environments and might even have the function of helping to "steel" children for the harshness of the world in which they must live. To take another example, parenting in Native American communities tends to be permissive and loosely structured, allowing for multiple caregivers to assume physical custody of the child. While this may be perceived as neglectful by observers from the dominant culture, to Natives such parenting reflects cultural values of respect for the child's autonomy and reliance on the extended family (Malley-Morrison & Hines, 2004). Therefore, it is essential that investigators be culturally competent in order to accurately judge the intent and impact on the child of various parenting practices (Korbin, 2002).

Empirical evidence in support of a *cultural relativism* argument comes from Deater-Deckard and colleagues' (1996) study, which found that physical punishment was associated with increased child aggression in European American samples but not in African American samples. They interpret their results as suggesting the importance of the culturally derived *meaning* of parental behavior to the child. In particular, they argue, the emotional context of punishment is imperative, with the effects depending on whether discipline is carried out in an emotionally charged or controlled fashion (Deater-Deckard & Dodge, 1997). As they put it, "among European American families, the presence of harsh discipline may imply an out-of-control, parent-centered household for some, whereas a lack of discipline among African American parents may indicate an abdication of the parenting role to others" (p. 170). However, it is important to note that the Deater-Deckard et al. (1996) study was of *mild* physical punishment—in subsequent research, they found that effects of physical *abuse* were equally negative for both European American and African American children (Deater-Deckard, Dodge, & Sorbring, in press).

Box 14.1 | **Case Study: Munchausen by Proxy Syndrome**

Munchausen Syndrome was named for Baron von Munchausen, a 17th-century nobleman famous for concocting wild tales. This is a disorder in which adults repeatedly seek medical attention for fictitious illnesses. *Munchausen by proxy syndrome* involves a parent's simulating illness in a child in order to attract the attention of medical professionals (Meadow, 1993). The effects of this are far from benign. The child may undergo painful and invasive medical procedures and suffer the emotional stress of repeated hospitalizations. Also, in the most extreme form, the parent may intentionally subject the child to injury in order to bring about an actual illness.

One case involved an 8-year-old girl whose mother repeatedly sought help for a string of vague physical problems. While the physicians sought in vain to find a cause, the girl's health rapidly deteriorated. Although previously a slender and vivacious child, she became enormously obese and apathetic. Examination showed that her bones were under such severe stress that hairline fractures were developing throughout her body. Clearly, something was terribly wrong, and she was brought into the hospital. With more opportunity to observe mother and child, the staff began to notice other peculiarities. While previous reports indicated that this child had been progressing well in development, she now behaved immaturely and had no interest in school or peer relationships.

She and her mother were inseparable, spending long periods gazing adoringly into one another's eyes in a way that the staff found unnerving. The mother was initially unwilling to cooperate with the clinical psychologists brought in to consult on the case, but slowly her trust was won. As she began to reveal more information about herself, the psychologists learned a number of peculiar facts. For example, the mother believed that her milk was the only proper sustenance for her child, and therefore years ago, when breast-feeding her younger child, she froze a large supply of breast milk "popsicles." These were now a part of her school-age child's regular diet. Curious about the younger child, the psychologists

Next we review each of the types of maltreatment and describe their effects on child development.

Physical Abuse

Definition and Characteristics

Definition

Physical abuse involves acts that result in actual or potential physical harm to a child and that are perpetrated by a caregiver who reasonably could be expected to be in control of those actions (World Health Organization [WHO], 1999). Physical abuse can range widely in terms of severity and potential to cause lasting physical harm. Injuries may be relatively minor, such as bruises or cuts, or major, such as brain damage, internal injuries, burns, and lacerations. A rare form of physical abuse is *Munchausen by proxy syndrome,* in which a parent fabricates or even creates physical illness in a child,

causing psychological or physical harm through subjecting the child to repeated and unnecessary medical procedures. (See Box 14.1.)

Prevalence

Prevalence rates vary widely from study to study because of the different definitions and measures used. A telephone survey of a nationally representative sample of 2,030 U.S. children ages 2 to 17 discovered that during the past year, approximately 3 percent of children had been subjected to physical abuse at the hands of a caregiver (Finkelhor et al., 2005). Physical abuse accounts for 23 percent of all cases of *substantiated* maltreatment (DHHS, 2001). However, it is believed that the *actual* rates are probably much higher. While over 1,200 abuse-related *fatalities* occur in the United States each year, this too is believed to be an underestimate because many child deaths are misattributed to "accidents" or "sudden infant death syndrome."

inquired further about him and learned that he had died of undiagnosed causes 2 years before, following prolonged treatment at the very same hospital.

The solution to the mystery came when a staff member observed the mother's giving the child some tablets during visiting hours. Her purse was searched, and steroids were found. Through administering massive doses of steroids to her child, this mother had created a severe and debilitating illness.

What could cause a parent to mistreat a child in such a way? Little research has been done in this area, although interest is increasing as we come to recognize that the syndrome might not be as rare as originally thought. For example, one survey of 316 pediatricians uncovered 273 confirmed cases, with 192 more suspected (Schreier & Libow, 1993). More recently, Sheridan's (2003) review uncovered 451 cases described in the empirical literature. Of these, 7 percent were considered to have suffered long-term disability; a further 6 percent had died. Victims were most likely to be infants and toddlers, but these were equally likely to be girls or boys. On average, 21 months passed between the onset of symptoms and diagnosis, and in over 60 percent of cases siblings also had suspicious symptoms. While the perpetrating parent is usually the mother (76 percent of cases), fathers are sometimes described as playing an enabling role. In terms of perpetrator psychopathology, 29 percent had characteristics suggestive of Munchausen Syndrome, 22 percent had another psychiatric diagnosis, usually of depression or personality disorder, and another 22 percent had suffered abuse themselves in childhood. Further, clinical descriptions paint a picture of the marital relationship as a distant one (Bools, Neale, & Meadow, 1994). Sometimes older victims are coached to participate in the deception and falsify their own symptoms, further contributing to the difficulty in detecting and treating the disorder (Parnell, 2002).

Child Characteristics

The incidence of physical abuse varies by *age*. The majority of abused children are young: 51 percent are 7 years of age or younger, while 26 percent are 3 or younger. Adolescents account for 20 percent of the sample, the third-largest group. Serious injuries are more common among the older children, but most child fatalities occur in those under the age of 2. In addition, age interacts with *gender*. Boys between the ages of 4 and 8 are the most likely to be physically abused, while girls are more likely to be abused between the ages of 12 and 15 (DHHS, 2001). With regards to *ethnicity*, it appears that, among maltreated children, European American children are more likely than African American children to be the victims of physical abuse (Office of Juvenile Justice, 2000).

Children at greater risk for abuse are those who are difficult or have special needs, including those who are premature or mentally retarded. For example, Sullivan and Knutson (1998) found that *disabled* children were almost twice as prevalent among those who are physically maltreated than those who are not maltreated. Children with *behavior disorders*, such as oppositional-defiant disorder, also are at risk for physical abuse (Ford, Racusin, Ellis, Davis, Reiser, Fleischer, et al., 1999). Behaviorally or developmentally challenging children may overtax the resources of the parent, who then parents poorly, thus increasing child difficulty— which in turn further stresses the parent, with the downward spiral ultimately leading to violence.

Developmental Course

(Our review integrates information from exhaustive reviews by Kolko, 2002; Trickett and McBride-Chang, 1995; and Wekerle and Wolfe, 2003, unless otherwise noted.)

The Biological Context

Recent research in neuropsychology demonstrates that child abuse has significant and adverse effects on the developing brain. Magnetic resonance imaging (MRI) has uncovered negative consequences of maltreatment-related trauma, including smaller brain volume, a smaller corpus collosum and right temporal lobe, and less white matter in the prefrontal cortex (Beers & De Bellis, 2002). These deficits are likely to affect executive functions and efficient communication between the parts of the brain, interfering with such important developmental capacities as emotion regulation, impulse control, and reasoning. Moreover, these structural differences are related to the *age of onset* of abuse: Trauma is associated with the most negative consequences when it occurs early in development.

A proposed explanation for these effects is that prolonged traumatic stress stimulates the production of catecholamines—neurotransmitters, including norepinephrine, epinephrine, and dopamine—and activates the limbic-hypothalamic-pituitary-adrenal (LHPA) axis of the brain. These events lead to the hypersecretion of cortisol from the adrenal gland and stimulate the sympathetic nervous system, causing behavior activation and intense arousal. When this activation continues unabated for long periods of time, excessive cortisol essentially has toxic effects on brain development (De Bellis, 2001). (See Figure 14.3.) On an encouraging note, evidence also

Figure 14.3   Effects of Trauma on the Developing Brain.

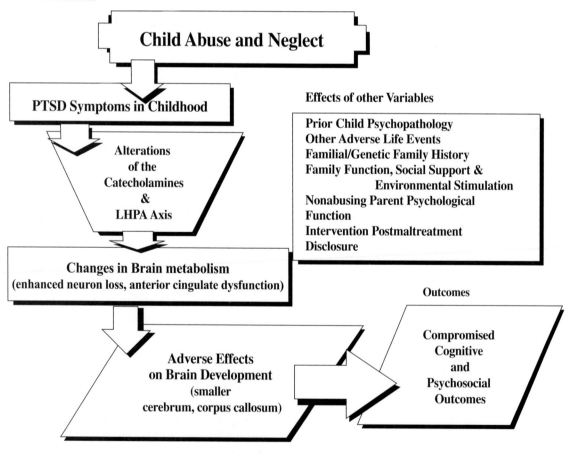

From D. De Bellis, 2001.

suggests that children who are rescued from abusive environments also are able to show recovery and normalization of their cognitive processes.

The neuropsychological research generally has grouped together children who have experienced diverse forms of maltreatment. Therefore, these findings are not specific to physical abuse and will be relevant to our discussions of other forms of abuse that follow.

Cognitive Development

Young maltreated children show significant delays in *cognitive* and *language* development, particularly expressive language. As they enter middle childhood, physically abused children continue to demonstrate cognitive delays in all areas, scoring 20 points lower than nonabused children on standardized IQ tests. Similarly, school achievement tests show that physically abused children perform 2 years below grade level in verbal and math abilities, with one-third of them requiring special education. They are also overrepresented among those with learning disorders. In adolescence, lower achievement and more grade retention is seen.

Emotional Development

The intrapersonal and interpersonal contexts intersect in the major stage-salient task of infancy—the formation of a secure attachment relationship—which is necessary for providing the child with a sense of security, mutuality, and self-esteem. Significantly, from 70 to 100 percent of maltreated infants demonstrate insecure attachments with their caregivers. Physically abused children are most likely to show a pattern of *avoidant attachment,* in which they refrain from seeking attention or contact when under stress (Crittenden, 1992). This behavior may be adaptive in that it reduces the likelihood of maternal anger by keeping bids for attention minimal and low-key. However, because avoidant children's needs for security and comforting are not met, their future development is negatively affected.

Problems of *externalizing,* such as aggression, noncompliance, and conduct disorder, are frequently seen in abused boys. *Internalizing* problems such as depression and low self-esteem also emerge during the school-age years, especially, but not exclusively,

in girls. Toth, Manly, and Cicchetti (1992) found that 22 percent of a sample of physically abused children evidenced clinical levels of *depression,* in contrast to 3 percent of those who had been neglected and 6 percent of the nonmaltreated group. A depressive cognitive style is particularly likely to develop if maltreatment begins prior to age 11, when young children depend on their parents to provide them with a sense of interpersonal trust and personal efficacy.

There is also evidence that physical abuse interferes with the normal development of the *self* in the early years. One of the tests of the early development of the self as an independent entity is toddlers' ability to recognize their reflection in a mirror. Such visual self-recognition is delayed in maltreated toddlers. Moreover, they react with neutral or negative affect when they do inspect their faces in the mirror, rather than with the positive affect that nonabused children show. While deficits in self-esteem most often take the form of the maltreated children's underestimating their capacities, some maltreated children also demonstrate unrealistically *inflated self-esteem.* This emphatic assertion that "I am the best at everything!" may serve as a primitive defense against deeper feelings of powerlessness and inadequacy (Vondra, Barnett, & Cicchetti, 1989). However, because it is not based on actual competence, this defensive overestimation of self is brittle and easily shattered. Thus, overestimation of self serves not as a protective mechanism but rather as a new source of vulnerability (Cicchetti & Howes, 1991).

The development of the self in the early years also is inextricably tied to the ability to recognize and talk about emotions in oneself and others. Beeghly and Cicchetti (1994) found that maltreated toddlers had a poor *internal state lexicon*—that is, that they had fewer words for describing emotional states, particularly regarding negative emotions. The long-term consequences are a lack of access to emotions and the ability to regulate them. Thus, in the school years physically abused children continue to be deficient in the ability to detect and respond to emotions in others. In addition, they demonstrate poor *emotion regulation,* resulting in either overcontrol or undercontrol of emotions. For example, in a sample of 325 Chinese children and their families, Chang and colleagues (2003) found that the relationship between harsh parenting and child peer aggression was mediated by emotion dysregulation. Parental anger, the authors of the study argue, is a form of affective communication that both socializes children into negative patterns of emotion exchange and disrupts their ability to manage upsetting feelings. "The expression of anger, coldness, or hatred that accompanies the physical act of parental aggression could well be more detrimental than the act itself" (p. 603).

Far from abating, the emotional and behavioral problems of abused children intensify in adolescence. Childhood abuse is a significant predictor of adolescent *depression, low self-esteem, conduct disorder,* and *antisocial behavior.*

Social Development

Abused toddlers respond to peers in ways that parallel the behavior of their own parents. For example, when exposed to a peer in distress, abused toddlers are less likely to respond with sympathy or concern than are other toddlers and are more likely to react with *fear,* and *physical aggression.* Similarly, Egeland's (1991) longitudinal research showed that physically abused children were more aggressive in preschool when compared to neglected, psychologically abused, and nonabused children.

Peer relationships become of increasing importance in the school-age years; therefore, it is significant that one of the most consistent consequences of physical abuse is increased *hostility* and *aggression* against others. Maltreated children are reactive to the slightest provocation and are more likely than other children to retaliate against perceived slights with aggression. Like conduct-disordered children (see Chapter 10) they have poor *interpersonal problem-solving skills* and demonstrate a *hostile attribution bias.* Abused children assume that others harbor negative intentions toward them and thus deserve the same in kind. The problem behavior of abused children contributes to the development of a negative reputation in the peer group. They are more likely to experience *peer rejection.* For example, they are least often nominated as a choice of playmate and receive less social support from their classmates (Salzinger et al., 1993). And, as we saw in Chapter 10, peer rejection fuels further aggression.

Adolescence is a time when young people begin to develop significant romantic relationships, and often their family provides them with the blueprint for intimacy. Wolfe and colleagues (1998) investigated the effects of childhood abuse on adolescents' dating relationships. They found that youths who experienced abuse at the hands of their own parents were more likely to be verbally and physically *abusive toward dating partners.* The imitation of their parents' behavior occurred despite the fact that those who were physically abused held negative attitudes about their parents and blamed them for the abuse. Victimization in childhood, therefore, appears to set the stage for violence in later intimate relationships and thus for the intergenerational transmission of abuse.

Summary

Recasting the findings concerning physical abuse in terms of the personality variables we have been using in this text, we have found that attachment, emotional development, cognition, and interpersonal relationships are all adversely affected. Avoidant *attachment* sets the stage by denying the child the opportunity to have needs for security met and to develop a positive working model of self and other. Physical abuse is a particular risk factor for the development of poor emotion regulation, which reveals itself in such varied forms as *aggression* with peers and family members and *internalizing* problems such as withdrawal and depression. Cognitively, abused children evidence a depressive cognitive style and hostile attribution bias. In terms of interpersonal development, abused children have *poor social skills,* fewer friends, and a lack of emotional sensitivity to others.

Etiology: The Physically Abusive Parent

Parents perpetrate 77 percent of child maltreatment, while other family members account for another 12 percent (Wolfe & McEachran, 1997). Because they are the primary providers of child care, mothers are the most frequent perpetrators of abuse; however, fathers and male caregivers are responsible for the majority of child fatalities (National Center on Child Abuse and Neglect, 2001). Child deaths are caused by extreme forms of assault, such as beating children about the head or violently shaking, suffocating, or scalding them.

The Individual Context

Who would abuse a child? A simple explanation might be that these parents are mentally ill; however, the facts are not so simple. Almost nothing is known about male abusers; however, what can be said about the typical abusing mother is that she is young, having usually had her first child while still in her teens. Her life stress is high: She often has many young children in the home, enjoys few advantages, has little social support, and lives in poverty. She may struggle with depression or substance abuse and be irritable and quick to anger (Black, Heyman, & Smith-Slep, 2001).

While poverty is a risk factor and stressful life events increase that risk, most poor, stressed mothers do not abuse their children. Instead, there are individual differences in parents' vulnerability to stress. For example, Pianta, Egeland, and Sroufe (1990) found that the amount of stress did not predict maternal abusiveness, but certain personality characteristics and competencies did. The abusing mothers were highly *anxious, angry,* and *defensive,* while the nonabusing ones were better able to take stress in stride. The mothers' emotional instability was the most important factor contributing to maltreatment in the early preschool period, while stress and social support were of secondary importance.

There are many ways in which abusing mothers appear to be ill equipped for the parenting role. Dukewich, Borkowski, and Whitman (1996) found that lack of *preparation for parenting*—knowledge about child development, child-centeredness, and appropriate expectations for the parenting role— was the strongest predictor of abusiveness in adolescent mothers. Physical abusers also tend to have low *impulse control* and *frustration tolerance.* These mothers may be unable to tolerate even the run-of-the-mill demands of childrearing; further, they are rigid in their choice of childrearing strategies and have few alternatives to physical punishment in their repertoire (Black, Heyman, & Smith-Slep, 2001).

The abusive parents' cognitive processing of child behavior also appears to be problematic. For example, abusive parents engage in *cognitive distortions* regarding their children. These might take the form of misattributing behavior problems to the child's *intentionality* (e.g., "He *knew* it would get to me") or to *internal and stable* negative traits (e.g., "She's a sneak"), or of *discrimination failures* when the parent allows negative feelings toward others to color perceptions of the child (e.g., "He's just like his father—no good!") (Azar, 1997). The parent who perceives child misbehavior as willful and wicked is more distressed by it, and these negative attributions provide a self-justification for responding in a highly punitive way. Parental *depression* may play a role in these distorted attributions by reducing the parent's tolerance for stress and increasing the tendency to appraise events in negative ways.

Much has been made of the statement that abusing parents were themselves abused as children. While it is true that abusers often were abused, those maltreated as children are not "doomed to repeat." An estimate of the *intergenerational transmission* of abuse is that around 30 percent of children will go on to repeat the cycle of maltreatment in adulthood (Egeland, 1988). *Protective factors* have been identified. Parents who do not become abusers are likely to have had a supportive relation with the nonabusing parent while growing up. They also are apt to have a supportive adult relationship currently and to be experiencing fewer stressful events. Additionally, they are more openly angry about the abuse they received and more explicit in recounting their past and their determination not to repeat it (Egeland et al., 2000).

The Cultural Context

While found at all levels, abusive families on average are considerably below national norms on several socioeconomic indicators such as income and employment. *Poverty, family disorganization, crowded housing,* and frequent *disruptions* in living arrangements increase the likelihood of parent-to-child violence, with the risk increasing as the number of indicators increases (Kolko, 2002). Abuse also tends to co-occur with many sources of *family dysfunction,* including parental substance abuse, divorce and separation, frequent moves, and marital violence. The fact that there are so many negative influences operating at the same time in these families makes it difficult to isolate the specific effects associated with abuse. As noted earlier, while abuse rates vary with ethnicity, these findings are difficult to disentangle from the effects of social class and their interpretation is controversial (Malley-Morrison & Hines, 2004).

Taking an even broader perspective, some have pointed out that the United States has the highest level of *violence* of any Western society, as evidenced by statistics on crime and murder. Moreover, the rate of violence is higher among family members than among any other social group. As shocking as physical abuse of children is, it is even more

disturbing to consider that it is just one manifestation of aggression in a society marked by violence.

Integrative Model

Wolfe (1999) has conceptualized the research findings on physically abusing parents in terms of deviations from the normal pattern of authoritarian childrearing. Physical abuse itself is not viewed as an inexplicable outburst but as the result of forces that tip the delicate balance between anger and control. Though conceptualized in terms of a series of stages, the transitions are not inevitable and the parents can move back and forth among them. (See Figure 14.4.)

The *first stage* is marked by a *reduced tolerance for stress* and a *disinhibition of aggression.* There are three *destabilizing* or risk factors contributing to this state of affairs. The first is *poor preparation for parenting.* This may be related to the parents' own

Figure 14.4   Wolfe's Model of the Development of Child Abuse.

Stage	Destabilizing (risk) factors	Compensatory (protective) factors
I. Reduced tolerance for stress and disinhibition of aggression	Poor preparation for parenting Low control and lack of coping strategies Stressful life events	Social support Economic stability, success in work or school Exposure to models of successful coping
II. Poor management of acute crises and provocations	Conditioned emotional arousal Appraisals of threat, harm, or loss Attributing intentionality to child	Improved child behavior Relief from stress Better coping responses
III. Habitual patterns of arousal and aggression	Short term: Parent reinforced for abusiveness by child compliance Long term: Child habituates to punishment; child misbehavior increases due to parents' punitiveness	Parent gains insight into own role in pattern Child responds to noncoercive measures Crisis intervention

Source: Wolfe, 1987.

childhood experiences, in which their parents relied upon punitive authoritarian discipline and were deficient in empathy, reasoning, and the cultivation of problem-solving and social skills. Thus, the parent has learned that the principal way to cope with frustration is aggression. The next component is *low control,* which may be viewed as another untoward consequence of punitive, authoritarian childrearing. An impoverished repertoire of coping strategies is accompanied by a feeling of vulnerability to losing control: If saying no does not work, what can I do then? The final component is *stressful life events,* usually an accumulation of the common, everyday problems of parenting, marriage, and work.

Counterbalancing the three destabilizing factors are *compensatory,* or protective factors: a supportive spouse, friends or organizations, socioeconomic stability, success at work or school, or people who can serve as models of effective coping.

The *second stage* is characterized by *poor management of acute crises and provocations.* The punitive, authoritarian parent uses short-term and possibly self-defeating solutions to problems, such as excessive alcohol or drug use, relocation to escape from debtors, or, in the case of children, harsh punishment.

Three *destabilizing factors* turn punishment into abuse. The first is *conditioned emotional arousal.* The potentially abusive parent has had many experiences of being angry with the child. By a process of classical conditioning, specific aspects of the child's behavior or appearance, such as a facial expression or whining, can come to be associated with irritation or rage. In the future, similar behaviors on the child's part will arouse similar affects in the parent. The second destabilizing factor involves *attribution,* whereby the parent misattributes to the child anger related to any source of irritation in day-to-day life. This is akin to the defense mechanism of displacement: For example, the man who feels irritable after a hard day at work spanks his son for leaving the tricycle in the driveway. The third destabilizing factor is an intensification of aggression by the attribution of *intentionality:* The parent views the child's acts as purposely defiant or provocative, thereby justifying excessive punishment.

Compensatory factors in the second stage include *improvements in the child's behavior,* say,

through maturation or a positive experience in school or with peers. There may be *community resources* that can offer relief from the home situation, such as day-care facilities. Finally, *parental coping resources* can be increased through the intervention of concerned individuals or professionals so that stress is perceived as less overwhelming.

The *third stage* is characterized by *habitual patterns of arousal and aggression.* Here the preceding pattern of increased stress, arousal, and overgeneralized response to the child becomes habitual. In part the change comes about because some children easily *habituate* to existing levels of intensity of punishment so that harsher measures are required to maintain a given level of compliance. In part, parents are immediately *reinforced* by venting their anger and making the child comply. (Recall our discussion of coercive family processes in Chapter 10.) However, in the long run, they are paving the way for further escalation of punishment while concomitantly failing to help the child find alternative modes of behaving that would decrease or eliminate the necessity of punishment. Thus, the parents' complaint, "No matter what I do, he won't listen" and "He only listens if I get really mad," is justified to a certain extent. What the parents have failed to grasp is their own role in this impasse.

Compensatory factors in this final stage, unfortunately, are minimal. Parents, either on their own or through help from others, may come to realize the self-defeating nature of their behavior. The child in turn may respond positively to noncoercive measures. Finally, community services such as crisis intervention centers may help change the pattern of parental behavior.

Neglect

Definition and Characteristics

Definition

The definition of **neglect** includes the failure to provide for a child's physical or mental health, education, nutrition, shelter, or safe living conditions that

Neglect may be more devastating than physical abuse.

are within the resources of the caregiver to provide (WHO, 1999). Neglect is an act of *omission* rather than *commission* and thus may be difficult to detect. For example, many "accidental" deaths and injuries occur because children were left unsupervised, which may be a consequence of neglect. The most frequently detected form of neglect in children age 2 and younger is called *failure to thrive,* which is characterized by a significant delay in growth resulting from inadequate caloric intake (Wren & Tarbell, 1998).

Prevalence and Child Characteristics

Neglect is the most prevalent form of maltreatment in the United States, accounting for 58 percent of all reported cases (National Center on Child Abuse and Neglect, 2001). In a recent national survey, Finkelhor et al. (2005) found that about 2 percent of children in the United States had experienced neglect in the past year. *Age differences* are significant. Neglect is most prevalent in the infant and toddler period and decreases substantially as children get older. No gender differences have been found. With regards to *ethnicity,* it appears that, among maltreated children, African American children are more likely than European American children to be the victims of neglect (Office of Juvenile Justice, 2000).

Developmental Course

For this discussion we integrate information from exhaustive reviews by Erickson and Egeland, 2002; Trickett and McBride-Chang, 1995; and Wekerle and Wolfe, 2003, unless otherwise noted.

The Biological Context

The research cited earlier on neuropsychological dysfunctions in maltreated children includes those who have been neglected as well (De Bellis, 2001).

Cognitive Development

Cognitive development and *language* development are more severely affected by neglect than by other forms of maltreatment. This is not surprising, because neglect generally occurs in an environment that is low in stimulation and responsiveness from the earliest years, with parents who show little interest in the child's achievements. Deficits in cognitive ability persist from early childhood to school age, with neglected children demonstrating more deleterious effects when compared to other abused children or controls. Neglected children have fewer basic skills at school entry and perform as much as 2 years below grade level on measures of language, reading, and math throughout their school years. Similarly, neglected adolescents achieve the lowest school grades of all abused children and are the most likely to repeat a grade (Veltman & Browne, 2001). As neglected children approach adolescence, adverse effects on achievement motivation and initiative are seen. For example, Steinberg and colleagues (1994) found that over the period of a year neglected adolescents evidenced decreasing interest in work and school and increasing involvement with delinquency and substance abuse.

Emotional Development

Neglected children demonstrate deficits in the processing of emotion-related information. They are less accurate in discriminating between emotional expressions (e.g., a happy versus sad face) perhaps because of the limited affective range they have been exposed to in the parent-child relationship (Pollak et al., 2000).

Insecure attachment also is a major consequence of neglect. Neglected infants relate to their mothers in ways that articulate clearly their sense of insecurity and their view of their mothers as unreliable and unavailable. They are less able to tolerate the stress of separation, to modulate their own affect and distress, and to cope with new situations. While their *passivity* toward their mother differentiates neglected children from those who have been physically abused, increasing *anger and resistance* are seen through the toddler years.

Compared to other maltreated children, neglected preschoolers and school-age children demonstrate a number of difficulties with *internalizing* problems, such as anxiety, sadness, and social withdrawal (Manly et al., 2001).

Social Development

Neglected children's *passivity* with mothers extends to their peer relationships in the preschool years. They are generally described as avoidant, withdrawn, unassertive, lacking in social competence, and unable to cope with challenging interpersonal situations. Observations of neglected preschoolers show that they *lack persistence* and enthusiasm, demonstrate *negative affect,* and are highly *dependent* on caregivers and teachers for support and nurturance. As with preschoolers, neglected school-age children are more likely than either nonmaltreated or physically abused children to remain *isolated* and passive with peers, to withdraw from social interactions, and to make fewer initiations for play (Erickson et al., 1989).

A Longitudinal Perspective

Data from the Minnesota Mother-Child project provide an integrative summary of the findings reported in the previous section. The investigators identified a group of 267 at-risk pregnant women and followed their children into adulthood. (See Egeland, 1997, and Erickson and Egeland, 2002.) In infancy, two-thirds of neglected children demonstrated an avoidantly anxious attachment to their mothers. At 2 years of age, they showed a lack of enthusiasm, poor frustration tolerance, and noncompliance during a problem-solving task. In their 4th year, they were observed to have low impulse control, rigidity, and negative affect. In their 1st year, they exhibited poor self-control, dependence on their teachers, and general poor adjustment in the classroom. Neglect during the preschool years had a more pernicious effect than other forms of maltreatment and was associated with inattention, withdrawal from learning, anxiety, aggression, peer rejection, and poorer scores on tests of intellectual functioning and academic achievement.

Follow-up of these children in grades 1, 2, 3, and 6 showed that children neglected in their first 2 years were rated lower than other children in overall emotional health. Teachers described them as more socially withdrawn and unpopular than normative peers, and more withdrawn and inattentive than children who had been physically abused. Neglected children also were rated high in both internalizing and externalizing problems, and their achievement scores were lower than those of their peers. For example, only 1 neglected child out of 13 was not receiving some kind of special education in the first three grades of school.

In adolescence, those neglected in early childhood demonstrated a myriad of academic, social, behavioral, and emotional problems. They had low scores on achievement tests, rated high in delinquent behaviors, substance abuse, and school dropout, and were more aggressive and more likely to have made a suicide attempt than their peers. While maltreated children as a whole were more likely to meet criteria for a psychiatric diagnosis at age 17, the highest rate was for children whose parents were emotionally neglectful, all but one of whom received a psychiatric diagnosis.

Summary

The domains of development affected by neglect parallel those affected by physical abuse in many ways. However, *attachment* takes an avoidant form, and *emotional development* and *interpersonal* development are characterized by passivity and avoidance.

Cognitive development is more negatively affected by neglect than by any other form of maltreatment. As Erickson and Egeland (2002) put it, neglected children do not expect to have their needs met in relationships, and so they do not even try to solicit care or affection; they do not expect to be effective, and so they do not even try to succeed. Significantly, the effects of neglect do not appear to be moderated by the presence or absence of physical abuse; neglect derails children's development regardless. While the drama of violence receives the most attention, the effects of indifferent parenting are insidious yet devastating.

Etiology: The Neglecting Parent

Despite the prevalence and adverse effects of neglect, it is one of the least well-studied forms of child maltreatment. Therefore, less is known about the perpetrators of neglect than of other forms of abuse (Schumacher, Smith-Slep, & Heyman, 2001). Perhaps because women are likely to be the primary caregivers of young children, the research focuses exclusively on neglecting mothers to the exclusion of fathers.

The Individual Context

Like physical abusers, neglectful parents are characterized by high rates of stress, low social support, difficulties with substance abuse, and impulsivity. As with physical abuse, mothers are the most frequent perpetrators due to their role as primary caregivers to children. However, there are a number of ways in which parents who neglect their children differ from those who are physically abusive. Neglecting parents tend to have a greater degree of *global distress*, as indicated by the presence of multiple psychiatric symptoms. Also, in contrast to the impulsive and intermittent nature of physical abuse, neglect occurs in the context of *chronic inadequacy.* Neglecting mothers experience more stress, failure, unmet needs, loneliness, and discontent in all aspects of their lives. They tend to have few friends and to lack *social support.* In addition, neglecting mothers may have a general coping style that relies on such unhelpful strategies as *withdrawal, passivity,* and *mental disengagement* to cope with life problems (Schumacher et al., 2001).

Neglecting mothers are likely to have *negative views about relationships* and to dismiss the importance of them. Thus, they see little significance in their parenting behavior and have little motivation to change it. Further, these mothers are also more likely to have personality characteristics—such as *low self-efficacy, self-preoccupation, depression,* and developmentally *inappropriate expectations* regarding children—that interfere with their sensitivity to the child's signals or emotional distress (Crittenden, 1993). One explanation for this may lie in the histories of these parents, many of whom were maltreated in childhood. Those who were powerless to elicit care from others may be ill-equipped to provide it. They may even defensively block awareness of the child's distress just as they had to inure themselves to their own childhood unhappiness.

The Cultural Context

Although *poverty* is associated with increased risk for all forms of maltreatment, neglect is the *most* strongly predicted by economic distress (Erickson & Egeland, 2002). For example, Drake and Pandy (1996) found that incidents of neglect were 18 times more frequent in communities with high rates of poverty (88 reports per 1,000 families) versus those with low rates of poverty (5 reports per 1,000 families). As noted earlier, the overlap with poverty must be considered when we evaluate *ethnic differences* in rates of neglect. Some data suggest that, among children reported to Child Protective Services, 70 percent of African American children are reported for neglect as opposed to 58 percent of European American children (Office of Juvenile Justice, 2000).

Psychological Abuse

Definition and Characteristics

Definition

A widely cited definition of **psychological abuse** (also termed emotional abuse) is the one proposed by Hart, Germain, and Brassard (1987):

> Acts of commission and omission which are judged on a basis of a combination of community standards and professional expertise to be psycho-

logically damaging. Such acts are committed by individuals . . . in a position of differential power that renders a child vulnerable. Such acts damage immediately or ultimately the behavioral, cognitive, affective, or physical functioning of the child. (p. 6)

Psychologically damaging acts are those that convey the message that the child is worthless, inadequate, unloved, endangered, or only valuable in so far as he or she meets someone else's needs (Hart, Binggeli, & Brassard, 1998). Such acts might include *rejecting* (e.g., rejection, criticism, and hostility); *degrading* (e.g., publicly insulting or humiliating a child); *terrorizing* (e.g., threatening violence against a child or the child's loved ones, placing a child in dangerous situations); *isolating* (e.g., confining a child to the home, refusing to allow a child to interact with others outside the family); *missocializing or corrupting* (e.g., modeling or encouraging criminal or developmentally inappropriate behavior); *exploiting* (e.g., treating a child as a servant, involving a child in pornography or prostitution, coercing a child into playing a parentified role and meeting the parent's emotional needs); and *denying emotional responsiveness* (e.g., interacting with a child only when necessary and failing to express affection, caring, and love).

Prevalence and Characteristics

Because psychological maltreatment is the most difficult to detect and to substantiate, rates are relatively low, accounting for less than 1 percent of substantiated cases (DHHS, 2001). However, it is worth noting that the category of "Other Abuse," which accounted for more than a third of the reports in the National Center on Child Abuse and Neglect's database, includes acts such as "abandonment" and "threats of harm" that would fit under Hart and colleagues' (1987) definition of psychological maltreatment. In Finkelhor et al.'s (2005) national survey, psychological abuse was experienced by 10 percent of U.S. children in the past year.

Moreover, it has been argued that psychological maltreatment is intrinsic to all forms of abuse. Physical abuse, neglect, and sexual molestation all constitute major disruptions in the parent-child relationship that deprive the child of emotional security and thus involve psychological harm. However, despite the fact that psychological maltreatment *co-occurs* with other forms of abuse, evidence suggests that it has *specific* and *independent* consequences over and above those associated with its comorbid forms of maltreatment (Hart, Binggeli, & Brassard, 1998).

Developmental Course

Our review integrates information from Hart, Binggeli, and Brassard (1998) and Hart et al. (2002) unless otherwise noted.

Cognitive Development

There is a correlation between psychological maltreatment and *cognitive delays* in young children. For example, Erickson and colleagues (1989) found that cognitive skills declined from ages 9 to 24 months for children of psychologically unavailable mothers. In addition, just as with children maltreated in other ways, psychologically abused school-age children demonstrate lower scores on achievement tests and poorer school performance when compared to nonabused children (Crittenden, Claussen, & Sugarman, 1994).

Emotional Development

Egeland and colleagues' (1990) longitudinal study assessed two parenting styles that fall under the heading of psychological maltreatment: *verbal abuse* and *psychological unavailability*. These forms of psychological maltreatment in the toddler and preschool period had different effects from physical abuse and neglect. While all maltreated children were noncompliant, had low self-control, and lacked persistence and enthusiasm for tasks, psychologically unavailable mothering was associated with the most devastating developmental consequences throughout the early years. These included declines in *competence* and increases in *self-abusive behavior* as well as other serious forms of psychopathology.

A number of studies have suggested that psychological abuse is related to the development of the cognitive style associated with *depression* in middle childhood, including low self-esteem, hopelessness,

external locus of control, and a pessimistic view of life. Further, Stone (1993) found that depression was more strongly associated with psychological abuse than with other forms of maltreatment. Externalizing problems may also result. Herrenkohl, Egolf, and Herrenkohl (1997) found that children subjected to parental criticism, rejection, and terrorization demonstrated both *low self-esteem* and heightened *aggressiveness* during the school-age period.

Similarly, in adolescence, psychologically maltreated youths are at risk for *externalizing problems* such as conduct disorder, aggression, and juvenile delinquency, as well as *internalizing problems* such as depression, learned helplessness, and low self-esteem. In addition, *emotional instability* has emerged as a consequence of psychological maltreatment. Thus, it is not surprising that other disorders of impulse control and emotion regulation, such as substance abuse and eating disorders, are seen in psychologically maltreated adolescents.

In late adolescence, psychologically abused females report frequent hospitalizations, somatic complaints, and poor overall sense of well-being. Emotional maltreatment in childhood also predicts the development of eating disorders (Rorty et al., 1994) and personality disorders (Braver et al., 1992) in the college years.

Social Development

Psychologically maltreated children demonstrate *poor social competence*. They are likely to withdraw from social interaction or to respond with hostility toward others (Crittenden et al., 1994). For example, data from a longitudinal study found that psychologically abused preschoolers were more aggressive than peers in elementary school and were more likely to engage in assaultive behavior in adolescence (Herrenkohl et al., 1997).

Summary

While frequently overlooked by child protection agents and psychological investigators alike, psychological maltreatment is embedded in the experience of all other forms of abuse and may even account for many of their effects (Hart, Binggeli, &

Brassard, 1998). However, psychological maltreatment has *unique effects,* with pervasive and insidious consequences for development. While aggression is seen increasingly over the course of development, *depression* and *internalizing disorders* appear to be most strongly related to psychological maltreatment. The resulting negative views of self and others—feelings of worthlessness, self-loathing, and insecurity—compromise the ability to get emotional needs met in current or future relationships.

Sexual Abuse

Definition and Characteristics

Definition

Sexual abuse is defined as the involvement of a child in sexual activity that the child does not comprehend, is unable to give informed consent to, or is not developmentally prepared for; or that violates the laws and social norms of the community (WHO, 1999). The perpetrator may be an adult or an older child, typically when there is an age difference of 5 years or more. The sexual act itself may range from actual penetration to acts that involve no physical contact with the child, such as viewing pornography. The context may be sudden and violent, as in the case of rape, or may involve a long period of seduction and "grooming." The abuse may be acute or chronic over a period of years and the perpetrator may be a stranger or a family member, in which case the abuse is labeled *incest.* What constitutes sexual abuse varies from locality to locality, depending on the age at which laws specify that a young person is able to give consent. (See Berliner and Elliott, 2002.)

Prevalence and Child Characteristics

Sexual abuse accounts for 11 percent of substantiated child maltreatment cases in the United States (National Center on Child Abuse and Neglect, 2001). Reports of sexual abuse rose more dramatically than any other category of maltreatment in the period between 1976 and 1993, with an increase of 300 percent (National Center on Child Abuse and Neglect, 1995). However, there is some indication that the numbers have leveled off in recent years.

Once again, evidence is strong that these rates underestimate the *actual* prevalence rates. In a national survey of 2,626 American men and women, Finkelhor and colleagues (1990) found that 27 percent of the women and 16 percent of the men reported at least one of four kinds of childhood sexual abuse—sexual intercourse, touching or kissing their body, taking nude photographs or exhibitionism, and oral sex or sodomy. Sixty-two percent of male victims and 49 percent of female victims experienced actual or attempted intercourse. The majority of encounters were one-time events for both sexes; however, a significant minority had experiences lasting more than a year. Most of the abusers were men, who comprised 98 percent of those who abused girls and 83 percent of those who abused boys, although boys were more likely to be abused by older adolescents. Strikingly, 42 percent of males and 33 percent of females never disclosed the abuse to anyone, again pointing to the unreliability of official prevalence data. In their recent telephone survey, Finkelhor et al. (2005) found that 1 in 12 children ages 2 to 17 years had experienced sexual abuse in the past year.

There are clear *gender differences* in sexual abuse, as Finkelhor's data suggest. In general, girls are overwhelmingly more likely to be victims. According to the 1999 data (DHHS, 2001), sexual abuse rates occurred in 0.4 percent of male children per 1,000 and 1.6 percent of females. *Age-related* differences reveal that older children and adolescents are most at risk, and the ratio of girls to boys also increases with age: 2:1 for infants, 3:1 for school-age children, and 6:1 for adolescents (Sedlak, 1997).

Social class also enters into prevalence rates. Children growing up in violent and disadvantaged communities are disproportionately represented among the victims of sexual abuse (Boney-McCoy & Finkelhor, 1995). With regards to *ethnicity,* it appears that among maltreated children European American children are more likely than African American children to be the victims of sexual abuse (Office of Juvenile Justice, 2000), while other studies suggest that children in the Native American community are disproportionately at risk (see

Malley-Morrison & Hines, 2004). Again, however, the data are inconsistent.

Developmental Course

For our discussion we integrate information from Berliner and Elliott, 2002; Trickett and McBride-Chang, 1995; and Wekerle and Wolfe, 2003, unless otherwise noted.

Cognitive Development

Children who have been sexually abused are rated by teachers as having poor overall *academic competence,* including low task orientation, school avoidance, and distractibility. Sexually abused teenagers demonstrate lower academic performance as well as more learning disorders (Trickett, McBride-Chang, & Putnam, 1994).

The *cognitive attributions* children make about the sexual abuse have important implications for development. The abused children face the difficult task of processing the experience in such a way that they can make sense of it and integrate it into their developing schemata about themselves and others. Reaching an adequate understanding of the experience can be further complicated by the distorted rationales given by the abuser: Sexual violation is "love"; abuse is "normal"; a painful and degrading act is "pleasurable"; betraying the secret makes the child "bad." The resulting attributions of *powerlessness, external locus of control,* and *self-blame* predict the severity of symptoms in sexually abused girls (Cohen, Berliner, & Mannarino, 2000), particularly posttraumatic stress disorder (PTSD) (Deblinger, Steer, & Lippmann, 1999).

Emotional Development

Most studies find that sexually abused children have *internalizing* problems, including fears, anxiety, depression, low self-esteem, and excessive shyness. In the preschool years, the most frequent symptoms are anxiety and withdrawal. In young children, other emotional problems may include regression and loss of developmental achievements (e.g., bedwetting, clinging, tantrums, fearfulness) and sleep disturbances. By middle childhood, many sexually abused

children meet criteria for a diagnosis of *depression.* In adolescence, almost half evidence *suicidal ideation,* and suicide attempts and self-harming are more prevalent in this group than in nonabused controls (Wagner, 1997). In adolescence, other signs of severe disturbance linked to sexual abuse include *eating disorders* and *substance abuse* (see Chapter 12) and *running away.*

Many of the acute symptoms of sexual abuse resemble general *stress reactions.* Signs include headaches, stomachaches, loss of appetite, enuresis, vomiting, sensitivity to touch, and hypersecretion of cortisol (see Chapter 9). Further, one-third or more of sexually abused children meet the criteria for *posttraumatic stress disorder* (Cohen et al., 2000; see Chapter 8), and PTSD is more prevalent among sexually abused children than among those who have suffered other forms of maltreatment (Dubner & Motta, 1999). One of the features associated with PTSD is utilization of the defense mechanism of *dissociation* to shut out awareness of upsetting thoughts and feelings related to sexual abuse (Trickett et al., 2001). The resulting fragmentation of self has negative implications for all domains of development (Fischer & Ayoub, 1994).

Social Development

A behavioral sign highly specific to sexual abuse is *inappropriate sexual behavior,* including excessive masturbation, compulsive sexual play, seductive behavior toward adults, and victimization of other children. McClellan and colleagues (1996) found that over 70 percent of sexually abused preschoolers demonstrated such behavior, while the prevalence was also related to the age of onset of the abuse. Inappropriate sexual behavior was most common in the *preschool period* and declined somewhat in middle childhood. Sexually inappropriate behavior reemerges in adolescence in the form of *promiscuity* in girls, *sexual coercion* in boys, and increased likelihood to engage in unprotected and risky sex (Elze et al., 2001).

One of the dynamics of a sexually abusive relationship is that it is a psychologically controlling one in which the child is coerced to participate through manipulation or fear. Thus, sexually abused children are likely to develop an *internal working model* of others as untrustworthy and the self as shameful and bad. For example, victims of sexual abuse tend to believe that such abuse is pervasive and that adults are generally exploitative of children (Wolfe, 1998). This has negative implications for their self-esteem and capacity for forming satisfying relationships. Consequently, their social competence tends to be less well developed, as is their trust in others and sense of belonging to the peer group (Mannarino & Cohen, 1996).

In addition, the sense that such abuse is inevitable increases the likelihood that sexually abused children will not be able to correctly identify or respond to risky situations in the future and that they will feel that they have no right to defend themselves against unwanted sexual attention. This is borne out by the fact that sexually abused children are highly likely to be *revictimized* over the course of development (Boney-McCoy & Finkelhor, 1995; Irwin, 1999).

Long-Term Course

No one symptom characterizes the entire population and there is no pattern of symptoms that can define a "sexual abuse syndrome." In general, approximately one-third of child victims are *asymptomatic* over the long term. The number of children who either show no symptoms or recover may seem surprisingly high in light of the inferred traumatic nature of the experience. Remarkably, Rind, Tromovitch, and Bauserman (1998) conducted a meta-analysis that showed that once all other variables were accounted for, university students who had been sexually abused in childhood looked little different from their peers. An important caveat to this meta-analysis is that it was based solely on studies of university students, who may be better functioning overall than the general population of abuse survivors.

On the one hand, much of the variation in outcome may be related to the variation in the kinds of experiences that fall under the heading of sexual abuse, which range from a one-time experience of fondling to repeated violent sexual assaults. As might be expected, the factors that lead to the greatest number of symptoms are a *high frequency* and *long duration* of sexual contacts, the use of *force;* a close *relationship to the perpetrator;* and oral, anal, or vaginal *penetration* (Kendall-Tackett, Williams, & Finkelhor, 1993).

In addition, there is a phenomenon called the "*sleeper effect*" in which the impact of an event occurs sometime later rather than immediately after an experience (Beitchman, Zucker, Hood, & DaCosta, 1992). For example, the effects of sexual abuse in early childhood may not emerge until adolescence when the youth attempts to cope with the stage-salient issues of sexuality and intimate relationships.

On the other hand, there is evidence for long-lasting effects of sexual abuse. Between 10 and 24 percent of sexually abused children either do not improve or get worse with time (Berliner & Elliot, 2002). One prospective study that followed sexually abused children over a 5-year period found that, overall, there were no changes in symptoms of depression, low self-esteem, and behavior problems (Tebbutt et al., 1997). However, a closer inspection of the data revealed that this average was misleading. In fact, an equal number of children had deteriorated as had improved. Further, retrospective studies of adult women sexually abused as children show significantly higher lifetime and current episodes of *suicide, anxiety,* and *conduct disorders* (Fergusson & Horwood, 1996), as well as *depression, substance abuse,* and *posttraumatic stress disorder* (Duncan et al., 1996). Strikingly, Rodriguez and colleagues (1997) found that, among women seeking treatment, 87 percent of adult female survivors of childhood sexual abuse met criteria for a diagnosis of posttraumatic stress disorder in comparison to 19 percent of those who had not been sexually abused. By the same token, by the time they reach manhood, boys sexually abused in childhood are at risk for *substance abuse, conduct problems,* and *suicidal behavior* (Garnefski & Arends, 1998).

Integrative Model

Finkelhor and Browne (1988) conceptualize the effects of sexual abuse in terms of four trauma-causing or *traumagenic dynamics.*

1. *Traumatic sexualization.* Sexual abuse shapes the child's sexuality in a developmentally inappropriate and interpersonally dysfunctional manner. The child may be repeatedly rewarded by affection, privileges, and gifts for sexual behavior and may also learn that sex is a means of manipulating others into meeting inappropriate needs. Traumatic sexualization may occur when certain parts of the child's body are given distorted importance and when the offender transmits misconceptions about sexual behavior and sexual morality to the child.

   The psychological impact of traumatic sexualization includes an increased salience of sexual issues, a confusion of sex with care, and negative associations concerning sex or intimacy. The behavioral consequences might include sexual preoccupations, precocious or aggressive sexual behavior, or promiscuity, on the one hand, and sexual dysfunctions and avoidance of sexual intimacy on the other.

2. *Betrayal.* Betrayal concerns the children's discovery that a trusted person on whom they depend has done them harm. During or after abuse, for example, children can come to realize that they have been manipulated through lies or misrepresentations about proper standards of behavior, or they can realize that a loved adult treated them with callous disregard. Children can also feel betrayed by other family members who are unwilling to protect or believe them or who withdraw support after the disclosure. Betrayal can lead to a number of diverse affective reactions, such as depression and grief or anger and hostility. Young children in particular can become clingy because of an intense need to regain a sense of trust and security. Betrayal can produce a mistrust of others and subsequently can impair the adult's ability to judge the trustworthiness of others.

3. *Powerlessness.* When a child's will, desires, and initiative are constantly opposed, disregarded, or undermined, the result is a feeling of powerlessness. In sexual abuse, this can result when a child's body is repeatedly invaded against the child's will and when the process of abuse involves coercion and manipulation on the part of the offender. Powerlessness is strongly reinforced when the child's attempts to halt the abuse are frustrated and when efforts to make adults understand what is happening are ignored. Finally, a child's inevitable dependence on the very adults who abuse and ignore them produces a feeling of being trapped.

   Powerlessness can have two opposite effects. Children may feel anxious or helpless and perceive themselves as victims. As a protection against such terrifying feelings, they may go to the opposite extreme of identifying with the aggressive abuser or, less dramatically, may have an exaggerated need to dominate and be in control of every situation. The behavioral manifestations of powerlessness may include a number of symptoms such as nightmares, phobias, and eating disorders, along with running away from home and truancy. There may also be learning and employment difficulties because victims feel unable to cope with the usual demands of life. At the other extreme, children might attempt to manage anxiety by "turning passive into active," taking on the role of abuser themselves through aggressive and antisocial behavior and even the perpetration of sexual abuse on other children.

4. *Stigmatization.* Stigmatization refers to the negative connotations such as badness, shame, and guilt that are communicated to the child and then become incorporated into the child's self-image. Such negative meanings can come directly from the abuser, who may blame or denigrate the victim, or they may be implicit in the pressure for secrecy with its implication of having done something shameful. Positive feelings attached to the abuse (enjoyment of special attention and rewards, sexual stimulation) may further contribute to the child's feelings of being bad and blameworthy. Stigmatization may result from the child's prior knowledge that the sexual activity is deviant and taboo, and it may result from the reaction of others who hold the child responsible or regard the child as "damaged goods" because of the molestation.

   The psychological impact on the child consists of guilt, shame, and lowered self-esteem.

Behaviorally, stigmatization may be manifested by isolation, and, in extreme cases, suicide. The child may gravitate to various stigmatized levels of society and become involved in drug abuse, criminal activity, or prostitution. Stigmatization may result in a sense of being different from everyone else and a constant concern over being rejected if the truth were discovered.

Protective Factors

The most consistently identified protective factor for sexually abused children is a *supportive relationship with the nonoffending mother* (Kendall-Tackett, Williams, & Finkelhor, 1993). Contrast the experience of a child whose revelation is greeted with empathy and concern to the child who is disbelieved, held responsible, or criticized for getting the family in trouble. Accordingly, perceived support from the mother is found to be the most important mediator of the effects of sexual abuse on children's adjustment over time.

Controversies in the Study of Sexual Abuse

False Allegations

As awareness of the prevalence of sexual abuse has grown, the legal system has responded in a number of ways to give children their "day in court." (Our review follows Bruck, Ceci, and Hembrooke, 1998.) In the past couple of decades, courts have begun to allow children to provide uncorroborated testimony about sexual abuse, since often the only available evidence is the child's own report. With this increase in the availability of children's testimony, however, has come increasing concern about its reliability and validity.

Of the greatest concern are *false allegations*—fabricated reports of sexual abuse. Overall, estimates of the prevalence of false reports vary from 5 to 35 percent. They are more common in such situations as a conflictual divorce, during which a parent might coach a child to make false allegations in order to wrest custody from the other parent. In other cases, false reports may arise from suggestive questions, including those made by child abuse investigators.

Researchers investigating the *suggestibility* of children's testimony typically have children witness an event and, on subsequent questioning, suggest that they witnessed something different. The results of this research can be summarized as follows. As one would predict from studies of memory, children are more apt to accept an interviewer's suggestions the longer the delay between event and interview. Children between 3 and 5 years of age are more vulnerable to suggestion than are older ones. Suggestions tend to be accepted when children feel intimidated by the interviewer, when the interviewer's suggestions are strongly stated and frequently repeated, and when more than one interviewer makes the same suggestion (Bruck & Ceci, 1999).

Many of the early studies on children's suggestibility had limited ecological validity. They were carried out in the artificial conditions of the laboratory and often involved questions—such as whether or not a cabinet door was open—that had little relevance to sexual abuse. Recently, investigators have improved on this methodology by conducting more naturalistic investigations. For example, Saywitz and colleagues (1991) interviewed 72 five- to seven-year-old girls who underwent a medical checkup, half of whom had an external genital examination. First, regarding errors of omission, or *false negatives,* only 40 percent of the children who had been touched in the genital area mentioned it when asked the open-ended question, "Tell me everything that happened." However, they were more likely to do so when asked specific questions. Secondly, regarding errors of commission, or *false positives,* only three girls who had not had a genital exam gave a false positive response when asked a leading question. Ornstein and colleagues (1995) conducted a similar study by assessing 3- to 5-year-olds about their visits to the pediatrician. In general, preschool children could provide fairly accurate information about bodily touching. However, preschoolers were more likely than the older children to report events that did not happen when asked leading questions (e.g., "Did the doctor lick your knee?" "Did the nurse sit on top of you?").

In sum, the research presents the clinician with a dilemma. While specific questions may increase the likelihood of false positives, interviewing that is limited to open-ended questions may allow a preponderance of sexual abuse to go undetected. Therefore, it is important to navigate between two types of error: that of manufacturing abuse reports and that of dismissing all child abuse as fabrication.

Etiology: The Sexual Abuser

As noted previously, the overwhelming majority of sexual abusers are *male* (82 percent of substantiated cases), in contrast to perpetrators of other forms of abuse. However, as was true of physical abuse, there is no specific type of person who sexually abuses children, nor is there a simple cause. To begin with, child sexual abuse might be just one manifestation of a more general state of being sexually aroused by children, or **pedophilia.** Pedophiles may experience sexual excitement only in relationship to children; some become sexual predators, while others may confine themselves to masturbating to magazine advertisements of children. Other sexual abusers also engage in relations with adult women.

A little-recognized fact is that the significant proportion of perpetrators are other *youths.* In fact, up to 40 percent of sexual abusers are teenagers (Berliner & Elliott, 2002). Juvenile offenders also perpetrate their crimes on the youngest children—43 percent of molestations of children under the age of 6 are perpetrated by adolescents (National Center for Juvenile Justice, 1999). (A general guideline used to distinguish sexual abuse from normal childhood sexual exploration is an age difference of 5 years between the perpetrator and the victim.) In many cases—in some studies more than half—the victim is a sibling. The ratio of male to female adolescent sex offenders is about 20 to 1.

The Individual Context

To date, no psychiatric profile has been established that reliably characterizes the sexual abuser (Black, Heyman, & Smith-Slep, 2001). In their extensive review of the literature, Chaffin, Letourneau, and Silovsky (2002) note that some abusers are described as timid and unassertive while others are described as charming, articulate, and socially skilled.

While child molesters are not significantly more likely to exhibit psychopathic traits (see Chapter 10) than others in the criminal justice system, those with *psychopathy* are more likely to reoffend. Some evidence suggests that men who sexually abuse children have *substance abuse* problems and a substantial proportion report using alcohol immediately prior to committing an offense; however, the data are not consistent.

Like adults, juvenile sex offenders are a heterogeneous population (Chaffin, Letourneau, & Silovsky, 2002). However, they have in common that they are more likely than their nonoffending peers to have *poor social skills* and *low impulse control. Language and learning problems* are prevalent, perhaps contributing to their social isolation (Becker, 1998). Many evidence significant *depression,* often related to their own histories of *sexual or physical abuse:* Family violence and early sexual victimization are strong predictors of sexual aggression (Vizard, Monch, & Misch, 1995).

The Family Context

Characteristics of the families of sexually abused children include a more distant mother-child relationship, presence of a nonbiological parent, lack of cohesion, and general dysfunction (Berliner & Elliott, 2002). Madonna, Van Scoyk, and Jones (1991) conducted an observational study of families in which father-daughter incest had taken place. Family characteristics included a *weak parental coalition, enmeshment* and the discouragement of autonomy, and a *rigid* family belief system. Parents were described as being *emotionally unavailable* and showing an inability to appreciate the child's needs apart from their own.

Integrative Model

Finkelhor (1984) identifies four predictors that increase the potential for an adult to sexually assault a child, integrating the intrapersonal, interpersonal, and sociocultural contexts:

1. *Motivation to sexually abuse.* Adults more likely to offend are those who are sexually aroused by children and are blocked from other, more

appropriate sexual outlets. In addition, their emotional needs are sexualized, such that they seek love, care, and attention solely through sexual gratification. Other emotional needs may include the need for power and control over another person, as well as the need to reenact their own experiences of abuse and trauma. At the sociocultural level, the availability of erotic portrayals of children in advertising and pornography can foster these impulses.

2. *Disinhibition of internal constraints.* Characteristics of perpetrators that can overcome internal constraints include mental retardation, impulsivity, lack of empathy, use of alcohol, and a family belief system that legitimizes incest or the use of children for sexual purposes. Further, the abuser may cognitively distort cause and effect in order to self-servingly rationalize the abuse as a response to the child's initiation. Superordinate factors might include weak legal sanctions against sex offenders and an ideology that supports adults' absolute rights over children.

3. *Disinhibition of external constraints.* The major factor here is the accessibility of a child to the abuser. Children most vulnerable to sexual assault are those who receive inadequate supervision, whether through parental stress, illness, or intentional indifference. Living situations that provide opportunities for the abuser to be alone with the child contribute (e.g., children left unattended, sleeping arrangements that place an adult in a child's room). Superordinate contributions include the erosion of social support networks for single mothers.

4. *Overcoming the child's resistance.* Although an adult is physically capable of forcing a child to engage in sexual activity, many abusers avoid physical force, instead using patience and sophisticated psychological strategies to overcome the child's will to resist. Often the abuse takes place only after a prolonged period of "grooming" and gradual indoctrination. The abuser's power over the victim is enhanced when he is in a position of trust and responsibility—for example, as a coach, babysitter, or stepparent—with which the child has been socialized to comply.

Exposure to Domestic Violence

As we noted earlier, a child does not have to receive a physical blow in order to be negatively affected by violence in the family. Witnessing domestic abuse, especially when it is perpetrated against the mother, in itself is a traumatic experience, and investigators are increasingly coming to recognize its deleterious effects on child development (Geffner, Igelman, & Zellner, 2003; Graham-Bermann & Edleson, 2001; Jaffe, Wolfe, & Wilson, 1990; Rossman, Hughes, & Rosenberg, 1999).

Definition and Characteristics
Definition

There is as yet no universally accepted definition of exposure to domestic violence, and different terms and typologies are used from study to study. In addition, unlike other types of child maltreatment, exposure to domestic violence is as yet not universally recognized as a form of child abuse (Graham-Bermann, 2002). Some states, such as Utah, classify as a separate crime domestic assault that occurs in the presence of a child.

Just as child abuse takes many forms, domestic violence may involve physical aggression, verbal threats, sexual assault, and psychological abuse, all of which may be witnessed by the child in the home. The child need not be a visual witness to the violence in order to be affected by it. Hearing the cries—or even, in the case of a deaf child, feeling the thuds of the mother's body as she is thrown against the door of the room in which the child is hiding—is sufficient to inspire terror (Kerig, 2003b).

Prevalence and Child Characteristics

In terms of *prevalence,* rates appear to be high worldwide. Recognizing the importance of woman abuse to the well-being of children, UNICEF (2000) reports global data on rates of physical assault against women by male partners, which range from an astonishing 58 percent in Uganda to 5 percent in the Philippines (see Figure 14.5). A nationally representative survey in the United States found that one child in 28 had witnessed domestic violence (Finkelhor et al., 2005).

Figure 14.5   Prevalence of Violence Against Women by an Intimate Male Partner.

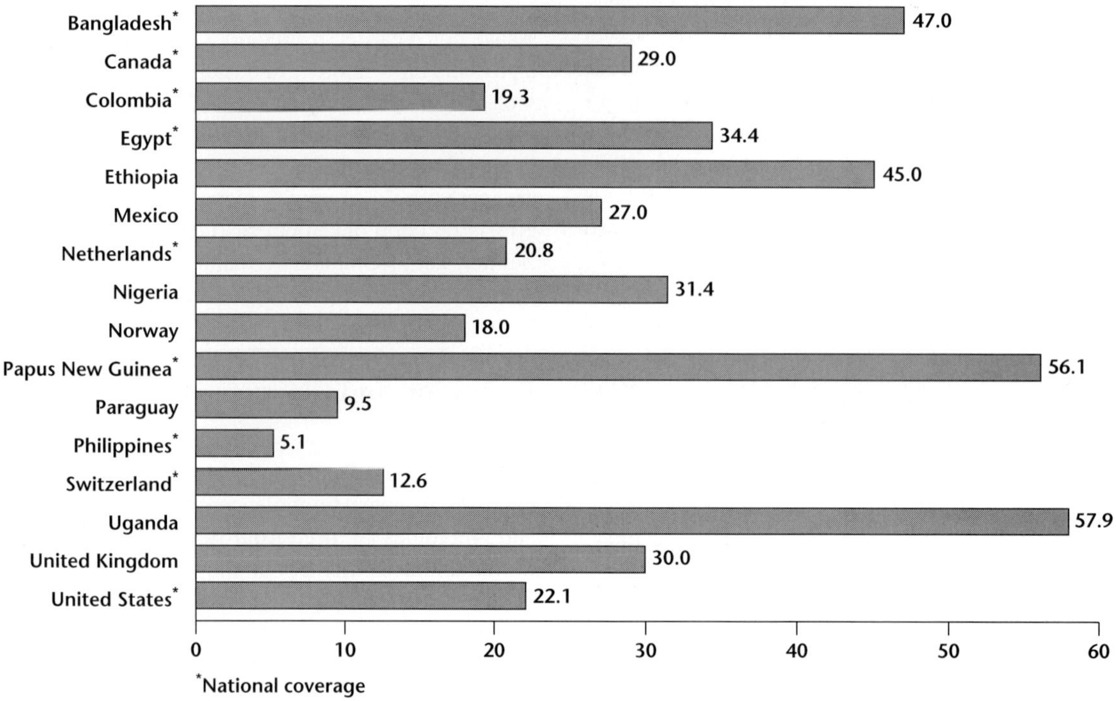

Source: WHO database on violence against women, 1948–1998.

Ethnic differences also are found within the United States. A nationally representative survey of almost half a million households found that European American and Hispanic women were abused by intimate partners at a rate of approximately 8 per 1,000 while rates for African American women were 35 percent higher (11.1 per 1,000). Native American women experienced the highest rates of all (23 per 1,000) while reported woman abuse in Asian American families was the lowest (2 per 1,000) (Rennison, 2001).

While these data do not take into account whether a child was present as a witness, other studies suggest that they are likely to be. Fantzuzzo and his colleagues (1997) examined police reports of domestic violence complaints in five U.S. cities and found that these households were twice as likely to contain children as would be expected on the basis of census data and included a disproportionate number of children under age 5. Overall, it is estimated that approximately 10 million children in the United States witness domestic violence each year (Straus, 1992).

Child *age* comes into play in two ways. Young children are not only the most likely to be present when their mothers are abused but also are the most negatively affected by exposure (Rossman, Hughes, & Rosenberg, 1999). This stands to reason in that the younger children are the most dependent on their parents and have the least well-developed capacities to process information, regulate emotions, and muster coping resources. Data are not conclusive about whether girls or boys are more at risk.

There is *comorbidity* between exposure to domestic violence and other forms of maltreatment, and children who both observe and are the victims of violence in the home are the most negatively affected (Osofsky, 2003; Wolfe et al., 2003). However, rates of overlap between exposure to violence and child abuse differ widely from study to study. While in clinical

Exposure to interparental conflict.

samples the co-occurrence of wife abuse and child abuse ranges from 30 to 60 percent (Edleson, 1999), in community samples it is as low as 6 percent (Appel & Holden, 1998). When there is co-occurrence of child witnessing and victimization, some data suggest that boys may be more at risk. It is hypothesized that boys tend to respond to family violence with externalizing disorders that, in turn, increase parental irritation that spills over onto the child in the form of abuse (Jouriles & Norwood, 1995).

Developmental Course

Our overview integrates information from extensive literature reviews by Graham-Bermann, 2002; Jouriles et al., 2001; and Rossman, Hughes, and Rosenberg, 1999.

Cognitive Development

Although children growing up in violent homes do not consistently show cognitive deficits, they often display academic problems (Hughes & Graham-Bermann, 1998). Distractibility and inattention in school may occur as a result of the trauma that is associated with exposure to violence.

Children's cognitive processing of the violence also plays a role in how they are affected by it. Studies of children's *appraisals* show that children who per-

ceive the violence between their parents as frequent, intense, and threatening are most likely to become distressed, as are those who engage in self-blame (Grych et al., 2001). Similarly, children may develop unrealistic expectations of their own ability to control their parents' quarreling (Rossman & Rosenberg, 1992). Dangers of *perceived control* include that children may put themselves in harm's way by attempting to physically intervene in the fight (Kerig, 2001), or that children may be left with feelings of guilt and inadequacy when they find they are unable to actually control the situation (Osofsky & Scheeringa, 1997). A particular dilemma for children may be the combination of high self-blame and low control: the perception that they are responsible for causing the violence but can do nothing about it (Kerig, 1998a).

Emotional Development

Research suggests that children exposed to domestic violence show a range of emotional and behavioral problems. In younger children, these include *insecure attachment* and, in the school years, both *externalizing* and *internalizing* problems are seen, including depression, anxiety, and aggression. In adolescence, these behavioral problems intensify and are combined with delinquent behavior and suicidal thoughts. One of the most sophisticated studies to date was conducted by

Yates et al. (2003), who examined whether exposure to domestic violence had effects on children over and above any effects related to physical abuse, neglect, socioeconomic status, and general life stress. Using data from a prospective, longitudinal study of a sample of 155 children followed from birth through adolescence, they found that exposure to violence in the home was an independent predictor of *externalizing* problems in *boys* and *internalizing* problems in *girls*. The *timing* of the experience mattered as well. While exposure to violence during the preschool years was the best predictor of maladjustment in adolescent boys and girls, the misbehavior of boys during middle childhood was best predicted by *contemporaneous* violence in the home. Further, over the long term, prospective longitudinal research shows that childhood exposure to violence is one of the best predictors of adult criminal activity in men (McCord, 1979).

While it might be assumed that children exposed to chronic violence in the home would become inured to it, in fact evidence points toward increasing *sensitization* (Cummings, 1998). For example, Hennessy et al. (1994) found that children exposed to violence, in comparison to peers, were more fearful and emotionally reactive to videotaped scenes of anger between adults. Sensitization may be related to *hypervigilance,* the tendency to anxiously scan the environment for possible threat that is one of the hallmarks of posttraumatic stress. And, indeed, children from violent homes show symptoms of *PTSD,* including nightmares, exaggerated startle response, intrusive thoughts, and dissociation; and as many as 50 percent meet full criteria for a PTSD diagnosis (Rossman & Ho, 2000).

Not surprisingly, when children are exposed to uncontrolled anger and distress in the very figures they would turn to for soothing and solace, deficits in *emotion regulation* also are observed (Graham-Bermann & Levendosky, 1998).

Social Development

Across the course of development, violence exposure has negative effects on children's interpersonal relationships. Preschoolers exposed to violence in the home display aggression and negative affect in interaction with others (Graham-Bermann & Levendosky, 1998). In the school-age years, they report more interpersonal distrust and poorer social skills than other children and are more likely to endorse the belief that violence against women is normal and justified (Jaffe et al., 1986; Kerig, 1999). Consequently, in the adolescent years, it is not surprising that teenagers from violent homes are the most likely to become involved in violent dating relationships, thereby replicating the very abusive patterns they witnessed in the home (Wolfe et al., 1998).

Resilience and Protective Factors

Although the research shows that children overall are adversely affected by exposure to domestic violence, there is a great deal of heterogeneity in their response. For example, Hughes and Luke (1998) conducted a study of 58 children living in a battered women's shelter and found significant variability among them. More than half the children in the study were classified as either "doing well" or "hanging in there." Children "hanging in there" were found to exhibit some anxiety symptoms but average levels of behavior problems and self-esteem. The remaining children in the study did evidence maladjustment: Nine showed "high behavior problems," another nine evidenced "high general distress" and four were labeled "depressed kids."

In a larger-scale study, Grych and his colleagues (2000) obtained parents' and children's reports of children's internalizing and externalizing symptoms. The investigators found that, of 228 children living in a shelter, 31 percent could be labeled "no problems reported," in that they exhibited no significant behavioral or emotional difficulties. A further 18 percent were termed "mild distress" in that they demonstrated low self-esteem, a few acting-out problems and mild depression and anxiety. Another 21 percent were characterized as "externalizing," evidenced by clinically high levels of acting-out behaviors but no problems with self-esteem or internalizing disorders. Another group, comprising 19 percent of the sample, was labeled "multiproblem-externalizing." These children were characterized by severe conduct problems as well as some depression, anxiety, and low self-esteem. In contrast, the 11 percent termed "multiproblem-internalizing" evidenced high levels of depressive symptoms, low self-esteem, and some conduct problems.

What *protective factors* account for the significant proportion of children who are resilient in the face of interparental violence? Grych and colleagues (2000) found that the children who demonstrated no or few measurable symptoms were distinguished from their peers by virtue of having been exposed to less-severe interparental violence, less child abuse at the hands of the father, and less child abuse at the hands of the mother. Children's appraisals of the interparental conflict also differentiated among the groups but in complex ways. While children in the "mild distress" or "multiproblem-internalizing" groups perceived the fighting between their parents as more threatening than did the other children, children in the "no problem" and "externalizing" groups were the least likely to blame themselves for the violence. It appears that, while the absence of self-blame might protect children from violent homes from developing internalizing disorders, it does not protect them from developing externalizing problems.

Another important protective factor for children exposed to domestic violence is the quality of their *relationship with the mother* and her ability to provide structure, warmth, and a prosocial model of relationships in the face of trauma and family disruption (Kerig, 2003).

Etiology: The Batterer

Dutton (2000) has noted that the clinical profile of the abusive man is remarkably similar to that of the victim of *childhood trauma.* Men who abuse their intimate partners evidence many of the symptoms of PTSD and have childhood histories that are marked by physical abuse, parental shaming and psychological abuse, and—significantly for our present discussion—exposure to domestic violence. Consequently, as we would expect, given our review of the literature on developmental psychopathology and child abuse, these men have difficulties with affect regulation, interpersonal problem solving, maladaptive appraisals and expectations, and aggression (Dutton, 1999).

The underlying mechanism linking childhood maltreatment to adult intimate violence, Dutton (2000) proposes, is that of *insecure attachment.* Children who lack secure attachments are unable to soothe themselves in the face of threat, which may lead to unregulated emotion and, ultimately, to aggression.

Consistent with this model, a specific attachment-related risk factor for spousal violence is *rejection sensitivity,* the anxious expectation that others will fail to fulfill one's needs for acceptance and belonging (Downey, Khouri, & Feldman, 1997). Downey and her colleagues (2000) have found that men who are high in rejection sensitivity are more likely to misperceive the actions of others as rejecting and are more likely to respond to perceived rejection with hostility and physical aggression toward their intimate partners.

Emery and Laumann-Billings (1998) suggest we expand the frame of reference further, considering individual factors as only one of four interacting sets of variables that increase the risk of domestic violence. Their model suggests that violence is best conceptualized as a product of (1) individual personality characteristics, such as internal working models of attachment; (2) the immediate social context, including family structure and acute stressors, such as job loss or death in the family; (3) community characteristics, including poverty, inadequate housing, social isolation, and neighborhood violence; and (4) societal factors, including cultural beliefs such as those promoting the use of aggression in intimate relationships, and the prevalence of violence in the media.

Comparison of Maltreatment Types

Two kinds of data are available to allow us to distinguish the effects of different types of maltreatment. Most of the studies cited so far are *noncomparative*—that is, they are based on samples of children who experienced one or another form of abuse. A significant weakness of this research, however, is that frequently it asks only about a particular form of abuse. The children may have experienced multiple forms of maltreatment, but we do not know because the investigators failed to ask. This might muddy the waters if, for example, a sample of children identified as sexually abused actually comprises several subgroups, some of whom have also been neglected or physically abused. Our ability to observe whether any observed outcomes are specific to the effects of sexual abuse, therefore, will be clouded.

Table 14.3

Developmental Summary of the Effects of Different Forms of Maltreatment

	Physical Abuse	Neglect	Psychological Abuse	Sexual Abuse	Exposure to Domestic Violence
Infancy and Early Childhood					
Cognitive	Cognitive delays	Most severe cognitive and language delays	Cognitive delays	Cognitive delays	Cognitive delays
Emotional	Avoidant attachment, limited understanding of emotions	Ambivalent attachment	Anger and avoidance, serious psychopathology	Anxiety, withdrawal	Anxiety, separation fears
Social	Fearfulness, aggression	Avoidance, dependence	Withdrawal, aggression	Inappropriate sexual behavior	Aggression
Middle Childhood					
Cognitive	Cognitive, language delays, learning disorder	Most severe cognitive deficits	Low achievement and IQ, poor school performance	School avoidance, learning problems	Poor academic performance
Emotional	Poor affect recognition, externalizing (boys), internalizing (esp. girls)	Dependence, lowest self-esteem	Depression most likely, aggression	PTSD, fears, low self-esteem, depression, regression	Depression, anxiety, externalizing, PTSD
Social	Aggression, peer rejection	Isolation, passivity	Poor social competence, aggression, withdrawal	Inappropriate sexual behavior, revictimization	Aggression
Adolescence					
Cognitive	Low academic achievement	Lowest grades, most likely to be retained	Low achievement	Poor academic performance	Truancy, poor performance in school
Emotional	Depression, low self-esteem, conduct disorder, violence	Internalizing, externalizing, low initiative	Delinquency, depression, poor emotion regulation, eating disorders, personality disorder	Depression, suicide, substance abuse, running away	Depression, suicidal thoughts, delinquency
Social	Aggression	Poor social skills	Pessimism	Revictimization	Violence in dating relationships

Despite these limitations, as the summary of this research presented in Table 14.3 suggests, trends can be found suggesting unique effects of specific forms of maltreatment. While *physical abuse* is associated with *aggression, neglect* is most likely to be linked to

social withdrawal. Neglected children also show the most serious *developmental and cognitive delays. Sexual abuse,* in turn, is associated with *sexualized behavior* and internalizing disorders, particularly *depression.* In general, the symptoms linked to sexual abuse center around trauma-related emotional and behavioral problems rather than the cognitive and interpersonal problems that follow from physical abuse and neglect. In turn, *psychological maltreatment* is associated with the most significant levels of *depression,* as well as increasing *aggression* over the course of development. Lastly, *exposure to domestic violence* is related to the *intergenerational transmission* of violence in relationships with intimate partners.

Comparative studies, which directly assess the degree to which children have been exposed to various forms of maltreatment, are rare. Moreover, such research is often based on small samples and idiosyncratic measures; therefore, it is not surprising that the findings are not always consistent. For example, Manly, Cicchetti, and Barnett (1994) found child *neglect* to have more detrimental consequences than physical or sexual abuse. Kaufman and colleagues (1994) conducted another study that directly compared different forms of maltreatment, although they did not include sexual abuse. The authors summarize the results as follows: (1) *Neglect* was associated with the greatest deficits in *intellectual functioning;* (2) *physical abuse* was associated with *aggressive behavior;* and (3) *psychological maltreatment* was the best predictor of *depression.*

The most comprehensive study to date was that conducted by McGee, Wolfe, and Wilson (1997), who found that *psychological abuse* overall had more pernicious effects on adolescents' mental health than neglect, sexual abuse, physical abuse, or exposure to domestic violence. Moreover, psychological abuse exacerbated the effects of all other forms of maltreatment. Their study also shed light on developmental and gender differences in the effects of maltreatment. For boys, current adjustment was predicted by the interaction of physical and psychological abuse, and the interaction of neglect and witnessing domestic violence, when those experiences occurred in early childhood. Instead, for girls, adolescent well-being was most affected by an increase in neglect or psychological abuse from early to middle childhood. While boys appeared to be affected more by concrete manifestations of maltreatment, such as physical abuse and violence in the home, girls appeared to be more affected by

damage to the parent-child relationship, such as nonnurturing or psychological abusive parenting.

Intervention and Prevention

Physical Abuse, Neglect, and Psychological Abuse

Interventions for Abused and Neglected Children

Friedrich (2002) has developed an integrative model for interventions with maltreated children, focusing on three developmental domains affected by abuse: attachment, emotion regulation, and self-perception. In the domain of *attachment,* targets for intervention include poor differentiation of self and other, the tendency to recapitulate the role of victim or victimizer, distrust, and distorted perceptions of others. These issues can be addressed in therapy through establishing clear and appropriate boundaries between the child and therapist, as well as the therapist's consistent kindness and trustworthiness.

Emotion regulation is hampered by the experience of overwhelming negative emotions without the benefit of a soothing caregiver. Consequently, children who cannot tolerate strong emotions are likely to veer away from uncovering thoughts and feelings related to their abuse—just what is required of them in therapy. Techniques for addressing this problem include giving children control over the process, such as scheduling when and for how long they will talk about the abuse, or utilizing anxiety-reduction strategies such as relaxation training.

Lastly, abuse is a threat to the child's development of an accurate perception of *self.* Strategies for addressing this include fostering the child's development of an understanding of his or her own inner world. This may require refraining from rushing to offer blanket reassurances or offering effusive praise—although well meaning, these may ring false to a child who does not experience himself or herself as good-looking, smart, or fun to be with. At the same time, the child can be encouraged to take progressive steps away from an "all bad" view of self and to develop authentic realms of competence and mastery.

Studies of the *effectiveness* of interventions with abused children are sparse. Many of the approaches tried have a "catch-as-catch-can" quality and have not been adequately evaluated. However, improvement in a number of areas of functioning has resulted from placing preschoolers in a day treatment program, as well as from counseling school-age children and enhancing their problem-solving skills and self-esteem (Mannarino & Cohen, 1990).

Interventions for Abusive Parents

Most intervention efforts involve the physically abusive parent rather than the abused child. Various strategies have been utilized, including parenting education, problem-solving skills training, stress reduction, group discussion and support, and individual psychodynamic therapy. Azar (1997) describes a promising *cognitive-behavioral* approach aimed at restructuring the distorted cognitions that lead parents to abuse. The intervention was highly successful. At a 1-year follow-up, none of the parents in the cognitive-behavioral group had abused their children, while 21 percent of those treated with insight-oriented therapy had done so.

Prevention of Abuse

Prevention programs are the most promising of all in that their goal is to keep abuse from ever occurring. *Primary prevention* strives to alter maladaptive patterns of parent-child interactions, as well as addressing the larger family and community context within which abusive parenting arises (Guterman, 1997). At-risk parents are targeted either during the mother's pregnancy or at the time of birth. The prevention programs provide them with assistance at a number of levels: meeting concrete needs such as obtaining food, diapers, child care, or job skills training; enhancing parenting skills and efficacy through parenting education and support; increasing the quality of parent-child interaction through relationship-oriented interventions; and, in some cases, providing cognitive stimulation for the infant or individual therapy for the mother.

The most successful programs are those that offer *home-based interventions* (Emery & Laumann-Billings, 1998). A premier example is the Prenatal

and Infancy Home Visitors Program (Olds, 1997). Four hundred low-income, adolescent and single mothers were contacted when pregnant with their first child. Home-based support was carried out by a nurse practitioner, who provided parent education regarding child development, involved the family and friends of the mother in providing an extended network of help and support, and linked the family to other medical and social services. Follow-up 2 years and even 10 to 15 years later showed that, in comparison to control group mothers, those who received home visits were less likely to be reported to child protection agencies, had fewer subsequent children, spent less time on welfare, and were less likely to be arrested or engage in substance abuse. Inspired by the success of this work, the National Committee to Prevent Child Abuse initiated a program called Healthy Families America, the goal of which is to create a universal system of home visitation for *all* new parents. Currently, the program is in place in over 240 communities across the United States.

Sexual Abuse

Interventions with Sexually Abused Children

The very nature of the problem of sexual abuse challenges our ability to treat it. While sexual abuse may lead to psychopathology, it is not a disorder in and of itself. Sexually abused children may have undergone different kinds of experiences, and they may be brought to treatment for different kinds of problems. Also, some may evidence no symptoms at all. Although the majority of sexually abused children are female, a significant number of males may need treatment sensitive to their particular symptoms and experiences. (Friedrich, 1997, describes treatment of sexually abused boys.) This diversity makes it difficult to define one correct approach to intervention. However, Finkelhor and Berliner (1995) outline the common elements to interventions designed for sexually abused children. These include: (1) encouraging expression of feelings about the experience; (2) altering erroneous beliefs and negative attributions, such as self-blame; (3) teaching abuse-prevention skills; and (4) diminishing a sense of isolation and stigmatization.

Meta-analytic studies confirm that treatments for sexually abused children are helpful in reducing symptoms, with the strongest evidence in favor of cognitive-behavioral treatments (CBT) that target specific abuse-related appraisals (Saywitz et al., 2000). For example, Celano and colleagues (1996) developed an intervention designed to reduce *"traumagenic beliefs"*—self-blame and powerlessness—in girls who had been sexually abused. A sample of 32 primarily low-income African American girls aged 8 to 13 were randomly assigned to the experimental treatment or an unstructured comparison program. While both interventions were successful in reducing symptoms of posttraumatic stress disorder, the experimental treatment was more effective in reducing traumagenic beliefs and increasing overall adjustment. Another unique aspect to this study is that mothers underwent a parallel intervention. Following treatment, mothers were more supportive of their children, were less likely to engage in self-blame, and exhibited fewer exaggerated fears about the effects of the abuse. Other investigators have found that inclusion of the nonoffending parent increases the therapeutic power of abuse-specific CBT (Deblinger, Stauffer, & Steer, 2001).

Interventions with Sexual Abusers

Chaffin et al. (2002) review the available research on interventions with sexual abuse perpetrators. Many different types of intervention have been implemented: One survey revealed that 338 different therapies were being used in various correctional institutions throughout the United States. Some unifying themes in the goals of treatment can be identified: (1) confronting denial, (2) identifying risk factors, (3) decreasing cognitive distortions, (4) increasing empathy for the victim, (5) increasing social competence, (6) decreasing deviant arousal, and, when appropriate, (7) addressing the perpetrator's own history of victimization (Vizard, Monch, & Misch, 1995). Most use a group format under the assumption that confrontations are more powerful when voiced by a chorus of peers; however, the relative effectiveness of group versus individual treatment has not been established.

Reviews of the intervention research literature paint a mixed picture of the effectiveness of treatments for adult sexual offenders. The best that can be said, it seems, is that the likelihood of reoffending is decreased for *some* child molesters who complete the treatment program. Overall, recidivism rates range from 3 to 39 percent for molesters who undergo treatment, versus 12 to 57 percent for those without treatment (Chaffin et al., 2002).

Empirical evidence for treatment efficacy for juvenile offenders also is lacking, given that no published studies have randomly assigned youths to treatment versus nontreatment conditions. However, one promising intervention is multisystemic therapy (MST), which targets multiple aspects of the adolescent's social ecology, including school, family, and peer relationships (see Chapter 10). Research with a 10-year follow-up suggests the effectiveness of MST with teenage sexual offenders (Bourdin et al., 1990; Henggeler et al., 2002).

Prevention of Sexual Abuse

Most preventive programs involve children and are aimed at teaching certain key concepts and skills. Among these are that children own their bodies and can control access to them; there is a continuum from good to bad touching; and trusted adults should be informed if someone makes a child feel uncomfortable or strange. Children are also informed that potential abusers are apt to be familiar individuals rather than strangers and are taught ways of coping with attempted molestation such as saying no or running away (Wurtele, 1997).

Prevention programs are effective in increasing children's knowledge of sexual abuse concepts and self-protection skills (Rispens, Aleman, & Goudena, 1997). Younger children, such as those under age 5, are particularly likely to benefit. However, evidence that such knowledge is effective in preventing sexual abuse or increasing its reporting is still lacking. Critics of these prevention efforts have pointed out that children who participate become more worried and fearful about the possibility of abuse (Melton, 1992). On the other hand, those children appear to gain the most from the programs; thus, their worry may have a function (Finkelhor & Dziuba-Leatherman, 1995). On the positive side, there is evidence that sexual abusers are deterred by children who indicate that they would tell a specific adult about an assault. Thus, there may be significant benefits to teaching children, especially those who are passive, lonely, or troubled, the simple strategy of telling an adult about attempted abuse.

Exposure to Domestic Violence

Interventions with Battered Women and Their Children

Developmentally sensitive and empirically supported interventions have been developed for children from violent homes (Graham-Bermann & Hughes, 2003). Noting that children under the age of 5 are disproportionately represented among those exposed to interparental violence, Jouriles and colleagues (1998) developed a home-based intervention that focused on providing support and parent training to the mothers. Eight months later, mothers showed better coping strategies and more effective parenting skills while children's behavior problems were reduced (Jouriles et al., 2001).

A well-supported program for school-age children is the Kids Club (Graham-Bermann, 2000), which provides parallel interventions for children and their mothers. The child groups provide children with information about family violence; address maladaptive beliefs and attitudes; and provide prosocial strategies for coping with emotional, behavioral, and interpersonal problems. The intervention for mothers includes education about the effects of violence on children's development, parenting skills, and provision of support to increase empowerment and self-esteem. The investigators put their program to a vigorous empirical test, randomly assigning participants to child-only, mother-plus-child, or comparison "treatment-as-usual" conditions. Data from a sample of over 200 families showed that children who participated in the 10-week Kids Club improved more than those in the comparison treatment on such variables as social skills, safety planning, emotion regulation, and internalizing and externalizing symptoms; and these gains were enhanced by participation of the mother in the parent group.

Interventions with Batterers

When it is safe to do so, fathers are sometimes included in the same groups that are attended by battered women. Aims are to increase fathers' understanding of the effects of domestic violence on children, challenge attitudes that normalize wife abuse, and improve parenting skills (Peled & Edleson, 1995). Key issues that must be addressed for fathers include: (1) resistance and denial, (2) knowledge about child development, (3) perceived shame and ways of coping with it, (4) empathy for children, (5) stepparenting issues, and (6) willingness to make a commitment to nonviolent parenting (Matthews, 1995).

Prevention of Domestic Violence

Group treatments have proven to be powerful tools in the prevention of interpersonal violence across the life span (Rossman, Hughes, & Rosenberg, 1999). For example, Wolfe and colleagues (1997) developed the Youth Relationships Project to prevent the development of violent dating relationships among teenagers. Peer groups are used to address the history of exposure to family violence that characterizes so many of the teens who go on to abuse their partners and attempt to counter the maladaptive beliefs that justify the use of force in intimate relationships. An evaluation of the program was conducted with teenagers aged 14 to 17 years who were referred from social service agencies due to their exposure to violence in the home. Following participation in the groups, the investigators saw positive changes in the youths' attitudes, knowledge, and endorsement of the use of violence in relationships with girlfriends or boyfriends (Wekerle & Wolfe, 1999).

Having explored factors in the biological, intrapersonal, and interpersonal contexts that place children and adolescents at risk for developing problem behavior, we now move onward in our developmental timeline and begin to explore the late adolescent transition into adulthood. In Chapter 15 our concern will be with extreme disturbances in the development of self, namely the emergence of personality disorders.

Late Adolescence to Early Adulthood: Emergent Personality Disorders

Our next topic marks a dramatic shift. While substance use may be a part of normative adolescent exploration, and substance abuse the extreme end of a continuum, **personality disorders** represent profound deviations from normal self-development. DSM-IV-TR (2000) defines a personality disorder as *"an enduring pattern of inner experience and behavior that deviates markedly from the expectations of the individual's culture"* (p. 686). The disorder must be manifested in at least two of the following areas: *cognition, affectivity, interpersonal functioning,* or *impulse control.* Further, this pattern is *inflexible and pervasive across a broad range of personal and social situations, leads to significant distress and functional impairment, is stable and of long duration,* and has an *onset in adolescence or early adulthood.*

In DSM-IV-TR, the personality diagnoses are grouped into three clusters, based upon their common characteristics. Cluster A comprises disorders in which individuals appear odd or eccentric, including *paranoid,* characterized by pervasive distrust and suspiciousness of others; *schizoid,* in which the person is detached from social relationships and expresses limited emotion; and *schizotypal,* involving pervasive interpersonal deficits, social discomfort, cognitive and perceptual distortions, and eccentric behavior. Cluster B comprises disorders in which individuals appear dramatic and emotional, including *histrionic,* which features excessive emotionality and attention-seeking behavior; *narcissistic,* involving grandiosity, a need for admiration, and a lack of empathy; *antisocial,* which, as we encountered in Chapter 10, involves a pervasive pattern of disregard for the rights of others; and *borderline,* marked by instability in self-image, emotions, and relationships. Cluster C comprises disorders in which individuals appear anxious or fearful, and includes *obsessive-compulsive,* featuring a preoccupation with orderliness, perfectionism, and personal control; *avoidant,* characterized by social inhibition, feelings of inadequacy, and hypersensitivity to criticism; and *dependent,* distinguished by a pattern of clinging submissive behavior, and fear of separation. To focus our discussion in this chapter, however, we will target the personality psychopathology that to date has gleaned the most extensive developmental theory and research, namely *borderline personality disorder.*

Should Personality Disorder Diagnoses Be Applied to Youths?

Before we proceed, however, given the emphasis on "enduring patterns," "stability," and "inflexibility" in the DSM criteria described in the previous section, our knowledge of development requires that we stop to ask: *can* and *should* youths be described as having personality disorders? Children and adolescents, as we have seen, change dramatically over the course of normal development, their levels of functioning waxing and waning over time. Adolescence in particular is a developmental period marked by inconsistency, volatile emotions, and deviant behavior, which might lead to an excess of "false positives" in the diagnosis of personality disorder (Geiger & Crick, 2001). Moreover, over the course of childhood, many factors might intervene to change the trajectory of a child's developmental path; therefore, considerable hesitation is warranted before we conclude that a child's personality is a fixed or immutable "type." For example, one study found that among adolescents diagnosed with personality disorders, less than half retained the diagnosis over the course of 2 years (Bernstein et al., 1993). Given the negative stigma and pessimistic prognosis associated with a diagnosis of personality disorder, there is concern

among some clinicians that the diagnosis might do more harm than good.

For all of these reasons, only under exceptional circumstances may a person under age 18 be given a diagnosis of personality disorder. DSM-IV-TR specifies that personality disorders may be applied to children and adolescents in *unusual instances* in which the maladaptive personality traits are *pervasive and long-lasting* (at least 1 year) and are *likely to persist across developmental periods.*

Keeping these cautions in mind, there are a number of reasons why it is appropriate for us to explore the topic of personality disorder in our discussion of the late adolescent transition. First, over the course of adolescence there is an increasing coherence and predictability in emotions, attitudes, and behavior, and thus stability in personality. In addition, one of the stage-salient issues of adolescence is the development of a sense of identity. Thus, we should consider the plight of those who fail to develop a coherent sense of self, as is the case in borderline personality.

Definition and Characteristics

DSM-IV-TR Criteria

A common thread running through all of the characteristics associated with Borderline Personality Disorder (BPD) is *inconsistency:* in interpersonal relationships, emotions, behavior, and self-image. Nine specific criteria are listed in DSM-IV-TR (see Table 15.1). For example, those with BPD evidence an *unstable sense of self,* with pervasive feelings of being empty, damaged, or less than human. *Impulsivity* and *self-destructiveness* are often seen, including such extreme behavior as *self-mutilation.* In addition, the relationships of individuals with BPD are marked by excessive *fear of abandonment,* and extreme shifts between the opposite poles of *idealization* and *devaluation* of other people. Affects are *intense and unregulated,* and therefore the experience of strong emotions, particularly anxiety and anger, can be highly disruptive to functioning. Anxiety quickly escalates to panic and anger to unmodulated rage.

This description makes apparent why BPD is called a disorder of the *self.* Such dramatic and rapid shifts in mood, and in perceptions of self and others,

Table 15.1

DSM-IV-TR Criteria for Borderline Personality Disorder

A pervasive pattern of instability of interpersonal relationships, self-image, and affects, and marked impulsivity beginning by early adulthood and present in a variety of contexts, as indicated by five or more of the following:

   (1) Frantic efforts to avoid real or imagined abandonment.

   (2) A pattern of unstable and intense interpersonal relationships characterized by alternating between extremes of idealization and devaluation.

   (3) Identity disturbance: Markedly and persistently unstable self-image or sense of self.

   (4) Impulsivity in at least two areas that are potentially self-damaging (e.g., spending, sex, substance abuse, reckless driving, binge eating).

   (5) Recurrent suicidal behavior, gestures, or threats, or self-mutilating behavior.

   (6) Affective instability due to a marked reactivity of mood (e.g., intense episodic dysphoria, irritability, or anxiety usually lasting a few hours and only rarely more than a few days).

   (7) Chronic feelings of emptiness.

   (8) Inappropriate, intense anger or difficulty controlling anger (e.g., frequent displays of temper, constant anger, recurrent physical fights).

   (9) Transient, stress-related paranoid ideation or severe dissociative symptoms.

Source: Adapted from DSM-IV-TR, 2000.

interfere with the individual's ability to maintain a consistent sense of identity. A description of an adolescent diagnosed with BPD is presented in Box 15.1.

Prevalence

Recent research suggests that personality disorders occur in adolescents at about the same rates as in adults (Johnson, Cohen, Skodol, Oldham, Kasen, & Brook, 1999). BPD is estimated to be present in about 2 percent of the general population, 10 percent of outpatients in mental health centers, and 20 percent of psychiatric inpatients. Among those diagnosed with personality disorder, 30 to 60 percent carry the borderline label. The disorder is diagnosed predominantly in *females* (about 75 percent). No information is available about differences in prevalence associated with ethnicity or social class.

Criteria Specific to Children and Adolescents

While clinicians only apply the label of BPD to young people with great caution, those who have observed extremely disturbed children in clinical settings have argued that some of them do show

characteristics consistent with the adult diagnosis. However, because the DSM criteria are adult oriented, others have proposed specific criteria to help us identify youths with borderline pathology (Cicchetti & Olsen, 1990; Goldman et al., 1992).

For example, Bemporad et al. (1982) describe five features common to children with borderline personality. The first of these is *rapid shifts in levels of functioning.* The developmental level of children with BPD is uneven and unpredictable, sometimes age-appropriate, and at other times immature or even primitive. Secondly, there is a *chronic presence of anxiety* as well as an inability to regulate affect. These children appear to be in a state of constant distress and may develop obsessions, rituals, phobias, and other so-called "neurotic" behaviors in an attempt to manage their emotions. However, they lack effective defense mechanisms and coping strategies with which to calm themselves. Therefore, they are vulnerable to being overwhelmed by their negative feelings and may experience episodes of panic and disorganization that look almost psychotic. Thirdly, their thought content and processes show excessive *fluidity between reality and fantasy.* Although children with BPD are not schizophrenic, their fantasies intrude on their reality testing to an

Box 15.1 | **Case Study in Borderline Personality Disorder**

Wendy was described as a charming and coy 17-year-old upon her admission to Chestnut Lodge Hospital. She had been transferred from another private psychiatric institution after attempting to choke her latest therapist. Hospitalized the prior three years for cutting herself and assaulting others, Wendy had exhausted numerous therapists and defeated all treatment interventions. Having fired one doctor after another, Wendy set personnel against one another and displayed a genius for finding the sensitive areas of staff member's psyches and exploiting them. In defeat, the institution recommended a transfer to Chestnut Lodge, a long-term residential treatment center.

Wendy's developmental history was a troubled one. She was the third of four siblings born to a wealthy family. Although the father was trained as an engineer, he never worked because Wendy's mother demanded that he stay home with her. However, their married life was colored by quarreling, heavy drinking, physical fights often culminating in bloodshed, and sexual promiscuity with others. When drunk, the father was physically and emotionally abusive while the mother retreated to her bed—cared for by a private nurse—and left the children to fend for themselves. While the mother frequently was emotionally unavailable, when present she was disapproving, mean, and frightening,

behaving in a sexually seductive and inappropriate manner with Wendy and her brothers.

From age 4 onwards, Wendy was frequently sent away to camp, where she inevitably became ill and was extremely accident prone. Wendy's behavioral problems emerged in grade school and took the form of temper tantrums and holding her breath when upset. Despite her behavior problems, however, she managed to make good grades and score in the average to above-average range on achievement tests. After school, her main playmate was her elder brother Eric, whose favorite game took the form of strangling birds to the edge of death and then

extent that is disruptive. One reason borderline children may find it difficult to avoid preoccupation with their internal worlds is that their fantasies tend to be extremely anxiety-arousing, concerned with disturbing images of self-annihilation, body mutilation, and catastrophe. Fourth, their relationships with others show an *excessive need for support* and reassurance that is sought in all interactions, not only from attachment figures. Bemporad and his colleagues describe these children as having an "as-if" personality in which they overidentify with the other person, as though they are trying to merge with the other in order to avoid feeling separate and alone. Fifth, children with BPD demonstrate a *lack of control over impulses*. They find it difficult to delay gratification and tolerate frustration, which may lead to extreme rage and temper tantrums inappropriate for their developmental level.

Similar criteria for diagnosing BPD in children were proposed by Vela, Gotlieb, and Gotlieb (1983), including: (1) disturbed interpersonal relationships,

(2) distortions in reality-testing, (3) excessive anxiety, (4) impulsive behavior, (5) neurotic-like symptoms, and (6) uneven or distorted development.

Multiple Complex Developmental Disorder

An alternative perspective places children with these characteristics in the spectrum of the Pervasive Developmental Disorders rather than in the personality disorder classification. Towbin and colleagues (1993) argue that we do not have enough evidence to support the idea that childhood-onset symptoms are continuous with the adult version of borderline personality disorder. Moreover, they point out that personality in children is dynamic and fluid and the diagnostic category of personality disorder is not likely to be appropriate. The early onset of the symptoms in children and the significant social deficits suggested to them a pervasive development disorder with a long-range deleterious effect on development. Consequently, they propose a attempting resuscitation. The neighboring families forbade their children to play with Wendy and her brother.

By the age of 10 Wendy was cutting herself in reaction to anger and humiliation. As she approached puberty, her father's friends made sexual advances to her at drunken parties on the family compound. When Wendy was 13, what little family life existed was shattered by her mother's death in a fire that resulted from a lit cigarette the mother held while passed out in a drunken stupor. Wendy's behavior became increasingly disorganized and unmanageable after her mother's funeral. She rampaged through the house breaking furniture, refused to attend school, and assaulted playmates. Her father arranged treatment with a psychoanalyst, who quickly recommended boarding school. Once there, Wendy beat up the younger children at the slightest provocation. Any form of reprimand from her teachers further inflamed her rage. After a year in the school, Wendy pleaded successfully to be allowed to return to live with her newly remarried father. Within weeks, however, Wendy decided that she hated her stepfamily and hit her stepsisters at every opportunity.

At this time, when Wendy was 14, her father placed her in a home for emotionally disturbed children. Upon entering the home, Wendy purposefully cut her leg. The wound became infected and her leg was put in traction. The wrong splint was used and she developed gangrene in her heel; in addition, while in the splint, Wendy developed appendicitis. Once recuperated, she jumped across the net while playing tennis, fell, and broke her wrist. Her father visited and accused her of breaking her wrist on purpose. In response, Wendy cut the bottoms of her feet. After only 2 months in the home, the headmistress informed Wendy that the staff was incapable of providing further care for her and Wendy's first psychiatric hospitalization was arranged.

Adapted from Judd and McGlashan, 2003.

---

separate category specific for children, which they termed Multiple Complex Developmental Disorder (MCDD).

The core diagnostic criteria for this disorder, which is proposed for inclusion in DSM-V, are presented in Table 15.2. MCDD is defined by the presence, before 5 years of age, of significant functional impairments that represent a consistent, enduring pattern of deficit. Features include *dysregulated emotions* (intense anxiety, episodic behavioral disorganization, extreme emotional lability), *interpersonal deficits* (disturbed attachments to adults, inability to initiate or maintain relationships with peers), and *impaired cognitive functioning* (irrationality, magical thinking, confusion of reality, and fantasy).

In their empirical work, Towbin and colleagues (1993) have shown that children who fit the MCDD label are easily distinguished from children with other diagnoses. Further, those with MCDD have an early onset of symptoms, poorer overall adjustment, more troubled peer relationships, and mothers with higher levels of psychopathology than other psychiatrically disturbed children. Subsequently, Van der Gaag and colleagues (1995) demonstrated that these diagnostic criteria could be used to distinguish children with MCDD from those with autism, externalizing problems (conduct disorder, ADHD), and internalizing problems (depression, anxiety disorders). The symptoms that were most effective in differentiating MCDD were *fluctuations in level of functioning, thought disorder,* and *primitive anxiety.*

Comorbidity and Differential Diagnosis

Many youths diagnosed with borderline personality present to the clinic with problems related to aggression and *conduct disorder.* Symptoms consistent with *anxiety disorders* also are often found in those diagnosed with BPD, particularly Posttraumatic Stress Disorder (*PTSD*). However, the symptom picture is dissimilar enough that it does not appear that BPD in children can be subsumed within

Table 15.2

Suggested Diagnostic Criteria for Multiple Complex Developmental Disorder

A. Regulation of affective state and anxiety is impaired beyond that seen in children of comparable mental age manifested by two of the following:
  1. Intense generalized anxiety, diffuse tension, or irritability.
  2. Unusual fears and phobias that are peculiar in content or in intensity.
  3. Recurrent panic episodes, terror, or flooding with anxiety.
  4. Episodes lasting from minutes to days of behavioral disorganization or regression with the emergence of markedly immature, primitive, and/or self-injurious behaviors.
  5. Significant and wide emotional variability with or without environmental precipitants.
  6. High frequency of idiosyncratic anxiety reactions such as sustained periods of uncontrollable giggling, giddiness, laughter, or "silly" affect that is inappropriate in the context of the situation.
B. Consistent impairments in social behavior and sensitivity (compared with children of similar mental age) manifested by one of the following:
  1. Social disinterest, detachment, avoidance, or withdrawal in the face of evident competence (at times) of social engagement, particularly with adults. More often attachments may appear friendly and cooperative but very superficial, based primarily on receiving material needs.
  2. Inability to initiate or maintain peer relationships.
  3. Disturbed attachments displaying high degrees of ambivalence to adults, particularly to parents/caregivers, as manifested by clinging, overly controlling, needy behavior, and/or aggressive, oppositional behavior. Splitting affects with shifting love-hate behavior toward parents, teachers, or therapists are common.
  4. Profound limitations in the capacity of empathy or to read or understand others' affects accurately.
C. Impaired cognitive processing (thinking disorder) manifested by one of the following:
  1. Thought problems that are well out of proportion with mental age, including irrationality, sudden intrusions on normal thought process, magical thinking, neologisms or nonsense words repeated over and over, desultory thinking, blatantly illogical bizarre ideas.
  2. Confusion between reality and fantasy life.
  3. Perplexity and easy confusability (trouble with understanding ongoing social processes and keeping one's thoughts "straight").
  4. Delusions, including fantasies of personal omnipotence, paranoid preoccupations, overengagement with fantasy figures, grandiose fantasies of special powers, and referential ideation.
D. No diagnosis of autism.
E. Duration of symptoms longer than 6 months.

Source: Reprinted from Towbin et al, 1993.

a diagnosis of either conduct disorder or PTSD (Guzder et al., 1996; Paris, 1994).

Mood disorders are often seen in those with BPD. While the disorders may be truly comorbid, the self-dramatizing quality of "parasuicidal" self-harming behavior (Linehan et al., 1991; see Chapter 9) differs from the typical suicidal ideation seen in simple depression. Similarly, while BPD and bipolar disorder may co-occur, the recklessness and impulsive behavior seen in BPD is of a more habitual and chronic nature than the short-lived episodes seen in mania. *ADHD* also has been found to co-occur with BPD in young persons (Greenman et al., 1986; Wenning,

1990). Borderline personality also has been found in *eating disorders*. (See Chapter 12.) This is not surprising, given that binge eating is one example of impulsive behavior included in the DSM-IV criteria for the diagnosis of BPD. In addition, the two disorders share etiological factors such as disturbed parent-child relationships, as well as common symptoms including distorted self-perceptions and self-abusive behavior. However, BPD is distinguished by its pervasive effect on all aspects of functioning, particularly interpersonal relationships, and is not limited to, or generally focused on, issues of eating and weight.

On the other hand, some developmental phenomena that might give the appearance of borderline pathology need to be distinguished from true borderline personality disorder. DSM-IV-TR cautions that adolescents and young adults struggling with *identity formation,* especially when involved with *substance use,* may show transient symptoms consistent with BPD, including emotional instability, anxiety, identity confusion, and "existential dilemmas." We are reminded here of the second criterion necessary to the diagnosis of a personality disorder listed previously, that the symptom is unlikely to be limited to a particular developmental period—one such developmental phase involves the search for self and meaning associated with adolescence.

Gender Differences

In addition to the preponderance of females diagnosed with BPD, other important *gender differences* have emerged. Female children with BPD have more severe symptoms than males, and their symptoms are more likely to persist over time. Consequently, there is greater continuity of BPD in females during the transitions from childhood to adolescence and from adolescence to adulthood. Boys who display similar symptoms, in contrast, are more likely to end up on a trajectory toward *antisocial personality disorder,* an adult diagnostic category consisting largely of males (Guzder et al., 1996).

Gender differences in the symptoms of adolescents with BPD were examined by Bradley, Conklin, and Westen (in press). The investigators identified 81 youths ages 14 to 18 who had been diagnosed with BPD (55 females and 26 males) and asked the youths' clinicians to rate the patients on 200 statements describing personality characteristics associated with psychological disturbance in adolescents (e.g., "tends to fear she will be rejected or abandoned by those who are emotionally significant"; "expresses emotion in exaggerated and theatrical ways"; "tends to feel life has no meaning; "tends to become irrational when strong emotions are stirred up"). After analyzing the clusters of symptoms, Bradley and colleagues found that they could identify four distinct subtypes of BPD in adolescent females. The first category, termed

high-functioning internalizing, included tendencies to be self-critical, anxious, guilty, self-blaming, and self-punishing, while still demonstrating creativity and insightfulness. The second grouping, termed *histrionic,* showed tendencies toward provocative, overly dramatic, manipulative, and attention-seeking behavior, as well as idealized and unrealistic expectations of relationships. The third category, termed *depressive internalizing,* was characterized by loneliness, feelings of being an outcast, lack of pleasure and meaning in life, and expectations of abusiveness from others. The fourth category, *angry externalizing,* included such characteristics as defiance, oppositionality, projection of unacceptable impulses and feelings onto others, sensation seeking, and explosive anger.

Although the sample of boys was too small to allow for such a fine-grained analysis of subtypes, Bradley and colleagues found that the cluster of symptoms on which males scored highest was strikingly different from those of females—and strikingly different from the DSM-IV criteria, even those criteria were the ones used to identify the patients. Whereas the male and female profiles had in common symptoms of emotion dysregulation and unstable identity, males with BPD were considerably more *aggressive, disruptive, and antisocial* than their female counterparts. For example, males but not females were ranked high on gaining pleasure from being aggressive, sadistic behavior, bullying, taking advantage of others, and having a sense of entitlement and exaggerated self-importance. While noting that their data are preliminary and based on a small sample, Bradley and colleagues suggest that future research explore the question of whether the gendered characteristics of BPD represent two manifestations of the same underlying disorder versus whether the DSM-IV criteria for BPD are inaccurate and thus lead to an erroneous diagnosis of males who would be placed more appropriately in the antisocial spectrum. In either case, they argue, the identification of such distinct subtypes in females has important implications for treatment, in that interventions might be more effective if they are modified to address the particular vulnerabilities and needs of each borderline personality disorder style.

Etiology

There is as yet little agreement on the etiology of borderline personality disorder, nor even how to conceptualize the core deficits that characterize this disorder—the so-called "basic fault" (Balint, 1968). How has development gone awry in this extreme deviation from the normal sense of self? There are two issues on which theorists tend to disagree. The first concerns how BPD is best characterized: In other words, what are the *defining features* of the disorder and how will we recognize it? The second issue concerns how the disorder comes about: In other words, what is its *etiology* and what are the developmental processes that account for it? As we will see, individual theorists characterize the disorder somewhat differently, focusing on some features amongst those listed in DSM as opposed to others. Moreover, because theorists' speculations about how the disorder develops are linked to how they view its defining features, there are many different models of borderline personality. While interest in this disorder has a long history in the psychodynamic tradition, cognitive-behavioral models have recently come to the fore.

The Individual Context

Psychodynamic Perspectives

Mahler's (1975) *separation-individuation* theory (see Chapter 1) provides a bedrock for much of psychodynamic thinking about the origins of BPD. Mahler focuses on the first 3 years of life, during which time children develop their identity through their experiences with their caregivers (Mahler, Pine, & Bergman, 1975). Children who experience warm and sensitive care internalize an image of the loving parent—the "good object"—and therefore of themselves as lovable. In contrast, children who experience poor parenting internalize an image of their caregiver as angry and rejecting and come to see themselves as unworthy and incapable of inspiring love.

All children sometimes feel anger or frustration with their caregivers, and all parents are sometimes "bad objects" who disappoint their children. Therefore, some negative feelings are inevitable during development. However, the magical thinking of pre-operational children leads them to mistakenly believe that their negative thoughts and feelings can have real consequences. For example, young children are likely to believe that their anger can actually harm someone, destroying the loving mother or transforming her into the bad object of their fears. Because the child has trouble holding onto a sense of security about the mother when she is absent, rage at the mother can be frightening. A child who thinks "I wish she'd go away" might worry "What if she does go away?" In such a case, angry feelings toward the mother interfere with the ability to sustain a positive image of her in the child's mind, threatening the internal image of the good mother and with it the child's positive self-image and sense of security.

In order to protect positive internal representations from these strong negative feelings, Mahler proposes that during rapprochement children defensively split their experience of the caregiver into good and bad images, as if there were two caregivers in the child's emotional world—the one who is the source of comfort and good feelings and the one who is frustrating and depriving. Similarly, the sense of self is split in two—the child who is good and lovable and the child who is bad and evokes the caregiver's ire. Thus, **splitting** is a defense mechanism that protects the infant's positive internal representations from feelings of anger and aggression. Thoughts of the loved and loving caregiver—and the lovable self—are safely locked away from negative emotions. (See Figure 15.1.)

While splitting is a normal part of the young child's development, it is a primitive defense that does not allow us to experience ourselves and others as fully fleshed, complete persons. Therefore, the final stage of separation-individuation requires that we overcome it in order to achieve emotional **object constancy:** the ability to integrate both positive and negative feelings into a single representation. Thus, it is possible to be angry with the caregiver and yet still love her or him, to be disappointed with oneself and yet still believe one is a worthwhile human being. Like Piaget's concept of object permanence, object constancy depends on the *cognitive* capacity to recognize that an object out of sight still exists. However, object constancy requires the recognition

Figure 15.1

Splitting—perceiving others as "all good" or "all bad"—keeps us from seeing them as they really are.

Source: Reprinted by permission of Marian Nenley.

that the *emotion* we are not currently experiencing—for example, affection for someone who has just enraged us—still exists.

As Mahler theorizes, young children use the defense mechanism of splitting to protect their internal image of their loving parent—and lovable self—from their negative feelings. Over the course of development, most children can overcome the need to compartmentalize their positive and negative experiences in order to achieve emotional object constancy and to be able to integrate both loving and hostile feelings toward themselves and others. However, psychodynamic theorists believe that the development of children with BPD is arrested during this process. Children with BPD fail to develop emotional object constancy, and are unable to overcome the need to use the defense mechanism of splitting when dealing with difficult emotions (Mahler, 1971).

Why is this process arrested in children with BPD? The reason that some children find it difficult to achieve emotional object constancy, Kernberg (1967) believes, is that they are temperamentally prone to experiencing *excessive rage.* These intense emotional experiences interfere with the development of a stable internal world; because their negative emotions are so violent, it is more difficult for these children to hold onto positive internal images in the face of them. In their rage, they lose all sense of the positive self and loving caregiver that is so important to their sense of security. To lessen the anxiety engendered by such threatening feelings, therefore, these children rely on the defense mechanism of splitting to pathological extent.

Pine (1974) has a somewhat different perspective on BPD, which emphasizes particular defining features of the disorder: failures in ego functions, such as the ability to *modulate anxiety;* and failures in object relations, such as poor differentiation of the *boundary between self and other.* Like Kernberg, Pine believes that splitting plays a role in borderline pathology; however, Pine emphasizes anxiety as its precipitant more than rage. Because of neglectful parenting, children with BPD are often left alone with their emotional distress. Thus, they fail to develop effective defense mechanisms for coping with feelings of anxiety, which they experience as overwhelming panic. These intense and unregulated emotions, in turn, interfere with their ability to integrate positive and negative experiences, and to maintain stable internal representations of themselves and their caregivers (Pine, 1986). Therefore, they cannot tolerate being separated from their caregivers, or acknowledging negative feelings toward them, because they cannot hold onto a sense of being loved and cared for when distressed or alone.

However, in Pine's (1974) view, not only do these children "stand still" in development, utilizing the defense mechanism of splitting long past the point at which it is developmentally appropriate, but when panicked they regress even further back in development, to an early state of merger or enmeshment with their caregiver. Therefore, Pine believes that children with BPD are arrested at a very early stage in the separation-individuation process, when self and other are not clearly differentiated. Pine sees borderline personality not just as failure to integrate positive and negative internal experiences, but as a fundamental problem in maintaining the distinction between self and other.

In addition, according to Pine (1979), relationships with others are perceived as being fraught with terrifying consequences. Although borderline children find separation anxiety-arousing, the experience of merging with the other and losing their sense of individual selfhood is also frightening. Therefore, Pine presents the child with BPD as being caught in a double-bind, vacillating fear of *abandonment* and unbearable aloneness on the one hand, while also struggling against *enmeshment* with the other and the loss of a sense of self.

What might happen during development to account for these distorted perceptions of self and other? Object relations theorists such as Pine believe that children with borderline personality BPD are the product of abusive and traumatic caregiving that interferes with the development of healthy object relations. More specifically, Masterson and Rinsley (1975) hypothesize that children with BPD are parented by caregivers who are unable to tolerate their children's development of an autonomous self. Rather than continuing to be *emotionally available*

to the toddler who is aggressive, frustrating, and willful in the course of normal development, these parents turn away; they are emotionally rejecting when their children express negative feelings or independent-mindedness. According to object relations theory, this is the worst fear of the preoperational child, who believes that angry feelings might actually destroy the loving parent: "If I get mad at you, you will go away."

According to this theory, the parents of children with BPD demand that their children mirror them and strive to meet the parents' needs at all times. It is as if the parent conveys to the child, "If you are not what I need you to be, you don't exist for me" (Ogden, 1982, p. 16). Masterson (1976) believes that the reason for this is that these caregivers have difficulty tolerating separation themselves, and thus desperately need their children to provide them with a sense of security and to calm their *own* abandonment fears. The picture we are presented is one of adults who interpret their children's growing up as an abandonment of themselves, and thus have difficulty tolerating their children's attempts at individuation. Not surprisingly, Masterson's own clinical observations suggest to him that the parents of children with BPD have borderline features themselves.

Psychodynamic theorists are often purely speculative and have been faulted for neglecting the need for corroborating research. However, an interesting series of studies conducted by Westen and his colleagues (Westen et al., 1990; Westen & Cohen, 1993) lends some validation to the picture of borderline personality presented to us by object relations theory. Based on their review of psychoanalytic and cognitive perspectives on the development of the self, they devised a coding system to analyze the responses made by adolescents with BPD to projective tests (see Chapter 16). For example, they noted that the phenomenon of splitting was evident in the "all-good" or "all-bad" responses of these youths (e.g., "I was always a person who could do anything and now I can't do nothing"). The researchers also found these adolescents' representations of themselves to be unstable, severely negative, and lacking in clear differentiation of self and other. They were also described as losing their sense of self and becoming caught up in the emotions and drama of the moment. Again consistent with object relations theories, relationships with others were represented as malevolent, victimizing, and unempathic.

Much of psychodynamic thinking about the origins of borderline personality concerns the quality of parent-child relationships. This overlaps with theories of etiology concerned with family factors, which we will return to later in this chapter.

Cognitive-Behavioral Theory

An important contribution to our understanding of BPD is provided by Linehan's (1993a) cognitive-behavioral model. Linehan focuses her attention on a particular subset of those who come to be diagnosed with the disorder, "those with histories of multiple attempts to injure, mutilate, or kill themselves" (p. 10), behavior she terms *parasuicidal.* The core characteristics she perceives in these individuals are outlined in Table 15.3 and include (1) *emotional vulnerability,* including high emotional intensity, reactivity, and poor affect regulation; (2) *self-invalidation;* (3) *perpetual crises;* (4) *inability to tolerate grief and loss;*

(5) *passivity* in the face of life problems; and (6) an *appearance of competence* that belies the functional deficits under the surface.

Linehan believes that temperamental factors, negative events, and self-generated dysfunctional beliefs combine to create the soil in which borderline pathology can grow. Specifically, she proposes that those vulnerable to BPD are temperamentally prone to low distress tolerance and are thus highly uncomfortable with their own strong emotions. Further, they have inadequate coping strategies, including deficiencies in emotion regulation, interpersonal problem solving, and self-management skills. Lastly, irrational beliefs are held, including that life stresses are intolerable and inescapable and that dysfunctional behaviors such as self-mutilation are the only available strategies for solving one's problems.

Similarly to object relations theorists, Linehan views BPD as arising within the context of pathological parent-child relationships. The key deficit in caregiving she identifies is an *invalidating environment,* "one in which communication of private experiences is met by erratic, inappropriate, and extreme

Table 15.3

Behavioral Patterns in BPD

1. *Emotional vulnerability:* A pattern of pervasive difficulties in regulating negative emotions, including high sensitivity to negative emotional stimuli, high emotional intensity, and slow return to emotional baseline, as well as awareness and experience of emotional vulnerability. May include a tendency to blame the social environment for unrealistic expectations and demands.
2. *Self-invalidation:* Tendency to invalidate or fail to recognize one's own emotional responses, thoughts, beliefs, and behaviors. Unrealistically high standards and expectations for self. May include intense shame, self-hate, and self-directed anger.
3. *Unrelenting crises:* Pattern of frequent, stressful, negative environmental events, disruptions, and roadblocks—some caused by the individual's dysfunctional lifestyle, others by an inadequate social milieu, and many by fate or chance.
4. *Inhibited grieving:* Tendency to inhibit and overcontrol negative emotional responses, especially those associated with grief and loss, including sadness, anger, guilt, shame, anxiety, and panic.
5. *Active passivity:* Tendency to passive interpersonal problem-solving style, involving failure to engage actively in solving of own life problems, often together with active attempts to solicit problem solving from others in the environment; learned helplessness, hopelessness.
6. *Apparent competence:* Tendency for the individual to appear deceptively more competent than she actually is; usually due to failure of competencies to generalize across expected moods, situations, and time, and to failure to display adequate nonverbal cues of emotional distress.

Source: Linehan, 1993.

responses" (p. 49). Linehan believes that the parents of children destined for BPD are unable to tolerate the expression of negative emotions such as fear or anxiety and therefore invalidate, ignore, or trivialize their children's emotional experiences. While invalidation may take place in the context of overt maltreatment, it also takes subtle forms that might be seen in families without overt psychopathology. For example, a family member might express impatience that the individual with BPD "just can't control herself."

First among the consequences of an invalidating environment is that the children do not learn to recognize or understand their internal states. Second, because their parents do not help to comfort or soothe them, these young people do not internalize the capacity to soothe themselves, and therefore do not develop the ability to regulate their emotions and tolerate stress. Third, when the usual emotional displays are met with indifference, children learn that intense emotions may be the only way to evoke a response from the caregiver; thus, extreme emotional responses are reinforced. Fourth, an invalidating environment fails to teach the children to trust their own emotional and cognitive reactions. Instead, children learn to invalidate their own experiences and to look to the social surroundings to provide cues about how to think, feel, and behave. No matter how aversive the invalidating environment, the child is its prisoner—the child does not have the capacity to leave the family. Unable to change his or her environment, the child cannot do anything other than to try to change his or her inner experience to meet its demands.

At the heart of the matter in borderline pathology, Linehan argues, is a failure of *dialectics*—the ability to tolerate and participate in the normal give and take of relationships and to achieve a sense of wholeness and balance that incorporates all of the rich distinctions and contradictions of reality. Individuals with BPD vacillate between rigidly held points of view, polarizing reality and relationships into "either-or" categories, without the ability to synthesize them into a realistic and well-rounded whole.

Research evidence in support of Linehan's perspective comes primarily from intervention studies, in which she has tested the effectiveness of a treatment designed according to her model. These will be reviewed in the section on intervention.

Emotion Regulation and Deliberate Self-Harm

The inability to tolerate and modulate emotions is a key feature of all of the models of a borderline personality that we have discussed. Affect dysregulation also may play a role in the development of one of the most prevalent and disturbing symptoms of the disorder, deliberate self-harming. Unlike a simple suicidal "gesture," the self-injurious behavior of parasuicidal youths with BPD can be quite serious and disfiguring. It is not uncommon for cutting of the body to become habitual, with cuts repeatedly made in the same areas of the arms or hands so that permanent scars are left. Adolescents and adults with BPD often report that cutting themselves is a way of relieving tension—indeed, the only way they know to achieve relief.

In the clinical literature, it has been suggested that this type of self-mutilation has addictive qualities. Nixon, Cloutier, and Aggarwal (2002) set out to empirically test this hypothesis in a sample of 42 self-injurious adolescents admitted to a hospital over a 4-month period. Almost 79 percent of adolescents reported the urge to engage in self-injury on a daily basis, and 83 percent gave in to the urge more than once a week. Cutting, scratching, hitting oneself, hairpulling, biting, and interfering with the healing of wounds were among the most common forms of self-injury. The two primary reasons given for harming themselves were "to cope with feelings of depression" and "to release unbearable tension." Moreover, among the adolescents in this sample, almost 98 percent endorsed three or more symptoms consistent with addictive behavior in relationship to their self-injury, as defined by DSM (e.g., the individual continues despite knowledge the behavior is harmful, uncomfortable symptoms arise when the individual attempts to discontinue, the behavior causes social problems, the frequency or intensity must be increased to achieve desired effect, and the behavior is time consuming and disrupts normal activities).

Just as substance abuse or binge-purging might be used as a method of regulating emotions by some adolescents, as we learned in Chapter 12, so might self-injury become a pathological addiction.

The Family Context

Childhood Trauma and Maltreatment

Troubled parent-child relationships are the major risk factor for borderline personality disorder. A number of studies have confirmed that *child maltreatment* is implicated in the development of BPD. Looking retrospectively, as many as 91 percent of adults diagnosed as borderline report having been maltreated in childhood (Zanarini et al., 1997), particularly in the form of *sexual abuse* (Ogata et al., 1990; Wagner & Linehan, 1994).

Recently, powerful data sets have begun to speak to the significance of childhood maltreatment in the developmental psychopathology of personality disorders, including BPD. The Collaborative Longitudinal Personality Disorders Study (Gunderson et al., 2000) is a multisite project that, since 1996, has been studying 668 adults aged 18 to 45 who carry diagnoses of avoidant, obsessive-compulsive, schizotypal, or borderline personality disorder. In one study published by the group, retrospective interview data regarding childhood trauma revealed that the severity of personality disorder symptoms was related to the frequency and severity of childhood trauma in general (Yen et al., 2002). The findings were particularly striking for those with BPD, who reported the highest rates of traumatic experiences, the earliest ages of exposure, and the most symptoms of PTSD. A full 91.6 percent of those with BPD had a significant trauma history; 55.1 percent had undergone some form of sexual abuse in their early years and 36.5 percent had been raped.

Looking concurrently, data also indicate the significance of maltreatment in childhood BDP. In comparison to those with other psychiatric disorders, children with BPD have higher rates of physical abuse, sexual abuse, severe neglect, and parent

dysfunction (Guzder, Paris, & Zelkowitz, 1999). The maltreatment experienced by these children tends to have an onset very early on in life and to be cumulative over the course of childhood.

Of course, one of the limitations of retrospective and concurrent data is that they cannot speak to whether the personality disorder emerged as a consequence of maltreatment; it is even possible that the direction of effects is reversed, such that characterological problems make the young people vulnerable to becoming the victims of abuse. However, another data set is available that has the advantage of providing a prospective view. Johnson and colleagues (1999) have been following a sample of 639 New York State families and their children for 2 decades. In an initial study, the group found that children with documented evidence of maltreatment were more than 4 times more likely than others to develop a personality disorder by early adulthood (Johnson et al., 1999). In a subsequent study, now including a sample size of 793 families, the investigators focused on *psychological abuse*—whether the mother had screamed at the child, said she did not love the child, or threatened to send the child away. Children who experienced such psychological maltreatment in childhood were 3 times more likely than others to develop a personality disorder. The effects of psychological abuse remained significant even when the contributions of child temperament, physical abuse, sexual abuse, neglect, parent psychopathology, and comorbid disorders were taken into account.

In addition to physical, sexual, and psychological abuse, youths with BPD are disproportionately likely to have undergone other forms of traumatic family experiences. These include *chaotic, unstable,* and *violent* family environments, *separations* and *disrupted attachments* in early childhood, and parental *rejection* (Bemporad et al., 1982; Ludolph et al., 1990). Guzder and colleagues (1996) describe a pattern of "grossly inappropriate" parenting behavior in youths with BPD: For example, one father and daughter double-dated and watched one another's sexual activities; other parents threatened to maim the family pet; and one mother handed her daughter a loaded gun, saying, "Shoot me if you hate me that much."

The importance of family risk factors was confirmed in Zanarini and colleagues' (1997) large-scale study of 358 adults diagnosed with BPD. Four risk factors were identified, the first of which was *female gender*. In addition, three significant childhood experiences distinguished those with BPD from individuals with other personality disorder diagnoses: *sexual abuse, emotional neglect* by a male caregiver, and *inconsistent parenting* by a female caregiver. Participants with borderline diagnoses were also more likely to describe having had a caregiver withdraw from them emotionally, negate their thoughts and feelings, place them in a parenting role, and fail to provide for their safety and security.

Parent Psychopathology

Masterson's hypothesis that parents of these children have borderline pathology themselves has met with some support (Links, Steiner, & Huxley, 1988), although the evidence is not consistent. More common is the finding that family members of children with BPD demonstrate higher rates of *severe psychopathology in general* (Feldman et al., 1995; Guzder et al., 1996). For example, Goldman and colleagues (1993) found that 71 percent of children with BPD had a parent who met DSM criteria for a psychiatric disorder, including substance abuse, depression, and antisocial personality disorder (curiously, the authors did not document the prevalence of BPD among family members).

The Family System

Turning to the whole family system, psychodynamic theories of borderline personality disorder—with their use of terms such as *boundaries* and *enmeshment*—are reminiscent of Minuchin's (1974) ideas about the systemic family processes underlying the development of psychopathology (see Chapter 1). Like object relations theory, the structural family model emphasizes the importance of maintaining healthy psychological boundaries between individuals in the family. Therefore, we might expect that the family relationships associated with BPD would be those that interfere with the child's attainment of a separate and

cohesive identity (Combrinck-Graham, 1989; Slipp, 1991). Systemic family hypotheses were tested by Shapiro, Zinner, Shapiro, and Berkowitz (1975), who observed the family interactions of children diagnosed with BPD. Consistent with both family systems and object relations theories, the investigators found that children's assertions of independence were met by emotional withdrawal in the family; however, this was characteristic of all family members—not just mothers.

The Social Context

Youths with borderline personality are difficult to engage socially—they engender uncomfortable feelings in others because of their high anxiety, extreme mood changes, fluctuations between good reality-testing and disorganization, and erratic shifts in positive or negative attitudes toward others. Because this unpredictable and extreme behavior is difficult for others to tolerate, their interpersonal relationships are often volatile and transient.

In an attempt to better explain this phenomenon, some theorists have proposed that individuals with BPD characteristically engage others in a process of **projective identification** (Ogden, 1982; see Chapter 2). Projective identification is a complex defense mechanism that requires an interaction between two people. The process takes place in three steps (Lieberman, 1992). First, unwanted thoughts and feelings are attributed to, or *projected* onto, the other person. For example, someone who defends against acknowledging his or her own angry feelings might project those onto another person. Second, the other person is *pressured to comply* with the projection (e.g., by behaving in ways that are subtly irritating and anger-arousing, one might begin to make the other person begin to feel irritable and angry). Lastly, *identification* takes place when the recipient of the projection comes to feel that these thoughts and feelings actually *are* his or her own. Through the process of projective identification, individuals with BPD can engender in others their most intolerable and distressing emotions—worthlessness, unreality, terror, rage, and desolation. (See Box 15.2.)

| Box 15.2 | **Projective Identification in Borderline Personality Disorder** |

In a revealing essay, psychotherapist Mark Rhine (Adler & Rhine, 1988) writes about his long-term work with a young woman with borderline personality disorder: "Many times in the following years I wondered why I had chosen to work with this patient, questioned my ability to help her, wondered if she were treatable, and dreaded seeing her during the lengthy treatment that often left both of us confused, angry, hurt, bewildered, despairing, and feeling as if each of us was going stark raving mad because of the other" (p. 476).

The patient was a 22-year-old college graduate, working as a file clerk, who came for therapy because of chronic feelings of being less than human, lack of pleasure in life, fear of rejection, and suicidal thoughts. She formed a very hostile attachment to her therapist, referring to him as "the Gestapo" (particularly hurtful to the therapist, given that he was Jewish), criticizing his interpretations, and complaining that he was a lousy therapist because she wasn't getting better.

Dr. Rhine felt guilty about the anger and negative feelings he experienced toward his patient and made every effort to repress them. When she insulted him, he would respond mildly, offering a platitude such as, "I am sorry that you hold me in such contempt." In fact, he felt quite hurt, but tried to forbear to remain "therapeutic" and to be accepting of the patient's need to express this negative transference. When she threatened to quit therapy, he would be as neutral as possible, stating, "Although I would like you to continue, I'll respect your decision," and so forth. In response, she pressed him, asking, "How does it *really* make you feel?"

Her attacks escalated until one day Dr. Rhine succumbed to exasperation and finally let his true feelings show. He complained that the patient was unfair to him and that it was quite painful to him to be berated constantly. Her reaction surprised him. In a calm and sober voice, she stated, "It isn't you I am berating; it is myself. I need to know what a human being would feel and do under an attack like that." Together, they went on to discover the fact that she needed the therapist to speak for a part of herself "that had never spoken up, that was terrified and didn't know how to be human" (p. 479)—the part of herself that suffered in silence the beatings and humiliation she received from her parents. In short, through projective identification, the patient was engendering in her therapist her own feeling state, provoking him to experience a part of her that she needed to learn more about and to master.

Projective identification is a process that can occur in any relationship. What distinguishes it in healthier people is their capacity to reality-test and recognize when they are projecting onto others. At its highest level, projective identification may even be related to empathy and the capacity to feel for and with another person.

Therefore, viewed *transactionally,* the way in which youths with borderline pathology relate to others increases the likelihood that they will experience the very rejection and abandonment they fear. Peer relationships are often completely absent, because agemates find it difficult to tolerate this unusual and demanding behavior. And because of their inability to cope with the demands of the normal school environment, youths with BPD are likely to be placed in inpatient settings or day treatment programs, further isolating them from opportunities to engage in normative peer relationships.

The Biological Context

As noted previously, many theorists, including those from the psychoanalytic perspective, believe that there is biological predisposition toward borderline personality disorder. The exact nature of the biological underlay is a matter of speculation, although suggestive data are beginning to emerge.

Genetics

Evidence for a genetic component in BPD was found in a twin study of adults (Torgerson et al., 2000). Heritability rates were estimated at 0.69 for

BPD and 0.60 for personality disorders in general. (See Posner et al., 2003, for further suggestive research on possible genetic contributions to BPD.)

Neurochemistry

After reviewing the available research, Figueroa and Silk (1997) hypothesize that at least two neurochemical systems may be implicated in the development of BPD. One dimension of borderline pathology, impulsivity, may be linked to constitutionally based abnormalities in the regulation of the neurotransmitter *serotonin* (Siever, Koenigsberg, & Reynolds, 2003). A second biologically mediated borderline trait, hyperreactivity to the environment, is associated with irregularities in the *hypothalamic-pituitary-adrenal* (HPA) system. This system is associated with the "flight or fight" response and is involved in the development of stress-related disorders, particularly PTSD. Therefore, Figueroa and Silk propose that borderline pathology is a function of two factors: an inherent physiological vulnerability, and experiences of traumatic stress that act on the individual's biological functioning to produce the disorder.

Neuropsychology

A number of studies of BPD adults have indicated the presence of neuropsychological deficits (Judd & McGlashan, 2003). These include neurological soft signs, difficulties in auditory-visual integration, and learning disorders. For example, Kimble et al. (1997) found some form of neurological difficulties in the histories of 87.5 percent of adult patients with BPD, including childhood speech and language problems, learning disabilities, ADHD, and prenatal and postnatal complications.

As the dysregulation and poor self-control seen in BPD would suggest, *executive functioning deficits* are implicated. In their studies of adults with BPD, Posner and colleagues (2003) have found consistent deficits on measures of executive attentional control, an index of the individual's ability to resolve problems regarding conflicting cognitions and emotions. Brain scan studies confirm that adults with BPD display structural abnormalities that are consistent with deficits in executive control and self-regulation. For example, when exposed to stimuli representing negative or even neutral events, adults with BPD show overactivity in the amygdala, an area of the brain that is important in the regulation of affect.

Because the studies of the brain have not been developmental in nature, it is not yet clear whether these neuropsychological deficits precede the disorder or whether they are the consequences of the same negative environmental factors that contribute to the disorder. For example, a reduced hippocampal volume is characteristic of individuals with PTSD as well as those with BPD (Driessen et al., 2000). The same is true of other findings in the study of BPD, such as deficits in the serotonergic and HPA systems, which are known to be related to the trauma of child maltreatment (Beers & DeBellis, 2002; Cicchetti & Rogosch, 2001).

Integrative Developmental Model

Based on their 30 years of clinical and research experience as part of the Chestnut Lodge Follow-up Study, Judd and McGlashan (2003) offer a rich and intriguing integrative developmental psychopathology model of BPD. (See Figure 15.2.) True to the developmental psychopathology framework, their model takes as its basis the organizational perspective, in which the development of the child takes places through a process of increasing differentiation and hierarchical organization of emotional, social, and cognitive competencies. Each successive adaptation is a product of the integration of new experiences and previous development. Borderline personality disorder, they suggest, is one with its origins in the very earliest stages of life. Consequently, development is set off course in infancy and the effects are cascading and cumulative across all domains of development throughout childhood and adolescence and into adulthood.

Their model focuses on four key phenomenological characteristics of borderline pathology. First,

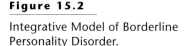

Figure 15.2

Integrative Model of Borderline
Personality Disorder.

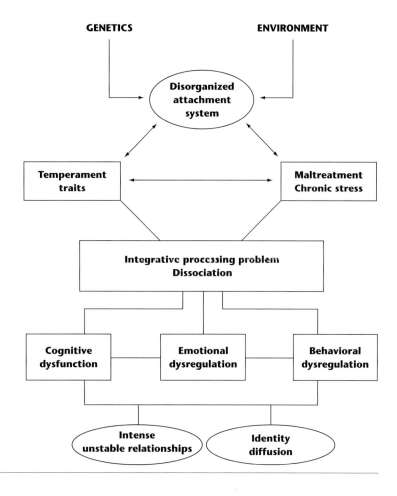

From Judd and McGlashan, 2003.

insecure and disorganized attachments lead to unstable and intense interpersonal relationships, identity disturbances, and impediments to achieving interpersonal intimacy. Second, *cognitive processing* dysfunctions take such forms as dissociation, poor metacognitive functioning, splitting, and stress-related psychotic states. Third, *emotional dysregulation* is indicated by affective instability and hypersensitivity; numbness; chronic feelings of emptiness; and inappropriate, intense anger. Fourth, *behavioral dysregulation* takes such forms as reenactments of traumatic experiences; frantic efforts to avoid real or imagined abandonment; impulsivity; recurrent suicidal behavior, gestures, or threats; and self-mutilating behaviors.

Biological and Environmental Contributions

Initially, Judd and McGlashan propose, the child who will develop BPD comes into the world with a genetically derived *neurodevelopmental predisposition.* Temperamental traits, such as impulsivity and affective instability, equip the child poorly to cope with stress. Zanarini and Frankenburg (1997) term this temperament "hyperbolic," by which they mean a temperament that is overreactive, attention-seeking, and dysregulated. The environment, which includes family, friends, and the community, acts on these vulnerabilities and potentiates them by subjecting the child to various forms of *maltreatment.*

Other dysfunctions and negative events in the family system further interfere with the environment's ability to provide the child with the kinds of nurturance, structure, and support that could act as buffers or protective factors.

Insecure Attachment and Trauma

Both biologically based vulnerabilities and adverse life experiences contribute to the development of an *insecure attachment* relationship that, Judd and McGlashan posit, is the key pathway through which the disorder develops. Through their early attachment relationships, children develop a number of capacities fundamental to good adaptation: self-soothing and emotion regulation, positive self-evaluation, and the ability to communicate needs in a relationship and to trust that those needs will be met (Carlson & Sroufe, 1995; see Chapter 2). However, pathological family relationships interfere with the attainment of a secure sense of self, as well as the ability to regulate emotions and to perceive others in ways not distorted by distrust (Linehan, 1991; Sabo, 1997). In the case of the child with BPD, the caregiving environment is terrifying and unpredictable; the child's source of security is also the source of the threat. The result is an impossible paradox, which, Judd and McGlashan propose, the child can only resolve by retaining two separate schemas of relationship: one in which the parent is safe and another in which the parent is frightening and abusive. The result is a *disorganized attachment,* which has been conceptualized as a breakdown of any coherent strategy for maintaining proximity under conditions of threat. Further evidence for the link between attachment and BPD is suggested by the association of disorganized attachment with extreme forms of child maltreatment; distortions in the parent-infant relationship, such as parentification (van IJzendoorn et al., 1999); and with the development of dissociation in middle childhood and adolescence (Carlson, 1998), all of which also are characteristics of those with borderline pathology: in summary, the disordered attachments of those who go on to develop BPD. Consequently, the development of insecure, disorganized, and poorly integrated internal working models in turn leads to unstable interpersonal relationships, identity confusion, and deviations in cognitive, emotional, and behavioral development.

Judd and McGlashan (2003) liken BPD to a form of "developmental internalized PTSD." Unlike other forms of PTSD, in which trauma is linked to a memory of a specific incident, the trauma of the child with BPD is associated with the entire caregiving relationship. Because of the child's experience of overt abuse and covert forms of grossly inappropriate parenting, closeness to another person brings with it the perceived or actual threat of emotional neglect, abuse, or abandonment. This trauma is not one the child recalls when exposed to a specific traumatic cue, but rather an experience that the child lives with every moment of the day.

The chronic psychological and physiological state of stress becomes part of the child's characteristic response to others and forms a core feature of his or her personality. Further, traumatic stress interferes with cognitive and emotional development, leading to significant informational processing deficits. These deficits arise particularly when the individual is required to process complex emotional, sensory, and motor information; translate nonverbal cues into verbal codes; and discriminate and prioritize divergent visual and verbal interpersonal responses. These cognitive skills are central to the ability to develop stable and coherent representational schemas of relationships. Instead, however, characteristics of borderline thinking are odd and fragmented, resulting in developmentally immature forms of reasoning such as magical thinking, superstitiousness, absolutist (black-and-white) thinking, dissociation, and transient psychotic states.

Cognitive Dysfunction

Another important developmental failure that results from the breakdown in cognitive and emotional coherence is a lack of metacognitive monitoring in interpersonal relationships. *Metacognitive monitoring,* also termed reflective functioning, is the ability to observe oneself, to detect errors in one's thinking or inconsistencies in one's speech, and to understand that things may look different from another's perspective—in other words, to "think about thinking." Without metacognition and the ability to integrate thoughts, feelings, and perspectives in relationship with others, individuals with BPD are left to fall back on more developmentally primitive cognitive processes, such as denial, splitting, and projection—defenses that are reality distorting and fragmenting.

Emotional and Behavioral Dysregulation

Emotion dysregulation is a core feature of BPD and permeates all areas of functioning. Having lacked the experience of the kind of parental empathic attunement that helps children to develop an understanding of emotions and ability to self-regulate, the emotional and behavioral development of the child with BPD is early on set off course in fundamental ways. Due to the lack of coherence, integration, and stability in their internal worlds, individuals with BPD are unable to progress in emotional development. They do not develop the ability to differentiate among emotions or to experience complex and blended emotions as part of a single experience, nor are they able to modulate or cope with strong emotions without yielding to the impulse to act on them. They lack skills to read subtle emotional cues accurately and to react adaptively in emotion-laden situations. In short, "they face adult situations with a child's emotional repertoire" (p. 30).

Frequently misreading situations, those with BPD tend to overreact or underreact, based on their misinterpretations, experiencing dramatic swings between hyperarousal and underarousal. Their affective instability is seen in shifts between states of feeling "empty," emotionally numb, "miserable," and intensely angry. Once their affects are aroused, they return only slowly to baseline and this is particularly true for the emotion of anger. Because of their experiences of frustration and helplessness throughout childhood, individuals with BPD harbor a deep current of inarticulate, wounded, disowned rage that is easily provoked. However, the perceived danger of expressing this rage—rejection, abandonment, or attack by the caregiver—generates intense anxiety, shame, dysphoria, and a feeling of being less than human.

The impulse to act on these intense and unstable emotional states contributes to behavioral dysregulation, which takes such forms as overreactivity, erratic behavior, and recklessness. In particular, emotions that trigger traumatic memories are distressing and disorganizing. When overwhelmed with emotions, and without healthy defenses to cope with them, individuals with BPD tend to act out traumas with behaviors that endanger the safety of themselves or others—these might include risky sexual behavior, substance abuse, suicidal behavior, and self-mutilation.

Intense and Unstable Personal Relationships

All of the factors described in the previous section—disorganized models of attachment, cognitive dysfunctions, and emotional and behavioral instability—understandably wreak havoc with the ability to form stable intimate relationships. The shifting states of mind of individuals with BPD are extreme and absolute; Judd and McGlashan believe that these individuals are dimly if at all consciously aware of the fact that their emotions and perceptions dramatically shift from one moment to the next. Their experience of the world and of themselves is fragmented and compartmentalized. Each state of mind is all the reality there is, in the present moment, and memory is mood-dependent and cannot be retrieved when the person's state of mind changes again. Not only are experiences of others shifting, disorganized, and incoherent, but so is the individual's experience of self—there is no "me" that is consistent across situations and social contexts. Thus, there is a lack of a continuous self with which to engage others in a relationship.

The cumulative effect of these multiple developmental deficits, Judd and McGlashan state, is an inability to sustain meaningful relationships with others. The ability to form a truly intimate and deep attachment, which requires a mutually reciprocal, empathic relationship, is impeded by all of the developmental failures that have gone before.

As the life course of children with borderline personality proceeds, their inability to cope with their negative emotions contributes to an ongoing inability to master new developmental challenges (Pine, 1983). If the experience of even the slightest anxiety threatens to escalate to panic and overwhelm the child, exploration of the environment is impeded and new learning experiences cannot take place. As new developmental challenges arise, failure to successfully navigate earlier stage-salient issues related to basic trust and self-individuation impedes the development of competence in other realms. For example, in the social domain the skills necessary for the formation of peer relationships are absent, and in the realm of initiative preoccupation with their internal world interferes with their ability to function in performance contexts such as the classroom.

Borderline personality organization, therefore, represents an extreme source of vulnerability during adolescence. The challenges that arise during this developmental period—separation from the family, achievement of a sense of individual identity, and autonomous functioning—may precipitate a crisis for those youths whose psychological makeup ill-equips them to cope with even the normal stresses of development.

Developmental Course

Evidence is accumulating that adolescent-onset personality disorders in general are predictive of personality pathology and major mental illness during adulthood (Johnson et al., 1999, 2000). However, few follow-up studies have been conducted concerning children and adolescents with BPD specifically. Those that exist suggest that BPD constitutes a severe deviation in development that, like all personality disorders, is highly resistant to change. Wenning (1990) conducted follow-up interviews with 28 children who had been treated for BPD on an inpatient unit. Approximately 10 years later, many continued to show signs consistent with a diagnosis of BPD, although diagnoses of *antisocial* and *schizotypal* personality also were common. One-

third fit criteria for generalized *anxiety disorder,* while two-thirds showed symptoms of *depression,* half having undergone a major depressive episode. In contrast, Lofgren and colleagues (1991) report that, while children given the borderline label are likely to develop personality disorders in adulthood, these are not necessarily in the form of borderline personality. Thomsen (1996) also reports a wide range of adult diagnoses for children with BPD, including antisocial personality disorder and *schizophrenia.*

Although focused on adults and adolescents, perhaps the richest dataset comes from the Chestnut Lodge Follow-up Study, which tracked the outcomes of patients treated at the Chestnut Lodge Hospital, a renowned psychoanalytically oriented long-term treatment center once located in Rockville, MD (Judd & McGlashan, 2003; McGlashan, 1992). Among the 81 patients who had been diagnosed with BPD, most were single and female. The onset of their disorder was usually in late adolescence, with first treatment contact in their 20s; however, there was generally a long-standing history of dysfunction in all spheres of adaptation. Treatment at the hospital was as brief as 2 years or as prolonged as 32 years. Fifteen years after discharge, follow-up interviews were conducted, most consisting of telephone interviews about 2 hours in length. The majority of those with BPD were rated as having a positive outcome, with most achieving a score of "good," indicating that they were unimpaired by symptoms most of the time, had been seldom and only briefly rehospitalized since discharge from Chestnut Lodge, and were employed and socially active. Their outcomes compared favorably with those achieved by patients who were treated for schizophrenia or unipolar depression (see Figure 15.3). Therefore, it appears that, at least for those on a late-starter pathway to BPD and those who receive long-term, intensive treatment, the outcome is far from dire.

However, there was evidence of persisting clinical symptoms in those who had been treated for BPD, particularly in the form of depression and substance abuse. Moreover, given the centrality of unstable relationships in the psychopathology of

Figure 15.3   Fifteen-Year Outcomes of the Chestnut Lodge Follow-up Study.

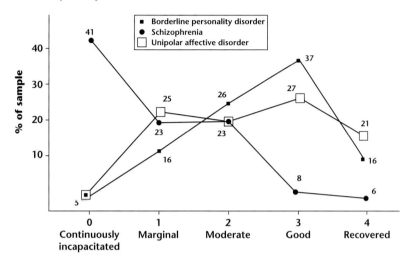

Note: Frequency Distribution of Clinical Global Functioning Scale Scores Since Discharge for Patients with Borderline Personality Disorder and Comparison Groups.

From Judd and McGlashan, 2003.

BPD, the investigators took a closer look at the interpersonal functioning of the individuals in the study. One group was described as having managed to form and maintain meaningful relationships over time: some with friends only, others with intimate partners but no children, and some with spouses and families of their own. However, another large proportion handled the problem of interpersonal relationships by studiously avoiding them. No longer were their relationships stormy and intense, but they had achieved that emotional equilibrium by remaining superficial, isolated, or avoidant.

Intervention

Psychodynamic Perspectives

Psychodynamic psychotherapy with borderline children and adolescents focuses on providing them with a different kind of relationship than the one that brought about the disorder—a "corrective emotional experience" (A. Freud, 1964). In particular, the therapist encourages the child to over-come the need for splitting by maintaining a consistent level of positive engagement that is not disrupted by the child's anger, projective identification, and acting out. Pine (1983) writes that this approach requires the therapist to "absorb the child's rage attacks and 'hold' them within the affectionate working relationship" (p. 97). In addition, the therapist helps the child to establish better interpersonal boundaries by assisting the child to recognize and express his or her own thoughts and feelings and to differentiate them from the therapist's. While expression of feelings is encouraged, emotion regulation is also fostered so that children will not be overwhelmed by their intense emotions. (See also Bleiberg, 2001.)

However, Goldstein (1997) cautions that strictly psychoanalytic approaches are often not tolerated well by those with borderline pathology, who tend to regress in unstructured situations and have difficulty tolerating intense relationships. Therefore, he recommends that more supportive approaches be used to help them stabilize their internal and external worlds.

To this end, Westen (1991) has integrated cognitive-behavioral and psychoanalytic approaches in the treatment of BPD with adolescents. For example, he suggests bolstering self-regulation by teaching impulse control strategies to children. He also uses cognitive strategies to counter distorted thinking. For example, Westen helped an adolescent with BPD to develop a series of "red flags" that would alert him to the fact that he was engaging in pathological thought processes; the boy's internal flag would be raised when he used words suggestive of escalating emotional distress, or words such as "perfect" and "total" that reflected black-and-white thinking. Other strategies Westen recommends include using drawing tasks to help adolescents differentiate their representations of self and other and having the therapist provide a model of emotion regulation and self-awareness.

Cognitive-Behavioral Approaches

A systematic cognitive-behavioral approach to treating BPD has been developed by Linehan (1993b), based on her theory of etiology. Dialectical Behavior Therapy (DBT) combines cognitive behavioral techniques with those derived from Zen philosophy and meditation practices. DBT requires the therapist to maintain an accepting attitude toward the erratic behavior and distorted beliefs of the patient with borderline pathology, responding matter-of-factly to suicidal gestures and other bizarre behaviors, while supporting and modeling healthy behaviors. The focus is on changing behavior through helping individuals to trust and validate their own inner experiences, modulate their emotions, and learn more adaptive ways of solving interpersonal problems. Weekly individual treatment is supplemented by group therapy, in which behavioral skills are taught in the areas of interpersonal problem solving, distress tolerance, acceptance of reality, and emotion regulation. A key to these strategies is the practice of *mindfulness,* the cultivation of the ability to be engaged but dispassionately present with what *is,* in the here and now.

The success of Linehan's approach has been documented in several carefully controlled empirical studies with adults (Koerner & Linehan, 2000). Recently, a team of clinicians who trained with Linehan have extended DBT to their work with parasuicidal adolescents. Rathus and Miller (2002) note that the key issues targeted by DBT—emotion regulation, interpersonal effectiveness, impulse control, self-validation, and identity—correspond to key developmental tasks of the adolescent period, thus making this intervention an eminently appropriate one. However, the authors adapted Linehan's intervention in two key ways to further meet the developmental needs of adolescents. First, while the therapy retains its focus on the four skills of mindfulness, distress tolerance, emotion regulation, and interpersonal effectiveness, the language and the content of the DBT modules are simplified and made more developmentally appropriate. Second, in recognition that teens are living in the context of the very problematic parent-child relationships implicated in the etiology of the disorder, an important innovation is that a parent or other family member is included in the treatment. In addition to the individual therapy, the adolescent and family member participate in a multifamily skills training group.

In their work with the parents of parasuicidal adolescents, Rathus and Miller (2000) identified four "dialectical dilemmas" that need to be addressed in the family treatment. (See Table 15.4.)

The first is a dilemma between *excessive leniency versus authoritarian control.* Just as with Patterson's (1982) model of antisocial behavior, many parents of parasuicidal children report feeling coercively controlled by the child, whose extreme emotional reactions to limit-setting tempt the parent to relinquish authority and adopt a permissive, laissez-faire style of parenting. However, the youth's uncontrolled and self-destructive behavior subsequently compels the parent to overreact and impose restrictive limits, such as by imposing overly strict rules or unrealistic standards. "The parents' dialectical dilemma here involves vacillating between the extremes of being overly permissive with their adolescent and feeling ineffectual, coerced, and partly responsible for their adolescent's continued difficulties on the one hand, and setting unreasonable, overly restrictive limits on the other, often to compensate for a period of

Table 15.4

Dialectical Dilemmas in DBT for Adolescents and Their Families

Dilemma	Targets
Excessive leniency versus authoritarian control	Increasing authoritative discipline; decreasing excessive leniency Increasing adolescent self-determination; decreasing authoritarian control
Normalizing pathological behaviors versus pathologizing normative behaviors	Increasing identification of pathological behaviors; decreasing normalization of pathological behaviors Increasing recognition of normative behaviors; decreasing pathologizing of normative behaviors
Forcing autonomy versus fostering dependence	Increasing effective reliance on others; decreasing excessive autonomy Increasing individuation; decreasing excessive dependence

Source: Miller & Rathus, 2000.

perceived overpermissiveness" (p. 428). The therapist's dialectical dilemma, in turn, is to find a balance between supporting the parent in appropriate limit-setting while allowing the youth a reasonable level of freedom.

The second dilemma concerns *normalizing the pathological versus pathologizing the normative.* Parents of parasuicidal youths may become so desensitized to high-risk behaviors that they fail to recognize when they are truly dangerous, to overlook them out of relief that the adolescent is not engaging in even more destructive activities, or to ignore such behavior out of the parent's own anxiety and guilt. While the parent's perspective on what is truly dangerous may become jaded by their experiences with multiple suicide attempts, hospitalizations, and self-mutilation, the parent's job is made more difficult by virtue of the fact that normative adolescent development includes such features as unstable identity, experimentation with risky behaviors, and emo-

tional lability. "In this case, the dialectical dilemma for the parent involves identifying those behaviors that are linked to severe negative consequences so as to properly address them, while at the same time, recognizing normal adolescent behavior so as to not impart unrealistic expectations and limitations" (p. 429). The therapist shares the same dilemma as the parent and must help both parent and youth to discriminate where behaviors lie on the continuum between the normative and pathological.

The third dilemma concerns *forcing autonomy versus fostering dependence* and involves regulating emotional distance with the adolescent in order to allow for both connection and independent functioning. Parents of adolescents with borderline characteristics frequently forge overly close, dependent relationships with the child that are characterized by an intense, special bond. Ambivalence about separation and confusion about how to foster it in a healthy way may lead the parent to erratically push the adolescent toward independence, sometimes by inappropriately thrusting upon the youth responsibilities that are beyond his or her developmental capacities. "For the parent, the dialectical dilemma here necessitates finding the middle way between pushing away or letting go precipitously, and clinging or caretaking to the point of stifling the adolescent's separation and individuation process" (p. 430). For the therapist, the dilemma is to help both parent and child achieve a balance between autonomy and relatedness.

Rathus and Miller (2002) empirically tested the effectiveness of their intervention in a study of 110 consecutive admissions to an inpatient treatment program for parasuicidal youths. Twenty-nine adolescents were provided with 12 weeks of DBT, including weekly individual sessions and a weekly multifamily skills group, while 82 received 12 weeks of supportive-psychodynamic "treatment as usual." Despite the fact that the adolescents in the DBT condition had higher pretreatment symptom levels, following treatment they underwent fewer psychiatric hospitalizations and were more likely to have completed treatment than youths in the other condition. Further, youths who received DBT evidenced significant reductions in suicidal ideation, symptoms of borderline personality, and general psychiatric symptoms at the end of treatment.

Family Therapy

Techniques also have been developed for working with borderline pathology in the family system. For example, Slipp's (1991) object relations family systems approach involves working with the entire family in order to reinforce the boundaries between family members and increase their differentiation from one another, striving to change the family dynamics that interfere with the youth's development of an autonomous sense of self. In particular, work with the parents focuses on helping them to get their own emotional needs met in ways that do not compromise their children's individuation.

We have now explored psychopathologies as they emerge over the life span, from infancy to early adulthood. Now that we know the characteristics and consequences of these disorders, our next concerns will be, How will the clinical child psychologist know that a given child has a disorder, and how will the clinician help to remediate it? These are the issues that will concern us next as we turn to in-depth discussions of assessment and intervention.

Psychological Assessment

U p to this point our goal has been the scientific one of investigating the factors that help us to understand the development of psychopathology. Clinical assessment, while guided by scientific principles, has a practical focus somewhat different from that of empirical inquiry. The clinician's primary role is that of a help-giver. Therefore, the ultimate goal of child assessment is to develop an effective treatment plan.

We will take the point of view of a clinician who seeks a comprehensive understanding of the child's psychopathology, noting how different theoretical orientations, such as psychodynamic or behavioral, might influence the assessment process. In addition, in order to bring these concepts alive, we will follow a hypothetical assessment of a boy named Rudy. Coverage of specific techniques will be selective. We will assume that readers have an understanding of test construction, reliability, and validity commensurate with that gained in an introductory course in psychology.

(For more detailed coverage, see Sattler, 2001, 2002.)

Assessment from a Developmental Psychopathology Perspective

When conducting an assessment, the clinician looks for data that will confirm or rule out various hypotheses about the nature of the child's problems and the processes that account for their development. Therefore, assessment cannot be divorced from theory. The *theoretical perspective* of the clinician influences which hypotheses come most readily to mind and which kind of data will be useful for testing them. For example, *behaviorally* oriented clinicians believe that psychopathology can be understood in terms of social learning principles. Therefore, they tend to study the antecedents and consequences of children's problem behavior in order to determine what in the environment might be reinforcing it. *Cognitively* oriented clinicians are more interested in children's reasoning processes and the appraisals that lead them to respond maladaptively. *Psychoanalytically* oriented clinicians focus on the unconscious determinants of children's symptoms, which cannot be observed directly but must be inferred from children's projections and fantasies. Clinicians with a *systemic* orientation believe that children's problems arise within the context of the family system and thus want to assess the ways that all the members of the family interact with one another in the here and now. In contrast, *humanistic* clinicians do not want to interfere with self-discovery by imposing their interpretations on children, and therefore they reduce assessment to a bare minimum.

However, developmental psychopathologists argue that each of these clinicians is only obtaining a piece of the puzzle. The *organizational perspective* (see Chapter 1) suggests that a complete assessment of a child needs to *integrate* information from a number of domains, including the behavioral, cognitive, emotional, psychodynamic, interpersonal, and systemic (Achenbach, 1995). Moreover, developmental psychopathologists view children not as a sum of these separate parts, but as integrated, organized, and dynamic systems (Cicchetti & Wagner, 1990).

For example, even when children are working on what is ostensibly a cognitive task, such as solving a math problem, they are also engaged at the emotional, behavioral, and interpersonal level. Is the child happy to be challenged, anxious to please the examiner, crushed by failure, irritated at the task's difficulty? Is the child bright but oppositional, determined to fail as a way of "getting the goat" of the examiner? Is the child striving to compete with peers or, quite the reverse, to underachieve in order to be perceived as "one of the gang"? And there is a family context: Is the child worried about parental reaction should the child fail, or about upsetting the balance in the family if the child succeeds too well?

Yet another way in which an assessment needs to be integrative is in terms of the need to obtain reports on children's behavior from a number of different perspectives. As we discussed in Chapter 3, multiple sources of information may help us obtain a more accurate picture of the child, "triangulating"

perspectives much the way a surveyor does (Cowan, 1978). Teachers have unique knowledge of the child's classroom behavior, while parents have a long-span view of their child that is invaluable. And only children have access to their own innermost thoughts and feelings. Therefore, each perspective may have something to contribute. Parents and teachers might be particularly good informants in regard to observable behavior, such as hyperactivity and conduct problems, while children's reports may be more informative about subjective symptoms such as anxiety and depression (Cantwell, 1996).

Lastly, because our goal is to understand the child as a whole person, we must identify not only deficits, but also strengths and *competencies* that can be used to help the child overcome any areas of disadvantage. Therefore a comprehensive assessment of many different aspects of functioning is required.

The *developmental dimension* plays an important role in child assessment. First, there are the challenges to developing rapport and communicating clearly with children of different ages, which we will discuss next. Further, standardized tests incorporate development into the assessment technique itself. Such tests define the age of the population for which they are used, such as tests of infant cognition or high school achievement. Only age-appropriate items are included and items progress in difficulty according to age. Consequently, the clinician can compare the developmental status of a given child with the norms established on a population of children his or her age. Even nonstandardized tests, such as projective techniques, are scored in terms of normative information about what is appropriate for children at different ages. In sum, results of any assessment measure always carry the implicit proviso, "for a child at this developmental level."

The Assessment Process

Assessment is like a hypothesis-testing enterprise. In attempting to assimilate, integrate, and interpret the massive amount of data they collect, clinicians implicitly proceed just like any other scientist (Johnson & Goldman, 1990). No single bit of behavior is definitive, but each is suggestive. As these bits accumulate, certain initial hunches are confirmed and others discarded. By the end of the assessment process, the clinician can make some statements concerning the child's problem with a reasonable degree of assurance; other statements will be tentative and qualified, and a number of questions will remain unanswered.

Clinicians never assume that within the space of a few hours they will be able to fully apprehend the nature and origin of the problems that bring a particular child to their attention. They realize they are viewing parent and child under special circumstances that both limit and bias the data they will obtain. The child who is frightened by a clinic waiting room may not be a generally fearful child, just as one who is hyperactive in school may be a model of cooperation when taking an intelligence test. Parents may have their own misperceptions and blind spots in regard to their child's behavior, along with varying degrees of willingness to reveal information about themselves. Standardized tests also have limitations in terms of reliability, validity, or appropriateness for different populations. Thus, as much as clinicians strive toward achieving an understanding of the child and family, they also must be duly mindful about the limitations of the assessment techniques they use (American Psychological Association, 2002).

Purposes of Assessment

While the medical model might strive toward the end product of a static, one-dimensional diagnosis (see Chapter 3), the goal of assessment from a developmental psychopathology perspective is a **case formulation.** A case formulation is a succinct, dynamic description of the child that incorporates the clinician's interpretation of how the problem came about and how it might be remediated (Shirk & Russell, 1996). The case formulation helps to synthesize all of the information the clinician obtained and to put it into a form that will be useful to those who requested the assessment. An effective assessment report helps its reader to understand the child and generates ideas about how to intervene effectively (Friedberg & McClure, 2002). (We will have more to say about how the case formulation informs treatment in Chapter 17.) Table 16.1 displays the

Table 16.1

Components of the Case Formulation

1. Presenting problem: Define in a way that reflects unique situation of this child and family
   a. Physiological
   b. Mood
   c. Behavioral
   d. Cognitive
   e. Interpersonal
2. Testing data
3. Cultural context variables
   a. Racial identity
   b. Level of acculturation
   c. Ethnocultural beliefs, values, and practices
   d. Experiences of prejudice or marginalization
4. History and developmental milestones
   a. Temperament; emotional and behavioral dysregulation
   b. Developmental delays and deviations
   c. Family relationships and attachment processes
      i. Interparental relationship: conflict, coparenting cooperation
      ii. Dyadic parent-child relationships: closeness, role clarity, boundary dissolution
      iii. Individual parenting styles: warmth, structure, overprotectiveness, demandingness, perceived parenting competence/anxiety, parenting stress
      iv. Attachment
      v. Whole-family processes: Enmeshment-distance, triangulation; coalitions; scapegoating
   d. Functioning in extra-familial environments (e.g., school, peer relationships)
   e. Strengths, skills, and competencies
5. Cognitive variables
   a. Automatic thoughts
   b. Schemata
   c. Cognitive distortions
6. Behavioral antecedents and consequences
7. Provisional formulation
   a. Coordinates the components in a dynamic and interrelated way
   b. Paints a portrait of the child's environment and inner world
   c. Relates pathogenic processes that led to disorder to change processes that will be used to intervene
8. Treatment plan
9. Expected obstacles and impediments to treatment

Source: Adapted from Friedberg and McClure, 2002.

elements that might be included in a comprehensive case formulation. While the case formulation helps the clinician to find a path through the forest of information collected during the assessment, it should not be a rigid one. Like all hypotheses, the case formulation is open to new information and can be revised in the face of disconfirming data.

Initial Sources of Data

Referrals

The first data concerning the child come from the *referring person*—teacher, parent, physician, and so on—who can provide information about the problem as perceived by concerned adults, its duration and onset, its effects on the child and on others, and what measures, if any, have been taken to remedy it. Parents and teachers are the major sources of referrals.

In contrast to adults, children rarely refer themselves to treatment, a fact that has important psychological implications. Seeking help is very different than being told one needs help. Children may not feel the need to change and may not understand why they are being brought for an evaluation. Sometimes parents give children reasons the children disagree with, or even fail to tell them why they are being brought to the clinic. Therefore, during the first telephone contact, it can be helpful to discuss with parents how they might introduce the topic of the assessment with their children.

You are a clinical child psychologist who has been asked to assess Rudy, an 8-year-old boy. His teacher suggested an evaluation because of academic and behavioral problems in the classroom. Specifically, his mother tells you that Rudy is failing reading and arithmetic and that his teacher describes him as "lazy," withdrawn, and uncooperative in class. A neighbor suggested that Rudy sounded just like her own boy, who was diagnosed with ADHD. The first questions in the back of your mind concern the reasons for this referral and the constructions being placed on this problem by the mother, the teacher, and Rudy himself. Is this a learning problem, a conduct problem, attention-deficit

related, or the consequence of a negative interaction between this family and the school? Are the teacher and the parents going to be supportive of Rudy during the assessment process, or have they taken a blaming attitude that will complicate your work? Is Rudy willing to come to the clinic or will he be angry and oppositional with you? As your consultants, we'll follow the evaluation of Rudy throughout this chapter in order to see how an assessment like this might play out.

Parent Interviews

Information concerning the child and the family usually comes first from an interview with the parents. Typically, the interview begins with an account of the presenting problem. Next, a detailed *developmental history* is obtained in order to explore the antecedent conditions that might have contributed to the child's present difficulties. Among the topics covered are the child's prenatal and birth history and early development. The subsequent adjustment of the child within the family and with peers is explored, along with social and academic performance. For teenagers, information is obtained concerning sexual development and work history, as well as possible drug and alcohol use and delinquent behavior. The clinician also inquires about major illnesses and injuries and stresses experienced by the child and family. To complete the picture, the parents may be asked about their own individual, marital, and occupational adjustment; their specific goals, satisfactions, and dissatisfactions; and the attempts they have made to deal with the problem in the past.

What about the studies showing the *unreliability* of retrospective reports? While parents may not always report accurate information concerning many aspects of the child and family, it is still important for the clinician to know the parents' perception of the facts. Whether the child was a "difficult" infant and a "bad" toddler may not be as important as the parents' perception or memory of the child as difficult and bad.

In the process of interviewing, the clinician is beginning to know the parents, while the parents are also beginning to know the clinician. Since there is no hard and fast line between assessment and therapy, skilled interviewers can use this initial contact to lay the groundwork for the trust and respect that will be so crucial in the future. The establishment of *rapport* between the parent and the clinician is an important part of the process. Parents may feel shamed about bringing their child for an assessment and may have concerns either that their parenting is at fault or that the clinician will blame them for causing the problem. Thus, the interviewer wants to take care to put parents at ease, support them for their obvious concern for their children, and establish that the parents and the assessor are "rowing on the same team."

In addition, the parent interview provides the clinician the opportunity to gather information about the present family system of relationships, as well as the possible role that the parents' own family histories might play in their difficulties with their child. To accomplish this, McGoldrick, Gerson, and Shellenberger (1997) suggest asking parents to complete a family *genogram* as part of the assessment. The genogram is a pictorial representation of the relationships among the people in a family, usually spanning three generations to include the child, parents, and grandparents. First, demographic information is recorded, such as birth and death dates, places of origin, and career paths. Second, critical events are indicated, such as divorces, moves, or traumatic experiences. Third, interaction patterns are represented by special lines connecting various family members. For example, lines can indicate relationships that are close, enmeshed, distant, conflictual, or cut off. (See Figure 16.1.) The genogram can help the clinician to identify coalitions and triangles in the family, as well as intergenerational patterns of conflict, estrangement, role-reversal, and so forth that interfere with parents' ability to respond appropriately to their children's developmental needs. (See McGoldrick and Gerson, 1985, for a number of intriguing examples, including a genogram of Sigmund Freud's family.)

Rudy's mother Christina is 20 minutes late for her first meeting with you, arriving flustered and disheveled. She explains that as a single parent she found it difficult to manage the complications of getting off work early and arranging day care for her youngest son,

Eddie. She divorced the boys' father, Rudolfo, 2 years ago, and they have rarely heard from him since he returned to his native Argentina. "Everything was fine with Rudy up until then," she says. "Sometimes I wonder if we should've stayed together for the boys. But Rudolfo is no good—nothing but a drunken brute. Rudy is nothing like him, thank goodness. He's a terrific kid—my little man." In contrast, she seems to have little to say about little Eddie. He is described as a "handful," and she states she is glad to have Rudy's help with managing her younger son's behavior.

Christina's description of Rudy's early history includes nothing remarkable. She reports no major illnesses or deviations from expected development until the time of the divorce, which, you note, also occurred the year that Rudy entered first grade. She doesn't believe that there is anything "wrong" with Rudy; she suspects that the teacher "just can't relate to him." She acknowledges that she and the teacher are not on particularly good terms. She explains that she herself had a lot of difficulty in school, and, with some humor, states that she looks back on her teachers as "torturers."

Christina is uncomfortable at first with the idea of completing a family genogram, commenting that she doesn't understand "what this has to do with anything." However, as your rapport improves, she agrees. What emerges is a history of broken relationships across the generations. (See Figure 16.1.) Rudy's father cut off contact with his own parents and little is known about them. Christina also has nothing to do with her own family of origin. Her father August was a violent but charming man who died of cirrhosis of the liver when she was about Rudy's age. She was his "favorite" when drink made him affectionate, and the special target of his abuse when he was "mean drunk." She says, "I adored him and hated him in equal amounts." Following the father's death, Christina's mother abandoned the children, leaving Christina in the care of her older sis-

ter, Theresa. *The two sisters, always rivals for the little affection there was in the family, had a falling out about the disposition of their mother's will a couple of years ago and have not spoken since. When asked about current sources of support in her life, Christina pauses and then confides that she attends AA*

meetings. This is your first intimation that, like her father and Rudy's father, she has a problem with alcohol.

Informal Observations

The clinician's assessment begins when first seeing the child and parents. Their appearance and inter-

Figure 16.1   Genogram: Three Generations of Rudy's Family.

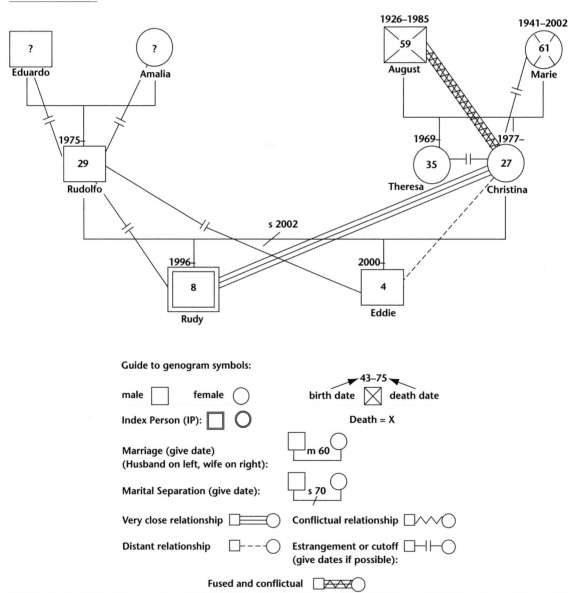

actions provide clues about *family characteristics* and the relationships among its members. First impressions furnish information concerning the family's social class and general level of harmony or disharmony, as well as its stylistic characteristics— reserved, expressive, authoritarian, intellectual, and so on. As always, the clinical child psychologist evaluates behavior in terms of its age appropriateness or inappropriateness, the former providing clues about assets and resources; the latter providing clues to possible disturbances.

Once with the child, the clinician systematically gathers certain kinds of information. The overall impression of the child's *personality* is always worth noting: "A funny, fun-loving boy"; "he already has the worried look of an old man"; "she has a sullen look, like she is spoiling for a fight"; "a direct, honest, no-nonsense preadolescent girl, who doesn't want to be coddled." While it is important not to prejudge children on the basis of initial impressions, these first reactions might give the clinician clues about the child's social-stimulus value, which may be a potent elicitor of positive or negative reactions from others.

The child's *manner of relating* to the clinician furnishes information concerning his or her perception of adults. It is natural for children to be reserved initially, since the clinician is a stranger. As they discover that the clinician is an interested and friendly adult, they should become more relaxed and communicative. However, certain children never warm up; they sit as far back in their chair as possible, speak in an almost inaudible monotone, either rarely look at the examiner or else watch intently, as if he or she were a kind of monster who might strike out at any minute. Provocative children "test the limits," mischievously peeking when told to close their eyes or destroying a puzzle when asked to leave it intact.

Generally speaking, clinical observations such as these are nearer an art than a science because the procedures are not standardized and the target behaviors are so wide-ranging. However, observation per se is not unscientific. Behavioral clinicians, as we will see later, bring to assessment the structure and reliability that the more open-ended approach lacks.

Upon first spotting Rudy in the waiting room, you have the impression that he is a handsome and healthy-looking boy, although you are struck by the fact that he is neater and more carefully groomed than is usual for a youngster his age. When you enter the room, he is disciplining his little brother, cautioning him not to handle the magazines too roughly. He greets you brightly but checks back with his mother before he goes with you, asking her if she will be "okay."

Child Interviews

Structured, Semistructured, and Unstructured Interviews

The clinician wants to be able to see things from the child's-eye point of view, which can be facilitated by conducting an interview. Interviews confer a number of advantages, such as giving children a chance to present their *own perspective* on the problem, allowing the interviewer to assess areas of functioning that might not be accessible through other means, enabling the interviewer to *observe* children's behavior and attitudes relevant to the problem, and providing an opportunity to establish the *rapport* that will be necessary if a therapeutic relationship is to develop (McConaughy & Achenbach, 1994). In addition, the interview gives the clinician the opportunity to clarify with children why they are there and to explain what the assessment process will be like. (For more information, see Sattler, 1998.)

Interviews can be conceptualized along a continuum based on how structured they are. In *unstructured interviews,* clinicians encourage children to put in their own words their views about the problem; the family, school, and peers; interests, hopes, and fears; self-concept; and, for adolescents, career aspirations, sexual relations, and drug or alcohol use.

In contrast to unstructured interviews, which allow the interviewer considerable leeway for improvising and following up unexpected leads, *semistructured interviews* consist of a series of open-ended questions followed by specific probes to help the interviewer determine the presence or absence of diagnostic symptoms. An example is the Semistructured Clinical Interview for Children and Adolescents (SCICA; McConaughy & Achenbach, 1994), which was developed for children ages 6 through 18. A series of open-ended questions is interspersed with nonverbal tasks, such as drawings and play activities, designed to set children at ease and to encourage them to reveal their thoughts, feelings, and behavior through their interaction with the examiner. The interviewer uses both child self-reports and his or her own observations of the child in order to rate psychopathology.

Structured interviews also consist of a series of specific questions or statements, but the child's response is structured as well, whether as a "yes-no" choice or as a point on a scale ranging from "strongly agree" to "disagree." Structured interviews devised for children include the *Diagnostic Interview for Children and Adolescents* (DICA-IV; Reich, Welner, & Herjanic, 1997); the *Schedule for Affective Disorders and Schizophrenia for School-Age Children* (K-SADS-IVR; Ambrosini & Dixon, 1996); the *Diagnostic Interview Schedule for Children and Adolescents* (DISC-IV; Shaffer, Fisher, Lucas, & Comer, 2003); and the *Children's Interview for Psychiatric Syndromes* (ChIPS; Weller et al., 1999). Each of these interviews has both a child and parent version, and all generate DSM diagnoses for most disorders seen in childhood. (See Hodges, 1993, and Kamphaus and Frick, 2002, for reviews.) Figure 16.2 on p. 498 presents excerpts from the K-SADS and DISC illustrating the questions used to elicit information about impulsive/inattentive behavior.

Rapport

In order for any assessment technique to be of use, the child must at least be minimally cooperative; ideally, the child should participate wholeheartedly. Therefore, essential to the assessment process is good *rapport*. The establishment of rapport requires clinical skills, sensitivity, and experience. Moreover, the clinician must be prepared to deal with a variety of obstacles at different ages—a crying infant; a toddler fearful of leaving the mother; a provocative, defiant school-age child; a sullen teenager who resents all questioning by adults. But aside from such dramatic challenges, there is always the question of how one goes about establishing oneself as an interested, friendly adult to children of

different ages. For example, while a preschool child might be set at ease by meeting the clinician in a playroom and using puppets or drawings to express thoughts and feelings, an adolescent might feel insulted by being interviewed in such a setting. In addition, older youths may warm more readily to an examiner who is candid and direct, treating them as competent young persons whose active participation in the assessment process is invited.

Barker (1990) makes a number of helpful suggestions for enhancing rapport with children. He recommends that the interviewer adopt a *warm, interested,* and *respectful* attitude that engages the child, without being overly formal. He also suggests that the interviewer attempt to match the *pace* and *interpersonal style* of the child. A shy and reticent child may be more comfortable with an examiner who talks softly and slowly, while a rough-and-tumble or streetwise child may respond best to a lively and fast-paced interviewing style. Children can also be set at ease by some side conversations that establish common ground or mutual interests between themselves and the examiner, even if it is only to discuss the child's "cool" T-shirt or to satisfy the child's curiosity about how the tape recorder works. In addition, Barker suggests that interviewers be willing to adopt a *"one-down"* position with children, allowing them to play the experts with their special knowledge regarding the latest video games, television shows, or music. (For further reading, see Garbarino, Stott, and Faculty of the Erikson Institute, 1992, and Greenspan, 2003.)

Developmental Considerations

For any interview to be valid, it must be tailored to the child's level of understanding. At the very least, it is important for the interviewer to match the vocabulary level of the child in order to be understood and to help the interview go smoothly (Barker, 1990). However, the child's developmental level will affect many other aspects of the interview process.

During the *preschool* years, children's self-understanding is expressed primarily in terms of *physical characteristics* and *actions* ("I have brown hair"; "I play ball"; "I have a dog"). (Here

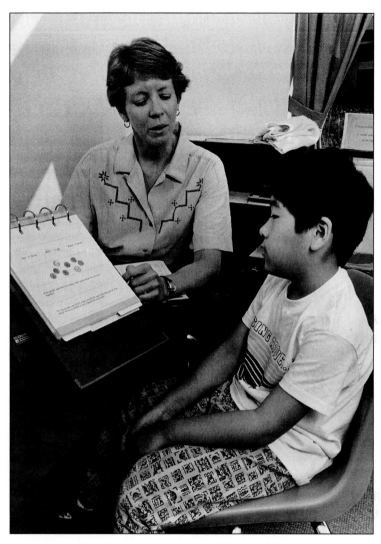

The importance of good rapport in assessment: Will this child give his best performance?

we follow Harter, 1988; Steward et al., 1993; Stone and Lemanek, 1990.) Consequently, questions about the nature of the problem that brought them to see a psychologist are apt to elicit responses couched in terms of specific behaviors ("I hit my brother") rather than internal experiences. These, in turn, probably echo what parents or other adults have said to them about being "bad." Recall that young children are never self-referred

and often do not see themselves as having problems. In a like manner, children's view of the cause of the problem is apt to be specific and external ("I hit my brother because he takes my things").

Preschoolers' evaluations of their own emotions and those of other people are also *concrete* and *situational;* for example, being happy is having a birthday party. Consequently, interview questions must

Figure 16.2   Examples of Questions Used in Structured and Semistructured Interviews.

K-SADS

Impulsivity: Refers to the child's characteristic pattern of acting before thinking about the consequences. It does not refer to "bad" actions only but to a behavioral characteristic spanning all types of behavior independent of moral significance.

Are you the kind of person who tends to get into trouble, or maybe even gets hurt, because you rush into things without thinking what might happen?	0 No information
	1 Not present
	2 Slight: May occur on occasion when excited (party, etc.) but not typical and no bad consequences.
Are you often wrong in school because you answer with the first thing that comes to your mind instead of thinking it over first?	3 Mild: Definitely present. Acts impulsively at least 3 times a week in at least 2 settings.
Do you get into trouble in school because you often speak out when you're supposed to be quiet?	4 Moderate: Impulsive in all settings.
Does your teacher often have to tell you what you are supposed to do after the rest of the class has started doing it?	5 Severe: Impulsive in all settings and has gotten into dangerous situations for lack of foresight in a few instances (more than 3 times in a year).
Do you have trouble organizing your work?	6 Extreme: Very impulsive; it is an almost constant characteristic of child's behavior. Gets into danger at least once a week.
Do you often do things on a dare or just because the idea popped into your head or just for the heck of it?	

DISC

Impulsivity	No	Sometimes	Yes
Does your teacher often tell you that you don't listen?	0		2
(if yes) Does he/she say that to you more than to most kids?	0	1	2
(if yes) How long has that been happening?	Months:		
(if yes) Have you been like that since you started school?	0		2
Does your teacher often tell you that you're not keeping your mind on your work?	0		2
(if yes) Does he/she say that to you more than to most kids?	0		2
(if yes) How long has that been happening?	Months:		
(if yes) Have you been like that since you started school?	0		2
Sometimes kids rush into things without thinking about what may happen. Do you do that?	0	1	2
(if yes) Have you always been like that?	0		2
(if yes) How long have you been like that?	Months:		
Some kids have trouble organizing their schoolwork. They can't decide what they need. They can't plan what to do first, what to do second. Are you like that?	0	1	2
(if yes) How long have you been like that?	Months:		
Do you start your schoolwork and not finish it?	0	1	2
(if yes) How long has that been happening?	Months:		
(if yes) Have you always had trouble finishing it?	0		2
(if yes) Is that because you don't know how to do it?	0	1	2

Source: K-SADS (Puig-Antich and Chambers, 1978); DISC (Costello et al., 1984).

be similarly concrete and action oriented ("Do you cry?" rather than "Do you feel sad?"). The interviewer should also expect people to be described in terms of what they do rather than what they think or how they feel.

In *middle childhood* children are able to express ideas about the self-concept that are "psychological" and more differentiated; for example, instead of being judged "smart" or "dumb," the child can be "smart" in some things and "dumb" in others. In this period children are able to provide accurate reports of their own emotions by using *internal, psychological* cues. They also begin to attribute psychological characteristics to others and realize other people have perspectives different from their own. Along with these cognitive advances goes the ability to recognize deviance. However, even in early adolescence there is still the tendency to attribute cause to external, typically social, events, such as family quarrels and conflicts.

Cognitive development determines how the child will understand the helping relationship, including the concept of the psychologist as helper as well as the concept of being helped. The *preschooler* is apt to view the former in terms of general traits, such as being "kind" or "nice," along with the psychologist's specific behaviors, such as "playing games." In *middle childhood* references to competence begin to appear, such as "She knows what she is doing," while the early *adolescent* recognizes the role of inner qualities of empathy and a desire to help. Being helped itself changes from denoting some form of direct action in the preschool period (for example, "Buy me a new game to play and tell my brother to quit picking on me") to a recognition of the importance of support, validation, regard, and other kinds of indirect help in early adolescence.

Ethnic Diversity

Cultural competence, an ethical mandate for psychologists (American Psychological Association, 2003; Sue, 1998), is an important part of rapport and effective interviewing with children and families. (See also Gibbs and Huang, 2003; McGoldrick, 2002; and Sattler, 1998.) Comprehension of cultural values and norms can assist the interviewer to engage with the family and appreciate rather than pathologize their differences. For example, understanding the courtesies and conventions of conversation is important (Tharp, 1991). While an informal approach in which the psychologist greets the parents on a first name basis might set at ease a middle-class European American family, a traditional Asian family might perceive this friendly approach as a sign of disrespect (Ho, 1992). To take another example, Native American children prefer to wait before responding to questions, and so it is important that the clinician understand that a long lag time is neither an indication of insecurity nor resistance (Tharp, 1989).

Being an expert in all cultural groups and their norms is not a prerequisite for becoming a clinical child psychologist, however. Awareness of one's own cultural expectations and recognizing that they are not universal norms is key to remaining open minded, receptive, and nonjudgmental (McIntosh, 1998). In addition, a therapist's sensitive and honestly interested inquiries into the family's cultural beliefs and practices may be quite well received (Ho, 1992).

Sue and Sue (1999) have identified three variables that are important when assessing ethnic minority families: *culture-bound* (e.g, cultural beliefs and practices), *language-bound* (e.g., facility with the vocabulary and linguistic conventions of the interviewer's language), and *class-bound* (e.g., the effects of socioeconomic status on the family's lifestyle, community, and aspirations). Issues to explore in interviews with ethnic minority children and their families include the level of *acculturation* of the family as a whole, and where there might be differences among individual family members, particularly between the generations. For example, immigrant children often become quickly assimilated into U.S. culture through their exposure to peers during the school day, even when their parents continue to hold fast to traditional values derived from the home country. *Cultural strain* may also be evident when children experience conflict between meeting the demands of the old and new culture. *Ethnic identity* reflects the child's internalization of a sense of belonging to a specific cultural group.

While the development of a secure sense of *bicultural identity* (e.g., identification with one's ethnic group as well as a feeling of membership in the larger culture) is believed to be linked to positive adjustment (Ogbu, 1999), many factors might interfere with its development, including prejudice, racism, and experiences of marginalization. Lastly, *social class* differences among ethnic minority families are vast and belie stereotypes that automatically equate minority status with lack of privilege. Just as middle-class African American families create different contexts for child development than those who struggle with poverty, immigrants from the elite classes may have little in common with impoverished refugees from the same country.

Ho (1992) presents a transcultural framework for assessing children from diverse cultural backgrounds. (See Table 16.2.) His model integrates influences in the individual, family, school, peer, and community spheres. Within each area of functioning, one of the clinician's key tasks is to determine to what extent the child's adaptation is a reflection of culturally appropriate norms that are in conflict with those of the majority norms.

Because Rudy is in middle childhood, you decide to equip the interview room with colored pens and paper, clay, checkers, and a few other games that might help to set him at ease. Your first observation is that Rudy ignores all of the toys and attends carefully to you, eager to answer all your questions. While most children are cautious initially, and rightly so, from the beginning of the interview Rudy is unusually open and communicative. As the interview progresses, he continues to impress you as a bright, alert, open youngster. You mentally note Rudy's behavior and wonder what it might represent. Perhaps this is a basically well-functioning boy whose problems have been exaggerated; perhaps he has been overly close to adults at the cost of developing appropriate peer relationships; perhaps he is a charming psychopath; perhaps his social skills are a defense against some unknown fear.

Rudy offers his own perspective on the problem. "I don't like school," he says, and when asked what he doesn't like about it, he replies with a downcast face, "Schoolwork is boring. And the other kids are jerks. I don't like any of them." He spends most of his time after school helping his mother around the house and taking care of his little brother. "I like to help out," he says. He states that if he could have three wishes, they would be "to stay home instead of going to school," "to buy a big house for us to live in," and "to have a billion dollars so that my mom wouldn't have to go to work anymore."

When you ask Rudy about his father, his initial reaction is flat and dismissive. He describes him as "no good," echoing his mother's words and sentiments in a way that is striking. However, as you inquire more about the father's return to his South American homeland, Rudy expresses some wistful longing to see for himself the land that his father's family hailed from. He begins to talk with animation about the things he has learned about Argentinian culture from the books he checked out of the library. Rudy seems at first taken aback and then puzzled when you ask about his own ethnic identity. "I don't know. I never really thought about it. My dad is Argentinian," he says, "but I guess I'm just American like my mom."

Psychological Tests

Of all professionals dealing with disturbed children, clinical psychologists have been the most concerned with developing assessment techniques that can be objectively administered and scored, that have norms based on clearly defined populations, and that have established reliability and validity. While many different tests have been developed, our coverage here will focus only on a few of the more widely used tests. (For more extensive and detailed reviews of a variety of psychological tests for children, refer to Sattler, 2001 and 2002.)

Table 16.2

Transcultural Guidelines for the Assessment of the Child and Family

To what extent is the individual child's adjustment a function of the following?

Individual Level of Psychosocial Adjustment

1. Physical appearance, which can be affected by malnutrition, improper diet, height, weight, skin color, and hair texture and unfavorably compared with preferred Anglo norms
2. Affect expression, which may be culturally appropriate but may be in direct conflict with the mainstream norms which emphasize directness and overt assertiveness
3. Self-concept and self-esteem, which are germane to the child's native culture and are appropriate criteria for self-evaluation but are in conflict with the mainstream criteria for self-concept and self-esteem
4. Interpersonal competence, which differs according to different sociocultural milieu
5. Definition of and attitudes toward autonomy, which may be in serious conflict with the norms of the child's school or community milieu or is adaptive within the child's overall life situation
6. Attitudes toward achievement, which are culturally appropriate but are in conflict with the traditional channels of educational achievement enforced by the public school system
7. Management of aggression and impulse control, which can enhance or impede his or her school performance and interpersonal competence
8. Coping and defense mechanisms that may be dysfunctional in certain sociocultural contexts and environments

Relationships with Family

9. Family structure that is in transition because of immigration, acculturation, or life-cycle processes
10. Roles within the family, which are in conflict with the traditional structure favoring older-age and male-gender hierarchies
11. Family communication conflict from hierarchical to egalitarian caused by acculturation and family life processes
12. Parental use of discipline, which may enhance or impede the child's performance at school or at home
13. Culturally defined dominant dyad, which is in conflict with the Anglo-American nuclear family ideals that define father-mother as the dominant dyad
14. Culturally defined autonomy, which is in conflict with the Anglo-American nuclear family ideals that define autonomy as physical departure from family of origin and financial independence

School Adjustment and Achievement

15. Psychological adjustment, which may be attributed to parental lack of education, parental negative attitudes toward the school, the child's unfamiliarity with the norms and expectations of the classroom and school environment, social-class differences, and/or language difficulties
16. Social adjustment, which may require moving away from a familiar neighborhood school to a larger school where there are greater cultural, racial, and economic differences
17. Behavioral adjustment, which may be related to an unstable home situation, poor nutrition, poor physical health, or the inability to handle overwhelming anxiety and stress
18. Academic achievement as measured by culturally biased achievement tests and/or verbal skills, motivation for learning, attitudes toward a particular class or toward the school in general, study habits, and family support

Relationships with Peers

19. Ability to display empathy, to form friendships, to engage in cooperative and competitive activities, and to manage aggressive and sexual impulses
20. Social skills to form peer relationships at school and within the child's own community and the effects of these peer relationships on overall psychosocial functioning

Adaptation to the Community

21. Quality participation in church activities, youth groups, and language- and ethnic-related classes
22. Quality participation in organized sports, arts activities, volunteer activities, or part-time jobs
23. Inappropriate or excessive activities that create family conflicts or dysfunctional behavior, such as delinquency, drug abuse, or poor academic behavior

Source: Ho, 1992.

Cognitive Testing from Infancy to Adolescence

Infant Cognitive Testing

Infant testing requires that the examiner have special skills in *accommodation* in order to elicit the child's optimal performance. The examiner must know how to intrigue the infant with the test material, allow for distractions, temporarily become a comforting caretaker in response to fretting, postpone testing when distress becomes too great—in short, the good examiner must have the sensitivity, flexibility, and warmth of a good parent.

One of the best constructed standardized infant tests is the *Bayley Scales of Infant Development—Second Edition* (Bayley, 1993), which evaluates cognitive, language, motor, and social functioning of children 1 to 42 months of age. The Mental Scale evaluates the infant's perceptual acuity, object constancy, memory, learning, problem solving, and verbal communication and yields a normalized standard score, the Mental Development Index. The Motor Scale evaluates fine and gross motor coordination and body control and also yields a standard score, the Psychomotor Development Index. The Behavior Rating Scale assesses the infant's attention and arousal, social engagement with others, and emotional regulation.

The Bayley can help to identify areas of development in which there are delays or impairments and can be used to design interventions to address those problems. However, while scores on the Bayley are associated with children's current developmental status, unless the scores are extremely low, they are not strong predictors of future intelligence (Nellis & Gridley, 1994). Therefore, unless concerns emerge very early in a child's life, such as the possibility of mental retardation, autism, or developmental disability, it is more common for cognitive testing to occur in the preschool or school-age years. (For a more detailed presentation of infant assessment, see Wyly, 1997.)

The Wechsler Scales

The *Wechsler Intelligence Scale for Children—Fourth Edition* (WISC-IV; Wechsler, 2003) is the most widely used intelligence test for children aged 6 through 16. The Wechsler Preschool and Primary Scale of Intelligence—Revised (Wechsler, 1989) is used for children aged 3 to 7.

The WISC-IV consists of 10 core subtests and 5 supplemental subtests, the items in each being arranged according to increasing difficulty. The subtests are grouped into four composite indices (See Figure 16.3.) The *Verbal Comprehension Index,* which requires facility in using verbal symbols, consists of three basic subtests (Similarities, Vocabulary, and Comprehension) and two supplemental subtests (Information and Word Reasoning). The *Perceptual Reasoning Index,* which involves concrete material

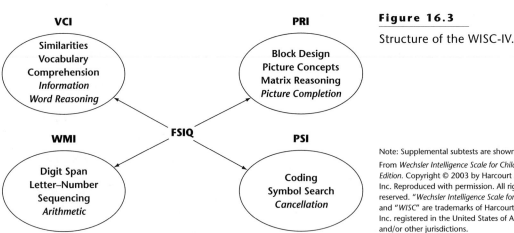

Figure 16.3

Structure of the WISC-IV.

Note: Supplemental subtests are shown in italics.
From *Wechsler Intelligence Scale for Children—Fourth Edition.* Copyright © 2003 by Harcourt Assessment, Inc. Reproduced with permission. All rights reserved. *"Wechsler Intelligence Scale for Children"* and *"WISC"* are trademarks of Harcourt Assessment, Inc. registered in the United States of America and/or other jurisdictions.

such as pictures, blocks, and jigsaw puzzles, consists of three basic subtests (Block Design, Picture Concepts, Matrix Reasoning) and one supplemental subtest (Picture Completion). The *Working Memory Index* comprises Digit Span and Letter-Number Sequencing with Arithmetic as a supplemental subtest. Finally, the *Processing Speed Index* consists of two basic subtests (Coding and Symbol Search) and one supplementary subtest (Cancellation). (See Figure 16.4 for examples of WISC-IV-like items.) In addition, scoring yields a *Full-Scale IQ* with a mean score of 100 and a standard deviation of 15. For example, a child with a total score of 115 will be one standard deviation above the mean or in approximately the 84th percentile.

While the IQ score is important, it is only one of many pieces of information gained from an intelligence test. First, the assessor examines the *discrepancies* among the composite index scores on the WISC-IV to determine whether they are statistically significant. These discrepancies furnish clues about the child's differential ability to handle the various kinds of tasks; for example, the child who has a Full-Scale IQ of 100, a Verbal Comprehension Index of 120, and a Perceptual Reasoning Index of 80 is quite different from a child with the same overall IQ but with a Verbal Comprehension Index of 80 and a Perceptual Reasoning Index of 120. The second child may be particularly penalized in school, where the manipulation of verbal symbols becomes increasingly important, while being quite talented on tasks that require minimal verbal facility.

Analysis of successes and failures on individual items may provide further clues to intellectual strengths and weaknesses. A child may do well on problems involving rote learning and the accumulation of facts but do poorly on ones requiring reasoning and judgment. As another example, an otherwise bright child may be weak in visual-motor coordination, which might make learning to write difficult (Sattler, 2001).

Stanford-Binet Intelligence Scales, Fifth Edition

The *Stanford-Binet Intelligence Scales, Fifth Edition* (SB5) (Roid, 2003) covers the age span of 2 to 85 or

more years. It consists of 10 tests, organized into five broad areas of cognitive abilities that follow from the Cattell-Horn-Carroll theory of intelligence (Carroll, 1993). Further, each factor is evaluated in Verbal and Nonverbal domains. (See Figure 16.5.) The *Fluid Reasoning* factor involves novel tasks that are relatively free of dependence on knowledge learned in school or through previous experience. For example, the Early Reasoning subtest requires the child to observe pictures of humans in action and to deduce the underlying problem or situation by telling a story, while the Matrix subtest requires the child to determine the rules or relationships underlying a series of changes in the appearance of a visual stimulus. *Knowledge,* or Crystallized Intelligence, in contrast, involves information that is accumulated through schooling and general life experience. Subtests include Vocabulary (e.g., "What does envelope mean?) and Procedural Understanding, which requires the child to describe the steps involved in solving an everyday problem. *Quantitative Reasoning* assesses the child's facility with numbers and numerical problem solving, using either verbally or pictorially depicted stimuli. *Visual-Spatial Processing* assesses the child's ability to comprehend patterns, spatial relationships, or the gestalt whole among separate elements. For example, the Form Board requires the child to duplicate familiar patterns using puzzle pieces, and Position and Direction requires the understanding of spatial concepts such as "behind" or "under." *Working Memory* involves the child's ability to store either verbal or spatial information in short-term memory while performing a cognitive operation on it.

The items in each test are arranged according to difficulty; thus, the more items children successfully complete, the higher their abilities are when compared with children their own age. Like the WISC-IV, the index factors combine to form a Full Scale IQ, with a mean of 100 and a standard deviation of 15. In addition, Verbal IQ and Nonverbal IQ scores can be derived to compare the child's functioning in these two modalities.

Observations During Cognitive Testing

The purpose of cognitive testing is not simply to derive an IQ score. The testing situation can also provide

Figure 16.4   WISC-IV-Like Items.

Information

How many wings does a bird have?
How many nickels make a dime?
What is steam made of?
Who wrote "Tom Sawyer"?

Comprehension

What should you do if you see someone forget his book when he leaves a restaurant?
What is the advantage of keeping money in a bank?
Why is copper often used in electrical wires?

Arithmetic

Sam had three pieces of candy and Joe gave him four more. How many pieces of candy did Sam have altogether?
Three women divided eighteen golf balls equally among themselves. How many golf balls did each person receive?
If two buttons cost $.15, what will be the cost of a dozen buttons?

Similarities

In what way are a lion and a tiger alike?
In what way are a saw and a hammer alike?
In what way are an hour and a week alike?
In what way are a circle and a triangle alike?

Vocabulary

This test consists simply of asking, "What is a _____ ?" or "What does _____ mean?" The words cover a wide range of difficulty.

Digit Span

Digits Forward contains seven series of digits, 3 to 9 digits in length (Example: 1-8-9).
Digits Backward contains seven series of digits, 2 to 8 digits in length (Example: 5-8-1-9).

Picture Completion (26 items)

The task is to identify the essential missing part of the picture.
A picture of a car without a wheel.
A picture of a dog without a leg.
A picture of a telephone without numbers on the dial.
An example of a Picture Completion task is shown below.

Courtesy of The Psychological Corporation.

Picture Arrangement (12 items)

The task is to arrange a series of pictures into a meaningful sequence.

Block Design (11 items)

The task is to reproduce stimulus designs using four or nine blocks. An example of a Block Design item is shown below.

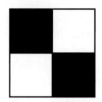

Object Assembly (4 items)

The task is to arrange pieces into a meaningful object. An example of an Object Assembly item is shown below.

Courtesy of The Psychological Corporation.

Coding

The task is to copy symbols from a key (see below).

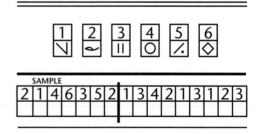

Courtesy of The Psychological Corporation.

Mazes

The task is to complete a series of mazes.

Note. The questions resemble those that appear on the WISC-IV but are not actually from the test.

Figure 16.5   Organization of the Stanford-Binet, Fifth Edition.

		Domains	
		Nonverbal (NV)	Verbal (V)
Factors	**Fluid Reasoning (FR)**	*Nonverbal Fluid Reasoning** Activities: Object Series/Matrices (Routing)	*Verbal Fluid Reasoning* Activities: Early Reasoning (2–3), Verbal Absurdities (4), Verbal Analogies (5–6)
	Knowledge (KN)	*Nonverbal Knowledge* Activities: Procedural Knowledge (2–3), Picture Absurdities (4–6)	*Verbal Knowledge** Activities: Vocabulary (Routing)
	Quantitative Reasoning (QR)	*Nonverbal Quantitative Reasoning* Activities: Quantitative Reasoning (2–6)	*Verbal Quantitative Reasoning* Activities: Quantitative Reasoning (2–6)
	Visual-Spatial Processing (VS)	*Nonverbal Visual-Spatial Processing* Activities: Form Board (1–2), Form Patterns (3–6)	*Verbal Visual-Spatial Processing* Activities: Position and Direction (2–6)
	Working Memory (WM)	*Nonverbal Working Memory* Activities: Delayed Response (1), Block Span (2–6)	*Verbal Working Memory* Activities: Memory for Sentences (2–3), Last Word (4–6)

Note: Names of the 10 subtests are in **bold italic.** Activities include the levels at which they appear.

* = Routing subtests

From Roid, 2003.

important clues about the child's *style of thinking.* Note the responses of two equally bright 8-year-olds to the question, "What should you do when you lose a ball that belongs to someone else?" One child answered, "I'd get him another one." The other said, "I'd pay money for it. I'd look for it. I'd give him another ball. I'd try to find it, but if I couldn't, I'd give him money for it because I might not have the kind of ball he wants." Both answers receive the same high score, but one is clear, simple, and to the point, while the other is needlessly cluttered.

Styles of thinking are closely related to psychological health or disturbance. Intelligence is not some kind of disembodied skill existing apart from the rest of the child's personality. On the contrary, a psychologically well-functioning child tends to think clearly, a child with poor self-control tends to think impulsively, and an obsessive child (like the one just quoted) tends to think in terms of so many possible alternatives that it becomes difficult to decide on one

and act on it. A schizophrenic child tends to think bizarrely, as is revealed in this rambling, fantasy-saturated answer to the simple question, "Why should one tell the truth?" "If you don't tell the truth, you get into trouble; you go to court; like teenagers who don't tell the truth; they're usually armed, guys who run around the forest and woods, the woods near the house. We go there to catch frogs, and we always have to have older people go with us because of the teenagers with guns and knives. A child drowned there not long ago. If you don't tell the truth, they start a gang and drown you."

The intelligence test also allows the clinician to evaluate the child's *work habits.* Some children are task oriented and self-motivated; they need almost no encouragement or help from the examiner. Others are uncertain and insecure, giving up readily unless encouraged or prodded, constantly seeking reassurance that they are doing well, or asking to know whether their response was right or wrong.

Finally, the tests yield information concerning the child's capacity for *self-monitoring,* which is the ability to evaluate the quality of the responses. Some children seem to be implicitly asking, "Is that really correct?" or "Is that the best I can do?" while others seem to have little ability to judge when they are right or wrong, an incorrect response being given with the same air of uncritical assurance as a correct one.

Strengths and Limitations of Cognitive Testing

Intelligence tests can play a useful role in child assessment. The IQ score itself is related to many aspects of the child's life—success in school, vocational choice, peer relations—and IQ is a better predictor of future adjustment than any score on a personality test. In addition, the test provides data concerning general areas of strength and weakness; the kind and degree of impairment of specific intellectual functions, such as immediate recall or abstract reasoning; the child's coping techniques, work habits, and motivation; stylistic characteristics of thinking that may well be related to personality variables; and the presence of distorted thinking that might indicate either organic brain pathology or psychosis (Sattler, 2001).

Yet care must be taken that an intelligence test is used *appropriately* and that results are properly understood. As IQ became a household term, so did the misconception that the score represents an index of the child's unalterable intellectual potential existing independent of background and experience. In particular, concerns have been expressed that these tests might do more harm than good by underestimating the abilities of children from cultural groups other than the mainstream (see Bender et al., 1995, and Kaminer and Vig, 1995, for both sides of the issue). For this reason, the ethical guidelines of the American Psychological Association (2002) require that clinicians develop *cultural competence* and demonstrate the ability to interpret test data in the light of the unique cultural and environmental factors that affect the child (see also Valencia and Suzuki, 2000).

In contrast to his friendly and open manner during the interview, Rudy's behavior changes markedly during the WISC-IV. His brow is furrowed and he responds to the tasks as though they are stressful and even irritating to him. In addition, he tends to make self-derogatory remarks at the beginning of each new task. He says "I don't know" too readily when items become difficult, and he quickly destroys a puzzle he had put together incorrectly, as if trying to cover up his mistake. At times he seems to use his conversational skills to divert attention away from the test material. He is willing to try the first arithmetic problems, which are easy for him and allow him to be certain about the right answer. As they get more difficult, however, he refuses even to try. He states that he "hates" this test. When he is encouraged to respond to difficult items, it is clear that he does not know the correct answer.

The test scores add a significant bit of data: While he has high expectations for himself, Rudy has only average intelligence. In addition, there is significant scatter among his index scores. While he shows strengths on verbal comprehension tasks, he demonstrates deficits on tasks assessing working memory. You begin speculating, "If his sociability misled me into thinking he was intellectually advanced, his mother and teachers might have also been misled into setting unrealistically high goals and pressuring him to achieve them." This hypothesis naturally would have to be checked by interviewing the parents and teacher. Clearly there is more to be learned about Rudy's abilities to achieve in school and how they mesh with expectations that others have of him and that he has for himself.

Tests of Achievement

An assessment of academic achievement is important in deciding whether a child has a learning disability and in evaluating the effectiveness of a remedial program. Low academic achievement may also contribute to the development of a behavior problem. As with intelligence tests, individually administered *achievement tests* allow the clinician to make behavioral observations of the child and to analyze the nature of the child's failures. These data may provide helpful clues about motivational and academic problems; for example, a boy who gives up without trying is different from one who fails after trying his best, just as a girl who fails multiplication problems because of careless mistakes is different from another who fails because she has not grasped the basic process of multiplying. A comprehensive battery is provided by the *Woodcock-Johnson III Tests of Achievement* (WJ III; Woodcock, McGrew, & Mather, 2001a). The tests cover 10 areas, including the child's mastery of grade-level reading, math, written language, oral language, and academic knowledge, skills, and fluency in subjects such as social studies, science, and the humanities.

In order to assess the possibility that Rudy has learning problems, you administer the WJ III. Rudy's scores indicate that his achievement in most areas is about average, while his mathematics skills are far below what is expected of children at his age. Apparently, therefore, there are reasons for Rudy to report that he "hates" math. However, you note that his reading skills are at age level, and therefore the explanation for his failing reading does not seem to lie in the direction of a learning disorder. Taken together with the IQ tests results, these data also raise further questions, such as the effects of being regarded as "lazy" on the boy's self-image. There is more to learn about Rudy the person and the ways his learning problems are affecting him emotionally.

Neuropsychological Assessment

A neuropsychological assessment usually begins with tests of intelligence and achievement. These tests not only provide information about the children's intellectual level and academic progress; but, more important, they also provide clues about what psychological functions might be affected by organic brain damage. As we have seen, the manifestations of brain damage may range from a slight deficit in sensorimotor abilities to a pervasive disruption of every aspect of a child's intellectual and personality functioning. It follows that there can be no single diagnostic test for organicity.

If brain damage potentially affects a variety of functions, then a battery of tests casting a wide psychological net would seem to provide a reasonable strategy for capturing the elusive problem. One such comprehensive test is the *NEPSY*, a test specifically designed for the assessment of neuropsychological functions in children ages 3 to 12. Based on the Russian psychologist Luria's (1980) model of cognition, the NEPSY assesses functioning in five core domains: *Attention/Executive Functions, Language, Sensorimotor, Visuospatial,* and *Memory/Learning.* Each domain is assessed via a set of core subtests, while additional expanded subtests can be added to further clarify the referral question.

The diversity of the tests may be seen in the following sampling. Among the *Attention/Executive Function* tasks is the *Tower,* a board with three pegs on which an array of differently colored beads is placed. The child must move the beads to match the display represented by a model, but in no more—and no less—than a prescribed number of moves. Thus, the child is required not only to use good planning and nonverbal problem-solving skills but to inhibit the impulse to solve the problem too quickly. In turn, the *Auditory Attention and Response Set* subtest presents the child with a box of colored tiles and an audiotaped voice that reads off random words interspersed with the word "red." At first, each time the child hears the word "red," the task is to put a red tile in a box. The second phase is more difficult in that in this pass through, each time the child hears the word "red," the task is to put a yellow tile in the box, whereas the word "yellow" is the signal to put in a red tile, and the word "blue" indicates that a blue tile should be placed. The test allows for observation of errors of *commission* (false positives: that is, placing a red tile in the box when "red" is not called) and *omission* (false negatives: that is, failing to place a tile when "red" is called). While acts of commission generally reflect impulsivity, acts of omission are related to inattentiveness.

Among the *Language* subtests, Comprehension of Instructions requires the child to demonstrate good receptive language skills by following the examiner's directions, while Verbal Fluency assesses facility of verbal skills by asking the child to name quickly as many objects as possible that fit into a given semantic or phonemic category (e.g., types of food or words that start with the letter "J"). Sensorimotor functions are assessed by subtests such as Imitating Hand Positions, in which the child must demonstrate good motor coordination and imitation, while Memory tasks include memory for faces, names, sentences, and lists. Among the *Visuospatial Processing* tasks is Route Finding, in which the child must show an understanding of directionality, orientation, and spatial relationships by tracing the pathway that one would take to get from one point to another.

Another addition to the neuropsychologists' armamentarium is the Delis-Kaplan Executive Function System (*D-KEFS*) (Delis, Kaplan, & Kramer, 2001). This test is designed to measure important executive functions that have been implicated in many of the psychopathologies we have discussed, such as flexibility of thinking, problem solving, planning, impulse control, inhibition, concept formation, and creativity in individuals aged 8 to 89. For example, similar to the well-known Wisconsin Cart Sorting Test (Heaton, Chelune, Talley, Kay, & Curtiss, 1993), the D-KEFS *Card Sort* presents the child with a set of cards with both perceptual stimuli and printed words. First, the child is invited to sort the cards into two groups using as many different concepts or rules as possible. Then, the examiner sorts the cards and the child is required to identify and describe the rules or concepts that were used. The *Trail Making Test* assesses flexibility of thinking by asking the child to connect marks on a page according to shifting rules (e.g., by connecting just the letters, just the numbers, or switching between the letters or numbers) while the *Proverb Test* assesses the child's ability to abstract the interpretation of a familiar saying. The D-KEFS also includes a *Tower Test* that parallels the NEPSY.

The *Woodcock Johnson III Tests of Cognitive Abilities* (Woodcock, McGrew, & Mather, 2001b) also assesses a number of cognitive functions of interest to the neuropsychologist, including verbal comprehension, short-term memory, long-term storage and retrieval, visual-spatial thinking, auditory processing, auditory attention, fluid reasoning, processing speed, working memory, comprehension and knowledge, and executive processing.

Tests of Attention Although tests of attention are included in most of the comprehensive neuropsychological batteries, there are several stand-alone tests of attentional processes that are frequently used by psychologists who are asked to rule out the diagnosis of ADHD. Conner's *Continuous Performance Test* (CPT II; Conners, 2000) is a computer-based instrument that assesses visual attention by asking the child to click the mouse button every time an "X" appears on the screen. Indices are scored related to inattentiveness (e.g., omission errors, slow reaction time), impulsivity (e.g., commission errors, fast reaction time), and lack of vigilance (e.g., slowing reaction time as the test progresses). The *Test of Variables of Attention-Auditory* (Greenberg & Waldman, 1993) is another computer-based assessment tool that also tests auditory attention by asking the child to respond every time a specific tone is heard.

Given the discrepancies between Rudy's performance on tasks assessing different areas of intelligence on the WISC-IV, you decide to follow up with a neuropsychological screening. Given that Christina wants to know if her neighbor was correct in saying that ADHD was the explanation for his behavior problems in the classroom, you select an instrument that will allow you to assess his attention as well. On the NEPSY, you find that his skills are in the average range overall. However, the pattern of scores is of interest. Although still in the average range, Rudy's scores on tests of executive functions are a relative weakness for him in comparison to his strengths on language and sensorimotor tasks. His most significant deficit, however, is in the areas of auditory attention. While his ability to attend to auditory information is adequate when the stimuli presented are simple and unambiguous, his attentional efficiency is markedly reduced when stimuli become more complex. His errors generally are those of commission (responding with false positives), which generally is considered a sign of impulsivity.

Socioemotional Assessment

Parent and Teacher Report Scales

One of the most widely used adult-report inventories is the *Child Behavior Checklist* (CBCL; Achenbach & Rescorla, 2001), which was described in Chapter 3.

There are different forms for parents (CBCL) and teachers (Teacher Report Form), and norms are provided for children from 4 to 16 years of age. Figure 16.6 presents a segment of the parent-report version of the CBCL.

The *Behavior Assessment System for Children* (BASC; Reynolds & Kamphaus, 1992) similarly includes both parent- and teacher-report versions. The *Parent Rating Scale* (PRS) includes scales of Adaptability, Anxiety, Aggression, Attention Problems, Atypicality, Conduct Problems, Depression, Hyperactivity, Leadership, Social Skills, Somatization, and

Figure 16.6   Excerpt from the Parent Version of the Child Behavior Checklist.

Please print. Be sure to answer all items.

Below is a list of items that describe children and youths. For each item that describes your child **now or within the past 6 months**, please circle the **2** if the item is **very true or often true** of your child. Circle the **1** if the item is **somewhat or sometimes true** of your child. If the item is **not true** of your child, circle the **0**. Please answer all items as well as you can, even if some do not seem to apply to your child.

0 = Not True (as far as you know)   1 = Somewhat or Sometimes True   2 = Very True or Often True

0 1 2   1. Acts too young for his/her age
0 1 2   2. Drinks alcohol without parents approval (describe): _____

0 1 2   3. Argues a lot
0 1 2   4. Fails to finish things he/she starts

0 1 2   5. There is very little he/she enjoys
0 1 2   6. Bowel movements outside toilet

0 1 2   7. Bragging, boasting
0 1 2   8. Can't concentrate, can't pay attention for long

0 1 2   9. Can't get his/her mind off certain thoughts; obsessions (describe): _____

0 1 2   10. Can't sit still, restless, or hyperactive

0 1 2   11. Clings to adults or too dependent
0 1 2   12. Complains of loneliness

0 1 2   13. Confused or seems to be in a fog
0 1 2   14. Cries a lot

0 1 2   32. Feels he/she has to be perfect
0 1 2   33. Feels or complains that no one loves him/her

0 1 2   34. Feels others are out to get him/her
0 1 2   35. Feels worthless or inferior

0 1 2   36. Gets hurt a lot, accident-prone
0 1 2   37. Gets in many fights

0 1 2   38. Gets teased a lot
0 1 2   39. Hangs around with others who get in trouble

0 1 2   40. Hears sound or voices that aren't there (describe): _____

0 1 2   41. Impulsive or acts without thinking

0 1 2   42. Would rather be alone than with others
0 1 2   43. Lying or cheating

0 1 2   44. Bites fingernails
0 1 2   45. Nervous, highstrung, or tense

0 1 2   46. Nervous movements or twitching (describe): _____

From Achenbach and Rescorla, 2001.

Table 16.3

BASC Parent Rating Scale

Scales and Key Symptoms	
Adaptability	Adjusts to changes in routines and plans, adjusts well to new teachers, shares toys or other possessions with others
Aggression	Argues with, bullies, teases, hits, threatens, and blames others
Anxiety	Exhibits nervousness, worry, guilt, dread, fear, and sensitivity to criticism
Attention Problems	Does not complete work, has difficulty concentrating and attending, forgets things, and does not listen to directions
Atypicality	Has urges to hurt self, hears name when alone, cannot control thoughts, and hears voices
Conduct Problems	Drinks alcohol, uses illegal drugs, or chews tobacco; steals and lies, has been suspended from school, or is in trouble with police
Depression	Complains that no one listens to or understands him or her; cries, is sad, pouts, whines, and complains of loneliness
Hyperactivity	Acts impulsively, interrupts others, and has tantrums: is restless, leaves seat, and climbs on things
Leadership	Is creative, energetic, and good at facilitating the work of others; joins clubs and participates in extracurricular activities
Social Skills	Compliments and congratulates others, and makes suggestions tactfully; has good manners and smiles at others
Somatization	Complains about health, dizziness, heart palpitations, pain, shortness of breath, and being cold; has headaches and stomach problems
Withdrawal	Avoids others and competition: is extremely shy and refuses to join group activities

Source: Adapted from Reynolds and Kamphaus, 1992.

Withdrawal. There are separate versions for preschoolers, school-age children, and adolescents. (See Table 16.3 for a description of the items loading on each scale.) The BASC Teacher Rating Scale (TRS), in turn, includes scales assessing *Externalizing Problems* (aggression, hyperactivity, conduct problems), *Internalizing Problems* (anxiety, depression, somatization), *School Problems* (inattention, learning difficulties), *Other Problems* (atypicality, withdrawal), and *Adaptive Skills* (adaptability, leadership, social skills, study skills). There are separate forms for preschool, elementary, and middle/high school students, with 109, 148, and 138 items, respectively. The PRS and TRS have good psychometric properties and include indices of adaptive functioning (e.g., social skills) that are missing from many measures of children's behavior (Kamphaus & Frick, 2002).

An alternative rating scale, which uses the same form for either teachers' or parents' reports, is the *Devereux Scales of Mental Disorders* (Naglieri, LeBuffe, & Pfeiffer, 1994). There are two versions, one for children ages 5 to 12 and one for ages 13 to 18; each version has 110 items. Three composite scales are derived: *Internalizing* (anxiety, depression), *Externalizing* (conduct problems, delinquency, attention problems), and *Critical Pathology* (autistic features, self-harming, substance abuse, fire-setting, hallucinations).

The *Personality Inventory for Children—Revised* (PIC-R; Wirt et al., 1990), designed for children ages 3 through 16, asks the parent to rate the presence or absence of 420 characteristics (shorter forms are also available, which include fewer items). Scales include depression and poor self-concept; worry and anxiety; reality distortion; peer relations; unsocialized aggression; conscience development; poor judgment; atypical development; distractibility, activity level, and coordination; speech and language; somatic complaints; school adjustment; and family discord. Factor analysis was used to derive four broad-band scales: *Undisciplined/Poor Self-Control, Social Incompetence, Internalization/Somatic Symptoms,* and *Cognitive Development.*

His mother's responses on the CBCL place Rudy well below the clinical cutoff for the disruptive behavior scales, consistent with her description of him as a "terrific kid." However, what emerges on the CBCL profile that was not revealed by your interview with her are a significant number of internalizing symptoms: She indicates that Rudy often worries, feels tense and anxious, has trouble sleeping, and complains of headaches and stomachaches. The fact that the mother is aware of these problems indicates that she has the capacity to be empathic and sensitive to her son, a source of strength that you note.

His teacher's responses on the Teacher Report Form paint a very different picture of Rudy. The teacher rates him high in oppositionality and inattention and describes him as having poor interpersonal skills. Clearly, either Rudy's behavior—or adults' perception of it—is markedly different in the classroom than at home.

Child Self-Report Scales

Syndrome-Specific Measures   Commonly used child-report measures are those that assess specific kinds of symptoms. Particularly useful are measures of internalizing symptoms, about which children's reports may be the most informative. One of the most widely used of these, the *Children's Depression Inventory* (CDI; Kovacs, 1992), is a 27-item paper-and-pencil measure for children ages 6 through 17 that assesses sadness, cognitive symptoms of depression, somatic complaints, social problems, and acting out. The *Revised Children's Manifest Anxiety Scale* (RCMAS; Reynolds & Richmond, 1985), used for children 6 through 17, includes 37 items assessing physiological anxiety, social concerns, worry, and oversensitivity, as well as defensive responding. The *Multidimensional Anxiety Scale for Children* (MASC; March, Parker, Sullivan, Stallings, & Conners, 1997) expands the assessment of anxiety to include Physical Symptoms, Social Anxiety, Perfectionism, Separation, and Panic.

Multidimensional Measures   An example of a multidimensional child self-report measure is the *Personality Inventory for Youth* (PIY; Lachar & Gruber, 1994). The PIY parallels the parent-report measure, the Personality Inventory for Children, and is designed to assess academic, emotional, behavioral, and interpersonal adjustment in children 9 through 19 years of age. Four broad factors are derived: *Externalizing/Internalizing, Cognitive Impairment, Social Withdrawal,* and *Social Skills Deficit.* In addition, three scales were developed to assess the validity of children's responses, including inattentive or provocative responses, as well as inconsistent or defensive responding. While this measure is promising, it is new on the scene and so its utility is still unknown.

The *Self-Report of Personality* (SRP) is part of the multifaceted Behavior Assessment System for Children (BASC; Reynolds & Kamphaus, 1992). The SRP is designed to assess children's perceptions of school, parents, peers, and self. Factor analysis was used to develop four scores. *Clinical Maladjustment* includes scales assessing anxiety, atypical feelings and behaviors, social stress, locus of control, and somatization. *Personal Adjustment* includes scales assessing self-esteem, self-reliance, peer relations, and positive parent-child relationships. Another scale assesses *School Maladjustment,* which includes items tapping problems that might interfere with academic functioning, such as negative attitudes toward school and teachers, and sensation-seeking for adolescents. *Emotional Symptoms* is a composite score that gives an indication of general psychopathology. A lie scale detects "fake good" response sets by assessing whether children deny even the most ordinary, run-of-the-mill misbehavior (e.g., "I never get angry"). Forms are available for children age 8 through 11, as well as adolescents 12 through 18. Norms are available for different age groups as well as for clinical samples.

Strengths of the SRP include a large standardization sample matched demographically to 1990 U.S. census figures, good reliabilities, and some evidence for validity derived from comparisons between the SRP and similar scales of more established measures.

Because fairly good reading ability is required, the measure might not be appropriate for mentally retarded or learning disabled youths at any age. Again, this measure has not been widely used to date.

Other measures have been developed specifically for adolescents. The *Minnesota Multiphasic Personality Inventory—Adolescent* (MMPI-A; Butcher et al., 1992) is a downward extension of the well-known adult measure, the MMPI-2. Scales assess such symptoms as depression, psychopathy, paranoia, schizophrenia, anxiety, obsessiveness, conduct problems, low self-esteem, alcohol and drug abuse proneness, and school and family problems, among others. Validity scales also assess attempts to present oneself in a good or bad light, as well as defensiveness and inconsistent responding. Like the original adult version, the MMPI-A requires English literacy, and it is extremely long, preventing some youths from completing it in one sitting.

The *Youth Self-Report* (YSR; Achenbach & Rescorla, 2001) is used to obtain self-report ratings from adolescents ages 11 through 18 regarding *internalizing* and *externalizing* symptoms, paralleling parents' reports on the CBCL. Scales include Withdrawn, Somatic Complaints, Anxious/Depressed, Social Problems, Thought Problems, Attention Problems, Delinquent Behavior, and Aggressive Behavior. Social Competence scales also assess participation in social activities and peer relationships.

Projective Techniques

In all the assessment instruments discussed so far, the stimulus material is as clear and unambiguous as possible. **Projective techniques** take the opposite tack by using ambiguous or unstructured material; either the stimulus has no inherent meaning, such as an inkblot, or it has a number of potential meanings, such as a picture that is to be used as the basis of a story. Theoretically, the particular meaning attributed to the unstructured material is a reflection of the individual's unique personality. The disguised nature of the responses allows the individual to express ideas that would be too threatening to talk about directly; for example, a girl who is too frightened to talk about her anger toward her mother may feel free to tell a story about a daughter being angry with and defying a parental figure.

The Rorschach

The *Rorschach* is a series of 10 inkblots, which are presented to the child one at a time with the question, "What could this be?" The child's responses are recorded verbatim; and after the cards have been viewed once, the examiner asks the child to look at each card again and to explain what part of the blot was used ("Where did you see it?") and what suggested each particular response ("What made it look like that?").

Although the validity of the Rorschach has been the subject of much debate, in recent years Exner (1993) made three important contributions to Rorschach analysis. First, he took the numerous scoring systems available and *integrated* them into a single comprehensive one. Second, he reviewed the available research and conducted a number of additional studies of the Rorschach in order to develop an *empirically based* interpretation scheme. Third, he provided separate *norms* for adults and for children 5 to 16 years of age, so that clinicians can evaluate the deviancy of a given child's responses in comparison to those of his or her peers.

Exner's system requires the examiner to code each response on seven different criteria. The first of these is *location,* or where on the blot the percept is seen. For example, it might be based on a small detail ("this little spot looks like a peephole"), or the whole blot might be used to create a complex and elaborated response ("this is an aquarium with lots of exotic plants and fish swimming around"). Second, each response is scored in terms of the *determinants,* or features that contribute to the percept described. These include such features as the form of the blot ("it is a bat because it is shaped like one") or its color or shading ("this gray part makes it look fuzzy and furry, like a bear skin rug"). Third, *form quality* is assessed, which concerns how well the percept actually fits the blot; for example, poor form quality would be indicated by a response that in no way follows the outline or features of the blot presented. The *content* of the percept is also recorded—that is, whether the percept involves humans, animals, or objects.

Popularity is noted in terms of whether the percept is one that is commonly seen by others. *Organizational activity* concerns the degree of cognitive effort required to organize and integrate the parts of the blot into a coherent response; for example, the "aquarium" response quoted previously would be rated as high in organization. Lastly, *special scores* are given to certain responses, such as those that include violent or morbid themes ("two cannibals eating the brains out of their victim's head").

After scoring the child's responses, the examiner first uses the norms obtained from other children of the same age in order to gauge the developmental appropriateness of the child's response. While some ways of responding to the Rorschach are indicative of psychopathology in adolescents and older children, they are normal for younger children. For example, young children are highly reactive to the color of the inkblots and thus tend to use color as a determinant of their responses rather than form. Because this reactivity to color is believed to represent emotional liability, this is a response style that, while perhaps a sign of immaturity in an adult, is not at all surprising to find in children. In fact, a young child who does *not* give many color-based responses might warrant concern, because this could suggest pseudomaturity and excessive control of emotions (Exner, 1994).

Exner has also constructed a number of scales that allow the assessor to gauge the likelihood that a child's Rorschach responses are indicative of a particular psychopathology, such as schizophrenia, anxiety, conduct disorder, or depression. For example, characteristics of depressed children's responses include a high number of morbid responses (sad or damaged images—for example, "an abandoned house that is falling apart because no one cares about it anymore"); responses based on white space in the inkblots rather than the shaded or colored portions; and a low ratio of responses based on color as opposed to black and white features. Characteristics of psychotic thought processes include poor form quality, incongruous combinations ("a bird holding a basketball" or "a man with three heads"), and bizarre or gruesome content.

It should be noted that, despite Exner's efforts, not all psychometricians are satisfied that the Rorschach

has proven its validity and utility. While there have been a sufficient number of positive research findings to reassure its advocates (see Bornstein and Masling, 2005), there have also been a sufficient number of negative ones to bolster the arguments of its detractors (see Garb, Wood, Cilienfeld, and Nezworski, 2005). The use of the Rorschach, therefore, is still subject to controversy.

Rudy engages readily with the Rorschach, and his responses are well elaborated and imaginative. However, he strives too hard to integrate every detail of each inkblot into his responses, sometimes at the expense of accuracy; and the themes of his percepts are not as highly sophisticated as the effort he puts into them warrants. His responses also include a significant use of white space and few responses based on color. In addition, morbid themes emerge in many of his responses, which tend to involve helpless victims that have been "blasted," "knocked down," and "squished" by sadistic monsters. You note that these responses suggest a child who is striving to accomplish beyond his abilities, and they also are consistent with the key indicators of depression.

Projective Drawings

The *Draw-A-Person* (DAP) is one of the most widely used of the projective drawing techniques. According to Machover's (1949) original procedure, the child is first asked to draw a person, then to draw a person of the other sex. Next, a series of questions follows, such as What is the person doing? How old is he or she? What does the person like and dislike? although the questions asked are not standard across clinicians.

Theoretically, the child's drawing is a projection of both the self-image and the body image. Various characteristics of the drawing are interpreted in terms of psychological variables—a small figure indicating inferiority, faint lines suggesting anxiety or an amorphous identity, an overly large head indicating excessive intellectualization—while the child's answers to the assessor's questions are interpreted thematically; for example, a figure who is "just standing there" suggests passivity, while one who is a cheerleader suggests energy and extroversion. The figure may represent either the "real" self or the idealized self.

The *House-Tree-Person* (HTP) drawing is a variation on this theme in which the child completes three drawings—of a person, a house, and a tree—in order to provide a richer source of data. In theory, the house represents the individual's home life and family situation, while the person represents the self-image and the tree represents aspects of the self-concept that are less consciously accessible (Hammer, 1958).

Yet another projective drawing task is the *Kinetic Family Drawing* (KFD; Burns, 1982). Children are instructed to draw their family "doing something—some kind of action." The active, or kinetic, aspect of the drawing is intended to elicit material related to the emotional quality of relationships among family members. Children's drawings are scored in terms of actions (e.g., cooperation, nurturance, tension, or sadism); positions (e.g., whether figures are facing one another); physical characteristics (e.g., sizes of figures, details, and facial expressions); styles (e.g., whether the figures are placed in separate "compartments," or lined up at the top or bottom of the page); and whether there are distances separating family members or barriers blocking their access to one another.

Validity of Drawing Interpretations While their popularity attests to their intuitive appeal, projective drawing tasks such as the DAP, HTP, and KFD only rarely withstand empirical scrutiny. In general, the scoring systems developed lack sufficient norms and have not been subjected to adequate tests of validity. In some cases the research simply has not been done; in other cases the research has been nonsupportive (Handler & Habenicht, 1994).

There is one point in particular on which considerable research converges. Studies of the DAP and KFD indicate that the *individual details* in children's drawings on which most scoring systems base their interpretations are *not* linked to specific kinds of psychopathology and are not predictive of behavior. Therefore, glossaries to drawing features

that make such interpretations as "large eyes = suspiciousness," "a hole in the tree signifies abuse has taken place," or "family members placed higher on the page are more significant" have not been found to be valid.

However, scoring systems based on more *global* screenings of children's drawings have demonstrated some success in empirical research. For example, Naglieri and Pfeiffer (1992) established a scoring procedure for human figure drawings (the DAP Screening Procedure for Emotional Disturbances, or DAP:SPED) that indexes a large array of possible indicators of psychopathology and successfully differentiates emotionally disturbed from normative children. Significant scores are given to such unusual features as transparencies, missing body parts, shading, vacant eyes, nude figures, and aggressive symbols in the drawing.

In sum, children's drawings are probably most useful as means of generating ideas for further exploration rather than as providing definitive data in and of themselves. As Knoff (1990) concludes, "Projective drawings are probably best used *to generate hypotheses* about the referral situation rather than *to validate those hypotheses*" (p. 101).

A clinical use of projective drawing tasks with children is to focus on the *process* rather than the content of the creation. Drawing is an inherently enjoyable activity, which can help the clinician to establish rapport with children who might be shy or uncommunicative. In addition, through showing active interest in children's drawings (e.g., "Tell me about your family picture. What is everyone doing?"), the clinician encourages children to describe their private worlds in a less threatening way than by direct questioning.

Using the DAP:SPED procedure, you ask Rudy to create three figure drawings in turn: of a man, a woman, and of himself. Initially, Rudy is reluctant to draw a picture of a person, complaining that he's "not a good drawer" and "it will look stupid." Although the quality of his drawing of a man is age-appropriate, it is somewhat sparse and lacking in detail. In addition, his picture is small and shows many erasures and hesitations. He frets over getting the man's hands right, finally giving up and saying, "His hands are in his pockets. He doesn't care." His drawing of a female figure is larger and more elaborated, including many small details, such as eyelashes, jewelry, and hairstyle. When asked to complete the drawing of himself, Rudy balks and protests that it is "just too hard." Finally, he creates an almost unrecognizable squiggle at the bottom of the page and announces, "There!" in a defiant tone of voice. It is the first time you have seen the oppositional side of Rudy that his teachers complain about.

On a subsequent visit, during which your rapport seems stronger and Rudy appears less self-conscious, you ask him to complete a Kinetic Family Drawing. Rudy agrees but this picture too is sketchy and hesitantly drawn. Rudy depicts his little brother high on a Ferris wheel, while he and his mother stand on the ground waving at him. He wistfully describes this as representing a fun day when they went to the fair together "a long time ago."

Many different observations might be made of these drawings. For instance, we might remark on Rudy's attitude toward the tasks themselves. His reluctance to draw may derive from his own harsh criticism of what he will produce. A negative self-perception also is suggested by the odd and inhuman depiction of himself. Moreover, both the process and the content of his drawings reflect an incapacity to play and to be the carefree boy he wishes he could be.

Apperception Tests

The *Thematic Apperception Test* (TAT) consists of a set of pictures about which the child is instructed to tell a story. Each of the pictures is intentionally ambiguous, with the assumption that in attempting to impose meaning or structure, the child will project onto the pictures his or her own needs, desires, and conflicts. For example, a sketchy figure depicted leaning against a couch may be male or female, exhausted or relaxed, suicidal, in a state of bliss, or

merely resting. Because any of these responses is equally plausible, the only determinant of the child's own perception is his or her frame of mind. In this way, the technique is designed to allow unconscious aspects of personality to be expressed. About 10 pictures are selected for a particular child. Specific cards are designed for males or females, children, adolescents, or adults. The child is instructed to make up a story about the picture, including a beginning, middle, and end, and to describe what the people in the story are thinking and feeling. The examiner records the story verbatim and asks questions concerning any elements that may have been omitted.

When interpreting the TAT, most clinicians report that in actual practice they do not use a standard procedure (Rossini & Moretti, 1997). The commonly accepted assumption underlying TAT interpretation is that the protagonists of the stories represent various aspects of the individual's *self-concept,* both conscious and unconscious. Thus, special attention is paid to the protagonists' needs, interests, traits, strivings, and competencies. In the *interpersonal* sphere, themes concerning parent-child and family relationships are of special interest, with the stories analyzed for the extent to which others are represented as nurturing, trustworthy, hostile, or unreliable. Stories are also examined for their overall *emotional tone,* along with the effectiveness of *coping strategies* used to deal with the problems generated in the stories.

Westen (1990) has contributed an empirically validated system for TAT interpretation. The Social Cognition and Object Relations Scale (SCORS) integrates psychodynamic theory and knowledge of social-cognitive development to assess individuals' representations of interpersonal relationships. Four dimensions are rated. The first of these concerns the *complexity* of representations of people. A low score indicates a lack of differentiation between self and others while a high score indicates that others are seen in complex and multidimensional ways. Second, the *affective tone* of relationships is rated. A low score indicates that the social world is perceived as hostile and depriving, while a high score is given to responses that include a range of affects but, on balance, present others as positive and trustworthy. Third, the capacity for *emotional investment* in relationships and *moral standards* is rated. A low score indicates that people are represented as being motivated solely by self-interest, with relationships simply as means to achieving self-serving ends; a high score indicates a reciprocity and valuing of relationships with others. The fourth dimension concerns the understanding of *social causality.* A low score indicates an absence of apparent interest in interpreting the internal motivations underlying others' behavior, while a high score indicates an understanding of the thoughts, feelings, and unconscious conflicts that underlie the behavior of people. The SCORS has fared well in reliability and validity studies and differentiates various psychopathological groups, including youths with psychosis, delinquency, borderline personality disorder, and a history of sexual abuse. (For further information, see Alvarado, 1994.)

An effort to adapt the apperception approach to children is the *Roberts Apperception Test for Children* (RATC; McArthur & Roberts, 1992). There are 16 stimulus cards depicting common situations, conflicts, and stresses in children's lives—for example, interparental arguments, child misbehavior, sibling rivalry, and peer conflicts. Four sets of cards are provided, which depict boys or girls with either light or dark skin. The RATC provides criteria and examples for scoring the stories in terms of six *adaptive scales,* including such dimensions as reliance on others, support provided to others, self-sufficiency and maturity, limit-setting by parents and authority figures, the ability to formulate concepts about the problem situation, and the child's ability to construct positive and realistic solutions to conflicts. Five *clinical scales* are rated, including anxiety, aggression, depression, rejection, and lack of resolution. Critical indicators are also assessed, including atypical responses, maladaptive outcomes, and card rejections. Advantages of the RATC include high agreement between assessors, and the existence of norms for children ages 6 to 15 that aid the clinician in evaluating an individual child's adjustment.

You ask Rudy to respond to a TAT card that depicts a boy looking at a violin on a table in front of him, an ambiguous expression on his face. The following is Rudy's story:

"Well, there is a little boy, and his teacher told him to practice the violin, and he doesn't want to practice the violin, so he just sits there staring at it. After a while he fell asleep, and he has a dream and—now I have to think up a dream. He dreamed he was the greatest violinist in the world, and fame and success brought him riches and happiness. He bought his mother beautiful things, and they like lived in luxury. Um . . . these are hard to figure out. He had a special violin, and he couldn't play no other violin because this was the only one that ever worked for him, because there was only one that could play the right tunes. It seemed like magic that it played all right. He kept it by his bedside because if he lost the violin, he would lose his wealth and everything. It was almost like magic. Finally, there came a time when his worst rival realized he could only play that one violin, and he sent some bandits to break up his violin and ruin his career. Just as the bandits were going to break the violin in half, he woke up."

What can we make of Rudy's story? First, it is important to keep in mind that no one story is definitive in itself; it is merely suggestive. Only as themes occur repeatedly and can be fitted together does the clinician have confidence in the interpretation of the data. Keeping that caveat in mind, it is useful to know that this particular picture often elicits stories concerning achievement and initiative, which seem to be important themes in Rudy's life. Rudy's version contains the familiar theme of a child having to do something he does not want to do because an adult says he must. Rudy's method of coping with this conflict is to flee into a dream. Further, most striking is the contrast between the initial picture of the put-upon boy and the grandiose world-famous virtuoso in the dream. However, instead of bringing security, success is accompanied by a state of heightened vulnerability, since a competitive rival sets out to destroy him. These story themes fit with some of the formulations we have derived from other

*data. We might hypothesize that Rudy's striv-
ings to meet unrealistic expectations—to
achieve impossible academic goals and to act
as the "man of the house"—have generated
feelings of inadequacy. In addition, Rudy seems
to perceive aggression and hostile competitiveness to be an integral part of achievement. Perhaps because his actual abilities do not fit with
his expectations of himself, and he fears hostility and rejection from his peers, Rudy with-
draws from the whole enterprise. On the positive side, Rudy's assets include a lively
imagination and an ability to express thoughts
and feelings in a disguised form when they are
too painful to face directly. These characteristics suggest that he might be a good candidate
for psychotherapy.*

Behavioral Assessment

As we have noted, a key purpose of clinical assessment is to understand the basis of the child's psychopathology sufficiently so that the clinician can
design an effective intervention. A prime example of
tailoring the inquiry to a therapeutic procedure is
behavioral assessment. Since behavior therapy
concerns the current situation, assessment aims at
obtaining a specific account of a child's problem
behaviors along with their immediate antecedents
and consequences.

Behavioral assessment utilizes many traditional
diagnostic procedures, but the emphasis differs. In
obtaining referral information, the clinician focuses on the question of who has seen what behaviors in which situations. Similarly, the *behavioral
interview* aims primarily at obtaining behavior-
specific accounts of the problem and the environmental factors that may be eliciting and maintaining it. The behavioral clinician also inquires into
attempts to change the troublesome behavior and
the results obtained. Adults directly involved
with the child's problem, such as parents, teachers,
and relatives, are interviewed. Generally speaking,
obtaining historical information is minimized,
since the clinician is only incidentally interested in
reconstructing etiology.

Some of the main features of the behavioral interview deserve to be presented in detail. To begin
with, the interviewer *operationalizes* general descriptions of the child, such as "uncooperative,"
"withdrawn," or "lazy," by translating them into
concrete *behaviors*. Specificity is of the essence:
"Rudy misbehaves in class" is not as helpful as
"Rudy stares out the window, doesn't answer when
he's called on, and gets into arguments with the
other children." Next, the interviewer inquires concerning *antecedents* (a description of the situations
in which the problem behavior occurs). Next, the
clinician inquires about events that occur immediately following the problem behavior—namely, its
consequences. Here, as in every aspect of the interview, behavioral specificity is sought in terms of exactly who is present and what is done: "When Rudy
doesn't answer me, I call him up to the front of the
class and he always says he heard something rude
from the boy who sits in the second row."

Certain ancillary information is helpful. The clinician may obtain an initial inventory of potential
reinforcers to be used in therapy by asking what the
child enjoys, such as favorite foods, recreational
activities, or pastimes. The parents or teachers may
be asked what behavior they would wish to have as
a replacement for the present objectionable ones.
The clinician may assess the amount of time the parent has to participate in a therapeutic program if one
were deemed desirable and may evaluate the parent's ability and willingness to do so. Finally, the
child may be interviewed to obtain his or her perception of the problems as well as a list of likes and
dislikes.

The interviewer's emphasis on specific behavior
in no way eliminates the problems inherent in conducting any clinical interview. Parents and teachers
are personally involved rather than objective reporters; for example, in the preceding illustration,
the teacher may have cited only Rudy's behavior as
an antecedent and omitted the other child's provocation out of prejudice or honest obliviousness. Thus,
the behavioral clinician must be as skilled as any
other in establishing rapport, constructively handling
negative feelings, judging the accuracy of the information and when it is suspect, finding ways of

eliciting a realistic account without antagonizing or alienating the parent.

Behavior Rating Scales

A number of scales have been developed for rating observed child behavior. While they are reliable and robust, considerable time and effort is often required to train coders to use these systems.

One example is the *Behavioral Coding System* (BCS; Reid, 1978), which was designed to rate children's behavior both at home and at school. Specific positive and negative behaviors are rated, including verbalizations (such as laughing, whining, complying, and teasing) and nonverbal behaviors (such as destructiveness, ignoring, or touching another person). Good interrater reliabilities have been demonstrated, and the BCS successfully differentiates clinical and normative samples, such as aggressive and prosocial boys, as well as revealing significant changes in rates of negative behavior before and after behavioral treatment.

The Child Behavior Checklist *Direct Observation Form* (DOF; Achenbach, 1991) has the advantage of directly paralleling the parent and teacher versions of the CBCL. Ninety-six behavior items are rated, of which 86 overlap with the parent-report form and 73 overlap with the teacher-report form. The DOF requires the assessor to observe a child for six 10-minute sessions, during which a narrative description of the child's behavior is recorded, including the occurrence, duration, and intensity of any problem behaviors. At the end of each session, each behavior is rated on a 4-point scale. Good interrater reliabilities have been demonstrated, as well as correspondence between parents' and teachers', and other observers' reports.

Behavioral Observation

The behavioral approach has made a unique contribution by adapting the technique of naturalistic observation—previously used primarily for research purposes—to assessment goals and placing it at the heart of the process. It is easy to understand this emphasis on direct observation, since abnormal behavior is assumed to develop and to be maintained by environmental stimuli, while behavior modification corrects problem behaviors by altering the environmental conditions maintaining them.

To begin with, the clinician identifies the *target behaviors* to be observed. These are derived from the information obtained from the referral, checklist, and interview, but also should be behaviors for which specific treatment goals can be specified. These behaviors are, in effect, the operational definition of the child's problem. "Uncooperative," for example, might be translated into "not answering the teacher when called on." Other disruptive behaviors in the classroom might include the child's being out of his or her chair without permission; touching, grabbing, or destroying another child's property; vocalizing, speaking, or noisemaking without permission; hitting other children; and failing to do assignments.

The behavioral clinician's next task is to determine the frequency of the target behavior in order to establish a *baseline* for its natural occurrence against which to evaluate the effectiveness of the therapeutic intervention. Observations are scheduled for the specific periods in which the problem behavior is most likely to happen. Depending on the natural occurrence of the target behavior, the period may last half an hour to an entire day, while observations may be made daily or only on particular days. Rudy, for example, may need to be observed for only about 30 minutes in the classroom.

There are a number of different methods for quantifying behavioral observations. *Frequency* involves counting the number of times the target behavior occurs within a specific period. Frequency divided by time yields a measure called *response rate;* for example, a disruptive boy may leave his seat without permission five times in a 50-minute class period, and his response rate would be recorded as 5/50, or 0.10. In *interval recording* an observer has a data sheet divided into small time units, such as 20 seconds. Aided by a timing device (such as a stopwatch) attached to a clipboard, the observer indicates whether the target behavior occurred in a given time unit. Frequently, a *time-sampling* method is used in which the observer observes the child's behavior for 10 seconds, for example, and spends the next 5 seconds recording the target behaviors that occurred in that 15-second interval. This sequence is repeated for the duration of the observational period. Typically, only the presence or absence of this target behavior is recorded. Some data are lost if a behavior occurs more than once during an interval, but such losses are often unimportant. Interval recording is usually more practicable than the frequency method when the observer wishes to record a number of behaviors. Finally, *duration* consists of measuring the interval of time between the onset and termination of the target behavior, a useful method for assessing the amount of time spent in a particular behavior, such as head banging or socializing with peers during class time.

In addition, observation is used to carry out a *functional analysis* of the target behavior. A common strategy for accomplishing this is the A-B-C method, which requires attending to *antecedents, behavior,* and *consequences* that might perpetuate problem behavior (see Figure 16.7 for an example). These data are more qualitative than quantitative, with a description of the child's behavior provided in a narrative form. As always, the observer is aware

Figure 16.7   A Hypothetical Example of Simple A-B-C Observational System of an 8-Year-Old Boy (B).

Time/Setting	Antecedent	Behavior	Consequence
8:30/Math class – copying from board		B takes pencil from another child	Child ignores him
	Child ignores him	B tears paper on child's desk	Child tells teacher and teacher reprimands B
	Teacher reprimands B	B sulks	Teacher allows B to erase board
8:35/Math class – doing seatwork		B leaves seat to sharpen pencil	Teacher asks B to raise hand to leave seat
		B raises hand	Teacher continues to work with other student
	Teacher ignores B	B gets out of seat and pulls on teacher's shirt to get attention	Teacher scolds B for leaving seat and places name on board
	Teacher puts B's name on board	B starts to cry	Child teases B
	Child teases B	B tries to hit other child	B sent to office
8:55/Math class – completing seatwork	B returns to class	B sullen and refuses to work	Teacher allows B to collect assignments

Source: Kamphaus and Frick, 1996.

of the situation-specific nature of the relationships observed and is alert to the possibility that the setting may significantly alter the functional meaning of behavior. For example, a teacher's reprimand may tend to decrease provocative behavior when teacher and child are alone, but it may increase such behavior when other children are present, particularly if they tease or egg on the target child.

Theoretically, the baseline phase should continue until the target behavior has become stable. Because of the variability of human behavior, such an ideal is often difficult to achieve. The general consensus is that there should be a minimal baseline period of one week of data collection. (For a more extended presentation, see La Greca and Stone, 1992.)

Reliability

In order to ensure reliability, researchers using naturalistic observation have found it necessary to train observers. Typically, two or more trainees observe, record, and score the behavior of the same child. Disagreements are discussed and reconciled. Additional observations are made and scored until agreement between observers is at least 80 to 85 percent. Even after training is completed, it is highly desirable to "recalibrate" the observers periodically by repeating the training procedures. Such intensive training further attests to the fact that, the emperor's new clothes notwithstanding, the untrained eye is an inaccurate observational instrument.

Behavioral clinicians rarely have the time or the personnel to train for accurate observation. Consequently, they must rely on untrained adults such as parents and teachers, whose reliability, as might be expected, is significantly lower (Achenbach & McConaughy, 1997). In general, a given individual is consistent with himself or herself over a period of 1 week to 1 month; even after 6 months, consistency is marginal but adequate. Reliability between similar observers, such as between parents or between teachers, is satisfactory but not so high as to prevent disagreements between mother and father or between teachers. Reliability plunges precipitously between adults who view the same child in different situations, such as parents and teachers, teachers and mental health workers, or even teachers who see the child in different settings. This last finding suggests that many problem behaviors may be situation-specific. Thus, reliability is affected both by the implicit definitions and biases of the observers and by the different information input they have in terms of the situations in which they have observed the child.

The Developmental Dimension in Behavioral Assessment

Developmental considerations, while often neglected, need to be integrated into the behavioral assessment process (Ollendick & King, 1991). It is important to be able to compare the child's behavior to *normative information* about what can be expected of a child this age. For example, while a teacher may perceive a school-age child who does not stay in his seat as overly active and disruptive, knowledge of developmental norms will help the behavioral assessor to recognize whether it is the child's behavior that is deviant or the adult's expectations. A second way in which developmental norms for behavior need to be understood is in terms of *patterns of behavior*. Behaviors associated with the same disorder might differ across gender and age. For example, while depression in older boys is associated with "uncommunicativeness," depressed girls are more likely to exhibit "social withdrawal." Similarly, older children with separation anxiety are characterized by physical complaints and school refusal, while younger children show behaviors such as sleep disturbances and excessive anxiety about their attachment figures. Therefore, behavioral assessors must be sensitive to the fact that the signs and symptoms rated change with gender and development. Finally, establishing *rapport* with children is a universal feature of assessment that requires developmentally relevant knowledge and skills.

Rudy's teacher is eager to be of help and agrees to allow your colleague to conduct a behavioral assessment by observing Rudy in the classroom. She makes note of the antecedents and consequences of Rudy's behavior in four specific categories: on-task behavior (doing the work assigned, raising his hand to contribute to the class discussion, asking relevant questions about the material); off-task behavior (staring off into space, engaging in activities other than the one assigned by the teacher); oppositionality (refusing to answer the teacher when called on); and peer conflicts (negative exchanges with other children, including verbal or physical aggression, and incidents in which Rudy is the initiator or the victim). During one half hour, she observes one brief moment of on-task behavior, six incidents of off-task behavior, three of oppositionality, and three peer conflicts. Each off-task incident seems to occur when other students are responding to the teacher's questions, something Rudy never volunteers to do. The episodes of oppositionality occur during arithmetic lessons, and the teacher's response each time is to call him to the front of the room. As he passes one particular boy near the front, she observes subtle provocative behaviors by this other youngster, such as murmured insults, attempts to trip Rudy, and so forth. Rudy's retorts to these provocations are neither subtle nor quiet—his attempts to strike back verbally catch the teacher's attention and land Rudy in even more trouble. The other children seem to watch these little dramas with glee and even to look forward to them.

Clinical Assessment: Art and Science

While differences in assessment procedures can best be understood in terms of clinicians' different theoretical and therapeutic allegiances, there is another related source of disagreement. As scientists, psychologists strive for objectivity and precision, which require, among other things, clearly delineated procedures that are available to the scientific community. It is no accident that psychologists in the past championed the use of standardized assessment techniques over impressionistic evaluations. Nor is it by chance that behavioral assessment, with its explicit procedures for observation and avoidance of inferences about personality characteristics and

motivations, is exercising a similar appeal. Concomitantly, there is a mistrust of the hypothesis-testing clinician initially described in this discussion. While utilizing theoretical and experiential guides, the process by which the clinician generates, tests, accepts, and discards ideas is nearer to an art than a science. He or she may indeed come up with impressive insights but also may be seriously in error; more important—and this is what concerns the critical psychologist—there is no clearly established procedure for deciding in favor of one outcome over the other.

Certain clinicians might answer that scores are only one kind of information to be gained from a test, as we have seen in discussing intelligence tests. To limit assessment to such scores would be to eliminate the added behavioral data so vital to understanding an individual child. If such data have yet to be standardized and are of unknown reliability, their clinical utility justifies their use for the present. These clinicians rightly claim that there are a number of important areas for which no standardized, clinically useful instruments exist. Thus, they can do no more than put the pieces of assessment data together as best they can. Moreover, it is just such efforts to understand complex, heretofore unsystematized data that can ultimately serve as the basis for objective assessment techniques.

While techniques and goals may vary, all clinical assessment requires a high degree of *professional competence*. Clinicians must be skillful and sensitive in handling the many interpersonal problems inherent in dealing with troubled parents and children; they must be knowledgeable concerning the procedures they use and the problems they are called on to evaluate; they must be well acquainted with and abide by the ethical principles of their profession; and they must have received adequate academic and professional preparation, which for a clinical child psychologist typically involves a PhD or PsyD from an accredited university and at least 2 years of supervised experience (American Psychological Association, 1985).

Another aspect of assessment that is more art than science is the *integration* of various discrete findings into a meaningful whole. To return to the case of Rudy, the data we gathered illustrate the fact that children's emotional and behavioral problems have multiple dimensions. Therefore, there is no simple statement that will capture all the richness of the data. There is a *cognitive* component, as evidenced by Rudy's learning difficulties in the area of arithmetic; an *emotional* or psychodynamic component, as seen in his tendency to internalize his distress as well as his conflicts over achievement and aggression; a *family system* component, suggested by the caregiving role he plays with his mother; and a *behavioral* component, seen in his difficulties interacting with teachers and peers.

Which of these provides the "right" hypothesis? Clinicians from different theoretical orientations will focus on the data that present them with the most plausible case formulation and treatment plan for a given child. However, the clinician operating from a developmental psychopathology perspective has an advantage in that no one theory dictates to him or her what evidence is to be gathered nor which data warrant attention. Instead, the develop-

mental psychopathologist will evaluate each bit of evidence and data—regardless of what theoretical orientation it derives from or supports—in order to construct a mosaic that best depicts this most interesting and complex young person. Further, each of these orientations suggests particular avenues for intervention—for example, with Rudy, his family, or the school—that might be integrated into an effective multidimensional treatment plan. Rudy's response to these different interventions, in turn, will provide the clinician with feedback about the accuracy of his or her formulation of the problem and the possible need for further psychological testing. Therefore, just as assessment informs intervention, intervention can inform assessment.

The dovetailing of assessment and psychotherapy that we have emphasized throughout this chapter will become even clearer after we explore the major intervention techniques themselves. This is the topic of our final chapter.

Chapter **Seventeen**

Intervention and Prevention

Conceptualizing and Evaluating Child Interventions

It is estimated that over 200 psychotherapies are currently in use with children and adolescents (Kazdin & Weisz, 1998). (See also Burns, Hoagwood, and Mrazek, 1999, for an extensive overview.) These interventions derive from different assumptions about the nature of psychopathology and different ideas about the means necessary to alleviate it. How is the clinician to choose the best course of action? Our consideration of the topic of intervention requires that we come full circle and return to the theme first introduced in Chapter 1: the various theories of psychopathology. Theory guides the clinician's understanding of what causes—and what might alleviate—children's mental health problems.

In the past, it was often the case that therapists adhered rigidly to a theoretical point of view, whether psychoanalytic, behavioral, or systemic. Adherence to their "brand" of psychotherapy led clinicians to see all cases through only one set of lenses and, in many instances, to recommend the same form of treatment for everyone (Matarazzo, 1990). Following this kind of thinking, clinical researchers set out to determine which was the overall best therapy by conducting studies in which they pitted various kinds of intervention against one another. Overall, the results of these "horse race" studies were not very discriminating. While treatment was consistently associated with improvement, and treated participants fared better than those in the no-treatment group, few differences among therapies were found. As the Dodo in Lewis Carroll's *Alice in Wonderland* declared, "*Everybody* has won and *all* must have prizes" (Luborsky, Singer, & Luborsky, 1975).

These earlier studies were predicated on an assumption—called the *"uniformity myth"*—that one form of therapy would be the treatment of choice for all psychopathologies. Increasingly, the movement is toward asking more complex and sophisticated questions, such as *which* therapy is most effective for *whom, when* (Roth & Fonagy, 1996). Therefore, a better approach is to find the "best fit" for a given child, depending on his or her developmental stage, psychopathology, and intrapersonal and family characteristics. In the same light, another current trend in psychotherapy practice is toward developing *integrative* models that take a multifaceted approach to solving child and family problems. Integration can take place by combining individual and family treatment or by utilizing a variety of techniques drawn from psychodynamic, cognitive, and behavioral theory (see Wachtel, 1994).

Finally, there is a movement afoot to promote the use of *empirically supported* or *evidence-based* treatments (Chambless & Ollendick, 2001). This is particularly the case in the field of clinical psychology, where the Ethical Principles of Psychologists (American Psychological Association, 2002) explicitly call for psychologists to use interventions for which there is some evidence of effectiveness.

In this chapter we discuss ways in which psychopathologies of childhood can be ameliorated or even prevented. Our presentation is selective, offering examples of only a few of the 200 treatment techniques available. (For more extensive overviews, see Kazdin and Weisz, 2003; Mash and Barkley, 1998; and Steiner, 2004.) In the realm of *intervention* we present five of the major therapeutic approaches—psychoanalytic, humanistic, behavioral, cognitive, and systemic—along with the conceptualization of psychopathology that provides the rationale for the therapeutic techniques each employs. As we consider *prevention,* we discuss programs that target at-risk populations in order to prevent psychopathology from developing. Following the movement for evidence-based treatments, we examine the available research regarding the major forms of intervention used with children and focus our attention on those that have received empirical support. First, however, we must consider

how we can determine whether a given treatment is effective.

Empirical Validation: Methods and Challenges

While it might seem a simple matter to prove that an intervention "works," there are actually a number of challenges to this endeavor. For example, a large number of children with the same diagnosis must be recruited. The parents must be willing to allow their children to be assigned to either the treatment or control groups. The assignment to condition must be done on a random basis, and yet these groups should not differ significantly from one another in terms of such characteristics as severity of the disturbance, age, ethnicity, family constellation, and social class. A number of therapists expert in the intervention of choice must be available, and the treatment protocol must be laid out specifically so that all of the therapists carry out the prescribed treatment in the same way. The outcome must be operationalized clearly, reliably, and validly and should indicate that the treatment has made a difference that is lasting and of real-world significance.

Kazdin (1997c) illustrates the ways in which the majority of child therapy outcome studies have failed to hit the mark. Most of the research on child interventions consists of *analogue* studies that only approximate the way that psychotherapy is carried out in the real world. Generally, an analogue study involves the delivery of an intervention to nonclinical samples by inexperienced therapists, often graduate student research assistants. Thus, the therapies are a far cry from the actual practice of skilled professionals, and the children treated do not evidence the high *levels of disturbance* and *comorbidity* that are characteristic of real clinical samples and present significant challenges to psychotherapy. Willingness to remain in treatment is another important factor, and the more disturbed and disruptive children and families are more likely to fail to stay the course; *attrition,* or treatment dropout, is a major problem with real clinical samples. In addition, most of the studies use *narrow outcome criteria* such as symptom relief that, while statistically significant, often lack clinical significance in terms of their impact on the child's life outside of therapy. *Follow-up* is generally only short-term, with a median length of 5 months after termination, so that little evidence is presented for therapy's effectiveness over the long haul.

Further, few studies have made an effort to demonstrate that the intervention *processes* themselves are what account for the change associated with therapy. Whether the intervention targets the acquisition of a skill, insight into an internal conflict, or change in maladaptive cognitions, research should establish that alterations in these particular processes are what lead to improvement. Without such evidence, intervention studies are vulnerable to the challenge that *nonspecific effects,* such as attention from a caring adult—or unintended effects, such as inadvertent positive reinforcement provided by a psychoanalysts' smiles and nods—are what lead to the positive outcome. Finally, the majority of studies neglect to attend to the many *mediating factors*—for example, age, family constellation, quality of the therapeutic relationship—that might influence the impact of treatment on individual children.

Despite these limitations, the research on psychotherapy outcome in general paints an encouraging picture. Effective interventions for children have been developed, and increasing attention is being paid to the need to document their effectiveness with specific problems and across samples. In fact, Kazdin (1997c) makes the following bold assertion: "The basic question about whether psychotherapy 'works' has been answered affirmatively and can be put to rest" (p. 115). The most convincing evidence for the effectiveness of child interventions comes from *meta-analysis,* which aggregates data from a number of studies. The outcome of a meta-analysis is an estimation of *effect size:* Overall, in all these different samples studied in all these different settings, how much difference did treatment make?

A comprehensive meta-analysis of the child intervention research included 150 studies published between 1967 and 1993, involving children 2 to 18 years of age (Weisz et al., 1995). The effect size indicated that the average child who underwent

treatment was less symptomatic at follow-up than 76 percent of the untreated children. This is considered to be a significant effect, in the medium to large range, comparable to that found in psychotherapy outcome studies conducted with adults.

On the one hand, Weisz and colleagues found that *behavior therapies* consistently were the most effective interventions for children, contradicting the "Dodo verdict" reached with adults. On the other hand, only 10 percent of the studies they reviewed involved nonbehavioral interventions. Given the dearth of empirical research conducted on other forms of therapy, therefore, the jury may still be out. In general, *adolescents* tended to improve more than younger children. Curiously, *females,* especially female adolescents, gained the most from intervention. *Experienced* therapists were more effective than well-trained paraprofessionals in treating overcontrolled problems, such as anxiety and depression, but the *paraprofessionals* were equally as effective in treating undercontrolled problems such as conduct disorder. Further, effects were overwhelmingly stronger for *laboratory-based* interventions than for those conducted in "real-life" settings. Finally, effects were strongest for outcome measures that were *specifically matched* to the treatment technique, arguing against the idea that the effectiveness of child therapy can be accounted for by nonspecific effects.

The APA Task Force Criteria

With the move toward using empirically supported treatments, APA Division 12 (Clinical Psychology) launched a task force to define, promote, and disseminate psychological treatments that meet scientific standards. Later refined by Chambless and Hollon (1998), the criteria are presented in Table 17.1. In order to be considered empirically supported, treatments must be tested in studies that meet a number of standards of scientific inquiry. First, the experimental treatment must be compared to a *control group,* whether defined as no treatment, placebo, or an alternative treatment. Second, studies must involve *random assignment* of participants to treatment conditions so that selection biases cannot color the results. Third, the intervention must be carried out with the use of a *treatment manual* that insures

Table 17.1

Summary of Criteria for Empirically Supported Psychological Therapies (EST)

1. Comparison with a no-treatment control group, alternative treatment group, or placebo (a) in a randomized control trial, controlled single case experiment, or equivalent time-samples design and (b) in which the EST is statistically significantly superior to no treatment, placebo, or alternative treatments or in which the EST is equivalent to a treatment already established in efficacy, and power is sufficient to detect moderate differences.
2. These studies must have been conducted with (a) a treatment manual or its logical equivalent; (b) a population, treated for specified problems, for whom inclusion criteria have been delineated in a reliable, valid manner; (c) reliable and valid outcome assessment measures, at minimum tapping the problems targeted for change; and (d) appropriate data analysis.
3. For a designation of efficacious, the superiority of the EST must have been shown in at least two independent research settings (sample size of 3 or more at each site in the case of single case experiments). If there is conflicting evidence, the preponderance of the well-controlled data must support the EST's efficacy.
4. For a designation of possibly efficacious, one study (sample size of 3 or more in the case of single case experiments) suffices in the absence of conflicting evidence.
5. For a designation of efficacious and specific, the EST must have been shown to be statistically significantly superior to pill or psychological placebo or to an alternative bona fide treatment in at least two independent research settings. If there is conflicting evidence, the preponderance of the well-controlled data must support the EST's efficacy and specificity.

Source: Chambless and Hollon, 1998.

each therapist is adhering to the procedures and principles of the particular treatment under study. Fourth, there must be a *defined population* on which the study was based, with clear selection criteria that will allow the investigators to know for whom specifically the treatment was proven successful. Fifth, *outcome measures* must be reliable and valid, rather than being based on subjective or impressionistic ratings of therapist or client. Sixth, *data analyses* must be carried out in an appropriate and valid way. In short, each of these procedures is designed to assure that the study in question is carried out in an empirically sound manner, that the effects observed are due to the treatment and not some chance or confounding factor, and that it is well-enough designed and described that its methods could be replicated easily by another set of investigators.

Further, the task force established three levels of empirical support: possibly efficacious, efficacious, and efficacious and specific. In order to be considered *possibly efficacious,* there must be one well-designed study evident that shows the superiority of the treatment in comparison to the control condition. To meet the higher standard of *efficacious,* the superiority of the treatment must have been demonstrated in at least two independent research

laboratories. To meet the highest standard, *efficacious and specific,* the intervention must be shown to be more effective than a bona fide alternative treatment by at least two separate sets of investigators.

Although the criteria generated a fair amount of controversy (Chambless & Ollendick, 2001; Fonagy & Target, 1996a; Garfield, 1996), they have become increasingly accepted and referred to in the literature on psychotherapy's effectiveness.

Ethnic Diversity and Interventions with Children

As Vargas and Willis (1994) note, despite efforts to increase the representation of ethnic minorities in training programs for mental health providers, it is still the case that most ethnic minority children and families will be treated by clinicians who are not members of their race. Therefore, specific training in culturally sensitive and responsive treatments is a necessity (American Psychological Association, 2003).

In addition, the effectiveness and acceptability of treatments can be increased when they are adapted to the needs and experiences of ethnically diverse populations. We have encountered a number of excellent examples so far, including Santisteban and colleagues' (2003) adaptation of traditional family therapy for substance-abusing Hispanic youths (Chapter 12), Berry's (2001) MALE intervention for delinquent African American youths (Chapter 10), and Rosello and Bernal's (1999) modification of interpersonal therapy for use with depressed Puerto Rican teens (Chapter 8).

As Tharp (1991) points out, cultural issues may be relevant to child therapy on a number of levels. One of these is *cultural differences in pathology:* Particular disorders may be more prevalent in particular ethnic groups, whether because of characteristic social problems, sociocultural practices, or culturally specific definitions of normalcy and psychopathology. For example, hostility and prejudice associated with racism may increase the risk of conduct disorder in African American children; stresses associated with immigration may increase the risk of anxiety in Indochinese refugee children; repeated losses associated with high rates of death and family dislocation may precipitate depression in Native American youths. On the other hand, parents' beliefs about socialization and proper child behavior may lead to cultural differences in rates of disorders. For example, in Thailand, where the culture encourages inhibition, deference, and peacefulness, children are more likely to be referred for internalizing problems, whereas in the United States, where independence and competitiveness are fostered, rates of child referrals for externalizing problems are more common.

Cultural differences in treatment relate both to access and effectiveness. For example, lower-income minority families may be less likely to seek help from mental health professionals, especially from unfamiliar, majority-culture-dominated agencies and professional staff. In addition, research shows that, once they have entered treatment, ethnic minority families are more likely to drop out, often after the first session. Therefore, treatments that are accessible and responsive to minority clients are essential. Furthermore, techniques that are effective in one culture may not "fit" with another. For example, behavior therapists working with Chinese families

report that cultural beliefs about parenting and family structure generate significance resistance from Chinese parents who are asked to play with or contingently ignore their children. (A contrary point of view is expressed by Webster-Stratton and Taylor, 1998, who report good success in overcoming culturally based resistance to their parent training program with low SES, ethnic minority families in the United States.)

Cultural differences in knowledge come into play when the clinician and client hail from different cultural backgrounds. The likelihood that such knowledge deficits will arise is a function not only of the majority status of most mental health professionals, but of the lack of attention to diverse children and families in the clinical and research literatures. Consequently, armed only with an understanding of their own cultures, therapists are highly vulnerable to misunderstanding or even pathologizing culturally normative childrearing practices and values. For example, we encountered this problem in the study of physical discipline versus abuse in the context of African American and European American families. Obtaining such cultural knowledge, however, is complicated by the great *diversity* among and between ethnic groups. For example, the term "Native American" comprises many different tribal groups, each with its own history and practices, just as "Hispanic" families may hail from such diverse cultures as Cuba, Mexico, and Puerto Rico, to name only a few.

To address the issues of cultural diversity, some clinicians advocate the development of *culturally specific* interventions that are addressed to the unique needs and perspectives of the individual culture. A good example of such a culturally specific approach is the Canoe Family substance-abuse prevention program for Northwestern tribal groups developed by Hawkins and colleagues (2004), which we encountered in Chapter 12. However, in general, the thrust is toward the development of *culturally compatible* treatments that can be modified in ways that create a better fit with the child's and family's cultural pattern. (For further reading about interventions for children and families from a variety of ethnic and cultural groups, see Boyd-Franklin and Bry,

2000; Fong, 2003; Gibbs and Huang, 2003; Ho, 1992; Sue and Sue, 1999; and Webb, 2001.)

The Developmental Psychopathology Approach

A number of authors have suggested that an understanding of developmental psychopathology might inform our interventions with children (Cicchetti & Toth, 1992; Shirk, 1999; Steiner, 2004). At the most fundamental level, knowledge of *normal development* is essential (Holmbeck, Greenley, & Franks, 2003). First, familiarity with what is typical for children of a given age allows the clinician to *distinguish normal from pathological* behavior (Forehand & Wierson, 1993). Second, an understanding of the developmental tasks the child faces may help to put the behavior in *context* and explain its etiology. Further, the child's level of *cognitive and emotional development* must be taken into account when selecting an appropriate intervention technique (Shirk, 1988). While the need to adapt to the child's developmental level is obvious, few therapies have actually attended to the cognitive and linguistic differences between, for example, a preschooler or school-age child.

Other principles of developmental psychopathology also have implications for intervention. Attention to *stage-salient issues* may help tailor treatments to be maximally effective for children at particular developmental periods (Cicchetti et al., 1988). For example, individuals may be more amenable to change during times of *developmental transitions,* such as first entry into school, or when poised at the cusp of adolescence. Therefore, interventions might be more effective if timed to take such transitions into account. As Rutter (1990) states: "Particular attention needs to be paid to the mechanisms operating at key turning points in individual's lives, when a risk trajectory may be redirected onto a more adaptive path" (p. 210).

Finally, because problems emerge as a function of *transactional processes,* intervention in those processes provides a powerful way of inducing change (Rutter, 1990). Accordingly, interpersonal relationships are likely to provide a key to therapeutic change in the developmental psychopathology perspective.

An Integrative Developmental Psychopathology Model of Intervention

Shirk and Russell (1996) offer an intriguing reconceptualization of child psychotherapy. Influenced by the developmental psychopathology perspective, they argue for therapists to relinquish adherence to "brands" of psychotherapy and instead link intervention planning to an understanding of *pathogenic processes.* This term refers to the clinician's theoretical formulation of the developmental issues underlying the child's problems, which we encountered in Chapter 16 as the *case formulation.* The case formulation goes beyond simple diagnosis. Because there are divergent pathways to specific psychopathologies, children who share the same diagnosis may not have reached the therapist's doorway via the same road and thus may not share the same underlying pathogenic processes.

Shirk and Russell focus on three major domains of development: cognitive, emotional, and interpersonal. Within the *cognitive* realm, pathogenic processes might take the form of deficits in knowledge or skills, such as a lack of understanding of how to solve interpersonal problems, cognitive distortions and maladaptive schema about the self or others, or simply lack of insight into one's own motivations and behavior. In the *emotional* realm, pathogenic processes might include blocked access to feelings, lack of understanding of emotions, or an inability to regulate and cope with affective states. In the *interpersonal* realm, pathogenic processes might include caregivers who fail to validate the child's self-worth, deprive the child of support and structure, or contribute to the development of insecure models of attachment relationships.

A clear understanding of the pathological processes that brought the disorder about can help the clinician to develop a treatment plan. The strategy is to match the formulation of the pathological process to the most relevant *change process.* These change processes are derived from the major

Table 17.2

Integrating Theories, Case Formulations, and Change Processes in Child Psychotherapy

Theory	Model	Pathogenic Process	Change Process
Psychodynamic	Internal conflict	Symptoms are a compromise between an unacceptable impulse and the defense against its expression.	Interpretation and insight
	Ego deficit	Developmental deficits arise as a function of failure of the environment to meet child's emotional needs.	Corrective emotional experience
Humanistic	Low self-esteem	Psychopathology arises as a function of feelings of inadequacy, low self-worth, lack of self-acceptance.	Validation and emotional support
	Emotional interference	Psychopathology arises as a function of feelings that are not expressed or not accepted.	Encouragement of emotional expression
Behavioral	Maladaptive conditioning	Problem behavior occurs when a maladaptive link is made between a stimulus and a response.	Classical conditioning to trigger more adaptive responses
	Inappropriate contingencies	Problem behavior learned through reinforcement, punishment, and/or modeling.	Operant conditioning to change contingencies in the environment
Cognitive	Cognitive skill deficit	Psychopathology arises when child lacks necessary cognitive skills to cope with life problems.	Skill development
	Cognitive distortion	Psychopathology arises due to distorted, maladaptive, or irrational interpretations.	Schema transformation
Systemic	Enmeshment-disengagement	Overly rigid or diffuse boundaries prevent family members from achieving closeness to or individuation from one another.	Restructuring to strengthen or loosen boundaries
	Triangulation	Triangles and cross-generational coalitions have formed that place children in developmentally inappropriate roles.	Detriangulation child, strengthening marital coalition

Source: Adapted from Shirk and Russell, 1996, with additions.

theoretical orientations, with which we are familiar (see Table 17.2). For example, the formulation that an aggressive child's difficulties are a product of inadequate attachments would suggest that the therapist strive to provide a "corrective emotional experience" via a psychodynamically nurturing relationship. In contrast, the formulation that the child's difficulties derive from a lack of social skills would suggest that the therapist play a cognitively educative function and help the child to learn those skills.

Shirk and Russell limit their discussion to *psycho*therapies, defined as therapies directed at changing internal factors that mediate between the environment and the child's behavior. Thus, they distinguish psychotherapies from *behavior* therapies and *family systemic* therapies, both of which are directed toward changing the environment itself.

However, their scheme can easily be expanded to include behaviorally oriented and systemic interventions; therefore, we have added these two conceptualizations to Table 17.2. For example, the formulation that the child's aggression is being positively reinforced by poor parenting practices suggests that intervention should take a behavioral bent. In contrast, the formulation that the child's behavior is an attempt to distract the parents from their marital difficulties suggests a systemic orientation.

To illustrate their approach to treatment formulation, Shirk and Russell offer the case of "Jack." Jack was a 10-year-old boy brought to the clinician by his single mother, who was concerned about his short temper and inability to tolerate frustration. Struggles at home revolved around Jack's refusal to complete his chores, and teachers complained that despite Jack's good intelligence he seldom completed school assignments. Increasingly, Jack was coming home with bruises and scrapes that testified to his aggressive behavior with peers. Jack showed all the signs of oppositional-defiant disorder and was in danger of sliding down the slope toward more serious conduct problems.

An empirically based approach to treatment planning suggested that Jack was a prime candidate for interpersonal problem-solving skills training (see Chapter 10), one of the most effective techniques for curbing child misbehavior. However, a trial of this kind of therapy made little headway. Jack quickly grasped the necessary concepts and demonstrated the ability to execute the requisite social problem-solving skills, but there was no apparent change in his behavior outside of the therapy room.

Going back to the drawing board, the therapist took into consideration Jack's developmental history, which suggested an alternative formulation regarding the pathogenic processes that led to his behavior problems. During his first 2 years, Jack's mother was the target of physical abuse by his father and was consequently an anxious, depressed, and preoccupied parent. Jack's early life, therefore, was marked by turmoil, unpredictability, and violence. Thus, he developed a set of negative expectations of others, viewing them as unreliable, self-centered,

and uncaring. Sensitized to this issue, the therapist began to notice other evidence of Jack's cognitive distortions: His problems at school were due to his teachers' "unfairness," his mother's motivation to help Jack was to "look good to her boyfriends," the therapist met with the boy only because "he was paid to." A new formulation was developed that centered on the negative schemata that interfered with Jack's ability to utilize adaptive social skills. Accordingly, the target of the treatment plan shifted to the need to change his maladaptive cognitions.

Shirk and Russell's perspective is a promising one. In the short term, they provide a useful guide to case formulation and treatment planning in child psychotherapy. For the future, their work promises to revitalize research on psychotherapy with children by contributing to the development of clear and testable hypotheses regarding the link between pathological processes and the interventions used to address them. Next, we take a closer look at how each of these formulations is put into action.

The Psychoanalytic Approach

Classical Psychoanalysis

The Conceptual Model

Psychoanalytic theory presents us with an inherently developmental model, with the *psychosexual stages* defining the pivotal conflicts to be mastered on the way to maturity. (Our presentation is based on the writings of Anna Freud, 1965.) Consequently, the focus of therapy is on the particular psychosexual stage or stages presumed to be responsible for the psychopathology (see Chapter 1).

Classical psychoanalysis grows directly out of the psychoanalytic theory of neurosis. According to this theory, psychopathology originates in the psychosexual stages, in which the child who is unable to master psychosexual anxieties defends himself or herself against them. The essence of psychoanalysis consists of reversing the *defensive process,* reconfronting the individual with the original trauma so that it can be mastered belatedly. Successful psychoanalysis is epitomized by Freud's aphorism, "*Where id was, there shall ego be.*" The once-overwhelming

A play therapy session.

hates, jealousies, and fears of the oedipal period, for example, can now be revived and viewed from a more mature perspective. The ensuing insight into the root of the problem exercises it. The result is a "*widening of consciousness*" in two senses: The individual can face previously unacceptable aspects of his or her personality, and the energy used for defensive maneuvers can now be employed in growth-promoting activities.

The Therapeutic Process

A general feature of psychoanalysis is the maximizing of free expression during the psychoanalytic hour. With adult patients, this is accomplished through verbal **free association,** which involves speaking freely about whatever comes to mind. However, classical psychoanalysis with children requires major changes in procedures and techniques. In particular, because children cannot verbally free-associate, *play* is substituted.

The use of play presents special challenges to the therapist. Through verbal associations, adults provide the key to the idiosyncratic meaning of events or dreams; since children provide no such key, the analyst is left with the task of decoding the meaning of their fantasies. In order to ensure that the play is rich in the kind of material that will be useful to the analyst, the child is introduced to play material that is *projective,* such as a doll family, crayons, or clay. Such play materials tap into fantasies rather than skills. The analyst watches for signs that a theme is of special importance—signs such as repetition, excessive affect, regression in the form of more infantile play or speech, loss of control such as scattering the toys around, or a "they lived happily ever after" dismissal of a conflict situation.

As with adult psychoanalysis, a major goal of child psychoanalysis is the undoing of the *defense mechanisms* that inhibit self-awareness and emotional growth. One technique for overcoming defenses is to analyze the **transference.** This term refers to the patient's displacing, or transferring, to the therapist his or her feelings toward the parents. The analyst calls attention to transferences so that by exploring them patients can begin to gain access to the distressing relationships that played a decisive role in their neurosis. However, children's transferences, unlike those of adults, do not involve feelings toward shadowy parental figures dating back to the distant past. Instead, the child's current relationships with parents may be acted out with the analyst in a direct and immediate way.

A second technique for dealing with defenses is by analyzing the *resistance.* Since defenses protect the patient from anxiety, he or she will find numerous ways to retain them. The analyst gently and persistently makes **interpretations** that call attention to such maneuvers and help the patient to focus on the threatening material that prompted them. Often this is done through the metaphor of the child's play rather than by confronting the child directly with his or her own feelings (e.g., "I bet that family was really scared when the hurricane started coming toward their house." "Being locked in a closet for 2 years after misbehaving does seem a long time." "The girl doll got angry at her mommy and then suddenly ran away. I wonder if it is scary for her to feel angry"). As therapy progresses, the analyst can build bridges from the safe disguise of make-believe to the child's own feelings; for example, "That hurricane sounds like what you told me about your mom and dad fighting." Through such interpretations the child is led back to the original traumatic situation and is helped to recognize, reevaluate, and master it.

Correctly timed, interpretations produce **insights;** prematurely timed, they are rejected and fuel the patient's resistance. A therapeutic cure does not come in one blinding flash of insight, however. Instead, the same material has to be approached again and again from many different directions and through many different experiences in order for the insight to be firmly established—a process called **working through.** Again, however, children differ from adults in terms of their tolerance for this process. Children often lack the capacity for self-observation

or self-monitoring that enables adults to participate in an intense emotional experience while at the same time observing themselves reacting. Finally, during times of developmental stress such as adolescence, children are reluctant to add to their emotional burdens by confronting their anxieties. Thus, psychoanalysis with children is a challenging enterprise.

Ego Psychology

The next stage in the development of psychoanalytic theory is *ego psychology,* associated with the work of Erik Erikson (1950). Erikson's perspective emphasizes the ego and healthy, reality-oriented aspects of development, as opposed to Freud's emphasis on the primitive drives of sex and aggression. We offer only a brief presentation of ego psychology here.

The Conceptual Model

Erikson's theory of development is familiar to us (see Chapter 1). He delineates stages of *ego development* from infancy to late adulthood, as well as the issues or crises that must be resolved at each step in order for development to proceed. (See Table 3.5.) Psychopathology results when the tasks of a given stage are not mastered and the individual cannot progress to the next stage in development, or when the individual resolves the conflict in a negative way. For example, as in the case of Jack presented earlier, a boy who experiences unreliable care in the early years may develop a sense of basic mistrust that colors his future relationships.

Erikson's model epitomizes the *stage-salient* approach recommended by developmental psychopathology. One of the implications of this approach is that children's behavior problems are not thought of in terms of diagnoses as much as in terms of the stage-salient issues that underlie them. Therefore, whether a school-age child is diagnosed with depression or conduct disorder, Erikson would hypothesize that underlying the behavioral problem is a struggle over feelings of inferiority and lack of industry, while an adolescent with the same diagnosis might be hypothesized to be struggling with identity confusion.

The Therapeutic Process

Consistent with his emphasis on ego functioning and adaptive strivings, Erikson sees the key to change in child therapy as the opportunity to gain *mastery* over conflicts, and the medium for this mastery is play. Play gives the child the opportunity to act out disturbing events and feelings in a safe environment with objects that are under the child's control. As Erikson (1950) states, play allows the child "to deal with experience by creating model situations and to master reality by experiment and planning. . . . To 'play it out' is the most natural self-healing measure childhood affords" (p. 222).

The therapist's role is that of a facilitator of healthy ego functioning. Sometimes this role is played by being unobtrusive and *emotionally available,* allowing the child's natural self-healing processes to unfold. The therapist's acceptance and understanding give the child the opportunity to play out secret fears or hates in order to gain internal peace. Ultimately, however, like the classical psychoanalyst, the ego psychologist strives to facilitate children's awareness of their repressed feelings through the means of *interpretation.*

Erikson made many significant contributions to the psychodynamic understanding of children through his observations of play behavior (Erikson, 1964a). For example, one of his insights had to do with the significance of *play disruptions,* those moments when children abruptly change the themes of their play or cease playing altogether (Erikson, 1964b). A therapist who attends carefully to the process of the session, noting what leads up to and follows after a play disruption, gains insight into the sources of conflict in the child's internal world.

Object Relations Theory

In its third wave, psychoanalytic theory supplemented its traditional concern with the intrapsychic variables (id, ego, and superego) with an emphasis on interpersonal relations. This is the realm of *object relations theory,* which we will describe briefly here.

The Conceptual Model

As we encountered in Chapter 1, the object relations model posits that psychopathology results from arrests in the separation-individuation process due to negative experiences with caregivers. (See Masterson, Tolpin, and Sifneos, 1991.) In more severe forms of psychopathology, inadequate parenting may interfere with the development of an autonomous *self.* The child without a secure and stable sense of his or her own individual selfhood is unable to move beyond the need to use primitive defense mechanisms such as *splitting.* Further along in the separation-individuation process, after children have learned to discriminate the boundary between self and other, threats to healthy development hinge on the valence, or emotional coloring, of *internal representations* of self and other. Affectionless, abusive, or inconsistent parenting may deprive the child of appropriate self-esteem as well as the capacity for interpersonal trust. The result is an internal model of others as unreliable and unloving and of the self as unlovable. The therapist's task, therefore, is to assess the point in development at which the child is arrested and to supply a *corrective emotional experience* that will help development return again to its normal course.

The Therapeutic Process

As with classical psychoanalysis, the therapist understands the children's internal world through *transference.* Children's feelings and expectations about relationships come to life in the therapy session as they are reenacted with the therapist. However, just as the role of relationships is crucial in the etiology of psychopathology, the *therapeutic relationship* is critical to the effectiveness of object relations therapy. In contrast to the Freudian model, the psychoanalyst is more than a detached observer and interpreter. The therapist's real, human presence is an important part of object relations therapy's curative power: "Psychoanalytic interpretation is not therapeutic *per se,* but only as it expresses a personal relationship of genuine understanding" (Guntrip, 1986, p. 448).

An object relations therapist who epitomizes this approach is D. W. Winnicott (1975). Although much of Winnicott's work was with children, a revealing portrait of his therapeutic style was presented by one of his adult analysands, Harry Guntrip (1986), who contrasted Winnicott's warm and personable manner with the "blank screen" presentation of his previous, more classically styled psychoanalyst.

Winnicott's technique is difficult to summarize and only a flavor of it can be given here. One of Winnicott's techniques to engage children in the therapy relationship is the "squiggle game," in which child and therapist take turns drawing a random squiggle and then asking the other to make something out of it. The squiggles and their transformations introduce playfulness into the interaction and supply the therapist with projective material regarding children's concerns. As part of the ongoing therapy process, the squiggle game allows the therapist to work with unconscious material at a nonverbal level, more appropriate for children than the cognitively and linguistically demanding "talking cure" of classical psychoanalysis.

Again in contrast to classical psychoanalysis, the therapist's own emotional reactions are not considered to be sources of interference in the therapeutic process but rather to be meaningful sources of data. Here the concept of *projective identification* (Chapter 2) comes into play. (See Ogden, 1979; Silverman and Lieberman, 1999.) Children may evoke in the therapist feelings that they themselves are unable to tolerate as a way of attempting to master them. Therefore, an object relations therapist who finds herself feeling stressed and confused during a session with an anxious child, or who feels hurt and angered by the jibes and insults of a conduct-disordered child, might wonder, "What do these feelings tell me about this child's internal world?" As therapy progresses, the therapist's ability to tolerate the child's negative emotions helps the child to overcome the need to use the defense mechanism of splitting in order to keep those feelings from consciousness.

Object Relations in the Family Context

Selma Fraiberg (1980) is another psychoanalyst who exemplifies the object relations approach. She takes to heart the idea that relationships are causal in the development of psychopathology and that they provide the key to ameliorating it. Accordingly, Fraiberg

recommends treating relationships rather than individuals. *Parent-infant psychotherapy* (Lieberman & Pawl, 1993) strives to prevent psychopathology in young children through banishing from the nursery the "ghosts" of the mother's troubled childhood. Through remembering and resolving their childhood traumas, adults can avoid reenacting them with their own children. "In each case, when our therapy has brought the parent to remember and reexperience his childhood anxiety and suffering, the ghosts depart, and the afflicted parents become the protectors of their children against the repetition of their own conflicted past" (p. 196). (See Box 17.1.)

Erickson and colleagues (Erickson, Korfmacher, & Egeland, 1992; Erickson & Kurtz-Reimer, 2002) have continued this line of work by providing home-based interventions for at-risk mothers and young children. The *STEEP* (Steps Toward Effective, Enjoyable Parenting) program is designed to offset the risk of an insecure attachment. The target population is mothers pregnant with their first child who are at risk for parenting problems due to poverty, youth, lack of education, social isolation, and stressful life circumstances. Individual sessions are offered with the goal of helping the mother achieve insight into how her own early experiences of being inadequately cared for triggered her current feelings of sadness, loss, and anger and then to help her deal with these feelings. The therapist also serves an educative function by providing information about child care and helping the mother with issues regarding personal growth, education, work, and general life management. There are also group sessions, which allow the mothers to confront their defense mechanisms, air problems, and gain confidence from mutual support.

Psychodynamic Developmental Therapy

One of the most recent developments in psychoanalytic psychotherapy is Fonagy and Target's (1996b) *psychodynamic developmental therapy for children (PDTC).* Their work is conducted at the Anna Freud Center in London, which, as the name implies, is inspired by Anna Freud's thinking. Fonagy and colleagues were particularly interested in developing

Box 17.1 | A Psychoanalytic Infant-Parent Psychotherapy Session

Annie, age 16, came to the attention of the Infant Mental Health Program when she refused to care for her baby Greg. She avoided physical contact with him, often forgot to buy milk, and fed him Kool-Aid and Tang. Annie herself was the product of an abusive upbringing, and while she could remember the facts of what had occurred to her, she blocked off all awareness of the emotions she suffered—just as she seemed unable to empathize with her baby's distress. The team speculated that Annie's abusive parenting arose from a defense mechanism—identification with the aggressor—that allowed her to keep from awareness of her childhood feelings of anxiety and terror. Her therapist, Mrs. Shapiro, visited her at home.

Greg, 17 months old, was in his high chair eating his breakfast. Mother kept up a stream of admonitions while he ate: "Don't do that. Don't drop the food off." Then suddenly, responding to some trivial mishap in the high chair, Annie screamed, "Stop it!" Both Greg and Mrs. Shapiro jumped. Annie said to

the therapist, "I scared you, didn't I?" Mrs. Shapiro, recovering from shock, decided this was the moment she was waiting for. She said, "Sometimes, Annie, the words and sounds that come out of your mouth don't even sound like you. I wonder who they do sound like?" Annie said immediately, "I know. They sound just like my mother. My mother used to scare me." "How did you feel?" Annie said, "How would you feel if you were in with a bull in a china shop? . . . Besides, I don't want to talk about that. I've suffered enough. That's behind me."

But Mrs. Shapiro persisted, gently, and made the crucial interpretation. She said, "I could imagine that as a little girl you might be so scared that, in order to make yourself less scared, you might start talking and sounding like your mother." Annie said again, "I don't want to talk about it right now." But she was deeply affected by Mrs. Shapiro's words.

The rest of the hour took a curious turn. Annie began to collapse before

Mrs. Shapiro's eyes. Instead of a tough, defiant, aggressive girl, she became a helpless, anxious little girl for the entire hour. Since she could find no words to speak of the profound anxiety which had emerged in her, she began to speak of everything she could find in her contemporary life that made her feel afraid, helpless, alone.

In this way, and for many hours to come, Mrs. Shapiro led Annie back into the experiences of helplessness and terror in her childhood and moved back and forth, from the present to the past, identifying for Annie the ways in which she brought her own experiences to her mothering of Greg, how identification with the feared people of her childhood was "remembered" when she became the frightening mother to Greg. It was a moment for therapeutic rejoicing when Annie was able to say, "I don't want my child to be afraid of me."

Source: Fraiberg, 1980.

a treatment model that would lend itself to the demands of empirical investigation. Their program of research represents a step forward in terms of its clarification of the underlying theory, its operationalization of slippery psychoanalytic concepts, and its explicit links between theory and intervention techniques.

The Conceptual Model

Influenced by the work of John Bowlby, Fonagy and colleagues consider disturbed *self-development* to lie at the heart of childhood psychopathology.

Failures in the early attachment relationship with the parent deprive the child of the kind of social experiences that lead to a positive, undistorted view of self and relationships.

Further, Fonagy and Target (1996b) utilize concepts from social cognitive theory to describe the ways children's assumptions about themselves and others are internally represented. For example, they use the term *theory of mind*, which we encountered in relation to autism (see Chapter 5) to refer to the child's capacity to understand mental states in the self and others. This capacity is deficient in children whose parents lack empathy and emotional responsiveness. Other important mental functions that are disrupted in psychopathology include the ability to *tolerate emotions* and *control impulses* rather than being overwhelmed by them, a *reality organization* that allows the child to explore the world and act in it, and *stable representations* of the self and others.

The Therapeutic Process

The focus of PDTC is to remove the obstacles that prevent children from progressing on a healthy developmental course. This is accomplished by providing children with *corrective experiences* that help them to develop more complete and accurate representations of self and others. The therapist strives to increase children's capacity to reflect on mental states in self and others, to bring their feelings and actions under conscious control, and to develop a "metacognitive mode"—that is, to be able to think about their own thought processes. We now turn to describing how these aims are accomplished.

In order to *enhance reflective processes,* the therapist helps children to observe their own emotions, to understand and label them, and to recognize the relationship between their behavior and their feelings. Next, in order to *strengthen impulse control* the therapist may employ a variety of techniques. One such technique involves the use of metaphor. For example, one child acted out the part of the "most powerful train engine in the world," going so far as to threaten to jump out the window in order to prove his indestructibility. The therapist suggested that really powerful trains have good brakes and interested the child in the challenge of finding his.

Next, the psychoanalytic relationship gives the PDTC therapist the opportunity to help the child develop *awareness of others,* such as an understanding of the motivations underlying people's actions. Children who have experienced disturbed attachment relationships may find the mental states of adults to be confusing or frightening. The supportive and accepting environment of the therapy relationship provides children with a safe place to explore their ideas about interpersonal relationships and correct their faulty internal models. Lastly, PDTC

aims to help children develop the *capacity to play.* The capacity to play is central to the acquisition of metacognitive capacities because it requires the child to hold in mind two different realities: the pretend and the actual. The therapist facilitates playfulness by exaggerating actions in order to indicate that they are "just pretend," and by encouraging the use of play materials (e.g., wooden blocks) that do not make reference to real-world concerns.

Empirical Support

Psychoanalytically oriented psychotherapies do not lend themselves readily to empirical research. Neither the technique nor the outcome it strives to achieve is easily standardized. For example, the mechanism of change is the creation of an intense relationship between patient and therapist; interpretations must be timed just so, so that the patient is ready to receive them. The subtleties of these techniques are not easily put into a treatment manual for therapists to follow in a uniform way. Further, the outcome of a successful psychoanalysis is a change in such hypothetical constructs as defense mechanisms, ego strengths, and internal representations that are difficult to observe or quantify. Thus, it comes as no surprise that efforts to empirically test the effectiveness of psychoanalysis with children are few and far between. By the same token, the difficulties inherent in research on psychoanalysis with children make the efforts that have been made all the more noteworthy.

Psychodynamic developmental therapy is the only psychoanalytically oriented child treatment to be subjected to rigorous and programmatic research. To date, Target and Fonagy (1997) have documented the success of their approach with a wide range of disorders, including depression, anxiety, phobias, posttraumatic stress disorder, oppositional-defiant disorder, conduct disorder, and ADHD. As described in Chapter 10, children and adolescents with *internalizing disorders* tend to respond to psychodynamic developmental therapy better than those with externalizing disorders. For example, Fonagy and Target (1994) found that over 85 percent of children treated for anxiety and depression were no longer diagnosable at outcome, whereas this was the case for only

69 percent of children with conduct disorder and 30 percent of those with obsessive-compulsive disorder. *Younger* children (less than 12 years old) benefited the most, particularly when therapy was *intensive* (four to five times per week).

Next, research on the *STEEP* program (Erickson, Korfmacher, & Egeland, 1992) for preventing attachment disorders (described earlier) is worth consideration, since it approximates a test of the object relations model. A follow-up evaluation conducted a year after the intervention ended, when the children were 2 years old, showed that the treated mothers provided a more appropriately stimulating and organized home environment for their children than did mothers in the control group. In addition, mothers had fewer symptoms of depression and anxiety and better life management skills. Attachment security was not increased in the 1st year, but a trend in that direction was detected in the 2nd year. Finally, van IJzendoorn, Juffer, and Duyvesteyn (1995) conducted a *meta-analysis* of a number of attachment-based interventions for mothers and young children. Results indicated that they were effective, especially when treatment was intensive and long-lasting.

The Humanistic Approach

The **humanistic therapy** approach, also called client centered or nondirective, differs radically from the psychoanalytic and behavior therapies. The humanistic therapist never interprets as does the analyst and never tells clients how to solve their problems as does the behavior therapist. Instead, the therapist strives to create a nonjudgmental and nurturing atmosphere in which the client can grow. While on the face of it the humanistic approach seems simple, in reality, the therapy is based on an explicit developmental model of psychopathology and is one of the most demanding for its practitioners.

The Conceptual Model

Our discussion is based on the ideas of Carl Rogers (1959), founder of humanistic therapy. Rogers stresses the primacy of the individual's *self,* the concept of who one is and of one's relations with

others. As awareness of the self emerges in the toddler period, the individual develops the universal need for warmth, respect, sympathy, and acceptance. It is essential that the people the child loves and values foster the child's need to experience and decide things for himself or herself. This can be done only if the child receives **unconditional positive regard.** Here no aspect of the child is perceived as more or less worthy of positive regard. Children are intrinsically valued, and their experiences are not viewed judgmentally as being "good" or "bad" by adult standards.

Normal development goes awry because of what Rogers calls **conditions of worth.** Instead of unconditional positive regard, significant adults, particularly parents, say, in essence, "I will love you on the condition that you behave as I want you to." Because of the strong need for positive regard, children eventually make parental values into self-values. At this point children are no longer in touch with their true selves, no longer open to experience and capable of deciding for themselves whether an experience is growth promoting. By incorporating alien values they become alienated from themselves. Because of alienation, children begin to distort experiences in order to fit the imposed model of a "good boy" or a "good girl": Perhaps the aesthetic boy believes he has to be a competitive go-getter because this is his father's ideal, or the bright girl is hounded by feelings of inadequacy because her mother disparages intellectual achievement.

The Therapeutic Process

In light of what we have explored in our discussions, we can understand how the humanistic therapist, by offering the child unconditional positive regard, can help undo the damage of conditional love. The focus is continually on feelings because these hold the key to maturity. In addition, the process of therapy is client centered, allowing the child to take the lead in choosing the themes to be explored.

Virginia Axline (1969) is the figure most closely associated with the application of Rogers' principles to child therapy. The major change in the client-centered procedure is the introduction of

Box 17.2 | **A Humanistic Play Therapy Session**

Joanne, age 6, comes into the playroom. She sits quietly at the table and uses clay to make the same thing she does every session: a figure of a man carrying a cane [Joanne's mother's new boyfriend also carries a cane]. Each time, after he is finished, awful things happen to him.

Therapist:	Here comes that man again.
Joanne:	Yes. *(her voice is tense, determined)*
Therapist:	The man with the cane.
Joanne:	Yes. *(she begins to punch him full of holes)*
Therapist:	You're putting holes in the clay man.
Joanne:	Stab! Stab! Stab!
Therapist:	You're stabbing him.
Joanne	*(in a small voice):* Ouch, you hurt me. *(voice changes)* I don't care. I want to hurt you.
Therapist:	The clay man is crying because he is hurt.
Joanne:	*(interrupting):* I *want* to hurt him.
Therapist:	You want to hurt him.
Joanne:	I don't *like* him.
Therapist:	You don't like him.

Joanne:	I don't like him. I hate him. Look this hole went clear through him. It went in his front and out his back.
Therapist:	He gets holes punched clear through him. You'll fix him.
Joanne:	Yes. I'll tear his head off.
Therapist:	You'll even tear his head off.
Joanne:	I know, I know. I'll put him clear down in the bottom of the jar and then I'll put the clay in on top of him and he'll smother.
Therapist:	*(following child's actions):* You tore him into little pieces and buried him in the bottom of the jar.

Joanne nods and smiles at the therapist. Then she goes over to the baby doll, pretends to feed it, holds it tenderly in her arms, puts it to bed, and plays house very quietly.

Source: Axline, 1969.

play material for children below the preadolescent age range. The material is simple and conducive to self-expression—dolls, animals, clay, sand, building materials. Construction toys and games of skill are avoided as being too structured to produce varied and individualized behavior. While the formal arrangement resembles that of psychoanalysis, the purpose is quite different. Rather than using play as the basis for interpretation, therapists limit their activity to reflecting the themes and affects the child introduces. (See Box 17.2 for an example of Axline's technique.)

The technique of *reflection* of the child's feelings is at the heart of the humanistic approach. While easily parodied in the form of mindlessly parroting back what another person says, reflection is a powerful technique, especially for working with children. Children often have the experience of talking with adults who are busy or distracted or who listen with only half an ear. The therapists' reflection of the child's own thoughts and feelings communicates that the therapist is actively listening and taking

the child's concerns seriously. What is more, in the permissive atmosphere of the therapeutic session, the child begins to explore feelings that formerly had to be banished from conscious awareness. In fact, some of these feelings may never have been clearly recognized for what they were. Thus, reflection also serves a defining function rather than being a mere echo of what the child already knows.

The therapist's nonjudgmental reflection also communicates *acceptance* of formerly banished feelings, which encourages the child's self-acceptance. As feelings are explicitly defined and accepted, they become congruent. For example, as the boy realizes his resentment for being pushed into the alien role of a go-getter, and as the girl can face her fear of being rejected by a nonintellectual mother, such feelings become part of the self. The once-divided self is whole again.

The therapist has complete confidence in the client's ability to solve his or her own problems with the minimum of direction—hence, the humanistic child therapist is *nondirective*. After discussing the ground rules for the therapeutic hour and describing the procedure in general terms, humanistic therapists leave the direction of the sessions up to the child. As we have seen, therapists do not interpret the meaning of the child's behavior, nor do they introduce any material from the child's past, from the reality of the child's present situation or from previous sessions. If, for example, they learn that the child has started setting fires, they wait until the child is ready to make such behavior part of the therapeutic session. Thus, responsibility is always on the child's shoulders. What therapists communicate implicitly is a faith in the child's ability to decide what is best for his or her own growth.

Understandably, it is demanding to be a nondirective therapist. First it means relinquishing the role of the authoritative adult who "knows better." Moreover, the therapist's acceptance of and respect for the child must be *genuine*. However, when children are given freedom to do what they like, many of them begin to gravitate toward destructive acting out. Not only that, but they also have a genius for finding ways of teasing, testing, and provoking adults. For the therapist to maintain an attitude of acceptance and understanding rather than self-defense and retaliation requires a forbearing disposition and self-discipline.

Play Therapy

Landreth (2002) has further elaborated the client-centered approach with children in his approach to play therapy. Play has an important role in child development, providing a bridge between concrete experience and abstract thought (Piaget, 1962), allowing children a secure, self-directed means for organizing their experiences, and providing a natural means by which children express and learn about their inner worlds. For example, Landreth illustrates, following the terrorist attacks on September 11, 2001, adults told and retold their experiences, sharing verbally their shock and anxiety. Children, however, rarely talked about their experience, but rather acted out their feelings through their play. Towers were built only to be felled by crashing airplanes, buildings burned, people were hurt, and sirens wailed as the ambulances and fire trucks came to

rescue them. Landreth describes a 3-year-old patient who repeatedly crashed a helicopter into a wall and said vehemently, "I hate you, helicopter!"

In order to help children to communicate about their inner experiences, the client-centered therapist engages the child in a process of sharing that child's world. The therapist is nondirective, allowing the child to fully express and explore feelings, thoughts, behaviors, and experiences through the symbolic medium of play, with the expectation that "playing it out" in itself is a self-healing process. "Child-centered play therapy is both a basic philosophy of the innate human capacity of children to strive toward growth and maturity and an attitude of deep and abiding belief in children's ability to be constructively self-directing" (p. 65).

Consistent with Rogers, Landreth describes three essential conditions for therapeutic growth. The first is that the therapist is *real;* "Genuineness is a basic and fundamental attitude that is for the therapist a way of being rather than a way of doing" (p. 70). Second, the therapist must offer to the child *warm caring and acceptance,* by which the therapist communicates unconditional regard and respect for the child's worth. Third, the therapist must provide *sensitive understanding* of the child's internal world and subjective frame of reference. As the children experience this therapeutic relationship, they gradually come to feel free to be themselves and to value who they are.

One feature that sets this approach to child therapy apart from others, particularly the cognitive and behavioral approaches that we will discuss, is that the focus of attention is on the *child* rather than the "problem." There is no concern with diagnosis because the therapist does not vary the approach depending on the definition of the presenting problem. Instead, the conditions are set for the child to generate within him- or herself the processes that lead to growth and change. As self-healing takes effect, the behaviors or symptoms that brought the child to treatment should naturally drop away.

Empirical Support

While Rogers had an interest in assessing the effectiveness of his therapeutic approach, little programmatic research has been carried out on humanistic therapy with children. However, psychotherapy process research is consistent in showing that therapist-offered conditions, such as warmth, empathy, and acceptance, are related to positive outcomes with children. (See Shirk and Russell, 1996, for a review of the research.)

Behavior Therapies

The Conceptual Model

Behavior therapies are characterized by attention to specific, *currently observable behaviors* of the client, by a concern with *objective measures* of the outcomes of their interventions, and by a reliance on the research laboratory to provide *general principles of behavior change* that can be used as the basis of therapeutic intervention and as a place to put clinical findings to rigorous experimental tests. Rather than being a special set of techniques, behavior therapies are "an *approach* to abnormal behavior . . . characterized by [an] empirical methodology" (Ross & Nelson, 1979, p. 303).

To elaborate: Pragmatic considerations have dictated the emphasis on current behaviors, since these are most amenable to change. Behavior therapists would not deny that such behaviors may be rooted in the past, but the past cannot be altered, whereas the present and the future can. Among ongoing behaviors, the therapists deal with three response systems: *overt-motor, physiological-emotional,* and *cognitive-verbal.* All must be considered in a comprehensive treatment program, since they are not necessarily correlated; for example, a boy who is constantly fighting in school may tell the therapist that "everything is OK" and he only fights "a little every now and then."

In the constant interplay between the clinic and the laboratory, principles of learning have been extensively used to generate therapeutic procedures, while both social psychology and developmental psychology have provided conceptual underpinnings for therapeutic techniques, although to a lesser degree. Perhaps even more significant than the application of laboratory findings is the incorporation of *experimental procedures* into psychotherapeutic practice. The behavior therapist reasons very much like his or her experimental counterpart: If behavior X is due to antecedent Y and consequent Z, then as Y and Z are changed, so should X. The therapeutic intervention, like an experiment, consists of testing out the hypothesis, the crucial measure being a change in the base rate of the target behavior X in the desired direction.

The simplest design in evaluating therapeutic effectiveness is the *A-B design,* in which the dependent measure is evaluated both before intervention (baseline, or A) and during intervention (B). If, for example, a therapist hypothesized that temper tantrums in a 3-year-old were being sustained by maternal attention, he might advise the mother to ignore them. If the base rate went down, the therapist would have evidence that the hypothesis was correct. Such a design is adequate for clinical work because it demonstrates whether change occurs. However, for a more stringent test of the hypothesis that change was caused by the intervention rather than by other variables, the reversal, the *A-B-A-B design,* is used, in which the therapeutic procedure is repeatedly applied and withdrawn. If change in the target behavior occurs only in the presence of the intervention, then a causal relationship can be more readily assumed (see Figure 17.1).

The Developmental Dimension

We have integrated discussion of developmental issues into our description of other forms of therapy. However, behavioral thinking is by definition *ahistorical*—current contingencies for behavior are all that matters and the past is irrelevant. Are developmental considerations irrelevant to behavior therapy? While roundly criticizing behaviorists for their insensitivity to developmental issues in their conceptualization and treatment of psychopathology, leading figures in the field have taken on the task of filling the gap. For example, Forehand and Wierson (1993) present an overview of developmental factors to be considered in designing behavioral interventions for children. They review the literature on stage-salient issues and emotional, cognitive, social, and moral development, as well as considering

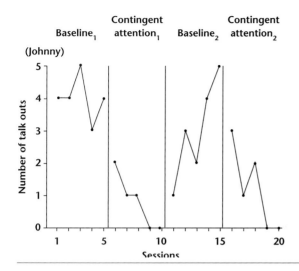

Baseline₁   Contingent   Baseline₂   Contingent
(Johnny)   attention₁   attention₂

Source: Hall et al., 1971.

Figure 17.1

A Record of Talking-Out Behavior of an Educable Mentally Challenged Student.

Baseline₁—before experimental conditions. Contingent Teacher Attention₁—systematic ignoring of talking out and increased teacher attention to appropriate behavior. Baseline₂—reinstatement of teacher attention to talking-out behavior.

changes in the environmental context of development from infancy to adolescence.

From their review, Forehand and Wierson derive three major areas for the behavioral therapist to consider. The first of these is the *cognitive capacity* of the child. For example, younger children require concrete, present-oriented language and cope best with nonverbal modes of interaction, such as drawings and play. With the onset of more sophisticated cognitive abilities, older children may be able to benefit from learning more sophisticated, verbally based control techniques, such as problem-solving skills.

The second area concerns the child's *developmental tasks*. For behavior therapy to be maximally effective, the behaviors targeted for change should be consistent with the developmental tasks the child is currently facing, such as to achieve mastery in middle childhood or to achieve individuation in adolescence. In addition, intervention must target tasks the child has failed to accomplish at previous developmental transitions. This means that the child therapist may need to go beyond the simple presenting problem in order to determine what might have gone awry in earlier developmental periods.

Third is the *developmental context*. Not only do children change over the course of development, but their environments change also, as the social world broadens from the family to include peers, school, and the larger society. The individuals in each of these settings provide contingencies for children's behavior, acting as reinforcers, punishers, and models. Individuals outside the family increasingly have the capacity either to contribute to problem behavior or to help to reduce it. Thus, over the course of development, behavior therapists need to widen their scope of intervention from the narrow focus on parent-child relationships in order to incorporate peers and teachers into the intervention plan.

The Therapeutic Process

Principles of learning—specifically, classical conditioning, operant learning, and imitation—form the bases of behavior therapy procedures. We examine here exemplars of the application of each principle. (For an account of how behavior therapies are applied to various psychopathologies, see Morris and Kratochwill, 1998.)

Classical Conditioning

Systematic desensitization, as developed by Wolpe (1973), is a procedure for eliminating anxiety-mediated problems. In such problems, initially neutral stimuli come to elicit powerful anxiety responses as a result of classical conditioning. The bond between the conditioned stimulus and the anxiety response can be broken, however, by **reciprocal inhibition,**

in which the stronger of two incompatible responses tends to inhibit the weaker. The therapist's task, therefore, becomes one of pairing anxiety-eliciting stimuli with a more powerful, incompatible response. The response Wolpe uses is deep muscle relaxation, since an individual cannot be simultaneously anxious and relaxed.

Two preliminary steps are needed to implement the therapy. First, the child must be instructed in the technique of relaxing various muscle groups throughout the body. The child is also required to make up a graduated sequence of anxiety-eliciting stimuli, going from the least to the most intense. A girl with a school phobia, for example, may feel no anxiety when she awakens and dresses, mild anxiety at breakfast, increasingly strong anxiety while waiting for the bus and approaching school, and the most intense anxiety during the free period before classes start.

In the therapy proper, the children imagine each of the steps, pairing them with the relaxation response. If the anxiety is too strong at any particular step and they cannot relax, they return to the preceding step. Over a series of sessions the children gradually are able to relax in response to even the most intense anxiety-producing stimuli. While Wolpe's rationale has been questioned and the specific variables responsible for improvement have not been satisfactorily isolated, the therapy itself has been successful in treating a host of problems. Systematic desensitization is a mainstay of many empirically supported interventions for child anxiety disorders, including phobias, social and generalized anxiety, PTSD, and separation fears (Amaya-Jackson et al., 2002; Kendall et al., 2004; Morris & March, 2004).

Operant Conditioning

Behavior therapists have made extensive use of the operant principle that behavior is controlled by specific antecedent and consequent stimulus events. **Contingency management,** or the manipulation of rewards and punishments that follow or are contingent upon the response, is particularly potent in decreasing the strength of undesirable behaviors or increasing the strength of adaptive ones. There are two kinds of positive consequences: reward, or **positive reinforcement,** and removal of an aversive stimulus, or **negative reinforcement.** There are also two kinds of negative consequences: *positive punishment,* or the administering of an aversive stimulus, and *negative punishment,* or the removal of a pleasant stimulus.

Examples of the application of operant principles are legion, with some involving a therapist and others involving parents, who not only can be taught how to implement a therapeutic program with relative ease but who also are in a position to control a wider range of behaviors than can be elicited in a therapeutic setting. For example, the language skills of 2- and 3-year-old children were enhanced when their mothers reinforced naming of objects with praise or bits of food, while the tantrums of a 21-month-old were extinguished when the mother ignored them, thereby withdrawing the attention that had been sustaining them.

Instead of direct reinforcement, a child can be given a *token,* which subsequently can be redeemed for rewards such as prizes or privileges. In one therapeutic program children were given tokens for cooperative behavior and doing chores but lost them for undesirable social behavior. In **time out,** the child is isolated for a brief period, thereby being punished by the withdrawal of reinforcers. In one complex program an acting-out boy was isolated for 2 minutes when he was aggressive and disobedient, while less severe misbehavior was ignored and cooperative behavior was rewarded by special attention and treats.

Observational Learning

Observational learning, or **modeling,** has not been extensively employed as a primary therapeutic technique. However, having fearful children observe fearless children interacting with a phobic stimulus, such as a snake or a dog, has successfully eliminated some phobias. The model may be presented either in real life or on film. Modeling is often combined with reinforcement of the desired behavior; for example, in teaching verbal behavior to children with autism, the child is immediately rewarded with food upon each successful imitation of the therapist's vocalization. Another good example of this technique is the pain management modeling described in Chapter 13.

Behavior Therapy in the Family Context

Behavior therapists have also begun expanding their interventions to include various contexts in their treatment plan, such as the family, the school, and peers. It makes little sense to change a deviant behavior while leaving a child in a disharmonious or dysfunctional setting.

Parent management training (PMT), introduced in Chapter 10, is one of the most successful and best-documented programs based on social learning principles. PMT was developed by Patterson (1982), who saw maladaptive parent-child relationships as central to the etiology of conduct disorder. PMT focuses on altering the interactions between parent and child so that prosocial behavior, rather than coercive behavior, is reinforced. As the name implies, this is accomplished by training the parents to respond more effectively to the child. The principles of operant conditioning are central to parent training therapies, primarily used for families in which children display conduct problems (Kazdin, 2003; Webster-Stratton & Hancock, 1998).

First, parents learn how to think about their child-rearing problems in *behavioral terms.* They are trained to identify, define, and observe problem behavior, as well as its precipitants and consequences. In this way, they are better able to perceive their roles in perpetuating child misbehavior and to abandon such unhelpful attributions as personalizing the problem ("I'm a lousy parent") or psychopathologizing their children ("He's a bad seed").

Second, parents learn a number of behavior modification techniques, including the use of *positive reinforcement.* Often, parents who have become caught in repetitive cycles of coercive exchanges neglect the need to provide any sort of positive feedback to their children and seldom spend pleasurable time with them. The fundamental goals of behavior modification are not only to reduce problem behavior but to increase prosocial behavior as well. Therefore, parents learn to use social praise ("Good job!")

and tokens that can be exchanged for rewards when children have behaved well. Reinforcement for positive behavior ("Try to catch the child doing something good") also counteracts the child's experience of the family as a kind of boot camp.

As a parallel to increasing positive reinforcement, parents are also trained to use *mild punishment.* Rather than using such aversive techniques as yelling, hitting, or "nattering" (repetitive nagging complaints without any follow-through) that only exacerbate the problem, parents are encouraged to provide *time out* from reinforcement or *loss of privileges* in response to misbehavior. Typically, these skills are first applied to relatively simple, easily observed behavioral sequences. As parents become more adept, the focus shifts to more difficult and involved behaviors. As children's behavior improves, parents learn higher-level skills such as *negotiation* and mutual problem solving with children. In this way, the overall tone of family relationships becomes more positive and collaborative, as well as being more supportive of children's increasing self-control over their own behavior.

Empirical Support

Behavior therapists have been the most active in documenting the effectiveness of their approach. Outcome studies report success with a wide variety of child behavior problems, ranging from phobias to bed-wetting to conduct disorder.

For example, many outcome studies conducted over the past 2 decades attest to the effectiveness of parent management training (PMT) (Kazdin, 1997c; Webster-Stratton & Reid, 2004). Marked improvement is shown in the behavior of conduct-disordered children, which is sustained as long as 4½ years after treatment ends. In addition, the impact of PMT is broad, with many other problem behaviors improving in addition to the specific ones targeted for treatment. Sibling behavior also improves and ratings of maternal psychopathology, particularly depression, decrease after PMT. Overall, family members report feeling more positive emotions with one another. Thus, PMT seems to alter multiple aspects of dysfunctional family relationships.

Despite its proven effectiveness, there are *limitations* to PMT (Patterson, 1982). For one thing, the treatment is relatively time-consuming: 50 to 60 hours seems to be optimal. Further, not everyone benefits equally. Patterson finds that he is unable to help about a third of the families who come to his clinic. Often these are parents who have serious psychopathology or families that are in crisis. PMT is also relatively demanding: Parents must be willing and able to engage in the extensive training, to implement a consistent routine, and to work intensively with the behavior therapists. A considerable number of parents are too disturbed or too despairing to make such a commitment. Finally, the failure of several studies to find treatment effects has led to the suggestion that parent training should be supplemented by other techniques, such as those that address academic problems or cognitive skill deficits. (See Vuchinich, Wood, and Angelelli, 1996, for an innovative intervention program that integrates Patterson's approach to parent training with cognitive problem-solving skills training for children.) It is to those therapies inspired by the cognitive model that we turn next.

Cognitive Therapies

The Conceptual Model

Cognitive therapies can be distinguished from behavior therapies by their attention to the *mental processes* that mediate between stimulus and response. Rather than changing the environmental contingencies that reinforce child behavior problems, cognitive therapists target the dysfunctional and maladaptive *beliefs* that guide behavior. The basic goal is to change the way the child thinks. When this has been accomplished, behavior will also change.

There is not actually a strict dichotomy between behavior and cognitive therapies. Behavior therapists employ cognitive elements as a means of achieving behavioral change; in desensitization, for example, children imagine various situations and instruct themselves to relax, both of which are cognitive activities. For their part, cognitive therapies are consistent with their behaviorist roots in that they concern themselves with changing specific observ-

able behaviors, systematically monitor the relation between intervention and behavioral change, and retain allegiance to the scientific method. Many therapists combine the techniques under the rubric of "cognitive-behavioral therapy." For the sake of clarity, however, we limit our discussion here to the specifically cognitive dimension of these therapies.

Cognitive therapies have been developed to address a wide variety of childhood psychopathologies, including depression, substance abuse, ADHD, anxiety, sexual abuse, conduct disorder, and autism, among others. We select for presentation three treatment programs—two for internalizing problems (anxiety and OCD), and one for an externalizing problem, conduct disorder. (For presentations of cognitive techniques applied to various disorders in children, see Reinecke, Dattilio, and Freeman, 2003.)

The Therapeutic Process

Cognitive Therapy for Anxiety Disorders

Kendall and his colleagues (Kendall, 2000; Kendall et al., 2004) developed a cognitive intervention program called Coping Cat for treating anxiety disorders in children. The core principle underlying the model is that *cognitive representations* of the environment determine children's response to it. In the case of anxiety disorders, exaggerated perceptions of *threat*—the fear of devastating loss, harsh criticism, or catastrophic harm—dominate the child's reactions to events. The therapist's job is to alter these maladaptive cognitions, as well as the behavioral patterns and emotional responses that accompany them, by designing new *learning experiences* for the child.

The therapists' goals are to teach children to identify anxious feelings and to calm themselves when anxious, to modify their thoughts, to develop a plan for coping with anxiety-arousing situations, and to reward themselves for coping well. Children are taught to accomplish these goals in a series of steps identified with the acronym *FEAR*.

The first step in the FEAR sequence—*Feeling Frightened?*—focuses on helping children to recognize when they are experiencing anxiety. (See Box 17.3 for an example.) Often children do not perceive the connection between physical

Box 17.3 | **A Cognitive Therapy Session for Childhood Anxiety**

Allison, aged 9, was referred to treatment for separation anxiety disorder. During this session Allison and her therapist discuss how she coped with an anxiety-provoking situation one morning when she forgot to bring her homework to school. Annotations identify the FEAR steps.

Therapist: So tell me, how did you know that you were feeling frightened? *(Feeling Frightened?)*

Allison: My heart started pounding.

Therapist: What else?

Allison: Umm . . . let's see. I started biting my nails.

Therapist: Uh-huh. That's a sign isn't it?

Allison: Yeah.

Therapist: So then what did you notice? What were you thinking about? *(Expecting Bad Things to Happen?)*

Allison: I could get in real big trouble here—get punished.

Therapist: That's what you were thinking about. Well, what bad things were going to happen to you? What were you worried about?

Allison: I was gonna get yelled at.

Therapist: You were gonna get yelled at, and if you got yelled at, what?

Allison: I would probably have to stay in for recess.

Therapist: Okay, what about your teacher? What would your teacher be thinking if you lost your health homework?

Allison: Boy, is she forgetful. He'd say, "Why did you take it home in the first place?"

Therapist: He would think you were forgetful?

Allison: Yeah, and he yells. You can hear him all the way down the hall. And when he yells, the kids down the hall can hear him.

Therapist: You might get yelled at, and other kids would know. What would they think?

Allison: They'd just think I was weird.

Therapist: They'd think you were weird. Well, no wonder you were feeling a little scared! Okay, so what did you do about that? How else could you have thought about that? *(Attitudes and Actions That Can Help)*

Allison: Maybe he won't want to go over them today, because he didn't. I asked him at lunch, and he said he didn't want to go over them until tomorrow.

Therapist: That was an action you took to help yourself out. Good for you, Allison; you went and asked the question! How could you have changed your scary thoughts around a little bit?

Allison: I don't know. Maybe he'll just forget about going over them or something, and maybe if he doesn't, he won't yell at me.

Therapist: Well, I think that you should really be congratulated for that action that you took! That's like the best idea I could have thought of—go check it out, you found out what's going to happen. *(Results and Rewards)*

Allison: Before you start worrying your head off.

Therapist: Before you start getting so upset and worried. Yeah, that was excellent!

Source: Levin et al., 1996.

sensations—trembling, stomachache, and so forth—and their emotional distress in a given situation. Recognizing that they are anxious cues them to the fact that it is time to put into place their problem-solving skills.

The second stage is *Expecting Bad Things to Happen*? Here the child is helped to identify the negative expectancies that generate the fear. For example, a child might fear riding an elevator because a "bad man" might get on it or because her parents might disappear while she is gone. However, many young children have difficulty with this step. Their cognitive capacities are limited such that it is difficult for them to observe their own thought processes. The therapist might assist by suggesting possible expectations rather than requiring the child to come up with them (e.g., "Some kids are afraid that the elevator will get stuck"). The therapist uses cartoons with empty "thought bubbles" to help the child identify anxious thoughts and their alternatives in various situations (see Figure 17.2).

The third stage is *Attitudes and Actions That Can Help.* Here the therapist assists the child to come up with more realistic attitudes about the feared event, as well as actions to cope with it. For example, the therapist might ask the child to think about the likelihood of being locked in an elevator or to conduct a poll to find how many times others have ridden in an elevator without incident. Then the child is encouraged to generate possible solutions to the problem. For example, the child might be encouraged to talk about how she could differentiate "bad men" from harmless ones; alternatively, the child might be taught how to use the emergency phone to bring help. New coping strategies are tried out as "experiments," a word that has a playful and nonthreatening air.

The fourth stage is *Results and Rewards.* Here children evaluate the success of their problem-solving attempts and are encouraged to think of possible rewards for coping with the anxiety-arousing situation, such as having a snack, telling parents about their accomplishment, or praising themselves for doing a "good job."

After children have learned the FEAR steps, the next phase of treatment involves *practicing* their new skills in imaginary and real-life situations. Exercises are tailored to the specific fears of a child and are called *Show That I Can* tasks. For example, the child who is anxious about riding an elevator might be exposed to one in increasingly proximal steps, while a child who believes he alone worries might be assigned to interview classmates and report back regarding what they worry about. *Reinforcements* are provided for children who complete their "homework" assignments. The completion of treatment is celebrated with a special session in which child and therapist create a videotaped commercial for the FEAR steps they have learned. Not only does this activity introduce an element of fun

and creativity, but it also helps to reinforce the collaborative and positive relationship that is an important component of the therapy.

While the focus on the intervention is with children, *parents* play an important role as well. Parents often inadvertently reinforce children's withdrawal from anxiety-arousing situations by giving in to their fears. The therapist works with parents to help them support their child's independence from them and to increase their capacity to tolerate the child's short-term discomfort with facing the feared situation. The therapist is also sensitive to the ways in which the parents' own concerns—such as their own anxieties or marital difficulties—might contribute to the child's problems. Consequently, Kendall has expanded the scope of his approach in the form of cognitive-behavioral family therapy (see Howard et al., 2000).

Cognitive Therapy for Obsessive-Compulsive Disorder

Cognitive techniques also are at the heart of empirically demonstrated treatments for childhood OCD (March & Mulle, 1998). After a careful assessment, treatment begins with *psychoeducation* about OCD, in which the child is helped to understand that the disorder is like a "hiccup" in the brain—it causes unwanted things to happen, but it is a problem that can be cured. The child also is given the opportunity to make up a silly name for the disorder (e.g., "Mr. Germy"), in order to externalize it and minimize its seeming power. Next, the therapist and child work together to "*map*" *OCD*; that is, to identify the times and places when OCD "wins," the child "wins," or the outcome is fairly even. This third spot on the map is called the *transition zone,* and it is here that the therapist and child will concentrate their work, gradually expanding the territory that is the child's rather than the disorder's. Further, situations and stimuli are ranked on a hierarchy of anxiety so that the therapist can be guided where to begin, looking for tasks that are challenging but not too threatening.

The next step in treatment involves *cognitive training,* in which the child is taught how to "talk back" to OCD by engaging in positive self-talk.

Self-talk 1: Seeing a big dog in the street

Figure 17.2

Identifying Anxious and Alternative Thoughts.

Self-talk 2: Mom is home late

Source: *Children and Adolescents: An Evidence-Based Approach,* by R. M. Rapee, A. Wignall, J. L. Hudson, and C. A. Schniering, 2000, Oakland, CA: New Harbinger.

Box 17.4 | Cognitive Therapy for Obsessive-Compulsive Disorder

Kristin is a 6-year-old girl who experiences many intrusive thoughts about harm coming to herself, her family, or the planet. In order to prevent these fears from become actualities, she believes that she must compulsively tell her mother and repeatedly seek reassurance. To assist her in developing cognitive coping strategies, such as positive self-talk, the therapist decides to take her through an experiential exercise in the distinction between thoughts and reality.

Therapist: OK, Kristin, remember we said today we'd try to work on the scary pictures that come into your head?

Kristin: How are we going to do that?

Therapist: Well, first I want to show you a trick. Last time you were here you said that "Tummy Tickle" (OCD) tells you that if you have one of those scary pictures in your head and you didn't tell Mommy that maybe it would happen and it would be your fault?

Kristin: I still think that.

Therapist: Well, let's see if we can mess with it a bit.

Therapist: First, I want you to look at that soda bottle on my desk. See it there?

Kristin: Yeah, I see it.

Therapist: Well, I want you to get a good picture of it in your head, and then close your eyes and imagine it in your head. Can you do that?

Kristin: Yeah.

Therapist: OK, good. Now I want you to move the soda bottle in you head from one side of the desk to the other.

Kristin: Do I have to move the real one too?

Therapist: No, just the one in your head.

Kristin: OK, I did it.

Therapist: Great, now make it grow wings and fly across the room like a butterfly.

Kristin: What color should the wings be?

Therapist: Any color you like.

Kristin: OK, it's flying now.

Therapist: Can you make it smile?

Kristin: It doesn't have a face.

Therapist: OK, give it a face and make it smile.

(See Box 17.4 for an example.) For example, a boy who fears contamination by germs and is feeling the impulse to engage in ritualistic behavior might say to himself, "You're not the boss of me!" Humor also is a helpful strategy. For example, a boy who was obsessed with fears of the devil made up his own rhyme to use in exposure situations: "What I once feared will become a bore; the devil is just a metaphor" (Franklin et al., 2003, p. 173).

With these coping strategies in hand, the child then begins, slowly and carefully and with the therapist's help, to move up the hierarchy of fears by engaging in exposure and response prevention. In *exposure,* the child is encouraged to remain in contact with the feared stimulus—initially, this might need to involve very distal exposure, such as being willing to hear the word "snake," or to look at a picture of one. In *response prevention,* the children are helped to use their coping skills to refrain from engaging in the obsessional or compulsive rituals that have bound their anxiety in the past. The goal is for the child to remain in the exposure situation long enough that the anxiety subsides and, a revelation for many children with OCD, the stimulus actually becomes boring. Increasingly, exposures take place *in vivo* and *in situ,* with the therapist's taking the child on "field trips" in which they encounter the feared stimulus in a real-life setting. The last step of the treatment is *relapse prevention,* in which the child is asked to anticipate challenges that might present themselves in the future and to describe ways in which the child might cope.

Interpersonal Problem-Solving Skills Training (IPS)

IPS was introduced in Chapter 10 as a treatment of choice for conduct disorder. As described, Shure and Spivack (1988) focus on building competence in

Kristin:	It's smiling now.
Therapist:	Can you see it really clearly now?
Kristin:	Yes, I can see its bright blue wings and its big happy teeth.
Therapist:	Great, now open your eyes. Where's the soda bottle now?
Kristin:	(Laughs) It's still on your desk, silly!
Therapist:	I thought it was flying around the room like a smiling butterfly?
Kristin:	No, that's just the one in my head.
Therapist:	So even if you see something really clearly in your head, it doesn't mean that it's real, right.
Kristin:	Right.
Therapist:	Let's go back to it now—close your eyes, and give the soda bottle back its mouth.
Kristin:	OK.
Therapist:	Can you make it bite my hand?
Kristin:	That wouldn't be very nice.
Therapist:	Well how about a little bite.
Kristin:	OK, I guess so.

Therapist:	Did it bite me?
Kristin:	Yup, right on the finger.
Therapist:	Which finger?
Kristin:	The little finger.
Therapist:	Why don't you have it bite me on the thumb now, OK?
Kristin:	OK.
Therapist:	OK, now open your eyes again. Do you see any teeth marks?
Kristin:	No.
Therapist:	How come?
Kristin:	Because it was only pretend.
Therapist:	And what does this say about the scary pictures that come into your head, like the one you had today while driving in with your parents?
Kristin:	Well, maybe they're pretend too, and I don't have to make them go away any more.

Source: Franklin, Rynn, Foa, and March, 2003.

five skills found to be deficient in aggressive children. The first of these is to *generate alternative solutions* to a problem. Children are encouraged to brainstorm and explore different ideas without fear of censorship or premature closure. The goals are to assemble a repertoire of solutions that children can draw from and to develop the habit of thinking before acting. One of the hallmarks of IPS training is that the focus is not so much on *what* children think but on *how* they think. Rather than the children's relying on external support for their behavior, the idea is to bring behavior under children's control by helping them think through interpersonal problems and arrive at solutions on their own.

Second, children are trained to *consider the consequences* of social acts. Aggressive children do not generally think beyond the present to consider the possible negative consequences of misbehavior or, for that matter, the positive consequences of

prosocial behavior. Therefore, children learn to consider the consequences of acts of self and other and to develop a less-impulsive response style. The third goal is to develop *means-ends thinking,* to learn to engage in the step-by-step process needed to carry out a particular solution. This may require considering several possible actions and their consequences along the way. The next stage involves the development of *social-causal thinking,* an understanding of how the people in a problem situation feel and what motivates them to act the way they do. For example, this may involve recognizing the fact that aggressive behavior may anger other children and cause them to retaliate.

Fourth, children are helped to develop *sensitivity to interpersonal problems.* Children with poor social skills lack the sensitivity to the cues that indicate that there is a relational conflict between themselves and another person, and they often fail to

Box 17.5 | **An Interpersonal Problem-Solving Skills Training Session**

The following is a dialogue between a kindergarten-age child and a teacher trained in IPS. Annotations identify the IPS techniques used at each step in the process.

Teacher: What's the matter? What happened? *(eliciting child's view of problem)*

Child: Robert won't give me the clay!

Teacher: What can you do or say so he will let you have the clay? *(eliciting a problem solution)*

Child: I could ask him.

Teacher: That's one way. And what might happen next when you ask him? *(guiding means-end thinking)*

Child: He might say no.

Teacher: He might say no. What else could you try? *(guiding child to think of alternative solutions)*

Child: I could snatch it.

Teacher: That's another idea. What might happen if you do that? *(not criticizing child's solution; continuing to guide consequential thinking)*

Child: He might hit me.

Teacher: How would that make you feel? *(encouraging social-causal thinking)*

Child: Mad.

Teacher: How would Robert feel if you grabbed the clay? *(encouraging social-causal thinking)*

Child: Mad.

Teacher: Can you think of something different you can do or say so Robert won't hit you and you both won't be mad? *(guiding child to think of further solutions)*

Child: I could say, "You keep some and give me some."

Teacher: That's a different idea. *(reinforcing idea as different rather than "good," thus avoiding adult judgment)*

Source: Spivack and Shure, 1982.

recognize when a problem is an interpersonal one. Finally, at the highest level of IPS skills training, children develop a *dynamic orientation*. This refers to the ability to look beyond the surface of human behavior and to appreciate that there may be underlying motives that arise from the unique perspective of that person, based on his or her experience in life. For example, a bully may be construed as a bad person who likes to hurt others, as someone who is insecure and trying to prove he is good enough, or as someone who is mistreated at home and is taking his frustrations out on others. The issue is not the validity of the interpretation but rather the ability to see that surface behavior often masks underlying concerns and motivations, an understanding of which can guide a more effective response.

Another contribution to understanding the cognitive basis for children's aggression and behavior problems has been made by Shure and Spivack (1988). They delineate the following cognitive components to *interpersonal problem solving:* a

sensitivity to human problems, an ability to imagine alternative courses of action, an ability to conceptualize the means to achieve a given end, consideration of consequences, and an understanding of cause and effect in human relations. (See Box 17.5.)

There is a developmental unfolding of the components related to IPS. In the preschool period, *generating alternative solutions* to problems such as "What could you do if your sister were playing with a toy you wanted?" is the single most significant predictor of interpersonal behavior in a classroom setting. Children who generate fewer alternatives are rated by their teachers as disruptive, disrespectful, and defiant and unable to wait to take turns. In middle childhood, alternative thinking is still related to classroom adjustment, while *means-end thinking* emerges as an equally important correlate. For instance, when presented with the problem of a boy's feeling lonely after moving to a new neighborhood, the well-adjusted child can think not only of different solutions but also of ways to implement the solutions and overcome the obstacles involved, such as saying, "Maybe he could find someone who liked to play Nintendo like he does, but he'd better not go to a kid's house at suppertime or his mother might get mad!" Again, impulsive and inhibited children are deficient in these cognitive skills.

The data on adolescence are meager but suggest that means-end thinking and alternative thinking continue to be correlated with good adjustment. The new component to IPS involves *considering consequences* or weighing the pros and cons of potential action: "If I do X, then someone else will do Y and that will be good (or bad)." Thus, the developing child is able to utilize progressively advanced cognitive skills to solve interpersonal problems.

Using Manuals Creatively, Flexibly, and Developmentally Appropriately

Having described the content of cognitive interventions, let us take a closer look at the *process* of cognitive therapy and consider how it differs—or might not differ—from more unstructured approaches. One of the advantages of cognitive behavioral therapies, and one of the reasons why they are so amenable to empirical validation, is that they are manualized. A *treatment manual* presents clear guidelines for the therapist and ensures that treatment is carried on in a standardized way across a variety of therapists and clients. However, one of the objections made by psychodynamically and humanistically oriented therapists to manualized treatments is that they run the risk of being rigid, impersonal, and not individually tailored to the needs of the client. However, Kendall and his colleagues (1999) dispel the "cookbook" stereotype of manualized treatments by arguing that they can—and, in order to be effective they *must*—be used flexibly and creatively, with the needs, interests, culture, and developmental status of the individual child in mind.

For example, Kendall and colleagues (1998) describe techniques used to bring Kendall's manualized treatment for anxiety disorders, Coping Cat, "alive" in the United States, Netherlands, Ireland, and Australia. They present a number of illustrations of how therapists bring to bear all their creativity,

clinical skills, and not a little humor in order to personalize the intervention for each individual child. For example, they describe one girl who complained that the acronym FEAR, standing for the steps in the cognitive behavioral procedure, was "boring." Rather than run the risk of losing the child's motivation and interest, the therapist readily invited the child to rename the procedure, which she chose to call "The Happy Helper Steps." However, noticing that both he and the child were now having difficulty remembering what the steps were, the therapist suggested the child create definitions for the new acronym, "THHS." Intrigued and excited, the child created her own steps ("Thou art feeling frightened?" "Hey! Expecting bad things to happen?" "Happy actions and attitudes that can help" "So? Results and rewards") and discovered a new level of excitement and mastery in teaching them to the therapist.

Maintaining the child's active interest and motivation is crucial to the success of manualized treatments, especially those like Coping Cat that challenge children to go outside of their comfort zone and face exposure to what they most fear. The therapist can assist the child by making sure that the tasks are relevant, intriguing and, whenever possible, fun. As the authors state, "being both scary and dull is a lethal combination" (p. 188).

In summary, cognitive interventions, while they do not focus on the relationship as the main avenue for change, rely on the same relationship components that are attributed to the success of other therapies: warmth, engagement, and a therapeutic alliance between client and therapist.

Empirical Support

The cognitive therapies described previously have received empirical support. For example, Kendall and colleagues (1997) randomly assigned 47 anxiety-disordered children to cognitive treatment or a wait-list control group. Those children who underwent treatment showed significant decreases in anxiety on self-report measures, as well as on measures obtained from parents, teachers, and observers. Two-thirds of the treated children were no longer diagnosable after treatment, and treatment gains were maintained at follow-ups conducted 1 year and then 3½ years later. Moreover, 7 years later, children who had undergone successful cognitive treatment for their anxiety disorders were at decreased risk for substance abuse in adolescence (Kendall et al., 2004).

Even more impressive, Kazdin's (1996, 2004) studies of cognitive problem-solving skills training have been singled out as a model of research into therapeutic effectiveness. He and his colleagues randomly assigned a sample of school-age boys with conduct disorder to one of three treatments. The first group received problem-solving skill training. The second group received the same training, but it was supplemented by in vivo practice; for example, they were given "homework" involving applying what they learned in the treatment session to situations with parents, peers, and teachers. The third group received relationship therapy that emphasized empathy, warmth, and unconditional positive regard on the therapists' part, along with helping the boys express their feelings and discuss their interpersonal problems. The children in the two cognitive problem-solving skills training groups showed significantly greater reductions in antisocial behavior and overall behavior problems and greater increases in prosocial behavior than did the children in the relationship group. The effects were present in a 1-year follow-up in the home and at school. In spite of their improvement, however, the children were still outside the normal range for antisocial behavior. Further, gains of this kind of intervention do not always generalize beyond the treatment situation (Southam-Gerow et al., 1997).

Meta-analyses demonstrate that, taken as a whole, the various cognitive therapies for children are effective. However, some questions remain about how this effectiveness comes about. For example, Durlak, Fuhrman, and Lampman (1991) analyzed 64 studies of various kinds of cognitive therapies. Most of the studies involved 9-year-old boys with externalizing problems in brief treatment. The results showed that treated children changed significantly as compared with untreated controls, although their behavior was still not within normal limits. Improvement was maintained over a 4-month follow-up period. Effectiveness was a function of

the children's cognitive level, those functioning at the formal operational level (ages 11 to 13) showing twice as much change as those at less advanced stages (ages 5 to 10). However, contrary to what the rationale of cognitive behavior therapy would predict, improvement was not related to changes in cognition. Thus, the underlying mechanism responsible for change remains to be discovered.

Further, in general, cognitive treatments are more effective with adolescents than with younger children, perhaps because cognitive treatments are modeled on those developed for adults and require a fairly high level of verbal skill, self-monitoring, and abstraction. Indeed, Weisz and colleagues (1995) argue that the effectiveness of cognitive treatments could be improved if they were better integrated with what is known about child development. For example, sensitivity to children's cognitive and language development could help to increase their capacity to understand and utilize the skills being taught to them.

The Family Systemic Approach

Given the importance of the family system in the etiology of psychopathology, it is not surprising that therapists from most schools of psychotherapy, including behaviorists, cognitive therapists, and psychoanalysts, have adapted their techniques to treating families. However, these approaches to working with individuals in the context of the family can be distinguished from approaches that specifically treat the whole family as a system. Our discussions of anorexia nervosa (Chapter 12) and schizophrenia (Chapter 11) introduced the basic premise and some of the concepts generated by the family systemic approach. Here we will examine both in greater detail.

The Conceptual Model

The basic premise is that the family is a *dynamic system*, an entity over and above the interaction of its individual members. Further, the family system has certain characteristics that define whether it is functioning adequately. As we saw in Chapter 1, Minuchin's structural approach (1974; Minuchin,

Lee, & Simon, 1996) introduces two important concepts, those of boundaries and triangulation. For example, in malfunctioning families, *boundaries* may be blurred, resulting in an enmeshed system in which family members are overly involved with one another in an intrusive way; or *triangulation* may result when rigid patterns have formed in which certain family members ally with one another to the exclusion of other family members.

These patterns, once established, are difficult to change. The reason for this resistance to change, however, lies at the heart of the systemic theory of psychopathology: These troublesome patterns serve a *function* in the family system. To take a concrete example, consider the child in the *detouring-attacking* family (see Chapter 1). This is the child whose misbehavior serves the function of distracting the parents from their marital problems. Because there is such a significant payoff for the child's symptoms—the family stays intact—there will be strong ambivalence on the part of family members about relinquishing them.

The disturbed child is merely the *identified patient*—the symptom, as it were, that something has gone wrong. The pathology itself is in the system. Consequently, treatment of one individual within the family system is not going to be effective in bringing about change, because the family will tend to reorganize in order to reestablish the old pattern. Thus, the focus of treatment must be the entire family.

The Therapeutic Process

How does the therapist facilitate change? First, in order to change the system, the therapist must become a part of it. The initial step in the process of forming a therapeutic system is *joining.* Minuchin himself joins the family through his use of self. He emphasizes aspects of his personality and life experience that are consistent with the family's, such as by sharing with an immigrant family the fact that he, too, had to struggle with adapting to life in the United States. He accepts the family's organization and style and accommodates to them, showing respect for their way of doing things. In this way, the family therapist behaves much like an anthropologist taking the role of participant-observer, accepting the way that people define their problems, using their language, and openly enjoying their humor.

The next stage in the process is *enacting transactional patterns.* Here the family therapist encourages family members to show, rather than to tell, so that the therapist can observe their interactions directly. This can be informative in diagnosing the problem. For example, the therapist might note the small smile on the father's face as the conduct-disordered boy describes his pranks, or the way the mother always interrupts to qualify her anxious daughter's comments. The therapist might re-create problematic family scenarios by instructing family members to enact them in the therapy session: For example, if a child is complaining that his father never spends time with him, Minuchin might ask him to turn to his father and talk with him about it. Enacting patterns in the therapy session not only allows the therapist to see family members in action, but also can help family members to experience their own interactions with a heightened awareness. A prototypical example of this technique is the family lunch session used in treating families of adolescents with anorexia, which was described in Chapter 12.

Once accepted into the family system, and with sufficient observation to develop a formulation of the problem, the therapist moves into action. **Restructuring techniques** are the tools of the trade used to alter family patterns of interaction. For example, the therapist acts to *re-create communication channels* among family members who resist talking directly to one another and attempt to route all their comments through the therapist. The therapist may avoid making eye contact, refuse to respond when addressed, insist that family members talk to one another, or even leave the room and observe behind a one-way mirror. Like an orchestra conductor, the therapist signals family members when to speak or be silent. The family therapist also uses *repositioning,* which involves manipulating the physical space between family members in order to alter their interactions, perhaps by moving chairs to physically separate family members who need more psychological

Box 17.6 | **A Family Therapy Session**

When the MacLean family sought help for an "unmanageable" child, a terror who'd been expelled from two schools, Dr. Minuchin uncovered a covert split between the parents, held in balance by not being talked about. The ten-year-old boy's misbehavior was dramatically visible; his father had to drag him kicking and screaming into the consulting room. Meanwhile, his seven-year-old brother sat quietly, smiling engagingly. The good boy.

To broaden the focus from an "impossible child" to issues of parental control and cooperation, Minuchin asked about seven-year-old Kevin, who misbehaved invisibly. He peed on the floor in the bathroom. According to his father, Kevin's peeing on the floor was due to "inattentiveness." The mother laughed when Minuchin said "Nobody could have such poor aim."

Minuchin talked with the boy about how wolves mark their territory, and suggested that he expand his territory by peeing in all four corners of the family room.

Minuchin:	Do you have a dog?
Kevin:	No.
Minuchin:	Oh, so you are the family dog.

In the process of discussing the boy who peed–and his parents' response–Minuchin dramatized how the parents polarized each other.

Minuchin:	Why would he do such a thing?
Father:	I don't know if he did it on purpose.
Minuchin:	Maybe he was in a trance?
Father:	No, I think it was carelessness.
Minuchin:	His aim must be terrible.

The father described the boy's behavior as accidental; the mother considered it defiance. One of the reasons parents fall under the control of their young children is that they avoid confronting their differences. Differences are normal, but they become toxic when one parent undercuts the other's handling of the children. (It's cowardly revenge for unaddressed grievances.)

Minuchin's gentle but insistent pressure on the couple to talk about how they respond, without switching to focus on how the children behave, led to their bringing up long-held but seldom-voiced resentments.

distance from one another. For example, the therapist may sit between a mother and parentalized child in order to block the child from interfering while the mother and the identified patient talk. (See Box 17.6 for an example of Minuchin's structural techniques.)

Another restructuring technique is called *marking boundaries.* The therapist may promote clear boundaries between individuals by ensuring that family members refrain from talking for one another. In addition, the therapist encourages differentiation of individual family members by interacting differently with each of them according to their age and developmental status. The therapist may also work to emphasize boundaries between subsystems, such as between the marital and child subsystems. For example, a boy was referred for therapy because of a dog phobia so severe he could

not leave the house. After interacting with the family, the therapist's formulation was that the mother and son were enmeshed and that the father was being excluded from their intimate twosome. The therapist decided to restructure the family interaction by increasing the affiliation between father and son. Recall that this boy had a dog phobia. As it happened, the father was a mailman and therefore an expert in dealing with dogs. Therefore, the therapist assigned the father the task of teaching his son how to cope with strange dogs. The intervention was a great success. Ultimately, the child, who was himself adopted, asked to adopt a dog; and the father and son spent time together training their new pet. As the father-son bond strengthened, a healthy separation between mother and son was promoted, and the parents embarked on marital therapy.

Mother: Bob makes excuses for the children's behavior—because he doesn't want to get in there and help me find a solution for the problem.

Father: Yes, but when I did try to help, you'd always criticize me. So after a while I gave up.

Like a photographic print in a developing tray, the spouses' conflict had become visible. Minuchin protected the parents from embarrassment (and the children from being burdened) by asking the children to leave the room. Without the preoccupation of parenting, the spouses could face each other, man and woman–and talk about their hurts and grievances. It turned out to be a sad story of lonely disengagement.

Minuchin: Do you two have areas of agreement?

He said yes; she said no. He was a minimizer; she was a critic.

Minuchin: When did you divorce Bob and marry the children?

She turned quiet; he looked off into space. She said, softly: "Probably ten years ago."

What followed was a painful but familiar story of how a marriage can drown in parenting and its conflicts. The conflict was never resolved because it never surfaced. And so the rift never healed; it just expanded.

With Minuchin's help, the couple took turns talking about their pain–and learning to listen. By unbalancing, Minuchin brought enormous pressure to bear to help this couple break through their differences, open up to each other, fight for what they want, and, finally, begin to come together–as husband and wife, and as parents.

Source: Excerpted from Nichols and Schwartz, 2004.

The therapist can also use *positive reframing* to give family members a new perspective on the problem and new lenses through which to see themselves. For instance, the therapist might praise overprotective parents for their desire to be supportive and nurturing, reframing their behavior in positive terms. In this way, the therapist underlines the good intentions behind problematic interaction patterns, thus reducing resistance to finding new and better ways to achieve those ends.

Empirical Support

Robbins and colleagues (2003, 2004; Santisteban et al., 2003) have in progress an extensive program of research on the effectiveness of structural family therapy in contexts of cultural diversity. In particular, their work focuses on treatment of Hispanic families with conduct-disordered and drug-involved

adolescents. In one study, families were randomly assigned either to structural family therapy or to a control condition in which they received "treatment as usual" as it would be delivered in an outpatient setting. Results showed that youths in both conditions improved significantly, with no differences between the types of intervention. However, there were dramatic differences in retention rates. Families in the family therapy condition were overwhelmingly more likely to complete the treatment program: Only 17 percent dropped out of treatment as compared to 44 percent of those in the control condition.

In regard to the effectiveness of family therapies overall, Hazelrigg, Cooper, and Borduin's (1987) review of the available research showed that family therapy had positive effects when compared with no treatment and with alternative treatment controls.

Follow-up studies showed that positive effects continued over time, but the effects were weaker and more variable than at the end of treatment. Again, however, family therapies were more effective than alternative treatments in reducing recidivism.

Prevention

Definition

First, we need to define **prevention.** Preventive efforts can be conceptualized along a continuum. (See Figure 17.3.) At one end are those programs put into place before a problem develops, designed to prevent it from occurring in the first place. This is known as *primary prevention.* An example of this is the home-based visiting program for first-time mothers, designed to prevent child abuse, as described in Chapter 14. In contrast, *secondary prevention* efforts focus on early identification of problems in order to prevent them from blossoming into full-blown disorders. An example of this is a crisis line for stressed parents who are demonstrating poor parenting skills. Lastly, *tertiary prevention* intervenes somewhat later, in order to prevent a burgeoning problem from getting worse or reoccurring. In fact, the line between tertiary prevention and intervention is not a strict one, because most child therapies also have the goal of preventing problems from intensifying or relapsing.

Recall that when we first discussed developmental psychopathology in Chapter 1, we noted that the concepts of risk and developmental pathways could furnish guides for prevention. Developmentally oriented research has been sufficiently fruitful that some of those guides are now available. We have already discussed one prevention program, STEEP, designed to prevent insecure attachment (Erickson, Korfmacher, & Egeland, 1992). Here we will present another preventive program informed by the research on the developmental psychopathology of conduct disorder.

The Fast Track Program

Fast Track (Conduct Problems Prevention Research Group, 1992) is based on the developmental pathway that identifies the early signs of conduct disorder and the contribution of parents, school, and peers to its fruition (see Chapter 10). The target population is first-graders evidencing disruptive behaviors such as noncompliance, aggression, impulsivity, and immaturity. The techniques used are ones that had been tried already with some degree of success. However, the unique feature of the program is the integration of such techniques. In this way the separate components, such as dealing with parents and teachers, can be coordinated and can reinforce one another, and the chances of generalizing across settings can be maximized.

We have already presented two of the interventions: changing parents' ineffectual disciplinary practices and increasing the child's social skills in order to circumvent peer rejection (see Chapter 10). Therefore, in this discussion we concentrate on the more novel components of the program aimed at avoiding school failure. Sessions with the family focused on setting up a structured learning environment in the home and encouraged parental involvement in the child's learning as well as communication with the school. The importance of establishing a positive relation with the child's teacher was particularly emphasized. At school, teachers were trained by Fast Track staff in strategies for effective

Figure 17.3   The Continuum of Prevention and Intervention.

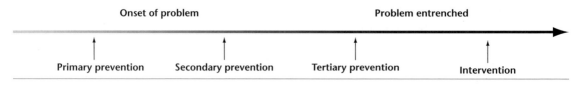

Box 17.7 | **Can Interventions Harm?**

Like the Hippocratic oath for physicians, a prevailing principle in the American Psychological Association's (2002) code of ethics is to *do no harm.* Is it possible that well-meaning therapies could actually make children worse? We have encountered one example so far, in the school-based suicide prevention programs that were found to have the unfortunate effect of increasing distress in the students most vulnerable to suicide (see Chapter 9). Such unwanted negative outcomes of treatment are termed *iatrogenic effects.* Two more examples are offered by Dishion, McCord, and Poulin (1999) who uncovered iatrogenic effects of peer-group interventions designed to decrease youth problem behavior. In the Adolescent Transitions Study, Dishion and colleagues (1988) randomly assigned 119 high-risk youths to one of four treatment conditions: parent only, teen only, parent and teen; and an attention-only condition. The teen-only treatment consisted of group sessions in which youths with behavior problems met together to address issues

such as setting prosocial goals and self-regulation. While both the parent- and teen-focused treatments initially seemed to be beneficial, longer-term outcomes were disconcerting. One year later, increases in tobacco use and teacher reports of externalizing behavior were found for the adolescents who had been involved in the teen-focused groups. Three years later, these iatrogenic effects had persisted, with tobacco use and delinquency being consistently higher for those in the teen intervention than the other conditions, whether or not parents had been involved. Older youths were the most susceptible to the negative influences of their antisocial peers.

A similar effect was found in the Cambridge-Somerville Youth Study (McCord, 1978), in which boys at high risk for delinquency were randomly assigned to a control group or an intervention that involved a number of components, a key one of which was group activities and involvement in summer camps. Treatment, which began when the boys were about age 10 and ended when

they were 16, had a disconcerting iatrogenic effect: Boys who received the most attention in the treatment had the *worst* outcomes. Dishion and colleagues (1999) took a closer look at the boys' participation in the program and found that most of the damaging effects of the intervention were accounted for by the boys who had been sent to summer camp more than once.

Based on these data, Dishion and colleagues urge that interventions be informed by the developmentally psychopathology of the disorder under investigation. For example, association with deviant peers is a strong predictor of delinquent behavior in youths, and interventions that prescribe just that may do more harm than good. On the other hand, they point out, successful group treatments for antisocial youths have been developed but differ from those described earlier in one important way: They included a mix of prosocial and antisocial youths, which appears to have a dampening effect on problem behavior.

management of disruptive behaviors, such as establishing clear rules, rewarding appropriate behavior, and not rewarding—or punishing—inappropriate behavior. Teachers also implemented special classroom programs designed to strengthen the children's self-control, to build and maintain friendships, and to enhance problem-solving abilities. Finally, children who needed it were tutored, especially in reading.

Fast Track, along with recognizing the multidetermined nature of conduct disorder, is both integrated and solidly based on research. Thus, it avoids the rather piecemeal, improvisational quality of many previous attempts at prevention. While studies of effectiveness are not available at present, it is a prime example of the practical application of developmental psychopathology.

G l o s s a r y

accelerated longitudinal approach (Also known as the longitudinal, cross-sectional approach.) A research technique in which data on the origins of a psychopathology are obtained from different age groups that are subsequently followed until the children in the younger groups are the same age as those in the next older group.

accommodation In Piaget's theory, the process of changing an existing cognitive schema in order to take into account new information from the environment.

adaptational failure A conceptualization of psychopathology in which disorder is viewed as stemming from the child's inability to adapt to the expectations of the environment.

adaptive behavior The ability to cope with environmental demands, such as those for self-care, conventional social interactions, and independent functioning in the community, at an age-appropriate level.

adjustment disorder Deviant behavior that is a reaction to a specific event or events, such as parental death or divorce.

anaclitic depression The infant's reaction of despair following the loss of a loved and needed caregiver.

anal stage In Freud's psychosexual theory, the second stage of development, in which pleasure is derived from retaining and evacuating feces and the toddler confronts the issue of autonomy versus compliance.

anorexia nervosa A voluntary restriction of food and/or an involvement in purging in an active pursuit of thinness that results in at least a 15 percent loss of body weight. The *restricting* type relies solely on strict dieting to lose weight; the *binge-eating/purging* type alternates between dieting and binge eating, followed by self-induced vomiting or purging.

anxiety disorders A group of disorders characterized by intense, chronic anxiety. Formerly called psychoneurotic disorders.

assimilation In Piaget's theory, the process of transforming information so as to make it fit with an existing cognitive schema.

asynchrony Disjointed or markedly uneven rates of progression among developmental variables.

attention-deficit/hyperactivity disorder Developmentally inappropriate inattention accompanied by motor restlessness and impulsivity.

attrition Attrition is the loss of subjects during longitudinal studies.

authoritarian parenting Discipline requiring strict, unquestioning obedience.

authoritative parenting Discipline requiring compliance with standards for mature behavior, accompanied by love, communication, and respect for the child.

autism A severe disorder of the infancy and toddler period marked by extreme aloneness, a pathological need for sameness, and mutism or noncommunicative speech.

avoidance learning A form of learning in which an organism, having experienced an aversive stimulus, behaves in order to prevent future encounters with that stimulus.

avoidant attachment A form of insecure attachment marked by precocious independence from the caregiver.

behavior deficit or excess The behaviorists' conceptualization of psychopathology as behaviors occurring at a lower or at a higher frequency or intensity than is expected within a given society.

behavior therapies A group of therapies characterized by attention to specific, current behaviors, objective measurement, and reliance on principles of behavior change derived from the laboratory.

behavioral assessment Procedures designed to locate specific behaviors—along with their antecedents and consequences—that subsequently can serve as targets for modification through behavioral techniques.

behavioral inhibition A temperamental predisposition for children to react to novelty with avoidance or distress and to be shy and fearful.

bipolar disorder (Also known as manic-depression.) A severe form of psychopathology characterized by depression alternating with states of euphoria or overactivity.

borderline personality disorder A disorder characterized by a pervasive pattern of instability in interpersonal relationships, self-image, and affect.

boundaries The separation between individuals or subsystems within the family, such as between marital and parent-child relationships.

brain damage Damage to the brain can be defined neurologically in terms of the nature, site, and size of the damage, behaviorally in terms of impaired functions, or etiologically in terms of the source of the damage.

bulimia nervosa An eating disorder characterized by recurrent episodes of binge eating (i.e., the rapid consumption of large quantities of food in a brief time), followed by attempts to prevent weight gain either through self-induced vomiting or misuse of laxatives in the purging type or through fasting or excessive exercise in the nonpurging type.

case formulation A succinct description of the child that incorporates the clinician's interpretation of how the problem came about and how it might be remediated.

casual attribution Beliefs concerning whether events are the result of factors within the self (internal vs. external), are likely to persist (stable vs. unstable), or are pervasive across situations (global vs. specific).

coercion In parent-child interactions, use of negative reinforcement to influence the other's behavior; e.g., the child who ceases to tantrum once the parents capitulate to his or her demands.

cognitive triad In Beck's cognitive theory of depression, attributions about the self involving worthlessness, helplessness, and hopelessness.

cohort effect The possibility that childrens' behavior might be different because they were born in different eras and therefore had different experiences.

comorbidity The co-occurrence of two or more psychopathologies.

compulsion An irrational act that an individual is compelled to do.

computerized axial tomography (CAT scan) (Also called computer-assisted tomography or CT scan.) Uses computer-driven X-ray machines to produce detailed images both of the brain's surface and of the levels below, making it possible to locate lesions at any level of the brain.

concrete-operational stage In middle childhood, the emergence of the ability to understand the world in terms of reason rather than naive perception.

conditions of worth Carl Rogers' term for conditions set by parents under which they will grant their love and respect for the child.

conduct disorders Behaviors in which children act out their feelings or impulses toward others in an antisocial or destructive fashion.

contingency management Decreases the strength of undesirable behaviors and increases the strength of adaptive ones by manipulating the rewards and punishments that follow or are contingent upon such behaviors.

continuity Consistency in the presence or absence of a disorder from one developmental period to another.

defense mechanisms Unconscious strategies for reducing anxiety. See also *repression, reaction formation, projection,* and *displacement.*

delusion A firmly held, irrational belief that runs counter to reality and to the individual's culture or subculture.

detouring Salvador Minuchin's term for parents' avoidance of their own conflicts by regarding their child as their sole problem.

developmental delay Development that proceeds at a significantly slower pace than normal.

developmental deviation Emergence of a behavior that is so qualitatively different from the normative that it would be considered inappropriate at age stage of development.

developmental pathway The risk and protective factors responsible for diverting development from its normal course, maintaining the deviation, or returning development to its normal course.

developmental psychopathology The study of the developmental processes that contribute to the formation of, or resistance to, psychopathology.

developmental transformation A change in the outward manifestation of a disorder due to age-related changes in individuals or their environments.

discontinuity Inconsistency in the presence or absence of a disorder from one developmental period to another.

discrepancy model Defining learning disability as the difference between what students should achieve in terms of their ability and their actual achievement.

disorganized/disoriented attachment A form of insecure attachment marked by inconsistent and odd behavior.

disorganized or catatonic behavior In schizophrenia, behavior marked by extreme deviance, such as grimacing, odd posturing, long periods of immobility, or self-mutilation.

disorganized speech In schizophrenia, speech characterized by loose associations, illogical reasoning, fragmentation, and bizarreness.

displacement A mechanism of defense in which an impulse is directed toward a target that is safer than the original one.

Down syndrome A form of mental retardation caused by having three number 21 chromosomes instead of the normal two.

DSM   The *Diagnostic and Statistical Manual of Mental Disorders,* published by the American Psychiatric Association, providing diagnostic criteria for mental disorders. The latest edition is DSM-IV-TR.

dysthymic disorder   Characterized either by a depressed mood or by irritability in children, along with at least two other specific symptoms of depression. The disturbance persists for at least a year.

ego   In Freud's structural theory, the psychic component responsible for learning the nature of reality in order to gratify the id's demands for maximal pleasure, on the one hand, and to avoid the painful censure of the superego, on the other hand.

egocentrism   In Jean Piaget's theory, the tendency to view the physical and social world exclusively from one's own point of view.

ego control   The extent to which individuals inhibit or give free expression to their impulses.

ego psychology   Associated with Erik Erikson, an outgrowth of psychoanalytic theory that focuses on the reality-oriented, adaptive aspects of the psyche.

ego resilience   The ability to adapt resourcefully to changes in the environment.

electroencephalogram (EEG)   A device for recording the electric activity of the brain.

emotion regulation   The ability to monitor, evaluate, and modify one's emotional reactions in order to achieve one's goals.

encopresis   Involuntary soiling with feces in a child age 5 and older.

enuresis   (Also called functional enuresis.) Involuntary urination during the day or night in children 5 years of age or older.

equilibration   In Piaget's theory, the balance between assimilation and accommodation.

etiology   The study of the causes or of the necessary and sufficient conditions for producing various psychopathologies.

event-related potential (ERP)   An electroencephalographic technique that records the brain response to a given stimulus so that one can tell whether the response is characteristic (normal) or deviant.

executive functions   The functions underlying flexible, goal-directed behavior; specifically, planning, working memory, set shifting, and inhibition of competing behaviors.

externalizing   See *internalizing-externalizing.*

extinction   The gradual disappearance of a learned behavior through the removal of reinforcements.

familial or familial cultural retardation   Retardation characterized by a mild degree of retardation with no clear organic cause, a greater prevalence among minorities and individuals of low socioeconomic status, and a tendency to blend in with the general population after school.

fixation   The persistence of normal behavior beyond the point where it is developmentally appropriate. This arrest of development may be psychopathological, depending on the degree or intensity.

follow-back strategy   A research technique in which the origins of a psychopathology are reconstructed by obtaining data from records made at a previous time period, such as school or court records.

follow-up strategy   A research technique involving following children for a considerable period of time in order to obtain data on

the antecedents of various psychopathologies.

formal operational stage   In adolescence, the ability to think in terms of general ideas and abstract concepts.

free association   The basic psychoanalytic technique for uncovering unconscious material by encouraging the patient to say whatever comes to mind.

functional magnetic resonance imaging (fMRI)   A brain imaging technique that tracks increases and decreases in oxygen in the brain as an individual performs a given task and subsequently can locate where the greatest areas of activation occur.

gender constancy   The recognition that gender is permanent and does not change.

gender identity   Self-classification as male or female.

gender identity disorder   A disorder characterized by a strong and persistent desire to be, or belief that one is, a member of the other sex.

gender role   Society's prescriptions for appropriate behaviors and feelings for boys and girls.

generalized anxiety disorder   A disorder characterized by excessive worry and anxiety that significantly interferes with functioning across a variety of situations.

genital stage   In Freud's psychosexual theory, the last stage of development, during which mature sexuality and true intimacy are achieved.

goodness of fit   The optimal match between the child's temperament and the demands that the environment places on the child.

hallucination   A sensory perception occurring in the absence of any appropriate external stimulus.

id   In Freud's structural theory, the biologically based pleasure-seeking source of all psychic energy.

identity   In Erik Erikson's theory, the search for inner continuity and interpersonal mutuality that begins in adolescence and is evidenced by a vocational choice.

imitation   (Also called *modeling*.) Learning by observing the behavior of others (models).

insecure attachment   There are three types: in *resistant attachment* there is an ambivalent mixture of demands for and rejection of maternal attention; in *avoidant attachment,* the child ignores the mother; and in *disorganized/ disoriented attachment* there are contradictory responses to the mother such as approaching her with depressed or flat affect.

insight   In psychoanalytic psychotherapy, the patient's conscious awareness of anxiety-producing thoughts and feelings that had been in the unconscious.

intelligence quotient (IQ)   A measure of intelligence derived either (1) from the relation between the child's mental age and chronological age or (2) from the deviation of a child's score from the mean score of children his or her age.

intelligence tests   Standardized techniques for measuring intellectual functioning.

internalization   The process by which behavior that was once dependent on environmental factors for its maintenance comes to be maintained by intraindividual factors.

internalizing-externalizing   A classification of psychopathologies based on whether the child suffers (internalizing) or the environment suffers (externalizing).

internalizers   See *internalizing-externalizing*.

interpretation   In psychoanalytic theory, interpretation consists of the therapist pointing out the meaning of material the patient is not aware of.

latency stage   In Freud's psychosexual theory, the fourth stage of development, in which concerns about sexuality diminish and the child's attention is drawn to mastery of social and academic environments.

learning disabilities   (Also called learning disorders.) Learning problems due to a disorder in one or more of the basic psychological processes involved in understanding or in using spoken or written language and not due to mental retardation, emotional disturbance, environmental disadvantage, or specific perceptual or motor handicaps.

magnetic resonance imaging (MRI)   A brain imaging technique that generates three-dimensional images of various brain structures by using images from successive layers of the brain.

major depression   An acute, debilitating disorder characterized by five or more symptoms, one of which is depressed mood in adults or irritability in children.

maltreatment   Behavior that is outside the norms of conduct and entails a substantial risk of causing physical or emotional harm.

masked depression   Underlying depression in children in middle childhood that is masked by a wide variety of deviant but nondepressive behaviors.

mastery motivation   The drive to interact with the environment for the intrinsic pleasure of learning about it.

mediator   A variable that accounts for the effects of one variable upon another.

mental retardation   A condition characterized by subnormal intelligence, deficits in adaptive behavior, and onset typically under the age of 18 years.

modeling   See *imitation*.

moderator   A variable that affects the strength or direction of the relationship between one variable and another.

multiaxial classification   A diagnostic system whereby individuals are assessed in terms of a number of dimensions rather than in terms of a single classification.

multideterminism   The idea that psychopathology is determined by a number of causes rather than a single cause.

multifinality   The idea that a single risk factor may have a number of different consequences depending upon contextual and intraindividual factors.

myelination   The formation of an insulating sheath of white matter around the axon of the nerve cell.

negative affectivity   Subsuming anxiety and depression under their shared negative affects such as fear, sadness, and guilt.

negative reinforcement   Increasing the probability that behavior will occur by removing unpleasant or aversive consequences.

neglect   Deficiencies in provision of caregiving that compromise the child's physical and/or psychological health.

neglectful parenting   Parents who are indifferent to their children or uninvolved and self-centered.

neuroendocrines   Processes involved in the interaction between neural and hormonal (endocrine) systems.

neurotransmitters   The "chemical messengers" responsible for communication among nerve cells.

object constancy   In object relations theory, the ability to integrate both positive and negative feelings into a single representation of the self or other.

object permanence   In Piaget's cognitive theory, the understanding that physical objects exist independently even when we are not in direct contact with them or observing them.

object relation   In Freudian theory, the term used for an emotional attachment to another person.

obsession   An irrational thought, the repeated occurrence of which is beyond the individual's conscious control.

obsessive-compulsive disorder   See *obsession* and *compulsion.*

Oedipus complex   In Freud's psychosexual theory, the universal desire of the preschool boy to take possession of the mother and eliminate the rivalrous father.

omnipotent thinking   Belief that one can control events that, in reality, lie beyond one's power.

operant conditioning (instrumental conditioning)   A form of conditioning in which the persistence of a response depends on its effects on the environment.

oppositional-defiant disorder   Purposeful defiance of adults' requests resulting in violation of minor rules.

oral stage   In Freud's psychosexual theory, the first stage of development, in which pleasure is derived from sucking and biting and attachment to the caregiver is formed.

organic MR   (mental retardation): Significantly below-average intellectual abilities combined with deficits in adaptive functioning prior to 18 years of age that is caused by biological factors.

overinclusiveness   A thought disorder in which ideas flit from one tangential association to another.

overprotectiveness   Excessive and unrealistic concern over another's welfare.

parasuicidal behavior   (Also referred to as suicidal gestures.) Non-lethal self-harming behavior such as superficial cuts to the extremities.

parent-child coalition   Salvador Minuchin's term for a family pattern in which a child sides with one parent against the other.

parent management training (PMT)   The use of social learning principles such as positive reinforcement and mild punishment to alter parent-child interactions in a prosocial direction.

pediatric psychology   The study of the interplay between organic factors on the one hand and psychological, social, and cultural factors on the other in the etiology, course, and treatment of disease. Pediatric psychology is also concerned with prevention and health maintenance.

pedophilia   A state of being sexually aroused by children.

permissive parenting   Parents who are undemanding, accepting, and child centered but who make few attempts at control.

personality disorders   Deeply ingrained, maladaptive behaviors that, while more pervasive than the anxiety disorders, still do not significantly diminish the individual's reality contact.

phallic stage   In Freud's psychosexual theory, the third stage of development, in which the preschooler is expansive and assertive and wishes to be the exclusive love object of the other-sex parent.

phobia   An intense, persistent, irrational fear of an animate or inanimate object or of a situation.

phonemes   The sound units of speech.

phonological awareness   Recognition of the fact that words are made up of separate sounds, or phonemes, an important function underlying the ability to read.

positive reinforcement   Use of rewards to increase the probability that a desired behavior will occur.

positron-emission tomography (PET scan)   A brain scan technique that detects abnormal functioning in brains that might look structurally intact by recording the rate of metabolizing radioactive glucose that has been introduced into cerebral arteries.

posttraumatic stress disorder   A disorder resulting from experiencing an event involving actual or threatened death or injury to the self or others.

potentiating factor   A variable that increases the impact of a risk factor.

precocity   As applied to psychopathology, precocity is an accelerated rate of development that leads to an attempt to take on adult roles and responsibilities before the child is prepared to do so successfully.

preoperational stage   In the preschool period, the literal belief in what is seen so that, for example, things that look different are in fact different.

prevention   Programs initiated before a problem develops (*primary* prevention), in the early stages of a problem to forestall its development into a full-blown disorder (*secondary* prevention), or to prevent a problem from worsening or reoccurring (*tertiary* prevention).

projection   A mechanism of defense in which anxiety-provoking impulses are denied in oneself and attributed to others.

projective techniques   Personality assessment methods using ambiguous or unstructured stimuli. The most popular are the *Rorschach,* consisting of a series of ink blots; the *Thematic Apperception Test (TAT),* consisting of a series of ambiguous pictures; and human figure drawing.

protective factors   Factors that promote healthy development and counteract the negative effects of risks.

protective mechanisms   The underlying developmental processes that account for the positive effects of protective factors.

pruning   The process of the brain ridding itself of redundant or unnecessary neural cells.

psychopathy   A psychopathology marked by callousness, egocentricity, shallow emotions, superficial charm, manipulativeness, impulsiveness, and an absence of meaningful relations.

psychosexual theory   Freud's developmental theory in which each stage—the oral, anal, and phallic—is marked by a change in the source of erotic bodily sensations: personality development.

punishment   Presentation of an aversive stimulus that decreases the probability that the response leading to it will occur.

reaction formation   A mechanism of defense in which a child's thoughts and feelings are diametrically opposed to an anxiety-provoking impulse.

reactive attachment disorder   A disorder characterized by disturbed social relations due to pathological caregiving in the first three years of life.

reciprocal determinism   In social learning theory, the idea that both the individual and the environment influence one another rather than the individual's being the passive recipient of environmental influences.

reciprocal inhibition   The inhibition of the weaker of two incompatible responses by the stronger one. Utilized in systematic desensitization.

regression   The return of behaviors that once were developmentally appropriate but no longer are. Whether or not the behaviors are psychopathological depends on the degree or intensity of regression.

reinforcement   An increase in the probability that a response will occur to a contiguously presented stimulus.

reliability   The consistency with which an assessment instrument performs.

repression   The basic mechanism of defense in which anxiety-provoking impulses and ideas are banished from consciousness.

resilience   A child's ability to make a good adjustment in spite of being at high risk for developing a disturbance.

resistant attachment   A form of insecure attachment in which the infant is preoccupied with the caregiver while relating in an ambivalent manner.

respondent conditioning (Also called classical conditioning.)   A form of conditioning in which a previously neutral stimulus takes on the properties of a stimulus that innately evokes a response.

restructuring techniques   Techniques for altering faulty patterns of family interaction.

retrospective strategy   A research technique involving reconstructing the origins of a psychopathology through inquiring about the past history of the disturbed child.

rigidity   Excessive and unrealistic resistance to change.

risk mechanisms   The underlying developmental processes that account for the negative effects of risk variables.

risks   Factors that increase the probability that development will be diverted from its normal path, resulting either in clinically significant problem behavior or psychopathology.

schema (plural, schemata)   For Piaget: cognitive structures comprising children's developing understanding of their experience of the environment and of themselves. For social cognitive theories: stable mental structures incorporating perceptions of self and others and including past experiences and future expectations.

schizophrenia   A severe, pervasive disorder consisting of delusions, hallucinations, disorganized speech, inappropriate affect, disorganized or bizarre behavior, and the negative symptoms of flat affect, avolition, alogia, and anhedonia.

self-constancy   The sense of the self as continuous and "going on being" despite changes in one's mood or the environment.

self-efficacy   An individual's estimation of the likelihood of achieving a given outcome.

self-regulation   The autonomous initiation and control over one's own behavior.

sensorimotor stage   The infant's and toddler's reliance on sensations and motor actions as vehicles for understanding the environment.

separation anxiety disorder   Excessive anxiety concerning separation from those to whom the child is attached.

separation-individuation   In object relations theory, the development of a sense of the self as distinct from the caregiver and the achievement of a sense of uniqueness.

sexual abuse   Involving children in incest, sexual assault, fondling, exposure to sexual acts, and pornography.

sexual orientation   Attraction to same-sex or other-sex partners.

social phobia (Also known as social anxiety disorder.)   A disorder characterized by excessive anxiety and avoidance of social situations.

stage-salient issues   At each age period, the key developmental tasks that the child must accomplish in order to successfully move forward in development.

substance abuse   A pattern of excessive use of a chemical substance to the extent that it interferes with work or school and interpersonal relationships.

substance dependence   A pattern of continual use of a substance despite significant substance-related problems, resulting in symptoms such as tolerance, withdrawal, and a lifestyle consumed with activities revolving around substance use.

superego   The moral component, or conscience, in Freud's structural theory. Initially, it is perfectionistic, requiring absolute obedience and punishing transgressions with guilt feelings.

sustained attention   The ability to continue a task until it is completed.

syndrome   A group of behaviors or symptoms that tend to occur together in a particular disorder.

systematic desensitization   A behavior therapy for extinguishing anxiety by pairing a graded series of anxiety stimuli with the incompatible response of relaxation.

theory of mind   A child's understanding that others have intentions, motivations, and perspectives different from one's own.

time out   In behavior therapy, isolating the child from reinforcement for brief periods in order to extinguish undesirable behaviors.

transaction   A series of dynamic, reciprocal interactions between the child, the family, and the social context.

transference   In psychoanalytic therapy, the projection onto the therapist of intense feelings once directed toward significant figures, typically the parents.

triangulation   Salvador Minuchin's term for a family pattern in which the child is forced to side with one parent against the other.

unconditional positive regard   In Carl Rogers' theory, the parents' intrinsic valuing and acceptance of the child.

validity   The degree to which an instrument evaluates what it intends to evaluate.

vulnerability   A factor that increase the likelihood that a child will succumb to risk.

working through   In psychoanalytic theory, the process by which the patient gains insight into the many ways in which a single conflict is expressed.

References

Abela, J. R. Z., & Seligman, M. E. P. (2000). The hopelessness theory of depression: A test of the diathesis-stress component in the interpersonal and achievement domains. *Cognitive Therapy & Research, 24,* 361–378.

Aber, J. L., Brown, J., & Jones, S. (2003). Developmental trajectories toward violence in middle childhood: Course, demographic differences, and response to school-based intervention. *Developmental Psychology, 39,* 324–348.

Aboud, F. E. (1987). The development of ethnic self-identification and attitudes. In J. S. Phinney & M. J. Rotheram (Eds.), *Children's ethnic socialization: Pluralism and development* (pp. 32–55). Newbury Park, CA: Sage Publications.

Abramson, L. Y., Seligman, M. E. P., & Teasdale, J. D. (1978). Learned helplessness in humans: Critique and reformulation. *Journal of Abnormal Psychology, 87,* 49–74.

Achenbach, T. M. (1990). Conceptualization of developmental psychopathology. In M. Lewis & S. M. Miller (Eds.), *Handbook of developmental psychopathology* (pp. 3–14). New York: Plenum.

Achenbach, T. M. (1991). *Manual for the Child Behavior Checklist/4-18 and 1991 Profile.* Burlington: University of Vermont Department of Psychiatry.

Achenbach, T. M. (1995). Developmental issues in assessment, taxonomy, and diagnosis of child and adolescent psychopathology. In D. Cicchetti & D. J. Cohen (Eds.), *Developmental psychopathology, Vol. I: Theory and methods* (pp. 57–80). New York: Wiley.

Achenbach, T. M. (2000). Assessment of psychopathology. In A. J. Sameroff, M. Lewis, & S. M. Miller (Eds.), *Handbook of developmental psychopathology* (pp. 41–56). New York: Kluwer Academic.

Achenbach, T. M., Howell, C. T., McConaughy, S. H., & Stanger, C. (1995). Six-year predictors of problems in a national sample of children and youth, Vol. II: Signs of disturbance. *Journal of the American Academy of Child and Adolescent Psychiatry, 34,* 488–498.

Achenbach, T. M., & McConaughy, S. H. (1997). *Empirically based assessment of child and adolescent psychopathology: Practical applications.* Newbury Park, CA: Sage.

Achenbach, T. M., & Rescorla, L. A. (2001). *Manual for the ASEBA school-age forms and profiles.* Burlington: ASEBA.

Adler, G., & Rhine, M. W. (1988). The selfobject function of projective identification. *Bulletin of the Menninger Clinic, 52,* 473–491.

Agbayani-Siewert, P., & Enrile, A. V. (2003). Filipino American children and adolescents. In J. T. Gibbs & L. N. Huang (Eds.), *Children of color: Psychological interventions with culturally diverse youth* (2nd ed., pp. 229–264). San Francisco: Jossey-Bass.

Aguilar, E. J., Leal, C., Acosta, F. J., Cejas, M. R., Fernandez, L., & Gracia, R. (2003). A psychopathological study of a group of schizophrenic patients after attempting suicide. Are there two different clinical subtypes? *European Psychiatry, 18,* 190–192.

Ahrons, C. R., & Wallisch, L. S. (1987). The relationship between former spouses. In D. Perlman & S. Duck (Eds.), *Intimate relationships: Development, dynamics, and deterioration* (pp. 269–296). Newbury Park, CA: Sage.

Ainsworth, M. D. S., Blehar, M., Waters, E., & Wall, S. (1978). *Patterns of attachment.* Hillsdale, NJ: Erlbaum.

Akiskal, H. S. (1995). Developmental pathways to bipolarity: Are juvenile-onset depressions prebipolar? *Journal of the American Academy of Child and Adolescent Psychiatry, 34,* 754–763.

Albano, A. M., Chorpita, B. F., & Barlow, D. H. (1996). Childhood anxiety disorders. In E. J. Mash & R. A. Barkley (Eds.), *Child psychopathology* (pp. 196–241). New York: Guilford.

Allen, J. P., & Hauser, S. T. (1996). Autonomy and relatedness in adolescent-family interactions as predictors of young adults' states of mind regarding attachment. *Development and Psychopathology, 8,* 793–809.

Altman, H., Collins, M., & Mundy, P. (1997). Subclinical hallucinations and delusions in nonpsychotic adolescents. *Journal of Child Psychology and Psychiatry, 38,* 413–420.

Altmann, E. O., & Gotlib, I. H. (1988). The social behavior of depressed children: An observational study. *Journal of Abnormal Child Psychology, 16,* 29–44.

Alvarado, N. (1994). Empirical validity of the Thematic Apperception Test. *Journal of Personality Assessment, 63,* 59–79.

Amato, P. R. (2001). Children of divorce in the 1900s: An update of the Amato and Keith (1991) meta-analysis. *Journal of Family Psychology, 15,* 355–370.

Amato, P. R., & Keith, B. (1991). Parental divorce and well-being of children: A meta-analysis. *Psychological Bulletin, 110,* 26–46.

Amaya-Jackson, L., & March, J. (1995). Posttraumatic stress disorder. In J. March (Ed.), *Anxiety disorders in children and adolescents* (pp. 276–300). New York: Guilford.

Amaya-Jackson, L., Reynolds, V., Murray, M., C., McCarthy, G., Nelson, A., Cherney, M. S., et al. (2003). Cognitive-behavioral treatment for pediatric posttraumatic stress disorder: Protocol and application in school and community settings. *Journal of Cognitive Behavioral Practice, 10*(3), 204–213.

American Academy of Pediatrics. (2000). Diagnosis and evaluation of the child with Attention-Deficit/Hyperactivity Disorder. *Pediatrics, 105,* 1158–1170.

American Associative of Child and Adolescent Psychiatry (AACAP) Official Action. (1997). Practice parameters for assessment and treatment of children, adolescents and adults with attention-deficit/hyperactivity disorder. *Journal of the American Academy of Child and Adolescent Psychiatry, 36*(Suppl. 10), 85S–114S.

American Association on Mental Retardation. (1992). *Mental retardation: Definition classification and systems of support* (9th ed.). Washington, DC: Author.

American Psychiatric Association. (1968). *Diagnostic and statistical manual of mental disorders* (2nd ed.). Washington, DC.

American Psychiatric Association. (1994). *Diagnostic and statistical manual of mental disorders. 4th ed.-Text Revision.* Washington, DC: Author.

American Psychiatric Association. (2000). *Diagnostic and statistical manual of mental disorders* (4th ed.). Washington, DC: Author.

American Psychological Association. (1985). *Standards for educational and psychological testing.* Washington, DC: Author.

American Psychological Association. (2002). Ethical principles of psychologists and code of conduct. *American Psychologist, 57,* 1060–1073.

American Psychological Association. (2003). Guidelines on multicultural education, training, research, practice, and organizational change for psychologists. *American Psychologist, 58,* 377–402.

Ammerman, R. T., & Campo, J. V. (1998). *Handbook of pediatric psychology and psychiatry, Vol II: Disease, injury, and illness.* Boston: Allyn & Bacon.

Anastopoulos, A. D. (1998). A training program for parents of children with Attention-Deficit/Hyperactivity Disorder. In J. M. Briesmeister & C. E. Schaefer (Eds.), *Handbook of parent training* (pp. 27–60). New York: Wiley.

Anderson, C. A., & Hammen, C. (1993). Psychosocial outcomes of children of unipolar depressed, bipolar, medically ill, and normal women: A longitudinal study. *Journal of Consulting and Clinical Psychology, 61,* 448–454.

Anderson, I. M., Parry-Billings, M., Newsholme, E. A., Fairburn, C. G., & Cowen, P. J. (1990). Dieting reduces plasma tryptophan and alters brain 5-HT function in women. *Psychological Medicine, 20,* 785–791.

Andrews, J. A., Hops, H., & Duncan, S. C. (1997). Adolescent modeling of parent substance use: The moderating effect of the relationship with the parent. *Journal of Family Psychology, 11,* 259–270.

Andrews, T. K., Rose, F. D., & Johnson, D. A. (1998). Social and behavioural effects of traumatic brain injury in children. *Brain Injury, 12,* 133–138.

Annegers, J. F., Grabow, J. D., Kurland, L. T., & Laws, E. R. (1980). The incidence, causes, and secular trends of head trauma in Olmsted County, Minnesota, 1935–1974. *Neurology, 30,* 912–919.

Appel, A. E., & Holden, G. W. (1998). The co-occurrence of spouse and physical child abuse: A review and appraisal. *Journal of Family Psychology, 12,* 578–599.

Applegate, B., Lahey, B. B., Hart, E. L., Waldman, I., Biederman, J., Hynd, G. W., Barkley, R. A., Ollendick, T., Frick, P. J., Greenhill, L., McBurnett, K., Newcoren, J., Kerdyk, L., Garfinkel, B., & Shaffer, D. (1997). Validity of the age-of-onset criterion for ADHD: A report of the DSM-IV field trials. *Journal of the American Academy of Child and Adolescent Psychiatry, 36,* 1211–1221.

Apter, A., & Freudenstein, O. (2000). Adolescent suicidal behaviour: Psychiatric populations. In K. Hawton & K. van Heeringen (Eds.), *The international handbook of suicide and attempted suicide* (pp. 261–273). Chichester, UK: Wiley.

Apter, A., & Wasserman, D. (2003). Adolescent attempted suicide. In R. A. King & A. Apter (Eds.), *Suicide in children and adolescents* (pp. 63–85). Cambridge, MA: Cambridge, University Press.

Arseneault, L., Cannon, M., Poulton, R., Murray, R., Caspi, A., & Moffitt, T. E. (2002). Cannabis use in adolescence and risk for adult psychosis: Longitudinal prospective study. *British Medical Journal, 325,* 1212–1213.

Ary, D. V., Duncan, T. E., Duncan, S. C., & Hops, H. (1999). Adolescent problem behavior: The influence of parents and peers. *Behavior Research and Therapy, 37,* 217–230.

Asarnow, J. R., & Asarnow, R. F. (2003). Childhood-onset schizophrenia. In E. J. Mash & R. A. Barkley (Eds.), *Child psychopathology* (2nd ed., pp. 455–485). New York: Guilford.

Asarnow, J. R., Carlson, G. A., & Guthrie, D. (1987). Coping strategies, self-perceptions, hopelessness, and perceived family environments in depressed and suicidal children. *Journal of Consulting & Clinical Psychology, 55,* 361–366.

Asarnow, J. R., Goldstein, M., Carlson, G., Perdue, S., Bates, S., & Keller, J. (1988). Childhood-onset depressive disorders: A follow-up study of rates of rehospitalization and out-of-home placement among child psychiatric inpatients. *Journal of Affective Disorders, 15,* 245–253.

Asarnow, J. R., Jaycox, L. H., & Tompson, M. C. (2001). Depression in youth: Psychosocial interventions. *Journal of Clinical Child Psychology, 30,* 33–47.

Asarnow, J. R., Tompson, M., Hamilton, E. B., Goldstein, M. J., & Guthrie, D. (1994).

Family-expressed emotion, childhood-onset depression, and childhood-onset schizophrenia spectrum disorders: Is expressed emotion a nonspecific correlate of child psychopathology or a specific risk factor for depression? *Journal of Abnormal Child Psychology, 22,* 129–146.

Asarnow, J. R., Tompson, M. C., & McGrath, E. P. (2004). Childhood-onset schizophrenia: Clinical and treatment issues. *Journal of Child Psychology and Psychiatry, 45,* 180–194.

Asarnow, R. F., Nuechterlein, K. H., Fogelson, D., Subotnik, K. L., Payne, D. A., Russell, A. T., et al. (2001). Schizophrenia and schizophrenia-spectrum personality disorders in the first-degree relatives of children with schizophrenia: The UCLA Family Study. *Archives of General Psychiatry, 58,* 581–588.

Asperger, H. (1944). Die autistichen Psychopathen in Kindesalter. *Archiv fur Psychatirie und Nervenkrankheiten, 117,* 76–136.

Attie, I., & Brooks-Gunn, J. (1995). The development of eating regulation across the life span. In D. Cicchetti & D. J. Cohen (Eds.), *Developmental psychopathology: Vol. 2. Risk, disorder and adaptation* (pp. 332–368). New York: Wiley.

Attwood, A., Frith, U., & Hermelin, B. (1988). The understanding and use of interpersonal gestures by Down's syndrome children. *Journal of Autism and Developmental Disorders, 18,* 241–257.

Aube, J., Fichman, L., Saltaris, C., & Koestner, R.

(2000). Gender difference in adolescent depressive symptomatology: Towards an integrated social-developmental model. *Journal of Social and Clinical Psychology, 19,* 297–313.

Avenevoli, S., Stolar, M., Li, J., Dierker, L., & Merikangas, K. R. (2001). Comorbidity of depression in children and adolescents: Models and evidence from a prospective high-risk family study. *Biological Psychiatry, 49,* 1071–1081.

Axline, V. (1969). *Play therapy.* New York: Ballantine.

Aytaclar, S., Tarter, R. E., Kirisci, L., & Lu, S. (1999). Association between hyperactivity and executive cognitive functioning in childhood and substance use in early adolescence. *Journal of the American Academy of Child & Adolescent Psychiatry, 38*(2), 172–178.

Azar, S. T. (1997). A cognitive behavioral approach to understanding and treating parents who physically abuse their children. In D. A. Wolfe, R. J. McMahon, & R. D. Peters (Eds.), *Child abuse: New directions in prevention and treatment across the lifespan* (pp. 79–101). Thousand Oaks, CA: Sage.

Bailey, D. S. (2003). Who is learning disabled? Psychologists and educators debate over how to identify students with learning disabilities. *Monitor on Psychology, 34,* 58.

Baird, G., Charman, T., & Baron-Cohen, S. (2000). A screening instrument for autism at 18 months of age: A 6-year follow-up

study. *Journal of the American Academy of Child and Adolescent Psychiatry, 39,* 694–702.

Bakan, D. (1966). *The duality of human existence: Isolation and communion in Western man.* Boston: Beacon Press.

Bakermans-Kranenburg, M. J., van IJzendoorn, M. H., & Juffer, F. (2003). Therapy: Parent-child relationships. In J. Ponzetti (Eds.), *International encyclopedia of marriage and family* (pp. 1642–1645). New York: Macmillan.

Balint, M. (1968). *The basic fault: Therapeutic aspects of regression.* London: Tavistock.

Ballaban-Gil, K., & Tuchman, R. (2000). Epilepsy and epileptiform EEG: Association with autism and language disorders. *Mental Retardation & Developmental Disabilities Research Reviews, 6,* 300–308.

Ballon, B. C., Courbasson, C. M., & Smith, P. D. (2001). Physical and sexual abuse issues among youths with substance use problems. *Canadian Journal of Psychiatry, 46,* 617–621.

Baltaxe, C. A. M., & Simmons, J. Q., III. (1995). Speech and language disorders in children and adolescents with schizophrenia. *Schizophrenia Bulletin, 21,* 677–687.

Bandura, A. (1977). *Social learning theory.* New York: Holt, Rinehart & Winston.

Bandura, A. (1986). *Social foundations of thought and action: A social cognitive theory.* Englewood Cliffs, NJ: Prentice-Hall.

Bandura, A., Pastorelli, C., Barbaranelli, C., & Caprara, G. V. (1999). Self-efficacy pathways to childhood depression. *Journal of Personality and Social Psychology, 76,* 258–269.

Barber, B. K. (Ed.) (2002). *Intrusive parenting: How psychological control affects children and adolescents.* Washington, DC: American Psychological Association.

Bardone, A. M., Moffitt, T. E., Avshalom, C., Dickson, N., & Silva, P. A. (1996). Adult mental health and social outcomes of adolescent girls with depression and conduct disorder. *Development and Psychopathology, 8,* 811–829.

Barker, P. (1990). *Clinical interviews with children and adolescents.* New York: Norton.

Barkley, R. A. (1990). *Attention-deficit hyperactivity disorder: A handbook for diagnosis and treatment.* New York: Guilford.

Barkley, R. A. (1997). *ADHD and the nature of self-control.* New York: Guilford.

Barkley, R. A. (1998). Attention-deficit/hyperactivity disorder. In E. J. Mash & R. A. Barkley (Eds.), *Treatment of childhood disorders* (pp. 55–110). New York: Guilford.

Barkley, R. A. (2002). International consensus statement on ADHD. *Clinical Child and Family Psychology Review, 5,* 89–114.

Barkley, R. A. (2003). Attention-Deficit/ Hyperactivity Disorder. In E. J. Mash & R. A. Barkley (Eds.), *Child* psychopathology (2nd ed., pp. 75–143). New York: Guilford.

Barkley, R. A., Fischer, M., Smallish, L., & Fletcher, K. (2002). The persistence of attention-deficit/hyperactivity disorder into young adulthood as a function of reporting source and definition of disorder. *Journal of Abnormal Psychology, III,* 279–289.

Barkley, R. A., Fischer, M., Smallish, L., & Fletcher, K. (2004). Young adult follow-up of hyperactive children: Antisocial activities and drug use. *Journal of Child Psychology and Psychiatry and Allied Disciplines, 45,* 195–211.

Barnett, D., Manly, J. T., & Cicchetti, D. (1993). Defining child maltreatment: The interface between policy and research. In D. Cicchetti, S. L. Toth, & I. E. Sigel (Eds.), *Child abuse, child development, and social policy: Advances in applied developmental psychology* (pp. 7–73). Norwood, NJ: Ablex.

Baron-Cohen, S. (2001). The Autism-Spectrum Quotient (AQ): Evidence from Asperger Syndrome/high-functioning autism, males and females, scientists and mathematicians. *Journal of Autism and Developmental Disorders, 31*(1), 5–17.

Baron-Cohen, S. (2003). *The essential difference: The truth about the male and female brain.* New York: Basic Books.

Baron-Cohen, S., Wheelwright, S., Spong, A., Scahill, V., & Lawson, J. (2001). Are intuitive physics and intuitive psychology independent? *Journal of Developmental*

and Learning Disorders, 5, 47–78.

Barry, C. T., Frick, P. J., Deshazo, T. M., McCoy, M. G., Ellis, M., & Loney, B. R. (2000). The importance of callous-unemotional traits for extending the concept of psychopathy to children. *Journal of Abnormal Psychology, 109,* 335–340.

Bartels, L., & Crowder, D. (1999, August 22). Fatal friendship: How two boys traded baseball and bowling for murder and madness. *Rocky Mountain News;* http://denver. rockymountainnews.com/ shooting/0822fatal.shtm

Bateson, G., Jackson, D., Haley, J., & Weakland, J. (1956). Toward a theory of schizophrenia. *Behavioral Science, 1,* 251–264.

Batsche, G. M. (1998). Bullying. In G. G. Bear, K. M. Minke, & A. Thomas (Eds.), *Children's needs II: Development, problems, and alternatives* (pp. 171–179). Bethesda, MD: National Association of School Psychologists.

Baumeister, R. F., Bushman, B. J., & Campbell, W. K. (2000). Self-esteem, narcissism, and aggression: Does violence result from low self-esteem or threatened egotism? *Current Directions in Psychological Science, 9,* 26–29.

Baumrind, D. (1991a). Effective parenting during the early adolescent transition. In P. A. Cowan & E. M. Hetherington (Eds.), *Family transitions* (pp. 111–163). Hillsdale, NJ: Erlbaum.

Baumrind, D. (1991b). The influences of parenting style on adolescent competence and substance

use. *Journal of Early Adolescence, 11,* 56–95.

Bauserman, R. (2002). Child adjustment in joint-custody versus sole-custody arrangements: A meta-analytic review. *Journal of Family Psychology, 16,* 91–102.

Bayley, N. (1993). *Bayley Scales of Infant Development* (2nd ed.). San Antonio, TX: Psychological Corporation.

Beck, A. T. (1987). Cognitive models of depression. *Journal of Cognitive Psychotherapy, 1,* 5–37.

Beck, A. T. (2002). Cognitive models of depression. In *Clinical advances in cognitive psychotherapy: Theory and Application* (pp. 29–61). New York: Springer Publishing Co.

Becker, J. V. (1998). What we know about the characteristics and treatment of adolescents who have committed sexual offenses. *Child Maltreatment, 3,* 317–329.

Beeghly, M., & Cicchetti, D. (1994). Child maltreatment, attachment, and the self system: Emergence of an internal state lexicon in toddlers at high social risk. *Development and Psychopathology, 6,* 5–30.

Beers, S. R., & De Bellis, M. D. (2002). Neuropsychological function in children with maltreatment-related posttraumatic stress disorder. *American Journal of Psychiatry, 159,* 483–486.

Beidel, D. C., & Turner, S. M. (1998). *Shy children, phobic adults: Nature and treatment of social phobia.* Washington, DC: American Psychiatric Association.

Beidel, D. C., Turner, S. M., & Morris, T. L. (1999). The psychopathology of childhood social phobia. *Journal of the American Academy of Child and Adolescent Psychiatry, 38,* 643–650.

Beidel, D. C., Turner, S. M., & Morris, T. L. (2000). Behavioral treatment of childhood social phobia. *Journal of Consulting and Clinical Psychology, 68,* 1072–2080.

Beitchman, J. H., Zucker, K. J., Hood, J. E., & DaCosta, G. A. (1992). A review of the long-term effects of child sexual abuse. *Child Abuse & Neglect, 16*(1), 101–118.

Bell, C., & Jenkins, E. (1993). Community violence and children on Chicago's southside. *Psychiatry, 56,* 46–53.

Bell-Dolan, D. J., Reaven, N. M., & Peterson, L. (1993). Depression and social functioning: A multidimensional study of the linkages. *Journal of Clinical Child Psychology, 22,* 306–315.

Bemporad, J. R., & Schwab, M. E. (1986). The DSM-III and clinical child psychiatry. In T. Millon & G. L. Klerman (Eds.), *Contemporary directions in psychopathology: Toward the DSM-IV* (pp. 135–151). New York: Guilford.

Bemporad, J. R., Smith, H. F., Hanson, G., & Cicchetti, D. (1982). Borderline syndromes in childhood: Criteria for diagnosis. *American Journal of Psychiatry, 139,* 596–602.

Bender, S. L., Ponton, L. E., Crittenden, M. R., & Word, C. O. (1995). For underprivileged children, standardized intelligence testing can do more harm than good: Reply. *Journal of Developmental and Behavioral Pediatrics, 16,* 428–430.

Benoit, D., & Parker, K. C. (1994). Stability and transmission of attachment across three generations. *Child Development, 65,* 1444–1456.

Bennett, D. S., & Bates, J. E. (1995). Prospective models of depressive symptoms in early adolescence: Attributional style, stress, and support. *Journal of Early Adolescence, 15,* 299–315.

Berliner, L., & Elliott, D. M. (2002). Sexual abuse of children. In J. E. B. Myers, L. Berliner, J. Briere, C. T. Hendrix, C. Jenny, & T. A. Reid (Eds.), *The APSAC handbook on child maltreatment* (2nd ed., pp. 55–78). Thousand Oaks, CA: Sage.

Berman, A. L. (2003). An idiographic approach to understanding suicide in the young. In R. A. King & A. Apter (Eds.), *Suicide in children and adolescents* (pp. 198–210). Cambridge, England: Cambridge University Press.

Berman, A. L., & Jobes, D. A. (1991). *Adolescent suicide: Assessment and intervention.* Washington, DC: American Psychological Association.

Bernstein, A. C., & Cowan, P. A. (1975). Children's concepts of how people get babies. *Child Development, 46,* 77–91.

Bernstein, D. P., Cohen, P., Velez, C. N., Schwab-Stone, M., Siever, L. J., & Shinsato, L. (1993). Prevalence and stability of the DSM-III-R personality

disorders in a community-based survey of adolescents. *American Journal of Psychiatry, 150,* 1237–1243.

Berry, J. D. (2001). An outcome evaluation of the Making Atttitude Adjustments in order to Lead more Effective lives (MALE) program. *Dissertation Abstracts International, 61,* 6124.

Bettelheim, B. (1967). *The empty fortress: Infantile autism and the birth of the self.* Oxford, England: Free Press.

Bettelheim, B. (1983). *Freud and man's soul.* New York: Knopf.

Beyer, H. A. (1991). Litigation involving people with mental retardation. In J. L. Matson & J. A. Mulick (Eds.), *Handbook of mental retardation* (pp. 451–467). New York: Pergamon.

Biederman, J. (2003). Pharmacotherapy for attention-deficit/hyperactivity disorder (ADHD) decreases the risk for substance abuse: Findings from a longitudinal follow-up of youths with and without ADHD. *Journal of Clinical Psychiatry, 64,* 3–8.

Biederman, J., Faraone, S. V., Milberger, S., Jetton, J. G., Chen, L., Mick, E., et al. (1996). Is childhood oppositional defiant disorder a precursor to adolescent conduct disorder? Findings from a four-year follow-up study of children with ADHD. *Journal of the American Academy of Child and Adolescent Psychiatry, 35,* 1193–1204.

Biederman, J., Rosenbaum, J. F., Chaloff, J., & Kagan, J. (1995). Behavioral

inhibition as a risk factor for anxiety disorders. In *Anxiety disorders in children and adolescents* (pp. 61–81). New York: Guilford Press.

Biederman, J., Santangelo, S. L., Faraone, S. V., Kiely, K., Guite, J., Mick, E., et al. (1995). Clinical correlates of enuresis in ADHD and non-ADHD children. *Journal of Child Psychology and Psychiatry, 36,* 865–877.

Bifulco, A., Harris, T., & Brown, G. W. (1992). Mourning or early inadequate care? Reexamination of the relation of maternal loss in childhood with adult depression and anxiety. *Development and Psychopathology, 4,* 433–449.

Black, D. A., Heyman, R. E., & Smith-Slep, A. M. (2001). Risk factors for child sexual abuse. *Aggression and Violent Behavior, 6,* 121–188, 203–229.

Blagg, N., & Yule, W. (1994). School phobia. In T. H. Ollendick, N. J. King, & W. Yule (Eds.), *International handbook of phobia and anxiety disorders in children and adolescents* (pp. 169–186). New York: Plenum.

Blanck, R., & Blanck, G. (1986). *Beyond ego psychology: Developmental object relations theory.* New York: Columbia University Press.

Blatt, S. J. (2004). *Experiences of depression: Theoretical, clinical and research perspectives.* Washington, DC: American Psychological Association.

Blatt, S. J., & Homann, E. (1992). Parent-child interaction in the etiology of

dependent and self-critical depression. *Clinical Psychology Review, 12,* 47–91.

Blatt, S. J., Zohar, A., Quinlan, D. M., & Luthar, S. (1996). Levels of relatedness within the dependency factor of the Depression Experience Questionnaire for Adolescents. *Journal of Personality Assessment, 67,* 52–71.

Blazer, D. G., Kessler, R. C., McGonagle, K. A., & Swartz, M. S. (1994). The prevalence and distribtuion of major depression in a national community sample. *American Journal of Psychiatry, 151,* 919–986.

Block, J., Block, J. H., & Keyes, S. (1988). Longitudinally foretelling drug usage in adolescence: Early childhood personality and environmental processes. *Child Development, 59,* 336–355.

Block, J., & Gjerde, P. F. (1990). Depressive symptoms in late adolescence: A longitudinal perspective on personality antecedents. In J. Rolf, A. S. Masten, D. Cicchetti, K. H. Nuechterlein, & S. Weintraub (Eds.), *Risk and protective factors in the development of psychopathology* (pp. 334–360). Cambridge, England: Cambridge University Press.

Block, J. H. (1973). Conceptions of sex role: Some cross-cultural and longitudinal perspectives. *American Psychologist, 28,* 512–526.

Block, J. H. (1983). Differential premises arising from differential socialization of the sexes: Some conjectures. *Child Development, 54,* 1335–1354.

Block, J. H., & Block, J. (1980). The role of ego-control and ego-resiliency in the organization of behavior. In W. A. Collins (Ed.), *Minnesota symposia on child psychology* (pp. 39–101). Hillsdale, NJ: Erlbaum.

Bloom, D. R., Levin, H. S., Ewing-Cobbs, L., Saunders, A. E., Song, J., Fletcher, J. M., et al. (2001). Lifetime and novel psychiatric disorders after pediatric traumatic brain injury. *Journal of the American Academy of Child and Adolescent Psychiatry, 40,* 572–579.

Boergers, J., & Spirito, A. (2003). Follow-up studies of child and adolescent suicide attempters. In R. A. King & A. Apter (Eds.), *Suicide in children and adolescents* (pp. 271–294). Cambridge, England: Cambridge University Press.

Bohart, A. C., & Stipek, D. J. (2001). *Constructive and destructive behavior: Implications for family, school, and society.* Washington, DC: American Psychological Association.

Bolger, K. E., Patterson, C. J., & Thompson, W. W. (1995). Psychosocial adjustment among children experiencing persistent and intermittent family economic hardship. *Child Development, 66,* 1107–1129.

Boll, T. J., & Stanford, L. D. (1997). Pediatric brain injury. In C. R. Reynolds & E. F. Fletcher-Janzen (Eds.), *Handbook of clinical child neuropsychology* (2nd ed., pp. 140–157). New York: Plenum.

Bolton, D., Luckie, M., & Steinberg, D. (1995). Long-term course of obsessive-compulsive disorder treated in adolescence. *Journal of the American Academy of Child and Adolescent Psychiatry, 34,* 1441–1450.

Bond, M. P. (1995). The development and properties of the Defense Style Questionnaire. In H. R. Conte & R. Plutchik (Eds.), *Ego defenses: Theory and measurement* (pp. 202–220). New York: John Wiley & Sons.

Boney-McCoy, S., & Finkelhor, D. (1995). Prior victimization: A risk factor for child sexual abuse and for PTSD-related symptomatology among sexually abused youth. *Child Abuse and Neglect, 19,* 1401–1421.

Bools, C. N., Neale, B. A., & Meadow, S. R. (1994). Munchausen syndrome by proxy: A study of psychopathology. *Child Abuse and Neglect, 18,* 773–788.

Bornstein, M. H., & Bradley, R. H. (2004). *Socioeconomic status, parenting, and child development.* Mahwah, NJ: Erlbaum.

Bornstein, M. H., & Cote, L. R. (2004). Mothers' parenting cognitions in cultures of origin, acculturating cultures, and cultures of destination. *Child Development, 75,* 221–235.

Bornstein, R. F., & Masling, J. M. (Eds.). (2005). *Scoring the Rorschach: Seven validated systems.* Mahwah, NJ: Erlbaum.

Botvin, G. J., Griffin, K. W., Pul, E., & Macaulay, A. P. (2003). Preventing alcohol use among elementary school students through life skills training. *Journal*

of Child and Adolescent Substance Abuse, 12, 1–17.

Bourdin, C. M., Henggeler, S. W., Blaske, D. M., & Stein, R. (1990). Multisystemic treatment of adolescent sex offenders. *International Journal of Offender Therapy and Comparative Criminology, 33,* 161–172.

Bourdin, C. M., Mann, B. J., Cone, L. T., Henggeler, S. W., Fucci, B. R., Blaske, D. M., et al. (1995). Multisystemic treatment of serious juvenile offenders: Long-term prevention of criminality and violence. *Journal of Consulting and Clinical Psychology, 63,* 569–578.

Bowlby, J. (1960). *The psychoanalytic study of the child. Vol. 15: Grief and mourning in infancy and early childhood.* New York: International Universities Press.

Bowlby, J. (1982). *Attachment and loss. Vol 1: Attachment* (2nd ed.). New York: Basic Books.

Bowlby, J. (1988). Developmental psychiatry comes of age. *American Journal of Psychiatry, 145,* 1–10.

Boyd-Franklin, N., & Bry, B. H. (2000). *Reaching out in family therapy: Home-based, school, and community interventions.* New York: Guilford.

Bradley, R., Conklin, C. Z., & Westen, D. (2005). The borderline personality diagnosis in adolescents: Gender differences and subtypes. *Journal of Child Psychology and Psychiatry.*

Bradley, R. H., & Corwyn, R. F. (2002). Socioeconomic status and child development. *Annual Review*

of Psychology, 53, 371–399.

Bradley, R. H., Corwyn, R. F., Burchinal, M., McAdoo, H. P., & Coll, C. G. (2001). The home environments of children in the United States part II: Relations with behavioral development through age thirteen. *Child Development, 72,* 1868–1886.

Bradley, S. J. (2000). *Affect regulation and the development of psychopathology.* New York: Guilford.

Braver, M., Bumberry, J., Green, K., & Rawson, R. (1992). Childhood abuse and current psychological functioning in a university counseling center population. *Journal of Counseling Psychology, 39,* 252–257.

Bray, J. H., Adams, G. J., Getz, G., & Baer, P. E. (2001). Developmental, family, and ethnic influences on adolescent alcohol usage: A growth curve approach. *Journal of Family Psychology, 15,* 301–314.

Brennan, P. A., Hall, J. A., Bor, W., Najman, J. M., & Williams, G. M. (2003). Integrating biological and social processes in relation to early-onset persistant aggression in boys and girls. *Developmental Psychology, 39,* 309–323.

Brenner, R., Azbel, V., Madhusoodanan, S., & Pawlowka, M. (2000). Comparison of an extract of hypericum (LI 160) and sertraline in the treatment of depression: A double-blind, randomized trial. *Clinical Therapeutics, 22,* 411–318.

Brenner, R., Madhusoodanan, S., Pawlowka, M., &

(Eds.), *Handbook of early childhood intervention* (pp. 246–277). Cambridge, MA: Cambridge University Press.

Cicchetti, D., & Walker, E. (2003). *Neurodevelopmental mechanisms in psychopathology.* New York: Cambridge.

Clark, D. M. (2001). A cognitive perspective on social phobia. In W. Crozier & L. E. Alden (Eds.), *International handbook of social anxiety: Concepts, research and interventions relating to the self and shyness* (pp. 405–430). New York: Wiley.

Clark, R., Anderson, N. B., Clarke, V. R., & Williams, D. R. (1999). Racism as a stressor for African Americans: A biopsychosocial model. *American Psychologist, 54,* 805–816.

Clarke, G. N., DeBar, L. L., & Lewinsohn, P. M. (2003). Cognitive-behavioral group treatment for adolescent depression. In A. E. Kazdin & J. R. Weisz (Eds.), *Evidence-based psychotherapies for children and adolescents* (pp. 120–134). New York: Guilford.

Coatsworth, D. J., Pantin, H., & Szapocznik, J. (2002). Familias Unidas: A family-centered ecodevelopmental intervention to reduce risk for problem behavior among Hispanic adolescents. *Clinical Child and Family Psychology Review, 5,* 113–132.

Cobham, V. E., Dadds, M. R., & Spence, S. H. (1998). The role of parental anxiety in the treatment of childhood anxiety. *Journal of Consulting &*

Clinical Psychology, 66, 893–905.

Cohen, D., Nisbett, R. E., Bowdle, B. F., & Schwarz, N. (1996). Insult, aggression, and the Southern culture of honor: An "experimental ethnography." *Journal of Personality and Social Psychology, 70,* 945–960.

Cohen, D., & Strayer, J. (1996). Empathy in conduct-disordered and comparison youth. *Developmental Psychology, 32,* 988–998.

Cohen, J. A., Berliner, L., & Mannarino, A. P. (2000). Treating traumatized children: A research review and synthesis. *Trauma, Violence, and Abuse: A Review Journal, 1,* 29–46.

Cohen, P., Cohen, J., Kasen, S., Velez, C. N., Hartmark, C., Johnson, J., et al. (1993). An epidemiological study of disorders in late childhood and adolescence—I: Age- and gender-specific prevalence. *Journal of Child Psychology and Psychiatry, 34,* 851–867.

Cohen, P., Slomkowski, C., & Robins, L. N. (1999). *Historical and geographical influences on psychopathology.* Mahwah, NJ: Lawrence Erlbaum Associates.

Coie, J., Terry, R., Lenox, K., Lochman, J., & Hyman, C. (1995). Childhood peer rejection and aggression as predictors of stable patterns of adolescent disorder. *Development and Psychopathology, 7,* 697–714.

Cole, D. A., Martin, J. M., Powers, B., & Truglio, R. (1996). Modeling casual relations between academic and social competence and depression: A multitrait-multimethod

longitudinal study of children. *Journal of Abnormal Psychology, 105,* 258–270.

Cole, D. A., Peeke, L. G., Martin, J. M., & Truglio, R. (1998). A longitudinal look at the relation between depression and anxiety in children and adolescents. *Journal of Consulting and Clinical Psychology, 66,* 451–460.

Cole, P. M., Michel, M. K., & Teti, L. O. (1994). The development of emotion regulation and dysregulation: A clinical perspective. In N. A. Fox (Ed.), *Monographs of the Society for Research in Child Development, 59,* 73–102.

Cole, P. M., Zahn-Waxler, C., Fox, N. A., Usher, B. A., & Welsh, J. D. (1996). Individual differences in emotion regulation and behavior problems in preschool children. *Journal of Abnormal Psychology, 105,* 518–529.

Cole, P. M., Zahn-Waxler, C., & Smith, K. D. (1994). Expressive control during a disappointment: Variations related to preschoolers' behavior problems. *Developmental Psychology, 30,* 835–846.

Coll, C. G., Akerman, A., & Cicchetti, D. (2000). Cultural influences on developmental processes and outcomes: Implications for the study of development and psychopathology. *Development and Psychopathology, 12,* 333–356.

Coll, C. G., & Garrido, M. (2000). Minorities in the United States: Sociocultural context for mental health and developmental psychopathology. In A. J. Sameroff, M. Lewis, &

S. M. Miller (Eds.), *Handbook of developmental psychopathology* (pp. 177–196). New York: Kluwer Academic.

Coll, C. G., & Pachter, L. M. (2002). Ethnic and minority parenting. In M. H. Bornstein (Ed.), *Handbook of parenting: Vol. 4. Social conditions and applied parenting* (2nd ed., pp. 1–20). Mahwah, NJ: Erlbaum.

Collinson, S. L., Mackay, C. E., James, A. C., Quested, D. J., Phillips, T., Roberts, N., & Crow, T. J. (2003). Brain volume, asymmetry and intellectual impairment in relation to sex in early-onset schizophrenia. *British Journal of Psychiatry, 183,* 114–120.

Comas-Diaz, L. (1995). Puerto Ricans and child sexual abuse. In L. A. Fontes (Ed.), *Child abuse in nine North American cultures: Treatment and prevention* (pp. 31–66). Thousand Oaks, CA: Sage.

Combrinck-Graham, L. (1989). Family models of childhood psychopathology. In L. Combrinck-Graham (Ed.), *Children in family contexts: Perspectives on treatment.* New York: Guilford.

Compas, B. E. (1997). Depression in children and adolescents. In E. J. Mash & L. G. Terdal (Eds.), *Assessment of childhood disorders* (pp. 197–229). New York: Guilford.

Compton, S. N., Nelson, A. H., & March, J. S. (2000). Social phobia and separation anxiety symptoms in community and clinical samples of children and adolescents. *Journal of the American*

Academy of Child and Adolescent Psychiatry, 39, 1040–1046.

Conduct Problems Prevention Research Group. (1992). A developmental and clinical model for the prevention of conduct disorder: The FAST Track Program. *Development and Psychopathology, 4,* 509–528.

Conger, J. J., & Galambos, N. L. (1997). *Adolescence and youth* (5th ed.). New York: Longman.

Conger, R. D., Ge, X., Elder, G. H., & Lorenz, F. O. (1994). Economic stress, coercive family process, and developmental problems of adolescents. *Child Development, 65,* 541–561.

Conger, R. D., Patterson, G. R., & Ge, X. (1995). It takes two to replicate: A mediational model for the impact of parents' stress on adolescent adjustment. *Child Development, 66,* 80–97.

Conger, R. D., Wallance, L. E., Sun, Y., Simons, R. L., McLoyd, V. C., & Brody, G. H. (2002). Economic pressure in African American families: A replication and extention of the family stress model. *Developmental Psychology, 38,* 179–193.

Conners, C. K. (2000). *Conners' Continuous Performance Test (CPT II).* Toronto, Ontario, Canada: MHS.

Cooper, M. L. (1994). Motivations for alcohol use among adolescents: Development and validation of a four-factor model. *Psychological Assessment, 6,* 117–128.

Cooper, M. L., Frone, M. R., Russell, M., & Mudar, P. (1995). Drinking to regulate positive and negative emotions: A motivational

model of alcohol use. *Journal of Personality and Social Psychology, 69,* 990–1005.

Copans, S. A., & Kinney, J. (1996). Adolescents. In J. Kinney (Ed.), *Clinical manual of substance abuse* (pp. 288–300). St. Louis, MO: Mosby.

Costello, E. J., Angold, A., Burns, B. J., Erkanli, A., Stangl, D. K., & Tweed, D. L. (1996a). The Great Smoky Mountains Study of youth: Functional impairment and serious emotional disturbance. *Archives of General Psychiatry, 53,* 1137–1143.

Costello, E. J., Angold, A., Burns, B. J., Stangl, D. K., Tweed, D. L., Erklani, A., et al. (1996b). The Great Smoky Mountains Study of Youth: Goals, design, methods, and the prevalence of DSM-III-R disorders. *Archives of General Psychiatry, 53,* 1129–1136.

Costello, E. J., Angold, A., & Keeler, G. P. (1999). Adolescent outcomes of childhood disorders: The consequences of severity and impairment. *Journal of the American Academy of Child and Adolescent Psychiatry, 38,* 121–129.

Costello, E. J., Edelbrock, L. S., Dulcan, M. K., Kalas, R., & Klaric, S. H. (1984). *Report on the NIMH Diagnostic Interview Schedule for Children (DISC).* Washington, DC: National Institute of Mental Heath.

Costello, E. J., Erkanli, A., Federman, E., & Angold, A. (1999). Development of psychiatric comorbidity with substance abuse in adolescents: Effects of

timing and sex. *Journal of Clinical Child Psychology, 28,* 298–311.

Costello, E. J., Farmer, E. M. Z., Angold, A., Burns, B. J., & Erkanli, A. (1997). Psychiatric disorders among American Indian and White youth in Appalachia: The Great Smoky Mountains study. *American Journal of Public Health, 87,* 827–832.

Costello, E. J., Loeber, R., & Stouthamer-Loeber, M. (1991). Pervasive and situational hyperactivity: Confounding effect of informant *Journal of Child Psychology and Psychiatry, 32,* 367–376.

Costello, E. J., Mustillo, S., Erklani, A., Keeler, G., & Angold, A. (2003). Prevalence and development of psychiatric disorders in childhood and adolescence. *Archives of General Psychiatry, 60,* 837–844.

Cott, J. M., Rosenthal, N., Blumenthal, M., Fomous, C. M., Cardelina, J. H., Cohen, H. W., et al. (2001). St. John's wort and major depression. *JAMA: Journal of the American Medical Association, 286.*

Cowan, P. A. (1978). *Piaget with feeling.* New York: Holt, Rinehart, and Winston.

Cox, M., & Klinger, E. (1990). Incentive motivation, affective change, and alcohol use: A model. In M. Cox (Ed.), *Why people drink* (pp. 291–311). New York: Gardner Press.

Crago, M., Shisslak, C., & Estes, L. (1996). Eating disturbances among minority groups: A review. *International Journal of Eating Disorders, 19,* 239–248.

Craig, K. D., & Grunau, R. V. E. (1991). Developmental issues: Infants and toddlers. In J. P. Bush & S. W. Harkins (Eds.), *Children in pain: Clinical and research issues from a developmental perspective* (pp. 171–193). New York: Springer-Verlag.

Cramer, P. (2000). Defense mechanisms in psychology today: Further processes for adaptation. *American Psychologist, 55,* 637–646.

Cramer, P., & Block, J. (1998). Preschool antecedents of defense mechanism use in young adults: A longitudinal study. *Journal of Personality and Social Psychology, 74,* 159–169.

Crawford, T. N., Cohen, P., Midlarsky, E., & Brook, J. S. (2001). Internalizing symptoms in children and adolescents: Gender differences in vulnerability to parental distress and discord. *Journal of Research on Adolescence, 11,* 95–118.

Crick, N. R., & Dodge, K. A. (1994). A review and reformulation of social information-processing mechanisms in children's social adjustment. *Psychological Bulletin, 115,* 74–101.

Crick, N. R., & Dodge, K. A. (1999). "Superiority" is in the eye of the beholder: A comment on Sutton, Smith, and Swettenham. *Social Development, 8,* 128–131.

Crick, N. R., & Grotpeter, J. K. (1995). Relational aggression, gender, and social-psychological adjustment. *Child Development, 66,* 710–722.

Crisp, J., Ungerer, J. A., & Goodnow, J. J. (1996). The impact of experience on children's understanding of illness. *Journal of Pediatric Psychology, 21,* 57–72.

Crittenden, P. M. (1988). Relationships at risk. In J. Belsky, & T. Nezworski, *Clinical implications of attachment* (pp. 136–174). Hillsdale, NJ, Erlbaum.

Crittenden, P. M. (1992). Treatment of anxious attachment in infancy and early childhood. *Development and Psychopathology, 4,* 575–602.

Crittenden, P. M. (1993). An information-processing perspective on the behavior of neglectful parents. *Criminal Justice and Behavior, 20,* 27–48.

Crittenden, P. M., Claussen, A. H., & Sugarman, D. B. (1994). Physical and psychological maltreatment in middle childhood and adolescence. *Development and Psychopathology, 6,* 145–164.

Crow, T. J., Done, D. J., & Sacker, A. (1995). Childhood precursors of psychosis as clues to its evolutionary origins. *European Archives of Psychiatry and Clinical Neurology, 245,* 61–69.

Crowell, J. A., Treboux, D., Gao, Y., Fyffe, C., Pan, H., & Waters, E. (2002). Assessing secure base behavior in adulthood: Development of a measure, links to adult attachment representations, and relations to couples' communication and reports of relationships. *Developmental Psychology, 38,* 679–693.

Crowell, J. A., & Waters, E. (1990). Separation anxiety. In M. Lewis & S. M. Miller (Eds.), *Handbook of developmental psychopathology*

(pp. 209–218). New York: Plenum.

Crowley-Jack, D. (1999). Silencing the self: Inner dialogues and outer realities. In T. Joiner & J. C. Coyne (Eds.), *The interactional nature of depression: Advances in interpersonal approaches.* Washington, DC: American Psychological Association.

Cuddy-Casey, M., & Orvaschel, H. (1997). Children's understanding of death in relation to child suicidality and homicidality. *Clinical Psychology Review, 17,* 33–45.

Cullen, D. (2004). The depressive and the psychopath: At last we know why the Columbine killers did it. *Slate, http://slate.msn.com/id/2099203/.*

Cummings, E. M. (1998). Children exposed to marital conflict and violence: Conceptual and theoretical directions. In G. W. Holden, R. A. Geffner, & E. N. Jouriles (Eds.), *Children exposed to marital violence: Theory, research and applied issues* (pp. 55–93). Washington, DC: American Psychological Association.

Cummings, E. M., & Cummings, J. S. (2002). Parenting and attachment. In M. H. Bornstein (Ed.), *Handbook of parenting Vol. 5: Practical issues in parenting* (pp. 35–58). Mahwah, NJ: Erlbaum.

Cummings, E. M., & Davies, P. T. (1994). *Children and marital conflict: The impact of family dispute and resolution.* New York: Guilford.

Cummings, E. M., & Davies, P. T. (1994). Maternal depression and child

development. *Journal of Child Psychology and Psychiatry, 35,* 73–112.

Cummings, E. M., DeArth-Pendley, G., Schudlick, T. D., & Smith, D. A. (1999). Parental depression and family functioning: Towards a process-oriented model of children's adjustment. In S. R. H. Beach (Ed.), *Marital and family processes in depression* (pp. 89–110). Washington, DC: American Psychological Association.

Curran, P. J., & Hussong, A. M. (2002). Structural equation modeling of repeated measures data: Latent curve analysis. In D. S. Moskowitz & S. L. Hershberger (Eds.), *Modeling intraindividual variability with repeated measures data: Methods and applications* (pp. 59–85). Mahway, NJ: Erlbaum.

Curran, P. J., Stice, E., & Chassin, L. (1997). The relation between adolescent alcohol use and peer alcohol use: A longitudinal random coefficients model. *Journal of Consulting and Clinical Psychology, 65,* 130–140.

Dadds, M. R., Barrett, P. M., & Rapee, R. M. (1996). Family process and child anxiety and aggression: An observational analysis. *Journal of Abnormal Child Psychology, 24,* 715–734.

Dadds, M. R., & Roth, J. H. (2001). Family processes in the development of anxiety problems. In M. W. Vasey & M. R. Dadds (Eds.), *The developmental psychopathology of anxiety* (pp. 278–303). New York: Oxford University Press.

Dadds, M. R., Ryan, S., Barrett, P. M., & Rapee, R. M. (1993). *Family anxiety coding schedule procedures manual.* Brisbane, University of Queensland.

Dansky, B. S., Brewerton, T. D., & Kilpatrick, D. G. (2000). Comorbidity of bulimia nervosa and alcohol use disorders: Results from the National Women's Study. *International Journal of Eating Disorders, 27,* 180–190.

D'Augelli, A. R., Hershberger, S. L., & Pilkington, N. W. (1998). Lesbian, gay, and bisexual youth and their families: Disclosure of sexual orientation and its consequences. *American Journal of Orthopsychiatry, 68,* 361–371.

D'Augelli, A. R., Hershberger, S. L., & Pilkington, N. W. (2001). Suicidality patterns and sexual orientation-related factors among lesbian, gay, and bisexual youth. *Suicide and Life-Threatening Behavior, 31,* 250–265.

Davies, M., and Cunningham, G. (1999). Adolescent parasuicide in the Foyle area. *Irish Journal of Psychological Medicine, 16,* 9–12.

Davies, P. T., Dumenci, L., & Windle, M. (1999). The interplay between maternal depressive symptoms and marital distress in the prediction of adolescent adjustment. *Journal of Marriage and the Family, 61,* 238–254.

Davies, P. T., Harold, G. T., Goeke-Morey, M. C., & Cummings, E. M. (2003). Child emotional security and interparental conflict. *Monographs of the Society for Research in Child*

Development, No. 67, 1–131.

Davies, P. T., & Windle, M. (1997). Gender-specific pathways between maternal depressive symptoms, family discord, and adolescent adjustment. *Developmental Psychology, 33,* 657–668.

Davison, K. K., & Birch, L. L. (2001). Weight staus, parent reaction, and self-concept in five-year-old girls. *Pediatrics, 107,* 46–53.

Dawson, G. (1991). A psychobiological perspective on the early social-emotional development of children with autism. In D. Cicchetti, & S. L. Toth, *Rochester symposium on developmental psychopathology* (pp. 207–234). Rochester, NY: University of Rochester.

Dawson, G., Frey, K., Panagiotides, H., & Osterling, J. (1997). Infants of depressed mothers exhibit atypical frontal brain activity: A replication and extension of previous findings. *Journal of Child Psychology & Psychiatry, 38,* 179–186.

Dawson, G., & Osterling, J. (1997). Early intervention in autism. In M. J. Guralnick (Ed.), *The effectiveness of early intervention* (pp. 307–326). Baltimore: Brookes.

Dawson, G., Webb, S., Schellenberg, G. D., Dager, S., Friedman, S., Aylward, E., et al. (2002). Defining the broader phenotype of autism: Genetic, brain, and behavioral perspectives. *Development and Psychopathology, 14*(3), 581–611.

De Bellis, M. D. (2001). Developmental traumatology: The psychobiological development of maltreated children and its implications for research, treatment, and policy. *Development and Psychopathology, 13,* 539–564.

de Wilde, E. J., Kienhorst, I. C. W. M., & Diekstra, R. F. W. (2001). Suicidal behavior in adolescents. In I. M. Goodyer (Ed.), *The depressed child and adolescent,* 2nd ed. (pp. 267–291). New York: Cambridge University Press.

De Wolff, M. S., & Van IJzendoorn, M. H. (1997). Sensitivity and attachment: A meta-analysis on parental antecedents of infant attachment. *Child Development, 68,* 571–591.

Deater-Deckard, K., & Dodge, K. A. (1997). Externalizing behavior problems and discipline revisited: Nonlinear effects and variation by culture, context, and gender. *Psychological Inquiry, 8,* 161–175.

Deater-Deckard, K., Dodge, K. A., Bates, J. E., & Pettit, G. S. (1996). Physical discipline among African American and European American mothers: Links to children's externalizing behaviors. *Developmental Psychology, 32,* 1065–1072.

Deblinger, E., Stauffer, L., & Steer, R. (2001). Comparative efficacy of supportive and cognitive behavioral group therapies for young children who have been sexually abused and their nonoffending mothers. *Child Maltreatment, 6,* 332–343.

Deblinger, E., Steer, R. A., & Lippmann, J. (1999). Two-year follow-up study of cognitive behavioral therapy for sexually abused children suffering post-traumatic stress symptoms. *Child Abuse & Neglect, 23,* 1371–1378.

Deep, A. L., Nagy, L. M., Weltzin, T. E., Rao, R., & Kaye, W. H. (1995). Premorbid onset of psychopathology in long-term recovered anorexia nervosa. *International Journal of Eating Disorders, 17,* 291–297.

DeKlyen, M. (1996). Disruptive behavior disorder and intergenerational attachment patterns: A comparison of clinic-referred and normally functioning preschoolers and their mothers. *Journal of Consulting & Clinical Psychology, 64*(2), 357–365.

Delis, D. C., Kaplan, E., & Kramer, J. H. (2001). *Delis-Kaplan Executive Function System.* San Antonio, TX: The Psychological Corporation.

Denham, S. A., Mason, T., & Couchoud, E. A. (1995). Scaffolding young children's prosocial responsiveness: Preschoolers; responses to adult sadness, anger, and pain. *International Journal of Behavioral Development, 18,* 489–504.

Dennis, T. A., Cole, P. M., Zahn-Waxler, C., & Mizuta, I. (2002). Self in context: Autonomy and relatedness in Japanese and US mother-preschooler dyads. *Child Development, 73,* 1803–1817.

DeVane, C. L., & Sallee, F. R. (1996). Serotonin selective reuptake inhibitors in child and adolescent psychopharmacology: A review of published experience. *Journal of Clinical Psychiatry, 57,* 55–66.

Didden, R., Duker, P. C., & Korzilius, H. (1997). Meta-analytic study on treatment effectiveness for problem behaviors with individuals who have mental retardation. *American Journal of Mental Retardation, 101,* 387–399.

Dishion, T. J., French, D. C., & Patterson, G. R. (1995). The development and ecology of antisocial behavior. In D. Cicchetti & D. J. Cohen (Eds.), *Developmental psychopathology, Vol. 2. Risk, disorder, and adaptation* (pp. 421–471). New York: Wiley.

Dishion, T. J., McCord, J., & Poulin, F. (1999). When interventions harm: Peer groups and problem behavior. *American Psychologist, 54,* 755–764.

Dishion, T. J., & McMahon, R. J. (1998). Parental monitoring and the prevention of child and adolescent problem behavior: A conceptual and empirical formulation. *Clinical Child & Family Psychology Review, 1,* 61–75.

Dishion, T. J., & Owen, L. D. (2002). A longitudinal analysis of friendships and substance use: Bidirectional influence from adolescence to adulthood. *Developmental Psychology, 35,* 480–491.

Dissanayake, C., & Sigman, M. (2001). Attachment and emotional responsiveness in children with autism. *International Review of Research in Mental Retardation 23,* 239–266.

Dodge, K. (1990). Developmental psychopathology in children of depressed mothers. *Developmental Psychology, 26,* 3–6.

Dodge, K. (1993). Social-cognitive mechanisms in the development of conduct disorder and depression. *Annual Review of Psychology, 44,* 559–584.

Dodge, K. A., Bates, J. E., & Pettit, G. S. (1990). Mechanisms in the cycle of violence. *Science, 250,* 1678–1683.

Dodge, K. A., Lochman, J. E., Harnish, J. D., & Bates, J. E. (1997). Reactive and proactive aggression in school children and psychiatrically impaired chronically assaultive youth. *Journal of Abnormal Psychology, 106,* 37–51.

Dodge, K. A., & Petit, G. S. (2003). A biopsychosocial model of the development of chronic conduct problems in adolescence. *Developmental Psychology, 39,* 349–371.

Dodge, K. A., Pettit, G. S., & Bates, J. E. (1994). Effects of physical maltreatment on the development of peer relations. *Development and Psychopathology, 6,* 43–56.

Dodge, K. A., Pettit, G. S., Bates, J. E., & Valente, E. (1995). Social information-processing patterns partially mediate the effect of early physical abuse on later conduct problems. *Journal of Abnormal Psychology, 104,* 632–643.

Donahue, K. M., Perry, K. E., & Weinstein, R. S. (2003). Teachers' classroom practices and children's rejection by their peers. *Journal of Applied Developmental Psychology, 24,* 91–118.

Donaldson, D., Spirito, A., & Overholser, J. (2003). Treatment of adolescent suicide attempters. In *Evaluating and treating adolescent suicide attempters: From research to practice* (pp. 295–321). San Diego, CA: Academic Press.

Douglas, V. I. (1983). Attention and cognitive problems. In M. Rutter (Ed.), *Developmental neuropsychiatry* (pp. 280–329). New York: Guilford.

Douglass, H. M., Moffitt, T. E., Dar, R., McGee, R., & Silva, P. (1995). Obsessive-compulsive disorder in a birth cohort of 18-year-olds: Prevalence and prediction. *Journal of the American Academy of Child and Adolescent Psychiatry, 34,* 1424–1430.

Doussard-Roosevelt, J. A., Joe, C. M., Bazhenova, O. V., & Porges, S. W. (2003). Mother-child interaction in autistic and nonautistic children: Characteristics of maternal approach behaviors and child social responses. *Development and Psychopathology, 15*(2), 277–296.

Downey, G. (2000). Rejection sensitivity and male violence in romantic relationships. *Personal Relationships, 7,* 45–61.

Downey, G., & Coyne, J. C. (1990). Children of depressed parents: An integrative review. *Psychological Bulletin, 108,* 50–76.

Downey, G., Khouri, H., & Feldman, S. I. (1997). Early interpersonal trauma and later adjustment: The mediational role of rejection sensitivity. In D. Cicchetti & S. L. Toth (Eds.), *Developmental perspectives on trauma: Theory, research, and intervention* (pp. 85–114). Rochester, NY: University of Rochester Press.

Doyle, J., & Bryant-Waugh, R. (2000). Epidemiology. In B. Lask & R. Bryant-Wauch (Eds.), *Anorexia nervosa and related eating disorders in childhood and adolescence* (pp. 41–61). Philadelphia: Psychology Press.

Drake, B., & Pandey, S. (1996). Understanding the relationship between neighborhood poverty and specific types of child maltreatment. *Child Abuse and Neglect, 20,* 1003–1018.

Driessen, M., Herrmann, J., & Stahl, K. (2000). Magnetic resonance imaging volumes of the hippocampus amygdala in women with borderline personality disorder and early traumatization. *Archives of General Psychiatry, 57,* 1115–1122.

Drotar, D., Stein, R. E. K., & Perrin, E. C. (1995). Methodological issues in using the Child Behavior Checklist and its related instruments in clinical child psychology research. *Journal of Clinical Child Psychology, 24*(2), 184–192.

Dube, E. M., Savin-Williams, R. C., & Diamond, L. M. (2001). Intimacy development, gender, and ethnicity among sexual-minority youth. In A. R. D'Augelli & C. Patterson (Eds.), *Lesbian, gay and bisexual identities among youth: Psychological perspectives* (pp. 129–152). New York: Oxford University Press.

Dubner, A. E., & Motta, R. W. (1999). Sexually and physically abused foster care children and posttraumatic stress disorder. *Journal of Consulting and Clinical Psychology, 67,* 367–373.

Dujovne, V. F., Barnard, M. U., & Rapoff, M. A. (1995). Pharmacological and cognitive-behavioral approaches in the treatment of childhood depression: A review and critique. *Clinical Psychology Review, 15,* 589–611.

Dukewich, T. L., Borkowski, J. G., & Whitman, T. L. (1996). Adolescent mothers and child abuse potential: An evaluation of risk factors. *Child Abuse and Neglect, 20,* 1031–1047.

Dumas, J. E., LaFreniere, P. J., & Serketich, W. J. (1995). "Balance of power": A transactional analysis of control in mother-child dyads involving socially competent, aggressive, and anxious children. *Journal of Abnormal Psychology, 104,* 104–113.

Duncan, R. D., Saunders, B. E., Kilpatrick, D. G., Rochelle, F., & Resnick, H. S. (1996). Childhood physical assault as a risk factor for PTSD, depression, and substance abuse: Findings from a national survey. *American Journal of Orthopsychiatry, 66,* 437–448.

DuPaul, G. J., Barkely, R. A., & Connor, D. F. (1998). Stimulants. In R. A. Barkley (Ed.), *Attention deficit hyperactivity disorder: A handbook for diagnosis and treatment* (2nd ed., pp. 510–551). New York: Guilford.

DuPaul, G. J., McGoey, K. E., Eckert, T. L., & VanBrakle, J. (2001). Preschool children with attention-deficit/hyperactivity disorder: Impairments in behavioral, social, and school functioning. *Journal of the American Academy of Child and Adolescent Psychiatry, 40,* 508–515.

Durlak, J. A. (1997). Primary prevention programs in the schools. In T. H. Ollendick & R. J. Prinz (Eds.), *Advances in clinical child psychology Vol. 19* (pp. 283–318). New York: Plenum.

Durlak, J. A., Fuhrman, T., & Lampman, C. (1991). Effectiveness of cognitive-behavior therapy for maladapting children: A meta-analysis. *Psychological Bulletin, 110,* 204–214.

Dutton, D. (1999). Traumatic origins of intimate rage. *Aggression and Violent Behavior, 4,* 431–447.

Dutton, D. G. (2000). Witnessing parental violence as a traumatic experience shaping the abusive personality. *Journal of Aggression, Maltreatment, and Trauma, 3,* 59–67.

Dykens, E. M. (2002). Are jigsaw puzzle skills "spared" in persons with Prader-Willi syndrome? *Journal of Child Psychology and Psychiatry, 43,* 343–352.

Dykens, E. M., Leckman, J. F., & Cassidy, S. B. (1996). Obsessions and compulsions in Prader-Willi syndrome. *Journal of Child Psychology and Psychiatry, 37,* 995–1002.

Eaves, L. J., Silberg, J. L., & Meyer, J. M. (1997). Genetics and developmental psychopathology: 2. The main effects of genes and environment on behavioral problems in the Virginia Twin Study of Adolescent Behavioral Development.

Journal of Child Psychology and Psychiatry, 38, 965–980.

Ebata, A. T., Peterson, A. C., & Conger, J. J. (1990). The development of psychopathology in adolescence. In J. Rolf, A. S. Masten, D. Cicchetti, K. H. Nuechterlein, & S. Weintraub (Eds.), *Risk and protective factors in the development of psychopathology* (pp. 308–333). Cambridge, England: Cambridge University Press.

Edleson, J. L. (1999). Interventions and issues in the co-occurrence of child abuse and domestic violence. *Child Maltreatment, 4*(2), 91–182.

Egeland, B. (1988). Breaking the cycle of abuse: Implications for prediction and intervention. In K. D. Browne, C. Davies, & P. Stratton (Eds.), *Early prediction and prevention of child abuse* (pp. 87–99). New York: Wiley.

Egeland, B. (1991). A longitudinal study of high-risk families. In R. Starr & D. Wolfe (Eds.), *The effects of child abuse and neglect: Issues and research* (pp. 43–46). New York: Guilford.

Egeland, B. (1997). Mediators of the effects of child maltreatment on developmental adaptation in adolescence. In D. Cicchetti & S. L. Toth (Eds.), *Developmental perspectives on trauma: Theory, research, and intervention* (pp. 403–434). Rochester, NY: University of Rochester Press.

Egeland, B. R., Pianta, R. C., & O'Brien, M. A. (1993). Maternal intrusiveness in infancy and child

maladaptation in early school years. *Development and Psychopathology, 5,* 359–370.

Egeland, B. R., Weinfield, N. S., Bosquet, M., & Cheng, V. K. (2000). Remembering, repeating, and working through: Lessons from attachment-based interventions. In J. D. Osofsky & H. E. Fitzgerald (Eds.), *Handbook of infant mental health, Vol. 4: Infant mental health in groups at high risk* (pp. 35–89). New York: Wiley.

Eggers, C., & Bunk, D. (1997). The long-term course of childhood-onset schizophrenia: A 42-year followup. *Schizophrenia Bulletin, 23,* 105–116.

Eggers, C., Bunk, D., & Ropcke, B. (2002). Childhood and adolescent onset schizophrenia: Results from two long-term follow-up studies. *Neurology, Psychiatry, and Brain Research, 9,* 183–190.

Einfeld, S. L., & Aman, M. (1995). Issues in the taxonomy of psychopathology in mental retardation. *Journal of Autism & Developmental Disorders, 25*(2), 143–167.

Einfeld, S. L., & Tonge, B. J. (1996). Population prevalence of psychopathology in children and adolescents with intellectual disability. II: Epidemiological findings. *Journal of Intellectual Disability Research, 40,* 99–109.

Eisenberg, N., Fabes, R. A., Shepard, S. A., Murphy, B. C., Guthrie, I. K., Jones, S., Friedman, J., Poulin, R., & Maszk, P. (1997). Contemporaneous and longitudinal prediction of children's social

functioning from regulation and emotionality. *Child Development, 68,* 642–664.

Eisenberg, N., & Strayer, J. (1987). *Empathy and its development.* New York: Cambridge University Press.

Eisenberg, N., Valiente, C., Fabes, R. A., Smith, C. L., Reiser, M., Shepard, S. A., et al. (2003). The relations of effortful control and ego control to children's resiliency and social functioning. *Developmental Psychology, 39,* 761–776.

Eley, T. C. (2001). Contributions of behavioral genetics research: Quantifying genetic, shared environmental and nonshared environmental influences. In M. W. Vasey & M. R. Dadds (Eds.), *The developmental psychopathology of anxiety* (pp. 45–59). New York: Oxford University Press.

Eley, T. C., Deater-Deckard, K., Fombonne, E., & Fulker, D. W. (1998). An adoption study of depressive symptoms in middle childhood. *Journal of Child Psychology and Psychiatry and Allied Disciplines, 39,* 337–345.

Elkind, D. (1981). *The hurried child.* Reading, MA: Addison-Wesley.

Elliot, D. S., Huizinga, D., & Menard, S. (1989). *Multiple problem youth: Delinquency, substance use, and mental health problems.* New York: Springer-Verlag.

Elliott, S. N., Busse, R. T., & Shapiro, E. S. (1999). Intervention techniques for academic performance problems. In T. B. Gutkin & C. R. Reynolds (Eds.),

The handbook of school psychology (2nd ed., pp. 664–685). New York: Wiley.

Elze, D. E., Auslander, W., McMillen, C., Edmond, T., & Thompson, R. (2001). Untangling the impact of sexual abuse on HIV risk behaviors among youths in foster care. *AIDS Prevention and Education, 13,* 377–389.

Eme, R. F., & Kavanaugh, L. (1995). Sex differences in conduct disorder. *Journal of Clinical Child Psychology, 24,* 406–426.

Emery, N. J. (2000). The eyes have it: The neuroethology, function and evolution of social gaze. *Neuroscience and Biobehavioral Review, 24,* 581–604.

Emery, R. E., & Kitzmann, K. M. (1995). The child in the family: Disruptions in family functions. In D. Cicchetti & D. J. Cohen (Eds.), *Developmental psychopathology: Vol. I. Theory and methods* (pp. 3–31). New York: Wiley.

Emery, R. E., & Laumann-Billings, L. (1998). An overview of the nature, causes, and consequences of abusive family relationships: Toward differentiating maltreatment and violence. *American Psychologist, 53,* 121–135.

Emmons, S., Geiser, C., Kaplan, K., & Harrow, M. (1997). *Living with schizophrenia.* Washington, DC: Accelerated Development.

Emslie, G. J., Mayes, T. L., & Hughes, C. W. (2000). Updates in the pharmacologic treatment of childhood depression. *Psychiatric Clinics of North America, 23,* 813–835.

Emslie, G. J., Rush, J., Weinberg, W. A., Kowatch, R. A., Hughes, C. W., Carmody, T., et al. (1997). A double-blind, randomized, placebo-controlled trial of fluoxetine in children and adolescents with depression. *Archives of General Psychiatry, 54,* 1031–1037.

Endresen, I. M., & Olweus, D. (2001). Self-reported empathy in Norwegian adolescents: Sex differences, age trends, and relationship to bullying. In A. C. Bohart & D. J. Stipek (Eds.), *Constructive and destructive behavior: Implications for family, school, and society* (pp. 147–185). Washington, DC: American Psychological Association.

Epstein, J. N., March, J. S., Conners, C. K., & Jackson, D. L. (1998). Racial differences on the Conners Teacher Rating Scale. *Journal of Abnormal Child Psychology, 26,* 109–118.

Erickson, M. F., & Egeland, B. (2002). Child neglect. In J. E. B. Myers, L. Berliner, J. Briere, C. T. Hendrix, C. Jenny, & T. A. Reid (Eds.), *The APSAC handbook on child maltreatment* (2nd ed., pp. 3–20). Thousand Oaks, CA: Sage.

Erickson, M. F., Egeland, B., & Pianta, R. (1989). The effects of maltreatment on the development of young children. In D. Cicchetti & V. Carlson (Eds.), *Child maltreatment: Theory and research on the causes and consequences of child abuse and neglect* (pp. 647–684). New York: Cambridge University Press.

Erickson, M. F., Korfmacher, J., & Egeland, B. R. (1992).

Attachments past and present: Implications for therapeutic intervention with mother-infant dyads. *Development and Psychopathology, 4,* 495–508.

Erickson, M. F., & Kurz-Riemer, K. (2002). *Infants, toddlers, and families: A framework for support and intervention.* New York: Guilford.

Erikson, E. H. (1950). *Childhood and society.* New York: Norton.

Erikson, E. H. (1964a). Clinical observation of play disruption in young children. In M. R. Haworth (Ed.), *Child psychotherapy* (pp. 264–276). New York: Basic Books.

Erikson, E. H. (1964b). Play and cure. In M. R. Haworth (Ed.), *Child psychotherapy* (pp. 475–485). New York: Basic Books.

Erikson, E. H. (1968). *Identity: Youth and crisis.* New York: Norton.

Eron, L. D. (2001). Seeing is believing: How viewing violence alters attitudes and aggressive behavior. In *Constructive & destructive behavior: Implications for family, school, & society* (pp. 49–60). Washington, DC: American Psychological Association.

Eron, L. D., & Huesmann, L. R. (1990). The stability of aggressive behavior—Even unto the third generation. In M. Lewis & S. M. Miller (Eds.), *Handbook of developmental psychopathology* (pp. 147–155). New York: Plenum.

Esposito, C., Spirito, A., & Overholser, J. (2003). Behavioral factors: Impulsive and aggressive behavior. In A. Spirito & J. C.

Overholser (Eds.), *Evaluating and treating adolescent suicide attempters: From research to practice* (pp. 147–160). New York: Academic Press.

Evans, B., & Lee, B. K. (1998). Culture and child psychopathology. In S. S. Kazarian & D. R. Evans (Eds.), *Cultural clinical psychology: Theory, research, and practice* (pp. 289–315). New York: Oxford University Press.

Evans, G. W. (2004). The environment of childhood poverty. *American Psychologist, 59,* 77–92.

Exner, J. E. (1993). *The Rorschach: A comprehensive system: Vol. 1. Basic foundations* (3rd ed.). New York: Wiley.

Exner, J. E. (1994). *The Rorschach: A comprehensive system: Vol. 3. Assessment of children and adolescents* (2nd ed.). New York: Wiley.

Faedda, G. L., Baldessarini, R. J., Suppes, T., Tondo, L., Becker, I., & Lipschitz, D. S. (1995). Pediatric-onset bipolar disorder: A neglected clinical and public health problem. *Harvard Review of Psychiatry, 3,* 171–195.

Fairburn, C. G., Cooper, Z., Doll, H. A., Norman, P., & O'Connor, M. (2000). The natural course of bulimia nervosa and binge eating disorder in young women. *Archives of General Psychiatry, 56,* 468–476.

Fairburn, C. G., Cowen, P. J., & Harrison, R. J. (1999). Twin studies and the etiology of eating disorders. *International Journal of Eating Disorders, 26,* 349–358.

Fairburn, C. G., Norman, P. A., Welch, S. L., O'Connor, M. E., Doll, H. A., & Peveler, R. C. (1995). A prospective study of outcome in bulimia nervosa and the long-term effects of three psychological treatments. *Archives of General Psychiatry, 52,* 304–312.

Fairburn, C. G., Shafran, R., & Cooper, Z. (1999). A cognitive behavioral theory of anorexia nervosa. *Behaviour Research and Therapy, 37,* 1–13.

Fairburn, C. G., Welch, S. L., Doll, H. A., Davies, B. A., & O'Connor, M. E. (1997). Risk factors for bulimia nervosa: A community-based case-control study. *Archives of General Psychiatry, 54,* 509–517.

Fallon, A., & Bunce, S. (2000). The psychoanalytic perspective. In K. J. Miller & J. S. Mizes (Eds.), *Comparative treatments for eating disorders* (pp. 82–127). New York: Springer.

Fantuzzo, J. W., Boruch, R., Beriana, A., Atkins, M., & Marcus, S. (1997). Domestic violence and children: Prevalence and risk in five major US cities. *Journal of the American Academy of Child and Adolescent Psychiatry, 36,* 116–122.

Farrell, A. D., & White, K. S. (1998). Peer influences and drug use among urban adolescents: Family structure and parent-adolescent relationship as protective factors. *Journal of Consulting and Clinical Psychology, 66,* 248–258.

Farrington, D. P. (1992). Understanding and preventing bullying. In M. Tonry & N. Morris (Eds.), *Crime and justice: An annual review of research: Volume 17* (pp. 381–458). Chicago: University of Chicago Press.

Farrington, D. P. (1995). The development of offending and antisocial behavior from childhood: Key findings from the Cambridge study in delinquent development. *Journal of Child Psychology and Psychiatry, 360,* 929–964.

Faulkner, A. H., & Cranston, K. (1998). Correlates of same-sex sexual behavior in a random sample of Massachusetts high school students. *American Journal of Public Health, 88,* 262–266.

Federal Interagency Forum on Child and Family Statistics. (2002). *America's children: Key national indicators of well-being.* Washington, DC: U.S. Government Printing Office.

Feeney, T., & Ylvisaker, M. (1995). Choice and routine: Antecedent behavioral interventions for adolescents with severe traumatic brain injury. *Journal of Head Trauma Rehabilitation, 10,* 67–86.

Feigelman, S., Stanton, B. F., & Ricardo, I. (1993). Perceptions of drug selling and drug use among urban youths. *Journal of Early Adolescence, 13,* 267–284.

Feldman, R. B., Zelkowitz, P., Weiss, M., Heyman, M., Vogel, J., & Paris, J. (1995). A comparison of the families of borderline personality disorder mothers and the families of other personality disorder mothers. *Comprehensive Psychiatry, 36,* 1–8.

Ferguson, C. P., & Pigott, T. A. (2000). Anorexia and bulimia nervosa: Neurobiology and pharmacotherapy. *Behavior Therapy, 31,* 237–263.

Fergusson, D. M., & Horwood, L. J. (1996). The role of adolescent peer affiliations in the continuity between childhood behavioral adjustment and juvenile offending. *Journal of Abnormal Child Psychology, 24,* 205–221.

Fergusson, D. M., Horwood, L. J., & Beautrais, A. L. (1999). Is sexual orientation related to mental health problems and suicidality in young people? *Archives of General Psychiatry, 56,* 876–880.

Fergusson, D. M., Horwood, L. J., & Lynskey, M. T. (1995). The stability of disruptive childhood behaviors. *Journal of Abnormal Child Psychology, 23,* 379–396.

Fergusson, D. M., Horwood, L. J., & Lynskey, M. T. (1996). Childhood sexual abuse and psychiatric disorder in young adulthood II: Psychiatric outcomes of childhood sexual abuse. *Journal of the American Academy of Child and Adolescent Psychiatry, 34,* 1365–1374.

Fergusson, D. M., & Lynskey, M. T. (1996). Adolescent resiliency to family adversity. *Journal of Child Psychology and Psychiatry and Allied Disciplines, 37,* 281–292.

Fergusson, D. M., Lynskey, M. T., & Horwood, L. J. (1996). Factors associated with continuity and changes in disruptive behavior patterns between childhood and adolescence. *Journal of Abnormal Child Psychology, 24,* 533–553.

Fergusson, D. M. & Woodward, L. J. (2000). Educational, psychosocial, and sexual outcomes of girls with conduct problems in early adolescence. *Journal of Child Psychology & Psychiatry, 41,* 779–792.

Fergusson, D. M., Fergusson, I. E., Horwood, L. J., & Kinzett, N. G. (1988). A longitudinal study of detine lead levels, intelligence, school performance, and behavior. *Journal of Child Psychology and Psychiatry, 29,* 811–824.

Field, T. (1992). Infants of depressed mothers. *Development and Psychopathology, 4,* 49–66.

Figueroa, E., & Silk, K. R. (1997). Biological implications of childhood sexual abuse in borderline personality disorder. *Journal of Personality Disorders, 11,* 71–92.

Filipek, P. A., Accardo, P. J., Baranek, G. T., Cook, E. H., Dawson, G., Gordon, B., et al. (1999). The screening and diagnosis of autistic spectrum disorders. *Journal of Autism and Developmental Disorders, 29(6),* 439–484.

Finkelhor, D. (1984). *Child sexual abuse: New theories and research.* New York: Free Press.

Finkelhor, D. (1994). Current information on the scope and nature of child sexual abuse. *Future of Children, 4,* 31–53.

Finkelhor, D., & Berliner, L. (1995). Research on the treatment of sexually abused children: A review and recommendations. *Journal of the American Academy of Child and Adolescent Psychiatry, 34,* 1408–1423.

Finkelhor, D., & Browne, A. (1988). Assessing the long-term impact of child sexual abuse: A review and reconceptualization. In L. Walker (Ed.), *Handbook on sexual abuse of children* (pp. 55–71). New York: Springer.

Finkelhor, D., & Dziuba-Leatherman, J. (1995). Victimization prevention programs: A national survey of children's exposure and reactions. *Child Abuse and Neglect, 19,* 129–140.

Finkelhor, D., Hotaling, G. T., Lewis, I. A., & Smith, C. (1990). Sexual abuse in a national survey of adult men and women: Prevalence, characteristics, and risk factors. *Child Abuse and Neglect, 14,* 19–28.

Finkelhor, D., Ormrod, R., Turner, H., & Hamby, S. L. (2005). The victimization of children and youth: A comprehensive, national survey. *Child Maltreatment, 10,* 5–25.

First, M. B., Frances, A., & Pincus, H. A. (2002). *DSM-IV-TR handbook of differential diagnosis.* Washington, DC, American Psychiatric Press.

Fischel, J. E., & Liebert, R. M. (2000). Disorders of elimination. In A. J. Sameroff, M. Lewis, & S. M. Miller (Eds.), *Handbook of developmental psychopathology* (pp. 625–640). New York, Kluwer Academic.

Fischer, K. W., & Ayoub, C. (1994). Affective splitting and dissociation in normal and maltreated children: Developmental pathways for self in relationships. In D. Cicchetti & S. L. Toth (Eds.), *Rochester symposium on developmental psychopathology: Disorders and dysfunctions of the self* (pp. 149–222). New York: Rochester.

Fischer, M., & Barkley, R. A. (2003). Childhood stimulant treatment and risk for later substance abuse. *Journal of Clinical Psychiatry, 64,* 19–23.

Fischer, M., Barkley, R. A., Smallish, L., & Fletcher, K. R. (2002). Young adult outcome of hyperactive children as a function of severity of childhood conduct problems: Comorbid psychiatric disorders and interim mental health treatment. *Journal of Abnormal Child Psychology, 30*(5), 463–475.

Fitzgerald, H. E., Davies, W. H., Zucker, R. A., & Klinger, M. T. (1994). Developmental systems theory and substance abuse: A conceptual and methodological framework for analyzing patterns of variation in families. In L. L'Abate (Ed.), *Handbook of developmental family psychology and psychopathology* (pp. 350–372). New York: Wiley.

Flament, M. F., Whitaker, A., Rapoport, J. L., & Davies, M. (1988). Obsessive compulsive disorder in adolescence: An epidemiological study. *Journal of the American Academy of Child & Adolescent Psychiatry, 27,* 764–771.

Flannery, D. J., Vazsonyi, A. T., Liau, A. K., Guo, M. S., Powell, K. E., Atha, H., et al. (2003). Initial behavior outcomes for the PeaceBuilders Universal School-Based Violence Prevention Program.

Developmental Psychology, 39, 292–308.

Flisher, A. J. (1999). Mood disorder in suicidal children and adolescents: Recent developments. *Journal of Child Psychology & Psychiatry, 40,* 315–324.

Folstein, S. E., & Santangelo, S. L. (2000). Does Asperger syndrome aggregate in families? In A. Klin & F. R. Volkmar (Eds.), *Asperger syndrome* (pp. 159–171). New York: Guilford Press.

Fombonne, E., & Chakrabarti, S. (2001). No evidence for a new variant of measles-mumps-rubella induced autism. *Pediatrics, 108,* 56.

Fonagy, P., Gergely, G., Jurist, E., & Target, M. (2003). *Affect regulation, mentalization, and the development of the self.* New York: Other Press.

Fonagy, P., & Target, M. (1994). The efficacy of psychoanalysis for children with disruptive disorders. *Journal of the American Academy of Child and Adolescent Psychiatry, 33,* 45–55.

Fonagy, P., & Target, M. (1996a). Should we allow psychotherapy research to determine clinical practice? *Clinical Psychology: Science and Practice, 3,* 245–250.

Fonagy, P., & Target, M. (1996b). A contemporary psychoanalytical perspective: Psychodynamic developmental therapy. In E. D. Hibbs & P. S. Jensen (Eds.), *Psychosocial treatments for child and adolescent disorders: Empirically based strategies for clinical practice* (pp. 619–638). Washington,

DC: American Psychological Association.

Fonagy, P., & Target, M. (2000). Attachment and borderline personality disorder. *Journal of the American Psychoanalytic Association, 48,* 1129–1146.

Fonagy, P., Target, M., Steele, M., & Gerber, A. (1995). Psychoanalytic perspectives on developmental psychopathology. In D. Cicchetti & D. J. Cohen (Eds.), *Developmental psychopathology: Vol. I. Theory and methods* (pp. 504–554). New York: Wiley.

Fong, R. (2003). *Culturally competent practice with immigrant and refugee children and families.* New York: Guilford.

Foorman, B. R., Francis, D. J., Beeler, T., Winikates, D., & Fletcher, J. M. (1997). Early interventions for children with reading problems: Study designs and preliminary findings. *Learning Disabilities: A Multidisciplinary Journal, 8,* 63–72.

Ford, J. D., Racusin, R., Ellis, C. G., Davis, W. B., Reiser, J., Fleischer, A., et al. (2000). Child maltreatment, other trauma exposure, and posttraumatic symptomatology among children with oppositional defiant and attention deficit hyperactivity disorders. *Child Maltreatment, 5,* 205–217.

Forehand, R., & Wierson, M. (1993). The role of developmental factors in planning behavioral interventions for children: Disruptive behavior as an example. *Behavior Therapy, 24,* 117–141.

Foreyt, J. P., & Mikhail, C. (1997). Anorexia nervosa

and bulimia nervosa. In E. J. Mash & L. G. Terdal (Eds.), *Assessment of childhood disorders* (pp. 683–716). New York: Guilford.

Forgatch, M. S., & Patterson, G. R. (1998). Behavioral family therapy. In F. M. Dattilio (Ed.), *Case studies in couple and family therapy: Systemic and cognitive perspectives* (pp. 85–107). New York: Guilford.

Forth, A. E., Hart, S. D., & Hare, R. D. (1990). Assessment of psychopathy in male young offenders. *Psychological Assessment, 3,* 342–344.

Fosson, A., Knibbs, J., Bryant-Waugh, R., & Lask, B. (1987). Early onset anorexia nervosa. *Archives of Disease in Childhood, 62,* 114–118.

Fraiberg, S. (1980). *Clinical studies in infant mental health: The first year of life.* New York: Basic Books.

Franklin, M. E., Rynn, M., Foa, E. B., & March, J. S. (2003). Treatment of obsessive-compulsive disorder. In M. A. Reinecke, F. M. Dattilio, & A. Freeman (Eds.), *Cognitive therapy with children and adolescents: A casebook for clinical practice* (2nd ed., pp. 162–188). New York: Guilford.

Frazier, J. A., Alaghband-Rad, J., & Jacobsen, L. (1997). Pubertal development and the onset of psychosis in childhood onset schizophrenia. *Psychiatry Research, 70,* 1–7.

Freud, A. (1964). *The psychoanalytical treatment of children.* New York: Schocken.

Freud, A. (1965). *Normality and pathology in child-*hood. New York: International Universities Press.

Frick, P. J., Bodin, S. D., & Barry, C. T. (2000). Psychopathic traits and conduct problems in community and clinic-referred samples of children: Further development of the Psychopathy Screening Device. *Psychological Assessment, 12,* 382–393.

Frick, P. J., Cornell, A., Bodin, D., Dane, H., Barry, C. T., & Loney, B. R. (2003). Callous-unemotional traits and developmental pathways to severe conduct problems. *Developmental Psychology, 39,* 246–260.

Frick, P. J., & Ellis, M. (1999). Callous-unemotional traits and subtypes of conduct disorder. *Clinical Child and Family Psychology Review, 2,* 149–168.

Frick, P. J., & Jackson, Y. K. (1993). Family functioning and childhood antisocial behavior: Yet another reinterpretation. *Journal of Clinical Child Psychology, 22,* 410–419.

Frick, P. J., Lahey, B. B., Loeber, R., Tannenbaum, L., Van Horn, Y., Christ, M. A., et al. (1993). Oppositional defiant disorder and conduct disorder: A meta-analytic review of factor analyses and cross-validation in a clinic sample. *Clinical Psychology Review, 13,* 319–340.

Frick, P. J., O'Brien, B. S., Wootton, J. M., & McBurnett, K. (1994). Psychopathy and conduct problems in children. *Journal of Abnormal Psychology, 103,* 700–707.

Friedberg, R. D., & McClure, J. M. (2002). *Clinical practice of cognitive therapy with children and* adolescents: The nuts and bolts. New York: Guilford.

Friedrich, W. (1997). Psychotherapy with sexually abused boys. In D. A. Wolfe, R. J. McMahon, & R. D. Peters (Eds.), *Child abuse: New directions in prevention and treatment across the lifespan* (pp. 205–222). Thousand Oaks, CA: Sage.

Friedrich, W. N. (2002). An integrated model of psychotherapy for abused children. In J. E. B. Myers, L. Berliner, J. Briere, C. T. Hendrix, C. Jenny, & T. A. Reid (Eds.), *The APSAC handbook on child maltreatment* (2nd ed., pp. 139–140). Thousand Oaks, CA: Sage.

Fristad, M. A. (2002). *Assessing and treating early-onset bipolar disorder.* Chicago: American Psychological Association.

Fristad, M. A., Shaver, A. E., & Holderle, K. E. (2002). Mood disorders in childhood and adolescence. In D. T. Marsh & M. A. Fristad (Eds.), *Handbook of serious emotional disturbance in children and adolescents* (pp. 228–265). New York: Wiley.

Frith, U. (1989). *Autism: Explaining the enigma.* Oxford: Blackwell.

Frith, U. (2003). *Autism: Explaining the enigma* (2nd ed.) Malden, MA: Blackwell.

Fritz, G. K., & McQuaid, E. L. (2000). Chronic medical conditions: Impact on development. In A. J. Sameroff, M. Lewis, & S. M. Miller (Eds.), *Handbook of developmental psychopathology* (pp. 277–292). New York: Kluwer Academic.

Fuller, R., Nopoulos, P., Arndt, S., O'Leary, D., Ho, B. C., & Andreasen, N. C. (2002). Longitudinal assessment of premorbid cognitive functioning in patients with schizophrenia through examination of standardized scholastic test performance. *American Journal of Psychiatry, 159,* 1183–1189.

Gabel S. (1997). Oppositional defiant disorder. In J. Noshpitz (Ed.), *Handbook of child and adolescent psychiatry* (pp. 351–359). New York: Wiley.

Gaensbauer, T. J., Chatoor, I., Drell, M., Siegel, D., & Zeanah, C. H. (1995). Traumatic loss in a one-year-old girl. *Journal of the American Academy of Child and Adolescent Psychiatry, 34,* 94–102.

Gallo, C. L., & Pfeffer, C. R. (2003). Children and adolescents bereaved by a suicidal death: Implications for psychosocial outcomes and interventions. In R. A. King & A. Apter (Eds.), *Suicide in children and adolescents* (pp. 294–312.). Cambridge, England: Cambridge University Press.

Garb, H. N., Wood, J. M., Lilienfeld, S. O., & Nezworski, M. T. (2005). Roots of the Rorschach controversy. *Clinical Psychology Review, 25*(1), 97–118.

Garbarino, J., Stott, F. M., & Faculty of the Erikson Institute. (1992). *What children can tell us: Eliciting, interpreting, and evaluating information from children.* San Francisco: Jossey-Bass.

Garber, J. (1984.) Classification of childhood psychopathology: A developmental perspective. *Child Development, 55,* 30–48.

Garber, J., Braafladt, N., & Weiss, B. (1995). Affect regulation in depressed and nondepressed children and young adolescents. *Development and Psychopathology, 7,* 93–116.

Garfield, S. L. (1996). Some problems associated with "validated" forms of psychotherapy. *Clinical Psychology: Science and Practice, 3,* 218–229.

Garfinkel, P. E., & Garner, D. M. (1986). Anorexia nervosa and adolescent mental health. In R. A. Feldman & A. R. Stiffman (Eds.), *Advances in adolescent mental health* (Vol. 1, pp. 163–204). Greenwich, CT: JAI Press.

Garfinkel, P. E., Lin, E., Goering, P., Spegg, C., Goldbloom, D. S., Kennedy, S., et al. (1995). Bulimia nervosa in a Canadian community sample: Prevalence and comparison of subgroups. *American Journal of Psychiatry, 152,* 1052–1058.

Garland, A. F., & Zigler, E. (1993). Adolescent suicide prevention: Current research and social policy implications. *American Psychologist, 48,* 169–182.

Garland, E. J., & Weiss, M. (1996). Case study: Obsessive difficult temperament and its response to serotonergic medication. *Journal of the American Academy of Child & Adolescent Psychiatry, 35,* 916–920.

Garnefski, N., & Arends, E. (1998). Sexual abuse and adolescent maladjustment: Differences between male

and female victims. *Journal of Adolescence, 21,* 99–107.

Garner, D. M. (1993). Binge eating in anorexia nervosa. In C. G. Fairburn & G. T. Wilson (Eds.), *Binge eating: Nature, assessment, and treatment* (pp. 50–76). New York: Guilford.

Garner, D. M., Vitousek, K. B., & Pike, K. M. (1997). Cognitive-behavioral therapy for anorexia nervosa. In D. M. Garner & P. E. Garfinkel (Eds.), *Handbook of treatment for eating disorders* (2nd ed., pp. 94–144). New York: Guilford.

Garrido, M. (2000). Minorities in the United States: Sociocultural context for mental health and developmental psychopathology. In A. J. Sameroff, M. Lewis, & S. M. Miller (Eds.), *Handbook of developmental psychopathology* (pp. 177–196). New York: Kluwer Academic.

Garrison, C. Z., Jackson, K. L., Marsteller, F., McKeown, R., & Addy, C. (1990). A longitudinal study of depressive symptomatology in young adolescents. *Journal of the American Academy of Child and Adolescent Psychiatry, 29,* 581–585.

Gaster, B., & Holroyd, J. (2000). St. John's Wort for depression. *Archives of Internal Medicine, 160,* 152–156.

Ge, X., Conger, R., Lorenz, F., & Simons, R. (1994). Parents' stressful life events and adolescent depressed mood. *Journal of Health and Social Behavior, 35,* 28–44.

Ge, X., Conger, R. D., Cadoret, R. J., Nedierhiser, J. M.,

Yates, W., Troughton, E., et al. (1996). The developmental interface between nature and nurture: A mutual influence model of child antisocial behavior and parent behaviors. *Developmental Psychology, 32,* 574–589.

Geffner, R. A., Igelman, R. S., & Zellner, J. (2003). *The effects of intimate partner violence on children.* New York: Haworth.

Geiger, T., & Crick, N. R. (2001). Childhood features of personality disorders. In R. Ingram & J. Price (Eds.), *Handbook of vulnerability to psychopathology: Risks across the lifespan* (pp. 57–102). New York: Guilford.

Gelfand, D. M., Teti, D. M., Seiner, S. A., & Jameson, P. B. (1996). Helping mothers fight depression: Evaluation of a homebased intervention program for depressed mothers and their infants. *Journal of Clinical Child Psychology, 25,* 406–422.

Geller, B., Bolhofner, K., Craney, J. L., Williams, M., DelBello, M. P., & Gunderson, K. (2000). Psychosocial functioning in a prepubertal and early adolescent bipolar disorder phenotype. *Journal of the American Academy of Child and Adolescent Psychiatry, 39,* 1543–1548.

Geller, B., & DelBello, M. P. (2003). *Bipolar disorder in childhood and early adolescence.* New York: Guilford.

Geller, B., Fox, L. W., & Clark, K. A. (1994). Rate and predictors of prepubertal biopolarity during followup of 6- to 12-year-old depressed children. *Journal of the American Academy*

of Child and Adolescent Psychiatry, 33, 461–468.

Geller, B., & Luby, J. (1997). Child and adolescent bipolar disorder: A review of the past 10 years. *Journal of the American Academy of Child and Adolescent Psychiatry.*

Geller, B., Williams, M., Zimmerman, B., Frazier, J., Berringer, L., & Warner, K. (1998). Prepubertal and early adolescent bipolarity differentiated from ADHD by manic symptoms, grandiose delusions, utrarapid or ultradian cycling. *Journal of Affective Disorders, 51,* 81–91.

Geller, B., Zimmerman, B., Williams, M., Bolhofner, K., Craney, J, L., Del Bello, M. P., et al. (2000). Six-month stability and outcome of a prepubertal and early adolescent bipolar disorder phenotype. *Journal of Child and Adolescent Psychopharmacology, 10,* 157–164.

Geller, J., & Johnston, C. (1995). Predictors of mothers' responses to child noncompliance: Attributions and attitudes. *Journal of Clinical Child Psychology, 24*(3), 272–278.

Gershon, J. (2002). A meta-analytic review of gender differences in ADHD. *Journal of Attention Disorders, 5,* 143–154.

Gibbons, F. X., Gerrard, M., Cleveland, M. J., Wills, T. A., & Brody, G. (2004). Perceived discrimination and substance use in African American parents and their children. *Journal of Personality and Social Psychology, 86,* 517–529.

Gibbons, F. X., Gerrard, M., & Lane, D. (2003). A social

reaction model of adolescent health risk. In J. M. Suls & K. Wallston (Eds.), *Social psychological foundations of health and illness* (pp. 107–136). Malden, MA: Blackwell.

Gibbs, J. T., (2003). Biracial and bicultural children and adolescents. In J. T. Gibbs & L. N. Huang (Eds.), *Children of color: Psychological interventions with culturally diverse youth* (2nd ed., pp. 145–182). San Francisco: Jossey-Bass.

Gibbs, J. T., & Huang, L. N. (2003). *Children of color: Psychological interventions with culturally diverse youth* (2nd ed.). San Francisco: Jossey-Bass.

Giedd, J. N. (2003). The anatomy of mentalization: A view from developmental neuroimaging. *Bulletin of the Menninger Clinic, 67,* 132–142.

Gil, K. M., Anthony, K. K., Carson, J. W., Redding-Lallinger, R., Daeschner, C. W., & Ware, R. E. (2001). Daily coping practice predicts treatment effects in children with sickle cell disease. *Journal of Pediatric Psychology, 26,* 163–173.

Gillberg, C. (1991). Outcome in autism and autistic-like conditions. *Journal of the American Academy of Child and Adolescent Psychiatry, 30,* 375–382.

Gjerde, P. F. (1995). Alternative pathways to chronic depressive symptoms in young adults: Gender differences in developmental trajectories. *Child Development, 66,* 1277–1300.

Gjerde, P. F., & Block, J. (1991). Preadolescent antecedents of depressive symptomatology at age 18:

A prospective study. *Journal of Youth and Adolescence, 20,* 217–231.

Gladstone, T. R., & Kaslow, N. J. (1995). Depression and attributions in children and adolescents: A meta-analytic review. *Journal of Abnormal Child Psychology, 23,* 597–606.

Gogtay, N., Sporn, A., Clasen, L. S., Greenstein, D., Giedd, J. N., Lenane, M., et al. (2003). Structural brain MRI abnormalities in healthy siblings of patients with childhood-onset schizophrenia. *American Journal of Psychiatry, 160,* 569–571.

Goldberg, S. (1997). Attachment and childhood behavior problems in normal, at-risk, and clinical samples. In L. R. Atkinson, & K. J. Zucker, *Attachment and psychopathology.* New York: Guilford.

Goldman, S. J., D'Angelo, E. J., & DeMaso, D. R. (1993). Psychopathology in the families of children and adolescents with borderline personality disorder. *American Journal of Psychiatry, 150,* 1832–1835.

Goldman, S. J., D'Angelo, E. J., DeMaso, D. R., & Mezzacappa, E. (1992). Physical and sexual abuse histories among children with borderline personality disorder. *American Journal of Psychiatry, 149,* 1723–1726.

Goldstein, M. J. (1987). The UCLA High-Risk Project. *Schizophrenia Bulletin, 13,* 505–514.

Goldstein, M. J. (1990). Family relations as risk factors for the onset and course of schizophrenia. In J. Rolf, A. S. Masten, D. Cicchetti,

K. H. Nuechterlein, & S. Weintraub (Eds.), *Risk and protective factors in the development of psychopathology* (pp. 408–423). Cambridge, England: Cambridge University Press.

Goldstein, W. N. (1997). Dynamically-oriented psychotherapy with borderline patients. *American Journal of Psychotherapy, 51,* 14–30.

Golombok, S., & Fivush, R. (1994). *Gender development.* Cambridge, UK: Cambridge University Press.

Gooding, D. C., & Iacono, W. G. (1995). Schizophrenia through the lens of a developmental psychopathology perspective. In D. Cicchetti & D. J. Cohen (Eds.), *Developmental psychopathology, Vol. I: Theory and methods* (pp. 535–580). New York: Wiley.

Goodman, S. H. (2003). Genesis and epigenesis of psychopathology in children with depressed mothers: Toward an integrative bipsychosocial perspective. In D. Cicchetti & E. Walker (Eds.), *Neurodevelopmental mechanisms in psychopathology* (pp. 428–460). New York: Cambridge.

Goodman, S. H., & Gotlib, I. H. (1999). Risk for psychopathology in the children of depressed mothers: A developmental model for understanding mechanisms of transmission. *Psychological Review, 106,* 458–490.

Goodman, S. H., & Gotlib, I. H. (2002). *Children of depressed parents: Mechanisms of risk and implica-*

tions for treatment. American Psychological Association.

Goodman, S. H., Schwab-Stone, M., Lahey, B., Shaffer, D., & Jensen, P. (2000). Major depression and dysthymia in children and adolescents: Discriminant validity and differential consequences in a community sample. *Journal of the American Academy of Child and Adolescent Psychiatry, 39,* 761–770.

Goodyer, I. M., Herbert, J., Tamplin, A., & Altham, P. M. E. (2000). Recent life events, cortisol, dehydroepiandrosterone and the onset of major depression in high-risk adolescents. *British Journal of Psychiatry, 177,* 499–504.

Gordon, I., Lask, B., Bryant-Waugh, R., Christie, D., & Timimi, S. (1997). Childhood onset anorexia nervosa: Toward identifying a biological substrate. *International Journal of Eating Disorders, 22,* 159–166.

Gould, M. S., Shaffer, D., & Greenberg, T. (2003). The epidemiology of youth suicide. In R. A. King & A. Apter (Eds.), *Suicide in children and adolescents* (pp. 1–40). Cambridge, MA: Cambridge University Press.

Grados, M., Scahill, L., & Riddle, M. A. (1999). Pharmacotherapy in children and adolescents with obsessive-compulsive disorder. *Child & Adolescent Psychiatric Clinics of North America, 8,* 617–634.

Graham-Bermann, S. A. (2000). Evaluating interventions for children exposed to family violence. *Journal of Aggression,*

Maltreatment, and Trauma, 4, 191–216.

Graham-Bermann, S. A. (2002). Child maltreatment in the context of domestic violence. In J. E. B. Myers, L. Berliner, J. Briere, C. T. Hendrix, C. Jenny, & T. A. Reid (Eds.), *The APSAC handbook on child maltreatment* (2nd ed., pp. 119–130). Thousand Oaks, CA: Sage.

Graham-Bermann, S. A., & Edleson, J. L. (2001). *Domestic violence in the lives of children: The future of research, intervention, and social policy.* Washington, DC: American Psychological Association.

Graham-Bermann, S. A., & Hughes, H. M. (2003). Intervention for children exposed to interparental violence: Assessment of needs and research priorities. *Clinical Child and Family Psychology Review, 6,* 189–204.

Graham-Bermann, S. A., & Levendosky, A. (1998). The social functioning of preschool-age children whose mothers are emotionally and physically abused. *Journal of Emotional Abuse, 1,* 57–82.

Granboulan, V., Rabain, D., & Basquin, M. (1995). The outcome of adolescent suicide attempts. *Acta Psychiatrica Scandinavica, 91,* 265–270.

Grandin, T. (1996). *Thinking in pictures.* New York: Vintage.

Green, J., Gilchrist, A., Burton, D., & Cox, A. (2000). Social and psychiatric functioning in adolescents with Asperger syndrome compared with conduct disorder. *Journal of Autism and Developmental Disorders, 30,* 279–293.

Greenberg, L. M., & Waldman, I. D. (1993). Developmental normative data on the Test of Variables of Attention (T. O. V. A.). *Journal of Child Psychology and Psychiatry, 34*(6), 1019–1030.

Greenberg, M. T., DeKlyen, M., Speltz, M. L., & Endriga, M. C. (1997). The role of attachment processes in externalizing psychopathology in young children. In L. R. Atkinson & K. J. Zucker (Eds.), *Attachment and psychopathology.* New York: Guilford.

Greenberg, M. T., Speltz, M. L., & DeKlyen, M. (1993). The role of attachment in the early development of disruptive behavior problems. *Development and Psychopathology, 5,* 191–214.

Greenberg, R. P., & Fisher, S. (1996). *Freud scientifically reappraised.* New York: Wiley.

Greene, R. W., & Doyle, A. E. (1999). Toward a transactional conceptualization of oppositional defiant disorder: Implications for assessment and treatment. *Clinical Child and Family Psychology Review, 2*(3), 129–148.

Greening, L., & Dollinger, S. J. (1989). Treatment of a child's sleep disturbance and related phobias in the family. In M. C. Roberts & C. E. Walker (Eds.), *Casebook of child and pediatric psychology* (pp. 94–111). New York: Guilford.

Greenman, D. A., Gunderson, J. G., Cane, M., & Saltzman, P. R. (1986). An examination of the borderline diagnosis in children. *American Journal of Psychiatry, 143,* 998–1003.

Greenspan, S. I. (2003). *The clinical interview of the child* (3rd ed.). Washington, DC: American Psychiatric Press.

Grigorenko, E. L. (2001). Developmental dyslexia: An update on genes, brains, and environments. *Journal of Child Psychology and Psychiatry, 42,* 91–125.

Grolnick, W. S., & Farkas, M. (2002). Parenting and the development of children's self-regulation. In M. H. Bornstein (Ed.), *Handbook of parenting: Vol. 5. Practical issues in parenting* (pp. 89–110). Mahwah, NJ: Erlbaum.

Group for the Advancement of Psychiatry Committee on the Family (1996). Global Assessment of Relational Functioning scale (GARF): I. Background and rationale. *Family Process, 35*(2), 155–172.

Grych, J. H., & Fincham, F. (2001). *Child development and interparental conflict.* New York: Cambridge University Press.

Grych, J. H., Fincham, F. D., Jouriles, E. N., & McDonald, R. (2001). Interparental conflict and child adjustment: Testing the mediational role of appraisals in the cognitive-contextual framework. *Child Development, 71,* 1648–1661.

Grych, J. H., Jouriles, E. N., Swank, P. R., McDonald, R., & Norwood, W. D. (2000). Patterns of adjustment among children of battered women. *Journal of Consulting and Clinical Psychology, 68,* 84–94.

Guerra, N. G., Huesmann, L. R., & Spindler, A. (2003). Community violence exposure, social cognition, and aggression among urban elementary-school children. *Child Development, 74,* 1561–1576.

Guerrero, A. P. S., Hishinuma, E. S., Andrade, N. N., Bell, C. K., Kurahar, D. K., Lee, T. G., et al. (2003). Demographic and clinical characteristics of adolescents in Hawaii with obsessive-compulsive disorder. *Archives of Pediatrics and Adolescent Medicine, 157,* 665–670.

Guertin, T. L. (1999). Eating behavior of bulimics, self-identified binge eaters, and non-eating-disordered individuals: What differentiates these populations? *Clinical Psychology Review, 19,* 1–23.

Gunderson, J. G., Shea, M. T., Skodol, A. E., McGlashan, T. H., Morey, L. C., Stout, R. I., et al. (2000). The Collaborative Longitudinal Personality Disorders Study: Development, aims, design, and sample characteristics. *Journal of Personality Disorders, 14,* 300–315.

Gunnar, M. R., Bruce, J., & Donzella, B. (2001). Stress physiology, health, and behavioral development. In *The well-being of children and families: Research and data needs* (pp. 188–212). Ann Arbor: The University of Michigan Press.

Guntrip, H. (1986). My experience of analysis with Fairbairn and Winnicott (How complete a result does psychoanalytic therapy achieve?). In

P. Buckley (Ed.), *Essential papers on object relations* (2nd ed., pp. 447–468). New York: New York University Press.

Gustafsson, P., Thernlund, G., Ryding, E., Rosen, I., & Cederblad, M. (2000). Associations between cerebral blood flow measured by single photon emission computed tomography (SPECT), electro-encephalogram (EEG), behavior symptoms, cognition and neurological soft signs in children with attention-deficit/hyperactivity disorder (ADHD). *Acta Paediatrica, 89,* 830–835.

Guterman, N. B. (1997). Early prevention of physical child abuse and neglect: Existing evidence and future directions. *Child Maltreatment, 2,* 12–34.

Gutierrez, P. M., Osman, A., Kopper, B. A., & Barrios, F. X. (2000). Why young people do not kill themselves: The Reasons for Living Inventory for Adolescents. *Journal of Clinical Child Psychology, 29,* 177–187.

Guyll, M., Spoth, R. L., Chao, W., Wichrama, K. A. S., & Russell, D. (2004). Family-focused preventive interventions: Evaluating parental risk moderation of substance use trajectories. *Journal of Family Psychology, 18,* 293–301.

Guzder, J., Paris, J., & Zelkowitz, P. (1999). Psychological risk factors for borderline pathology in school-age children. *Journal of the American Academy of Child and Adolescent Psychiatry, 38,* 206–212.

Guzder, J., Paris, J., Zelkowitz, P., & Marchessault, K.

(1996). Risk factors for borderline pathology in children. *Journal of the American Academy of Child and Adolescent Psychiatry, 35,* 26–33.

Häfner, H., & Nowotny, B. (1995). Epidemiology of early-onset schizophrenia. *European Archives of Psychiatry and Clinical Neuroscience, 245,* 80–92.

Haggiag, T. (2000). The broken jigsaw: A child's perspective. In B. Lask & R. Bryant-Wauch (Eds.), *Anorexia nervosa and related eating disorders in childhood and adolescence* (pp. 3–10). Philadelphia: Psychology Press.

Hale, C. A., & Borkowski, J. G. (1991). Attention, memory, and cognition. In J. L. Matson & J. A. Mulick (Eds.), *Handbook of mental retardation* (pp. 505–528). New York: Pergamon.

Hall, N. W., & Zigler, E. (1997). Drug-abuse prevention efforts for young children: A review and critique of existing programs. *American Journal of Orthopsychiatry, 67,* 134–143.

Hall, R. V., Fox, R., Willard, D., Goldsmith, L., Emerson, M., Owen, M., et al. (1971). The teacher as observer and experimenter in the modification of disputing and talking-out behaviors. *Journal of Applied Behavioral Analysis, 4,* 141–149.

Hallowell, E., & Ratey, J. (1994). *Driven to distraction: Recognizing and coping with Attention Deficit Disorder from childhood through adulthood.* New York: Simon and Schuster.

Hammen, C. (1991). The family-environmental context of depression: A perspective on children's risk. In D. Cicchetti & S. L. Toth (Eds.), Rochester symposium on developmental psychopathology (Vol. 4, pp. 251–281). Rochester: University of Rochester Press.

Hammen, C. (1992). Cognitive, life stress, and interpersonal approaches to a developmental psychopathology model of depression. *Development and Psychopathology, 4,* 189–206.

Hammen, C. (1999). Children of affectively ill parents. In H. C. Steinhausen & F. Verhulst (Eds.), *Risks and outcomes in developmental psychopathology* (pp. 38–53). Oxford: Oxford University Press.

Hammen, C., Burge, D., & Adrian, C. (1991). Timing of mother and child depression in a longitudinal study of children at risk. *Journal of Consulting and Clinical Psychology, 59,* 341–345.

Hammen, C., Burge, D., Daley, S. E., Davila, J., Paley, B., & Rudolph, K. D. (1995). Interpersonal attachment cognitions and prediction of symptomatic responses to interpersonal stress. *Journal of Abnormal Psychology, 104,* 436–443.

Hammen, C., Burge, D., & Stansbury, K. (1990). Relationship of mother and child variables to child outcomes in a high-risk sample: A casual modeling analysis. *Developmental Psychology, 26,* 24–30.

Hammen, C., & Compas, B. E. (1994). Unmasking unmasked depression in

children and adolescents: The problem of comorbidity. *Clinical Psychology Review, 14,* 585–603.

Hammen, C., & Rudolph, K. D. (1996). Childhood depression. In E. J. Mash & R. A. Barkley (Eds.), *Child psychopathology* (pp. 153–195). New York: Guilford.

Hammen, C., & Rudolph, K. D. (2003). Childhood mood disorders. In E. J. Mash & R. A. Barkley (Eds.), *Child psychopathology* (2nd ed., pp. 233–279). New York: Guilford.

Hammer, E. F. (1958). *The clinical application of projective drawings.* Springfield, IL: Charles C. Thomas.

Handler, L., & Habenicht, D. (1994). The Kinetic Family Drawing Technique: A review of the literature. *Journal of Personality Assessment, 62,* 440–464.

Hankin, B. L., & Abramson, L. Y. (2002). Measuring cognitive vulnerability to depression in adolescence: Reliability, validity, and gender differences. *Journal of Clinical Child and Adolescent Psychology, 31,* 491–504.

Hankin, B. L., Abramson, L. Y., Moffitt, T. E., Silva, P. A., McGee, R., & Angell, K. E. (1998). Development of depression from preadolescence to young adulthood: Emerging gender differences in a 10-year longitudinal study. *Journal of Abnormal Psychology, 107,* 128–140.

Hanson, R. F., & Spratt, E. G. (2000). Reactive attachment disorder: What we know about the disorder and implications for treatment. *Child Maltreatment, 5*(2), 137–145.

Happé, F., & Frith, U. (1996). Theory of mind and social impairment in children with conduct disorder. *British Journal of Developmental Psychology, 14,* 385–398.

Happé, F. G. (1994). An advanced test of theory of mind: Understanding of story characters' thoughts and feelings by able autistic, mentally handicapped, and normal children and adults. *Journal of Autism and Developmental Disorders, 24*(2), 129–154.

Happé, F. G. (1999). Autism: Cognitive deficit or cognitive style. *Trends in Cognitive Science, 3,* 216–222.

Harbeck-Weber, C., & Peterson, L. (1992). Elephants dancing in my head: A developmental approach to children's concepts of specific pains. *Child Development, 63,* 138–149.

Harbeck-Weber, C., & Peterson, L. (1993). Children's conceptions of illness and pain. *Annals of Child Development, 9,* 133–161.

Harbeck-Weber, C., & Peterson, L. (1996). Health-related disorders. In E. J. Mash & R. A. Barkley (Eds.), *Child psychopathology* (pp. 572–601). New York: Guilford.

Hare, R. D. (1993). *Without conscience: The disturbing world of the psychopaths among us.* New York: Pocket Books.

Hare, R. D. (1996). Psychopathy: A clinical construct whose time has come. *Criminal Justice and Behavior, 23,* 25–54.

Harkness, S., & Super, C. M. (2000). Culture and psychopathology. In A. J. Sameroff, M. Lewis,

& S. M. Miller (Eds.), *Handbook of developmental psychopathology* (pp. 197–216). New York: Kluwer Academic.

Harlow, H. F. (1958). The nature of love. *American Psychologist, 13,* 673–685.

Harrington, R., Bredenkamp, D., Groothues, C., Rutter, M., Fudge, H., & Pickles, A. (1994). Adult outcomes of childhood and adolescent depression: III. Links with suicidal behaviours. *Journal of Child Psychology and Psychiatry, 35,* 1309–1319.

Harrington, R., Fudge, H., Rutter, M., Pickles, A., & Hill, J. (1991). Adult outcomes of childhood and adolescent depression: II. Links with antisocial disorders. *Journal of the American Academy of Child Psychiatry, 30,* 434–439.

Harrington, R., Rutter, M., & Fombonne, E. (1996). Developmental pathways in depression: Multiple meanings, antecedents, and endpoints. *Development and Psychopathology, 8,* 601–616.

Harrington, R., & Saleem, Y. (2003). Cognitive behavioral therapy after deliberate self-harm in adolescence. In R. A. King & A. Apter (Eds.), *Suicide in children and adolescents* (pp. 251–270). Cambridge: England: Cambridge University Press.

Hart, B. I., & Thompson, J. M. (1996). Gender role characteristics and depressive symptomatology among adolescents. *Journal of Early Adolescence, 16,* 407–426.

Hart, C. H., Germain, R., & Brassard, M. (1987). The

challenge: To better understand and combat psychological maltreatment of children and youth. In M. Brassard, R. Germain, & S. Hart (Eds.), *Psychological maltreatment of children and youth* (pp. 3–24). New York: Pergammon Press.

Hart, E. L., Lahey, B. B., Loeber, R., Applegate, B., & Frick, P. J. (1995). Developmental changes in Attention-Deficit Hyperactive Disorders in boys: A four-year longitudinal study. *Journal of Abnormal Child Psychology, 23,* 729–750.

Hart, S. N., Binggeli, N. J., & Brassard, M. R. (1998). Evidence for the effects of psychological maltreatment. *Journal of Emotional Abuse, 1,* 27–56.

Hart, S. N., Brassard, M. R., Binggeli, N. J., & Davidson, H. A. (2002). Psychological maltreatment. In J. E. B. Myers, L. Berliner, J. Briere, C. T. Hendrix, C. Jenny, & T. A. Reid (Eds.), *The APSAC handbook on child maltreatment* (2nd ed., pp. 79–104). Thousand Oaks, CA: Sage.

Harter, S. (1986). Processes underlying the construction, maintenance, and enhancement of the self-concept in children. In J. Suls & A. Greenwald (Eds.), *Psychological perspectives on the self* (pp. 137–181). Hillsdale, NJ: Erlbaum.

Harter, S. (1988). Developmental and dynamic changes in the nature of the self-concept: Implications for child psychotherapy. In S. Shirk (Ed.), *Cognitive development and child psychotherapy*

(pp. 119–160). New York: Plenum.

Harter, S. (1990). Causes, correlates, and the functional role of global self-worth: A life-span perspective. In R. J. Sternberg & J. Kolligian (Eds.), *Competence considered* (pp. 67–97). New Haven: Yale University Press.

Harter, S. (1999). *The construction of the self: A developmental perspective.* New York: Guilford Publications.

Harter, S., Bresnick, S., Bouchey, H. A., & Whitesell, N. R. (1997). The development of multiple role-related selves during adolescence. *Development and Psychopathology, 9,* 835–853.

Harter, S. & Marold, D. (1991). A model of the determinants and mediational role of self-worth: Implications for adolescent depression and suicidal ideation. In G. R. Goethals & J. Strauss (Eds.), *The self: An interdisciplinary approach* (pp. 66–92). New York: Springer-Verlag.

Harter, S., & Marold, D. B. (1994). Psychosocial risk factors contributing to adolescent suicidal ideation. In G. G. Noam & S. Borst (Eds.), *Children, youth, and suicide: Developmental perspectives* (pp. 71–92). San Francisco: Jossey-Bass.

Harter, S., & Whitesell, N. R. (1989). Developmental changes in children's understanding of single, multiple, and blended emotion concepts. In *Children's understanding of emotion* (pp. 81–116). New York: Cambridge University Press.

Harter, S., & Whitesell, N. R. (1996). Multiple pathways to self-reported depression and psychological adjustment among adolescents. *Development and Psychopathology, 8,* 761–777.

Hartmann, T. (1997). *Attention deficit disorder: A new perception.* Grass Valley, CA: Underwood Books.

Harvey, P. D. (1991). Cognitive and linguistic functions of adolescent children at risk for schizophrenia. In E. F. Walker (Ed.), *Schizophrenia: A life-course developmental perspective* (pp. 139–156). San Diego, CA: Academic Press.

Hashima, P. Y., & Amato, P. R. (1994). Poverty, social support, and parental behavior. *Child Development, 65,* 394–403.

Hauser, S. T., & Safyer, A. W. (1995). The contributions of ego psychology to developmental psychopathology. In D. Cicchetti & D. J. Cohen (Eds.), *Developmental psychopathology: Vol. I. Theory and methods* (pp. 555–580). New York: Wiley.

Hawkins, E. H., Cummins, L. H., & Marlatt, G. A. (2004). Preventing substance abuse in American Indian and Alaska Native Youth: Promising strategies for healthier communities. *Psychological Bulletin, 130,* 304–323.

Hawkins, J. D., Catalano, R. F., & Miller, J. Y. (1992). Risk and protective factors for alcohol and other drug problems in adolescence and early adulthood: Implications for substance abuse prevention. *Psychological Bulletin, 112,* 64–105.

Hazelrigg, M. D., Cooper, H. M., & Borduin, C. M. (1987). Evaluating the effectiveness of family therapies: An integrative review and analysis. *Psychological Bulletin, 101,* 428–442.

Heatherton, T. F., & Baumeister, R. F. (1991). Binge eating as escape from self-awareness. *Psychological Bulletin, 110,* 86–108.

Heaton, R. K., Chelune, G. J., Talley, J. L., Kay, G. G., & Curtiss, G. (1993). *Wisconsin Card Sorting Test Manual—Revised and Expanded.* Odessa, FL: Psychological Assessment Resources.

Heim, C., & Nemeroff, C. B. (2001). The role of childhood trauma in the neurobiology of mood and anxiety disorders: Preclinical and clinical studies. *Biological Psychiatry, 49,* 1023–1039.

Helfer, M. E., Kempe, R. S., & Krugman, R. D. (1997). *The battered child* (5th ed.). Chicago: University of Chicago Press.

Henggeler, S. W., Schoenwald, S. K., Rowland, M. D., & Cunningham, P. B. (2002). *Serious emotional disturbance in children and adolescents: Multisystemic therapy.* New York: Guilford.

Hennessy, K. D., Rabideau, G. J., Cicchetti, D., & Cummings, E. M. (1994). Responses of physically abused and nonabused children to different forms of interadult anger. *Child Development, 65,* 815–828.

Henry, B., Moffitt, T. E., Caspi, A., Langley, J., & Silva, P. A. (1994). On the "remembrance of things past": A longitudinal evaluation of the retrospective

method. *Psychological Assessment, 6,* 92–101.

Herman, M. (2004). Forced to choose: Some determinants of racial identification in multiracial adoelscents. *Child Development, 75,* 730–748.

Hermelin, B. (2001). *Bright splinters of the mind: A personal story of research with autistic savants.* London: Jessica Kingsley.

Herrenkohl, R. C., Egolf, B. P., & Herrenkohl, E. C. (1997). Preschool antecedents of adolescent assaultive behavior: A longitudinal study. *American Journal of Orthopsychiatry, 67,* 422–432.

Hershberger, S. L., & D'Augelli, A. R. (1995). The impact of victimization on the mental health and suicidality of lesbian, gay, and bisexual youths. *Developmental Psychology, 31,* 65–74.

Hershberger, S. L., Pilkington, N. W., & D'Augelli, A. R. (1997). Predictors of suicide attempts among gay, lesbian, and bisexual youth. *Journal of Adolescent Research, 12,* 477–497.

Herzog, D. B., Keller, M. B., Sacks, N. R., Yeh, C. J., & Lavori, P. W. (1992). Psychiatric comorbidity in treatment-seeking anorexics and bulimics, *Journal of the American Academy of Child and Adolescent Psychiatry, 31,* 810–818.

Herzog, D. B., Sacks, N. R., Keller, M. B., Lavori, P. W., von Ranson, K. B., & Gray, H. M. (1993). Patterns and predictors of recovery in anorexia nervosa and bulimia nervosa. *Journal of Child Psychology and Psychiatry, 32,* 962–966.

Hesse, P., & Cicchetti, D. (1982). Perspectives on an integrated theory of emotional development. In D. Cicchetti & P. Hesse (Eds.), *New directions for child development: Emotional development* (pp. 3–48). San Francisco: Jossey-Bass.

Hetherington, E. M., Bridges, M., & Insabella, G. M. (1998). What matters? What does not? Five perspectives on the association between marital transitions and children's adjustment. *American Psychologist, 53,* 167–184.

Hetherington, E. M., & Parke, R. D. (2003). *Child psychology: A contemporary viewpoint.* New York: McGraw-Hill.

Hetherington, E. M., & Stanley-Hagen, M. (1999). The adjustment of children with divorced parents: A risk and resiliency perspective. *Journal of Child Psychology and Psychiatry and Allied Disciplines, 40,* 129–140.

Hetherington, E. M., & Stanley-Hagen, M. (2002). Parenting in divorced and remarried families. In M. H. Bornstein (Ed.), *Handbook of parenting, Vol. 5: Practical issues in parenting* (pp. 287–316). Mahwah, NJ: Erlbaum.

Hewitt, J. K., Silberg, J. L., & Rutter, M. (1997). Genetics and developmental psychopathology I: Phenotypic assessment in the Virginia Twin Study of Adolescent Behavioral Development. *Journal of Child Psychology and Psychiatry, 38,* 943–963.

Hill, K., White, H. R., Chung, I. J., Hawkins, J. D., & Catalano, R. F. (2000).

Early adult outcomes of adolescent binge drinking: Person- and variable-centered analyses of binge drinking trajectories. *Alcoholism: Clinical and Experimental Research, 24,* 892–901.

Hill, N. E., Bush, K. R., & Roosa, M. W. (2003). Parenting and family socialization strategies and children's mental health: Low-income Mexican-American and Euro-American mothers and children. *Child Development, 74,* 189–204.

Hill, S., Shen, S., Lowers, L., & Locke, J. (2000). Factors predicting the onset of adolescent drinking in families at high risk for developing alcoholism. *Biological Psychiatry, 48,* 265–275.

Hinshaw, S. P. (2000). Attention-deficit/hyperactivity disorder: The search for viable treatments. In P. C. Kendall (Ed.), *Child and adolescent therapy: Cognitive-behavioral procedures* (pp. 88–128). New York: Guilford.

Hinshaw, S. P., & Anderson, C. A. (1996). Conduct and oppositional defiant disorders. In E. J. Mash & R. A. Barkley (Eds.), *Child psychopathology* (pp. 113–149). New York: Guilford.

Hinshaw, S. P., & Lee, S. S. (2003). Conduct and oppositional defiant disorders. In E. J. Mash & R. A. Barkley (Eds.), *Child psychopathology* (2nd ed., pp. 144–198). New York: Guilford.

Hinshaw, S. P., & Park, T. (2002). Research problems and issues: Toward a more definitive science of disruptive behavior disor-

ders. In *Handbook of disruptive behavior disorders* (pp. 593–620). Dordrecht, Netherlands: Kluwer Academic Publishers.

Hinshaw, S. P., Zupan, B. A., Simmel, C., Nigg, J. T., & Melnick, S. (1997). Peer status in boys with and without attention-deficit hyperactivity disorder: Predictions from overt and covert antisocial behavior, social isolation, and authoritative parenting beliefs. *Child Development, 68,* 880–896.

Hirshfeld, D. R., Biederman, J., Brody, L., Faraone, S. V., & Rosenbaum, J. F. (1997). Expressed emotion toward children with behavioral inhibition: Associations with maternal anxiety disorder. *Journal of the American Academy of Child and Adolescent Psychiatry, 36,* 910–917.

Ho, M. K. (1992). *Minority children and adolescents in therapy.* Newbury Park, CA: Sage.

Hodapp, R. M., & Dykens, E. M. (2003). Mental retardation (intellectual disabilities). In E. J. Mash & R. A. Barkley (Eds.), *Child psychopathology* (2nd ed., pp. 486–519). New York: Guilford.

Hodapp, R. M., Dykens, E. M., & Masino, L. L. (1997). Families of children with Prader-Willi syndrome: Stress-support and relations to child characteristics. *Journal of Autism and Developmental Disorders, 27,* 11–24.

Hodapp, R. M., & Zigler, E. (1995). Past, present, and future issues in the developmental approach to mental retardation and developmental disabilities. In

D. Cicchetti & D. J. Cohen (Eds.), *Developmental psychopathology: Vol. 2. Risk, disorder, and adaptation* (pp. 299–331). New York, Wiley.

Hodges, K. (1993). Structured interviews for assessing children. *Journal of Child Psychology and Psychiatry, 34,* 49–68.

Hoge, R. D., Andrews, D. A., & Leschied, A. W. (1996). An investigation of risk and protective factors in a sample of youthful offenders. *Journal of Child Psychology and Psychiatry, 37,* 419–424.

Hollenbeck J., Dyl, J., & Spirito, A. (2003). Social factors: Family functioning. In A. Spirito & J. C. Overholser (Eds.), *Evaluating and treating adolescent suicide attempters: From research to practice* (pp. 161–192). New York: Academic Press.

Hollis, C. (2000). Diagnosis and differential diagnosis. In *Schizophrenia in children and adolescents* (pp. 82–118). New York: Cambridge University Press.

Hollis, C. (2003). Developmental precursors of child- and adolescent-onset schizophrenia and affective psychoses: Diagnostic specificity and continuity with symptom dimensions. *British Journal of Psychiatry, 182,* 37–44.

Holmbeck, G. N. (1997). Toward terminological, conceptual, and statistical clarity in the study of mediators and moderators: Examples from the child-clinical and pediatric psychology literatures. *Journal of Consulting and Clinical Psychology, 65,* 599–610.

Holmbeck, G. N., Greenley, R. N., & Franks, E. A. (2003). Developmental issues and considerations in research and practice. In A. E. Kazdin & J. R. Weisz (Eds.), *Evidence-based psychotherapies for children and adolescents* (pp. 21–41). New York: Guilford.

Hooper, S. R., & Baglio, C. (2001). Children and adolescents experiencing traumatic brain injury. In J. N. Hughes, A. M. La Greca, & J. C. Conoley (Eds.), *Handbook of psychological services for children and adolescents* (pp. 267–234). New York: Oxford University Press.

Hops, H. (1992). Parental depression and child behaviour problems: Implications for behavioural family intervention. *Behaviour Change, 9,* 126–138.

Hops, H., Andrews, J. A., Duncan, S. C., Duncan, T. E., & Tildesley, E. (2000). Adolescent drug use development: A social interactional and contextual perspective. In A. J. Sameroff, M. Lewis, & S. M. Miller (Eds.), *Handbook of developmental psychopathology* (pp. 589–606). New York: Kluwer Academic.

Houts, A. C. (2003). Behavioral treatment for enuresis. In A. E. Kazdin & J. R. Weisz, *Evidence-based psychotherapies for children and adolescents* (pp. 389–406). New York: Guilford.

Houts, A. C., Berman, J. S., & Abramson, H. (1994). Effectiveness of psychological and pharmacological treatments for noctural enuresis. *Journal of Consulting and Clinical Psychology, 62*(4), 737–745.

Howard, B., Chu, B. C., Krain, A. L., Marrs-Garcia, A. L., & Kendall, P. C. (2000). *Cognitive-behavioral family therapy for anxious children: Therapist manual.* Ardmore, PA: Workbook Publishing.

Howard, C. E., & Porzelius, L. K. (1999). The role of dieting in binge eating disorder: Etiology and treatment implications. *Clinical Psychology Review, 19,* 25–44.

Howlin, P. (2000). Outcome in adult life for more able individuals with autism or Asperger syndrome. *Autism, 4,* 63–83.

Howlin, P. (2002). Practitioner Review: Psychological and educational treatment for autism. *Journal of Child Psychology and Psychiatry, 39,* 307–322.

Hoyle, R. H., & Smith, G. T. (1994). Formulating clinical research hypotheses as structural equation models: A conceptual overview. *Journal of Consulting and Clinical Psychology, 62,* 429–440.

Huang, L. N., Ying, Y. W., & Arganza, G. F. (2003). Chinese American children and adolescents. In J. T. Gibbs & L. N. Huang (Eds.), *Children of color: Psychological interventions with culturally diverse youth* (2nd ed., pp. 187–228). San Francisco: Jossey-Bass.

Huesmann, L. R., Moise-Titus, J., Podolski, C., & Eron, L. D. (2003). Longitudinal relations between children's exposure to TV violence and their aggressive and violent behavior

in young adulthood. *Developmental Psychology, 39,* 201–221.

Huesmann, L. R., & Reynolds, M. A. (2001). Cognitive processes and the development of aggression. In A. C. Bohart & D. J. Stipek (Eds.), *Constructive and destructive behavior: Implications for family, school, and society* (pp. 249–269). Washington, DC: American Psychological Association.

Huey, S. J., Jr., & Weisz, J. R. (1997). Ego control, ego resiliency, and the five-factor model as predictors of behavioral and emotional problems in clinic-referred children and adolescents. *Journal of Abnormal Psychology, 106,* 404–415.

Hughes, H. M., & Graham-Bermann, S. A. (1998). Children of battered women: Impact of emotional abuse on adjustment and development. *Journal of Emotional Abuse, 1,* 23–50.

Hughes, H. M., & Luke, D. A. (1998). Heterogeneity in adjustment among children of battered women. In G. W. Holden, R. Geffner, & E. N. Jouriles (Eds.), *Children exposed to marital violence: Theory, research, and applied issues* (pp. 185–222). Washington, DC: American Psychological Association.

Hultén, A., & Wasserman, D. (1995). Suicide and attempted suicide among children and adolescents. In J. Beskow (Ed.), *Right to life; Lust for life: Suicidal behavior in the child and adolescent population.* Stockholm: Forskningrådsnämnden, Rapport 95:4.

Humphrey, L. (1989). Observed family interactions among

subtypes of eating disorders using structural analysis of social behavior. *Journal of Consulting and Clinical Psychology, 57,* 206–214.

Hundleby, J. D., & Mercer, G. W. (1987). Family and friends as social environments and their relationship to young adolescents' use of alcohol, tobacco, and marijuana. *Journal of Marriage and the Family, 49,* 151–164.

Hussong, A., & Chassin, L. (1994). The stress-negative affect model of adolescent alcohol use: Diaggregating negative affect. *Journal of Studies on Alcohol, 55,* 707–718.

Hussong, A., Hicks, R., Levey, S., & Curran, P. J. (2001). Specifying the relations between affect and heavy alcohol use among young adults. *Journal of Abnormal Psychology, 110,* 449–461.

Hutchinson, G., Takei, N., Fahy, T. A., Bhugra, D., Gilvarry, C., Moran, P., et al. (1996). Morbid risk of schizophrenia in first-degree relatives of White and African-Caribbean patients with psychosis. *British Journal of Psychiatry, 169,* 776–780.

Hyman, S. W. (2001). Mood disorders in children and adolescents: An NIMH perspective. *Biological Psychiatry, 49,* 962–969.

Hypericum Depression Trial Study Group. (2002). Effect of Hypericum perforatum (St. John's Wort) in major depressive disorder. *Journal of the American Medical Association, 287,* 1807–1814.

Ialongo, N., Edelsohn, G., Werthamer-Larsson, L.,

Crockett, L., & Kellam, S. (1993). Are self-reported depressive symptoms in first-grade children developmentally transient phenomena? A further look. *Development and Psychopathology, 5,* 433–457.

Ida, D. J., & Yang, P. (2003). Southeast Asian children and adolescents. In J. T. Gibbs & L. N. Huang (Eds.), *Children of color: Psychological interventions with culturally diverse youth* (2nd ed., pp. 265–296). San Francisco: Jossey-Bass.

Inclan, J. E., & Quinones, M. E. (2003). Puerto Rican children and adolescents. In J. T. Gibbs & L. N. Huang (Eds.), *Children of color: Psychological interventions with culturally diverse youth* (2nd ed., pp. 382–407). San Francisco: Jossey-Bass.

Ingoldsby, E. M., & Shaw, D. S. (2002). Neighborhood contextual factors and early-starting antisocial pathways. *Clinical Child and Family Psychology Review, 5,* 21–55.

Institute of Medicine. (1994). *Growing up tobacco free: Preventing nicotine addiction in children and youths.* Washington, DC: National Academy Press.

Irwin, H. J. (1999). Violent and nonviolent revictimization of women abused in childhood. *Journal of Interpersonal Violence, 14,* 1095–1110.

Izard, C. E., & Harris, P. (1995). Emotional development and developmental psychopathology. In D. Cicchetti & D. J. Cohen (Eds.), *Developmental psychopathology, Vol. I:*

Theory and methods (pp. 467–503). New York: Wiley.

Jablensky A., Sartorius, N., Ernberg, G., Anker, M., Korten, A., Cooper, J. E., & Bertelsen, A. (1992). Schizophrenia: Manifestations, incidence and course in different cultures: A World Health Organization ten-country study. *Psychological Medicine Monograph, 20.*

Jacob, T., & Johnson, S. L. (1997). Parent-child interaction among depressed fathers and mothers: Impact on child functioning. *Journal of Family Psychology, 11,* 391–409.

Jacobs, J. (1971). *Adolescent suicide.* New York: Wiley.

Jacobsen, L. K., & Rapoport, J. L. (1998). Research update: Childhood-onset schizophrenia: Implications for clinical and neurobiological research. *Journal of Child Psychology and Psychiatry, 38,* 101–111.

Jacobvitz, D., Hazen, N., Curran, M., & Hitchens, K. (2004). Observations of early triadic family interactions: Boundary disturbances in the family predict depressive and anxious symptoms in middle childhood. *Development and Psychopathology, 16,* 577–592.

Jacobvitz, D., Riggs, S., & Johnson, E. (1999). Cross-sex and same-sex family alliances: Immediate and long-term effects on sons and daughters. In N. D. Chase (Ed.), *Burdened children* (pp. 34–55). Thousand Oaks CA: Sage.

Jacobvitz, D. B., & Bush, N. F. (1996). Reconstructions of family relationships: Parent-child alliances, personal distress, and self-esteem. *Developmental Psychology, 32*(4), 732–743.

Jaffe, P., Wolfe, D., Wilson, S. K., & Zak, L. (1986). Family violence and child adjustment: A comparative analysis of girls' and boys' behavioral symptoms. *American Journal of Psychiatry, 143,* 74–77.

Jaffe, P. G., Wolfe, D. A., & Wilson, S. K. (1990). *Children of battered women.* Newbury Park, CA: Sage.

Jensen, P. S., & Hoagwood, K. (1997). The book of names: DSM-IV in context. *Development and Psychopathology, 9,* 231–249.

Jessor, R., Donovan, J. E., & Costa, R. M. (1991). *Beyond adolescence: Problem behavior and young adult development.* New York: Cambridge University Press.

Jessor, R., & Jessor, S. L. (1977). *Problem behavior and psychosocial development: A longitudinal study of youth.* New York: Academic Press.

Jessor, R., Van Den Bos, J., Vanderryn, J., Costa, F. M., & Turbin, M. S. (1995). Protective factors in adolescent problem behavior: Moderator effects and developmental change. *Developmental Psychology, 31,* 923–933.

Jewell, J. D., & Stark, K. D. (2003). Comparing the family environments of adolescents with conduct disorder or depression. *Journal of Child and Family Studies, 12,* 77–89.

Jimerson, D. C., Wolfe, B. E., Metzger, E. D., Finkelstein, D. M., Cooper, T. B., & Levine, J. M. (1997). Decreased serotonin function in bulimia nervosa. *Archives of General Psychiatry, 54,* 529–534.

Joergensen, J. (1992). The epidemiology of eating disorder in Fyn County, Denmark, 1977–1986. *Acta Psychiatrica Scandinavica, 85,* 30–34.

Johnson, C., & Larson, R. (1982). Bulimia: An analysis of mood and behavior. *Psychosomatic Medicine, 44,* 341–351.

Johnson, C. A., MacKinnon, D. P., & Pentz, M. A. (1996). Breadth of program and outcome effectiveness in drug abuse prevention. *American Behavioral Scientist, 39,* 884–896.

Johnson, J. G., Cohen, P., Brown, J., Smailes, E., & Bernstein, D. (1999). Childhood maltreatment increases risk for personality disorders during adulthood. *Archives of General Psychiatry, 56,* 600–606.

Johnson, J. G., Cohen, P., Skodol, A., Oldham, J., Kasen, S., & Brook, J. S. (1999). Personality disorders in adolescence and risk of major mental disorders and suicidality during adulthood. *Archives of General Psychiatry, 56,* 805–811.

Johnson, J. G., Cohen, P., Smailes, E., Kasen, S., Oldham, J. M., & Skodol, A. E. (2000). Adolescent personality disorders associated with violence and criminal behavior during adolescence and early adulthood. *American Journal of Psychiatry, 157,* 1406–1412.

Johnson, J. H., & Goldman, J. (1990). *Developmental assessment in clinical child psychology: A handbook.* Boston: Allyn & Bacon.

Johnson, M. H., Halit, H., Grice, S. J., & Karmiloff-Smith, A. (2002). Neuroimaging of typical and atypical development: A perspective from multiple levels of analysis. *Development and Psychopathology, 14,* 521–536.

Johnson, S. W., & Maile, L. J. (1987). *Suicide and the schools: A handbook for prevention, intervention, and rehabilitation.* Springfield, IL: Charles C. Thomas.

Johnston, C., & Mash, E. J. (2001). Families of children with Attention-Deficit/Hyperactivity Disorder: Review and recommendations for future research. *Clinical Child and Family Psychology Review, 4,* 183–207.

Johnston, L. D. (1985). The etiology and prevention of substance use: What can we learn from recent historical changes? In C. L. Jones & R. J. Battjes (Eds.), *Etiology of drug abuse: Implications for prevention* (pp. 155–177). NIDA Research Monograph 56. Rockville, MD: National Institute on Drug Abuse.

Johnston, L. D., O'Malley, P. M., & Bachman, J. G. (1988b). *National survey results on drug use from the Monitoring the Future study, 1975–1994: Vol. II. College students and young adults.* Bethesda, MD: National Institute on Drug Abuse.

Johnston, L. D., O'Malley, P. M., & Bachman, J. G. (2001). *Monitoring the*

Future National Survey Results on Drug Use, 1975–2000. Volume 1: Secondary School Students (NIH Publication No. 01-4924). Bethesda, MD: National Institute on Drug Abuse.

Johnston, L. D., O'Malley, P. M., & Bachman, J. G. (2003). *Monitoring the future: National survey results on adolescent drug use: Overview of key findings, 2002.* Bethesda, MD: National Institute on Drug Abuse.

Joiner, T. E., Jr., Catanzaro, S. J., & Laurent, J. (1996). Tripartite structure of positive and negative affect, depression, and anxiety in children and adolescent psychiatric inpatients. *Journal of Abnormal Psychology, 105,* 401–409.

Joiner, T. E., Metalsky, G. I., Katz, J., & Beach, S. R. H. (1999). Depression and excessive reassurance-seeking. *Psychological Inquiry, 10,* 269–278.

Jordan, K. M. (2000). Substance abuse among gay, lesbian, bisexual, transgender, and questioning adolescents. *School Psychology Review, 29,* 201–206.

Jouriles, E. N., McDonald, R., Stephens, N., Norwood, W., Spiller, L. C., & Ware, H. S. (1998). Breaking the cycle of violence: Helping families departing from battered women's shelters. In G. W. Holden, R. A. Geffner, & E. N. Jouriles (Eds.), *Children exposed to marital violence: Theory, research, and applied issues* (pp. 337–370). Washington, DC: American Psychological Association.

Jouriles, E. N., & Norwood, W. D. (1995). Physical aggression toward boys and girls in families characterized by the battering of women. *Journal of Family Psychology, 9,* 69–78.

Jouriles, E. N., Norwood, W. D., McDonald, R., & Peters, B. (2001). Domestic violence and child adjustment. In J. H. Grych & F. D. Fincham (Eds.), *Interparental conflict and child development* (pp. 315–336). Cambridge, England: Cambridge University Press.

Judd, P. H., & McGlashan, T. H. (2003). *A developmental model of borderline personality disorder.* Washington, DC: American Psychiatric Publishing.

Jurkovic, G. J. (1997). *Lost childhoods: The plight of the parentified child.* New York: Brunner/Mazel.

Kadesjo, B., Gillberg, C., & Hagberg, B. (1999). Brief report: Autism and Asperger syndrome in seven-year-old children: A total population study. *Journal of Autism and Developmental Disorders, 29*(4), 327–332.

Kaffman, M., & Elizur, E. (1977). Infants who become enuretics: A longitudinal study of 161 kibbutz children. *Monographs of the Society for Research in Child Development, 42*(2), 1–89.

Kagan, J., Reznick, J. S., & Snidman, N. (1988). Temperamental influences on reactions to unfamiliarity and challenge. In G. P. Chruousos, K. L. Louriaux, & P. W. Gold (Eds.), *Mechanisms of physical and emotional stress: Advances in experimental medicine and biology* (pp. 319–339). New York: Plenum.

Kameguchi, K., & Murphy-Shigetmatsu, S. (2001). Family psychology and family therapy in Japan. *American Psychologist, 56,* 65–70.

Kaminer, R., & Vig, S. (1995). Standardized intelligence testing: Does it do more good than harm? *Journal of Developmental and Behavioral Pediatrics, 16,* 425–427.

Kamphaus, R. W., & Frick, P. J. (1996). *Clinical assessment of child and adolescent personality and behavior.* Boston: Allyn & Bacon.

Kamphaus, R. W., & Frick, P. J. (2002). *Clinical assessment of children's personality and behavior* (2nd ed.). New York: Allyn & Bacon.

Kandel, D., Yamaguchi, K., & Chen, K. (1992). Stages of progression in drug use involvement from adolescence to adulthood: Further evidence for the gateway theory. *Journal of Studies on Alcohol, 53,* 447–457.

Kane, P., & Garber, J. (2004). The relations among depression in fathers, children's psychopathology, and father-child conflict: A meta-analysis. *Clinical Psychology Review, 24,* 339–360.

Kanner, L. (1943). Autistic disturbances of affective contact. *Nervous Child, 2,* 217–250.

Kaplow, J. B., Curran, P. J., Angold, A., & Costello, E. J. (2001). The prospective relation between dimensions of anxiety and the initiation of adolescent alcohol use. *Journal of Clinical Child Psychology, 30,* 316–326.

Kasari, C., Sigman, M., Baumgartner, P., & Stipek, D. J. (1993). Pride and mastery in children with autism. *Journal of Child Psychology and Psychiatry, 34,* 353–362.

Kasen, S., Johnson, J., & Cohen, P. (1990). The impact of school emotional climate on student psychopathology. *Journal of Abnormal Child Psychology, 18,* 165–177.

Kashani, J. H., & Carlson, G. A. (1987). Seriously depressed preschoolers. *American Journal of Psychiatry, 144,* 348–350.

Kaslow, F. W. (1996). *Handbook of relational diagnosis and dysfunctional family patterns.* New York: Wiley.

Kaslow, N. J., Deering, C. G., & Racusin, G. R. (1994). Depressed children and their families. *Clinical Psychology Review, 14,* 39–59.

Kaslow, N. J., McClure, E., & Connell, A. (2002). Treatment of depression in children and adolescents. In I. H. Gotlib & C. L. Hammen (Eds.), *Handbook of depression* (pp. 441–464). New York: Guilford.

Katz, P. A. (2003). Racists or tolerant multiculturalists: How do they begin? *American Psychologist, 58,* 897–909.

Kaufman, J., Jones, B., Steiglitz, E., Vitulano, L., & Mannarino, A. P. (1994). The use of multiple informants to assess children's maltreatment experiences. *Journal of Family Violence, 9,* 227–248.

Kaufman, J., Martin, A., King, R. A., & Charney, D.

(2001). Are child-, adolescent-, and adult-onset depression one and the same disorder? *Biological Psychiatry, 49,* 980–1001.

Kaukiainen, A., Salmivalli, C., Lagerspetz, K., Tamminen, M., Vauras, M., Maki, H., et al. (2002). Learning difficulties, social intelligence, and self-concept: Connections to bully-victim problems. *Scandanavian Journal of Psychology, 43,* 269–278.

Kavale, K. A. (1988). Learning disability and cultural disadvantage: The case for a relationship. *Learning Disability Quarterly, 11,* 195–210.

Kavale, K. A., & Forness, S. R. (1996). Social skill deficits and learning disabilities: A meta-analysis. *Journal of Learning Disabilities, 29,* 226–237.

Kavale, K. A., & Forness, S. R. (2000). History, rhetoric, and reality: Analysis of the inclusion debate. *Remedial and Special Education, 21,* 279–296.

Kaye, W. H., Barbarich, B. S., Putnam, B. S., Gendall, K. A., Fernstrom, J., Fernstrom, M., et al. (2003). Anxiolytic effects of acute tryptophan depletion (ATD) in anorexia nervosa. *International Journal of Eating Disorders, 33,* 257–267.

Kaye, W. H., Gendall, K., & Strober, M. (1998). Serotonin neuronal function and selective serotonin reuptake inhibitor treatment in anorexia and bulimia nervosa. *Biological Psychiatry, 44,* 825–838.

Kazak, A. E. (1992). The social context of coping with childhood chronic illness: Family systems and social support. In A. M. La Greca, L. J. Siegel, J. L. Wallander, & C. E. Walker (Eds.), *Stress and coping in child health* (pp. 262–278). New York: Guilford.

Kazak, A. E., Segal-Andrews, A. M., & Johnson, K. (1995). Pediatric psychology research and practice: A family/systems approach. In M. C. Roberts (Ed.), *Handbook of pediatric psychology* (2nd ed., pp. 84–104). New York: Guilford Press.

Kazak, A. E., Simms, S., & Rourke, M. T. (2002). Family systems practice in pediatric psychology. *Journal of Pediatric Psychology, 27,* 133–143.

Kazdin, A. E. (1996). Problem solving and parent management in treating aggressive and antisocial behavior. In E. D. Hibbs & P. S. Jensen (Eds.), *Psychosocial treatments for child and adolescent disorders* (pp. 377–408). Washington, DC: American Psychological Association.

Kazdin, A. E. (1997a). Practitioner review: Psychosocial treatments for conduct disorder in children. *Journal of Child Psychology and Psychiatry and Allied Disciplines, 38,* 161–178.

Kazdin, A. E. (1997b). A model for developing effective treatments: Progression and interplay of theory, research, and practice. *Journal of Clinical Child Psychology, 26,* 114–129.

Kazdin, A. E. (1997c). Conduct disorder across the life-span. In S. S. Luthar, J. A. Burack, D. Cicchetti, & J. R. Weisz (Eds.), *Developmental psychopathology: Perspectives on adjustment, risk, and disorder* (pp. 248–272). Cambridge, MA: Cambridge University Press.

Kazdin, A. E. (2003). Problem-solving skills training and parent management training for conduct disorder. In A. E. Kazdin & J. R. Weisz (Eds.), *Evidence-based psychotherapies for children and adolescents* (pp. 241–262). New York: Guilford.

Kazdin, A. E., Kraemer, H. C., Kessler, R. C., Kupfer, D. J., & Offord, D. R. (1997). Contributions of risk-factor research to developmental psychopathology. *Clinical Psychology Review, 17,* 375–406.

Kazdin, A. E., & Weisz, J. R. (1998). Identifying and developing empirically supported child and adolescent treatments. *Journal of Consulting and Clinical Psychology, 66,* 19–36.

Kazdin, A. E., & Weisz, J. R. (2003). *Evidence-based psychotherapies for children and adolescents.* New York: Guilford.

Kearney, C. A. (2003). *Casebook in child behavior disorders* (2nd ed.). Belmont, CA: Wadsworth.

Keel, P. K., Mitchell, J. E., Miller, K. B., Davis, T. L., & Crow, S. J. (1999). Long-term outcome of bulimia nervosa. *Archives of General Psychiatry, 56,* 63–69.

Keenan, K., Loeber, R., & Green, S. (1999). Conduct disorder in girls: A review of the literature. *Clinical Child & Family Psychology Review, 2*(1), 3–19.

Keith, R. W. (1994). *Auditory Continuous Performance Test.* San Antonio: Psychological Corporation.

Kellam, S. G., Rebok, G. W., Mayer, L. S., Ialongo, N., & Kalodner, C. R. (1994). Depressive symptoms over first grade and their response to developmental epidemiologically based preventive trial aimed at improving achievement. *Development and Psychopathology, 6,* 463–481.

Kelleher, M. J. C. D. & Chambers, D. (2003). Cross-cultural variation in child and adolescent suicide. In R. A. King & A. Apter (Eds.), *Suicide in children and adolescents* (pp. 170–197). Cambridge, England: Cambridge University Press.

Keller, A., Jeffries, N., Blumenthal, J., Clasen, L. S., Liu, H., Giedd, J. N., & Rapoport, J. L. (2003). Corpus callosum development in childhood-onset schizophrenia. *Schizophrenia Research, 62,* 105–114.

Keller, M. B., Herzog, D. B., Lavori, P. W., Bradburn, I. S., & Mahoney, E. M. (1992). The natural history of bulimia nervosa: Extraordinarily high rates of chronicity, relapse, recurrence and psychosocial morbidity. *International Journal of Eating Disorders, 12,* 1–9.

Keller, M. B., Ryan, N. D., Strober, M., Klein, R. G., Kutcher, S. P., Birmaher, B., et al. (2001). Efficacy of paroxetine in the treatment of adolescent major depression: A randomized, controlled trial. *Journal of the American Academy of Child and Adolescent Psychiatry, 40,* 762–772.

Kelly, J. B. (2003). Children's adjustment in conflicted marriage and divorce: A decade review of research. *Journal of the American Academy of Child and*

Adolescent Psychiatry, 39, 963–973.

Kelly, S. A., Brownell, C. A., & Campbell, S. B. (2000). Mastery motivation and self-evaluative affect in toddlers: Longitudinal relations with maternal behavior. *Child Development, 71,* 1061–1071.

Kendall, P. C. (2000). *Cognitive-behavioral therapy for anxious children: Therapist manual* (2nd ed.). Admore, PA: Workbook Publishing.

Kendall, P. C., Aschenbrand, S. G., & Hudson, J. L. (2003). Child-focused treatment of anxiety. In A. E. Kazdin & J. R. Weisz (Eds.), *Evidence-based psychotherapies for children and adolescents* (pp. 81–100). New York: Guilford.

Kendall, P. C., Chu, B., Gifford, A., Hayes, C., & Nauta, M. (1999). Breathing life into a manual: Flexibility and creativity with manual-based treatments. *Cognitive and Behavioral Practice, 5,* 177–198.

Kendall, P. C., Flannery-Schroeder, E., Panichelli-Mindel, S. M., Southam-Gerow, M. A., Henin, A., & Warman, M. (1997). Therapy for youths with anxiety disorders: A second randomized clinical trial. *Journal of Consulting and Clinical Psychology, 65,* 366–380.

Kendall, P. C., Safford, S., Flannery-Schroeder, E., & Webb, A. (2004). Child anxiety treatment: Outcomes in adolescence and impact on substance use and depression at 7.4-year follow-up. *Journal of Consulting and Clinical Psychology, 72,* 276–287.

Kendall-Tackett, K. A., Williams, L. M., & Finkelhor, D. (1993). Impact of sexual abuse on children: A review and synthesis of recent empirical studies. *Psychological Bulletin, 113,* 164–180.

Kerig, P. K. (in press). Revisiting the construct of boundary dissolution: A multidimensional perspective. *Journal of Emotional Abuse, 5(2/3).*

Kerig, P. K. (1995). Triangles in the family circle: Effects of family structure on marriage, parenting, and child adjustment. *Journal of Family Psychology, 9,* 28–43.

Kerig, P. K. (1998a). Gender and appraisals as mediators of adjustment in children exposed to interparental violence. *Journal of Family Violence, 15,* 345–363.

Kerig, P. K. (1999). Gender issues in the effects of exposure to violence on children. *Journal of Emotional Abuse, 1,* 87–105.

Kerig, P. K. (2001). Children's coping with interparental conflict. In J. H. Grych & F. D. Fincham (Eds.), *Interparental conflict and child development* (pp. 213–245). Cambridge, England: Cambridge University Press.

Kerig, P. K. (2003a). Boundary dissolution. In J. Ponzetti, R. Hamon, Y. Kellar-Guenther, P. K. Kerig, L. Scales, & J. White (Eds.), *International Encyclopedia of Marital and Family Relationships* (pp. 164–170). New York: Macmillan.

Kerig, P. K. (2003b). In search of protective processes for

children exposed to interparental violence. *Journal of Emotional Abuse, 3,* 149–182.

Kerig, P. K. (2004). Shedding light on our dark side. *Contemporary Psychology, 491,* 94–96.

Kerig, P. K., Fedorowicz, A. E., Brown, C. A., & Warren, M. (2000). Assessment and intervention for PTSD in children exposed to violence. In R. Geffner, P. Jaffe, & M. Sudermann (Eds.), *Children exposed to family violence: Current issues in research, intervention and prevention, and policy development* (pp. 161–184). Binghamton, NY: Haworth Press.

Kerig, P. K., Fedorowicz, A. E., Brown, C. A., & Warren, M. (2000). Assessment and intervention for PTSD in children exposed to violence. *Journal of Aggression, Maltreatment, and Trauma, 3,* 161–184.

Kernberg, O. (1967). Borderline personality organization. *Journal of the American Psychoanalytic Association, 15,* 641–685.

Kersel, D. A., Marsh, N. V., Havill, J. H., & Sleigh, J. W. (2001). Psychosocial functioning during the year following severe traumatic brain injury. *Brain Injury, 15,* 683–696.

Kessler, R. C., Avenevoli, S., & Merikangas, K. R. (2001). Mood disorders in children and adolescents: An epidemiological perspective. *Biological Psychiatry, 49,* 1002–1014.

Kessler, R. C., Borges, G., & Walters, E. E. (1999). Prevalence of and risk factors for lifetime suicide attempts in the National Comorbidity Study.

Archives of General Psychiatry, 56, 617–626.

Kessler, R. C., & Walters, E. E. (1998). Epidemiology of DSM-III major depression and minor depression among adolescents and young adults in the National Comorbidity Survey. *Depression and Anxiety, 7,* 3–14.

Killen, J. D., Hayward, C., Wilson, D. M., Taylor, C. B., Hammer, L. D., Litt, I., et al. (1994). Factors associated with eating disorder symptoms in a community sample of 6th and 7th grade girls. *International Journal of Eating Disorders, 15,* 357–367.

Kim, E. Y., & Miklowitz, D. J. (2002). Childhood mania, Attention Deficit Hyperactivity Disorder, and Conduct Disorder: A critical review of diagnostic dilemmas. *Bipolar Disorders, 4,* 215–225.

Kim, I. J., Ge, X., Brody, G. H., Conger, R. D., Gibbons, F. X., & Simons, R. L. (2003). Parenting behaviors and the occurrence and co-occurrence of depressive symptoms and conduct problems among African American children. *Journal of Family Psychology, 17,* 571–583.

Kimble, C. R., Oepen, G., & Weinberg, E. (1997). Neurological vulnerability and trauma in borderline personality disorder. In M. C. Zanarini (Ed.), *Role of sexual abuse in the etiology of borderline personality disorder* (pp. 165–180). Washington, DC: American Psychiatric Press.

Kim-Cohen, J., & Moffitt, T. E. (2004). Genetic and environmental processes in young children's resilience and vulnerability to socioeconomic deprivation. *Child Development, 75*(3), 651–668.

King, B. H., State, M. W., Shah, B., Davanzo, P., & Dykens, E. (1997). Mental retardation: A review of the past 10 years: Part I. *Journal of the American Academy of Child and Adolescent Psychiatry, 36,* 1656–1663.

King, S., Ricard, N., Rochon, V., Steiger, H., & Nelis, S. (2003). Determinants of expressed emotion in mothers of schizophrenia patients. *Psychiatry Research, 117,* 211–222.

Kitayama, S. (2000). Collective construction of the self and social relationships: A rejoinder and some extensions. *Child Development, 71,* 1143–1146.

Klein, R. G., & Mannuzza, S. (1991). Long-term outcome of hyperactive children: A review. *Journal of the American Academy of Child and Adolescent Psychiatry, 30,* 383–387.

Klimes-Dougan, B., Free, K., Ronsaville, D., Stilwell, J., Welsh, C. J., & Radke-Yarrow, M. (1999). Suicidal ideation and attempts: A longitudinal investigation of children of depressed and well mothers. *Journal of the American Academy of Child and Adolescent Psychiatry, 38,* 651–659.

Klinger, L. G., & Dawson, G. (1996). Autistic disorder. In E. J. Mash & R. A. Barkley (Eds.), *Child psychopathology* (pp. 311–339). New York: Guilford.

Klinger, L. G., Dawson, G., & Renner, P. (2003). Autistic disorder. In E. J. Mash, &

R. A. Barkley, *Child psychopathology* (2nd ed., pp. 409–454). New York: Guilford.

Klinnert, M. D., Campos, J. J., Sorce, J. F., Emde, R. N., & Svejda, M. (1983). Emotions as behavior regulators: Social referencing in infancy. In R. Plutchik & H. Kellerman (Eds.), *Emotion: Theory, research, and experience, Vol. 2: Emotion in early development* (pp. 57–86). New York: Academic Press.

Knoff, H. M. (1990). Evaluation of projective drawings. In C. Reynolds & R. Kamphaus (Eds.), *Handbook of psychological and educational assessment of children* (pp. 89–146). New York: Guilford.

Knudson, B., & Coyle, A. (2002). Parents' experiences of caring for sons and daughters with schizophrenia: A qualitative analysis of coping. *European Journal of Psychotherapy, Counselling and Health,* 169–183.

Kobayashi, R., Murata, T., & Yoshinaga, K. (1992). A follow-up study of 201 children with autism in Kyushu and Yamaguchi areas, Japan. *Journal of Autism and Developmental Disorders, 22,* 395–411.

Kochanska, G. (1997b). Mutually responsive orientation between mothers and their young children: Implications for early socialization. *Child Development, 68,* 94–112.

Kochanska, G. (2002). Committed compliance, moral self, and internalization: A mediational model. *Developmental Psychology, 38,* 339–351.

Kochanska, G., & Aksan, N. (1995). Mother-child mutually positive affect, the quality of child compliance to requests and prohibitions, and maternal control as correlates of early internalization. *Child Development, 66,* 236–254.

Kochanska, G., Aksan, N., & Koeing, A. L. (1995). A longitudinal study of the roots of preschooler's conscience: Commited compliance and emerging internalization. *Child Development, 66,* 1752–1769.

Kochanska, G., Coy, K. C., & Murray, K. T. (2001). The development of self-regulation in the first four years of life. *Child Development, 72,* 949–1286.

Kochanska, G., Gross, J. N., Lin, M. H., & Nichols, K. E. (2002). Guilt in young children: Development, determinants, and relations with a broader system of standards. *Child Development, 73,* 461–482.

Kochanska, G., & Murray, K. T. (2000). Mother-child mutually responsive orientation and conscience development: From toddler to early school age. *Child Development, 71,* 417–431.

Koerner, K., & Linehan, M. M. (2000). Borderline personality disorder: Research on dialectical behavior therapy for patients with borderline personality disorder. *Psychiatric Clinics of North America, 23,* 151–167.

Kog, E., & Vandereycken, W. (1988). The facts: A review of research data on eating disorder families. In W. Vandereycken, E. Kog, & J. Vanderlinden (Eds.), *The family approach to eating*

disorders (pp. 25–26). New York: PMA.

Kog, E., Vandereycken, W., & Vertommen, H. (1985). Toward a verification of the psychosomatic family model: A pilot study of ten families with an anorexia/bulimia nervosa patient. *International Journal of Eating Disorders, 4,* 525–538.

Kohlberg, L. (1976). Moral stages and moralization: The cognitive-developmental approach. In T. Lickona (Ed.), *Moral development and behavior: Theory, research, and social issues* (pp. 84–107). New York: Holt, Rinehart & Winston.

Kolb, B., & Whishaw, I. Q. (2003). *Fundamentals of human neuropsychology.* New York: Worth.

Kolko, D. J. (2002). Child physical abuse. In J. E. B. Myers, L. Berliner, J. Briere, C. T. Hendrix, C. Jenny, & T. A. Reid (Eds.), *The APSAC handbook on child maltreatment* (2nd ed., pp. 21–54). Thousand Oaks, CA: Sage.

Kolvin, I., Miller, F. J. W., Fleeting, M., & Kolvin, P. A. (1989). Risk/protective factors for offending with particular reference to deprivation. In M. Rutter (Ed.), *Studies in psychosocial risk: The power of longitudinal studies* (pp. 77–95). Cambridge, England: Cambridge, University Press.

Kopp, C. B. (2002). Self-regulation in childhood. In N. J. Smelser & P. B. Baltes (Eds.), *International encyclopedia of the social and behavioral sciences* (pp. 13862–13866). New York: Pergamon.

Korbin, J. E. (2002). Culture and child maltreatment: Cultural competence and beyond. *Child Abuse and Neglect, 26,* 637–644.

Korkman, M., Kirk, U., & Kemp, S. (1998). *NEPSY: A developmental neuropsychological assessment.* Psychological Corporation.

Kosterman, R., Hawkins, J. D., Spoth, R., Haggerty, K., & Zhu, K. (1997). Effects of a preventive parent training intervention on observed family interactions: Proximal outcomes from Preparing for the Drug Free Years. *Journal of Community Psychology, 25,* 277–292.

Kovacs, M. (1992). *Children's Depression Inventory manual.* Toronto, Ontario, Canada: Multi-Health Systems.

Kovacs, M. (1996). Prevalence and course of major depressive disorder during childhood and later years of the life span. *Journal of the American Academy of Child and Adolescent Psychiatry, 35,* 705–715.

Kovacs, M., Akiskal, H. S., Gatsonis, C., & Parrone, P. L. (1994). Childhood-onset dysthymic disorder: Clinical features and prospective naturalistic outcome. *Archives of General Psychiatry, 51,* 365–374.

Kovacs, M., & Beck, A. T. (1977). An empirical-clinical approach toward a definition of childhood depression. In J. G. Schulterbrandt & A. Raskin (Eds.), *Depression in childhood: Diagnosis, treatment and conceptual models* (pp. 1–25). New York: Raven Press.

Kovacs, M., & Devlin, B. (1998). Internalizing disorders in childhood. *Journal of Child Psychology and Psychiatry and Allied Disciplines, 39,* 47–63.

Kowatch, R. A., Suppes, T., Carmody, T. J., Bucci, J. P., Hume, J. H., Kromelis, M., et al. (2000). Effect size of lithium, divalproex sodium, and carbamazepine in children and adolescents with bipolar disorder. *Journal of the American Academy of Child and Adolescent Psychiatry, 39,* 713–720.

Kravariti, E., Morris, R. G., Rabe-Hesketh, S., Murray, R. M., & Frangou, S. (2003). The Maudsley Early-Onset Schizophrenia Study: Cognitive function in adolescent-onset schizophrenia. *Schizophrenia Research, 65,* 95–103.

Kruttschnitt, C., & Dornfeld, M. (1993). Exposure to family violence: A partial explanation for initial and subsequent levels of delinquency? *Criminal Behaviour and Mental Health, 3,* 63–75.

Kuczynski, L., & Kochanska, G. (1990). Development of children's non-compliant strategies from toddlerhood to age 5. *Developmental Psychology, 26,* 398–408.

Kuhne, M., Schachar, R., & Tannock, R. (1997). Impact of comorbid oppositional or conduct problems on attention-deficit hyperactivity disorder. *Journal of the American Academy of Child and Adolescent Psychiatry, 36,* 1715–1725.

Kuklinski, M. R., & Weinstein, R. S. (2001). Classroom and developmental differences in a path model of teacher expectancy effects. *Child Development, 72,* 1554–1578.

Kumpfer, K. L., Molgaard, V., & Spoth, R. (1996). Family interventions for the prevention of delinquency and drug use in special populations. In R. Peters & R. McMahon (Eds.), *Proceedings of the 1994 Banff International Conference.* Thousand Oaks, CA: Sage.

Kumra, S., Giedd, J. N., Vaituzis, A. C., Jacobsen, L. K., McKenna, K., Bedwell, J., et al. (2000). Childhood-onset psychotic disorders: Magnetic resonance imaging of volumetric differences in brain structure. *American Journal of Psychiatry, 157,* 1467–1474.

Kupersmidt, J. B., Burchinal, M., & Patterson, C. J. (1995). Developmental patterns of childhood peer relations as predictors of externalizing behavior problems. *Development and Psychopathology, 7,* 825–844.

La Greca, A. M., & Stone, G. (1992). Assessing children through interviews and behavioral observations. In C. E. Walker & M. C. Roberts (Eds.), *Handbook of clinical child psychology* (pp. 63–83). New York: Guilford.

Lachar, D., & Gruber, C. P. (1994). *The Personality Inventory for Youth.* Los Angeles: Western Psychological Services.

LaFromboise, T., & Dizon, M. R. (2003). American Indian children and adolescents. In J. T. Gibbs & L. N. Huang (Eds.), *Children of color: Psychological interventions with culturally diverse youth* (2nd ed., pp. 45–90). San Francisco: Jossey-Bass.

LaFromboise, T. D., Coleman, H. L. K., & Gerton, J. (1993). Psychological impact of biculturalism: Evidence and theory. *Psychological Bulletin, 125,* 470–500.

Lahey, B. B., Loeber, R., Hart, E. L., Frick, P. J., Applegate, B., Zhang, Q., et al. (1995). Four-year longitudinal study of conduct disorder in boys: Patterns and predictors of persistence. *Journal of Abnormal Psychology, 104,* 83–93.

Lahey, B. B., McBurnett, K., & Loeber, R. (2000). Are Attention-Deficit/Hyperactivity Disorder and Oppositional Defiant Disorder developmental precursors to Conduct Disorder? In A. J. Sameroff, M. Lewis, & S. M. Miller, *Handbook of developmental psychopathology* (pp. 431–446). New York: Kluwer Academic.

Lahey, B. B., Miller, T. L., Gordon, R. A., & Riley, A. W. (1999). Developmental epidemiology of the disruptive behavior disorders. In *Handbook of disruptive behavior disorders* (pp. 23–48). Dordrecht, Netherlands: Kluwer Academic Publishers.

Lahey, B. B., Moffitt, T. E., & Caspi, A. (2003). *Causes of conduct disorder and juvenile delinquency.* New York: Guilford.

Lainhart, J. E. (1999). Psychiatric problems in individuals with autism, their parents and siblings. *International Review of Psychiatry, 11,* 278–298.

Lake, A., Staiger, P., & Glowinski, H. (2000). Effect of Western culture on women's attitudes to eating and perceptions of body shape. *International Journal of Eating Disorders, 27,* 83–89.

Lamb, M. E. (1997). *The role of the father in child development* (3rd ed.). New York: Wiley.

Landa, R. (2000). Social language use in Asperger syndrome and high functioning autism. In A. Klin, F. R. Volkmar, & S. S. Sparrow (Eds.), *Asperger syndrome* (pp. 125–157). New York: Guilford.

Landreth, G. L. (2002). *Play therapy: The art of the relationship.* New York: Brunner-Routledge.

Langrock, A. M., Compas, B. E., Keller, G., Merchant, M. J., & Copeland, M. E. (2002). Coping with the stress of parental depression: Parents' reports of children's coping, emotional, and behavioral problems. *Journal of Clinical Child and Adolescent Psychology, 31,* 312–324.

Lansford, J. E., Deater-Deckard, K., Dodge, K. A., Bates, J. E., & Pettit, G. S. (2004). Ethnic differences in the link between physical discipline and later adolescent externalizing behaviors. *Journal of Child Psychology & Psychiatry, 45,* 801–812.

Lapalme, M., Hodgins, S., & LaRoche, C. (1997). Children of parents with bipolar disorder: A meta-analysis of risk for mental disorders. *Canadian Journal of Psychiatry, 42,* 623–631.

Larson, J., & Lochman, J. E. (2002). *Helping school-children cope with anger: A cognitive-behavioral intervention.* New York: Guilford.

Larson, R. W., & Richards, M. H. (1994). Family emotions: Do young adolescents and their parents experience the same states? *Journal of Research on Adolescence, 4,* 567–583.

Lask, B. (2000). Aetiology. In B. Lask & R. Bryant-Wauch (Eds.), *Anorexia nervosa and related eating disorders in childhood and adolescence* (pp. 63–79). Philadelphia: Psychology Press.

Last, C. G., & Francis, G. (1988). School phobia. In B. B. Lahey & A. E. Kazdin (Eds.), *Advances in clinical child psychology* (Vol. 11, pp. 193–222). New York: Plenum.

Last, C. G., & Perrin, S. (1993). Anxiety disorders in African-American and white children. *Journal of Abnormal Child Psychology, 21,* 153–164.

Last, C. G., Perrin, S., Hersen, M., & Kazdin, A. E. (1992). DSM-III-R anxiety disorders in children: Sociodemographic and clinical characteristics. *Journal of the American Academy of Child and Adolescent Psychiatry, 31,* 928–934.

Lau, E. (1995). An insatiable emptiness. *The Georgia Straight,* 13–14.

Laurent, J., & Ettelson, R. (2001). An examination of the tripartite model of anxiety and depression and its application to youth. *Clinical Child and Family Psychology Review, 4,* 209–230.

Leff, J. P., Sartorius, N., Jablensky, A., Anker, M., Korten, A., Gulbinat, W., & Ernberg, G. (1991). The International Pilot Study of Schizophrenia: Five-year follow-up of findings. In H. Hafner & W. F. Gattaz (Eds.), *Search for the causes of schizophrenia* (pp. 57–66). Berlin: Springer-Verlag.

Leffert, J. S., & Siperstein, G. N. (1996). Assessment of social-cognitive processes in children with mental retardation. *American Journal on Mental Retardation, 100,* 441–455.

Leon, G. R., Fulkerson, J. A., Perry, C. L., & Dube, A. (1994). Family influences, school behaviors, and risk for the later development of an eating disorder. *Journal of Youth and Adolescence, 23,* 499–515.

Leon, G. R., Fulkerson, J. A., Perry, C. L., & Early-Zald, M. B. (1995). Prospective analysis of personality and behavioral vulnerabilities and gender influences in the later development of disordered eating. *Journal of Abnormal Psychology, 104,* 140–149.

Leon, G. R., Lucas, A. R., Colligan, R. C., Ferdinande, R. J., & Kamp. J. (1985). Sexuality, body-image, and personality attitudes in anorexia nervosa. *Journal of Abnormal Child Psychology, 13,* 245–258.

Levin, M. R., Ashmore-Callahan, S., Kendall, P. C., & Ichii, M. (1996). Treatment of separation anxiety disorder. In M. A. Reinecke, M. Dattilio, & A. Freeman (Eds.), *Cognitive therapy with children and adolescents* (pp. 153–174). New York: Guilford.

Levy, F., & Hay, D. A. (2001). *Attention, genes, and ADHD.* Philadelphia: Brunner-Routledge.

Levy, F., Hay, D. A., McStephen, M., Wood, C., & Waldman, I. (1997). Attention-deficit hyperactivity disorder: A category or a continuum? Genetic analysis of a large-scale twin study. *Journal of the American Academy of Child and Adolescent Psychiatry, 36,* 737–744.

Lewandowski, L. M., Gebing, T. A., Anthony, J. L., & O'Brien, W. H. (1997). Meta-analysis of cognitive-behavioral treatment studies for bulimia. *Clinical Psychology Review, 17,* 703–718.

Lewinsohn, P. M., Clarke, G. N., Rohde, P., Hops, H., & Seeley, J. R. (1996). A course in coping: A cognitive-behavioral approach to the treatment of adolescent depression. In E. D. Hibbs & P. S. Jensen (Eds.), *Psychosocial treatments for child and adolescent disorders* (pp. 109–135). Washington, DC: American Psychological Association.

Lewinsohn, P. M., Clarke, G., Seeley, J., & Rohde, P. (1994). Major depression in community adolescents: Age at onset, episode duration, and time to recurrence. *Journal of the American Academy of Child and Adolescent Psychiatry, 33,* 809–818.

Lewinsohn, P. M., Gotlib, I. H., Lewinsohn, M., & Seeley, J. R. (1998). Gender differences in anxiety disorders and anxiety symptoms in adolescents. *Journal of Abnormal Psychology, 107,* 109–117.

Lewinsohn, P. M., Gotlib, I. H., & Seeley, J. R. (1997). Depression-related psychosocial variables: Are they specific to depression in adolescents? *Journal of Abnormal Psychology, 106,* 365–375.

Lewinsohn, P. M., Klein, D. N., & Seeley, J. R. (1995). Bipolar disorders in a community sample of older adolescents: Prevalence, phenomenology, comorbidity, and course. *Journal of the American Academy of Child & Adolescent Psychiatry, 34,* 454–463.

Lewinsohn, P. M., Pettit, J. W., Joiner, T. E., & Seeley, J. R. (2003). The symptomatic expression of major depressive disorder in adolescents and young adults. *Journal of Abnormal Psychology, 112,* 244–252.

Lewinsohn, P. M., Rohde, P., & Seeley, J. R. (1998). Major depressive disorder in older adolescents: Prevalence, risk factors, and clinical implications. *Clinical Psychology Review, 18,* 765–794.

Lewinsohn, P. M., Rohde, P., Seeley, J. R., Klein, D. N., & Gotlib, I. H. (2000). Natural course of adolescent major depressive disorder in a community sample: Predictors of recurrence in young adults. *American Journal of Psychiatry, 157,* 1584–1591.

Lewinsohn, P. M., Striegel-Moore, R. H., & Seeley, J. R. (2000). Epidemiology and natural course of eating disorders: Young women from adolescence to young adulthood. *Journal of the American Academy of Child and Adolescent Psychiatry, 39,* 1284–1292.

Lewis, M., Feiring, C., & Rosenthal, S. (2000). Attachment over time. *Child Development, 71,* 707–720.

Lieberman, A. F. (1992). Infant-parent psychotherapy with toddlers. *Development and Psychopathology, 4,* 559–574.

Lieberman, A. F. & Pawl, J. H. (1993). Infant-parent psychotherapy. In C. H. Zeanah (Ed.), *Handbook of infant mental health* (pp. 427–442). New York: Guilford.

Limber, S. P., & Wilcox, B. L. (1996). Application of the U.N. Convention on the rights of the child to the United States. *American Psychologist, 51,* 1246–1250.

Lincoln, A., Courchesne, E., Allen, M., Hanson, E., & Ene, M. (1998). Neurobiology of Asperger syndrome: Seven case studies and quantitative magnetic resonance imaging findings. In E. Schopler & G. B. Mesibov (Eds.), *Asperger syndrome or high-functioning autism?* (pp. 145–163). New York: Plenum.

Lincoln, A. J., Courchesne, E., Kilman, B. A., & Elmasian, R. (1988). A study of intellectual abilities in high-functioning people with autism. *Journal of Autism & Developmental Disorders, 18*(4), 505–524.

Lindahl, K. M., & Malik, N. M. (1999). Marital conflict, family processes, and boys' externalizing behavior in Hispanic American and European American families. *Journal of Clinical Child Psychology, 28,* 12–24.

Lindahl, K. M., & Malik, N. M. (2001). The System for Coding Interactions and Family Functioning. In P. K. Kerig & K. M. Lindahl (Eds.), *Family observational coding systems: Resources for systemic research* (pp. 77–92). Hillsdale, NJ: Erlbaum.

Linde, K., Ramirez, G., Mulrow, C. D., Pauls, A., Weidenhammer, W., & Melchart, D. (1996). St. John's wort for depression: An overview and meta-analysis of randomized clinical trials. *British Medical Journal, 313,* 253–258.

Linehan, M. M. (1991). *Cognitive-behavioral treatment for Borderline Personality Disorder: The dialectics of effective treatment.* New York: Guilford.

Linehan, M. M. (1993a). *Cognitive-behavioral treatment of borderline personality disorder.* New York: Guilford.

Linehan, M. M. (1993b). *Skills training manual for treating borderline personality disorder.* New York: Guilford.

Linehan, M. M., Armstrong, H. E., Suarez, R. A., Allmon, D., & Heard, H. L. (1991). Cognitive-behavioral treatment of chronically parasuicidal borderline patients. *Archives of General Psychiatry, 48,* 1060–1064.

Links, P. S., Steiner, M., & Huxley, G. (1988). The occurrence of borderline personality disorder in the families of borderline patients. *Journal of Personality Disorders, 2,* 14–20.

Lish, J. D., Meenan, S., Whybrow, P. C., & Price, R. A. (1994). The National Depressive and Manic-Depressive Association (DMDA) survey of bipolar members. *Journal of Affective Disorders, 31,* 281–294.

Little, M., & Kobak, R. (2003). Emotional security with teachers and children's stress reactivity: A comparison of special education and regular education classrooms. *Journal of Clinical Child and Adolescent Psychology, 32,* 127–138.

Lizardi, H., Klein, D. N., Ouimette, P. C., Riso, L. P., Anderson, R. L., & Donaldson, S. K. (1995). Reports of the childhood home environment in early-onset dysthymia and episodic major depression. *Journal of Abnormal Psychology, 104,* 132–139.

Lochman, J. E., & Wells, K. C. (2003). Effectiveness of the coping power program and of classroom intervention with aggressive children: Outcomes at a 1-year follow-up. *Behavior Therapy, 34,* 493–515.

Lock, J., LeGrange, D., Agras, W. S., & Dare, C. (2002). *Treatment manual for anorexia nervosa: A family-based approach.* New York: Guilford.

Loeber, R. (1988). Natural histories of conduct problems, delinquency, and associated substance use: Evidence for developmental progression. In B. B. Lahey & A. E. Kazdin (Eds.), *Advances in clinical child psychology* (Vol. 11, pp. 73–118). New York: Plenum.

Loeber, R., & Farrington, D. P. (1994). Problems and solutions in longitudinal and experimental treatment studies of child psychopathology and delinquency. *Journal of Consulting and Clinical Psychology, 62,* 887–900.

Loeber, R., Green, S. M., Lahey, B. B., Christ, M. A., & Frick, P. J. (1992). Developmental sequences in the age of onset of disruptive child behaviors. *Journal of Child and Family Studies, 1,* 21–41.

Loeber, R., Green, S. M., Lahey, B. B., Frick, P. J., & McBurnett, K. (2000). Findings on disruptive behavior disorders from the first decade of the Developmental Trends Study. *Clinical Child & Family Psychology Review, 3,* 37–60.

Loeber, R., & Hay, D. (1997). Key issues in the development of aggression and violence from childhood to early adulthood. *Annual Review of Psychology, 48,* 371–410.

Loeber, R., & Keenan, K. (1994). Interaction between conduct disorder and its comorbid conditions: Effects of age and gender. *Clinical Psychology Review, 14,* 497–523.

Loeber, R., Lahey, B. B., & Thomas, C. (1991). Diagnostic conundrum of oppositional defiant disorder and conduct disorder. *Journal of Abnormal Psychology, 100,* 379–390.

Loeber, R., & Stouthamer-Loeber, M. (1998). Development of juvenile aggression and violence: Some common misconceptions and controversies. *American Psychologist, 53,* 242–259.

Loeber, R., Stouthamer-Loeber, M., & White, H. R. (1999). Developmental aspects of delinquency and internalizing problems and their association with persistent juvenile substance use between ages 7 and 18. *Journal of Clinical Child Psychology, 28,* 322–332.

Loeber, R., Wung, P., Keenan, K., Giroux, B., Stouthamer-Loeber, M., VanKammen, W. B., et al. (1993). Developmental pathways in disruptive child behavior. *Development and Psychopathology, 5,* 103–134.

Lombardo, G. T. (1997). BDP and ADHD. *Journal of the American Academy of Child and Adolescent Psychiatry, 36,* 719–720.

Lonigan, C. J., Carey, M. P., & Finch, A. J. (1994). Anxiety and depression in children and adolescents: Negative affectivity and the utility of self-reports. *Journal of Consulting and Clinical Psychology, 62,* 1000–1008.

Lonigan, C. J., & Phillips, B. M. (2001). Temperamental influences on the development of anxiety disorders. In *The developmental psychopathology of anxiety* (pp. 60–91). London: Oxford University Press.

Lorion, R. L., & Satzman, W. (1995). Children's exposure to community violence: Following a path from concern to research to action. *Psychiatry, 56,* 55–65.

Loue, S. (2003). *Diversity issues in substance abuse treatment and research.* New York: Kluwer.

Lourenco, O., & Machado, A. (1996). In defense of Piaget's theory: A reply to 10 common criticisms. *Psychological Review, 103,* 143–164.

Lovaas, O. I., & Smith, T. (2003). Early and intensive behavioral intervention in autism. In A. E. Kazdin, & J. R. Weisz (Eds.), *Evidence-based psychotherapies for children and adolescents* (pp. 325–340). New York: Guilford.

Lovett, M. W., Lacerenza, L., Borden, S. L., Frijters, J. C., Steinbach, K. A., & De Palma, M. (2000). Components of effective remediation for developmental reading disabilities: Combining phonological and strategy-based instruction to improve outcomes. *Journal of Educational Psychology, 92,* 263–283.

Luborsky, L., Singer, B., & Luborsky, L. I. (1975). Comparative studies of psychotherapies: Is it true that "Everyone has won and all must have prizes?" *Archives of General Psychiatry, 32,* 995–1008.

Lucas, A., Beard, C., O'Fallon, W., & Kurland, L. (1991). 50 year trends in the incidence of anorexia nervosa in Rochester, Minnesota: A population based study. *American Journal of Psychiatry, 148,* 917–922.

Ludolph, P., Westen, D., Misle, B., Jackson, A., Wixom, J., & Wiss, F. C. (1990). The borderline diagnosis in adolescents: Symptoms and developmental history. *American Journal of Psychiatry, 147,* 470–476.

Luria, A. R. (1980). *Higher cortical functions in man.* New York: Basic Books.

Luthar, S. S. (1993). Annotation: Methodological and conceptual issues in research on childhood resilience. *Journal of Child Psychology and Psychiatry, 34,* 441–453.

Luthar, S. S., & Becker, B. E. (2002). Privileged but pressured? A study of affluent youth. *Child Development, 73,* 1593–1610.

Luthar, S. S., Cicchetti, D., & Becker, B. (2000). The construct of resilience: A critical evaluation and guidelines for future work. *Child Development, 71,* 543–562.

Luthar, S. S., Cushing, G., & McMahon, T. J. (1997). Interdisciplinary interface: Developmental principles brought to substance abuse research. In S. S. Luthar, J. A. Burack, D. Cicchetti, & J. R. Weisz (Eds.), *Developmental psychopathology: Perspectives on adjustment, risk, and disorder* (pp. 437–456). Cambridge, MA: Cambridge University Press.

Luthar, S. S., & Latendresse, S. J. (2002). Adolescent risk: The costs of affluence. In R. M. Lerner & C. S. Taylor (Eds.), *Pathways to positive development among diverse youth* (pp. 101–121). San Francisco: Jossey-Bass.

Lynam, D. R. (1997). Pursuing the psychopath: Capturing the fledgling psychopath in a nomological net. *Journal of Abnormal Psychology, 106,* 425–438.

Lynch, M. (2003). Consequences of children's exposure to community violence. *Clinical Child and Family Psychology Review, 6,* 265–274.

Lyon, G. R., Fletcher, J. M., & Barnes, M. C. (2003). Learning disabilities. In E. J. Mash & R. A. Barkley (Eds.), *Child psychopathology* (pp. 520–587). New York: Guilford.

Lyon, M., Chatoor, I., Atkins, D., Silber, T., Mosimann, J., & Gray, J. (1997). Testing the hypothesis of the multidimensional model of anorexia nervosa in adolescents. *Adolescence, 32,* 101–111.

Lyons-Ruth, K., Alpern, L., & Repacholi, B. (1993). Disorganized attachment classification and maternal psychosocial problems as predictors of hostile-aggressive behavior in the preschool classroom. *Child Development, 64*(572), 585.

Lyons-Ruth, K., Easterbrooks, M. A., & Cibelli, C. D. (1997). Infant attachment strategies, infant mental lag, and maternal depressive symptoms: Predictors of internalizing and externalizing problems at age 7. *Developmental Psychology, 33*(4), 681–692.

Lyons-Ruth, K., Zeanah, C. H., & Benoit, D. (1996). Disorder and risk for disorder during infancy and toddlerhood. In E. J. Mash & R. A. Barkley (Eds.), *Child psychopathology* (pp. 457–491). New York: Guilford.

Lytton, H. (1990). Child and parent effects in boys' conduct disorder: A reinterpretation. *Developmental Psychology, 26,* 683–697.

Maccoby, E. E. (1999). *The two sexes: Growing up apart, coming together.* Cambridge, MA: Harvard University Press.

Maccoby, E. E., & Mnookin, R. H. (1992). *Dividing the child: Social and legal dilemmas of custody.* Cambridge, MA: Harvard University Press.

MacFie, J., Houts, R. M., McElwain, N. L., & Cox, M. J. (in press). The effect of father-toddler and mother-toddler role reversal on the development of behavior problems in kindergarten. *Social Development.*

Machover, K. (1949). *Personality projection in the drawing of the human figure.* Springfield, IL: Charles C Thomas.

MacTurk, R. H., & Morgan, G. A. (1995). *Mastery motivation: Origins, conceptualization, and applications.* Westport, CT: Ablex.

Madonna, P. G., Van Scoyk, S., & Jones, D. P. H. (1991). Family interactions within incest and nonincest families. *American Journal of Psychiatry, 148,* 46–49.

Maggs, J. L., & Galambos, N. L. (1993). Alternative structural models for understanding adolescent problem behavior in two-earner families. *Journal of Early Adolescence, 13,* 79–101.

Mahler, M. S., Pine, F., & Bergman, A. (1975). *The psychological birth of the human infant.* New York: Basic Books.

Mahoney, A., Donnelly, W. O., Boxer, P., & Lewis, T. (2003). Marital and severe parent-to-adolescent physical aggression in clinic-referred families: Mother and adolescent reports on co-occurrence and links to child behavior problems. *Journal of Family Psychology, 17,* 3–19.

Main, M., & Goldwyn, R. (1988). *Adult attachment scoring and classification systems.* Unpublished manuscript, University of California at Berkeley.

Main, M., & Weston, D. R. (1982). Avoidance of the attachment figure in infancy: Descriptions and interpretations. In C. M. Parkes & J. Stevenson-Hinde (Eds.), *The place of attachment in human behavior* (pp. 31–59). New York: Basic Books.

Malatesta, C. Z., & Haviland, J. M. (1982). Learning display rules: The socialization of emotion expression in infancy. *Child Development, 53,* 1001–1003.

Malla, A., Norman, R., McLean, T., Scholten, D., & Townsend, L. (2003). A Canadian programme for early intervention in non-affective psychotic disorders. *Australian and New Zealand Journal of Psychiatry, 37,* 407–413.

Malley-Morrison, K., & Hines, D. (2004). *Family violence in a cultural perspective: Defining, understanding, and combating abuse.* Thousand Oaks, CA: Sage.

Malphurs, J. E., Field, T. M., Larraine, C., Pickens, J., Pelaez-Nogueras, M., Yando, R., et al. (1996). Altering withdrawn and intrusive interaction behaviors of depressed mothers. *Infant Mental Health Journal, 17,* 152–160.

Manassis, K. (2001). Child-parent relations: Attachment and anxiety disorders. In W. K. Silverman & A. Treffers (Eds.), *Anxiety disorders in children and adolescents: Research, assessment, and intervention* (pp. 255–272). New York: Cambridge.

Manly, J. T., Cicchetti, D., & Barnett, D. (1994). The impact of subtype,

frequency, chronicity, and severity of child maltreatment on social competence and behavior problems. *Development and Psychopathology, 6,* 121–143.

Manly, J. T., Kim, J. E., Rogosch, F. A., & Cicchetti, D. (2001). Dimensions of child maltreatment and children's adjustment: Contributions of developmental timing and subtype. *Development and Psychopathology, 13,* 759–782.

Mannarino, A. P., & Cohen, J. A. (1990). Treating the abused child. In R. T. Ammerman & M. Hersen (Eds.), *Children at risk: An evaluation of factors contributing to child abuse and neglect* (pp. 249–268). New York: Plenum.

Mannarino, A. P., & Cohen, J. A. (1996). A follow-up study of factors that mediate the development of psychological symptomatology in sexually abused girls. *Child Maltreatment, 1,* 246–260.

Mannuzza, S., Klein, R. G., Bessler, A., & Malloy, P. (1998). Adult psychiatric status of hyperactive boys grown up. *American Journal of Psychiatry, 155,* 493–498.

Mannuzza, S., Klein, R. G., Bessler, A., Malloy, P., & Hynes, M. E. (1998). Educational and occupational outcome of hyperactive boys grown up. *Journal of the American Academy of Child and Adolescent Psychiatry, 36,* 1222–1227.

Mannuzza, S., Klein, R. G., & Moulton, J. L. (2003). Does stimulant treatment place children at risk for adult substance abuse? A controlled, prospective follow-up study. *Journal of Child and Adolescent Psychopharmacology, 13,* 273–282.

March, J. S. (1995). Cognitive-behavioral psychotherapy for children and adolescents with OCD: A review and recommendations for treatment. *Journal of the American Academy of Child and Adolescent Psychiatry, 34,* 7–18.

March, J. S., Amaya-Jackson, L., Terry, R., & Costanzo, P. (1997). Post-traumatic stress in children and adolescents after an industrial fire. *Journal of the American Academy of Child and Adolescent Psychiatry, 36,* 1080–1088.

March, J. S., & Mulle, K. (1998). *OCD in children and adolescents: A cognitive-behavioral treatment manual.* New York: Guilford.

March, J. S., Parker, J., Sullivan, K., Stallings, P., & Conners, C. (1997). The Multidimensional Anxiety Scale for Children (MASC): Factor structure, reliability and validity. *Journal of the American Academy of Child and Adolescent Psychiatry, 36,* 554–565.

Marcia, J. E., Waterman, A. S. M. D. R., Archer, S. L., & Orlofsky, J. I. (1993). *Ego identity: A handbook for psychosocial research.* New York: Springer-Verlag.

Markon, K. E., Krueger, R., Bouchard, T. J., & Gottesman, I. I. (2002). Abnormal and normal personality traits: Evidence for genetic and environmental relationships in the Minnesota Study of Twins Reared Apart. *Journal of Personality, 70,* 661–695.

Mash, E. J., & Barkley, R. A. (1998). *Treatment of childhood disorders* (2nd ed.) New York: Guilford Publications.

Mash, E. J., & Dozois, D. J. A. (2003). Child psychopathology: A developmental-systems perspective. In E. J. Mash & R. A. Barkley (Eds.), *Child psychopathology* (pp. 3–71). New York: Guilford.

Masten, A. S., & Coatsworth, J. D. (1998). The development of competence in favorable and unfavorable environments. *American Psychologist, 53,* 205–220.

Masten, A. S., & Curtis, W. J. (2000). Integrating competence and psychopathology: Pathways toward a comprehensive science of adaptation in development. *Development and Psychopathology, 12,* 529–550.

Masterson, J. F. (1976). *Psychotherapy of the borderline adult.* New York: Brunner/Mazel.

Masterson, J. F., & Rinsley, D. B. (1975). The borderline syndrome: The role of the mother in the genesis and psychic structure of the borderline personality. *International Journal of Psychoanalysis, 56,* 163–177.

Masterson, J. F., Tolpin, M., & Sifneos, P. E. (1991). *Comparing psychoanalytic psychotherapies: Developmental, self, and object relations; self psychology; short-term dynamic.* New York: Brunner/Mazel.

Matarazzo, J. D. (1990). Psychological assessment versus psychological testing: Validation from Binet to the school, clinic, and courtroom. *American Psychologist, 45,* 999–1017.

Matthews, D. J. (1995). *Ending the cycle of violence: Community responses to children of battered women.* Thousand Oaks, CA: Sage.

Maughan, B. (1995). Annotation: Long-term outcomes of developmental reading problems. *Journal of Child Psychology and Psychiatry, 36,* 357–371.

Maughan, B., Pickles, A., Hagell, A., Rutter, M., & Yule, W. (1996). Reading problems and antisocial behaviour: Developmental trends in comorbidity. *Journal of Child Psychology and Psychiatry, 37,* 405–418.

Max, J. E., Sharma, A., & Qurashi, M. I. (1997). Traumatic brain injury in a child psychiatry inpatient population: A controlled study. *Journal of the American Academy of Child and Adolescent Psychiatry, 36,* 1595–1601.

McAdoo, W. G., & DeMyer, M. K. (1978). Personality characteristics of parents. In M. Rutter & E. Schopler (Eds.), *Autism: A reappraisal of concepts and treatment* (pp. 251–267). New York: Plenum.

McArdle, P., O'Brien, G., & Kolvin, I. (1995). Hyperactivity: Prevalence and relationship with conduct disorder. *Journal of Child Psychology and Psychiatry, 36,* 279–303.

McArthur, D. S., & Roberts, G. E. (1982). *Roberts Apperception Test for Children.* Los Angeles: Western Psychological Services.

McCabe, K. M., Rodgers, C., & Yeh, M. (2004). Gender differences in childhood onset conduct disorder. *Development and Psychopathology, 16,* 179–192.

McClellan, J., McCurry, C., Ronnei, M., & Adams, J. (1996). Age of onset of sexual abuse: Relationship to sexually inappropriate behaviors. *Journal of the American Academy of Child and Adolescent Psychiatry, 35,* 1375–1383.

McClellan, J. M., Werry, J. S., Bernet, W., Arnold, V., Beitchman, J. H., Benson, S., Bukestein, O., Kinlan, J., Rue, D., & Shaw, J. (2001). Practice parameters for the assessment and treatment of children and adolescents with schizophrenia. *Journal of the American Academy of Child and Adolescent Psychiatry, 40,* 4S–23S.

McClure, E., Connell, A., Zucker, M., Griffith, J. R., & Kaslow, N. J. (2005). The Adolescent Depression Empowerment Project (ADEPT): A culturally sensitive family treatment for depressed African American girls. In E. D. Hibbs & P. S. Jensen (Eds.), *Psychosocial treatment for child and adolescent disorders: Empirically based strategies for clinical practice.* Washington, DC: American Psychological Association.

McConaughy, S. H., & Achenbach, T. M. (1994). *Manual for the Semistructured Clinical Interview for children and adolescents.* Burlington, VT: University Associates in Psychiatry.

McConnell, M. C., & Kerig, P. K. (2002). Assessing coparenting in families of school age children:

Validation of the Coparenting and Family Rating System. *Canadian Journal of Behavioural Science, 34,* 56–70.

McCord, J. (1978). A thirty-year follow-up of treatment effects. *American Psychologist, 33*(3), 284–289.

McCord, J. (1979). Some child rearing antecedents to criminal behavior in adult men. *Journal of Personality and Social Psychology, 37,* 1477–1486.

McCord, J. (1990). Long-term perspectives on parental absence. In L. Robins & M. Rutter (Eds.), *Straight and devious pathways from childhood to adulthood* (pp. 116–135). Cambridge: Cambridge University Press.

McCord, J. (1992). The Cambridge–Somerville Study: A pioneering longitudinal-experimental study of delinquency prevention. In J. McCord & R. E. Tremblay (Eds.), *Preventing antisocial behavior: Interventions from birth through adolescence* (pp. 196–206). New York: Guilford.

McCord, J., Tremblay, R. E., Vitaro, F., & Desmarais-Gervais, L. (1994). Boys' disruptive behaviour, school adjustment, and delinquency: The Montreal Prevention Experiment. *International Journal of Behavioral Development, 17,* 739–752.

McEachlin, J. J., Smith, T., & Lovaas, O. I. (1993). Long-term outcome for children with autism who received early intensive behavioral treatment. *American Journal on Mental Retardation, 97,* 379–372.

McGee, R., Feehan, M., Williams, S., & Anderson, J. C. (1992). DSM-III disorders from age 11 to age 15 years. *Journal of the American Academy of Child and Adolescent Psychiatry, 31,* 50–59.

McGee, R. A., Wolfe, D. A., & Wilson, S. K. (1997). Multiple maltreatment experiences and adolescent behavior problems: Adolescent's perspectives. *Development and Psychopathology, 9,* 131–150.

McGlashan, T. H. (1992). The Chestnut Lodge Follow-up Study. In D. Silver & M. Rosenbluth (Eds.), *Handbook of borderline disorders* (pp. 53–83). New York: International Universities Press.

McGoldrick, M. (2002). *Re-visioning family therapy: Race, culture, and gender in clinical practice.* New York: Guilford.

McGoldrick, M., & Carter, B. (2003). The family life cycle. In F. Walsh (Ed.), *Normal family processes: Growing diversity and complexity* (pp. 460–489). New York: Guilford.

McGoldrick, M., & Gerson, R. (1985). *Genograms in family assessment.* New York: Norton.

McGoldrick, M., Gerson, R., & Shellenberger, S. (1997). *Genograms: Assessment and intervention* (2nd ed.). New York: Norton.

McGorry, P. D., & Yung, A. R. (2003). Early intervention in psychosis: An overdue reform. *Australian and New Zealand Journal of Psychiatry, 37,* 393–398.

McGrath, J. J., Feron, F. P., Burne, T. H. J., Mackay-Sim, A., & Eyles, D. W. (2003). The neurodevelopmental hypothesis of schizophrenia: A review of recent developments. *Annals of Medicine, 35,* 86–93.

McGrath, P. J., & Pisterman, S. (1991). Developmental issues: Adolescent pain. In J. P. Bush & S. W. Harkins (Eds.), *Children in pain: Clinical and research issues from a developmental perspective* (pp. 231–250). New York: Springer-Verlag.

McGue, M., Elkins, I., & Ianoco, W. G. (2000). Genetic and environmental influences on adolescent substance use and abuse. *American Journal of Medical Genetics, 96,* 671–677.

McHale, J. P., Kuersten-Hogan, R., Lauretti, A., & Rasmussen, J. L. (2000). Parental reports of coparenting and observed coparenting behavior during the toddler period. *Journal of Family Psychology, 14,* 220–236.

McIntosh, P. (1998). White privilege: Unpacking the invisible knapsack. In M. McGoldrick (Ed.), *Re-visioning family therapy: Race, culture, and gender in clinical practice* (pp. 147–152). New York: Guilford.

McLoyd, V. C., Cauce, A. M., Takeuchi, D., & Wilson, L. (2000). Marital processes and parental socialization in families of color: A decade review of research. *Journal of Marriage and Family, 62,* 1070–1093.

McMahon, R. J., & Estes, A. M. (1997). Conduct problems. In E. J. Mash & L. G. Terdal (Eds.),

Assessment of childhood disorders (pp. 130–193). New York: Guilford.

McMahon, R. J., & Forehand, R. L. (2003). *Helping the noncompliant child: Family-based treatment for oppositional behavior* (2nd ed.). New York: Guilford.

McNeil, T. F., Cantor-Graae, E., & Blennow, G. (2003). Mental correlates of neuromotoric deviation in 6-year-olds at heightened risk for schizophrenia. *Schizophrenia Research, 60,* 219–228.

Mead, G. H. (1932). *Mind, self and society.* Chicago: University of Chicago Press.

Meadow, S. R. (1993). False allegations of abuse and Munchausen syndrome by proxy. *Archives of Disease in Childhood, 68,* 444–447.

Mednick, S. A., Machon, R. A., Huttunen, M. O., & Bonett, D. (1988). Adult schizophrenia following prenatal exposure to an influenza epidemic. *Archives of General Psychiatry, 45,* 189–192.

Mehlenbeck, R., Spirito, A., Barnett, N., & Overholser, J. (2003). Behavioral factors: Substance abuse. In A. Spirito & J. C. Overholser (Eds.), *Evaluating and treating adolescent suicide attempters: From research to practice* (pp. 113–146). New York: Academic Press.

Melamed, B. G. (2002). Parenting the ill child. In M. H. Bornstein (Ed.), *Handbook of parenting, Vol. 5: Practical issues in parenting* (pp. 329–348). Mahwah, NJ: Erlbaum.

Mellin, L. M., Irwin, C., & Scully, S. (1992). Prevalence of disordered eating in girls: A survey of middle class children. *Journal of the Amercian Dietetic Association, 92,* 851–853.

Mellon, M. W., & Stern, H. P. (1998). Elmination disorders. In R. T. Ammerman, & J. V. Campo, *Handbook of pediatric psychology and psychiatry. Vol. 1: Psychology and psychiatric issues in the pediatric setting* (pp. 182–198). Needham Heights, MA: Allyn & Bacon.

Melton, G. B. (1992). The improbability of prevention of sexual abuse. In D. J. Willis, G. W. Holden, & M. S. Rosenberg (Eds.), *Prevention of child maltreatment: Developmental perspectives* (pp. 168–179). New York: Wiley.

Menzies, R. G., & Clarke, J. C. (1995). The etiology of phobias: A nonassociative account. *Clinical Psychology Review, 15,* 23–48.

Mesibov, G., Shea, V., & Adams, L. W. (2001). *Understanding Asperger syndrome and high functioning autism.* New York: Kluwer Academic/Plenum.

Messer, S. C., & Gross, A. M. (1995). Childhood depression and family interaction: A naturalistic observation study. *Journal of Clinical Child Psychology, 24,* 77–88.

Meyer, C., Blissett, J., & Oldfield, C. (2001). Sexual orientation and eating psychopathology: The role of masculinity and femininity. *International Journal of Eating Disorders, 29,* 314–318.

Meyer, R. G. (1989). *Cases in developmental psychology and psychopathology.* Boston: Allyn & Bacon.

Miklowitz, D. J. (1994). Family risk indicators in schizophrenia. *Schizophrenia Bulletin, 20,* 137–147.

Miklowitz, D. J., George, E. L., Richards, J. A., Simoneau, T. L., & Suddath, R. L. (2003). A randomized study of family-focused psychoeducation and pharmacotherapy in the outpatient management of bipolar disorder. *Archives of General Psychiatry, 60,* 904–910.

Miklowitz, D. J., Goldstein, M. J., Nuechterlein, K. H., Snyder, K. S., & Mintz, J. (1998). Family factors and the course of bipolar affective disorder. *Archives of General Psychiatry, 45,* 225–231.

Milich, R., Balentine, A. C., & Lynam, D. R. (2001). ADHD combined type and ADHD predominantly inattentive type are distinct and unrelated disorders. *Clinical Psychology: Science and Practice, 8,* 463–488.

Miller, A. L., Wagner, E. E., & Rathus, J. H. (2004). Dialectical behavior therapy for suicidal adolescents: An overview. In H. Steiner (Ed.), *Handbook of mental health interventions in children and adolescents* (pp. 659–684). New York: Jossey Bass.

Miller, K. (1993). Concommitant nonpharmacologic therapy in the treatment of primary nocturnal enuresis. *Clinical Pediatrics,* 32–37.

Miller, K. J., & Mizes, J. S. (2000). *Comparative treatments for eating disorders.* New York: Springer.

Minnes, P. (1988). Family stress associated with a developmentally handicapped child. *International Review of Research on Mental Retardation, 15,* 195–266.

Minuchin, S. (1974). *Families and family therapy.* Cambridge, MA: Harvard University Press.

Minuchin, S., Lee, W. Y., & Simon, G. (1996). *Mastering family therapy: Journeys of growth and transformation.* New York: Wiley.

Minuchin, S., & Nichols, M. P. (1998). Structural family therapy. In F. M. Dattilio (Ed.), *Case studies in couple and family therapy: Systemic and cognitive perspectives* (pp. 233–256). New York: Guilford.

Minuchin, S., Rosman, B. L., & Baker, L. (1978). *Psychosomatic families: Anorexia nervosa in context.* Cambridge, MA: Harvard University Press.

Mistry, R. S., Vandewater, E. A., Huston, A. C., & McLoyd, V. C. (2002). Economic well-being and children's social adjustment: The role of family process in an ethnically diverse low-income sample. *Child Development, 73,* 935–951.

Mitchell, J., McCauley, E., Burke, P. M., & Moss, S. J. (1988). Phenomenology of depression in children and adolescents. *Journal of the American Academy of Child and Adolescent Psychiatry, 27,* 12–20.

Moffitt, T. E. (1993). Life-course persistent and adolescence-limited antisocial behavior: A developmental taxonomy. *Psychological Review, 100,* 674–701.

Moffitt, T. E., & Caspi, A. (2001). Childhood predictors differentiate life-course persistent and adolescence-limited antisocial pathways among males and females. *Development and Psychopathology, 13,* 355–376.

Moffitt, T. E., Caspi, A., Dickson, N., Silva, P., & Stanton, W. (1996). Childhood-onset versus adolescent-onset antisocial conduct problems in males: Natural history from ages 3 to 18 years. *Development and Psychopathology, 8,* 399–424.

Moffitt, T. E., Caspi, A., Harrington, H., & Milne, B. (2002). Males on the life-course-persistent and adolescence-limited pathways: Follow-up at age 26 years. *Development and Psychopathology, 14,* 179–207.

Moffitt, T. E., Caspi, A., Rutter, M., & Silva, P. A. (2001). *Sex differences in antisocial behavior: Conduct disorder, delinquency, and violence in the Dunedin longitudinal study.* New York: Cambridge University Press.

Moffitt, T. E., & Lynam, D. (1994). The neuropsychology of conduct disorder and delinquency: Implications for understanding antisocial behavior. In D. C. Fowles, P. Sutker, & S. H. Goodman (Eds.), *Progress in experimental personality and psychopathology research* (pp. 233–262). New York: Springer.

Moldin, S. O., & Gottesman, I. J. (1997). At issue: Genes, experience, and chance in schizophrenia: Positioning for the 21st century. *Schizophrenia Bulletin, 23,* 547–561.

Molfese, V. J., & Molfese, D. L. (2000). *Temperament and personality across the life span.* Mahwah, NJ: Erlbaum.

Morris, R. J., & Kratochwill, T. R. (1998). *The practice of child therapy* (3rd ed.). Boston: Allyn & Bacon.

Morris, T. L., & March, J. S. (2004). *Anxiety disorders in children and adolescents.* New York: Guilford.

Morrison, D. R., & Coiro, M. J. (1999). Parental conflict and marital disruption: Do children benefit when high-conflict marriages are dissolved? *Journal of Marriage and the Family, 61,* 626–637.

Mortensen, P. B., Pedersen, C. B., Melbye, M., Mors, O., & Ewald, H. (2003). Individual and familial risk factors for bipolar affective disorders in Denmark. *Archives of General Psychiatry, 60,* 1209–1215.

Morton, T. D. (1999). The increasing colorization of America's child welfare system: The overrepresentation of African-American children. *Policy and Practice of Public Human Services, 57,* 23–30.

Moss, E., & St. Laurent, D. (2001). Attachment at school age and academic performance. *Developmental Psychology, 37,* 863–874.

Mowbray, C. T., & Oyserman, D. (2003). Substance abuse in children of parents with mental illness: Risks, resiliency, and best prevention practices. *Journal of Primary Prevention, 23,* 451–482.

MTA Cooperative Group. (1999). A 14-month randomized clinical trial of treatment strategies for Attention-Deficit/Hyperactivity Disorder. *Archives of General Psychiatry, 56,* 1073–1086.

Mufson, L., & Dorta, K. P. (2003). Interpersonal psychotherapy for depressed adolescents. In A. E. Kazdin & J. R. Weisz (Eds.), *Evidence-based psychotherapies for children and adolescents* (pp. 165–185). New York: Guilford.

Mufson, L., Dorta, K. P., Moreau, D., & Weissman, M. M. (2004). *Interpersonal psychotherapy for depressed adolescents.* New York: Guilford.

Muris, P., Merckelbach, H., Gadet, B., & Moulaert, V. (2000). Fears, worries, and scary dreams to 4- to 12-year-old children: Their content, developmental patterns, and origins. *Journal of Clinical Child Psychology, 29,* 43–52.

Murphy, L. M. B., Thompson, R. J., & Morris, M. A. (1997). Adherence behavior among adolescents with type I insulin-dependent diabetes mellitus: The role of cognitive appraisal processes. *Journal of Pediatric Psychology, 22,* 811–825.

Murray, L., Woolgar, M., Cooper, P., & Hipwell, A. (2001). Cognitive vulnerability to depression in 5-year-old children of depressed mothers. *Journal of Child Psychology and Psychiatry and Allied Disciplines, 42,* 891–899.

Murry, V. M., Bynum, M. S., Brody, G. H., Willert, A., & Stephens, D. (2001). African American single mothers and children in context: A review of studies of risk and resilience. *Clinical Child and Family Psychology Review, 4,* 133–155.

Musun-Miller, L. (1993). Social acceptance and social problem solving in preschool children. *Journal of Applied Developmental Psychology, 14,* 59–70.

Nader, K., & Pynoos, R. S. (1991). Play and drawing techniques as tools for interviewing traumatized children. In C. E. Schaefer, K. Gitlin, & A. Sandgrund (Eds.), *Play diagnosis and assessment* (pp. 375–389). New York: Wiley.

Naglieri, J. A., LeBuffe, P. A., & Pfeiffer, S. I. (1994). *Devereux scales of mental disorders.* New York: The Psychological Corporation.

Naglieri, J. A., & Pfeiffer, S. I. (1992). Performance of disruptive behavior disordered and normal samples on the Draw A Person: Screening procedure for emotional disturbance. *Psychological Assessment, 4,* 156–159.

Nassau, J. H., & Drotar, D. (1997). Social competence among children with central nervous system-related chronic health conditions: A review. *Journal of Pediatric Psychology, 22,* 771–793.

Nasser, M., Katzman, M. A., & Gordon, R. A. (2001). *Eating disorders and cultures in transition.* New York: Brunner-Routledge.

National Center for Health Statistics. (1999). *Vital statistics of the United States, 1993: Volume I Natality (Center for Disease Control Publication No. PHS 99–1100).* Hyattsville, MD: Centers for Disease Control.

National Center for Health Statistics. (2002). *National Vital Statistics Reports, 50* (No. 16). Hyattsville, MD: Author.

National Center for Juvenile Justice. (1999). *Juvenile offenders and their victims: 1999 national report.* Washington, DC: Office of Juvenile Justice and Delinquency Prevention.

National Center on Addiction and Substance Abuse. (2004). *Criminal neglect: Substance abuse, juvenile justice and the children left behind.* New York: Author.

National Center on Child Abuse and Neglect. (1995). *Child maltreatment 1993: Reports from the states to the National Center on Child Abuse and Neglect (Contract Number ACF-105-91-1802).* Washington, DC: U.S. Government Printing Office.

National Center on Child Abuse and Neglect. (2001). *Child maltreatment 1999: Reports from the states to the National Center on Child Abuse and Neglect.* Washington, DC: U.S. Government Printing Office.

National Coalition to Abolish Corporal Punishment in Schools. (2001). *Facts about corporal punishment.* Retrieved from http://www.stophitting.com

National Institute of Mental Health Research Roundtable on Prepubertal Bipolar Disorder. (2001). *Journal of the American Academy of Child and Adolescent Psychiatry, 40,* 871–878.

National Joint Committee on Learning Disabilities (1988, April). Austin, TX: Author.

Nechmad, A., Ratzoni, G., Poyurovsky, M., Meged,

S., Avidan, G., Fuchs, C., Bloch, Y., & Weizman, R. (2003). Obsessive-compulsive disorder in adolescent schizophrenia patients. *American Journal of Psychiatry, 160,* 1002–1004.

Neff, J. A., & Hoppe, S. K. (1993). Race/ethnicity, acculturation, and psychological distress: Fatalism and religiosity as cultural resources. *Journal of Community Psychology, 21,* 3–20.

Neiderman, M. (2000). Prognosis and outcome. In B. Lask & R. Bryant-Wauch (Eds.), *Anorexia nervosa and related eating disorders in childhood and adolescence* (pp. 81–101). Philadelphia: Psychology Press.

Neitzel, C., & Stright, A. (2003). Mothers' scaffolding of children's problem solving: Establishing a foundation of academic self-regulatory competence. *Journal of Family Psychology, 17,* 147–159.

Nellis, L., & Gridley, B. E. (1994). Review of the Bayley Scales of Infant Development-Second Edition. *Journal of School Psychology, 32,* 201–209.

Newacheck, P. W., & Taylor, N. R. (1992). Childhood chronic illness: Prevalence, severity, and impact. *American Journal of Health, 82,* 364–371.

Newcomb, M. D., & Bentler, P. M. (1988). *Consequences of adolescent drug use: Impact on the lives of young adults.* Newbury Park, CA: Sage Publications.

Newman, D. L., Caspi, A., Moffitt, T. E., & Silva, P. A. (1997). Antecedents of adult interpersonal functioning: Effects of individual differences in age 3 temperament. *Developmental Psychology, 33,* 206–217.

NICHD Early Child Care Research Network. (1999). Chronicity of maternal depressive symptoms, maternal sensitivity, and child functioning at 36 months. *Developmental Psychology, 35,* 1297–1310.

Nicolson, R., Brookner, F. B., Lenane, M., Gochman, P., Ingraham, L. J., Egan, M. F., Kendler, K. S., Pickar, D., Weinberger, D. R., & Rapoport, J. L. (2003). Parental schizophrenia spectrum disorders in childhood-onset and adult-onset schizophrenia. *American Journal of Psychiatry, 160,* 490–495.

Nicholson, R. M., Giedd, J. N., & Lenane, M. (1999). Clinical and neurobiological correlates of cytogenic abnormalities in childhood onset schizophrenia. *Schizophrenia Research, 41,* 55.

Nicholson, R. M., Lenane, M., & Singaracharlu, S. (2000). Premorbid speech and language impairments in childhood onset schizophrenia: Association with risk factors. *Schizophrenia Research, 41,* 55.

Niemi, L. T., Suvisaari, J. M., Tuulio-Henriksson, A., & Loennqvist, J. K. (2003). Childhood developmental abnormalities in schizophrenia: Evidence from high-risk studies. *Schizophrenia Research, 60,* 239–258.

Niendam, T. A., Bearden, C. E., Rosso, I. M., Sanchez, L. E., Hadley, T., Nuechterlein, K. H., & Cannon, T. D. (2003). A prospective study of childhood neurocognitive functioning in schizophrenic patients and their siblings. *American Journal of Psychiatry, 160,* 2060–2062.

Nihira, K. (1976). Dimensions of adaptive behavior in institutionalized mentally retarded children and adults: Developmental perspectives. *American Journal of Mental Deficiency, 81,* 215–226.

Nihira, K., Foster, R., Shellhaas, M., & Leland, H. (1974). *AAMD Adaptive Behavior Scale* (1974 revision). Washington, DC: American Association on Mental Deficiency.

Nixon, M. K., Cloutier, P. F., & Aggarwal, S. (2002). Affect regulation and addictive aspects of repetitive self-injury in hospitalized adolescents. *Journal of the American Academy of Child and Adolescent Psychiatry, 41,* 1333–1341.

Nock, M. K., & Kazdin, A. E. (2002). Examination of affective, cognitive, and behavioral factors and suicide-related outcomes in children and young adolescents. *Journal of Clinical Child & Adolescent Psychology, 31,* 48–58.

Nolen-Hoeksema, S. (2002). Gender differences in depression. In I. H. Gotlib & C. Hammen (Eds.), *Handbook of depression* (pp. 492–509). New York: Guilford.

Nolen-Hoeksema, S., Girgus, J. S., & Seligman, M. E. P. (1991). Sex differences in depression and explanatory style in children. *Journal of Youth and Adolescence, 20,* 233–245.

Obeidallah, D. A., McHale, S. M., & Silbereisen, R. K. (1996). Gender role socialization and adolescents' reports of depression: Why some girls and not others? *Journal of Youth and Adolescence, 25,* 775–785.

Ocampo, K. A., Knight, G. P., & Bernal, M. E. (1997). The development of cognitive abilities and social identities in children: The case of ethnic identity. *International Journal of Behavioral Development, 21,* 479–500.

O'Connor, T. G., Neiderhiser, J. M., Reiss, D., Hetherington, E. M., & Plomin, R. (1998). Genetic contributions to continuity, change, and co-occurrence of antisocial and depressive symptoms in adolescence. *Journal of Child Psychology & Psychiatry, 39,* 323–336.

O'Connor, T. G. & Plomin, R. (2000). Developmental behavioral genetics. In A. J. Sameroff, M. Lewis, & S. M. Miller (Eds.), *Handbook of developmental psychopathology* (pp. 217–236). New York: Kluwer Academic.

O'Donnell, J., Hawkins, J. D., & Abbott, R. D. (1995). Predicting serious delinquency and substance use among aggressive boys. *Journal of Consulting and Clinical Psychology, 63,* 529–537.

Office of Juvenile Justice. (2000). *Children as victims (1999 National Report Series, Juvenile Justice Bulletin).* http://ncjrs.org/html/ojjdp/2000_5_2/child_09.html

Ogata, S., Silk, K. R., Goodrich, S., Lohr, N. E., Westen, D., & Hill, E. (1990). Childhood sexual and physical abuse in adult patients with borderline personality disorder. *American Journal of Psychiatry, 147,* 1008–1013.

Ogawa, J. R., Sroufe, L. A., Weinfield, N. S., Carlson, E. A., & Egeland, B. (1997). Development and the fragmented self: Longitudinal study of dissociative symptomatology in a non-clinical sample. *Development and Psychopathology, 9,* 855–879.

Ogbu, J. V. (1999). A cultural context of children's development. In H. E. Fitzgerald, B. M. Lister, & B. S. Zuckerman (Eds.), *Children of color: Research, health, and policy issues* (pp. 73–92). New York: Garland.

Ogden, T. (1979). On projective identification. *International Journal of Psychoanalysis, 60,* 357–373.

Ogden, T. H. (1982). *Projective identification and psychotherapeutic technique.* New York: Academic.

Oldenburg, C. M., & Kerns, K. A. (1997). Associations between peer relationships and depressive symptoms: Testing moderator effects of gender and age. *Journal of Early Adolescence, 17,* 319–337.

Olds, D. (1997). The prenatal early infancy project: Preventing child abuse and neglect in the context of promoting maternal and child health. In D. A. Wolfe, R. J. McMahon, & R. D. Peters (Eds.), *Child abuse: New directions in prevention and treatment across the lifespan* (pp. 130–154). Thousand Oaks, CA: Sage.

Olin, S. S., & Mednick, S. A. (1996). Risk factors of psychosis: Identifying vulnerable populations permorbidly. *Schizophrenia Bulletin, 22,* 223–240.

Ollendick, T. H., & King, N. J. (1991). Developmental factors in child behavioral assessment. In P. R. Martin (Ed.), *Handbook of behavior therapy and psychological science: An integrative approach* (pp. 57–72). New York: Pergamon.

Ollendick, T. H., & King, N. J. (1998). Empirically supported treatments for children with phobic and anxiety disorders: Current status. *Journal of Clinical Child Psychology, 27,* 156–167.

Ollendick, T. H., & Schroeder, C. S. (2003). *Encyclopedia of clinical child and pediatric psychology.* New York: Kluwer.

Ollendick, T. H., Yang, B., King, N. J., Dong, Q., & Akande, A. (1996). Fears in American, Australian, Chinese, and Nigerian children and adolescents: A cross-cultural study. *Journal of Child Psychology and Psychiatry, 37,* 213–220.

Olweus, D., Limber, S., & Mihalic, S. (1999). *The bullying prevention program: Blueprints for violence prevention.* Boulder, CO: Center for the Study and Prevention of Violence.

Oosterlaan, J. (2001). Behavioural inhibition and the development of childhood anxiety disorders. In W. K. Silverman & A. Treffers (Eds.), *Anxiety disorders in children and adolescents: Research, assessment, and intervention* (pp. 45–71). New York: Cambridge.

Orbach, I. (2003). Suicide prevention for adolescents. In R. A. King & A. Apter (Eds.), *Suicide in children and adolescents* (pp. 227–250). Cambridge, England: Cambridge University Press.

Organista, K. C. (2003). Mexican American children and adolescents. In J. T. Gibbs & L. N. Huang (Eds.), *Children of color: Psychological interventions with culturally diverse youth* (2nd ed., pp. 344–381). San Francisco: Jossey-Bass.

Ornitz, E. M., Hanna, G. L., & de Traversay, J. (1992). Prestimulation-induced startle modulation in attention-deficit hyperactivity disorder and nocturnal enuresis. *Psychophysiology, 29,* 437–451.

Ornstein, P. A., Baker-Ward, L., Myers, J., Principe, G. F., & Gordon, B. N. (1995). Children's long-term retention of medical experiences: Implications for testimony. In F. E. Weinert & W. Schneider (Eds.), *Memory performance and competencies: Issues in growth and development* (pp. 349–371). Hillsdale, NJ: Erlbaum.

Osofsky, J. D. (1995). The effects of exposure to violence on young children. *American Psychologist, 50,* 782–788.

Osofsky, J. D. (2003). Prevalence of children's exposure to domestic violence and child maltreatment: Implications for prevention and intervention. *Clinical Child and Family Psychology Review, 6,* 161–170.

Osofsky, J. D., & Scheeringa, M. S. (1997). Community and domestic violence exposure: Effects on development and psychopathology. In D. Cicchetti & S. L. Toth (Eds.), *Developmental perspectives on trauma: Theory, research, and intervention* (pp. 180). Rochester: University of Rochester Press.

Osterling, J., & Dawson, G. (1994). Early recognition of children with autism: A study of first birthday home videotapes. *Journal of Autism and Developmental Disorders, 24,* 247–257.

Ott, S. L., Roberts, S., Rock, D., Allen, J., & Erlenmeyer-Kimling, L. (2002). Positive and negative thought disorder and psychopathology in childhood among subjects with adulthood schizophrenia. *Schizophrenia Research, 58,* 231–239.

Overholser, J. (2003). Predisposing factors in suicide attempts: Life stressors. In A. Spirito & J. C. Overholser (Eds.), *Evaluating and treating adolescent suicide attempters: From research to practice* (pp. 42–54). New York: Academic Press.

Overholser, J., Hemstreet, A. H., Spirito, A., & Vyse, S. (1989). Suicide awareness programs in the schools: Effects of gender and personal experience. *Journal of the American Academy of Child and Adolescent Psychiatry, 28,* 925–930.

Overholser, J., & Spirito, A. (2003). Precursors to

adolescent suicide attempts. In A. Spirito & J. C. Overholser (Eds.), *Evaluating and treating adolescent suicide attempters: From research to practice* (pp. 19–41). New York: Academic Press.

Ozonoff, S., & Cathcart, K. (1998). Effectiveness of a home program intervention for young children with autism. *Journal of Autism and Developmental Disorders, 28,* 25–32.

Ozonoff, S., & Griffith, E. M. (2000). Neuropsychological function and the external validity of Asperger Syndrome. In A. Klin, F. R. Volkmar, & S. S. Sparrow (Eds.), *Asperger syndrome* (pp. 72–96). New York: Guilford.

Ozonoff, S., & McEvoy, R. (1994). A longitudinal study of executive function and theory of mind development in autism. *Development and Psychopathology, 6,* 415–431.

Ozonoff, S., South, M., & Miller, J. N. (2000). DSMIV-defined Asperger syndrome: Cognitive, behavioral and early history differentiation from high-functioning autism. *Autism, 4,* 29–46.

Pagani, L., Tremblay, R. E., Vitaro, F., Boulerice, B., & McDuff, P. (2001). Effects of grade retention on academic performance and behavioral development. *Development and Psychopathology, 13,* 297–315.

Pantelis, C., Velakoulis, D., McGorry, P., Wood, S. J., Suckling, J., Phillips, L. J., Yung, A. R., Bullmore, E. T., Brewer, W., Soulsby, B., Desmond, P., & McGuire, P. (2003).

Neuroanatomical abnormalities before and after onset of psychosis: A cross-sectional and longitudinal MRI comparison. *Lancet, 361,* 281–288.

Paris, J. (1994). *Borderline personality disorder: A multidimensional approach.* Washington, DC: American Psychiatric Press.

Parke, R. D. (2004). Development in the family. *Annual Review of Psychology, 53,* 365–399.

Parker, J. G., Rubin, K. H., Price, J. M., & DeRosier, M. E. (1995). Peer relationships, child development, and adjustment: A developmental psychopathology perspective. In D. Cicchetti & D. J. Cohen (Eds.), *Developmental psychopathology, Vol. II: Risk, disorder, and adaptation* (pp. 96–161). New York: Wiley.

Parnell, T. F. (2002). Munchausen by proxy syndrome. In J. E. B. Myers, L. Berliner, J. Briere, C. T. Hendrix, C. Jenny, & T. A. Reid (Eds.), *The APSAC handbook on child maltreatment* (2nd ed., pp. 131–138). Thousand Oaks, CA: Sage.

Patterson, G. R. (1982). *Coercive family process: A social learning approach.* Eugene, OR: Castalia.

Patterson, G. R., & Capaldi, D. M. (1990). A mediational model for boys' depressed mood. In J. Rolf, A. S. Masten, D. Cicchetti, K. H. Nuechterlein, & S. Weintraub (Eds.), *Risk and protective factors in the development of psychopathology* (pp. 141–163). Cambridge, England: Cambridge University Press.

Patterson, G. R., DeBaryshe, B. D., & Ramsey, E. (1989). A developmental perspective on antisocial behavior. *American Psychologist, 44,* 329–335.

Patterson, G. R., & Dishion, T. J. (1988). Multilevel family process models: Traits, interactions, and relationships. In R. A. Hinde & J. Stevenson-Hinde (Eds.), *Relationships within families: Mutual influences* (pp. 283–310). Oxford, England: Clarendon Press.

Patterson, G. R., Reid, J. B., & Dishion, T. J. (1992). *Antisocial boys.* Eugene, OR: Castalia.

Patterson, G. R., & Yoerger, K. (2002). A developmental model for early- and late-onset delinquency. In J. B. Reid, G. R. Patterson, & J. J. Snyder (Eds.), *Antisocial behavior in children and adolescents: A developmental analysis and model for intervention.* (pp. 147–172). Washington, DC: American Psychological Association.

Patton, G. C., Selzer, R., Coffey, C., Carlin, B., & Wolfe, R. (1999). Onset of adolescent eating disorders: Population-based cohort study over 3 years. *British Medical Journal, 318,* 768.

Peled, E., & Edleson, J. L. (1995). Process and outcome in small groups for children of battered women. In E. Peled, P. G. Jaffe, & J. L. Edleson (Eds.), *Ending the cycle of violence: Community responses to children of battered women* (pp. 77–96). Thousand Oaks, CA: Sage.

Pelham, W. E., Wheeler, T., & Chronis, A. (1998).

Empirically supported psychosocial treatments for attention deficit hyperactivity disorder. *Journal of Clinical Child Psychology, 27,* 190–205.

Pelphrey, K. A., Sasson, N. J., Reznick, J. S., Paul, G., Goldman, B. D., & Piven, J. (2002). Visual scanning of faces in autism. *Journal of Autism and Developmental Disorders, 32*(4), 249–261.

Pennington, B. F. (2002). *The development of psychopathology: Nature and nurture.* New York, Guilford.

Perrin, E. C., Newacheck, P., Pless, B., Drotar, C., Gortmaker, S. L., Leventhal, J., et al. (1993). Issues involved in the definition and classification of chronic health conditions. *Pediatrics, 91,* 787–793.

Perry, C. L., Williams, C. L., Veblen-Mortenson, S., Toomey, T. L., Komro, K. A., Anstine, P. S., et al. (1996). Project Northland: Outcomes of a communitywide alcohol use prevention program during adolescence. *American Journal of Public Health, 86,* 956–965.

Peterson, A. C., Compas, B. E., Brooks-Gunn, J., Stemmler, M., Ey, S., & Grant, K. E. (1993). Depression in adolescence. *American Psychologist, 48,* 155–168.

Pfeffer, C. R. (2000). Suicidal behavior in prepubertal children: From the 1980s to the new millennium. In *Review of suicidology, 2000* (pp. 159–169). New York: Guilford Press.

Pfeffer, C. R. (2003). Assessing suicidal behavior in children and adolescents. In R. A.

King & A. Apter (Eds.), *Suicide in children and adolescents* (pp. 211–226). Cambridge, England: Cambridge University Press.

Pfeffer, C. R., Hurt, S. W., Kakuma, T., Peskin, J. R., Siefker, C. A., & Nagabhairava, S. (1994). Suicidal children grow up: Suicidal episode and effects of treatment during follow-up. *Journal of the American Academy of Child and Adolescent Psychiatry, 33,* 225–230.

Pfefferbaum, B. (1997). Posttraumatic stress disorder in children: A review of the past 10 years. *Journal of the American Academy of Child and Adolescent Psychiatry, 36,* 1503–1511.

Pfiffner, L. J., & McBurnett, K. (1997). Social skills training with parent generalization: Treatment effects for children with attention deficit disorder. *Journal of Consulting and Clinical Psychology, 65,* 749–757.

Phares, V. (1992). Where's Poppa? The relative lack of attention to the role of fathers in child and adolescent psychopathology. *American Psychologist, 47,* 656–664.

Phillips, L. J., Curry, C., Yung, A. R., Yuen, H. P., Adlard, S., & McGorry, P. D. (2002). Cannabis use is not associated with the development of psychosis in an 'ultra' high-risk group. *Australian and New Zealand Journal of Psychiatry, 36,* 800–806.

Phinney, J. S., Ong, A., & Madden, T. (2000). Cultural values and intergenerational value discrepancies in immigrant and non-immigrant families.

Child Development, 71, 528–539.

Piaget, J. (1932). *The moral judgment of the child.* London: Kegan Paul.

Piaget, J. (1962). *Play, dreams, and imitation in childhood.* New York: Norton.

Piaget, J. (1967). *Six psychological studies.* New York: Random House.

Piaget, J. (1981). *Intelligence and affectivity: Their relationship during child development.* Palo Alto, CA: Annual Reviews.

Pianta, R. C., Egeland, B., & Sroufe, L. A. (1990). Maternal stress and children's development: Prediction of school outcomes and identification of protective factors. In J. Rolf, A. S. Masten, D. Cicchetti, K. H. Nuechterlein, & S. Weintraub (Eds.), *Risk and protective factors in the development of psychopathology* (pp. 215–235). Cambridge, England: Cambridge University Press.

Pike, A., Hetherington, E. M., McGuire, S., Reiss, D., & Plomin, R. (1996). Family environment and adolescent depressive symptoms and antisocial behavior: A multivariate genetic analysis. *Developmental Psychology, 32,* 590–603.

Pike, K. M., & Rodin, J. (1991). Mothers, daughters, and disordered eating. *Journal of Abnormal Psychology, 100,* 198–204.

Pilgrim, C., Luo, Q., Urberg, K. A., & Fang, X. (1999). Influence of peers, parents, and individual characteristics on adolescent drug use in two cultures. *Merrill-Palmer Quarterly, 45,* 85–107.

Pilkington, N. W., & D'Augelli, A. R. (1995). Victimization of lesbian, gay, and bisexual youth in community settings. *Journal of Community Psychology, 23,* 33–56.

Pilling, S., Bebbington, P., Kuipers, E., Garety, P., Geddes, J., Orbach, G., & Morgan, C. (2002). Psychosocial treatments in schizophrenia: I. Meta-analysis of family intervention and cognitive behaviour therapy. *Psychological Medicine, 32,* 763–782.

Pine, F. (1974). On the concept "borderline" in children. *Psychoanalytic Study of the Child, 29,* 341–368.

Pine, F. (1979). On the pathology of the separation-individuation process as manifested in later clinical work: An attempt at delineation. *International Journal of Psychoanalysis, 60,* 225–242.

Pine, F. (1983). Borderline syndromes in childhood: A working nosology and its therapeutic implications. In K. Robson (Ed.), *The borderline child* (pp. 84–100). New York: McGraw-Hill.

Pine, F. (1986). On the development of the "borderline-child-to-be." *American Journal of Orthopsychiatry, 56,* 450–457.

Pliszka, S. R. (2002). *Neuroscience for the mental health clinician.* New York: Guilford.

Plunkett, M., & Mitchell, C. (2000). Substance use rates among American Indian adolescents: Regional comparisons with Monitoring the Future high school seniors. *Journal of Drug Issues, 30,* 593–620.

Poal, P., & Weisz, J. R. (1989). Therapists' own childhood problems as predictors of their effectiveness in child psychotherapy. *Journal of Clinical Child Psychology, 18,* 202–205.

Pollak, S. D., Cicchetti, D., Hornung, K., & Reed, A. (2000). Recognizing emotion in faces: Developmental effects of child abuse and neglect. *Developmental Psychology, 36,* 679–688.

Ponzetti, J., Hamon, R. R., Kellar-Guenther, Y., Kerig, P. K., Scales, T. L., & White, J. M. (2003). *International encyclopedia of marriage and family* (2nd ed.). New York: Macmillan.

Posner, M. I., Rothbart, M. K., Vizueta, N., Thomas, K. M., Levy, K. N., Fossella, J., et al. (2003). An approach to the psychobiology of personality disorders. *Development and Psychopathology, 15,* 1093–1106.

Post, R. M. (1992). Transduction of psychosocial stress into the neurobiology of recurrent affective disorder. *American Journal of Psychiatry, 149,* 999–1010.

Post, R. M., & Weiss, S. R. (1997). Emergent properties of neural systems: How focal molecular neurobiological alterations can affect behavior. *Development and Psychopathology, 9,* 907–929.

Power, P. J. R., Bell, R. J., Mills, R., Herrman-Doig, T., Davern, M., Henry, L., Yuen, H. P., Khademy-Deljo, A., & McGorry, P. D. (2003). Suicide prevention in first episode psychosis: The development of a randomised controlled trial of cognitive therapy for acutely suicidal patients with early psychosis. *Australian and New Zealand Journal of Psychiatry, 37,* 414–420.

Powers, S. W. (1999). Empirically supported treatments in pediatric psychology: Procedure-related pain. *Journal of Pediatric Psychology, 24,* 131–145.

Powers, S. W., Mitchell, M. J., Gaumlich, S. E., Byars, K. C., & Kalinyak, K. A. (2002). Longitudinal assessment of pain, coping and daily functioning in children with sickle cell disease receiving pain management skills training. *Journal of Clinical Psychology in Medical Settings, 9,* 109–119.

Prince-Hughes, D. (2002). *Aquamarine Blue 5: Personal stories of college students with autism.* Athens, OH: Ohio University Press.

Prinstein, M. J. (2003). Social factors: Peer relationships. In A. Spirito & J. C. Overholser (Eds.), *Evaluating and treating adolescent suicide attempters: From research to practice* (pp. 193–215). New York: Academic Press.

Prinstein, M. J., Boergers, J., Spirito, A., Little, T. D., & Grapentine, W. L. (2000). Peer functioning, family dysfunction, and psychological symptoms in a risk factor model for adolescent inpatients' suicidal ideation severity. *Journal of Clinical Child Psychology, 29,* 392–405.

Prinstein, M. J., Boergers, J., & Vernberg, E. M. (2001). Overt and relational aggression in adolescents: Social-psychological adjustment of aggressors and

victims. *Journal of Clinical Child Psychology, 30,* 479–491.

Puig-Antich, J., & Chambers, W. (1978). *The Schedule for Affective Disorders and Schizophrenia for School-Age Children (Kiddie-SADS).* New York: New York State Psychiatric Institute.

Pynoos, R. S., Steinberg, A. M., & Wraith, R. (1995). A developmental model of childhood traumatic stress. In D. Cicchetti & D. J. Cohen (Eds.), *Developmental psychopathology: Vol. II. Risk, disorder, and adaptation* (pp. 72–95). New York: Wiley.

Radke-Yarrow, M. (1998). *Children of depressed mothers: From early childhood to maturity.* New York: Cambridge University Press.

Radke-Yarrow, M., McCann, K., DeMulder, E., Belmont, B., Martinez, P., & Richardson, D. T. (1995). Attachment in the context of high-risk conditions. *Development and Psychopathology, 7*(2), 247–265.

Ramey, C. T., & Campbell, F. A. (1991). Poverty, early childhood education, and academic competence: The Abecedarian experiment. In A. C. Huston (Ed.), *Children in poverty: Child development and public policy* (pp. 190–221). Cambridge: Cambridge University Press.

Randall, J., & Cunningham, P. B. (2003). Multisystemic therapy: A treatment for violent substance-abusing and substance-dependent juvenile offenders. *Addictive Behaviors, 28,* 1731–1739.

Rapee, R. M., & Sweeney, L. (2001). Social phobia in children and adolescents: Nature and assessment. In W. Crozier & L. E. Alden (Eds.), *International handbook of social anxiety: Concepts, research and interventions relating to the self and shyness* (pp. 505–524). New York: Wiley.

Rapee, R. M., Wignall, A., Hudson, J. L., & Schniering, C. A. (2000). *Treating anxious children and adolescents: An evidence-based approach.* Oakland, CA: New Harbinger.

Rapoport, J. L., Inoff-Germain, G., Weissman, M. M., Greenwald, S., Narrow, W. E., Jensen, P. S., et al. (2000). Childhood obsessive-compulsive disorder in the NIMH MECA study: Parent versus child identification of cases. *Journal of Anxiety Disorders, 14,* 535–548.

Rapoport, J. L., & Ismond, D. R. (1996). *DSM-IV training guide for diagnosis of childhood disorders.* NY: Brunner/Mazel.

Rapport, M. D., Scanlan, S. W., & Denney, C. B. (1999). Attention-deficit/hyperactivity disorder and scholastic achievement: A model of dual developmental pathways. *Journal of Child Psychology and Psychiatry, 40,* 1169–1183.

Rasmussen, P., & Gillberg, C. (2001). Natural outcome of ADHD with developmental coordination disorder at age 22 years: A controlled, longitudinal, community-based study. *Journal of the American Academy of Child and Adolescent Psychiatry, 39,* 1424–1431.

Rasmussen, S. A., & Eisen, J. L. (1992). The epidemiology and clinical features of obsessive compulsive disorder. *Psychiatric Clinics of North America, 15,* 743–758.

Rastam, M. (1992). Anorexia nervosa in 51 Swedish adolescents: Premorbid problems and comorbidity. *Journal of the American Academy of Child and Adolescent Psychiatry, 31,* 819–828.

Rastam, M., & Gillberg, C. (1991). The family background in anorexia nervosa: A population-based study. *Journal of the American Academy of Child and Adolescent Psychiatry, 30,* 283–289.

Rathus, J. H., & Miller, A. L. (2000). DBT for adolescents: Dialectical dilemmas and secondary treatment targets. *Cognitive and Behavioral Practice, 7,* 425–434.

Rathus, J. H., & Miller, A. L. (2002). Dialectical behavior therapy adapted for suicidal adolescents. *Suicide and Life-Threatening Behavior, 32,* 146–157.

Redfield-Jamison, R. (1995). *An unquiet mind.* New York: Knopf.

Reich, W., Welner, Z., & Herjanic, B. (1997). *Diagnostic Interview for Children and Adolescents-IV (DICA-IV).* North Tonawanda, NY: Multi-Health Systems.

Reid, J. B. (1978). *A social learning approach to family intervention: Observations in the home setting.* Eugene, OR: Castalia Publishing.

Reid, J. B., Patterson, G. R., & Snyder, J. J. (2002). *Antisocial behavior in children and adolescents: A developmental analysis and model for intervention.* Washington, DC: American Psychological Association.

Reinecke, M. A., Dattilio, F. M., & Freeman, A. (2003). *Cognitive therapy with children and adolescents: A casebook for clinical practice* (2nd ed.). New York: Guilford.

Reinhertz, H. Z., Gianconia, R. M., Pakiz, B., Silverman, A., Frost, A. K., & Lefkowitz, E. S. (1993). Psychological risks for major depression in late adolescence: A longitudinal community study. *Journal of the American Academy of Child and Adolescent Psychiatry, 32,* 1155–1163.

Reiss, D., Neiderhiser, J. M., Hetherington, E. M., & Plomin, R. (2000). *The relationship code: Deciphering genetic and social influences on adolescent development.* Cambridge, MA: Cambridge University Press.

Remschmidt, H. E., Schulz, E., Martin, M., & Warnke, A. (1994). Childhood-onset schizophrenia: History of the concept and recent studies. *Schizophrenia Bulletin, 20,* 727–745.

Rende, R., & Plomin, R. (1995). Nature, nurture, and the development of psychopathology. In D. Cicchetti & D. J. Cohen (Eds.), *Developmental psychopathology: Vol. I. Theory and methods* (pp. 291–314). New York: Wiley.

Rende, R. D., Plomin, R., Reiss, D., & Hetherington, E. M. (1993). Genetic and environmental influences on depressive symptomatology in adolescence: Individual differences and extreme scores. *Journal of Child Psychology and Psychiatry, 8,* 1387–1398.

Rennison, C. M. (2001). *Violence victimization and race, 1993–1998.* Retrieved February 12, 2003, from http://www.ojp.usdoj.gov/bjs/abstract/ipv.htm

Rey, J. M. (1993). Oppositional defiant disorder. *American Journal of Psychiatry, 150*(12), 1769–1778.

Reynolds, C. R., & Kamphaus, R. W. (1992). *Behavior assessment system for children (BASC).* Circle Pines, MN: American Guidance Services.

Reynolds, C. R., & Richmond, B. O. (1985). *Revised Children's Manifest Anxiety Scale (RCMAS).* Los Angeles: Western Psychological Services.

Richters, J. E., Arnold, L. E., Jensen, P. S., Abikoff, H., Conners, C., Greenhill, L., et al. (1995). NIMH collaborative multisite multimodal treatment study of children with ADHD: I. Background and rationale. *Journal of the American Academy of Child and Adolescent Psychiatry, 34,* 987–1000.

Richters, J. E., & Cicchetti, D. (1993). Mark Twain meets DSM-III-R: Conduct disorder, development, and the concept of harmful dysfunction. *Development and Psychopathology, 5,* 5–30.

Richters, J. E., & Martinez, P. E. (1993). Violent communities, family choices, and children's chances: An algorithm for improving the odds. *Development and Psychopathology, 5,* 609–627.

Rind, B., Tromovitch, P., & Bauserman, R. (1998). A meta-analytic examination of assumed properties of child sexual abuse using college samples. *Psychological Bulletin, 124,* 22–53.

Rispens, J., Aleman, A., & Goudena, P. P. (1997). Prevention of child sexual abuse victimization: A meta-analysis of school programs. *Child Abuse and Neglect, 21,* 975–987.

Robbins, M. S., Szapocznik, J., Santisteban, D. A., Hervis, O. E., Mitrani, V. B., & Schwartz, S. J. (2003). Brief strategic family therapy for Hispanic youth. In A. E. Kazdin & J. R. Weisz (Eds.), *Evidence-based psychotherapies for children and adolescents* (pp. 407–437). New York: Guilford.

Roberts, R. E., Chen, Y. R., & Roberts, C. R. (1997). Ethnocultural differences in prevalence of adolescent suicidal behaviors. *Suicide and Life-Threatening Behavior, 27,* 208–217.

Roberts, R. E., Roberts, C. R., & Chen, Y. R. (1997). Ethnocultural differences in prevalence of adolescent depression. *American Journal of Community Psychology, 25,* 95–110.

Robertson, J., & Robertson, J. (1971). Young children in brief separation. *Psychoanalytic Study of the Child, 26,* 264–315.

Robertson, J., & Robertson, J. (1989). *Separation and the very young.* London: Free Association Books.

Robin, A. L., Seigel, P. T., Moye, A., Gilroy, M., Dennis, A. B., & Sikand, A. (1999). A controlled comparison of family versus individual therapy for adolescents with anorexia nervosa. *Journal of the American Academy of Child and Adolescent Psychiatry, 38,* 1428–1489.

Robins, L. N. (1966). *Deviant children grown up: A sociological and psychiatric study of sociopathic personality.* Baltimore, MD: Williams & Wilkins.

Robins, L. N. (1972). Follow-up studies of behavior disorders in children. In H. C. Quay & J. S. Werry (Eds.), *Psychopathological disorders of childhood* (pp. 483–513). New York: Wiley.

Rodin, J., Striegel-Moore, R. H., & Silberstein, L. R. (1990). Vulnerability and resilience in the age of eating disorders: Risk and protective factors for bulimia nervosa. In J. Rolf, A. S. Masten, D. Cicchetti, K. H. Nuechterlein, & S. Weintraub (Eds.), *Risk and protective factors in the development of psychopathology* (pp. 361–383). Cambridge, England: Cambridge University Press.

Rodkin, P. C. (2000). Heterogeneity of popular boys: Antisocial and prosocial configurations. *Developmental Psychology, 36,* 14–24.

Rodriguez, N., Ryan, S. W., Vande Kemp, H., & Foy, D. W. (1997). Posttraumatic stress disorder in adult female survivors of childhood sexual abuse: A comparison study. *Journal of Consulting and Clinical Psychology, 65,* 53–59.

Roeyers, H., Van Oost, P., & Bothuyne, S. (1998). Immediate imitation and joint attention in young children with autism. *Development and Psychopathology, 10*(3), 441–450.

Roff, J. D., & Fultz, J. M. (2003). Childhood antecedents of schizophrenia: Developmental sequencing and specificity of problem behavior. *Psychological Reports, 92,* 793–803.

Rogers, C. R. (1959). A theory of therapy, personality, and interpersonal relationships as developed in the client-centered framework. In S. Koch (Ed.), *Psychology: Study of a science: Vol. 3. Formulations of the person and the social context* (pp. 184–256). New York: McGraw-Hill.

Rogers, S. J. (1998). Empirically supported comprehensive treatments for young children with autism. *Journal of Clinical Child Psychology, 27*(2), 168–179.

Roid, G. H. (2003). *Stanford Binet Intelligence Scales, Fifth Edition.* Itasca, IL: Riverside Publishing.

Romans, S. E., Gendall, K. A., Martine, J. L., & Mullen, P. E. (2001). Child sexual abuse and later disordered eating: A New Zealand epidemiological study. *International Journal of Eating Disorders, 29,* 380–392.

Rorty, M., Yager, J., & Rossotto, E. (1994). Childhood sexual, physical, and psychological abuse in bulimia nervosa. *American Journal of Psychiatry, 151,* 1122–1126.

Rose, D. R., & Abramson, L. Y. (1991). Developmental predictors of depressive cognitive style: Research and theory. In D. Cicchetti, & S. L. Toth (Eds.), *Rochester symposium on developmental psychopathology, No. 4* (pp. 323–349).

Rosen, K. S., & Rothbaum, F. (2003). Attachment: Parent-child relationships. In J. Ponzetti (Ed.), *International encyclopedia of marriage and family* (pp. 105–111). New York: Macmillan.

Rosenblith, J. F., & Sims-Knight, J. (1992). *In the beginning: Development in the first two years of life.* Monterey, CA: Brooks/Cole.

Rosenthal, P. A., & Rosenthal, S. (1984). Suicidal behavior by preschool children. *American Journal of Psychiatry, 141,* 520–525.

Ross, A. O., & Nelson, R. O. (1979). Behavior therapy. In H. C. Quay & J. S. Werry (Eds.), *Psychopathological disorders of childhood* (2nd ed.). New York: Wiley.

Rossello, J., & Bernal, G. (1999). Treatment of depression in Puerto Rican adolescents: The efficacy of cognitive-behavioral and interpersonal treatments. *Journal of Consulting and Clinical Psychology, 67,* 734–745.

Rossini, E. D., & Moretti, R. J. (1997). Thematic Apperception Test (TAT) interpretation: Practice recommendations from a survey of clinical psychology doctoral programs accredited by the American Psychological Association. *Professional Psychology: Research and Practice, 28,* 393–398.

Rossman, B. B. R., & Ho, J. (2000). Posttraumatic response and children exposed to parental violence. In R.Geffner, P. G. Jaffe,

& M. Sudermann (Eds.), *Children exposed to domestic violence: Current issues in research, intervention, prevention, and policy development* (pp. 85–106). New York: Haworth.

Rossman, B. B. R., Hughes, H. M., & Rosenberg, M. S. (1999). *Children and interparental violence: The impact of exposure.* New York: Brunner/Mazel.

Rossman, B. B. R., & Rosenberg, M. S. (1992). Family stress and functioning in children: The moderating effects of children's beliefs about their control over parental conflict. *Journal of Child Psychology and Psychiatry, 33,* 699–715.

Rossman, B. B. R., & Rosenberg, M. S. (1997). *Multiple victimization of children: Conceptual, research, and treatment issues.* New York: Haworth Press.

Rosso, I. M., & Cannon, T. (2003). Obstetric complications and neurodevelopmental mechanisms in schizophrenia. In D. Cicchetti & E. Walker (Eds.), *Neurodevelopmental mechanisms in psychopathology* (pp. 111–137). New York, NY, US: Cambridge University Press.

Roth, A., & Fonagy, P. (1996). *What works for whom: A critical review of psychotherapy research.* New York: Guilford.

Rothbart, M. K., Derryberry, D., & Hershey, K. (2000). Stability of temperament in childhood: Laboratory infant assessment to parent report at seven years. In V. J. Molfese & D. L. Molfese (Eds.), *Tempera-*

ment and personality across the life span (pp. 85–119). Mahwah, NJ: Erlbaum.

Rotheram-Borus, M. J., & Langabeer, K. A. (2001). Developmental trajectories of gay, lesbian, and bisexual youths. In A. R. D'Augelli & C. Patterson (Eds.), *Lesbian, gay and bisexual identities among youth: Psychological perspectives* (pp. 97–128). New York: Oxford University Press.

Rourke, B. P., & Tsatsanis, K. D. (2000). Nonverbal learning disabilities and Asperger Syndrome. In A. Klin, F. R. Volkmar, & S. S. Sparrow (Eds.), *Asperger syndrome* (pp. 231–253). New York: Guilford.

Rowa, K., Kerig, P. K., & Geller, J. (2001). The family and anorexia: Examining parent-child boundary problems. *European Eating Disorders Review, 9,* 97–114.

Roza, S. J., Hofstra, M. B., Van der Ende, J., & Verhulst, F. C. (2003). Stable prediction of mood and anxiety disorders based on behavioral and emotional problems in childhood: A 14-year follow-up during childhood, adolescence, and young adulthood. *American Journal of Psychiatry, 160,* 2116–2121.

Rubin, K. H. (1993). The Waterloo longitudinal project: Correlates and consequences of social withdrawal from childhood to adolescence. In K. H. Rubin & J. B. Asendorpf (Eds.), *Social withdrawal, inhibition, and shyness* (pp. 291–314). Hillsdale, NJ: Earlbaum.

Rubin, K. H., & Mills, R. S. L. (1991). Conceptualizing developmental pathways to internalizing disorders in childhood. *Canadian Journal of Behavioural Science, 23,* 300–317.

Ruble, D. N., & Martin, C. L. (1998). Gender development. In W. Damon & N. Eisenberg (Eds.), *Handbook of child psychology (5th ed.): Vol. 3. Social, emotional, and personality development* (pp. 933–1016). New York: Wiley.

Rudolph, K. D. (2002). Gender differences in emotional responses to interpersonal stress during adolesence. *Journal of Adolescent Health, 30,* 3–13.

Rudolph, K. D., & Clark, A. G. (2001). Conceptions of relationships in children with depressive and aggressive symptoms: Social-cognitive distortion or reality? *Journal of Abnormal Child Psychology, 29,* 41–56.

Rudolph, K. D., & Hammen, C. (1999). Age and gender as determinants of stress exposure, generation, and reaction in youngsters: A transactional perspective. *Child Development, 70,* 660–677.

Rudolph, K. D., Hammen, C., & Burge, D. (1994). Interpersonal functioning and depressive symptoms in childhood: Addressing the issues of specificity and comorbidity. *Journal of Abnormal Child Psychology, 22,* 355–371.

Rudolph, K. D., Kurlakowsky, K. D., & Conley, C. S. (2001). Development and social-contextual origins of depressive control-related beliefs and behavior. *Cognitive Therapy and Research, 25,* 447–475.

Rumbaut, R. G. (1994). The crucible within: Ethnic identity, self-esteem, and segmented assimilation among children of immigrants. *International Migration Review, 28,* 748–794.

Runyan, D. K., Hunter, W. M., Socolar, R. R. S., Amaya-Jackson, L., English, D., & Landsverk, J. (1998). Children who prosper in unfavorable environments: The relationship to social capital. *Pediatrics, 101,* 12–18.

Russell, A. T., Bott, L., & Sammons, C. (1989). The phenomenology of schizophrenia occurring in childhood. *Journal of the American Academy of Child & Adolescent Psychiatry, 28,* 399–407.

Rutter, M. (1977). Brain damage syndromes in childhood: Concepts and findings. *Journal of Child Psychology and Psychiatry, 18,* 1–21.

Rutter, M. (1981). Psychological sequelae of brain-damaged children. *American Journal of Psychiatry, 138,* 1533–1544.

Rutter, M. (1990). Psychosocial resilience and protective mechanisms. In J. Rolf, A. S. Masten, D. Cicchetti, K. H. Nuechterlein, & S. Weintraub (Eds.), *Risk and protective factors in the development of psychopathology* (pp. 181–214). Cambridge, England: Cambridge University Press.

Rutter, M. (1994). Beyond longitudinal data: Causes, consequences, changes, and continuity. *Journal of Consulting and Clinical Psychology, 62,* 928–940.

Rutter, M. (2000). Psychosocial influences: Critiques, findings, and research needs. *Development and Psychopathology, 12,* 375–405.

Rutter, M., Silberg, J., O'Connor, T., & Simonoff, E. (1999). Genetics and child psychiatry II: Empirical research findings. *Journal of Child Psychology and Psychiatry and Allied Disciplines, 40,* 19–55.

Saarni, C. (1999). *The development of emotional competence.* New York: Guilford Publications.

Sabo, A. N. (1997). Etiological significance of associations between childhood trauma and borderline personality disorder: Conceptual and clinical implications. *Journal of Personality Disorders, 11,* 50–70.

Sachs, H. T., & Barrett, R. P. (2000). Psychopathology in individuals with mental retardation. In A. J. Sameroff, M. Lewis, & S. M. Miller (Eds.), *Handbook of developmental psychopathology* (pp. 657–670). New York: Kluwer Academic.

Sagrestano, L., Paikoff, R. L., Holmbeck, G., & Fendrich, M. (2003). A longitudinal examination of familial risk factors for depression among inner-city African American adolescents. *Journal of Family Psychology, 17,* 108–120.

Saigh, P. (1992). *Posttraumatic stress disorder: A behavioral approach to diagnosis and treatment.* Needham Heights, MA: Allyn & Bacon.

Sallee, F. R., & March, J. S. (2001). Neuropsychiatry of paediatric anxiety disorders. In W. K. Silverman & A. Treffers (Eds.), *Anxiety disorders in children and adolescents: Research, assessment, and intervention* (pp. 90–125). New York: Cambridge.

Salzinger, S., Feldman, R. S., Hammer, M., & Rosario, M. (1993). The effects of physical abuse on children's social relationships. *Child Development, 64,* 169–187.

Sameroff, A. J. (1990). Neoenvironmental perspectives on developmental theory. In R. M. Hodapp, J. A. Burack, & E. Zigler (Eds.), *Issues in the developmental approach to mental retardation* (pp. 93–113). Cambridge, England: Cambridge University Press.

Sameroff, A. J. (1994). Models of development and developmental risk. In C. H. Zeanah (Ed.), *Handbook of infant mental health* (pp. 3–13). New York: Guilford.

Sameroff, A. J. (1995). General systems theories and developmental psychopathology. In D. Cicchetti & D. J. Cohen (Eds.), *Developmental psychopathology: Vol. I. Theory and methods* (pp. 659–695). New York: Wiley.

Sandfort, T. G. M. (2000). *Childhood sexuality: Normal sexual behavior and development.* New York: Haworth Press.

Sandfort, T. G. M., & Cohen-Kettenis, P. (2000). Sexual behavior in Dutch and Belgian children as observed by their mothers. In T. G. M. Sandfort & J. Rademakers (Eds.),

Childhood sexuality: Normal sexual behavior and development (pp. 105–116). Binghamton. NY: Haworth.

Sandler, I. N., Tein, J., & West, S. G. (1994). Coping, stress, and the psychological symptoms of children of divorce: A cross-sectional and longitudinal study. *Child Development, 65,* 1744–1763.

Sanson, A., Prior, M., & Smart, D. (1996). Reading disabilities with and without behaviour problems at 7–8 years: Prediction from longitudinal data from infancy to 6 years. *Journal of Child Psychology and Psychiatry, 37,* 529–541.

Santisteban, D. A., Coatsworth, D. J., Perez-Vidal, A., Kurtines, W., Schwartz, S., LaPerriere, A., et al. (2003). Efficacy of brief strategic family therapy in modifying Hispanic adolescent behavior problems and substance use. *Journal of Family Psychology, 17,* 121–133.

Satterfield, J. H., & Schnell, A. (1997). A prospective study of hyperactive boys with conduct problems and normal boys: Adolescent and adult criminality. *Journal of the American Academy of Child and Adolescent Psychiatry, 36,* 1726–1735.

Sattler, J. M. (1992). *Assessment of children* (3rd ed.). San Diego: J. M. Sattler.

Sattler, J. M. (1998). *Clinical and forensic interviewing of children and families.* San Diego, CA: Jerome M. Sattler.

Sattler, J. M. (2001). *Assessment of children: Cognitive applications* (4th ed.). San Diego, CA: Jerome M. Sattler.

Sattler, J. M. (2002). *Assessment of children: Behavioral and clinical applications* (4th ed.). San Diego, CA: Jerome M. Sattler.

Savin-Williams, R. C., (2001). *Mom, Dad, I'm gay: How families negotiate coming out.* American Psychological Association.

Savin-Williams, R. C., & Ream, G. L. (2003). Suicide attempts among sexual-minority male youth. *Journal of Clinical Child and Adolescent Psychology, 32,* 509–522.

Saywitz, K. J., Goodman, G., Nicholas, G., & Moan, S. (1991). Children's memory of a physical examination involving genital touch: Implications for reports of child sexual abuse. *Journal of Consulting and Clinical Psychology, 59,* 682–691.

Saywitz, K. J., Mannarino, A. P., Berliner, L., & Cohen, J. A. (2000). Treatment for sexually abused children and adolescents. *American Psychologist, 55,* 1040–1049.

Scarr, S. (1992). Developmental theories for the 1990s: Development and individual differences. *Child Development, 64,* 1333–1353.

Schaeffer, C. M., Petrras, H., Ialongo, N., Poduska, J., & Kellam, S. (2003). Modeling growth in boys' aggressive behavior across elementary school: Links to later criminal involvement, conduct disorder, and antisocial personality disorder. *Developmental Psychology, 39,* 1020–1035.

Schneider, B. H., Atkinson, L., & Tardif, C. (2001). Child-parent attachment and children's peer relations: A quantitative review. *Developmental Psychology, 37,* 86–100.

Schreibman, L., & Charlop-Christy, M. H. (1998). Autistic disorder. In *Handbook of child psychopathology* (3rd ed., pp. 157–179). New York: Plenum Press.

Schreier, H. A., & Libow, J. A. (1993). *Hurting for love: Munchausen by proxy syndrome.* New York: Guilford.

Schuhrke, B. (2000). Young children's curiosity about other people's genitals. In T. G. M. Sandfort & J. Rademakers (Eds.), *Childhood sexuality: Normal sexual behavior and development* (pp. 27–48). Binghamton. NY: Haworth.

Schulsinger, F. (1980). Biological psychopathology. *Annual Review of Psychology, 31,* 583–606.

Schultz, R. T., Romanski, L. M., & Tsatsanis, K. D. (2000). Neurofrontal models of autistic disorder and Asperger syndrome: Clues from neuroimaging. In A. Klin, F. R. Volkmar, & S. S. Sparrow (Eds.), *Asperger syndrome* (pp. 172–209). New York: Guilford.

Schulze, B., Richter-Werling, M., Matschinger, H., & Angermeyer, M. C. (2003). Crazy? So what! Effects of a school project on students' attitudes towards people with schizophrenia. *Acta Psychiatrica Scandinavica, 107,* 142–150.

Schumacher, J. A., Smith-Slep, A. M., & Heyman, R. E. (2001). Risk factors for child neglect. *Aggression and Violent Behavior, 6,* 231–254.

Schwalberg, M. D., Barlow, D. H., Alger, S. A., & Howard, L. J. (1992). Comparison of bulimics, obese binge eaters, social phobics, and individuals with panic disorder on comorbidity across DMS-II-R anxiety disorders. *Journal of Abnormal Psychology, 101,* 675–681.

Schwartz, J. A., Kaslow, N. J., Racusin, G. R., & Carton, E. R. (1998). Interpersonal family therapy for childhood depression. In V. B. Van Hasselt & M. Hersen (Eds.), *Handbook of psychological treatment protocols for children and adolescents.* Mahwah, NJ: Lawrence Erlbaum Associates.

Schwartz-Kenney, B. M., & McCauley, M. (2003). Physical abuse and neglect. In J. Ponzetti, R. Hamon, Y. Kellar-Guenther, P. K. Kerig, L. Scales, & J. White (Eds.), *International Encyclopedia of Marital and Family Relationships* (pp. 215–221). New York: Macmillan.

Sedlak, A. J. (1997). Risk factors for the occurrence of child abuse and neglect. *Journal of Aggression, Maltreatment, and Trauma, 1,* 149–187.

Seidman, L. J., Biederman, J., Faraone, S. V., Weber, W., & Ouellette, C. (1997). Toward defining a neuropsychology of attention deficit-hyperactivity disorder: Performance of children and adolescents from a large clinically referred sample. *Journal of Consulting and Clinical Psychology, 65,* 150–160.

Seiner, S. H., & Gelfand, D. M. (1995). Effects of mothers' simulated withdrawal and depressed affect on mother-toddler interactions. *Child Development, 66,* 1519–1528.

Selman, R. L., & Schultz, L. H. (1988). Interpersonal thought and action in the case of a troubled early adolescent: Toward a developmental model of the gap. In S. R. Shirk (Ed.), *Cognitive development and child psychotherapy* (pp. 207–246). New York: Plenum.

Selman, R. L., Schultz, L. H., & Yeates, K. O. (1991). Interpersonal understanding and action: A developmental psychopathology perspective on research and prevention. In D. Cicchetti & S. L. Toth (Eds.), *Models and integrations. Rochester symposium on developmental psychopathology, Vol. 3* (pp. 289–326). Rochester: University of Rochester Press.

Serafica, F. C. (1997). Psychopathology and resilience in Asian American children and adolescents. *Applied Developmental Science, 1,* 145–155.

Shaffer, A., & Sroufe, L. A. (in press). The developmental and adaptational significance of boundary dissolution: Findings from a prospective, longitudinal study. *Journal of Emotional Abuse.*

Shaffer, D., Fisher, P., Lucas, C., & Comer, J. (2003). *Scoring Manual: Diagnostic Interview Schedule for Children (DISC-IV).* New York: Columbia University.

Shaffer, D., Garland, A., Vieland, V., Underwood, M., & Busner, C. (1991). The impact of curriculum-based suicide prevention programs for teenagers.

Journal of the American Academy of Child and Adolescent Psychiatry, 30, 588–596.

Shafii, M., & Shafii, S. L. (1992). *Clinical guide to depression in children and adolescents.* Washington, DC: American Psychiatric Press.

Shaloub-Kevorkian, N. (1999). The politics of disclosing female sexual abuse: A case study of Palestinian society. *Child Abuse and Neglect, 23,* 1275–1293.

Shapiro, E. R., Zinner, J., Shapiro, R. L., & Berkowitz, D. A. (1975). The influence of family experience on borderline personality development. *International Review of Psycho-Analysis, 2,* 399–411.

Shapiro, E. S., DuPaul, G. J., & Bradley Klug, K. L. (1998). Self-management as a strategy to improve the classroom behavior of adolescents with ADHD. *Journal of Learning Disabilities, 31,* 545–555.

Shaw, D. S., & Bell, R. Q. (1993). Developmental theories of parental contributors to antisocial behavior. *Journal of Abnormal Child Psychology, 21,* 493–518.

Shaw, D. S., Bell, R. Q., & Gilliom, M. (2000). A truly early starter model of antisocial behavior revisited. *Clinical Child and Family Psychology Review, 3,* 155–172.

Shaw, D. S., Gilliom, M., Ingoldsby, E. M., & Nagin, D. S. (2003). Trajectories leading to school-age conduct problems. *Developmental Psychology, 39,* 189–200.

Shaw, D. S., Owens, E. B., Vondra, J. I., Keenan, K., & Winslow, E. B. (1996). Early risk factors and pathways in the development of early disruptive behavior problems. *Development and Psychopathology, 8,* 679–699.

Shaw, D. S., Vondra, J. I., Hommerding, K. D., Keenan, K., & Dunn, M. (1994). Chronic family adversity and early child behavior problems: A longitudinal study of low income families. *Journal of Child Psychology and Psychiatry, 35,* 1109–1122.

Shaw, D. S., Winslow, E. B., Owens, E. B., & Vondra, J. I. (1998). The development of early externalizing problems among children from low-income families: A transformational perspective. *Journal of Abnormal Child Psychology, 26,* 95–107.

Shedler, J., & Block, J. (1990). Adolescent drug use and psychological health. *American Psychologist, 45,* 612–630.

Sheeber, L., Davis, B., & Hops, H. (2002). Gender-specific vulnerability to depression in children of depressed mothers. In S. H. Goodman & I. H. Gotlib (Eds.), *Children of depressed parents: Mechanisms of risk and implications for treatment* (pp. 253–274). Washington, DC: American Psychological Association.

Sheeber, L., Hops, H., Alpert, A., Davis, B., & Andrews, J. (1997). Family support and conflict: Prospective relations to adolescent depression. *Journal of Abnormal Child Psychology, 25,* 333–344.

Shelton, R. C., Keller, M. B., Gelenberg, A., Dunner, D. L., Hirschfeld, R., et al. (2001). Effectiveness of St. John's Wort in major depression: A randomized controlled trial. *Journal of the American Medical Association, 285,* 1978–1988.

Sheridan, M. S. (2003). The deceit continues: An updated literature review of Munchausen by proxy syndrome. *Child Abuse and Neglect, 27,* 431–451.

Shirk, S. R. (1988). Introduction: A cognitive-developmental perspective on child psychotherapy. In S. R. Shirk (Ed.), *Cognitive development and child psychotherapy* (pp. 1–16). New York: Plenum.

Shirk, S. R. (1999). Developmental therapy. In W. K. Silverman & T. H. Ollendick (Eds.), *Developmental issues in the clinical treatment of children* (pp. 60–73). Boston: Allyn & Bacon.

Shirk, S. R., & Russell, R. L. (1996). *Change processes in child psychotherapy: Revitalizing treatment and research.* New York: Guilford.

Shochet, I. M., Dadds, M. R., Holland, D., Whitefield, K., Harnett, P. H., & Osgarby, S. M. (2001). The efficacy of a universal school-based program to prevent adolescent depression. *Journal of Clinical Child Psychology, 30,* 303–315.

Shortt, J. W., Capaldi, D., Dishion, T. J., Bank, L., & Owen, L. D. (2003). The role of adolescent friends, romantic partners, and siblings in the emergence of the adult antisocial lifestyle. *Journal of Family Psychology, 17,* 521–533.

Shure, M. B., & Spivack, G. (1988). Interpersonal cognitive problem-solving. In R. H. Price, E. L. Cowen, R. P. Lorion, & J. Ramos-McKay (Eds.), *Fourteen ounces of prevention: A casebook for practitioners* (pp. 69–82). Washington, DC: American Psychological Association.

Siegler, R., DeLoache, J., & Eisenberg, N. (2003). *How children develop.* New York: Worth.

Siever, L. J., Koenigsberg, H. W., & Reynolds, D. (2003). Neurobiology of personality disorders: Implications for a neurodevelopmental model. In D. Cicchetti & E. Walker (Eds.), *Neurodevelopmental mechanisms in psychopathology* (pp. 405–427). New York: Cambridge.

Silberg, J., Pickles, A., Rutter, M., Hewitt, J., Simonoff, E., Maes, H., et al. (1999). The influence of genetic factors and life stress on depression among adolescent girls. *Archives of General Psychiatry, 56,* 225–232.

Silk, J. S., Nath, S. R., Siegel, L. R., & Kendall, P. C. (2000). Conceptualizing mental disorders in children: Where have we been and where are we going? *Development and Psychopathology, 12,* 713–735.

Silverman, R. C., & Lieberman, A. F. (1999). Negative maternal attributions, projective identification, and the intergenerational transmission of violent relational patterns. *Psycho-*

analytic Dialogues, 9, 161–186.

Silverman, W. K., & Ginsburg, G. S. (1998). Anxiety disorders. In T. H. Ollendick & M. Hersen (Eds.), *Handbook of child psychopathology* (pp. 239–268). New York: Plenum.

Silverman, W. K., & Rabian, B. (1994). Specific phobias. In T. H. Ollendick, N. J. King, & W. Yule (Eds.), *International handbook of phobic and anxiety disorders in children and adolescents* (pp. 87–110). New York: Plenum.

Silverthorn, P., & Frick, P. J. (1999). Developmental pathways to antisocial behavior: The delayed-onset pathway in girls. *Development and Psychopathology, 11,* 101–126.

Simic, M., & Fombonne, E. (2001). Depressive conduct disorder: Symptom patterns and correlates in referred children and adolescents. *Journal of Affective Disorders, 62,* 175–185.

Simmons, R. G., & Blyth, D. (1987). *Moving into adolescence: The impact of pubertal change and school context.* Hillsdale, NJ: Erlbaum.

Simons, R. L., Murry, V., McLoyd, V., Lin, K. H., Cutrona, C., & Conger, R. D. (2002). Discrimination, crime, ethnic identity, and parenting as correlates of depression symptoms among African American children: A multilevel analysis. *Development and Psychopathology, 14,* 371–393.

Simons, R. L., Whitbeck, L. B., Beaman, J., & Conger, R. D. (1994). The impact of mothers' parenting,

involvement by nonresidential fathers, and parental conflict on the adjustment of adolescent children. *Journal of Marriage and the Family, 56,* 356–374.

Simons-Morton, B. (2004). Prospective association of peer influence, school engagement, drinking expectancies, and parent expectations with drinking initiation among sixth graders. *Addictive Behaviors, 29,* 299–309.

Simos, P. G., Breier, J. I., Fletcher, J. M., Foorman, B. R., Bergman, E., Fishbeck, K., et al. (2000). Brain activation profiles in dyslexic children during non-word reading: A magnetic source imaging study. *Neuroscience Reports, 290,* 61–65.

Simos, P. G., Fletcher, J. M., Bergman, E., Breier, J. I., Foorman, B. R., Castillo, E. M., et al. (2002). Dyslexic-specific brain activation profile becomes normal following successful remedial training. *Neurology, 58*(8), 1203–1213.

Simpson, D., & Reilly, P. (1982). Pediatric coma scale. *Lancet, 2,* 450.

Siperstein, G. N., & Leffert, J. S. (1997). Comparison of socially accepted and rejected children with mental retardation. *American Journal of Mental Retardation, 101,* 339–351.

Siperstein, G. N., Leffert, J. S., & Wenz-Gross, M. (1997). The quality of friendships between children with and without learning problems. *American Journal of Mental Retardation, 102,* 111–125.

Skara, S., & Sussman, S. (2003). A review of 25

long-term adolescent tobacco and other drug use prevention program evaluations. *Preventive Medicine, 37,* 451–474.

Skodol, A. E., Oldham, J. M., Hyler, S. E., Kellman, H. D., Doidge, N., & Davies, M. (1993). Comorbidity of DSM-III-R eating disorders and personality disorders. *International Journal of Eating Disorders, 14,* 403–416.

Slipp, S. (1991). *The technique and practice of object relations family therapy.* New York: Aronson.

Smart, D., Sanson, A., & Prior, M. (1996). Connections between reading disability and behavior problems: Testing temporal and causal hypotheses. *Journal of Abnormal Child Psychology, 24,* 363–375.

Smetana, J. G. (1990). Morality and conduct disorders. In M. Lewis & S. M. Miller (Eds.), *Handbook of developmental psychopathology* (pp. 157–180). New York: Plenum.

Smith, K. A., Fairburn, C. G., & Cowen, P. J. (1999). Symptomatic relapse in bulimia nervosa following acute tryptophan depletion. *Archives of General Psychiatry, 56,* 171–176.

Smith, P. K., & Brain, P. (2000). Bullying in schools: Lessons from two decades of research. *Aggressive Behavior, 26,* 1–9.

Smolak, L., & Striegel-Moore, R. H. (2001). Challenging the myth of the golden girl: Ethnicity and eating disorders. In R. H. Striegel-Moore & L. Smolak (Eds.), *Eating disorders* (pp. 111–132). Washington, DC: American Psychological Association.

Snow, J. H., & Hooper, S. R. (1994). *Pediatric traumatic brain injury.* Thousand Oaks, CA: Sage.

Solantaus, T., Leinonen, J., & Punamaki, R. L. (2004). Children's mental health in times of economic recession: Replication and extension of the family economic stress model in Finland. *Developmental Psychology, 40,* 412–429.

Southam-Gerow, M. A., Henin, A., Chu, B., Marrs, A., & Kendall, P. C. (1997). Cognitive-behavioral therapy with children and adolescents. *Child and Adolescent Psychiatric Clinics of North America, 6,* 111–136.

Sowell, E. R., Toga, A. W., & Asarnow, R. (2000). Brain abnormalities observed in childhood-onset schizophrenia: A review of the structural magnetic resonance imaging literature. *Mental Retardation & Developmental Disabilities Research Reviews, 6,* 180–185.

Spangler, D. L. (1999). Cognitive-behavioral therapy for bulimia nervosa: An illustration. *Journal of Clinical Psychology, 55,* 699–713.

Spauwen, J., Krabbendam, L., Lieb, R., Wittchen, H. U., & van Os, J. (2003). Sex differences in psychosis: Normal or pathological? *Schizophrenia Research, 62,* 45–49.

Speier, P. L., Sherk, D. L., Hirsch, S., & Cantwell, D. P. (1995). Depression in children and adolescents. In E. E. Beckham & W. R. Leber (Eds.), *Handbook of depression* (pp. 467–493). Homewood, IL: Dorsey Press.

Speltz, M. L., DeKlyen, M., Greenberg, M. T., & Dryden, M. (1995). Clinic referral for oppositional defiant disorder: Relative significance of attachment and behavioral variables.

Spence, S. H., Donovan, C., & Brechman-Toussaint, M. (2000). The treatment of childhood social phobia: The effectiveness of a social skills training based cognitive behavioral intervention, with and without parental involvement. *Journal of Child Psychology and Psychiatry, 41,* 713–726.

Spence, S. H., Sheffield, J. K., & Donovan, C. (2002). Problem-solving orientation and attributional style: Moderators of the impact of negative life events on the development of depressive symptoms in adolescence. *Journal of Clinical Child Psychology, 31,* 219–229.

Spencer, M. B., & Markstrom-Adams, C. (1990). Identity processes among racial and ethnic minority children in America. *Child Development, 61,* 290–310.

Spencer, T., Biederman, J., Wilens, T., Harding, M., O'Donnell, D., & Griffin, S. (1996). Pharmacotherapy of attention-deficit-hyperactivity disorder across the life cycle. *Journal of the American Academy of Child and Adolescent Psychiatry, 35,* 409–432.

Spencer, T., Wilens, T. E., Biederman, J., Wozniak, J., & Harding-Crawford, M. (2000). Attention-defiict/hyperactivity disorder with mood disorders. In T. E. Brown (Ed.), *Attention*

deficit disorders and co-morbidities in children, adolescents, and adults (pp. 79–124). Washington, DC: American Psychiatric Press.

Spirito, A. (2003). Understanding attempted suicide in adolescence. In A. Spirito & J. C. Overholser (Eds.), *Evaluating and treating adolescent suicide attempters: From research to practice* (pp. 1–18). New York: Academic Press.

Spitz, R. A. (1946). Anaclitic depression. *Psychoanalytic Study of the Child, 2,* 313–342.

Sporn, A., Greenstein, D., Gogtay, N., Jeffries, N. O., Lenane, M., Gochman, P., Clasen, L. S., Blumenthal, J., Giedd, J. N., & Rapoport, J. L. (2003). Progressive brain volume loss during adolescence in childhood-onset schizophrenia. *American Journal of Psychiatry, 160,* 2181–2189.

Sroufe, L. A. (1990a). An organizational perspective on the self. In D. Cicchetti & M. Beeghly (Eds.), *The self in transition: Infancy to childhood* (pp. 281–307). Chicago: University of Chicago Press.

Sroufe, L. A. (1990b). Considering normal and abnormal together: The essence of developmental psychopathology. *Development and Psychopathology, 2,* 335–348.

Sroufe, L. A. (1997). Psychopathology as an outcome of development. *Development and Psychopathology, 9,* 251–268.

Sroufe, L. A., & Rutter, M. (1984). The domain of developmental psychopathology. *Child Development, 55,* 17–29.

Sroufe, L. A., & Ward, M. J. (1980). Seductive behavior of mothers of toddlers: Occurrence, correlates and family origins. *Child Development, 51,* 1222–1229.

Stack, S. (2000). Media impacts on suicide: A quantitative review of 293 findings. *Social Science Quarterly, 81,* 957–971.

Stanger, C., Achenbach, T. M., & Verhulst, F. C. (1997). Accelerated longitudinal comparisons of aggressive versus delinquent syndromes. *Development and Psychopathology, 9,* 43–58.

Stanton, M. D., & Shadish, W. R. (1997). Outcome, attrition, and family-couples treatment for drug abuse: A meta-analysis and review of the controlled, comparative studies. *Psychological Bulletin, 122,* 170–191.

Stark, K. D. (1990). *Childhood depression: School-based interventions.* New York: Guilford.

Stark, K. D., Sander, J. B., Yancy, M. G., Bronik, M. D., & Hoke, J. A. (2000). Treatment of depression in childhood and adolescence. In P. C. Kendall (Ed.), *Child and adolescent therapy: Cognitive-behavioral procedures* (pp. 173–234). New York: Guilford.

Stark, K. D., Schmidt, K. L., & Joiner, T. E. J. (1996). Cognitive triad: Relationship to depressive symptoms, parents' cognitive triad, and perceived parental messages. *Journal of Abnormal Child Psychology, 24,* 615–631.

State, M. W., King, B. H., & Dykens, E. (1997). Mental retardation: A review of the past 10 years (Part II).

Journal of the American Academy of Child and Adolescent Psychiatry, 36, 1664–1671.

Statham, D. J., Heath, A. C., Madden, P. A. F., Bucholz, K. K., Bierut, L., Dinwiddie, S. H., et al. (1998). Suicidal behaviour: An epidemiological and genetic study. *Psychological Medicine, 28,* 839–855.

Steele, R. G., & Forehand, R. (2003). Longitudinal correlates of depressive symptoms among urban African American children II: Extensive of findings across 3 years. *Journal of Clinical Child and Adolescent Psychology, 32,* 606–612.

Steele, S. L., & Eccles, J. S. (1995). *Predicting adolescents' academic expectations over time: Understanding the roles of gender, ethnicity, and SES.* Indianapolis, IN: SRCD.

Stein, D., Williamson, D. E., Birmaher, B., Brent, D. A., Kaufman, J., Dahl, R. E., et al. (2000). Parent-child bonding and family functioning in depressed children and children at high risk and low risk for future depression. *Journal of the American Academy of Child and Adolescent Psychiatry, 39,* 1387–1395.

Steinberg, L., Dornbusch, S. M., & Brown, B. (1992). Ethnic differences in adolescent achievement: An ecological perspective. *American Psychologist, 47,* 723–729.

Steinberg, L., Lamborn, S. D., Darling, N., Mounts, N. S., & Dornbusch, S. M. (1994). Over-time changes in adjustment and competence among adolescents from authoritative, authoritarian, indulgent, and neg-

lectful families. *Child Development, 65,* 754–770.

Steinberg, L., & Scott, E. S. (2003). Less guilty by reason of adolescence: Developmental immaturity, diminished responsibility, and the juvenile death penalty. *American Psychologist, 58,* 1009–1018.

Steiner, H. (2004). *Handbook of mental health interventions in children and adolescents.* New York: Jossey Bass.

Stern, D. N. (1985). *The interpersonal world of the infant.* New York: Basic Books.

Steward, M. S., Bussey, K., Goodman, G. S., & Saywitz, K. J. (1993). Implications of developmental research for interviewing children. *Child Abuse and Neglect, 17,* 25–37.

Stewart, S. M., Rao, N., Bond, M. H., McBride-Chang, C., Fielding, R., & Kennard, B. D. (1998). Chinese dimensions of parenting: Broadening Western predictors and outcomes. *International Journal of Psychology, 33,* 345–358.

Stice, E. (1999). Clinical implications of psychosocial research on bulimia nervosa and binge-eating disorder. *JCLP/In Session: Psychotherapy in Practice, 55,* 675–683.

Stice, E., & Bearman, S. K. (2001). Body-image and eating disturbances prospectively predict increases in depressive symptoms in adolescent girls: A growth curve analysis. *Developmental Psychology, 37,* 597–607.

Stice, E., Burton, E. M., & Shaw, H. (2004). Prospective relations between

bulimic pathology, depression and substance abuse: Unpacking comorbidity in adolescent girls. *Journal of Consulting and Clinical Psychology, 72,* 62–71.

Stice, E., & Whitenton, K. (2002). Risk factors for body dissatisfaction in adolescent girls: A longitudinal investigation. *Developmental Psychology, 38,* 669–678.

Stice, E., Ziemba, C., Margolis, J., & Flick, P. (1996). The dual pathway model differentiates bulimics, subclinical bulimics, and controls: Testing the continuity hypothesis. *Behavior Therapy, 27,* 531–549.

Stipek, D. J. (1995). The development of pride and shame in toddlers. In J. P. Tangney & K. W. Fischer (Eds.), *Self-conscious emotions: The psychology of shame, guilt, embarrassment, and pride* (pp. 237–252). New York: Guilford.

Stipek, D. J. (2001). Pathways to constructive lives: The importance of early school success. In A. C. Bohart & D. J. Stipek (Eds.), *Constructive and destructive behavior: Implications for family, school, and society* (pp. 291–315). Washington, DC: American Psychological Association.

Stone, N. (1993). Parental abuse as a precursor to childhood onset depression and suicidality. *Child Psychiatry and Human Development, 24,* 13–24.

Stone, W. L., & Lemanek, K. L. (1990). Developmental issues in children's self-reports. In A. M. La Greca (Ed.), *Through the eyes of the child:*

Obtaining self-reports from children and adolescents (pp. 18–56). Boston: Allyn & Bacon.

Storr, A. (1989). *Churchill's black dog.* London: Harper Collins.

Straus, M. A. (1992). Sociological research and social policy: The case of family violence. *Sociological Forum, 7,* 211–237.

Straus, M. A., & Gelles, R. J. (1990). *Physical violence in American families.* New Brunswick, NJ: Transaction.

Straus, M. A., Sugarman, D. B., & Gile-Sims, J. (1997). Spanking by parents and subsequent antisocial behavior of children. *Archives of Pediatrics and Adolescent Medicine, 151,* 761–767.

Straus, M. A., & Yodanis, C. L. (1996). Corporal punishment in adolescence and physical assaults on spouses in later life: What accounts for the link? *Journal of Marriage and the Family, 58,* 825–841.

Striegel-Moore, R. H. (1993). Etiology of binge eating: A developmental perspective. In C. G. Fairburn & G. T. Wilson (Eds.), *Binge eating: Nature, assessment, and treatment* (pp. 144–172). New York: Guilford.

Strober, M. (1995). Family-genetic perspectives on anorexia nervosa and bulimia nervosa. In K. Brownell & C. G. Fairburn (Eds.), *Eating disorders and obesity: A comprehensive handbook* (pp. 212–218). New York: Guilford.

Strober, M., Freeman, R., Lampert, C., Diamond, J., & Kaye, W. (2000).

Controlled family study of anorexia nervosa and bulimia nervosa: Evidence of shared liability and transmission of partial syndromes. *American Journal of Psychiatry, 157,* 393–401.

Strober, M., Freeman, R., & Morrell, W. (1997). The long-term course of severe anorexia nervosa in adolescents: Survival analysis of recovery, relapse, and outcome predictors over 10–15 years in a prospective study. *International Journal of Eating Disorders, 22,* 339–360.

Strober, M., & Humphrey, L. (1987). Familial contributions to the etiology and course of anorexia nervosa and bulimia. *International Journal of Eating Disorders, 5,* 654–659.

Stromme, P., & Hagberg, G. (2000). Aetiology in severe and mild mental retardation: A population-based study of Norwegian children. *Developmental Medicine and Child Neurology, 42,* 76–86.

Sue, D. W., & Sue, D. (1999). *Counseling the culturally different: Theory and practice* (3rd ed.). New York: Wiley.

Sue, S. (1998). In search of cultural competence in psychotherapy and counseling. *American Psychologist, 53,* 440–448.

Sullivan, H. S. (1953). *The interpersonal theory of psychiatry.* New York: Norton.

Sullivan, P. M., & Knutson, J. F. (1998). Maltreatment and behavioral characteristics of youth who are deaf and hard-of-hearing. *Sexuality & Disability, 16,* 295–319.

Sutton, J., Smith, P. K., & Swettenham, J. (1999). Bullying and "theory of mind": A critique of the "social skills deficit" view of anti-social behaviour. *Social Development, 8,* 117–127.

Swarr, A. E., & Richards, M. H. (1996). Longitudinal effects of adolescent girls' pubertal development, perceptions of pubertal timing, and parental relations on eating problems. *Developmental Psychology, 32,* 636–646.

Sweeney, L., & Rapee, R. M. (2001). Social phobia in children and adolescents: Psychological treatments. In W. Crozier & L. E. Alden (Eds.), *International handbook of social anxiety: Concepts, research and interventions relating to the self and shyness* (pp. 525–537). New York: Wiley.

Szatmari, P. (1992). The epidemiology of attention-deficit hyperactivity disorders. *Child and Adolescent Psychiatric Clinics of North America, 1,* 361–372.

Szatmari, P., Offord, D. R., & Boyle, M. H. (1989). Ontario Child Health Study: Prevalence of attention deficit disorder with hyperactivity. *Journal of Child Psychology & Psychiatry, 30,* 219–230.

Tager-Flusberg, H. (2000). Language and understanding minds: Connections in autism. In S. Baron-Cohen, H. Tager-Slusberg, & D. Cohen (Eds.), *Understanding other minds: Perspectives from developmental cognitive neuro-*

science (pp. 124–149). Oxford: Oxford University Press.

Tager-Flusberg, H. (2001). A reexamination of the Theory of Mind hypothesis of autism. In J. A. Burack, T. Charman, N. Yirmiya, & P. R. Zelazo (Eds.), *The development of autism: Perspectives from theory and research* (pp. 173–194). Mahwah, NJ: Erlbaum.

Tangney, J. P. (2001). Constructive and destructive aspects of shame and guilt. In A. C. Bohart & D. J. Stipek (Eds.), *Constructive and destructive behavior: Implications for family, school, and society* (pp. 127–145). Washington, DC: American Psychological Association.

Tangney, J. P., & Fischer, K. W. (1995). *Self-conscious emotions: The psychology of shame, guilt, embarrassment, and pride.* New York: Guilford.

Tannock, R. (2000). Attention-deficit/hyperactivity disorder with anxiety disorders. In T. E. Brown (Ed.), *Attention deficit disorders and comorbidities in children, adolescents, and adults* (pp. 125–170). Washington, DC: American Psychiatric Press.

Tantam, D. (2000). Adolescence and adulthood of individuals with Asperger syndrome. In A. Klin, F. R. Volkmar, & S. S. Sparrow (Eds.), *Asperger syndrome* (pp. 309–339). New York: Guilford.

Target, M., & Fonagy, P. (1994). The efficacy of psychoanalysis for children: Prediction of outcome in a developmental context. *Journal of the*

American Academy of Child and Adolescent Psychiatry, 33, 1134–1144.

Target, M., & Fonagy, P. (1997). Research on intensive psychotherapy with children and adolescents. *Child and Adolescent Psychiatric Clinics of North America, 6,* 39–51.

Tarter, R. E., Kirisci, L., & Mezzich, A. (1997). Multivariate typology of adolescents with alcohol use disorder. *American Journal on Addictions, 6,* 150–258.

Tarter, R. E., Moss, H. B., & Vanyukov, M. W. (1996). Behavior genetic perspective of alcoholism etiology. In H. Begleiter & B. Kissin (Eds.), *Alcohol and alcoholism* (Vol. 1, pp. 294–326) New York: Oxford University Press.

Tarter, R. E., Vanyukov, M., Giancola, P., Dawes, M., Blackson, T., Mezzich, A. C., et al. (1999). Etiology of early age onset substance use disorder: A maturational perspective. *Development and Psychopathology, 11,* 657–683.

Tassone, F., Hagerman, R. J., Ilke, D., Dyer, P. N., Lampe, M., Willemson, R. et al. (1999). FMRP expression as a potential prognostic indicator in fragile X syndrome. *American Journal of Medical Genetics, 84,* 250–261.

Taylor, H. G., Drotar, D., Wade, S., Yeates, K., Stancin, T., & Klein, S. (1995). Recovery from traumatic brain injury in children: The importance of the family. In S. H. Broman & M. E. Michel (Eds.), *Traumatic head injury in children* (pp. 188–217). New York: Oxford University Press.

Taylor, L., & Ingram, R. (1999). Cognitive reactivity and depressotypic information processing in children of depressed mothers. *Journal of Abnormal Psychology, 108,* 202–210.

Tebbutt, J., Swanston, H., Oates, R. K., & O'Toole, B. I. (1997). Five years after child sexual abuse: Persisting dysfunction and problems of prediction. *Journal of the American Academy of Child & Adolescent Psychiatry, 36,* 330–339.

Teeter, P. A., & Semrud-Clikeman, M. (1997). *Child neuropsychology.* Boston: Allyn & Bacon.

Tein, J. Y., Sandler, I. N., & Zautra, A. J. (2000). Stressful life events, psychological distress, coping, and parenting of divorced mothers: A longitudinal study. *Journal of Family Psychology, 14,* 27–41.

Terr, L. C. (1988). What happens to early memories of trauma? A study of twenty children under age five at the time of documented traumatic events. *Journal of the American Academy of Child and Adolescent Psychiatry, 27,* 96–104.

Terr, L. C. (1991). Childhood traumas: An outline and overview. *American Journal of Psychiatry, 148,* 10–20.

Teti, D. M., Gelfand, D. M., Messinger, D. S., & Isabella, R. (1995). Maternal depression and the quality of early attachment: An examination of infants, preschoolers, and their mothers. *Developmental Psychology, 31,* 364–376.

Tharp, R. G. (1989). Psychocultural variables and constants: Effects on teaching and learning in schools. *American Psychologist, 44,* 349–359.

Tharp, R. G. (1991). Cultural diversity and treatment of children. *Journal of Consulting and Clinical Psychology, 59,* 799–812.

Thomas, A., & Chess, S. (1977). *Temperament and development.* New York: Brunner/Mazel.

Thompson, A. H., Stuart, H., Bland, R. C., Arboleda-Florez, J., Warner, R., & Dickson, R. A. (2002). Attitudes about schizophrenia from the pilot site of the WPA worldwide campaign against the stigma of schizophrenia. *Social Psychiatry and Psychiatric Epidemiology, 37,* 475–482.

Thompson, P., Vidal, C., Giedd, J. N., Gochman, P., Blumenthal, J., Nicolson, R., Toga, A. W., & Rapoport, J. L. (2001). Mapping adolescent brain change reveals dynamic wave of accelerated gray matter loss in very early-onset schizophrenia. *Proceedings of the National Academy of Sciences, 98,* 11650–11655.

Thompson, R. A. (1987). Empathy and emotional understanding. The early development of empathy. In N. Eisenberg & J. Strayer (Eds.), *Empathy and its development* (pp. 119–145). Cambridge, MA: Cambridge University Press.

Thompson, R. A. (1994) Emotion regulation: A theme in search of definition. In N. A. Fox, *Monographs of the Society for Research in Child Development, 59,* 25–52.

Thompson, R. A. (2001). Childhood anxiety disorders from the perspective of emotion regulation and attachment. In M. W. Vasey & M. R. Dadds (Eds.), *The developmental psychopathology of anxiety* (pp. 160–182). New York: Oxford University Press.

Thompson, R. A., & Amato, P. R. (1999). *The postdivorce family: Children, parenting, and society.* Thousand Oaks, CA: Sage.

Thompson, R. J., & Gustafson, K. (1996). *Adaptation to chronic childhood illness* (pp. 271–287). Washington, DC: American Psychological Association.

Thompson, S. & Rey, J. (1995). Functional enuresis: Is desmopressin the answer? *Journal of the American Academy of Child and Adolescent Psychiatry, 34,* 266–271.

Thomsen, P. H. (1996). Borderline conditions in childhood. *Psychopathology, 29,* 357–362.

Tienari, P., Lahti, I., Sorri, A., Naarala, M., Moring, J., Kaleva, M., et al. (1990). Adopted-away offsprings of schizophrenics and controls: The Finnish adoptive family study of schizophrenia. In L. E. Robins & M. Rutter (Eds.), *Straight and devious pathways from childhood to adulthood* (pp. 365–379). Cambridge: Cambridge University Press.

Tienari, P., Sorri, A., Naarala, M., Lahti, I., & Pohjola, J. (1983). The Finnish adoptive study: Adopted-away offspring of schizophrenic mothers. In H. Stierlin, L. C. Wynne, & M. Wirsching (Eds.), *Psychological intervention in schizophrenia* (pp. 21–34). Berlin: Springer-Verlag.

Tolan, P., Gorman-Smith, D., & Henry, D. (2003). The developmental ecology of urban males' youth violence. *Developmental Psychology, 39,* 274–291.

Toner, B. B., Garfinkel, P. E., & Garner, D. M. (1988). Affective and anxiety disorders in the long-term follow-up of anorexia nervosa. *International Journal of Psychiatry in Medicine, 18,* 357–364.

Tonge, B. (1994). Separation anxiety disorder. In T. H. Ollendick, N. J. King, & W. Yule (Eds.), *International handbook of phobic and anxiety disorders in children and adolescents* (pp. 145–168). New York: Plenum.

Torgerson, S. (2000). Genetics. In M. Hersen & A. S. Bellack (Eds.), *Psychopathology in adulthood* (2nd ed., pp. 55–76). Needham Heights, MA: Allyn & Bacon.

Toth, S. L., Manly, J. T., & Cicchetti, D. (1992). Child maltreatment and vulnerability to depression. *Development and Psychopathology, 4,* 97–112.

Towbin, K. E., Dykens, E. M., Pearson, G. S., & Cohen, D. J. (1993). Conceptualizing "borderline syndrome of childhood" and "childhood schizophrenia" as a developmental disorder. *Journal of the American Academy of Child and Adolescent Psychiatry, 32,* 775–782.

Tremblay, R. E., Pagani-Kurtz, L., Masse, L. C., Vitaro, F., & Pihl, R. O. (1995). A bimodal preventive intervention for disruptive kindergarten boys: Its impact through mid-adolescence. *Journal of Consulting and Clinical Psychology, 63,* 560–568.

Treuting, J. J., & Hinshaw, S. P. (2001). Depression and self-esteem in boys with attention-deficit/hyperactivity disorder: Associations with comorbid aggression and explanatory attributional mechanisms. *Journal of Abnormal Child Psychology, 29,* 23–39.

Trickett, P. K., & McBride-Chang, C. (1995). The developmental impact of different forms of child abuse and neglect. *Developmental Review, 15,* 311–337.

Trickett, P. K., McBride-Chang, C., & Putnam, F. W. (1994). The classroom performance and behavior of sexually abused girls. *Development and Psychopathology, 6,* 183–194.

Trickett, P. K., Noll, J. G., Reiffman, A., & Putman, F. W. (2001). Variants of intrafamilial sexual abuse experience: Implications for short- and long-term development. *Development and Psychopathology, 13,* 1001–1019.

Tully, L.A., Arseneault, L., Caspi, A., Moffitt, T. E., & Morgan, J. (2004). Does maternal warmth moderate the effects of birth weight on twins' attention-deficit/hyperactivity disorder (ADHD) symptoms and low IQ? *Journal of Consulting & Clinical Psychology, 72*(2), 218–226.

Turkheimer, E., Haley, A., Waldron, M., D'Onofrio, B., & Gottesman, I. I. (2003). Socioeconomic status modified heritability of IQ in young children. *Psychological Science, 14,* 623–628.

Turner, S. M., Beidel, D. C., & Wolff, P. L. (1996). Is behavioral inhibition related to the anxiety disorders? *Clinical Psychology Review, 16,* 157–172.

Umbarger, C. C. (1983). *Structural family therapy.* New York: Grune & Stratton.

Underwood, M. K. (2003). *Social aggression among girls.* New York: Guilford.

United Nations. (1989). *Adoption of a convention on the rights of the child (U.N. document No. A/44/736).* New York: Author.

United Nations Children's Fund. (1999). *The state of the world's children 2000.* New York: Author.

United Nations International Children's Emergency Fund. (2000). *Domestic violence against women and girls.* Florence, Italy: UNICEF Innocenti Research Center.

United Nations International Children's Emergency Fund. (2003). *A league table of child maltreatment deaths in rich nations.* Florence, Italy: UNICEF Innocenti Research Center.

Urban, J., Carlson, E., Egeland, B., & Sroufe, L. A. (1991). Patterns of individual adaptation across childhood. *Development and Psychopathology, 3,* 445–460.

U.S. Bureau of the Census. (2003). *We the first Americans.* Washington, DC: Author.

U.S. Department of Education. (2002). *Exemplary and promising school-based programs that promote safe, disciplined and drug-free schools.* Washington, DC: U.S. Department of Education.

U.S. Department of Health and Human Services (DHHS). (2001). *Child maltreatment 1999: Reports from the states to the National Center on Child Abuse and Neglect.* Washington, DC: U.S. Government Printing Office.

U.S. Food and Drug Administration. (2004). Suicidality in children and adolescents being treated with antidepressant medications. *FDA Public Health Advisory,* http://www.fda.gov/cder/drug/antidepressants/SSRIPHA200410.htm.

U.S. Office of Education. (1992). Individuals with Disabilities Education Act (IDEA). *Federal Register, 57,* 44842–44843.

Usiskin, S. I., Nicolson, R., Krasnewich, D. M., Yan, W., Lenane, M., & Wudarsky, M. (1999). Velocardiofacial syndrome in childhood-onset schizophrenia. *Journal of the American Academy of Child and Adolescent Psychiatry, 38,* 1536–1543.

Vaden-Kiernan, N., Ialongo, N. S., Pearson, J., & Kellam, S. (1995). Household family structure and children's aggressive behavior: A longitudinal study of urban elementary school children. *Journal of Abnormal Child Psychology, 23,* 553–568.

Valencia, R. R., & Suzuki, L. A. (2000). *Intelligence testing and minority students.* Thousand Oaks, CA: Sage.

Van Der Gaag, R. J., Buitelaar, J. K., Van Den Ban, E., Bezemer, M., & Van Engeland, H. (1995). A controlled mulitvariate chart review of multiple complex developmental disorder. *Journal of the American Academy of Child and Adolescent Psychiatry, 34,* 1096–1106.

van IJzendoorn, M. H. (1995). Adult attachment representations, parental responsiveness, and infant attachment: A meta-analysis on the predictive validity of the adult attachment interview. *Psychological Bulletin, 117*(3), 387–403.

van IJzendoorn, M. H., Juffer, F., & Duyvesteyn, M. G. C. (1995). Breaking the intergenerational cycle of insecure attachment: A review of the effects of attachment based interventions on maternal sensitivity and infant security. *Journal of Child Psychology and Psychiatry and Allied Disciplines, 36,* 225–248.

van IJzendoorn, M. H., & Sagi, A. (1999). Cross-cultural patterns of attachment: Universal and contextual dimensions. In J. Cassidy & P. Shaver (Eds.), *Handbook of attachment* (pp. 713–734). New York: Guilford.

van IJzendoorn, M. H., Schuengel, C., & Bakermans-Kranenburg, M. J. (1999). Disorganized attachment in early childhood: Meta-analysis of precursors, concomittants, and sequelae. *Development and Psychopathology, 11,* 225–249.

Vargas, L. A., & Willis, D. J. (1994). Introduction to the special section: New directions in the treatment and assessment of ethnic minority children and adolescents. *Journal of Clinical Child Psychology, 23,* 2–4.

Varni, J. W., Blount, R. L., Waldron, S. A., & Smith, A. J. (1995). Management of pain and distress. In M. C. Roberts (Ed.), *Handbook of pediatric psychology* (2nd ed., pp. 105–122). New York: Guilford.

Varni, J. W., La Greca, A. M., & Spirito, A. (2000). Cognitive-behavioral interventions for children with chronic health conditions. In P. C. Kendall (Ed.), *Child and adolescent therapy: Cognitive-behavioral procedures* (pp. 291–333). New York: Guilford.

Vasey, M. W., Crnic, K. A., & Carter, W. G. (1994). Worry in childhood: A developmental perspective. *Cognitive Therapy and Research, 18,* 529–549.

Vasey, M. W., & Dadds, M. R. (2001). An introduction to the developmental psychopathology of anxiety. In M.W.Vasey & M. R. Dadds (Eds.), *The developmental psychopathology of anxiety* (pp. 3–26). New York: Oxford University Press.

Vasey, M. W., & MacLeod, C. (2001). Information processing factors in childhood anxiety: A review and developmental perspective. In M.W.Vasey & M. R. Dadds (Eds.), *The developmental psychopathology of anxiety* (pp. 253–277). New York: Oxford University Press.

Vasey, M. W., & Ollendick, T. H. (2001). Anxiety. In A. J. Sameroff, M. Lewis, & S. M. Miller (Eds.), *Handbook of developmental psychopathology* (pp. 511–530). New York: Kluwer.

Vega, W. A., Gil, A. G., Warheit, G. J., Zimmerman, R. S., & Apospori, E. (1993). Acculturation and delinquent behavior among Cuban American adolescents: Toward an empirical model. *American Journal of Community Psychology, 21,* 113–125.

Vela, R. M., Gottlieb, E. H., & Gottlieb, H. P. (1983). Borderline syndromes in childhood: A critical review. In K. S. Robson (Ed.), *The borderline child: Approaches to etiology, diagnosis, and treatment* (pp. 31–48). New York: McGraw-Hill.

Veltman, M. W. M., & Browne, K. D. (2001). Three decades of child maltreatment research: Implications for the school years. *Trauma, Violence, and Abuse: A Review Journal, 2,* 215–239.

Verdoux, H., Liraud, F., Gonzales, B., Assens, F., & van Os, J. (2001). Predictors and outcome characteristics associated with suicidal behaviour in early psychosis: A two-year follow-up of first-admitted subjects. *Acta Psychiatrica Scandinavica, 103,* 347–354.

Verhulst, F. C., Van der Ende, J., Ferdinand, R. F., & Jasius, M. C. (1997). The prevalence of DSM-III-R diagnoses in a national sample of Dutch adolescents. *Archives of General Psychiatry, 54,* 329–336.

Vik, P. W., Brown, S. A., & Myers, M. G. (1997). Adolescent substance abuse problems. In E. J. Mash & L. G. Terdal (Eds.), *Assessment of childhood disorders* (pp. 717–748). New York: Guilford.

Vitaro, F., Tremblay, R., Kerr, M., Pagani, L., & Bukowski, W. M. (1997). Disruptiveness, friends' characteristics, and deliquency in early adolescence: A test of two competing models of development. *Child Development, 68,* 676–689.

Vizard, E., Monch, E., & Misch, P. (1995). Child and adolescent sex abuse perpetrators: A review of the research literature. *Journal of Child Psychology and Psychiatry, 36,* 731–756.

Vlach, N. (2003). Central American children and adolescents. In J. T. Gibbs & L. N. Huang (Eds.), *Children of color: Psychological interventions with culturally diverse youth* (2nd ed., pp. 301–343). San Francisco: Jossey-Bass.

Volbert, R. (2000). Sexual knowledge of preschool children. In T. G. M. Sandfort & J. Rademakers (Eds.), *Childhood sexuality: Normal sexual behavior and development* (pp. 5–26). Binghamton. NY: Haworth.

Volkmar, F. R. (1996). Childhood and adolescent psychosis: A review of the past 10 years. *Journal of the American Academy of Child and Adolescent Psychiatry, 35,* 843–851.

Volkmar, F. R., Becker, D. F., King, R. A., & McGlashan, T. H. (1995). Psychotic processes. In *Developmental psychopathology, Vol. 2: Risk, disorder, and adaptation* (pp. 512–534). Oxford, England: John Wiley & Sons.

Volkmar, F. R., & Klin, A. (2001). Asperger's disorder or high-functioning autism: Same or different? *International Review of Research in Mental Retardation, 23,* 83–110.

Volkmar, F. R., & Schwab-Stone, M. (1996). Annotation: Childhood disorders in DSM-IV. *Journal of Child Psychology and Psychiatry and Allied Disciplines, 37,* 779–784.

Volkmar, F. R., & Woolston, J. L. (1997). Comorbidity of psychiatric disorders in children and adolescents. In *Treatment strategies for patients with psychiatric comorbidity* (pp. 307–322). New York: John Wiley & Sons.

Vondra, J. I., Barnett, D., & Cicchetti, D. (1989). Perceived and actual competence among maltreated and comparison school children. *Development and Psychopathology, 1,* 237–255.

Vourdas, A., Pipe, R., Corrigall, R., & Frangou, S. (2003). Increased developmental deviance and premorbid dysfunction in early onset schizophrenia. *Schizophrenia Research, 62,* 13–22.

Vuchinich, S., Wood, B., & Angelelli, J. (1996). Coalitions and family problem solving in the psychosocial treatment of preadolescents. In E. D. Hibbs & P. S. Jensen (Eds.), *Psychosocial treatments for child and adolescent disorders* (pp. 497–520). Washington, DC: American Psychological Association.

Vygotsky, L. S. (1978). *Mind in society.* Cambridge MA: Harvard University Press.

Wachtel, E. F. (1994). *Treating troubled children and their families*. New York: Guilford.

Wagner, A. W., & Linehan, M. M. (1994). Relationship between childhood sexual abuse and topography of parasuicide among women with borderline personality disorder. *Journal of Personality Disorders, 8,* 1–9.

Wagner, B. M. (1997). Family risk factors for child and adolescent suicidal behavior. *Psychological Bulletin, 121,* 246–298.

Wagner, K. D., & Ambrosini, P. J. (2001). Childhood depression: Pharmacological therapy/treatment (pharmacotherapy of childhood depression). *Journal of Clinical Child Psychology, 30,* 88–97.

Waldron, H. B. (1997). Adolescent substance abuse and family therapy outcome: A review of randomized trials. In T. H. Ollendick & R. J. Prinz (Eds.), *Advances in clinical child psychology* (Vol. 9, pp. 199–234). New York: Plenum.

Walker, C. E. (1995). Elmination disorders: Enuresis and encopresis. In M. C. Roberts (Ed.), *Handbook of pediatric psychology* (2nd ed., pp. 537–557). New York: Guilford.

Walker, E. F., & Lewine, R. J. (1990). Prediction of adult-onset schizophrenia from childhood home movies of the patients. *American Journal of Psychiatry, 147,* 1052–1056.

Walker, E. F., Neumann, C. C., Baum, K., Davis, D. M., DiForio, D., & Bergman, A. (1996). The developmental pathways to schizophrenia: Potential moderating effects of stress. *Development and Psychopathology, 8,* 647–665.

Walker, E. F., Savole, T., & Davis, D. (1994). Neuromotor precursors of schizophrenia. *Schizophrenia Bulletin, 20,* 441–451.

Walker, E. F., & Walder, D. (2003). Neurohormonal aspects of the development of psychotic disorders. In D. Cicchetti & E. Walker (Eds.), *Neurodevelopmental mechanisms in psychopathology* (pp. 526–544). New York: Cambridge.

Walker, J. L., Lahey, B. B., Russo, M. F., Frick, P. J., Christ, M. A., McBurnett, K., et al. (1991). Anxiety, inhibition, and conduct disorder in children: I. Relations to social impairment. *Journal of the American Academy of Child and Adolescent Psychiatry, 30,* 187–191.

Walker, N. W. (1997). *Best practices in assessment and programming for students with traumatic brain injury*. Raleigh, NC: Public Schools of North Carolina.

Wallander, J. L., & Varni, J. W. (1998). Effects of pediatric chronic physical disorders on child and family adjustment. *Journal of Child Psychology & Psychiatry, 39,* 29–46.

Walsh, T., & Menvielle, E. (1997). Disorders of elimination. In J. M. Weiner (Ed.), *Textbook of child and adolescent psychiatry* (pp. 613–615). Washington, DC: American Psychiatric Association.

Warren, S. L., Huston, L., Egeland, B., & Sroufe, L. A. (1997). Child and adolescent anxiety disorders and early attachment. *Journal of the American Academy of Child and Adolescent Psychiatry, 36,* 637–644.

Waters, E., Merrick, S., Treboux, D., Crowell, J., & Albersheim, L. (2000). Attachment security in infancy and early adulthood: A twenty-year longitudinal study. *Child Development, 71,* 543–562.

Watkins, J. M., Asarnow, R. F., & Tanguay, P. E. (1988). Symptom development in childhood schizophrenia. *Journal of Child Psychology and Psychiatry, 29,* 865–878.

Watson, J. B., & Rayner, R. (1920). Conditioned emotional reactions. *Journal of Experimental Psychology, 3,* 1–14.

Watt, N. F., Anthony, E. J., Wynne, L. C., & Rolf, J. E. (Eds.). (1984). *Children at risk for schizophrenia: A longitudinal prospective*. New York: Cambridge University Press.

Webb, N. B. (2001). *Culturally diverse parent-child and family relationships: A guide for social workers and other practitioners*. New York: Columbia University Press.

Webster-Stratton, C. (1998). Preventing conduct problems in Head Start children: Strengthening parenting competencies. *Journal of Consulting and Clinical Psychology, 66*(5), 715–730.

Webster-Stratton, C., & Hancock, L. (1998). Training for parents of young children with conduct problems: Content, methods, and therapeutic process. In J. M. Briesmeister & C. E. Schaefer (Eds.), *Handbook of parent training* (pp. 98–152). New York: Wiley.

Webster-Stratton, C, & Herbert, M. (1994). *Troubled families—problem children: Working with parents: A collaborative process*. New York: Wiley.

Webster-Stratton, C., & Reid, M. J. (2004). The Incredible Years parents, teachers, and children training series: A multifaceted treatment approach for young children with conduct problems. In A. E. Kazdin & J. R. Weisz (Eds.), *Evidence-based psychotherapies for children and adolescents* (pp. 224–240). New York: Guilford.

Webster-Stratton, C., & Taylor, T. K. (1998). Adopting and implementing empirically supported interventions: A recipe for success. In A. Buchanan (Ed.), *Parenting, schooling, and children's behavior: Interdisciplinary approaches* (pp. 1–25). Hampshire England: Ashgate Publishing.

Wechsler, D. (1989). *Wechsler Preschool and Primary Scale of Intelligence—Revised*. San Antonio, TX: The Psychological Corporation.

Wechsler, D. (2003). *Wechsler Intelligence Scale for Children—Fourth Edition*. San Antonio, TX: The Psychological Corporation.

Weinberger, D. R. (1987). Implications of normal brain development for the pathogenesis of schizophrenia. *Archives of General Psychiatry, 44,* 660–669.

Weiner, I. B. (1992). *Psychological disturbances in adolescence* (2nd ed.). New York: Wiley.

Weinfield, N. S., Sroufe, L. A., & Egeland, B. (2000). Attachment from infancy to adulthood in a high-risk sample, continuity, discontinuity, and their correlates. *Developmental Psychology, 71,* 695–702.

Weinstein, C. S., Apfel, R. J., & Weinstein, S. R. (1998). Description of mothers with ADHD with children with ADHD. *Psychiatry: Interpersonal and Biological Processes, 61,* 12–19.

Weinstein, R. S. (2002). *Reaching higher: The power of expectations in schooling.* Cambridge, MA: Harvard University Press.

Weiss, B., & Garber, J. (2003). Developmental differences in the phenomenonology of depression. *Development and Psychopathology, 15,* 403–430.

Weiss, D. D., & Last, C. G. (2001). Developmental variations in the prevalence and manifestation of anxiety disorders. In M. W. Vasey & M. R. Dadds (Eds.), *The developmental psychopathology of anxiety* (pp. 27–43). New York.

Weiss, G., & Hechtman, L. T. (1993). *Hyperactive children grown up: ADHD in children, adolescents, and adults.*

Weissman, M. M., Wolk, S., Goldstein, R. B., Moreau, D., Adams, P., Greenwald, S., et al. (1999). Depressed adolescents grown up. *JAMA: Journal of the American Medical Association, 281,* 1707–1713.

Weisz, J. R., Donenberg, G. R., Han, S. S., & Weiss, B. (1995). Bridging the gap between laboratory and clinic in child and adolescent psychotherapy. *Journal of Consulting and Clinical Psychology, 63,* 688–701.

Weisz, J. R., & Weiss, B. (1991). Studying the "referability" of child clinical problems. *Journal of Consulting and Clinical Psychology, 59,* 266–273.

Weisz, J. R., Weiss, B., Han, S. S., Granger, D. A., & Morton, T. (1995). Effects of psychotherapy with children and adolescents revisited: A meta-analysis of treatment outcome studies. *Psychological Bulletin, 117,* 450–468.

Weisz, J. R., Weiss, B., Suwanlert, S., & Chaiyasit, W. (2003). Syndromal structure of psychopathology in children of Thailand and the United States. *Journal of Consulting and Clinical Psychology, 71,* 375–385.

Wekerle, C., & Wolfe, D. A. (1999). Dating violence in mid-adolescence: Theory, significance, and emerging prevention initiatives. *Clinical Psychology Review, 19,* 435–456.

Wekerle, C., & Wolfe, D. A. (2003). Child maltreatment. In E. J. Mash & R. A. Barkley (Eds.), *Child psychopathology* (pp. 632–695). New York: Guilford.

Weller, E. B., Weller, R. A., & Fristad, M. A. (1995). Bipolar disorder in children: Misdiagnosis, underdiagnosis, and future directions. *Journal of the American Academy of Child & Adolescent Psychiatry, 34,* 709–714.

Weller, E. B., Weller, R. A., Fristad, M. A., & Teare, M. (1999). *Children's Interview for Psychiatric Symptoms (ChIPS).* Washington, DC: American Psychiatric Publishing Group.

Weller, R. A., Weller, E. B., Fristad, M. A., & Bowes, J. M. (1991). Depression in recently bereaved prepubertal children. *American Journal of Psychiatry, 148,* 1536–1540.

Wenning, K. (1990). Borderline children: A closer look at diagnosis and treatment. *American Journal of Orthopsychiatry, 60,* 225–232.

Wenar, C., Ruttenberg, B. A., Kalish-Weiss, B., & Wolf, E. G. (1986). The development of normal and autistic children: A comparative study. *Journal of Autism & Developmental Disorders, 16(3),* 317–333.

Werner, E., Dawson, G., Osterling, J., & Dinno, N. (2000). Brief report: Recognition of autism spectrum disorder before one year of age: A retrospective study based on home videotapes. *Journal of Autism and Developmental Disorders, 30(2),* 157–162.

Werner, E. E., & Smith, R. S. (1992). *Overcoming the odds: High risk children from birth to adulthood.* Ithaca, NY: Cornell University Press.

Westen, D. (1990). *Social cognition and object relations scale (SCORS): Manual for coding TAT data.* Department of Psychology, University of Michigan.

Westen, D. (1991). Cognitive-behavioral interventions in the psychodynamic psychotherapy of borderline personality disorders. *Clinical Psychology Review, 11,* 211–230.

Westen, D. (1998). The scientific legacy of Sigmund Freud: Toward a psychodynamically informed psychological science. *Psychological Bulletin, 124,* 333–371.

Westen, D., & Cohen, R. (1993). The self in borderline personality disorder: A psychodynamic perspective. In Z. V. Segal & S. J. Blatt (Eds.), *The self in emotional distress: Cognitive and psychodynamic perspectives* (pp. 334–360). New York: Guilford.

Westen, D., Ludolph, P., Lerner, H., Ruffins, S., & Wiss, F. C. (1990). Object relations in borderline adolescents. *Journal of the American Academy of Child and Adolescent Psychiatry, 29,* 338–348.

Whalen, C. K., Jamner, L. D., Henker, B., Delfino, R. J., & Lozano, J. M. (2002). The ADHD spectrum and everyday life: Experience sampling of adolescent moods, activities, smoking, and drinking. *Child Development, 73,* 209–227.

Whitaker, A., Johnson, J., Shaffer, D., & Rapoport, J. L. (1990). Uncommon troubles in young people: Prevalence estimates of selected psychiatric disorders in a nonreferred adolescent population. *Archives of General Psychiatry, 47,* 487–496.

White, J. L., Moffitt, T. E., Caspi, A., Bartusch, D. J., Needles, D. J., & Stouthamer-Loeber, M. (1994). Measuring impulsivity and examining its relationship to delinquency. *Journal of Abnormal Psychology, 103,* 192–205.

White, L., & Rogers, S. J. (2000). Economic circumstances and family outcomes: A review of the

1990s. *Journal of Marriage and Family, 62,* 1035–1051.

White, T., Andreasen, N. C., Nopoulos, P., & Magnotta, V. (2003). Gyrification abnormalities in childhood- and adolescent-onset schizophrenia. *Biological Psychiatry, 54,* 418–426.

Whiteside, M. F. (1998). The parental alliance following divorce: An overview. *Journal of Marital and Family Therapy, 24,* 3–24.

Wicks-Nelson, R., & Israel, A. C. (2000). *Behavior disorders of childhood.* New York: Prentice Hall.

Wilens, T. E., Biederman, J., Abrantes, A. M., & Spencer, T. J. (1997). Clinical characteristics of psychiatrically referred adolescent outpatients with substance use disorder. *Journal of the American Academy of Child and Adolescent Psychiatry, 36,* 941–947.

Willcutt, E. G., & Pennington, B. F. (2000). Comorbidity of reading disability and attention-deficit/hyperactivity disorder: Differences by gender and subtype. *Journal of Learning Disabilities, 33,* 179–191.

Willcutt, E. G., Pennington, B. F., Boada, R., Ogline, J. S., Tunick, R. A., Chhabildas, N. A., et al. (2001). A comparison of the congitive deficits in reading disability and attention-deficit/ hyperactivity disorder. *Journal of Abnormal Psychology, 110,* 157–172.

Williams, P., Lorenzo, F. D., & Borja, M. (1993). Pediatric chronic illness: Effects on siblings and mothers. *Maternal-Child Nursing Journal, 21,* 115–121.

Williamson, D. A., & Netemeyer, S. B. (2000). Cognitive-behavior therapy. In K. J. Miller & J. S. Mizes (Eds.), *Comparative treatments for eating disorders* (pp. 61–81). New York: Springer.

Williamson, S. E., Harpur, T. J., & Hare, R. D. (1991). Abnormal processing of affective words by psychopaths. *Psychophysiology, 28,* 260–273.

Wilson, G. T. (2002). The controversy over dieting. In C. G. Fairburn & K. D. Brownell (Eds.), *Eating disorders and obesity: A comprehensive handbook* (2nd ed., pp. 93–97). New York: Guilford.

Wilson, G. T., Becker, C. B., & Heffernan, K. (2003). Eating disorders. In E. J. Mash & R. A. Barkley (Eds.), *Child psychopathology* (pp. 687–715). New York: Guilford.

Wilson, G. T., & Fairburn, C. G. (2002). Eating disorders. In P. E. Nathan & J. M. Gorman (Eds.), *Treatments that work* (pp. 559–592). New York: Oxford University Press.

Wilson, G. T., Heffernan, K., & Black, C. M. (1996). Eating disorders. In E. J. Mash & R. A. Barkley (Eds.), *Child psychopathology* (pp. 541–571). New York: Guilford.

Windle, R. C., & Windle, M. (1997). An investigation of adolescents' substance use behaviors, depressed affect, and suicidal behaviors. *Journal of Child Psychology and Psychiatry and Allied Disciplines, 38,* 921–929.

Wing, L. (1981). Asperger's syndrome: A clinical account. *Psychological Medicine, 11,* 115–129.

Wing, L. (1991). The relationship between Asperger's syndrome and Kanner's autism. In U. Frith (Ed.), *Autism and Asperger Syndrome* (pp. 93–121). Cambridge, UK: Cambridge University Press.

Wing, L., & Attwood, A. J. (1987). Severe impairments of social interaction and associated abnormalities in children: Epidemiology and classification. *Journal of Autism and Developmenal Disorders, 9,* 11–30.

Wing, L., & Potter, D. (2002). The epidemiology of autistic spectrum disorders: Is the prevalence rising? *Mental Retardation and Developmental Disabilities Research Reviews, 8*(3), 151–161.

Winnicott, D. W. (1975). *Through paediatrics to psycho-analysis.* New York: Basic Books.

Winnicott, D. W. (1987). *The child, the family, and the outside world.* Reading, MA: Addison-Wesley.

Wintre, M. G., & Vallance, D. D. (1994). A developmental sequence in the comprehension of emotions: Intensity, multiple emotions, and valence. *Developmental Psychology, 30,* 509–514.

Wirt, R. D., Lachar, D., Klinedinst, J. K., & Seat, P. S. (1990). *Personality Inventory for Children— 1990 edition.* Los Angeles: Western Psychological Services.

Wolfe, D. A. (1999). *Child abuse* (2nd ed.). Newbury Park, CA: Sage.

Wolfe, D. A., Crooks, C. V., Lee, V., McIntyre-Smith, A., & Jaffe, P. G. (2003). The effects of children's exposure to domestic violence: A meta-analysis and critique. *Clinical Child and Family Psychology Review, 6,* 171–187.

Wolfe, D. A., & McEachran, A. (1997). Child physical abuse and neglect. In E. J. Mash & L. G. Terdal (Eds.), *Assessment of childhood disorders* (pp. 523–568). New York: Guilford.

Wolfe, D. A., Wekerle, C., Reitzel-Jaffe, D., Grasley, C., Pittman, A. L., & MacEachran, A. (1997). Interrupting the cycle of violence: Empowering youth to promote healthy relationships. In D. A. Wolfe, R. J. McMahon, & R. D. Peters (Eds.), *Child abuse: New directions in prevention and treatment across the life span* (pp. 102–129). Thousand Oaks, CA: Sage.

Wolfe, D. A., Wekerle, C., Reitzel-Jaffe, D., & Lefebvre, L. (1998). Factors associated with abusive relationships among maltreated and nonmaltreated youth. *Development and Psychopathology, 10,* 61–85.

Wolfe, V. V. (1998). Child sexual abuse. In E. J. Mash & R. A. Barkley (Eds.), *Treatment of childhood disorders* (pp. 545–597). New York: Guilford.

Wolpe, J. (1973). *The practice of behavior therapy* (2nd ed.). New York: Pergamon.

Wolraich, M. L., Felice, M. E., & Drotar, D. (1997). *The classification of child and adolescent mental diagnoses in primary care: Diagnostic and statistical manual for primary care*

Cambridge University Press. **Box 9.3** From An Unquiet Mind, by Kay Redfield Jamison. Copyright © 1995 by Kay Redfield Jamison. Used by permission of Alfred A. Knopf, a division of Random House, Inc. **Box 9.5** From A. Spirito, J. Kurkjian, & D. Donaldson, 2003, Case Examples, in A. Spirito & J. C. Overholser (Eds.), *Evaluating and Treating Adolescent Suicide Attempters: From Research to Practice*, pp. 284–295. New York: Academic Press, pp. 287–289. Copyright © 2003 by Elsevier. Reprinted with permission. **Table 9.1** Adapted with permission from *Diagnostic and Statistical Manual of Mental Disorders*, Text Revision, Fourth Edition, 2000. Copyright © 2000 American Psychiatric Association. **Table 9.2** Adapted with permission from *Diagnostic and Statistical Manual of Mental Disorders*, Text Revision, Fourth Edition, 2000. Copyright © 2000 American Psychiatric Association. **Table 9.3** Adapted with permission from *Diagnostic and Statistical Manual of Mental Disorders*, Text Revision, Fourth Edition, 2000. Copyright © 2000 American Psychiatric Association. **Table 9.4** From S. H. Goodman, 2003, "Genesis and Epigenesis of Psychopathology in Children with Depressed Mothers: Toward an Integrative Bipsychosocial Perspective," in D. Cicchetti & E. Walker

(eds.), *Neurodevelopmental Mechanisms in Psychopathology,* pp. 428–460. New York: Cambridge. Reprinted with the permission of Cambridge University Press. **Table 9.5** Adapted with permission from *Diagnostic and Statistical Manual of Mental Disorders,* Text Revision, Fourth Edition, 2000. Copyright © 2000 American Psychiatric Association. **Table 9.6** "Youth Suicide Rates, by Age, Sex, and Country," data from the World Health Organization website at: http://whqlibdoc.who.int/hq/1999/WHO_MNH_MBD_99.1.pdf. Reprinted with permission. **Figure 9.6** From S. R. Pliszka, 2002, *Neuroscience for the Mental Health Clinician,* p. 201. New York: Guilford Press. Reprinted with permission.

Chapter 10

Table 10.1 Reprinted with permission from *Diagnostic and Statistical Manual of Mental Disorders,* Text Revision, Fourth Edition, 2000. Copyright © 2000 American Psychiatric Association. **Table 10.2** From R. L. Selman, & L. H. Schultz, 1988, "Interpersonal Thought and Action in the Case of a Troubled Early Adolescent: Toward a Developmental Model of the Gap," in S. R. Shirk (Ed.), *Cognitive Development and Child Psychotherapy,* pp. 207–246. NY: Perseus. Reprinted with permission. **Figure 10.1** From P. J. Frick, et al., 1993, "Oppositional Defiant

Disorder and Conduct Disorder: A Meta-Analytic Review of Factor Analyses and Cross Validation in a Clinical Sample," *Clinical Psychology Review,* 13, pp. 319–340. Copyright © by Elsevier. Reprinted with permission. **Figure 10.2** From L. M. Broidy, D. S. Nagin, R. E. Tremblay, J. E. Bates, B. Brame, K. A. Dodge, et al., 2003, "Developmental Trajectories of Childhood Disruptive Behaviors and Adolescent Delinquency: A Six-Site, Cross-National Study," *Developmental Psychology,* 39(2), pp. 222–245. Copyright © 2001 by the American Psychological Association. Reprinted with permission.

Chapter 11

Box 11.1 From S. Emmons, C. Geiser, K. Kaplan & M. Harrow, 1997, *Living With Schizophrenia,* Taylor & Francis. Reprinted with permission. **Table 11.1** Reprinted with permission from *Diagnostic and Statistical Manual of Mental Disorders,* Text Revision, Fourth Edition, 2000. Copyright © 2000 American Psychiatric Association. **Figure 11.2** From M. S. Keshavan, 2003, "Toward Unraveling the Premorbid Neurodevelopmental Risk for Schizophrenia," in D. Cicchetti & E. Walker (eds.) *Neurodevelopmental Mechanisms in Psychopathology,* p. 367. New York: Cambridge University Press. Reprinted with the permission of Cambridge University Press. **Figure 11.3** From P. Thompson, C. Vidal,

J. N. Giedd, P. Gochman, J. Blumenthal, R. Nicolson, et al., 2001, "Mapping Adolescent Brain Change Reveals Dynamic Wave of Accelerated Gray Matter Loss in Very Early-Onset Schizophrenia," *Proceedings of the National Academy of Sciences,* 98(20), 11650–11655. Copyright © 2001 National Academy of Sciences, U.S.A. **Figure 11.4** From J. R. Asarnow & R. F. Asasrnow, 2003, "Childhood-Onset Schizophrenia," in E. J. Mash & R. A. Barkley, *Child Psychopathology,* 2nd ed., p. 463. New York: Guilford Press. Reprinted with permission.

Chapter 12

Box 12.1 From T. Haggiag, 2000, "The Broken Jigsaw: A Child's Perspective," in B. Lask & R. Bryant-Wauch (eds.), *Anorexia Nervosa and Related Eating Disorders in Childhood and Adolescence,* pp. 3–10. Philadelphia: Psychology Press. Reprinted by permission of Taylor & Francis. **Box 12.2** From E. Lau, 1995, "An Insatiable Emptiness," *The Georgia Straight,* pp. 13–14. Copyright © Evelyn Lau. First published in *The Georgia Straight,* 1995. Reprinted with permission. **Table 12.1** Reprinted with permission from *Diagnostic and Statistical Manual of Mental Disorders,* Text Revision, Fourth Edition, 2000. Copyright © 2000 American Psychiatric Association. **Table 12.3** Reprinted with permission from

Box 17.3 From M. R. Levin, S. Ashmore-Callahan, P. C. Kendall & M. Ichii, M, 1996, "Treatment of Separation Anxiety Disorder," in M. A. Reinecke, M. Dattilio, & A. Freeman (eds.), *Cognitive Therapy with Children and Adolescents,* pp. 153–174. New York: Guilford. Reprinted with permission. **Box 17.4** From M. E. Franklin, M. Rynn, E. B. Foa & J. S. March, 2003, "Treatment of Obsessive-Compulsive Disorder," in M. A. Reinecke, F. M. Dattilio, & A. Freeman (eds.), *Cognitive Therapy with Children and Adolescents: A Casebook for Clinical Practice,* 2nd ed., pp. 162–188. New York: Guilford. Reprinted with permission. **Box 17.5** From G. Spivack & M. B. Shure, 1982, "Interpersonal Cognitive Problem Solving and Clinical Theory," in B. Lahey & A. E. Kazdin (eds.), *Advances in Child Clinical Psychology: Vol. 5,* pp. 323–372. New York: Plenum. Reprinted with

permission from Elsevier Academic/Plenum Publishers. **Box 17.6** From Michael P. Nichols and Richard C. Schwartz, *Family Therapy: Concepts and Methods,* 6th ed. Published by Allyn & Bacon, Boston, MA. Copyright © 2003 by Pearson Education. Reprinted by permission of the publisher. **Table 17.1** From D. L. Chambless & S. D. Hollon, 1998, "Defining Empirically Supported Therapies," *Journal of Consulting and Clinical Psychology,* 66, pp. 7–18. Copyright © 2001 by the American Psychological Association. Reprinted with permission. **Table 17.2** From S. R. Shirk & R. L. Russell, 1996, *Change Processes in Child Psychotherapy: Revitalizing Treatment and Research.* New York: Guilford. Reprinted with permission. **Figure 17.1** From R. V. Hall, R. Fox, D. Willard, L. Goldsmith, M. Emerson, M. Owen, T. Davis, T. & E. Porcia,

1971, "The Teacher as Observer and Experimenter in the Modification of Disputing and Talking-out Behaviors," *Journal of Applied Behavioral Analysis,* 4, pp. 141–149. Reprinted by permission. **Figure 17.2** From R. M. Rapee, A. Wignall, J. L. Hudson C. A. Schniering, 2000, *Treating Anxious Children and Adolescents: An Evidence-Based Approach,* Oakland, CA: New Harbinger. Reprinted with permission from New Harbinger Publications, Inc.

Photo Credits

Name Index

Subject Index

Italicized page numbers refer to boxes, figures, illustrations, and tables.

Coercion theory, 320–321, 322
Cognitive-behavioral therapy (CBT), 7–8
  for attention-deficit/hyperactivity disorder, 198–199
  for borderline personality disorder, 474–476, *475, 486–488, 487*
  for child maltreatment, 462–463
  for chronic illness, 427–428
  for conduct disorder, 327–328
  for depressive spectrum disorders, 274, *275*
  for obsessive-compulsive disorder, 233–234
  for posttraumatic stress disorder, 238
  for schizophrenia, 356–357
Cognitive biases, 240, 242, *243*
Cognitive delays, 448, 460
Cognitive development, 34, 39–43, 61, 81, 360
  and autistic spectrum disorders, 149–151, *150*
  and child maltreatment
    neglect, 445–446
    physical abuse, 439
    psychological abuse, 448
    sexual abuse, 450
  and chronic illness, 421–423
  and depressive spectrum disorders, 263
  and mental retardation, 121–125, *122*
  and oppositional-defiant disorder, 173
  and schizophrenia, 340–341
  and substance abuse, 393
  and suicide, 288
  and traumatic brain injury, 412–413
Cognitive developmental theory, 8–9, *16*
Cognitive distortions, 42, 463
  and child maltreatment, 441
  and eating disorders, 365–367, 374–375
  and oppositional-defiant disorder, 173
Cognitive dysfunction, 482
Cognitive models, 8–9, 258–260, *260*

Cognitive schemata, 8–9, 259, 263, 317, 393–394, 564
Cognitive skills, 393–394
Cognitive symptoms, 219, 252–253
Cognitive testing, 502–506
  infant cognitive testing, 502
  observations during, 503–506
  Stanford-Binet Intelligence Scales, Fifth Edition, 503, *505*
  strengths and limitations of, 506
  Wechsler Intelligence Scale for Children, 502–503, *502, 504*
Cognitive therapies, 178, 212, 381, *529,* 544–552
  conceptual model of, 544
  empirical support for, 551–552
  therapeutic process in, 544–551
    for anxiety disorders, 544–546, *545, 547*
    interpersonal problem-solving skills training, 548–551, *550*
    for obsessive-compulsive disorder, 546–548, *548–549*
    using manuals in, 551
Cognitive triad, 258–259, 559
Cohort effect, 29, 559
Collaboration (family systems pediatric interventions), 426
Collaborative Longitudinal Personality Disorders Study, 476
Collaborative partnerships with parents, 213
Columbine shootings, *298–299,* 304–305
Coma, 410
Communalism, 80
Communication deficits, 135–136, 349–350
Community factors, 75, 110, 403, 443
Comorbid clinical disorder (DSM), 418
Comorbidity, 22, 86, 89, 559

Comorbidity—*Cont.*
  of anorexia nervosa, 217, 225, 363
    and attention-deficit/hyperactivity disorder, 186
    and autistic spectrum disorders, 140
    and bipolar disorder, 280
    and child maltreatment, 448
    and conduct disorder, 306
    and mental retardation, 115
    and oppositional-defiant disorder, 170, 173
  of anxiety disorders, 217
    and anorexia nervosa, 363, 365
    and attention-deficit/hyperactivity disorder, 186
    and autistic spectrum disorders, 140
    and bipolar disorder, 280
    and borderline personality disorder, 469, 483
    and bulimia nervosa, 372
    and child maltreatment, 450–451
    and conduct disorder, 306
    and mental retardation, 115
    and oppositional-defiant disorder, 170, 173
    and posttraumatic stress disorder, 237
    and substance abuse, 388, 395
  of Asperger's disorder, 142
  of attention-deficit/hyperactivity disorder, 184–187, 189, 191, 195, 197
    and bipolar disorder, 278–281
    and borderline personality disorder, 470
    and conduct disorder, 306, 309
    and depressive spectrum disorders, 255
    and obsessive-compulsive disorder, 233

Comorbidity—*Cont.*
    and reading disorders, 206
    and schizophrenia, 336–337, 343, 349
    and social phobia, 225
    and substance abuse, 388
    and traumatic brain injury, 187, 411
  of autism, 140
  of bipolar disorder, 186, 280, 335, 350, 470
  of borderline personality disorder, 469–471
  of bulimia nervosa, 372
  of child maltreatment, 456–457
  of conduct disorder, 306–307
    and bipolar disorder, 279
    and borderline personality disorder, 469
    and child maltreatment, 440, 451
    and depressive spectrum disorders, 255
    and oppositional-defiant disorder, 169, 170
    and schizophrenia, 334
    and substance abuse, 387–388, 391
    and suicide, 287
    and traumatic brain injury, 413
  of depressive spectrum disorders, 217, 225, 255–256
    and anorexia nervosa, 363
    and anxiety disorders, 217, 219–220
    and attention-deficit/hyperactivity disorder, 186
    and bipolar disorder, 280–281
    and borderline personality disorder, 483–484
    and bulimia nervosa, 372
    and child maltreatment, 439–440, 441, 448–449, 460–461
    and conduct disorder, 255–256, 306–307, 327
    and mental retardation, 115

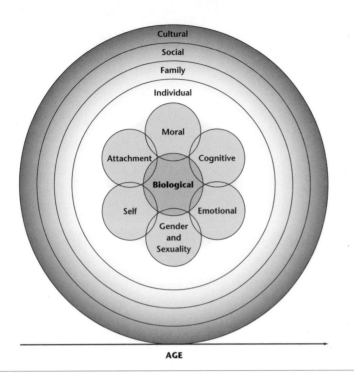

Figure 1.2

A Developmental Framework.

Note: All contexts and variables interact at each point in time as well as over time.

Figure 2.1   Map of the Human Brain.

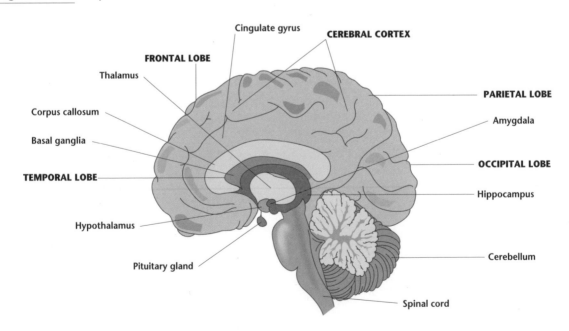